HISTORY OF PERQUIMANS COUNTY

As Compiled from Records Found There
and Elsewhere

Abstracts of Deeds from 1681 through the Revolution—Petitions, Divisions, and Marriages Found in Perquimans and Adjacent Counties—A brief Summary of the Settling of Perquimans, with the kind and manner of settlers—Two Maps, One of the Old Order, and, One a Present Day Map—Illustrations of a Few Old Residences and Several More Modern Ones.

By
Mrs. Watson Winslow

This volume was reproduced from
An 1931 edition located in the
Publisher's private library,
Greenville, South Carolina

All rights reserved. No part of this publication may be reproduced,
stored in a retrieval system, transmitted in any form, posted
on to the web in any form or by any means without the
prior written permission of the publisher.

Please direct all correspondence and orders to:

www.southernhistoricalpress.com
or
SOUTHERN HISTORICAL PRESS, Inc.
PO BOX 1267
375 West Broad Street
Greenville, SC   29601
southernhistoricalpress@gmail.com

Originally published: Raleigh, NC. 1931
Reprinted by:
Southern Historical Press, Inc.
Greenville, SC
ISBN #0-89308-975-3
All rights Reserved.
Printed in the United States of America

To my Husband
WATSON WINSLOW
OF WHOM I HAVE NOTHING BUT SWEET MEMORIES
KIND, FAITHFUL, TRUE, HONEST
GOOD CITIZEN, AND GENTLEMAN
SON OF PERQUIMANS

ABBREVIATIONS
(Official)

Alb.	Albemarle
Capt.	Captain
Clk.	Clerk of Court
Com.	Commission (ed)
Com'd	Command (ed)
Con. (con)	Consideration
Dept.	Deputy
Exrs.	Executors
E.	East
Gen'l	General
Gov.	Governor
Leg.	Legatee
N.	North
Perq.	Perquimans
Pre'ct	Precinct
Pro'	Province
Reg.	Register of Deeds
S.	South
Test'	Testator
Val'	Valuable
W.	West
adj.	adjoining
afsd.	aforesaid
agst	against
b.	born
d.	died
grt.	grant
m.	married
p.	pence
p.	probated
pt.	part
s.	shilling
sd.	said

FOREWORD

In writing a history of any county, the first consideration should be the perpetuation of valuable data found in the records, of which there can be no doubt, that Perquimans County possesses one of the richest fields of investigation in the State of North Carolina.

The State of Virginia has yielded, much interesting matter, leading up to the settlement of Perquimans, and many marriages between residents of that mother State and the immigrants coming to the new country of Carolina.

The Quaker records in Lower Monthly Meeting, Isle of Wight, Burleigh, and other meetings in Virginia, teem with marriages of Quakers who came to Perquimans. They also give other very important items of interest, which I have endeavored to weave into this history, thereby making a more complete record.

Much credit should be given the kind ladies in the Archives, Richmond, Va., for their patience and material aid in the undertaking; also Mrs. Nugent of the Land Office, Richmond, Va., who, through one whole week rendered her time and sweet interest to the success of my searchings, in her office, for which I feel the greatest gratitude and appreciation.

Of the county officers in Virginia, who have always been courtesy itself, I shall always have the highest esteem. Nowhere I am sure can one go and find a readier welcome, or more willing assistance in any individual, or official, undertaking.

This work represents years of untiring labor, trips to various counties in Virginia, days spent in Guilford College, for Quaker data, and over a year's work on the Perquimans records. I think I can say without egotism, that I am well acquainted with Perquimans County, from the beginning to the present day. And yet there is much more that ought to be done to make this work complete. One person could not in justice to the wonderful storehouse of information contained in the records here, make a finished job of them alone. So it is my earnest hope that a younger person, with enthusiasm and love for his, or her, native county, will take up the work where I am leaving off, and carry it through to a more satisfactory end. My work only takes these grand records to and through the Revolutionary period, and much of interest could be added.

Perquimans has sent out to the four winds, sons and daughters who have helped to make history in other parts of the world. Some have elected to remain and make history in their own little domain. Chief among these have been General William Skinner of Revolutionary fame, and Congressman T. G. Skinner, who spent a useful and efficient life

FOREWORD

in our county, and lies buried in the Episcopal Cemetery in Hertford, beloved and honored by all.

This work is in a way a supplement to Grimes' *North Carolina Wills,* a book of wide circulation and well established integrity; and Mr. J. R. B. Hathaway's grand contribution to the history of our country at large, the *North Carolina Historical and Genealogical Register,* also a work of renown, both found in all large libraries, in probably every State in the Union.

My efforts are sent out with an earnest desire to *help somebody.* If if does not accomplish this wish, then I have failed in the most strenuous work of a lifetime. Errors may be herein found, for which I crave leniency, but no stone has been left unturned to come at the truth, sometimes, however, not so clear as to be positively *certain.* In such cases I have tried to always use the doubtful phrase, "thought to be" or "probably," so as to print nothing misleading. It is not possible to find all that is necessary to fill out *everything* in a work of this kind, but my efforts have been ceaseless and untiring in that direction, though sometimes without *avail.*

My purpose to faithfully reproduce the records of the past has forbidden me to "spell out" abbreviations. I have adhered to the rule that it is best to let the records speak for themselves.

To the Perquimans officials great credit is due, from the fact that they have given me free use of everything contained in the two offices, and turned over the "loose papers," a very valuable collection, for my unmolested inspection, for a month or more. Those papers are now securely stored and protected by fireproof rooms in the North Carolina Hall of History, where they can be seen by any one searching for data. The custodians of this institution are all that could be wished for in courtesy and consideration.

The history of Perquimans is the child of my declining years, and when it is launched on the world, I will feel that it is my last effort, and will send it out hoping for a welcome from the public, and with a sincere desire that it may accomplish its purpose, by being of undying service to posterity.

The matter following was checked and gone over by the author many times before releasing it for publication.

Perquimans is of Indian origin, and means "Land of fair women."

Very sincerely yours,

Ellen Goode Winslow.

Hertford, March, 1931.

TABLE OF CONTENTS

	PAGE
Early Inhabitants	1
Religion and Churches	28

Records of Deeds:

Deed Book A	38
Deed Book B	69
Deed Book C	95
Deed Book D	119
Deed Book E	135
Deed Book F	151
Deed Book G	187
Deed Book H	211
Deed Book I (first part)	244
Petitions	285
Division of Estates	293
Marriages (at random)	299
Clerks of Court	311
Sheriffs	313
Representatives	314
The Family Bible of Perquimans County	314

Families:

Albertson	315
Arnold	317
Baker	318
Barrow	320
Bartlett	321
Bateman	323
Beasley	324
Bentley	324
Belman	325
Blanchard	325
Blitchenden	326
Blount	326
Bundy	327
Calloway	330
Charles	331
Chesson	332
Clare	333
Cox	334

TABLE OF CONTENTS

Families—*Continued*   PAGE

Davis	336
Draper	338
Durant	340
Elliott	341
Fleetwood	349
Fletcher	350
Godfrey	351
Gordon	352
Granbery	356
Gregory	360
Hollowell	361
Hoskins	362
Jessop	363
Jones	364
Jordan	366
Lamb	373
Lawrence	373
Layden	374
Leigh	375
Jacocks	376
Lillington	376
Long	377
Maudlin	379
McMullen	380
Mayo	382
Moore	383
Morgan	384
Morris	385
Newby	388
Nicholson	394
Nixon	396
Pearson	398
Perry	401
Phelps	403
Pierce	404
Pritlow-Pricklove	406
Ratcliffe	408
Scott	410
Skinner	411
Snoden	412

TABLE OF CONTENTS

Families—*Continued*   PAGE
   Speight 413
   Spivey 414
   Sutton 415
   Swann 418
   Toms 420
   Tucker 424
   White 425
   Williams 432
   Wilson 434
   Winslow 437
   Wood 445
   Woolard 447
   Wright 448
Rent Roll 449
Original Wills 450
Index to Deeds 452
General Index 481

EARLY INHABITANTS

From the Settlement of Perquimans to the Revolutionary Period

At what date the first white man set foot on Perquimans soil, staked a claim and erected his humble abode, no one can say with any degree of certainty. Foote in his notes claims that a band of settlers moved down on the Chowan River shortly after the Indian massacre in 1622. Where they took root he does not vouchsafe. As Chowan River has its headwaters in Virginia, with the Blackwater River as one of its tributaries, the inference may well be drawn that those early settlers followed the water courses, in their journey down to the new country instead of overland migration, as it is a well known fact that the forest and land adjoining the Dismal Swamp was at that time an impenetrable tangle of trees and undergrowth, full of danger for man and beast, with but a few Indian paths, and no man knew where they led. Therefore the immigrants fought shy of the interior, and clung to the river banks, where escape was more easy in case of attack by hostile tribes, fish could be procured for the daily fare, and houses built on high ground.

The settlement spoken of by Foote was most probably in what is now Gates County, and was then Chowan, or still in the unnamed wilderness called Carolina. Orapeak (Corapeak) in Gates County was certainly one of the first, if not the first settlement in Carolina, and the records in Perquimans prove beyond a single doubt that Perquimans County at that time ran all the way to the Virginia line, taking in this old landmark. This line was changed in 1779, and Perquimans shrank to its present boundary.

Roger Green, a clergyman from Virginia, started with a colony to settle on lower Chowan River in 1653. He came vested with power to possess lands in Carolina, but there has always been some doubt about the location of his settlement, and as the name of Green appears on the early records in Perquimans we are led to believe that some of his followers may have drifted over into the bordering county and taken up land there. As the names of his followers are not mentioned there is no authoritative way by which they can be traced, or the locality of their destination be determined. Green no doubt allowed full freedom to his countrymen, and they naturally selected land where it best suited them to "squat." As no record remains to show where they did take up claims, the Rivers and high lands adjoining afforded the most charming sites for homes, with the waterways as an outlet to market, a place to fish, the land less hard to clear, and last but not least, a better water supply, which was a very strong inducement, considering the health of the colony. This migration preceded the advent of George Durant by eight years, and there can be little doubt in the mind of any one versed in the early history of Albemarle, that many settlers were well established on their own land in Perquimans Precinct before said Durant decided to come to North Carolina. Among these early settlers, no doubt can be enumerated such men as Samuel Pricklove, whose land adjoined the land sold to George Durant by the Indian Chief Kilcoconewen King of Yeopim, on March 1, 1661, and Caleb Calloway, who appears as a witness to said deed. The land of said Samuel Pricklove lay around, or just below where the town of New Hope now stands. This made him a near neighbor of Durant, and they became fast friends. Pricklove was a Quaker, but it did not prevent him from following Durant in the Rebellion of 1677-79, even when his associations strictly forbade one of the sect to take up arms, and other Quakers followed his example, being also a part of the "rabble" that helped to depose acting Governor Thomas Miller. The rebellion caused a great deal of unrest in the colony and the county breathed easier, and sat more at ease when Miller finally took passage for Virginia, and later went home to England. All unwittingly George Durant struck the first note for American Independence, and routed the first unjust tax collector to appear on American soil, when he with his "rabble" drove out Miller, and stopped the unlawful Custom receipts in 1677-79.

So much has been written and said about being *first* that it has become somewhat a sore subject, especially when it is done without undisputed authority, therefore the writer feels it a real duty to bring before the reading public the fact that in Perquimans precinct, at the mouth of Little River came into being the *first authenticated* town in Albemarle, called "Little River." This town was situated on the west side of the mouth of Little River and by act of Assembly became one of the "Ports of Entry" for Albemarle, where "ships shall laid, and unlaid." Precinct Court was held in this town for forty years, and near this place a "Gran Court House" was built about 1701, where Court was held for only one time on October 14, 1701. The Court House stood on the Sound, and was probably burned between the time of the holding of the October Court, and the date of its next session, as it is not mentioned on any record after that date. The Precinct Courts came to order at the houses of old residents before, and afterwards, the first recorded being at the house of one Harris (Thomas Harris) who was the first Clerk of Perquimans, and later after his death at the house of Thomas White, who had married the widow of Harris, September 4, 1694. In every precinct a court consisted of a Steward (Judge) and four justices, who were inhabitants of said precinct, owning 300 acres of land as a freehold. No man could serve on the jury unless he held a freehold of fifty acres of land in the county, and a grand juryman had to be the possessor of 300 acres, the petty jurymen having 200 acres, a constable 100 acres, and no man was called a freeman who did not acknowledge God. Divers persons in Carolina were possessed of land by reason of grants from Sir William Berkeley.

The deed to George Durant being the oldest recorded in North Carolina, has led the general public to the wrong impression that he brought into Perquimans its first settlers, and planted the first colony, while as a matter of fact many persons were well rooted, even in the neck now called "Durants" before his arrival in the colony. This deed, however, was not recorded on the deed book in Perquimans until 1716, when the then Register of Deeds, John Stepney made a copy of it, calling himself "Register of all Writings for Perquimans Precinct." Durant, as the deed shows, took up all the land between Perquimans and Little River and immediately began to *build,* when one George Catchmaid arose and claimed the said land by a prior grant from Sir William Berkeley, thereupon Durant after starting his home in the new land "desisted" and quit building. George Catchmeyed was an Englishman, who at a council "At James Citty Virginia," September 25, 1663, is styled as Gent, "coming from Treslick England," and he received a grant from the Virginia government of 1500 acres, "in a Bay of ye River Carolina (Sound) adjoining Captain Jenkins (John) by ye River piquimins, due for transpotation of thirty persons into this Collony." His land was either increased by purchase or other grants, as the deeds in Perquimans prove he was possessed of 3,333 acres, which descended to his niece, Elizabeth Chandler, of London, he having died in Nansemond County, Virginia, without heirs. His widow married second Timothy Biggs of Perquimans, who set up a counter claim for the land called "Birkswear" which was situated in the lower end of Durants Neck, and later became known as "Stevensons Point."

At a Council held at St. Mary's, Maryland, October 17, 1666, the Assembly of the Province of North Carolina "sent hither William Drummond, Esq., Governor thereof and George Catchemeyed Gent Speaker of the Assembly." George Catchmaid, who lived his last days in Virginia, and was at his death Clerk of Nansemond County in said State.

William Drummond, a sober Scotch gentleman of good repute, was appointed Governor of Albemarle in the fall of 1664, and served until 1676, when he was summarily recalled by Sir William Berkeley, who had him executed in an hour after his arrival, for his sympathy with Bacon in the rebellion. It is a well established fact that Governor Drummond lived in Durant's Neck, Perquimans County, somewhere near the Sound and Little River, but sad to relate every vestage of the site has disappeared, old residents claiming that the land at that point caved in, and has been engulfed by the greedy waters of the Sound. He was no doubt buried in Virginia, and his wife lies sleeping the last sleep in the graveyard at Jamestown.

George Durant of whom so much has been written and said, came to America from London, and landed first in Northumberland County, Virginia. While it is admitted that he came from England, some writers claim he was of Scotch parentage, and also that he was by faith a Presbyterian, although an opinion has erroneously been spread abroad that he adhered to the Quaker faith, which can not be proven by any record, either county or Friends Church Register. He was married by an Episcopal minister (David Lindsay) in Northumberland County, Virginia, and the records in Perquimans are ample proof of the fact that he never affiliated with the Friends in a religious way, only one of his many children having married in the last named society, that being a daughter, who married Joseph Sutton. (See Sutton family in this book.)

George Durant in a deed Perquimans County, calls himself "Mariner" therefore he may have been master of some sailing vessel, which calling he probably abandoned on coming to Perquimans, where he was undoubtedly engaged in rather extensive farming operations for the time, becoming one of the most influential planters in all Albemarle. He was evidently far above the average in educational advantages, possessed of pronounced political opinions, added to other good qualities fine executive ability. He swayed the masses at his will, and according to Colonial Records "used Jenkins (John) as his property" being called by those opposed to him in the rebellion, "the most uncontrollable man in the country." With the Indians he was just, and according to records now on file in Perquimans not one thing can be brought against him, as to honesty and fair dealing with his neighbors, or fellowmen. His home has faded from the memory of man, and not even the location of his last resting place can be found, but tradition has it that he was buried by the side of a large lead drain, in Durants Neck, and that repeated cutting of the drain caused an accumulation of soil to be heaped up on the mound, thereby obscuring it from sight, until the very place has been lost where he lies buried. Beloved of men, honored by the Indians, his memory still lives in the hearts of descendants, and those interested in the history of Perquimans.

EARLY INHABITANTS

To encourage emigration every settler was granted 100 acres for his own transportation, and fifty acres for every servant he brought in. "All persons who doe come to plant in Carolina before December 25, 1672, above the age of sixteen" were granted fifty acres of land. The Register of each precinct had to be the owner of 300 acres, and was charged to "well behave himself." Each precinct was ordered to keep a record of all marriages, birth, and deaths, "in a book" in his own respective limitations. Such a "book" was painstakingly kept by the Register of Perquimans, which was called "Births, Deaths, and Marriages in Berkeley" being the name of the parish, which seems to have taken into its bounds the whole confines of Perquimans Precinct, as then surveyed. This "book" is still to be seen at the Hall of History, Raleigh, N. C., in a fairly good state of preservation.

Among some of those who received grants from Sir William Berkeley are to be found, John Harvey, who was granted 250 acres, on River Carolina (Sound) adjoining Roger Williams, which land was granted "att James Citty" September 5, 1663; and John Jenkins in like manner received 700 acres, "being a Neck of land, bounded on the South by River Carolina (Sound) and on the North by Pyquomons River, and on the West by land of Thomas Jarvis." Granted at same place.

John Harvey whose land was situated in what is now called "Harveys Neck" lay on a sunny bluff, fronting on both the Sound, and the River, one of the choice possessions in the county. The founder of this illustrious family became one of the early Governors, 1678-79, lived and died in the Neck that bears his name, and was buried in the old cemetery on the Sound. This graveyard after many years caved in, and the stones were washed into the Sound. Some of them (three) were recovered, and placed in another cemetery further inland, where numerous Harveys, all of good repute lie buried. This family held every office that the county could bestow on any citizen, from Justice to Governor, and the flower of them all became Moderator at New Bern 1774, who unfortunately died just at the beginning of the Revolutionary War, thereby the county lost one of its strongest supporters, and the State a great patriot. Not a vestage is left of the old Harvey mansion, called "Harvey Hall" and the underbrush and weeds are growing where statesmen once walked. The old cemetery nearby is pitifully neglected, forsaken and desolate in the extreme, where rest the remains of Col. Thomas Harvey, and others with only the song of night birds, and a requiem of the trees to keep them company. Of all the many Harvey sons not one remains in Perquimans who bears the name, but there are still living a few collateral branches, and only one strictly speaking lineal descendant in the person of Miss Emily Skinner of Hertford. As this family has been well written up in the *North Carolina Historical and Genealogical Register,* the writer feels that it has been fully taken care of, and that no addition made could improve that splendid contribution to posterity.

No minister being stationed in the Province of Carolina prior to January 20, 1669, an Act of Assembly was passed making it lawful for those wishing to be joined in marriage to appear before the Governor, or some Councilor, and there declare themselves as man and wife having several friends, or neighbors present as witnesses, whereupon the marriage was declared legal and the Register of the Precinct in which such marriage took place inscribed their names on the book used for that purpose.

A "Grand Councell for ye County of Albemarle" was held at the house of "Gen'l Mr George Durant November 6, 1679" at which time John Nixon, who was a member of said Council, declared his age to be fifty-four years. George Durant's house was on the Sound. (*Colonial Records*, Vol. I, page 355.)

Mr. Seth Sothel, a sober, moderate man, in no way concerned with the rebel factions of 1677-79 took the helm as Governor of Carolina November 20, 1680. Pirates had already begun their nefarious work in the waters of Albemarle, and the English government were cognizant of the state of affairs, ordering suppression of all sea rovers, at Whitehall February 27, 1683. One Jacob Hall came from La Vera Cruz, who "belonged not to the place, having no Inhabitants of Carolina with him sayled for Virginia" when he was questioned by the authorities in Albemarle about his sailing papers. He was sailing under orders from Van Horn with a commission from the French government, nevertheless he was indicted, found guilty and hung with two others as a privateer at the entrance of the port. Soon after this occurrence grave charges were preferred against Seth Sothel (1691) for which he was imprisoned. He was accused of seizing two persons who came from Barbados, "charging them with Pyracy" though they produced clearance papers from the government, and did "imprison unlawfully Robert Cannon, and arbitrarily detained two servants of John Stewart, and out of malice did imprison George Durant upon some reflecting words of yo self, and compelled him to give you a sum of money while in durance." He also took from John Tomlin his plantation, and detained unlawfully cattle belonging to George Mathews, and would not deliver them even after an Order of Court was secured by said Mathews for their liberation. From John Harris (son of Thomas first Clerk of Perquimans) he took possession of a plantation, for which offence he was ordered to "come speedily to England" where the home government dealt in a lenient manner with his misdemeanors, being "unwilling to make of him a publick shame" May 12, 1691. Finally he was accused of being in sympathy with the pirates to the limit of extending commissions to them, which accusation brought about his impeachment, and he was deposed from the governorship, taking refuge in South Carolina. In the last Province he was again lifted to the high office of governor, and again suffered impeachment for the identical nefarious practices, and returned to Perquimans where he died in shame. The records give the fact that "there was no vice known to man that he had not been guilty of." Dying without descendants his bad nature died with him, and Anne, his wife, took for her fourth husband, John Leah, of Nansemond County, Virginia.

On November 8, 1691, instructions were received from England to "use ye uttmost endeavor to make a settm't of a Towne, remote from the Sea, as a Seat of Government in Carolina" at which date Edenton was made the seat of government for Carolina, it is supposed.

The Colonial Records of North Carolina have excellent copies of the old precinct court proceedings in Perquimans, showing the earliest extant to be that at the house of —— Harris (Thomas) May, 1693. According to the same source the fact is gained that the *oldest* records were burned during the rebellion of 1677-79. A few old papers escaped this tragic fate by being lodged with the Secretary of State, the old wills of Perquimans having been fortunate in that respect, have been beautifully abstracted by Mr. J. Bryan Grimes, Secretary of State, in his book, *Grimes' North Carolina Wills*. All wills prior to 1762 are there found in abstract form, and the later ones Mr. J. R. B. Hathaway did the same for in his Quarterlies, now procurable in all libraries in book form. These Quarterlies are a wonderful contribution to the collection of any library, giving as they do such a fund of information about the entire history of eastern North Carolina. If a person in search of data from these counties will work this book in conjunction with the two mentioned he or she will be well repaid for the trouble.

The Court held May, 1693, shows sitting as Justices, Alexander Lillington, Caleb Calloway, and John Barrow. The will of Robert Smith was proven at this court, and Jonathan Bateman and John Durant (son of George) were appointed to appraise his estate. Mrs. Sarah Woolard secured an order of court, demanding estate due her, "now in the hands of Mr. Edward Smythrick in Chowan county." On the grand jury are found the names of "Timo Pead, Mr Rich Evins, Mr Antho Dawson, Mr Geo Branch, Mr Israel Snelling, Mr Thomas Tondle (Toddy), Mr Jno Little, Mr Jno Stepne, Mr James Hogg. The pettit jury consisted of Mr Ralph Fletcher, Mr Christopher Butler, Mr Timo Clare, Mr James Thigpen, Mr Tho. Pierce, Mr Patrick Kenedy, Mr Ste. Mannering (Manwarring), Mr Robert Brightwell, Mr Geo

Eames, Mr Isac Wilson, Mr John Willoughby, Mr Francis Foster." Robert and Johanna Beasley were paid for six days attending court, and Caleb Calloway received 30 shillings from the estate of "Guyles Long deceased" for what reason is not specified.

Diana (Manners) Harris, wife of Thomas, married second William Foster, 1675, hence the next precinct court came to order at the house of "Diana Foster in February 1694/4, with same justices present. The proceeding of this court show that Mr. John Davis was dead, and John Philpott withdrew an action against Richard Nowell. Rights were proven by Thomas Lepper for ten persons as follows: Thomas (twice) Ann, Sarah, Rebecca Lepper, Ann Kent, John Thomas, William Brown, William Brickstone, and Nicholas Roberson. Caleb Calloway proved rights for "Dan'll Pembroke, Tho. Merett (an Indian) and Arthur Long." The last captain in Bacon's Rebellion. Roger Snell by gift conveyed land to Jonathan Taylor. The will of Mr. George Durant was probated during the session of this court, "by oath of Mr. John Philpott and Mr. Francis ffoster." Seth Sothel had also passed away, and his will was proven by Col. William Wilkinson, Capt. Henderson Walker, and Sarah Woolard, all residents of Perquimans. Lawrence Arnold, deceased, his widow, Elizabeth, was sworn in as his Administratrix. Rights were proven by Thomas Pierce, for himself, John, Susanna, Ruth, Dorothy, Mary, and John Pierce. Hannah Gosby proved rights for her son, John Gosby, Jno. Anderson, Jean Anderson, Katherine Kinsey, Jeremiah White and Henry Clayton. (John Kinsey came to North Carolina from Nansemond County, Virginia, and wedded Katherine, daughter of Francis Toms, having one son, John, born 1692, his death occurring soon after, she married second John Nicholson.) John Bentley entered land for importations, Jean, Mary, and Sarah Bentley. Jenkins Williams proved rights for himself. Timothy Clare imported Edmond Rodman, and Richard Fox, Junior. Samuel Nicholson rights for Christopher Nicholson, and Hannah his wife (who came from New England) Deliverance Sutton (daughter of said Christopher, and wife of Joseph Sutton) Francis Simons, Hannah Nicholson. Thomas Harloe proved rights for himself, Mary (twice) and John Harloe, probably his son. John Durant rights for himself and wife Sarah (Jooke). William Godfrey rights for himself and Sarah Godfrey. James, Ann, Alice, and John Wilson came to Carolina as headrights of James ffewox. Edward Mayo, Senior, transported himself and children, Edward, Sarah, Ann, Elizabeth Mayo, also Em John, and Ann Nixon, and Samuel and Affica Pike. William Butler rights for himself and wife Diana. Richard Nowell rights for himself Joan, Ellinor, Alice, and Olliver Nowell, John Smith, Charles, George, and Mary Taylor. (Richard Nowell settled on Little River.) Tabitha

Haskeet (Hasket) rights for John Gray and Tabitha his wife (her daughter), John Gray, Junior, and Thomas Gray. William Lacey proved rights for himself, his father, William Lacey, Sr., Grace, and John Lacey, probably his wife and brother, and Jean Davis. James Loadman rights for himself (twice) and his mother, Jean Buyard. Stephen Manwaring rights for Edward Berry, and John Deadman (who died at the house of John Harris July 15, 1692, for whom Deadman's Swamp in Perquimans was named). The name of Manwarring appears on the records of Richmond County, Virginia, and one Stephen Manwarring came to Carolina from Surry County, Virginia, apparently.

Thomas Hassold (Hassell) came from Pennsylvania about this time bringing with him Thomas Snowden, Mary and Thomas Hassold, Jr. William Barclift proved rights for himself, Sarah Beasley, James, and Johanna Beasley, Richard and Sarah Chastone (Chesson).

The third court held in the precinct of Perquimans, convened at the same residence, with Justices present; Major Alexander Lillington, Mr. Henry White (a Quaker who came to Perquimans from Surry County, Virginia, where he purchased land from John Troy of Surry, June 9, 1655), Mr. Thomas Lepper, Mr. John Barrow, Esquires. At this sitting of court Ann Parish, formerly Jacocks (wife of Thomas of Little River), acknowledged a deed of gift to her son, John Huffton. Thomas Hassold entered land on Northeast side of Perquimans River, between the lands of Samuel Pricklove, and Thomas Attoway. During the session of the court Elizabeth Arnold petitioned the court to the effect that Lawrence Arnold her deceased husband had bequeathed his estate unto their son John, which was to be turned over to him when he reached the age of thirteen years, prayed for a guardian to be appointed in the person of Jonathan Bateman, whom she later married for her second husband. Thomas Hassold presented a petition showing that Thomas Snoden, a child, was left with him by his father-in-law, Edmund Pirkins, and that said child was bound to him until he was twenty-one years old.

Court November 6, 1694, at Mrs. Diana Fosters; same Justices present. Petition presented by Mr. John Hunt (who lived in Little River), showing that "Mrs Ann Durant held in her possession books and papers belonging to the estate of Mr William Therrill," prayed that they be turned over to him, he being the only living Executor, which was granted. George Durant, husband of said Ann, in his life time was Executor for Mr. William Therrill, who was one of his followers during the rebellion of 1677-79. William Therrill in his will probated in Perquimans County, speaks of George Durant of "Berty Point," and said Therrill himself lived on Little River.

Thomas Gilliam appeared in the court and accused Robert White and Vincent, his son, with grand larceny. The court ordered that a penalty be imposed upon the two of having the letter "T" branded in the hand which was duly executed. Augustine Scarbrough entered 300 acres of land on Powells Point Neck. Thomas Haskins (Hoskins) appeared in court for the first time. Elizabeth Banks of London appointed "beloved friends ffrancis Tomes and John Hawkins" attorneys to recover money and goods due from the estate of Seth Sothel, late Governor of Carolina. Thomas White, and Diana, his wife (late wife of William Foster), entered a suit against John Wilson. These two were continually in litigation with some one in the precinct. Jurors appointed for their case; William Jackson, Robert Moline (Modlin), John Belman (who immigrated to Perquimans from Surry County, Va.), Uriah Cannon, John Raper, Thomas Gilliam, and John Barrow, foreman. (Thomas Gilliam also came from Surry County, Va., to Perquimans.)

A General Court was held at the house of Mr. Thomas White (he having married Diana Foster, widow of William Foster, nee Manners), September 25, 1694, with Honorable Thomas Harvey, presiding. Major Alexander Lillington in behalf of John Wright of Virginia brought suit against Thomas Haskins (Hoskins) for debt. On September 26, Honorable Thomas Harvey, Esquire, present Deputy Governor of this Province, and Councilors; "ffrancis Tomes, Benjamin Lakar, Major Samuel Swann, Coll. Thomas Pollock, Daniel Akehurst, Esquires, and Captain Anthony Dawson, and Mr. John Durant, assistants. At this sitting of court the will of Coll. Francis Hartley was probated, and Mrs. Susanna Hartley chosen as Administratrix of his estate.

Mary Lamb, widow of Joshua, who had migrated to Perquimans from New England in court on legal business. Thomas Welch, indentured servant of Mr. Joseph Commander prayed for his freedom, which was granted.

September 28, 1694. Major Samuel Swann proved rights, himself, wife, Sarah (daughter of William Drummond), William, Samuel, Samson, Henry, and Thomas Swann, and Elizabeth Hunt; negroes Tom, Mary, Hanah, Eliza, and Jane, for transportation of which he received 650 acres of land on the Sound in Perquimans precinct.

November 29, 1694, Daniel Phillips received an appointment and became Deputy Marshall of Perquimans. A list of tithables was exhibited in court numbering 787 souls, and a levy of five shillings was imposed upon each person therein named. On February 25, 1694/5 Anne Ward petitioned the court for administration on estate of her deceased husband Francis Ward, which was granted. Elizabeth Bateman, widow of Jonathan, craved her third part of her husband's estate, his son **Jonathan** being Executor. Jacob Overman proved rights for himself, Dorothy, Jacob, Junior, Tho., Ephrim, Margery, Charles, and Ann Overman. Diana White (petition) for her son, John Harris, same court, prayed for his estate.

February 27, 1695, the will of Mrs. Ann Durant was proven by oath of Jno. Clapper and Elinor Moline (Modlin), and Thomas Durant was made Executor, March 1, 1695.

James Ward and Hanah', his wife, relict of Richard Stiball were granted Execution the estate of said Stiball. Major Samuel Swann, Surveyor, for the Province of Carolina, brought suit against Benjamin Laker for non-payment of his fee, he having surveyed 1500 acres for said Laker, which was dismissed.

In 1696 the records show that there were in Carolina sixty or seventy scattered families, settled principally along the water front for twenty miles up Little River shore, and around to Perquimans River. The inlet of Roanoke was frequented by small vessels trading to and from the West India Islands, and pirates and run-away slaves resorted to this place from Virginia. (*Colonial Records,* Vol. I, page 467.)

John Archdale was Governor of Carolina at this time, the only Quaker to hold such a high office. He favored his own sect, and his constituents became flush with appointments to every known position in his power to bestow, but he made a wise forbearing just reign with the colony enjoying peace and security under his benign rule. Honorable Francis Jones, Benjamin Laker, Major Samuel Swann, and Thomas Harvey, Esquires, Lords Deputies during the incumbency of Archdale.

January Court, 1696/7 was "holden" at the house of Thomas Nichols, with Justices present; Mr. John Godfrey, Caleb Calleway, Captain Ralph Fletcher, John Barrow, and Samuel Nicholson. James Oates appeared for the first time at this court. Rights were proven by Thomas Speight, for himself, John Morres (Morris), Elizabeth, John, Junior, William, and Mare Morres. Denis Maclenden proved rights for himself, Rebecca Carpenter, Elizabeth Brient, Denis Francis, and Thomas Maclenden. Abraham Williams rights for himself, wife Anne, and Edward, and John Williams. Peter Jones brought suit in this court. In March, 1696/7, John Stepney took oath as Clerk of Perquimans.

Court at the house of Mr. Thomas Blount April, 1697, with Justices present; Caleb Calleway, Judge Captain Ralph Fletcher, Mr. John Barrow, Mr. John Godfrey, Mr. John Whedby and Mr. Samuel Nicholson. Richard Nowel and Ellener, his wife, acknowledged a deed of gift to their daughter, Allis. Mr. John Whedby did the same for his two children, Richand and Deborah. John Lilly, Robert Harmon and Jonathan Tailor were appointed constables of the precinct.

Court met at the house of James Oates January, 1698, at which time Timothy Clare was appointed "Keeper of the Toole Bookes of Piquemons on West sid, and Isaack Wilson on ye East Sid." Tolls had become necessary on account of vagrant persons pilfering cattle from the herds of their neighbors, and driving them into Virginia for sale, therefore a law was passed that each animal, cattle, hog or sheep should be marked to prevent thievery.

April, 1698, court at same place. William Bogue appointed constable "from ye Narrows of piquemons to Suttens Creek, and to Mr. Lakars Crick on ye West Side."

Court at Mr. James Oates October, 1698, with Hon'ble Thomas Harvey, Deputy Governor, presiding. The Court of January, 1699, came to order at the same house. John Parish was appointed overseer of the highway "from the ferry to Mr Whedbys path." It is to be deplored that the "ferry" here spoken of is not better designated. In October of the same year a "Grate brig" is mentioned over the head of Perquimans River, where James Perrisho served as overseer. This bridge was probably the same later called "Newbys Bridge" and crossed the River beyond Belvidere going to Piney Woods.

An Assembly was held at the house of Mr. James Oates January, 1699-1700. Mr. James Cole received permission to build a "Mill at the head of Indian Crick" during the sitting of this court.

Court at Mr. James Oates house April, 1700, when William Moore proved rights for transporting himself, and wife Elizabeth into this country. Court at same place October, 1700. Daniel Hall and wife Rose appeared in court. James Oates was dead October 6, 1703. His will was probated January, 1704, and names son Joseph, and wife, Elizabeth, another legatee Jonathan Evins. Elizabeth Oates was a daughter of John Wyatt and wife Rachel Calloway. The ages of their children are given in Berkeley Parish Register as follows: John, born August 7, 1697; John (first by name), born February 4, 1667; Jesse, born August 31, 1669; Mary, born November 16, 1672. Joseph Oates moved from Perquimans to Beaufort County.

Court at the house of Captain Anthony Dawson April 8, 1701, at which time Captain Ralph Fletcher had been advanced to the office of Judge of the precinct. Justices Samuel Nicholson, Francis Foster, James Cole, and Samuel Charles. The next court July 8, 1701, at same house, Robert Inkrsone "sheweth that Walter Sestion is ded Haven Made No Will" prays for administration on his estate "having married Rellock of said Sestion." John Pricklo petitioned the court that "ffrancis Bedson (Belson) Lay Sick at His—— (House). A long time, who died and was Buried At His on Cost, now prays for Custodie of his Estate."

EARLY INHABITANTS

Court was "Holden at ye Gran Court House for ye precinct of Perquimons ye Secont tues In October 1701." Major Samuel Swann and Elizabeth, his wife (second wife, daughter of Alexander Lillington), acknowledged a deed to Samuel Swann, Jr. John Hecklefield petitioned the court "Shewen that George Prody Is dead Haven Maide No Will" and prays for management of his estate. Samuel Philips and James Chesen petitioned the court for their share of a crop made while living with John Lilly, and it was ordered that said Samuel should have "full Sheare and Chesen a Halfe Sheare." John Hecklefield had just arrived in Carolina and he made choice of Little River as his future home. Court was held at his house for a number of years and an Assembly in 1707. On April, 1702, court at the house of Captain James Coles. Peter Albertson "sheweth that John Lilly was indebted to Ann Jones Now his Wife, and James Oates was ordered to pay to said Albertson Tenn Shillings and six pence." At same session of court Sarah Harris chose as her guardian her uncle, Nathaniel Albertson. Mrs. Mary Swann (wife of Samuel Swann, Jr.), proved his will in Court at Capt. James Coles' October, 1702. The will of Albert Albertson was probated during the same Court by Mary, his widow, and sons, Albert, Peter, and Nathaniel. At this Court Thomas Winslow "Proved on Write for his freedom An Assigned it to Timothy Clar." Soon after this date he married Elizabeth Clare, daughter of Timothy, and it seems certain he was an apprentice to said Clare, and had just come of age.

A "Gen'll Court was held at the House of Captain John Hecklefield in Little River, October 27, 1702. The function of this Court appears to have been on the same basis of our present day Supreme Court. Those of note present at this session were Honorable Samuel Swann, Esquire; Honorable William Glover, Esquire; John Jenkins, Esquire; William Duckenfield (whose home was in Bertie County), who came to prosecute a suit against Thomas Evins.

Henderson Walker was Governor of the Province, April 24, 1703. Peter Godfrey was appointed Clerk of Perquimans, January 1702/3, at which time Captain John Stepney turned over the books, while Samuel Swann administered the oath to the new Clerk, being secretary of the Court. Governor Walker had sworn in three new justices, Samuel Swann, Frances Toms, and William Glover.

Court at Captain James Coles February 2, 1703. Hannah Snellen, widow of Israel, acknowledged a deed to her "Chelldren," Rachel and Esther. Soon after this date she became the wife of Timothy Clare, his *third* and *last* wife. Sarah Harris made choice of her grandmother, Mary Albertson, as her guardian.

Court at same place March 9, 1703, when William Turner made over a patent of land unto James Newby and wife, Sarah, and they sold it to James Foster. At the same court the orphans of Thomas and Mary Hancocke were bound to Gabriel Newby. This is the first mention of any one by the name of Newby in the court proceedings of Perquimans, and from that fact they seem to have recently arrived in Carolina.

At this court Eza (Esau) Albertson was "Sworne Constable, from the hithermost part of Little River to the lower side of Suttons Creeke." Lawrence Arnold (2) had the embarrassing experience of having a child sworn to him out of wedlock by Jeane Richards, servant of John Hecklefield. John West, brother-in-law of the orphans of Lewis Alexander and Esther Knight, was ordered to take them with Emanuel Knight under his care.

A second General Court came to order on March 29, 1703, at the house of Captain John Hecklefield; Councilors present: Honorable William Glover, Thomas Symons, Richard Plater and William Collins, Esquires. An account of the estate of John Harvey, Esquire, was presented in Court by Mr. Christopher Gale. The will of Samuel Pricklove was probated by oath of Francis Penrice and John Anderson. Mr. Henry Baker of Virginia brought suit against William Early for debt; thereupon he appointed his "good friend" Samuel Swann, Esquire, of Carolina attorney to collect all delinquencies due him from said Early. Another General Court at Captain John Hecklefield's house on July 27, 1703, when said Hecklefield sued Captain Richard Sanderson for £10 due him. He also attached the estate of Daniel Phillips, and levied a second attachment against William Nicholson's estate. John Eavans made petition in this court. Thomas Dewham (Derham) of Bath was arraigned in Court for the murder of William Hudson, who had been slain September preceding, for which crime he was sentenced to be branded on the brawn of the left hand with the letter M, but he appears to have been released from the cruel punishment by the following Court.

Court was held on April 11, 1704, at the house of Dennis Macclenden. Some of the inhabitants of Carolina mentioned as being in Court were James Beesley (Beasley) and Mary, his wife, Francis Wells and David Harris, and wife, Elizabeth. Constance Snowden, wife of Thomas relinquished her dower right in land unto John Bateman, and Thomas Evans and Mary, his wife, acknowledged a deed made by them to Thomas Snowden. A petition was presented in Court by James Thigpen, showing the need of a road "to be cleared from the ferry out to the High Road."

Court same house July 11, 1704. William Morgan brought suit against David Harris for "Defamacon and Aspersing words, he having said Thee art a Rogue and Ile prove itt." This defamation of character proving to be pure slander, the court ruled that the defendant should cast himself upon the mercy of the Court and pay all cost. John White and Alice were defendants in a case. About this time roads became a crying need and many resolutions appear on the Court records authorizing new roads or clearing and straightening old ones, therefore the old road from Lakars Creek was ordered to be cleared and Caleb Calleway was appointed overseer. William Williams proved rights for himself and at the next session of court his wife Susannah appointed friend Dennis Macclenden her attorney.

On January 1, 1704/5, Colonel William Wilkinson and Hester, his wife, by Thomas Snowden, their attorney, brought suit against Johannah Taylor, Executor of the estate of William Boyce, deceased, for two rings belonging to said Susannah. Richard Skinner became overseer of the highway "in Room of Francis Beasley."

Court at the house of Dennis Macclenden April 1, 1705, at which date Thomas Snowden was appointed "Clearke of Court for Perquimans precinct." The Court records name the fact that about this date Deborah Whidby (daughter of John), became the wife of Henry Bonner.

January 6, 1705. Court at Dennis Macclenden's. Isaac Wilson proved rights, for "Importacon" of Mary Brasinan (Brassuer) Elizabeth Brasman, John Morris, James White, Anne Barker, George Baite and wife, Rebeccah Ratcliffe, Joseph Canerle, Richard Turner, William Barnstable, John Hooks, Isaac and Abraham Ricks, for which he was awarded 1200 acres of land in Perquimans Precinct. Ralph Boasman, who immigrated to Perquimans from Surry County, Virginia, had rights proven for importing Samuel, Elizabeth, Mercy, and Susannah Bond, Matthew Potter, Sarah Johnson, and Luke Grace. James Nuby was allowed 300 acres of land for the transportation of John, Magdalen, Elizabeth, and James Newby. He took up land in Pasquotank County where he died. As soon as this 300 acres was entered he immediately conveyed it to Isaac Wilson of Perquimans.

Mrs. Deborah Whedbee, widow of John, married second Dennis Macclenden, and it was at her house that Court was held July 9, 1706, the presumption being admissible that she was a widow for the second time. The Justices present at this Court were James Cole, Thomas Long, Joseph Sutton, Senior, William Long, Esquires. Ezekiel Maudlin, deceased, his wife, Hannah, being Administratrix. Ralph Bosman was appointed Constable. Ordered that John Parish, Francis Beesley and Samuel Phelp be "packers" for this precinct, "John Parish from the head of Little River to the mouth thereof and soe around up Pequimins River to Lillys Creek," and Francis Beasley and Samuel Phelps for the remainder of the precinct. Plainly this demonstrates the fact that along the bank of Little River and the mouth of Perquimans the settlers were more thickly congregated than further up towards the interior. Samuel Phelps was ordered to "keep the Toll Booke att the Head of Pequimins River."

Mr. James Minge appears for the first time at a Court August 8, 1696, held at the house of James Thigpen, proving rights for himself, his wife, Ruth (nee Laker), and eight negroes for which he secured 1000 acres of land. His land situated in Harveys Neck ran along the bank of what is now called "Minsie" Creek then and later named in deeds as Ming Creek. Richard Turner proved rights and had 450 acres of land turned over to him for importing himself, wife, Bridget, William Barnstable, Elizabeth Turner (who married —— Newby), John Turner and John Hooks. Edward Wilson was appointed constable "in Room of John Davenport." Among the Justices present only two, James Cole and John Stepney, could sign their own names, all the others making marks.

A letter written by John Holden March 21, 1707, to the Lords of Trade, deplores the fact that "Carolina was barred by Inlets which spoil trade, as none but small vessels from New England and Barbadoes are able to cross these obstructions." He further asserts that "the soil of Albemarle is more lusty" than that of South Carolina, producing in abundance tobacco, corn, wheat, and that the cattle, hogs and sheep thrive in the open all winter. This could have been no exaggeration as the same is the case at the present day. Commodities such as hides, tar, furs, beaver, otter, fox, wild cat, and deer skins were plentiful. Leather, herbs and drugs were some of the exportations at quite an early date. An affidavit made by Robert Lawrence of Nansemons County, Virginia, asserted that he was 69 years old, being seated about 47 years upon a plantation on South West side of Chowan River, where he had lived for the past seven years and that he was well acquainted with the boundary lines of those rivers.

An Assembly met at the House of Captain John Hecklefield in Little River October 11, 1708, where were gathered nine representatives from Chowan, two from Pasquotank of Quaker choosing, five from Currituck, with the number from Perquimans not designated. Mr. Edward Moseley was chosen Speaker of the House. The country became torn and rent with dissatisfaction as another rebellion called the Cary Rebellion arose like a monster causing distrust and discontent among the struggling colonists. This rebellion was at its height in 1709-10, when the country had hardly recovered from the dissention of 1677-79, proved a great hardship on those peacefully minded and disrupted the governemnt.

Rev. John Rainsford who had been selected to serve the Church of England in Carolina received a letter of warning from Mr. Hyde about this time which purported in part "that he would not have him discouraged by misrepresentations made by Mr. Urmstone (John), who will be loud in complaining, but the dissatisfaction of said person is in the greater part owing to himself, as his unfortunate temper in no way suits the natual born people of America, who were not to be won by any thing but gentle methods, and he by his railings and morose disposition had driven the people from the Church." This dissatisfaction on the part of Church of England people had augmented the ranks of the Quakers, and numbers of Church people had gone over to the new religion.

The last Council to convene in Perquimans was held at the house of Captain John Hecklefield in Little River July 4, 1712. No date appears to justify the assertion but it was probably about this date that "Phelps Point" became the seat of Precinct Court. However the earliest authenticated sitting of Court on the Point is 1735, but the Assembly passed an Act for a Court House to be erected thereon in 1722. Many persons were summoned to Court on Phelps Point soon after this date.

A Council was held at the house of Honorable Edward Hyde, Governor, and Captain General, June 2, 1712, in Chowan County. Governor Hyde died September 8, 1712, of a violent fever. His death left the colony in a deplorable condition at a time when they were facing a barbarous enemy, confronted with a scarcity of provisions, and worst of all a divided people. A great misfortune had befallen them, with no strong hand to lead through the troubled waters.

September 12, 1712, Edward Wilson "Dead without a will," his wife, Sarah, and daughter, Elizabeth Wiatt, nearest of kin with Daniel Jones (who had married another daughter), Executors.

For a period of nine years no precinct Court records are to be found while the precinct was readjusting its broken order into some form of stability, after recent disorders. The house of Mrs. Elizabeth French was honored by the sitting of this Court, as John Hecklefield had passed to his great reward, and her home became the regular meeting place for several years. She may have been the widow of John Hecklefield, but if so this made her fourth marriage.

The Minute books and loose papers give ample proof that a well organized ferry was in use between two points of land called Phelps Point, and Newbys Point before 1735. On Newbys Point Nathan Newby supervised the "setting over" of persons who wished to cross the River and in like manner Jonathan Phelps dispensed the same act of courtesy, both being paid a stipend by the county for their services. The town of Hertford was laid out on land sold to the county by Jonathan Phelps in 1749, which by Act of Assembly had been authorized to be called

Hertford, having as Directors of said town John Harvey, John Clayton and Nathan Newby. Jonathan Phelps had died before this date, and his son Benjamin now had charge of the "Ferry." Nathan Newby lived at "Bear Garden on the opposite side from Hertford, and here it was that Gideon Newby in 1784 made a deed for land (75 acres) Nigh the Float Bridge Road" showing that a float bridge was in use across Perquimans River at that date.

By Act of Assembly October, 1739, a tax of 2 shillings 6 pence was levied upon each "Tythable for the purpose of building a Publick Goal" and Nathan Newby was ordered to make a "Good sufficient double Door to the Prison of Oak Planks and provide a Good Lock to be fixed in the Middle of the Door with a Good Bolt" April, 1754, and John Weeks was appointed "Keeper of the Common Goal on November 12, 1760.

Zachariah Chancey made a charge against Gabriel Newby of Perquimans in Court August 6, 1735, his petition setting forth; that said Newby had used "wicked Boastful Malitious Scanderlous and Oprobius English words" against said Chancey thereby causing him great unrest, and that he felt himself to be "in danger of much harm of his good name and Office, praying the Court to administer Punishment either Corporal or Pecuniary" that he be hereafter deterred from like libelious words.

Another Act of Assembly provided that each person in Perquimans Precinct should be taxed for the "'Building of a publick warehouse as by Law Directed" of the following dimensions: 12 feet high, 18 feet wide, 25 feet long, and Macrora Scarbrough and Nathaniel Caruthers were appointed to "Manage" and agree with proper persons to build said warehouse as soon as possible.

Nathan Newby (2) was deceased on October 18, 1762, when Seth Sumner was chosen in his place as one of the Directors of the town of Hertford.

An Act of Assembly July, 1755, for "Establishing a Ferry from Newbys Point to Phelps Point Whereon the Courthouse Now Stands on Perquimans River" makes plain the fact that the Court had moved from Little River to Hertford some time before this date, in fact no Court had convened in a private dwelling since the one held in the house of Mrs. Elizabeth French in 1721.

Jonathan Phelps and Nathan Newby were each allowed by the county £4 per annum for "Setting over ferry free Inhabitants of this county at Court times Elections Members of Assembly, Vestrymen and Musters in said county." Jonathan Phelps was granted "Lycences to keep an Ordinary at his Now Dwelling house on Phelps Point on same date."

Nathan Newby (2) was ordered by the Court to "Erect and Compleat a warehouse on the Courthouse Lot for Inspection of Tobacco on

Phelps Point" the dimensions of same to be as follows: "30 feet long, 20 feet wide with 7½ pitcht, a Squair Roof weather boarded with half Inch plank well Nailed with tenpenny Nails, well Shingled with hart Sypress Shingles two feet long Nailed with 8 penny Nails to be Completed by November 1, 17—" for which he received £37. William Skinner and James Sitterson were appointed Inspectors of tobacco. John Harvey and Joseph White were ordered to "Supply Steel yards and other Necessary Materials for said Inspectors." (Minute book, Perquimans County, 1755.)

A motion was made by Richard Cheston in Court July 3, 1740, for laying out a road from Newbys Point to the main road leading to Morgans. Granted.

This road appears to be the same which now runs from the Causeway to Winfall. Zachariah Nixon, Richard Cheston and James Morgan, Senior, were appointed to lay off the road. On the same date Mary Newby, widow, petitioned the court that her "Tithables be taken off the main road to labour on the ferry road, it being more Convenient to me than the main road and I can better tend the ferry if any person Comes to be Set over my lands being on that road Can Set them over so shall get no Blame." (Petition granted.) Mary Newby (nee Toms, wife of Nathan first) was required to give bond after the death of her husband in 1735 for the maintenance of the ferry between her Point and where the ferry landed on the Phelps Point side. She exhibited her husbands will in Court, July, 1735. Soon after his death she married Samuel Moore. Her son, Nathan (2), continued to operate the ferry, which was later cared for by Samuel Pretlow who married his widow. Jonathan Phelps, who had charge of the ferry on the Hertford side, died before January, 1769, when Francis Nixon in behalf of Benjamin Phelps, his son, petitioned the Court showing that about January 1, 1767, he had rented the ferry and ferry house in the town of Hertford and by Order of Court for six years on condition that the highest bidder should pay the rent yearly which had been bid off to Hatten Williams in behalf of William Newbold, now in possession, who failed to pay the rent, and said Nixon now prayed for the use of said premises for four years. This Francis Nixon had married the widow of Nathan Newby (2). She being Kesiah Pierce, daughter of Thomas, and having for her third husband Samuel Pretlow. Dorothy Phelps (nee Jordan daughter of Matthew Jordan of Isle of Wight County, Virginia), wife of Jonathan had by him son, Benjamin, and a daughter, Dorothy. The widow of Jonathan Phelps married second John Skinner, and he is found at a later date keeping the ferry.

A petition was brought in Court by Evan Skinner (no date) praying for leave to build a "House of Entertainment on the Lott and a half of ground Laid out for Publick Buildings, as are convenient and Necessary for Man or Horse," which was granted. The location of this house is uncertain.

Thomas Nicholson, being guardian for Joseph McAdams, prayed the Court for an Order to "run a ferry over to Nixonton which might prove of great ease to the publick," and also petitioned the Court "that said Orphans' slaves be exempt from working on the publick road rather putting their labor on the road" that leads to Nags Head Chappel. (No date.) The "Inhabitants of Old Neck complained that they were at great hardship for want of a road, and prayed the Court to have one cleared from Francis Toms Bridge to the mouth of Suttons Creek." The following persons were assigned to keep the road in order: Richard Sanders, Aaron Albertson, Joseph Ratcliff, Samuel Parks, Christopher Sutton, Thos. Pierce, and Joseph Newby. The records mention a "Landing" at the mouth of Suttons Creek on the south side, and it is possible that the road here spoken of is the same still traceable through the woods past the Martin Towe home straight to the Creek. The road is now impassable.

The "Inhabitants on the North side of Orepeak Swamp" prayed the Court for a road to be cleared "at the path Now going over the Swamp to the County line by James Sumners into the main road" which was granted.

Benjamin Phelps gave bond July 20, 1774 "to keep an Ordinary (Lodging house) at his now dwelling house" and pledged himself to "Constantly Provide good wholesome Cleanly Lodging and Dyet for Travellers and Stable foder and corn for horses," for the term of one year.

Petitioners: Joseph Robinson, Thomas Newby, Nathan Newby, Cornelius Moore, John Murdaugh, Francis Newby, Merchants and traders from Perquimans to the Colony of Virginia, Sheweth: that Moses Eason, a planter obtained an order of Court for turning up the road below the Mill dam, over Bassetts Swamp on the main road leading to Virginia, claiming it would shorten the way, and said petitioners find it is at least a mile and a half further, and before the winter will be impassable, prays for an order for the road to have its former position. July, 1760. This road passed through what is now Gates County and may have been the same route taken by the present road called "the Virginia Highway."

The Kings Quit Rents were paid at Deep Creek and Charles Denman was treasurer of Perquimans precinct. Macrora Scarbrough, one-time treasurer, was accused of being "a high criminal" by a complaint laid

EARLY INHABITANTS 21

before the Assembly, 1744. James Castellaw preferred the charge and the next day Scarbrough appeared in Court and resigned.

A petition from citizens of Perquimans brought before the Assembly, 1756, praying the body to lay off 100 acres on Phelps Point for a town and town common, but the town does not appear to have been really incorporated until 1759. The Point boasted a Court House long before this date which seems to have stood on the point where the warehouse was built, but no positive proof can be found to substantiate the fact. It is claimed by old citizens that in their memory a deep depression like a large ditch came up from the River as far as the business section of the town, and that a wharf built at the end of Grubb street brought and carried the commerce to and from outside cities. If this be true the "warehouse" above mentioned may very well have been located on the River back of the present Court House and still have been on the Court House lot, which public ground was not at so long a period of time ago much larger than it is at the present time, embracing all the land from the corner of Grubb Street to the corner where Blanchards store now stands. The County gradually sold off lots of the public ground, and streets and sidewalks took up more until the Court House Green became a square, surrounded by business structures as at present.

Public warehouses doing business in Perquimans in 1764 appear to have been at Cypress Bridge, Hertford, Sanders Landing, John Barrows, Yeopin Creek, Seth Sumners, Little River Bridge, Judge Barclifts (Durants Neck), and Joseph Suttons, the last at the mouth of Suttons Creek.

Col. John Harvey commanded the Militia in 1776. Rev. Charles Pettigrew writing to the Home Mission Board in England, said he was taken into Perquimans and officiated in Berkeley Parish where there were five Chapels, at which he preached and was paid by voluntary contribution. Miles Harvey was appointed Colonel of Militia by the September Congress, 1775; William Skinner, Lieutenant Colonel; Thomas Harvey and Richard Clayton, Majors. Perquimans County raised a Company of Minute Men in the Revolutionary War.

This county was a stronghold of Quakers, and was one of the four which was divided in 1672, becoming at that date Perquimans Precinct. In April, 1776, Benjamin Harvey, Junior, and Edmund Blount were appointed to gather all arms to be found in the county for the use of troops, fifty of which were sent under guard, commanded by Captain William Moore to the defense of Wilmington. John Harvey was Speaker of the Provincial Congress at New Bern, 1774, 1775, 1776. Other members from Perquimans: Andrew Knox, Thomas Harvey, John Whedbee, Junior, Joseph Jones, Miles Harvey, Benjamin Harvey, William

Skinner, Charles Blount, Charles Moore, William Hooper. Councilors: 1776-1868, John Skinner, Henry Skinner; State Treasurer, William Skinner; Superior State Judge Jonathan B. Albertson; State Senator, 1777, William Skinner; Representatives, Benjamin Harvey, John Harvey; Members of Constitutional Convention, 1788-1875, Samuel Johnson, William Skinner, Joshua Skinner, Thomas Harvey, John Skinner, Joseph Harvey, Benjamin Perry, Ashbury Sutton, Jonathan H. Jacocks. Members of the Assembly: Joseph Jessop, Thomas Speight, Charles Denman, Samuel Phelps, Macrora Scarbrough, Richard Skinner, Marmaduke Norfleet (He lived in that part of Perquimans cut off into Gates), Zebulon Clayton, Richard Sanderson, Joshua Long, Thomas Weeks, Joseph Sutton, James Sumner, Nathaniel Caruthers, William Wiatt, Tully Williams, George Durant, Luke Sumner, John Harvey, Benjamin Harvy, Francis Brown, Thomas Bonner, William Mackey, Charles Blount, Seth Sumner, Andrew Knox, John Skinner, Nathaniel Williams, John Whedbee. Before 1740.

The first Tax list found in Perquimans was one taken by Edward Hall in 1729. This list is interesting from the fact that it mentions the acreage of each person named on the list. They are given in rotation as follows: Jeremiah Sutton with 50 acres; John Leary, 100 acres; Edward Hall, Jr., ——; Nathan Long, 150 acres; Zebulon Pratt, 46 acres; John Smith, 75 acres; Ann Wilson, 100 acres; Robert Roe, 50 acres; Elisha Stone, ——; William Arkill, 167 acres; Thos. Thatch, 96 acres; Zebulon Calleway, 50 acres; Joseph Barrow, 300 acres; Luke White, 50 acres; Spencer Thach, 100 acres; Andrew Donaldson, 175 acres; John Wyatt, ——; Mary Whidbee, 66½ acres; William Clemons, 240 acres; Benjamin Sanders, 1019 acres; William Creecy, 250 acres; William Arrington, 160 acres; John Barrow, 200 acres; Nathan Skinner, 55 acres; Thos. Simmons, 130 acres; William Stepney, 350 acres; John Sanders, 162 acres; Frederick Luten, 223½ acres; Willis Butler, 140 acres; Richard Cale, 140 acres; Bailey Forbes, 399 acres; Lemuel Forbes, ——; Thomas Harmon, 209 acres; Leven Thach, 72½ acres; John Johnson, 50 acres; John Nixon, 236 acres; Jesse Bunch, 50 acres, Malachi Deal, ——; James Brinkley, 507 acres; Levy Creecy, 231½ acres; William Mullen, 50 acres; James Bush, 50 acres; Nathaniel Bratton, 152 acres; Francis Sutton, 50 acres; Leven Scot, 100 acres; William Long, 466 acres; Lemuel Long, 50 acres; Richard Hatfield, 207 acres; Jeremiah Doe, ——; William Jones, Jr., 113½ acres; Thos. Long, 103½ acres; Reuben Long, 143 acres; Joseph Thach, 100 acres; John Collins, 120 acres; Christopher Collins, 104 acres; Joseph Mathias, 125 acres; Isacher Branch, 50 acres; William Branch, 156½ acres; Benjamin Bratton, 210 acres; John Lumsford, 100 acres; Henry Hall, 125 acres; John Wingate, ——; Richard

Skinner, 492½ acres; Thos. Stacey, 50 acres; Thos. Creecy, 337 acres; Eri Barrow, 200 acres and six negroes; Edward Wingate, 50 acres; Job Miller, 260 acres; William Jones Joiner, Thos. Whedbee, 133 acres; Frederick Halsey, 100 acres; William Standin, 286 acres; Joseph Norcom, 322 acres; Joseph Harvey, 297 acres; Peleg Lawton, 200 acres; Burton (?) Harvey, 500 acres; Robert Harvey, 300 acres; William Jones, Sr., 130 acres; Ezekeil Arrenton, 170 acres; Stephen Skinner, 15 acres; Isaac White, 133½ acres, Charles W. Miller, ———; Delight Nixon, 416 acres; William Weston, 50 acres; Arodi Barrow, 25 acres; James White, 150 acres; Benjamin Smith, 139 acres; Jeremiah Collins, 100 acres; Ann Skinner, 200 acres; Gray Spruel, 226 acres; James McClenny, 50 acres; Mary Pratt, 33½ acres; William White, 477 acres; Sarah White, 800 acres; Thos. Parramore, 100 acres; Richard Hatfield, 69½ acres; John Skinner, 850 acres; Mary Harvey, 800 acres; Joshua Skinner, 550 acres; Jonathan Pearson, 52 acres; Thomas Harvey, Esquire, 379 acres and 18 town lots, 15 blacks, Thomas Harvey, 588 acres; Benjamin Harvey, 700 acres; (12 blacks each); Joseph Gilbert, 100 acres; Sarah Skillings, 2 town lots and two blacks; Charles Moore, Jr., 242 acres and six blacks; Samuel Penrice, ———; Joshua Long, 621½ acres, Charles Pettigrew, 750 acres and ten blacks; William Skinner, 851½ acres; Thos. Jones Estate, 400 acres.

A list of house-holders as taken by John Perry, 1744: Francis Jones, Ralph Fletcher, Zachariah Nixon, Samuel Moore, Thomas Jessop, Thomas Pierce, Joseph Ratclift, Aaron Albertson, Richard Sanders, John Anderson, Thomas Bateman, Arthur Albertson, Josiah Boswell, Mary Newby, Moses Elliott, John Stone, Thomas Winslow, Jr., John Mardlen, Abraham Elliott, Roger Kennion (Kenyon), Joseph Elliott, John Henby, Joseph Newby, Thomas Elliott, Ezekiell Maudlen, Sr., John Lacey, Joseph and James Henby, Edward Maudlen, Robert Bogue, John Morgan, Jobe Hendrickson, John Byrom, John Gyor, Arthur Croxton, Rachell Peirson, Thos. Bagley, William Bogue, John More, Josioue Bugue, Moses Wood, Thomas Hollowell, Peter Peirson, Joseph Mayow, John Roberson, Joseph Winslow, Thomas Winslow, Sr., Thomas White, Truman Moore, John Wilson, William White, Richard Rainer, John Griffin, Francis Jones, John Hutson, Evan Jones, Timothy Winslow, Jacob Perry, John Winslow, Sr., Jacob Elliott, John White, John Lilly, Benjamin Perry, Phillip Perry, John Middleton, James Field, John Hollowell, William Hollowell.

List of Taxables taken by Thomas Weeks, J.P., 1742: Robert Cock, George Gording, and sons, William and Nathaniel, Jeremiah Hendrick, Joseph Robinson, Thos. Knoles, Samuel Moore, Francis Toms, John Morris, John Guyer, Mary Newby, widow, and son, Thomas, Ezekiel

Maudlin, Jane Morgan, widow, John Henby and son, Silvanus, Arthur Albertson, John Lacey, James Henby, Jr., Edward Maudlin, and sons, William and Ezekiel, Thos. Jessop, Jesse Newby, Thos. Barclift, John Mann, John Barclift, Sr., and son, John, Solomon Hendrick, David Huffton, Michael Murphy, Thos. Montague, Josiah Raper, Benjamin Monday, and son, Thomas, Thos. Stafford, William Tomblin, Margaret Stanton, and sons, Moses and Aaron Jackson, Charles Overman, John Robinson, William Hasket, Nathaniel Welch, Isaac Hendrick, William Colson, Phineas Nixon, John Winslow, William Knoles, Thos. Godfrey and son, Thomas, Samuel Right (Wright) William Arnold, Jno. Nixon, Jno. Moore, Thos. Sharbo, Thos. Winslow and son, Job, and six slaves (Thomas Winslow, Senior), Thos. Winslow, Jr., Joseph Ratcliff, Aaron Albertson, Jno. Anderson, Rachel Pearson, widow, and son, Jonathan, John Perrishaw, Josiah Bundy, John Wilson, William Bundy.

As has already been mentioned John Skinner, married Dorothy, widow of Jonathan Phelps, who owned the land at the ferry and operated it as long as he lived. A stipend of £5 s5 p10 was paid to said John Skinner July 18, 1763, by Andrew Knox, Sheriff, of Perquimans for maintenance of the Ferry. "Having attended the ferry Duly for the Year past over Perquimans River at Publick times According to Order of Court." John Skinner and Keziah Newby petitioned the court for their "Sallery."

At a Precinct Court April 18, 1754, Jacob Docton prayed the Court to exempt him from further taxation on account of "mind being impaired." Joshua Hobart did the same thing on account of a broken *Shoulder* April, 1762.

The inhabitants on North East Side of the head of Vossess Creek petitioned the Court same date setting forth that they had "a long bad Road to make and maintain from the county Road by Joseph Outlands up said Creek to a branch of the Creek known by the name of Reedy Branch to be laid off from John Laceys to said Branch and all the inhabitants that are or may Settle within said Boundaries are expected to make and repair said Road, therefore they said petitioners pray to be exempt from Service on any other Road."

No history of Eastern North Carolina could be complete without mentioning the notorious pirate Teach who frequented it is supposed every navigable River that emptied its waters into the Sound. He was an Englishman by birth and first settled in Virginia where he married a lady of quality in Alexandria of said state. He soon after began to show his brutal character and was known to have kicked this sweet lady down the stair of their home when in a white rage. His first unlawful venture proved to be blockade running, a favorite trade with him being bringing in negroes free of duty. When he had worn himself out in these nefarious practices and incensed the Virginia authorities to such a pitch that they were ready to execute him on speedy apprehension, he fled to North Carolina and for a while conducted himself in an exemplary manner even pruning himself before the Church of England as a very pious good fellow, which caused the people of his new home to half way believe he had been much traduced and he made many strong friends in Carolina who were later to repent of the association but could not entirely shake it off from fear. On land he appeared to be like other sea-faring men and he paid religiously the dues that were levied upon him and spent with a free hand among his neighbors and cohorts. But this good behavior vanished as soon as the sails were spread to the breeze, his natural cruelty becoming rampant. Of all sea rovers he was the most brutal, gaining for himself the title of being the "thug of the sea." Perquimans records do not show any sign of his having ever lived or done any trading in the precinct and this county does not lay claim to residence of his or to his having any buried treasure stored away in the soil of Perquimans. It is a fact, however, that two of his sons lived apparently in this county and conveyed property in Perquimans. It is also said that he has descendants still living in the district but the writer does not give much credence to the fact.

Among prominent sons of Perquimans mention must be made of General William Skinner who saved the day at Great Bridge when the Continental troops were so hard pressed by the British. This splendid man served his county as faithfully in peace as he did in war and lies buried on a farm not far from Hertford.

John Harvey, one of the early Provincial Governors, and his no less prominent son, Col. Thomas Harvey, Deputy Governor, are well established in the minds of historians.

Perquimans County has produced many representative men, one of whom was Congressman T. G. Skinner. Another, Mr. Harry Skinner of Greenville, N. C., who has distinguished himself in many fields. Also Judge Harry Whedbee, born in Perquimans, of Greenville, N. C., of whom the county is very proud. Judge Ward is another and he rose from an humble beginning which gives him that much more to be grateful for. In an old house near the Chowan line the mother of Judge Ward first saw the light of day. This house is built of boards over a foot broad and two and one-half inches thick put together without studdings, dovetailed at the corners and has withstood the weather for several generations; a most remarkable piece of workmanship in the way of architecture. There are in Perquimans many other old homes, some of them so far off the beaten path of travel that they are never seen unless they are specially sought. The history of most of these places is shrouded in mystery and no one at the present day can give a detailed account of their age or occupants. In Durants Neck still in a livable condition is standing the old Whedbee home said to have been built in 1722. Another beautiful old home, that of Mr. James P. Whedbee, on the road to New Hope, burned not many years ago, is said to have had the loveliest woodwork on the interior to be found in the county. Just a few years ago the old Wood home near Hertford went up in flames. This house was built by a family of Cannons and there is an old burying ground near by with members of the family sleeping the long sleep.

Too much can not be said for the old County of Perquimans but space forbids enumerating all the virtues of past, present and future possibilities of this land lying between Perquimans and Little Rivers.

Out of the past arise forms long still storking before the present with dignified applause waving unlimited approval toward the growing altitude of the small corner of the earth which they formerly called home. And grateful hearts remember the stark necessity of these tillers of the soil and how they dug out of the Swamps a splendid prosperity; the brawn and sinew of the land her pioneer men, bent with heavy toil, bronzed by the sun, pinched with cold, ravaged by dread malaria, yearning over little ones and sickly wife who helped to bear and share their burdens, carving out of the bare wilderness a home where the future generations might live at ease. Truly may it be said that our forefathers in Perquimans laid the foundations of the progress that followed. Every soul with an ounce of patriotism should take off the hat in lowly reverence by the side of a grave where is silently lying the remains of one of these who labored so long and so well that coming descendents could possess the land in freedom.

Scores of these have vanished from our recollection by reason of their names ceasing to be recorded on the pages of time. Where they went and whence they came is one of the unsolved secrets of the past. Some can be traced to other parts of the world and others dropped out like a pebble dropped into the sea, but they all did their utmost to reclaim an unknown land and make it safe for us. Such names as Clare, Oates, Thigpen, Manwarring, Cheaston, Branch, Peele, Pettiver, Woolard and others too numerous to mention have long ago disappeared from the records. Some of them died out for lack of male issue, and the greater majority migrated south, west and to every part of the then known land. The trend being ever westward carried many to the middle west and not a few went with the gold rush to California in 1849. Sons of Perquimans have taken root in almost every clime, New York having claimed some of the best, with the National Capital a close runner for precedence. The tropics have swallowed up several of the most promising of our sons, and South America has taken toll of a few, in fact every corner of the earth has claimed one or more who have distinguished themselves each in his own way. From sturdy seed has sprung good fruit, and it is a great comfort to know the sons of Perquimans wherever found have done nothing to shame a good mother.

Among those who from the beginning have elected to remain in the county can be cited such names as White, Wilson, Skinner, Whedbee, Blount, Wood, Modlin, Evans, Winslow, Jessop, Cox, Hollowell, Nixon, Toms, Newby, Leigh, Morgan, Smith, and many more whose names were first found on the page of history when Perquimans first opened its doors to settlers. For over two hundred years these people have considered the home land of their forefathers good enough for them, and they continue to bless the old fireside with their presence.

RELIGION AND CHURCHES

As Found Mentioned in County Records and Other Data

The Friends have every right to claim that it was their denomination that first flourished in Perquimans, and the Colonial records are proof of the fact. It may also be a fact that the Church of England here was established simultaneously, but no documentary proofs can be found to establish the claim, and the letters of ministers sent out by the English Church bear out the point, testifying as they do that Friends had four well appointed Churches in Perquimans before a single one of any other denomination was erected. It is claimed that Henry Phillips was the first Quaker to set foot in the precinct, coming from New England in 1665, and it is a well known fact that the first religious service held in Perquimans was that of William Edmundson in the spring of 1672. Tradition coming down through Quaker sources has it that Henry Phillips wept for joy on seeing the Quaker minister, and well he may have, had he realized how strong his society would grow in the new land. Old records show that this "meeting" of Friends was held on the banks of Perquimans River, under several large Cypress trees, two of which are still standing by the side of beautiful Perquimans. Henry Phillips, so the story goes, lived on the "Point." His humble dwelling offered to the great preacher for the service of God being too small to accommodate the crowd of worshipers who came to hear this noted speaker, and some probably coming through curiosity, they gathered in the spring sunshine under the venerable trees to hear him expound the "truth" as he understood it, and many converts were there made. In his Journal Edmundson states that "many received the truth gladly," chief among them being one "Tems" (Toms) who embraced the new religion on the spot and requested them to "meet" at his home the next day, which house is reported to be two miles away across the water. The records of Perquimans show that the lands of Francis Toms here mentioned were on the head of Vosses Creek, somewhere in the vicinity of the present Mount Sinai Church neighborhood, which is about two miles from Hertford and the water they had to cross was none other than Perquimans River, a rather formidable stream to get over in that day. The supposition is plausible that up to that date Francis Toms had not embraced Quakerism, but from that day he became one of the most influential in the county, his son Francis, Junior, following in his footsteps. In fact all the early Tomses were of that belief, and married into families of the same persuasion. Edmundson was followed in the

A. Baptist Church, Hertford, remodeled, which replaced the church built in 1854, an offshoot from Bethel. First trustees: Charles W. Skinner and Richard Felton.
B. Episcopal Church, Hertford. Built 1859. Replaced the old one on the corner of Main and Grubb streets.
C. Methodist Episcopal Church. Built before July 23, 1838, on Lots No. 80 and 82. An offshoot of New Hope in Durant's Neck.
D. Modernized Piney Woods Friends Church, which was in use before the Revolution.

same year by the noted Quaker minister, George Fox, who came in the fall, giving in his Journal a most interesting account of his visit to Perquimans. Four years later Edmundson returned to the precinct and wrote in his Journal afterward that he found "Friends finely settled" in the county, and "things well among them."

From records still extant it seems certain that Little River "meeting" was the earliest to be "set up" in Perquimans, and the Virginia records are authority for the fact that Henry White built the first "Meeting House." He, it appears, was already a resident of Perquimans Precinct as early as 1699, at which time a "meeting" was held at his house, where Quaker marriages were solemnized. Taking into consideration the fact that he lived in that part of Perquimans bordering on Little River, somewhere near the present town of Woodville just across the line from Pasquotank County, makes it all the more evident that the church he built was somewhere in the vicinity of his own home, then too records show that part of Perquimans was the earliest and most thickly settled. Hertford and its environment had not then come into prominence, although there were no doubt settlers in and around the "Point." Deeds in Perquimans are authority for the fact that "Little River Meeting House" stood at the turn of the road going over Weeks Bridge, which is just beyond the village of Woodville, and it is spoken of as being "at the head of Little River" where today a Quaker burying ground can be seen on a small eminence on the right side of the road going toward the old Weeks home across Little River, on the Pasquotank side. A large sycamore tree marks the location and many small grave stones lift their mute testimony for all to see. Here in tranquil peace lie numbers of old residents of Quaker faith, probably in their midst the renowned Herny White, and certainly Joseph Jordan.

Why the Quaker settlers abandoned the Little River neighborhood and finally congregated in the Piney Wood section is one of the unsolved problems of the past, but it is true nevertheless that they did move, in and around Belvidere which has from early times been the stronghold of that faith. At the present date not any or very few live anywhere else in the county, and a large proportion of this once flourishing sect have moved away, some to Baltimore, others to Raldolph County, North Carolina, from which section they went west to Indiana, Illinois, Iowa, and even as far as California. These good people in their new homes have made for themselves a name that makes those remaining in Perquimans proud. Among the families given in this book will be found the names of many who so migrated, who still keep up with the doings in the old State and county. Joseph Jordan, one of that splendid family of Nansemond County, Virginia, came early to Perquimans and lived on Little River, where he taught school in the first place of learning mentioned in the precinct. He was also a Quaker minister, being named in the Quaker Records in Virginia as "that great and worthy man and Minister" according to Lower Monthly Meeting, Nansemond County, Virginia. He was a son of Thomas Jordan, a prominent Quaker of said county and state, and his wife Margaret Brasurre (French Huguenot) who took an active part in the Church and civic activities in Virginia.

Vosses Creek meeting was probably the next to be "set up" and was built on land donated by Francis Toms (second) but the location is not definitely certain, however, as his land can be traced and the location of that is proven, there is not much doubt that this chucrh was built near his home, probably near Boswell Fork. The record of Vosses Creek meeting was carried west by one of the old residents of Perquimans where it reposed for many years, finally being copied by an old gentleman in Richmond, Indiana, who sent the old record back home, but in some way it was lost and no one knows what became of it. As represented to the writer the copy made by the Richmond gentleman is a wonderful piece of recording, and posterity should and will be undyingly grateful to him for his labor in years to come.

Suttons Creek Meeting house stood on ground where Newbolds school house now stands. Just back of it in the woods is the old Quaker burying ground, and Quaker records show that numbers of their dead are buried there, among whom if stones could be found would probably be found Albertsons, Nixons, Townsends, Suttons, Tomses, Hollowells, Newbys, Morrises, Henbys, Moores, Morgans, and many more whose names appear on Suttons Creek Register, who attended and affiliated with the personnel of this particular "meeting."

The location of Wells Meeting house is well authenticated, but the time it was built is not indicated by any record so far found in Perquimans. The place where this old house once stood remains in the memory of some of the oldest citizens of the county, being on Perquimans River across from the old Jessop residence not far from Blanchands Bridge. After a number of years for some unexplained reason the church was moved out on the road across from the Peele place, going towards Belvidere and here it still stands as part of a barn on the property of Mrs. Jack Trueblood who was before her marriage a daughter of Mr. Thomas Jessop. The old structure was for many years used as a school house, called "Jessops Schoolhouse" and here the children of the neighborhood went to study the Blue-back Speller, where formerly their ancestors came to worship God. It is claimed by old residents in Perquimans that there was at one time a "float bridge" across Perquimans River where the old Blanchard place stands, which was later replaced by a ferry. At this time it seems that part of the county was more prosperous than it is at the present day, and Ephrim Blanchard, himself a Quaker, probably lived there and gave the place its name. A store of thriving trade did business at the crossing and Mr. Blanchard accumulated there a handy sum, from which some descendant of his laid by enough to come to the town of Hertford and set up a store, from which has emerged "Blanchard Brother since 1832" still going strong. Mr. Blair who arrived in Carolina January 24, 1704, in an epistle written later mentions the fact, "that the roads were deep and difficult in Perquimans, and that there were seven great Rivers over which no passing was possible with horses, over one of which the Quakers had settled a ferry for their own conveniency and no body but themselves had the privilege of it." From the fact that Wells meeting house stood near this point and further that Quakers were settled on both sides of the river at that date the "ferry" here named was probably the same as that spoken of as being at Blanchards Bridge. Wells was probably a rather weak "meeting" and was absorbed by the stronger sister "Piney Woods" at what date can not be ascertained. As in other sections of the precinct this "Meeting" was kept up and attended by those near by and among those lifting their hearts to God in this sanctuary are to be found the names of Pritlow, Nicholson, Elliott, Lamb, Cannon, Haskit, Saint, Fletcher, Cosand, Draper, Anderson, Copeland, Albertson, Chappel, Sanders, Ratcliff, Munden Jordan, Barrow, Charles, Jessop, Guyer. It may be that this "meeting" was named for Francis Wells, an influential Quaker residing in this neighborhood.

The most staple of them all appears to have been "Piney Woods" which is the only remaining Friends meeting in the county except "Up River" a place of much less importance. This meeting was probably "set up" about the time Wells came into being, and unlike the others has kept its light burning through all the changes that have laid low the others, and up to the present time Belvidere continues to dominate the section in which it is situated. According to old deeds in Perquimans it appears that the town derived its name from an old farm belonging to Ann Scott of Nansemond County, Virginia, who left to her nephew an estate called "Belvidere" which was just across the River from the site of the town, and later became the property of Exum Newby, for whom Newby's Bridge was named. It is thought with good authority that this estate was the same as that now called "the old Lamb place" and it is said that the house thereon was built in 1767. The land of this place is said to have joined the land of Pleasant Winslow, who was the widow of Joseph (2) Winslow, son of Thomas (1) Winslow and wife, Elizabeth Clare.

Among Quakers who were imprisoned for not bearing arms, are found the names of William Bundy, John Pierce, Jonathan Phelps, James Hogg, Samuel Hill, who suffered confinement for six months. 4, 5mo, 1680. The book of suffering would add much to the history of Perquimans, but the writer has not had the good fortune to consult said book for data.

The first Episcopal Church in Perquimans was undoubtedly Nags Head Chapel which has more mention than any other on account of the deeds using it as a boundary for lands in and around its location. Every deed without exception speaks of it as "Old Nags Head Chapple" showing that it was considered "Old" even when the county was young. Mr. William Gordon in writing to the Society for the Propagation of the Gospel, on May 13, 1709, states that "there was in Perquimans at that date a compact little Church which was still unfinished by reason of the death of Major Samuel Swann" who was dead September, 1707. When all facts are reviewed no dubious opinion can arise to question this fact, for Major Swann labored long and dilligently to establish his faith on a firm foundation in Perquimans during his life as a citizen of the colony. The sons of Major Swann probably carried on their father's zealous work after his death but as they later moved from the county to Swann Quarter, Hyde County, their support was withdrawn. This Church was said to have been "beter contrived" than the one in Chowan County of same date, and we feel sure promoted religion "where there was none in the county." In this small house of God worshiped the gentry of Durants Neck. Here came in stately carriages the bewigged gentlemen and the furbelowed and flounced ladies who graced their homes. Outside sat the well trained negro servant to lift down his old-fashioned mistress or do some humble service for his dignified master. From neighboring plantations gathered such men as Richard Sanderson, Charles and Edmund Blount, Thomas Jacocks, Gilbert Leigh, with his young son James (who had not thought of then the beautiful brick house he was to build and give the Neck fame), John Whidby and later his son, Richard, the Stevensons, Durants, Hecklefields, both father and son here raised up thankful hearts for liberty in the new country, Joseph and Christian Reed (brothers), who had married daughters of George Durant (2) grandson of George in all the trappings of fine gentlemen came here to worship, and here Thomas Corprew got his early training in religion, and many others of substance who lived in the Neck, or on the outer fringe of its boundary. Old citizens are agreed on the fact that Nags Head Chapel stood on ground which was conveyed by Mr. James P. Whedbee to the Methodists, and they claim the site is identical with the one where now stands New Hope Methodist Church, and it is

RELIGION AND CHURCHES   33

further stated that the Methodist Church arose on the foundations of the old Chapel. Could it be possible that this gave to the town its name? A new hope on an old foundation, a new church on crumbling walls, a new beginning out of past failure. Why Nags Head Chapel was abandoned no one knows but it may be that this church suffered the same fate of others, notably in Virginia, being left to fall into decay after the Revolutionary War. When Hertford became a town many old residents of Durants Neck flocked to the new center where educational facilities were better and others moved out of the county, thereby Nags Head Chapel lost its strongest supporters, and some others went over to the newer religion then introduced and joined either the Methodist or Baptist churches. It is a very comforting thought, however, that the sacred place is still used for a sacred purpose, and that prayer still ascends as of old from the same spot.

Land was donated by Elizabeth Mathias, daughter of Jeremiah Pratt, one-half acre for the "worship of God after the order of The Church of England" which was called Yeopim Chapel. From the deed giving this site and other records in Perquimans it is learned that the present Baptist Church at Bethel in said county occupies the exact site of old Yeopim Chapel. That also fell into disuse after the Revolution and was probably like Nags Head abandoned, when the Baptists acquired the property. Yeopim supplied the need of a place for calling on the Lord in all time of need, mothers came with infants to be baptized, the young to be wedded and many a sad funeral procession wended its way from the doors of this Chapel to the last resting place. Here worshiped dwellers in historic Harveys Neck. Statesmen and Councilors sat with silent attention riveted on the face of the Rev. Daniel Earl who served in Perquimans as well as in Chowan, while mothers nodded their disapproving heads at some wayward child and coaxed them into good behavior during the long and tedious service.

Berkeley Parish was created in 1715, and embraced every part of the present county and part of what is now Gates County extending as far north as the Virginia line.

An Act of Assembly of 1669 for the promotion of morality authorized the civil officers of each precinct to perform marriages as no ordained ministers were at that time living in Carolina. In a letter written by Governor Walker to the Bishop of London, October 21, 1703, he says in part, "we have been settled here near fifty years and for the most part of twenty-one years without priest or altar, for which cause the Quakers continued to grow very numerous." In 1709 they constituted one-tenth of the population in Carolina. Mr. William Gordon, another Episcopal minister sent out as a missionary by the English Church in making his report to the home station bewailed the fact that the Quakers were "constant opposers of the Church of England" which can be easily accounted for by their own persecution in other parts of the country before coming to Perquimans and as they had become well rooted in Perquimans before the church began to really assert herself, it was but natural that they should not be very hospitable to a doctrine which they had learned by ill usage to distrust.

All persons by Act of Assembly were charged to enter the births, deaths and marriages of their families in the county register kept for the express benefit of such unregistered persons and a fine was imposed upon such careless residents as failed to comply with the regulations laid down.

Henderson Walker wrote to the Bishop of London April 24, 1703, deploring the fact that "Mr Brett after a half year of modest manner had broken out in a way shameful to all of the faith, which gave the dissenters much to charge us with." He also stated that one church had been built and another was in course of construction, Francis Nicholson of Virginia having contributed to the building of same £10 to each. Mr. Blair who came to Carolina in January, 1704, said "'he married no one that seeming to be the perquisite of the Magistrate." There were in Carolina at this date three Glebes and a fund of £30 per annum was appropriated by the Assembly for the support of a minister.

The church people were few in number but were said to be of the "better sort." The ministers complained that the people were "planted only on the Rivers" and that it took the greater part of twelve weeks to make the rounds of any minister's parish. Far the greater inhabitants were dissenters and, according to all reports, lived in great peace, being willing to give to even the Church of England some support. Carolina gave to every man the freedom of religious belief, under the great Charter given the Earl of Clarendon March 24, 1663, when toleration and indulgence to all Christians in the free exercise of their opinions were made into one clause of the Constitution, and no person could be excluded from the Assembly on account of his faith.

The Rev. Richard Marsden, on his way to South Carolina, passed through the province of North Carolina, and on September 25, 1708, administered the "Holy Supper on Trinity Sunday for the first time in Carolina, when forty five persons were baptized." Soon after this (1709) the records show there were twelve vestrymen in Perquimans but, according to Rev. William Gordon, "very ignorant loose in life and unconcerned about religion and their ill example caused many to stray from the mother Church" and become affiliated with the Friends who appear to be more circumspect. The country was described to be at that date "wild and imperfect in circumstances with here and there a gentleman of sunstance" whose methods and managing qualities lifted them far above the ordinary settler.

The first school mentioned is that established at Sarum under the management of Mr. Mashburn July, 1712, which school Perquimans can not rightfully lay any claim to, it being in Chowan County, but no doubt the youth of the precinct sought knowledge there under the tutelage of said Mashburn. Sarum is now in Gates County since the division in 1779.

Vestrymen as appointed by Act of Assembly in 1715 were as follows: Francis Foster, Maurice Moore, John Hecklefield, Thomas Hardy, Richard Sanderson, James Minge, Samuel Phelps, Rich. Whedbee, William Kitching (Kitchin) and John Stepney. Three of these were residents of Durants Neck, probably affiliated with "Old Nags Head Chapel" and the others with the exception of Maurice Moore were all land owners and members of the little "Chapel" called Yeopim. William Kitchin lived in what is now Gates County, his land being well up in said county near the Virginia line. The Tithables taken in 1739 numbered 755. Church wardens in Perquimans at different periods of time were found in the loose papers, and a list as far as resurrected shows that Benjamin Perry and Nathaniel Caruthers had that honor, serving January 20, 1741, for what length of time the record did not specify, most probably for six years as they were followed by Thomas Weeks and John Harvey in April, 1747, and they in like manner were superseded by Jesse Eason; Thomas Weeks continuing to serve, November 2, 1753. Several vestry meetings are recorded on the deed books of Perquimans, giving the then Vestrymen. It seems a little strange to see the name of Benjamin Perry as one of the Church Wardens from the fact that that family adhered strongly to the Quaker faith. This shows that the Church augmented its ranks from the Friends equally as often as the Friends from other denominations. Friends were extremely strict and they churched their men and women for every trivial offense and no doubt this habit drove out some of rebellious nature. If a man happened to be of a convivial nature and attended a dance or took one drink too much he had to give reason why to the next Friends monthly meeting and women also came in for their share of chastisement by being called before the woman's monthly meeting where she was required to give a strict account of her shortcomings. At a day like that when all men were breaking away from restraint of every kind, it is not to be supposed that free thinkers would long submit to punishment submissively when an outlet stood right at the door.

Tradition gives the fact that the first Episcopal Church in Hertford at one time stood on the corner diagonally across from the Post Office, where a funeral parlor and Service Station now stand. This church so it is claimed, stood on ground now in the street, and the cemetery came across the street and extended into the yards of several residents. When the church occupied this location the records do not mention, but there must be truth in the old story for not many years ago while having a flower pit dug a human skull was unearthed in the back yard of Mrs. G. D. Newby who owned the home directly in front of the supposed location of the old church, and in the yard next door no depth can be penetrated without digging up bricks. Two large stones, one on each side of the sidewalk, mark the spot where it is claimed an Indian chief lies buried, and they have been ever thus without molestation as long as the memory of man can reach. It has been suggested by some imaginarily inclined that this might be the resting place of Kilcoconen, King of Yeopim Indians, who made the deed to George Durant but of course it can not be verified. Since he was a proven friend to the whites in the colony it would not be such a bad guess that they in return wished to repay him for his loyalty and naturally in first line of endeavor along that line would want to make a Christian of him. If that effort had proved to be a success and he had embraced Christianity as many did, the church people would have gone further and honored him by having his remains given a Christian burial in consecrated ground. Furthermore as the family of George Durant were Episcopalians they would most surely wish to put away this chief in their own churchyard, seeing that he had so abundantly favored their father. The present Episcopal Church was built in 1855, Benjamin Skinner making a deed for land for that purpose in that year and the Rev. Mr. Snowden offered his services to the Church Wardens of Holy Trinity parish for the stipend of $300 per annum, which was accepted.

The Baptist Church at Bethel is the oldest church now in use in Perquimans, being built about 1806. One of the early deacons of this church was Joshua Skinner who had come up in a Quaker family and he married Martha Ann Blount who was raised an Episcopalian so they both compromised by becoming Baptists. He with his numerous family sleeps the sleep that knows no waking close beside Bethel Church. Except for the deed conveying land for the church to the trustees by William Creecy and the fact that Martin Ross was the first preacher who officiated in the new church we have no knowledge of when the church was really built. A celebration was held here in 1906 commemorating the founding of Bethel Church and it is known that such men as Charles Skinner, Job Pettijohn and the family of Richard Felton were instrumental in bringing about a building for the worship of God according to the doctrine of the Baptist faith at this spot. The Church

RELIGION AND CHURCHES

stood in a community of strong Baptist persuasion and still makes its appeal to the brethren congregated about. This church was built on land given by Elizabeth Mathias, nee Pratt, daughter of Jeremiah Pratt, and wife of John Mathias, the deed bearing date of July 17, 1732, and reads in part "To the Parish of Perquimans ½ acre square of land for the Worship called the Church of England by Yawpim Creek bridge where a Chapple is now built, land formerly belonging to my father, Jeremiah Pratt." The Chapel was still standing and in use for said "worship" in 1745. Yeopim Chapel was named as a boundary many times for land lying in that neighborhood. The bridge here mentioned probably fell into decay or was replaced by a new and modern one as the roads grew to be improved and new ones were constantly being made. Probably Yeopim Chapel continued to do its work of service for the good to the surrounding country until the Revolutionary War when the Church of England became taboo. Having done the work appointed for it to do the little structure either became too small or the congregation moved away or changed with the times whichever was the case, in some way, the land fell into the hands of private citizens who sold it to the trustees for the erection of Bethel Church in 1806.

William Creecy of Perquimans conveyed to Joshua Skinner of Perquimans and Job Pettyjohn of Chowan, Deacons of the Baptist Church, "out of Respect goodwill and affection which he hath toward the Baptist Society whereof Martin Ross, Joshua Skinner and said Pettyjohn are members do grant to them land called Creecy's Mill tract formerly called Yoppim Chapel" for the use of a church called Bethel. Martin Ross, first minister so far as records prove, made his home on a farm near Hertford now owned by Mr. John O. White, a prosperous farmer, and he, with his good wife, lie buried on the land not far from Mr. White's house.

The Methodist Church in Hertford came into being about 1838 and records are extant showing the Hertford Baptist Church was of much later date than Bethel and was a child of Bethel. It was built in 1854.

RECORDS OF DEEDS

ABSTRACTS COMPILED FROM BOOKS IN THE COUNTY REGISTER'S OFFICE

DEED BOOK A

No. 1. Albemarle Co of Berkley. John Chesson within said Co, to William Wilkson. 100a on the Sound, adj Thomas Hart, for 10,000 Lbs of Tobacco. June 10, 1681. Test' John Lewis, Jonathan Ashford.

No. 2. Robert Marlow, "Warrants, & makes good the above Sale of Land unto William Wilkerson when he shall come of age." Jan 12, 1681. Test' Jonathan Ashford, Robert Marlow.

No. 3. Albemarle. William Wilkerson, "Warrents above sale of Land" unto Cornelius Lerre (Leary). July 15, 1682. Test' Francis Hartley, Peter Simpson, Emanuel Alberry.

No. 4. April 7, 1686. Henderson Walker (Clerk of Albemarle Co) & John Philpots of Yeopim, to Alexander Moore, "Land in Yeopim," formerly belonging to James Long. Test' Lawrence Gonsolvo, Charles Prows.

No. 5. July 2, 1686. Thomas Harvey of Perq Pre'ct, Co of Albemarle, Esq' & Joanna his wife, to Wm Hughes of afore' 700a "a Neck of Land" adj Land of Richard Bentley. Test' Charles Jones, Richard Bentley, Henderson Walker.

No. 6. Albemarle Co. June 12, 1686. Valentine Barton of Yeopim River, Planter- sold Land on Yeopim River.

No. 7. John Hipkins, joint deed with Valentine Barton. Oct. 7, 1686. Test' John Philpots, Richard Fountain.

"Personally there appeared before me one George Foredice Exor of the last will, & test' of Valentine Barton, & Ack' said bill of Sale." Edward Mayo, Clk.

No. 8. Feb. 2, 1688. Wm Stephens of Perq, planter- to Stephen Manwaring of same, Carpenter—a plan' on West-side of Perishos Creek," with Entry, & right of said Stephens, & Joanna his wife," for 650 lbs of Merchantable Tobacco. His trusty friend Alexander Lillington, of Yeopim Gent- to present this Deed in Court. Test' Wm Stewart, Wm Chapman. Edward Mayo, Reg'r.

No. 9. Nov. 15, 1684. Thomas Atoway of Albemarle, unto William Chapman, "Plan' on the North-side of Perq River. 150a, with Labour done upon it." Test' Henderson Walker, Nicholas Cropp.

No. 10. William Chapman, unto Roger White, Land. Oct. 2, 1685. Test' Thos Godrom (probably Gordon) Ed Norwood.

No. 11. Joane White assigns "Right, of Bill of Sale," to John Hallum. Dec. 1, 1686. Test' Sam'l Pricklove, Charles Jones.

No. 12. Albemarle. Richard Bentley, of Perq Pre'ct, & Co afore' Lawyer— for £10 pd by Richard Williams, of said Co, Mill Wright—"doth sell plan' on Deep Creek, where Richard Bentley now lives." Dec. 1, 1686. Test' Thomas Harvey, Henderson Walker. Henderson Walker Clk.

No. 13. John Lilly of Perq, in Co of Albemarle, Province of N. C. planter— for 1940 lbs of Pork pd by Wm. Foster of Afore' Planter—"do sell my plan'

150a on North-side of the mouth of Perq River." Jan. 31, 1682. Test' Samuel Woodrove, Alex Speed, John Thurstone.

No. 14. William Foster, "do give unto my son Francis Foster, within mentioned title, to him, & his heirs forever." Dec. 24, 1683.

Dec 2, 1686. Wm Foster, & Dianah his wife, sold Land unto Jonathan Bateman. Test' Wm Wilkinson, Alex Lillington, Edward Mayo.

No. 15. Wm Morrison, assigned all right, of a Plan' unto "Right Hon'ble Seth Sothel Esq, Gov of this Province" Nov 17, 1696.

No. 16. Timothy Burton, of the City of London, "doth sell 3333a. English Measure, late Mr George Catchmaids, in poss' of Timothy Biggs, & Mary his wife, granted by the Lords Pro' to sd Mary, on North side of Roanoke Sound, & Katherine River, now called Little River," con' 5 shillings. Test' Obadiah Kendall, Edward Loe, Sam Slight, Edward Smith, Wm Collings.

No. 17. Timothy Burton, to Seth Sothel of Albemarle Co, for £50 sold 3333a on North side of Roanoke Sound (Albemarle Sound), & westerly side of Katherines River, which was grt to Mary Biggs by the Lords Pro'. April 26, 1686. Test' Jonathan Kendall, Obadiah Kendall, Edward Lee, Sam Slight, Edward Smith, Wm Collins.

No. 18. John Kellum, & Prudence his wife, for "5 shillings, & one Bay Mare," pd by Richard Williamson of same, Carpenter-sold plantation at the upper end of Tylers Creek. Dec 2, 1686. Test' Henderson Walker, John Hurt.

No. 19. Charles Prows of Pasquotank, planter-Ex of the last will of Ann Prows, late of sd precinct, widow; relict of Henry Prows Dec'd, sold unto Francis Toms of Perq 260a, adj Wm Vosses, & Wm Charles. June 11, 1683. Test' Henderson Walker, Josiah Slocum, Wm Charles.

No. 20. Grant from Lords Pro' unto Francis Toms, planter-478a on West side of Perq River, adj Robert Wilson, "due sd Toms for Trans' of eleven persons into the Country." Feb 6, 1687. Seth Sothel Gov, & Comd-in-Chief. Councillors; Thomas Miller, Anthony Slocum, James Blount, Thomas Harvey.

No. 21. Wm Charles of Yeopim, "in con' of a plan' where I now live, 300a up Perq River, now in poss' of my brother Daniel (formerly John Lacys) delivered to us by our father-in-law Francis Toms, do assign to sd Francis 140a on East side of Perq River." April 11, 1687. Test' John Stepney, Anthony Heathcott, Edward Mayo Sen'r.

No. 22. Francis Toms of Perq River, in con' of a plan' on East side of sd River delivered to me by Wm Charles, do covey to sd Daniel, & Samuel Charles, Brother of sd William, 300a on West side of Perq River, "taken out of my Dividend of 580a," adj land of Robert Wilson. Mar 26, 1687. Test' John Stepney, Anthony Heathcoatt. Edward Mayo Sec'r.

No. 23. June 6, 1683. Francis Toms, with consent of Abigail my wife, (John Lacy Dec'd, her former husband) do give right of land at the head of Yeopim Creek, 300a called "John Lacys Plantation" unto William Charles. Test' Joseph Goodman, Samuel Pricklove.

No. 24. William Vose of Perq River, planter-sold to Thomas Kent of Albemarle Co, parcel of land in Perquimans, on East side of the River, adj William Charles. 100a by an assignment of a Pattent from Wm West. Mar

11, 1668. Test' Herman ———wick, Arnold White. Thomas Harris Clk Court.

No. 25. Thomas Kent of Perq, Planter—"do assign all right to Land mentioned in Bill of Sale unto Ralph Fletcher." June 27, 1672. Test' Samuel Pricklove. Thomas Harris Clerk Court.

No. 26. Samuel Pricklove of Perq River, Planter—in con' of £45 pd by John Durant of same, sold a patent of land given from Thomas Lepper to John Davis, from him to sd Durant, & from him to myself. April 25, 1687. Test' Wm Chapman, Richard Eivens.

No. 27. Wm Earl of Craven, one of the Lords Pro' grant unto Josiah Fendall, 100a in Perq Precinct, on N. Side of Albemarle River, "At Mr George Durants house," under Seal of the Co of Albemarle, 3d of May 1684. Seth Sothel Gov. Councellors; Anthony Slocum, Thomas Harvey, James Blount.

No. 28. Lords Pro' unto Josiah Fendall 100a on N. side of Albemarle River, in Perq Precinct, "due for trans' two persons." At Mr George Durants house, same date. May 3, 1684. (Court at Mr. Durant's house.)

No. 29. Tabitha Gray, widow of John Gray Dec' bound as an apprentice her son Robert, one year old, to Daniel Snuke, for 20 years, "to do all manner of work his said Master Shall Employ him in, Said Snuke to be dilligent in bringing up said Robert Gray, & to maintain him in sickness, & health, & to find him good Wholesome meat, drink, Washing, lodging, & apparel, & at age of 21 years to pay sd apprentice 2000 lbs of Tobacco." Aug 22, 1687. Test' Peter Gray, Thomas Long.

No. 30. Tabitha Gray, widow of John, bound two children, Thomas, & Elizabeth, 1st seven, 2d four years old, unto Thomas Long of sd County. Thomas to serve until he is 21 years old, & Elizabeth until she be 16, or marries. Aug 22, 1687. Test' Peter Gray, Daniel Snuke.

No. 31. "I Jean Loadman, do give to my son James, one cow & calf." Test' Peter Gray, Richard Buyer.

No. 32. Grant from Lords Pro' unto Joseph Sutton of Albemarle, planter—300a on east side of Perq River, adj Debora Sutton, "due sd Sutton for trans' six persons into the Country." Seth Sothel Gov. Councillors; Anthony Slocum, Thomas Harvey, James Blount.

No. 33. George Castleton, to Richard Evins 150a "upon a Creek out of Perq River, called Perishoes Creek, adj James Perisho, & William Steward, sd land Surveyed by Wm James, Deputy Surveyor for the Co." Entered May 24, 1688. Test' Dan'l Snuke, Wm Chapman.

No. 34. Grant from Lords Pro' to Thomas Long, planter—168a English Measure, on West side of Perq River, adj Lands of Lawrence Noggins, due sd Long for Trans' three persons into said Co. At Mr George Durants House Feb 6, 1668.

No. 35. Thomas Long, & Alce my wife, for £60 Sterling pd by Edward Mayo, have assigned sd Patent. Feb 18, 1689. Test' Em Nixon, Sarah Mayo.

No. 36. Grant from Lords Pro' to Richard Eavans, of Carolina, planter—240a on west side of Perq River, "by a small Swamp, & the River Side," adj Thomas Long, due sd Eavans for Trans' five persons. Feb 5, 1678.

No. 37. Richard Evans, & Elizabeth his wife, for £26 pd by Edward Mayo, "assigns within mentioned Patent." Mar 27, 1684.

No. 38. Grant from Lords Pro' to Lawrence Noggins, planter—230a, on West side of Perq River, in Pre'ct of Perq, adj Joshua Scott. Due said Noggins for Trans of five persons into said Co. At Mr George Durants house, Feb 6, 1678.

No. 39. Jeane Nogell, Widow & relict of Lawrence, Dec'd, for the sum of £18 pd by Edward Mayo, of Perq River, "assigned my right to said Patent." May 20, 1686.

No. 40. Elizabeth Hews, of Perq precinct, widow—late wife of Wm Hews dec'd to Thomas Harvey Esq of same, 700a English Measure. "A Neck of Land" bounded on South by River, on West by a great Swamp, which parteth this land from Richard Bentleys, & on East by mouth of Perq River." Ack in Court June 6, 1688. Test' Benj Laker, Cornelius Leary, Jonathan Ashford, John Spellman, Henderson Walker.

No. 41. Thomas Jacocks of the Co of Albemarle, "do give to Walter Senicer, & his heirs, a plan' at the head of Deep Creek, on south side of Swamp." Dec 20, 1688. Thomas & Ann Jacocks. Test' James Davis, Henry White.

No. 42. Albemarle. June 17, 1688. Samuel Pricklove, of Perq, to Thomas Jacocks, "all right to Land, on the head of Deep Creek" 600a. Test' Richard Craigg, Thomas Downs. Samuel Pricklove, Clerk, & Reg.

No. 43. Albemarle. Feb 15, 1689. Patrick Kenedy planter—assigns to Timothy Clare, of same Co, planter—right to Plan' on Franks Creek. Patrick & Elizabeth Kenedy. Test' Peter Gray, James Loadman.

No. 44. John Bellman of Albemarle, assigns to Richard Byar "houses, clear Ground on Franks Creek, on North side of River." 25day 8mo 1687. Test' Peter Gray, Robert Wilson.

No. 45. Thomas Sanford of Perq, to Wm Bogue, his right to Land in the "Narrows" of Perq River, on Northeast side thereof—adj lands of Richard Byar. June 29, 1689. Test' Sam'l Pricklove, Israel Snellin.

No. 46. Cornelius Leary, of Perq precinct, & Mary his wife, to Benj Laker of same 200a on the Sound, "on West side of Wm Tettertons line." April 22, 1689. Test' John Bentley, Edward Mayo Senior. "Samuel Pricklove, Reg of writings."

No. 47. John Bentley of Perq precinct, "for a sum in hand" pd by Cornelius Leary of same, sold 200a, being part of Land I live on, in lieu of 200a given him by my father Richard Bentley, as a dowry with his wife; which land was sold by my father, to Mr Benj Laker, whereon he now liveth, fronting on the Sound, adj Land whereon I now live." April 22, 1689. Test' Benj Laker, Edward Mayo Sen'r.

No. 48. John Eldin, to Wm Steward, & Samuel Green, "a parcel of Land adj Lands of James Perisho, with two sows, & five shoats, now running on said Land." Feb 27, 1678/9. Test' Sam'l Pricklove, Geo Harris.

No. 49. Albemarle. 21—3 Mo 1689. "I Francis Toms, do sell my right to Land, adj Joshua Lamb, & Wm Lawrence," to line of Anthony Haskit. Test' John Harlow, Mary Toms.

No. 50. David Blake of Perq, sold to Robert Beasley of same, all right to a Tract of Land—adj Peter Gray, on North side of Perq River. Mar 5, 1687. Test' Peter Gray, Stephen Mannering.

HISTORY OF PERQUIMANS COUNTY

No. 51. Wm Vose of Albemarle, planter—for £30 pd by Israel Snellin, sold 100a on North side of Perq River, between land of Ralph Fletcher, & Wm Lawrence. William & Joan Vose. Nov——1663. Test' Wm Bundy, John Whedbee, Robert Wilson.

No. 52. Wm Vose, "for love I bear my dau' Margaret," wife of Jonathan Jones, do give 100a where I now live, on the "Point" of the River. Wm Vose, & Joan Vose. Aug 20, 1690. Test' Ralph Fletcher, James Morgan.

No. 53. Daniel Snooke, & Margaret his wife, of Perq Pre'ct, "for a sum of money" pd by Cornelius Leary, & Jonathan Ashford, of same-sold plan' on Castletons Creek, adj Wm Steward," where we now live," 150a. Sept 16, 1690. Test' Wm Steward, John Bentley, Walter Cassell.

No. 54. Hannah Edge, for a valuable con' pd by James Johnson, sold 200a, "which was entered by John Taylor dec'd." Nov 2, 1690. Richard Plater Clerk. Test' Richard Pope, Jonathan Bateman.

No. 55. Oct 5, 1690. James Johnson, & Rachel his wife, to Robert Beasley, Land. Test' Charles Macdaniel, Samuel Nicholson Sen'r.

No. 56. Thomas Jacocks, & Ann his wife, of the Co of Albemarle, "assigned within mentioned Sale of land" unto Wm Bartlett. 29-11mo 1689. Test' Henry White, James Davis. (Wm Bartlett above, married Elizabeth Durant, dau of George, & Ann Moorwood.)

No. 57. Charles Prows of Pasq, Precinct, sold to John Hodgson, all right to land on South side of Deep Creek, adj Richard Bentley. 4, 8mo 1686. Test' Judith Sprie, ——Mether.

No. 58. John Hodgson, assigns right to land, unto Robert Smith. Oct 30, 1688. Test' Henry White.

No. 59. Robert Smith assigns right to within mentioned "bill of Sale" to Wm Bartlett. April 18, 1689. Robert, & Ann Smith. Test' Henry White. Samuel Pricklove Reg of writings for Perq Pre'ct.

No. 60. Richard Evans, assigned Land, unto Stephen Manoring, "for the use of James Perrishaw, & his heirs." Ack in Court July 7, 1690. Test' Richard Dorman, Stephen Manoring.

No. 61. Edward Mayo of Perq River, for £40 pd by Anthony Dawson, of same-sold 590a, on South west side of Perq River, "as by three Patents," under Seal of the Hon'ble Seth Sothel Esq, Gov of this Province. Aug 20, 1690. Ack at a "Grand Counsel" at the house of Mr John Harris, Feb 5, 1690-1. Test' John Stepney, John Taylor. Richard Playtor Clerk.

No. 62. Humphrey Willis of Albemarle, Carpenter—for a con' pd by Henry Jenkins, of sd Co, sold tract of Land on North side of Yeopim River, adj Thomas Houghton Nov 4, 1789. Henderson Walker Clerk. Test' Henderson Walker, Thomas Houghton.

No. 63. Henry Jenkins, assigned "bill of Sale unto George Mathews, of Yeopim River." Oct 7, 1690. Richard Plater Clerk. Test' John Tormey, John Harlow.

No. 64. Thomas Attoway of Perq, in Co of Albemarle, for a con' pd by Patrick Kenedy, of same-sold plan' "bequeathed to me by Thomas Long Dec'd" Oct 2, 1690. Thomas, & Elizabeth Attoway. Test' Stephen Manoring, Jos Hollford.

No. 65. Samuel Nicholson, for love I bear my brother, Joseph, do give 200a on North east side of Perq River, adj land formerly Joseph Scotts.

called "Log house Land" when it shall come into my hands by the death of Ann Dorman, the Relict of Christopher Nicholson Dec'd. Oct 5, 1691. Test' Peter Gray, John Kinse, John Lawrence.

No. 66. Grant from Lords Pro' unto Samuel Stephens Esq, Gov of Albemarle, as by "our instructions, & Commission, Annexed, wherein he is given Authority to Convey, & grant Land." Oct A,D. 1667.

No. 67. John Bentley, Cooper—(son of Richard, of Perq Pre'ct, Cooper, Dec'd) sold 100a (part of a grt unto his father Richard Bentley, 15000a, Mar 29, 1680) unto Joyas (Josiah) Fendall, adj Cornelius Leary, & Henry Norman. Feb 4, 1691. Test' John Harvey, John Philpotts, Alexander Lillington.

No. 68. Julianna Taylor, "hath engaged to deliver unto Capt Anthony Dawson, one heifer, in Ballance of all account between sd Parties, which Heifer sd Dawson freely gives to Jone Taylor." Aug 29, 1692. John Stepney Reg, & Clerk. Test' Stephen Manwarring, John Hollford.

No. 69. James Loadman of Perq, sold to Charles Macdaniel a plan' adj Patrick Kenedy. June 21, 1692. Test' Peter Gray, Patrick Kenedy.

No. 70. Articles of agreement; between John Foster, of Perq Pre'ct, planter—& Stephen Paine of afsd—"Joint Partners from henceforth, during their natual lives" each binds himself unto the other, in the sum of £50 Sterling. Test' Peter Gray, Richard Davenport. Ack in Court Aug 7, 1693.

No. 71. *George Durant of Albemarle, Mariner-assigned to Hon'ble Seth Sothel right of Land, "at a Creek called Lilleys Creek, which issueth out of Perq River," down sd River to Perq Point, & along Sound side, "Eastward of his now Cleared Ground, by virtue of a certain writing of George Catchmeyd, dated Mar 13, 1662, now upon Record" 200a. Dec 20, 1687. At a Court at Capt Woolards, Jan 6, 1689-90. John Wingate Clerk. Test' Wm Wilkerson, John Hartley, John Davis, Henderson Walker.

No. 72. James Johnson of Perq, assigned right of within mentioned "Bill of Sale" unto Ralph Fletcher. April 17, 1693. Rachel Johnson Ack'her dower right. Test' John Whedbee, Elizabeth Fletcher, Jun, Ralph Fletcher Jr. Edward Mayo Clerk.

No. 73. Caleb Bundy, & Jean his wife, sold to Timothy Clare a plan' on North side of Perq River "towards the head thereof." John Stepney Clerk. 25-2 mo 1692-3. Test' Henry White, Thomas Symonds.

No. 74. John Foster, & Stephen Paine, in Co of Albemarle, Planters—for £27½ s10 pd by Alex Lillington of same—sold 150a on Yeopim Creek, adj John Barrow. Sept 2, 1693. Test' Henderson Walker, John Blount, John Spelman.

No. 75. Wm Turner of "Little River" do give to my son-in-law (step-son) John Kinsie, two thirds of a Plan' which did belong to my Predecessor John Kinsie father of sd John, on North side of Perq River, when he comes of age, "after Decease of my wife Catherine," 150a. 6-2 mo 1694. Test' Francis Toms, Joseph Nicholson.

---

* (This was probably the land George Durant deeded to Seth Sothel, "*unlawfully taken from him, while in durance*." One of the charges brought against said Seth Sothel, when he was impeached.)

No. 76. Wm Turner, "binds himself" to pay to son-in-law John Kinse (son of wife Catherine) a "debt due him from me," £20 Sterling, at age of 21 years. April 9, 1694. Test' Francis Toms, Joseph Nicholson.

No. 77. Francis Toms assigned right of within mentioned Patent, to Gabriel Newby. 278a. 22-5 mo 1693. Test' Israel Snellen, Samuel Nicholson.

No. 78. *Thomas Lepper, of Albemarle, for £20 pd by James Hogg of same-sold 166a on Yeopim Creek, "being Wester-most side of Land grt to me by Lords Pro' April 1, 1694." Thomas, & Ann Lepper. Test' Robert Beasley, Elizabeth Cook, Wm Glover.

No. 79. Joseph Trowel of Perq precinct, to Thomas Horton, 640a adj James Long, on North East side of Yeopim River. Jan 1, 1693-4. Test' John Stepney, Peter Gray.

No. 80. John Flowers, & Susanna his wife, sold a plan' to Timothy Clare, on North side of Perq River, adj Wm Bundy, & sd Flowers. Nov 2, 1693. Test' Patrick Kenedy, Wm Bogue. Edward Mayo Clerk.

No. 81. Timothy Clare assigned sd "Bill of Sale, within Specified" unto Robert Fraser. June 25, 1694. Test' Peter Gray, Charles Macdaniel.

No. 82. Wm Godfrey of Albemarle, sold unto Wm Bentley 150a on West side of Little River, adj John Hawkins, & Lawrence Arnold. April 6, 1693. Test' Henry White, Robert White, Arnold White.

No. 83. John Hawkins, doth "Engage myself never to molest, nor trouble Wm Bentley Sen'r, of a seat of Land, sd Bentley hath now bought of Wm Godfrey." April 6, 1693. Test' Henry White, Robert White.

No. 84. John Tomlin of Little River, planter—for "love I bear my sons: John, & William Tomlin, do give unto them, six cows each, with increase" when they are of age. To dau' Elizabeth "six cows, two pewter dishes, & to my sd sons, & dau' one Mare." 20-11mo 1693-94. Test' Thomas Twede, John Baker.

No. 85. Hannah Gosby, for Natural love I bear my son John Gosby, & dau' Sarah Gosby, do give £30 when they are 16 years of age." Aug 13, 1694. Test' Stephen Manwarring, Jonathan Bateman, John Stepney.

(Note, Sarah Gosby above married *Joshua Toms*, son of Francis, & Priscilla.)

No. 86. Elizabeth Evans, of Perq precinct, widow—for "love I bear my youngest dau Sarah, to make her equal with her Brothers, & sisters do give 20 lbs of Pork, to be paid the 20 day of Dec after sd Sarah be married, or at 18 years of age." Aug 23, 1694. Test' Elizabeth Davis, Wm Glover.

No. 87. Peter Foure of Albemarle, sold to John Flowers a plan' on North side of Alligator Creek, adj James Caron. Reg Oct 11, 1694. Test' Francis Delamare, Patrick Kenedy.

No. 88. John Flowers, assigned right of "Bill of Sale" unto Cornelius Giles. Sept 28, 1694. John Stepney Clerk, & Reg of writings for Perq Pre'ct.

No. 89. Cornelius Giles of Perq, assigned right of a certain tract of Land, bought of Jonathan Jones, on East side of Voses Creek, at a place called

---

*(Note, Thomas Lepper moved from Perquimans to Beaufort Co, where he died.)

"Doctors Plaines." Cornelius, & Hannah Giles. Test' Richard Flowers, Jonathan Jones.

No. 90. John Wallis of Albemarle, sold 400a to Thomas Phillips, "by Entry of sd Phillips" June 1, 1693-4. Test' Anthony Dawson, James Fisher.

No. 91. Thomas Phillips of Perq River, sold unto Daniel Snooke right of "within bill of Saile with Consent of my wife Mary." Oct 8, 1694. Test' Anthony Dawson, John Lille.

No. 92. Samuel Nicholson of Albemarle, for £20 pd by Joseph Nicholson of same—sold 300a West side of Suttons Creek, "to me grt by the Lords Pro'" May 22, 1694. Seal Aug 13, 1694. Test' John Whedbee, John Stepney.

No. 93. Wm Bundy of Albemarle, Cordwainer—for £25 pd by Timothy Clare of same, planter—sold 100a on North side of Perq River, adj Joseph Sutton Dec'd, called "Finkles Point." Ack in Gen'l Court Nov, 1694. Test' George Deare, Wm Glover, Richard Craigg.

No. 94. Richard Chaston of Albemarle, for a con' pd to me by Anthony Haskit, of same—sold land called "Canoe Landing." Ack' April 8, 1695. Test' Peter Gray, Gabriel Newby, Mary Newby.

No. 95. Jan 7, 1694. Charles Tailor of N. C. Cordwainer—to Jacob Overman, Bricklayer—of same, 132a "abutting on Land of John Tomlin, & Wm Jackson, & East side of Little River." Ack' in Gen'l Court Feb 26, 1694. Test' Henry Whitr, Arnold White.

N. 96. Cuthbert Philps of Albemarle, planter—unto Roger Snell of same, Cooper all "my labour upon a tract of Land, on Alligator Creek, called Cedar Land." Cuthbert, & Frances Philps. Test' Richard Ward, Samuel Payen, Jacq lu Caron. Jan 22, 1694.

(Note, This land was in what is now Dare Co N. C.)

No. 97. Jenkins Williams, & Joanna his wife, for £5 pd by Joseph Sutton, sold 158a, & one half, (pt of a patent recorded May 15, 1694) on Perq River, adj said Sutton. Feb 7, 1694. Test' Stephen Manwarring, James Perishow.

No. 98. Articles of agreement; between Alex Lillington, & Anthony, "Alias Tony" a Negro Slave of sd Lillington, sd negro to serve for ten years (to Dec 1705) & sd Lillington "doth oblige himself to set sd negro free at the Expiration of sd time, provided sd negro shall truely serve sd Lillington." Aug 20, 1794. Test' John Luigger, John Stepney.

No. 99. John Lilly of Albemarle, for £16 pd by John Godfrey of Little River, "conveyed ten cows, & five calves, being all the cattle that doth belong to me, & my Brother William Lilly, running between Little River, & Perq River." Sept 3, 1695. Test' Anthony Dawson, Francis Foster, John Whedbee.

No. 100. Wm Tetarton, (son of William, planter Dec'd, & Margaret Peavall his mother, Spinster) "doth bind himself an apprentice, to Benj Laker of Albemarle, precinct of Perq, planter—with Consent of his Natual Mother, Margaret Peavall, to serve sd Laker, & his wife Jane, for the term of 9 years." Reg Nov 1, 1695. Test' William Gardner.

No. 101. Peter Gray, sold to Anthony Haskit, a "Piece of cleared ground," 1a adj a Plan' called David Blakes. Oct 14, 1695. Test' Alex Lillington, Wm Glover.

No. 102. Stephen Manwaring, for £16 pd by Jonathan Jones, sold land in Perq. Ack' Oct 14, 1695. Test' Elizabeth Thigpen, Mary Bolles.

No. 103. Jonathan Bateman of Perq, Planter, sold unto Samuel Parsons, of afsd planter—300a on "Beaver Cove" adj Ralph Fletcher, & sd Parsons. Sept 22, 1695. Test' Richard Bayle. John Stepney Reg of all writings for Perq Pre'ct.

No. 104. John Bentley, (son of Richard Dec'd), with "consent of his Natual Mother Lede Hare, doth bind himself, an apprentice to Anthony Dawson, Carpenter—for five years (to Dec 3, 1700) to learn the Art, & Mistery of his Trade." Dec 3, 1695. Test' John Hare, John Stepney.

No. 105. Richard Bentley, sold to Wm Ray 640a "at the Bottom of the bay of Perq River" Mar 11, 1696. Test' John Peirs, James F—nox.

No. 106. Wm Collings, of Pasquotank Precinct, for £22 s18 p8 pd by Samuel Swann, of Perq precinct, sold half of 300a "Late the property of Joshua Lamb Dec'd, called Finkleys Point." Feb 25, 1695-6. Test' Daniel Akehurst, Thos Pollock. Wm Glover Clerk.

No. 107. Jeane Byer of Perq, "for love I bear my son Wm Moore, do give 150a out of my Patent" adj Timothy Clare, & Wm Bogue, on South west side of "Narrows of Perq River." July 13, 1696. Test' Thos Abington, John Stepney.

No. 108. Jeane Byer of Albemarle, sold to Wm Butler 50a on North side of Perq River, "part of a pat for 266a taken up by me, (widow) May 1, 1694." Seal 1—5mo 1696. Test' Isaac Wilson, Gabriel Newby, Richard Cheston.

No. 109. Peter Gray, & Mary my wife, for £26 pd by Charles Macdaniel, sold land in Perq, "Excepting a small parcel, sold to Anthony Haskit." Oct 13, 1696. Test' Ralph Fletcher, John Stepney.

No. 110. Charles Macdaniel, & Elizabeth his wife, sold to Peter Gray Plan' in Perq. Oct 13, 1696. Test' John Stepney, Clerk of all writings for Perq Pre'ct.

No. 111. Joseph Pierce of Albemarle, for £10 pd by Peter Gray of same—sold 150a, adj 300a grt to my Brother Thomas Pierce by the Lords Pro' Oct 12, 1696. Test' Caleb Calloway, Ralph Fletcher.

No. 112. Oct 12, 1696. James Oates of Albemarle, "Mary Stroud doth bind to sd Oates, her Eldest dau, Easter Stroud, for 15 years." Test' Anthony Dawson, Cornelius Leary.

No. 113. Lords Pro' to "our trusty, & well beloved Samuel Swann Esq, Gov of Albemarle, do give to him full Authority, by consent of Counsel, to grant Lands, as by Instructions annexed, A.D. 1667." Given under our hand, & Seal May 1, 1668. John Archdale.

No. 114. Hon'ble Francis Toms Esq, Dept to Thomas Amy Esq, one of the Lords Pro', "deposed that about 1669 he did see the Lords Pro' grant to the Co of Albemarle Authority for holding Lands, with their Lordships great Seal affixed" & Hon'ble Thomas Harvey Esq Dept to John Earle of Bath, one of the Lords Pro', deposed that "about 1670 he did see the Lords Pro' grant to the Co of Albemarle Authority for holding Lands." Before John Archdale Gov. (1696-7.)

No. 115. Stephen Manwarring of Perq, "Entitled to a tract of Land, 640a as by Patent, May 1, 1695, in con' of a bill of Sale under the hand of James Perishow of same—assigns 240a, pt of sd tract, in possession of sd Stephen, at the lower End of Bear Garden along the Swamp to the Creek." (Vosses

Creek) Jan 9, 1696-7. Test' Anthony Dawson, Patrick Kenedy, Cullum Flyn.

No. 116. James Perishow of Perq, planter-in con' of a Deed of Sale, from Stephen Manwaring of same—do assign unto sd Manwaring, plan' on South west side of Perq River, down to a Creek called "Perishows" adj Wm Steward. Jan 9, 1696. Test' Anthony Dawson, Patrick Kenedy, Cullum Flyn.

No. 117. Jonathan Jones of Pasquotank Co, for £15 pd by Stephen Manwaring, sold "Land formerly purchased from sd Manwaring, with his assignment on back of sd Patent, formerly belonging to Charles Macdaniel." Oct 13, 1696. Test' James Perishow, Cullum Flyn, Nicholas Johnson.

No. 118. John Haughkins (Hawkins) of Perq, planter—for 1200lbs of Sound Merchan-table Pork, do sell to John Godfrey of same 300a on South side of Little River. Sept 25, 1693. Test' John Pell, Francis Penrice.

No. 119. Thomas Lepper, & Ann his wife, "do Alienate from us, our plan' on Yeopim Creek where we now live," 304a, unto Thomas Long. Jan 13, 1696/7. Test' James Hogg, Alex Lillington, Robert Harmon.

No. 120. Richard Nowell of Little River, Perq precinct, for £9 pd by Albert Albertson Jun, assigned a patent dated Sept 1, 1694. Seal Dec 20, 1694. Test' Richard Rooke, John Tomlin, Richard & Eleanor Nowell. John Stepney Clerk.

No. 121. Wm Vose, & Johannah his wife, for a valuable con' pd by Stephen Manwaring, do assign our right to a plan' whereon I now live, 50a on North side of Perq River. June 6, 1696. Test' Wm Stewars, Edward Woodhara, Mary Long.

No. 122. April 6, 1697. Wm Chebsey of Albemarle, "doth Covenant with Robert Auston, to bind his son Francis Auston to sd Chebsey, for 12 years." Test' Thomas Norcom, John Stepney.

No. 123. John Whedby of Albemarle, for "Natual love, I bear my son Richard, do give to him a Plan' on North side of Suttons Creek—stock of Hoggs, & 3 negroes, belonging to sd plantation, 4 cows, & calves, 4 ewes, & lambs, one feather bed boulster, & 2 blankets, one ring, 29 lbs of pewter, & one iron pott." To dau Debro "one woman named Sarah, 3 cows, & calves, 6 ewes, & lambs, one feather bed & boulster, two blankets, & one ring, 20lbs of pewter, one iron Porrage pott, & an oval table. To sd son & dau; two mares, & colts, & one horse, with their increase, to be divided between them when dau Debro is 16 years of age, but if they die in Minority, to sons of my Brother George Whedby." Ack' April 13, 1697. Test' Caleb Calaway, Ralph Fletcher.

No. 124. Richard Nowell of Perq; in "Lawfull possession of a plan' on South west side of Little River, by a patent Sept 1, 1694, for love I beare my dau Alis, do give, with consent of my wife Elenor, 200a of sd Land." April 12, 1697. Test' Stephen Manwaring, John Stepney.

No. 125. Richard Batchler, & Katherine my now wife, (Admix of John Spellman Dec'd) for a valuable con' sold to John Jenkins a plantation. April 12, 1697. Test' John Barrow, Stephen Manwaring.

No. 126. Patrick Beasley, "of the upper part of Little River," sold to John King 400a "where I now live, on South west side of Little River," upon Little Creeks Mouth, for £50 in hand. Jan 13, 1693. Test' Richard Craigg, Charles Tellow.

Little River was the first town settled in Perquimans, & was for many years the seat of all the precinct Courts. Here were held many General Courts, and an Assembly met in said place in 1713, at the house of John Hecklefield. This Town was situated on the South west side of the mouth of the River, & is named as one of "four Ports of Entry" for the Province of N. C. In its confines dwelt all the early notables of the Colony, such as Wm Glover, Richard Sanderson, John Hecklefield, & Thomas Jacocks. Near or in Little River lived the redoubtable George Durant, & Court was held at his house, 1677-79 during the trial of acting Gov Thomas Miller. James Oates in whose house numerous Courts were held probably lived near, as also Thomas Blount where Court met.

No. 127. 10, 3-mo 1697. Lawrence Hunt, & Elizabeth his wife, unto John Morgan, a Patent of Land of Perq. Test' James Perishow, Ralph Fletcher.

No. 128. James Hibens, & Eleanor his wife, & Jane Harbort, widow— doth sell a Plan' 280a, at the mouth of Indian Creek, & Yeopim River, adj James Fisher, & Sarah Johnson. July 12, 1697. Test' Ralph Fletcher, John Stepney.

No. 129. Daniel Snuke of Albemarle, for a Con' pd by John Lilly of afsd-sold 200a at the head of John Pricklos Land, adj Samuel Phelps, & David Sharwood. A patent to me Feb 25, 1696. Seal Aug 7, 1697. John Stepney Clerk, & Reg. Test' Caleb Caleway, John Whedbee.

No. 130. Jenkins Williams, assigns right of 150a unto Joseph Bennett. Oct 18, 1697. Test' Caleb Caleway, John Whedby.

No. 131. John Hancock of Perq, sold tract of Land unto Richard Woolard of same, adj sd Woolard. Sept 8, 1697. Test' Arthur Charlton, John Foster.

No. 132. William Butler, unto Wm Moore, all right "of within Bill of Sale" for 50a of Land, which was purchased by me of Jane Byer. July 30, 1697. Test' Richard Cheston, Mary Newby, Gabriel Newby.

No. 133. David Sharwood of Carolina, for a Valuable Con' pd by John Prickloe, Weaver—of same, sold 100a "on Wide of Perq River" adj Samuel Phelps, & sd John Prickloe, taken up by me Jan 1, 1698. Jane Sharwood Ack' her Dower right. Ack' Jan 10, 1697/8. Test' Samuel Charles, Charles Scott, Gabriel Newby.

No. 134. 14-10mo 1697. Wm Edwards, with Consent of wife Elizabeth, doth assign 200a "upon the Wide of Little River, up Deep Creek" to a Branch called "Sheltons Gut" adj Arnold White, & John Cartrite. Test' Henry White, Robert White.

No. 135. John Fisher of Albemarle, for a Con' pd by Wm White of same—sold 400a on North side of Yeopim River, adj Land formerly Richard Williams. Jan 12, 1693. Test' Thomas Hassold, John Long.

No. 136. Samuel Charles of Car, Planter—to Charles Scott, planter of same—60a purchased by sd Charles of "my father" (step father) Francis Toms, as per Deed Mar 27, 1687, "on Wide of Perq River," adj West Land of Gabriel Newby, & sd Samuel. Jan 1, 1698-9. Test' John Pricklove, David Sharwood. Gabriel Newby.

RECORDS OF DEEDS 49

No. 137. Charles Scott of Car, planter—for a con' pd by Gabriel Newby of same—Wheelwright; sold 10a on North west side of sd Newbys line. Ack Jan 10, 1698/9. Test' John James, Wm Rivers.

No. 138. Gabriel Newby of Car, to Charles Scott of same—10a adj sd Newby, & Scott. Jan 8, 1698. Test' John James, Wm Rivers, Thomas Nicholson.

No. 139. Samuel Nicholson, & John Nicholson, (Ex of Joseph Nicholson Dec'd) assign right of a Conveyance, unto Andrew Reed, "for a con' pd by Joseph Nicholson, before his death." Jan 11, 1698. Test' Caleb Caleway, John Barrow.

No. 140. Mary Peterson, of Perq precinct, widow—to my dau Ann, "New feather bed, & Boulster, 2 Blankets, & a Rugg, 1 doz Pewter plates, & 2 Pewter Dishes, & 1 Iron Pott." At 16 years of age "1 negro man, £40, & 4 young Sows, as a gift from me." July 9, 1698. Test' Caleb Calleway, John Barrow.

No. 141. Caleb Callaway, by power of Att' from James Hogg, & Ann his wife, sold Land to Thomas Long. Oct 10, 1698. John Stepney Clk, & Reg of writings, Perq.

No. 142. James Coles Jun'r. of Nanseymond Co, in Virginia, "am firmly bound to Ann Peterson, of the Precinct of Perq, for the sum of £200 Lawful Money of Eng, & bind my self to deliver every thing mentioned in a deed of Gift made by her Mother, Miss Mary Paterson, Widow—whom I intend to marry this day." July 16, 1698. Test' John Whedby, John Watts, Wm Hall, James Fugett.

No. 143. May 18, 1698. Samuel Swann of Perq precinct Esq, to Henderson Walker of Chowan precinct; Whereas "a marriage is shortly to be Solemnized, between Samuel Swann, & Elizabeth Fendall, widow"—to Henderson Walker a plan' whereon said Samuel Swann now lives, for the use of said Elizabeth, her natual life & two negroes. Ack Oct 10, 1698. Test' Samuel Swann, Mary Lillington, Robert Harmon, Robert Fendall. (Elizabeth Fendall widow of Johnnee Lillington.)

No. 144. John Watts, Ship Carpenter—of N. C., "Thomas Cockery, doth bind himself unto said Watts, as an apprentice, to learn his trade," for the term of four years. Sept 14, 1698. Test' James Coles, Samuel Payen.

No. 145. N. C. James Hogg, & Ann my wife, Thomas Pierce, & Mary my wife, Fornyfield Green, & Hannah my wife, for £40 s8 pd by Wm Long, "do jointly sell a tract of Land, formerly belonging to Lawrence Consellver, lately dec'd" 250a on Indian Creek, & Yeopim River. Aug 15, 1698. Test' James Long, Thomas Long, Wm Keeter.

No. 146. Roger Snell, for a Val' Con' pd by Hon'ble Thomas Harvey Esq, assigned a "Patent." Nov 17, 1694. Test' John Fendall, Robert Fendall, Wm Garner.

No. 147. N. C. At a Counsel Holden June 6, 1698, at the house of Mrs Elizabeth Godfrey, Present; Hon'ble Thomas Harvey Esq, Dept Governor; Hon'ble Daniel Akehurst, Francis Toms, Major Samuel Swann, Capt Henderson Walker, Lords Pro' Dept' "Benj Laker Esq came before this Board, & conveyed to his dau Ruth Laker 538a of Land, on the Sound side, adj a Creek that parteth this Land from Edward Wilson," said Land being now in poss' of John Watts. Wm Glover Cleark of Court.

No. 148. James Cole, & Mary his wife, for £30 in hand pd by John Stepney, assigns a Patent. April 11, 1699. Test' Ralph Fletcher, John Whedby, John Barrow Justice.

No. 149. Anthony Hasket of Perq, to John Henby, a small parcel of Land, adj plan' formerly Richard Attkins, & along Peter Grays line, next to the "Canoe Landing." Reg Apl 15, 1699. Anthony, & Tabytha Haskett. Test' Peter Gray, Robert Beasley, Mary Gough.

No. 150. George Deare, & Elizabeth my wife, for £5 paid by Richard Davenport, assigns a Patent of Land. April 11, 1699. Test' Richard Plater, James Fisher.

No. 151. Samuel Charles, & Elizabeth his wife, of the Co of Albemarle for a Val' Con' pd by Gabriel Newby, of same, sold 240a on West-side of Perq River, adj Robert Wilson. "Land purchased by me of my father (step father) Toms." Mar 26, 1699. Test' John Stepney, John Nicholson.

No. 152. "We the subscribers at the house of Richard Williams Nov 26, 1692. Said Williams being very sick," said how he would "settle his Estate Giving all to his wife, except the Plan', which he gave to his Dau Ruth," after the decease of his wife. He left to Dau Jane one heifer, with all increase, given her by Richard Bentley. (Richard Williams died suddenly after the 26 of Nov 1692.) Test' John Foster, Richard Williams, Elizabeth Brooke.

No. 153. John Pierce, for a Val' Con' unto Jacob Peterson Senior, of Perq. Land "Patent to me granted" Feb 25, 1696. Wm. Glover Clerk. Test' Alex Lillingon, Caleb Callaway.

No. 154. John Stepney, & Marcy his wife, for £40 pd by James Coles, sold 300a on West-side of Perq River—"a patent granted to John Pierce Sept 1, 1694." Seal July 11, 1699. Test' Isaac Wilson, Daniel Phillips.

No. 155. Wm Hall of Perq precinct, assigns right of an Estate, (given to Ann Peterson, by Jacob Peterson her father Dec'd)—to James Coles of same, Con £10 to be paid to said Hall Oct 10, 1699. Test' Daniel Phillips, Robert Fendall.

No. 156. Thomas Norcom, & Mary my wife, assigns right of within deed, to William Long. Nov 20, 1699. Test' Mary Chew, Margaret Pafelm, John Stepney.

No. 157. Edward Holmes of Car, sold 200a "for a Val' Con' pd by John Lilly" Said Land taken up by Daniel Snoke, & sold to said Lilly by said Snuke, Feb 25, 1696, on lines of John Pricklove, Phelps, & David Sharwood. Elizabeth Holmes Ack her dower right. Test' Callum Flin, Peter Gray.

No. 158. James Thigpen Att' to Stephen Manwaring, late of N. C. sold to John Lilly of same, 30a formerly belonging to Wm Voss, purchased of said Wm Voss by Stephen Manwaring, Jan 16, 1696, on line of Francis Toms & Jonathan Jones. Oct 1, 1700. Test' Gabriel Newby, Mary Newby.

No. 159. Robert Fendall of Perq precinct, for a Val' Con' pd by John Bennett of same, 300a, "part of tract granted to me by Hon'ble Henderson Walker, formerly granted to John Fendall dec'd, & lapsed for want of settling," on West-side of Perq River, adj James Coles. Aug 30, 1700. Test' Francis Beasley, Wm Pargiter.

RECORDS OF DEEDS 51

No. 160. John Bennett, "assigns right of within mentioned Contents," unto Wm Hall. Oct 8, 1700. Test' Ralph Fletcher, John Barrow.

No. 161. Robert Fendall of Perq precinct, to Francis Beasley of same, 340a "to me granted by Hon'ble Henderson Walker Esq." Formerly patented by John Fendall & Lapsed for want of settling, adj Lands of Mr Anthony Alexander, on South-west side of Perq River. Oct 8, 1700. Test' James Fugett, John Yates.

No. 162. Daniel Hall assigns to John Bennett, my Plan' & House, on my Entry of 200a of Land. Sept 30, 1700. Test' William White, James Coles.

No. 163. John Lilly, & Hannah his wife, for a sum of Money pd by James Thigpen sold a "plan' formerly belonging to Wm Voss," & sold unto me by James Thigpen, Att for Stephen Manwaring. Oct 1, 1700. Nath'l Chevin Clk Court. Test' Gabriel Newby, Mary Newby.

No. 164. Wm Glover of Pasquotank Pre'ct, in Albemarle Co, Gent; for £5 pd by Isaac Wilson, of same, 490a in Perquimans percinct, adj Robert Wilson. Nov 20, 1699. Test' John Porter, Daniel Akehurst, Thos Abington.

No. 165. George Matthews of Perq precinct, unto Wm Wilkerson, "my whole Estate both real, & Personal." Nov 18, 1699. In the Eleventh year of the Reign of our Sovereign Lord William III, King of England. Jan 14, 1700. Test' Argell Simons, Thos Houghton, Samuel Heeree.

No. 166. William Long of Perq precinct, assigns right of Land on Northside of Yeopim River, called "Bennets" on lines of James Fisher, & Peter Jones. Jan 9, 1700. Test' Christ' Butler, Peter Gray, Thos Long.

No. 167. Anthony Alexander, & Ann his wife of Perq, to Thomas Harvey of afsd, 75a "on Southwest side of Perq River, adj Francis Beasley, & Jonathan Taylors Survey." Ack' July 8, 1701. Test' Wm Pargits, James Coles.

No. 168. Anothony Alexander, & Ann his wife, sold to Frances Beasley of Perq, 275a on Southwest side of Perq River, adj sd Francis. Ack July 8, 1701. Test' Wm Pargiter, John Falconer.

No. 169. Wm Fryly of Perq precinct, Joiner—& Grace his wife; Thomas Blount, & Mary his wife of Chowan precinct, to Edmond Peirce of Chowan Gent, sold 1050a called "Old Scotts" on North side of Perq River, formerly Joshua Scotts Land. June 6, 1701. Test' Daniel Bret, Richard Smith, Henderson Walker.

No. 170. Wm Barrow, & Elizabeth his wife of Albemarle, for £20 pd by John Hopkins of same—sold 140a on North side of the Sound, & Cypress Swamp, adj Gov Harvey, & Cornelius Learie, "Land Surveyed for John Bentley, & by him given to his wife, which by Inheritance came to me." Mar 20, 1699. Test' Sarah Long, John Stepney.

No. 171. Edmond Peirce of Chowan & Sarah his wife, for a con' pd by Wm Farly of Perq, sold Plantation called "Old Scotts" 1050a on North side of Perq River. Test' James Blount, Kathran Taylor. June 8, 1701.

No. 172. Joshua Lamb of Roxborough, Co of Suffolk, province of Massachusetts Bay, in New England, Yeoman—Eldest son of Joshua Lamb of same, Merchant Dec'd, for £27 s10 pd by Samuel Swann Esq of Perq, sold 300a on North east side of Perq River, adj Timothy Clare, & John Lawrence. Nath'l Chevin Clek. Ack' in Gen'l Court July 30, 1701. Test' John Tucker, Moses Abott, Simon Daniel, Eliezer Moody.

No. 173. Jeane Bier, widow—"do give to my son Wm Moore a Patent of Land, from me and my Now husband William Newby, after the death of both of us." Aug 12, 1701. Test' Ralph Fletcher, John Barrow, Isaac Wilson.

No. 174. James Thigpen Att' to Stephen Manwaring of Perq, for a Valuable con' pd by John Flowers of same—sold 80a on Western side of "Long Reach, in the Narrows of Perq River" adj Francis Toms Sr. Aug 12, 1701. Test' John Barrow, Francis Foster.

No. 175. Samuel Swann Esq, & Elizabeth his wife, to our son Samuel Swann, 100a bounded on the South by the Sound, on West by Henry Normans land, & on East by land of Cornelius Leary. Aug 28, 1701.

No. 176. Oct 14, 1701. John Anderson, unto James Laeton (Layden) Land. Jane Anderson Ack' her dower. John Stepney Clk.

No. 177. Robert Latton of Perq, planter—for a con' sold 200a adj Arthur Carlton," & plan' where Mary Rucks Now dwelleth" upon the head of Deep Creek. Feb 13, 1701. Test' Richard Plater, Hugh Campbell.

No. 178. Ann Wilson, widow, & Relict of Robert Wilson Dec'd,* doth assign "my Interest in Estate, both Real, & Personal unto John Belman, & Isaac Wilson, (her son, & son-in-law) jointly to possess, & Enjoy." 11-5mo 1701. Test' David Sherwood, Joseph Smith, George Bion.

No. 179. Christopher Butler, Att' to Stephen Manwaring, sold to John Anderson Land on North-east side of Perq River, called "Pricklows plan'" adj Thomas Atterway, & Francis Foster, formerly Edward Norwoods land—209a. Reg Oct 16, 1701. Test' James Ward, Joannah Ward.

No. 180. Wm Godfrey of Perq precinct, "Released unto John Arnold, of same, all right to Land—150a on Little River." Aug 26, 1701. Test' Wm Glover, Robert White, Joseph Glover. Hon'ble Wm Glover Esq Governor.

No. 181. John Stepney of Albemarle, Att' to John Slocum of Pamlico River, Co of Beath (Bath) province of N. C. for £25 pd by Thomas Norcum of Albemarle, assigned Patent to said Norcum. Jan 13, 1701/2. Test' Ralph Fletcher.

No. 182. Richard Davenport of Perq, Carpenter—with "Consent of my wife Joanna, but more Especially for the Love we bear our Dau, wife of John Foster, of said place"—do give to said John & Elizabeth Foster—170a, "between the great Marsh," & Land of Archibald Holmes. Ack At Genl. Court July 20, 1701. Test' John Stepney, Caleb Callaway. Nath'l Chevin Clk.

No. 183. Richard Fox assigns all Right to above mentioned Patent, unto Daniel Oneel. Nov 1, 1700. Test' Timotry Cleare, Francis James.

No. 184. Daniel Oneel doth Assign my Right of this Patent, unto William Bogue. Mar 12, 1702. Test' David Elder, Daniel Jones, Richard Cheston.

No. 185. Samuel Swann Jun'r, for a Val' Sum of Money, pd by Major Samuel Swann, assigned a Plantation. Reg April 16, 1702. Test' Francis Foster, James Coles.

No. 186. "Thomas Harvey, & Margaret my wife," assigns right of Land, to Mary Coffin. April 14, 1702. Test' Ralph Fletcher, John Stepney.

---

*Robert Wilson came to Perquimans precinct, from Chuckatuck, Nansemond Co. Va. He was a Quaker, and lived on "The Narrows of Perq River" where he died "at his own house Dec 21, 1696." His wife Ann (née Blount, dau of Thomas) went back to Va. after the death of her husband, where her will may be found in Surry Co Va. Isaac Wilson son of above, married Ann Parker, who married 2d John Pettiver.

No. 187. Robert Fendall of Perq precinct, for £5 pd by Samuel Swann Esq of said precinct, do "Release 100a on North-side of Roanoak Sound," in said Precinct, adj Lands of Henry Norman, & Cornelius Leary. April 14, 1702. Test' Samuel Swann Jun'r, Francis Beasley.

No. 188. James Coles, & Mary my wife, of Perq precinct, Carpenter—for £30 pd by Lewis Alex Knight, & Emanuel Knight, (Brother, of afore) planters; sold plan' bought of Wm Hall, heir to Ann Peterson Dec'd, on North-east side of Perq River—100a, adj Land of Christopher Nicholson, into the woods to "Mile End," & on South adj Land of John Kinsey. Bill of Sale dated Mar 14, 1672, & was sold to Thomas Kent by Wm Voss, being part of 200a Patent from his Majesty, & signed by Sir William Berkeley, Sept 26, 1663. April 4, 1702. Test' Samuel Swann, Jun'r, Ralph Fletcher.

No. 189. Wm Godfrey of Perq precinct, to Thomas Bartlet of same, for £30 pd by said Bartlett, assigns plan' upon the Banks of Little River, now in poss' of said Godfrey, adj lands of said Bartlet on the North, & on the South the Dower Lands of Mrs. Elizabeth Hecklefield—300a. Test' John Falconer, Wm Barclift, Wm Glover, Joseph Glover. Ack in Gen'l Court Mar 3, 1702. Nath'l Chevin Clk.

No. 190. Jenkins Williams, & Joanna his wife, for a Val' Con' pd by Mr John Bire (Bier assigns "our Plan' between lands of Mr Ralph Fletcher, & Joseph Sutton," 150a. Ack in Gen'l Court Aug 2, 1700. Test' John Wiloby, Lenard Lafton.

No. 191. Thomas Bird, assigns Right to within Conveyance, to Thomas Harvey. Feb 10, 1701. Test' Samuel Persons, Geo Fletcher.

No. 192. Ralph Fletcher Sr, of Perq, to dau Margaret 170a on North west side of land seated by Jenkins Williams, & South west side of "Grassy Point Gut." Mar 21, 1702. Test' Ralph Fletcher, Jane Fletcher, Orphans Court Aug 11, 1702.

No. 193. July 23, 1701. Wm Friley, & Grace his wife, dau of Joshua Scott Dec'd, for £15 pd by Ezekiel Moadley (Modlin) sold 66a on North side of Perq River, being one third of 200a formerly belonging to sd Joshua Scott. Test' Daniel Hall, Joseph Sutton, John Bird.

No. 194. Richard Woolard, & Ann his wife, for a con' pd by Thomas Haires (Hare) sold 150a on North side of the head of Yeopim River. July 24, 1702. Test' Christopher Butler, Joanna Ward. Peter Godfrey Clk.

No. 195. Patrick Kanidy, (Kenedy) doth assign Right of a Patent, unto James Fugett, for £14. Oct 29, 1700.

No. 196. "Parties to this Indenture, have set their hands, day, & year written." In presence of Thomas Snoden, Francis Foster, Jan 14, 1702-3. Thomas Snoden Reg of Perq.

No. 197. Francis Beasley, & Hannah his wife of Perq, for a con' sold to Thomas Gray of afsd—190a adj South east side of Wm Halls land, on South west side of Perq River. Sept 2, 1702. Test' John Anderson, Richard Ross. Peter Gray Clk.

No. 198. Hannah Snelling,* widow of Israel, of Perq Pre'ct, "for Love I bear my Daughters; Richel, & Esther Snelling, do give part of my Estate

---

* Hannah Snelling, (née Larance, dau of William, & Rachel Welch) married 2d Timothy Clare, shortly after this deed was made. She was his third, & last wife; having issue by him one dau Hannah, who married Benjamin

one young mare bought of Samuel Nicholson, with her increase," To dau Rachel one cow, named "Tulip" to dau Esther one cow, & calf named "Meele," to Rachel my great Bible, & to each "one Iron Pot." 8-12mo 1702. Test' Francis Toms, Timothy Clare.

No. 199. July 13, 1702. John Hufton of Perq, for £20 pd by John Parish, sold 524a on Little River, at the mouth of Deep Creek, adj sd Parish, & Wm Man. Land grt to me Sept 1, 1694. Seal Aug 1, 1702. Test' James Newby, Wm Glover.

No. 200. William Turner of Perq, & Ann his wife, assigned a Patent, to James Newby of Pasquotank precinct. Reg Mar 10, 1702-3. Test' Wm Barclift, Peter Godfrey.

No. 201. James Newby of Pasq, sold within Patent unto James Foster of Perq. Mar 9, 1702-3 Sarah Newby Ack' her Dower right. Test' Wm Barclift, Peter Godfrey.

No. 202. John Hopkins of Perq, for £3 to be pd in Pork, by John Hare Jr, sold 10a on North east side of Yeopim River, adj John Hare Sr, & John Hopkins. Nov 26, 1702. Test' James Coles, John Stepney.

No. 203. Mar 23, 1703. Robert Hosea of Perq, & Mary Rooks of same—assigned to "Robert Hosea, & heirs of his body, by my dau his wife, 150a on North west side of Deep Creek, formerly Surveyed by Richard Rooks." Test' John Anderson, John Foster.

No. 204. Isaac Wilson of Perq Pre'ct, planter—for £5 pd by Ralph Bosman, sold 150a "on East-side of great Pond, to the small Ponds, & the head of Robert Wilsons Creek, & down said Branch to Horse Bridge, being line between Isaac Wilson & Samuel Phelps." Mar 9, 1702/3. Isaac Wilson, & Ann Wilson. Test' James Coles, Peter Godfrey.

No. 205. Mar 9, 1702/3. "In the first year of the Reign of our Sovereign Lady Anne, of England." Peter Gray of Chowan Pre'ct, planter—& Peter Godfrey of Perq Pre'ct, Merchant—for £3 paid by said Peter Gray, "all my Tenement" 144a on North-side of the "Narrows" of Perq River, adj on one side Plan' formerly Patrick Kenedies, & on the other, land of Wm Bogue, said land lately in the tenure of Peter Gray, father of said Peter Gray, since Dec'd, of which Peter Gray now hath part there-of. At a Court held at the house of Capt James Coles ——— 1702/3. Test' John Falconer, Thomas Snoden.

No. 206. Oct 28, 1702. John Willoby of Perq precinct, to John Anderson, of same, for £19 11 pence, pd by said Anderson, assigns Plan' on Banks of Perq River—248a, now in poss' of said Willoby. Ack in Gen'l Court Oct 20, 1702. Test' Thomas Twedie, Wm Stephens, George Kinzerly.

207. Mary Coffin, Widow—of Perq Pre'ct, for £3 Sterling, pd by James Anderson, of Same, assigns Land. Court at Capt James Coles, Mar, 1702. Test' James Coles, Peter Godfrey.

Bundy. Esther Snelling was wife of John Winslow, thought to be a brother of Thomas Winslow, who married Elizabeth Clare, eldest dau of Timothy Clare, by his first wife Mary Bundy, dau of William Bundy. There were three other Clare children, all children of the first wife, respectively; Mary (twin to Elizabeth) who married Edward Mayo, Sarah who married John White, m 2d Jacob Elliott, Jane married 1st —— Robinson & 2d Thomas Jessop, & Ann, thought to be the wife of William Newby. (2) of Perq Co.

No. 208. Richard Davenport, of the Precinct of Perq, for "Natual Love & Aff' I bear to my son John Davenport, of same," assigns plan' on Yeopim Creek, where said Richard now lives—300a. Also one small Island, called "Bats grave," by Estimation 27a. July 3, 1703. Test' John Stepney, Ralph Fletcher.

No. 209. John Davenport of Perq Pre'ct, planter—for the "Yearly Rent of one ear of Indian, payable at the feast of pentecost, have sold to Richard Davenport, my father, all that plan' whereon said Richard now lives," with the Island called "Batts Grave," 317a. July 13, 1703. Test' John Stepney, Peter Godfrey.

No. 210. July 13, 1703. Anthony Alexander, & Anne his wife, of Perq Pre'ct, to Thomas Evans of same, Boatright—for £26 assigned 359a, on Perq River. Test' James Foster, Peter Gray.

No. 211. Richard Burtonshall, & Priscilla my wife, of N. C. for £12 pd by John Yates, of same—220a on West-side of Perq River. July 13, 1703. Test' John Stepney, Peter Godfrey.

No. 212. Ralph Fletcher Sen'r of Perq Pre'ct, for "Love, & Natual Aff' that I do bear to my Son Ralph Fletcher Jun'r, Bequeath to said son all my plan' lying betwixt land of Francis Toms Sen'r, & Land of Rachel Snelling," dau of Israel Dec'd. Jan 12, 1703/4. Thomas Snoden Clerk of Court. Test' Francis Foster, James Coles.

No. 213. Ralph Fletcher Jun'r of Perq Pre'ct, for Love & Aff' I bear My father Ralph Fletcher Sen'r, "do give to him half of that plan', between land of Francis Toms Sen'r, & Rachel Snelling," dau of Israel Dec'd. Jany 14, 1703/4. Test' Francis Foster, James Coles.

No. 214. Jan 10, 1703. Capt Ralph Fletcher of Perq Pre'ct, for £20 to Richard Burtonshall, Planter—assigns plan', now in poss' of said Burtonshall, 300a. Reg Jan 13, 1703/4. Test' Thomas Snoden, Thomas Houghton.

No. 215. Jan 10, 1703/4. Francis Foster of Perq precinct, Gent—& Hannah his wife; to Thomas Snoden of same, Planter—for £8, assigns Land, "at the head of Thomas Atteways Land," on Pocoson, & Lillys Creek. Reg Jan 13, 1703/4. Test' Denis Macklenden, Thos Houghton, John Stepney.

No. 216. Wm Fryley of the Precinct of Chowan, Carpenter—& Grace his wife, to Capt James Coles of Perq Pre'ct, Carpenter—& Mary his wife—640a on Wide of Perq River. Con' £70 Sterling. Reg Jan 13, 1703/4. Test' Richard French, Henry Sprig, Jno Brown.

No. 217. Aug 13, 1730. Bartholomew Phelps, & Elizabeth his wife, of Scuppennong, in Perq Pre'ct, Co of Albemarle, to Anthony Alexander of same, for £12 pd by said Anthony—380a in Scuppennong, on the Sound, formerly owned by Benj Massagay. Reg Jan 13, 1703/4. Test' Thos Snoden, John Falconer.

No. 218. John Shaw assigns all Right to "within Contents," to James Newby. April 11, 1704. Test' Thos Snowden, John Stepney.

No. 219. April 11, 1704. James Morgan Sen'r of Perq Pre'ct, Planter— "for Love & Aff' I have to my son Williiam Morgan," hath given 100a to him, on Vosses Creek, adj James Thigpen, & Thomas Harveys plan'. Test' Anthony Haskins Sen'r (Haskit), Peter Gray.

No. 220. Jan 9, 1703. Peter Godfrey of Perq Pre'ct, Merchant—to Anthony Haskins Sen'r of same, planter—for £3 s5—pd by said Haskins, 140a on North side of Narrows of Perq River, adj plan' formerly Patrick Kennedies, & Wm Bogue, lately in tenue of Peter Gray dec'd. Test' John Brown, Richard Grey.

No. 221. July 13, 1702. John Anderson, & Jeane his wife, of Perq precinct, to John Hawkins of same, planter—150a on North-east side of Perquimans River, called "Norwoods Old field" Test' John Willoughbee, Robert White.

No. 222. Feb 22, 1703/4. Thomas Evins of Perq precinct, to Jeremiah Goodridge of same, for £30 in hand, assigned plan' purchased of Anthony Alexander—359a late in the tenue of Thomas Evans. Test' Caleb Calleway, Thomas Snoden.

No. 223. Ralph Fletcher "the Elder," of Perq, "for Love & Aff, I do bear by Dau Margaret Harvey, wife of Thomas Harvey," of afore' have given Land, adj that seated by Jenkins Williams, & East by Grassy point Gut. 170a. April 11, 1704. Test' John Stepney, Tho Snoden.

No. 224. David Harris, & Elizabeth his wife, to Thomas Harvey, 200a on Vosses Creek, adj John Morgan, Wm Morgan, & Francis Toms. Jan 2, 1703/4. Test' Ralph Fletcher, John Flowers.

No. 225. Thomas Harvey & Margaret his wife, for a Val' Con' in hand, pd by David Harris, assigns whole plan' (328a) on Grassy Point, on North-west side, "with all things there-unto, Except my Stock, & Movables." Jan 22, 1703/4. Test' Ralph Fletcher, John Flowers.

No. 226. James Beasley of Chowan Pre'ct, for a Val' Con' pd by Francis Wells of same, 282a upon Perq River, adj Pete Gray—a patent Granted Robert Beasley dec'd may 1, 1694. With Consent of my Wife Mary Beasley. April 10, 1704. Test' John Anderson, Peter Godfrey.

No. 227. Archibald Holmes Att' to Wm Barrow, assigns "all right of within premises," to Anthony Wherry. April 11, 1704. Test' John Anderson.

No. 228. Wm Jackson assigns all Right of 208a, part of 312a named in Patent to Richard Nowell. July 11, 1704. Test' Tho Snoden, Denis Macklenden, John Anderson.

No. 229. John Winbury, by virtue of a Power, given me by Richard Nowell, assined Right of 200a part of 400a in Patent to Wm Jackson. July 11, 1704. Test' Tho Snoden, Denis Macklenden, John Anderson.

No. 230. Thomas Cartright Sen'r, to Samuel Right—95a on South-side of Deep Creek, adj Wm Godfrey, & Wm Hunt, "belonging to me Wm Terrell, in New England." April 25, 1704. Test' Thomas Twedie, Wm Twedie.

No. 231. Thomas Ayres, assigns "Right of within mentioned Deed of Sale," to Wm Williams. July 14, 1704. Test' John Stepney Reg of Perq.

No. 232. Anthony Haskit Sen'r, of Perq, assigns "all Right, wife Tabitha Joining with me" to land, unto son Anthony Haskitt Jun'r. July 11, 1704.

No. 233. James Anderson & Debrow, my wife, to John Volloway, both of Perq precinct, 275a, surveyed by Samuel Swann Jr, for Anthony Alexander, & sold by him to Thomas Harvey, by him unto Mary Coffin, & by said Mary to me. Land on South-west side of Perq River, adj Francis Beasley. May 9, 1704. Test' John Anderson.

No. 234. Wm Williams of Chowan Pre'ct, Carpenter—for £10 s7 pd by Thomas Norcom, of same, planter—sold 150a in Perq precinct, Surveyed in the name of Richard Woolard, & sold by him to Thomes Ayres, & by said Ayres to me. Oct 7, 1704. Test' Thos Snoden, Aughter (Arthur) Carlton, Richard Woolard.

No. 235. Thomas Norcom of Perq precinct, planter—for a sum of money pd by Thos. Snoden of same, "assigns within mentioned Deed of Sale." Oct 7, 1704. Test' Arthur Carlton, Smethwick Warburton.

No. 236. *Wm Bogue of Albemarle, for a Val' Con' pd by Wm Newby, conveyed to said Newby, Isaac Wilson, John Prickloe, & Wm Moore, one a of Land, to belong to a Society of Protestant Desenters; Vulgarly called "Quakers" living in Perq precinct, "upon which a House of Worship has already been Built." Land formerly belonging to James Lodman, & now leased to Anthony Haskit, on Perq River. 2 day 6 mo 1704. Test' Francis Toms, Francis Wells, Francis Toms, Jr.

No. 237. John Davenport of Perq Pre'ct, planter—for a Val' Sum pd by Alexander Ray, assigned 100a "on Albemarle Sound, Opposite Batts Grave." Reg Oct 12, 1704. Test' Archibald Holmes, John Anderson.

No. 238. John Foster, with Consent of my wife Elizabeth, assigns Right of within mentioned Deed of gift to John Davenport. Oct 10, 1704. Test' Dennis Macklenden, John Yates.

No. 239. Richard Burtonshall, assigns "Right to within Bill of Sale," to David Harris. 11 of 7 mo 1704. Test' Francis Toms, Ralph Fletcher.

No. 240. Jan 8, 1704/5. James Coles of Perq precinct, to John Pettiver of same, for £60 assigns "Dividend of Land Granted to John Peire, under the hand of Phillip Ludwell Gov; & Thomas Harvey, Francis Toms, Benj Laker, & Thomas Pollock, of the Counsel. By said John Peairee "Conveyed to Jacob Peterson, & said Peterson Dying left it to Mary wife of James Coles, she being widow of said Peterson." Test' John Falconer, John Foster.

No. 241. John Vollway & Jean my wife, for a Val' Con' assigns Land to David Right 50a. Surveyed by Samuel Swann Jr, for Anthony Alexander, & sold by him to Thomas Harvey, & by him to Mary Coffin, on South-west side of Perq River. Dec 27, 1704. Test' John Vallway, Jan Vallway.

No. 242. John Yates & Elizabeth my wife, assigns "Bill of Sale," to Richard Burtonshall. Jan 5, 1704/5.

No. 243. John Norcom, & Elizabeth his wife of Perq precinct, for a Sum of Money pd by Henry Warring of same, sold Land on Sound side, adj Henry Norman, & Mr Mins (Ming) called the "Gore" 122a. Jan 6, 1704/5. Test' George Kinisle, Richard Leary.

No. 244. Henry Warring, & Elizabeth his wife, sold 400a on Yeopim Creek, to John Norcom, adj Land of Robert Harmon, & Anthony Wherry. known as "Walter Greens Plantation," on West-side of Creek. Reg April 11, 1705.

No. 245. Richard Burtonshall of Perq Pre'ct, for a Val' Con' pd by Andrew Reed of same, assigned Plantation. April 9, 1705. Test' Dennis Macklenden, Tho Snoden.

No. 246. John N. Norcom, assigned unto Richard Skinner all Right to within Patent. April 10, 1705. Test' Wm Hall, Jno Falconer.

No. 247. Archibald Holmes, assigns within Patent, unto Edward Wilson. April 9, 1705.

No. 248. Alexander Ray, assigns "Right of within Deed of Sale" unto Archibald Holmes. April 10, 1705.

No. 249. Ezekiel Mauldin, for £7 s10 to me pd by Timothy Clear, assigns Land. April 26, 1705.

---

*(Wells Mo Meeting)

No. 250. Oct 26, 1704. Esau Albertson of Perq Pre'ct, planter—to Mary Rooks, Widow of Richard Rooks, for £5 pd by said Mary, assigns 150a at the head of Deep Creek, "now in Occupation of Me" by order of Counsel, Mar 29, 1701. Test' Samuel Norton, Tho Snoden, Geo Harris.

No. 251. Henry Warren, & Elizabeth his wife, for £10 s10 pd by James Minge, sold Land called the "Gore" 122a, adj Henry Norman, & James Minges own Land. Mar 27, 1705. Test' Richard Leary, Jeremiah Banns.

No. 252. John Haire, assigns "Right of within Bill of Sale," to John Bennett Sen'r. Aug 29, 1705. Test' Jno Falconer, Samuel Hearse.

No. 253. John Hair, for £14 pd by John Bennett Sen'r, assigns 100a on North-east side of Yeopim River, adj Geo Matthews, & Hopkins plantations. "Except a Nursery growing in my Corn field, & all my Corn, Peas, beans, & Cotton* growing in my fields." Aug 29, 1705. Test' Jno Falconer, Samuel Hearse.

No. 254. Wm White of Perq Pre'ct, for a Sum of Money, pd by Wm Pargeter, of same, sold "my Dividend of Land," on North-east side of Yeopim River—200a adj Lands Surveyed for the Dau of Richard Williams Dec'd, at a place called "Deep Branch." Oct 6, 1705. Test' Tho Snoden, Tho Houghton.

No. 255. John Falconer, of Chowan Pre'ct, for a Sum of Money, pd by John Gray of Perq Pre'ct—assigns Land, "in the Narrows of Perq River," formerly property of Patrick Kenedy. Sept 3, 1705. Test' Tho Snoden, Tho Houghton.

No. 256. Arnold White, & Parthene his wife, to John Cartrett (Cartright) of Albemarle Co, for £6 pd by Aughter (Arthur) Carlton, of same, sold 200a on West-side of Little River, up Deep Creek, on a Branch called "Sheltons Gut." Reg Jan 10, 1705. Test' Tho Snoden, John Stepney.

No. 257. The "Subscribers assign Right of within Deed of Sale," to Gilbert Goodale. Jan 8, 1705/6. Aughter (Arthur) Carlton. Test' John Stepney, Tho Snoden.

No. 258. Arther Carlton, of Chowan precinct, Wheelmaker—for £7 pd by Gilbert Goodale, of Perq Pre'ct, planter—sold 60a of Land called "Dogwood Neck." Jan 5, 1705/6. Arthur Carlton. Test' John Stepney, Tho Snoden.

No. 259. John Parish of Perq, for a "Val'" sum of Money" pd by John Newby, of the Pre'ct of Pasquotank, sold Land. Jan 8, 1705. Test' Christopher Nichols, Samson Swann.

No. 260. Francis Toms of Albemarle, to Thomas Pierce, Wm Bogue, Isaac Wilson, & Gabriel Newby, one acre of Land, "to belong to a Society of Protestant Desenters, Vulgarly called Quakers, living in Perq Precinct" where on a "house is there built to Worship God in." Jan 11, 1705. Francis Toms Sen'r. Test' Mary Toms, John Stepney, James Coles.

No. 261. David Harris of Perq River, to Daniel Jones—180a on Voss's Creek, & Long Branch, adj John Morgan, & Francis Toms. June 10, 1706. Test' Francis Toms Jun'r, Margaret Toms.

No. 262. Francis Wells of Albemarle. for a Val' Con' pd by Gabriel Newby—sold 50a of Land, adj Peter Gray, "part of Tract formerly belonging to Robert Beasley, & left to his son James Beasley." 17 d 7 mo 1706. Test' Richard Cheston, Wm Moore.

---

*(Note: This is the first mention of Cotton being grown in Perquimans Precinct.)

No. 263. John Bennett of Perq precinct, planter—for £13 pd by Daniel Hall of afore', planter—"Plantation on Wide of Indian Creek"—120a. July 5, 1706.

No. 264. Thomas Pollock of Chowan precinct, to Samuel Bond of Perq, planter—"Right of Land on Perq River—128a, where said Samuel now lives." July 2, 1706. Test' Wm Johnson, John Yates.

No. 265. Peter Baudrey of Perq precinct, Millwright—& Rachel my wife. for £13 p8 paid by Wm Long of afore'. sold a Plantation. Sept 17, 1706. Test' Ann Stiball, Tho Snoden.

No. 266. Feb 6, 1705/6. Wm White of Perq precinct, planter—& Anne his wife. to Peter Baudry of same, Millwright—for £10 pd by said Baudry sold Land "on East-side of Indian Creek, in Yeopim River"—200a adj Land of Wm Parqittor, & Maj Alex. Lillington, now in poss' of said Wm White. Test' John Falconer, Tho. Snoden.

No. 267. Robert Douglas of Chowan precinct, planter—& Anne my wife, for a sum of money pd by Edward Berry, of Perq precinct," assigns plan' on North-east side of Yawpim River," adj Land belonging to dau of Richard Williams Dec'd, & John Hopkins—200a. Surveyed in the name of Robert Inkinson dec'd, & now in the tenure of Edward Berry. Jan 15, 1705/6. Test' Tho's Clark, Tho Snoden.

No. 268. Edward Berry, for a Val' Con' sold to Peter Jones of Perq Pre'ct, "all right to within mentioned Deed," At a Court held for Perquimans Feb 1, 1705/6. Test' Wm Long, Tho. Snoden.

No. 269. Wm Glover of Perq precinct, Esq—for £28 pd by Jonathan Stanley, of same, Mariner—"all my Plan" 316a on South-west side of Little River, between Lands of John Arnold, & Thomas Holloway. Reg April 15, 1707. Test' Robert Hosea, John Arnold, Joseph Glover, John Willoughby.

No. 270. Samuel Bond of Perq precinct, unto Susanna Robinson of same, part of Tract of Land where I now live, called "cuthrs" (Cruthers) 640a April 3, 1707. Test' Wm Carman, Timothy Winslo.

No. 271. Edward Phelps of Chowan precinct sold to Wm Stevens of Perquimans, 264a of Land. Jan 4, 1705/6. Test' Godfrey Spruiel, Geo Durant. Thomas Abington C. C. (Pasq Pre'ct).

No. 272. Edward Phelps of Albemarle, appoints Mr. James Fox of same, Att to this Court, in a sale of Land to Mr. Wm Stevens, of same, called "Whiteoak Land" on South-side of Albemarle Sound, "between Scupernong, & Alegater." Aug 26, 1706. Frances Phelps, her dower right.

No. 273. Richard Leary, for a Val' Con' assigns a Patent, taken in the name of Jane Charles, lately in poss' of Tho's Norcom, & now in my possession. Aug 22, 1707. Test' John Stepney, Wm Long.

No. 274. Thomas & Mary Norcom doth make over unto Richard Leary, our right in Lands, in the Neck, between Yawpim Creek, & River. April 8, 1707. Test' John Lillington, Thomas Snoden. (Harveys Neck.)

No. 275. Richard Leary of Perq precinct, appoints Mr. James Ming, of same place, merchant—Att' to sell Land to John Wyatt, on west-side of Yawpim Creek—288a adj John Barrows line. Sept 22, 1707. Test' Edward Wilson, Wm Wilson.

No. 276. John Wyatt, & Rachel my wife, assign our right of within patent unto Richard Leary. Aug 22, 1707. Test' John Stepney, Wm Long.

No. 277. John Bennet, assigns right to within deed of sale of John Bennet Sen'r. Aug 13, 1707. Test' Tho. Horton, Wm Houghton. George Lumley Clk Court.

No. 278. John Benet, assigns right to John Yelverton. Aug 13, 1707.

No. 279. John Bennet assigns right to within Deed, to John Yelverton. Aug 13, 1707. Test' Tho Houghton, Wm Houghton.

No. 280. Daniel Guthry of Perq precinct, assigns Right of a Patent of Land, to Edward Ellston, of Gloster Co in Virginia. Jan 12, 1708/9. Test' Richard French, Isaac Wilson.

No. 281. John Flowers Sen'r assigns Right, to David Harris. Jan 12, 1708. Test' Timothy Clare, John Stepney.

No. 282. David Harris, assigns Right, to Peter Howerd. Jan 10, 1708/9. Test' Timothy Clare, John Stepney.

No. 283. Daniel Jones of Albemarle, for a Val' Con' sold unto Timothy Clare, 180a in Perq Pre'ct, "upon Vosses Creek, adj Land of John Morgan, & Francis Toms. Land purchased by me of David Harris." June 10, 1706. Seal Jan 8, 1708. Test' Gab'l Newby, Wm Newby Jun'r.

No. 284. "Samuel Bond, & Elizabeth my wife of Perq precinct, to John Pricklowe of same, all Right in a Tract of Land on Cypress Swamp—625a, adj land of Gabriel, & Nathan Newby." 13d, mo 1708. Test' Wm Bogue, Peter Albertson.

No. 285. Samuel Nicholson of Perq River, "in Con' of the Love I bear my Dau Abigal Albertson, do give to her my Plan' at the River side, next to Ezekiel Modlins line, the other part being possessed by Ann Dorman. Said Dau to have one half of said Land—200a, & if she die without issue, to dau Hannah Nicholson." 12d, 2mo 1708. Samuel & Elizabeth Nicholson.

No. 286. John Hallum of Perq Pre'ct, for a Val' Con' in hand, to Thomas Bartlett, "Right of Land at the head of Lilleys Creek," adj Wm Godfrey—150a. Mar 10, 1709. Test' Harris Willoughby, I. Darm.

No. 287. John Hopkins, with Consent of Sarah his wife, deed to Thomas Long. Con' £27 pd by said Long. Jan 6, 1708/9. Test' John stepney, Richard Leary.

No. 288. Christopher Nicholson, & Mary his wife, "of the North-side of Suttons Creek, on the Road of Perq," assigns Right of a Patent to Nathaniel Albertson. May 3, 1709. Test' Orlando Payne, Nathaniel Nicholson.

No. 289. Charles Wilkins planter—& Elizabeth my wife to Patrick Eggerton, 15a on North-east side of Yeopim River, Pattented in the name of James Fisher dec'd, & since in Occupation of Patrick Eggerton, planter. Feb 1, 1708/9. Test' Nicholas Crisp, Daniel Cox.

No. 290. John Lillington of Chowan Pre'ct, Gent—for £35 pd by John Bennett of Perq precinct, 170a of Land in Perq, upon Yeopim Creek. Surveyed in the name of Maj Alex Lillington. April 1, 1709. Test' Thomas Snowden, Mary Jackson.

No. 291. John Yelverton, & Elizabeth my wife, "do assign our Right of within Pattent to Patrick Eggerton." July 12, 1709. Richard Leary Clk.

No. 292. John Yelverton & Elizabeth my wife. (To same) July 12, 1709. Test' Lemuel Taylor, Peter Hord.

No. 293. John Yelverton & wife Elizabeth. (Same Parties) July 14, 1709.

No. 294. Thomas Harvey of Perq Pre'ct, Planter—for £25 pd by Timothy Clare of same, sold Land on Upper Vosses Creek, adj Land of John Morgan, William Morgan, & Francis Toms— 200a. "An Estate of Inheritance." Test' Wm Moore, Joseph Jessop. Thomas & Margaret Harvey. Samuel Nicholson, Att to Margaret Harvey. Ack in Gen'l Court Mar 31, 1709. Go Lumly Clk.

No. 295. John Newby assigns "Right to within Bill of Sale"—333a purchased by me of John Parish," unto Barneba Nixon, 9d 2mo 1707. Test' Christopher Nicholson, John Flower.

No. 296. Daniel Right, "in behalf of Mysel, heirs, & Exors sold Land, as to me granted" 14 of 8 mo 1707. Daniel, & Anne Right.

No. 297. Sept 3, 1707. Anthony Rawlings, & Katherine his wife, John Peirson & Rebeckah his wife, & Rachel Dawson of the Co of Dawchester, in Maryland, to Isaac Wilson of Albemarle, for 15,000 lbs of Tobacco Land called "Dawsons" on South-west side of Perq River, adj Capt James Coles, & Jonathan Evens, 600a. Test' John Rawlings, Joseph Kennerly, Thomas Taylor.

No. 298. Maryland, Dorchester Co. Sept 3, 1707. "Before her Magesties Justices, Sitting, the within Named Anthony Rawlings, & Katherine his wife, John Peirson & Rebeckah his wife, and Rachel Dawson did Ack deed, unto said Isaac Wilson." Reg Oct 11, 1709. John Stepney Reg of Perq. Her Enleston Clk.

No. 299. Anthony Rawlings, & Catherine his wife, John Peirson & Rebeckah his wife, & Rachel Dawson, of Dorchester Co, in the Pro' of Maryland, appoints our Friend James Thigpen, & John Stepney, Lawful Att. Sept 3, 1707. Test' John Rawlings, Thos Taylor, Joseph Kennerly. Thomas Evenden. Reg Oct 14, 1709. Her Eventon Clk.

No. 300. Peter Jones, assigns "Right of within Deed of Gift, to Henry Coggwell," for £4 s5. Jan 10, 1709. Peter, & Anne Jones. Test' John Falconer, Sam'l Philps. Richard Leary Clk.

No. 301. John Woolard of Perq Pre'ct, Labourer—for £25 pd by Wm Eggerton, of afore' Planter—200a part of Tract, (300a) "Pattented in the name of Rich'd Woolard, my dec'd Father," now in the tenure of said Eggerton. April 6, 1710. Test' Anne Stiball, Thomas Snoden. Edward Bonwick Clk.

No. 302. Dec 18, 1707. Thomas Houghton of Perq Pre'ct, Taylor—to Thomas Snowden Sen'r of afore' Gentleman—for £25 assigns 196a on North-side of Yawpim River, called "Philpotts old field." Cavey Houghton, her dower rights. Test' Wm Brethett, Thomas Legrave. Go Lumley Clk.

No. 303. Thomas Snowden, assigns "Right of Within Deed of Sale" to Wm Phillips. Jan 5, 1709/10. Test' Rich'd Morris, Wm Brethett. Edward Bonwick Clk.

No. 304. Wm Phillips assigns "Right of within Deed of Sale unto John Wiatt." Dec 15, 1711. Test' Joseph Sutton, John Stepney. Richard Leary Clk.

No. 305. John Hopkins, & Sarah his wife, for £100 sold to Joshua Calloway Right to Land, "except 10a" sold to John Hare. Feb 15, 1710. Test' Henry Cookson, John Stepney.

No. 306. May 22, 1711. Peter Horde of Perq Pre'ct, Carpenter—to James Coles of same, Carpenter—for £30 pd by said Coles (with Consent of his wife Elizabeth) sold 200a on North-east side of Perq River, adj Grassy Point, purchased by said Peter of David Harris. Test' Francis Beasley, Thomas Grayling, John Vallaway.

No. 307. Aug 13, 1711. Anthony Dawson of Newton in the Co of Glocester, & Providence of New Jersey, Yeoman—to Isaac Wilson of Perq Pre'ct in N. C. for £25 pd by said Wilson 590a of Land on South-side of Perq River, now in poss' of said Isaac Wilson. Test' Joseph Jessop, John Kay Jun'r, John Kay.

No. 308. Anthony Dawson of Newton New Jersey, appoints beloved friend Francis Toms, the Elder; & Francis Toms, the Younger both of Perq River, in N. C. Lawful Att, to ack deed in open Court unto Isaac Wilson, for 590a of Land. Test' Joseph Jessop, John Kay Jun, John Kay. Reg Jan 14, 1712/13.

No. 309. We the Subscribers do make over within deed of Sale unto Thomas Blitchenden. Test' John Norcom. Samuel Taylor. Ack in open Court Jan 13, 1712.

No. 310. James Coles of Perq, assigns "Rite" of a Patent, to James Perishoe, of afore'. Aug 12, 1712.

No. 311. Daniel Garrant, & Jane his wife, assigns Right of Land, to Daniel Hall. April 14, 1712/13. Test' Mathias Giles, John Bennet. Henry Clayton Clk.

No. 312. Wm Tetterton, assigns his Right of Land to James Sitterson, for £9. William & Sarah Tetterton. Test' Thomas Blitchenden, John Stepney. Reg Apl 15, 1713.

No 313. John Bennet Sen'r & "Rose my wife," for a Val' Con' unto Peter Jones; a tract of Land. Sept 20, 1709. Test' Thomas Snoden, Robert Jones.

No. 314. Edward Arvingdile, & Comfort his wife of Chowan precinct, for £8 "doth convey unto Rich'd Morris of same, Land Surveyed & Entered for Jesterling Petite"—264a in Perq Pre'ct, at the head of Maj Lillingtons Creek. Oct 3, 1712. Test' Wm Breathwaile, Robert Jones.

315. Richard Cheston of Perq precinct, Cooper—Atty of George Fox, of Isle of Wight Co, Virginia, planter—" Whereas the Lords Pro' of N. C. did Grant unto Richard Fox father of said George, 200a in Perq precinct on Perq River," adj Land of Joseph Jessop, formerly Land of Timothy Clear, as by pattent upon record, Richard Cheston Att' for George Fox the Elder, son & heir of Richard Fox, Con' £5 pd by Wm Bogue of Perq precinct, sold plan' on Perq River, now in poss' of Wm Moore, & Thomas Winslow. April 10, 1713. Test' Thomas Pierce, Francis Toms, John Barrow.

No. 316. George Fox of Isle of Wight, in Virginia, Appoints friend Richard Cheston of N. C. Lawfull Att' to Ack' to Wm Bogue of Perq, sale of land, pattented by my father Richard Fox, in the "Narrows" of Perq River. Test' Thomas Perry, Joseph Jessop. Mar 1, 1711. Henry Clayton Clk.

No. 317. George Fox of Isle of Wight Co in Vir', am firmly bound unto Wm Bogue of N. C. for the sum of £100, in Con' of a plan' on the "Narrows" of Perq River, now in poss' of said Bogue. Mar 1, 1710/11. Test' Thomas Perry, Joseph Jessop.

No. 318. "I do assign right of within Bond" to Wm Moore. April 14, 1713. Test' Francis Toms, Joseph Jessop. William Bogue.

No. 319. Wm Bogue assigns Right of within mentioned Deed of Sale, to Wm Moore for a valuable Con.' July 14, 1713. Test' John Stepney, Joseph Jessop.

RECORDS OF DEEDS 63

No. 320. Timothy Clear, for the sum £40 "Silver Money," pd by Joseph Jessop, sold Land mentioned in Pattent. 9 day of June, 1713. Test' Wm Carman, Elizabeth Carman. Hannah Clear, her dower Right.

No. 321. John Johnson of Perq Pre'ct, for a Con' pd by James Anderson of same, 15a, being "part of a tract" belonging to John Thurston, (63a) at the mouth of Suttons Creek, adj Joseph Sutton Jun'r, & John Kinsey. Dec. 12, 1711. Test' Edward Sweeney, Joseph Sutton.

No. 322. Timothy Clear of Albemarle, Planter—for a Con' assigns unto Wm Carman, of ye same Co, Planter—265a on North-side of Perq River "adj Timothy Clears own Land," on North-side of "Brambly Branch," the line of Wm Butler, called "Round House." July 8, 1713. Test' Sarah Clear, Joseph Jessop.

No. 323. John Lillington of the Per'ct of Chowan; Whereas the Lords Pro' of Carolina (by Grant Mar 31, 1691) "did give to Alex. Lillington Esq, Father of said John 640a On easternmost side of Indian Creek, in Perq precinct," do sell to John Banks, for £56 said Land, "now in his possession." Apl 10, 1713. Test' Jonathan Ashford, Thomas Cook.

No. 324. Aug 11, 1713. Robert Moore of Perquimans, & Hannah my wife, assign "our Right of within Patent," to William Lacy. Test' Henry Clayton.

No. 325. Thomas Meriday & Elizabeth my wife, dau of John Larance (Lawrence) Dec'd "son of Old William Larence, the first in the Co of Albemarle, N. C." for £35 pd by Francis Toms, assign our Right of ½ acre of Land on North-side of Perq River," on line formerly Thomas Finkles, now in Possession of Elizabeth Goodlet." Reg Aug 13, 1713. Test' Caleb Bundy, Edward Mayo, John Henly.

No. 326. April 1, 1713. Jonathan Stanley of Perq Pre'ct. & Elizabeth his wife, to Cornelius Ratcliff, of same, for £35 sold a Plan'. which "I purchased of Hon'ble Wm Glover Esq"—313a between lands of John Arnold & Thomas Holloway. Reg Aug 13, 1713. Test' T Knight, Richard Sanderson.

No. 327. John Norcom, & "Elizabeth my wife" of Perquimans, for £40 pd by Samuel Wiatt, Planter—do Sell Plan' 440a on West-side of Yawpim Creek, adj Robert Harmon, & Anthony Wherry, called "John Norcom Plantation," an Est' of Inheritance. Reg Oct 20, 1713. Test' Richard Leary, John Wiatt.

No. 328. William Moore of Perquimans, assigns Right of within Patent, to Timothy Clar. Jan 12, 1713. Reg Jan 20, 1713.

No. 329. Daniel Hall & Rose "ye wife of said Daniel," of Perq Pre'ct, for £8 pd by Daniel Garrant, Late of the Pre'ct of Chowan, Weaver—conveyed 100a, where said Hall now lives, adj John Hopkins. An Est' of Inheritance. Oct 10, 1712. Test' John Falconer, George Land.

No. 330. I do assign my Right of within mentioned Deed of Sale to Francis Carpenter Jun'r. Jan 12, 1713/14. Test' James Minge, Joshua Calleway.
                                                                Daniel Hall.

No. 331. Nov 9, 1709. John Lillington of Chowan Pre'ct, Abraham Warren, Mary Evens of Perq Pre'ct, for £55 pd by said Warren, & Mary, Sold 301a upon Little River, adj Lands of Capt John Hecklefield, & George Kinsley, said land formerly Capt. George Cleerke's of afore', & was Surveyed for George Lillington Nov 26, 1697, Wm Swann being Dept Surveyor, but now in the tenure of said Warren, Mary Evans, & Francis Pennis (Penrice), said Mary being widow of George Clerke. Test' George Lumley, John Hecklefield.

No. 332. Albert Albertson for £14 pd by William Jackson Jun'r, of Perq Pre'ct, Planter—assigns Land. April 8, 1712. Test' Richard French, Edward Bonwick.

No. 333. Elizabeth Scott, (dau of Charles Scott, Late of Albemarle,) for £8 pd by Gabriel Newby of same, 60a, on said Newbys line, purchased by my father Samuel Charles (father-in-law) Jan 1, 1696/7. Seal April 13, 1714. Test' Richard French, Jno Middleton, Richard Skinner.

No. 334. Peter Jones of the Pre'ct of Perq. Planter—to Wm Tetterton of afore' for £15 sold 200a on North-side of Yeopim River. "Land belonging to the Daus of Richard Williams Dec'd," lately in poss' of John Hopkins. Surveyed in the name of Robert Inkinson, Dec'd, and now in the tenure of Peter Jones. Mar 8, 1711-12. Test' Anne Stiball, Thomas Snoden.

No. 335. Richard Sanderson Jun'r of Currituck Pre'ct Gent—to Thomas Robinson of Perq Pre'ct, Carpenter—400a on Little River, formerly Land of John King, & lately land of William Glover Esq, Con' £50. Reg July 15, 1714. Test' Benia West, J. Palin.

No. 336. Perq Pre'ct. Wm Tetterton, & "Sarah my wife," for a Con' pd by John Norcom of same, assigns Plantation. Reg. July 15, 1714. Test' Henry Clayton, Margaret Pevell.

No. 337. Wm Tetterton & Sarah my wife, James Cittison & Hannah my wife of Perq Pre'ct: Whereas; John Lilly in his life time did for a sum due from Charles Macdaniel, Late of afore' obtained a Judgement against said Macdaniel, "on a Moyrty of Land" belonging to said Macdaniel on North-side of the Narrows" of Perq River—500a to Thomas Blitchenden for £3 pd by said Blitchenden, our Right in aforesaid Land, "Entered by said John Lilly. April 14, 1713. Test' John Stepney, Tho Snowden. Court at the house of Mr Richard French. (Thomas Blitchenden assigned said Land to Anthony Haskitt.)

No. 388. Samuel Bond of Perq Pre'ct, for £25 s5 pd by Henry Grace, of afore' sold 640a on South-west side of Perq River, adj Francis Toms. Reg July 15, 1714. Test' Joseph Jessop, Wm Kitching.

No. 339. Henry Grace of Perq, for £20 sold Tract of Land in said Co to Thomas Blitchenden, "of ye said place"—on South-side of "Mulberry Branch," by joint Consent of Samuel Bond, & Henry Grace. Reback Grace her dower right. Reg Aug 12, 1714. Test' Richard French, John Stepney.

No. 340. Wm Kitching & Margaret Snook of Perq, for £4 s10 pd by Wm Carman of afore' 100a adj the Bridge, on Isaac Wilsons line, called "Cabin Point Except Ground Sufficient, for a House 20 foot square at Bridge Landing." Our Right as by Patent April 1, 1713. Seal Aug 17 1714. Test' Wm Brem, Samuel Bond, Thomas Lilly.

No. 341. Wm Moore assigns Land to Richard Gray for £16. June 11, 1714. Test' Anthony Haskit, Joseph Jessop. John Lillington Clk.

No. 342. Ruth Parieter, widow, "for Love, doth give a Plan' formerly belonging to my father Richard Williams," & given by him to me, & my husband Wm Parieter, to his son William, Also four head of cattle, two cows, that his father gave him, & the other given by Wm White, also one Young mare, negroes & Land—one pair of Mill Stones, bought of John Falconer, one great Chest, one Iron Pot, & Pot-Hooks, to my son Wm Parieter when he comes of age." Aug 27, 1714. Test' Lemuel Taylor, John Stepney.

No. 343. Ann Wilson Widow—of Perq Pre'ct do Give unto Ralph Boseman of same—for £50 900a on South-west side of Perq River, adj Samuel Bond & Henry Grace, & the line of Joseph Smith. Another Parcell of Land 300a on said Bosemans line, & the line of Benj Wilson, called "Little Neck," given to said Benj by his father, on Robert Wilsons line. Oct 12, 1714. Test' John Falconer, Thomas Blitchenden.

No. 344. James Foster doth sell to Samuel Right (Wright) Land, adj Thomas Robeson. Reg 13 —— 1714. Test' Thomas Snoden, George Lo.

No. 345. Oct 12, 1714. James Foster to Wm Jackson, 290a of Land. Test' Edward Jackson, Samuel S. Wright. Richard Leary Clk.

No. 346. Ralph Bosman for £50, assigns Right unto Ann Wilson widow. Jan. 14, 1714. Test' John Pettiver, Henry Clayton.

No. 347. John Pettiver of Perq Pre'ct, Gent—in consideration of a Negro Girl Named Philis, delivered by Thomas Pierce of same, Planter—doth give & grant to him 300a on Wide of Perq River. Said Land purchased of the late Mr James Coles Dec'd, Now in the tenure of John Mason. "Except ten-foot square, where Jacob Peterson, & James Cole lies intered." Reg Jan 25, 1714/15. Test' Thomas Long, Henry Clayton.

No. 348. Archibald Holmes of the Co of Bath, Cooper—in Con' of the Love I bear Sarah Jones, late wife of Daniel Jones dec'd do give Tract of Land on South-side of Perq River, adj Land said Holmes sold to Edward Wilson Dec'd, known by the name of "Rays Old field." James Minge Att to Archibald Homes. Reg June 25, 1714.

No. 349. Richard Gray for £10 received of Wm Carman, assigns "Within Patent of Land." Feb 25, 1714. Test' Joseph Jessop.

No. 350. Mary Spellman, (dau of John Spellman, of Perq River, Dec'd) for "12 Barrels of Pitch, Received of John Pettiver," sold 300a in the fork of Lakers Creek, adj to Capt Guttery & Land of Andrew Reed. Mary Spellman 21 years of age Aug 2, 1715. Deed Aug 9, 1715. Test' Jno Falconer, James Williamson. At an Orphans Court at the House of Mr. Richard French, on Perq River.

No. 351. Mary Spellman a single woman, is firmly bound to John Pettiver, for the sum of £30. Sale of Land. Aug 9, 1715. Test' Jno Falconer, James Williamson.

No. 352. Samuel Wiatt of Perq Pre'ct, Planter—to his brother Thomas Wiatt of same, For £12 have "given a Tract of Land on ye mouth of Yeopim River, & Creek," adj Land of John Wiatt, left me by my father William Wiatt, dec'd. April 6, 1714. Elizabeth Wiatt, her dower right. Test' John Stepney, John Wiatt.

No. 353. Wm Kitching for £10 pd by —— Harell, assigns "Right to Remaining part of within mentioned Tract of Land." Oct 10, 1715. Margaret Kitching her dower right. Test' Thomas Blitchenden, Joseph Jessop.

No. 354. Wm Carman of Perq Pre'ct, for Love & good will I bear to my —— George Simons of same, & Susanna his wife, and their Dau Elizabeth, do give 90a of Land called "Butlers Neck." A Patent from Lords Pro' to George Simons, & wife Susanna, & at their Decease to their dau Elizabeth. Oct 10, 1715. Test' Wm Kitching, Joseph ——.

No. 355. Ann Wilson Sen'r, Widow—of Perq Pre'ct for Love I bear my son Isaac Wilson, do give to him 900a on West-side of Perq River, adj Samuel

Bond, & Henry Grace, on line of Joseph Smith. Another Parcell of Land 300a on South-west side of Perq River, adj Benj Wilson, called "The Little House Neck" being upon Robert Wilsons line, running to Cypress Swamp. At a Court at Mr. Richard French, Perq River Oct 11, 1715. Test' John Falconer, Wm Kitching.

No. 356. Timothy Clear, of Albemarle, for £15 s5 pd by Francis Smith, of afore' sold 300a in the "Narrows" of Perq River, commonly called "Sanders Dock" Patented in the name of Ezekiel Maudlin, & assigned by him to me July 10, 1705. Seal Aug 25, 1715. Court at Mr Richard French Oct 11, 1715.

No 357. "I Charles Overman & Ann my wife, for £9 pd by Ephrim Overman, "our brother," assigns Right of a Patent. Jan 10, 1715/16. John Mackey Att' for Ann Overman. Test' Jno Falconer, Richard Leary. At a Court held at the House of Elizabeth French, in Perquimans Jan 10, 1715/16.

No. 358. Thomas Williams & Sarah my wife, for £37 pd by Richard Bound 500a on the Sound, called "Homes." Feb 1, 1715/16. Test' James Minge, John Barrow.

No. 359. Oct 1, 1715. Richard Ratcliffe, Planter—of Perq Pre'ct, to Wm Hall, Blacksmith—by order of my Brother Cornelius Ratcliffe, Carpenter—Late of Perq Pre'ct for £40 pd by said Hall assigns Plan' which my Brother Cornelius bought of Jonathan Stanley, & Elizabeth his wife—313a on Westside of Little River, between Lands of John Arnold, & Thomas Holloway. Test' Daniel Guthrie, Christopher Dudley.

No. 360. John Pettiver, of Perq Pre'ct, Merch't—am firmly bound unto Daniel Richardson Esq, of ye afore' in the Penal Sum of £500 to be pd in "either good Pitch, or Pork," sealed with my Seal, & dated Jan ye 2, 1715/16. In Con' of a Marriage to be Solumnized between said John Pettiver, & Ann Wilson (Widow, & Relict of Isaac Wilson Late of Perquimans Dec'd) "said Marriage has been Solumnized." Test' John Lovick, Francis James. Reg May 4, 1716.

No. 361. Thomas Blitchenden of Perq Pre'ct for £20 pd by Charles Denman, of afore', Merchant—Convey to said Denman 100a called the "Gore" adj Henry Norman, James Minge, & the Sound side. April 10, 1716.

No. 362. Nathaniel Nicholson, & Sarah his wife, assigns Right of Land to Abraham Warren. Mar 31, 1709. Test' George Lumley.

No. 363. Abraham Warren, & Mary his wife assigns Right of within mentioned Land to Benjamin Nicholson. Mar 31, 1709. Entered by George Lumley Clk Of Gen'l Court.

No. 364. Nathaniel Nicholson, assigns "Right of said Patent" to Abraham Mullen, 210½a April 10, 1716. Test' Jo Jessop, Rich'd Whidby.

No. 365. Harris Willoby, & "Mary my now wife," for a valuable Con' pd by Francis Layden, assigned Land, which belonged to George Kinserly Dec'd, of which said Harris is now possessed. Reg May 4, 1716. Henry Palin Clk Of Gen'l Court. Test' Thomas Collins, Roger Middleton.

No. 366. Richard Bound of Perq pre'ct for the sum of £16 s15 pd by Francis Beasley of same, sold 200a, which I bought of Richard Morris, of said Pre'ct, on East-side of Maj Lillingtons Land, on Yeopim Creek, where said Beasley now lives, "with Consent of Abigall my wife." April 10, 1716. Test' Jo Oalst (Oats), Timothy Truelove.

No. 367. Joshua Calleway of Perq Pre'ct, for £36 pd by John Davis of same, conveyed Right to one half of Plan' on Lillies Creek, in the mouth of Perq River, Patented in the name of Ann, & Elizabeth Walker, 350a, now in the tenure of said John Davis. Aug 14, 1711. Test' Thomas Harvey, Richard Leary.

No. 368. May 7, 1716. I do hereby assign all my Right of the within Deed of Sale, to Wm Archdeacon. John Davis, & Mary Davis. Test' Callum Flyn.

No. 369. John Davis of Bath Co, for £30 s10 pd by Wm Archdeacon, of ye Co of Albemarle, in the mouth of Perq River, on a Creek called "Lillys Creek" 175a purchased by me of Joshua Calleway, being part of 350a Patent to Ann & Elizabeth Walker. June 12, 1716. Test' Jo Drinkwater, Ellener Melloyn, Arthur Harris.

No. 370. Wm Carman of Perq in N. C. for a sum of Money, pd by Joseph Jessop, "do Convey Land in the Narrows of Perq River," 318a on South-west side, on line of Ann Wilson, at the head of Indian Creek. July 5, 1716. Test' Jonathan Evens, Joseph Oates.

No. 371. Henry Hill "of ye upper Parish of Nansemond Co" for 5,000 lbs of Tobacco, to me pd by William Eason, assigns Right of 600a on ye main desert of Perq River, on line of Christopher Givens. Patented by me Aug 30, 1714. Deed Feb 16, 1714/15. Henry Hill & Mary Hill. Test' John Sutton, Farlow Quinn, Henry Hill.

No. 372. Sept 1, 1715. Thomas Long, & Elizabeth his wife of ye Pre'ct of Chowan, to Richard Widby of Perq Pre'ct for £20 Tract of Land 125a, called "ye Rich Land," adj said Whidby. Test' Joseph Sutton Sen'r, Wm Havett.

No. 373. Thomas Williams & Sarah his wife, for £5 sold to John Stepney, & Joshua Callaway, of Perq Pre'ct, 100a on ye Sound side, fronting "Batts Grave," & joining Land where Matthew Giles formerly lived, also where Archibald Holmes formerly lived, & sold to Edward Wilson Dec'd. Feb 21, 1715. Test' John Falconer, James Stepney.

No. 374. "Know all men that I Kilcocanen King of Yeopim, for a Val' Con' Received, with the Consent of my People, have sold to George Durant, a parcell of Land on Roanoke Sound, on a River called Perquimans, which issueth out of the North side of the Sound," adj Land formerly sold to Samuel Pricklove. 1 day of March, 1661. Kilcocanen or Kistotanew. Test' Thomas Weamouth, Caleb Calleway. Reg Oct 24, 1716.

No. 375. "I Kiskitando King of Yeopim, do sell to George Durant, a Parcell of Land on Perquimans River, Aug 4, 1661. Cuscutenew. Test' Thomas Weamouth, Caleb Calleway. Reg Oct 24, 1716. John Stepney Reg.

No. 376. Whereas George Durant hath Seated a Plan' on Roanoke Sound, "on a Point" known by name of "Wicocombe" between two Rivers, called Perquimans & Kototine, (Indian name for Little River) & George Catchminy has obtained a Grant of the Hon'ble Gov of Va, for the whole Neck of Land, betwixt the two Rivers, part of which is claimed by said George Durant, George Catchmany assigns Land "on ye Neck," on a small Creek which divideth Land from Neck called "Langleys" to a small "Piece of Ground where said Durant did begin to Clear, but desisted, George Catchmany doth assign Pattyn." Mar 13, 1662. Test' John Jenkins, Edward Remington.

*No. 377. Albemarle. 1673/4. Have settled with Mr. George Durant, & "there is not any thing Else betwixt us" Mar ye 11, 1673. Timo Biggs.

No. 378. "At a Court Holden ye 26 of Nov 1679;" present, John Harvey Esq Gov'r, John Willoughby Esq, Richard Foster Esq, John Jenkins Esq,

---

*Note—Timothy Biggs, m widow of George Catchmaid (Catchmany).

Anthony Slocum Esq, Robert Holden Esq, Lords Dept' Wm Cracofard Esq, James Blount Esq, John Varnham Esq, Assistants; ordered that Mr. George Durants Land "Comprehended in said Catchmanys Pattyn, be Surveyed, & his Rights in his own name drawn to effect same." A true copy of the Original. Henderson Walker Clk. Edward Mayor Register. Reg ye 24 Oct, 1716. John Stepney Reg.

No. 379. Grant from Lords Pro' to Mr George Durant, "that Parcell of Land in a certain Neck Betwixt two Rivers, called Perquimans, & Katatine," which divideth land from a Neck called "Langleys." Dec 26, 1673. Reg Oct 24, 1716. John Stepney, Reg of Writings for Perq Pre'ct.

No. 380. Deposition of Richard Watrey, age 51 years, "designed to go Southwards about 1662, to see how he might like the Place" At which time Mr. George Catchmany desired the Dept' to go to the Place, where Mr. George Durant was Seated, & was shown the Land, Intended by him for Mr. Catchmany, & returned to Va. About a Month later Mr. Catchmany employed the Dept' to go with three hands, to settle, & Seat said Land, & went with us himself. Coming to the House of Mr George Durant, he heard, & saw them conclude A line, dividing Between them, at a pine on the Sound, extending toward Land Seated by Coll Caltropp, & agreed that Catchmany have Land East-ward, & Durant Land on the West-ward. Also heard that Sir William Berkeley lately arrived from England had resolved that the Inhabitance of the South should hold no longer by Indian Titles. Dec 5, 1687. Richard Watrey appeared Before me & made Oath. Jno. Leary.

No. 381. (Deposition) Dep. of John Barrow "aged 50 years, saith; to his knowledge George Durant was Seated upon the Neck of Land, where his widow now lives, on or before George Catchmaid came into the Country for to Seat, & that Catchmaid did obtain A Pattent from Sir Wm Berkeley, for the Whole Tract." July 8, 1693.

No. 382. Dep. of Caleb Caloway aged 48, "that George Durant was Seated upon ye Neck of Land where his Widow now lives," before George Catchmaid; & the Dept was a witness to the Bill of Sale, by which Durant bought it of the King of Yawpim Indians, & that he had been informed that Mr. Catchmaid had a Pattent from Sir Wm Berkeley for the Whole Tract. July 13, 1693. Before us, Wm Wilkinson, Henderson Walker. Reg Oct 24, 1716. John Stepney Reg.

No. 383. Robert Harman of Perq Pre'ct, "do Revoke a deed of Gift from me to my son-in-law Anthony Wherry," bearing date April 10, 1715, "we both being well agreed it should be so." Seal May 24, 1716. Test' ——— Smith, Samuel Wiatt.

No. 384. Richard Wedby "Doe assign Right of Pattent," with my wife (Sarah) to John Arnold. Sarah Whedbee her dower right. Test' Wm Hill, Richard Whedbee. Court at the House of Mrs. Elizabeth French.

No. 385. Perquimans. Wm Godfrey of afore' for £30 s10 pd by Thomas Holloway, of same, "assigns Pattent, with all appurtenances belonging" to William Godfrey "as heir of John Godfrey." Aug 28, 1712. Test' Wm. Norris, Susanna Norris.

No. 386. Lewis Alex Knight of Pasquotank Pre'ct, for £30 pd by Joseph Sutton Jun'r, of Perq Pre'ct, "assigns Right of within Deed of Sale." Oct 9, 1716. Test' Francis Toms, Richard Leary. Court at the House of Mrs Eliz. French.

No. 387. Thomas Elliott of N. C. "for Love I bear my son Wm Elliott of Afore' Have given, Part of Tract, Granted to me Aug 27, 1714, in Perq Pre'ct, on Nathan Newbys line, & the line of James Thigpen—200a "with all appurtenances." 8d 8mo 1716. Test' Jo. Jessop, Richard Leary. Margaret Elliott her dower right.

No. 388. Wm Kitching of Perq Pre'ct, "to fulfill the will of Daniel Snook Dec'd "do give to Thomas Lilly of afore' "Parcell of Land, in the Narrows of Perq River, Above ye Bridge," adj Isaac Wilsons Land, whereon Thomas Lilly now liveth—100a, in poss' of said Lilly. Reg Oct 24, 1716. Test' Jo. Jessop, Richard Whedbee.

No. 389. James Thigpen Sen'r, & Margaret his wife of Perq Pre'ct, Planter—for £11, to be pd by Richard Morris of same, Planter—sold 100a "taken out of Pattent" of 300a granted 1696, at a Place called "Chinquopin Orchard" up the Branch of Cypress Swamp, adj Ann Wilson. Oct 9, 1716. Test' Wm Havett, Elizabeth Nixon.

"A true Copy made by order of Court, of Deed book A, from the Originals."
Nov 8, 1808. By William Jones, Benjamin Albertson.

DEED BOOK B

No. 1. Thomas Bagley of Perq for £3 pd by Peter Pearson, of Nansemond Co Va, assigns 50a, Part of Tract in Perq Pre'ct, adj John Burkehead, on "Burnt Pocoson" granted to me by Lords Pro' Aug 12, 1716. Seal Jan 7, 1716.

No. 2. Joseph Jessop "Doe assign within Pattent," unto John Sampson. Jan 8, 1716. At a Court at Mrs. Elizabeth French. Margaret Jessop her Dower right. Joshua Calleway her Att'.

No. 3. Richard Morris, & "Hannah my wife" assigns Right, to James Thigpen Jun'r. Jan 8, 1716.

No. 4. Wm Therell Sen'r "of the Town of Albington in New Eng, Pro' of Mass Bay" for £65 pd by Anthony Hatch, of Albemarle, Planter—Tract of Land in Perquimans, adj Cap'n Rich'd Sandersons. 277a. Mar 31, 1716. Test' John Gray, Sam'l Therall, Will Brothers.

No. 5. Richard Chaston of Perq, for ye sum of £40 pd by Thomas Bagley of afore' sold Land on North-side of Cypress Swamp," whereon I now live." 4a. Jan 7, 1716.

No. 6. Thomas Bagley of Perq, for a sum of Money pd by Richard Cheaston of same, "do sell Parcell of Land" in Perq—30a on "Burnt Pocoson," on line of Thomas Blitchenden. Granted to me Aug 16, 1716. Seal Jan 8, 1716/17.

No. 7. Robert Barnes of Perq Pre'ct, for a Con' "pd by Charles Wilkes of ye said Place"—sold a Parcell of Land, on Thomas Brooks line. A patent from the Lords Pro' Jan 19, 1715/16. Elizabeth Barnes her dower right. Test' Francis Toms, Peter Denman. Seal Jan 7, 1716/17.

No. 8. Joshua Toms of Perq Pre'ct, Planter—& Sarah his wife for £5 pd by Francis Foster Esq, of same, assigns 50a "now in Occupation of said Foster," by the side of Bull Branch; Tract laid out for John Gosby, "being part of his Land, on Suttons Creek, which came by will, & descent unto my wife, only surviving Dau of said Gosby." Jan 8, 1716/17. Test' Wm Havett, Sam'l Phelps.

No. 9. Richard Leary, & Sarah my wife, assign Right of Pattent, unto John Barrow Jun'r. Aug 12, 1712.

No. 10. 15 day of Mar 1716. Elizabeth Angly of Chowan Pre'ct, Widow—to John Falconer of same, for £10, sold Land on North-side of Yeopim River, "an Est' of Inheritance." Test' Richard Trant, John Hopkins. John Norcom Att' for Elizabeth Angley. April 9, 1719.

No. 11. Samuel Charles of Perq Pre'ct, Planter—for £5 pd by Hon'ble Francis Foster Esq, "do Sell a Parcell of Land, on N. E. side of Perq River," adj Lands of said Foster, 40a. April 9, 1717. Test' John Stepney, Richard Leary.

No. 12. Sarah Long Widow—of Perq for ye sum of £20 pd by Jonathan Taylor, of afore' 184a adj Land where said Sarah now Doth live, on ye W-side of Indian Creek," called "The old field," an Est' of Inheritance. April 6, 1717. Test' Sam'l Taylor, John Stepney.

No. 13. Jonathan Taylor, of Perq Pre'ct, for "Love & good will I do bear, unto Sarah Long, of same, Widow—& £10 pd by said Sarah; Sold Plan on W-side of Indian Creek, which I purchased of said Sarah—220a for "the time of her Natual Life." April 9, 1717.

No. 14. John Hopkins, for £55 pd by Samuel Taylor, of afore—assigned "Right of ye Within Patent." Jan 6, 1713. Test' Richard Leary, Alex Oliver, Daniel Hall. John Falconer Att' for John Hopkins.

No. 15. John Hopkins of Perq, Planter—for £55 pd by Samuel Taylor of same, Carpenter—sold 300a on S. W. side of Indian Creek, "to a Creek which divides said Land from the Land of Sarah Long." An Est' of Inheritance. Jan 11, 1714. Test' John Stepney, John Lillington.

No. 16. John Flowers, Cordwainer, of Perq Pre'ct, for "Natual Love I bear unto Wm Steward, & Joseph Steward," assigns to them Land upon Vosses Creek. April 9, 1717. Test' Richard Leary, James Williamson.

No. 17. Abraham Hobs Jun'r, of Perq Pre'ct, for £25 pd by Richard Leary, of same—Sold 400a called "Hobs Plantation" on N. E. side of Mill Swamp, adj Thomas Long, an Est' of Inheritance. Test' Francis Carpenter, John Norcom. Apl 12, 1715.

No. 18. Richard Leary of Perq Pre'ct, for £30 pd by Mrs. Joanner Peterson of same, assigns "Right of within Deed of Sale," Except 50a, already sold to my father-in-law Thomas Long, below "Horse-pen Branch." Feb 16, 1716/17. Test' John Falconer, Elizabeth Longlader.

No. 19. Richard Leary, Planter—for £60 pd by Miss Johanna Peterson of Perq, Widow—"Sold Dividend of Land, Surveyed for Abraham Hobs," also a parcel of Land which was given me by my father-in-law Thomas Long, as a Dowry with his Dau, being part of a greater Tract Surveyed in the name of said Thos Long—(500a) on Eastern side of "Mill Swamp," beginning on the upper side of "Horse Pen Branch," now in the tenure of said Richard Leary. April 9, 1717. Test' John Falconer, Jonathan Evens.

No. 20. John Porter of N. C. Merchant for £10 paid by Francis Toms of Perq, Planter—"do Sell 100a, on said Toms line," & the Line of James Thigpen, to me from my father John Porter Dec'd. Said Porter being "Compelled to Travail abroad Twelve English Miles, from the Place of his Usual abode." Aug 1, 1716. Test' Jon'r (Jonathan) Jacocks, Joseph Jessop. C. Gale. C. C.

No. 21. Joseph Smith of Perq, "for a certain sum" pd by Thomas Ellitt, of afore' 200a, being part of Tract, Granted by Patent to Joseph Smith April 1, 1713. (The whole Patent 1000a.) Seal April 7, 1717. Joseph Smith. Leah Smith. Test' Joseph Jessop, John Stepney.

No. 22. Joseph Smith "for a sum of Money" pd by Samuel Phelps, of Perq, sold part of a Grant, to me April 1713, (for 1000a) from my line to line of Samuel Bond, along lines of Thomas Blitchenden, Henry Grace, Francis Toms, Isaac Wilson, & Thomas Ellit, 400a. April 11, 1717. Leah Smith her dower right. Test' Jo. Jessop, Jo. Stepney.

No. 23. April 20, 1716. *Robert Moore, & Hannah his wife in the Pre'ct of Perq for £14, pd by James Thigpen, assigns Land, "on Which said Thigpen now lives," on the Perq River, (200a) which did formerly belong to Stephen Manwaring, Late of N. C. Purchased by said Stephens of Wm Vose, Jan 16, 1696, upon lines of Francis Toms, & Jonathan Jones. Test' Jno. Falconer, Jonathan Evens.

No. 24. Wm Archdeacon, assigns "All Right of ye Within Deed" to Simon Trombal. Dec 31, 1716. Test' Rich'd Sanderson, Anthony Hatch.

No. 25. Zachariah Nixon of Perq Pre'ct, Planter—for £13 s10 pd by Thomas Montague, of same, 133a of Land. Part of 504a on South-side of Little River "as by Patent unto said Zachariah." July 9, 1717. Test' Sam'l Nichols, Christo Nichols, George Lumley.

No. 26. John Morris assigns "Right to my Part of Within mentioned Tract of Land, Granted to Zachariah Nixon." Reg July 10, 1717.

No. 27. Wm Bogue of Perq Pre'ct, for £29 pd by Joseph Jessop, of afore' sold 143a, Surveyed for James Loadman, & "Bequeathed to me by said James Loadman, in his will, "on ye Banks of Perq River. (Granted May 1, 1694.) Seal July 6, 1717. William & Elliner Bogue. Test' William Moore.

No. 28. Charles Denman, Merchant—for £16 Received of John Pettiver, do Sell 100a. July 2, 1717. Test' John Cake, Will Hall.

No. 29. Richard Morris, "for Good causes & £30 Received, do assign Within Land." Test' Wm Dowers, Jno Falconer. Reg July 10, 1717. Henry Clayton, Mary Clayton.

No. 30. Jonathan Jones, of Pasquotank, for £16 Paid by Wm Moore of Perq, Sold 100a, on ye N. E. side of Perquimans River, called "Voses Point." April 6, 1717. Test' Marg' Jessop, Joseph Jessop.

No. 31. Zachariah Nixon, of Perq, Planter—for £3 10s pd by Christopher Nichols of same, sold 50a (Part of Tract for 504a) on South-side of Little River. July 9, 1717. Test' Sam'l Nichols, George Lumley.

No. 32. Harris Willougby of Albemarle, for £16 pd by Thomas Collinge, of afore' Planter—sold half of Tract of Land, on North-side of Perq River, 203a adj Land of John Bateman, & Elliner Atteway, dau of Thomas Dec'd, as by Patent assigned, 104a. an Est of Inheritance. Reg Sept 22, 1717. Test' Elizabeth Gale, Elizabeth Armer.

No. 33. Elleaner Attaway of Perq, Spinster—Whereas "my father Thomas Attaway Dyed Seized of a Tract of Land" 208a on North-side of Perq River, on lines of John Bateman, & James Perishow, "which fell to me & my Sister Mary, as coheirs of said Thomas," in Con' of £15 pd to me by Harris Willoby, Planter—have sold half of said Tract, adj other half, "now in possession of my mother Elizabeth," which belonged to my sister Mary. May 27, 1716. Test' Rich Smith, Dan'l Guthrie.

No. 34. Thomas Harvey of Perq, yeoman—& Elizabeth my wife, for £18 pd by Jonathan Evens, of afore' Planter—sold 275a "On ye S. W. side of Perq

---

*Note.—Hannah Manwaring dau of Stephen m Wm Moore.

River," adj Henry Clayton, Elizabeth French, & John Pettiver. Jan 15, 1717/18. Court at the House of Mrs. Elizabeth French.

No. 35. Elliner Attaway of Perq, assigns Pattent unto Richard Gray. April 8, 1718.

No. 36. Thomas Collins for the Sum of £6 pd by Peter Dovewiner, assigns "Right of Pattent." April 8, 1718. Test' Wm Havett, Rich'd Leary.

No. 37. Jonathan Evens of Perq, Gent—for £16 pd by Wm Dowers of afore' Blacksmith—sold 100a called "Benjamin Giddins old field" on S. W. side of Req River, adj Mr. Henry Clayton, & John Pettiver. April 8, 1718. Test' Wm Havet, John Falconer.

No. 38. April 8, 1718. Timothy Clear of Albemarle, Pre'ct of Perq, & Hannah my wife, to Thomas Rountree of Chowan* for £15 pd by Wm. Moore, of the Co & Pre'ct above, "doth Acquitt said Rountree, & sold 101a on North side of Perq River, at the Mouth of Cypress Swamp" being part of Tract Granted to Timothy Clare (203a), Sept 4, 1714. Reg April 10, 1718. Test' J. Jessop, Jacob Hill, Luke Hollowell.

No. 39. Thomas Rountree of Chowan Pre'ct, & Elizabeth his wife, & Francis Rountree Sen'r of afore' other part' for £7 s10, sold 50a on N. E. side of Perq River, "part of Tract Granted to Timothy Clare Sept 4, 1714." Seal April 8, 1718. Test' James Griffin, Will Hill, Luke Hollowell.

No. 40. Gabriel Newby, & Mary my wife, of Albemarle, for the Sum of £25 pd by Ralph Bufkin, of same, conveyed 300a on West-side of Cypress Swamp, & West-side of Perq River. 13 day 6 mo 1717. Test' John Henly, Benjamin Sanders. Wm Newby.

No. 41. Timothy Clare assigns unto Luke Hollowell, one half of "Within Mentioned Pattent," of 203a, for £13. April 8, 1718.

No. 42. Wm White of Chowan, Planter—unto Thomas Snoden of Perq; Planter—"Right of Within Pattent." April 8, 1718. Test' Jno Falconer, Francis Layden.

No. 43. Wm White of Chowan, unto Thomas Snoden, of Perq, Right of Pattent, & "oblige myself that my wife shall Relinquish her Dower Right." April 8, 1718. Test' Jno Falconer, Francis Layden.

No. 44. Francis Smith assigns Land unto James Griffin. April 8, 1718.

No. 45. John Sampson, & Isaac Sampson, "of Charles City Co in Virginia," for £14 pd by Timothy Cleare of Perq in N. C. sold 200a (willed to us by our father Stephen Sampson Dec'd) in Perq Pre'ct. Reg April 11, 1718. Test' Jo Jessop, Arthur Croxton.

No. 46. Timothy Cleare of Perq, assigns "Within Pattent" to John Winslow, "Having Received £20 as full satisfaction for same." April 7, 1718.

No. 47. Thomas Rucks, "of Nansemum In Virginia," for £15 pd by John Parish of Perq Pre'ct, N. C. 150a on the Head of Deep Creek, in said Co. June 25, 1718. Test' George Gordon, Wm Colson, Wm Knowles.

No. 48. Nathaniel Nicholson, "For a Con' Received by me, do let over unto Abraham Jewett," my Right of Patent. July 8, 1718.

No. 49. Francis Beasley for £75 pd by Charles Denman, assigns 605a bought of Mr. Robert Fendall, & Mr Anthony Ellexander, on S. W. side of Perq River. Feb 19, 1718. Test' William Kenedy, William Hall.

No. 50. Benjamin Wilson of Perq, for £10 pd by William Bastable of afore' sold 60a, part of Tract on S. W. side of Perq River. July 8, 1718. Test' Will Kitching, Jonathan Evens.

No. 51. Edward Mauldin of Perq, for a "Val' Con' pd by John Henby" of afore' sold 104a, & ½, being "one half of the Land of my wife Mary, & the said John Henbys wife Hannah" on Gum Swamp, Perq River, & Suttons Creek. Test' Rich'd Ratlif, Rich'd Cheston, Ezekiel Maudlin. Reg July 12, 1718.

No. 52. James Thigpen of Perq, for £80 pd by Francis Toms of afore' sold 200a on N. E. side of Perq River, adj line of said Toms. Jan, 1717/18. Test' William Moore, Joseph Jessop. "At a Court at the House of Mrs. Elizabeth French on Jan 15, 1717.18. came James Thigpen, & Margarett his wife, & Ack said deed."

No. 53. Lemuel Taylor of Perq, Carpenter—for £45 pd by Jeremiah Pratt of afore' sold 100a on N. E. side of Indian Creek, between Land of John Wiatt, & John Banks, "including Land on each side of stream." Jan 15 1717/18. Test' William Low, Rich'd Leary.

No. 54. Wm Hall of Perq Pre'ct, Cooper—for £40, "& one Negro woman," to me in hand by Henry Clayton of same, sold 640a on So West side of Perq River, said "Land Granted unto Joseph Scott," & later (Sept 17, 1703) was conveyed by Wm Frilie, & Grace his wife, (dau of Joshua Scott) to James Coles & Mary his wife, & their heirs. Wm Hall "only proper heir" of Mary late wife of said Henry Clayton. Feb 19, 1718/18. Test' Zachariah Ellson, Charles Denman. Deed ack by Ann wife of Wm Hall at a Court at Mrs. Elizabeth French 1719.

No. 55. Henry Grace of Perq for £27 pd by John Hudler (Hurdle) of afore' sold 300a "part of Tract Granted to Samuel Bond," on Francis Toms line, now in possession of Maurice Walker. Sept in the 4th year of the Reign of King George 1718.

No. 56. Richard Cheston of Perquimans, for £15 in hand, sold——— and ——— (torn)

No. 57. John Banks, & Sarah my wife, of Perq, for £15 pd by Samuel Taylor of same, sold "our Right in a Parcell of Land" on North-side of Indian Creek, "where the Water-Mill now stands," & where the said Banks now lives. Oct 11, 1709. —st' John Stepney, Isaac Wilson.

No. 58. Sarah Banks Appoints "Friend Richard Leary" Att' to Ack her Dower Rights. Sept 10, 1709. Test' John Hare, Henry Cokson.

No. 59. ———Flowsers Jun'r of Perq, assignment to Sa——— ——— & his heirs forever. Mar 8, 1707. Test' William Horton, Thomas Horton.

No. 60. Thomas Snoden of Perq, for £6 pd by Samuel Cretchington of afore' "assigns Right of 210a on the Narrows of Perq River," Pattented in the name of Patrick Canidy, & now in the tenure of said Samuel. April 8, 1707. Test' John Lillington, Richard Leary.

No. 61. Samuel Cretchington of Perq, assigns Right to within Deed unto Abraham Mullen, of same, for £10. April 8, 1707.

No. 62. ——————— unto John Bass 300a, in the Pre'ct of Perq, July 14, 1709. Thomas Spigh (Probably Speight). Test' Thomas Blitchenden, Richard Leary.

No. 63. Robert Barnes ——— of Albemarle, in Con' ——— to Lewis Skinner Land adj Land ——— which I ——— of Charles Wilkes ——— Running along line "towards the Dwelling House of me Robert Barnes"—£35 ——— as ample Manner ——— 15 day of July in the Reign of ——— George ———. Test' J. Jessop ———. Court at the House of Mrs. ———. July 14, 1719.

No. 64. Timo—————— of Perq, for £6 pd by John Hudson of afore' sold "part of Tract," adj Timothy Clear's line, 20a Granted ———— June 20, 1703, & assigned to me 1704 ———— & that said John ———— July 1719. Timothy Clear.

No. 65. Richard Bounds of Perq, Taylor—one pt & Humphrey Felt (Phelps) of afore' Carpenter—other pt, for £6, assigns 50a of Land. Sept 2, 1718. Test' Francis Smith, Elizabeth Horner.

No. 66. Feb 20, 1719. ———— Pettiver (John) & Ann his wife of N. C. to James Smith, Cordwainer—of same, for £58, "Received" sold 300a, known by the name of "Davenports Plan'" on Roanoke Sound, (Albemarle) Running up the Mouth of Yeopim Creek. Mar 4, 1719/20. Test' Thomas Parris, Henry Clayton. Will Havet Cl Co.

No. 67. Thomas Bagley in Albemarle, for £40, pd by William Bogue of afore' sold 250a, part of "Tract, on North-side of Cypress Swamp, whereon I now live," to a Place called "Little Ridge." Susan Bagley her dower right. Reg April 13, 1720.

No. 68. Thomas Bagle of Perq, to Anthony Haskitt Jun'r of afore', "Part of Tract" 200a on Peter Pearsons line, & lines of Thomas Blitchenden, & Rich'd Cheston." Oct 12, 1720. Test' Gabriel Newby, Thomas Peters. (Peirce) West-side of Perq River. 12-10 mo, 1719. Test' Tho Harvey, Joseph Newby.

No. 69. Edward Moseley, of Chowan Pre'ct, Gent—"for affection I have for Samuel Swann, (Grand-son of Maj Samuel Swann, late of N. C. Dec'd) have given my Plan' in Perq, on the Sound-side, between Perq and Little Rivers, called "Moseleys Gut Plantation" 400a, which was purchased by me of Mr. Thomas Swann, April 1, 1715, & "for want of heirs" of said Samuel Swann, to come to Moseley Vail, half brother of said Samuel, for "want of heirs" of said Moseley Vail, to come to John Vail, brother of said Moseley Vail. Dec 25, 1718. Test' Elizabeth Swann, Richard Wilson, Tho Swann.

No. 70. Richard Skinner Sen'r, "in Con' of Natrill aff' I Bear unto my Dau' Margarett Wattson, have given, A Tract of Land at the Punch Bowel" 100a, adj Mr. Henry Hill. Nov 6, 1718. Test' Ja Oates, Richard Skinner Jun'r.

No. 71. Wm Dowers, late of Perq, assigns "Right of Within Deed of Sale," of Land, unto Thomas Bagley. April 12, 1720. Test' Thomas Herman, Joseph Jessop.

No. 72. Anthony Harkins (Hawkins) Sen'r of Perq, for £30 pd by Joseph Newby, of afore' sold 143a of Land. Jan 23, 1719/20. Test' Rich'd Cheston, Wm Bogue.

No. 73. James Thigpen of Perq, for £13 pd by James Thigpen, of afore', sold to him "Half a Tract of Land," 640a in Chowan Pre'ct, adj Richard Skinner, Nathan Newby, Thomas Ellit, & Thomas Bray, (320a being half of said Land) Granted to me Aug 16, 1716. Seal Oct 12, 1719. Test' Tho Harvey, Francis Smith.

No. 74. Thomas Bagley of Perq, assigns "Right of Within Patent," to Anthony Haskitt Jun'r, "save a small quantity passed to Peter Pearson, & Rich'd Cheston." Oct 12, 1720. Test' Gabriel Newby, Thomas Peters. (Peirce)

No. 75. Thomas Bagley, assigns "Right of Within Deed of Sale," to Rich'd Cheston. July 12, 1720. Test' Jo Jessop, Jacob Hill.

No. 76. James Newby assigns "Right of Within Contents," unto Christopher Nicholson. Jan 10, 1720/21. Test' Tho Blitchenden, Joseph Barrow, George Lumley.

RECORDS OF DEEDS 75

No. 77. James Perishew, for £44 pd by Timothy Clear, sold Land, "with Appurtenances." Oct 12, 1710. Test' Edward Mayo, Jos Jessop.

No. 78. Joseph Jessop, for £9 pd by Timothy Clear, assigns "Right of Patent, to me Granted." Jan 10, 1720.

No. 79. Francis Toms, of Perq, in Con' of a "Plan' adj one where Arthur Jones Lately lived," (now in my possession) secured to me by Stephen Gibson, & Jane his wife, sold to said Gibson, "Part of said Tract," 128a, on N. E. side of Voses Creek, beg' at "Bull Branch," & running to lower "Great Pond," on James Henbys line, to me Grt by Pat'. 11 of 9 mo 1719. Test' Wm Moore, Jos Jessop.

No. 80. Richard Turner, of Perq, for "Love I do bear my son-in-law William Bairstable, do give to him part of my Tract of Land, whereon I now live"—50a next to "Bull Branch." Oct 13, 1714. Test' Mary Jessop, Joseph Jessop.

No. 81. Thomas Penrice, of Perq, in Con' of a "Sum of money" paid by Francis Lading (Layden) of same, sold 6a, taken out of Patent for 165a, adj said "Laydens Corner Tree." April 7, 1721. Thomas & Sarah Penrice. Test' Thomas Snoden, John Bateman, Anthony Hatch.

No. 82. Thomas Penrice, Planter—assigns unto Francis Layden, of afore' weaver—"Right of Patent." April 10, 1721. Test' Jno Bateman, Thomas Snoden.

No. 83. I assign my "Right of within Patent" to James Henby of Perquimans. April 11, 1721. Thomas Boswell. Test' Richard Leary Clk Co.

No. 84. Thomas Penrice of Perq, Planter—assigns unto Thomas Snoden of afore', Planter—"Right of Patent." April 10, 1721. Test' John Bateman, Francis Layden.

No. 85. James Thigpen Jun, for £50 pd by Abraham Sanders, assigns Right to Land. April 10, 1721. Test' Samuel Phelps, Rich'd Leary.

No. 86. James Thigpen Sen'r of Perq, for £15 pd by may son James Jun'r, sold Part of Tract, beg' at Nathan Newbys Corner. 100a, same to me Grt, Aug 16, 1716. Seal April 6, 1721. Test' Jo Jessop, Pave Palmer.

No. 87. Thomas Bagley of Perq, for £40 pd by Wm More of afore' 100a called "Benjamin Giddings old field" on S. W. side of Perq River, adj Henry Clayton, & Capt Jno Pettiver, & Jonathan Evens, April 10, 1721. Test' Jo Jessop, Joseph Oates.

No. 88. Wm Moore, of Perq, for £30 pd by Thomas Lilly of afore' sold 50a at a Place called "Hills," Betwixt it & a Place called "Great Neck." April 10, 1721. Test' Rich'd Leary, Sam'l Phelps.

No. 89. Francis Toms of Perq, for £5 pd by Wm Moore Sen'r of afore' "Sold Part of Tract," adj his own line, 2a. April 10, 1721. Test' Jo Jessop, Jo Oates.

No. 90. James Thigpen Sen'r, to John Edwards, "Part of Tract," on Branch called "Homes Branch," to Chinquapin Orchard Branch, for £20 Sterling. 50a April 11, 1719. Test' Samuel Branch, Jo Jessop.

No. 91. Nathanell Albertson, of Perq, in Con' of a "Certain Covenant Between me & Samuel Sherer of same, "assigned Part of Tract, of my father Albert Albertson," 95a on S. W. side of Suttons Creek, adj Andrew Reads, "Swamp side," being Peter Albertsons line. April 10, 1721. Test' Ezekiel Maulding, James Newby.

No. 92. Wm Moore Sen'r of Perq, for £50, Sold to Thomas Bagley 150a on N. E. side of Perq River, on Lines of Timothy Cleare, & Wm Booge, down said line to "Cypress Swamp," a Grt to me. April 10, 1721. Test' J. Jessop, Paul Palmer.

No. 93. James Thigpen Jun'r of Perq, Planter—for £10 pd by Gabriel Newby, of same, Wheelright—320a on lines of Richard Skinner, Nathan Newby, Thomas Elletts, & Thomas Brays Land, "One half of which was taken up by my father James Thigpen Aug 16, 1716." Seal April 6, 1721. Test' Wm Trotter Jun'r, Jesse Newby.

No. 94. I do assign "Right of this Deed of Sale," unto Mr Thomas Speight. July 11, 1721. Test' Jo Jessop, Sam'l Phelps. Robert Barnes.

No. 95. Robert Barnes for £25 pd by Tho Speight, assigns Patent. July 10, 1721. Test' Jos Jessop, Sam'l Phelps. Court at the House of Mrs. Elizabeth French.

No. 96. I do assign unto Mr. Thomas Commander "Right of Patent." July 11, 1721. Test' Thos Harvey, James Henby. William Jackson.

No. 97. Thomas Collins, & wife Alexandris, assigns "Right of Patent," unto John Gibson. July 12, 1721. Test' Albert Albertson, Richard Whedby. Received of John Gibson £10 for said Land.

No. 98. Wm Ellett, & Elizabeth my wife, for £11 pd by Thomas Elliott, 200a "in fork of Cypress Swamp," on John Prickloes line, granted to me Oct 19, 1716. This deed Ack July 11, 1721. Test' James Henby, Wm Bogue.

No. 99. Oct 8, 1720. Robert Barnes of Perq, & Elizabeth my wife, to Thomas Speight Esq, of afore' 200a "on a Place called Sandy Ridge" adj Middle Swamp, that issueth out of "Catherines Creek Swamp," part of Land conveyed by Wm Citchen "to John Hurdle of Nansemond Co Va," on line of Thomas Docton. Which Survey was Grt to Thomas Speight Esq, being "part of two Patents, one to Citchen (Kitchen), & the other to Snook (Daniel)," & left by will of Wm Citchen, & Margaret Snook, by Deed of Gift. Test' J. Jessop, Sam'l Phelps.*

No. 100. July 14, 1719. Francis Toms of Perq, for £20 Received of James Henby of afore' assigns Right of Patent. Test' Henry Clayton.

No. 101. John Lillington, of Bath Co, Gent; for £70 pd by Thomas Cary, of Bath, Esq—Sold Tract of Land in Perq, "whereon my father lately Dwelt" on a Branch of Yeopim Creek, 640a adj land of Mr. Calloway, & Peter Jones. April 9, 1715. Test' Cha Gale, Edward Moseley, Edmund Porter, John Moor. C. Gale, Ch Just.

No. 102. Thomas Cary Esq for £90 pd by James Williamson, "Sold Plan'" in Perq 640a on Branch of Yeopim Creek, purchased of Mr. John Lillington." Feb 17, 1716. Test' Thomas Cooke, James Ward, Edward Moseley.

No. 103. James Williamson of Perq, for £62 s10 pd by Richard Leary, of afore' Sold 640a on a Branch of Yeopim Creek, "Surveyed, & Patented in the name of Mr. Alexander Lillington." April 11, 1717. Test' John Shailer, Thomas Long, Thomas Wiatt.

No. 104. John Woolard of Perq, for £22, pd by John Welch of Afore' Planter—Sold 110a on N. E. side of Yawpim River, adj Joshua Calloway, & John Wiatt. 10 day 8 mo 1721. Test' Rich'd Leary, Jos Oates.

No. 105. Sept 7, 1722. John Williams of Perq, Planter—to Nicholas Crisp of Chowan, Gent—for £100, Sold 200a in Perq on Albemarle Sound, by the "Great Swamp," adj Lands of Maj Thomas Harvey, & Mary Norman (Widow

---

*Note—Wm Kitchen m Margaret Snook (either wife or dau of Daniel).

of Henry) part of 340a "Patent to said John Williams." Nov 11, 1719. Test' Thomas Parris, Will'm Badham.

No. 106. Lewis Scinner (Skinner) of Perq, for the Sum of ———— pd by "Lott Stallings of the Co Of Nansemond in Virginia," 35a adj Land of Charles Wilks. Oct 10, 1721. Test' Daniel Smith, Joseph Gibson.

No. 107. Charles Wilks, of Perq, Planter—for £20 pd By Lott Stallings of Va, Planter—100a on Thomas Brooks line. Oct 10, 1721. Test' Daniel Brooks, Joseph Gibson.

No. 108. Jan 9, 1721. Albert Albertson Sen'r, assigns "Right of within deed," to son Albert Albertson Jun'r.

No. 109. James Thigpen Jun'r of Albemarle, for £12 pd by John Edwards, 50a of Land, at a Branch called "Homes Branch" up "Chinquapin Orchard Branch." Dec 27, 1721. Test' Joseph Newby, Gabriel Newby.

No. 110. John Edwards, & Elizabeth my wife, for £10 pd by Benjamin Sanders ————. Dec 28, 1721. Test' James Thigpen, Gabriel Newby.

No. 111. Ralf Bufkin for £50 pd by Francis Newby ————. 9th 11mo 1721. Test' Zachariah Elton, Richard Cheston.

No. 112. Gabriel Newby for £12 pd by James Thigpen Jun'r, assigns 320a of Land. Jan 9, 1721. Test' Richard Cheaston, Timothy Clare.

No. 113. Thomas Collings, of Albemarle, Planter—for £33 pd by Ralph Fletcher, of afore' Weaver—Sold 203a on No side of Perq River, adj John Bateman, & John Flowers. Jan, 1722. Test' Charles Denman, Jeremiah Symons.

No. 114. John Woolard of Perq, "with Consent of Alce my wife," for £15 pd by Wm Eggerton, of afore' Planter"—100a Given by Richard Woolard unto his son Richard, & he Dying in Minority, fell to said John Woolard," adj Land of Thomas Snoden Dec'd. Test' John Woolard, John Falconer. Reg April 16, 1722.

No. 115. Lords Pro' of N. C. Grant unto Capt Stepney 293a on "Yawpim Creek," in Perq Pre'ct, by a Branch in Jeane Charles line, to a pine in Maj Alex. Lillingtons line. Seal of Colony Feb 13, 1696. Wit' our Well beloved John Archdale Esq, Gov of Carolina, & our Councillors; Daniel Akehurst, Francis Toms, Thomas Pollick, Samuel Swann, Henderson Walker. Reg May 17, 1722.

No. 116. John Stepney Sen'r of Perq, "appoints friend Jonathan Evens" of afore' Att' to Ack' unto my son John Stepney the "Assignment of a Patent of Land, where I now live." April 19, 1722. Test' Wm Tederton, John Hare

No. 117. John Stepney Sen'r, "for Natual Love I do bear unto my son John, & his wife Sarah, in Consideration that they live on my Plan' & assist me in my affairs During my life, do assign Patent to him, to me Grt, as his proper Estate & Birthright." April 4, 1722.

No. 118. John Stepney Sen'r, to his son John. Ack by Jonathan Evens Att' to John Stepney Sen'r. April 14, 1722.

No. 119. Jonathan Taylor, of the Pre'ct of Perq, Planter for £50 pd by James Cheson, of Afore' sold 184a, "where said Cheson now doth live," on west side if Indian Creek; being "Dividend of Land" purchased by said Taylor of Sarah Long Dec'd. Oct 11, 1721. Test' Paul Palmer, Richard Leary.

No. 120. Richard Leary, of Perq, Planter—for £39 pd by Nicholas Crisp, of Chowan, Sold 27a called "Batts Grave Island" at the "Mouth of Yawpim

River," in Albemarle Sound. April 10, 1722. Test' Richard Whedby, Thomas Peirce.

No. 121. John Pettiver of Perq, for £50 pd by Capt Nicholas Crisp, of Chowan., Sold 200a. "Original Patent from Lords Pro' May 8, 1684 to William Tetterton," Test' Thomas Beterly, Henry Speller, Wm Older. C. Gale Ch Just.

No. 122. Joseph Jessop, of Perq, for £10 pd by Capt Allston, of Chowan, sold to said Capt John Alston, 200a in Perquimans, on N. E. side of the River, adj Land of John Gooding. "Part of 400a Grt to me April 4, 1720." Seal July 9, 1722.

No. 123. Benjamin Willson, & Judith My Wife, of Perq, for "Natual Aff" we bear to our Sister Ann Elliott (wife of Thomas afore') do Give to said Thomas part of Tract given me by my Dec'd father Isaac Willson, where John White lived, 100a to him for life, & at his Dec' to his son Joseph, that he had by my Sister Ann, & to his son Thomas also son of Ann, & for want of heirs back of me." April 9, 1722. Test' Gabriel Newby, Wm Barstable.

No. 124. Lords Pro' grant unto Richard Gray of Perq 45a, in fork of "Beaver Cove Swamp," adj John Tomlin. Which Land was "granted Jan 8, 1714 to Elinder Atteway & lapsed for want of Seating." April 4, 1721. Councillors; Wm Reed, C. Eden, Tho Pollock, Rich'd Sanderson, John Hackelfield. Reg Sept 20, 1722.

No. 125. Richard Leary assigns "Right of this Patent" unto Alber—— Albertson. Feb 3, 1721/2. Richard Gray R. G.

No. 126. July 2, 1722. Thomas Davis of Perq, & Elizabeth his wife, to John Bogue of afore' for £213, sold 80a on the "Great Pocoson," where Perq River Heads, at a tree on Henry Hills Land, to line of Thomas Docton, "being part of Patent to said Docton," & conveyed by him to Thomas Davis, 550a. Test' Thomas Docton, Paul Phillips.

No. 127. April 9, 1722. Thomas Docton of Perq, & Elizabeth his wife, to Thomas Davis of afore' for £10 Sold 275a, adj the "Great Pocoson," & Henry Hill. Test' John Falconer, Richard Leary.

No. 128. Joseph Sutton, Jun'r of Perq, for £5 pd by Richard Wedby, of afore' sold 235a adj said "Whedbys own Land," formerly Benjamin Nichilsons, "one half of Tract Surveyed Jan 25, 1719/20." Seal Oct 10, 1721. Test' Jo Jessop, Rich' Leary.

No. 129. Gabriel Newby, of Albemarle, Conveyed unto Anthony Haskitt 50a of Land, "formerly Peter Grays," Land Grt to me Nov 11, 1720. Seal July 9, 1722. Test' Thos Harvey, Richard Ratlif.

No. 130. James Coles, Carpenter, & Mary my wife, of Perq—for £30 to Lewis Alexander Knight, & Emanuel Knight (his brother) of Afore' Planters— sold Plan' (bought of Wm Hall, heir to Ann Peterson Dec'd) on N. E. side of Perq River, 100a adj Land of Christopher Nicholson, & the land of John Kinsey, "which was sold Mar 14, 1672 to Thos Kent, by one Wm Vose of said Pre'ct, being part of 200a Granted Sept 25, 1663, & signed by Sir William Berkeley." Seal April 14, 1702. Test' Samuel Swann Jun'r, Ralf Fletcher.

No. 131. Lewis Alex. Knight, of Pasquotank, for £30 pd by Joseph Sutton Jun'r of Perq, assigned "Right of Within Deed." Oct 9, 1716. Test' Francis Toms, Richard Leary.

No. 132. Joseph Sutton Jun'r of Perq, for £45 pd by Richard Ratlif, assigned "Right of within Deed of Sale." July 10, 1722. Test' Tho Speight, Rich'd Whedbee.

RECORDS OF DEEDS

No. 133. Henry Norman, of Chowan, Planter—for £100 pd by John Crisp of same, Gent—assigned 200a on N. side of Albemarle Sound, "In Perq Pre'ct," adj Land formerly Capt Fendals, but now belonging to John Swann, son of Maj Samuel Swann. Jan 16, 1722. Test' E. Moseley, Chris'er Heidlbery, Wm Coward.

No. 134. Lords Pro' Grant to Thomas Bozell (Boswell) 51a on N. side of "Long Branch" in Perq, adj Samuel Nicholson, & Nathaniel Albertson. Said Land was Surveyed for Peter Albertson, & assigned by him to said Bizell. Councillors; Fran' Foster, Charles Eden, Richard Sanderson, Thomas Pollock, Wm Reed.

No. 135. I do assign "Right of Patent," to James Henby of Perquimans. April 9, 1721. Thomas Bosell.

No. 136. I assign my "Right of Patent," unto Thomas Bozell of Perquimans. April 9, 1723. Test' Arthur Croxton, J. Jessop. James Henby.

No. 137. Samuel Wiatt, & Elizabeth my wife of Perq, for £111 pd by Richard Sutton of same, Planter—Sold our Plan' on the Sound, near "Batts, his grave," on a small Creek called "Benby Creek," on line of Abigail Bounds. 250a, said "Land Grt to Edward Wilson Feb 17, 1696," an Estate of Inheritance. Oct 3, 1722.

No. 138. Richard Sutton of Perq, Planter—for £200 pd by Joseph Sutton Jun'r, of afore' Sold 344a on N. E. side if Suttons Creek, "a Patent in the name of George Sutton my father, June 20, 1703." Seal Oct 9, 1722. Test' T. Sweeney, Richard Ratlif. Richard & Mary Sutton.

No. 139. Lords Pro' unto George Sutton, of Albemarle Co N. C.—344a in the Precinct of Perquimans, on S.west side of Suttons Creek, "due said Sutton for Trans' of persons in the Colony," June 20, 1703. Test' Our well beloved Henderson Walker Esq, President, of our Councell; & Com'd in Chief, of our Province; & Councellors, Samuel Swann, Francis Toms, Thomas Pollock.

No. 140. Richard Sutton of Perq, Planter—for the Sum of £200 pd by Joseph Sutton, do assign "Right of the Within mentioned Patent." Aug 28, 1722. Test' Charles Denman, Rich'd Leary.

No. 141. Richard Sutton of Perq, Planter—for £10 pd by Joseph Sutton Jun'r, sold "half of Tract," on N. east side of Perq River—107a adj Land of said Joseph Richard Whedby, & Wm Wood, "same being Grt to me, & Nathaniel Sutton Oct 8, 1717, I the Sole, & lawful owner in mine own proper Right. April 9, 1723. Richard & Mary Sutton.

No. 142. Edward Maudlin of Perq, for £20 pd by Richard Ratlif of afore' Sold part of Tract, 60a on N. east side of Perq River, adj said Richard, it being the third part of 200a, of which said Richard hath the other two thirds. Test' Ezekiel Mauldin, Francis Croxton. Edward & Mary Maudlin. Reg May 20, 1723.

No. 143. Mary Evens of Perq, Spinster—for £50 pd by Abraham Warren of same—Sold 150a, adj Land I now live on, "whereon Abraham Warren father of said Abraham dwelt." Half of 300a Grt to me April 3, 1719. Seal Oct 3, 1722. Test' Charles Denman, Danbey Briant.

No. 144. Oct 8, 1723. Daniel Smith of Perq, & Sarah his wife, "to John Powell of upper parish of Nansemond Co in Va," for £23, assigned 250a on S. W. side of Perq River, adj Timothy Clare, on River Pocoson, to Thomas Roundtrees line, "to me Grt April 1, 1720." Test' Ezekiel Maudling, Wm Bastable.

No. 145. Richard Davenport of Perq, planter—with consent of Joanah my wife "for tender love which we have for our Dau Elizabeth, now wife of John Foster of said place, do give to them 270a between the great marsh, & Land now in possession of Archibald Holmes." July 20, 1700. Test' John Stepney, Caleb Calloway.

No. 146. John Foster, "with the consent if Elizabeth my wife," assigns right of this deed of gift unto John Davenport. Oct 10, 1704. Test' Dennis Macklenden, John Yates.

No. 147. John Davenport, of Chowan precinct, & Anne my wife, for £12 pd by Hugh Davis, of Perq, conveyed 150a in Perq, on Albemarle Sound, opposite "Batts Grave" formerly belonging to Richard Davenport, in line of Archibald Holmes. Aug 1, 1717. Test' John Falconer, William Winson.

No. 148. Nathaniel Albertson, of Perq, planter—for £36 pd by Nathaniel Nicholson, of afore' sold "part of tract on west-side of Suttons Creek," to a dividing line between me & my brother Albert," Land granted to my father Albert Albertson dec'd, by patent May 22, 1694." Seal Aug 24, 1722. Test' Cornelius Leary, Richard Leary.

No. 149. Lords Pro' Grant to Gabriel Newby, 374a in Perquimans, on N. E. side of the River, on lines of Peter Gray, & Francis Wells. Nov. 20, 1720. Charles Eden Esq, Gov; Councellors; Richard Sanderson, Fred'k Jones, John Heckelfield, Tho Pollock. J. Lovick Sec'y

No. 150. Gabriel Newby, wheelwright—"doth assign" 324a of this patent, unto Peter Person, of same place, shoemaker—for £40 in hand, "the other 50a I have sold to Anthony Haskitt." 8 day 6 mo 1723. Test Wm Trotter, Wm Bogue

No. 151. Nov 1, 1722. Robert Wilson of Albemarle, to Francis Newby 300a, on lines of Sam'l Phelps, Gabriel Newby, Ben J Wilson, & the River of Perq, as by patent to said Gabriel Oct 16, 1722 (450a) for £50 with "house buildings, & all appurtenances." Test' Wm Little, Roger Hager.

No. 152. Francis Newby of Perq, planter—for £40 in hand, sold 300a unto Robert Wilson. 9 day 5 mo 1723. Test' Timothy Clare, Richard Whedbee.

No. 153. Nathaniel Nicholson, of Perq, planter—to George Sutton Jun'r of afore', for £20 s10 sold 105a, adj Joseph Sutton Sen'r, & Richard Whedbee, "patented in my name July 20, 1703." Seal July 10, 1722. Test' Joseph Jessop, Sam'l Phelps.

No. 154. Richard Whedbee, of Perq, Gent—for £10 pd by John Anderson, (son of James of said precinct) planter—assigns 50a on N. E. side of Perq River, part of "350a granted to me Oct 20, 1716." Reg Aug 20, 1723. Test' Richard Leary, John Arnell Jun'r.

No. 155. Lords Pro' grant unto John Norcom, 450a on S. W. Side of Yeopim Creek, at the "mouth of a small gutt," which parts the said Land from Anthony Wherry, adj Robert Harmon, Nov 22, 1714. Charles Eden Esq Gov; Francis Foster, T. Knight, Wm Reed. Wit' N. Chevin, C. Gale. Recorded Nov 29, 1714. T. Knight Sec.

No. 156. John Norcom for £45 pd by Samuel Wiatt of Perq precinct, sold right of within pattent. Jan 10, 1720. Test' Joseph Oates, John Banks.

No. 157. John Williams, of Perq, for £25 pd by Thomas Long, Planter, sold 140a on N. east side of Cypress Swamp, adj Maj Thomas Harvey, & Thomas Norcom, being "Land given by John Bentley, to Wm Barrow," & now patented in the name of John Williams. Sept 2, 1721. Test' Cornelius Leary, David Lewellin.

No. 158. Robert Moore, & Hannah his wife, of Perq, for "love we bear our friend Joseph Jessop" of afore' do give a plan' which "our father Stephen Manwaring dec'd purchased of Charles Mackdaniel, on the "Narrows" of Perquimans, S. W. side, & "willed to his Dau Hannah Manwaring, now Hannah Moore." April 9, 1723. Test' Thomas Jessop, James Newby.

No. 159. Abraham Sanders, of Perq, for £60 pd by Benjamin Sanders, of afore' sold 100a on S. W. side of the "Narrows" of Perq River, & Cypress Swamp, at the mouth of "Chinquepin Orchard" branch, to Ralph Bosmans line. Aug 19, 1723. Test' Robert Wilson, Nathan Newby.

No. 160. Mary Evens of Perq, Spinster—for £50 pd by Abraham Warren, of same—sold 150 adj "Land I now live on" where the late "Abraham Warren, father of said Abraham lately dwelt," granted to said Mary April 3, 1719. Seal Oct 3, 1722. Test' Charles Denman, Darby O. Briant.

No. 161. Perquimans. Abraham Warren, for the Sum of £100 pd by Mr William Stevens, assigns Land. April 23, 1723. Test' William Jones.

No. 162. Abraham Warren, of Perq, Planter—for £100 pd by Wm Stevens of same, joiner—do sell part of Tract of (300a) granted to Mary Evens. "Land on which my father lived." April 3, 1724. Test' Richard Whedbee, George Sutton.

No. 163. Gabriel Newby, of Albemarle, "for a con' in hand," sold unto Francis Newby, of same, 50a at the mouth of "Holy branch swamp," to head line of my 640a reserving 100 yards breadth, "to begin at a Valley next to Toms House." 14 day 11 mo 1723/24. Test' Thomas Trotter, Ralf Bufkin.

No. 164. Francis Newby, of Albemarle, sold to Gabriel Newby 300a, on east side of Perq River, at the head of "Vosses Creek Swamp," on lines of John Flowers, & Francis Toms, "Land given me by my Grand-father Francis Toms in his will." 7 day 11 mo 1723/24.

No. 165. Joshua Calloway, of Perq, Gent—for £30 pd by Abraham Warren, of afore' planter—290a on N. side of Yeopim River, "by pattent Feb 7, 1698 unto John Hopkins." Seal Sept 15, 1723.

No. 166. John Pettiver, of Perq, until Thomas Blitchenden of same—60a adj Henry Norman dec'd, which was his home Plan' at the head of "Spelmans Creek," part of a Pattent to me 1720/21. Seal April 10, 1722. (Called "Gore Land.") Test' Jo Jessop, Jonathan Evens.

No. 167. Robert Wilson, of Perq, for 2100-lbs of Tobacco in hand, by Benjamin Sanders, of afore' sold 200a on "Wilsons Creek," up Ralph Boozmans line to Cypress Swamp, "along a division line between said Sanders & Isaac Wilson." Rachel Wilson "doth surrender her right of dower." Test' Joseph Oates, John Williams. June 23, 1724.

No. 168. George Durant, of Perq, Joiner—for £5 pd by Thomas Snoden, of afore' do sell 36,&½a, "part of 73a pattented Nov 2, 1723," on west-side of Little River, to a pine on Thomas Bartlifs line. April 22, 1724. Test' Richard Whedbee, George Sutton.

No. 169. Isaac Wilson, of Perq; "my father Isaac Wilson left unto my brother Robert Wilson, 200a, by his will, my mother making it fee simple in my Minority, I now being Twenty years, & past," to perform my Fathers will have given, unto my brother Robert, said Land on east-side of Cypress

Swamp, adj Robert Wilson, & Ralf Boazman. 9 day of Mar 1723/24. Test' Benj Willson, Abraham Sanders.

No. 170. Joseph Oates, of Perq, for £10 pd by William Houghton, of Chowan, Planter—Sold 200a on S. side of "Mill Swamp." Ack April 23, 1724. Test' Wm Peirce, Mary Havett.

No. 171. Oct 3, 1723. Thomas Commander, of Pasquotank, for £22 pd by Robert Hosea, of Perq, "doth Sell 260a on S. side of Deep Creek, in Little River." Test' Edm'd Gale, Anna Skings.

No. 172. Lords Pro' grant to Thomas Roberts, 566a in Chowan, & Perq precincts, on line of Mr. Garrett, Mitchell Bentley, & Christopher Dudley; formerly Grt to John Pettiver, & lapsed for want of seating." Nov 11, 1720. Charles Eden Gov; Councellors; Thomas Pollock, Wm. Reed, Rich'd Sanderson, Francis Foster. J. Lovick Secty.

No. 173. Thomas Roberts, of N. C. "for a valuable Con' "pd by John Pettiver of this Province, "do sell to him my right of within Pattent." May 20, 1722.

No. 174. John Pettiver, of N. C. "for a valuable con' " pd by John Rice, of Chowan, "do sell my right of Land granted to Thomas Roberts, & made over to me." May 10, 1722. Test' Samuel Wigins, Edward Rice.

No. 175. Perquimans. John Rice, assigns "Pattent, unto Richard Berriman," 220a that I have sold "out of this pattent to John Burkett." April 23, 1724. Test' Rich'd Leary, Joseph Oates.

No. 176. John Winberry, of Pasquotank, planter—for £50 pd by Elijah Stanton, 208a on S. W. side of Little River, "on which I lately lived," bounded by George Gordins, Thomas Robinson, & Robert Cox. May 13, 1724.

No. 177. Francis Wells of Perq, for £100 pd by Joseph Jessop, of afore' sold 282a, "surveyed by Robert Beezley, & James Beezley his son, & sold to me." Oct 13, 1724. Test' Thomas White, Robert Moore.

No. 178. Luke Hollowell, of Perq, & Elizabeth my wife, "for a sum of money in hand, & also for love to Joseph & John Allston of Chowan, do assign our Right of a Pattent," to us granted (400a), 200a on Jessops, & 200a on Allstons line. July 13, 1724. Test' Jacob Perry, John Stepney.

No. 179. Wm Moore, of Perq, for £40 pd by Jacob Perry, of afore' sold 400a on north East side of the River, adj Thomas Lilly, "to me granted Aug 6, 1719." Seal July 14, 1724. Test' Joseph Jessop, John Stepney.

No. 180. Mary Lacy, of "Isle of Wight Co in Va" for £15 pd by Smith Kelly, "late of Va," Sold 100a called "Huckeltout" on North side of Vosses Creek, adj "Land willed to my Brother Francis, & Brother William," & Land of my sister Elizabeth, "which was Pattented by Stephen Manwaring," & sold by his "heirs to my Father Wm Lacy, & given to me in his will." Sept 19, 1724. Test' Thom White, John Williams.

No. 181. Wm Tomlin of Perq, Planter—for £15 Pd by Solomon Henry, of afore' sold 50a on S. W. side of Little River, binding on Land of Robert Cox. Pattented July 3, 1694.

No. 182. Lords Pro' grant to Timothy Clare, of Perq, 330a, adj said Timothys, & Wm Moores lines. April 15, 1720. Charles Eden Gov; Counsellors Richard Sanderson, Thomas Pollock, John Hecklefield, Fred Jones. John Lovick Sec'y.

No. 183. Thomas Winsloe, & Elizabeth his wife for £30 pd by Thomas White, "all inhabitants of Perq," do assign our right of patent, "within granted, April 5, 1720, to our Father Timothy Clare dec'd, & by his will to us," 330a. Jan 10, 1724. Test' Thomas Walsh, Jos Jessop.

RECORDS OF DEEDS 83

No. 184. Lords Pro' grant to Joseph Jessop, of Albemarle, 190a in Perq, on Newbegun Creek, "running up to Timothy Clares line." Feb 4, 1713/14. Thomas Pollock Esq President of Councill; & Commander in Chief. Councellors; Thos Boyd, T. Knight, Na Chevin, C. Gale. T. Knight, Sec.

No. 185. Joseph Jessop, assigns "Pattent to John Sampson." Jan 8, 1716. Court at the House of Mrs Elizabeth French, "Margaret wife of Joseph Jessop Esq" Ack' deed. John Stepney Reg.

No. 186. John Sampson, & Isaac Sampson "both of Westover Parish Charles City Co Va" assigns unto Wm Moore of N. C. "our Right of within Pattent." Nov 15, 1720. Test' Thomas Bagley, Wm Moore Jun'r.

No. 187. James Perisho, of Perq, for £15 pd by "my Brother John Perisho" of afore' sold half of Tract Grt to John Anderson 29 ———— 1703 (Whole tract 209a) "assigned by said Anderson, to James Layton, & by Layton, to Daniel Guthrie, who assigned same to Edward Ellson, by him to James Coles, & said Coles to me." Land on N. side of Perq River. Dec 11, 1714/15. Test' J. Jessop, John Morgan.

No. 188. Ephrim Overman, Yeoman, & Sarah his wife, for £100 pd by Henry, & Arnold White Jun'r, of afore' sold 245a on S. W. Side of Little River Swamp, adj Wm Jackson. Dec 26, 1724. Test' Sam'l Charles, Robert Cox Jun'r, Jeremiah Symonds.

No. 189. Lemuel Taylor, of Perq, Glazier—for £80 pd by Joshua Long, of afore' planter—sold 300a on S. W. side of Indian Creek, adj Land of James Chesson, & Daniel Hall. Pattent dated Feb 17, 1696. Seal Nov 22, 1723.

No. 190. Joshua Long, of Perq for £50 pd by Jeremiah Pratt, of same, "Jentleman" sold 100a "Purchased of Lemuel Taylor," on W. side of said "Pratts Mill Pond," adj Daniel Hall. Dec. 23, 1723. Test' Zach Fields, John Pratt, Samuel Taylor.

No. 191. Ruth Minge, of Perq, "Widow, & relict of Mr. James Minge, late of this precinct dec'd," for £100 pd by John Wiatt, of afore' sold 300a on Eastermost side of Bentleys Creek, known as "Mr James Minges quarter plan' "part of Tract" on which I now live, Land granted to my father Benjamin Lakhare (Laker)." April 29, 1724. Test' Humphrey Phelts (Phelps), Samuel Wiatt.

No. 192. John Morgan Sen'r, of Perq, for "aff' I bear unto my dau Mary Elliott wife of Thomas Jun'r," of afore' do give to said Thomas, Land "on which I now dwell, 50a on a branch coming out of Vosses Creek, through a Neck known as broad Neck." Jan 12, 1724/25. Test' Thomas Elliott Sen'r, Francis Newby.

No. 193. Thomas Norcom, & Mary his wife, sold to Richard Leary, of afore' 287a, a "pattent to Jean Charles, & now in the Tenure of said Richard," on W. Side of Yeopim Creek, called "Jane Charles Land." April 8, 1707. Test' Robert Fendal, Thomas Long.

No. 194. Richard Leary, for £15 pd by John Wiatt, assigns "right of within deed of sale." April 12, 1725. Test' Joshua Long, Thomas Long.

No. 195. John Hudler (Hurdle), of Perquimans, for £50 pd by Thomas Blitchenden, of afore' sold 299a on S. W. side of Perq River, adj Francis Toms, "down said River to Reedy Branch," Land granted to Samuel Bond, & "conveyed by him to Henry Grace, & by said Grace to me." Dec 9, 1724. Ann Hudler Ack her dower. Test' Thomas Harvey, John Stepney.

No. 196. Lords Pro' of N. C. to Thomas Blitchenden, 200a in Perq Pre'ct, on Thomas Lillys line, to Timothy Taylors corner, & Wm Brinns line. Grt Aug 16, 1716 to Benj Willson, & by him "elapsed for want of seating." Seal of Colony Dec 6, 1720. Charles Eden Esq Gov; Councellors; Fred. Jones, Tho. Pollock, Rich'd Sanderson, J. Lovick.

No. 197. Thomas Blitchenden, assigns "right of said patent," unto Martin Asbille. April 14, 1725. Test' James Smith, John Stepney.

No. 198. Thomas Stafford, of Perq, for £25 pd by Edward Turner of afore' sold 115a on S. West side of Little River, & on N. W. side of Deep Creek, "near the head thereof," formerly Thomas Collins. Mar 16, 1723. Test' Henry Raper, Wm Turner. Thomas & Amey Stafford.

No. 199. Thomas Harvey, of Perq Esq, & Elizabeth his wife, "dau & heir of Maj James Cole dec'd" for £180 pd by Richard Sciner of afore', Planter—sold plan' on Perq River, 216a part of "Larger parcell of Land formerly James Coles, father of said Elizabeth, laid out Jan 15 last, by Edward Moseley Esq Surveyor Gen'l for N. C." adj Peter Jones, & Henry Clayton. Test' Sam' Phelps, Charles Denman. July 24, 1725.

No. 200. Thomas Commander, of Albemarle, Yeoman—for £16 pd by John Parish, of the precinct of Perq, yeoman sold 290a on S. W. side of Little River. Sept 14, 1704. Test' Edward Evens, Anne Bartlift, Jonathan Hobbs.

No. 201. Wm Boswell, of Albemarle, for £30 pd by Thomas Trowbell, of afore' sold 175a in the "mouth of Perq River," on a Creek called "Lillys" half of Tract "pat" by Anne, & Elizabeth Walker," in the year 1694, the other half belonging to Joshua Calloway. April 13, 1725. Test' John Perishoe, William Wood.

No. 202. Lords Pro' of N. C., to Joseph Sutton Sen'r, 175a in Perq precinct, adj James Newby, & Thomas Boswell. Seal of the Colony 1 day of Sept 1712. Thomas Pollock Esq President of the Councill, & commander in Chief; Councellors; N. Chevin, Thomas Boyde, T. Knight, C. Gale. Rec in Sec office Sept 4, 1713.

No. 203. George Sutton, Eldest son of Joseph: for £20 pd by Edward Maudlin, of same, assigns "right of Land in said Pattent." Test' Robert Hicks, Jo—— Oates. Jan 12, 1724.

No. 204. Wm Tomlin of Perq, for £15 rec'd sold unto Dennis Collings, of same, 80a on Little River, adj Wm Jackson; part of "grant to me 1694." April 10, 1722. Test' Jonathan Evens, John Pettiver.

No. 205. July 13, 1725. "I do assign right of within Deed of Sale," unto William Davis. Dennis Collings. Test' John Falconer, Wm Wood, Wm Bogue.

No. 206. Francis Newby, for £50 pd by Wm Moore Sen'r, of Perq, conveyed 300a on W. side of Perq River, to Samuel Bons corner (formerly Gabriel Newbys), & conveyed by him to Ralf Bufkin, & by him to said Francis. July 13, 1725. Test' Jo Jessop, Paull Phillips.

No. 207. James Smith, Cordwinder—& "Ann my wife" of Perq, appoints John Pettiver Att' to "make Sale of our Lands in Perq, also Cattle, All our Right to properties, truely invested in said Pettiver." Aug 4, 1725. Test' Thomas Peirce, Jun'r, Thomas Collins, Thomas Horton.

No. 208. James Smith, of Perq, Cordwinder—appoints Thomas Peirce Jun'r, Att' to "Ack deed for Land in Perq, & also to collect debts." Aug 10, 1725. Test' Wm Smith, Thomas Horten, Thomas Bennett.

No. 209. James Smith, of Perq for £60 pd by Anthony Alexander Sen'r, of Chowan, planter—sold 300a part of larger Tract—570a, formerly called "Devenports" of which 250a is now "in possession of the Orphans of Hugh Davis dec'd," bounding on Land of Wm Long, "down Franks Creek, to the mouth of Yeopim Creek," along the Sound side, purchased by me of John Pettiver. Aug 17, 1725. Test' Thomas Pierce, Wm Smith, Thomas Horton.

No. 210. Wm Moore, for £50 pd by Francis Newby, of Perq, sold 100a on S. W. side of Perq River, called "Benjamin Gideons old field," adj Henry Clayton, Isaac Willson, & John Williams, "now in possession of John Pettiver," July 13, 1725. Test' Paul Phillips, J. Jessop.

No. 211. John Flowers, Shoemaker, & wife Mary, of Perq—for £30 pd by John Pettiver, of same, sold 200a—100a on N. E. side of the River, adj Ralph Fletcher & 100a adj Land of Wm Lacy dec'd, near a Mill Dam, called "Isaac Willsons" upon Vosses Creek, now in possession of Thomas Sharbo, a planter. July 30, 1725. Test' Charles Denman, John Falconer.

No. 212. "We appoint Mr John Falconer, our Att' to ack' deed of Sale before the Hon'ble Christopher Gale Esq, unto Mr. John Pettiver of Perquimans." July 30, 1725. Test' Charles Denman, John Lockey. John & Mary Flowers.

No. 213. Jan 9, 1724/25. John Parish of Perq, for "love I bear my dau' Ann, do give to her 200a where she now dwelleth," on Deep Creek, adj Wm Manns, between Wm Godfreys, & Robrt Hoseas lines. "If she die to fall to my son John."

No. 214. James Smith, & Ann his wife, of Perq, for £10 pd by Richard Cheston of afore' 100a on N. E. side of Perq River, called "Grassy Point" the "manner plan' on which David Harris lived, & left to me Ann Smith, dau' of said Harris in his will," between Lands of Sarah, & Elizabeth Harris, sisters of said Ann. Oct 12, 1725.

No. 215. Wm Harris, & Sarah his wife, of Chowan precinct, for £8 pd by Richard Cheston of Perq, "the receipt whereof we do hereby"———

No. 216. ——— Oct 12, 1725. Richard Cheston. Test' Paul Palmer, Zach Elton.

No. 217. July 22, 1725. John Dudley, & Elizabeth his wife, of Bath, to Stephen Gibbons of Perq, planter—for £15, do convey 300a pattented by David Harris dec'd, on N. E. side of Perq River, adj "Grassy Point" now in possession of Richard Cheston, & Land of Joseph Sutton, on Cypress Swamp. 100a. Reg Nov 4, 1725. Test' Richard Cheston, Christopher Dudley, John Pettiver.

No. 218. John Dudley of Bath, & Elizabeth, his wife, Apts' John Williams of Perq Att' to ack' "Conveyance unto Stephens Gibbins of Perq." July 22, 1725. Test' Richard Cheston, Christopher Dudley, John Pettiver.

No. 219. Lords Pro' of N. C. unto Thomas Collins, 280a in Perquimans, adj Esau Albertson, to Deep Creek, & John Tomlins line. July 20, 1717. Hon'ble Charles Eden Capt Gen'l, & Admix of our province; Councellors; Thomas Pollock, Wm. Reed, Nath Chevin, T. Knight.

No. 220. Thomas Collins, for £65 pd by Peter Dovewiner, assigns pattent. April 8, 1718. Test' Wm Havett, Richard Leary.

No. 221. Peter Dovewiner, for £6 pd by Thomas Stafford, assigns "right of within pattent." Test' Jeremiah Pratt, Lemuel Taylor.

No. 222. Thomas Stafford, assigns "one half of Pattent" unto Edward Turner. Test' Peter Jones, Jeremiah Barnes.

No. 223. Oct 26, 1724. Henry Clayton Esq of Perq, & Col Thomas Harvey of afore' & Elizabeth his wife; Whereas Wm Fryley late of Perq, & Grace his wife sold for £70, 640a, on West-side of Perq River Dec 17, 1703, to James Cole, & Mary his wife; (Wm Hall heir of said Mary) "& Elizabeth only child of James Cole," now wife of said Thomas Harvey: "Henry Clayton claiming under said Wm Hall, heir of said Mary Cole, by Survivorship," hereby agreed between parties—one third to Thomas Harvey, & Elizabeth his wife, & Henry Clayton, & his heirs the other 2 thirds, "in Con' of 5 shillings pd by said Harvey, hath sold unto him one third of afore'." Test' Wm Little, Ro Forster. C. Gale Ch Just.

No. 224. Thomas Winsloe, of Perq, for £3 pd by John Hudson, of same, sold 2a "part of a grant to me from Lords Pro' of Car." Nov 4, 1707. Test' J. Jessop, Robert Willson, Jacob Hill.

No. 225. Lords Pro' of N. C. grant to Richard Scinner (Skinner), 170a "where he now lives," adj Wm Steward, & Samuel Phelps (due for trans'), "50a for each person" imported into the Colony. Sept 22, 1714. Charles Eden Esq Gov, & Commander in Chief; Councellors; N. Chevin, C. Gale, W. Reed, Francis Foster, To Knight.

No. 226. Richard Skinner, "with my wife Sarah," assigns right of pattent, unto Mrs Juliannah Lakers. Mar 2, 1724/25. Test' John Pettiver, Jonathan Evens, John Falconer.

No. 227. Richard Skinner of Perq, Planter—for £80 pd by Mrs Laker of afore' Widow—sold 27a, adj John Flowers, John Simpson, Samuel Phelps, & Paul Palmer. Mar 2, 1724. Test' John Pettiver, Jonathan Evens, John Falconer.

No. 228. Wm Coleston, of Perq, Cooper—conveyed unto Robert Hosea, of same, planter—58a on N. side of Deep Creek, adj Land of said Hosea, & John Arnold, "willed by Gibert Goodale unto said Colestons father." Jan 11, 1725. Test' Richard Whidbee, Thomas Weeks.

No. 229. Charles Denman, of Perq, "Jentleman" for £40 pd by Daniel Huntwagger of afore' planter—sold part of "Land whereon I now live," on S. W. side of Perq River, granted to Francis Beasley May 9, 1713. Seal Jan 11, 1725/26. Test' Richard Leary, Joseph Oates.

No. 230. Lords Pro' of N. C. grant to William Tomlin, 540a in Perquimans, adj Thomas Robinson, on River line, of Wm Jackson. April 4, 1720. C. Eden, Thomas Pollock, Richard Sanderson, John Hecklefield.

No. 231. "I assign right of within pattent, unto Thomas Weeks." Jan 11, 1725/26. William Tomlin. Test' Joseph Oates, Richard Cheston.

No. 232. Mary Evens, of Perq, for "love I do bear my son William Evens, of same, have given plan' 150a "where I now live," adj William Godfreys Land. Jan 4, 1723/4. Test' George Durant, William Stevens, Joseph Pette.

No. 233. Ann Pettiver, of Perq for £20 "to us in hand" from Wm Moore, of afore' (my husband John Pettiver) convey part of Tract on S. W. side of Perq River, on Joseph Smiths line, to lines of Thomas Blitchenden, & Francis Toms, "on uppermost Branch of Paley Bridge," 1380a, granted to Isaac Wilson Jan 5, 1712/13, & willed to his wife Ann Wilson, now Ann Pettiver. July 5, 1726.

No. 234. Wm Moore, of Perq, for £30 pd by John White, of afore' sold 30a "on New Begun Creek," part of 190a Grt to Joseph Jessop, Feb 14, 1713/14,

& "assigned by said Jessop to John Sampson, & by said Sampson to me." April —, 1726.

No. 235. Wm Moore, of Perq, for £30 pd by John White, of same, sold two Tracts of Land, "joining on said Whites own Land, & Bounds of Thomas Lilly," & Perq River Swamp, being part of two patents to Wm Moore (1st) Aug 6, 1719. Other part joining Thomas Lilly, John White, & Jacob Perry, being part of Pattent Mar 30, 1721., both parts 116a to him John White. July, 1726. Test' Jos Jessop, Tho Roundtree.

No. 236. Ann, & John Pettiver, of Perq, for £5 pd by Joseph Jessop, of afore' sold 50a on S. west side of Perq River, on Isaac Wilsons line, & said Jessops corner. Part of 1380a Grt to Isaac Wilson (Sr) Jan 5, 1712/13, & "willed to Ann his wife, now wife of said Pettiver." July 7, 1726.

No. 237. Jan 10, 1725/6. Joseph Jessop, Gent, of Perq, & Margaret his wife, to Thomas Rountree of Chowan, for £10 sold 200a "on N. east side of the Head of Perq River Swamp," adj Land formerly Timothy Clares, & now Luke Hollowells. Test' John White, Wm Moore, John Stepney.

No. 238. Jacob Hill, of Perq, & Elizabeth his wife, for £60 pd by Thomas Hollowell of same, sold 100a on N. east side of Perq River, at the mouth of Wolf Pit Branch; said Land was "Patented for our father William Bogue Dec'd Nov 22, 1714." The whole of which was willed to his Dau' Elizabeth Bogue. July 11, 1726. Test' Wm Moore, Edmond Hollowell.

No. 239. Benjamin Wilson, of Perq, for £70 pd by Robert Wilson, of same, Conveyed to him 150a on S. west side of the River, adj Samuel Phelps, & along said Wilsons line, called "Little House Neck land." July 2, 1724. Test' Jesse Newby, Thomas Hollowell.

No. 240. Christopher Gale, John Lovick, & William Little, Esquires; Exors, & Trustees Apt' in the last will of Henry Clayton, late of Chowan Pre'ct, Esq; said will Jan 20, 1725/6, "did bequeath to them" his Plan' in Perq, called the "Vineyard" for the use of his Dau' Sarah Clayton, & did empower them to sell same: One Abraham Sanders being the Highest Bidder, do sell same for £400 "where Henry Clayton formerly lived," being two thirds of 640a Patented Feb 6 —— One half bought by Maj James Coles Dec'd, of Wm Fryley, & Grace his wife, & by said James Coles in his will "divided between his dau' Elizabeth, & his wife Mary," & was by Henry Clayton purchased of Wm Hall of Perq, Planter—"also heir of said Mary Dec'd." July 12, 1726. Test' Jo Jenure, Robert Foster, Wm Badham.

No. 241. Lords Pro' of Car. Grant unto Francis Toms, 200a on Perq River, at the mouth of "Reedy Branch," formerly Surveyed for Samuel Bond, & by him sold to said Francis, "due for transportations." C. Eden, T. Knight, N. Chevin, Francis Foster, Wm Reed. Nov 25, 1714.

No. 242. Francis Toms of Perq, for £50 pd by Thomas Winslow, of afore' sold 200a, Pattented Nov 25, 1714. Seal July 12, 1726.

No. 243. Mary Mayo, Relict of Edward, of Albemarle, for Love which I bear towards my Children, do Give, Goods, Chattels, & Real Estate." To son Joseph half of my "Land where I now Dwell," 100a when he comes of age. The rest of Plan' I give the use of same to "Joseph Newby my Intended Husband," his Natual life, then to my son. Bequest to daughters, Ann, Elizabeth, & Sarah Mayo, "each a negro girl." 8 da 5 mo 1726. Test' Nathan Newby, William Moore.

No. 244. Thomas Blitchenden, of Perq, for £7 pd by Thomas Gray, of afore' sold Tract of Land on S. west side of Perq River, on line of Thomas Bagley, & ———— Newby, to Ann Pettivers line, 100a. April 30, 1726. Test' J. Jessop, Thomas Roundtree.

No. 245. Thomas Blitchenden, of Perq, for £25 pd by Edward Hollowell, of same, conveyed 200a, on S. W. side of Perq River, adj Thomas Lilly, Thomas Gray & Ann Pettivers line. Oct 11, 1726. Test' William Moor, Chas Wilks.

No. 246. William Man, of Perq, Planter—sold unto John Bartlet of same, Planter—"An Island known by the name of William Mans old Plan'" on S. W. side of Little River, part of 120a "Due said Man for Trans" three persons, by Patent May 1, 1694. Seal Feb 20, 1724. Test' Tho. Weeks, Anne Weeks.

No. 247. John Bartlet, of "Little River," in Perq Pre'ct, Planter—for £25 pd by John Parish, of same, sold 599a, adj John Newby, & Jacob Overman, a patent from Lords Pro' of N. C. Oct 11, 1726. Test' Jo. Oates, William Man.

No. 248. John Parish, of Perq, Planter—for £25 pd by John Barelift, assigns Land, "on the Head" of Deep Creek. 150a. Oct 11, 1726.

No. 249. Oct 10, 1726. William Godfrey, of Perq, Planter—to Thomas Godfrey, of afore' for a "certain sum of money," sold 175a, on S. side of Deep Creek, whereon he "now Dwelleth," being one half of Tract taken up by William Godfrey Dec'd, in 1694. Said Wm Godfrey being "Seized in fee Simple" of said Parcell of Land. Richard Leary Clk.

No. 250. William Godfrey, of Albemarle, for a sum of money pd by John Godfrey, of Perq, Planter—sold 175a on S. side of Deep Creek, known by name of "New Ground," "one half of Patent taken up by Wm Godfrey Dec'd in the year 1694." Seal Oct 10, 1726. Test' Jeremiah Sweeney.

No. 251. William Moor, of Perq, for £10 pd by Nathan Newby, of "Place afore'" sold 100a on N. east side of River of Perq, on said Newbys own line, "fronting on the River," also 2a adj same, which I purchased of Francis Toms, April 10, 1721. Seal Jan 9, 1726. Test' John Hudson.

No. 252. Lords Pro' of Car, Grant unto Jonathan Evens, 194a in Perq, on S. east side of Castletons Creek. (No date.)

No. 253. ———— unto said John Williams, 300a in Perq, on the ———— side of Castletons Creek, adj Isaac Wilson Dec'd, "now in possession of John Pettiver," on lines of Francis Newby, Henry Clayton, & Peter Jones Sen'r. "I the said Jonathan Evens, & Mary his wife ——" Seal ———— (torn)

No. 254. Francis Newby, for £50 pd by William Moor Sen'r, of Perq, sold 300a on West side of Perq River, & west side of Cypress Swamp, adj Samuel Bond, said Land "formerly Gabriel Newbys," & was sold by him to Ralf Bufkin, & by said "Bufkin to me." July 13, 1725. Test' J. Jessop, Paul Phillips.

No. 255. "I assign within mentioned Land, to Caleb Elliott." April 17, 1732. William Moore. Test' Joseph Oates, Joshua Elliott.

No. 256. Wm Boswell of Perq, Planter—for 30lbs "in good Pork," pd by Wm Bundy of same, Merchant—sold 75a, on So Wt side of Little River. Land Grt May 16, 1702 to John Shaw, & by him sold to James Newby, by said Newby sold to Christopher Nicholson, & by said Nicholson "in his will given to Margaret his dau' now wife of said Wm Boswell," April 17, 1732. Test' Jacob Chancy, Thos Weeks.

No. 257. Elijah Stanton, of Perq, Planter—for £28 pd by Solomon Hendrick, of same, Planter—sold 200a, on S. W. side of Little River, "where said Elijah now liveth," part of 312a Grt to Wm Jackson Jun'r; 208 of which "was sold to Richard Nowells July 11, 1704, & by said Nowell given to his dau Alice, since which time the said Alice became the wife of John Winberry, & said Land was sold by them to me May 13, 1724." 8a of which said Elijah hath sold to George Gooding. July 4, 1727. Test' David Baley, Nath'l Hall.

No. 258. John & Ann Pettiver, of Perq, for £100 pd by James Griffin, of Chowan, Sold 600a at the mouth of a small "branch out of Perq River, dividing him & Thomas Winslow," to Wm Moores Land, along back line to Joseph Jessop, & down Perq River. Part of 1380a "Grt to Isaac Wilson Jan 5, 1712/13." Seal April 10, 1727. Test' Tho Harvey, Sam'l Phelps.

No. 259. Thomas Gray, of Perq, for £4 pd by John Lacky, of same, sold 100a, on So West side of River, adj Thomas Bagley, (to Ann Pettivers line) part of 528a "Grt to Thomas Blitchenden July 14, 1725." Seal July 9, 1727. Test' R. Wilson, John Williams.

No. 260. Rich'd Cheston, of Perq, for £4 pd by Charles Wilks, of afore' sold 30a on So West side of Perq, adj "Burnt Pocoson," & line of Isaac Willson. Patented by Thos Bagley. July 8, 1727.

No. 261. Thomas Blitchenden, of Perq, for "32 Barrels of Tarr," pd by Charles Wilks, of afore' sold 150a on So West side of Perq River, adj Nath'l Williams, John Arline, & Martin Asbell. Grt to Thomas Blitchenden July 14, 1725. Test' Francis Newby, Nathan Newby.

No. 262. April 5, 1727. Wm Godfrey, of Perq, & Mary his wife, to Joseph Godfrey, of afore', for a "certain Plan' Delivered" by said Joseph, "Ack' ourselves Paid," & sold to said Joseph, a plan' on So Wt Side of Little River, 300a 'Patented by John Godfrey 1694, "to us said William & Mary Godfrey." Test' F. Sweeny, Nath'l Welch.

No. 263. Thomas Winslow, of Perq, For £15 pd by James Field of afore' sold part of Tract, on No East side of Perq River, adj Sarah Robinson, & Luke Hollowell; Part of 400a Grt to Thomas Winslow Nov 11, 1719, "next the River," & the said Tho Winslows Land. 100a. Oct 9, 1727. Test' Wm Moore, James Morgan.

No. 264. April 8, 1718. Thomas Rountree, of Chowan, & Elizabeth his wife, to Francis Rountree Sen'r, 50a on No West side of Perq River, on a Swamp called "Cypress" to River Pocoson. "Grt to Timothy Clear of Perq, 203a—Sept 4, 1714. Sold by said Timothy to Thomas Rountree party of these presents." Test' James Griffin, Wm Hill, Luke Hollowell.

No. 265. Francis Rountree, of Chowan, for £7 11s pd by James Field of Perq, assigns "Right of within Deed of Sale." Oct 10, 1727. Test' Jno Brasier, J. Jessop.

No. 266. John Lackee, of Perq, for £20 pd by Joseph Jessop, sold 100a on So West side of River, adj Thomas Bagley, to a pine on Ann Pettivers. Part of Tract Pat' by Thomas Blitchenden, & sold by him to Thomas Gray. Oct 9, 1727. Test' Matthew Gums, John Simson.

No. 267. Joseph Jessop, am firmly bound unto John Lackee, of Perq, for the Sum of £100, "do bind myself" to the payment. Obligation: "Joseph Jessop to John Lackee, & Mary his wife, to hold, & enjoy During thier natual lives a Plan' in the Narrows of Perq River, whereon said Lacky, & Mary his wife did formerly live, for the yearly Rent of 5 shillings." Test' Tho Bell, Ralf Bufkin.

No. 268. Wm Moore, of Perq, for £20 pd by James Morgan, of afore' sold 100a on No East side of Perq River, adj Timothy Clears dec'd, & Wm Morgans line, "Grt to Wm Bogue, & by him Elapsed," now Grt to me on June 8, 1725. Oct 9, 1727. Test' Jos Jessop, John Falconer.

No. 269. John Alston, of Chowan, for £10 pd by Thos Norfleet, of "upper Pre'ct of Nansemond Co in Virginia," 200a on No East side of the head of Perq River, adj John Gooding, now in possession of Thomas Rountree, 400a "to be divided by joint contract" by said Thos Norfleet, & Thos Rountree, according to a sale July 9, 1722. Seal Jan 9, 1727/8. Test' Gabriel Newby, R. Everard.

No. 270. Ralf Bufkin, of Perq Prec't, for £40 pd by Thomas Jessop, of afore' sold 100a on Southwest side of Perq River, on line of Wm Moore, "Grt to Isaac Wilson Mar 9, 1718, & willed by said ——— to Ralf Boseman, & assigned by said Boseman to said Bufkin," Mar 1, 1726. Seal Oct 9, 172—. Test' J. Jessop, Jno Brasier.

No. 271. John Henby, of Perq, for £5 pd by Peter Pearson, of afore' 10a on No E side of Perq River, on line formerly Peter Grays, now in possession of Anthony Haskitt, "where my father formerly lived." Jan 9, 17——(27). Test' R. Wilson, Nicholas Rawlins.

No. 272. Jan 8, 1727/8. Thomas Blitchenden, of Perq, & Mary his wife, to Moses Rountree, of Chowan, for £20 sold 182a on S. W. side of the head of Perq River, by the River Pocoson, adj James Field, & Thos Rountree. Test' James Pagit, Rebeccah Phillips.

No. 273. Lords Pro' of N. C. to Wm Moore Jun'r, of Perq Co, 300a on No East Side of Perq River, adj Wm Moore Sen'r, "for the importation of one person for every 50a, he paying yearly on the 29 day of Sept the fee Rent of 1 shilling for every 50a." Seal of the Colony Feb 25, 1725. Richard Everard, Wm Reed, C. Gale, Rd Sanderson, E. Moseley, Francis Foster (Sec'y), Thomas Harvey, Edm'd Gale.

No. 274. Wm Moore Jun'r for £25 pd by Benj Perry, assigns 300a "as by patent dated Feb 25, 1725." Seal July 5, 1727. Test' Wm Moore Sen, J. Jessop.

No. 275. Jacob Perry of Perq, for £50 pd by Benj Perry of afore' sold 200a "part of two tracts Patented by Wm Moore, & sold by him to me," adj Thomas Lilly, John White, & Wm Moore, Jun. April 11, 1727. Test' ——— Brasier, Jo. Jessop.

No. 276. John Lackke, of Perq, for £20 pd by Joseph Jessop, of afore' sold 100a on So Wt Side of the River, adj Thomas Bagley, & Ann Pettiver. Pattented by Thomas Blitchenden, & sold by him to Thos Gray July 19, 1727, passed by said Gray to said Lackky Oct 9, 1727. Test' Matthew Gums, John Simson.

No. 277. Joseph Jessop of Perq, for £20 pd by Charles Wilkes of afore' assigns Right in within Plan'. Jan 8, 1727.

No. 278. Ralf Bufkin of Albemarle, for ——— sold 130a to Wm Foster, (on Cypress Swamp) adj Gabriel Newby. "Divided by a Branch on the lower side of the Virginia Road," from James Packets land, to Holmes Branch. Nov 23, 1727. Test' Gabriel Newby, Francis Newby, Ralph Bufkin, Mary Bufkin.

No. 279. John Minge, Att' to my "Coz Valentine Minge, of Charles City Co Vir' Gent'm"—for £30 pd by Thos Blitchenden of N. C. in Perq Planter—sold 100a "on east side of Mr James Minge dec'd," & west side of Henry Norman dec'd called "Gore Land," Grt to Capt John Pettiver 1720/21, said John Minge doth bind my self to Defend said Thos Blitchenden in above assignment. Sept 30, 1727. Test' Thomas Harvey, John Harloe.

No. 280. Joshua Calleway, of Perq, Gent—for £12 pd by Francis Penrice, of Chowan, sold "Parcell of land on No side of Albemarle Sound," in Perq, 50a, adj John Stepney. Test' Joseph Oates, John Falconer.

No. 281. Valentine Minge, of Westover Parish in Charles City, Co Vir' Planter—appoints John Minge of same Att' in the "Estate of my uncle James Minge Dec'd late of N. C." of which he "Died Possessed in said Province." Sept 20, 1727. Test' Thomas Blitchenden, John Minge Jun'r.

No. 282. Samuel Warner, of Chowan, for £20 pd by Wm Standing, of Perq, Planter—sold 400a which was "Grt to Thomas Pierce Nov 11, 1719," adj James Cheston, John Barrow, & Spelmans Corner, "on fork of Bentleys Creek," to Edward Wilson, & John Davenports lines. Sept 28, 1725. Test' Geo Allen, John Pettiver, John Harloe.

No. 283. James Thigpen Sen'r, in Albemarle, for £45 pd by Ralph Bufkin, of same, sold 200a "at River Pocoson," adj Gabriel Newby, to Holmes Branch. Test' Jesse Newby, Thomas Trotter. Oct 10, 1722.

No. 284. Lords Pro' of N. C. unto Isaac Wilson, 640a in Chowan Precinct, on lines of Wm Carman, Col Edward Moseley, John Jordan, John Exum, James Thigpen, Thos. Elliott, & Josiah Smith. "Due for Importations." Mar 9, 1717/18. Hon'ble Charles Eden Gov; Test' Wm Reed, Fred Jones, Rich'd Sanderson.

No. 285. Ralph Boseman, for £20 pd by Ralph Bufkin of Perq, assigns 640a "in the within Pattent." Mar 9, 1726. Test' Francis Foster, Ann Pettiver.

No. 286. Thomas Penrice, of Perq, for £30 pd by Richd Sanderson, of afore' Esq—"sold my Manner Plan'" 400a on a small creek, "issuing out of Lillys Creek," down to the mouth of the Creek. Nov 22, 1727. Test' Tho Betterley, Tho Lovick.

No. 287. John Pettiver of Perq, for 25 Sheep to me pd by Capt Rich Sanderson Jun'r Esq, of afore' sold to said Sanderson, a certain Island at the mouth of Yeopim, in Albemarle Sound, called "Battes Grave" 27a a Patent to George Deer (Odear) & assigned by him to Richd Davenport, by him given to his son John Davenport, & by said John sold to me. April 9, 1728. Test' Thomas Harvey, Charles Denman, Terence Sweeney.

No. 288. Terence Sweeney, of Perq, Sadler—for £28 pd by Col Richd Sanderson Esq, of same, sold 100a on S. W. side of Little River, adj Thomas Holloway, & Thos. Collins, to the River, called "Graces Point." April 9, 1728. Test' C. Clayton, Thomas Morgan.

No. 289. Eliz'b Carman, of Perq, for "love I bear my Cousen James Smith of afore' do Give 218a in the Pine Woods, on So W. side of Perq River, a Grt to my Dec Husband Wm Carman, Jan 19, 1715/16, & given to me in his will," Aug 1725. Seal Nov 2, 1727. Test' Edm'd Gale.

No. 290. Thomas Winslow, & Elizabeth his wife, John White & Sarah his wife, of Perq, for love we have to our Cousin Joseph Mayo, of afore' have given our Right of 50a adj Land of Thomas Jessop, & Joseph Newby. April 6, 1728. Test' Joseph Newby, Joseph Winslow.

No. 291. James Ward, & Timothy Trulove, of Chowan, (agreement) "said Ward will give a Plan'" called "Bridge Neck" 120a, & Timothy Trulove to give 120a, adj same unto James Minge, the son of Joseph Minge, & Rachel his wife, & "we do bind ourselves," in the Penal sum of £20. Dec 21, 1727. Test' David Butler, Thomas Penrice.

No. 292. April 5, 1728. Richd Sanderson Esq, of Perq, Gent—to Mr. Zebulon Clayton, for £14 sold 50a on S. W. side of Little River, taken up by Terence Sweeney in the year 1724. Seal April 9, 1728. Test' T. Sweeney, Thomas Morgan.

No. 293. Aug 28, 1725. Joshua Callaway of Perq, for £60 received of John Pettiver of afore' Planter—300a on N. side of Albemarle Sound, at the mouth of Yeopim Creek, adj "Battis Grave Island" lately belonging to James Smith, & his wife Ann, with 13 head of cattle, & 1 horse. Test' Richd Leard, Caleb Calleway.

No. 294. John Pettiver of Perq, to James Smith of same, assigns land sold to me by Joshua Calleway. May 12, 1727. Test' Ann Hall, Emme Jones.

No. 295. John Pettiver of Perq, Planter—for £123 pd by Mary Gilbert, Josiah Gilbert, & Joseph Gilbert of Perq, sold 240a, on Perq River, adj John Spelman, a Patent to me Dec 10, 1712, "to said Mary her natual life, & at her Decease to Josiah, & Joseph Gilbert equally." Dec 23, 1727. Test' John Charlton, Thos Pierce.

No. 296. Arthur Croxton, of Perq, for £27 pd by Thomas White, of afore' sold Land on Newbegun Creek, adj said Thomas, & Daniel Smith, to me Grt Nov 7, 1723. Seal July 9, 1728. Test' Wm Trotter, John Moore.

No. 297. April 8, 1728. Charles Wilkes, of Perq, to John Rice, of Chowan, for £20 assigns 150a, near a Swamp called "Warrick Swamp" adj Nath'l Williams, a Patent to Thomas Blitchenden (528a) July 14, 1725, & conveyed by him to Charles Wilkes. Test' Thos Blitchenden, John Winslow.

No. 298. James Beasley, of Bertie precinct, Cooper—for £12 pd by Tho. Pierce, Jun'r of Chowan, Planter—sold 435a on So Wt Side of Perq River, adj Wm Hall, Henry Clayton, & John Hancock, & Maj Lillingtons corner, called "Morris's." Nov 6, 1727. Test' John Bentley, John Barten.

No. 299. Francis Pettit, of Chowan, Planter—for £10 pd by Thos Pierce, Jun of same, sold 200a on S. W. side of Perq River, adj Thos Commander, Wm Jones, Charles Denman, & Francis Beasley, "which came to said Francis from his uncle Jesse Pettit by death," called "Morrises." Jan 2, 1727. Test' Edward Orindell, Wm Smith, Cornelius Leary.

No. 300. Jan 1, 1715/16. Wm Evens, of Perq, Planter—to Joseph Pottle, of afore' Tayler—"Devised Land" called "Mary Evens Old field," adj John Stevens, "for his natual life, for the annual Rent of one ear of Indian Corn." Test' Ter Sweeney, Joseph Godfrey.

No. 301. Wm Moore, of Perq, for £20 pd by Nicholas Stallings, of Nansemond Co in Vir, do sell 100a part of tract Pat' for Joseph Jessop, & sold by him, to John Sampson, & by said Sampson to said Moore. On Newbegun Creek, adj John White, Thos. Jessop, & said Moore. Oct 8, 1728. Test' Arthur Croxton, J. Jessop.

No. 302. Thomas Norcom (son of John), of Chowan, Planter—to Paul Palmer, of Perq, 150a adj Wm Steward, & Paul Palmer, on No side of Castletons Creek. July 8, 1728. Test' Jno Falconer, Charles Denman.

No. 303. Antego. 8 ber 5, 1719 (Letter from Dan Mackinen) Sirs: "I wrote you by way of Boston. Having no opportunity for your Country Directly, to inform you that I had Rec'd part of our Money, & I should have Shipped it to you by this opportunity, but ye orders Bound me up in Such a manner that I could not, unless I had transgressed, or acted contrary, if you Shall give me orders to ship it to you when any opportunity Presents, either for ye Country, or Boston I Shall not fail, either in Cotton, Rum, Sugar, or Molasses; it so falls out Sometimes, that Negro Ships are not here when Passage do Present, but if you are for negroes, I will buy them, keep them till Passage do offer. Another thing is that the power of Att' you Sent me is of no force, because I could not prove it. You must get a power new Drawn. And get the master, & one of the men Belonging to the Sloop, to be Witnesses to it, that they may prove it When it comes here, that I may have it in my power to oblige him if he Should scruple to pay the Exchange, & Charges. I have received £32, the rest he promises, but I doubt Whether he would, or not, if he knew the Defect of the Power, that the Sloop that you Wrote to me by, when to St. Christophers, & never came near this Island, And I do not hear Whether Tof, Designs to your Country, or not, tho he told me he Should go hence last June, but was not so good as his promise.

I am Sr your most Humble Serv't.

Reg Jan 2, 1728.   Dan Mackiner.

No. 304. John, & Jane Padgett, of Scuppernong & Chowan, Planter—for £12 s10 pd by Thomas Bell of afore' sold 125a in Yawpim. Mar 27, 1725. Test' John Padgett, Jos Turner, Susanner Phelps.

No. 305. Jan 20, 1728/9. Joseph Godfrey, of Perq, to Eziekiel Maudlin, of afore' Merc't—for £30, with Wm Godfrey, my brother, "Confirm unto said Maudlin, 100a on So West side of Little River, on line of Wm Evens, taken up by John Godfrey year 1694." Test' Richd Sanderson, Jun'r, Nathan Newby. Thos Crew Clk.

No. 306. Francis Toms, of Perq, for £25 pd by Jonathan Phelps, of afore' sold 100a on No E. side of Perq River, adj Samuel Swann. Jan 18, 1728. Test' Will'm Moore, J. Jessop.

No. 307. Jan 20, 1728/9. Joseph Godfrey, of Perq, to Wm Evens, of afore' for a "certain sum," Assigned 50a, on So West side of Little River, adj said Wm Evens, "taken up by John Godfrey year 1694." Test' Richd Sanderson Jr, Ezekiel Maudlin.

No. 308. Stephen Gibson, of Perq sold Plan "secured to me by Francis Toms," of afore' do "Ack' myself fully Satisfied, also to the Satisfaction of my wife Jane Gibson," land on No E side of Perq River, adj Arthur Jones line, to "Bridge Branch," along Branch to John Lawrence, & along his line to the River. 75a. 11mo 9ber, 1719. Test' Wm Moore, Jos Jessop.

No. 309. Wm Bogue, of Perq, Planter—for £17 s10, sold to Sam'l Phelps of afore' 443a on East side of Cypress Swamp, known by name of "Ballihack," an Estate of Inheritance. Test' Wm Havett, Peter Denman.

No. 310. Grant to Wm Kichen, & Margarett Snooks, Widow—300a on the head of Perq River, adj Thomas Doctons, "surveyed for Daniel Snook, & devised to said William & Margarett." Seal of Colony July 1, 1713. Thos Pollock Esq Pres, of Councill.

No. 311. Benj Newby, of Perq, Planter—for £110 pd by Thomas Ratcliff, of same, "do set over" unto Joseph Rattiff 215a on So W. side of Little River, on lines of Mr. Joseph Sutton, & Jacob Overman, "an Est of Inheritance." July 19, 1727. Test' Thos Hollowell, Nathan Newby.

No. 312. June 27, 1729. Edward Maudlin, of Perq, Planter—to Arnold White, of afore' for £30 "doth sell 175a," on James Newbys line, "by a forked Branch," & Swamp, adj Thomas Boswell. Test' Ezekiel Maudlin, Wm ———.

No. 313. John White, & Sarah his wife (née Clear), for £25 pd by Thos Price, of Nansemond Co, Vir, "do sell 50a on S. W. side of Perq River, at the mouth of a "Crooked Branch," adj John Powell. "A Grt from the Lords Pro' to our Father Timothy Clear Dec'd. Dec 1, 1712. & by our said Father willed to us." Oct 25, 1729. Test' Joseph Jessop, Joseph Riddick.

No. 314. Wm Godfrey, of Albemarle, for a Certain sum pd by Joseph Godfrey, of afore' Planter—do set over 50a of land in Perq, between Wm Evens, & line Run by John Anderson, "taken up by Mr. John Godfrey 1694." July 12, 1728. Test' Ter Sweeney, Antho Hatch.

No. 315. Joseph Godfrey, of Perq, for £180 pd by Ezekiel Maudlin, of afore' "Doth sell 150a," All that said Joseph now holds, called "Hacklefield land" surveyed by John Godfrey 1694, on So W. side of Little River, by a Small Creek Issuing out of Little River, adj Thos Bartlets, & Maudlins. April 21, 1729. Test' Thos Weeks, Henry Wise.

No. 316. John White, & Sarah his wife, for £25 pd by Joseph Riddick, & Robert Riddick, of Nansemond Co Vir, sold 125a, on So W. side of Perq River, to line of Thos Price, "Grt to Timothy Clear Dec 1, 1712, & willed to us." Oct 20, 1729. Test' J. Jessop, Thos Pris (Price).

No. 317. July 28, 1729. Thomas Rountree, of Chowan, & Elizabeth his wife, to Robert Chapple, of afore' for "love we bear our Friend Robert Chaple, Have Given" 84a on So Wt. side of the head of Perq River. Test' John Freeman, Sen, George White Jr.

No. 318. Robert Cock, of Perq, for £4 pd by Zachariah Nixon, of Afore' sold 100a, adj land "where he now lives." Robert Cock, & Elizabeth my wife. July 9, 1722. Test' Robt Cock Jr, Ann Cocks.

No. 319. ——————— Grant ——————— (torn).

No. 320. John Harrell, of Upper Parish of Nansemond Co. in Vir, unto Richd Harrell, of afore' for £10 "Right, as by Assignment, of Wm Kitchen, to whom the Pattent was Grt." ——— 1728.

No. 321. Aug 5, 1728. Joseph Godfrey, of Perq, to Thos Barclift, of same, for £50, sold 50a on So Wt side of Little River, adj land where said Barclift, now lives. Test' Elizth Clayton, Chas Conwall.

No. 322. Oct 27, 1728. John Keaton Jr, of Chowan, & Hannah his wife, to John Perry, & Sarah Bond (late wife of Richd, Dec'd), of afore' for £15 sold 158a, on So East side of Perq River, adj Nath'l Sutton, "Granted by deed of Gift from John Stepney to Joseph Sutton, late father of said Hannah, & left by will of said Joseph to his dau." Test' Tho Rountree, Jun, Wm Ashley Jun.

No. 323. Thos Blitchenden of Perq, for £10 pd by Moses Rountree, of Chowan, sold 50a on No Wt Side of Perq River, "remaining part of Land I sold to Thos. Hobbs." Jan 20, 1728. Test' Edward Howcott, Thos Weeks.

RECORDS OF DEEDS

DEED BOOK C

No. 1. Richd Leary, of Perq, Planter—for £300 pd by Thos Commander, late of Pasquotank, Gent—sold 640a on a branch of Yawpim Creek, adj Joshua Calloway, & Wm Jones, "where Maj Alex Lillington formerly dwelt." Mar 7, 1726/7. Test' Thos Harvey, Thos Suton (Sutton).

No. 2. John Bass, of Bertie, for £25 pd by James Field, of Perq, sold 310a bought of Thos Speight, July 14, 1719, adj Timothy Clare. Jan 13, 1728. Test' Wm Little, Thos Jones.

No. 3. Wm Moore Sen, of Perq, for "love I do bear my son John Moore" of afore' have given 216a now in possession of said John, "a Pat' to Jane Beyard 1694," adj Wm Bogue, Timothy Clare, & Thomas Bagley, & binding on the River. Jan 20, 1729/30. Test' J. Jessop, Thos. Jessop.

No. 4. John Swann, of New Hanover, in Bathe Co, Gent—for £100 pd by Geo Durant, of Perq, sold 100a on Albemarle Sound, adj "Land formerly Henry Normans, & where Thos Norcom Now dwelleth, willed, to me by my father Samuel Swann Esq." Nov 8, 1729. Test' Thos Ashley, Giles Hicks, E. Moseley.

No. 5. Wm. Evens, of Albemarle, for £29 s10 pd by John Stephens, sold 25a of Land "patented by my mother Mary Evens April 20, 1719." Seal Nov 5, 1729.

No. 6. John Simpson, of Perq, for £25 pd by Wm Townsend, sold 50a on Southwest side of River, on main Road, adj Phelps line. Elizabeth Simpson "her dower Right." Mar 2, 1729/30. Test' Wm Sanders, Robt Willson.

No. 7. Joseph Glison, of Perq, for £10 pd by Wm Rountree, sold 100a, adj John White, said Joseph & Wm Rountree. April 19, 1729. Test' Christ Arrington, Gilbert Scott.

No. 8. Joseph Newby, Mary Newby, Thos Winslow, Elizabeth Winslow, Thomas Jessop, Jane Jessop, John White, Sarah White & Hannah Bunday, "all of Perq," for £10 pd by Nicholas Stallings, late of Vir, assigns 169a "granted to Timothy Clare Dec 1, 1712, & given to his children Parties in these present." July 21, 1729. Test' R. Cheason, James Parishoe.

No. 9. Joseph Jessop, of Perq, for £150 pd by Arthur Croxton, of afore' sold 260a in the "Narrows of Perq River," adj Abraham Mullen "betwixt this & the old field on which the Meeting house now Standeth." Jan 26, 1729. Test' Thos Jessop, Nathan Newby.

No. 10. Thos Commander, "for a Con" pd by Joshua Calloway, of Perq, planter—sold "all my Plan" on a branch of Yawpim Creek, adj Wm Jones, "where Richd Leary formerly dwelt." Dec 17, 1728. Test' Charles Denman, Thos Callaway.

No. 11. Thos Blitchenden, of Perq, for £10 pd by Thos Hobbs, of Chowan, sold 50a on N. W. side of Perq River, adj James Field, & Moses Rountree. Jan 20, 1728. Test' Edm'd Howcott, Thomas Waters.

No. 12. Jan 20, 1728/29. Joseph Godfrey, of Perq, to Wm Evins, of afore' a parcel of Land, on So West side of Little River (50a), adj Said Wm Evins, "taken up by John Godfrey in year 1694." Test' Richd Sanderson Jr, Ezekiel Maudlin.

No. 13. Wm Evens, for £100 pd by Coln'l Richd Sanderson, assigns "right of within Mentioned Tract." Nov 8, 1729. Test' E. Maudlin, Tho Weeks.

No. 14. Wm Tetterton, of Perq, planter—for £130 pd by Thomas Long, of same, planter—sold 580a on the "Swamp of Yawpim Creek," adj Thomas Pierce Jr. Jan 6, 1729/30. Test' Samuel Warner, Samuel Standin.

No. 15. April 8, 1707. "We the Subscribers do assign the within deed of the late Thomas Norcom, & his heirs forever." Richard Leary. Test' John Lillington, James Cole, Thomas Snoden.

No. 16. Wm Jackson Jr of Perq, Planter—"do swap a Plan' of Joseph Robinsons," on So Wt side of Little River, 200a, on a Long branch, that "lies between Plan'" where the above said Wm Jacksons "Father now lives," Richd Nowell the first Pattentee. Feb 17, 1729. Test' Tho Weeks, John Nixon. William & Margaret Jackson.

No. 17. Grant, unto John Falconer, 200a on N. side of Yawpim River, at the mouth of a Creek, which "divides this land from Robert Inkerson," formerly Elizabeth Angley's, & by her assigned to said Falconer; due for importations. Seal of Colony Dec 6, 1720. Charles Eden Esq Gov; Councillors; Fred'k Jones, Richd Sanderson, Tho Pollock, J. Lovick Secty.

No. 18. John Falconer of Chowan, assigns unto John Norcom, of Perq, all "right in within Pattent." Dec 13, 1721. Test' Thos Harvey, Chris'r Butler, David Butler.

No. 19. John Norcom of Chowan, for £55 assigns "title of the within Pattent," unto John Stepney of Perq. Feb 10, 1725/6. Test' John Falconer, Thomas Falconer.

No. 20. Wm Evens, of Perq, planter—for £200 pd by Col Richard Sanderson of afore' sold 225a, adj "Lands of Col Hecklefield dec'd." Nov 8, 1729. Test' E. Maudlin, Tho Weeks.

No. 21. Feb 16, 1727. Wm Draper, of Pasquotank, to Able Ross, of same, for £100 220a in Perq, on the east side of Cuppernong River, "betwixt Riders, & the second Creek," Grt to Geo Cooper June 24, 1704, & assigned by said Cooper to my Father Charles Draper. Nov 2, 1705. Test' Wm Stephens, John Wallies.

No. 22. Mar 15, 1716. Elizabeth Angley, of Chowan, widdow—to John Falconer, of same, for £10 sold 200a on No side of Yawpim River, "at the mouth of a Creek that divides said Land from Robert Inkerson." Test' Richd Trant, John Hopkins.

No. 23. John Falconer, of Chowan, unto John Norcom, of Perq, "assigns within deed." Jan 9, 1721. Test' Thos Rountree, Richd Leary.

No. 24. John Norcom, of Chowan, for £55 pd by John Stepney, of Perq, "assigns deed of Sale." Feb 10, 1725/6. Test' John Falconer, Thomas Falconer.

No. 25. Wm Morgan Sen, of Perq, Planter—"For love I bear my son James Morgan of same," do give 200a out of a Tract (328a), "now in possession of said William," on Voses Creek, adj Francis Toms. Jan 20, 1728/9. Test' James Morgan Jr, Wm Morgan Jr.

No. 26. Ralph Fletcher, of Perq, for £24 pd by Richd Cheston, of afore' sold 30a on So East side of Perq River, "in middle Swamp," known by the name of "Frog Hall" down said Swamp to a Branch, to line of Francis Toms, along his line to Wm Jones 6a, between me, & Wm Jones, to line of Francis Toms Jun. April 20, 1730. Test' ——— Oates, ———bert (Gilbert) Scot.

No. 27. William Jones, of Perq, for £30 pd by Richd Cheaston, of afore' sold 20a "in the middle of a Swamp" called "Frog Hall" at a line which divides him, & Ralph Fletcher. April 20, 1730. Test' Ralph Fletcher, Isaac Elliott.

No. 28. At a Gen'l Biennial Assembly, Held at Edenton, Nov 4, 1723, An Act was passed, to empower Robert West, of Bertie, Gent—to make sale of "Sundry Lands in Perq, entailed on Mary his wife, the mother of Martha, Sarah, & Mary West." Whereas; Robert West should have full power to sell said lands (540a at Faulks point, Perq precinct, on West side of Perq River) formerly belonging to Thomas Harvey, late of Perq dec'd, "who by his will divised same to Mary, wife of said Robert West, & her heirs, doth sell same to Col Thomas Harvey of Perq Esq," for £150. Dec 2, 1727. Test' Edm'd Gale, Thos. Pollock.

No. 29. Inventory, of all goods, & chattels belonging to the Estate of Coln'l John Hecklefield, dec'd, as produced by the Exors; Mr Edmund Gale, & George Durant. Among said effects, "1 Silver hilted Sword, ditto buckles" Sold at Publick Vendure. Reg June 1, 1721.

No. 30. June 4, 1730. Robt Cock Sr, of Perq, planter—to Thomas Weeks, of same, schoolmaster—for £110 assigned plan' on So Wt side of Little River. "Where I now dwell," by pattent, Sept 1, 1694, to Charles Taylor, 132a, & sold by him to Jacob Overman, & by said Overman to me, adj Wm Jackson. Test' Solomon Hendrick, Job Hendrick.

No. 31. Joshua Elliott, of Perq, planter—for £50 pd by Benj Sanders, of same, planter—assigns 200a in "Little house Neck," along lines of Joseph, & Francis Newby, at a place called "body of reeds." July 20, 1731. Test' Zachariah Nixon, Francis Newby.

No. 32. July 20, 1731. John Goodwin, of Chowan, to John Pettiver of Perq, for "48 barrels of Tarr" pd by said Goodwin, sold 100a on So Wt side of Perq River on line of Coln'l Thomas Harvey, along River to a small Cove, by a field called "Fosters Old field," part of tract granted to me, Dec 20, 1720. Test' Thomas Garrett, John Goodwin Jr.

No. 33. July 20, 1731. Thomas Garrett, of Chowan, Gent—to John Pettiver, of Perq, for "90 barrels of Tarr," sold 200a on So Wt side of Perq River, "adj the widow Gilbert," down the River taking in an old field called "Yates old field" granted to me, Dec 20, 1720. Test' John Goodwin, sen'r, John Goodwin Jr.

No. 34. Stephen Gibbens, of Perq, planter—for £45 pd by James Henby, of same do sell 42a "by the lower pond," adj former line of Francis Toms Sen'r, up "Reedy Branch." July 19, 1731. Test' Thos Jessop, Thos Weeks, John Henby.

No. 35. Stephen Gibbens, & Jane his wife, of Currituck, for £35 pd by Dan'l Smith, of Perq sold 100a, on No Est side of River, adj "Land where said Daniel now lives," & John Perry, to line of James Anderson. April 19, 1731. Test' Ralph Fletcher, James Fletcher.

No. 36. Stephen Gibbens, of Perq, for £60 pd by Sarah Morgan Jun, of afore' sold "part of two Tracts," on No Et side of River, & lower side of Voses Creek, & on "upper side of Horse branch," adj Francis Toms, called "James Henby's" 100a to me "granted, as well as by a deed of sale from Francis Toms," Mar 1, 1719. Seal 11 of 9br 1731. Test' Jonathan Phelps, Ralph Fletcher.

No. 37. Stephen Gibbens, of Perq, for £20 pd by John Henby, of afore' sold 100a "at the mouth of long branch, up the Creek to Horse branch." Jane Gibbons her dower right. Oct 12, 1727. Test' Richard Cheaston, Richd Skinner, Ralph Fletcher.

No. 38. John Stepney, of Perq, planter—for £90 pd by Nathaniel Carruthers, sold plan' purchased of John Norcom, on No Est side of Yawpim River. Oct 18, 1731. Test' Charles Denman.

No. 39. Thomas Winslow, of N. C. planter—for "great love I bear to my son Thomas, do give 150a" at the mouth of Reedy branch, upon the pocoson of the River. 18th 8br 1731. Test' Francis Newby, Joshua Elliott.

No. 40. Abraham Jennet, of Perq, for £40 s10 pd by Richd Whedbee, of afore' do sell 380a on Suttons Creek, "on said Whedbees own line, & the head of lower gum Swamp," to line of Joseph Sutton. Jan 11, 1730/1. Test' Wm Williams, Chas Denman.

No. 41. Thomas Docton, of Perq Esq, for "love I bear my son-in-law Samuel Perry" of same, planter—have given 180a on S. side of Indian branch, "where he now dwells" to a line between him & Benj Willson, at his death to gr-child Rachell Perry. Oct 18, 1731. Test' Thomas Davis, Eliz'b Davis.

No. 42. Thomas Docton, of Perq, for "love to my son-in-law Benj Willson, & to Judith his wife (my Daughter)" of same, planter—do give unto him 180a on South Side of Indian branch, running to Wm Kitchings line, "where they now dwell." I give unto my Dau' Elizabeth Price the 4th part of said Land, during her natual life, after her death to my said son-in-law & dau Judith, & at their death to Gr-son Jacob Willson. Oct 15, 1731. Test' Sarah Docton, Gilbert Scott.

No. 43. James Perishoe, of Perq, planter—for £40 pd by Clement Hall, of afore' assigns 104a on No East side of Perq River" being the manner Plan' on which my Father James Perishoe formerly dwelt" adj Land where Jon'a. Bateman formerly lived, along John Andersons line. Oct 18, 1731. Test' Richard Whedbee, John Bateman.

No. 44. Samuel Wiatt, of Perq, planter—for "Natual love I bear unto my brother Thomas Wiatt" of same, planter—for £12 paid "have given 450a on the mouth of Yawpim River, & Creek, adj Land of John Wiatt, Land left me by my dec Father William Wiatt, with consent of Elizabeth my wife." April 6, 1714. Test' John Stepney, John Wiatt.

No. 45. Thomas Wiatt, for £150 pd by Mackrora Scarborough Gent, assigned right of "within deed of Sale," except part given by "old James Longs father, Thomas Long, unto Andrew Wolard" Jan 29, 1729. Test' John Stepney, Thomas Long, Mangus Ploman.

No. 46. Grant unto Isaac Wilson, of Perq, 138a at the mouth of a small branch, out of Perq River, said Branch dividing him, & Samuel Bond, adj Joseph Smith, to River, on Snooks corner. Jan 5, 1712. T. Knight Sec'y. Hon'ble Thomas Pollack Esq, president of the council, & Com'd in Chief, & the Councillors; Thomas Boyd, N. Chevin, C. Gale, Wm Reed, T. Knight.

No. 47. John Pettiver, & Ann my wife, for "a val' con" pd by Jacob Perry, of Perq, "assigns right of within Pattent" 480a, to Wm Moore Sen'r, & Joseph Jessop, said "land given by Isaac Willson Sr, to his dau Ann Willson. July 19, 1731. Test' Joseph Haynes, Payrance Steward, Elizabeth Flowers.

No. 48. John White, of Perq, for £20 pd by Robert Rountree, of Nansemound Co in Vir, assigns 100a on W. Side of the River, adj Daniel Snooks, now in possession of Wm Kitchen. "A Patent to Timothy Clare Dec 1, 1712, & by said Clare given to me in his will." July 20, 1730.

No. 49. Wm Moore, of Perq, for £20 pd by Nicholas Stallings, of Nansemond Co in Va, sold 100a "Pattented by Joseph Jessop," & assigned by him to John Simpson, & by said Simpson to me, on Newbegun Creek, adj John White, & Thomas Jessop. Oct 8, 1728. Test' Arthur Croxton. J. Jessop.

No. 50. Nicholas Stallings, for £20 pd by James Stallings, assigns right of 100a. Oct 19, 1731. Test' Thomas White, Jacob Perry.

No. 51. At a Vestry held at the House of Mr Wm Hall, Mar 8, 1730/31. Present: Mr Samuel Swann, Mr. James Sitterson, Francis Foster Esq, Colln'l Richard Sanderson, Esq, Mr Richard Whedbee, Charles Denman, Mr Robert Moore, Mr Joshua Calloway, Mr Albert Alderson, Mr Joshua Long, Mr John Stevens. Charles Denman Clk.

No. 52. July 28, 1730. John Byrd, of Bertie, planter—to George Sutton, of Perq, for one negro male slave, & £10 in Publick bills of credit, sold 135a on No Et side of Perq River, & on east of Suttons Creek, adj "Land where said Sutton now liveth." Test' Thos Weeks, George Boswell. Edward Byrd Att' of John Byrd.

No. 53. John Flowers, & Mary his wife, for £100 pd by David Sherwood, of Perq, sold 104a on N. E. side of Perq River, adj Land of John Perishoe, George Fletcher, & John Bateman, "land left me by my Father Thomas Attoway." July 27, 1732. Test' Wm Suton, Samuel Swann.

No. 54. Jan 17, 1731. Wm Houghton, of Chowan, & Mary his wife, to John Brinkley, of afore' for £50 sold 200a, on S. side of Mill Swamp, adj Daniel Hall, "by a branch that parts the said Land from deadmans Neck." Test' Paul Palmer, John Goodwin, Zach'y Chancey.

No. 55. Jacob Perry, of Perq, for £22 pd by Phillip Perry, of afore' sold 200a on Perq River, adj Benj Perry. Land pattented for Wm Moore, & sold by him to me, July 14, 1724. Seal July 17, 1732. Test' Frances James, Thos Parker.

No. 56. Wm Taylor, "late from Boston in New Eng, but now Resident in Durants Neck, upon Little River, labourer, of his own free will, with consent of Jedidath Heggins of Boston, Mariner—his former Master—doth bind himself to be a servant unto Zebulon Clayton of Little River Gent—to dwell, & to serve, for the Term of Four years, & the said Zebulon will find, & Provide said servant good, Sifficient meat, drink, & aparrel, with lodging, according to Custom of the Country." Jan 18, 1731. Test' Charles Malone, Oliver Satter.

No. 57. Thomas Godfrey, of Perq, for £50 pd by Terrence Macardel, of same, Taylor—sold 50a on So Wt side of Little River, & on So side of deep Creek, along James Gibsons line, part of 350a Grt to Wm Godfrey Jan 1, 1694. Elinor Godfrey wife of said Thomas, her dower right. Nov 26, 1731. Test' Wm Hall, John Barclift, John Godfrey.

No. 58. John Pettiver, of Perq, to Mr. Jeremiah Pratt, Miller, of same, 275a on S. W. side of Perq River, adj Benj Sanders, Benj Willson, & Francis Newby, surveyed for "old Isaac Willson" by Richd Leary. Mar 1, 1731½. Test' Robert Boman.

No. 59. John Pettiver, of Perq, Gent—& Ann his wife, for £20 pd by Wm Moore, of same, planter—sold 900a on So West side of Perq River, on lines of Samuel Bond, Henry Grace, & Joseph Smith. Called "Little house Neck" Jan 8, 1724. Test' R. Hicks, Geo Sharrow.

No. 60. Wm Moore, for £50 pd by Joseph Haynes, assigns right of Land, "Except 150a according to deed I have for same." Feb 19, 1731. Test' Joseph Jessop, Jun'r, R. Hicks.

No. 61. Christopher Snoden, of Bertie, for £225 pd by Samuel Gregory, of Chowan sold 325a in Perq, on James Eggertons line, to the head of Yawpim Swamp, adj Joseph Minges line. April 3, 1732. Test' Samuel Warren, Thomas Ming.

No. 62. Thomas Plato, of Pasquotank for £8 pd by Thomas Wright, of Perq, "released forever right I had in Land" 100a—adj Land of Samiel Right, & John Robinson, on the River called "Little River." Feb 10, 1731. Test' Wm Tappan, Wm Keel.

No. 63. I William Hall, "do discharge my Mulatto man Andrew, of all service to me, or any one that shall lay Claim after my death." July 3, 1731. Test' James Foster, Terence Cardell.

No. 64. Charles Wilks, of Perq, for £30 pd by James Collins, of Pasquotank, sold 100a, "in the Pine Woods, near the burnt pocoson." Pattented by Thos Blitchenden, & sold by him to Thos Gray, by said Gray, to John Lackey, & by said Lackey, to Joseph Jessop, & by him to said Wilks, also 30a passed from Thomas Bagle to Richd Cheaston, & by said Cheaston to me. Jan 26, 1729. Test' Thos Blitchenden, James Thigpen.

No. 65. Daniel Hall, of Perq, planter—for "good will I have towards Wm Aden, Elizabeth, Samuel, Aden & Jacob Hall, sons & daus of my dec'd wife Jane Hall," do give unto them, my dwelling plan" 20a of Land. The rest of my Land to be equally divided between Samuel Aden, & Jacob Hall, To Elizabeth Aden, all "Cattle, Hoggs, & Sheep of her recorded mark." Aug 3, 1732. Test' Charles Denman, John Powell, John Felt.

No. 66. Isaac Elliott, of Perq, for £50 pd by Wm Elliott of afore' sold 220a at "Chinquepin Orchard Branch" adj Land of Francis Newby, & Benj Sanders. Margaret Elliott her dower right. Jan 17, 1731/2. Test' Zach'y Chancy, Joshua Elliott.

No. 67. Samuel Bond, of Perq, for £20 pd by Henry Grace, of afore, sold 640a on So Wt side of Perq River, "at the head of Bull Branch," adj Francis Toms, by Pattent to said Samuel, 1714. Seal June 24, 1714. Test' Jo Jessop, Wm Kitching.

No. 68. Henry Grace, of Craven precinct, son of Henry Grace, of Perq dec'd, for £75 pd by Thomas Blitchenden, of Perq, assigns "right of remaining part of Land, 190a." Nov 11, 1731. Test' Arthur Croxton, Thomas Winslow, Jos Jessop.

No. 69. April 17, 1732. Thomas Blitchenden, of Perq, for "30 barrels of Tarr, pd by Wm Hurdle, of afore'" sold 150a on line of Edward Holloway, & John Rue, part of Tract called "Luckett." Aprill 17, 1732. Test' J. Jessop, J Perry, Zeb Clayton.

No. 70. Grant, unto James Thigpen 542a, adj Richard Skinner, to Bear Swamp, down said Swamp to line of Gabriel Newby, thence to Joseph Newbys line. Nov 8, 1728. Sir Richard Everard Bart, Gov. Councillors; Thomas Pollock, Edm'd. Gale, J. Lovick, E. J. Worley, C. Gale, E. Moseley, Rich'd. Sanderson.

No. 71. James Thigpen Jun'r, for £50 sold unto Thomas Newby, of Vir' 440a in Perq Pre'ct, "a Pattent of 542a to me," 100a being already sold to

Marthew Gews (probably Gums). Jan 17, 1731. Test' John Pettiver, Joshua Elliott.

No. 72. Peter Albertson, planter—for "love which I have for my son Arthur Albertson have given 145a on Suttons Creek," adj Nath'l Nicholson, & Wm Sherwood, now in possession of Alex Steward. July 5, 1732. Test' R. Cheaston, Ralph Fletcher.

No. 73. Thomas Jessop, of Perq, for £8 pd by James Stallings, of Afore' sold 250a on No Wt side, of Newbegun Creek, "a grant to me Nov 19, 1728." Seal April 16, 1732. Test' Chas Denman, John Pettiver, Joshua Moore.

No. 74. Edward Salter, of Beaufort precinct, Merch't—"Am firmly bound unto John Lovick Esq, & Capt Miles Gale, of Edenton," for the sum of £2000 & that said Edw Salter, shall pay unto Thomas, John, Benj, & Miles Harvey, as they come of age, (21 years) "one likely negro boy," & assign 3d part of Plan' whereon Elizabeth Harvey, now liveth, left by her dec'd husband Col Thos Harvey, said Elizabeth (Alias, Elizabeth Salter) shall sell, or give to Miles Gale (son of Capt Miles Gale), one Young mare, & colt, & two Young cows, & calves before Aprill 1st, 1732. Prover July 15, 1734. Test' Thomas Norcom, Chas Denman.

No. 75. July 15, 1732. Caleb Elliott, of Perq, & Mary His Wife, to Thomas Parker, of afore' for £60 assigns 50a at the mouth of "gum Branch," to line formerly, Thomas Elliotts. Test' Joshua Elliott, Ann Eliott.

No. 76. John Woolard, of Perq, for £22 pd by John Welch, of same, planter—sold 110a upon No Et side of Yawpim River, adj Joshua Calloway, & John Wiatt. 10th 8br 1721. Test' Richard Leary, Joseph Oates.

No. 77. John Arnold, for £40 pd by Elisha Stevens, assigns right—to Land, "due me by the will of my Father-in-law John Welch dec'd." May 8, 1732. Test' Charles Denman, Sarah Denman.

No. 78. Solomon Hendricks of Perq, planter—for £60 pd by Thomas Sharbo, of same, planter—"doth sell 200a on So Wt side of Little River, where Elijah Stanton formerly lived," adj on So Et George Gording, on So Wt by Thos Robinson dec'd, & on No Wt by Robert Cock, "Grt to Wm Jackson Jun Jan 1, 1694." 208a sold by said Jackson to Richd Novel (Nowell), July 11, 1704, & by said Novel, given to his dau Alee, who mar John Winberry, & by said Winberry, sold to said Stanton, by said Stanton, sold to Solomon Hendrick (Elijah Stanton & Elizabeth his wife). July 4, 1727, 200a. Seal Aprill 20, 1732. Test' Thomas Weeks, Wm Jackson, John Keaton Jun.

No. 79. John Mathias, & Elizabeth his wife, for "love we have for that Worship called the church of England do give to the Parish of Perq, a Moyety of Land ½ acre square, by Yawpim Creek bridge, on So Wt side of the Road, whereon a new chapel is now built" Land given me by my Father Jeremiah Pratt, Mar 4, 1730/1, "for the use & benefit of the said Chapple" July 17, 1732. Test' Charles Denman, John Stepney.

No. 80. Anthony Haskitt of Perq, assigns "right of within deed," unto Thomas Grey. July 18, 1732. Charles Denman Clk, & Reg.

No. 81. Anthony Haskitt, assigns "right of within pattent" to Thomas Grey, save a small quantity passed to Peter Person, & Richard Cheaston. July 18, 1732. Test' Clement Hall, Ralph Doe.

No. 82. Jeremiah Pratt of Perq, for "love I do bear my dau' Elizabeth do give 3a on S. side of the bridge, & Creek." Mar 4, 1730. Test' Joshua Long, John Pratt.

No. 83. Grant, unto Francis Smith, 92a in Chowan precinct, "at Yawpim River," along Edward Doringtons line, to line of Francis Pettit, down his line to a small Creek, "said Land formerly granted to John Pettiver, & by him lapsed," to said Francis. Dec 6, 1720. Charles Eden Esq Gov: Councillors: Fred Jones, Tho Pollock, Richd Sanderson.

No. 84. Francis Smith, assigns "Pattent unto me John Aymes." Dec 23, 1720. Test' Thomas Penrice, Jun'r, John Bennet.

No. 85. John Aymes assigns "within pattent unto Francis Penrice." Feb 17, 1722. Test' Thomas Pierce Jun'r, John Bennet.

No. 86. Sept 16, 1725. Francis Penrice assigns "unto John Ames the within Pattent." Test' William Smith.

No. 87. Nov 2, 1732. Joseph Haynes, of Perq, to Wm Mackey of Edenton, Gent—for £100 sold 300a on South side of Perq River, called "Little House." Test' Jno. Lacky Jun, Anderson Jugg, Jun. Wm Little Clk C.

No. 88. Samuel Swann, of New Hanover, for £800 pd by Joshua Moore, sold plan' on Perq River, "whereon my father Maj Samuel Swann dwelt," bounded on S. west by the River, on No Et by Land of Pargiter, & on So Et by Land lately Mr. Timothy Clares, 300a. Said Samuel "doth reserve one half acre where his Father lyes buried." Oct 24, 1732.

No. 89. Francis Newby, sold unto Samuel Newby, 50a on N. side of Cypress Swamp "in the pine woods," adj Buckets, & Bufkins lines. Jan 16, 1732. Test' Jesse Newby, Joshua Elliott.

No. 90. Peter Jones Sen'r, of Perq, "Att' to Cary Godbee, & Elizabeth his wife," for £25 pd by said Cary, & John Mathias, of said precinct, 100a called "Bennetts" on Yawpim River, adj James Cheston, which Land became due said Elizabeth by the death of her Father Henry Coddell. Jan 16, 1732/3.

No. 91. Joseph Bucket, of Perq, for £60 pd by Humphrey Griffin, of afore' sold 120a "on Minges Creek," at the mouth of a branch, "below a settlement which Epafraditus Brinkley hath made, said Land given me by my Father John Burket dec'd." Aprill 15, 1733. Test' Zachariah Elton, Thomas Blitchenden.

No. 92. Joshua Moore, of Perq, for £450 pd by Robert Willson, of same, planter—sold 150a on So Wt by Perq River, & on No Wt by Land "in occupation of Elizabeth Phelps." Aprill 16, 1733. Test' Charles Denman, Zach'h Elton.

No. 93. Abraham Warren, of Perq, for £1 s10 pd by Elisha Stephens, of afore' sold 2a of Swamp land. Feb 20, 1732. Test' Nath'll Caruthers, Jos Oates.

No. 94. Aprill 14, 1733. Nicholas Stallings, of Perq, for £6 pd by Elias Stallings, assigned 50a part of a pattent to Thimothy Clare Dec 1, 1712. 169a by his will descended to Joseph Newby, & Mary his wife, Thomas Winslow & Elizabeth his wife, John White & Sarah his wife, & Hannah Bundy, "heirs of said Timothy, & by them sold to said Nicholas." July 21, 1729. Test' Thos White, John Riddick.

No. 95. Aprill 14, 1733. Nicholas Stallings, of upper parish of Nansemond Co, in Vir, & Christian his wife, & Henry Stallings of Perq, for £4 sold to Jesse Riddick, of "same parish & Co." 50a near the So West side of the head of Perq River; "part of a pattent to Timothy Clare dec'd, 169a Dec 1, 1712," & willed to Joseph & Mary Newby, Thomas & Elizabeth Winslow, John & Sarah White, & Hannah Bundy his heirs, & sold by them to said Stallings. July 21, 1729. Test' Thomas White, John Riddick.

RECORDS OF DEEDS

No. 96. Aprill 14, 1733. Nicholas Stallings, of Upper Parish Nansemond Co, Va & Christian his wife, to Simon Stallings, of Perq, for £3 pd by said Simon, sold 69a on So Wt side of Perq River, "part of a pattent to Timothy Clare 196a, & sold by his heirs to said Nicholas." Test' Thomas White, John Riddick.

No. 97. John Henby, of Perq, planter—for £20 pd by Zachariah Nixon, of same, farmer—sold 300a between Samuel Nicholson, & Wm Morgan, "formerly Surveyed by his brother James Henby." July 16, 1733. Test' Thos Weeks, R. Cheaston.

No. 98. John Gilbert, & Elizabeth his wife, for £35 pd by Elixander Steward, of Perq, Hatter; sold 60a joining "his now plan." Oct 16, 1733. Test' Charles Denman, Zach Chancy.

No. 99. Grant, unto Mary Evens, of Perq, 300a adj to the lands of Cor'll John Hecklefield, "in Little River," surveyed "for George Lillington, & by him Assigned to Mary Evens." Charles Eden Esq Gov: Councillors: Wm Reed, Richd Sanderson, Fred Jones, T. Knight.

No. 100. Col Richards Sanderson, for £64 pd by Tully Williams, of afore' Gent—"do sell my right of within Patent." Mar 27, 1733. Test' Sam'll Hall, James Carithers.

*No. 101. Ruth Ming (Minge) of Perq, Widow, for £70 pd by Col Richard Sanderson, of same, assigns "right of a Plan" on No East side of Albemarle Sound, & on lower side of Bentleys Creek, commonly called "Gore land" 200a whereon "I now live." Dec 21, 1726. Test' Ralf Doe, Richd Leary.

No. 102. Col Richard Sanderson, for £55 pd by Tully Williams, of Perq Gent—"sold my right of Land within mentioned." Mar 27, 1733. Test' Sam'll Hall, James Caruthers.

No. 103. George the Second, by the Grace of God, King of Great Britain: To the Provost Marshall; (or Deputy) Whereas "Joseph Haines late of Perq, at our Gen'l Court, Held at Edenton on Oct last, was Convicted of the Murder of John Pettiver, & for the same was Executed on the Gallows at Edenton, by which Conviction his Goods & Est were forfeited." Test' Wm Little Esq, our Chief Justice. April 14, 1733.

No. 104. Wm Mackey, Esq Deputy Mars'll of the Co of Albemarle, appointed Robt Hatton Esq; Provost Marshall of said Province. Mar 9, 1730. Whereas; Joseph Haynes late of Perq, Labourer—"as by Proceedings of Gen'l Court was Convicted, & Executed, at Edenton, said Wm Mackey hath received from Wm Little Esq, C. J. of afore' April 14 last orders declaring said Haynes Est forfeited, & Commanding the Provost Marshall, to Seize Same, in Obedience the afore' did Seize one Tract of Land in Perq, which one Wm Moore, planter—sold to said Haynes in 1732, & the same was sold by outcry at the Court House in Perq 16 April last. Joshua Elliott of Perq being the highest Bidder," £165 pd for 270a called "Little House Neck" adj Jonathan Sherwood, Benj Willson, Benj Sanders, on E. side of Cypress Swamp Bridge. May 18, 1733. Test' Zach Chancy, W. Badham, Jos Anderson.

No. 105.' Oct 19, 1733. John Goodwin, of Chowan, to Charles Jordan, of afore' for £60 conveyed 100a on So Wt Side of Perq River, adj Thomas Harvey, "to a Small Cove, called Fosters old Field part of a Grt to John Pettiver,

---

*Note: Ruth Minge (dau of Benj Laker) widow of James Minge, m 2d Col Richard Sanderson.

Dec 10, 1720," & sold to said Goodwin. July 2, 1731. John & Mary Goodwin. Test' John Burkett, Rich'd Goodwin.

No. 106. James Sitterson, of Perq, Planter—for £20 pd by Wm Moore, of afore' sold 61a on Southside of Perq River. July 16, 1733. Test' Charles Denman, Nathan Newby, Joshua Moor.

No. 107. James Sitterson, of Perq, for £10 pd by Wm Townsend, of afore, assigned 50a "whereon" I now live, on No Et Side of main Road, that leads from Cypress to Castletons Creek Bridge." Pattented by Daniel Snook, Feb 25, 1694, & sold by him to Edw'd Homes, & John Lilly, by the Death of said Lilly, Descended to his Dau Sarah Tedderton, & Hannah Sitterson, & by said Tedderton, sold to James Sitterson. July 15, 1734. Test' J. Jessop, Thomas Jessop.

No. 108. Robert Hosea Junior, of Perq, Planter—for "5 barrels of Pork pd by Abraham Riggs" of same, Planter—sold 521a on No east Side of Perq, called "Hill levels" part of Pattent (for 421a) Grt to Nathniel Nichols, & Joseph Sutton, June 20, 1703, & since "divided between them by Samuel Swann Surveyor." 110a "given by Joseph Sutton to his Daus Sarah, & Elizabeth in his will," 52a being said Sarahs part. Sarah Hosea her dower right. April 15, 1734. Test' John Bartlet, Thomas White, Thomas Weeks.

No. 109. Grant, unto John Norcomb, 200a, on Yawpim River, formerly Surveyed for Robert Inkerson, & assigned by him to said John Norcomb. Nov. 23, 1723. Wm Reed Esq, President of Councell, & Com'd in Chief.

No. 110. John Norcomb, for £100 pd by Joseph Oates, "assigns Pattent." Jan 12, 1724. Test' Abraham Warren.

No. 111. Joseph Oates, for £100 pd by Nath'l Curruthers, assigns "Right of said Land." April 15, 1734. Test' Tully Williams, John Moor.

No. 112. Robert Barnes, of Perq, Planter—for "love I do bear my son Joseph, & my Dau Mary Barnes, do Give Bed, & furniture, Pot & pot Hooks, Small pewter Dish, 1 Pewter Bason, 3 Pewter Plates, 6 new pewter Spoons, & 1 Pewter Tankard, & all the Rest of my Goods & Chattels, Hogs, Cattle, Sheep, & Household Goods now in my Dwelling, on plan' known by name of "Anthony Wharys Plan'." April 16, 1733. Test' Thomas Callaway, Abra'm Warren.

No. 113. Ephroditus Boyce, of Perq, assigns "part of Tract," on No East Side of the Narrows of Perq River, & on No Wt side of "Bramley Branch," by joint consent of Timothy Clare, & Wm Carman, Dividing this part from part belonging to Joseph Jessop, on upper side the land of John Brasier, 260a said land Pattented by Timothy Clear, & by said Clear, sold to Wm Carman July 8, 1713, & said Wm Carman, our Gr-father Willed to us." July 29, 1732. Test' John Waters, Abraham Odom, John Waters Jun.

No. 114. Wm Kitching of Perq, for "love I bear my friend Daniel Rogerson" of same, Have Given, 50a Upon Northside of Perq, called "Mount Mesery" part of 400a. Jan 10, 1733. Test' Thomas Docton, Gilbert Scott.

No. 115. Daniel Rogerson, assigns unto Martin Assple (Asbell) of Perq "within 50a according to Deed of Gift." Jan 15, 1732/3. Test' Gilbert Scott, Joseph Glitons.

No. 116. Ann Harrington, of Perq; Whereas "my Father Humphrey Harrington, by his Will did give me 300a on Perq River," adj Land of Ralph Doe, & Josiah Gilbert, sold said Land to Abraham Jennet, Oct 1, 1733.

COVE GROVE, THE SKINNER HOME IN OLD NECK

Built by Benjamin Skinner in 1833. Now owned by his grandson, J. J. Skinner, of Washington, D. C.

No. 117. Mary Hunley, for 30 Shillings, pd by Francis Lacy of afore' to be paid "in Indian Corn, & Pork each year," sold 120a being my third of the "Long Reach Land." Sept 8, 1733. Test' Charles Denman Clk.

No. 118. July 14, 1733. James Stallings, of Perq, Planter—for £13 pd by William Rountree, sold 190a on east Side of Newbegun Creek, laid off for Joseph Jessop, & 50a adj it, being part of land, taken up by Thomas Jessop. July 16, 1733. Test' Daniell Rogerson, Gilbert Scott.

No. 119. Charles Denman, of Perq, for "good will, & aff' I bear my Dau Ann Moor," do assign 100a, adj land "I now live on," upon the Pocoson, & the River. April 15, 1734. Test' Nath'll Caruthers, Tulle Williams.

No. 120. Joseph Oates, of Perq, Cordwinder—for £20 pd by Nath'l Caruthers, of same, assigns Land, "Granted to me by John Norcom," 20a. July 21, 1733. Test' C. Hall, John Powel.

No. 121. Isaac Elliott, of Perq, "in Exchange for a parcel of Land with James Morgan, I do ack' myself Contented," "assigned 15a before the said Morgans Door" between that, & Isaac Elliotts Land. Margaret Elliott her dower Right. Oct 15, 1733.

No. 122. Caleb Stevens, age about 40, saith "about 20 years past, before Wm Stewarts Death (Sen'r) said Stewart, took several of his Neighbors, John Bennet, & Rose his wife, John Bennet his son & your Deponent being present, we went from said Stewarts, up his Swamp that leads to "Frogg Hall," & marked off land, for his daus Elizabeth, & Patience, on Frogg Hall land." Oct 15, 1733. Test' Charles Denman Clk.

No. 123. James Morgan (son of Wm), of Perq, "in Exchange for a small parcell of land, from Isaac Elliott, do ack' myself contented," & do confirm unto said Isaac, 15a next to John Henbys. Oct 15, 1733. Test' Nathan Newby, W. Sanders.

No. 124. Francis James, & Sarah his wife, of Perq, in Con' of a feather bed & furniture, to us pd by James Field of afore' Ack' ourselves "Contented," & sold 40a in Cypress Swamp, on said James Fields, Back line, same Grt by Deed April 8, 1723, from Thomas Winslow to Sarah Roberson, now Sarah James." Oct 15, 1733. Test' J. Jessop, Zach Nixon.

No. 125. Joseph Robertson, of Perq, Planter—in Con' of an "Exchange of a Plan' on So Wt side of Little River, with Wm Jackson Jun," of same, planter—do Ack' myself Contented, & Assigns Plan' 210a on line of George Gording & John Robinson. Feb 17, 1729. Test' Zachariah Nixon, Edw'd Maudlin.

No. 126. Mar 28, 1720. Cap'n John Pettiver, of Perq, & Ann, his wife, to John Burket Sen'r, of Chowan, for £50 pd, sold 350a "upon a point, where Mr. Lakures (Lakers) Creek Divides, up little Creek," on No Wt side of the Great Creek, 350a being "Land Grt to John Spellman April 20, 1694, & by Mary Spellman, dau of said John conveyed to John Pettiver." Test' Thos Herman, James Bates.

No. 127. James Smith, of Perq, "by power of Att'" to me, assigns right to within Deed, to Joseph Bucket Sen'r, & Joseph Oates. Jan 22, 1733. Test' Paul Palmer, John Pratt.

No. 128. Wm Jones, of Perq, Planter—for £140 pd by Elizabeth Phelps, of Mass Bay, in Boston, "widow of Jonathan Phelps Dec'd, of place afore'" Confirm to her 100a, part of a tract, on No East Side of the River, & down the River to Wm Lawrence, "Saving a Reserve as by Deed to Richard Cheaston." Aug 8, 1733. Test' Zach'ry Nixon, John Moor, Nathan Newby.

No. 129. John Willoby, of No Car, for £75 pd by Tully Williams, "do Confirm" unto said Williams 147a, a pattent to said Willoby Nov 27, 1727. Seal April 12, 1734. Test' Peleg Rogers, Job Rogers.

No. 130. Richard Sanderson, & Tully Williams, of Perq, for £30 pd by James Gibson, of same, sold 50a on So Wt Side of Little River, called "Graces point." April 15, 1734/3. Test' R. Cheaston, Joshua White.

No. 131. April 15, 1734. John Wimberly, & Elizabeth his wife of Perq, to Nicholas Stallings of Afore' (with Consent of John Powell of same)—for a "Val' Con" assigns 125a on So Wt Side of the head of Perq River, now in occupation of Thomas Rountree, to River Swamp, or Pocoson. Test' Benj Perry, Simon Stallion (Stallings).

No. 132. John Ward Jun'r, & Mary his wife, of Perq, Planter—for £19 pd by Jesse Newby, of afore' Wheelwright; assigns 30a adj lands of Robert Willson, & said Jesse, on Perq River. April —, 1734. Test' Mac Scearbrough, Paul Palmer.

No. 133. John Bartlet, Sen'r, of Perq, "for 13 Barrels of Pork, & a half Barrel of Hoggs fatt" pd by Jacob Mullen, of same, Planter—sold 150a on head of Deep Creek, "Pattented by Richard Rooks, & became due to his son Thomas, & of him purchased by John Parish, of whom I purchased said land." July 23, 1733. Test' John Parish, Charles Denman.

No. 134. Julianna Lakers, of Perq, for "love I bear my Friends Macrora Scarbrough & Anna his wife, (my Gr-Dau of afore') Have Given part of tract whereon I now dwell, bounded by "Barn Bridge Swamp," the path to Indian Creek, & Logghouse Land, at the head of Perishaws Creek, a pattent to me April 10, 1704." Seal July 20, 1731. Test' Zachariah Nixon, Thomas Weeks, Zachariah Elton.

No. 135. Grant, unto Thomas Wyatt, 286a at Yawpim. Seal of the Colony April 5, 1720. Charles Eden Esq Gov, & Com'd in Chief: Wm Reed, Richard Sanderson, Thos. Pollock, John Hecklefield, J. Lovick Sec'y.

No. 136. Thomas Wyatt, for £150 pd by Macrora Scarbrough, Gent—assigned within Pattent, "except part Given by old James Long, Father to Thomas Long, unto Andrew Wolard." Jan 29, 1729/30. Test' Thomas Long, Madgness Plowman.

No. 137. Thomas Godfrey, of Perq, Planter—for £50 pd by Wm Turner, of Pasquotank, Planter—sold 60a on So West Side of Little River. Ellinor Godfrey "Doth give all her Right of Dowry." Aug 5, 1732. Test' Thomas Weeks, John Parish, William Godfrey.

No. 138. William Stevenson, of Perq, yeoman—for £100 pd by John Willcocks, of afore' sold 50a at the "So Et Corner of land formerly belonging to George Durant, Dec'd, on the No Side of Albemarle Sound." Mar 20, 1732/3. Test' John Stevenson, Jeremiah Willcox, Ter Sweeney.

No. 139. Abraham Warren, "Personally came before me, and hath taken Corporal Oath that he never knew any thing of Mr. Thomas Norcoms killing, or Stealing, a Ram of Capt John Pettiver, nor any thing of any bodys Else." Sept 16, 1734. "Before me Mac Scarbrough, J. P."

No. 140. Feb 24, 1733/4. Received of James Smith, "full Satisfaction Conserning A Bond I have of his," Ack' a title to land of Jos Burkets, "whereon I now live." Jos Oates. Test' Mac Scarborough.

No. 141. Richard Whedbee, of Perq, for 30 Barrels of Pork, pd by Samuel Parsons of same, assigns 153a on No east Side of Perq River, adj said Parson,

& James Anderson. "Pattented by me Oct 19, 1716, & Divided between said Parson, & Abraham Mullen by a line of marked trees." Oct 19, 1734. Test' Abraham Moulin, Charles Denman.

No. 142. Richard Whedbee, of Perq, for 30 Barrels of Pork, pd by Abraham Moulin, (Modlin) of said Precinct, 153a on No east Side of Perq River, Called "Beaver Cove," adj land "he now lives on. a pattent to me Oct 19, 1716." Seal Oct 19, 1734. Test' Charles Denman, Samuel Parsons.

No. 143. Peter Albertson, of Perq, for £40 pd by Martin Parsons, of afore' sold 200a on a small Branch, "out of the Side of the Ponds, belonging to Voses Creek," adj Wm Lacys, & Francis ———, along Toms line, to Francis Newby, & John Flowers line. Jan 20, 1734. Test' Richd Cheaston, Ralph Fletcher.

No. 144. Grant, unto John Norcomb, of our said Co, 200a at Yawpim River, surveyed for Robert Inkerson, & by him assigned to said John Norcomb. Seal of the Colony Nov 23, 1723. Wm Reed, President of the Councell; & Com'd in Chief of our said province. Councillors; Richard Sanderson, T. Pollock, C. Gale, J. Lovick Sec.

No. 145. John Norcome, for £100 pd by Joseph Oates, assigns "Right to land in the within Pattent." Jan 12, 1724. Test' Abraham Warren.

No. 146. Joseph Oates, for £100 pd by Nathaniel Caruthers, assigns right of said land. April 15, 1734. Test' Tully Williams, John Moore.

No. 147. Joseph Oates, of Perq, Cordwiner, for £100 pd by Nathaniel Currut'ers, of same, sold Plan' on Yawpim River, "whereon I lived," 200a. April 15, 1734. Test' Tully Williams, John Moor.

No. 148. "I Mary Caly do give to my son Nicholas Caly, 1 Iron pot holding 5 gallons." June 18, 1734. Test' John Stone, Roger Kenyon.

No. 149. Joseph Glisson, of Perq, Cordwiner—for £40 pd by Joseph, & Robert Riddick of N. C. sold 269a on North Side of Perq River, adj Wm Kitchen, James Field, & Timothy Clear. July 11, 1734. Test' William Rountree, Elias Stallings.

No. 150. James Stallings, of Perq, for £30 pd by Francis Rountree, of Nansemond Co in Vir', sold 100a, "Pattented by Joseph Jessop," & sold by him to John Sampson, & by him to Wm Moore Sen'r; on Newbegun Creek, adj John White, Thomas Jessop, & Wm Rountree. Oct 21, 1734. Test' Thos Rountree, Benj Perry.

No. 151. Wm Moore, of Perq, Planter—for £80 pd by Wm Sanders, of afore' Planter—assigned 80a on "No East Side of Ballahack Swamp," bought of James Sitterson, part of tract taken up by said Moore, adj Samuel Phelps, & Wm Moore. Ack July 15, 1734. Test' Paul Palmer, Jos Jordan, Zach Chancey.

No. 152. Thomas Flowers, of Perq (son & heir of John), for £200 pd to "my Father before his Decease in land," now assigns unto Elixander Steward of said precinct, Hatter—tract of land on East Side of Perq River, adj John Flowers Sen'r, "Gave by Will to Elizabeth Flowers Dau of said John" Dec'd. 175a. June 8, 1734. Test' Joshua Moore, Josiah Bundy.

No. 153. Francis James, & Sarah his wife, of Perq, for £20 pd by James Field, above said—sold 400a "near the head of Perq River, on South side of same, adj Thomas Rountree, part of a Pattent unto Thomas Winslow," half of same made over unto Sarah Roberson, now wife of Francis James. Oct 20, 1734. Test' Thomas Rountree, Francis Rountree.

No. 154. Wm Bundy, of Perq, Merc't for £30 pd by Henry Raper of same, Planter—assigns 50a on S. W. Side of Little River, "whereon said Wm Bundy now lives," along his line to Joseph Robinson, part of a Pattent May 16, 1702. Seal Mar 4, 1733. Test' Thomas Weeks, David Huffton.

No. 155. Joshua Moore, of Perq, for £100 pd by John Wilson, of afore' sold 100a on No East Side of the River, adj Joseph Jessop, up "Camp Branch" to Wm Moore's old line. Sept 18, 1734. Test' Zachariah Nixon Jun, Samuel Chandler, Francis Toms.

No. 156. Oct 19, 1734. John Simson of Perq, & Elizabeth his wife. for £25 pd by John Harris, sold 150a on "No East Side of the main Road, that leads from Cypress Swamp to Skinners Bridge," adj Wm Townsend, along line of Zach'y Chancey, to Jon'a. Phelps, & along his line to Robt. Moore, which land "Descended to said John Simpson by Marriage, his wife being Dau of Wm Steward." Test' Thos Rountree, Francis James.

No. 157. James Morgan, of Perq, for £120 pd by Samuel Moore of same, sold 50a at the mouth of "Reedy Branch," on Wm Morgans line, adj Moses Elliott, to line of Thomas Jessop, "along the old path called Stephen Gibbens." Jan 20, 1734/5.

No. 158. Thomas Montigue, of Perq, "out of love I bear my friend Joseph Winslow," of the above-said, Planter—Have given 100a surveyed by Michall Morfohey (Murphey), on So West Side of Little River. Oct 1, 1734. Test' Jacob Docton, Moses Davis.

No. 159. Paul Palmer, & Joshua Palmer, of Perq, for "love we do bear toward our Children, Our son Samuel Palmer, our Dau Martham Palmer." To Samuel lands on Castletons Creek, reserving the maner Plan' to ourselves our natual lives. Land bought of Richard Leary to our Dau Martham Palmer, on No East Side of Indian Creek, called "Mill Swamp." If both die without issue, to Descend to Anna Scarbrough." July 13, 1734. Test' T. Callaway, Sam'l Gregory, Joseph Steward.

No. 160. Eliz'th Phelps, of Perq, Widow—for "aff' I do bear my Dau Morning Phelps, do give 80 odd a bought of Wm Jones last year," between land I now live on & Ralph Fletcher, if my Intended Husband Zachariah Nixon Jun'r, shall see meet to live there during his Natual life, he shall by no means be molested, but if he see not meet to live thereon, this Deed of Gift to take place." July 9, 1734. Test' Chas Denman, Joshua Moore.

No. 161. Terence Maccardel, of Pasquotank, Taylor—"am firmly bound" unto Thomas Godfrey of same, Planter—for £100 July 14, 1732. Whereas; said Maccardel did purchase 50a of land from said Godfrey, Nov 20, 1731, & Ack' the same before Hon'ble John Palin Esq, Chief Justice of province, "now said Maccardel do Disannul & make Void said Deed, his Right to said 50a. Reg Feb 5, 1734/35. Test' Thos Weeks, Wm Turner.

No. 162. John Parish, of Perq, in "Con' of Paternal aff' I bear my Dau Anne Barclift Have given one Negro Wench, called Kate, & One Negro Child, called Phillis, one Negro Child called Hagar, one Negro Child, called Nanny with all said Kates increase," & one Negro Wench, called Old Sue." Mar 18, 1734. Test' Thos Weeks, John Parish.

No. 163. James Smith, of Perq, for £10 pd by Thomas Blitchenden, Planter—"in Merchantable Barrel Pork, assigns 50a at the head of "Spellmans Creek," bought of Henry Norman Aug 5, 1732. Seal July 21, 1735. Test' Mac Scarbrough, Charles Denman, Geo Sharrow.

RECORDS OF DEEDS

No. 164. John Parish Sen'r, of Perq, "in Con' of Paternal aff' I bear my son John do give, one Negro called Robin, one Negro called Bess, one Negro boy called Robin, one Negro Child called Priscilla, & one Negro child called Quomine." Mar 18, 1734. Test' Thos Weeks, John Barclift.

No. 165. Francis Newby, for £150 pd by Josiah Gilbert, of Perq, sold 125a on So Wt Side of Perq River, called "Benj Gidings Old Field" adj Abraham Sanders, & Isaac Wilson, "now in possession of John Pettiver." Dec 6, 1736. Test' Thomas Gilbert, Wm Townsend.

No. 166. John Hawkins, of Perq, for £105 pd by John Anderson, of afore' sold 150a on No East Side of Perq River, "which fell to said Hawkins from his Father John Hawkins." Jan 17, 1736/7. Test' Arthur Albertson, Joseph Perisho, Chas Denman.

No. 167. We Mary, & Josiah Gilbert, of Perq, Planters—for £150 pd by Joseph Barrow, Planter—assigns plan' (240) on No Side of Albemarle Sound, by the side of Perq River, adj Spellman's line, on So Wt side of River, Jan Court, 1736. Test' John Millard, Thomas Callaway, Zachariah Chancey.

No. 168. John Pettiver, of Perq, Planter—sold to Zachariah Chancey, of same, Planter—4 Negroes, named Tom, Buck, Princess, & "a girl now at Hannah Phelpses," for "Love Respect, & good Will I owe & received." April 19, 1732. Test' Wm Moore, John Powell. Mac Scarbrough Reg.

No. 169. His Excell'y, Gabriel Johnson, Esq Gov, & Comd' in Chief: to James Craven, Do hereby appoint you Publick Reg, of the Precinct of Perquimans, "to Reg all Deeds, & other Conveyances, for land in said Precinct." Seal of Colony Mar 29, 1735.

No. 170. Jonathan Sherwood, in Perq, Planter—in "Con' of a parcel of land in the fork of Cypress Creek Swamp, on Southwest side of Perq River, adj Samuel Phelps, up each side of Ballahack Swamp, to Wm Moore's 63a which I sold to Wm Moore." April 22, 1735. Test' Joshua Elliott, John Townsend, Samuel Newby.

No. 171. Wm Moore, in Perq, Planter—in "Con' of a parcell of land of Jonathan Sherwoods, in Ballehak, Ack' all my Right" to 370a in fork of Cypress Swamp, adj Joseph Newby, & Nathan Newby. April 22, 1735. Test' Joshua Elliott, John Townsan, Samuel Newby. James Craven Clk, & Reg.

No. 172. Thomas Jones, & Sarah his wife, for £100 pd by Thomas White, of same, sold 265a on Northwest Side of the River, & west side of "Brambly Branch," which divides tract from Joseph Jessop, adj land lately John Brasiers, "same willed to us by Wm Carman, & his gr-Dau Ann Boice, & passed by Epohroditus Boice, & Ann his wife, to said White." April 15, 1732. A patent from Lords Pro' to Timothy Clear, Oct 1, 1712, & was by said Clear assigned to Joseph Jessop. April 21, 1735. Test' Zach Elton, Christo Jefferys.

No. 173. Joseph Jessop, of Perq, for "10 Barrels of Tarr, pd by James Smith, Brickmaker—of afore' Conveyed 100a, adj land now in possession of said Smith, to a Branch called Sweet Creek part of a Patent to Wm Carman Jan 19, 1715/16, & by him conveyed to Joseph Jessop." April 20, 1735. Test' Zachariah Elton, Christo'r Jeffry.

No. 174. James Boswell, of Perq, Planter—for £15 pd by Charles Overman, of Afore' Planter—"in Merchantable pork," sold 50a on Southwest of Little River, part of tract given by Thomas Boswell to his son James. April 4, 1735. Test' John Overman, Thomas Overman, Joseph Robinson.

No. 175. Robert Hosea Sen'r, of Perq, Cordwinder—in "Con' of Aff' I do bear to my son Robert Hosea Jun'r, do give 130a on Deep Creek," part of tract bought of Mr Thomas Commander, binding on Mr. Albert Albertsons land. April 21, 1735. Test' Wm Heritage, Charles Denman.

No. 176. Anthony Hatch, & Elizabeth Dickson, "was Joined together in Holy Estate of Matrimony, on the 12 day of June, by Joseph Sutton, one of his Majesties Justices of the Peace—1735." Test' James Craven Reg.

No. 177. Inventory, of William Barclift, Jun'r Dec'd, June 5, 1734. Negroes 5, six pewter plates, 1 pewter dish, 1 Doz pewter spoons, &c. Appraised by John Arnell, Thomas Holloway, John Barclift. April 15 1735. "This day came Sarah Barclift before me & proved above account." Simon Bryan. He had in Specie £272 s18 p11. In Bills £1091 s12.

No. 178. Martin Parsons of Perq, for £25 pd by Roger Keny, of afore' sold 200a on a small Branch "out of the South Side of Ponds of Voses Creek, nigh Francis Toms line," to Francis Newby, & John Flowers line. A Patent to Peter Albertson. July 21, 1735. Test' R. Chestin, Jos Oates.

No. 179. Thomas White, of Perq, for £21 s15 pd by Wm White, of afore' sold 165a, on No east Side of the River, & No West Side of "Brambley Branch." to line of Joseph Jessop, "lately in possession of John Brasiers, to me Indented by a Deed from Ephroditus Boyce, & Ann his wife, Oct 15, 1722," & a deed from Thomas Jones & Sarah his wife, Ack April 21, 1735. Seal, July 21, 1735. Test' Arthur Croxton, J. Jessop.

No. 180. June 18, 1735. "I do here assign my whole right of within Deed" to Edward Turner. Test' Sam'l Swann, Albert Albertson. John Hufton.

No. 181. Robert Boyce, of Perq, Planter—for £45 pd by James Morgan, of afore' sold 140a, on No east Side of the River, "part of a Patent to Wm Moore Sen'r, June 8, 1725, & sold by him to James Morgan Sen, Oct 9, 1727. An Est of Inheritance." July 1, 1735. Test' Wm Bogue, R. Cheston.

No. 182. Foster Toms, of Perq, for 40 Barrels of pork, pd by Joseph Perishoe, of afore' Sold 250a, on No east Side of Perq River, adj "Beaver Cove Swamp," part of a larger "Survey to my Gr-father Francis Toms Esq," by a pattent grt by John Archdel (Archdale) Esq, Gov, & Com' in Chief, of No Car, "with advice of Lords Pro' at six pence per hundred quit Rents, Dated Feb 25, 1695." Seal June 25, 1735. Test' Richd Cheaston, Ralph Fletcher.

No. 183. James Morgan, of Perq, for £50 pd by John Henbe Jun, of afore' Conveyed 50a at the head of "Dirty Branch" to James Morgans line, along his line to Isaac Elliott, & Thomas Jessop lines. Oct 20, 1735. Test' Zach Nixon, Jun, J. Jessop.

No. 184. John Godfrey, of Deep Creek Perq Pre'ct, for £120, & "300 lbs of Pork pd by Thomas Godfrey, my Brother," sold 125a (one half of land) a Patent to my Father William Godfrey, Jan 1, 1694, & "assigned by my Brother Wm Godfrey to me, & My Brother Thomas, on Deep Creek," adj John Barclift. Nov 1, 1732. Test' Jer Symonds, Wm Bracke.

No. 185. James Morgan Jun, of Perq, for £25 pd by Mary Newby, widow of Nathan Dec'd, of afore' Sold 90a part of tract "at the main Road, of the path formerly Called Stephen Gibsons" along Wm Morgans line, to Francis Toms. Jan 19, 1735/6. Test' R. Cheaston, R. Fletcher.

No. 186. Peter Albertson, of Perq, Planter—for £45 pd by John Morgan Jun, of afore' sold 40a on No east Side of Vosses Creek Swamp, adj said Morgan. Jan 19, 1735/6. Test' Wm Ambler, James Morgan Jun.

No. 187. Thomas Blichenden, of Perq, for £200 pd by Edward Rice of afore' sold 200a on South west Side of Perq River, at the mouth of "Reedy Branch," along Pocoson to Gum Swamp, & Perq River, "Pattented by Samuel Bond Dec'd, & lapsed to Henry Gray, & by said Gray sold to John Hurdle, & by said Hurdle to me." Jan 19, 1735. Test' Jos Jessop, John Powell, James Dickey.

No. 188. Wm Sanders, of Perq, for £80 pd by John Townsend, Assigns "Right to the within Deed." Jan 19, 1735. Test' Paul Palmer, Wm Townsend, Moses Elliott.

No. 189. Zebulon Clayton, of Perq, Esq, for £30 pd by James Gibson, of same, Planter—sold "Right to 50a mentioned in Deed." Jan. 19, 1735. Test' Samiel Dowding, James Craven.

No. 190. Jan 15, 1735. Martin Aspell (Asbell), & Richard Felton, for £10 pd by said Felton, "doth acquit, & sell Plan' with all appurtenances Belonging," 200a Plan' called "Sandy Ridge," adj Thomas Lilly, & Thomas Blitchenden, Timothy Taylor, & Wm Brinns. "Sarah Asbell wife of Martin her dower." Test' Charles Denman, Thos Hobbs.

No. 191. Jan 19, 1735/6. Foster Toms, of Perq to Joseph Perishoe, of afore' 250a on lower Side of Suttons Creek, "where said Toms now lives." A Pattent to John Gosby, son of Hannah Gosby, for 300a "50a of which belongs to Francis Foster, & 8a to Joseph Sutton Esq," dated Mar 1, 1693/4. "An Est of Inheritance." Test' R. Cheston, Ra. Fletcher.

No. 192. Feb 26, 1735/6. Christopher Jackson, of Upper Parish of Nansemond Co, in Vir' "Clerk of said Co"—to John Gourden (Gorden), of Perq, for £12 assigns 169a "part of a greater parcell taken up by Charles Drury in 1700," adj Pattent Grt to William Jones, to John Powells Corner, & mouth of a Branch by line of Marmaduke Norfleet. Mary, wife of said Chris'r, her dower. Test' Thomas Pugh, Wm Hughs, John Powell, Wm Taylor.

No. 193. Mar 21, 1736. Thomas Speight Esq, of Perq, & Mary his wife, sold to Lott Sterlings (Stallings) of afore' for £30 235a, a plan' called "Sandy Ridge" adj "middle Swamp" that issueth out of "Carerene" (Katherine), Creek Swamp, to a dividing line of Charles Wilks, & Robert Barnes, on line of Kitchen & Snooks. "A Survey made for Thomas Blitchenden, as by Pattent, to Robert Barnes, Jan 19, 1715 & sold by him to said Speight." Test' Elias Stallings, Lewis Skinner.

No. 194. John Pratt Esq, for £100 pd by Jobe Pratt, of Perq, Wheelright—sold 100a "part of tract which my Father Jeremiah, purchased of Joshua Long, on South west of the Mill pond." April 16, 1736. Test' James Eggerton, Richard Skinner.

No. 195. John Pratt, of Perq, Carpenter—for £100 pd by my Brother Jeremiah Pratt, Planter—of same, sold 120a "part of tract that my Father Jer. Pratt Purchased of Lemuel Taylor, (where John Banks now lives) on North side of Indian Creek, adj land where the Water Mill now Stands." April 16, 1736. Test' Richard Skinner, James Eggerton.

No. 196. John Pratt, for £100 pd by my Brother, Joshua Pratt, sold 150a called "Hargans" Grt to my Father Jer. Pratt, Planter—Aug 10, 1720. Seal April 16, 1736. Test' James Eggerton, Richard Skinner.

No. 197. Mar 8, 1736. Robert Chappel, of Chowan, & Elizabeth his wife for £10 pd by Elias Stallings, of Perq, assigns 84a on Southwest Side, of the head of Perq River, "part of tract Grt to Thomas Rountree of Chowan (250a)

Aug 10, 1720," & by said Rountree given to Robert Chappel, & Elizabeth, wife of same. July 28, 1720. Test' Nicholas Stallings, Thomas Rountree.

No. 198. Elisha Stevens, of Perq, Carpenter—for £80 pd by John Wiatt, of afore' Cooper—sold 112a on Northeast Side of Yeopim River. Bought by said Stevens, of Abraham Warring. Jan 19, 1735/6. Test' Joshua Long, Abraham Warrin, Sarah Warrin.

No. 199. James Henby Sen'r, of Perq, for £23 pd by Edward Maudlin, of same, sold 150a part of land "whereon I now Dwell," near the head of Vosses Creek, by the Side of "Goose Pond," adj John Morgan Jun. Elizabeth Henby, her dower right. Jan 24, 1735. Test' Thos Weeks, Anne Weeks.

No. 200. Wm Elliott, of Perq, for £80 pd by Francis Newby, of same, sold 220a at the "Chinquapin Orchard Branch along land where said Newby Dwells, adj land that Benj Sanders Dwells upon," April 17, 1736. Test' Jesse Newby, Joseph Newby, Sam'l Newby.

No. 201. John Parish Sen, for £23 pd by Wm Arnold, of Perq, sold land on Southwest side of Little River, on line of John Perishoe. Feb 28, 1735. Test' James Gibson, James Foster.

No. 202. John Parish Sen, of Perq, Plan'r—for £1 pd by Edward Dowdy, Plan'r—of afore' sold 500a, adj Esau Albertson. June 6, 1735. Test' Tho Weeks, Sam'l Bundy.

No. 203. Tully Williams, of Perq, Gent—for 50 Barrels of Pork, & 4 Barrels of Hoggs lard, pd by Thomas Norcomb, of same, Gent—Sold Plan' on Sound Side, & on lower side of Bentleys Creek, called "Gore land" 200a being Plan' I bought of "my Father-in-law Col Richard Sanderson," Aug 25, 1733. Seal June 2, 1736. Test' Sam'l Swann, Mathew Divit.

No. 204. April 5, 1726. John Parish, of Perq, sold to Thomas Weeks of same, "Plan' on Little River," 599a by Patent April 1, 1723. Test' John Parish, Elinor Godfrey.

No. 205. Nov 13, 1736. Michael Lawrence, of Upper Parish of Nansemond Co Vir, & Susannah his wife, to Thomas Wiggins of Perq, for £25 "doth assign part of tract granted unto Henry Plumpton April 16, 1683, & by said Henry sold to Michael Lawrence, by a Deed of Gift (in Perq Pre'ct) on the east Side of "Orepeak Swamp," adj John Lear, & John Powell. Test' John Powell, John Norfleet.

No. 206. Truman Moore, of Perq, Plan'r for a "Val' Con' received" of John Wilson, sold 100a on South West by Perq River, adj Joseph Jessop, to "Camp Branch," & Wm Moores old line. July 19, 1736. Test' Timothy Winslow, Francis James.

No. 207. Jesse Newby, of Perq, for £50 pd by Francis Newby, of afore' Conveyed 40a on a Branch Called "Ralph Bosmans Cow Branch," up said Branch to Francis Newbys line, & down the Branch on So Wt Side of "Scotts old field" & the "Mill Pond." May 19, 1736. Test' Joseph Wilson, Wm Newby.

No. 208. Nov 10, 1735. Michael Lawrence, of Nansemond Co in Vir, to John Powell, of Perq, for £50 "Doth assign land granted by Pattent unto Henry Plumpton April 16, 1680, & by said Plumpton Conveyed unto Said Lawrence by Deed of Gift, at a place called Ore-Peak on Eastern side of said Swamp, to John Leahs Pattent." Test' Thomas Wiggins, John Norfleet.

No. 209. Henry Norman, of Tyrrel Pre'ct, assigns "right of this Pattent," unto Richd Wallis. Sept 4, 1736. Test' Joseph Spruill, Samuel Bounds.

No. 210. July 18, 1737. James Stallings, assigns "within Deed" to Francis Rountree, for £8 paid. Test' Lemuel Riddick, Thomas White.

No. 211. Joseph Oates, of Perq, Planter—for £190 pd by Richard Skinner Sener, of afore' Planter—sold 450a called "Mr Lacorses" (Lakers) Creek," a grant to John Spelman, April 20, 1694, & by Mary Spelman Dau of said John, sold to John Pettiver, Mar 20, 1720, & Ack by said Pettiver, "for the use of John Burket before Frederick Jones Chief Justice, Mar 30, 1720," & sold by said Burket to me. May 21, 1737. Test' Richd Cheaston, James Skinner.

No. 212. Wm Moore of Perq, to James Thomas, late of afore' 50a on So west Side of Balahack Swamp, on line of John Townsend, through a Branch called "Deep Branch" a Pattent to Wm Moore. Mar 14, 1737. Test' Zachariah Chancey, Zachariah Allson, John Townson.

No. 213. Wm Turner, of Pasquotank, Planter—For 9 Barrels of Pork, pd by Joshua Barclift of Perq, sold 60a on Southwest Side of Little River. April C. 1737. Test' James Gibson, John Barclift, Noah Bishop.

No. 214. Wm Mann of Perq, Planter—for £5 pd by Elizabeth Knoles, Widow—sold 25a on South west Side of Little River, "unto William Knoles, son of said Elizabeth, & his assigns forever." April 16, 1737. Test' Thos Weeks, Ann Weeks.

No. 215. Lott Stallings, of Perq, Planter—for £10 22 Barrels of Tarr, pd the 25 Dec next, by Richard Harrel of afore' Planter—sold 170a, adj John Harrel. "Now in possession of said Richard," formerly Wm Kitchens, as by Deed July 15, 1719, sold by Robert Barnes to Lewis Skinner, & by him to Lott Stallings. July 9, 1737. Test' Gilbert Scot, James Scot.

No. 216. Patience Creasey, widow of Perq, for £40 pd by Macrora Scarbrough, of afore' assigned Right of Plan' "given unto me by my Father Wm Stewart in his will," 230a on west Side of Lakers Creek, "where John Simson now lives as a tenant." Dec 24, 1735. Test' Paul Palmer, Samuel Palmer.

No. 217. John Pettiver, late of London, now in N. C. "Heir-at-law of John Pettiver of Perq Co Dec'd" for £50 pd by Mackrora Scarbrough, sold 310a on Perq River, adj Thomas Garret, John Gooding, & Joseph Burket." "Part of 610a a Pattent to my uncle John Pettiver Dec 20, 1720," out of which he sold 200a to Thomas Garrat, & 100a to John Gooding, "an Est in fee *Simpple*." Nov 17, 1735. Test' Paul Palmer, Patience Creasey.

No. 218. Feb 20, 1733. Elizabeth Chandler, of the parish of St George, Bloomsberry, in Co of Middlesex, Widow—"only surviving Dau of Edward Catchmaid Dec'd, who was the Eldest son, of Thomas Catchmaid Dec'd, who was the Brother, & Devisee in the will of Geo Catchmaid of Nanciman (Va) in Carolina Dec'd," one pt, & John Humpage, of Gravesend, Co Kent, Marriner—& Ann Hinds, of the parish of Great St Hellens, London, Widow— of the other pt, for 5 Shillings pd to said Elizabeth, sold Seat of land called "Birkswear" in Car, to said John & Ann. Reg Aug 20, 1737. James Craven, P. R.

No. 219. Feb 20, 1733. Elizabeth Chandler (to same parties), for £10 "doth Release (in their actual possession) all her Seat of land Called "Birkswear" in Car. Sealed, & Delivered (the parchment being first duly Stampt) in presence of us: Archibald Wynne, Thos Wensley." Reg in Office of Perq Aug 20, 1737. James Craven P. Reg'r.

No. 220. John Humpage, & Ann Hinds, for £10 s10 "Rec'd by us." Elizabeth Chandler. Test' Archibald Wynn, Thos Wensley.

No. 221. "I Sir Edward Bellamy, Knt, Lord Mayor of London, Do hereby Certify that on the Date Hereof—appeared before me Archibald Wynne of the parish of St Hellens, London, Gent—being a person of good Credit, & by Oath did Solemnly Declare things in affidavit annexed." I said Lord Mayor of London "Caused the Seal of Office of said City, to be affixed to Deed of Release." London Mar 25, 1735.

No. 222. Archibald Wynne, of St. Hellens, London Gent—"did see Elizabeth Chandler duly Execute, Seal, & Deliver Deeds of Release." Sworn Mar 25, 1735. Edward Bellamy Mayor.

No. 223. Whereas; release bearing date Feb 20, 1733, & Release dated Feb 20, 1733 made between Elizabeth Chandler (and same parties) sold same land in Car. Feb 3, 1735. Test' Archibald Wynne, Gamaliel Gardner.

No. 224. "I Sir John Williams, Knight, Lord Mayor of London—Certifie that, on date affixed, appeared before me Archibald Wynne, Gent—& by Solemn oath Depos'd to be true, things in affixed deed." Feb 3, 1735.

No. 225. Archibald Wynne, of London Gent—"maketh oath on Feb 3, that he did see John Humpage of London & Ann Hinds, widow—Execute, Seal & Deliver the letter of Att' Hereunto annexed." Witness to same in his own proper hand writing.

No. 226. Wm Moore, of Perq, "for a Sum" pd by James Thomas, late of same, sold 50a on South west "Side of Balhacke Swamp," on John Townsens line, to Deep Branch. Mar 14, 1737. Test' Zach Chancey, Zach Elton, John Townsen.

No. 227. John Morris, of Pasquotank, Planter—for £110 pd. by Thomas Lands, of same, Planter—sold 200a on North east Side of Perq River, on line of David Smith. Oct 17, 1737. Test' Joseph Oates, Francis Harris.

No. 228. Joseph Steward, for £20 pd by Macrora Scarbrough, Gent—Sold right of plan' whereof "my Father was in his life time Seized, & at his Death gave to his Daus, Patience & Elizabeth, & now doth Descend unto me as heir-at-law, to said Patience, & Elizabeth." Oct 16, 1737. Test' Nicholas Rawlins, Sarah Toxcety.

No. 229. Richard Walless, of Perq, Cupper—for 32 Barrels of Pork pd by John Wiatt, of afore' Planter—assigned 150a on north Side of Albemarle Sound, by the Head of "Spellmans Creek Swamp," to Roger Snells corner, adj John Bentley, & Mrs Laker. May 10, 1737. Test' Thomas Pierce, Joshua Long, Abraham Warring.

No. 230. James Eggerton do give 1a unto John Pratt. Oct 17, 1737. Test' Joseph Oates, Richard Skinner.

No. 231. Jesse Newby, of Albemarle, for £81 pd by Francis Newby, of same, sold 50a "on South Side of the Mill Pond," to said Francis line. Oct 15, 1737. Test' Samuel Newby, Wm. Townsen, Joseph Wilson.

No. 232. John Robenson of Perq, Farmer—for £35 pd by Jeremiah Hendrick, of Pasq, Assigned 150a on S. W. Side of Little River, adj Solomon Hendricks, & "Heirs of Wm Jackson Jun." Jan 16, 1737. Test' Thos Weeks, Joseph Robinson.

No. 233. John Robinson, of Perq, for £35 pd by Solomon Hendrick, of same, farmer—sold 105a on South west Side of Little River, at the lower end of "Doctors Branch" along said side to River Pocoson. Jan 16, 1737. Test' Thomas Weeks, Joseph Robinson.

No. 234. Edward Dowdy, of Perq, Planter—for £5 s12 pd, "being sum due his Majesty at Michalmas past, for 8 years quit rent, for 100a of land, pd by Robert Hall," of afore' Planter—assigned 100a," South west part of 500a formerly belonging to John Parish Sen'r, near the Gut Branch of Deep Creek, on line of Esau Albertson (now John Huffton) along line of John Arnold, & John Perishoe. Jan 13, 1737. Test' John Huffton, Comfort Dowdy.

No. 235. Robert Hosea, of Perq, Planter—& Sarah his wife, for £42 pd by Potsefull Pierce, of same, Sold 50a, adj Abraham Mullen Sen'r, Abraham Riggs, & Isaac Mullens. April 17, 1738. Test' Wm Wood, Wm Townsen.

No. 236. Moses Speight, of Bartee (Bertie) Gent—for £90 pd by Mr Jacob Docton, of Perq, sold 114a "at the Head of Perq River, adj said Docton. Land Surveyed for Thos Blitchenden, & by him assigned to said Speight. May 17, 1738. Test' Isaac Speight, Gilbert Scott.

No. 237. Alex. Steward, of Perq, Hatter—"in Con' of the Exchange of 100a Wood land & Clear ground to me," by Thos Sharbo of same, farmer—"do acquit said Sharbo, & assign Plan' on Upper Side of Vosses Creek," on Joseph Newbys line, to Branch called "deep bottom" where said Steward formerly lived. Feb 17, 1738. Test' Thos Weeks, Anne Weeks.

No. 283. Anthony Wherry, of the Co of Bathe, Cooper—for £128 pd by John Stepney, of Perq, Planter—sold 300a that was "given me by my Brother Joshua," on South west Side of Yawpim Creek, at the mouth of "Greens Swamp," called "Wherrys Old field" Granted to John Cooke May 1, 1695. Seal Jan 24, 1737/8. Test' Thomas Price, Thomas Long.

No. 239. Samuel Right, of Perq, farmer—for 17 Barrels of Pork pd by Nathaniel Welch, of Pasq, farmer—Sold 100a on South West Side of Little River. Feb 13, 1738. Test' Thos Weeks, Anne Weeks.

No. 240. Thomas Lands, of Perq, planter—for £100 pd by Wm Ambler, of same, Gent—Conveyed 200a on north east Side of Perq River, adj Daniel Smith. Jan —, 1738. Test' Tulle Williams, Sam'l Swann, Chris'r Reed.

No. 241. Moses Elliott, & Hannah his wife, of Perq, for £250 pd by Joseph Newby, of afore' Sold 100a "upon Vosses Creek," adj John Morgan Sen, along the dividing line of Moses Elliott, & Joseph Winslow. Year 1738. Test' Thos Pierce, Robt Willson, Zachariah Nixon.

No. 242. Gabriel Johnson Esq, Gov, & Com'd in chief, over the Pro' of N. C. To Coll'o Macrora Scarbrough, "Out of knowledge I have of you, said Macrora Scarbrough—do hereby appoint you publick Reg of the precinct of Perquimans." Seal of the Colony at Newton, Sept 10, 1737. Edenton Sept 30, 1737, "Macrora Scarbrough appeared before me, & took the Oaths by law appointed." J. Montgomery.

No. 243. "Ann Newby, Relict of Wm Newby Dec'd, do give unto my son William Newby, "what was willed to him by his Father." 1 Negro called Jouah, 20 lbs Pewter, 2 Silver Spoons, 2 Cows, & Calves, also 1 Negro Girl called Judah, with increase, but if he die without issue, then said Negro Girl shall return to me." 23d 1mo 1720. Test' Benj Pritchard, Francis Newby. April C. 1739.

No. 244. Jan 22, 1738. Jesse Newby, of Perq, Wheelright—& Benj Pritchard, of Pasq for £100 sold 50a on Robert Wilsons line, to County Road, along said

Road "to Samuel Newbys New Road," to a tract formerly sold to my Brother Francis Newby, called "Scottsfield," at the head of Deep Branch. Test' Sam'l Newby, Francis Newby, Richd McClure.

No. 245. Wm Standing, of Chowan, Planter—for £160 pd by Joseph Barrow, of Perq, Weaver—assigned 240a, on the head of Minzes Creek (Minge) & on South west side of Perq River, & the North side of Albemarle Sound, adj Abraham Gennett, along said line to John Felts, & Samuel Bond. April 16, 1739. Test' Thos Peirce, Thos Harvey, Francis Wells.

No. 246. Jesse Newby, of Perq, Planter—for £150 pd by Samuel Newby, of same, planter—sold 100a at the Road, on Robt Wilsons line, up the Road to Jesse, & Francis Newby. Dec 10, 1736.

No. 247. Andrew Davis, of Perq, planter—for £8 pd by John Parish, of afore' sold 100a on Deep Creek, Pattented in the name of Joseph Commander, April 1, 1708. Test' Wm Jackson, Thos Snoden.

No. 248. John Barclift, & Anne my wife, of Perq, for 12 Barrels of Pork to us pd by James Foster, of afore' assigns "our right of within Deed." April 17, 1739. Test' James Gibson, John Parish.

No. 249. Henry White, of the Co of Onslow, "upon Nuse River," planter—for £300 pd by Josiah Bundy, of Perq, planter—sold 122a part of Tract granted to Ephrim, & Charles Overman, in 1709, on South west Side of Little River, adj Wm Jackson, & a line between "my Brother Arnold White, & myself," to a Branch called "Overmans great Branch." Feb 12, 1738/9. Test' Wm Bundy, Thos Nicholson.

No. 250. John Davenport, of Chowan, & Ann his wife, for £12 pd by Hugh Davis, of Perq, sold 150a on Albemarle Sound, Opposite "Batts Grave" part of a tract, "belonging to Rich'd Davenport." Aug 1, 1716. Test' John Falconer, Wm Winson.

No. 251. John Harmon, of Perq, Weaver—for £120 pd by Rich'd Walless, of same—Cooper, sold 150a unto Joshua Deal, of Currituck, planter. Feb 14, 1737/8. Test' Jno Falconer, Abraham Warren.

No. 252. Wm Haskit, of Perq, for £150 pd by Francis James, of afsd—sold 435a on North East Side of Perq River, which was grt to Anthony Haskit, by two deed, 30a from Richard Cheston, May 3, 1694, & the other from Gabriel Newby, 50a July 9, 1722, the whole 80a. Jan 11, 1736/7. Test' Thomas Jessop, Thomas Hollowell, Richard Cheston.

No. 253. Thomas Pierce, of Chowan, for £100 pd by Joseph Pierce of Perq, planter, sold 435a on South west Side of Perq River, adj Wm Hall, John Pierce, & Henry Clayton, from his line to John Hancock, & Maj Lillington lines, due sd Thomas from James Beasley, & Francis Pettitt. Mar 7, 1736. Test' Joseph Barrow, Sam'l Wiatt, Peter Jones Jr.

No. 254. James Smith, of Perq, for £20 pd by Wm White, planter—sold 50a now "in possession of Stephen Thomas," & land sd Smith bought of Joseph Jessop, purchased by sd Jessop of Wm Carman. July 16, 1739. Test' R. Cheston, Thos Hill.

No. 255. John Phelps, of Perq, planter—for £150 pd by Joseph Smith, of same, sold 200a on "Ballahack Swamp" adj Elizabeth Phelps. July 16, 1739. Test' R. Cherston, Jos Ratliff.

No. 256. John Phelps, for £100 pd by Elizabeth Phelps, of Perq, sold 200a, on Cypress Swamp, adj Joseph Smith, which "Land was Pattented by Samuel

Phelps, dec'd, in behalf of himself, Jonathan Phelps, dec'd, & Joseph Smith, dec'd to be equally divided between them, & "this part was given by Jonathan Phelps, to his dau' Elizabeth." July 16, 1739. Test' R. Cheston, Joseph Ratliff,

No. 257. John Charles, of Perq, for 14 Barrels of Pork, pd by Edw'd Maudlin, of same—sold 200a on N.East Side of Suttons Creek, adj Francis Foster, & Nathaniel Nicholson, thence to Gum Swamp, down sd Swamp to line of John Henby, & Samuel Charles, dec'd. July 6, 1734. Test' William Bogue, Thos Weeks.

No. 258. April 14, 1733. Nicholas Stallings, of Upper Parish of Nansemond Co, in Vir' & Christian his wife, for £4 pd by Henry Stallings of Perq, & Jesse Riddick of sd Parish in Vir' "doth assign to sd Stallings 50a, on Southwest Side of the head of Perq River," being part of a Patent to Timothy Clare (late of Perq, dec'd), Dec 1, 1712, & by his will descended to Joseph Newby, & Mary his wife, Thos Winslow, & Elizabeth his wife, Thos Jossop, & Jane his wife, John White, & Sarah his wife, & Hannah Bundy (wife of Benj), by them sold to sd Nicholas. July 21, 1729. Test' Thos White, John Riddick.

No. 259. Wm Taylor, of the Co of Bath, precinct of Cartaret, planter—for £110 pd by Joshua Long, of Perq Gent, sold 150a, "by the Mill Pond" on line of Daniel Hall, & sd Joshua. "Land willed to my father Samuel Taylor." Feb 13, 1739.

No. 260. Grace Frayley (Friley), for £60 pd by Thomas Pierce, of Chowan, sold 133a, on North East Side of Perq River, between land of Thomas Jessop, & Richard Ratliff. Feb 22, 1738. Test' John Worley, Josh Worley, Thos Leary.

No. 261. Samuel Hall of Perq, Planter—for £150 pd by Abraham Warren of afsd—sold 300a adj Mr Charles Denman Dec'd, on South Side of Perq River. Oct 8, 1739. Test' Narh'l Caruthers, Jacob Caruthers.

No. 262. John Banks, of Perq, for £200 pd by Joshua Long, planter, of afsd—sold 185a on East Side of Indian Creek, adj Wm Long. Oct 11, 1739.

No. 263. Arnold White, of Perq, for £130 pd by Wm Haskit, of afsd—sold 50a on South West Side of Little River. Mar 2, 1736.7.

No. 264. Samuel Moore, of Perq, for $120 pd by Abraham Elliott of same—sold 50a adj Wm Morgan, & Moses Elliott, along sd lines to "Reedy Branch." Jan 17, 1736/7. Test' James Morgan, Abram Sanders.

No. 265. Edward Maudlin, of Perq, planter—for "love I bear my Cousin Thomas Nicholson," of Pasquotank, planter—have given 183a, on Fork Swamp, called "Passimon tree land," as per Patent. Oct 15, 1739. Test' Zach. Nixon, R. Cheston.

No. 266. Moses Eliott, of Perq, planter—for £100 pd by James Morgan, of same, sold 50a on South west Side of Perq River, called "Camponds" adj Ralph Bufkin now Caleb Elliotts, to "Union Road," & the head line of John Smith. Oct 15, 1739. Test' R. Cheston, Joshua Elliott.

No. 267. Wm Moore, of Perq, planter—for £10 pd by Benjamin Sanders of afsd—sold 50a on North Side of "Ballihack Swamp" adj John Townsing, & James Thomas, across Swamp to Samuel Phelps line. Aug 2, 1739. Test' Zach. Elton, John Phelps, J. Pearson.

No. 268. Edward Maudlin, of Perq, for 7 Barrels of Pork pd by Wm Bogue, of afsd—sold 100a, on North East Side of Suttons Creek, & South Side of

Gum Swamp, adj Nathaniel Nicholson, part of 200a sold to sd Maudlin by John Charles, July 6, 1734. Seal Jan 5, 1734/5. Test' Joseph Riddick, Wm Hasket, Thos. Jessop.

No. 269. Ephroditus Boice, & Ann his wife, Thomas Jones, & Sarah his wife, of N. C. for a Val' Con' pd by James Smith of Perq, Brick-maker—sold to sd Smith, & Susanna his wife, (during their Natual lives, & at their Decease, to their son Thomas Smith) 109a on South west Side of Perq River, adj Joseph Jessop, & Wm Simmons, "part of a Patent to Wm Carman, Jan 19, 1715/16, & by sd Carman in his will bequeathed to us." April 25, 1735. Test' Zach. Elton, Jos. Jessop.

No. 270. Thomas Nicholson, of Pasquotank Co, for £100 pd by Thomas Hollowell, of Perq, sold 91a adj Joseph Ratliff, & Arnold White, being ½ of land grt to my father, Christ'r Nicholson, Nov 22, 1714. Seal Oct 16, 1739. Test' John Nixon, R. Cheaston, Jeremiah Barns.

No. 271. Feb 25, 1721. John Moseley, of Upper Parish of Nansemond Co, Vir' for £5 pd by Joseph Radden of afsd—sold 50a on the "Main Desert" on the South side of "Loosing Swamp" adj John Glissom, part of a tract, grt unto John Harris, & John Larkum, & by them conveyed to me. Feb 12, 1700. Test' Wm. Sumner, Wm. Sumner Jr, Elizabeth Sumner Jr.

No. 272. Feb 26, 1721. John Moseley, to Joseph Radden, for 350 lbs of Tobacco, sold 50a on "Main Desert" & South Side of "Loosing Swamp." (Same Testators)

No. 273. May 18, 1713. John Moseley, for £5, pd by Joseph Radden, sold 50a in Upper Parish of Nansemound Co Vir' (Patented by same parties, 888a April 21, 1695), 100a of which was conveyed to sd Moseley Feb 12, 1701, sd land adj lines of Wm Woodley, & Dennis Glissom. Test' Wm. Sumner, J. Sumner, Will. Sumner Jr.

No. 274. May 19, 1713, for 2000 lbs of Tobacco, pd by John Radden, sold 50a in Upper Parish of Nansemond Co, Vir' (part of 888a grt to John Harris, & John Larkum, April 21, 1695) 100a of which was conveyed to sd Moseley Feb 12, 1701. Test' Wm. Sumner, J. Sumner, Wm. Sumner Jr.

No. 275. Macrora Scarbrough, Treasurer of Perq Co; for £200 pd by John Stone, of afsd—Carpenter—sold 100a on Vosses Creek, "which was Mortgaged by Smith Cella, Late of sd Co dec'd," & for want of several payments in Public Bills of Credit, land adj Moses Elliott, & Roger Kinyon, "where sd Cella did Dwell." Jan 21, 1739/40. Test' James Morgan, James Craven.

No. 276. John, & Joshua Pratt, of Perq, for £180 pd by William Wyatt, of afsd—sold 400a on North side of Yeopim River, adj George Mathews, "land given us by our father Jeremiah Pratt, known by the name of Sturgins Point." Jan 21, 1739/40. Test' Robt Harmon, Caleb Calloway, Jeremiah, Pratt, John Creecy.

No. 277. Jan 29, 1739. Thomas Bagley, of Perq, planter—for £300 pd by Theophilus Pugh, of Nansemond Co, Va, Merchant—sold 100a formerly Wm Moores, & sold by sd Moore to sd Bagley, & by sd Bagley to his son Thomas, "according to the most Ancient Bounds." Test' Ja. Everard, William Pugh. Ack' before W. Smith C. J.

No. 278. John Low, & Hannah his wife, of Pasquotank, Planter—for £16 pd by Moses Wood of Perq, Planter—sold 260a adj Josiah Bogue, & Thomas

Hollowell, in Perq Co. 2-6mo 1739. James Craven Clk. Test' Samuel Bundy, James Bundy, Josiah Bundy, Thomas Nicholson. Macrora Scarbrough Reg.

DEED BOOK D

No. 1. James Thigpen, of Perq, planter—for £150 pd by Zachariah Nixon, of same, planter—sold 450a next to Thomas Elliott. Jan 22, 1729. Test' William Townsen, Joseph Willson.

No. 2. James Boswell, of Pasquotank, planter—for a con' sold 50a, near the head of Little River, "part of tract, Thomas Boswell Dec'd gave his son James," on the back line of Charles Boswell, & Joseph Overman, adj John Boswell, & George Boswell. July 14, 1737. Test' Joseph Robinson, John Robinson.

No. 3. Thomas Nicholson, of Pasquotank, planter—for an Exchange of a Plan' in the fork of Little River, on North East side of same, sold unto William Bundy of Perq, planter 134a on South west side of Little River, adj James Newby, River swamp, & John Nixon. A patent to Christopher Nicholson, 1716 & bequeathed to his son Thomas. Mary Nicholson "doth Surrender her Dower." April 8, 1740. Test' Thomas Overman, Joseph Robinson.

No. 4. Foster Toms, of Perq, for £225 pd by Samuel Barclift, of afsd—sold 125a on "Beaver Cove Swamp, & Dirt Bridge Branch" part of tract Surveyed for Francis Toms Esq, Oct 2, 1698, on North East side of Perq River, adj Joseph Perishoe called "Beaver Cove Land." April 21, 1740. Test' James Gibson, Joseph Sutton.

No. 5. Joseph Oates of Perq, Cordwinder—for £100 pd by Nathaniel Caruthers, of same—sold 200a "whereon I lived." April 15, 1734. Test' Charles Denman Clk.

No. 6. Nathaniel Caruthers Esq, for "Natual love I bear my son Jacob, of Perq Co, planter have Transferred within Deed." April 20, 1740. Test' Zach Chancey, Samuel Barclift.

No. 7. Grant unto Nath'l Caruthers, 156a in Perq, on Deep Branch, adj John Wyatt, & the Side of Indian Creek. Gabriel Johnson Esq, Gov, at Newton. Feb 16, 1737. Nath Rice Sec.

No. 8. Nath'l Caruthers, for "love I bear my son James" of Perq, Blacksmith—have "transferred Within Patent" April 21, 1740. Test Zach Chancey, Samuel Barclift.

No. 9. Jan 2, 1738, Mary Pierce (Widow of Thomas Dec'd), Thomas Pierce, and Peter Jones, "Exors of sd Dec'd Will" sold to Thomas Norcom Jr. "one Negro boy named Sam, for 20 Barrells of Pork." Test' Geo. Sharrow, Jos. & Sarah Barrow.

No. 10. William Tomlin, of Perq, for £200 pd by Albert Albertson of same—sold 200a on West side of land, whereon sd Albertson now lives, near the mouth of "Tomlins Branch" part of 300a, grt unto John Tomlin, father of sd William, 1694. Feb 23, 1739. Test' Jas Pierce, Joseph Perisho, William Tomlin.

No. 11. Arnold White, of Perq, planter—for £35 pd by William Haskit, of afsd—sold 11a adj sd Arnold, & William White. Elizabeth White "doth Surrender her right of Dowery." Feb 1, 1739/40. Test' Thomas Nicholson, Josiah Bundy, Benjamin Mundin.

No. 12. James Griffin Sr, of Chowan, for "love I bear my son John" of Perq, do give 150a on North East side of Perq River, at the mouth of a Branch, called "Plum Tree Branch" part of a Patent to Ezekiel Maudlin, 300a, June 20, 1703, by sd Maudlin assigned to Timothy Clare, dec'd, by sd Clare sold to Francis Smith late of Perq, & by him assigned to sd Griffin. July 19, 1740. Test' Tho Rountree Sr, Charles Rountree, Thomas Rountree Jr.

No. 13. William Barrow, of the Co of Hyde, for £5 pd by John Barrow, of Perq, sold 100a on East side of Yopim Creek, adj John Barrow Jr, dec'd, "part of 525a pattented by Joseph Barrow." June 26, 1740. Test' Thomas Peirce, Ann Barrow, Joseph Barrow.

No. 14. William Barrow, of Hyde Co, for £10 pd by Joseph Barrow, of Perq, Planter—sold 200a on East side of Yopim Creek, adj John Barrow, part of 300a, one hundred of which, was conveyed to sd John. June 26, 1740. Test' Thomas Peirce, Ann Barrow, John Barrow.

No. 15. Jane Davis, of Perq Widow—"being aged, & unable to get my own living, and especially, for Christian-like Maintenance, during my Natual life, by my Son-in-law, John Boyse, & his wife Susanna, have delivered unto my sd Son-in-law, all part, & parcel, given me by my late husband, Thomas Davis of Upper Parish Nansemond Co Vir' dec'd, in his will, Jan 28, 1705. The following now in actual possession of sd Boyse; 3 pewter dishes, 1 pewter tankard, 1 feather bed, & bedstead, 1 Iron pot, 1 Iron pestle, 2 Iron wedges, 6 chairs, & a Round Table, also 10 Barrels of Tar, due from my son Thomas Davis, over Orapeak Swamp, upon demand." April 4, 1739. Test' William Townsend, Elias Stallings.

No. 16. Isaac Stallings, of Perq, Planter—for £10 pd by Jacob Docton, of afsd—sold unto Elizabeth Price, 50a, part of a patent to Timothy Clare, dec'd, Dec 1, 1712, & by his will descended to Joseph Newby, & Mary his wife, Thos Winslow, & Elizabeth his wife, which was sold by them, to Nicholas Stallings, July 21, 1729. Seal Sept 20, 1740. Test' Isaac Speight, Lewis Bond.

No. 17. Abraham Mullen Sr, of Perq, for £150 pd by John Gohyer (Guyer), sold 210a adj Atthur Croxton, on the River side, & the supper side of land, belonging to Orphans of William Lacey. Oct 20, 1740. Test' Alb't Albertson, Jas Pierce.

No. 18. Joseph Ellitt, of Perq, for £27 pd by Jacob Perry, of afsd—sold 480a on South west side of Perq River, at a Branch called "Elder Branch," formerly land of Daniel Snooke, part of a patent to Isaac Wilson, Jan 5, 1712, & by sd Mary to her dau' Elizabeth, "now wife of John Wilson." Oct 20, of sd Joseph. Oct 20, 1740. Test' Robt Wilson, John Wilson.

No. 19. Abraham Mullen, of Perq, Planter—for "love I bear my son Isaac Mullen of same—do give 105a on North side of Beaver Cove Swamp, adj Foster Thomas, Christopher Sutton, & Abraham Rigs, where we now live." Oct 17, 1740. Test' Abraham Moullen, Jr, Abraham Hosea, Jos Sutton.

No. 20. John Willson, of Perq, for £13 pd by Jacob Perry, of afsd—sold 200a on North Side of Perq River, adj Jacob, & John Winslow, sd land grt to Timothy Clare, dec'd, Dec 1, 1712, & given by him to his dau' Mary Mayo, & by sd Mary to her dau' Elizabeth, "now wife of John Wilson." Oct 20, 1740. Test' Rt Willson, Joseph Elliott.

No. 21. Thomas Collins (son of James dec'd), of Chowan Co, for £6 pd by John Reddick, of Perq, sold 100a in the "Pine Woods" near the "burnt pocoson" which was patented by Thomas Blitchenden, & sold to Thomas Gray, by sd Gray to John Lackey, & by sd Lackey to Joseph Jessop, by sd Jessop, to Charles Wilkes, with 30a adj purchased of Thomas Bagley, & sold to Richard Cheston, who sold all the sd land, 130a to Charles Wilkes. Oct 20, 1740. Test' Jacob Perry, Zach'h Chancey.

No. 22. Sarah Elliott, & Jacob Elliott, Planters—of Perq, for £50 pd by John Perry, of afsd—Sadler; sold 50a on Vosses Creek, adj Joseph Newby, John Morgan Sr, Thomas Jessop, & Samuel Moore, to line of Francis Toms, "Land given me sd Sarah by my father Timothy Clare, my husband Jacob Elliott, having good authority to sell same." Oct 20, 1740. Test' Rt Wilson, Jacob Perry.

No. 23. Samuel Newby, of Perq, planter—for £25 pd by Henry Lamb, of afsd—sold 100a "at the Country Road, thence to Cypress Swamp, up Deep Branch, to Thigpens line." 12—8mo 1740. Test' Francis Newby, Huldah Newby.

No. 24. April 14, 1733. Nicholas Stallings, of Upper Parish of Nansemond Co, Vir', & wife Christian, for £4 pd by Henry Stallings of Perq, to Jesse Reddick of same Parish & Co, sold 50a near the South Westward side of the head of Perq River, "part of a patent to Timothy Clare late of Perq, dec'd, Dec 1, 1712—169a, which by the will of sd Clare, descended to Joseph Newby, & Mary his wife, Thomas Winslow, & Elizabeth his wife, Thomas Jessup & Jane his wife, John White, & Sarah his wife, & Hannah Bundy, heirs of sd Clare, & sold by them to sd Nicholas." July 21, 1729. Test' Thos White, John Reddick.

No. 25. July 16, 1739. Henry Stallings, "doth assign, within deed" unto Isaac Stallings. Test' James Scott, William Ambler.

No. 26. Jesse Newby, of Perq, Wheelright, or planter—for £73 pd by Samuel Newby of same, planter, sold 50a "where I now dwell, on a branch, running out of sd Samuel Newbys Mill Pond, that divides land of Francis, & Jesse Newby, to Sam'l Newbys New Road to Deep branch, along sd branch to Perq River, & up the sd River to Samuel Newbys Mill Creek." Jan 6, 1740. Test' Zach Chancey, Zach Elton, Jos Willson.

No. 27. Margaret Barrow, Spinster, of Perq—for a "Sum pd to my Mother," by Jonathan Phelps, Merchant—sold to Henry Phelps, son of afsd, 20a, adj land formerly belonging to William Lawrence, on North East of land taken up by Francis Toms, now in possession of Zachariah Nixon. Jan 19, 1740/1. Test' Joseph Wilson, Joseph Ratliff.

No. 28. Ann Hall of Perq, for £65 pd by John Creasy of same, planter—sold 100a on North East side of Yopim River, part of land formerly belonging to George Matthews, father of sd Ann, adj William Wyatt. April 20, 1741.

No. 29. Thomas Nicholson of Pasq Co, planter—for £100 pd by Thomas Hollowell, of Perq, sold 91a, adj James Newby, & Joseph Sutton. Nov 22, 1740. Test' John Perry, Will'm Haskitt, Michael Murphy.

No. 30. James Henby of Perq, for £120 pd by Edward Maudlin of afsd—sold 100a on "Bee Tree ponds" at the head of Vasies (Vosses) Creek, adj Upper part of sd Henbys land, a patent to Francis Toms Jr, 1716. Seal July 16, 1740.

No. 31. Arnold White of Perq, planter—for an "Exchange of land, with George Boswell," on South west side of Little River, doth acquit sd Boswell, & sold 61a, where sd White now dwells, adj Joseph Ratliff, & William Haskett, to River Pocoson, Elizabeth wife of sd White her dower right. Sept 13, 1740. Test' Thomas Nicholson, Stephen Hall, Michael Murphy.

No. 32. George Boswell of Perq, planter—for an "exchange of land, with Arnold White" on South west side of Little River, sold 100a on a division line, of sd Boswell, & James Boswell, to River Pocoson. Jane Boswell wife of George. Test' Thomas Nicholson, Stephen Hall, Michael Murphy. Sept 13, 1740.

No. 33. Francis Rountree of Vir, Planter—for £25 pd by John Smith of Perq, Planter—sold "near 100a" on Newbys Creek, formerly land of John White, adj Thomas Jessop, to a branch called "Great Branch" being bounds between sd land, & William Rountree. Test' Thomas White, Joshua White, Jacob Elliott. Apl Court 1741.

No. 34. Francis James of Perq, for £180 pd by William Moore, "of the Co of Isle of Wight, parish of Newport, in Vir," sold 80a on North East side of Perq River, same granted to Anthony Hasket, by two deeds, one from Richard Cheaston, May 3, 1694, & the other from Gabriel Newby, July 9, 1722, adj River Pocoson, formerly Peter Grays. Test' Jos Barnes, Richd Cheaston. May 14, 1741.

No. 35. Moses Speight of Bertie Co, planter—for a con' pd by Thomas Winslow of Perq, planter—sold 230a on Little River, adj Thomas Weeks, & Solomon Henry, on one side, & Dennis Collins, on the other, part of a patent to William Tomlin, July 23, 1724, due for transportations. April 25, 1741. Test' Will'm Litgram, Truman Moore, Thos Bagley.

No. 36. John Banks of Perq, planter—for £265 pd by Joshua Long of afsd, planter—sold 355a on East side of Indian Creek, or Mill Pond, down sd Creek to a small Gut, near Jeremiah Pratts house, adj William Wyatt. May 21, 1741. Test' Nath'l Carathers, Thos Long, Robert Harmon.

No. 37. Surveyor Genl', or his Dept; You are to lay out to Colonel Edward Moseley 640a in Chowan, "by virtue of within warrent." (No date) Wm Maule Surveyor Gen'l.

No. 38. Lords Pro' of N. C. grt to Col Edward Moseley 40a in Chowan Co, adj John Jackson, John Jordan, & William Carman, on Indian Creek, up sd Creek, Nov 20, 1716. Cha. Eden, Tho. Pollock, N. Chevin, Fras. Foster, T. Knight.

No. 39. Edward Moseley Esq, of N. C. for s5 pd by Francis Newby, of Perq, sold 640a in Chowan, on Indian Creek, a grt to me by Lords Pro' Nov 2, 1716. Seal Mar 13, 1741. Test' Sam'l James, Robert Wilson.

No. 40. Thomas Overman, of Perq, Planter—for £15 pd by Jonathan Sharwood, of afsd—sold 100a which Richard Turner "gave in his will to his Gr-son Samuel Newby, & sd Newby in his will bequeathed to his kinsman, Thomas Overman." On North East side of Cypress Swamp, adj Benj Wilson, & William Phillips. 19—8mo 1741.

No. 41. William Wyatt, of Perq, Planter—for £125 pd by Joseph Creasy, of afsd—Shoemaker—sold 200a, purchased by sd Wyatt, of John, & Joshua Pratt, on North side of Yopim River, adj George Matthews, called "Sturgeons Point." Oct 19, 1741. Test' Samuel Standin, Henderson Standin.

No. 42. Thomas Jessop, Sr of Perq, planter—to his son Thomas Jessop Jr, of afsd—100a, on West side of Perq River, adj William Moore. Oct 19, 1741. Test' Evan Jones, Nathan Pearson.

No. 43. James Morgan, Esq, of Perq, for £300 pd by Thomas Winslow, of afsd—sold 150a, adj William Morgan, on "Morgans Swamp." Sept 29, 1741. Test' Richard Cheaston, John Henby.

No. 44. Thomas Nicholson, of Pasq, planter—for £12 pd by John Moore, of Perq, planter—sold 183a, called "Persimon tree land" adj Joshua Boswell, & Thomas Hollowell. "John Moore to have the upper half, 90a & Thomas Hollowell to have the other Moytey thereof." Oct 19, 1741. Test' Francis Toms, Thomas Winslow, Nathan Pearson.

No. 45. John Lacy, of Perq, for £100 pd by John Maudling, of afsd—sold 50a on Voices, (Vosses) Creek. May 10, 1741. Test' Joseph Barnes, R. Cheston.

No. 46. Stephen Thomas, of Perq, for £60 pd by Robert Redick, sold 150a on the "Narrows" of Perq River, on South west side, 100a formerly William Carmans, & by him sold to Joseph Jessop, 50a of which sd Jessop, sold to Ann Pettiver, sd 50a part of 1380a grt unto Isaac Wilson, Jan 5, 1712. 100a bequeathed by said Jessop in his will. Oct 19, 1741. Test' Zach Elton, Wm Moore, Edward Rice.

No. 47. Jacob Perry, of Perq, Planter—for a con' sold to John Winslow of same, 90a on Perq River, "binding on land formerly Timothy Clares dec'd," unto sd John Winslow Sr. Oct 19, 1741. Test' Joseph Reddick, Thomas Calloway.

No. 48. Joseph Winslow, of Perq, planter—for £200 pd by Ezekiel Maudlin, of same—sold 125a, on Voices (Vosses) Creek, adj Gabriel Newby. Oct 19, 1741. Test' Zachariah Nixon, Nathan Pearson.

No. 49. William Wiat, of Perq, planter—for £75 pd by John Banks, of afsd—sold 100a on Yopim River, part of 400a called "Stergeons point," at the mouth of "Broad Creek," on North side of Albemarle Sound. Nov 3, 1741. Test' Joseph Oats, Thomas Pierce, Joseph Ashley.

No. 50. Edmund Jackson, of Pasq Co, planter—for £280 pd by John Robinson, of afore' planter—sold 200a, on South west side of Little River, adj William Tomblin, Joseph, & said John Robinson, a patent bearing date May 1, 1694. Seal Jan 19, 1741/2. Test' Thomas Pierce, Richard Skinner, Joseph Robinson.

No. 51. Thomas Hollowell, of Perq, planter—in Con' of "love I do bear unto my dau Elizabeth Barclift" of afore' have given 100a, on Wallers Line. Aug 26, 1738. Test' James Gibson, William Arnold.

No. 52. Elizabeth Simson, of Perq, for £104 pd by Robert Moore, sold 100a on South west by the "County road," on line of Jonathan Phelps, now in possession of Zach Nixon, adj Zach Chancey, & William Townsend. Mar 12, 1742. Test' Mc Scarbrough, Samuel Moore, William Townsend.

No. 53. Christopher Jackson, of Nancimund Co, in Va, "do grant unto my trusty friend Nicholas Stallings," power to Ack' unto John Hollowell, a tract of land, devised to said John, this 25 Oct, 1741. Test' Elias Stallings Jr, Wm Price.

No. 54. Christ Jackson, of Vir, Gent—for £10 pd by John Hollowell, of Perq Co, sold land on west side of Perq River, "left to me by the will of Wm Jackson." Oct 28, 1741. Test' Elias Stallings Jr, William Price.

No. 55. William Moore, of Perq, for £150 pd by Thomas Bagley, of afore' sold 88a, "granted to Anthony Haskett by two deeds," one from Richd Cheaston, for 30a May 3, 1694, & "ye other from Gabriel Newby" for 50a July 9, 1722. Seal Dec 10, 1741. Test' William Bogue, Moses Wood, Sarah Bogue.

No. 56. John Brinkley, of Chowan, planter—for £25 pd by William Foxworth, of Perq, planter—sold 50a on West side of a Plan' belonging to "heirs of Daniel Hall dec." Jan 18, 1741. Test' Nathan L. Crothers, John Stepney, John Pratt.

No. 57. James Boswell, of Pasq, for £11 s 15 pd by George Boswell, of Perq, sold 50a on S. W. side of Little River, "near the head thereof," adj Charles Overman; to line of Jacob Overman, along his line to Arnold White, & from his line to River pocoson. Nov 21, 1741. Test' John Overman James Overman, Joseph Robinson.

No. 58. Zachariah Chancey, of Perq, "for a sum" pd by William Townsend, of afore' sold 100a on S. W. side of Perq River, "near Balehak swamp," over said Swamp to Phelps line. Jan 16, 1741. Test' Robert Wilson, Samuel Newby.

No. 59. Elizabeth Simpson, of Perq, for £14 pd by William Townsend, of afsd' sold 100a on South West side of Perq River, called "Frog Hall" part of 450a "patented by Edward Holmes Feb 25, 1696," adj James Sitterson, & Phillips, to land of Paul Palmer. Along his line to Wm Stewarts, "ye old plan" now belonging to Mac Scarbrough, along his line to Robert Moore. Mar 12, 1741/2. Test' Mc Scarbrough, Zach'h Chancey, Samuel Moore.

No. 60. Zachariah Chancey, of Perq, for £150 pd by William Moore of afore' sold 79a in Ballahak "on ye South west side of ye swamp, on ye branch called ye great branch" down said branch to Wm Townsends line, along said line to William Bogue. Jan 15, 1741/2. Test' Robert Wilson, Samuel Newby.

No. 61. Richard Cheaston, of Perq, for £400 pd by Zachariah Nixon of afore' sold 330a on ye No East side of Perq River, in a swamp called "Frog Hall" to lines of Francis Toms, Ralph Fletcher, & William Jones. 13d 1mo 1742. Test' Samuel Moore, Joshua Davis, John Wilson.

No. 62. Robert Wilson, for an "Exchange of land" of Joseph Newbys, on S. W. side of Perq River, at the head of Cypress Creek, sold unto said Newby, Mill wright—50a on N. E. side of Perq River, adj Robert & Samuel Moore, formerly land of Jonathan Phelps. April, 1742. Test' Thomas Hollowell, John Anderson.

No. 63. Thomas Elliott, of Perq, planter—for £55 pd by Joseph Newby, of same, Millwright—sold 30a, adj Thomas Newby "in ye fork of Cypress Swamp, called "Aarons old field." Reg April Court, 1742. Test' Edmund Hatch, Richard McClure.

No. 64. Joseph Newby, Millwright; in con' of an "exchange" of land, with Robert Wilson, of Perq, planter—sold 200a on Gum Branch, "which runs out of Cypress Swamp," on each side of Mill Swamp, adj Thomas

Newby, & 130a "at ye head of sd land" adj William Elliott, John Pearson, & land called "Aarons old field" 7—2mo 1742.

No. 65. Caleb Elliott, of Perq, Planter—for £50 pd by Joseph Smith, of ye same—planter, sold 250a, on ye north side of Cypress Swamp, to "bounds of Luke Hollowell, by ye head of Liles branch." July 19, 1742. Test' Joseph Wilson, Abram Sanders, Nathan Pearson.

No. 66. Francis Penrice, & Elizabeth his wife, Christopher Arrington, & Abigail his wife, for £50 pd by William Long, all of Perq—sold 100a, adj Samuel Standin, Joseph Barrow, & John Felt. (Phelps) April 18, 1742. Test' John Callaway, Thomas Callaway.

No. 67. William Phelps, of Perq, for £50 pd by Richard Goodwin, of afsd—sold 50a on South west side of Perq River, & North side of Ballahak Swamp, adj Wm Townsend. July 19, 1742. Test' Joshua Hobart, Thomas Herreandeen, William Moore.

No. 68. Joseph Smith, of Perq, Planter—for an "exchange" unto me by Caleb Elliott, conveyed 150a, "three quarters of a tract, made over to me by John Phelps, because it belonged to my Father, & Samuel Phelps, both dying, before a division was made, this part came to me as heir of sd Father, "on East side of Ballahack Swamp, adj sd Phelps, & Elizabeth Phelps. July 19, 1742. Test' Joseph Wilson, Abram Sanders, Nathan Pearson.

No. 69. April 29, 1742. Thomas Sharbo, of Perq, planter—for £30 pd by Thomas Weeks, of same—sold 100a on South west side of Little River, "where said Thos. Weeks, now dwells" adj Alexander Steward, part of land sd Sharbo, bought of Solomon Hendricks. Rebecca Shrabo, assigns her Dower. Test' William Ward, Anne Harrison.

No. 70. Grant. Unto William Stewart, of Perq. planter—230a, "due for Trans', & for a" yearly rent of s1 for each 50a, "every 29 day of Sept, sd land lying on Perishaws Creek," adj James Perishaw. Co of Albemarle, Jan 1, 1694.

Phillip Ludwell Esq, Gov, & Capt Gen'l, & Councellors: Daniel Akehurst, Francis Toms, Thomas Pollock, Thos ————. Rec by Wm Glover, Clk of Sec Office.

No. 71. Joseph Stewart, of Perq, for £20 pd by Macrora Scarbrough, Esq of afsd—"conveyed said patent," 230a, granted to my Father William Stewart, Jan 1, 1694. Seal Nov 31, 1741. Test' Lemuel Hatch, Elizabeth Rud.

No. 72. Robert Hosea, of Pasq, for "12 barrels of Pork," pd by my brother William Hosea, of Perk, sold 130a on Deep Creek, binding on Mr Albert Albertsons land, part my father bought of Thomas Commander. Jan 17, 1742. Test' Robert Hosea, Thomas Hosea.

No. 73. William Moore, of Perq, planter—for £110 pd by Benjamin Sanders, of afsd—sold 50a on north side of Ballahack Swamp, adj John Townsend, & James Thomas, across Swamp to line of Samuel Phelps. Aug 2, 1739. Test' Zach Elton, John Pearson, John Phelps.

No. 74. Benjamin Sanders, planter—for £35 pd by William Moore, sold 50a, in Perq Co. Sept 5, 1741. Test' Zach Elton, John Pearson, John Phelps.

No. 75. Samuel Bond, of Perq, for £200 pd by James Pagitt, of afsd—sold 104a on South west side of Perq River, adj Thomas Blitchenden, which was given me, by my father. Oct 18, 1742. Test' Mac Scar———, Thomas Weeks, Edmund Hatch.

No. 76. Dec 18, 1741/2. Daniel Rogerson, of Perq, & Hannah his wife, for £96 pd by John Reddick of afsd—sold 50a on South west side of Perq River, on a branch Called "Willifords," now in the tenure of Thomas Foones, dec'd, adj Martin Asbell, & Swamp, part of a grt to Wm Kitching dec'd, April 1, 1713, 450a, & by sd Kitching "given to me" June 19, 1735. Test' Jacob Perry, Thomas Lilly.

No. 77. Mar 18, 1740. Mary Hall, widow—of Perq, for £71 s17 p9, sold land, "being full satisfaction, of the Est belonging to Anne Bedgood." William, & Ann Bedgood. Test' James Gibson.

No. 78. Thomas Parker, of Perq, for a con' sold unto Caleb Elliott, of afsd—20 head of cattle—36 hogs—1 white horse (bought of Zachariah Chancey) 1 gray mare—& colt—1 bay horse—3 sheep—2 ewes—1 ram—2 beds—& furniture—3 Iron pots—2 kettles, & 1 skillet—4 pewter dishes—2 basons—2 plates—, his corn, & meat, & all House-hold goods." Feb 11, 1742/3. Test' Peter Parker, John Parker.

No. 79. William Wyatt, of Perq, for £65 pd by Peter Jones Jr, of afsd—sold 50a on North side of Albemarle Sound, & South west side of Perq River, "which was given me by my father John Wyatt" adj Anthony Alexander, & Thomas Blitchenden, at the head of "Spellmans Creek." Jan 17, 1742. Test' Sam'l Swann, Silv'r Sweet, John Pierce.

No. 80. John Morgan Sr, of Perq, for £400 pd by Joseph Newby of afsd—sold 150a on East side of Bosses (Vosses) Creek, "according to Lawrence Hunts Patent 1696" by the side of the Swamp, "50a of which I gave to my dau' Mary Elliott." Feb 25, 1741/2. Test' Jos Robinson, Samuel Jackson Jr, Mary Robensin.

No. 81. Elizabeth Anderson, & John Anderson, Sarah, & John Jones, Sarah, & Jacob Mullen, & Thomas Nicholson, for £236 pd by Richard Sanders, of Perq, sold 100a on North east side of Perq River, "land that Samuel Nicholson, at the request of his father Christopher Nicholson, made over to his brother Joseph," & sd Joseph in his will gave to his brother John, who died without heirs, "in like manner," left it to Nathaniel Nicholson, he also having no heirs, left it to Benjamin Nicholson, "all failing of heirs" sd Joseph in his will, gave sd land to his five brothers, (Sam'l, John, Nath'l, & Christopher) called "Log house" land. Jan 17, 1742/3. Test' Joseph Robinson, Joseph Ratliff, Abram Sanders.

No. 82. Edward Modlin, of Perq, for £31 s10 pd by George Eason, of afsd—sold 100a on North east side of Suttons Creek, adj Nath'l Nichols, & Wm Bogue. Jan 14, 1742/3. Test' John Sumner, Christopher Sutton, Lott Stallings.

No. 83. William Elliott, of Perq, for £50 pd by Jules Bunch, of Chowan, planter—sold 200a on South west of Nathan Newbys line in Perq, adj James Thigpen. Dec 13, 1742. Test' Robert Wilson, Isaac Wilson, Joseph Newby.

No. 84. Joseph Newby of Perq, Millwright; for £10 pd by Lott Stallings, of afsd—sold 150a, part of 300a grt to sd Newby Jan 1, 1730, on N. E. side of Cypress Swamp, & "Balls branch" adj Nathan Newby. Jan 17, 1742. Test' Benj Perry, George Eason.

No. 85. Joseph Newby, for £10 pd by John Boyce, sold 150a on North east side of Cypress Swamp, on a branch called "Duck ponds." Jan 17, 1742. Test' Benjamin Perry, George Eason.

No. 86. Richard Wood, Farmer—for £160 pd by Aaron Wood, planter—sold 100a adj Thomas Hollowell, & John Perishoe, along said line to Wm Bogue, & Josiah Bogue. Jan 10, 1742/3. Test' Thomas Hollowell, Josiah Bogue, John Guyer.

No. 87. Elizabeth Simpson, for £104 pd by Zachariah Chancey, sold 100a, on South west side of Perq River, on Robert Moore, & Jonathan Phelps lines, to Zach Chancey, & up his line to Wm. Townsend, commonly called "Frog Hall." Mar 11, 1741. Test' James Morgan, Thomas Carte, Zach Elton.

No. 88. George Snoden, of Perq, farmer—for £200 pd by Joshua Barclift, of afore' sold 73a at the head of "Lilies Creek," betwixt land formerly held by Thomas Boswell, & Samuel Pritlow. Jane Snoden her Dower right. Jan 17, 1742/3. Test' James Gibson, John Barclift.

No. 89. Robert Rountree, of Nancemund Co, Vir, for £29 pd by Benjamin Perry, of Perq Co, sold part of tract, on West side of Perq River, adj Daniel Snooks line, (now in possession of John Riddick) to a Swamp called "Dennises" pattented by Timothy "Hare" (Clare) Dec 1, 1712 & given by him in his will to his dau Sarah White, & sold by said Sarah, & John White (her husband) to said Rountree. July 20, 1730. Robert Rountree & Elizabeth his wife "do bind ourselves to defend said deed." Jan 17, 1742. Test' Jacob Perry, Thomas White.

No. 90. Jacob Perry, of Perq, "have given" to Thomas White of afore' (his Nephew) 40a "which I took from him, by cources of an Old Patent," said land adj John Winslow, "pattented by Timothy Clare April 5, 1720, & given in his will to his dau Elizabeth, wife of Thomas Winslow," & by said Winslow sold to said White. Jan 17, 1742. Test' Benj Perry, Robert Rountree, Phillip Perry.

No. 91. Jeremiah Barne, of Perq, for £200 pd by Joseph Perishoe, of afore' sold 286a on N. E. side of Perq River, between Clement Hall, & Joseph Anderson, adj John Tomlin, Albert Albertson, & John Barclift, thence to John Batemans line. April 15, 1742. Test' John Anderson, William Wood, John Whidbee.

No. 92. Pierce Ashball (Asbell), for £95 pd by John Reddick, assigned 50a, part of a grant to Wm Kitching 1716, & by said Kitching made over to Daniel Rogerson, by deed of gift Jan 10, 1732/3, & by said Daniel sold to Martin Ashball Jan 15, 1732/3, "from said Martin to his son Pierce Ashball." Jan 3, 1742. Test' James Morgan, James Sumner, William Lacey.

No. 93. Andrew Woodley, of Perq, planter—for £100 pd by Samuel Moore, of afore' sold 100a on Sharrows line, to Arthur Albertsons, along said line, to the head land in Old Neck, thence to Ralph Fletcher. Jan 17, 1742/3. Test' Zachariah Nixon, Thomas White.

No. 94. Aaron Wood, of Perq, for £40 pd by Thomas Hollowell, of afore' Farmer—sold 5a at the mouth of a branch running down Cypress Swamp, to Josiah Bogues line. Jan 17, 1742/3. Test' Joseph Robinson, Josiah Bogue, Thomas Nicholson.

No. 95. Elizabeth Simson, of Perq, for £200 pd by Zachariah Chancey, of afore' sold 200a on West side of Perq River, upon a Creek running out of said River, called "Castletons Creek" said plan' formerly William Stewards, adj Robert Moore, & Wm Townsend, down said Creek to "Skinners bridge." Mar 31, 1742. Test' William Phelps, Thos Carte, Zach Elton.

No. 96. Zachariah Chancey, of Perq, planter for £20 pd by Mac Scarbrough, Esq, of afore'—sold 230a, conveyed to me "by Elizabeth Simson late of said Co," her whole right to the "Old plan" on Castletons Creek, "formerly William Stewarts," granted to said Stewart Jan 1, 1694. Seal Jan 17, 1742

*No. 97. April 1, 1743. Henry Wensley, formerly of London, gent—"but now of Perq Co," to Christian Reed, of afore' 500a, on Albemarle Sound, by the great swamp between said land, & "Harveys landing," adj Thomas Norcom, "down Sound to Thomas Blithenden," & also 200a, formerly "in possession of George Durant." April 1, 1743. "Whereas; Elizabeth Chandler, of St Marys parish, at Lambert, Co of Surry, in Great Britain, Widow"—only surviving dau, of Edward Catchmeyd, heretofore of St Clements, Danes, Co of Middlesex, fishmonger dec—who was the son of Thomas Catchmayd dec, who was brother, & devisee, of George Catchmayd, late of N. C. dec, who did appoint said Wensley Att', to dispose of land in Perq called "Tullick" 1500a, to which said Elizabeth hath claim, as heir-at-law of said George," & hath agreed to sell same to said Reed. Test' J. Montgomery, Joseph Anderson.

No. 98. April 1, 1743. Henry Wensley Gent, Att', for Elizabeth Chandler, to Samuel Standing 300a, (part of 1500a) for £300 on Eastermost side of Bentleys Creek, issuing out of the Sound, at a branch which issueth out of "Bridge Creek," on Thomas Norcoms line. Test' Christian Reed, Zach Chancey.

No. 99. Henry Wensley Att', for Elizabeth Chandler, sold Plan' called "Trillick" (part of 1500a) to Thomas Norcom, 500a for £100, "300a of which was bought of John Bentley, by Cornelius Larry (Leary), & was conveyed by Cornelius, son of said Larry, to Thomas Norcom, father of said Thomas," & 200a was sold by Tulle Williams, to said Thomas last mentioned, on northside of Albemarle Sound & Bentley, & Bridge Creeks, called "Goor Land." Test' Christian Reed, Zach Chancey.

No. 100. April 2, 1743. Henry Wensley, gent, Att', for Elizabeth Chandler, agreed to sell 425a part of a plan' called "Berkswear" in Perq Co (the whole 1700a) for £450 pd by Samuel Swann, of N. C. gent—near the mouth of Perq River, on Albemarle Sound, along Thomas Durants line, adj land formerly Richard Sandersons. Test' J. Montgomery, Christian Reed, Jos Anderson.

No. 101. Thomas Houghton, of Chowan, & Elizabeth, his wife, dau of Jonathan Evans dec, for £100 pd by Richard Skinner, Abram Sanders &

---

* This was land, conveyed by George Catchmaid of Nancemond Co Vir, to George Durant 1st.

QUAKER ENVIRONMENT

A. Piney Wood Quaker Meeting House. In use before the Revolutionary War.
B. First Friends Academy in Belvidere, where Dr. Thomas Nicholson taught school. Now a private residence.
C. Present High School building. Formerly Belvidere Academy. Built about 1824.
D. A corner of the "old Lamb place" just across the river from Belvidere, showing the hand-carved woodwork. This house was built in 1767 by Exum Newby.

Zachariah Nixon, (all of Perq), planter—, & John Wilcocks, of said Co, Millwright—sold 150a on Southeast side of "Castletons Creek," up Creek Swamp, between said Thomas, & his brother William Houghton, "a dividing line between Peter Jones Jun, & the Orphans of John Williams dec," over a Branch called "Beaver Dam Swamp" formerly belonging to "Jonathan Evans, father of said Elizabeth," April 18, 1743. Test' Samuel Swann, Samuel Standin.

No. 102. John White, of Perq, for £5 pd by Thomas White, of afore' "do sell 150a on mill swamp, out of a tract formerly belonging to Timothy Clerr (Clare)" patented 1707, from Lords Pro' of N. C. April 18, 1743. Test' Joshua White, John Winslow, Joseph Winslow.

No. 103. Daniel Rogerson, of Perq, planter—for £18 s10, pd by John Hollowell of afore' sold "part of tract," a patent to Wm Kitchen, & Margaret Snuke in 1713. 50a on North side of River pocoson, "on ye east side of a branch at the mouth of Willifords Branch." April 18, 1743. Test' Nicholas Stallings, Thomas White.

No. 104. William Bedgood, & Ann his wife, of Perq, for £300 pd by John Barclift, of afore' farmer—sold 100a on South west side of Little River, on line of John Arnold dec. April 15, 1743. Test' James Gibson, Thomas Noles, John Barclift Jr.

No. 105. Richard Whidbee, of Perq, gent—for £73 pd by John Whidbee, of afore' sold 417a, adj Joseph Sutton, along his own line to William Woods, thence to Benj Nicholson, & "Rattle Snake Ridge," as by patent. July 30, 1724. Test' Samuel Swann, Aaron Moses, William Collins. Richard & Hannah Whidbee.

No. 106. Thomas Parker, of Perq, planter—for £30 pd by John Boyce, sold 50a at the mouth of Gum branch, thence to Cypress Swamp. Feb 2, 1742/3. Test' Nicholas Stallings, Isaac Bogue, Sarah Parker.

No. 107. James Anderson, of Craven Co, planter—for £60 pd by John Anderson, sold 15a, near Suttons Creek, adj said John Anderson. Mar 29, 1743. Test' Thomas Hosea, Joseph Ratliff.

No. 108. Joshua Barclift, of Perq, farmer—for "15 barrels of pork," pd by James Gibson, of afore' sold 60a on South west side of Little River, adj said Gibsons line. Mar 28, 1743. Test' Peter Wren, John Barclift, Elizabeth Barclift, Joshua & Sarah Barclift.

No. 109. John Henby, of Perq, farmer—for £50 pd by Thomas Montague, of afore' farmer—assigned 200a, adj Thomas Overman, said John Henby, Thomas Hollowell, & Joseph Ratliffe, on N. E. of Francis Newbys land. April 14, 1743. Test' John Nixon, Dorothy Nixon, Thomas Nicholson.

No. 110. John, & Ann Barclift, of Perq, for £250 pd by Sarah Mc Adams, of Pasq, sold 200a, on South West side of Little River, adj William Mann, toward "Deep Creek," on line of John Parishoes land. April 12, 1743. Test' Thomas Nicholson, John Parish, Joshua White.

No. 111. Francis Laden, of Perq, planter—for £125 pd by William Layden, of afore' conveyed 100a, adj Samuel Pritlow, & Harry Willoughby, "to Mary Evans, & Godfreys bounds." Jan 5, 1743. Test' Benj Baptist, Anthony Hatch, Lemuel Hatch.

No. 112. John Riddick (son of Thomas), of Perq, for £7 pd by Timothy Lilly, of same, sold 100a, "in the pine Woods," near the burnt pocoson. Part of a patent to Thomas Blitchenden, & sold by him to Thomas Gray, by said Gray conveyed to John Lackey, & by said Lackey to Thomas Jessop, by said Jessop to Charles Wilkes. July 18, 1743. Test' Joseph Morris, Gideon Bundy.

No. 113. Samuel Snoden, of Perq, farmer—for £125 pd by Joshua Barclift, of afore' farmer—sold 65a, on Lillies Creek, "part of George Snodens patent." July 18, 1743. Test' James Gibson, Sarah Barclift.

No. 114. July 15, 1743. Andrew Woodley, of Perq, to William Hunter, of Chowan, for £30 sold 131a, on "north side of horse pool swamp." Test' James Sumner, John Wilcock.

No. 115. June 1, 1743. Henry Wensley, Att' for Elizabeth Chandler, widow—to Jeremiah Pratt, of Perq, Planter—for £50 sold 150a on North East side of Cypress Swamp, adj lands of "the late Thomas Harvey," Thomas Norcom, William Barrow, & John Williams. "Whereas; Joshua Long of Perq died possessed of 140a, (15000a, belonging to said Elizabeth) & devised the same to his son Thomas Long Junior, "under care & tuition of said Jeremiah, who intermarried with Elizabeth widow of said Joshua, & mother of said minor," & said Jeremiah "hath agreed to purchase all the Estate of the heirs of George Catchmayd." June 1, 1743. Test' Joseph Anderson, Richard Mc Clure.

No. 116. Andrew Woodley, & Ann his wife, of Perq. to Alex Ross, of afore', for £20 assigned 185a on North side of "Basses Creek Swamp," adj Joseph Reading, John Gordan, & John Harrison. July 16, 1743. Test' Jos Wilcock, John Wilcock.

No. 117. John Brinkley of Chowan, planter—for £200 pd by Zachariah Nixon, of afore' sold 100a on South West side of Perq River, adj Robert Moore, Jonathan Phelps, Zach Chancey, & Wm Townsend, called "Frog Hall." Mar 11, 1741. Test' James Morgan, Thomas Carte, Zach Elton.

No. 118. William Foxworth of Perq, planter—for £35 pd by Michael Brinkley of Bertie Co, planter—assigned 50a of land in Perq. Jan 6, 1742. Test' Mac Scarbrough, Elizabeth Scarbrough.

No. 119. James Henby of Perq, planter—for £200 pd by Zachariah Nixon, of afore sold 132a on North East side of "Voices Creek" (Vosses). Oct 17, 1743. Test' William Ambler, Joshua Davis.

No. 120. Elizabeth Simson of Perq, for £104 pd by Zach Chancey, of afore' sold 100a on South West side of Perq River, adj Robert Moore, Jonathan Phelps, & sd Chancey, to line of William Townsend, called "Frog Hall." Test' James Morgan, Thomas Carte, Zach Elton. Mar 11, 1741.

No. 121. Zachariah Chancey, for £15 pd by Daniel Rogerson, assigned "within contents." Aug 3, 1743. Test' Thomas Lilly, William Moore.

No. 122. Elizabeth Brasier, (Relict of John) of Perq, & Susannah Smith, (Relict of James) in con' of £45 pd by John Griffin, of afore' doth ack' myself satisfied, & sold, with consent of my mother sd Susannah, 40a on North East side of Perq River, part of 90a patented by William Moore first, & assigned by him to Richard Gray, & sold by sd Gray to William Carman, who made a deed of gift of sd land to George Simmons, "who bequeathed same to his dau Elizabeth Brazier, whereon I now dwell." Oct 17, 1743. Test' Truman Moore, Josiah Bogue, Luke Bond.

No. 123. John Pratt of Perq, Millwright conveyed to Jeremiah Pratt, a "Grist Mill, with utensils belonging." Oct 4, 1743. Test' Robert Beasley, David Butler.

No. 124. Christopher Sutton of Perq, farmer—for £240 pd by Edward Turner, of same—sold 200a, at the head of "Rattle Snake Ridge" part of which was granted to George Sutton Nov 11, 1719, & 36a out of a survey, for 260a belonging to me. Test' Thomas Weeks, Anne Weeks. Aug 6, 1743.

No. 125. Peter Jones Sr. of Perq, planter—for love I bear my son Peter Jones Jr, do give 150a whereon I now dwell, adj Thomas Pierce dec'd, & Richard Skinner, on Perq River, "which land came to me by the will of Richard Standrick dec'd, & became due to him out of a patent of 300a, by Thomas Pierce dec'd, & by him conveyed." July 18, 1743. Test' Thomas Pierce, James Sitterson.

No. 126. Oct 11, 1742. Timothy Lilly of Perq, for £7 s 10 pd by Richard Felton Jr of same—sold 125a on west side of the County road, which road parts land of sd Lilly, & his brother William Lilly, a grant to Thomas Lilly, father of sd Timothy, 500a Oct 9, 1712/13, & came by will to sd party. Test' Thomas Rountree Sr, James Scott.

No. 127. Thomas Jessop Jr, of Perq, for s 10 pd by John Lilly of same, sold 100a on South west side of Perq River, adj William Moses, part of a patent to Isaac Wilson, Mar 9, 1717/18, & willed to Ralph Bozman, & sold by sd Bozman to Ralph Bufkin, Mar 1, 1726. Seal Oct 20, 1742. Test' Evan Jones, Benj Perry, William Price.

No. 128. Aug 15, 1743. Samuel Gregory, of Edenton, Innholder; to Benj Simson, of Perq, planter—for £100 sold 107a, on north side of Yeopim River, one half, of 115a, by a patent. Mar 25, 1743, Test' John Wobatten, Richard Mc Clure.

No. 129. Zachariah Chancey, gent—to Truman Moore, for £100 sold 100a, in Ballahack, on Phillips line, thence to Creek Neck, called "Beefscull neck." Aug 9, 1743. Test' William Moore, John Chancey, Joshua Hobard.

No. 130. Abraham Mullen, of Perq, planter—for "Parental love I bear my son Abraham, have given 105a, on north east side of Perq River, near the head of beaver cove swamp," part of land taken up by Nathan'l Nicholson, & Joseph Sutton, June 20, 1703, for 421a, being the "manner plan' whereon said Abraham Mullen Sen now dwells," also another tract, adj 153a, called "beaver cove," part of place "Richard Whidbee Surveyed Oct 19, 1716," & sold by him to me, Oct 19, 1734. Seal Sept 30, 1743. Test' John Anderson, William Wood, Abraham Riggs.

No. 131. James Padget, of Perq, planter—for £10 pd by Henry Lamb, of afore' planter—sold 50a, on South Side of Cypress Creek, part of 400a, granted to James Thigpen. Aug 24, 1743. Test' James Sumner, Thomas Wiggens.

No. 132. Joseph Winslow, of Perq, for £100 pd by Robert Bogue, of ye afore', sold 100a, on "ye North west side of Vasses Creek," adj Ezekiel Maudlin. 17d 11mo 1743. Test' Henry Phelps, Nathan Pearson.

No. 133. Zachariah Chancey, of Perq, for £50 pd by Jacob Doctor, of afore' sold 50a in Balahak, adj Turner, John Goodwin, & Benj Wilson, to the line of Sherwood. Oct 8, 1743. Test' William Cullin, William Moore, Francis Jones, John Chancey.

No. 134. Josiah Bogue, of Perq, planter—for a "parcel of land made over to me by Moses Wood of afore planter—do sell 50a on ye North east side of ye River, & on South side of Cypress Swamp, up beaver dam, & down Swamp to a dividing line between my brother Wm Bogue, & me." June 17, 1743. Test' Thomas Hollowell, Joseph Winslow, Joseph Mayo.

No. 135. Thomas Jessop Sen, of Perq, for £100 pd by John Lacey, of afore' sold 100a, adj Joseph Newby, John Henby, & "his son Thomas Jessop." Jan 16, 1743/4. Test' Thomas Jessop Jun, Mary Jessop.

No. 136. Thomas Norfleet, of Perq, for £10 pd by Samuel Powell, of afore' sold 200a, on North East side, near the head, of Perq River, part of a grant of Luke Hollowell, Aug 4, 1720, for 400a, said 200a, now in possession of Thomas Rountree, "to be divided by Joint consent of ye said Samuel," as per deed Jan 9, 1727. Seal Oct 28, 1743. Test' James Sumner, Luke Sumner.

No. 137. Joseph Newby, Millright—of Perq, for "a piece of land to me sold by John Morgan Jun" of same—sold part of tract on North west side of Vosses Creek swamp, "being the upper part," next to Ezekiel Modlings. 70a. 16d 4mo 1743/4. Test' Henry Phelps, Nathan Pearson.

No. 138. Isaac Wilson, of Perq, planter—for a plan', & "Water Mill, to me made over in Open Court, by my Father Robert Wilson," have conveyed 590a on North East by Perq River, adj Josiah Gilbert, & by a Creek up to the bridge, to John Wilcocks, land. Jan 16, 1743/4. Test' Samuel Newby, William White.

No. 139. Robert Wilson, of Perq, planter—in Exchange of a plan' from Isaac Wilson of afore' planter—"do convey two parcels of land," a survey called "Aarons Old field" 195a on Gum branch, adj Thomas Newby, & 130a on the head of above, adj William Elliott, & John Pearson. 16d 11mo 1743/4.

No. 140. Thomas Jessop, of Cartrite Co (Cartaret) planter—for £40 pd by William White, of Perq, planter—sold 200a, on South west side of Perq River, adj said White, & John Wilson. Jan 16, 1743/4. Test' Zachariah Nixon, Thomas Newby, Josiah Bogue.

*No. 141. Jan 14, 1743. John Norfleet, of Chowan, to John Powel, of Perq, for £10 assigned 636a "at a place called Corepeak." Test' Lemuel Powell, Dinah Simson.

No. 142. Moses Wood, of Perq, planter—for an "exchange of land" by Josiah Bogue, sold land running along said Josiahs line, 200a next to Thomas Hollowell. June 17, 1743. Test' Thomas Hollowell, Joseph Winslow, Joseph Mayo.

No. 143. Abraham Saunders, Zachariah Nixon, of Perq, planters—& John Wilcocks, of same, Millright—to Richard Skinner, of said Co, planter—for £75 assigned "our right in a plan" on Southeast side of Castletons Creek, which we bought of Thomas, & Elizabeth Haughton, adj Peter Jones Jun, &

---

* Corepeak now in Gates Co., N. C. Perquimons line until 1779 ran to, or very near the Va. line.

John Williams dec, 150a part of a tract "formerly Jonathan Evans." Jan 17, 1743. Test' Nathan Pearson, Malichi Salter Jun, John Pierce.

No. 144. April 14, 1744. Zachariah Chancey, of Perq, for £30 pd by John Goodwin, of Chowan, sold 150a on North west side of Perq River, commonly called "Balla-Hack," near land in the tenure of Jonathan Sherwood, & Benj Wilson, to line of Richard Goodwin. Test' Richard Goodwin, Isaac Wilson, William Moore.

No. 145. April 14, 1744. Thomas Winslow, of Perq, for £25 pd by Robert Chappel, of afore' sold 100a, on North West side of Perq River, at the mouth of "Reedy branch" a grant to Francis Toms late of said Co, and by him conveyed unto said Winslow. July 20, 1726. Test' William White, Simon Stallings.

No. 146. Thomas Blitchenden, of Perq, planter—for "love I bear my son John," Planter—have given 60a bought of John Pettiver, April 10, 1722, & 122a bought of John Norcomb, & Samuel Taylor Jan 13, 1712/13, (on the Sound) adj Thomas Norcomb Sen, called "Gore Land." April 16, 1744. Test' Nath'l Courthers, Zachariah Chancey.

*No. 147. Thomas Overman, "for the love I have for ye Truth professed by the people called Quakers, do give a parcel of land around the Meeting house on ye head of Little River, on lower side of River pocoson" to Phinehas Nixon, Thomas Nicholson, & Joseph Robinson, "for the promotion of Truth, & ye Religious worship of God do give above land to peacefully hold, & enjoy, & do warrant & secure same granted premises." 15d 2mo 1744. Test' Francis Mace, Josiah Bundy, Michael Murphrey.

No. 148. Josiah Bogue, & Deborah, his wife, of Perq, for £30 pd by William Haskit, of afore' sold 50a, which "Christopher Nicholson purchased, of Zach Nixon, & gave to his dau Deborah, wife of said Josiah, on North side of land where Phinehas Nixon now dwells." Feb 22, 1743/4. Test' Thomas Hollowell, Joseph Munden, Samuel Bagley.

No. 149. Christopher Sutton, of Perq, for £20 pd by Samuel Barclift, of afore' assigned 100a, on North East side of Perq River, part of tract surveyed for George Sutton Sen, Nov 15, 1722, called "Rattle Snake Ridge." Dec 5, 1743. Test' Abraham Rigs, Joseph Perisho.

No. 150. Feb 16, 1743. Joseph Creecy, of Chowan Co, cordwinder—to William Standing, of Perq, planter—for £200 assigned "parcel of land" that William Wyatt purchased of John Pratt, on North side of Yeopim River, adj George Mathews, & said Creecy purchased of said Wyatt. Test' Henderson Standing, Levi Creecy.

No. 151. William Moore, of Perq, for £16 s17 p6 pd by Joseph Reddick, of Perq, sold plan' on "ye South west side of Ballahack Swamp, granted unto Zachariah Chancey Mar 6, 1740," on a branch called "great branch" adj William Townsend. April 16, 1744. Test' John Morgan, Joseph Wilson.

No. 152. David Huffton, of Perq, planter—for "six barrels of Pork, & 65 bushels of Indian corn to me," by Thomas Hosea of same, bricklayer—sold 75a, on South west side of Little River, at the mouth of a branch, issuing out of Deep Creek Swamp, part of a patent Aug 6, 1719 to Esau Albertson,

---

* This land was about where the village of Woodville is now situated and the Meeting house "Little River."

& by him sold to John Huffton Jan 17, 1722/3, "plan' whereon I now live." Jan 4, 1743/4.

No. 153. Thomas Blitchenden, of Perq, "in con' that it is every ones duty to Worship his Great Creator, ye maker of Heaven, & Earth, for conveniency thereof must have a place to meet in: I have given 1a of land on ye South west side of Perq River, near a mile from the bridge, on ye North side of the road, close in ye fork of Gum Swamp, to their use, & benefit, unto Thomas Winslow, John Hudson, Thomas White, Ephrim Blanchard, & Benjamin Wilson." (Trustees) April 13, 1743. Test' Abraham Blitchenden, William Blitchenden, Pritlow Elliott. (Piney Woods Meeting).

No. 154. William Bundy, of Perq, farmer—for £20 pd by Thomas Nicholson, of Pasq, farmer—sold a parcel of land in Perq, "near Little River bridge," between Wm Bundy & Thomas Overman, "on the main road, above the Meeting house," at the head of a branch, by said Bundy, to River pocoson. Feb 24, 1743/4. Test' Phinehas Nixon, Josiah Bogue, Josiah Bundy.

No. 155. Samuel Gregory, of Chowan, "Ordanary keeper" for £600 pd by Joseph Creecy, of afore' cordwinder—sold 325a on North side of Yopim Swamp, in Perq Co, adj James Eggerton, & up Swamp to Joseph Mings line. May 2, 1744. Test' James Egerton, Caleb Caloway.

No. 156. Francis Newby, of Perq, farmer—for an "exchange of land with Thomas Montague, on ye S. W. side of Little River," have sold 100a, adj Thomas Overmans land, on head of said Montagues line, adj Josiah Bogue, Christ. Nicholson; said land purchased of Zachariah Nixon. 22d 8mo 1743. Test' Joseph Ratliff, Aaron Hill, Thomas Nicholson.

No. 157. William Bundy, & Mary his wife, of Perq, for "30 lbs of pork," pd by Thomas Overman, of afore' planter—sold 50a, & half where said "Overman now dwells," & 25a out of tract I now dwell on, "according to Christopher Nicholson ye first patentee," (Oct 1716) 134a on S. W. side of Little River, adj Rapers line, near said Bundys line, & the line of Joseph Robinson. April 14, 1744. Test' Jeremiah Symons, Joseph Robinson.

No. 158. John Henby, of Perq, planter—for £30 pd by Francis Newby, of same—sold 100a, on line of Joseph Ratliff, and sd Francis Newby. Nov 8, 1742. Test' Zach Nixon, Joseph Ratlif.

No. 159. Thomas Monticue, of Perq, for £100 pd by Francis Newby, of afore' sold 100a, on S. W. side of Little River, adj Thomas Overman, John Henby, & Thomas Hollowells lines. 20d 8mo 1743. Test' Zach Nixon, Joseph Ratlif.

No. 160. Thomas Blitchenden, of Perq, planter—for £15 pd by Evan Jones, of same—sold 100a on Southwest side of Perq River, to the mouth of Gum Branch, adj Thomas Leane. (Lane probably.) June 5, 1744. Test' Jacob Perry, William Blitchenden.

No. 161. Zachariah Chancey, of Perq, planter—sold unto John, & Joseph Winslow, of same—100a in Ballahack, adj place called "the Island" Sept 5, 1743. Test' Evan Jones, William White.

No. 162. Aug 1, 1744. Thomas Weeks Gent, of Perq, & Anne his wife, to Joseph Roberison of same, farmer—for £5 pd by said Joseph, sold 546a on S. W. side of Little River, called "Pine Glade" adj Thomas Robinson, &

Robert Cox. "Part of a grant to William Tomblin, & by him assigned to said Weeks." Test' Thomas Stafford, Josiah Raper.

No. 163. Sept 21, 1744. James Wanrite, of "Cour" (Core) Sound, to Samuel Moore, of Perq, for £90, pd by said Moore, assigned 70a, in Perq Co, on Westermost side of Suttons Creek, adj Nathan Nichols, "commonly called Nath'l Albertsons corner" to a beech, on Albert Albertsons line, along Timothy Clares line to survey on River. Test' William Symons, William Bundy, Peter Symons.

No. 164. John Morgan Jun, & James Henby, of Perq, Cooper—for an "exchange, delivered by Joseph Newby of same, Mill wright"—do convey 70a on North East side of Vosses Creek, called *"bepon fork."* 15d 10mo 1743. Test' Zach Nixon, Elizabeth Hudson.

No. 165. William Elliott, of Perq, for £400 pd by John Pearson, & Pritlow Elliott, of afore' sold 200a, on Cypress Swamp, on North west side, adj Nathan Newby. 16d 5mo 1744.

No. 166. George Durant, of Perq, planter—& Christian Reed, of afore' planter—for £200 pd by said Reed, sold 300a, on Albemarle Sound, adj Thomas Norcom, by John Harveys line, (formerly belonging to Mr Nicholas Crisp) Mr Swann, & the Westermost corner, commonly called "Petefers," & by said Crisp, left to said Durant. The Eastermost part called "Findals" was sold to George Durant by Samuel Swann. Oct 10, 1744. Test' John Stephenson, Sam Hatch.

No. 167. George Durant, of Perq Gent—for £11 s2 p5 pd by John Barclift Jun' of afore' sold 187a on west side of Little River, adj William Godfrey. Oct 15, 1744. Test' James Gibson, Samuel Barclift, Christopher Sutton.

DEED BOOK E

No. 1. We Zachariah Chancey, & William Townsend, of Perq, for £125 pd by William Wingett, of same—sold 100a, on North East side of Ballahack swamp, adj Goodwins line, over swamp to line of Zach Chanceys new pattent, down middle of swamp to William Moores line. April 28, 1744. Test' Richard Gooding, Zach Chancey.

No. 2. Potsfull Pierce, of Currituck, planter—for £70 pd by Abraham Riggs, of Perq, planter—"doth assign unto said Riggs 50a adj William Wood, Abraham Mullen, Isaac Mullen, & Abraham Riggs, part bought of Robert, & Sarah Hosea, which Joseph Sutton left by will to his two daus Sarah Hosea, & Elizabeth, wife of Isaac Mullen, to be equally divided between the two Sisters," & was conveyed by them to Posefull Pierce. Oct 15, 1744. Test' James Gibson, John Parish.

No. 3. William Townsen, & Zachariah Chancey, of Perq, for £100 pd by William Wilson, of afore' sold 100a, in Ballahack, at the mouth of "ye great branch" adj William Moores line, to Chanceys back line on Ballahack Swamp, & Wingetts line. Jan 25, 1744/5. Test' Moses Elliott, John Stone, Robert Harmon.

No. 4. John Maudlin, & Abraham Elliott, "came before me, & declared on Oath that Hannah Charles Jun, ye 15 day of Nov last dec'd, before her departure, in her right & Proper Senses, gave all her worldly goods, &

chattels, to her mother Hannah Charles, except one year Old hiefer, to John Maudlens dau Mary." Perq Nov 14, 1744. Reg May 8, 1745. Before John Whidbee.

No. 5. (Marriage contract) Thomas Winslow, & Leah Smith Widow) both of Perq, doth agree that said Leah "shall reserve to her own proper use at all times, goods, & Chattels, and do hereby bind myself, in the sum of 1000 to be paid Sept 9, 1734. Test' Zach'h Chancey, Hannah Sitterson.

No. 6. Leah Winslow of Perq, "by virtue of within agreement, unto me by my husband Thomas Winslow, before our marriage, do assign unto my son John Smith 100a of land. To Samuel Smith (son) a negro boy named Job, 6 cows, & calves, 3 pewter dishes, & plates, 1 feather bed, & furniture, 1 Iron pot, 1 young mare. To dau Huldah Smith, 5 cows & calves, 1 feather bed, & furniture, 1 young mare, 3 pewter dishes, & plates, 1 Iron pot, for love I bear my children." Feb 20, 1742/3. Test' Mc Scarbrough, Zach. Chancey.

No. 7. Thomas Nicholson of Pasq, farmer—for 42 pd by Phillip Perry of Perq, sol 174a "upon the head of Little River, called Sandy Hook, on the upper side of gum Swamp, where ye sd Swamp makes out of the River" adj sd Nicholson. Test' Aaron Hill, Barnabe Nixon, Samuel Scott. 27, 9mo 1744.

No. 8. Thomas Pierce of Chowan, for "love I bear my Nephew Thomas Pierce of Perq have given 133a, bought of Grace Fryley, on North east side of Perq River, adj Thomas, Jessop, & Joseph Ratlif. Aug 15, 1744. Test' Phineas Nixon, John Pierce, Robert Davis.

No. 9. Ezekiel Maudlin, & Mary his wife of Perq, for 100 pd by Joseph Arnold, sold "part of land that Daniel Hall formerly lived on, 100a called carpenters old field," adj John Hoskins, Oct 16, 1744. Test' Zach Nixon, Joshua Jones.

No. 10. Zachariah Chancey, & William Phelps of Perq, for 45 pd by Richard Gooding of afore' sold 55a "at the mouth of a branch over Ballahack Swamp, below where William Moore now dwells" down the Swamp to Phillips line. Dec 11, 1744. Test' James Sitterson, William Wingate, William Moore.

No. 11. (Will of Timothy Clear) "Sick & weak of body, but of sound mind, & memory do make this my last will, in manner as follows: To wife Hannah, what was hers before I married her, one negro man named Sibbe, household goods, & furniture. To dau Mary Mayo 200a, whereon I now live, the upper part thereof, where J. Perry lives, and 200a next to John Winslow.* To John Winslow plan' whereon his father & mothr now live, after their decease. To son-in-law Thomas Winslow, 154a in long Branch. To his two sons: Timothy, & Jesse, part of tract, adj their father. To Elizabeth Winslow, land back of John Winslow. To dau Jane Jessop, & husband Thomas, plan' in old neck, bought of my bro-in-law William Bundy (brother

---

* John Winslow here mentioned, m Esther (Hester) Snelling (d of Israel, & Hannah nee Larence) who m 2d Timothy Clare, by whom she had one dau Hannah, named in his will above. (See Hannah Clares Will, (Grimes) p 1726.) John Winslow was probably brother of Thomas, who m Elizabeth Clare, but no actual proof can be found. They were certainly contemporaries.

of his first wife Mary Bundy.) To dau Sarah White, plan' whereon she now lives, on ye creek, and a tract on the River called "Passing Hall" To dau Hepzibah Perry, (thought to be step-dau,) land formerly Simpsons, 200a whereon she now lives. To dau Hannah (by 3d wife) plan' on Vosses Creek, on lower side of same, 200a bought of Thomas Harvey, and 130a at "Snodens dock." To dau Jane, & son-in-law Thomas Jessop, 100a adj Stephen Gibson. To gr-son John Robinson, land given him by his father Joseph Robinson, 200a on Mill Creek. To each dau a negro, "ye Meeting to value same out of remaining Estate." My five children: Mary, Elizabeth, Jane, Sarah, & Hannah. Gr-son & gr-dau John, & Sarah Robinson £20. To gr-son Thomas Winslow, my beaver hat. "Exrs: Son-in-laws Thomas Winslow, & Thos, Jessop. Probated Nov 10, 1724, before E, Moseley. Test' Thos. Bagley, Smith Cale.

No. 12. Timothy Clear. late of this province dec'd, hath appointed Thomas Jessop, & Thomas Winslow Exrs of his will. Nov 17, 1724. George Burington.

No. 13. Wm Bogue of Perq, for £110 pd by Zach Chancey, of afsd—sold 443a, "ye whole pattent of sd Bogue, in Ballahack" Jan 10, 1744/5. Test' Joshua Hobart, Thomas Bagley, William Moore.

No. 14. William Hosea, of Perq, for "8 barrels of pork," pd by my brother Abraham Hosea, of afsd—sold 20a on Deep Creek, "below horse bridge" part of a tract formerly Mr Thomas Commanders. April 10, 1745. Test' Joseph Hosea, Jeremiah Hendricks.

No. 15. Abraham Mullen, of Perq, for "Paternal love I bear my son Abraham, of afsd—do give one negro man named Samson, & goods, & chattels." Mar 17, 1744/5. Test' Abraham Hosea, Joseph Sutton.

No. 16. Thomas Norcom, of Perq, for "love I have for my mother, Susannah Norcom, Widow of same, do "give six negroes, which fell to me by the will of my father" & goods, & chattels. April 15, 1745. Test' James Caruthers, Henry Hall, David Hufton.

No. 17. July 10, 1745. John Reddick, of Perq, & Margaret my wife, to Elickander Machlenden, for £14, sold 50a on North west side of Perq River, at the mouth of a branch called, Deep branch, adj Solomon Wyatt, Jacob Perry, & Thomas Lilly. Part of a survey for Daniel Snook, "& by his will descended to Margaret Lilly, now Reddick," June 1, 1712. Test' Thomas Lilly, Daniel Rogerson.

No. 18. John Jordan Jr, of Chowan, planter—for £15 pd by James Pagett, of Perq, planter—sold 250a adj John Burkett, & Francis Toms. May 25, 1729. Test' John Burket, Samuel Bond.

No. 19. James Pagett, Cooper—for £65 pd by Thom's Lamb, of Perq, assigned 250a in Chowan Co, bought of John Jordan Jr. Feb 9, 1744. Test' Mc Scarbrough, Eliza Scarbrough.

No. 20. Thomas Jessop, of Perq, for £40 pd by Joseph Winslow, of afsd—sold 640a on North East side of Perq River, adj William Moore Sr. Mar 5, 1744/5. Test' Zach Nixon, Henry Phelps.

No. 21. Nathaniel Caruthers, of Perq, Blacksmith, for "Natual love I bear my son John, have given, part of land I now live on," 60a, adj William Wyatt, & John Stepney. May —, 1745. Test' James Caruthers, Jacob Caruthers.

No. 22. Foster Toms, of Perq, planter, & Martha his wife, for £300 pd by Joseph Sutton, of afsd—sold 37a on East side of Suttons Creek, (part of a grt unto Hannah Gosby, 500a, for her son, & dau John, & Sarah Gosby) adj sd Sutton. Granted Mar 1, 169¾. Seal April 25, 1745. Test' Isaac Roberts, Jno. Clayton.

No. 23. April 26, 1745. Foster Toms, of Perq, for £100 pd by Joseph Perishoe, of afsd—sold 250a, on East side of Suttons Creek, (granted to John Gosby Mar 1, 1693/4) between Joseph Sutton, & sd Toms, "near Nags head Chapple." Test' James Henby, Joseph Anderson.

No. 24. John Blitchenden, of Perq, planter—for £70 pd by William Blitchenden, sold 60a, "at ye Sound side, which was conveyed by my Father Thomas Blitchenden, to Christian Reed," called "Gore land." July 15, 1745. Test' R. Wilson, Evan Jones.

No. 25. Sarah Ashley, Widow, of Perq, in Con' of "Love I bear my two sons, John, & Joseph, have given, a plan' on east side of Yoppim Creek, which was given me by my brother John Barrow dec'd," adj David Saint. If my two sons die without issue, to my sons, Amarius, & William, or Aaron. May 18, 1745. Test' Daniel Saint, Jacob, Wyatt.

No. 26. Abraham Saunders, Sr, & Abraham Saunders Jr, of Perq, for £10 pd by Wm Townsen, of afsd—sold 10a adj sd Townsen, & Phelps, part of a tract I had of my "father-in-law John Pritlow" of same. Jan 25, 1744/5. Test' William Phelps, Samuel Sitterson, James Sitterson.

No. 27. April 25, 1745. Joseph Perishoe, of Perq, Sadler—for £5 pd by Joseph Sutton Esq, assigned 37a, on East side of Suttons Creek, part of 300a conveyed by Foster Toms to sd Sutton, a grt unto Hannah Gosby Mar 1, 1693. Jan 19, 1745/6. Test' Foster Toms, John Clayton.

No. 28. Zach Chancey, of Perq, for £100 pd by John Wilson, of afsd—sold 900a in Ballahack, which was grt me July 27, 1743. Mar 18, 1744/5. Test' Jesse Newby, Samuel Newby, William Moore.

No. 29. Edward Rice, of Perq, for £12 pd by John Davis, of afsd—sold 75a on South west side of Perq River, "at ye mouth of Ready branch" which was grt to Samuel Bond dec'd, & sold by him to Henry Grace, & by sd Grace, to John Hudler (Hurdle), & by sd Hudler to Thomas Blitchenden, & from sd Thomas to me. Test' Nicholas Stallings, Zach Chancey, Evan Jones. July 11, 1745.

No. 30. William Blitchenden, of Perq, for 60a of land "down the Sound side" do ack' my self pd, by John Blitchenden, of same—sold 70a on South west side of Perq River, "on ye edge of Mulberry Swamp" adj William Phelps, which was grt unto Samuel Bond, & sold by him to Henry Grace, & by sd Grace to "my Father, Thomas Blitchenden, & by him bequeathed to me in his will." July 15, 1745. Test' Richard Skinner, Evan Jones.

No. 31. John Smith, & Rachel his wife, of Perq, for £35 pd by David Reddick, of afsd—sold 150a on Newbegun Creek, adj John White, along "great branch" to patent of Joseph Jessop, 190a, Feb 14, 1713/14. 80a of which John White dec'd, purchased of William Moore, & gave to his dau Rachel, now Rachel Smith." Test' Robert Reddick, Elias Stallings, Henry Griffin. (No date)

No. 32. Samuel Wyatt, planter—of Perq, for "love I bear my son Jacob, of same—have given 250a on the Southermost part of my plan' near my house. Test' Elizabeth Wyatt, Daniel Saint. Sept 2, 1745.

No. 33. Joseph Winslow, of Perq, planter—for "ye half charges of taking up, & surveying 200a, to me pd by Timothy Winslow (his brother), of afsd—

sold 100a part of sd tract, adj Jacob Overman. Patented July 17, 1743. Seal July 15, 1745.

No. 34. William Wyatt, of Perq, planter—for £30 pd by Jeremiah Pratt, of afsd—planter—sold 75a, known by the name of "Felts" on the side of Pratts Mill Swamp known by name of "Dead Mans Swamp." Sept 14, 1745. Test' Joshua Worley, Daniel Saint, John Stepney.

No. 35. William Hosea, of Perq, for £20 s10 pd by my brother Abraham, of afsd sold 110a on Deep Creek, adj Albert Albertson, "at the mouth of a Creek." Test' Joseph Hosea, William Davis. Oct 20, 1745.

No. 36. Oct 21, 1745. Abraham Blitchenden, planter, & Samuel Standing, of Perq for "12 barrels of pork," pd by Christian Reed, sold 50a, commonly called "ye folly land," lately surveyed by Richard McClure, Dept Suveyor. Test' John Harvey, Joshua Skinner.

No. 37. Oct 21, 1745. William Davis Sr, (heir of William Davis, of Pasq Co, dec) Carpenter—"for one negro boy, & two barrels of Pork," pd by Thomas Winslow Sr, of Perq Co, sold 238a, on South west side of Little River, adj Thomas Weeks, Mary Hendricks, & John Robinson, part of a patent to William Tomblin July 23, 1694, "on ye upper side of the River, at a place called, ye pine glade" which was sold by sd Tomblin to Dennis Collings. Test' Samuel Newby, Joseph Ratcliff.

No. 38. Arnold White of Perq, for £100 pd by Thomas Elliott Sr, of afsd— sold 87a on South West side of Little River, adj William Boswell, & Radcliff." at ye head of Long branch." Test' Isaac Wilson, Edward Maudlin. ———1745.

No. 39. Oct 8, 1745. Lemuel Powell of Perq, for £3 pd by George Eason, of afsd—sold 25a "part of an Elapsed patent to Luke Hollowell dec'd, which became Elapsed by Joseph Jessop, dec'd, for want to seating," by sd Hollowell sold to sd Jessop, & by sd Jessop, to John Alston, & by him to Thomas Norfleet, who sold sd land to me. Test' John Powel, Jesse Eason.

No. 40. Thomas Price of Nansemond Co Vir' planter—for £5 pd by Robert Reddick, of Perq, sold 75a, adj John White, Joseph Glisson, & sd Reddick, a patent to sd Powel 1729. Seal Oct 16, 1745. Test' Nicholas Stallings, Elias Stallings, William Hollowell.

No. 41. Christian Reed of Chowan Co, for £800 pd by Richard Skinner, of Perq, sold 300a, on Albemarle Sound, adj Thomas Norcomb, John Harvey, & John Blitchenden, formerly belonging to Mr. Nicholas Crisp, & Mr. Swann, called "Pettifers" which 200a was left by Nicholas Crisp to George Durant, & the other part called "Findals" (Fendalls) was sold to sd Durant by sd Swann, & later descended to George Durant, son of afsd George, & was by him sold to sd Reed. Test' Edmund Hatch, John Harvey. Oct 25, 1745.

No. 42. Christian Reed, & Mary his wife, of Chowan—for £1000, pd by Eliz'a Caldom of Perq, sold unto Miles Harvey (a minor) 200a, on Albemarle Sound, "East by ye great Swamp, between lands of Thomas Harvey, & Thomas Norcom" part of a pat' to John Williams Nov 11, 1719, 340a which sd Williams sold to Nicholas Crisp, & was given by sd Crisp in his will, to his Gr-dau Mary Durant now wife of sd Reed. Test' Richard Skinner, John Harvey. Oct 20, 1745.

No. 43. Sept 21, 1745. Moses Jackson, of Perq, planter—for £170 pd by John Robinson, of same—sold 200a on ye South West side of Little River, "where sd Jackson dwells," adj Joseph Winslow, part of 400a granted to

Richard Nowell, & descended to sd Jackson, "by virtue of my Gr-father William Jacksons will." Test' Henry Reynolds, Moses Barber, Joseph Robinson.

No. 44. Sept 21, 1745. Received this day £170. Moses Jackson. Test' Joseph Robinson, Henry Reynolds.

No. 45. John Moore of Perq, planter—for £16 pd by Thomas Winslow Jr, planter—of afsd, sold "ye half tract, known by name of Persimmon tree land" adj Joshua Boswell, & Thomas Hollowell, sd Hollowells land being the "other moiety," of 183a. Nov 15, 1745. Test' Samuel Moore, Francis Newby, Joseph Ratliff.

No. 46. Mary Hawkins of Perq, for "love I bear my dau Mary, now an infant, for £5 pd by her, do confirm unto her, 1 feather bed, & furniture, 6 pewter dishes, & 6 plates, 2 pots, 2 basons. 1 young cow, & calf, 1 ewe, & lamb, 1 sow, & pigs when she is of age, or marries." Oct 26, 1745. Test' Foster Toms, Martha Toms, Robert Hedges.

No. 47. Isaac Wilson, of Perq, planter—for £25 pd by Jacob Perry, of same—sold 100a on East side of Cypress run, to mouth of Mill Swamp, & gum branch. Test' William Roberts, Israel Perry. Jan 20, 1745/6.

No. 48. William Wyatt of Perq, yeoman, for £27 s10 pd by Edward Maudlin, weaver; of same—sold 150a, "part of tract I now live on," adj John Stepney, & Banks. Which was grt to sd Wyatt April 15, 1745. Seal Dec 16, 1745. Test' John Stepney, John Carruthers.

No. 49. Joseph Perishoe of Perq, farmer—for £9 s16 pd by John Barclift Jr, of afore, farmer—sold 78¾a "on ye North side of ye main Road" adj Albert Albertson & sd Barclift. Test' Jno Clayton, Rebecca Clayton. Jan 20, 1745/6.

No. 50. William Wyatt of Perq, for £205 pd by John Stepney of afsd—sold 156a on North East side of Indian Creek, "part of a grant to sd Wyatt 1745." Test' John Carruthers, Edward Maudlin. Oct 29, 1745.

No. 51. Richard Harrell Sr, of Perq, planter—for £15 pd by James Scott, (his son-in-law) planter, of same—sold 210a, purchased by sd Harrell of Lott Stallings, sd land bought by sd Stallings of Lewis Skinner, who purchased sd land of Robert Barnes, & sd Barnes of Wm Kitchen July 19, 1719," "toward ye dwelling house of sd Stallings, where sd Scott now Dwells." Jan 13, 1745/6. Test' Richard Felton, Gilbert Scott.

No. 52. John Chesson of Terrell Co, planter—for £230 pd by Isachar Branch planter, of Perq, sold 184a which James Chesson purchased of Jothan Taler, on Indian Creek, "to ye mouth of Mattis Creek." Dec 20, 1745. Test' Isaac Davenport, Eliza Davenport, Thomas Ming.

No. 53. April 8, 1746. John, & William Blitchenden, (brothers) for £240 pd by Luke Sumner, sold parcel of land known by name of "Gore land" 182a on the Sound, adj Richard Skinner, & Lemuel Standing, where "it joins the land of Thomas Norcom dec'd" 122a thereof sold by Henry Warren, to James Ming ——— 1705, & was by sd Ming (Minge) sold to Thomas Norcom, who sold sd land to Thomas Blitchenden, (father of sd John, & William) & 60a of same was granted to John Pettiver 1720, & sold to sd Thomas Blitchenden 1722, which was bequeathed to his sd sons in his will, & sd 60a was sold by sd John Blitchenden to his brother Wm. Test' George Eason, Joshua Skinner, Thomas Calloway.

No. 54. Joseph Newby Sr, for £195 pd by Thomas Elliott Sr, conveyed 50a, on Voices (Vosses) Creek, "by the name of Broad Neck, upon a branch called bee branch" & up sd branch to line of John Lacy. April 16, 1746. Test' Joseph Wilson, Joseph Newby Jr, James Elliott.

No. 55. John Nixon of Perq, farmer—for £60 pd by Thomas Nicholson, farmer of afsd—sold 50a adj Wm Bundy, "& my own land." 11-7mo 1745. Test' Michael Murphy, Jesse Henly, Jemmima Pierce.

No. 56. James Anderson of Craven Co N. C. planter, for £125 pd by Christopher Sutton of Perq, sold 62a on North East side of Perq River, & North West side of Suttons Creek, "formerly the property of my brother John Anderson dec'd late of Perq Co." Mar 18, 1746. Test' Henry Smith, Jemmima Smith, Josiah Hart.

No. 57. James Morgan of Perq, Esq—for £20 pd by Ben'jn Elliott, of afsd— sold 50a called "Crain Ponds," on ye South West Side of Perq River, adj the main Road, & Ralph Bufkin "now in possession of Caleb Elliott, betwixt Moses Elliott & James Morgan, at ye head of John Smiths line." April 1, 1746. Test' John Perry, James Parker.

No. 58. . Susanna Norcom of Perq, widow, for "love I bear my son Thomas, of same—have given 7 negroes, given me by my sd son April last past, I do hereby relinquish all claim to same." Dec 19, 1745. Test' Mac Scarbrough, Cornelius Leary Jr.

No. 59. Robert Hosea of Pasq Co, farmer, "in Con' of 30 lbs in pork, at s45 per barrel," pd by David Hufton of Perq, farmer—sold 75a on South Side of Little River, at the mouth of a branch, out of Deep Creek Swamp, part of a grt to Isaac Albertson, Aug 19, 1719, & sold by him to John Hufton, Jan 17, 1722/3. Test' Elihu Albertson. Joseph Hosea. April 19, 1746.

No. 60. David Hufton of Perq, for £50 pd by Elihu Albertson of afsd, farmer—sold 175a on South West side of Deep Creek, which land was surveyed for Robert Layton (Layden). Test' James Gibson, Joseph Hosea. April 19, 1746.

No. 61. Moses Rountree of Chowan, planter—for £5 pd by Simon Stallings of Perq, sold 232a which was grt unto Thomas Blitchenden, by two patents, on lines of Thomas Hobbs, James Fields, & Thomas Rountree, to River pocoson. Nov 30, 1745. Test' Nicholas Stallings Jr, William Price Jr.

No. 62. April 1, 1746. John Man of Pasq Co, for £85 pd by Thomas Weeks of Perq gent—sold 50a on South West side of Little River, part of a grt Jan 1, 1694, to William Man, gr-father of sd John, bounded with an Island, called "William Mans old plan' adj John Hufton, to ye head of a branch, on ye side of which a house stands, within which Elizabeth Knols, widow dwells" & was assigned to Thomas Knols July 7, 1744, sd Weeks having purchased sd Knols title to sd land. Test' Edmund Hatch, Abraham Hosea.

No. 63. Foster Toms, planter—for £50 pd by Thomas Winslow, conveyed 95a on South West side of Suttons Creek, adj Andrew Woodley, & Arthur Albertson. Test' Abraham Elliott, Joseph Ratliff. Feb 20, 1745.

No. 64. April 21, 1746. John Perry of Perq, Sadler—for £120 pd by Peter Parker planter—sold 102a on Southwest side of Little River, near the head, on Gum Swamp, adj Thomas Boswell, "John Perry being the first patentee." Mar 21, 1742/3. Test' James Parker, James Morgan.

No. 65. Zachariah Chancey of Perq, for £100 pd by Zachariah Elton of same—sold 200a on South west side of Perq River, "a patent to me July 27, 1743 adj Abraham Saunders, including an Island in ye Swamp" 100a part of sd patent. Test' William Townsen, Joseph Wilson, Isaac Wilson. July 16, 1746.

No. 66. Zachariah Chancey, for £180 pd by Macrora Scarbrough of Perq, Gent—sold "one negro woman, named Joane, about 22 years of age, & a negro boy Seven years old named Pomp." Test' William Moore, Lemuel Hatch. Oct 22, 1740.

No. 67. Zachariah Chancey, Gent—for £50 pd by Samuel Newby of Perq, husbandman—sold 250a in Balahack, adj Joseph Winslow, & Truman Moore, John & William Moore, & William Wilson, down to the Creek. Jan 3, 1745/6. Test' Zachariah Elton, William Phelps, James Sitterson.

No. 68. John Wilcocks of Perq, Millwright—for £29 s8 p6 pd by Andrew Woodley, of afsd, planter—sold "28 head of cattle, in Durants Neck, also 3 feather beds, & all other household goods." Aug 8, 1745. Test' Joseph Sutton Jr, Jno Clayton.

No. 69. John Wilcocks, "am firmly bound unto Andrew Woodley, in ye sum of £58 s17, bounded to deliver unto sd Woodley, a likely negro of ye value of £29 s8 p6 before Nov 1, next, without further delay." Aug 8, 1745. Test' Joseph Sutton Jr, John Clayton.

No. 70. March 29, 1746. "I Joseph Hosea have Rec'd of Robert Hosea, my full part of Thomas Hoseas Estate, both real, & personal." Joseph Hosea. Test' Joseph Robinson.

Mar 29, 1746. "Rec'd of Robert Hosea, Admix of Estate of Thomas Hosea, dec'd my own, & my sister Eliz'h Gimonesons full part, both Real, & personal. John Hosea. Test' Joseph Robinson.

Mar 29, 1746. "Rec'd of Robert Hosea, Admix of Est of Thomas Hosea dec'd, my full part, both Real, & personal." Thomas Meedes. July Court, 1746. Test' Joseph Robinson.

No. 71. James Caruthers of Chowan, for £150 pd by John Rousham of same, bricklayer—sold 156a on North side of Yeopim River, & the mouth of Mill Creek, down Deep branch to John Wyatts land, "88a of which was grt my father Nathaniel Caruthers, & by him assigned to me." July 22, 1746. Test' William Wyatt, Richard Skinner Jr.

No. 72. Richard Banks of Perq, planter—for £30 pd by William Standing of afsd—planter, sold 40a on North side of Yeopim River. July 18, 1746. Test' John Pierce, John Rowsham, John Cresey.

No. 73. Zachariah Chancey, for £50 pd by William Moore, sold 100a adj William Phelps, part of a survey, 950a for sd Chancey. Mar 7, 1745/6. Test' ——————

No. 74. Simon Perishoe of Perq, planter—for an "Exchange agreed upon by sd Simon & Joseph Perishoe of afsd, Sadler—sold 100a near "Naggs head Chappel" adj Thomas Stafford, Elihu Albertson, & William Tomblin, part of a Grt unto James Perishoe Dec'd, 50a in sd Co. April 21, 1746. Test' Richard Wood, John Clayton.

No. 75. Joseph Perishoe, Sadler—for an "Exchange with Simon Perishoe, do grant to sd Simon 50a "on ye South East side of a branch which parts this land, & land of Samuel Barclift, for a parcel of land I hold in Exchange, at ye head of Long Branch." Test' Richard Wood Jr, John Clayton. April 21, 1746.

No. 76. Simon Perishoe, for "Love I bear my brother James, have given 100a on ye North side of ye Road," adj Thomas Stafford, & Samuel Barclift. April 21, 1746. Test' Richard Wood, John Clayton.

No. 77. James Chesson of Terrel Co, for £340 pd by Jeremiah Pratt of Perq, sold 260a on West side of Indian Creek, in Perq Co, adj Samuel, & Jonathan Taylor. Test' D. Butler, Thomas Ming Jr. Sept 8, 1746.

No. 78. Richard Chesson of Onslow Co, planter—for £10 pd by Thomas Hollowell of Perq, sold 50a adj Thomas, & Moses Wood, across "Racoon Ridge," a patent to sd Chesson Feb 22, 1719. Test' Thomas Nicholson, Phineas Nixon, Zach Nixon. 19-4mo 1746.

No. 79. "We William Snoden, Samuel Snoden, & Solomon Snoden, of Perq, farmers"—for £17 pd by John Barclift Jr of afsd, farmer—sold 36½a part of 73a patented Nov 2, 1723, on "ye west side of Little River" adj sd Barclift. Jan 20, 1745/6. Test' Edmund Hatch, Samuel Barclift Jr, William Trumbull.

No. 80. Ralph Bosman of Perq, for "love I bear my Nephew Thomas Bullock of afsd do give 75a, part of a tract pat by sd Bosman in 1718, adj Isaac Wilson, to southernmost fork of Robert Wilsons Creek, & down ye branch to Horse bridge" sd Creek being line between Isaac Wilson, & Samuel Phelps. Aug 8, 1746. Test' Joshua Hubart, Samuel Sitterson, Joseph Wilson.

No. 81. Arnold White of Perq, farmer—for £110 pd by John Wallis of Chowan, farmer—sold 87a "upon ye Swamp side, out of ye head of Little River, called Fork Swamp below ye plan' of James Parker," to Thomas Hollowells line, on Little Long branch. Test' James Parker, Peter Parker. July 1, 1746.

No. 82. John Lilly of Perq, planter—for £10 pd by Thomas Lilly of afsd—sold 50a "in ye mouth of a small branch, issuing out of River Pocoson, called Poplar Branch," on line of Isaac Wilson, part of a grt unto William Kitchen, & Margaret Snuke in 1713, down sd branch to percoson. Oct 18, 1746. Test' Nicholas Stallings, Elias Stallings.

No. 83. Nov 25, 1746. Richard Brothers, & Mary his wife, "of ye upper parish of Nancenund in Vir" for £30 pd by James Sumner of Perq Co N. C. sold 343a in Perq known by the name of "Orapeak Marsh" sd land grt Richard Brothers, father of sd Richard, Oct 23, 1728, & given in his will to his son, party to these presents. Test' Joseph Leadger, Abraham Brinkley, Luke Sumner.

No. 84. Dec 12, 1746. Samuel Gregory of Edenton, Chowan Co, Innholder—for £113 s10 pd by James Eggerton of Perq, sold 215a on North side of Yoppim River. Test' Charles Dent Jr, Benj Simpson Jr.

No. 85. Joseph Pritchard of Perq, for "brotherly love I have for my brother Mathew, have given 50a on ye South East side of Perq River" adj Robert Wilson, up County Road to Samuel Newbys new Road, "& down sd road to land Jesse Newby sold his brother Francis, called "Scotts old field," at the head of Deep branch. Test' Zach Nixon, Francis Toms, Joseph Wilson. 27-12mo 1745/6.

No. 86. Zach Chancey of Perq, planter—for £300 pd by Macrora Scarbrough, sold one negro woman, named Joan, & also agrees to pay to sd Scarbrough, "ye just sum afsd, upon ye 25 Dec next, with interest." Dec 26, 1746. Test' Joseph Wilson, Pritlaw Elliott.

No. 87. Robert Wilson, & Joseph his son, of Perq—for £20 pd by Thomas Bullock, Sr of afsd—sold 30a, "part of a patent to Robert Wilson, gr-father of sd Robert, in 1684, on a branch called ye Pond branch, down ye run to horse bridge Creek." Aug 18, 1746. Test' Joshua Hobart, James Sitterson, Samuel Sitterson.

No. 88. Richard Skinner of Perq, for £28 pd by Robert Reddick of afsd—sold 150a on South East side of Castletons Creek, adj William Haughton, Peter Jones Jr, & orphans of John Williams. Jan 19, 1746. Test' Joseph Reddick, William Standin, Joshua Deal.

No. 89. Joseph Winslow of Perq, for £40 pd by John Griffin of afsd—sold 160a adj ———— Hudson, land bought by sd Winslow, of Thomas Jessop. Jan Court, 1746. Test' Henry Phelps, Daniel Saint.

No. 90. Aaron Wood of Perq, farmer—for £190 pd by Samuel Bagley of same, planter sold 100a, adj Thomas Hollowell, Peter Pearson, Gideon Bundy, Moses Wood. Test' Thomas Bagley, John Moore. Dec 1, 1746.

No. 91. Aaron Wood, for £15 pd by Moses Wood, of Perq, planter—sold 10a on ye North East side of Perq River, & South side of Cypress Swamp, on line of Gideon Bundy, along Bogues line, to said Moses. Nov 6, 1746. Test' John Moore, Samuel Bagley, Joseph Ratliff.

No. 92. Mary Moore, formerly Mary Newby, widow of Nathan dec'd, by "ye advice of Samuel Moore my husband, in Con' of love we do bear unto Francis, & Nathan Newby, sons of said Nathan, & Mary afore', his then wife," have given ye within mentioned land, to be equally divided between them. Jan 20, 1746. Test' Daniel Grandin, Jno Stevenson.

No. 93. Feb 5, 1746/7. Alexander Ross, of Perq, for £40 pd by George Eason, sold 185a "in ye mouth of Basses Swamp at ye Vineyard point" adj Land of John Harris, John Gordon, & Joseph Redding. A grant in Vir to John Harris, & John Larcum April 21, 1695, for 888a, & by said Harris, & Larcum sold to William Woodley, & was Ack' in Nansemond Co by said Woodleys son Andrew, & sold by him to said Alex Ross, July 16, 1743. Test' James Sumner, Luke Sumner, Seth Sumner.

No. 94. Samuel Wyatt, of Perq, for "love I owe my son-in-law John Swain, & my dau Elizabeth Swain, have given 300a in Perq, on ye west side of Yoppim Creek," adj my son Jacob Wyatt, up the Creek to Robert Harmons. Mar 2, 1747. Test' Daniel Saint, Joseph Barrow, Sarah Barrow.

No. 95. Jan 26, 1746. William Standin, of Perq, & Henderson Standin, of Chowan, for £40, pd by Samuel Standin, of Perq, sold 200a on East of land now in possession of Humphrey Griffin, on West side of Joseph Barrows land, & South of William Long. Part of 400a patented by Thomas Pierce, & by him sold to "Sarah Standin, now invested in us by deed." Test' Samuel Skinner, John Harvey Jun.

No. 96. Abraham Elliott, of Perq farmer—for £27 pd by Moses Field, of same, sold 50a on William Morgans line, to Moses Elliott line, & the mouth of "Reedy branch." April 20, 1747. Test' Thomas Nicholson, John Perry, Joshua Elliott.

No. 97. Thomas Rountree Sen, of Chowan, for "love I bear towards my gr-son William Wallis of Perq, have given plan' whereon I now live 50a, which said Rountree had of Timothy Clare late of Perq," provided said Wallis does not sell any part of said land without consent of my sons, Charles, & Thomas Rountree." April 9, 1747. Test' Elias Stallings Jun, John Lilly Jun.

RECORDS OF DEEDS 145

No. 98. Samuel Standin, of Perq, for £20 pd by William Standin, of same, sold 200a, adj Wilson, & Davenports line, to line of Joseph Barrow, now in possession of said Barrow. April 21, 1747. Test' Jos Oates, Joseph Crecy.

No. 99. Joseph Winslow, farmer—for £10, pd by Moses Field, of ye same, Farmer—sold 10a on line of Francis Toms, adj Abraham Elliott, & Moses Elliott, & "ye main Co Road, part of 50a given my mother, & by me possessed." April 20, 1747.

No. 100. Jacob Docton, of Perq, for £6 pd by William Wilson, of same, sold 50a in Ballahack, on lines of Turner, & Benj Wilson, to "Sharwoods old plan." Feb 7, 1746. Test' Zach Elton, Hannah Elton, William Phelps.

No. 101. Zachariah Chancey, of Perq, sold unto Stephen Chancey, of Pasq Co, two horses, aged about 10, & 12 years, for £50, Jan 17, 1746/7. Test' Pritlow Elliott, Joseph Smith.

No. 102. James Smith, of Perq, for £50 pd by Joshua Deal, of afore' sold 50a, on North west side of Albemarle Sound, "part of ye manner plan' belonging to James Sitterson dec'd," adj said Deals line. Jan 22, 1747. Test' John Felt, Joshua Skinner, Thomas Roberts.

No. 103. Zachariah Chancey of Perq, sold unto Charles Jordan of Chowan, 45 head of cattle, & two young cows, for £150. Dec 15, 1746. Test' Pritlow Elliott, Joseph Smith.

No. 104. Zachariah Chancey, unto Charles Jordan, planter—for £50 "one negro man 28 years of age, named Peter." Jan 13, 1746. Test' Stephen Chancey, Joseph Smith, Pritlow Elliott.

No. 105. Samuel Newby of Perq, for £20 pd by Thomas Lamb of afsd—sold 150a on a branch called "ye Islands" adj Cypress Swamp, "including ye sd Island, & up ye Creek to Hugh Lambs line." Aug 25, 1746. Test' Robert Newby, Wm Moore, Demsey Conner.

No. 106. James Smith of Perq, for £80 pd by William Long of afsd—sold 50a adj Joshua Deal, on Albemarle Sound, up sd Sound to the mouth of Yoppim Creek, called "Smiths old plan'." July 10, 1747. Test' Daniel Saint, Edward Penrice, Wm Long Jr.

No. 107. Lords Pro' unto Thomas Pierce, grt 400a at the head of Bentley's Creek, adj James Chesson, John Barrow, & John Davenport. Granted Dec 19, 1712, unto John Pettiver, & by him Elapsed, April 5, 1720. Test' Wm Reed, John Hecklefield.

Thomas Pierce assigned sd land to Samuel Standing, Feb 21, 1746. Test' Joseph Barrow, Wm Standing, Joseph Barrow, Jr.

No. 108. Sarah Winslow, Zachariah Nixon, & Francis Toms of Perq, Exors of the will of Thomas Winslow, dec'd, in con' of £16 pd by John Moore of afsd—conveyed "according to the Express words of sd will" half of tract, known by name of "ye persimmon tree land, the whole 183a, Thomas Hallowells land being the other moiety thereof" sd John Moore to have the upper part, adj Joshua Boswell. Oct 14, 1747.

No. 109. James Sitterson Sr of Perq, for £110 pd by John Harmon of afsd, planter—sold 100a called "Pond land" patented by sd Sitterson 1736, adj Ralph Bozman, Jonathan Sherwood, & Benj Wilson. May 2, 1747. Test' Samuel Sitterson, William Townsen, Jas Sitterson.

No. 110. Oct 1, 1747. James Packitt of Onslow Co, Carpenter—for £100 pd by Samuel Bond of Perq, sold 104a on Perq River, adj William Blitchenden. Test' John Packett, James Henderson, Lewis Jenkins.

No. 111. John Moore of Perq, for £16 pd by Thomas Eason of afsd, planter—sold 91a part of a "moiety called Persimmon tree land" adj Joshua Boswell. Test' Ralph Fletcher, Josiah Bogue, Joseph Ratliff. Oct 19, 1747.

No. 112. Thomas Newby Sr, of Nancemund in Vir, for £25 pd by John Pearson, of Perq Co N. C. sold 320a "in ye fork of Isaac Wilsons Mill pond, & up ye Swamp to Indian Branch" adj Zachariah Nixon. Thomas, & Mary Newby. Test' John Smith, Caleb Elliott, Joseph Smith. 19-8mo 1747.

No. 113. William Winslow of Perq, for £17 pd by Joseph Redding of afsd—sold 50a adj Jonathan Sherrod, Richard Gooding, & Benj'n Wilson, "part of a grant to Zachariah Chancey July 27, 1743, & conveyed by him to Jacob Docton, who sold sd land to me." Test' Nicholas Stallings, Moses Eason, James Reading. Oct 16, 1747.

No. 114. Joseph Hosea of Perq, for £50 pd by Abraham Hosea (brother) of afsd—sold 65a on Deep Creek, "part of land formerly, Mr. Thomas Commanders, dec'd, & given to me by my father Joseph Hosea dec'd." April 22, 1747. Test' William Hosea, William Trumball.

No. 115. Gideon Bundy, & Miriam his wife, of Pasq Co, for £80 pd by Aaron Wood of Perq, sold 50a, on ye North East side of Perq River, adj Peter Gray, part of 200a patented by Richard Chesson Sr, & conveyed by his son Richard, to William Bogue, & given by sd Bogue to his dau Miriam Bundy. Dec 10, 1746. Test' Josiah Bundy, Michael Murphy, Abraham Bundy.

No. 116. David Houghton & Mary his wife of Chowan Co, for £100 pd by Henry Hall Mariner; of Perq, sold 62½a, which fell to sd Mary as heir of Richard Sutton dec'd. Jan 18, 1747. Test' Francis Penrice, Jonathan Skinner, Thomas Calloway.

No. 117. Edward Maudlin of Perq, for £200 pd by Zach Nixon of afsd, sold 100a "on ye North East side of Voices (Vosses) Creek Swamp, adj James Henby Sr, being ye upper part of land formerly sd Henbeys." Jan 19, 1746/7.

No. 118. April 1, 1745. Joseph Blount, & Sarah his wife, Thomas Corprew, & Ann his wife, Christian Reed, & Mary his wife, Joseph Reed, & Elizabeth his wife, all of Perq, for £100 pd by John Hall Esq, of Chowan, sold an Island called "Batts grave" 30a, at the mouth of Yeopim River. E. Moseley C. Just. Test' George Reed Jr, Edmund Hatch, Benjamin Pickett, Jesse Brenn, Robert Harmon.

No. 119. "We do ack' having rec'd within mentioned money." Thomas Corprew, Joseph Blount, Christian Reed, Joseph Reed. April 6, 1745.

No. 120. Feb 8, 1747. James Egerton of Perq, planter—for £1150 pd by Charles Blount, of Chowan Co, planter—sold 300a in Perq, adj William Halsey, & Joseph Crecy, on Yeopim pocoson, sold by John Woolard to William Egerton, "except ye burying place, 60 feet square." Test' Jacob Carruthers, Isachar Branch.

No. 121. Edward Maudlin of Perq, weaver; for £250 pd by Levi Creecy of afsd—cordwinder, sold plan' bought of William Wyatt Aprill 15, 1745, "in ye mouth of Yoppim Neck, near Bucks Branch." Oct 30, 1747. Test' William Wyatt, Jos Oates.

No. 122. John Stepney of Perq, planter—for £90 pd by Nathaniel Carruthers, of afore' farrier; sold plan' bought of John Norcom, on North side of Yoppim River. Test' Charles Denman, Thomas Weeks, Nicholas Rawlins. Oct 18, 1731.

No. 123. Nathaniel Carruthers of Edgecombe Co, blacksmith—in con' of "love I do bear my son John of Perq Co, planter, do give all right of land in

Perq Co," bought Oct 18, 1731. Seal May 22, 1747. Test' Jacob Carruthers, Ann Carruthers.

No. 124. Joseph Hosea of Perq, bricklayer—for £6 pd by James Pierce, of afsd—planter—sold 204a on North side of Deep Creek, adj widow Arnold. Apl 16, 1748. Test' James Gibson, William Trumball, Isaac Cox. Joseph, & Mary Hosea.

No. 125. Mar 5, 1747/8. Christopher Sutton of Perq, for £50 pd by James Sumner of afsd—sold 121a on North East side of Perq River, to a Creek called Suttons, & down sd Creek to Perq River. Test' Willie Reddick, John Gordon Sr, Timothy Lilly, Luke Sumner.

No. 126. April 19, 1748. Charles Blount of Perq, planter—for £600 pd by Edmund Hatch of afsd, planter—sold 150a, adj William Halsey, half of land sd Blount purchased of James Egerton, "with all appurtenances, except the Burying place, 60 feet square." Test' Mac Scarbrough, William Wood, Elizabeth Scarbrough.

No. 127. John Maudlin of Perq, for £120 pd by Joseph Newby of afsd, sold 54a on Voices Creek, an Elapsed patent, to John Lacey April 2, 1725. Test' John Perry, Joseph Hosea, Joseph Newby Jr. May 30, 1748.

No. 128. William Hollowell of Perp, planter—for £1 s8 p1, pd by Joel Hollowell, of afore' sold 130a in the mouth of Juniper Swamp, adj James Field, on Cypress Swamp. July 16, 1748. Test' Nicholas Stallings, Moses Field, Elias Stallings.

No. 129. Foster Toms of Perq, planter—for £500 pd by Joseph Perishoe, cooper—sold 250a, to be paid "before Dec 25, 1739, & sealed with my seal." June 23, 1735. Test' Richard Cheaston, Ralph Fletcher.

No. 130. William Bagley of Perq, for £40 pd by Josiah Bogue of same, sold 5a, on said Bogues line, to Cypress branch. 16d 2mo 1748.

No. 131. William Hollowell of Perq, for £1 s8 p1 pd by James Field, of afore' sold 130a on North East side of River pocoson, called Cypress Swamp. July 16, 1748. Test' Nicholas Stallings, Elias Stallings, Humphrey Griffin.

No. 132. William Hollowell of Perq, for £1 s8 p1 pd by William Wallis of Perq, sold 110a, on North east side of River pocoson called "Reedy branch." July 16, 1748. Test' Moses Field, Nicholas Stallings, Elias Stallings.

No. 133. Zachariah Chancey of Perq, sold unto Abraham Saunders, of afore' one negro boy named Cato, aged two years, for £100 "in open market." Jan 7, 1746. Test' Rt Wilson, Stephen Chancey.

No. 134. N. C. July Court 1748. Present his Majesties Justices. "Bill of sale of a negro boy Cato was assigned over by Abraham Saunders, to Mr Luke Sumner." Edmund Hatch Clk Ct.

No. 135. Abraham Saunders, assigns right of one negro boy Cato, unto Luke Sumner. April 19, 1748. Test' Samuel Moore, Jeremiah Pratt, John Parish.

No. 136. Samuel Wyatt of Perq, planter—"for love I bear unto my son Jacob of same—do give all my estate, of what sort or kind, reserving my said estate during my life, as if this deed had never been made, meaning that my son shall have no power to trouble, or hinder me from using said estate for my support duing my life, he to have the whole, at my death." April 9, 1748. Test' J. Halsey, Thomas Falconer.

No. 137. Joshua Deal of Perq, planter—for £35 pd by John Smith of same, planter—sold 200a on ye Sound, adj Archibald Holmes. Oct 6, 1748. Test' William Saunders, Samuel Smith.

No. 138. Jacob Caruthers of Perq, for £50 pd by Thomas Hicks of Chowan, sold 190a "where said Jacob now lives," on Yoppim River, Sept 28, 1748. Test' Joseph Dear, J. Halsey, Sarah Dear.

No. 139. Sept 29, 1748. David Huffton of Berkeley Parish, Perq Co, planter—for a "5 year old mare, & £7 pd by my Father John Huffton dec'd, to Edward Turner of same, planter—all that plan' 115a in said Parish, on the head of Deep Creek, that issueth out of the South West side of Little River, adj Esau Albertson. Granted unto Thomas Collins July 20, 1717, & by him sold to Peter Dove, & by said Dove sold to Esau Albertson, & by him assigned to my Father." Test' James Pierce, ——— Turner.

No. 140. John Ashley of Perq, for £300 pd by Joseph Newby, of ye same—sold 144a adj land of Mr. Daniel Saint. Dec 28, 1748. Test' Thomas Calloway, Thomas Biggs.

No. 141. John Hollowell of Norfolk Co Vir, for £6 pd by Raniel Rogerson of Perq Co N. C. sold 200a on South west side of Perq River, adj Timothy Lilly, a patent to Thomas Blitchenden, July 14, 1725, & by him sold to Edmund Hallowell, & was given by him to John Bacon, & he "being dead, falls to me by kinship." Aug 30, 1748. Test' John Perishoe, Jun, Thomas Hollowell.

No. 142. Edward Rice of Perq, planter—for £55 pd by Robert Wilson, of same—sold 125a on South west side of Perq River, between John Davis, & Gum Swamp, a "grant to Samuel Bond, & Elapsed to Henry Grace," sold by said Grace to John Hudler (Hurdle) & by said Hudler, sold to Thomas Blitchenden, & by said Thomas conveyed to me. Dec 28, 1748. Test' Timothy Winslow, Amos Wood.

No. 143. William Trumball of Perq, planter—for £50 pd by Joseph Hosea, bricklayer—sold 50a, "whereon said Trumball now lives," on Lillies Creek. Dec —, 1748. Test' Jas Gibson, William Hosea.

No. 144. Robert Wilson of Perq, planter—for £60 pd by Joseph White of "ye Collony of Vir," sold 200a on ye North East by Perq River, & on North west by "Tanks Creek," to line of Ann Wilson, South to line of Josiah Gilbert. Nov 28, 1748. Test' William White, Isaac Wilson.

No. 145. Joseph Mayo, planter—for £25 pd by John Robinson, carpenter—sold 3a out of a patent to Timothy Clear, April 21, 1694, & was a "division of land by said Clears will." Jan —, 1748. Test' Francis Toms, Josiah Bundy.

No. 146. Robert Wilson of Perq, for £30 pd by Macrora Scarbrough, of afore' sold 30a "on ye Eastermost side of Lakers Creek, formerly called Perishoes Creek, near Skinners bridge" a survey made by John Wilcocks, who took up same, but "now appears to be within patent for 240a granted to Richard Evans in the year 1684," & by him assigned to Edward Mayo, & by him transferred to Anthony Dawson, & by said Dawson in 1711, conveyed to Isaac Wilson, "who by will devised same to his Nephew Isaac," son of said Robert. April 9, 1748. Test' Joseph Wilson, Sylvanus Wilson.

No. 147. Joseph Winslow of Perq, planter—for £12 s10 pd by Robert Evans Jr, of ye same—sold 60a called New Neck, a patent to Thomas Jessop. Jan 16, 1748/9. Test' Daniel Saint, William Hollowell.

No. 148. John Rousham of Chowan, for £25 pd by Jacob Caruthers, of Perq, sold 156a & 88a on Deep branch, formerly John Wyatts. Oct 15, 1748. Test' Wm Standin, John Carruthers.

No. 149. Robert Wilson of Perq, planter—for £18 pd by Joshua Deal, of same—conveyed 145a, adj John Griffin, a "grant from John Earle of Granville," to said Robert Wilson, Dec 20, 1748. Seal Jan 16, 1748/9. Test' Daniel Saint, Josiah Bundy.

No. 150. Robert Wilson, for £110 pd by Thomas Newby of Perq, planter—sold 390a of "up land, & 100a marsh land on ye North East side of Perq River, & west side of Tanks Creek," on Ann Wilsons line, called "Wilcocks," the marsh between that & Castletons Creek. Oct 19, 1748. Test' Dempsey Conner, Francis Newby.

No. 151. Joseph Winslow of Perq, for £3 pd by Timothy Winslow, planter—of same, sold 100a, at "ye lower end of Hickory Neck," adj John Griffin, being land patented by Thomas Jessop. Jan 16, 1748/9. Test' Daniel Saint, Wm Hollowell.

No. 152. Aug 4, 1748. William Wallis of Perq, for £30 by Moses Rountree of Chowan, sold 110a, near the head of Perq River, adj James Field, "at the mouth of Reedy branch." Test' Davenport Gooding, John Hobs.

No. 153. Charles Blount of Perq, for £550 pd by James Eggerton of same, sold 150a, adj Mr Joseph Creecy, & land of Mr Edmund Hatch, "in the mouth of Deep branch." Feb 22, 1748/9. Test' Thomas Calloway, Joseph Creecy.

No. 154. Evan Jones of Perq, Glover—for "good will I have towards my neighbor Robert Chappel" of same, planter—have given 40a on west side of Perq River, a grant unto me. April 18, 1749. Test' Jos Blount, Edmund Hatch.

No. 155. John Ghyer of Perq, planter—for £50 pd by William Newby of same, Tarner—sold 10a on North East side of Perq River, on line of William Lacey. April 17, 1749. Test' Joseph Ratcliff, Joseph Mayo, Joshua Davis.

No. 156. James Field of Perq, for "love I bear my son Moses" have made over 100a, on north side of Cypress Swamp, & north west of Juniper Swamp. Feb 18, 1748/9. Test' Davenport Gooding, Reubin Field.

No. 157. William Moore of Perq, planter—for a val' con' pd by Lott Stallings, sold 98a, on South West side of Perq River, on line of Elizabeth Symons, in Balahack, commonly called "the Elbow" taken out of a grant to Edward Moseley, & Robert Hatton, surveyed by John Clayton. April 17, 1749. Test' Isaac Hill, William Wilson, Samuel Sitterson.

No. 158. Joseph Newby, Millright; for "love I bear my son Joseph" of afore' have given 150a, on North East side of Perq River, betwixt Sam'l Moore, & Henry Phelps. 17- 2mo 1749. Test' Thomas White, Henry Phelps.

No. 159. James Griffin of Chowan, for "natural aff" I bear unto my brother John because my Father James Griffin made a deed of gift unto said John for a parcel of land in Perq, on North east side of Perq River, I do assign all the land on North side of 'plum tree branch,' to said John Griffin where he now lives." April 17, 1749. Test' Robert Wilson, Truman Moore.

No. 160. Thomas Smith of Perq, planter—for £6 pd by Michael Smith, of ye same, Planter—sold 50a, adj Thomas & William White, "to ye head of Sewell Creek, part of land that James Smith father of said Thomas bought of Joseph Jessop." Jan 14, 1748/9. Test' William Saunders, James Goodin.

No. 161. Joseph Sanders of Perq, for "good will, & aff' I owe unto my brother John Sanders of afore' have given 183a, on ye East side of Cypress Swamp at ye mouth of "ye Holly branch" running to line of Samuel Newby, & Robert Newby." April 15, 1749. Test' Thomas White, Samuel Moore, Thomas Newby.

No. 162. Joseph Sanders, for "love I have for my brother Benj Sanders" of Perq, Have given 183a on ye east side of Cypress Swamp, Joining Samuel Newby, to Joshua Elliotts line, & along his line to said Swamp. April 15, 1749. Test' Thomas White, Samuel Moore, Thomas Newby.

No. 163. John Perry of Perq, sadler—for £200 pd by John Lacey, of same, planter—sold 100a on "ye South East side of Voices Creek," being part of 414a granted to said Perry Dec 20, 1748 binding on Thomas Elliotts line. April 17, 1749. Test' Joseph Newby, Jun, Moses Field, Jos Wilson.

No. 164. William Wyatt of Perq, for 5s pd by Jacob Carruthers, of afore' assigned "all right of land on South side of Pratts Mill Swamp" 10a. July 17, 1749. Test' Thomas Calloway, John Stepney.

No. 165. Elias Stallings of Perq, for "love & aff' I have for my Friends, Nicholas Stallings, Robert Reddick, Joseph Reddick, John Reddick, John Hollowell, Daniel Rogerson, Thomas Lilly, William Lilly, Timothy Lilly, Joseph Lilly, Simon Stallings, & James Pierce, of afore' Co, have given to them land on North East side of head of Perq River, 50a without any manner of condition." July 15, 1749. Test' Samuel Powell, William Weeks.

No. 166. Mar 1, 1748. John Hull Esq, for £50 pd by Charles Blount of Perq, sold "an Island of 30a known as "Batts Grave" at ye mouth of Yoppim River. Test' Geo Gould, Issachar Branch.

No. 167. "We Jacob, & Hepsibeth Perry of Perq, for love we bear our son Israel Perry of same, have given 150a bounded on ye North by ye River, & on ye East by line of John Winslow." Oct 16, 1749. Test' Jacob Perry Jun, Reuben Perry.

No. 168. "We underwritten subscribers, in con' of a tract of land which fell to our wives as coheirs of Mr. George Durant dec'd, to divide said land, hath agreed as follows: parcel 284a on ye Sound, that divides Catchmades land, near ye old house, Joseph Reed has agreed to take in right of his wife; next 310a with houses thereon Christian Reed has agreed to take, as his wifes ¼ part; third lot on ye Sound, near "dirty swamp" called "Beaver dam" adj Samuel Swann, (whereon Foster Bryan lives, & that whereon George Laden liveth) 650a, Joseph Blount agrees to take as his ¼ part, in right of his wife; fourth 284a on "dirty swamp" to line of Samuel Swann, & ye Sound, (whereon Oliver Salter now liveth) Thomas Corprew agrees to take, in right of his wife." June 19, 1745. Test' Bryant Forset.

No. 169. William Newby, for £5 assigns "all right of within deed," to John Guyer. July 17, 1749. Test' Thomas Newby, Jonathan Phelps.

No. 170. Alice Caloway of Perq, "have bound" unto Sylvanus Wilson of same, my son Caleb Calloway; "to abide with said Sylvanus, & Rebeccah his wife, as their son, until he be 21 years of age: which will be April 22, 1763." Nov 15, 1748. Test' Robert Wilson, Rachel Wilson.

No. 171. Robert, & Joseph Wilson, of Perq, are firmly bound unto Thomas Bullock of afore' in the sum of £150. Obligation; 30a conveyed by said Robert, & Joseph, Aug 18, 1746. Seal Dec 1, 1749. Test' Mac Scarbrough, Sam'l Sitterson.

No. 172. Jan 8, 1749. John Perry, Sadler—for £19 s5, pd by Joseph Anderson, sold 100a, on Voices Creek, "part of a grant unto me" Dec 20, 174—, on lines of William Morgan, & Joseph Newby, & said Perry. Jan 8, 1749.

No. 173. Thomas Overman of Perq, farmer—for £15 pd by Charles Overman, of said Co, Blacksmith—sold 2a "at the Easterly side of a branch, running out of Little River pocoson, Just below the Meeting house." 8d 12 mo 1748/9. Test' Thomas Nicholson, James Henby, Mary Nicholson.

DEED BOOK F

No. 1. Samuel Stallings of Perq, Planter—for £18 s1 pd by George Eason, of afore' sold 150a "on Middle Swamp," to lines of James Scott, & Richd Harrell, & Thomas Docton. Mar 17, 1749/50. Test' Luke Sumner, James Redding.

No. 2. Elizabeth Sutton of Perq, for £100 pd by Henry Hall, of afore' Mariner—sold 12½a, "which fell to sd Elizabeth by co-heirship," part of plan' formerly belonging to Richd Sutton. April 16, 1750. Test' Joshua Skinner, Wm Long Jr, Wm Skinner.

No. 3. Abraham Hosea of Perq, for £125 pd by John Hosea, of Pasquotank, sold 260a on south side of Deep Creek, adj Albert Albertson, a "patent unto Thomas Commander Dec 6, 1720." Seal April 16, 1750. Test' Joshua Maudling, Wm Weeks, Richd Whedbee.

No. 4. Jacob Mullen, of Berkeley Parish; Perq Co, Planter—for £30 pd by George Layden of same, sold 50a, on west side of Suttons Creek, adj Peter Albertson, part of a "patent to Albert Albertson dec'd, May 22, 1694," which was divided & laid off to his brother Nathaniel Albertson, & by him sold to Nathaniel Nicholson, & became due sd Mullen by marriage with Sarah only dau of sd Nicholson. Aug 9, 1749. Test' Albert Albertson, James Pierce.

No. 5. Macrora Scarbrough of Perq, Gent—for 5s pd by Joshua Hobard of afore', School Master—sold 300a adj land whereon I now dwell, to line of Paul Palmers Oak Ridge land. Feb 3, 1745. Test' ———

No. 6. April 14, 1750. Lemuel Powell of Perq, to Thos Wiggins of same, in con' of £3 paid, sold 150a at a place called "Orapeak." (Now in Gates Co. N. C.) Test' John Sumner, Richd Brothers, John Benton Jun.

No. 7. July 16, 1750. Joseph Winslow Sen, of Perq, to Guy Hill of Chowan, for £50 paid, sold 50a on North east side of Perq River, adj Elias Stallings, being part of 400a granted to Thos Winslow Nov 11, 1717. Test' Davenport Gooding, Moses Field.

No. 8. Joseph Mayo planter—of Perq, for £15 pd by John Robinson, Carpenter—sold 30a part of a patent unto Timothy Clear April 21, 1694. Seal July 16, 1750. Test' Jos Winslow, Thos Newby.

No. 9. John Hosea of Pasq, Cooper—for £62 pd by Joseph Hosea of Perq, Bricklayer sold 260a on south side of Deep Creek, on lines of Albert Albertson, Wm Godfrey & John Perishoe. Aug 4, 1750. Test' Abraham Hosea, John Royal.

10. Benjamin Perry for "love I bear my son Joseph Perry," both of Perq, do "give land whereon sd Joseph now liveth," on West side of Perq River, adj John Reddick, on "Denny Swamp" to the River 100a. July 7, 1750. Test' Josiah Granberry, John Murdaugh.

No. 11. Wm Long Sen, of Perq, for "love I bear my son William" of same, do give 160a adj land formerly Mr John Banks dec, on "Pratts Mill Swamp." Sept 15, 1750. Test' Thos Calloway, Joseph Ashley.

No. 12. Isaac Hill of Perq, planter—for £15 pd by Jonathan Sharrod, of same, planter—sold 150a on North side of Cypress Swamp, "near the Duck Pond," & down sd Swamp to line of Thos Newby, & John Boyce. Dec 14, 1749. Test' Thos Newby, Jos Elliott, Isaac Elliott.

No. 13. Sept 1, 1750. Robert Wilson, Merchant—to Thomas Newby, Farmer—for £60 sold 125a on south west side of Perq River, adj River bridge, to line of John Davis, & the head of Gum Branch. Test' Joseph Robinson, John Sumner.

No. 14. John Robinson of Perq, Farmer—for £35 pd by Solomon Hendrick of same, Farmer—& his heirs, Viz; William Magnienes who married Frances dau of sd Soloman, & John Jackson who married Sarah another dau, to whom sd Solomon dec'd bequeathed sd land bought of me, & by "reason of the Patent being burnt in Zach Nixons house, sd deed could not be found," sold 113a on South west side of Little River, on a Creek formerly called "Platters Creek" adj Nathaniel Welch & Thomas Weeks Esq. Oct 13, 1750. Test' John Overman, Joseph Robinson.

No. 15. William Rountree of Edgecombe Co, planter—for £25 pd by Joseph Reddick of Perq, planter—sold 100a adj Jos Gibson, & John White. Dec 30, 1750. Test' Jos Perry, Jesse Eason, Robt Reddick, Jas Peirce.

No. 16. James Griffin of Chowan, for £25 pd by Will'm Griffin of same, sold 400a being part of 600a conveyed to James Griffin Sen, by John Pettiver April 10, 1729, at the mouth of a small branch that issueth out of the west side of Perq River, which divideth sd land from that formerly Thos Winslows, & Wm Moores, to the River. Nov 3, 1750. Test' Davenport Gooding, Francis Newby.

No. 17. Thomas Bagley of Perq, farmer—for £5 pd by Jonathan Pearson of same—planter—sold 15a adj sd Bagleys line, to the River. Jan 15, 1750. Test' Samuel Bagley, Aaron Wood.

No. 18. Moses Elliott of Perq, for £45 pd by Caleb Elliott of same—sold 90a, on line of Thomas Elliott, & Jos Smith. Jan 21, 1750/1. Test' Joseph Robinson, Joseph Wilson.

No. 19. Thomas Bagley of Perq, planter—for £49 pd by Aaron Wood of same—sold 15a, upon North East side of Perq River, adj Peter Gray, running to line of Jonathan Pearson. Jan 15, 1750. Test' Samuel Bagley.

No. 20. Wm Wyatt, & Penelope his wife of Perq, for £15 pd by William Woolard, of Chowan, sold 125a on north side of "Jeremiah Pratts Mill Swamp," a patent to us 1745. Seal Jan 22, 1750. Test' Jacob Caruthers, Jacob Wyatt.

No. 21. John Perry sadler—of Perq, for £10 pd by Moses Field of afsd, farmer—sold 10a "near the main Road," a survey made by Jno Clayton, for 414a to sd Perry Dec 20, 1748. Seal Oct 6, 1750. Test' Matthew Pritchard, Davenport Gooding.

No. 22. Dec 5, 1750. Lawrence Arnold of Berkeley Parish, Perq Co, farmer—to Elihu Albertson of same, farmer—in con' of £25 s5, sold 270a, part of 440a grt to sd Arnold June 27 "in the 22 year of the reign of King George the Second." Test' Thos Weeks, Thos Weeks Jun.

No. 23. John Perry of Perq, for a "Val' sum pd by Joseph Newby" of afsd, Millwright, sold 140a on So East Side of Vosses Creek, adj Moses Elliott,

Jno Lacey, & Thos Elliott, to sd Newbys line, formerly John Morgans, a grt to sd Perry Dec 20, 1748. Seal Nov 1, 1750. Test' Thomas Lamb, John Sanders, Dorothy Jordan.

No. 24. Dec 17, 1750. Henry Warren of Chowan Co, to James Luten of Edenton, for £70 sold plan' on north side of Yeopim River in Perq Co, "whereon Abraham Warren father of sd Henry did live," 300a grt' to John Hopkins Feb 16, 1696. Test' ——— Barker, Frances Newman.

No. 25. Moses Field of Perq, planter—for £26 pd by Jos Outland of same, planter—sold 50a formerly Moses Elliotts, on Jos. Andersons line to "reedy branch." April —, 1751. Test' Francis Toms, Nathan Newby, Jos Ratliffe.

No. 26. Richd Cheaston, of Bladen Co, Farmer—in con' of £10 pd by Dan'l Saint of Perq, sold 100a on No East Side of Perq River, called "Grassy point" the "Manner plan" on which David Harris lived, & left to his dau Ann Smith, by will, (on the River side) between land left to Sarah, & Elizabeth Harris. April 14, 1751. Test' Elizabeth Nixon, Ralph Fletcher Jun.

No. 27. Samuel Newby of Perq, for £10 s10 pd by William Moore, sold land adj Joseph Wilson, John Moore, & Wm Moore, to line of Zach Chancey. Sept 30, 1750. Test' Joseph Wilson, Joseph Elliott, Francis Jones.

No. 28. John Harman of Perq, Weaver—for £5 pd by Thos Bullock, of afsd, Blacksmith, sold 20a, part of a patent Mar 6, 1740, on Boazmans line. July 15, 1751. Test' John Harvey, Samuel Sitterson.

No. 29. John Parrish of Perq, Blacksmith, unto John Barclift Sen, of same farmer—sold 361a on "Sheltons Gut," adj James Foster. Dec 31, 1750. Test' ———————.

No. 30. John Parrish unto John Barclift Sen 324a on Little River, at the mouth of Deep Creek, near the mouth of "Sheltons Gut." Dec 31, 1750. Test' James Gibson, John Barclift.

No. 31. Thos Newby of Perq, for £115 pd by Jno Murdaugh, sold 390a of marsh land, on No Et side of Perq River, & on No Wt side of "Tanks Creek," called "Wilcox" to bounds of Richd Evans patent, between that & Castletons Creek. Oct 19, 1748. Test' Charles Blount, John Harvey.

No. 32. William Blitchenden of Perq, for £10 s2 pd by Jos Smith, of afsd, sold 50a on line of Samuel Bond, Wm. Philps, to a line between sd William & John Blitchenden. June 7, 1751. Test' John Smith, Reubin Brasher.

No. 33. Michael Brinkley of Perq, for £12 s10 pd by James Brinkley, of afsd, sold 100a on line of Jacob Hall, & John Brinkley, down to the River Swamp. Dec 31, 1750. Test' Joshua Hobart, Ann Hobart.

No. 34. Wm Rountree of Edgecombe Co, for £18 pd by Jno. Winslow, of Perq, planter—sold 100a on North side of Newborne (Newbegun) Creek, up the branch "to the dismal." Feb 12, 1750. Test' Thos Reddick, John Filar.

No. 35. Henry Warren of Perq, planter—for £18 s15 pd by Jno Jones, of afsd, sold 300a adj line of Mr Charles Denman dec, on the South side of Perq River, which my father Abraham Warren bought of Samuel Hall dec'd. Oct 8, 1739. Seal April 29, 1751. Test' Mac Scarbrough, Ben Scarbrough.

No. 36. "We; Robert, & Isaac Wilson of Perq, are firmly bound unto Jno Murdaugh of afsd, in the sum of £500 sealed with our seal," April 28, 1750, John Murdaugh in possession of 100a of marsh land, conveyed by said parties to sd Murdaugh Oct 18, 1748. Test' Tho Newby, Joshua Jones.

No. 37. Robert & Isaac Wilson, to John Murdaugh for £150, "made settlement of a suit long pending." April 28, 175—. Arbitrators: Jos. Robinson,

Jos White, Jno. Harvey, "chosen in behalf of said Wilsons." Test' Jacob Perry, Abraham Sanders."

No. 38. Whereas; "divers contentions, & disputes have happened between Robert, & Isaac Wilson, & Jno Murdaugh, for making an end of sd difference, sd parties by their several bonds dated April 28, 1750 are bounden to the other in the sum of £150 to abide, & keep the final determination" of sd Jos. Robinson, Jos. White, & John Harvey.

No. 39. Jonathan Pearson of Perq, farmer—in con' of £5 pd by Thomas Bagley, of same, planter—sold 15a on lines of sd Pearson, & Aaron Wood. Jan 13, 1750. Test' Samuel Bagley, Aaron Wood.

No. 40. Jacob Hall of Perq, Planter—for "love I bear unto my brothers Wm & Sam'l Hall, do give to sd William my dwelling plan' that did belong to my father Dan'l Hall, & to Sam'l the remaining part of sd land, which my father did by deed of gift divide between my brothers, & myself," Aug 3, 1732. Seal Jan 13, 1750. Test' J. Halsey, Wm Halsey.

No. 41. Feb 28, 1751. George Layden of Perq, Wheelright—for £30 pd by Jacob Mullen of same, sold 50a on Suttons Creek. Test' John Martin, William Layden.

No. 42. Jacob Docton of Perq, for "love, & other causes, have given unto my son-in-law Abner Eason" 50a in Chowan, & part in Perq Co, part of 114a bought of Moses Speight May 21, 1738, the 50a being the "Westermost part of afsd, with all improvements." Oct 21, 1751. Test' J. Halsey, Moses Field.

No. 43. Ann Williams of Perq, in con' of £45 pd by Jno. Harman of afsd, planter—sold 300a on East side of Coltons (Castletons) Creek, adj land of John Murdaugh, Joseph White, & Josiah Gilbert, along the Creek. Sept 7, 1751. Test' Dan'l Saint, Joseph White.

No. 44. Elizabeth Anderson of Perq widow, in con' of "love I bear my dau Abigail Anderson," of same do give 50a at the mouth of Long branch, down to Suttons Creek Swamp. Oct 13, 1751. Test' James Gibson, Joseph Perisho.

No. 45. Robt. Harman of Perq, planter—in con' of "within mentioned grant, truly performed by me Jno. Williams" of same, Blacksmith—, sd Robt, & Elizabeth Harman sold 175a on west side of Yeopim Creek, adj John Stepney, down the branch to "Beaver Cove" swamp. Aug 13, 1751. Test' John Callaway, John Harman.

No. 46. Thomas Lillie of Perq, for £8 & 120a of land, pd by Joseph Lillie of afsd, sold 50a in "Piney Woods," on line of Isaac Wilson, & Dan'l Snuke, to main Co road. Sept 8, 1750. Test' Nicholas Stallings, Alex Farqaharson.

No. 47. John Harmon, Weaver—of Perq, for £40 pd by Dan'l Saint, carpenter—of afsd sold 80a called "pond land," part of patent to sd Harmon Mar 6, 1740, adj Ralph Boazman, & Wm Phelps, to line of Jonathan Sharrad, & Benj Wilson. Sept 7, 1751.

No. 48. Elizabeth Anderson, for "love I bear my son Samuel Anderson" of Perq, do give 150a, on Suttons Creek Swamp, on upper side thereof, near the bridge, "being half of a patent to Samuel Nicholson," adj Anderson Woodley. Oct 19, 1751. Test' James Gibson, Joseph Perisho.

No. 49. Elizabeth Anderson, for "love I bear my son John Anderson" of Perq, do give 150a, on the "other side of Suttons Creek," near the bridge, on Nathaniel Albertsons line, down the Swamp, on the East side, "being the upper part of land granted to Samuel Nicholson." Oct 19, 1751. Test' James Gibson, Joseph Perisho.

No. 50. Robert Cox, of Perq, Planter—for £10 pd by Benjamin Munden Jr, do grant to William Hasket planter, of afsd—90a in "Fork Swamp," on line of James Parker. Dec 11, 1751. Test' Benjamin Munden, John Weeks.

No. 51. William Moore, of Perq, for £100 pd by Dempsey Conner, of afsd, sold 50a in sd Co. Oct 19, 1748. Test' Robt Newby, Thos Newby, Wm Wilson.

No. 52. Joel Hollowell of Perq, farmer—for £2 s7 pd by Moses Field, of same, sold 50a on sd Fields line. Dec 17, 1751. Test' Nicholas Stallings, Reubin Field, Elias Stallings.

No. 53. John Davis of Perq, for £15 pd by Thomas Newby of afsd, sold 75a on So West Side of Perq River, at the mouth of "Reedy Branch," sd land grt to Sam'l Bond dec, & passed by sd Bond to Henry Grace, & by sd Grace to John Hudler, & by sd Hudler to Thos Blitchenden, & by him given to Edward Rice, & from sd Rice to me. Feb 19, 1752. Test' Evan Jones, Jonathan Sherod Jun, Joseph Murdaugh.

No. 54. Oct 15, 1752. Thomas Burket, & Mary his wife, for £26 s9 pd by Joseph White, sold 141a patented Nov 22, 1714 by Jonathan Evans, father of sd Mary, in the fork of Castletons Creek 170½a. Test' Joseph Barrow Jr, Thomas Nichols.

No. 55. Joseph Elliott of Perq, planter—& Hannah his wife, for £35 pd by James Elliott of afsd, planter—sold 50a on east side of Bosses (Vosses) Creek, adj Mary Elliotts plan', "on Joseph Newbys Mill Pond, on sd Creek Swamp, known by the name of "Bee branch" 200a which was grt unto Susanna Hunt Oct 31, 1695." Seal May 23, 1752. Test' Joseph Elliott, Jacob Wilson, Penninah Wilson.

No. 56. May 28. 1752. Thomas Long of Perq, "the younger"—for £100 pd by John Harvey Planter—sold 100a on No East Side of Cypress Swamp, adj lands of sd Harvey, & Thomas Nowcome dec, formerly in possession of John Bentley, William Barrow, & John Williams, "patented by sd Williams Nov 11, 1719, & by deed Sept 2, 1721 conveyed, to Thos Long dec, gr-father of sd Thomas the younger, who by his will conveyed same to son Joshua Long, & he in his will bequeathed it to his son Thos Long." Test' Jeremiah Pratt, William Skinner.

No. 57. Oct 4, 1752. Charles Jordan of Chowan, planter—to Benj Harvey of Perq for £22 s10 sold 100a in Perq Co, on So-W-Side of Perq River, adj sd Harvey, up the River to a small cove, near the upper end of plan' called "Fosters old field," being part of tract "grt unto John Pettiver Dec 10, 1720," & conveyed by him to John Goodwin of Chowan July 17, 1731, by sd Goodwin conveyed unto sd Jordan. Oct 19, 1732. Test' Jno Clayton Jun, Thos Nichols.

No. 58. John Murdaugh of Perq, for £7 s10 pd by Joseph White, of afsd, sold 50a on No East side of Perq River, to Castletons Creek. June 24, 1752. Test' Joseph Saunders, Thomas Pierce.

No. 59. Zach Nixon of Perq, for £35 s12 p6 pd by Joshua Davis of afsd, sold 190a on No East Side of Vosses Creek, at the mouth of a branch issuing out of sd Creek Swamp, & down the Creek to line of Joseph Newby, from sd line to "Bee pond Swamp." Jan 30, 1751. Test' Zachariah Morris, Samuel Moore.

No. 60. John Hudson of Perq, for "love I bear my brother Uriah Hudson" of afsd, do give plan' whereon my sd brother now lives, same being" grt unto Eziekiel Maudlin June 20, 1703, & was conveyed by him to Timothy Clare April 26, 1705, & was conveyed by Hannah Bundy (his daughter) unto my father John Hudson, July 29, 1729." 130a. Jan 5, 1753. Test' Davenport Goodwin, Mary Hudson.

No. 61. John Winslow Sen of Perq for "love unto my son John Jun, have given tract of land whereon I now live," at the mouth of "Great branch" on line of Thos White, to Creek Swamp. 4d 1mo 1753. Test' Joseph White, Jacob Elliott, Joshua White.

No. 62. Thomas Docton of Perq, for "love I bear my son Jacob" of afsd, have given 220a on my head line. July 16, 1752. Test' Joshua Hubbard, Abner Eason.

No. 63. Benjamin Elliott, (son of Moses of Perq) for £25 pd by Benj Elliott (son of Thomas dec) of afsd, sold 75a on the mouth of Vosses Creek, part of tract "whereon Moses Elliott my father now lives," & given by will of Timothy Clare to his dau Hannah, & descended to sd Benj Elliott, heir-at-law of sd Hannah. Jan 11, 1753. Test' Wm Flenry, Thos Bagley.

No. 64. Moses & Benjamin Elliott (my son) of Perq, for £32 pd by Benjamin Elliot Sen of afsd, sold 125a on north side of Vosses Creek. Sept 16, 1752. Test' Jacob Elliott, Joseph Ratliff.

No. 65. William Trumball of Perq, farmer—for £50 pd by Joshua Barclift of afsd, farmer—sold 75a adj land where sd Trumball lives. Oct 4, 1752. Test' James Gibson, Joseph Hosea.

No. 66. Feb 13, 1752. John Hosea of Pasquotank, planter—to Francis Layden of Perq, planter—for £60 sold 210a on So East Side of Deep Creek, adj Albert Albertson, John Barclift, & James Foster, "part of 260a grt unto Thomas Commander, Dec 6, 1720, & by him conveyed to Robert Hosea Oct 8, 1723, & from sd Robert to his son Robert by deed of gift April 21, 1735, & from sd Robert to his brother William Hosea Jan 14, 1741, & from sd William to his brother Abraham Hosea Oct 20, 1745, & from sd Abraham to Joseph Hosea, & from him to sd John." Mar 27, 1753.

No. 67. George Eason of Perq, for £33 s15 pd by Moses Barber of afsd, sold 100a, on lines of Francis Foster, Nathaniel Nicholson, Wm. Bogue, & John Henby, sd land sold to sd Eason by Edward Maudlin Jan 14, 1742, & was sold to sd Maudlin by Samuel Charles July 6, 1734. Seal Aug 15, 1752. Test' Abner Eason Jun, James Price, Simon Stallings.

No. 68. John Blitchenden of Perq, for £30 pd by Benjamin Wilson, sold 70a "part of a grt unto Samuel Bond dec, & by deed of sd Bond to Henry Grace, & by sd Grace to my father Thomas Blitchenden, & from him to William Blitchenden, & from sd William to me." Mar 31, 1752. Test' Joseph Winslow, Joseph Saunders, Joseph Elliott.

No. 69. Joseph Riddick of Perq, unto Robert Riddick of afsd, plan' whereon "he now lives, on the River Swamp, called "Hoosing pine branch," also my right to land betwixt us brothers," formerly patented by Thos Speight dec, to a run called Deep run, pat July 20, 1717, 275a. Jan 12, 1753. Test' John Hollowell, Jesse Eason.

No. 70. Robt Riddick of Perq, unto Joseph Riddick of afsd, all my right to land whereon he now lives, adj a line betwixt us, Jan 12, 1753. Test' John Hollowell, Jesse Eason.

No. 71. Thomas Knowles, & Elizabeth his Wife of Perq, for £5 pd by Adam Knowles, of afsd. sold 50a on So West Side of Little River, at the head of Sheltons Gut part of a grt unto "Richard Whedbee Sept 27, 1715." Seal Mar 10, 1752. Test' James Peirce, John Turner, Sarah Turner.

No. 72. Thomas White of Perq, for £20 pd by John Winslow Jr of afsd, sold 200a between sd Thomas, & John Winslow, "land that was given to sd Thomas by the will of Timothy Clare, & was granted to sd Clare April 15, 1720." Seal 4d 1mo 1753. Test' Joseph White, Joshua White, Joseph Murdaugh.

No. 73. Michael Smith of Perq, planter—for £12 pd by James Smith of afsd, planter—sold 50a adj Thos Smith, to a branch at the head of Sewells Creek, part of land formerly Jos. Jessops. Jan 12, 1735. Test' William Sanders, Abraham Jordan.

74. Moses Field, & James Price of Perq, Exors of the last will of James Field dec'd, in con' of £20 pd by Joseph Riddick & Robert Riddick, do sell 250a on the north side of Perq River, at the mouth of Deep run, a patent for 210a July 20, 1717. Seal April 18, 1752. Test' Benjamin Wilson, Abraham Wilson.

No. 75. Zach Nixon of Perq, for £34 s7 p6 pd by Zachariah Morris of afsd, sold 190a on No East Side of Vosses Creek swamp, on line of Job Hendricks, between sd Morris, & Joshua Davis, being conveyed out of his patent by Francis Toms in year 1716 for 100a, and the other by Zach Nixon, in 1731. 13d 11mo 1751/2. Test' Samuel Moore, Joshua Davis.

No. 76. April 21, 1752. Joseph Hosea of Pasq, to John Hosea of afsd, for £60 sold 210a in Perq, on So Side of Deep Creek, adj Albert Albertson. Test' Francis Layden, James Peirce.

No. 77. Moses Field of Perq, for £2 s3 pd by Joel Hollowell of afsd, sold 25a on sd Moses line. Feb 21, 1752. Test' Nicholas Stallings, Reubin Field, Elias Stallings.

No. 78. Jan 10, 1752. Nicholas Stallings of Chowan Co to Hardy Hunter of same, for £18 sold 65a in Perq on So Side of "Basses Swamp," one half of 130a Wm Hunter bought of Andrew Woodley July 15, 1743, & by him given to his son Nicholas, & by sd Nicholas Hunter was conveyed to Hardy Hunter. Test' Elisha Hunter, Sarah Hunter, William Hunter.

No. 79. Aug 29, 1752. Edmund Hatch of Perq, planter—for £50 pd by James Houghton, of Chowan, sold 150a in Perq, adj Mr. William Halsey, & Mr Jas Eggerton dec, one half of land bought by Mr Charles Blount of sd Eggerton, & conveyed to sd Hatch. Test' William Halsey, Joseph Champion.

No. 80. Feb 12, 1752. Samuel Wyatt, & Jacob Wyatt of Perq, Planters— for £60 pd by Robt Roe, of Chowan, Hatter—sold 250a in Perq, "land sd Samuel did give to his son Jacob." Test' Walter Kippen, Edmund Hatch.

No. 81. Solomon Smith, for £5 pd by Francis Penrice, of Perq, sold 100a on Yeopim Creek, adj Wm Long, & John Smith, sd land "left to me by my father James Smith." Mar 13, 1752. Test' Edward Penrice Jun, William Arrenton.

No. 82. Thomas Docton of Perq, for "love I do bear my gr-son James Price of afsd, do grant the privilege to cut, fall, sow, clear, where he shall see fit, on a piece of land on north side of Indian Branch, at the mouth thereof, & after my death I do give sd land to him forever." April 11, 1752. Test' Joshua Hubbard, Sarah Field.

No. 83. Ann Caruthers widow, in Perq, for £55 pd by John Caruthers, of afsd, sold 50a on "Roanoke Cahukey Swamp," adj sd John. May 14, 1751. Test' James Caruthers Jun, James Joneston.

No. 84. Sept 18, 1752. James Luten of Edenton, for £100 pd by Thomas Bonner, of Chowan Co, sold 300a on north side of Yeopim River in Perq Co, sd land purchased Dec 7, 1750, from Henry Warren. Test' Edmund Hatch, Thomas Bonner.

No. 85. Joseph Hosea of Perq, farmer—for £10 pd by Francis Layden, of afsd, farmer—sold 50a on South side of Deep Creek, adj Jas Foster. April 16, 1753. Test' James Gibson, Richd Clayton.

No. 86. John Winslow Jun, of Perq, planter—for £30 pd by Israel Winslow, of afsd planter—sold 100a on No East Side of Newbegun Creek, "at the mouth of a branch & running up into the dismal." Feb 26, 1753. Test' Thomas Winslow, Thomas White Jun, Rachel White.

No. 87. Mar 1, 1735. Charles Blount of Chowan Co, for £40 pd by Joseph Harron, of afsd, sold 30a called "Batts Grave," at the mouth of Yeopim River, on the "No Side of Albemarle Sound, with all houses, orchards, &c." Test' Jos Blount, Eliz'th Blount, William Reed.

No. 88. Thomas Hollowell of Perq, Yeoman—for £3 s7 p6 pd by Peter Draper, Yeoman—of afsd, sold 150a at the "Drinking Pond," on the mouth of "Plum Tree" branch, to the middle of Fork Swamp. April 16, 1753. Test' ———————.

No. 89. John Ashley of Perq, for £50 pd by Joseph Ashley, sold 144a on the East side of Yeopim Creek, "which my mother Sarah Ashley gave me," on line of Dan'l Saint, near a branch that comes out of "Chestons Cove," & down the branch to the middle of the Cove, to a tree on the old Road. Nov 21, 1751, Test' William Halsey, John Calloway.

No. 90. April 6, 1753. Alexander McClellan, of Perq, for £17 pd by Jacob Powell, sold 50a on No Side of Perq River, at the mouth of Deep branch, to a line that divides sd land from Thomas Lillies. Test' John Hollowell, Joseph Riddick, Josiah Granberry.

No. 91. June 23, 1753. Lords Pro' to Joseph Perisho of Perq, planter—for s3, paid by sd Perishaw, doth grant 65a, in the "Parish of Berkeley, Co of Perq," adj John Anderson, & sd Perishaw. E. Moseley. Robt Halton.

No. 92. Joseph Perrishaw, of Berkley Parish, in Co of Perq, planter—for £9 s15 pd by William Bateman, of same, planter—assigns "so granted premises." Nov. 3, 1752. Test' Thomas Weeks, John Weeks, Thos Weeks Jr, Joseph Weeks.

No. 93. Thomas Jessop, of Cartright Co (Carteret) farmer—for £5 s1 pd by Joseph Winslow sen, sold 64a on Newbegun Creek, & "Thomas Whites Mill swamp, at a place called New Neck, where Joseph Winslow lately lived, to empower Pleasant Winslow relict of sd Joseph dec, to make proper conveyance, as her late husband sold part of sd land; therefore do give unto sd Pleasant land on No East side of Perq River 640a, according to patent." 17d 3mo 1753. Test' William White, Joseph Mayo, Joseph Winslow.

No. 94. Pleasant Winslow (widow, & relict, of Joseph), of Perq, in Con' of a "mistake made in a deed Mar 5, 1744/5 proved to be the now piece of land sold to my late husband, by Thomas Jessop, sd Jessop for regulating sd mistake hath made proper deed, for right of land to Pleasant Winslow, my late husband having sold 160a of the right land, being the upper part to me granted, for £40 pd by John Griffin, I do hereby acquit sd Griffin, & confirm unto him sd land, conveyed by sd Jessop to me." April 16, 1753. Test' John Winslow, Ben'j Elliott, Joshua Perisho.

No. 95. Pleasant Winslow, in con' of a "mistake made by my husband Jos. Winslow, & for regulating sd mistake" (he having disposed of 100a of right land, to Timothy Winslow, for £3, Jan 16, 1748/9, & by sd Timothy given to his son Obed in his will, April 26, 1752) I do hereby sell unto sd Obed Winslow 100a called "Hickory Neck," adj John Griffin, part of land bought of Thomas Jessop." April 16, 1753. Test' John Winslow, Benjamin Elliott, Joshua Perisho.

No. 96. Pleasant Winslow, for "love I do bear towards my dau Miriam Winslow," have given 200a of Woodland called "Grassy Ridge" given to her in her fathers will Sept 26, 1750, & since in my power to confirm sd gift." April 16, 1753. Test' John Winslow, Joshua Perisho, John Griffin.

No. 97. Joseph Elliott of Perq, planter—for "brotherly love I do bear to my brother Thos Elliott, & for just intentions of my dec'd father Thomas Elliott of afsd, have given 87a on So West side of Little River, on fork swamp, up sd swamp to Long Branch, land formerly William Boswells." May 4, 1752. Test' Joshua Elliott, Jos Elliott, Thos Elliott.

No. 98. George Eason Sen, of Perq, for £30 pd by George Spivey of Chowan, planter—sold 128a, surveyed by sd Eason, & patented June 28, 1748 on the River Swamp. Dec. 11, 1752. Test' George Eason, Joshua Hobart, Sarah Field.

No. 99. April 16, 1753. Francis Penrice of Perq, planter—for £10 pd by James Sutton, of afsd, sold 100a on the Sound side, adj Wm Long, & John Smith, purchased of Soloman Smith Mar 1, 1752. His father James Smith. Test' John Harvey, Charles Blount.

No. 100. John Chancey of Bladen Co, for £125 pd by Charles Jordan Jr, of Perq, conveyed 260a of high land, & 40a of marsh, at the mouth of "wolf pit branch" on line of Jonathan Phelps, "a patent to John Pritlow year 1668." April 17, 1753. Test' Joseph White, Samuel Sitterson, John Murdaugh.

No. 101. Nov 6, 1752. John Hunter of Perq, in con' of £25 pd by John Gordon Jr, of Chowan Co, doth sell 65a in Perq on North Side of "Horse pool Swamp," patented by William Woodley June 4, 1703, & sold by him to William Hunter, July 15, 1743, sd land bequeathed by sd William Hunter to his son John, in his will, adj his brother Nicholas Hunter, which is part of afsd patent. Test' Josiah Granbery Jun, George Gordon.

No. 102. Hardy Hunter of Perq, planter—for £32 s55 pd by Moses Eason, of afsd, sold 65a on "Basses branch," adj John Gordon, to line of Thomas Fullerton, crossing sd swamp, & down swamp to the main desert. Feb 2, 1753. Test' George Eason, John Price Jr.

No. 103. Sarah Sutton of Perq, for £12 s10 pd by Henry Hall, of afsd, sold 62a which fell to sd Sarah by co-heirship from Richard Sutton dec. April 16, 1753. Test' Joshua Skinner, John Perry.

No. 104. Susannah Sutton of Perq, for £12 s10 pd by Henry Hall, sold 62a which fell to sd Susannah, by the death of Richard Sutton. April 16, 1753. Test' Joshua Skinner, John Perry.

No. 105. John Stepney of Perq, for £20 pd by Robert Roe, Hatter—of afsd, sold 150a "given me in my fathers will," on the So Wt side of Yeopim Creek, at the mouth of "Greens Swamp," adj sd Roe. May 28, 1753. Test' William Wyatt, Jacob Wyatt, John Calloway.

No. 106. William Hall, & Jacob Hall, the one of Perq, and the other of Johnston Co, for £40, pd by Thomas Long, sold 250a on Indian Creek in

Perq Co, called "Mill Swamp," adj Mr. Richard French, grt to Daniel Hall of Perq Aug 16, 1716, & by him "given to his three sons William, Samuel, & Jacob," & sd William made purchase of sd Samuel 90a, the whole 160a. Mar 12, 1753. Test' J. Halsey, Mary Halsey, John Smith Jun.

No. 107. Eliz'th Binford, & John Binford my son, of Charles City Co, in Vir, for £75, pd by Samuel Moore, of Perq Co, in N. C. planter—sold 150a on No East Side of Perq River, adj Joseph Ratliff, & on No East side of Seth Sumner, which formerly belonged to James Anderson. June 9, 1753. Test' Aaron Morris, Joshua Perisho, Jno. Outland.

No. 108. Joseph Creecy of Perq, farmer—for £3 s4 pd by Sarah Branch, widow of Isacher dec, sold to sd Sarahs three sons, Arkil, Isacher, & Joel Branch, 150a "in the edge of a Savannah near the head of Pitch hole branch, to forked branch." July 11, 1743. Test' Sarah Callaway, Jos. Ming, James Eggerton.

No. 109. Joseph Hosea of Perq, Bricklayer—for £50 pd by William Trumball, of afsd, Farmer—sold 50a "where sd Trumball now lives," on the head of Lillies Creek, adj Thos Holloway. July 10, 1753. Test' James Gibson, Sarah Barclift.

No. 110. Elizabeth Caruthers of Perq have "after my decease given unto my cousin Nathaniel Caruthers (son of Jacob, & Ann his wife) plan' whereon I now live" 100a on north side of Yeopim River, adj Jacob Caruthers Sen, & Mr Thos Hicks, "if sd Nathaniel should die without issue, I give same to Jacob Caruthers, or next male heir by Ann his wife." Feb 20, 1753. Test' Thomas Bonner, Richd Clemens, Elizabeth Wilkins.

No. 111. William Wilson of Perq, for £15 pd by Joseph Riddick, of afsd, sold 50a on South west side of Ballahack Swamp, on sd Josephs line, a patent to Zach Chancey Mar 6, 1740. Seal Oct 13, 1753.

No. 112. Elizabeth Pratt widow, of Perq Co—for "love I bear toward my children, have given. To Mary Pratt 1 negro called Will, To Deborah Pratt 1 negro called Jack, To Richd Pratt 1 negro called Welcome, To Joseph Pratt 1 negro called Tony, at the day of my death." Sept 12, 1753. Test' Joseph Creecy Jun, John Stepney.

No. 113. Moses Elliott, planter—of Perq, for £2 s17 p6 pd by my Brother Benj Elliott, of afsd, "convey all right of plan' whereon I live" 75a part of 200a which has been made over to him, by deed from myself, & son Benj, on North west side of Vosses Creek. Mar 27, 1753. Test' Joseph Ratliff, Mary Ratliff.

No. 114. Humphrey Griffin Sr, of upper Parish of Nansemond Co, Vir, for £10 pd by John Wallburton, of Chowan Co, N. C. sold land in Perq, on Ming (Minge) Creek, between settlement made by Ephraditus Brinkley, & line of Joseph Burket, sd land given sd Burket, by his father John Burket, & was conveyed by sd Joseph, to me April 15, 1733. Seal Sept. 29, 1753. Humphrey & Martha Griffin. Test' Elizabeth Griffin, Joseph Griffin.

No. 115. May 3, 1753. George Parsons, of Berkeley Parish, Perq Co, planter —for 9 Barrels of pork, pd by Abraham Mullen, of same, planter—sold 50a on No East Side of Perq River, "part of 356a grt to Richard Whidbee, Oct 19 1716" one half of which sd Whidbee, sold to Samuel Parsons, father of sd George, John, & Mary Parsons. Test' Thos Weeks, Abraham Riggs.

No. 116. Oct 12, 1753. Elihu Albertson, of Perq, planter—for £15 pd by Edward Turner Sr, of same—sold 125a "on branches of Deep Creek," out of the south-west side of Little River, surveyed by John Clayton Esq, Dept surveyor of sd Co. Test' Thos Weeks, William Weeks.

No. 117. Sept 18, 1753. Moses Davis, in Craven Co, N. C. for £35 pd by Joseph Hurdle of Perq, sold 175a on the main desert, & Long Branch, in Perq, & Chowan Co, part of land Thomas Davis, bought of Thomas Docton, April 19, 1722, & came to sd Moses by the death of his father sd Thomas. Test' Josiah Granbery, Jr, Hardy Hurdle, Thomas Coffield.

No. 118. Thomas Eason of Perq, for "love I bear my son William" of afsd—have given 175a on the main desert, south of my plan' adj "patten of John Perry." Test' Nicholas Stallings Jr, Jas Eason, Hardy Hurdle. Oct 10, 1753.

No. 119. A. Thomas Lamb of Perq, planter—for £9 s10 pd by William Wilson, of afsd—sold 50a on So Wt side of Perq River, which runs to Cypress Creek, between Henry, & Thos Lamb. July 16, 1753. Test' Samuel Sitterson, Ben Scarbrough.

No. 119. B. Mar 29, 1753. John Jones of Perq, planter—for £25 pd by Moses Baker, of afsd—sold 150a called "Mill branch" given me by my father Peter Jones, by him patented. Oct 19, 1716, whereon he did live." Test' Dan'l Barber, William White, Joseph Gilbert.

No. 120. William Middleton of Perq, farmer—& Sarah his wife, for "love we bear our son Joseph Arnold" of same—do give 110a on west side of Little River, pt of a tract, formerly belonging to Lawrence Arnold, adj Edward Dowdy, Edward Turner, & Elihu Albertson. Jan 17, 1754. Test' Samuel Parsons, Gabriel Cosand.

No. 121. Thomas Lane of Perq, planter—for £6 pd by James Sitterson, of afsd—Carpenter—sold 52½a, on West side of the Road, adj Mary Barker. Test' Ephrim Elliott, Samuel Sitterson. Sept 28, 1753.

No. 122. Samuel Newby of Pery, planter—for £70 pd by Francis Jones, of afsd—sold 50a on West side of Perq River, at the "old footway, going to the Island" on the edge of the Swamp, near the mouth of "Holloways Point." June 24, 1753. Test' Robt Newby, Wm Newby, James Townsen.

No. 123. Jan 15, 1754. William Middleton, & Sarah his wife, of Berkeley Parish, Perq Co, for £4 s13 pd by Elihu Albertson, of some—sold 440a, on line of Edward Dowdie, & Edward Turner, a grt to Lawrence Arnold. Test' Samuel Parsons, Gabriel Cosand.

No. 124. Jan 9, 1754. William Blitchenden, for £15 pd by Abraham Wilson, sold 20a near the corner of "Edwards old field, in Mulberry Swamp" adj Joseph Smith, & sd Wilson. Test' Joseph Murdaugh, Thomas Small.

No. 125. Aaron Wood of Pasq Co, planter—for £30 pd by Dan'l Saint, of Perq, Carpenter—sold 70a, on North East Side of Perq River, & Pocoson, patented by Rich'd Cheston Sr, year 1694, 50a of which was sold to Wm Bogue, Oct. 14, 1718, left in his will, to his dau Miriam, now wife of Gideon Bundy, who sold sd land to me. The other 20a conveyed to me by Thos Bagley. Jan 20, 1754.

No. 126. Pursuant to the will of Truman Moore, we have marked trees, on the "Manor lands," for a division, between sons of sd Truman; adj Pleasant Winslow, & William White. 18, 7mo 1754. John Moore, Wm White, Daniel Saint.

No. 127. April 1, 1754. Michael Lawrence, & Susannah his wife, for £20 s10, pd by Lemuel Riddick, sold 200a on "Loosing Swamp" in Chowan Co, & Perq, called "Mount Jolly" sd Susannah being the dau of Susannah Larcomb, late of Nansemond Co, in Vir, dec'd, division having been made between sd Susannah, & her sister Elizabeth, late wife of Hugh Morton dec'd. Test' Josiah Granbery, Jethro Darden.

No. 128. William Long of Perq, planter—for £13 s10 pd by Joshua Skinner, Exor of Est of John Felt dec'd, "do sell to Job Felt (a minor) son of sd John, 240a adj Edward Wilson, a grant to John Pettiver April 1, 1723" & by him elapsed, & was grt to sd Long Aug 4, 1726, & sold by him to sd Felt, which was never pd, & deed never executed. April 15, 1754. Test' Wm Wyatt, John Swain.

No. 129. Articles of agreement, between John Griffin, & Uriah Hudson, (over a division of land) have consented to allow William White, & Thomas Newby, to make division, & "do bind ourselves in the sum of £50, never to disturb, or molest each other, in the quiet possession of what is their side of the line laid out" Mar 4, 1754. Test' Thomas Newby, John Murdaugh.

No. 130. Hannah Sitterson of Perq, for "love I bear my son Samuel, have given 75a whereon he now lives" formerly held by Wm Phelps, & Ralph Boazman, adj William Townsend. Aug 24, 1753. Test' Jos White, Thos Bullock, John White.

No. 131. Henry Hall of Perq, planter—for "love I bear my son Edward," of afsd, planter—have given 125a, called "Lazy Point" adj land whereon I now live. Test' Joshua Skinner, Sarah Skinner. July 11, 1754.

No. 132. July 13, 1754. Samuel Charles of Perq, planter—for £14 pd by William Foster, of same, planter—sold 396a, the Southermost part of a grt to my gr-father, along Whedbees line. Test' John Whedbee, Richd Whedbee.

No. 133. Joshua Elliott of Perq, planter—for £11 s5 pd by Joseph Winslow, of same, planter—sold 30a, adj Jonathan Sherwood, Benjamin Wilson, & Joseph White. Test' Joseph Elliott, Thos Elliott. July 15, 1754.

No. 134. Thomas Wiggins of Chowan, & Christian his wife, for £40 pd by Willis Wilson, of Isle of Wight Co, Vir, sold 100a in Perq, according to its most "ancient bounds." Test' Robert Fry, John Twine. Narhan'l Field, Edmund Godwin.

No. 135. Samuel Sitterson of Perq, for £25 pd by William Townsend, of afsd, sold 75a between my brother James, & sd Townsend, patented by Daniel Snooks, Feb 25, 1696, & sold by sd Snooks to Edward Holmes, & by sd Holmes to John Lilly, & by sd Lilly dec'd, bequeathed to his daus Sarah, & Hannah Sitterson, sd land given me by my father James Sitterson, in his will. Aug 24, 1753. Test' Will Skinner, Thos Small, Charles Jordan.

No. 136. William Hollowell of Perq, for £55 pd by Abner Hollowell, of afsd—sold 130a on No East Side of Pocoson, running to Juniper Swamp, adj Rountree, & Field. Test' Nicholas Stallings, Moses Field, Sarah Field. Sept 2, 1754.

No. 137. Joseph Griffin of Chowan, for £3 pd by Jacob Perry Sr, of Perq, sold 50a "at a Marsh on So Side of Hickory Branch." Oct 21, 1754. Test' Jonathan Phelps, Francis Nixon.

No. 138. Oct 19, 1754. Mary Henby of Perq, for £18 pd by Gideon Maudlin, of afsd, farmer—sold 143a near Suttons Creek, "patented by John Henby, year 1741, 587a, & was divided between my self, & brother Sylvanus Henby, by our fathers will, 5, 3mo 1752, this being the lower part of sd land." Test' Sylvanus Henby, Joseph Barber, John Maudlin.

RECORDS OF DEEDS 163

No. 139. John Hollowell, of Perq, planter—for £6 pd by Joseph Perry, of afsd—sold 35a, part of a patent, to William Kitchen, 1719, adj John Hollowell, and Timothy Clare. Test' Joseph Winslow, Mary Perry. Oct. 14, 1754.

No. 140. July 29, 1754. John Jackson, of Tyrrel Co, St Andrews Parish, planter—for £22 pd by Charles Taylor, of Perq, Berkeley Parish, planter—sold 80a, on West Side of Little River, in Perq Co, & sd Berkeley Parish, part of 437a grt to Joseph, & John Robinson, Mar 25, 1750, & sold by them to me, & my wife Sarah, & William Magorm, & wife Francis, Oct 13, 1750. Test' William Weeks, Jeremiah Hendricks.

No. 141. John Lasey of Perq, planter—for £30 pd by John Stone, Carpenter, & his brother William Stone, planter—of afsd, sold 100a on north west side of Vosses Creek, adj Benj Elliott, Abraham Haskett, & Mary Kenyon, widow of John, "being land on which John Stone dec'd, dwelt," & gave to his sons, John & William Stone. Test' Jacob Elliott, James Elliott, Joseph Ratliff. Aug 17, 1754.

No. 142. Jacob Perry Sr, of Perq, for £3 pd by Israel Perry, of afsd—sold part of a tract of land, on "Tongue of Reeds" adj sd Jacob, & Joseph Griffin. Test' Jonathan Phelps, Francis Nixon. Oct Court, 1754.

No. 143. Dec 31, 1754. John Barclift, son of William, of Perq, planter—for £70 pd by Capt Joseph Wilson, "of White Haven, in Cumberland, in Great Brittain, Mariner"—sold 100a in Perq, on So West side of Little River, adj John Arnold dec'd. Test' Daniel Saint, Francis Nixon.

No. 144. William Trumball of Perq, farmer—for £40 pd by John Stanton, of afsd—farmer, sold 50a at the head of Lillies Creek, adj John Holloway. Test' John Holloway, Jonathan Sharbo. Feb 15, 1754.

No. 145. Lemuel Snoden of Perq, farmer—for s17 p6 pd by John Barclift, of same, farmer—sold 36½a, on west side of Little River, adj Thos Barclift. Test' Francis Layden, Tulle Williams. Jan 8, 1755.

No. 146. Dec 24, 1754. John Riddick of Perq, for £89 pd by John Twine, of afsd—sold 100a on So West Side of Perq River, down to River Swamp, part of 450a grt to William Kitchen, April 1, 1713, & by him given to Daniel Rogerson, June 15, 173—, & by sd Rogerson, sold to Martin Asbell, Jan 13, 1732, which descended by his death to his son Pierce Asbell, who sold sd land to sd Riddock. Test' Jas Norfleet, Luke Sumner.

No. 147. Oct 30, 1754. Abraham Blitchenden, planter—for £5 pd by Thomas Newby, Merchant—sold 100a on So West Side of Perq River, at the mouth of Mulberry Swamp, & the edge of the woods, running to "Drinking Hole Swamp," adj sd Newby, & Abraham Wilson. Test' Joseph Murdaugh, Thos Small, Luke Sumner.

No. 148. Reuben Field, & Sarah his wife, for £100 pd by Joshua White, of Perq, sold 330a in the mouth of "Reedy Branch" adj Elias Stallings, & Moses Field, 500a of which was grt to William Hollowell, June 9, 1748, & 200a to Thomas Winslow, 1719. Seal Mar 6, 1755. Test' Nichols Stallings, Josh'a White, Wm Harris.

No. 149. Moses, & Ann Field of Perq, for £50 pd by John White, (son of Thomas) of afsd—sold 50a in the mouth of a branch, issuing out of the north side of Cypress Swamp, adj Joel Hollowell. Mar 6, 1755. Test' Nicholas Stallings, Josh'a White, Wm Harris.

No. 150. Feb 28, 1755. John Holloway of Perq, planter—for £40 pd by Charles Blount, of Edenton, sold 200a in Perq, patented by my father Thos Holloway, adj Mr Jas Gibson, Mr. Thos Godfrey, & Mr John Barclift. Test' Jas. Pierce, John Blount.

No. 151. April 21, 1755. Joshua Maudlin of Perq, planter—for £65 pd by Charles Blount, of Edenton, sold 80a, adj Tully Williams, & sd Maudlin. Test' Ben Harvey, Jno Weeks.

No. 152. April 5, 1755. William Blitchenden, for £65 pd by Thomas Newby, Merch't sold 60a on So West side of Perq River, adj Sam'l Bond, John Smith, & Abraham Willson. Test' Sam'l Bond, Sarah Newby.

No. 153. Phenias Nixon of Perq, farmer—for s25 pd by Thos Overman, of afsd—sold 50a on the head of his plan' a patent to sd Nixon. 16, 4mo 1755. Test' Thos Nicholson, Sam'l Bentley, Josiah Bundy.

No. 154. Mary Winslow (relict of John, late of Perq) for "love I do bear my children Josiah, Miriam, Thomas, Samuel, Ruth, & John Winslow, do give to each, a cow, & calf, to be delivered when them come of age, or marry." Test' Joseph Robinson, John Robinson, Joshua Morris. 16-4mo 1755.

No. 155. Moses Elliott, & Judith his wife, of Perq, for £20 pd by Moses Barber, of afsd—sold 98a. 47a of which was grt to Abraham Saunders dec'd, & 41a a new patent, sd land "bequeathed to sd Judah Boice." April 22, 1755. Test' Francis Robbins, William Skinner.

No. 156. William Blitchenden, for £3 s15 pd by Thomas Lane, of Perq, sold 30a adj Benjamin Willson, & Abraham Blitchenden. June 8, 1754. Test' James Sitterson, Sam'l Sitterson.

No. 157. John Perry, Sadler, of Perq—for £24 s13 pd by Joseph Outland, planter—sold 64a "where I now dwell" on No east Side of Perq River, adj Jos Newby, John Lasey, Samuel Moore, Francis Toms, & sd Outland. Sept 9, 1754. Test' Mary Williams, Joseph Ratliff.

No. 158. John Stone of Perq, planter—for £15 pd by Ben Elliott Sr, of same—sold 40a, on No West Side of Vosses Creek, adj sd Elliott "at the Bear Garden Swamp." Mar 1, 1755. Test' Jos Ratliff, Mary Guyer.

No. 159. Benjamin Elliott of Perq, planter—for £15 pd by John Stone, of same—sold 40a on No West Side of Vosses Creek, at the "mouth of Atkins Swamp," where I now live. Test' Joseph Ratliff, Mary Guyer. Mar 1, 1755.

No. 160. Joseph Blount of Chowan, & Benjamin Scarbrough, of Perq, for £7 pd by John Harvey of Perq, sold one "dwelling house, on the Court House lot, on Phelps Point" which was built, on sd lot by Col Mac Scarbrough dec'd, & in his will directed to be sold, by public Vendue, & sd Blount has since married Elizabeth widow of sd Mac Scarbrough, Benjamin Scarbrough, eldest son of afsd, did sell sd house, unto John Harvey, he being the highest bidder. July 21, 1755. Test' Thos Bonner, Charles Moore. Miles Harvey Clk. John Harvey Reg.

No. 161. Abraham Blitchenden of Perq, for £6 pd by Richard Berryman, sold 30a on So Wt Side of Perq River, adj Evan Jones, & Thos Lane, "by the main drinking hole." Test' Richd Jones, John Hatfield, Wm Blitchenden. Oct 31, 1754.

No. 162. Benjamin Perry, & Elizabeth his wife, for "love we bear our son-in-law Joel Hollowell, & our dau Miriam his wife," do give a negro girl, named Lucy 8 years of age. Mar 3, 1755. Test' Benjamin Perry Jr, Joseph Perry, Nicholas Stallings.

RECORDS OF DEEDS

No. 163. Thomas White of Perq, for "love I bear my son Thomas Jr, of afsd—do give all the land I purchased of Daniel Smith, & Arthur Croxton, adj the land whereon my sd son now lives." 11, 4mo 1755. Test' Joshua White, John White, Joseph Winslow.

No. 164. Thomas White, for "love I bear my son Joseph, of Perq, do give 100a whereon he now lives" 24, 4mo 1755. Test' Joshua White, John White, Joseph Winslow.

No. 165. Thomas Overman of Perq, planter—& Miriam my wife, for "love we do bear our son John do give 75a, part of a patent to Christopher Nicholson, year 1714, & given by him to his dau Miriam, now wife of sd Overman, called "Folly land" at the mouth of Gum Swamp, on Suttons Creek," adj Phenias Nixon. 21, 7mo 1755.

No. 166. Benjamin, & Elizabeth Perry of Perq, for "love we bear our son-in-law John Taylor, & our dau Susannah, his wife, do give one Negro girl, named Dinah 6 years of age, & goods, & chattels in their possession." Mar 3, 1755. Test' Nicholas Stallings, Joseph Perry, Benjamin Perry.

No. 167. Moses Barber, & John Harmon of Perq, for £13 pd by Robert Avery, of afsd, sold 50a "on the main road, that goes to Edenton," adj Moses Elliott, and Abraham Saunders. Test' Charles Jordan, John Murdaugh. July 21, 1755.

No. 168. Jacob Caruthers of Perq, for £15 pd by John Simmons of Chowan, sold 150a on South side of "Jeremiah Pratts Mill Swamp" adj William Woolard. Test' Robt Sumner, Timothy Truelove. July 21, 1755.

No. 169. Benjamin Simpson Sr, of Yeopim, for "love I bear my son Benjamin Jr," do give one half of 106a on North Side of Yeopim River. Feb 17, 1755. Test' Nicholas Williams, John Wallburton.

No. 170. July 21, 1755. Thomas Newby, Merchant, for £65 pd by James Bacon, farmer—sold 80a on So West side of Perq River, adj Samuel Bond, "on Mulberry Branch." Test' Joseph Jordan, Francis Newby.

No. 171. Thomas Overman, & Miriam his wife, for £20 pd by Gabriel Cosand, of afsd, sold 75a, part of a tract, called the "Folly land" a patent to Christopher Nicholson, 1714, & by him given to his dau Miriam, wife of sd Overman, at the mouth of "Horsepen branch" along the main road to Henby's line. Test' Thomas Nicholson, Sarah Barrow, Miriam Nicholson. 21, 7mo 1755.

No. 172. Thomas Overman, for £7 pd by Joseph Jordan, Schoolmaster; of Perq, sold plan' on which sd Overman now dwells, in the fork of the Road, called "Weeks Road" a division between sd Overman, & Williiam Bundy dec'd. 21, 7mo 1755. Test' Thomas Nicholson, Thomas Newby, John Overman.

No. 173. Charles Overman Jr, of Perq, Blacksmith—for an exchange of a plan' with Hannah Boswell, "Widdow of John" in Pasq Co, sold 50a where sd Hannah now lives, on River Pocosin. May 6, 1755. Test' Thos Nicholson, Joseph Jordan, Thomas Overman.

No. 174. Lords Pro' grt unto Robert Wilson, planter, or Perq, for s3 paid, 145a on East side of Perq River. E. Moseley, Robert Halton. Test' William Moore, Truman Moore. Oct Court 1755.

No. 175. Thomas Lane of Perq, planter—for £5 s5 pd by James Sitterson, of afsd, Carpenter—sold 51a in Chowan Co, adj Mary Barker. Oct 14, 1755.

No. 176. Abraham Sanders of Bladen Co N. C. for £33 pd by William Lamb of Perq, sold 190a on So Wt side of Perq River, between lands of

166   HISTORY OF PERQUIMANS COUNTY.

Charles Jordan, & Col John Harvey, to line of John Pritlow. Oct 13, 1755. Test' Joseph White, Jno Sanders, Jno White.

No. 177. George Spivey of Chowan, planter—for £7 s15 pd by Moses Rountree, of Perq, sold tract of land, "which was grt unto George Eason." July 12, 1755. Test' Nicholas Stallings, Abraham Hill.

No. 178. Mary Kenyenon of Perq, for £10 pd by Joshua Hasket of afsd—sold 200a on Cypress Branch, adj Joseph Newby, Robt Bogue, & Edward Maudlin, to the middle of pond Swamp, a grt to Peter Albertson. Feb 19, 1755. Test' Jno Perisho, Sarah Perisho.

No. 179. Benjamin Sanders of Perq, for £17 s15 pd by Sam'l Smith of afsd—sold 34½a adj Joseph, & Joshua Elliott, & Samuel Newby. July 28, 1755. Test' John Smith, Joseph Smith, John Murdaugh.

No. 180. Joshua Elliott of Perq, for £22 s10 pd by Samuel Smith of afsd—sold 50a in "Little Horse Neck" adj Ben Wilson, & Ben Sanders. July 24, 1755. Test' Joseph White, Francis Nixon, Jno Smith.

No. 181. Feb 18, 1755. Lords Pro' grt unto John Perisho of Perq, planter; for s3 pd 235a, "in the Parish of Berkeley, Co of Perq, on No East side of Perq River" adj Joseph Scott. Granville. Francis Corbin. Test' James Campbell, Richard Niger.

No. 182. July 8, 1749. Lords Pro' grt unto Joseph Perisho, for s3 pd 140a on North Side of "Beaver Cove Swamp," Berkeley Parish, Perq Co, "being the surplus land within lines of Francis Toms patent." E. Moseley. Test' Thos Relfe, Jno Clayton.

No. 183. Jan 19, 1753. Lords Pro' grt unto Thomas Hollowell of Perq, 300a in Berkeley Parish, Perq Co, "at a Cypress in the Drinking Pond." Granville. James Innes. Francis Corbin. Test' James Campbell, Benjamin Munden.

No. 184. Jonathan Pearson of Perq, in con' of £35 pd by Samuel Bartlett, late of New England, Mariner—sold 50a on east side of Perq River, adj Thomas Bagley. Jan 19, 1756. Test' Joseph White, Cornelius Moore, Robert Bogue.

No. 185. Oct 14, 1755. Thos. Stafford of Perq, for £30 pd by Enoch Raper (planters) of afsd, sold 70a on branches of Deep Creek, being the "lower part of a tract," adj Elihu Albertson, & Jacob Mullen, across to sd Stafford, near Simon Perisho. Test' Joseph Robinson, Thos. Robinson.

No. 186. Oct 14, 1755. Enoch Raper, planter—of Perq, to Joseph Robinson, Merchant—of afsd, for £40 sold 50a on Sou't side of Little River, "where Christopher Nicholson formerly dwelt, after his death where Wm Bundy dwelt, on a large branch near sd Robinsons house." Test' Wm. Tomblin, Thos. Weeks, T. Roberson.

No. 187. Thos Overman of Perq, for £25 pd by Thos Nicholson of afsd, trader—sold 50a adj "Little River Bridge," sd land sold by Wm Bundy, to sd Overman April 14, 1744, at the mouth of a branch near the Pocosin, to the main public Road, "reserving three small parcels, one for the Meeting house, a deed to my brother Charles, & a deed to Charles Jordan." Thomas, & Miriam Overman. 27d, 11mo 1755. Test' Charles Taylor, John Overman, Christopher Nicholson.

No. 188. Cornelius Moore of Perq, for "love I do bear my brother Gideon," of afsd, have given 116a, adj Wm Bagley dec, "now in possession of Benjamin Maudlin, & Joseph Mayo, near the main Road, plan' where my father John Moore dec'd did live, but if he die without issue, to my brother Joseph, provided

RECORDS OF DEEDS 167

he deliver up land at Ballahack unto my sister Bettie Bartlett." Oct 27, 1755. Test' Benjamin Maudlin, Joseph Mayo, Joseph Ratliff.

No. 189. Cornelius Moore, in con' of love I do bear my brother Joseph, have given 150a in Balahac near sd Swamp, adj William Moore, & if he die to my sister Bettie Bartlett. Oct 27, 1755. Test' Benj Munden, Jos Mayo, Joseph Ratliff.

No. 190. Jonathan Sharbo of Perq, planter—for £25 pd by Thos Weeks of same, sold 100a on So West Side of Little River, adj George Gordon, Thos Weeks, & River Pocosin, "a grt to Wm Jackson Jan 1, 1694," for 312a. Jan 12, 1756. Test' Jno Weeks, Thos Weeks Jun, Rosamond Barclift.

No. 191. Robert Evans Jun, of Perq, planter—for £12 s10 pd by Pleasant Winslow, widow, of same, planter—sold 60a at the East corner of a tract patented by Thos Jessop, "being a Neck, called New Neck." Jan 20, 1756. Test' Jos White, Jos Murdaugh, Francis Toms.

No. 192. George Eason Sen of Perq, in con' of "love I do bear my son George," of afsd, have given 175a on South side of my plan', along a patent I bought of John Perry, to a line between me, & my Brother Thos Eason, dec, & the main Desert. Jan 13, 1756. Test' Jo Riddick, John Hollowell, Robt Riddick.

No. 193. Aug 29, 1747. Jno. Campbell of Edenton, Merchant—to John Stevenson, of Perq, planter—Whereas; Elizabeth Chandler of St Marys Parish, at Lambeth, in Co of Surry, Grt Britian, Widow—dau of Edward Catchmaid dec, only son of Thomas Catchmaid dec, who was brother, & devisee, named in the will of George Catchmaid dec, of Nancemon, in America, who died seized of land called "Birkswear," in Perq Co, N. C. (3333a) by virtue of a "grt April 1, 1663, from Sir Wm Berkeley, Gov of Vir," did by letter of Att', Feb 12, 1738, appoint Henry Winslow, Gent, of London att' to take possession of sd land who did by Gen'l Court, July 1740, recover 850a called "Stevensons point," part of sd land, & sd Elizabeth did "some time after recovery, departed this life," whereby it descended to William Berkeley, of St Pauls, Covent Garden, Co of Middlesex; eldest son of sd Elizabeth, by her former husband John Berkeley dec, & sd Berkeley, did release sd land unto John Humpage, of Gravesend, in Co Kent, & Ann Hinds, of St Helens London Widow—& they did sell same to George Low, of London, & sd Low did appoint John Campbell, Att' to dispose of sd land, for a Val' con' unto John Stevenson, for £25. Test' Jos. Anderson, John Nichols, Joseph Sutton.

No. 194. Joseph Sanders, & Mary his wife, in Perq, for £11 pd by Samuel Newby, of afsd, sold 52a of woodland, on Wst side of Perq River, between Benjamin, & Joseph Sanders, adj Joseph, & Samuel Standing, to line of Robt Newby, & down his line to Francis, & Samuel Newby. May 17, 1755. Test' Edward Robbins, Robt. Newby, Benjamin Sanders.

No. 195. Samuel Charles of Perq, planter—for £17 s10 pd by John Maudlin, planter—of afsd, sold 50a on North East side of Gum Swamp, on So East side of Suttons Creek, adj orphans of James Henby, & line of William Bogue, a piece of new land patented by Foster Toms. Oct 28, 1755. Test' William Albertson, William Maudlin, John Peirce.

No. 196. Jane Jones widow—relict of Jonathan dec' of Perq Co, for "love I bear my son Joseph Jones, have given one negro named David—1 feather bed, bolster, & 2 pillows—1 pr of sheets—1 pr of blankets—1 Rug—1 Bedstead, mat & cord, to be delivered to him when 21 years of age." Nov 13, 1755. Test' Thos Jones, John Bateman.

No. 197. Clement Hall of Chowan Co, Clerk—for £45 pd by John Perisho Sen, of Perq, planter—sold 104a on North East side of Perq River, being one pt of 208a formerly Jas. Perishos. April 15, 1756. Test' James Gibson, Samuel Barclift.

No. 198. Caleb White of Perq, for £10 pd by Julius Bunch, sold 31½a, adj Thos Newby, Thos Elliott, & Nathan Newby, pt of a survey taken up by sd Caleb, year 1755. April 12, 1756. Test' Reuben Perry, John Brinn.

No. 199. Thomas Godfrey, & Mary his wife of Perq, for £10 s10 pd by James Brinkley of afsd—sold 100a, being pt of land whereon Daniel Hall lived, called "Carpenters old Field" adj John Hopkins. April 19, 1756. Test' Joseph White, James Gibson, Thos Jones.

No. 200. Hannah Boswell of Perq, widow—in con' of a "marriage to be solemnized between George Taylor & me" have given unto him 50a in Berkeley Parish, Perq Co, on South side of Little River, near the head thereof, where Charles Overman, formerly lived, around line of John Boswell, now in possession of sd Hannah." April 17, 1756. Test' Thomas Weeks Jun.

No. 201. July 15, 1756. Elizabeth Calldrom, & John Harvey, of Perq, "for a con' sold to John Morris, of afsd 200a on No East side of Perq River, adj Edward Turner, (sd land bequeathed to sd Elizabeth by the will of her father James Cole dec). Said Elizabeth, in the year 1725, (together with her then husband Thos Harvey, Esq dec) did sell unto Richd Morris, of afsd, (father of sd John) a plan who after sd sale died, & shortly after Thos Harvey died. So sd land was never sold according to law, now sd Elizabeth, with John Harvey, eldest son of sd Thomas dec, do set over unto sd John Morris, sd land whereon he now lives." Test' Ben Harvey, Miles Harvey.

No. 202. May 26, 1756. Thos Garrett of Chowan, for £20 pd by John Harvey, of Perq sold 200a on South side of Perq River, near sd River, adj Joseph Barrow dec, "formerly in poss' of Widow Gilbert," to Samuel Skinner's line, formerly Joseph Burkets, & "Yates old field" pt of a grt unto John Pettiver Dec 20, 1720, & by him sold to sd Garrett, July 20, 1731. Test' Thos Garrett Jun, Jesse Garrett.

No. 203. Caleb Elliott of Perq, for £5 pd by Joseph Smith Sen of afsd, sold 135a out of a grt unto the said Elliott 1756. July 14, 1756. Test' John Smith, Benjamin Sanders.

No. 204. Caleb Elliott of Perq, for £40 pd by Reuben Perry, of afsd—sold 55a on Wst side of Cypress Swamp, adj John Boyce, & Gabriel Newby, to the middle of Gum Branch. Test' Joshua Skinner, John Boyce. July 19, 1756.

No. 205. Caleb Elliott, for £40 pd by John Boyce, of Perq, sold 63a, on sd Elliotts patent line, adj Gabriel Newby, up Gum Branch. July 19, 1756. Test' Joshua Skinner, Reuben Perry.

No. 206. James Pierce of Perq, Planter—for £10 pd by Jacob Mullen, of afsd—sold 79a, adj Thomas Knowles. Test' Jas Pierce, Peter Cartright. Mar 12, 1756.

No. 207. George Low of London, packer—Whereas: John Humpage, Mariner, & Ann Hinds, have made release of a plan' called "Birkswear" in Car, July 15, 1744, "now in occupation of one Henry Winslow, it being to my advantage to sell same, do appoint John Campbell, of Edenton, N. C. Merchant—my Att' to make suit for recovery of same, & do authorize him to sell to the highest bidder, & deliver, proceeds to me." Test' Archibald Wynn, Benjamin Sharp. July 20, 1746.

No. 208. John Smith of Perq, Merchant—for £42 s13 pd by Ephrim Luten, of Chowan Co, sold 200a in Perq, adj Archibald Holmes, "at the mouth of a small gut," thence to the Sound. Test' Jonathan Phillips, Jas Houghton, John Hinds. Oct 19, 1756.

No. 209. Samuel Perry of Perq, Planter—for £30 pd by Samuel Bagley, of afsd—sold 180a on So Side of Indian Branch, adj Benjamin Wilson, formerly given by Thomas Docton, to Samuel Perry. Oct 16, 1756. Test' James Hunter, Jesse Perry.

No. 210. Thomas Lane of Perq, Planter—for £6 s15 p5 pd by James Sitterson, carpenter—of afsd, sold 62½a formerly held by Wm Blitchenden, & 38a formerly the property of Wm Phelps, adj Abraham Wilson. Oct 15, 1756. Test' Jacob Wilson, Abraham Mullen.

No. 211. Benjamin Elliott of Perq, for £4 pd by Joshua Elliott, of afsd—sold 100a on So East side of Bosses (Vosses) Creek adj Charles Morgan, Joseph Outland & Joseph Newby, down to the Creek. Oct 18, 1756. Test' Joseph Sanders, Samuel Smith, Charles Jordan.

No. 212. William Munden of Perq, planter—for £12 pd by Joshua Perisho, Cooper, of afsd—sold 100a on So side of Little River, adj Overman & Winslow. Test' Obadiah Small, Thomas Robinson, William Barclift, Joseph Robinson. Aug 23, 1756.

No. 213. Wm Munden, for £11 pd by Obadiah Small, of Perq, Cooper—sold 65a on So side of Little River, adj Joshua Perishoe, part of a grt to sd Munden, Feb 17, 1756. Seal Feb 17, 1756. William, & Hannah Munden. Test' Joshua Perishoe, William Barclift, Thos Robinson, Joseph Robinson.

No. 214. Jan 22, 1756 "We, the subscribers; promise to pay unto Benjamin Weaver Jr, £13 s2 p11, one half in pork, & the other half, in Indian Corn, at market price, before Jan 1—next." Nathan Newby. Test' Nathan Simmons.

No. 215. Joseph Winslow of Perq, Yeoman—for £2 s10 pd by John White, son of Thomas White, of afsd—sold 50 on No East side of Perq River, adj Joshua White & Elias Stallings, part of 400a grt unto Thomas Winslow, my gr-father, Nov 11, 1719. Test' Joshua White, Joel Hollowell, Dan'l Saint. Jan 17, 1757.

No. 216. John Parish, of Tyrrell Co, St Andrews Parish, for £48 pd by John Barclift Sr, of Berkeley Parish, Perq Co, sold 685a, "which my late father John Parish of sd Co, & Parish, did by his will 1738, give to me, his only son," at the mouth of Deep Creek, except 100a already passed to Wm Colson, & Ann his wife, where he now lives." Jan 3, 1757. Test' John Weeks, Thos Weeks Jr.

No. 217. Israel Winslow of Perq, planter—for £5 s8 pd by Benjamin Winslow of afsd, planter—sold 200a, on No East side of Perq River, part of a tract, grt unto John Winslow, adj Jacob Perry, Timothy Winslow, & Thomas White. Test' Joseph Perry, John Smith. Jan 15, 1757.

No. 218. Richard Cheaston, of Bladen Co, N. C. for £10 pd by Dan'l Saint, (in behalf of Robert Wilson, of Perq) sold to sd Wilson 100a, on No East side of Perq River, called "Grassy Point" part of land, whereon David Harris lived, & left to dau's, Sarah, & Ann Harris, in his will, now in possession of John Morris. Test' Isaac Overman, Jno Chancey, Sam'l Saint. Nov 27, 1756.

No. 219. Daniel Saint of Perq, Carpenter—for £12 pd by Robt Wilson, of afsd—sold 100a, on No East side of Perq River, called "Grassy Point" the "Manor plan' on which David Harris lived, & left to his dau, Ann Smith, in his will, adj land left to her sisters, Sarah, & Elizabeth Harris. Jan 18, 1757. Test' Thos Newby, Aaron Morris, Joseph Riddick.

No. 220. Benjamin Scarbrough, of Perq, for £30 pd by John Hubbard, of afsd, sold 160a, called "Chinquapin Ridge," adj land sold to me by Wm Arrington, pt of a grt, to Juliana Laker, April 1, 1718/19. Seal April 19, 1757. Test' William Arrington, Charles Moore.

No. 221. Nov 9, 1755. Lords Pro', for £10 pd by John Hubbard, doth grant, 79a in the Parish of Berkeley, Co of Perq, on the West side of Perq River, "being the surplus land within bounds, of a patent, to Nathan Newby. Granville. Francis Corbin, Ben Wheatley. Test' Robert Kirshaw.

No. 222. Benjamin Scarbrough of Perq, for £30 pd by William Arrington, of afsd, Planter—sold 160a, on South Side of Perq River, by the side of Deep Branch, "near Castletons Creek Swamp." April 20, 1757. Test' John Hubbard, Charles Moore.

No. 223. April 7, 1757. Joshua Small, & Charity his wife, of Perq, for £25 pd by William Davis, of afsd—sold 50a, on "So Side of Loosing Swamp," pt of 888a grt to John Harris, & John Lackum, April 21, 1695, & sold by them to John Moseley, who conveyed sd land to Jas. Redding, who bequeathed it in his will, to his son James, he dying intestate, it came to John Redding, his brother, who bequeathed sd land in his will, to his sisters; Rachel Davis, Mary Davis, & Charity Small, which sd lot did fall, to sd wife of sd Joshua. Test' Henry Hill, Isaac Hill, Marmaduke Norfleet.

No. 224. Wm Woolard, & Mary his wife, of Chowan, for £30 pd by Joseph Williams, late of Vir', sold 175a on "north side of Mr. Jeremiah Pratts, Mill Swamp," patented by Mr Wm Wyatt, 1745, & sold by him to me. Oct 1, 1756. Test' John Vail, Thos Williams.

No. 225. Caleb Elliott of Perq, for £5 pd by Joseph Newby, sold unto James Wilson, son of Isaac, Dec'd, (a minor) 75a, adj Pritlow Ellott, & Thomas Newby, down Mill Swamp, to line of Gabriel Newby. Jan 17, 1757. Test' Haig Elliott, Penina Elliott.

No. 226. Sept 2, 1756. William Magound, & Frances, his wife, of Perq, for £30 pd by Aaron Jackson, of afsd, sold 52½a, on So West side of Little River, at the mouth of "Doctons Branch," to Thos Weeks back line. Test' John Bartlet, Isaac Sitterson, John Weeks.

No. 227. Aug 16, 1756. Joseph Harron of Chowan, Mariner—for £50 pd by Joseph Creecy, of Perq, Planter—sold 27a on North Side of Albemarle Sound, at the mouth of Yeopim River, known by the name of "Batts grave." Test' Andrew Knox, John Simmons, Argile Simmons.

No. 228. Thomas Bagley of Perq, Planter—for £10 s10 pd by Sam'l Bartlet, of afsd, Mariner—sold 14a on East Side of Perq River, on lines of sd Bartlet, & Bagley. Mar 31, 1757. Test' Dan'l Saint, Jos. Ratliff.

No. 229. Samuel Bagley, Bricklayer—for £50 pd by Robt Evans, Jun, Planter—of Perq sold 100a, adj Thomas Hollowell, Peter Pierson, & Gideon Bundy, to line of Aaron Wood. Nov 9, 1756. Test' Abner Eason, Jeremiah Bundy.

No. 230. Mar 19, 1751. Thos Lane Sen, Planter—for £4 pd by John Chappel, Planter—sold 30a, Between Richard Berryman, & James Sitterson. Test' Thomas Newby, John Murdaugh, Jos Jordan.

No. 231. Robert Riddick of Perq, for 5s pd by John Harmon, of afsd, sold "one grist mill, in the fork of Castletons Creek, with all appurtenances." April 19, 1757. Test' Jos White, Jas Sitterson, Ben Scarbrough.

232. May 13, 1753. Lords Pro' grant unto Joseph Creecy, of Chowan Co, Gent—for 3s paid "grt land in Parish of Berkeley Co of Perq," 290a on Eggertons line, for "the yearly rent of s11 p8, for every hundred acres, to be paid before the feast of St Michael," at the Court House of Perq. Granville, James Innes, Fra Corbin. Miles Gale, Jas Campbell.

No. 233. Abraham Wilson of Perq, Hatter—for £65 pd by Isaac Vic, Hatter—late of Craven Co, sold one Negro Wench, 15 years of age, Named Juda, & one Negro girl, Named Phillis. June 1, 1757. Test' John Lain, Joseph Lain.

No. 234. Simon Stallings of Perq, planter—for £21 s6 p8 pd by Isaac Lilly, of afsd, sold 232a, adj Thos Hobbs, James Field, Thos. Rountree, & sd Stallings, pt of a patent unto Thomas Blitchenden Dec 6, 1728, & 182a grt to sd Blitchenden, Nov 18, 1727, "an Est of inheritance." Mar 2, 1757. Test' Abraham Riddick, Nicholas Stallings, Joseph Lilly.

No. 235. July 8, 1757. Joseph Creecy, of Perq, to Joseph Outland, of afsd, planter—Whereas; Thos Nicholson of Perq, had an attachment agst the Est of George Taylor, for £3 13s 4p, & Joseph Robinson of same, prosecuted another attachment agst sd Est, (for debt due him in Oct Court) & likewise Joseph Outland, for £5 4s 4p in same Co; & obtained Judgment, for sd sums due them. Joseph Creecy, Sheriff of sd Co, made return "that there was no goods, or chattels of sd Taylor to be found," & did expose for sale a tract of land at public Vendue, which sd Joseph Outland purchased, for £25 being the highest bidder." Test' Jasper Charlton, Joseph Robinson.

No. 236. William Halsey, & Martha his wife, of Perq, for "love we bear our dau Christian Knox, "& in con' of 3s pd by sd Christian, gave 51a between Eggertons Mill & Pratts Mill," Northermost pt of plan' where sd Halsey lives," adj land of the late John Matthias. Aug 7, 1756. Test' Joseph Creecy, Thomas Ward.

No. 237. Richard Wood of Perq, Tayler—for £79 pd by John Clayton, of afsd, sold 99a, on East side of Suttons Creek, adj Whidbee, & Elizabeth Riggs, grt "unto George Sutton May 22, 1694, & by him in his will bequeathed to his dau *Deborah," & by heirship to her son Richard Wood. May 19, 1755. Test' John Wilkins, Richard Whidbee.

No. 238. Feb 3, 1756. Lords Pro' in con' of 10s pd by Caleb Elliott, of Perq, "hath grt land in Berkeley Parish, Co of Perq," 480a on the Wst Side of Perq River, adj Thos Newby, & Thomas Elliott. Granville. Frans Corbin, Ben Wheatley. Test' Richd. Vigers.

No. 239. Sarah Modlin of Perq, for "love I bear my children; Joseph, Ashley, dau Esbill, & Jethro Modlin, do give goods & chattels." Jan 21, 1757. Test' John Swain, George Nichols.

---

*Deborah m 2d Wm Wood, father of sd Richard.

No. 240. Nov 8, 1756. Joseph Smith of Perq, planter—for £20 pd by James Bacon, of Nansemond Co, Vir', Planter—sold 50a, adj Samuel Bond, & Abraham Wilson, to line of Mary Baker. Test' Thomas Newby, Joseph Murdaugh.

No. 241. William Arenton of Perq, planter—for £45 pd by Edward Penrice, of afsd, planter—sold 193a, "land that fell to me from my Mother, & Uncle Samuel Bond," on North side of Albemarle Sound, adj Henry, & Edward Hall, & along his line to Bentleys Creek, & Wm Longs line, pt of a tract "belonging to Edward Willson." Mar 5, 1757. Test' William Wyatt, Wm. Ashley.

No. 242. Feb 28, 1757. John Smith, of Beaufort Co, for £16 pd by Ephrim Sutton, of Perq, sold 100a, on "So Side of Franks Creek," adj James Sutton, & John Felt. Test' Arthur Allen, Robt. Turner.

No. 243. April 13, 1757. Peter Parker of Perq, Planter—for £16 pd by Darby Moore, of afsd, sold 50a, on Gum Swamp, adj Thos Boswell. Test' Elisha Parker, Thos Bozwell.

No. 244. Oct. 18, 1757. John Chancey, & Miriam his wife, of Bladen Co N. C. for £50 pd by Sylvanus Willson, sold 150a, in Perq Co, on So Wst Side of Perq River, adj Thos Jones, & John Jones, "with 150a (now belonging to Thos Jones) grt unto Thos Paine, April 20, 1694, & was given to his son Joseph, in his will," & sd Joseph, bequeathed same to his son Thomas, & sd Thomas dying intestate, sd land fell to Miriam Chancey, wife of sd John, & Rebecca Wilson, wife of sd Sylvanus, who were sisters, & co-heirs of sd Thomas Paine, dec'd. Test' Nath'n Newby, Robt Newby, Jas Sitterson.

No. 245. Sept 19, 1757. George Fletcher, of Hide Co, for £26 pd by John Harvey, of Perq, sold 104a, on No East Side of Perq River, adj Thos Bateman, up the Branch that divides sd land from Thos Sherrods, (orphan of David dec'd) sd land "with like quantity belonging to sd Sherrad was grt to Thos Attoway, July 26, 1708," & was sold after his death, by Elenor his dau, to Harris Willoby Mar 27, 1716, & by sd Willoby, conveyed unto Thomas Collins, April 15, 1717, & by sd Collins, to Ralph Fletcher, father of sd George, Jan 10, 1721/2, & was "bequeathed to his son in his will." Test' Joseph Ratliff, Joshua Fletcher.

No. 246. Joseph Lilly, of Chowan, Husbandman—for £8 pd by Daniel Rogerson, of Perq Husbandman—sold 50a, in the "Pine Woods," pt of a patent to Thos Lilly, adj Isaac Willson, & along Daniel Snooks line, to the main Road. Oct 17, 1757. Test' John Callaway, Solom Wyatt, Isiah Rogerson.

No. 247. John Barclift Sen, of Perq, for "love I bear my son John of same," Farmer—have given 324a, on So Wt Side of Little River, & the "upper side of Deep Creek, where John Parish formerly lived." Sept 17, 1757. John & Ann Barclift. Test' James Gibson, William Barclift.

No. 248. Oct 20, 1758. Luke, & Sam'l Bond, Jun, to Abraham Willson, for £40 sold 100a, on No Wst side of Cypress Creek, at the mouth of a Branch next to the Bridge, to the road, & Joseph Smiths line. Test' Jos Jordan, Jos Lain, Thos Newby.

No. 249. Aug 1, 1757. Samuel Bond Jun, for £60 pd by Joseph Murdaugh, sold 220a, on the west side of Cypress Creek, at the mouth of "Bull Branch," adj James Bacon, Joseph Smith, & Abraham Willson, to Branch called "Tarklin." Test' Thos Newby, Joshua Fletcher, John Pearson.

No. 250. Oct 18, 1757. John, & Miriam Chancey, of Bladen Co N. C. for £25 pd by John Jones, of Perq, sold 435a, on So West Side of Perq River, commonly called "Morrises" adj William Hall, "land whereon sd Jones now liveth," sd land purchased of James Beasley, by Thos Pain, Nov 17, 1727, & was conveyed unto Joseph Paine, Mar 7, 1736, & in his will "bequeathed unto his dau Miriam, the now wife of sd John Chancey." Test' Jno Harvey, John Murdaugh.

No. 251. Silvanus Henbe, of Perq, farmer—for £25 pd by Joshua Boswell, of afsd, farmer—sold 93½a, near "Long branch of Suttons Creek, pt of a tract patented in 1740, by my father John Henbe, sd land given me in his will," adj Sam'l Charles. 18d, 8mo 1757. Test' Gideon Modlin, Joseph Farmer, Wm Albertson.

No. 252. Sept 21, 1757. John Harvey of Perq, for £35 pd by Abraham Turner, of afsd, sold 104a, on No East Side of Perq River, adj Thomas Bateman, "sd land half of 208a grt to Thomas Attoway July 26, 1708, & was after his death sold by Ellena his dau to Harris Willoby, Mar 27, 1716," & by sd Willoby, conveyed unto Thos Collins, April 15, 1717, & by sd Collins, sold to Ralph Fletcher, Jan 10, 1721/2, & by sd Fletcher, in his will given to his son George, & by sd George, Sept 29, 1757 deeded to me. Test' Ben Harvey, Edward Turner.

No. 253. John Hubbard of Perq, Planter—for £12 pd by Timothy Walton, of Chowan Co, sold 60a, on So Side of Perq River, a grt unto Julianna Laker, called "Chinquepin Ridge," adj Benj'm Scarbrough. June 20, 1757. Test' William Arrenton, Richd Walton.

No. 254. Edward Turner of Perq, "for love I bear my son Joseph," of afsd, do give 53a, on Deep Creek, "being the middle pt of a grt unto Thomas Collins," July 20, 1717, adj Elisha Albertson, & Elihu Albertson. Oct 10, 1757. Test' Wm Bedgood, Abraham Turner, Joseph Ratliff.

No. 255. Edward Turner, for "love I bear my son John," do give 58a, on west side of Deep Creek, pt of a grt unto Thos Collins July 20, 1717, on line of Elihu Albertson. Oct 17, 1757. Test' Wm Bedgood, Abraham Turner, Joseph Ratliff.

No. 256. Robert Wilson, for "good will, & aff' I bear unto my gr-son William Townsen, do give one negro boy named Scipio, if he die without issue, to my gr-dau Rachel Townsend, & if she die, to any other child of William, & Rachel Townsen, & for want of such issue to de divided between children of Timothy Winslow," 9d, 4mo 1757. Test' Rachel Townsen, Benjamin Pike, John Mann, Wm Townsend.

No. 257. Will'm Willson of Perq, for £9 s10 pd by Thos. Lamb, of afore' sold 50a on So Wt side of Perq River, between Henry & Thomas Lamb, running to Cypress Creek, & the main Road. May 4, 1757. Test' Sam'l Sitterson, Thos Elliott.

No. 258. Joshua Elliott of Perq, for £80 pd by Samuel Smith, of afsd, sold 190a, plan' "whereon I live," on East side of Cypress Swamp, adj Benjamin Sanders, & up sd Swamp to Joseph Winslows, & along his line, to Joseph Elliotts. Oct 17, 1757. Test' John Smith, Joseph Smith, Charles Jordan.

No. 259. John Winslow of Perq, planter—for £5 pd by Benjamin Winslow, of afsd, Planter—sold "Moiety of land patented by Wm Moore 1668," on No East Side of Perq River, at the mouth of Great Branch, to line of sd Benjamin Winslow. Jan 17, 1758. Test' Hannah Winslow, Elizabeth Winslow.

No. 260. Abraham Willson of Perq, for £20 pd by Benjamin Wilson, of same, sold 80a, on So Wst Side of Perq River, near "Edwards old field" in Mulberry Swamp. Jan 17, 1758. Test' John Page, Jas. Sitterson, Elias Stallings.

No. 261. Jonathan Sharbo, of Pasquotank Co, for £23 pd by Joseph Newby, Millwright—sold 100a, on No Wst Side of Vosses Creek, adj Roger Kenynion dec'd, on line of sd Newby, which was formerly Francis Toms Sen, dec'd, & land where Thomas Sharbo formerly lived. Jan 7, 1758. Test' Joseph Outland, Micajah Jordan.

No. 262. Nov 12, 1757. Charles Taylor Sen, of Pasquotank Co, for £30 pd by Aaron Jackson, of Perq, sold 80a, on So Wst side of Little River, "being the lowermost pt of a grt unto Joseph, & John Robinson Mar 25, 1749," & conveyed by sd Joseph, & John, to John Jackson, & Sarah his wife, & William Magound, & Frances his wife, Oct 13, 1750, & sold by John Jackson to me, July 20, 1751. Charles & Ellender Taylor. Test' John Douglas, John Nixon, John Nichols.

No. 263. Mar 1, 1758. Sylvanus Willson, & Rebecca his wife, of New Hanover Co, N. C. for £150 pd by Joseph White, of Perq, sold 150a, on So Wst Side of Perq River, adj Thos Jones, Thos Paine, & John Jones back lines, which (with 150a belonging to Thos Jones) was "grt to Thomas Paine, April 20, 1694," & was given by him in his will, to his son Joseph, & by him to his son Thomas, & sd Thomas "dying intestate, did descend unto Miriam Chancey, wife of John, & Rebecca Willson, wife of sd Sylvanus." Test' William Bell, Hannah Bell, Edmund Chancey.

No. 264. John Mann, of Pasquotank Co, & Thomas Knoles, of Perq, for £19 pd by George Shell, of same, Tailor—sold 50a, in Perq, adj Joseph Weeks, & Samuel Wright, "where William Knoles dec'd formerly lived." April 17, 1755. Test' Joseph Jordan, Jesse Eason.

No. 265. John Riddick, of Tyrrel Co N. C. for 20s pd by Isaac Lilly, of Perq, sold 50a, in Perq, pt of "640a grt unto Elias Stallings, which is all the right I ever had in sd Patent." Oct 13, 1757. Test' Joseph Perry, Daniel Rogerson, Nicholas Stallings.

No. 266. Jan 1, 1758. Thomas Rountree, Sen, of Chowan Co, for £20 pd by Jacob Spive, of afore' sold 50a, on North side of Perq River, "on Hickory Ridge," pt of "land sold by Joseph Jessop, to Thos. Rountree, & by his will to sd Thomas." Test' Thomas Acon, Guy Hill.

No. 267. Mar 23, 1758. Edward Penrice, of Perq, for £35 pd by John Harvey, sold 200a, on West Side of Mings Creek, adj Henry Hall, sd land "patented by Edward Wilson June 24, 1704. & descended to his dau Sarah, who married Thos Williams," & was sold by sd Sarah, & Thomas to Richard Bounds, & by "him bequeathed to his sons, Edward & Samuel, who both died under age, when sd land descended to sd Edward Penrice, & William Arrington in right of their Mothers," & sd Arrington assigned his right to me. Test' Andrew McHenry, John Callaway.

No. 268. April 8, 1758. Benjamin Scarbrough, of Perq, for £60 pd by John White, of afsd, sold 475a, on the head of Perishoes Creek, sd land "patented by Julianna Lakers April 10, 1704, & by her given to Macrora Scarbrough, & by his will given to his son sd Benjamin," July —, 1731. Test' John Hubbard, Absalom Alphin.

No. 269. Robert Cocks, of Perq, Planter—for £12 s10 pd by Thomas Boswell, of afsd, planter—sold 50a, on So west Side of Little River. ——— 17, 1758. Test' Benjamin Munden, Joseph Jordan.

No. 270. Matthew Pritchard, of Perq, for £30 pd by Samuel Newby, of afsd, sold 50a of woodland on West side of Perq River, adj Robt Willson, to

RECORDS OF DEEDS 175

sd Newbys Mill road, & Deep branch. April 18, 1758. Test' Jos White, Geo Nichols, Wm Townsen.

No. 271. John Barclift of Perq, Planter—for £20 s5 p9, pd by Joseph Riddick, of afsd, sold 180a, on "Shitten Gut," adj James Foster. Nov. 21, 1757.

No. 272. Dec 16, 1757. Guy Hill of Chowan Co, for £3 pd by Thomas Rountree, Sen, of afsd, sold 50a, in Perq on No east side of Perq River, adj Elias Stallings, pt of 400a pattented by Thomas Winslow, Nov. 11, 1719. Test' Thomas Acon, Jacob Spive.

No. 273. William Lacey of Perq, Planter—for £60 pd by Joseph Newby, of afsd, millwright—sold 125a, on north east side of Perq River, being "plan whereon William Lacey Sen dec'd lived," adj land of Jas Lacey, & John Guyer dec'd, Joseph Newby, William Lacey, & Sarah Lacey. Nov 30, 1757. Test' George Shell, James Elliott, Matthew Jordan.

No. 274. William Eason of Perq, for £18 pd by Joshua Boswell, of afsd, sold tract, called "Persimmon tree land," adj Thomas Hollowell, sd land the "upper half of 183a, sd Boswell to have the upper part 91½a." Jan 23, 1758. Test' Elias Stallings, Dempsey Perry, Nicholas Stallings.

No. 275. John Goodwin of Chowan Co, for a val' con' assigns "right of within" deed (from Zach Chancey in the year 1744, & Reg in Perq Co), unto Richard Goodwin. May 23, 1757. Test' Sam'l Sitterson, Miriam Sitterson.

No. 276. Jacob Docton of Perq, for "love I bear my son-in-law Samuel Bagley," of same, Bricklayer—do give 25a, adj James Price, Abner Eason, & sd Docton. Jan 31, 1758. Test' Jno Page, Ben Wilson, Reuben Eason.

No. 277. April 9, 1758. Andrew Knox, of Perq, for £40 pd by William Flury, of afsd, sold 50a (which formerly belonged to William Halsey, dec'd, & was by him, & his wife Martha, given to Christian Knox, wife of sd Andrew), adj land of John Matthias, dec'd, & Thomas Halsey. Test' John Donnelson, Thos Halsey.

No. 278. Nov 20, 1758. John Harvey of Perq, for £200 pd by Isaac Sanders, of same, sold 400a, (except cleared, & enclosed dwelling plan' of James Sitterson, & William Townsen) on So Wst Side of Perq River, on a Creek formerly called "Robert Wilsons Creek," (on south side of same), along River side, sd land "grt unto Jonathan Phelps, Feb 6, in the 20 year of our province of N. C. who in his will, gave sd land to his son Samuel, & was by sd Samuel, given in his will to his sons, Jonathan, & James," sd two sons dying intestate, before they were of age, the land fell unto William Phelps, "only surviving brother of afsd," who in his will, gave sd land unto John Harvey. Test' Joseph White, Miles Harvey.

No. 279. July 17, 1758. Francis Toms of Perq, for £20 pd by Jacob Jacobs, of afsd, sold 100a, adj "4a, belonging to sd Jacobs." Test' Nicholas Collins, Nathan Newby.

No. 280. July 17, 1758. Nathan Newby of Perq, for £4 pd by Jacob Jacobs, of afsd, sold 4a, pt of land that "Mary Newby purchased of James Morgan," adj Francis Toms. Test' Francis Toms, Nicholas Collins.

No. 281. July 15, 1758. Wm. Flury of Perq, for £40 pd by Andrew Knox, of same, sold 50a, at the head of Yeopim Creek, adj John Matthias dec, & Thomas Halsey, "formerly belonging to William Halsey." Test' Joshua Skinner, John Calloway, Robert Turner.

No. 282. Joshua Maudlin of Perq, Farmer—for £19 pd by John Whedbee, of afsd, Gent, sold 170a, on "Rattle Snake Ridge" adj Turner, & Joseph Sutton Jun. May 22, 1758. Test' Henry Williamson, Richard Whedbee.

No. 283. Samuel Barclift, for £18 pd by John Whidbee, both of Perq, conveyed 100a, on north East side of Perq River, "surveyed for George Sutton Sen, Nov 15, 1722," adj Edward Turners new line. Oct 8, 1757. Test' Henry Williamson, Thos Nichols, George Reed.

No. 284. Isaac Lilly of Perq, for £2 pd by Thomas Hurdle, of Chowan Co, sold 50a, in Perq, pt of a grt unto Elias Stallings, who sold sd land to John Riddick, & he by "deed of gift" assigned same to sd Lilly. May 29, 1758. Test' Nicholas Stallings, Elias Stallings.

No. 285. Joshua Elliott Sen, of Perq, for "love I bear my son Joshua," of afsd, have given a negro boy (named Peter), 3 years old. May 13, 1758. Test' Samuel Smith, Leah Smith.

No. 286. Joseph Winslow of Perq, schoolmaster—for £20 pd by Jonathan Sharrod, of same, sold 30a, adj Benjamin Wilson, & Joseph Elliott. Jan 23, 1758. Test' Joshua Elliott, Sen, Joshua Elliott Jun, Isaac Elliott.

No. 287. Feb 23, 1758. Martha Ann Kippen, of Edenton, Innholder—for £100 pd by John Thatch, of Chowan Co, sold 350a, on Indian Creek, in Perq Co, (sd Creek issuing out of Yeopim River,) adj Thomas Long, 150a, of which was conveyed to Richd Leary, by sd Long as a dowery for his dau, wife of sd Leary, pt of a greater tract, surveyed for sd Long, on the "East side of Mill Swamp, & the upper branch of Horsepen branch, 500a." Test' Thomas Bonner, Henderson Standin.

No. 288. Isaac Lamb of Perq, for £25 pd by Pritlow Elliott, of afsd, sold 24a, on So Wst shore of Cypress Swamp, adj Gabriel Newby, & Reuben Perry. Oct 12, 1758. Test' Reuben Perry, Joseph Smith, John Boyce.

No. 289. Edward Turner, for £30 pd by John Widbee, Gent, sold 230a, on East Side of Perq River, in the Parish of Berkeley, & on Est side of "Beaver Dam Swamp," adj sd Whidbee, to Long Branch. Oct 16, 1758. Test' Michael Smith, Henry Williamson.

No. 290. Oct 16, 1758. William Skinner Esq, of Perq Sheriff; Whereas: Ann Cary, Henry Stephens, & Edward Woodcoc, Exors of the Est of Robt Cary Esq, of London, Mehch't—dec'd; hath an attachment, agst the Est of Theopholus Pugh, late of sd Co, dec'd (lately in the hands of Benjamin Hill, of Bertie Co, Ex of sd Pugh, but now in hands of Robert Jones Jr, Ex of sd Benjamin Hill dec'd) for the sum of £874, s 5 p 4, and sd parties, did obtain Judgment, (for money due them), & sd Sheriff of Perq, made returns;" that there is no goods, or chattels, of sd Pugh, to be found" & in order to satisfy same, did expose for sale, at public Vendue, 100a "property of sd Pugh," Joseph Moore being the highest bidder. Test' N. Collins, Isaac Saunders.

No. 291. Thomas Nicholson of Perq, for £30 pd by "my father-in-law William Bundy," of afsd, & acquit Sarah Pritchard, dau of sd William, sold 25a, one half of land bought of John Nixon by sd Thomas, adj sd Bundy. 16d, 10mo 1758. Test' William Albertson, Joseph Outland.

No. 292. Oct 12, 1758. John Wallburton of Chowan Co, Gent—for £40 pd by Joshua Elliott, of Perq, sold land on Ming Creek, below settlement made by Ephraditus Brinkley, pt of a tract given to Joseph Burket, by his

A. Ye Old Eagle Tavern. Built before the Revolutionary War. It is claimed that George Washington spent a night here.
B. Newby's Bridge, just beyond Belvidere.
C. Perquimans High School.

father John Burket, dec'd, & sd Joseph, conveyed unto Humphrey Griffin, April 15, 1733. Test' Robt Fletcher, Caleb Clurely, John Huges.

No. 293. Isaac Lamb for £3 pd by Joseph Smith, sold 15a, on Wst Side of Cypress Creek, being sd Lambs new survey. Oct 12, 1758. Test' Reu'n Perry, John Boyce, Pritlow Elliott.

No. 294. Isaac Lamb for £15 pd by John Boyce, sold land on west side of Cypress Creek, "where sd Boyce now dwells," adj Joseph Smith, & Reuben Perry. Oct 12, 1758. Test' Reuben Perry, Joseph Smith Pritlow Elliott.

No. 295. Timothy Lilly, of Chowan, for £35 pd by Joseph Winslow, of Perq, Schoolmaster—sold 130a, in Perq "on Burnt Pocosin," adj Dan'l Rogerson, & Jacob Perry, pt of a "patent unto Thomas Blitchenden." Oct 12, 1758. Test' Jacob Powell, Ann Powell.

No. 296. Lords Pro' grt unto Archibald Holmes, of Perq, 543a, on north side of Albemarle Sound, adj Edward Wilson, to Lakers Creek, due for trans'. June 24, 1704. Robt Daniel, Francis Toms, Thos Pollock, John Ardeme. Rec By Thos Snoden Clk of Sec office, July 21, 1704.

No. 297. Jan 16, 1759. Andrew Knox, Ex of James Haughton dec, of Perq, for £100 s 14, "doth acquit Edward Hall," who bought 150a, of land "directed to be sold, by sd Huoghton, whereon he did live, at public Vendue," sd land on North Side of Yeopim River. Test' Will Skinner, Seth Sumner.

No. 298. Jan 15, 1759. John Harvey for £42 s 10, pd by Andrew Collins, sold 200a, on the Wst side of Mings Creek, adj Henry Hall, pt of a patent unto Edward Wilson, June 24, 1704, which at his death descended to Sarah (his dau), the wife of Thomas Williams, & was sold by them, to Richd Bounds, & by sd Bounds bequeathed to his sons, Edward, & Samuel, "who died under age, when sd land fell by heirship, to Edward Penrice, & William Arrington, in right of their mothers," sd Arrington, sold his pt unto sd Penrice, & he sold same, to John Harvey. Test' Joseph Robinson, John Wallburton.

No. 299. William Davis, & Mary his wife, of Edgecombe Co, N. C. are bound unto Marmaduke Norfleet, of Perq, in the sum of £200, June 28, 1757, & sold to sd Norfleet 60a, on South side of Loosing Swamp, adj the Desert, sd plan' being "part of a grt which John Riddick, gave his sisters," Rachel, Charity, & Mary, the last, wife of sd William Davis. Reg Jan 31, 1759. Test' Arthur Bell, Marmaduke Norfleet Jun, Reuben Perry.

No. 300. Robert Riddick, of Perq, for £5 pd by James Price, of afsd, sold 95a, on west side of the head of Perq River, in the desert, adj Lemuel Powell, & "up River Swamp." Nov 29, 1758. Test' Samuel Bagley, Simon Stallings, Christian Reed.

No. 301. Benjamin Simpson of Perq, for "love I bear my son Samuel," of afsd, and s1 pd, hath given 53a on No East Side of "Browns Mill Swamp," whereon sd Benjamin now dwells, & the other half, being the property of Benjamin Simpson Jun. adj Jas Eggerton dec. Jan 9, 1759. Test' Andrew Knox, Jas Eggerton, John Crabb.

No. 302. Josiah Perrishoe of Perq, for "love & the effectual complying, with the will, of my brother John, do give unto my brother Joseph, plan', which sd John, purchased of Clement Hall, 104a on No East Side of Perq River, adj a parcel of land, given by my dec father, John Perrishoe, to his sons; Joseph, & Samuel, adj "Beaver Pond," being pt of 108a, belonging to Jas Perrishoe dec, sd Josiah the eldest son of sd John. Jan 15, 1759. Test' John Harvey, James Eggerton.

No. 303. Sept 13, 1758. John Foans, of Chowan Co, for £5, s 10, pd by John Twine, sold 100a, in Perq on "Willifords Branch," adj John Hollowell, & sd Twine. Test' Jos Riddick, Joseph Perry, Thos Acon.

No. 304. Oct 21, 1758. Joshua Albertson of Perq, for £49 pd by Nath'l Albertson of afsd, sold 70a, on No East side of Perq River, & upper side of Suttons Creek, "which my dec'd father, Arthur Albertson, of Berkeley Parish, gave me in his will, his eldest son," adj Jesse Winslow. Test' John Harvey, Albert Albertson.

No. 305. Jacob Perry Sen, of Perq, wheelwright—for "love I bear my son John," of afsd, have given 200a, on Deep Creek, adj Snooks line, to line of Isaac Perry. Jan 12, 1758. Test' Jacob Perry Jun, Dempsey Perry.

No. 306. Solomon Wyatt, & Sarah his wife, of Perq, for £25 pd by Jacob Powell, of afsd, sold 100a, on So West side of Perq River, adj Isaac Wilson, to Deep Branch, pt of a grt unto William Kitchen, & Margaret Snooks, April 1, 1713, & conveyed by them to William Carman, & by him in his will, to sd Sarah Wyatt. Dec 19, 1758. Test' John Hollowell, Daniel Rogerson, Rasiah Lilly.

No. 307. Isaac Lamb of Perq, for £25 pd by Reuben Perry, of afsd, sold 24a on West shore of Cypress Swamp, adj Gabriel Newby. Oct 12, 1758. Test' Pritlow Elliott, Joseph Smith, John Boyce.

No. 308. Oct 14, 1758. Lemuel Riddick, of Nansemond Co, Vir, for £100, pd by Luke Sumner, of Chowan Co N. C. sold 200a, part in Chowan, & part in Perq, called "Mount Folly," formerly Theophilus Pughs, & after his death, sold unto sd Lemuel, by William Halsey, Sheriff of Chowan Co. Test' ———Baker, Francis Brown.

No. 309. Andrew Knox; "have received of Martha Halsey relict of William late of Perq Co, one negro boy, named Jim—1 table—3 guns—, tools, & chattels, &c. Having married Christian, dau of sd dec'd, do release sd Martha, from all demands, out of sd Estate, of sd William Halsey, dec'd." Mar 15, 1759. Test' Thos. Bonner, Jeremiah Halsey.

No. 310. William Arrinton "have received of Martha Halsey, relict of William dec, late of Perq, one negro wench, named Phillis, chattels, &c. Having married Mary, dau of sd William Halsey, dec. Mar 15, 1759. Test' Thomas Bonner, Jeremiah Halsey.

No. 311. Dec 2, 1758 Richard Sanderson, of Perq, for £390 pd by Charles Blount, of Chowan, sold 400a in Perq, at the mouth of a Creek, issuing out of Lillies Creek. Test' Sarah Elbeck, Jno. Blount.

No. 312. Samuel Newby in Perq, planter—for £20 pd by Francis Jones, sold 100a in Balahac, adj Joseph Willson, & William Moore, to line of Truman Moore. Jan 1, 1759. Test' Robt. Newby, Francis Newby, Joseph Newby.

No. 313. Francis Jones of Perq, Planter—"moved" for £20 pd by Samuel Newby, sold 50a, on West Side of Perq River, "at the old foot way." April 16, 1759. Test' Samuel Smith, Joseph Saundres, Francis Newby.

No. 314. Mar 8, 1759. Abraham Turner of Perq, for £40 pd by Thomas Stafford, of same, sold 104a, on No East side of Perq River, adj Thos

Bateman, "to a branch that divides sd land, from like quantity, belonging to Thos Sherrod, orphan of David, which 208a, was grt unto Thos Attoway, July 26, 1708." Test' James Pierce, Edward Turner, Joseph Turner.

*No. 315. Isaac Eiilott of Perq, Planter—for £75 pd by Joseph Barber, of afsd, Sadler—sold 150a, on So East side of "Bull Branch," adj John Lacey, & Dempsey Henby, formerly belonging to James Henby, father of sd Dempsey, to Charles Morgans line. "Part of a patent unto Francis Toms dec'd, & by him willed to his dau Margaret, the mother of sd Isaac Elliott. Mar 13, 1759. Test' Thos. Coffield, John Cale.

No. 316. April 17, 1759. John Jones for £25 pd by John Hind, sold 100a, on "a Swamp at the head of Yeopim Creek," adj Thos Long, pt of a grt unto Peter Jones, Mar 20, 1718. Seal April 17, 1759. Test' Joshua Skinner, Jas Dunlevy.

No. 317. Thos Stafford of Perq, for £65 pd by Abraham Turner, of afsd, sold 163a, grt to Thos Stafford April 1, 1720, & in his will given to his son Thomas. Mar 9, 1759. Test' Jas. Pierce, Edward Turner, Joseph Turner.

No. 318. Josiah Perrishoe, for £100 pd by Mathew White, of Perq, sold 175a, at the mouth of "Wolf Pit branch," & the head of Cypress Swamp, pt of a patent unto William Booge, Nov 22, 1714, & Thos Bagley, July 12, 1717. Seal Feb 14, 1759. Test' Nicholas Stallings, John Hollowell, Elias Stallings.

No. 319. Joseph Lacey of Perq, for £10 pd by John Stone, Carpenter— of afsd, sold 10a, on No East side of "Adkins Swamp, formerly William Laceys all his land on this side of the Swamp." Mar 6, 1759. Test' Hannah Moore, Keziah Newby, Nathan Newby.

No. 320. John Brinkley of Perq, for "love I bear my son James, have given, 200a, whereon I now live on South Side of Mill Swamp, adj Thos Long (formerly Daniel Hall's) with personal Estate, negroes, cattle, hogs, & sheep in my possession." Test' Hannah Moore, Keziah Newby, Nathan Newby. Mar 6, 1759.

No. 321. James Brinkley, "am firmly bound unto my father John Brinkley, in the sum of £500, sd James shall not molest, sd John, & Ann his wife, in the quiet possession of sd Estate, during their natual lives." April 2, 1759. Test' John Harvey, John Burns.

No. 322. Lords Pro' unto James Fisher, grt 225a, due for trans' Land on Yeopim River. Feb 6, 1696. John Archdale Esq, Gov of Carolina. Councilors; Daniel Akehurst, Francis Toms, Thomas Pollock, Samuel Swann, Henderson Walker.

James Fisher, "doth assign sd patent," unto William Halsey, of Chowan, April 7, 1732.

**No. 333. Thomas Halsey of Perq, for £10 pd by Andrew Knox, of same— sold 20a at the head of Yeopim River, where sd Halsey now lives. Sept 4, 1758. Test' John Barnes, Charles Moore, Francis Toms.

No. 334. July 16, 1759. John Wilkins of Chowan, Ex of John Caruthers, late of Perq, & Timothy Truelove, (who intermarried with Elizabeth widow

---

* Bull Branch issued out of Suttons Creek.

**Note: Deed book F, is a copy, of the old book, & has missing eleven deeds, as seen above; from 322, to 333, there is a skip of these numbers. Mrs. Watson Winslow.

of sd John) of same—for £25 pd by Hatten Williams, of afsd, sold 60a, on North side of Yeopim River, pt of 200a grt to John Falkner, Dec 6, 1720, & conveyed by him to John Norcom, who sold sd land to John Stepney, & by him to Nath'l Caruthers, who conveyed sd land, to John Caruthers dec'd. Test' Wm. Wyatt, Jas. Dunlevy, Seth Sumner.

No. 335. Sept 8, 1658. Lords Pro' grt unto John Clayton, 100a in Berkeley Parish, Perq Co, for s10 paid, adj George, & Nathaniel Sutton, on "Brandy Branch." Granville. Francis Corbin, Josh'a Bodley.

No. 336. Joseph Newby of Perq, for £80 pd by Josiah Perrishoe, of afsd, "house carpenter"—sold 124a on Vosses Creek Swamp, pt of a grt unto Francis Toms, Aug 15, 1716, & pt surveyed for Peter Albertson, Mar 10, 1720, & the other, an elapsed patent, unto John Lacey, April 2, 1725. Seal Mar 22, 1759. Test' Joseph Ratliff, Jesse Winslow.

No. 337. John Stevenson Esq, of Perq, for "love I bear my son Thomas, have given, 360a" on west side of Little River, & Albemarle Sound, called "Stevensons Point." Test' John Clayton, Dan'l. Budgate, Joseph Sutton. Oct 17, 1758.

No. 338. John & Ann Brinkley, for "Love we bear our dau Rebecca Gilbert, do give one negro woman, named Cate, & a negro girl, named Rose." May 26, 1759. Test' Will'm Luten, Duncan Ross.

No. 339. John & Ann Brinkley, for "love we bear our Gr-son William Sherad, do give, one negro boy, named Venture, 3 years of age." May 26, 1759. Test' William Luten, Duncan Ross.

No. 340. July 29, 1754. Articles of agreement, between Robert Riddick, & Jacob Docton, of Perq; that Job Riddick, son of Robert, "may have liberty, to clear, build, settle, upon land that was given him, by his gr-father Thos. Docton when he comes of age, without molestation," the Manner Plantation whereon Thomas Docton Esq, dec'd dwelt, & the use of 4 negroes, from this date." Test' Luke Sumner, Michael Griffin, James Price.

No. 341. Joseph Sutton, (son of Nathaniel) of Perq, for £20 pd by Edward Tatlocke, of same—sold 100a, on No East side of Perq River. 1, 12mo 1759. Test' Joseph Price, Edward Turner, Joseph Wood.

No. 342. Thomas Hendrix of Perq, "am bound unto my father, Job Hendrix, & Sarah my mother, of afsd" in the sum of £1000, to be pd unto them, April 17, 1759. Test' John Harvey, Samuel Parsons.

No. 343. Job Hendrix, & Sarah his wife, for "love we bear our son Thomas, have given 100a on lower side of Vosses Creek, & upper side of "Horse Pen Branch" whereon we dwell which was deeded to Sarah Morgan, before her marriage, by Stephen Gibson, now wife of sd Job. Oct 16, 1759. Test' John Harvey, Samuel Parsons.

No. 344. William Ashley of Perq, Planter—for £50 pd by George Nichols, sold 100a on Yeopim Creek, "where Joseph Ashley dec'd, settled," adj William Long, & John Barrow, to "Chesons Cove," formerly William Long's. Oct 15, 1759. Test' Joshua Skinner, John White.

No. 345. Timothy Lilly of Perq, for £1 s10 pd by Joseph Perry, of afsd—sold 50a, part of 640a grt unto Elias Stallings, Sept 20 ———. Feb 14, 1759. Test' John Perry, Daniel Rogerson.

No. 346. Joseph Lilly, & Sarah his wife, for £13 s10 pd by Nicholas Stallings, of Perq, assigned plan' "whereon Moses Rountree dec'd did live." Oct 5, 1759. Test' Joel Hollowell, Benj'n Perry, Abner Hollowell.

No. 347. Samuel Smith of Perq, for £60 pd by Rachel Smith, of afsd—sold 50a, adj Benjamin Wilson, & Benjamin Sanders. Oct 15, 1759. Test' Robert Riddick, Joseph Smith.

No. 348. Jacob Caruthers, "am firmly bound unto Hatten Williams, in the sum of £200" conveyed 150a of land, on East side of "Pratts Mill Creek." Test' Andrew Knox, Jas Dunlevy. Sept 29, 1758.

No. 349. Ann Caruthers, widow of Jacob, for £76 pd by Hatten Williams, "unto my dec'd husband, Sept 29, 1758, do make over, 150a of land on Deep Branch, adj land formerly John Wyatts, a grt unto Nath'l Caruthers," 1737. Oct 15, 1759. Test' Thos Coffield, Thos Williams.

No. 350. William Godfrey of Perq, for £50 pd by Thos Godfrey, of same —sold 50a, on So East Side of Deep Creek. Oct 13, 1759. Test' James Foster, William Barclift.

No. 351. Thomas Godfrey of Perq, for £50 pd by William Godfrey, of same—sold 80a, on So East Side of Deep Creek, adj John Barclift. Oct 13, 1759. Test' James Foster, William Barclift.

No. 352. Jan 21, 1760. Joseph Bullock, of Isle of Wight Co, Va, for £26 pd by Jas Sitizen, of Perq Co, N. C. sold 45a, on So West Side of Perq River, adj Wm Townsend, Isaac Saunders, & Daniel Saint, "sd land with 121a was grt unto Ralph Bosman dec'd, Feb 1, 1718, & given in his will, Jan 1, 1744/5, to sd Bullock." Test' John Harvey, Fras Nixon.

No. 353. Ephrim Elliott, for "love I bear my children; Keziah, & Caleb Elliott do give to sd dau, a negro girl, named Peg, & to sd son a negro girl, named Grace, reserving them for the use of my wife, her life time." Jan 22, 1760. Test' Joshua Skinner, James Sitterson.

No. 354. Thos Childs, Att' Gen'l of N. C. lately appointed; by John Earl Granville, do appoint, Thomas Weeks Esq, of Berkeley Parish, Co of Perq, Receiver of all vacant lands, in sd County, & "authorize him to receive all dues, according to the table of fees." Test' Thos Jones, Richard Vigers. Oct 26, 1759.

No. 355. Thomas Weeks Esq, came before me, & took the oath. Oct 26, 1759. John Stevenson, Joseph Sutton; Justices.

No. 356. Thomas Weeks, Joseph Sutton, & John Stevenson, of Perq Esqrs; are bound unto Hon' John Earl Granville, in the sum of £1000. Oct 26, 1759. Test' Joseph Robinson, Thomas Stevenson.

No. 357. 1757. Darby Moore of Perq, for £30 pd by Benjamin Roberts, of afsd—sold 50a, on Gum Swamp, adj Thomas Boswell. Darby, & Margery Moore. Test' John Weeks, Joseph Weeks, John Stafford.

No. 358. John Hubbard of Perq, Planter—for £40 pd by Luke Sumner, of Chowan, sold 160a on South Side of Perq River, & the head of Lakers Creek, "half of a grt unto Julianna Laker, April 1, 1718, & given by her, to Benjamin Scarbrough, her Gr-son, who sold sd land to sd Hubbard." Nov 19, 1759. Test' John Bridger, William Arrinton, Josiah Sumner.

No. 359. Benjamin Wilson of Perq, for £75 pd by Thomas Newby of afsd, sold 90a on So West Side of Perq River, Jan 21, 1760. Test' Miles Harvey, Joseph Murdaugh.

No. 360. Dec 18, 1759. Caleb Elliott of Perq, for £90 pd by William Wilson, of same—sold 150a on Balahac Swamp, adj sd Elliott, & Elizabeth Nixon. Test' Cornelius Moore, Thos. Coffield, Abraham Wilson.

No. 361. John Perry of Perq, for £50 pd by Israel Perry, of afsd—sold 200a at the mouth of Deep Branch, adj sd Israel. Aug 13, 1759. Test' Benjamin Small, Jos Winslow.

No. 362. William Wilson of Perq, for £47 pd by John Stone, of same—sold 75a on South side of Cypress Creek Swamp, adj Caleb Elliott, & Elizabeth Nixon. Test' Samuel Newby, William Newby, Sam'l. Sitterson. Dec 24, 1759.

No. 363. April 19, 1758. Joseph Creecy, of Chowan, Planter—for £250 pd by Francis Brown, of Perq, Merch't—sold 325a adj James Eggerton, near Yeopim Swamp, on line of Joseph Ming, which was sold by Christopher Snoden, to Samuel Gregory, April 3, 1732, & conveyed by sd Samuel to sd Creecy, May 1744, & 150a, pt of another grt, May 30, 1753. Test' Will'm. Boyd, John Mann.

No. 364. May 17, 1759. Lords Pro' for s10, pd by Jacob Hall, hath granted 212a in Berkeley Parish, Perq Co, on west side of "Hopkins Pattent." Granville. Frans Corbin, Josh'a Bodley.

No. 365. Feb 6, 1760. Joseph Barber of Perq, Sadler—for £12 s10 pd by John Maudlin, of afsd—sold 25a near Vosses Creek, on each side of Long Branch, on sd Creek, adj Wm Albertson. Test' Charles Morgan, Wm Albertson.

No. 366. Rachel Smith of Perq, for £60 pd by John Smith, of afsd—sold 51a, adj Benjamin Wilson, & Benjamin Sanders, also 34½a pt of land formerly sd Sanders, & sold to Samuel Smith, adj sd land. April 21, 1760. Test' Miles Harvey, Thos Newby.

No. 367. John Pearson of Perq, for "love I bear my younger Brother Joseph" (a Minor) of afsd, have given 100a on the fork of Cypress Swamp, half of a patent to John Pearson dec'd, & Pritlow Elliott, called "Aarons Ridge." Test' Reuben Perry, Isaac Elliott. April 1, 1760.

No. 368. John Pearson, for "love I have to my younger Brother Eleazer Pearson," (a Minor), of afsd do give Plan' whereon my father dwelt, 120a. April 21, 1760. Test' Reuben Perry, Isaac Elliott.

No. 369. Cornelius Ratliff, of Isle of Wight Co, Vir, for "love I have unto my cousin Mary Ratliff, widow of Joseph, of N. C. (Perq Co) have given one negro man, named Auger." April 11, 1760. Test' Thos. Newby, Nathan Newby.

No. 370. Cornelius Ratliff, for "love I bear my cousin Mary Moore, widow of John, of N. C. (Perq Co), do give one negro woman, named Molly." April 12, 1760. Test' Thos. Newby, Nathan Newby.

No. 371. Cornelius Ratliff, for "love I bear Children of Joseph Ratliff," of N. C., have given, "one negro woman, named Judah, & all her children, now in possession of Mary, the widow of sd Joseph, to be divided between them when the eldest comes of age, of 21 years." April 11, 1760. Test' Thos. Newby, Nathan Newby.

No. 372. Thomas Boswell of Perq, Planter—for £47 pd by Benjamin Mundy, of afsd, sold 50a on Little River Swamp, adj Ichabod Boswell, sd land taken up by Thomas Boswell Sen, "of late belonging to John Boswell, who died without issue, his brother Thomas Boswell, his lawful heir." April 21, 1760. Test' Matthew Jordan, Frans. Newby. Elizabeth Boswell, widow of John, makes over her right. Test' Matthew Jordan, Peter Pearson, Frans. Newby.

No. 373. April 21, 1760. Samuel Stallings of Chowan, for £42 pd by Caleb Elliott, of Perq, sold 98a, on So West Side of Perq River, adj Elizabeth Simons, in Balahack, called "the elbow," pt of land grt Wm Moore. Test' Haig Elliott William Willson.

No. 374. James Elliott of Perq, for £50 pd by Isaac Elliott, of afsd, sold 64a on No East of Cypress Swamp, at a branch which issueth out of sd Swamp, called "Homes branch," which divides sd land, from a survey whereon Isaac Lamb dwells, pt of a tract patented by James Thigpen, 1668. April 21, 1760. Test' Joshua Elliott, Zach Toms, Jas Barber.

No. 375. June 14, 1760. John Holloway, & Hannah his wife, of Perq, for £150 pd by Vivion Brooking, in Pasquotank Co, sold 200a, of which sd John was seized, under the will of Thomas Holloway dec, on the West side of Perq River, adj James Gibson, & William Bedgood. Test' William Tomblin, Durant Barclift.

No. 376. Samuel White of Perq, for £35 pd by Jacob Overman, of afsd, Planter—sold 4a, pt of land Arnold White dec, gave his son Samuel, adj William Munden. July 19, 1760. Test' Thom's Boswell, Elisha Parker, Morgan Overman.

No. 377. Feb 6, 1760. Charles Morgan of Perq, in con' of £20 s 10, pd by John Maudlin, of afsd, sold 100a, near Vosses Creek, on East side of same, adj Sylvanus Henby, Joseph Barber, & Wm Albertson. Test' Joseph Barber, John Sanders, Wm Albertson.

No. 378. Feb 9, 1760. William Matthias for £50 pd by Andrew Knox, (both of Perq) sold 100a, called "Bennets," on the head of Yeopim River, "formerly conveyed by Peter Jones Sen, to one Coddel, & by his death, became property of his dau Elizabeth, wife of Cary Godbee, who sold sd land to John Matthias dec, who devised it to his son William, in his will." Test' Frans. Brown, Ed. Hall.

No. 379. Feb 9, 1760. William Matthias for £40 pd by Andrew Knox, sold 2½a on North Side of Yeopim River, "being pt of 3a, conveyed by deed of gift, from Jeremiah Pratt Sen, to John Matthias dec, one half of which, sd John gave for the use of a Chappell" & sd land became property of sd William, by the death of his father. Test' Frans Brown, Ed Hall.

No. 380. William Matthias "am bound unto Andrew Knox, in the sum of £200" sd William, did execute a deed, for 100a on the head of Yeopim River, unto sd Knox. Feb 9, 1760. Test' Francis Brown, Ed Hall.

No. 381. Peter Jones Sen, of Perq, "Att' of Cary Godbee, & Elizabeth his wife," for £75 pd by John Matthias, sold to him 100a, called "Bennets" on Yeopim River, which came due sd Elizabeth, by the death of her father Henry Coddell. Jan 16, 1732/3. Test' Samuel Swann, Moses Speight, Chas Denman.

No. 382. Sept 19, 1760. Lords Pro' for £10, pd by Samuel Sutton, hath grt 340a, in the Parish of Berkeley, Co of Perq, on East side of Suttons Creek, at the mouth of Fork Creek, to line of Richd & Nath'l Sutton, on Bridge Branch. Granville; by Thos. Child.

No. 383. Aug 6, 1759. Lords Pro' for s10 pd by Benjamin Elliott, hath grt 66a, in Berkeley Parish, Perq Co, on east side of Perq River, binding on Pocosin. Granville; by Frans. Corbin, Josh'a Bodly.

No. 384. John Stone of Perq, for £90 pd by Joseph Moore, of same, sold 60a, on No West Side of Vosses Creek, at the mouth of Adkins Swamp, adj Abraham Hasket, & Joseph Lacey, to line of Joseph Newby. Dec 22, 1759. Test' Cornelius Moore, Benjamin Munden, Moses Stone.

No. 385. Abraham Mullen of Perq, planter—for "love I bear my Dau Tamer Hassell," of Tyrrell Co, have given 135a, on No East Side of Perq River, near the head of Beaver Cove Swamp, (on So side of sd Swamp), being pt of a grt unto Richd Whidbee, (356a) Oct 19, 1716. Isaac Hassell, husband of sd Tamer. Oct 21, 1760. Test' James Pierce, Abram Hassell, Benj. Hassell.

No. 386. George Shell of Perq, for £25 pd by Francis Toms, of afsd, sold 50a, adj Thomas Weeks, & William Turner, "land where Thomas Wright lives, & where Wm Noles dec, formerly lived." Aug 25, 1760. Test' Thos. Ray, Frans. Nixon, Ralph Fletcher.

No. 387. Oct 20, 1760. Joseph, & Cornelius Moore, Merchants—Ann Cary, Henry Stephens, & Edward Woodcocke, Exors of Robt Cary Esq, of London, Merch't—by Attchment, agst Theophilus Pugh, lately in hands of Benj. Hill, of Bertie Co, (Ex of sd Pugh), now in hands of John Jones Jr, (Ex of sd Hill dec) for the sum of £877 s5, 4p (also £4 1s 9p, for their cost) sd parties obtained Judgment, 1758, for sum due, & William Skinner, Sheriff of Perq, made return "that no goods, & chattels, of sd Pugh are to be found, & did expose land for sale at public Vendue, property of sd Pugh dec'd, which Joseph Moore being the highest bidder bought for £87," sd Joseph, sold sd land to sd Cornelius, 100a. Test' Phenias Nixon, Nicholas Collins.

No. 388. Abraham Wilson of Perq, for £30 pd by "my father Benjamin Wilson, assigned right to a negro man, named Coffee, after the death of my father, & Mother Judith Wilson, by the will of my gr-father, Thomas Docton dec." Oct 5, 1759. Test' Ruth Willson, Jacob Willson.

No. 389. Oct 4, 1760. Samuel Sutton of Perq Esq, for £3 pd by John Clayton, Planter—sold 8a adj George Sutton, & Nathaniel Sutton. Test' Sarah Sutton. William Robins.

No. 390. Edward Turner of Perq for "love I bear my son Edward, do give 164a on Deep Creek, being a grt unto George Sutton, May 1, 1668." Seal Joseph Turner, Dempsey Turner, Abraham Hasket. Oct 15, 1760.

No. 391. William Wilson of Perq, for £5 s10 pd by William Townsen, of afsd, sold 50a on So West side of Wm Phelps, now in poss' of Jas. Siterson, on line of Paul Palmer, & Zach Chancey, A grt to sd Chancey, & sold by him to Wm Moore, & by sd Moore to sd Wilson. Aug 29, 1760. Test' Huldah Moore, Edward Wingate, William Wingate.

No. 392. Thomas Lamb, & Sarah his wife, of Perq, for £80 pd by Benjamin Wilson, of afsd, sold 150a, on West side of Perq River, adj Henry

RECORDS OF DEEDS

Lamb, & Samuel Newby. Sept 10, 1760. Test' Joshua Elliott, John Sanders, Jacob Wilson.

No. 393. Henry Lamb of Perq, for £100 pd by Caleb White, of afsd, sold 150a, on south side of Cypress Creek. July 29, 1760. Test' Zachariah Nixon, Joshua Fletcher, Thomas Newby.

No. 394. Jan 7, 1760. Thomas Halsey of Perq, Planter—for £19 s1 p8, pd by Edward Hall, of afsd, sold 50a, formerly belonging to William Halsey, father of sd Thos. Test' Thomas Burket, Jonathan Houghton.

No. 395. Feb 14, 1741. Mr Joseph Perishoe, "deposed on oath that he was riding with Mr Francis Foster, & heard him say, he could take two negroes he had given his dau Hannah dec, from his son-in-law, John Barclift, but he would not show himself so little." Justice Joseph Sutton.

No. 396. Mr Samuel Barclift, "deposed on oath Feb 14, 1741, he heard his father-in-law, Mr Francis Foster, say a negro girl named Jane, belonged to his dau Hannah, & her husband John Barclift." Justice, Joseph Sutton.

No. 397. Thomas Biggs of Chowan, for £20 pd by John Whidbee, of Perq, sold 97a, in Berkeley Parish, Perq Co, on So Wst side of "Dead mans Swamp." Dec 9, 1760. Test' Caleb Benbridge, Michael Smith.

No. 398. Dec 19, 1760. Joshua Maudlin of Perq, for £19 pd by Charles Blount, of afsd, sold 20a, adj Tully Williams. Test' Tulle Williams, Anderson Gillet.

No. 399. Jan 20, 1761. John Bartlet of Perq, for £200 pd by Jarvis Jones, of same, Merchant—sold 180a, whereon sd Bartlet now lives, pt of 386a patented by John Parish, Nov 22, 1714, & by him sold to John Bartlet, "on Shitten Gut." Test' Will. Cumins, Mathew Jordan, Samuel Smith.

No. 400. John Turner of Perq, & Sarah his wife, for £75 pd by John Barclift, sold 75a on So west Side of Little River. Jan 20, 1761. Test' Jas Gibson, John Barclift.

No. 401. Jan 20, 1761. Jarvis Jones of Perq, for £20 pd by William Colson, of same, sold 50a "by Shitten Gut." Test' John Roberts, John Barclift.

No. 402. Thomas Jessop, of Carteret Co, Shoemaker—for £2 pd by John White, of Perq, sold 100a, on "Bee tree Swamp." Dec 8, 1760. Test' Benjamin Perry, Joel Hollowell.

No. 403. Benjamin Winslow of Perq, planter—for £6 s7, pd by Jacob Winslow, of same, Planter—sold 8a on No East Side of Perq River, patented by John Winslow, between Israel & Benj Winslow, to sd Jacobs line. Jan 20, 1761. Test' John Winslow, Elizabeth Winslow.

No. 404. Joel Hollowell, of Berkeley Parish, Perq Co, for £8 s16 p8, pd by Joshua White, of same, sold 80a, on East side of Perq River, adj Moses Rountree. Jan 7, 1761. Test' Thos Weeks, Thos Weeks Jun.

No. 405. Sept 3, 1760. Francis Toms, Planter—of Perq, for £47 s10, pd by William Wood, of afsd, sold 50a, on So West side of Little River, adj William Turner, & Thomas Wright, "where William Knowles formerly lived, & at his death fell to his brother Thomas." Test' Joseph Robinson, Thomas Robinson, Mark Newby.

No. 406. Dec 9, 1752. Lords Pro' for s3 pd by Phenias Nixon, of Perq, grt 280a, in Pasquotank Co, "on a branch that parts this land from John Nixon." Granville; by James Innes, Frans. Corbin.

No. 407. Feb 7, 1755. Lords Pro' for 3s, pd by Phenias Nixon, Planter—grt 80a, in Perq Co, adj John Nixon. Granville; by Frans. Corbin.

No. 408. Feb 7, 1761. Lords Pro' for 10s pd by Phenias Nixon, grt Land in Perq, in Parish of Berkeley, on line of Wm Arnold, & Foster Toms. (421a) Granville; by Thos. Child.

No. 409. Jan 7, 1761. Lords Pro' for 10s, pd by David Riddick, grt land in Birkeley Parish, Perq Co, on East side of Perq River. (252a.) Granville, by Thos. Child.

No. 410. Feb 7, 1761. Lords Pro' grt unto Luke Sumner, of Perq, Planter—for 10s land in Birkeley Parish, on north side of "Orepeak Swamp," 300a. Granville; by Thos. Child.

No. 411. Abram Mullen of Perq, for "love I have for my son-in-law (& dau) Isaac, & Tamer Hassell," of Tyrrell Co, have given, 135a in Perq, at the mouth of "Tarr Kills Branch," adj John Parson. Jan 21, 1761. Test' Edward Turner, Joseph Mullen, Benjamin Hassell.

No. 412. Abraham Wilson, for £60 s13, pd by Joseph Murdaugh (both of Perq) sold 100a, on No Wst Side of Cypress Creek. Mar 3, 1761. Test' Thomas Newby, Jos. Smith.

No. 413. John Stone of Perq, for £60, pd by William Wilson, of same, sold 75a, on South side of Cypress Creek. Mar 14, 1761. Test' Jacob Willson, Samuel Willson.

No. 414. Lords Pro' grt unto John Godfrey, of Perq, Gent—640a on Little River, for trans'. Jan 1, 1694. Phillip Ludwell Gov; Councellors: Thomas Harvey, Daniel Akehurst, Francis Toms, Thos. Pollock.

No. 415. Benjamin Scarbrough, of Perq, for £200 sold 380a, on west side of Castletons Creek Swamp, "called in some of the writings, Perrishoes Creek Swamp" a patent unto Benjamin Lakers, May 15, 1697, & by will of Julianna Lakers, was bequeathed to sd Benjamin. Mar 14, 1761. Test' Joshua Hobart, John White, John Skinner.

No. 416. Joseph Sutton Esq, of Perq, for £100 pd by Charles Morgan, of afsd, sold 200a, on Wst side of Little River, in Perq Co, adj Peter Parker. April 21, 1761. Test' Robert Cox, Foster Toms.

No. 417. Joseph Saunders of Perq, for £80 pd by Abraham Wilson, of afsd, sold 133a, on So West Side of Perq River, & North east side of Cypress Creek Swamp. Mar 4, 1761. Test' John Perry, Caleb Benbridge.

No. 418. April 23, 1761. William Gooding, of Berkeley Parish, Perq Co, for a con' pd by Thomas Weeks, of same, sold 50a, on Southmost side of Little River, "given me by my dec father George Gooding." Aug 11, 1748.

No. 419. June 9, 1761. Richard Berryman, for £5 s10, pd by Thomas Newby, sold 30a, on "the Sinking hole on the Pocosin." Test' Millicent Murdaugh, John Trotter.

No. 420. June 2, 1761. Evan Jones of Perq, for 8s, pd by Robert Chappel, sold 40a, on West Side of Perq River, adj sd Chappel. Test' Thos Newby, Joseph Murdaugh.

No. 421. Feb 28, 1761. Simon Perrishoe, of Perq, Planter—for £100 pd by Joseph Perrishoe, of afsd, sold 50a, adj "Perrishoes Grave yard, on Dirt Bridge branch." Test' John Clayton, Wm Bidgood.

No. 422. Moses Boyce of Perq, planter—for £31 pd by Thomas Small, of Chowan, sold 80a in Perq, adj Henry Hill, & Joseph Hurdell, to a line of

RECORDS OF DEEDS 187

Thomas Docton, & Thomas Davis, part of a patent, unto sd Docton, Mar 13, 172—, & conveyed by him to Thomas Davis, & from him to John Boyce, who bequeathed it, in his will to his son Moses. Feb 13, 1761. Test' Elias Stallings, Moses Rountree, Nicholas Stallings.

No. 423. Mar 8, 1760. James Eggerton of Perq, planter—for £85 pd by Francis Brown, of afsd, Merchant—sold 150a on Yeopim Creek, adj Richard Hall, Arkill Branch, & sd Brown, pt of 300a grt to Richard Woolard, Feb 10, 1669, & transferred by sd Woolard, Nov 16, 1721, to William Eggerton, father of sd James. Test' Ed Hall, Ann Pomerry.

No. 424. John Brinkley of Perq, "give unto James Brinkley, of afsd, all my goods, chattels, & house-hold Stuff, as may be found." Oct 19, 1761. Test' John Thatch, Green Thatch.

No. 425. Daniel Rogerson of Perq, Planter—for £6 pd by John Hollowell, of afsd—sold 10a on No Side of the River Pocosin, pt of a patent, to William Kitchen, & Margaret Snooks, 1713. Test' Nicholas Stallings, Jacob Powell. Oct 17, 1761.

No. 426. Sept 10, 1761. Thos. Halsey of Perq, for £100 s10 p4, pd by Edward Hall, of afsd—sold 104a on the head of Yeopim River, adj Andrew Knox, "pt of 205a patented by one Fisher, & conveyed to William Halsey, who gave 50a of sd land, to his dau Christian Knox, a sd William dying intestate, the remainder, descended to sd Thomas." Test' Andrew Knox, Christian Knox.

No. 427. John Harriss of Tyrell Co, N. C. for £102 pd by Elijah Harriss, of same, sold 200a on Loosing Swamp, in Perq, adj John Gordon, Jesse Eason, & Luke Sumner. Test' Sam'l. Holaday, Sam'l Harriss, Mary Harriss. Sept 7, 1761.

No. 428. Phenias Nixon of Perq, Gent—for £8 pd by John Whedbee of same—sold 163a, on North East Side of Perq River, adj Richard Whedbee, & Lawrence Arnold, in Lower Gum Swamp." Feb 7, 1761. Test' Thos. Weeks, John Calloway.

No. 429. Joseph Godfrey of Perq, Farmer—for £20 pd by Thomas Stanton, of same, Farmer—sold 50a, adj James Gibson, & Charles Blount. Mar 14, 1761. Test' James Gibson, John Gibson.

DEED BOOK G

No. 1. Benjamin Wilson, & Judith his wife, of Perq, for £90 pd by Nathan Cullens, of Chowan—sold "a negro man, named Coffee, given us by our father Thomas Docton, in his will, at our death to our son Abraham." Dec 20, 1761. Test' Jacob Wilson, Sam'l Bagley.

No. 2. Benjamin Scarbrough of Perq, Farmer—for £220 pd by Joshua Skinner, of afsd, Farmer—sold two tracts of land, adj each other, "on west side of Castletons Creek, patented by Benjamin Laker, May 15, 1697, 137a on Deep Branch in the "Patent called Castletons Creek Swamp," land patented by Johanna Taylor, (mother of Julianna Laker) May 15, 1697, who gave sd land to her gr-son Benj Scarbrough, & 165a which was given to Macrora Scarbrough, July 20, 1731, & was by him bequeathed to his son Benjamin, in his will." Jan 19, 1761. Test' Charles Moore, Thomas Paine.

No. 3. Joshua Hubbard, Schoolmaster—for £40 pd by Joshua Skinner, sold 100a, formerly belonging to Benj Laker, where Macrora Scarbrough formerly lived, pt of 300a, belonging to said Scarbrough. Dec 12, 1761. Test' James Sanders, Robert Jones.

No. 4. Aug 26, 1761. John White, to William Arrenton, for £39, sold 160a, in the fork of Castletons Creek Swamp (where Deep branch issueth out of the Swamp) pt of 475a, on the head of Perrishows Creek, "which was a grant unto Julianna Laker, April 10, 1704, & by her given in her will, to Macrora Scarbrough, who by gift to his son Benjamin, & said Benj sold same to me." April 8, 1758. Test' Benj Scarbrough, Phillip Mason.

No. 5. Robert Avery, for £25 pd by Zachariah Jones, sold 50a, on "the main Road that goeth to Edenton" along line of land bought by Moses Baker, of Moses Elliott, & land formerly Abraham Sanders. Jan 20, 1761. Test' Joshua Skinner, Sam'l Standin, Zepaniah Jones.

No. 6. Christopher Nicholson, farmer—for £5 pd by Thomas Nicholson, Trader—sold 3 parcels of land, on the So west Side of Little River, 57a, adj sd Thomas Nicholsons Mill, & Little River Bridge—50a, given by John Nixon, to said Thomas, & 20a, on lines of Barrow, & Robinson, "pt of a gt to me Sept 7, 1761." 5d, 12mo 1761. Test' Charles Overman, Joseph McAdams, Chs. Overman Jr.

No. 7. Thomas Nicholson, for £40 pd by Charles Overman, sold land on So west Side of Little River, "across the main Road, just below the Meeting House." 5d, 12mo 1761. Test' John Morriss, Nicholas Nicholson, Joseph McAdams.

No. 8. Christopher Nicholson, for £5 pd by Ellis, & Joshua Bundy, sold 85a, on South Wt side of Little River, at the mouth of a branch, adj Francis Nixon, "where Josiah Bundy formerly lived," on line of William Hasket. 13d, 12mo 1761. Test' Thomas Nicholson, Phineas Nixon, Thomas Robinson.

No. 9. Christopher Nicholson, for £16 pd by Phineas Nixon, Farmer—sold a "parcel of woodland," on So West Side of Little River 22a, pt of 700a, gt "to me by Earl Granville Sept 7, 1761." 20d, 12mo 1761. Test' Thomas Nicholson, Thomas Robinson, Ellis Bundy.

No. 10. Christopher Nicholson, Farmer—for £12 pd by John Nixon, farmer—sold 27a, on South west Side of Little River, pt of 700a. 13d, 12mo 1761. Test' Thomas Nicholson, Phineas Nixon, Thomas Robinson.

No. 11. Christopher Nicholson, for £2 pd by William Hasket, Farmer—sold 27a, on South west Side of Little River, pt of 700a. 30d, 12m 1762. Test' Thomas Nicholson, Phineas Nixon, Thomas Robinson.

No. 12. July 30, 1760. Earl Granville, gt unto William Arnold of Perq, Planter—"a parcel of Vacant land in the Parish of Berkeley," on South Side of Little River, adj John Nichols, & Lawrence Arnold, 265a. Granville; by Tho. Child. Sept 17, 1744.

No. 13. John Jones of Perq, Planter—for £237 pd by Miles Harvey Esq, of afsd—sold 300a, on Perq River, adj Chas Moore, John White, & said Jones, "sd land conveyed to me by Henry Warren, April 29, 1751." Seal Jan 13, 1762.

No. 14. Joseph Perrishoe of Perq, Planter—for £30 pd by William Bateman, Planter—sold 2a, adj said Bateman. Jan 16, 1762. Test' James Paine, William Barclift, Benjamin Bateman.

No. 15. Martha Flewmen of Perq, for "love I bear my brother James, do give to him, one Negro girl named Nell, to be enjoyed by him forever." Aug 16, 1761. Test' Joshua Skinner.

No. 16. Benjamin Wilson of Perq, for "love I bear my son Jacob," of afsd—have given, pt of a tract on Wst Side of Perq River, in the fork of Wilsons Creek, 100a, where he now lives, adj Joseph Elliott, Moses & Thomas Wilson. Jan 18, 1761. Test' Benj. Wilson, Jon. Newby, Robt. Newby, Fras. Newby.

No. 17. Dec 12, 1761. Joshua Maudlin of Perq, Planter—for £98 pd by Charles Blount, of afsd—sold 97¾a on the North side of Tully Williams line, adj said Blount, & Little River, a gt unto Joseph Godfrey. Test' Jno. Clayton, Stokes Norment.

No. 18. Oct 24, 1761. Benjamin Simpson of Perq, for £55 pd by John Nixon, of Chowan, sold 53½a "where I now live, on the North Side of Browns Mill Swamp, adj Francis Brown, half of which my father (Benj Simpson) bought of Samuel Gregory, Aug 15, 1743, & by him given me." Feb 17, 1755. Test' Thomas Ming, Delight Nixon.

No. 19. Sept 12, 1761. Vivian Brooking of Perq, for £150 pd by John Stevenson, of same, sold 200a, on West Side of Little River, granted Feb 25, 1696 to Thos. Holloway dec'd, who "divised same to his son, John Hollowell." Test' Joseph Reed, Joseph Barclift, Andrew Miller.

No. 20. Joshua Elliott Jr, of Perq, for £50 pd by Joseph Outland, of afsd—sold tract of land on Mings Creek, "below a settlement made by Ephraditus Brinkley," adj land given by Joseph Burket, to his father John Burket dec. April 23, 1761. Test' Thomas Small, Ann Outland.

No. 21. Mar 17, 1762. Francis Newby of Perq, for £400 pd by John Murdaugh, Joseph Smith, & Andrew Knox; all of same—sold "4 negroes, 4 horses, 20 head of cattle, a quantity of hogs, 5 feather beds, & furniture, 1 Desk 1 table, chairs, pots, pewter, all household goods, & a quantity of European goods in his Store house." Test' Ed Hall, John Smith.

No. 22. John Lancaster, & Mary his wife, of Pasquotank Co, Merchant—for £5 pd by William Townsend, sold 50a, on South west Side of Perq River, pt of a tract pat' by Zachariah Chancey, & by him sold to William Moore, & by him sold to Dempsey Conner, which by his will fell to his widow, adj William Phelps, now in possession of James Sitterson. 20d, 1mo 1762. Test' Joshua Skinner, John Skinner.

No. 23. Sept 7, 1761. Earl Granville, for 10s pd by Andrew Knox, do grt 100a, "in the Parish of Berkeley, Co of Perq," at a place in the Desert, called "Oakland." Ja. Gibson, W. Cheston. Granville, by Tho. Child. May 3, 1762.

No. 24. John Simons of Chowan, for £25 pd by Joseph Williams, of Perq, sold 150a, on So Side of "Pratts Mill Swamp," bought of Jacob Caruthers, & pat by him, adj William Wyatt. May 4, 1762. Test' Jer Halsey, Hatten Williams, Ann Williams.

No. 25. Peter Cartright of Perq, Planter—for £400 pd by Jarvis Jones, Merchant—of Pasquotank Co, "doth sell 30a in Perq," on the head of Deep Creek, patented by Albert Albertson Sen, Jan 1, 1694, & Jan 7, 1721, assigned to Albert Albertson Jr (son of sd Albert), & by will of Albert Albertson Jr, given to said Cartright. Nov 12, 1760. Test' Jacob Madon, Daniel Koen, Edward Halstead.

No. 26. Peter Cartright, for £3 pd by Col Jarvis Jones, sold 200a, in Perq, "where said Peter now lives," near the mouth of Tomblins Branch, being pt of 300a, grt to John Tomblin, July 1694. April Court, 1762. Test' Jacob Madren (Madre), Daniel Roen, Edward Halstead.

No. 27. George Boswell of Perq, for £10 pd by Joseph Boswell of afsd—sold 120a on So west Side of Perq River. Dec 13, 1761. Test' Isaac Boswell, John Clayton.

No. 28. James Morgan of Pasquotank, for £5 pd by Betty Maudlin, of Perq, Widow—sold "parcel of Swamp," on So-west Side of Little River—30a, at the mouth of Fork Swamp. Feb 7, 1762. Test' Peter Maudlin, Mary Maudlin.

No. 29. James Morgan, for £5 pd by Peter Maudlin, of Perq, Planter—sold 25a, of Swamp land, on So-west Side of Little River, adj Joseph Boswell. Jan 20, 1762. Test' Thomas Boswell, George Boswell.

No. 30. James Morgan, for £10 pd by Thomas Boswell, of Perq, sold 96a, of Swamp land, on So Wt side of Little River, in Perq Co. Dec 13, 1761. Test' Joseph Boswell, Isaac Boswell.

No. 31. George Boswell of Perq, for £10 pd by James Morgan, of Pasquotank, sold 76a, on So-west Side of Little River, adj Joseph Boswell. Dec 13, 1761. Test' Joseph Outland, Jno Clayton.

No. 32. James Morgan of Pasq, for £10 pd by Samuel White, & Arnold White, of Perq, sold tract of Swamp land, on So Wst Side of Little River—52a, adj Isaac Boswell, "up the Swamp to George Boswells Grt." Dec 13, 1761. Test' John Hasket, Jno Clayton.

No. 33. George Boswell of Perq, for £10 pd by Thomas Boswell, of afsd—sold 65a on the So Wst Side of Little River, adj Robert Cox, near Fork branch. "In trust for heirs of Benj, Munden, & Elisha his son." Feb 22, 1762.

No. 34. George Boswell, for £10 pd by Peter Munden, sold 51a, on So Wst side of Little River, "in trust for an orphan, Lidah Boswell," dau of Thomas (now an infant), adj Joseph Boswell. Jan 13, 1762. Test' John Hasket, Thomas Boswell.

No. 35. George Boswell, for £10 pd by Jacob Overman, sold 118a, on So-wst side of Little River, adj Isaac Boswell, to line of George Boswell. Oct 13, 1761. Test' Jno. Clayton, Joseph Boswell.

No. 36. James Morgan, for £10 pd by Joseph Boswell, sold 53a, on So-Wst side of Little River, adj George Boswell. Dec 13, 1761. Test' Jno. Clayton, Isaac Boswell.

No. 37. Mar 20, 1762. Samuel Parsons of Perq, for £90 pd by Roger Kinyon, sold 190a on No side of Perq River, "along Beaver Cove Swamp, patented by Samuel Parsons, gr-father of said Samuel, July 6, 1721, who dying intestate, said land descended to Sam'l Parsons, father of said Sam'l, who by his will did bequeath same to me." Test' John Harvey, Joseph Kinyon.

No. 38. Joseph Moore of Perq, Merchant—for £76 pd by Benj Elliott, of afsd—sold 60a at the mouth of Atkins Swamp, adj Abraham Hasket, & Joseph Lacey, down the Swamp to the Creek. Jan 20, 1762.

No. 39. Joseph Robinson of Perq, Planter—"exchanged a tract of land," on So-wst Side of Little River—210a with Moses, & Aaron Jackson; adj George Gording, & John Robinsons lines. Mar 3, 1762. Test' Thomas Robinson, Reed Durant.

No. 40. Dec 12, 1761. William Gording of Perq, Planter—for £70 pd by Jarvis Jones, of same, Merch't—sold plan' 52a, where said Gording now lives, "by the side of Little River, to the head of Spring branch, & the old horse bridge." Test' Edward Halstead, John Turner.

No. 41. Mar 27, 1762. Jarvis Jones of Perq, for £50 pd by William Arnold, of same, sold 100a, of "Woodland whereon I now live," pt of 361a patented by John Parish, Nov 22, 1714, & left by him to his son, & said son sold same to John Barclift, who sold the land to me—180a, adj Wm Coleson, on "Shitten Gut." Test' Samuel Newby, Henry Bailey.

No. 42. Benjamin Perry Sr, of Perq, for "love I bear my son Benjamin, of afsd—do give a tract of land, bought of William Moore Jr, 300a, adj land where I now dwell. April 19, 1762. Test' Robert Riddick, Nicholas Stallings, Joseph Perry.

No. 43. Mar 24, 1763. Jarvis Jones of Perq, for £70 pd by Edward Holstead, of same—sold 52a bought of William Gording, on Little River Swamp, adj Aaron Jackson, to the head of Spring branch, & "old horse bridge." Test' John Roberts, Israel Scarfe (Scaff).

No. 44. Mar 20, 1762. John Barclift Jr, of Perq, planter—for £10 pd by Edward Holstead, of same, sold 100a, whereon sd Holstead now lives, adj William Godfrey, by the side of Deep Creek. Test' Jarvis Jones, Thomas Barclift.

No. 45. Nov 12, 1761. James Foster Sr, of Pasq, for £75 pd by John Barclift Jr, of Perq—"doth sell plan' where Edward Holstead now lives," on Deep Creek, 100a, a patent to Joseph Commander, adj Thomas, & William Godfreys lines. Test' Jarvis Jones, Joseph Reed, Caleb Roen.

No. 46. May 1, 1762. George Hendrickson, late of Perq, (son of Jeremiah) for £30 pd by John Campbell, of Bertie Co N. C. sold 105a on South west side of Little River, adj Moses Jackson. Test' John Davidson, Alex Ford.

No. 47. Jeremiah Bundy of Perq, for £75 pd by Cornelius Moore, Merch't—sold 50a on North Side of Perq River, & South Side of Cypress Swamp, to lines of Gideon Bundy, & William Bogue. Jeremiah & Susannah Bundy. Test' Duke Bogue, William Bogue, Matthew Jordan.

No. 48. Francis Newby of Perq, Trader—for £400 pd by Josiah Jordan, of Isle of Wight Co, Vir', & Matthew Jordan, of Perq Co N. C. "sold 105a in Piney Woods," 25a on Little River, one house, & lot in the Town of Hertford,* (No. 93) one sail boat, one canoe, all my books, bonds, bills, Notes, & Money, (if any in the hands of Joseph Outland), on account of a Partnership, between him, & said Newby." May 11, 1762. Test' Thos Wilson, Joseph Newby, Mary Elliott.

No. 49. John Barclift Jr, for £20 pd by Robert Wilson, of Nixonton, sold pt of tract, 100a, on the East by Little River. Sarah Barclift, wife of said John, relinquishes her dower right. Mar —, 1758. Test' Joseph Overman, John Overman.

No. 50. Abraham Riggs of Pasq, "doth forever release 100a, on the main Road in Perq Co, unto Capt Joseph Turner, whereon my uncle Abraham Riggs lived, & by will did bequeath to me." Dec 31, 1761. Test' Rebeccah Clayton, John Clayton.

No. 51. July 16, 1762. Joseph Perrishoe Jr of Perq, for £51 pd by William Bateman, of afsd—sold 102a on No East side of Perq River, "according to the most ancient, & reputed bounds." Said land purchased by John Perrishoe father of said Joseph, of Mr. Clement Hall, at whose death sd land descended to

---

*(Note: Said "lot in Hertford" was across the Street from the Court House, just about where Morgans furniture store now stands.)

Josiah Perrisho, who conveyed same to sd Joseph Jr. Test' Thomas Bateman, John Harvey.

No. 52. John Hawkins of Bertie Co, Planter—for £16 pd by Joseph Newby, of Perq, Millwright—sold 160a, adj John Kinions line, which he bought of William Lacey, & was formerly John Flowers. July 16, 1762. Test' Joseph Moore, John Leah, Joshua Sutton.

No. 53. April 3, 1762. John Raper, planter—for £30 pd by Thomas Bateman Jr (both of Perq), "doth sell land on No Wst side of Muddy Creek," 50a, adj William, & Thomas Bateman, pt of land taken up by Thomas Snoden, (280a) May 1, 1768. Test' Thomas Robinson, Aaron Jackson.

No. 54. James Morgan of Pasq, for £10 pd by Isaac Boswell, of Perq, sold 34a of Swamp land, on So Wst Side of Little River. Dec 30, 1761. Test' Joseph Boswell, Jno Clayton.

No. 55. Jarvis Jones of Pasq, Esq—for £150 pd by Samuel Sutton, of Perq, sold part of two patents, one called "Gut patent" to John Parish, Nov 22, 1714, & the other 500a, called "Glades Patent" Oct 10, 1725, taken out of the whole, 400a, on "Shitten Gut," adj Thomas Weeks, & William Arnold near the head of "Turkey Ridge." July 20, 1762. Test' Joseph Sutton, Thomas Stevenson.

No. 56. July 20, 1762. Jarvis Jones, for £175 pd by Joseph Sutton, sold 300a, grt unto Albert Albertson Jr, Jan 1, 1694, also 200a grt unto John Tomblin, July 3, 1694, purchased by Albert Albertson, of William Tomblin, July 23, 1739, "he being the only surviving son of his father dec, land on So Side of Deep Creek, near Nags Head Chappel," on the head of Tomblins branch. Test' Sam'l Sutton, Joseph Sutton, Thomas Stevenson.

No. 57. June 8, 1762. Joseph Boswell, for £14 pd by James Morgan, sold 24a on So Wst Side of Little River, "where said Joseph now dwells," sd land taken up by Thomas Boswell. Test' Christopher Nicholson, Thomas Robinson, William Hill.

No. 58. George Boswell, for £10 pd by Isaac Boswell, both of Perq, sold 67a on So Wst Side of Little River. July Court, 1762. Test' Joseph Boswell, John Clayton.

No. 59. Feb 5, 1762. Thomas Bagley Sen, of Perq, for £55 s2 p4 ½ penny, sold 60a on No Est side of Perq River, to Samuel Bartlet, adj Daniel Saint, & Jonathan Pearson, "with all houses, & appurtenances." Test' Jonathan Pearson, Benjamin Bagley, Thomas Bagley Jr.

No. 60. July 19, 1762. John Nichols, & wife Jemmima, of Perq, Planter—for £100 pd by Jarvis Jones, of Pasq Co, sold part of 500a, a patent to John Parish, 1722, & sold by him to Edward Dowdy, June 6, 1735 (100a, sold to Robert Hall). The remaining 400a, fell to sd Jemmima, only dau of sd Dowdy, land near the end of "Turkey Ridge," adj William Coleson. Test' Thomas Nicholson, Joseph Sutton, Edward Holstead.

No. 61. Dec 9, 1761. William Wilson, & Jonathan Shared, for £115 pd by said Sharod, sold 150a on So Wst Side of Balahack Swamp, adj Caleb Elliott; & Elizabeth Nixon. Test' Joseph Elliott, To Bullock, Jacob Wilson.

No. 62. Joseph Lilly of Chowan, Planter—for 20s pd by Jacob Powell, of afsd—sold 50a on East Side of Perq River, part of a patent to Elias Stallings, for 640a. Feb 23, 1762. Test' John Hollowell, Samuel Farler.

RECORDS OF DEEDS 193

No. 63. James Perrishoe Jr, of Perq, for £25 pd by Robert Evans, of afsd—sold 148a, adj Joseph Scott, & Peter Pearsons line. June 29, 1762. Test' Matthew Jordan, George Metcalf.

No. 64. Jarvis Jones Esq, for £25 pd by William Arnold, of Perq, sold 50a, called "Glade patent" pt of 500a, patented by John Parish, Oct 10, 1725, on Suttons line. July 20, 1762. Test' Joseph Sutton, Tho Nichols, Edw'd Holstead.

No. 65. Jan 25, 1762. William Albertson of Perq, for £8 pd by Samuel Anderson, of afsd—sold 70a on Henbys line, to Barbers corner. Test' John Anderson, Joshua Boswell, Jonathan Sherod.

No. 66. Joshua Maudlin of Perq, planter—for £50 pd by Joseph Outland, Merch't—of afsd, sold 80a adj Dempsey Barclift, & Charles Blount, to the head of Little River. Jan 30, 1762. Test' Joshua Fletcher, Foster Toms.

No. 67. Jan 25, 1762. Timothy Walton Esq, of Chowan Co, for £12 s10, pd by Andrew Knox, of Perq, sold 60a on South Side of Perq River, pt of a tract grt Julianna Laker, April 1, 1718/19 called "Chinqupin Ridge," binding on lands of Joshua Skinner, William Arrington, & the desert. Test' Ed Hall, Peter Bretton.

No. 68. Obadiah Small of Pasq Co, Cooper—for £16 pd by William Munden, of same, sold 65a on the side of Little River, & Spring Swamp, adj Joshua Perrishoe. Feb 22, 1762. Test' Thomas Boswell, Elisha Parker, William Lowe.

No. 69. Benjamin Scarbrough of Perq, Farmer—for £100 pd by John Thatch, of same, sold 500a, "where sd Thatch now lives," formerly the property of Richard Leary, by conveyance became the property of Paul Palmer, & Joanna his wife, given by them to Samuel, & Martha Ann Palmer, their Heirs by Deed, July 13, 1734, both dying without heirs, sd land descended to Anna Scarbrough, & from my mother, to me, son of sd Anna Scarbrough. July 1, 1762. Test' Thos Bonner, Hatten Williams.

No. 70. Rachel Smith of Perq, for "love I bear my son John, do give one negro boy, named Ishmael, & in case he die, to be equally divided between my dau's Rachel, & Penninah." July 21, 1761. Test' Thos. Newby, Joseph Murdaugh.

No. 71. Francis Toms of Perq, for £30 pd by Joseph Smith Jr, sold 100a "near a ditch called Samuel Newby's," in Balahack, adj Truman Moore's line. Jan 7, 1762. Test' Samuel Snith, Jonathan Sherod, Thomas Elliott.

No. 72. Joseph Smith Jr of Perq, for £159 pd by Haig Elliott, of Pasq Co, sold 200a "at the Mirey branch, & Chowan Road, to the Holy bridge," on line of Mary Barker, & Caleb Elliott. Sept 27, 1762. Test' Joseph Smith, Jeremiah Carmon, John Trotten.

No. 73. Sept 6, 1762. Jesse Newby, for £5 pd by Robert Newby, sold land "at the Mill Pond" next to land where Mark Newby formerly dwelt, on lines of Samuel, Robert, & Francis Newby, to the mouth of a branch, running out of the Mill Pond, "on the north side of Francis Newby's house." Test' Cornelius Moore, Fras. Nixon, Joshua Fletcher.

No. 74. Aug 25, 1762. Francis Newby for £107 pd by Robert Newby, sold "right in 60a of land at the Mill Pond, next to Mark Newby's house, where he formerly lived," to line of Samuel Newby, & the mouth of a branch, running out of the Mill Pond, "on the north side of the house where Francis Newby now lives." Test' Matthew Jordan, Frederick Norcom, Abraham Bennett.

No. 75. Joseph Outland, Merch't—for £220 pd by Zachariah Nixon, sold 124a "where I now dwell," on No Est Side of Perq River, adj Charles Morgan, Joseph Anderson, Samuel Moore, & Francis Toms. Aug 7, 1762. Joseph & Mary Outland. Test' Zach Toms, Mark Newby.

No. 76. Sept 9, 1762. Joseph Outland, for £110 pd by Charles Blount, sold 80a on So wst Side of Little River, adj Dempsey Barclift, & sd Blount, "land formerly Joshua Maudlin's dec'd, a grt to John Godfrey, 1694." Test' Tully William, Joseph Whedbee.

No. 77. Jan 17, 1763. Edward Penrice, & Francis Penrice, of Perq for £288 s15, pd by Joseph Creecy, of Chowan Co, sold 170a, part of 543a, patented by Archibald Holmes, June 24, 1704, by him sold to Edward Wilson, April 7, 1705 which by sd Wilsons death fell to his dau Sarah, and was conveyed by sd Sarah & her husband Thomas Williams, to Richard Bond, by his death became the property of his brother Sam'l Bond, he dying without issue, sd land descended to his sister Elizabeth Penrice, & Abigail Arrenton, & from them to sd Edward, & William Arrenton, sons of sd Abagail, said William Arrenton, on Mar 5, 1757 sold his right to sd Penrice, 75a on North Side of Albemarle Sound, opposite "Battes Grave Island" belonging to Francis Penrice, dec'd father of sd Francis. Test' Joshua Skinner, John Hall, Christ Moore.

No. 78. Earle Granville, gt unto Joe. Sutton Sen, 300a, on Suttons Creek, (a grt to Deborah Sutton, Nov 4, 1707, for 1s for every 50a). Wm Glover Esq President. Councillors; John Hawkins, Spear Foster. Test' John Porter, Gabriel Newby.

No. 79. Aug 26, 1762. John Jones of Perq, for £80 pd by Miles Harvey, sold 200a, adj Moses Barker, pt of a tract, (435a) purchased by sd Jones, of John, & Miriam Chancey. Oct 10, 1757. Test' Thomas Long, Zepaniah Jones.

No. 80. 1763. Benjamin Scarbrough of Perq, for £25 pd by Joshua Skinner, of same—sold plan' on West Side of Castletons Creek, north-ward from "Skinners Bridge" formerly belonging to William Stewart, up the Creek to sd Skinner, & a line formerly Samuel Phelps, now William Townsends, pat by Richard Skinner, Nov 22, 1714, & by him sold to Julianna Laker, by descent from her to me. Jan 3, 1763. Test' William Arrenton, Wm Townsend, Robert Jones, Henry Moore.

No. 81. Samuel Standin of Perq, Planter—for £100 pd by William Standin. sold 150a on Mings Creek, "whereon my dec'd father Sam'l Standin did live." April 5, 1762. Test' Joshua Skinner, Hatten Williams.

No. 82. "Samuel Standin dec'd Mar 28, 1752." To divide a "bequest of land to his two sons, Sam'l, & William, on upper side of dividing branch, from Mings Creek to the head of sd branch, 150a the property of sd Samuel with 150a below the dividing branch, to William Standin; we here-unto divide same." Jan 10, 1763. John Skinner, Benjamin Harvey.

No. 83. William Standin, for £100 pd by Samuel Standin, sold 150a, at the mouth of "dividing branch" to Ming Creek, adj land of "my dec father Samuel Standin." April 5, 1763. Test' Joshua Skinner, Hatten Williams.

No. 84. Jesse Henley, Farmer—for £12 pd by Mary Ratclift, (widow & relict of Joseph of Perq dec), sold unto Joseph Ratclift (her son) 225a, on So East Side of Little River, near Fork Swamp, adj land formerly Joseph

RECORDS OF DEEDS 195

Sutton's, now Elliotts "by a grt from Earl Granville to me," Nov 28, 1760. Seal 5d, 2mo 1763. Test' Jesse Newby, And'n Wilson, Ralph Fletcher.

No. 85. April 19, 1763. William Standin of Perq, Planter—for £25 pd by Joshua Skinner of same, sold 50a, adj Luke Sumner, "to a Mirey branch," down the branch to Bridge Creek, pt of land formerly Samuel Standin's. Test' Samuel Penrice, John Cale.

No. 86. Sept 13, 1762. Thomas Ming of Chowan, Richard Rogers, & Delight Nixon, of same, for £310 sold to sd Rogers, & Nixon 120a, a grt to James Ward, Sept 29, 1706, who conveyed same to his gr-son James Ming, he dying without issue, sd land became the property of his brother Thomas Ming, Joseph Ming dec, (land at the bridge Neck, on the head of Yeopim River) sd land devised to sd Thomas by the will of his father Joseph Ming, 258a, in the fork of Eggertons Mill Swamp, called "Bridge Neck" adj James Eggerton dec, Francis Penrice dec, & John Wilkins. Thomas & Ann Ming. Test' Thomas Ming, Thomas Pallarten.

No. 87. Joseph Perrishoe of Perq, for "love I bear my brother Samuel of afsd—do give all that plan' on No Est Side of Perq River, 100a, which was given me by the will of my dec father, John Perrishoe, Dec 17, 1755, land grt unto John Anderson dec, July 26, 1703 (200a), & purchased by my father of him." April 16, 1762. Test' John Harvey, Tho Jones.

No. 88. Frans Penrice, late of Perq, did give to us Francis, & Samuel Penrice, a plan' whereon he then lived, "with directions of division, by which we bind ourselves to abide." Jan 16, 1763. Test' Joshua Skinner, Charles Moore.

No. 89. Josiah Perrishoe of Perq, for £55, pd by James Perrishoe Jr, of afsd—sold 54a by the Pond side, a pat unto John Lacey, 1725. Seal June 26, 1762. Test' Joseph Perrishoe, Joshua Davis.

No. 90. Oct 17, 1762. Andrew Knox Esq, of Perq, Sheriff of sd Co—to George Eason Sen, of afsd, Planter—Whereas; Moses Eason of Perq, Mariner—"was indebted to Charles Moore, & Seth Sumner, Churchwardens of Berkeley Parish, in Co afsd, for the sum of £28 s16 p4, and to Thomas Jones of Chowan Co, the sum of £4 s12 p6, which sd parties did recover, at the Court House in Hertford, July 20, 1762, (by Writ of Execution, to sd Sheriff), agst goods, chattels, & land, of sd Moses, to satisfy above £33 s8 p10, & £7 s2 p8, "not being able to find such goods, & chattels, did expose for sale a tract of land, 65½a, which George Eason bought, for £313 being the highest bidder," adj John Gordon, on the main desert. Test' Charles Moore, Miles Harvey.

No. 91. Jan 22, 1763, Edward Holstead of Perq, Joiner—for £75 pd by John Stokes, of same, planter—sold 100a, on East Side of Deep Creek, adj William Godfrey. Test' Jno. Clayton, Rebecca Clayton.

No. 92. Jan 28, 1762. Joshua Guyer of Perq, Planter—for £150 pd by Cornelius Moore, of same, Merchant—sold 210a, adj Arthur Croxton, & Joseph Newby. "Land my father John Guyer bought of Abraham Mullen." Oct 13, 1740. Test' Andrew Knox, Matthew Jordan, John Pleace.

No. 93. April 17, 1762. Charles Morgan, for £16 pd by Ralf Fletcher, sold 50a "back of land, whereon sd Fletcher now lives." Test' Jesse Winslow, Joseph Outland, Elizabeth Boswell.

No. 94. Feb 19, 1763. Francis Newby of Perq, for £16 s8, pd by Gabriel Cosand, of same—sold 25a near Suttons Creek, pat by John Henby, in 1741

(587a) "conveyed to my father, Francis Newby, & given by sd Francis in his will, to my brothers Robert, Mark, Jesse, & myself," adj sd Cosand. Test' Matthew Jordan, Gideon Maudlin, Moses Wilson.

No. 95. Keziah Newby of Perq, for "love I bear my sons Francis, & Thomas Newby"—(Minors) for the fullfilling of the last will of my dec husband, do give unto Thomas Newby, in trust for sd minors, two tracts of land; once parcel 113a, on the Sound in Chowan Co, pt of land whereon my father Thomas Pierce dec, lived, & was laid off to me—second a parcel on Chickmachomack banks in Currituck Co, 200a a grt to my father 1748. Seal April 20, 1763. Test' Daniel Saint, Francis Nixon, Jeremiah Carruthers.

No. 96. Zachariah Lilly of Perq, planter—for £20 pd by Jacob Perry Sen, sold 50a on Great branch, & North Side of River Pocosin, adj Jacob Powell, & sd Perry, pt of a grt to William Kitchen, by sd Kitchen, given to John Lilly, (son of Thomas) conveyed by said John Lilly to his brother Thomas, who by death gave same to his son Zachariah. Jan 12, 1763. Test' Nicholas Stallings, John Hollowell.

No. 97. Dec 3, 1758. Earl Granville, to Joseph Sutton, of Perq Esq, for 10s, "doth grt parcel of land in the Parish of Berkeley, Co of Perq," 115a, on the "No Side of the main Road," adj Sutton, & Whedbee. Sept 17, 1744. Granville; by Fras. Corbin, & Joshua Bodley.

No. 98. Thomas Jessop, & Joseph Jessop, of Carteret Co N. C., for £43 pd by William White, of Perq, planter—sold 200a on South west side of Perq River, the "same given me sd Thomas, by Joseph Jessop, of Perq dec, in his will." Mar 12, 1735.

No. 99. July 13, 1760. Earl Granville, grt unto William Albertson of Perq, land in Berkley Parish, adj John Henby. Granville, by Tho. Childs.

No. 100. Jacob Perry Jr, of Perq, Planter—for £25 pd by Jacob Perry Sr, of afsd—sold 50a on "McClennys branch," pt of a grt unto William Kitchen, at the mouth of Deep branch, adj sd Jacob Perry Sr, to River Swamp." April 19, 1763. Test' Edward Hall.

No. 101. Jacob Powell of Perq, for £9 pd by Jacob Perry Jr, sold 150a "at the Cabbin Point," on Snookes line, to line of Thomas Lilly, down to the Swamp. Mar 7, 1763. Test' Jacob Winslow, Arthur Conner.

No. 102. Jacob Perry Jr, for 10s pd by Benjamin Winslow, of Perq, sold 5a on the main road, adj sd Perry's back line. April 19, 1763. Test' Israel Perry, Jacob Winslow.

No. 103. Israel Perry of Perq, for £6 pd by Benjamin Winslow, of afsd—sold 15a on lines of sd Perry, & John Winslow, along sd "Benjamins own line." Mar 7, 1763. Test' Jacob Perry, Jr, Jacob Winslow.

No. 104. Jacob Perry Jr, for £50 pd by Israel Perry, sold 25a on the "old dividing line between Israel, & Jacob Perry," on the River Swamp. Mar 7, 1763. Test' Jacob Winslow, Benjamin Winslow.

No. 105. Benjamin Winslow of Perq, for £30 pd by Jacob Winslow, of same—sold 100a on East Side of Perq River, adj Jesse Winslow, & John Hudson. Mar 7, 1763. Test' Israel Perry, Jacob Perry Jr.

No. 106. Israel Perry, for £50 pd by Jacob Perry Jr, sold 50a on Deep Creek branch, & Snookes line. Mar 7, 1762. Test' Jacob Winslow, Samuel Farlow.

No. 107. Oct 9, 1762. Andrew Knox, Sheriff of Perq. Whereas; Martha Kippen of Chowan Co dec, was indebted unto Clerk Pike, of sd Co, for £40 "which sd Pike did recover, & was Ack' in Edenton Court House, before Charles Berry Esq, Justice, on Nov 20, 1761, agst Thomas Bell Ex, of sd Martha Ann Kippen, & sd Pike presented a Writ, to sd Knox, agst sd goods, chattels & land of sd Martha Ann he not being able to find any, did expose for sale land in Perq, 640a on So Wst Side of Perq River," adj Mrs. Julianna Lakers, on the Chinquepin Ridge, a grant unto Joanna Patterson 1717, (by whom she had Martha Ann Kippen dec), bought by Benj Scarbrough, he being the highest bidder, for £5 s6. Test' Thomas Ward, Thomas McNider.

No. 108. Samuel Newby of Perq, for "love I bear my dau Jemmima, & her husband William Newby, have given pt of tract, on So Wst side of Perq River 175a, at the mouth of Deep branch, above the Haw-tree Island, along side of Tongue of Reeds," to line of Benjamin Wilson, & the River Swamp. July 18, 1763. Test' Phineas Nixon, Wm. Albertson, James Sitterson.

No. 109. "We, Thomas, & Elizabeth Knowles," of Perq, for £36 pd by John Turner, sold 75a on So Wst Side of "Shitten Gut," part of a grt unto Richard Whedbee, Sept 27, 1715, for 250a. July 19, 1763. Test' James Gibson, Tho. Nichols.

No. 110. May 28, 1762. Earl Granville, grt unto John Clayton Esq, of Perq, land "near the head of Little River, in the mouth of Gum Branch & Juniper Island branch," to line of Jesse Perry. 150a. Granville, by Tho. Child.

No. 111. Sept 7, 1762. John Campbell, of Bertie Co, Merchant—for £30 pd by Charles Blount, of Perq, merchant—sold 105a on So West Side of Little River, adj Aaron, & Moses Jackson. Test' Edward Telfair, Elex'r. Ford, James Campbell.

No. 112. Nov 11, 1751. Earl Granville, for s3 pd by Zachariah Nixon, on Perq, Gent—do grt 235a in Berkeley Parish, adj Hendricks, & Albertson. Granville by James Innes, Fras. Corbin.

No. 113. James Elliott, & Mary his wife, of Perq, Planter—for £15 pd by Isaac Lamb, of afsd—sold 50a on No East Side of Cypress Swamp, "all the land they had on sd Swamp." Oct 17, 1763. Test' Frans. Nixon, Cornelius Moore, Keziah Nixon.

No. 114. Oct 20, 1763. Isaac Sanders, & Mary his wife, of Perq, for £10 pd by Francis Brown, of afsd, Planter—sold Swamp called "Wilsons Creek Swamp," 6a of high land, adj Reuben Wilson, "whereon sd Sanders now lives, which he purchased of Col John Harvey." Test' Andrew Knox, Robert Avery. Mary Ann Sanders, relinquished her dower.

No. 115. Jan 1, 1763. Benjamin Scarbrough of Perq, for £10 pd by Andrew Knox, of same—sold 640a on S. W. Side of Perq River, adj Mrs Julianna Lakers land, on Chinquepin Ridge, and John Thatch, (formerly Richard Leary's) grt unto Joanna Patterson 1717, & became the property of Martha Ann Kippen dec, (her dau) sold at public Vendue, Oct 9, 1762. Test' Thomas Ward, Thomas McNider.

No. 116. Joshua Small of Perq, for £12 pd by Richard Gording, sold 50a, adj Jonathan Sherod, & Benjamin Wilson, part of a tract, grt unto Zachariah Chancey, July 27, 1743, by him sold to Jacob Docton, & sd Docton sold to William Wilson. (No date.) Joshua & Charity Small. Test' John Campbell, Jacob Goodwin.

No. 117. Jeremiah Bundah (probably Bundy), & Sarah his wife, of Perq, for £25 pd by Cornelius Moore, sold 50a on No East side of Perq River, adj Thomas Hollowell. Dec 22, 1763.

No. 118. Charles Jordan Jr, & Sarah his wife, of Perq, for £31 pd by Robert Newby, of afsd—sold 260a at the mouth of "Wolf Pit" branch, on line of Jonathan Phelps, "patented by John Pretlow in the year 1668." Seal Dec 21, 1763. Test' Nath'l Williams, John Skinner, Jon'a. Hearring (Herring).

No. 119. William Godfrey of Perq, for £90 pd by Joseph Snoden, of same—sold 80a on "Ware Creek" ad John Barclift. Oct 27, 1762. Test' James Gibson, Demson Barclift. (Dempsey)

No. 120. Charles, & Robert Jordan, of Perq, are firmly bound unto Robert Newby, of afsd—in the sum of £620, Jan 16, 1764—sd Charles has sold 260a of high land, Dec 1, 1763, unto sd Newby, whereon sd Jordan, now lives, & 40a of Marsh, adj the same, & sd Newby has pd £310 for same. Test' W. Skinner, Miles Harvey.

No. 121. Charles Jordan Jr, of Perq, for £30 pd by Thomas McNider, of Chowan, sold "one house, & store house," on lot No. 110, in the Town of Hertford. Dec 17, 1763. Test' John Calloway, William Standin.

No. 122. James Paistree, & Elizabeth his wife, of Perq, (Shoemaker)—for £10 pd by Jacob Powell, of Chowan, sold 44a on the desert; part of a tract belonging to Joseph Reddin, (given him by his son John) given by sd John, to Elizabeth Collenton, adj John Gordon, & Jesse Eason. Jan 16, 1764. Test' Jesse Eason, Elias Stallings.

No. 123. "We; John, Thomas, & Samuel Weeks, of Perq; are firmly bound each, to the other; (in the sum of £200). Our dec father Thomas Weeks Esq, by his will gave lands in Perq, to be divided amongst us: James & Wilson Weeks (Minors), to have only one share between them, do make choice of John Clayton, & Richard Sanderson Esq, Phineas Nixon, & Thomas Nicholson, or any three of them to divide sd land." Test' Joseph Barclift, Benjamin Whedbee. Sept 12, 1763.

No. 124. Andrew Donoldson of Perq, for "love I bear my son Andrew, of Massachusetts Bay, in New Eng, do give one negro boy named Daniel." Mar 5, 1764. Test' John Harvey, Ben. Harvey.

No. 125. Samuel White of Perq, for £20 pd by Cornelius Moore, of afsd—sold 113a on South west side of Little River, & the mouth of Forked branch. Test' Abraham Wilson, Arnold White. Feb 14, 1764.

No. 126. Delight Nixon, & Richard Rogers, did purchase, 258a at the head of Yeopim River, known by name of "Bridge Neck," & jointly held sd land, until the death of sd Rogers, "now to make partition, with Elizabeth Coe Rogers, widow of sd Richard, doth make division, in trust for Sarah, Elizabeth, & Ospee, Daughters, of sd Rogers," land bought of Thomas Ming. Jan 30, 1764. Test' Melvin Duke, John Nixon.

No. 127. Joseph Moore of Bertie Co, for £350 pd by Cornelius Moore, Merchant, of Perq, sold 180a at the mouth of Island branch, in the edge of Beaver Dam Swamp, adj William Bagley, whereon John Moore, formerly . dwelt. Feb 20, 1764. Test' Frans. Nixon, Keziah Nixon, Francis Newby.

No. 128. April 13, 1764. Benjamin Roberts of Perq, planter—for £111 pd by Joseph Robinson, of Nancymond Co, Vir' farmer—sold 111a on So West side of Little River, adj Joshua Moore, taken up by Wm Tomlin. April 4, 1720. Test' Thomas Weeks, Benjamin Weeks.

No. 129. Mar 3, 1762. John Pearse of Bertie Co, for £25 pd by Aaron Mizelle, sold land in Perq, "part of tract grt to Richard Pearse dec'd & conveyed to sd John, in his will." Test' Edmund Walton, Thomas Hunter, Elisha Hunter.

No. 130. April 16, 1764. Robert Riddick Esq, of Perq, for £153 s5 pd by Zepaniah Jones, of afsd—sold 150a on South East side of Castletons Creek, adj land, belonging to orphans of Peter Jones dec'd, & John Harmon. Test' W. Skinner, Mark Newby.

No. 131. Phineas Nixon of Perq, for £27 s10 pd by Thomas Nicholson, of afsd—Trader, sold 50a, adj William Arnold, & Joseph Robinson. 15 2mo 1764.

No. 132. John Maudlin, of Perq, for £45 pd by Foster Toms, of afsd—sold 50a on No Est Side of Gum Swamp, & So Est Side of Suttons Creek, adj William Bogue an "older patent to Samuel Charles."

No. 133. Feb 11, 1764. Job Riddick of Perq, for £15 pd by Joseph Hurdle, of afsd—sold 45a on the main desert, patented by Thomas Docton, July 21, 1717, by deed of gift from him, to sd Job. Test' Samuel Green, Ruth Davis.

No. 134. May 22, 1764. John Campbell Esq, of Bertie Co, Merchant—for £266 s13 p4 pd by Richard Sanderson, of Perq, sold land commonly called, Sanderson Sound side plantation now in his "actual possession" 424a on No East side of the mouth of Perq River, sd Campbell Att' for Elizabeth Chandler, of St Marys Parish, Lambeth, Co of Surry, Grt Britain, widow; dau of Edward Catchmaid dec'd, only son of Thomas Catchmaid dec'd, brother, & devisee, in the will of George Catchmaid, of Nanciman Co, Vir' dec'd, who died seized of land in Perq Co, N. C. called "Birkswear," 3333a granted by Sir Wm Berkeley, Gov of Va, Elizabeth dying, the land descended to Wm Berkeley, of St Pauls, Covent Garden, Co of Middlesex, eldest son of sd Elizabeth, by her husband John Berkeley dec'd, & sd William Berkeley, did release on May 10, 1744, unto John Humpage of Gravesend, Co Kent, Mariner—& Ann Hinds of St. Helens, London, all of sd land; who sold sd land to George Low of London, July 15, 1744, who did authorize sd Campell to dispose of sd land. Test' Jno. Clayton, Andrew Knox.

No. 136. July 17, 1764. Richard Clayton of Perq, for £80 pd by Richard Sanderson Esq, sold 31½a, part of land whereon sd Clayton dwells, called "Robin's old field" at the head of a branch on sd Sanderson's line. Test' Thos. Newby, W. Skinner.

No. 137. July 17, 1764. Richard Sanderson Esq, for £213 pd by Richard Clayton, sold 96½a, "being part of land conveyed by John Campbell, of Bertie Co, May 22, 1764 on Robins branch." Test' Thos. Newby, W. Skinner.

No. 138. July 16, 1764. William, & Samuel Standin, for £18 s10 pd by Joshua Skinner, of Perq, sold 53a on a "Mirey branch issuing out of Bridge Creek, & 24½, formerly belonging to Samuel Standin dec, given to us in his will." Test' Robert Avery, John Callaway.

No. 139. April 24, 1760. Joshua Skinner, planter—bought of John Jones 105a, on a branch of Yeopim Creek, called "the Great Swamp," adj Peter Jones (the elder), & 150a, adj John Callaway, called "Paines" a patent to John Paine, the other, a grt unto Peter Jones, Sept 25, 1726. Test' Thomas Jones, Thos. McNider.

No. 140. July 14, 1764. Richard Sanderson, for £24 s10, pd by Joseph Sutton, sold 12¼a on So Wst Side of Little River, patented by William Glover Esq, Oct 14, 1701, & by purchase patent, by sd Sanderson, from Sir

Richard Everard (Gov) to sd Sanderson, on River side, adj Catchmaids line. Test' Miles Harvey, Thos. Newby.

No. 141. Samuel Bartlet of Perq, Mariner—for £400 pd by Lawrence Leisly, Mariner—of afsd—sold 124a on East Side of Perq River, near Jonathan Pearsons plan', on lines of Daniel Saint, & Thos Bagley, to the River Pocoson; being land 50a, sold by Jonathan Pearson, to Samuel Barclift, Jan 9, 1756, & 14a, from Thomas Bagley to sd Barclift, Feb 4, 1762. Seal Feb 20, 1764. Test' Cornelius Moore, Richard Hatfield, Joseph Moore.

No. 142. July 17, 1764. Mary Winslow, dau of Timothy, (late of Perq Co, Dec'd) & Reuben Wilson, of afsd, for the sum of £3 pd by sd Mary assigned 100a, by the side of Little River, adj McAdams, Robert Wilson (now Reubens), & John Barclift. Test' Joshua Skinner, Thos. McAdams.

No. 143. Joseph Smith Jr, of Perq, for £30 pd by Francis Jones, sold 200a on east side of "meadow Bridge," up mirey Branch, to a Bridge on Chowan Road, & line of Mary Barker. Jan 7, 1762. Test' Sam'l Smith, Thos. Elliott, Jonathan Sharrad.

No. 144. May 21, 1764. Abraham Jennet of Perq, for £40 pd by James Chew, of Chowan, Wheelwright—sold 100a, part of 348a, grt unto Ann Herrington (Arrington), Aug 21, 1716, by her conveyed to Abraham Jennet, Oct 1733, (father of sd Jennet) land in Perq Co, on So Wst Side of Perq River. Test' Charles Horton, Josiah Mathias, Will'm Horton.

No. 145. Joshua Deal of Chowan, Planter—for £20 pd by Moses Boyce, of Perq, sold 140a in sd Co, adj John Griffin, granted to Robert Wilson, Dec 20, 1740. Dec 12, 1763. Test' Samuel Jones, Robert Chappel.

No. 146. Jesse Perry of Perq, Farmer—for £2 s10, pd by William Small, of afsd—sold 5a upon the head of Little River, adj Jesse, & Isaac Perry. Oct 20, 1762. Test' John White, Isaac Boswell.

No. 147. Samuel Charles of Perq, "for love I bear my Brother Will'm Charles, of afsd—do give 50a, part of a grt unto my Father Samuel Charles in 1720," on the upper side of Gum Swamp, adj John Nicholson. Oct 12, 1764. Test' William Albertson, Foster Toms.

No. 148. Oct 15, 1765. Edward Halstead of Perq, for £100 pd by Francis Brown, of afsd—sold 52a "where sd Halstead now lives," by Little River Swamp, adj Aaron Jackson, at the head of Spring Branch. Edward, & Mary Halstead. Test' Daniel Saint, Jno. Blount, William Robbins.

No. 149. May 25, 1753. Earl Granville, for s10 pd by Luke Sumner Esq, of Perq "hath granted a parcel of vacant land, in Berkeley Parish," adj Jesse Eason, 150a. Granville, by Thos. Child. Wm. Cheston, Jas. Edmundstone.

No. 150. Joseph White Sr, for £3 s10, pd by Moses Boyce, sold 5a, adj John Griffin. Jan 12, 1765. Test' Joseph White Jr, Joseph Barker.

No. 151. William Munden of Perq, for £20 pd by Hannah Munden, (widow of Joseph) of afsd—sold 65a on So Wt Side of Little River (other part thereof, sd Munden sold to Joshua Perrisho), "contents of a grt to Joseph Munden, by Francis Corbin, & Benjamin Wheatley, agents of Earl Granville, Feb 19, 1762." Seal Jan 10, 1765. Test' Isaac Boswell, Thomas Boswell, Jesse Perry, Elisha Parker.

No. 152. Dec 15, 1764. William Wallace of Chowan, for £8 pd by Thomas Rountree, (son of Charles, Dec'd) of afsd—sold 50a on East Side of Perq

River, part of 200a, purchased by Thomas Rountree dec, of Joseph Jessop, & "left by will to sd Wallace." Test' Aaron Hill, Charles Rountree.

No. 153. John, & Ann Barclift, and John Barclift Jr, (son of sd John, & Ann,) of Perq, for £250 pd by James, & Sarah McAdams also £4 s10, pd to John Barclift, Jr, by Joseph McAdams, (son of James, & Sarah) sold 200a on So West Side of Little River, adj William Means, & land formerly John Parishoes. Dec 3, 1764. Test' Joseph Mullen, Thos. Nicholson.

No. 154. John Stokes of Perq, Farmer—for £75 pd by William Godfrey, of same, sold 100a, adj Layden, & sd Godfrey. Dec 17, 1763. Test' James Gibson, John Gibson.

No. 155. Nov 27, 1764. John Perry, of Bertie Co, Planter—for £30 pd by Thomas Wright, of Edenton, (Ropemaker)—sold 158a on No Et Side of Perq River, adj Nath'l Sutton, on lower side of Suttons Creek, near Cypress Swamp (both issuing out of the North side of.Perq River) sd land formerly John Perry's, father of sd John. Test' George Brownrigg, Thomas Dare.

No. 156. Peter Munden of Perq, for £5 pd by Thomas Boswell, of afsd—sold 25a of Swamp land, on So Wt side of Little River, adj Benjamin Munden, & up the River to Joseph Boswell's. Sept 8, 1763. Test' Elisha Parker, William Munden.

No. 157. Mar 19, 1765. William Skinner of Perq, Sheriff; to Joseph Mullen, of afsd; Whereas: Thomas Nicholson, late of sd County, prosecuted a suit in Court, held at Edenton, agst Exors of Joseph Wilson, dec'd, & obtained judgment, agst goods, chattels, & lands, of sd dec'd, William Skinner, "to satisfy same, sold at public vendue, on Nov 30, 1764, parcel of land, property of sd Wilson," which Joseph Mullen bought, for £86, being the highest bidder. Test' William White, Thos. White.

No. 158. Jan 17, 1765. Elijah Harriss, of Pitt Co N. C. for £30 pd by James Jones, of Chowan, sold 200a in Perq, on "Loosing Swamp," whereon my father John Harriss, lived, grt unto John Harris, & John Larkum 1695. Test' Jesse Eason, George Eason, Jr, Joshua Small.

No. 159. April 9, 1765. James Parker of Chowan, Planter—for £10 pd by Jacob Jordan, of afsd—sold 300a on So Wt Side of Perq River, on the head of Cypress Creek, & Balahack Creek, called "Bear Swamp" a pat to John Parker, July 28, 1730. Test' Jeremiah Carman, Thos. Osborn.

No. 160. Articles of agreement. 23d 2mo 1765, Jeremiah Carman, of Chowan Co, weaver—Whereas; Rachel Smith, widow of John Smith, of Perq Trader; dec'd, did purchase two parcels of land of Samuel Smith, for £60, & pd for same, out of sd estate, & gave same to her son John (a Minor), & Jeremiah Carman, having intermarried with sd Rachel, "proposed to give negroes, to be divided at her death, between her eight children, viz; Leah Sanders (wife of John), Joseph Smith, Mary Hill (wife of William), Sarah Smith, Benjamin Smith, Rachel Smith, Penniah, & John Smith, to which they agreed." Test' Thos. Nicholson, Thos. Newby, Frans. Nixon.

No. 161. Feb 21, 1765. Joshua Skinner of Perq, for £130 pd by John Jones, of afsd—sold two tracts of land, on branches of Yeopim Creek, adj Peter Jones, 150a called "Paines," adj John Callaway, Thos. Pierce & William White. Test' John Harvey, Mary AppleWhite.

No. 162. Aug 18, 1764. Sarah Davis, Willis Jones, & Mary his wife, of Chowan, for £14 pd by Joshua Small, of Perq, sold 56a on the side of the desert, along patent line of Marmaduke Davis, to John Gordon's line, part of a patent to John Hariss, & John Larcum, April 21, 1695, (888a) & by them sold to John Moseley, by him sold to Joseph Redding, & by sd Redding, willed to his son James, & descended from him to his brother John Redding, who willed it to his sister, Rachel Davis, wife of John, who after his death, sold it to Joshua Small. Test' John Campbell, Jr, John Davis, Henry Speight.

No. 163. Mar 27, 1765. William Stokes, & Elizabeth his wife, of Perq, Planter—for £40 pd by Wm Barclift Jr, of afsd—sold 40½a, on a branch of Muddy Creek. Test' Jno. Clayton, William Robbins.

No. 164. July 15, 1765. Thomas Bullock, & Robert Bogue Exors, of the will of Arthur Croxton dec, did "expose for sale 260a, of land whereon sd dec' lived," & Benjamin Harvey, of afsd—being the highest bidder, bought same for £201 s15, land on No East side of Perq River. Test' W. Skinner, Miles Harvey.

No. 165. Joseph Robinson, of the Colony of Vir, Co of Nancymond, farmer —for £120 pd by Thos Nicholson, of Perq Co, N. C. trader—sold 120a called "Pine Glade." 22, 4mo 1764. Test' Thomas Robinson, Joseph Robinson Jr.

No. 166. April 19, 1765. Thomas Nicholson, Merchant—of Perq for £20 pd by Joseph Robinson of Nancymond Co, in Vir, sold 20a on So Wt Side of Little River, adj Nixons corner. Test' Thomas Robinson, Joseph Robinson Jr.

No. 167. June 18, 1765. Joshua Skinner of Perq, for £30 pd by Samuel Jones, of afsd—sold 50a, "northward from Skinners bridge, to Raccoon Swamp," being part of a patent to Richard Skinner, Nov 22, 1714. Test' James Bush, Thos White.

No. 168. April 19, 1765. Francis Brown of Perq, Planter—for £110 pd by William Arnold, of same—sold 52a, "by Little River Swamp side," being part of a plan', whereon Edward Halstead lived. Test' Seth Sumner, Jane Jordan.

No. 169. Thomas Nicholson, for £37 s10, pd by Phineas Nixon, of Perq, sold 50a, near "Goodins gum pond, in the great body," adj William Arnold, Joseph Robinson, & sd Nixon. 15d 7mo 1765. Test' Frans. Nixon, Zepaniah Jones.

No. 170. Jacob Jordan, of Chowan, planter—for £5 pd by Jeremiah Carman, of afsd—sold 50a in Perq Co, on So Side of Perq River, "Balahack Creek Swamp, between Mulberry Ridge, & Bellmans old field." July 12, 1765. Test' Robert Boyce, John Hollowell.

No. 171. John Barclift Jr of Pasq Co, for £140 pd by Dempsey Newby, of afsd—sold 224a on Little River (south west side), & on Northwest side of Deep Creek, a patent dated 1694. April 23, 1765. Test' Samuel Newby, Esau Lamb.

No. 172. Zachariah Nixon of Perq, for £60 pd by Mark Newby, of same— sold 26a on N. E. Side of Perq River, & Frog Hall Swamp, to Francis Toms corner. Oct 21, 1765. Test' Frans. Nixon, Zachariah Jones.

No. 173. Oct 16, 1764. Richard Sanderson of Perq, for £300 pd by George Reed of same, planter—sold 100a, on No East Side of Albemarle Sound, "near the mouth of Perq River," part of a tract conveyed to sd Sanderson, by John Campbell of Bertie Co, May 22, 1764, adj Richard Clayton, & running

RECORDS OF DEEDS 203

to a branch called "Robbins Branch." Oct 16, 1764. Test' Miles Harvey, W. Skinner.

No. 174. Joseph Mullen of Perq, for £136 pd by John Whedby of same—sold 105a near Beaver Cove Swamp, with one half of sd Swamp, adj Foster Toms Sr, binding on lands of Christopher Sutton, & Abraham Rigs. Joseph & Elizabeth Mullen. Mar 1, 1765. Test' James Gibson, Benjamin Sutton.

No. 175. Nov 18, 1751. Earl Granville for s3 pd by William White Gent, of Perq—grt land in sd Co 255a, near Ricks Fox. Reg Oct Court 1765.

No. 176. Cornelius Moore of Perq, for £100 pd by Robert Evans of afsd—sold 50a, on N. E. Side of Perq River, & S. Side of Cypress Swamp, adj Gideon Bundy, & William Bogue. Aug 19, 1765. Test' Frans. Nixon, Zachariah Nixon.

No. 177. James Sitterson of Perq, Carpenter—for £15 pd by Mark Chappel of afsd—sold 62½a, & 24½a, formerly held by William Blitchenden, & Will'm Phelps, on line of Thos. Newby, & Abra'm Wilson. Oct 15, 1765. Test' Thos. Newby, Benjamin Russell.

No. 178. Ezekiel Moore of Perq, for £6 pd by William Newby Jr, sold 50a, on lines of Joseph Wilson, John Moore, & William Moore, to the line of Will'm Wilson. June 23, 1765. Test' Jas. Smith, Thos. Wilson, Jacob Elliott.

No. 179. Chrales Jordan of Chowan, for "love I bear unto my dau Rachel White, & her husband John White, do give negroes viz: Dick, Tony, Rose, Sue, & Grace. Sealed with my seal this day." Aug 2, 1765. Test' Phillip Perry, Joseph Smith.

No. 180. Sept 6, 1765. Andrew Knox of Perq, for £50 pd by William Arrenton of afsd—sold 100a at a place called "Oakland" a grt to sd Knox, Sept 7, 1761. Test' Thomas Long, Richard Banks.

No. 181. Joshua White of Berkeley Parish, Perq Co N. C. Planter—for £7 pd by Moses Rountree of same, Planter—sold 42a, of low ground, on East side of Perq River, "in the mouth of Reedy Branch." Oct 19, 1765. Test' Nicholas Stallings, Isaac Lilly, Joseph Lilly.

No. 182. Zachariah Nixon of Perq, for £50 pd by Ralph Fletcher, of same —sold 24a on the N. E. Side of Perq River, adj sd Fletcher, & Mark Newby. Oct 19, 1765. Test' Frans. Nixon, Zachariah Jones.

No. 183. Cornelius Moore, Merchant—for £40 pd by Robert Evans, sold 50a on North East Side of Perq River, adj Thomas Hollowell, & Moses Bundy. Test' Fras Nixon, Zachariah Nixon, William Mitferth. Aug 19, 1765.

No. 184. Narhaniel Albertson of Perq, for £3 pd by John Moore, of afsd—sold 1a on No Est Side of Perq River, adj sd Moore. Oct 21, 1765. Test' Joshua Moore, Hannah Moore.

No. 185. William Bedford of Perq, for £60 pd by Joseph Mullen, of same —sold 213a, on So Wt Side of Little River, along lines of John Holloway, & John Stevenson, to the River. Aug 29, 1765. Test' James Gibson, John Gibson.

No. 186. Oct 25, 1764. Henry Lawrence, of Nancymond Co Vir, to Luke Sumner of Chowan Co, N. C. Merchant—"Whereas Henry Plumpton of Nancymond Co, was seized of 100a in Perq Co, N. C." (grt April 16, 1683) at a place called "Orepeak" on East side of said Swamp, adj John Lears land,

& gave sd land to Michiel Lawrence, June 12, 1704, (which was recorded in Nancymond Co), & after his death sd land descended to his eldest son Henry, & was conveyed to sd Lawrence, & Ack before William Skinner Sheriff of Perq, for which Luke Sumner pd £25, & was recorded, Persuant to an Act of Assembly. Test' Samuel Wiggins, Stephen Parker, James Jones, John Powell, Sam'l Sumner.

No. 187. William Halsey of Chowan Gent, for £125 pd by Hatten Williams, of Perq sold 200a on Yeopim River. April 9, 1764. Test' William Jackson, Mary Johnson.

No. 188. April 26, 1766. Marnaduke Norfleet of Perq, for £1200 pd by George Washington, & Fielding Lewis, of the Colony of Vir, Gentlemen; sold two parcels of land in Perq Co, at a place called "White Oak Springs," one parcel given sd Norfleet, by his father Thomas Norfleet dec, being half of a tract sd Thomas purchased of William Jones, 225a April 5, 1707, & the other, sd Thomas purchased of Charles Drury, 40a July 26, 1721, & another tract, grt unto sd Marmaduke by Earl Granville, July 23, 1760, for 450a, "according to the most ancient bounds." Test' Lemuel Riddick, Phil. Alston, Willy Riddick, John Wasington, William Pugh.

No. 189. Gideon Modlin, William Bateman, William Colson, Christopher Towe of Perq, for £10 pd each of us, by Joseph Turner of sd Co, sold 100a, held by Abraham Mullen, & now the property of his Dau's, on the South Side of Beaver Cove Swamp, adj sd Turners line, "part of land grt unto Christopher Nicholson, & Joseph Sutton, June 20, 1703, & the other part grt unto Richard Whedbee, Oct 20, 1716." Seal Oct 9, 1765. Test' Ezekiel Towe, Jno. Clayton.

No. 190. Edward Turner of Perq, for "love I bear my son Dempsey Turner," have given 68½a, on a branch of Deep Creek, a grt to Thomas Collins, July 20, 1717, & now the property of sd Edward Turner. April 19, 1766. Test' Joseph Sumner, Abraham Mullen, Edward Turner Jr.

No. 191. Samuel Newby of Perq, Gent; for £45 pd by Jacob Goodwin, of afsd—sold 100a in Balahack, adj Joseph Wilson, & John Moore, to line of Truman Moore, called "Bouges." July 27, 1765. Test' James Elliott, Joseph Newby, Ann Newby.

No. 192. Feb 4, 1766. Simon Perrishoe of Perq, Planter—for £100 pd by David Colson, of afsd—sold 100a, "near Joseph Perrishoes grave yard," to line of James Perrishoe, & from his line "to the main road that leads to Nags-head Chapel, along Samuel Barclift's line to Dirt branch." Test' Joseph Turner, Jno. Clayton.

No. 193. Gideon Maudlin, & Mary his wife, Jeremiah Caruthers, & Tamer his wife, William Colson, & Miriam his wife, William Bateman, & Betty his wife, Christopher Towe, & Debrah his wife, of Perq, "for £10 to each of us, pd by Joseph Turner the elder—sold plan' whereon Abraham Mullen formerly lived, who died intestate, when sd land descended to sd parties, in right of their wives, & Jane Turner wife of sd Joseph, all dau's of sd Mullen dec'd, 180a on Beaver Cove Swamp, which was conveyed to sd Abraham Mullen, by his Father Abraham Mullen, the pattentee of sd land." July 22, 1766. Test' William Albertson, Zebulon Snoden, John Stokes, John Gibson.

No. 194. Dec 14, 1765. Articles of Agreement between Elenor Mullen of Perq, widow—& Joseph Turner of afsd—sd Elenor "doth agree to assign all her right of Dower, in a plan' & sd Turner agrees to find her sufficient meat, drink, washing & the use of the Shed Room, the liberty of raising Stock, on sd plan' during her Natual life, to which we do bind ourselves in the sum of £100." Test' John Clayton.

No. 195. Richard Sanderson, for £330 pd by Joseph Barclift, (both of Perq) sold 110a on No Et Side of Perq River, "in the fork of Muddy Creek," adj Richard Means, in the head of Robins Branch, & the mouth of Robins Swamp.

No. 196. April 3, 1765. Benj'n Bagley of Perq, for £30 pd by Cornelius Moore, sold "his Dwelling Plan" in Perq, 100a. Test' Andrew Miller, J. Shannonhouse.

No. 197. James Perrisho, "am firmly bound unto Simon Perrisho, & David Colson, in the sum of £200 for causes agreed upon by sd parties, paying sd Simons debts, support, & maintain, sd Simon during his natual life." July 3, 1766. Test' Rebecca Clayton, John Clayton.

No. 198. July 21, 1766. Samuel & William Standin, of Perq, for £51 15s pd by Amos, & Penelope Stack, sold land called the "Folly land" 50a, which was conveyed by Al'm & Wm Blitchenden, to Samuel Standin, & by sd Samuel, given in his will to Edward Standin dec, who by his will bequethed same to sd Samuel, & William Standin, & Penelope, to be equally divided between them, Penelope now the wife of sd Stack. Test' Wm. Bateman, Gideon Maudlin.

No. 199. Joseph Turner, & Jane his wife, for 1/5 part of a parcel of land, formerly the property of Abraham Mullen dec, to me secured by Christ' Towe, & Deborah his wife, do acquit sd Tow, sold to sd Tow 50a on Beaver Dam Swamp, a grt to Richard Whedbee, Oct 20, 1716. Seal July 22, 1766. Test' Wm. Bateman, Gideon Maudlin.

No. 200. Jesse Bogue of Perq, for £70 pd by Matthew White, of afsd— sold 66¼a on Cypress Swamp, adj sd Jesse, & Job Bogue, formerly property of Josiah Bogue. Jan 16, 1776. Test' James Perrishoe, Jos. Davis.

No. 201. Oct 5, 1765. Joseph Smith Jr, of Perq, for £75 pd by Francis Brown, of same—sold 100a in Balahac, where sd Smith now lives, near John Newby's ditch, to Jos Wilson's corner. Test' Thos Newby, Mark Newby.

No. 202. John Barrow of Perq, for £55 pd by Joshua Skinner, of afsd— sold 178a, part of 400a grt unto Thos Pierce, Nov 11, 1719, on the head of a Creek, formerly called "Spellmans" to Joseph Outlands corner, & the lines of Thomas, & William White. May 17, 1766. Test' Ben. Harvey, Nathan Simmons Jr, John Harvey.

No. 203. Oct 1, 1766. Benj Scarbrough of Perq, for £20 pd by Joshua Skinner, of afsd—sold 160a on So side of Perq River, near the head of Castletons Creek, adj sd Skinners land, & Wm Arrenton, a grt to Julianna Laker, April 1, 1712. Test' John Hill, John Callaway.

No. 204. Frans, & Elizabeth Penrice, of Perq, for £83 pd by Edward Penrice, sold "our right to a tract of land on Yeopim Creek, whereon Wm Ashley formerly lived, & gave in his will to his wife Elizabeth, now wife of sd Penrice," sd land to be sold when his two dau' Sarah, & Rebecca, were

18 years of age, & the money divided between them. Oct 7, 1766. Test' Joshua Skinner, Ben. Scarbrough, Joseph Skinner.

No. 205. Sept 9, 1766. Wm Arrinton of Perq, for £26 pd by John Jackson, of afsd—assigned land, which was grt unto Andrew Knox, Sept 7, 1761. Test' John White, Sarah White.

No. 206. David Colson, of Perq & Mourning his wife, for £26 pd by Thomas Nichols, of same—sold 60a, on the main road that leads to Nagshead Chapel, adj Joseph Perrishoe, formerly belonging to Simon Perrishoe. Oct 20, 1766. Test' John Hall, William Robbins.

No. 207. Aug 9, 1766. Elizabeth Winslow of Perq, Spinster—for £40 sold (after a decree by Assembly, signed by Jacob, & Israel Perry, Josiah Rogerson, John Twine, John Hollowell, Joseph Perry, Benjamin Perry, Joseph Riddick, James Price, Samuel Bagley, Moses Rountree, & Phillip Perry, before William Skinner Esq, the Sheriff of sd Co) 100a, bequeathed to her by her father, Isarel Winslow in his will, Aug 14, 1765—unto John Winslow of afsd, Planter. Test' Jacob Perry Jr, Huldah Griffin. Miles Harvey C. C. John Harvey Reg.

No. 208. David Colson, & Mourning his wife, for £16 s10 pd by Wm Robbins, sold 8a on the main road, leading to Nags head Chapel, adj James, & Joseph Perrishoe. Oct 20, 1766. Test' Thomas Nichols, John Hall.

No. 209. Joshua Davis of Perq, for £15 pd by Thomas Saint, of afsd—sold 25a on the Swamp, adj Perrishoes line, "land patented by Zach Nixon, & conveyed by him to me." 12d 7mo 1766. Test' Joseph Draper, Millicent Draper.

No. 210. Oct 20, 1766. William Arrenton of Perq, for £30 pd by Benjamin Hatfield, of afsd—sold 100a in the Desert, called "Oakland," a patent unto Andrew Knox, Sept 7, 1761. Test' Ben. Scarbrough, John White.

No. 211. Oct 8, 1766. Benj'n Roberts of Perq, for £50 pd by Benj Hall, sold 50a on So Wt Side of Little River, on line of Thomas Boswell, to Gum Swamp. Test' Thomas Robinson, William Robinson.

No. 212. Aug 23, 1766. William Skinner, Sheriff of Perq; to John Creecy of afsd—Planter—for £30, sold Land belonging to Thomas Bell, of Tyrell Co, N. C., "sd Bell being indebted to Nathan Miers in the sum of £60 which he did recover at the Court House in Edenton, before James Hassell, Esq Chief Justice, on 27d of May 1766, also £4 s3, for his cost, presented a Writ of Ex, to sd Skinner, who oxposed for sale land in Perq (125a) which was bought by sd Creecy, for £30, land on the north side of Yeopim River, adj John Standin, sd land patented by George Matthews, Feb 19, 1696." Test' Johnua Skinner, Will'm. White.

No. 213. Jacob Jordan of Chowan, for "love I bear my friend Thomas Ward Sr," of Perq, do give 50a, in sd Co, in Bear Swamp, adj Jeremiah Carman, & "Bellmans old field." Nov 16, 1765. Test' Peter Parker, Isaac Williams, Phillip Parker.

No. 214. Oct 18, 1766, George Eason of Perq, Planter—for £5 pd by Jacob Pierce, of afsd—sold land in Perq. Test' Robt. Riddick, Benj'n Perry.

No. 215. Robert Wilson of Perq, for £25 pd by Reuben Perry, of afsd—sold 40a "on Mill Swamp, that issues out of Cypress Creek," adj Gabriel

Newby's patent, on the East side of Mill Pond, to Caleb Elliott's new survey, & Reuben Perry's line. Oct 21, 1766. Test' Joseph Smith, Thos. Jones.

No. 216. Joseph Turner, & Jane his wife, for £5 pd by Jeremiah Caruthers (House Carpenter)—sold 29a, on So Side of Beaver Cove Swamp. Oct 20, 1766. Test' Zebulon Snowden, Jesse Winslow.

No. 217. Oct 20, 1766, Benjamin Wilson, for £100 pd by Jacob Wilson, sold 100a, on So Wst Side of Perq River, along a dividing line, between sd Benj, & Moses Wilson, adj Jonathan Sherrod, near Bakahack Swamp, to land of Joseph Elliott, which land with 380a more, was grt unto Benj Wilson, Aug 16, 1716. Test' James Sitterson, James Price, Timothy Winslow.

No. 218. Oct 18, 1766. Jacob Pierce of Perq, for £5 pd by George Eason, (both of Perq) sold 9a on the Desert side, part of a grt unto Richard Pearse, dec'd & given in his will to sd Jacob. Test' Robert Riddick, Benjamin Perry, Robert Riddick.

No. 219. John Hatch of Craven Co, N. C. for £67 pd by Richard Sanderson, of Perq—sold 277a in Perq, adj Capt Richard Sanderson. Mar 4, 1765. Test' Joseph Blount, John Fonville, Charles Bondfield.

No. 220. Oct 20, 1766. William Skinner Esq Sheriff of Perq; Whereas: James Perishoe of afsd, "did owe unto Cornelius Moore £16 s12, & to Francis Toms, & son, £2 s1, also £28 s10 to sd Toms & son, for cost—which they did recover on July 22 last, having a Writ agst goods & chattels of sd Perrishoe, which was levied on a tract of land, (34a) on "the main road to Nags head Chapel," formerly David Colsons," which Thomas Nichols purchased, for £21 s11, conveyed by sd Wm Skinner Sheriff. Test' Joshua Skinner, Joseph Snowden.

No. 221. Jan 19, 1767. Richard Sanderson of Perq, for £375 pd by Charles Blount, of afsd—sold 125a on North Side of Albemarle Sound, at the mouth of Perq River, part of a tract, conveyed to sd Sanderson by John Campbell, of Bertie Co, Att' of George Low of London, where Benjamin Whidbee now lives, called "Sanderson's Sound Side Plantation" by various courses to Muddy Creek. Test' Joseph Reed, Durant Reed.

No. 222. Charles Blount Esq, of Perq, for £100 pd by Benjamin Whidbee, of afsd—Planter, sold 125a on No East Side of Perq River, & Lillys Creek, to Snowdens line, part of a patent to Thomas Penrice, 1722. Jan 19, 1767. Test' Joseph Reed, Durant Reed.

No. 223. Samuel Jones of Perq, Glover—for £200 pd by Thomas Newby, Merchant—sold 260a on west Side of Perq River, adj Robert Chappel, to the mouth of Gum Branch. Jan 19, 1767. Test' Moses——— Jesse Moore.

No. 224. Dec 5, 1766. Joseph Bogue, for £90 pd by Thomas Newby, sold 66a along line of Thomas Hollowell. Test' Matthew White, Jesse Moore.

No. 225. Jan 5, 1766. Elizabeth Reed, widow of Joseph, late of Perq, Gent—for "love she bears her son Joseph Reed, doth give one half of land in Durants Neck, left him by sd Joseph dec'd, also the new house on sd land, he not to dispose of sd land during the life of sd Elizabeth, & if she die before sd son, he to have the whole, as bequeathed by his father in his will." April 13, 1765. Test' Durant Reed, Charles Worth Jacocks.

No. 226. Joseph Perry of Perq, for £3 pd by John Twine, of afsd—sold 4a known by the name of "Daniel Snookes line" sd land taken up by Timothy Clare, May 1, 1668, & conveyed by him to John White, by sd White to

Robert Rountree, by sd Rountree sold to Benjamin Perry, & by him given to his son Joseph, in his will. Jan 20, 1767. Test' Jeremiah Carman, Richard Hatfield, Ben. Wright.

No. 227. David Colson, for £20 pd by James Perrishoe, sold, 46a, part of land sold sd David by Simon Perrishoe, on line of Wm Roberts, & Abra'm Turner. Test' Thomas Nicholson, William Robins. June 2, 1766.

No. 228. Joseph Newby of Perq, for £10 sold unto John Bogue, of afsd— 10a on So Wt Side of Vosses Creek, down the branch to "Log bridge" Morgans corner, & Reedy Branch. Oct 31, 1766. Test' Samuel Newby, Zach. Nixon.

No. 229. Dec 13, 1766. Jesse Moore of Perq, Gent—for £82 pd by Francis Brown, of afsd—sold 100a on Phelps line, called "Beef-scull Neck." Test' Thos. Newby, Haiges Elliott.

No. 230. Isaac Elliott of Perq, "for an exchange of land, (a certain piece of Swamp land) to me by Isaac Lamb, of afsd—have given 3a, on No East Side of Cypress Swamp, part of a dividing line, between sd Elliott, & Lamb." Oct 19, 1765. Test' Reuben Perry, John Pearson.

No. 231. Jan 20, 1767, David Rogerson of Perq, Planter—sold 65a, left sd David "in the will of his father Daniel Rogerson," adj land where sd Daniel formerly lived, & binding on John Hollowels land, conveyed to Israel Perry. Test' W. Skinner, John Hollowell, Phillip Perry.

No. 232. Joshua Davis of Perq, weaver—for £107 pd by Zachariah Nixon, Planter—of afsd—sold 200a, whereon I now live, on N. E. Side of Vosses Creek, to the Desert, & "Bee Pond Branch." Jan 9, 1767. Test' John Penrice, Josiah Elliott.

No. 233. George Boswell of Perq, for £10 pd by Arnold White, of afsd— sold 41a on South West Side of Little River, on the Swamp side. Sept 24, 1766. Test' Joseph Nicholson, Samuel White.

No. 234. Samuel White of Perq, "in exchange between my dec father, Arnold White, & George Boswell dec, of afsd—some of which through error proved to be vacant land, since entered by me, plan' where George Boswell, son of sd George dec, now lives, with which swap we are satisfied, & do acquit sd Boswell, & confirm unto him sd land," on So W. Side of Little River, (70a) adj Wm Hasket, at the Swamps side. 24d 9mo 1766. Test' Joseph Nicholson, John Nixon, Arnold White.

No. 235. Mar 5, 1767. James Price of Perq, for £190 pd by Job Riddick, of same—sold 200a, on north side of Indian Branch. Test' George Eason, John Lewis, Will. King, Jacob Riddick.

No. 236. Mar 20, 1767. Job Riddick, for £130 pd by George Eason, sold 205a, grt to Thomas Docton May 1, 1717, & given to sd Riddick in his will, land on the west side of the desert, at Joseph Hurdels corner. Test' Robt. Riddick, Samuel Bagley, Will'm King.

No. 237. April 20, 1767. Robert, & Mark Newby, for £25 pd by Ralph Fletcher, sold 75a near the head of Suttons Creek, "part of a grt unto our father Francis Newby, & given to us, & our Brothers, Francis, & Jesse Newby," adj Gabriel Cosand, Gideon Maudlin, Thomas Hollowell, & Francis Nixon. Test' Jas. Smith Jr, Joseph Perrisho.

No. 238. Mar 11, 1767. Isaac Speight of Perq, for £70 pd by John Gordon Sr, of Chowan Co, sold 130a, on the north side of "Horse-pool Swamp," a

THE OLD MULLEN PLACE
Now occupied by Mr. W. F. C. Edwards, Register of Deeds, Perquimans County

grt unto said Speight, Mar 1, 1718, adj Thomas Fullerton, sd Gordon, & the desert. Test' Elisha Hunter, Thomas Hunter, Jacob Gordon.

No. 239. Arnold White of Perq, for £92 pd by Reubin Griffin, of afsd—sold 67a on So Wst Side of Little River, adj Isaac Boswell, & Samuel White, to the River. Jan 31, 1767. Test' Joseph Nicholson, Robert Hosea.

No. 240. Jacob Perry Sr, of Perq, for "love I bear my son Israel" of same—have given 50a, opposite land my sd son, bought of my son, John Perry, on Perq River. April 18, 1767. Test' Phillip Perry, John Hollowell.

No. 241. John Hollowell of Perq, planter—for "contract between me & Dan Rogerson in 1743, & willed by sd Rogerson to his son David," we do make over to Israel Perry 10a, on So East Side of "Briery Meadows" adj Josiah Rogerson, part of grt unto Wm Kitchen 1719, & given by him to Christopher Jackson, of Nansemond Co, Vir' & conveyed by sd Jackson, to sd Hollowell. Jan 17, 1767. Test' Jacob Perry Sr, Zach. Lilly, Ruth Lilly.

No. 242. Caleb Elliott of Perq, for £50 pd by John Goodwin of afsd, sold 90a on So W. Side of Perq River, adj Elizabeth Simmons, in Balahack, part of a grt unto Wm Moore, called the "Elbow." April 22, 1767. Test' Jacob Goodwin, Mark Newby.

No. 243. John Pearson of Chowan, for £150 pd by Ephrim Elliott, of Perq—sold 170a, adj Elizabeth Pearson, up Mill Swamp, in Perq Co. (No date.)

No. 244. May 29, 1767. John Adams of Chowan, for £80 pd by Andrew Knox, of Perq merchant—sold 184a at the mouth of Indian Creek, & the head of Yeopim River, part of a grt unto Sarah Long, & sold by her to Jonathan Taylor, who sold sd land to James Cheson, & by John Chesson (son of sd James) conveyed to Issacher Branch, who assigned it to Peter Adams dec, father of sd John, called "Chessons plan" with all houses thereon. Test' Samuel Benbury, Thos. Wells.

No. 245. May 8, 1767. Thomas Newby, for £90 pd by Robert Evans, sold 66a, adj Thomas Hollowell. Test' Zachariah Nixon, Thomas White.

No. 246. John Corprew of Perq, for £300 pd by Demson (Dempsey) Barclift, of sd Co—sold 100a on North side of Albemarle Sound, "which descended to me, in right of my mother Anne Corprew," adj Joseph Blount, & Beaver Dam Branch. July 3, 1767. Test' Jno. Clayton, William Barclift, John Corprew, Sarah Corprew.

No. 247. Samuel Perrishoe of Perq, Planter—for £40 pd by Demson Barclift, planter sold 52a on No East Side of Perq River. Oct 16, 1767. Test' Zebulon Snoden, Joseph Barclift.

No. 248. Sept 14, 1767. Peter Parker, Planter—for £120 pd by Thomas Overman, of Perq, Tailor—sold 102a on South west side of Little River, near the head thereof. Test' Wm Boyd, Eisha Parker.

No. 249. Joseph Arnold of Perq, Planter—for £100 pd by Joseph Turner Jr, of same—sold 110a called "the Body" near a Branch of Deep Creek, part of a grt to Lawrence Arnold. Oct 16, 1767. Test' Zebulon Snoden, Abra'm Mullen.

No. 250. Richard Whedbee of Perq, Planter—for £200 pd by Zebulon Snoden, of afsd sold 200a, adj John Whedbee. Oct 17, 1767. Test' Joseph Turner, John Bateman.

No. 251. Oct 8, 1767. John Corprew of Perq, for £1120 pd by Seth Sumner, of the same—sold 200a on the Sound Side, at the mouth of Dirt Swamp, adj

Demson Barclift, "being the Westermost part of a grt to George Durant." Test' Jno. Clayton, Rich. Clayton, Demson Barclift, John, & Sarah Corprew.

No. 252. Oct 20, 1767. Cornelius Moore, & Assignees; Thomas Newby, Joshua Skinner, Andrew Knox, Benjamin Harvey, & William Skinner, of Perq for £130 pd by Francis Nixon, of afsd—sold 210a on N. W. by Perq River, adj Benjamin Harvey Esq & lands of Joseph Newby Sr, dec'd, sd land purchased of Abra'm Mullen, by John Guyer, Oct 20, 1740. Test' Mark Newby, Ralph Fletcher.

No. 253. Oct 19, 1767. William Bateman of Perq, Farmer—"for the better maintenance of Benjamin Bateman, & natual affection, I bear my son, hath given 65a, adj John Anderson, formerly Joseph Perrishoe's dec'd, & sd William Bateman's, a grt unto Edward Moseley, & Robert Hatton, Esqrs, Agents of the Hon'bl John Earl Granville, from them unto Joseph Perrishoe dec, & by him sold to sd Bateman." Test' J. Whidbee, John Raper.

No. 254. Feb 2, 1767. Abraham Jennett of Perq, for £3 pd by Jeremiah Doe, of afsd—sold 14a on South Side of Perq River, on James Crew's line, & Deep branch, part of a tract, whereon sd Abraham lives. Test' Joshua Skinner, Wm White.

No. 255. Aug 14, 1767. Cornelius Moore, & Francis Nixon, (one of the assignees of sd Moore) for £106 pd by William White the Elder, of Perq, sold 100a, which sd Moore bought of Benjamin Bagley, called "Bagleys." Test' Joshua Skinner, Joseph White. (Keron Happuck Moore, wife of sd Cornelius relinquished her dower right.)

No. 256. Wm Bateman, for £50 pd by Joseph Arnold, Planter—sold 80a on No East Side of Perq River, adj John Anderson. Oct 16, 1767.

No. 257. Samuel Perrishoe, for £40 pd by Joseph Arnold, sold 52a on No East Side of Perq River, Oct 16, 1767. Test' Zebulon Snoden, Joseph Barclift.

No. 258. Joseph Turner Jr, of Perq, for £20 pd by John Turner, of same—sold 7½a, part of a tract grt to Lawrence Arnod. Oct 19, 1767. Test' Dempsey Turner, Abraham Mullen.

No. 259. April 18, 1767. Sylvanus Henby, of Perq, for 50a "up Gum Swamp," pd by William-Charles, sd land conveyed to sd Charles by deed of gift, from Samuel Charles, & 50a a patent from the Agent of the land office, to Foster Toms, conveyed by William Charles, "I do assign 100a near Suttons Creek, to me given by my father John Henby in his will" Test' John——— Wm Albertson.

No. 260. Robert Hall, of Pasquotank Co, for £12 pd by John Turner Jr, of Perq, sold 50a "which I bought of Edward Dowdy," part of 500a, formerly belonging to John Parish Sr, near Deep Creek. Sept 15, 1767. Test' Abraham Mullen, Demsey Turner.

No. 261. John Harmon Sr of Perq, for "love I bear my dau Susannah, do give 50a, adj Zepaniah Jones, & the Orphans of Moses Baker dec, whereon now lives, Aaron Barber." July 27, 1767. Test' William Albertson, Joshua Hobard.

No. 262. Dec 29, 1767. John Weeks of Perq, planter—for £70 pd by William Arnold Jr, Planter—sold 52a on So West Side of Little River. John & Sarah Weeks. Test' Joshua Morris, Stephen Douglas, Benj Roberts.

No. 263. Jan Court 1768. Sale of land from John Corprew, & Sarah his wife, to Seth Sumner, was proved in Court. (Sarah relinquished her right of dower.) Feb 22, 1768.

No. 264. Joseph Snoden, of Pasq Co, Farmer—for £100 pd by Thomas Godfrey, of Perq sold 121a, "in Ware Neck Perq Co," adj John Barclift. Aug 29, 1767. Test' John Gibson, Francis Leyden.

No. 265. Nov 14, 1767. William Skinner, Sheriff of Perq; Whereas: John McAlister by Writ, agst goods, & chattels of Enoch Raper, & John Welch, for the sum of £25 s12 p10, before the Justice of Perq, & sd Sheriff "not being able to find any, did expose for sale, a tract of land belonging to sd Raper, & John McAlister agreed to take sd land, at 2/3 its valuation." Test' Charles Moore, John Goodwin.

No. 266. Zebulon Snoden of Perq, for £200 pd by Richard Sanderson, of afsd—sold 130a, which was surveyed for Thomas Snoden. Jan 19, 1768. Test' J. Whidbee, Francis Toms.

DEED BOOK—H

No. 1. John Pearson of Chowan Co, for £20 pd by Isaac Elliott, of Perq, "have set over" 50a in Perq, & part in Chowan, adj Eliza Pearson, & Ephrim Elliott, (part of same tract) bounded on west by land of William Simpson, & north by the land of Thomas Newby Jr. Oct 14, 1767. Test' Pritlow Elliott, Job Elliott. Miles Harvey C. S. C. John Harvey Reg'st.

No. 2. Jacob Caruthers of Perq, for £25 pd by Hatten Williams, (and Jacob Caruthers, my father of same) sold land, grt unto Nathan Caruthers, (gr-father of sd Jacob), Feb 18, 1737, 156a, on North Side of Yeopim River, on a branch called Deep branch, adj land formerly John Wyatt's, now belonging to heirs of John Stepney, Esq dec, running to Indian Creek, & the mouth of Little Creek. Dec 23, 1767. Test' Joseph Ming, Mary Ming.

No. 3. Abraham Turner of Perq, for £22 pd by Demsey Turner, of afsd, sold 20a in sd Co. Jan 19, 1768. Test' Joseph Turner, Joseph McAdams.

No. 4. Jan 19, 1768. Joseph Nichols, & Mehitable his wife, of Pasquotank Co, sold to Julius Bunch of Perq, 120a in sd Co, for £20, formerly land of James Thigpen, adj Zachariah Nixon, along line of sd Bunch, to Thomas Newby's line & lines of John Pearson, & William Simmons Sr. Test' John Williams, Daniel Saint.

No. 5. July 13, 1767. Cornelius Moore of Perq, Merchant—"being indebted to Thomas Newby, Francis Nixon, Benj Harvey, William Skinner, Timothy Walton, and Andrew Knox, by reason of losses, & incapable of paying his creditors, to make the most ample satisfaction in his power, hath agreed to assign all his goods, all his land, & one house, & lot in Nixonton," also 12 negroes—£902, & £565 due sd Moore, from Moses Neeve, of Pool in Great Britain, in bills of exchange, also £100 due by Thomas Outland, £93 s18, due by Emperor Moseleys Est, £140, due by Richard Garrett, £230, due by a suit in Edenton, agst John Ireland. A copartnership between sd Moore, & Andrew Knox, expired, "allowing sd Moore £600 for 216a, where he now lives, & £210 where the Shipyard is; bought of Joshua Guyer, & six negroes mortgaged to Joshua Skinner, worth £200." Francis Nixon, for Mary Moore.

No. 6. Nov 23, 1767. William Skinner Gent, Sheriff of Perq—"John Lilly, late of Perq dec, was indebted to James Sumner in the sum of £35, who by his will did appoint his son Joshua Lilly, his Exor, Luke Sumner, surviving Exor of sd James dec, a judgment was directed to sd Sheriff of Perq, who took into his poss' goods & chattels of sd Lilly, also a piece of land, (purchased by Thomas Lilly, father of sd John, of William Moore) & given him by his father, (50a) on East side of Perq River, at Upper River Bridge, adj Benj'n Perry Sr & John White. Test' Sam'l Johnson, Josiah Granvery, Mat. Brickwell.

No. 7. Oct 7, 1767. William Wilkinson, of Suffolk Parish, Nansemond Co, Va, Gent—son & heir of William Wilkinson, of Isle of Wight Co, Va Esq, dec—& Will Wilkinson (an infant) son of Willis Wilkinson, of Co & Parish afsd, sd William in his lifetime being seized of 1200a, at a place called "Orapeak," which he gave in his will to his two sons William, & Willis, sd will dated Mar 6, 1740, & recorded in Isle of Wight Co for £5 pd by sd Willis, & £5 already in hand, in behalf of his son Will, (an infant) sold sd land. Test' Samuel Swann, Wager Speed, John Wilkinson, Anthony Holladee.

No. 8. April 1, 1767. "Isaac Speight, & Ann his wife, of Perq, for £500 pd by Mills Riddick, of Nansemond Co, in the Colony of Vir, sold———in Perq, at a place called" the horse Pool "adj the Great Dismal Swamp, except 100a, which sd Speight sold John Gordon, on North Side of horse Pool Swamp, said land grt to Thomas Speight, Gr-father of sd Isaac, Mar 1, 1718, & devised by sd Thomas in his will to his son Isaac, & by sd Isaac dec, to sd Isaac, in his will." Test' Luke Sumner, Wm. Leadman, John Darden.

No. 9. Jan 19, 1768. William Skinner Esq, Sheriff of Perq, Whereas: George Nichols dec, was indebted to Amos Stark, & Penelope his wife, of afsd, & sd Amos did recover £20 in Court of common Pleas, in the Court House in Hertford, Oct 20, 1767, agst Est of sd Nichols, & £5-4s for cost, sd Sheriff, "not being able to find any goods, or chattels, exposed for sale 100a of land," (which Joshua Skinner bought for £76-10s) on the north-side of Yeopim Creek. Test' Thomas Nichols, John Hall, Fras. Penrice.

No. 10. Mar 16, 1762. John Earl Granville, grt unto Samuel White, of Perq, Planter—for s10 176a, in the Parish of Berkeley, Co of Perq, on So west Side of Little River, adj William Hasket, running to Fork Branch. Reg May 12, 1768. Test' W. Churton, Jas. Edmond Donne. Thos. Child Esq.

No. 11. Mar 4, 1768. Cornelius Moore, Thomas Newby, Francis Nixon, Joshua Skinner, Benjamin Harvey, William Skinner, & Andrew Knox, for £8-5s pd by Ralph Fletcher, (all of Perq) sold 113a, on South side of the head of Little River, adj William Hasket, & up Little River Swamp to Fork Branch, land grt unto Samuel White, Mar 16, 1762. Test' Wm. Standin, John Standin.

No. 12. Mar 7, 1761. Earl Granville, grt unto George Boswell, of Perq, for 23s "a parcel of vacant land," 575a, in Parish of Berkeley, on the west side of Fork Swamp, running to line of Robert Cox. Granville, by Thos. Child. Test' W. Lucas, Thos. Weeks Jr.

No. 13. James Price of Perq, for £25 pd by Jonathan Collins, of Chowan Co, Bricklayer—sold 50a in Perq, part of a grt unto Timothy Clear, dec, Dec 1, 1712. Sept 20, 1767. Test' Job Riddick, Will. King.

No. 14. Nov 19, 1767. William Albertson, & Samuel Charles, farmers, of Perq, Ex of the will of Sylvanus Henby dec, for £27-17s pd by Gideon Maudlin, of afsd—sold part of 587a, patented by John Henby 1740, & given by him in his will to his son Sylvanus, sd "woodland left to be sold," lying between sd Maudlin, & Joshua Boswell. Test' William Foster, Joseph Wells.

No. 15. Nov 28, 1760. John Lord Granville, for 10s, unto Jesse Henby 225a, in Berkeley Parish, Perq Co, on South Side of Little River, adj Josiah Bundy. Test' W. Lucas, W. Churton. Granville by, Thos. Child.

No. 16. John Hollowell, & James Price of Perq, for £5, pd by Joel Hollowell, of afsd—sold 100a on East side of Perq River, adj Elias Stallings, dec, "land taken up by sd Stallings (640a) out of which sd Stallings gave unto Nicholas Stallings 600a, July 15, 1749," Robert, Job, John Riddick, John Hollowell, Daniel Rogerson, Thomas, Timothy, Joseph, & William Lilly, & Simon Stallings, & James Price, "parties who have never divided sd land," agreed that "Joel Hollowell do now have his part," adj sd land. Oct 31, 1767. Test' Robert Riddick, Joseph Perry, Seth Riddick.

No. 17. Oct 10, 1767. Ephrim Etheridge, & Miriam his wife, of Perq—for £5 pd by Jacob Jacobs, "do sell unto him 10a, on No East Side of Perq River, a 5 pt of land, sold by James Morgan, unto John Henby Jr." Test' Fras. Newby, Cornelius Moore.

No. 18. Benjamin Whidbee of Perq, Planter—for £100 pd by John Stokes, Planter—sold 52a on East of Perq River, being the north pt of 125a, conveyed to sd Whidbee, by Charles Blount, Jan 19, 1767. Seal April 19, 1768. Test' Charles Blount, Tully Williams.

No. 19. Mar 2, 1768. William Skinner Esq, Sheriff of Perq, Cornelius Moore, Merchant—"did owe to James Gibson of the Colony of Vir, £590 s8 p8, which sd Gibson did recover at Court in Edenton," & sd Skinner not being able to find goods & chattels to satisfy sd Execution, did expose for sale 216a of land, which was purchased by Thomas Newby, for £320, "being pt of a tract patented by Jane Binard 1694," adj lands of William Bogue, Timothy Clare, Thomas Bagley, & the River. Test' Jo. Whidbee, Miles Harvey.

No. 20. Seth Sumner Esq of Perq, for £300 pd by Demson Barclift, of afsd, Planter—sold 100a on north side of Albemarle Sound, land conveyed to sd Sumner by John Corprew Oct 8, 1767, running to the middle of Beaver Dam Swamp, & said Barclifts corner. Feb 10, 1768. Test' Jno. Clayton, Richd. Sanderson, John Stokes.

No. 21. Mar 25, 1768. Gideon Maudlin of Perq, for £13-18s pd by Samuel Charles, sold 200a pt of land "given by John Henby in his will, to his son Sylvanus, & Dau Mary Henby, & by them sold to me," adj Joshua Boswell, & sd Charles. Test' Wm. Albertson, William Foster.

No. 22. Thomas Saint of Perq, for £15 pd by Robert Bogue of afsd—sold 25a pat' by Zach'r Nicholson, "conveyed by him to me," on the head of Cow branch, down the Swamp to Perrishoes line. Jan 19, 1768. Test' Zach. Toms, Jos. Barber.

No. 23. John Moore of Perq, Weaver—for £10 pd by Capt Joseph Sutton of afsd—12½a on west Side of Suttons Creek, adj Mullen, Ratcliff, Aaron Moore, & the Creek. July 18, 1768. Test' Joshua Moore, Wm. Robbins, Jesse Winslow.

No. 24. Mar 20, 1768. Job Riddick, & Prudence his wife of Perq, for £130 pd by George Eason Jr, of afsd—sold 205a on west side of the main Desert, pt of a grt unto Thomas Docton May 1, 1717, "& given in his will to his gr-son Job Riddock," adj Joseph Hurdle, & Joseph Pierson. Mar 20, 1768. Test' Benj'n Perry Jr, Joel Hollowell, Edward Benison.

No. 25. May 28, 1768. Jeremiah Pratt, Miller—being possessed of land on Indian Creek, at the head of Yeopim River, called "Chews Plantation" which Jeremiah Pratt, dec, father of sd Jeremiah, bought of James Cheson, "in order to settle bounds of sd land, sd Jeremiah, & Andrew Knoz doth agree on a line, beginning at the mouth of Deep Branch, that issues into Indian Creek, & doth assign all right to land to the Southward of sd Creek, & sd Knox doth assign all land to the northward of sd branch." Test' Nathaniel Ming, Thomas Williams.

No. 26. Oct 26, 1767. George Eason, & Mary his wife of Perq, for £27-13s pd by Joseph Hurdle, sold 44a pt of a tract pat' by Thomas Docton 1722, & by him given in his will to his gr-son Job Riddick, & sold by him to sd Eason, adj the land of Docton Riddick, & the main Desert. Test' Demsey Eason, Thomas Hurdle.

No. 27. July 4, 1768. Benjamin Hall of Perq, for £65 pd by Thomas Boswell, sold 50a on Gum Swamp, adj Peter Parker. Test' Levi Blomden, Samuel Stafford, Jesse Perry.

No. 28. Charles Blount of Perq, "for love I bear my son-in-law Thomas Harvey of afsd—do give one negro man called Cato, a negro woman called Jenny, a girl named Bridget, another woman named Jenny, & her child Esther—9 head of cattle, 2 beds, & furniture, six large silver spoons, one pr of tea tongs, & sundry other things already delivered." April 14, 1768. Test' Jos Reed, James Donaldson.

No 29. Sept 16, 1768. Jacob Hall of Perq, for £25-s17-p7 pd by Samuel Johnson Attorney-at-law of Chowan Co, sold 212a in Perq, adj John Hopkins, & Daniel Hall, where sd Jacob now lives. Test' Sam'l. Duncomb, Arn't. Elbeekson.

No. 30. June 18, 1768. James Eggerton of Perq, for £30 pd by William Wilson of Chowan Co, sold 108a on North Side of a Branch of the head of Yeopim River, in Perq Co, adj Francis Brown, & Delight Nixon. Test' Joseph Champion, Susannah Champion, Wm. Matthews.

No. 31. Oct 3, 1768. Daniel & Hercules Saint of Perq, for £150 pd by Joshua Skinner of same, sold 100a on the north side of Yeopim Creek, in the mouth of a Swamp near John Barrows house, by the Creek, to a corner of land formerly Joseph Ashleys, but now belonging to Orphans of William Ashley dec, pt of 525a pat' by Joseph Barrow May 23, 1728. Test' W. Skinner, Richard Skinner.

No. 32. "We William Lowther, Robert Hardy, & Andrew Little of Edenton," Merchant for £50 pd by Francis Nixon in behalf of John Moore (a minor) son of Cornelius of Perq "doth give a negro boy called Peter" Nov 28, 1767. Test' John McAllister, Jos Reed.

No. 33. William Skinner of Perq, for £39 s10 pd by Francis Nixon, in behalf of Cornelius Moore (son of Cornelius, a minor) "hath given a negro man called Jeremy." Oct 18, 1768. Test' Robert Newby, Thos. Newby.

No. 34. Daniel Saint, Carpenter—of Perq, for £150 pd by Hercules Saint, sold 80a, pt of a pat' unto John Harmon Mar 6, 1740, called "Pond land" adj Ralph Bosman, William Phelps, Jonathan Sherwood, & Benjamin Wilson. Oct 5, 1768. Test' W. Skinner, Joshua Skinner.

No. 35. Samuel & William Standin of Perq, for £55 pd by Joshua Skinner of afsd sold 178a on a creek, formerly called "Spellmans" adj Joseph Outland, & land formerly Edward Wilsons, but now belonging to Orphans of William

Long, & land now owned by Thomas, & William White. Part of 400a pat' by Thomas Pearse, Nov 11, 1719. Seal Oct 16, 1768. Test' John Calloway, Anthony Williams.

No. 36. Jacob Jordan of Chowan Co, for £32-s10 pd by Richard Goodwin Jr of Perq, sold 150a, adj Thomas Ward in Perq Co, at the mouth of "Mire Swamp." Sept 19, 1768. Test' Jacob Goodwin, William Gordon Jr, William Bond.

No. 37. Aaron Moore, Yeoman of Perq, for £75 pd by Daniel Saint, carpenter —of afsd—sold "land which was left to me by my Father Samuel Moore, in his will" 75a on the banks of Perq River, adj Seth Sumner, being pt of a conveyance to my sd Father from Thomas Bedford of Vir. Oct 17, 1768. Test Jonathan Phelps, Hercules Saint.

No. 38. Richard Goodwin of Perq, for "love I bear my son Richard of afsd—do give 50a which I bought of Joshua Small, June 14, 1763," adj Jonathan Sherwood, & Benjamin Wilson. Feb 24, 1768. Test' John Goodwin, Samuel Williams, Mary Williams.

No. 39. Theopholus White of Perq, for £16-s8 pd by John Skinner of afsd— sold 50a of Marsh land on north east Side of Perq River "near the foot of the Bridge that leads to sd Marsh, in a direct course to Castletons Creek." Oct 18, 1768. Test' Mark Newby, John Toms.

No. 40. Jan 8, 1768. Demsey Harrell, & Susannah his wife of Perq, for £125 pd by Joseph Hurdle of afsd—sold 165a adj Sam. Bagley, George Eason, along the main road to John Scotts corner. Test' Sam'l Harrell, Elisha Hunter.

No. 41. William Bateman, & Betty his wife of Perq: "Albert Albertson in his will did bequeath unto Bettie Mullen (dau of Abraham) a tract of land (purchased by sd Albertson, of Richard Grey) & sd Bettie did since marry sd Bateman, the sd parties obtained a Writ & sold 45a whereof sd Bettie is "seized in fee," for £45 pd by my son John Bateman, in the fork of "Beaver Cove Swamp." Oct 18, 1768. Test' William Tumball, Joseph Arnold.

No. 42. Sept 4, 1766. Abraham Hasket, & Jemima his wife, of Rowan Co N. C. and Patience Newby, & John Skinner Extrix, & Ex of the will of Matthew Jordan dec, of Perq; sd Jordan "did in his life time purchase 150a of sd Hasket, & paid £110 for same, who died before sd deed was recorded, to secure sd title of sd Jordan, sd Abraham & his wife Jemima do now confirm deed to sd Extrix, & Ex," 150a, adj Benjamin Elliott, John Stone, & Joseph Pacey, down to the River. Test' Jesse Henly, Christopher Nation.

No. 43. Dec 16, 1768. Marmaduke Davis of Perq, for £30 pd by Marmaduke Norfleet, sold 62a on South Side of "Loosing Swamp," which was conveyed by John Moseley, to Joseph Redden, adj John Gordon, & Joshua Small, to the Desert. Test' Jacob Gordon, Joseph Gordon, Willis Jones.

No. 44. Sept 5, 1768. Wm Reed of Perq, for £247 pd by Charles Blount (both planters) of afsd—sold 100a on the "Sound Side, near the mouth of Perq River, adj Richard Clayton, to a branch called "Robbins branch" & down sd branch to "London branch," being land Richard Sanderson, sold my brother George Reed, Oct 16, 1764." Test' Tully Williams, Edmond Blount.

No. 45. Benjamin Sutton, for £25 pd by Thomas Nichols of Perq, sold 100a "on the main road that leads to Naggs Head Chappel" adj Abraham Turner, John Whidbee, & Samuel Barclift, pt of land formerly belonging to Simon Perrishoe, & by him conveyed to David Colson, Feb 4, 1765. Seal Jan 14, 1769. Test' Wm. Robbins, Joseph Sutton.

No. 46. Dec 20, 1766. John Jackson of Perq, for £28 pd by Thomas Halsey of afsd—sold one half of a tract, (100a) grt unto Andrew Knox, Sept 7, 1761, at a place in the Desert, called "Oakland." Test' Jno Thatch, Jos Williams.

No. 47. John Whidbee of Perq, Gent—for s40 pd by Demsey Turner of afsd—sold 13a on No East Side of Perq River. Jan 26, 1769. Test' J. Whidbee, Zebulum Snoden.

No. 48. John Bateman of Perq, for £50 pd by my father Wm Bateman, "hath given 45a on North East Side of Perq River in the fork of Beaver Cove Swamp, being land that Wm & Bettie Bateman conveyed to sd John." Jan 16, 1769. Test' John Harvey, Andrew Knox.

No. 49. Thomas Hollowell of Perq, for £29 pd by Jos Guyer of same, sold 30a at "the Plum tree bridge." Jan 3, 1769. Test' Daniel Saint, Ralph Fletcher, Sarah Fletcher.

No. 50. July 20, 1767. William Stokes, & Elizabeth his wife, of Perq, Planter—for £24 pd by William Barclift, sold 24½a between lines of Charles Blount, & Wm Trumbal, & afsd Barclift, as by pat' Feb 11, 1716," whereon sd Stokes now lives, with all buildings thereon standing." Test' William Trumbull, William Layden.

No. 51. John Harmon Jr of Perq, for £40 pd by Macrora Scarbrough of Edenton, sold 50a in Perq, on "Beaver Cove Swamp," adj John Stepney, & James Williams. Aug 20, 1767. Test' Joseph Hewes, Charles Barfield.

No. 52. Sarah Chancey, Relict of Joseph Barrow of Perq Co, now the wife of Edmund Chancey; in con' of an exchange of land, by my bro-in-law Thomas Nicholson Trader—of Perq, sold 150a near Little River Bridge, 116a, of which was given me by Joseph Pritchard Sr, of Pasq Co (former husband) in his will, 12d 10mo 1749, "whereon he then lived." 2d 11mo 1768. Test' Thomas Pritchard, Jos. Pritchard, William Barrow.

No. 53. Nov 15, 1766. James Perrisho of Perq, sold 100a unto Benjamin Sutton, adj Thos Nicholson, Abraham Turner, John Whidbee, & Samuel Bartlet. Test' Jno. Clayton, John Corprew.

No. 54. John Mason of Swansey, Co of Bristol, Massachusetts Bay, New Eng: Mariner—appointed friend Joseph Skinner, of Perq, N. C. his Attorney, "to sell land belonging to me." Oct 3, 1768. Test' Abraham Simmons, John Caruthers.

No. 55. Benj. Sutton of Perq, for £50 pd by Will'm Robbins, of afsd—sold 12a, adj sd Robbins, "near the grave yard, on the road that leads to Nags-head Chappel," pt of a tract formerly owned by James Perrisho, & by him conveyed to sd Sutton, May 20, 1767. Seal Jan 14, 1769. Test' Thomas Nichols, John Bateman.

No. 56. April 15, 1769. Benjamin Whedbee of Perq, planter—for £150, pd by Edward Blount, Planter—sold 73a on North Side of Perq River, on a Branch of Lillys Creek, running to the line of John Stokes, & Charles Blount, "with all buildings thereon." Test' Tully Williams, William Barclift.

No. 57. May 20, 1767. James Perrishoe of Perq, sold to Benj Sutton, 12a of land, adj Wm Ribbins, & Samuel Barclift. Test' Joseph Sutton, Sarah Sutton.

No. 58. John Barclift, & Ann his wife, of Perq; "John Parish dec did give to his dau Ann, (now the wife of sd Barclift) land in Perq, in fee," & they having obtained a Writ, of Ex, William Skinner Esq, Sheriff of sd Co, examined 200a thereof, & sold same, to Joseph McAdams, for £75, land by Little

River, towards Deep Creek, on line of William Man." Mar 9, 1769. Test' Durant Barclift, John Knowles.

No. 59. Jonathan Collins of Chowan Co, Planter—for £16-s1 pd by Simon Stalling, of afsd—sold 50a in Perq, pt of a Pat' unto Timothy Clare, dec'd, Dec 1, 1712. Seal April 15, 1769. Test' Joseph Stallings, Will. King, Nathan Collins.

No. 60. Jan 16, 1769. Sam'l. Skinner of Perq, & Sarah his wife, for £5 pd by James Skinner, of afsd, "doth convey tract of land, "125a on Minsie Creek, adj John Harvey, William Scarbrough, & Luke Sumner, running to the mouth of "Haw tree branch." Test' Andrew Collins, Richard Skinner.

No. 61. Mar 30, 1769. Marmaduke Norfleet, of North Hampton Co, N. C. for £30 pd by Marmaduke Davis, sold 62a in Perq Co, on the South Side of "Loosing Swamp," being pt of land conveyed by John Moseley, to Joseph Redden, adj John Gordon, & Joshua Small. Test' Joseph Gordon, Moses Blanchard, Joshua Small.

No. 62. Mar 25, 1767. Hatten Williams of Perq, Ship Carpenter—for £142 s10 pd by Levi Creecy, of Chowan Co, Planter—sold 190a on Yeopim River, in Perq Co. Haten, & Ann Williams. Test' Jno. Bat Beasley, William Creecy.

No. 63. April 20, 1767. Joseph Farmer, & Mary his wife, of Perq, for £5 pd by Jacob Jacobs, of afsd—sold 10a on No East side of Perq River, pt of land "conveyed by James Morgan to John Henby Jr." Test' John Hogard, Joseph Sutton.

No. 64. Josiah Perrishoe of Perq, Carpenter—for "another piece of land delivered by Jesse Bogue of same," farmer—assigned 75a, on Vosses Creek, in the fork of the Swamp. 29d, 10mo 1768. Josiah & Mary Perrishoe. Test' Joseph Bogue, Josiah Bogue, James Perrishoe.

No. 65. Jesse Bogue, & Ruth his wife, of Perq, in con' of "an exchange of land with Josiah Perrishoe," of same conveyed 80a, on north west Side of Vosses Creek Swamp, adj Edward Maudlin. April 15, 1769. Test' Joseph Bogue, Joseph Perrishoe, James Perrishoe.

No. 66. Mar 11, 1769. Hatten Williams, & Ann his wife, of Perq; Whereas "Joseph Ming dec, of Chowan Co, former husband of sd Ann, died intestate, possessed of 120a known by name of "Bridge Neck" which became the property of his brother Thomas, sd Thomas sold sd land to Richard, & Delight Nixon, in con' of £15 to sd Hatten & Ann his wife, (her Dower right) do sell same to Delight Nixon." Test' Andrew Knox, Nathaniel Ming, Andrew Paynter.

No. 67. April 25, 1769. William Skinner Esq, Sheriff of Perq: Francis Brown late of afsd Co, "was indebted to Isaac Sanders, in the sum of £9 s18 p6, to recover sd sum, obtained a Writ of Ex, agst goods, & chattels of sd Brown, but not being able to find any, did expose for sale 53a, of land in Perq," on North-side of Browns Mill Swamp, between lands of John Nixon, & James Eggerton which sd Brown bought of Samuel Simpson, same sold to John Nixon. Oct 25, 1768. Test' Nath'l. Howcott, William Roberts, John Calloway.

No. 68. July 15, 1769. Joseph Turner of Perq, planter—Joseph Sutton Dec, "did by his will bequeath to his dau's Sarah, & Elizabeth a tract of land called "Edge Hill" to be equally divided between them, & sd Sarah intermarried with Robert Hosea, who sold her pt to Abraham Riggs, April 15, 1734, & Joseph Turner having married Jane Riggs (widow of Abraham), & Joseph Mullen only surviving son of Elizabeth (née Sutton) to whom sd bequest was made, to sd Mullen conveyed sd land." Test' John Calloway, Hatten Williams.

No. 69. Oct 24, 1768. Jacob Jordan of Chowan Co, for £25 pd by John Jackson, of Perq—sold 50a in Bear Swamp, called "Mulberry Ridge" adj Richard Bond, & Jeremiah Cannon, pt of a pat' to John Parker, July 28, 1730. Test' Wm. Bond, Joshua Bagley, William Lane.

No. 70. April 17, 1769. Patience Newby Extrix, & John Skinner Ex, of the will of Matthew Jordan dec, (all of Perq) "who by his will directed sd Ex, to sell land on North side of Perq River, (sd land purchased of Abraham Hasket, & Jemima his wife) sold same to Ichabod Delano," of afsd—for £150, (150a) adj Benj Elliott, in the River Pocosin. Test' Charles Moore, Thomas Nichols.

No. 71. Mar 6, 1769. Thomas MacKnight, of Pasquotank Co, Merchant—for £65 pd by Humphrey Parks, of Perq, planter—sold 100a, whereon Joseph Smith formerly lived, (in Balahack) adj Joseph Wilson, Wm Moore, & Samuel Newby, to line of Truman Moore. Test' Mathias Elligood, Samuel Harrell, Will, Cunningham.

No. 72. Charles Blount of Perq, for "love I bear my son Edmund, of afsd—do give 8 negroes, 3 beds, & furniture, 15 head of cattle, 15 sheep, 15 hogs, 6 large Silver spoons, 1 Silved Soup spoon, 6 Silver tea spoons, & one Silver tea tong." April 26, 1768. Test' Sarah Blount, Ann Hoskins.

No. 73. Pleasant Winslow, (widow, & relict of Joseph) of Perq—for £200 pd by Ezekiel Maudlin, of afsd—sold a "moiety of land 125a, to sd Ezekiel, (since dec) Oct 19, 1741 sd land now in possession of his Eldest son, Edmund Maudlin, assigned her dower right in sd land." June 24, 1767. Test' Joseph Draper, William White Jr.

No. 74. Jacob Spivey, & Ann his wife, Planter—for £30 pd by Sam'l Perry, of afsd—sold 50a on No East side of Perq River, on "hickory ridge pt of 200a purchased by Thos Rountree dec, of Joseph Jessop, & left by sd Rountree to Thomas Rountree." July Court 1769. Test' Joseph Stallings, Cader Hill.

No. 75. Isaac Lilly of Perq, for £25 pd by Charles Rountree, of Chowan Co—sold 232a, adj Thos Hobbs, & Simon Stallings, by the River Pocosin. May 16, 1769. Test' Thos. Newby, Joseph Perry, Elisha Hunter.

No. 76. John Barrow, & Martha his wife, of Perq, for £102 s5 pd by Thomas Pierce, of afsd—sold 184a on north side of Yeopim Creek, adj Joshua Skinner, & William White, pt of 419a pat' by Thomas Pierce, Nov 11, 1719, & 525a pat' by Joseph Barrow. June 10, 1769. Test' Joseph Skinner, William White, John Sanders.

No. 77. Jan 19, 1769. Thomas MacKnight, of Pasq Co, for £39 pd by John Goodwin, of Perq, sold 100a in Perq, called "Ballahack" on South side of Perq River. Test' John Skinner, Will. Cunningham, William Newbold.

No. 78. July 18, 1769. Cornelius Moore, in behalf of himself, & Joseph Moore dec, both of Perq, for £25 pd by William Wingate, unto sd Joseph, "do make over unto sd Wingate 150a, on So Wst Side of Balahack Swamp, & along Swamp to Richard Goodwins line, & the line of Joseph Smith, sd land grt unto John Moore, & descended to Joseph Moore, (who died without heirs) sd Cornelius being heir-at-law, of sd Joseph, & next of kin." Test' Jacob Wilson, Richard Hatfield, Jos. Elliott.

RECORDS OF DEEDS 219

No. 79. Pleasant Winslow (relict of Joseph) for £100, pd by Robert Bogue, "to my sd husband, sold 100a Jan 17, 1743, her dower right in same." June 24, 1769. Test' Joseph Draper, Wm White, Jr.

No. 80. Richard Whidbee of Perq; "On Sept 17, 1768 I met Joshua Skinner on his land, in the woods, & after some difference between us, did beat, wound, & cruelly treated sd Joshua, for which I sd Richard, do declare I am heartily sorry." Dec 16, 1768. Test' John Harvey, Miles Harvey.

No. 81. Joseph Henby, & Mourning his wife, of Pasquotank Co, for £40 pd by Samuel Williams, of Perq, sold 75a on a new line between Henby, & Toms, to the Swamp. Oct 16, 1769. Test' Richard Goodwin, William Goodwin.

No. 82. Sept 29, 1769. Benjamin Hatfield, of Tyrrell Co, for £31 pd by William Chesson of Perq, Carpenter—sold 50a, being half of a pat' unto Andrew Knox, Sept 7, 1761, (in Perq Co) called "Oakland," adj Thomas Halsey. Test' Andrew Knox, John Wyatt.

No. 83. Aug 18, 1769. James Jones of Perq, for £120 pd by Jacob, & William Hinton, Jr, of Chowan Co, sold 200a on "Loosing Swamp," pt of plan' whereon John Harris lived, & patented by sd Harris, & John Lockum, in 1695, "according to reputed, ancient bounds." Test' Timothy Walton, Timothy Hunter, George Eason.

No. 84. Haig Elliott of Perq, for £159 pd by Henry Thomson, of Chowan Co—sold 200a on East Side of Meadow bridge, at the mirey branch, up sd branch to Chowan Road, & line of Mary Barker, to line of Caleb Elliott. Oct 16, 1769. Test' Ephrim Elliott, Soloman Elliott, Sarah Holt.

No. 85. Caleb Elliott of Perq, planter—for "love I bear my gr-son Cornelius Elliott (son of Haig), of same, do give 108a. also to Micajah his brother." Feb 16, 1769. Test' John Smith, Ephrim Elliott, Charles Jordan, Johanna Kippen.

No. 86. Caleb Elliott, for "love I bear my son Solomon, of Perq, do give (after the death of my wife) the remainder of Land whereon I now live." Feb 16, 1769. Test' John Smith, Charles Jordan, Haig Elliott, Johanna Kippen.

No. 87. July 31, 1769. Joseph White Sr, & Gulielma his wife, of Perq, for £85 pd by Wm White Sr, of same, sold 95a, "which was given to us by Thomas White, April 24, 1755," adj on west Braziers land, & on north land of Moses Bogue. Test' John White, Joseph White Jr, John Taylor,

No. 88. Robert Newby of Perq, for £142 pd by Isaac Elliott, of afsd—sold 60a on So Wst Side of Perq River, at the mouth of a branch, issuing out of Samuel Newbys Mill Pond, called "Cow Bridge Branch" which land was laid off to Fras. Newby, "agreeable to the will of his father," & sold to sd Robert. Mar 24, 1769. Test' Samuel Newby, Reuben Perry, Kerenhappuck Moore.

No. 89. Nov 1, 1768. William Skinner, Sheriff of Perq; to Thomas MacKnight of Pasq Co, Merchant—for £1124 s9 p10, (to satisfy a Judgement brought by sd MacKnight agst Francis Brown) sold 600a on north Side of the head of Yeopim River, which was purchased by Thomas Brown, for £200. Test' Chs Bondfield, Wm McCormick.

No. 90. Nov 1, 1768. (Same) Writ of Ex, for same; brought by Francis Brown, who sold 100a on So Side of Perq River, "called Balahack," which was purchased by sd Brown from Jesse Moore, for £35 pd by sd MacKnight. Test' Chas. Bonfield, Wm. McCormick.

No. 91. (Same)

No. 92. Benjamin Scarbrough, & Sarah his wife, for £270 pd by Joshua Skinner, all of Perq, sold 680a near Castletons Creek, (three tracts). Jan 16, 1770. Test' Jacob Wilson, Mark Newby.

No. 93. Dec 20, 1769. Ben Scarbrough, & Sarah his wife, for £168 pd by Macrora Scarbrough, sold 140a, on north Side of Yeopim River, adj William Wyatt Esq dec, & my brother Macrora, at the mouth of a branch, issuing out of the River, near the mouth of Yeopim Creek, making out of Beaver Cove, pt of land "bequeathed by my father Macrora Scarbrough to me in his will." Test' John Skinner, Andrew Collins.

No. 94. Richard Banks of Perq, Planter—for £20 pd by Jesse Bunch, of Chowan Co, sold 100a on Yeopim River, pt of 400a called "Sturgins point" on broad creek, which 400a Wm Wyatt, bought of John Pratt. Dec 15, 1769. Test' George Wells, John Rodie, Paul Berham.

No. 95. Cader Rountree, of Dobbs Co, N. C. sold unto John White, of Perq 50a, adj John Winslow, "on Newbegun Creek Swamp." Nov 7, 1769. Test' John New——, Silas White.

No. 96. John White of Perq, for £15 pd by Richard Cale, of afsd—sold 50a in "Balahack," adj Jonathan Sherwood, called "the Island." July 8, 1769. Test' Caleb White, Caleb Toms.

No. 97. William Simpson of Chowan, for £30, pd by Enoch Jessop, of Perq, sold 150a called "Chinquepin Ridge" adj Thomas Newby Jr, "to the Narrow oak Ridge." Jan 15, 1770. Test' Reuben Perry, Robert Wilson, Susannah Hoskins.

No. 98. Jan 13, 1770. Thomas Hendricks of Perq, for £80 pd by his father, Job Hendricks, sold 100a "whereon sd Job now lives," on lower side of Vosses Creek, & the upper side of Hosea's branch, "by a deed of sale from Stephen Gibbons, to Sarah Morgan Jr, before her marriage to sd Job, April 15, 1731, sd Job, & Sarah gave to sd Thomas." Oct 16, 1769. Thomas & Elizabeth Hendricks. Test' Francis Nixon, Benjamin Sandres, John Pinner.

No. 99. Patience Earll of Perq, for "love I bear my son John Earll" of afsd— do give "a parcel of land in Duke Co, Province of New York." April 17, 1770. Test' Jonathan Skinner, Christopher Collins.

No. 100. Isaac Elliott of Perq, for £31 pd by Wm. Jackson, of Chowan— sold 50 on South Side of a branch, issuing out out Reuben Perrys Mill Pond, which sd Isaac purchased of John Pearson, near Eleazer Pearson, running to Ephrim Elliott, & William Simpsons line, & Sandy Ridge Road. April 17, 1770. Test' Pritlow Elliott, Benjamin Wright.

No. 101. Joshua Davis of North Hampton Co, N. C. for £20 pd by Robert Bogue, of Perq, sold 20a in the fork of Vosses Creek Swamp, adj Jesse Bogue, running to the middle of "Bee Pond Swamp" sd land "surveyed for Zachariah Nixon." Dec 16, 1769. Test' John Pinner, Jesse Bogue.

No. 102. Miles Pierce of Perq, for £12 s3 pd by Abraham Mullen, of afsd— sold 13½a in sd Co. Jan 3, 1770. Test' Dempsey Sumner, Jacob Mullen.

No. 103. Feb 26, 1770. John Whidbee of Perq, for £60 pd by Richard Sanderson, of afsd—sold 97a on "Deadmans Swamp," sd land "taken up by Timothy Biggs, Aug 16, 1759, by him conveyed to sd Whidbee." Test' Thomas Robinson, J. Whidbee, George Whidbee.

RECORDS OF DEEDS

No. 104. Feb 27, 1770. Christopher Tow of Perq, for £40 pd by Richard Sanderson, of afsd—sold 64a on No East Side of Perq River, at the head of Beaver Dam branch. Test' Thomas Robinson, George Whidbee.

No. 105. Feb 27, 1770. Joseph Turner of Perq, for £30 pd by Richard Sanderson Esq, of afsd—sold 31½a in the fork of Beaver Cove, pt of a tract which sd Joseph bought of Gideon Maudlin, Mary Maudlin, Jeremiah, & Tamar Caruthers, Wm Colson & Miriam Colson, Wm Bateman, & Betty Bateman, Christopher, & Deborah Towe. July 22, 1766. Test' J. Whidbee, Thomas Robinson, George Whidbee.

No. 106. Feb 27, 1770. John Whidbee of Perq, for £200 pd by Richard Sanderson, of afsd—sold 230a on East Side of Perq River, on Beaver Dam Swamp, running to Long Branch. Test' Thomas Robinson, J. Whidbee, George Whidbee.

No. 107. Jeremiah Caruthers, & Tamer his wife of Perq; "Abraham Mullen in his life, did give to his dau Tamer Hassell 135a, & sd Tamer since the death of her husband Isaac Hassell, married sd Caruthers," obtained a Writ of Ex, & sold 50a on Beaver Cove Swamp, to Richard Sanderson, for £250. April 16, 1770. Test' Charles Blount, Ben. Harvey.

No. 108. Feb 24, 1770. Charles Blount of Perq, for £75 pd by Richard Sanderson, of afsd—sold 105a on No Wst Side of Little River, between lands of Aaron, & Moses Jackson, sd land bought by sd Blount, of John Campbell of Bertie Co, Sept 26, 1762. Test' John Stokes, Demson Barclift.

No. 109. June 20, 1749. Lords Pro' unto Foster Toms, of Perq, Gent—for s3 to "Earl Granville in hand, pd by sd Toms, doth grant 400a, in the Parish of Berkeley, Co of Perq," near the head of Suttons Creek, adj Samuel Charles. E. Moseley. Test' William Cheston, John Artee.

No. 110. Mar 7, 1770. John Sanders of Perq, for £30 pd by his sister Elizabeth Sanders, sold 20a pt of land "given me in the will of my father Richard Sanders, Dec 4, 1774," adj Aaron Albertson. Test' Francis Nixon, Ralph Fletcher, Keziah Nixon.

No. 111. Thomas Rountree of Chowan, Yeoman—for £3 s15 pd by Thomas White, of Perq—sold 50a on No Est Side of Perq River, adj Elias Stallings, along pat' line of John White, pt of a grt unto Thomas Winslow, Nov 11, 1719. Feb 13, 1770. Test' Moses Rountree, Thomas Rountree.

No. 112. Oct 12, 1769. Rachel Davis of Perq, for £7 pd by Joshua Small, of afsd—sold "⅕ pt of 50a on the Desert side, adj Marmaduke Davis, & John Gordon, being pt of a grt in Vir to John Harris, & John Larcum, April 21, 1706, (888a) sold by them to John Moseley, who sold sd land to John Redding, & was willed by him to his son James, & descended from him to his brother John Redding, who willed same to his three sisters; Rachel who married John Davis (one of them) from him to his five dau's, one of whom is sd Rachel." Test' Marmaduke Davis, Willis Jones.

No. 113. 17d, 2m 1738. Zachariah Nixon: "Certify, that I have seen an old deed of gift, from old Joseph Scott, to his gr-son, son of Joseph Pearce, which was both writ, & signed by his own hand, & further I have read it, & had it in my possession, as Ex of sd Joseph, & I solemnly declare it was burnt in my house, & I do bear witness, & pray that it be recorded." Reg May 18, 1770.

No. 114. Aug 31, 1769. John Stoakes of Perq, planter—for £104 pd by Tully Williams, Planter—sold 50a on the East of Perq River, adj sd Williams, Stoakes, & Charles Blount. Test' John Warrington, Wm. Reed.

No. 115. Feb 28, 1770. Joseph Arnold of Perq, for £150 pd by Richard Sanderson, of afsd—sold 130a on No E'st Side of Perq River, adj Demson Barclift, & William Bateman, land formerly John Anderson's, which sd Arnold bought of Samuel Perrisho, & William Bateman, Oct 16, 1767. Test' Thomas Nichols, Joseph Perisho.

No. 116. April 17, 1770. Henry Hardin, & Martha His wife, of Perq, for £47 pd by Andrew Collins, of same—sold 100a, pt of a pat' to William Long, April 1, 1723, conveyed by him to John Felt, "which at his death fell to his son Job, & by his death, to his dau Martha Hardin." Test' Joshua Skinner, Joshua Bagley.

No. 117. April 10, 1770. Luke Sumner of Chowan Co, for £50 pd by Jacob Riddick, of Perq, sold 50a, formerly called "John Lilly's," now called "the Upper River Bridge," adj Benj Perry, & John White. Test' Joseph Brinkley, John Powell, Docton Riddick.

No. 118. Abraham Mullen of Perq, for £67 pd by Thomas Mullen, of afsd—sold 50a in Perq. Jan 13, 1770. Test' Dempsey Turner, Jacob Mullen.

No. 119. Francis Brown, to "satisfy a Judgement brought by Thomas MacKnight of Pasq Co, empowered William Skinner Esq, Sheriff of Perq; to sell all my Balahack land, whereon I now live, & two plan's in Currituck Co, a parcel of land in Tyrell Co, & all stock on Plan' whereon I live." May 11, 1768.

No. 120. Mary Moore, widow (of John) of Perq, for £50 pd by Thomas Newby, of afsd, Merchant—(assigned right of dower) "in a tract of land whereon my late husband did live, with all improvements, & houses thereon, made by my son Cornelius Moore." Jan 26, 1770. Test' Lawrence Leesly, Thomas Saint.

No. 121. July 12, 1770. Jacob Jacobs of Perq, for £150 pd by Zachariah Toms, of afsd—sold 5a—one a of which sd Jacobs bought of Francis Toms, on the head of Morgans Swamp, adj line of Nathan Newby, & the other 4a sd Jacobs purchased of sd Nathan. Jacob, & Elizabeth Jacobs. Test' Jesse Winslow, Caleb Toms.

No. 122. Josiah Perrisho, & Mary his wife, of Perq—for £50 pd by Jesse Bogue, of same—sold 60a on north west side of Vosses Creek Swamp, "up the branch to a log Bridge." Jan 24, 1770. Test' Ralph Fletcher, John Pinner, Edward Maudlin.

No. 123. Feb 23, 1770. Josiah Perrisho, Edward Maudlin, & Joseph Perrisho, for £35 pd by sd Joseph, sold 40a on north Side of Vosses Creek Swamp, adj sd Maudlin. Test' Joseph Draper, Jesse Bogue, Moses Bundy.

No. 124. June 2, 1770. Thomas Nichols of Perq, Ex of the will of William Ashley dec, dated Jan 21, 1762, "who directed his Exors to sell his plan' whereon he lived, hath sold same to Joshua Skinner, for £190." Test' W. Skinner, John Calloway.

No. 125. Mar 13, 1770. James Harrell, of Nansemond Co Vir, for £16 s16 pd by Samuel Skinner, of Perq Co, N. C. sold 100a in Bear Swamp, called "G——— Old Field, (Greys) adj Thomas Newby, near the "Broken down branch." Test' Evan Skinner, William Simpson.

No. 126. June 30, 1770. John Jackson of Perq, for £25 pd by Joshua Bagley, of same, sold 50a in Bear Swamp called "Mulberry Ridge," adj Richard Bods, & Jeremiah Cannon. Test' J. Stafford, John Colson, David Lippincot.

No. 127. Oct 7, 1770. John Stevenson of Perq, Planter—for £262 s10, to Joseph Sutton, of same, planter—sold 850a pt of a tract pat' by George Catchmaid, April 1, 1663, called "Birkswear" now called "Stevenson's Point" on So Wst Side of Little River, at the mouth of old Great Branch, where afsd Joseph lives, by courses of Durants line, to head of sd Branch. Test' Joseph Sutton, Holls Williams, Benj Sutton.

No. 128. Aug 10, 1770. Jonathan Jessop, & Mary his wife, of Perq, for £260, pd by Benj. Harvey, of afsd—sold 100a on north side of Perq River, in "Old Neck," adj Joshua & John Moore, & Thomas Pierce, where sd Jessop now lives. Test' Joshua Skinner, William Harvey.

No. 129. Samuel Williams of Perq, for £80 pd by Jacob Goodwin, of afsd—sold 50a in Balahack, bought of Joshua Toms. Aug 6, 1770. Test' William Goodwin, John Colson, Thomas Sitterson, Sam. Williams.

No. 130. Miles Pierce, & Susannah his wife, of Perq, for £200 pd by William Melbourn, of Tyrell Co, sold 114a on No Wst Side of Deep Creek, bought by James Pierce, of Joseph Hosea. Mar 9, 1770. Test' John Raper, James Barclift.

No. 131. Jacob Godwin of Perq, Gent—for £80 pd by Sam'l Williams, of afsd—sold 100a in Balahack, adj sd Williams, Jos Wilson, John Moore, & Humphrey Parks. Aug 6, 1770. Test' William Goodwin, John Colson, Thomas Sitterson. Jacob, & Peache Goodwin.

No. 132. Oct 10, 1770. Edward Penrice of Perq, for £12 pd by Joshua Skinner, of same—sold 50a on South Side of Mings Creek, adj sd Skinner, & Andrew Collins. Samuel Penrice.

No. 133. June 2, 1770. Edward Penrice, & Penelope his wife, for "a lease to us of a plan' for a term of years," sold to Joshua Skinner 144a on North Side of Yeopim Creek, formerly belonging to William Ashley, adj sd Skinner, "sold to us by Francis Penrice, & Elizabeth his wife, for a term of years." Test' Samuel Penrice, Elizabeth Penrice.

No. 134. Saint Croix: John Coakley, & Thomas Lilly, of the Island afsd—Esq's, Exors of James Lytton Sen, Esq, late of same Island, dec'd, do appt' Mr Charles Blount, & Mr Andrew Knox, of N. C. Att' for sd James Lytton dec. July 5, 1770. Test' Peter Adams, Geo. Osboune.

No. 135. Isaac Lamb of Perq, for an "exchange of land, set over by Isaac Elliot" of afsd, have set over to sd Elliott 10a, part of a tract of Swamp land, adj Pritlow Elliott, & up sd Swamp to Holmes branch. Oct 19, 1769. Test' Reuben Perry, John Pearson.

No. 136. Isaac Elliott of Perq, planter—for £70 pd by Francis Jones, of afsd—sold 75a on the north East Side of Cypress Swamp, near the mouth of Deep branch & "Balahack path," to Holmes branch. Sept 7, 1769. Test' Caleb White, Sam'l. Sitterson, Isaac Lamb.

No. 137. Oct 1, 1770. Moses Phelps, & Miriam his wife, of Chowan Co, for £14 pd by Joshua Small, of Perq, sold ⅕ pt of 56a in Perq, "pt of 888a grt in Vir to John Harris, & John Larcum, April 1, 1695, which descended to Rachel Redding who married John Davis (who sold sd land to sd Small) Miriam wife, of sd Phelps dau of sd John Davis, & his wife Rachel," land adj Marmaduke Davis, John Gordon, & Jacob Powell, along the Desert. Test' Marmaduke Davis, John Davis, Ann Davis.

No. 138. John Nixon of Perq, for "an exchange of land with Thomas Nicholson," of afsd—assigned 27a known as "Coxes glade" at the head of land, between my brother Zachariah, & Ezra Nixon, running to sd "Glade." 13d, 5mo 1770. Test' Thomas Winslow, Zachariah Nixon Jr.

No. 139. Thomas Nicholson of Perq, Trader—for an "exchange of land with John Nixon, of afsd—do confirm unto sd Nixon 27a, pt of land called "Nicholsons deaded ground" at the head of Zachariah, & Ezra Nixons, glade land. 13d, 5mo 1770. Test' Thomas Winslow, Zachariah Nixon Jr.

No. 140. Robert, & James Wilson, of Perq, for £40 pd by Elizabeth Winslow, of afsd—sold 130a called "Aarons old field," adj Thomas Newby Jr, along the Desert to Pritlow Elliott, & John Pearsons line, & the line of sd Robert. Oct 13, 1770. Test' Reuben Perry, John Winslow Sr.

No. 141. Aug 10, 1770. Benjamin Harvey, & Julianna his wife, of Perq, for £100 pd by Jonathan Jessop, of afsd—sold 261a in "Old Neck," at the River side, formerly Abraham Mullens, "to the Swamp dividing sd land, & the old field on which the Meeting house now standeth." Test' Joshua Skinner, William Harvey.

No. 142. Francis Jones, & Judah his wife, of Perq, Planter—for £80 s15 pd by Isaac Lamb, of afsd—sold 200a on East Side of "Meadow bridge to a poly bridge on Chowan road," & line of Mary Barker. Sept 9, 1769. Test' Thomas Newby, Caleb White.

No. 143. Elias Stallings of Perq, "do give unto Job Bogue" of afsd—150a on North East side of Cypress Swamp, at a branch called "the duck pond," half of 300a pat' by sd Stallings. Oct Court 1770. Test' Joseph White, Zach Toms.

No. 144. James Wilson of Perq, "do set over unto Robert Wilson" of afsd—140a in the fork of Cypress Swamp, adj Ganriel Newbys old patent, upon the North side of sd Swamp, to line of Pritlow Elliott, conveyed to me by Caleb Elliott, & 50a along "the old body of Reeds" to Reuben Perry's Mill Pond. April 27, 1770. Test' Reuben Perry, Enoch Jessop, Esther Perry.

No. 145. Jacob Pierce of Perq, for £27 s10 pd by George Eason Jr, of afsd—sold 2a (pt of tract grt unto Richard Pierce 1743, & by his will given to his sd son Jacob), in the mouth of Great Branch. May 27, 1770. Test' George Eason Sr, Abraham Eason, Sarah Eason.

No. 146. Francis Albertson of Perq, for £10 pd by William Charles, of afsd—sold 5a near Suttons Creek, "pt of a tract given me by my father Joshua Albertson, in his will, Aug 5, 1753," adj sd Charles dwelling house, & the main road. Oct 15, 1770. Test' William Albertson, Reuben Lamb.

No. 147. Dec 12, 1770. Robert Roe of Perq, for £20 pd by Joshua Skinner, of afsd sold 159a on South Side of Yeopim Creek, at the mouth of "Greens Swamp" one half of land pat' by John Cook, May 1, 1695, called "Wharys old field," which was sold by sd Whary, to John Stepney, the elder, & by his son John Stepney, to sd Roe's Father, & descended from him to sd Robert Roe. Test' John Hall, Samuel Penrice.

No. 148. Thomas Barclift, & Sarah his wife, of Perq, for £39 s13 p4 pd by Joseph McAdams, of afsd—sold 50a near a creek called "Connors," which Thomas Weeks Esq, Gr-father of above sd Sarah, bought of John Mann, April 1, 1746, on South west Side of Little River. Jan 19, 1771. Test' John Roberts, W. Bedford, Thomas Leyden.

No. 149. Robert Newby of Perq, for £3 s10 pd by Samuel Newby, of afsd—sold 1½a of woodland, adj Isaac Elliott. Feb 17, 1770. Test' Cornelius Moore, Joseph Bogue, Ann Newby.

No. 150. Zachary Lilly of Chowan, planter—conveyed to Samuel Perry, of afsd 75a in Perq, (in con' of a swap of land). Nov —, 1770. Zachary, & Ann Lilly. Test' Joseph Stallings, Isaac Lilly.

No. 151. Samuel & Ann Perry of Perq, "in Con' of a swap with Zachariah Lilly," do convey 50a, on North East side of Perq River, upon Hickory Ridge, pt of 200a purchased by Thomas Rountree dec, of Joseph Jessop, & left by his will to his son Thomas. Nov 8, 1770. Test' Joseph Stallings, William Lilly.

No. 152. William Charles of Perq, "in Con' of 50a conveyed to me" by Sylvanus Henby, April 18, 1767, assign unto sd Henby 50a, near Suttons Creek, sd land grt unto Samuel Charles, 1720, "on upper side of lower Gum Swamp." Nov 1, 1770. Test' Wm Albertson, Gabriel Cosand, Benj Albertson.

No. 153. Caleb Elliott of Perq, Planter—for "love I bear my son Ephrim" of same, do give, 171a. Feb 16, 1769. Test' John Smith, Hague Elliott, Joanna Kippen, Mary Elliott.

No. 154. Caleb Elliott, for "love I bear my gr-children (issue of Joseph Scott of Pasq Co, & Pennina my dau) do give one negro girl, named Rose, & her increase, one bed, & furniture, if sd children die without issue, to return to my children; Ephrim, Hage, (Pennina Scott) & Soloman Elliott." Feb 16, 1769. Test' John Smith, Haig Elliott, Johanna Kippen, Charles Jordan.

No. 155. Jan 16, 1771. Jacob Wilson of Perq, for £20 pd by Mordecai Elliott, of same—sold 20a, on Southwest side of Perq River, adj Joseph Elliott, near Balahack Swamp. Test' Samuel Sitterson, Moses Wilson, John Jackson.

No. 156. Thomas Boswell of Perq, for £20 pd by Spencer Williams, of Pasq Co, sold 50a, on South west Side of Little River, in Perq Co, formerly belonging to Robert Cox, dec'd. 4d, 12mo 1770. Test' Levi Munden, Morgan Overman, Isaac Boswell.

No. 157. Feb 17, 1769. Joseph Outland of Perq, for £20 pd by Luke Sumner, of Chowan Co, Merchant—sold 120a "on Minses Creek, Nigh the Sound side" near the mouth of a branch, below a settlement made by Ephroditus Brinkley, sd land given in the will of John Burkett, to his son Joseph, & by him conveyed to Humphrey Griffin, April 15, 1733, & by sd Griffin sold to John Warburton, & by him to Josh'a Elliott, & by sd Elliott sold to sd Outland, April 3, 1761. Test' Samuel Wiggins, William Brickley.

No. 158. Jan 27, 1767. John Jones of Perq, for £120 pd by Luke Sumner, of Chowan Co, sold 250a on So Wst Side of Perq River, at a point on Yeopim Creek, adj Thomas Calloway, Capt Miles Harvey, Jno. Calloway, & Zephaniah Jones, formerly called "Morrises," land of Thomas Pierce, who conveyed same to Joseph Pierce, who gave sd land to his dau Miriam, who married John Chancy, & by them sold to sd Jones. Test' William Lumford, James Jones (alias Sketo).

No. 159. May 2, 1770. John Jones, for £150 pd by Luke Sumner, sold 445a on So Wst Side of Perq River, adj Thomas Long, Malachi Jones, Zephaniah Jones, William White, Luke Sumner, & John Calloway, where sd John Jones now dwells. Test' Charles Bondfield, Will Brickell.

No. 160. Nov 1, 1770. Andrew Knox of Perq, Merchant—for £19 pd by Luke Sumner, of same—sold 60a, pt of a grt to Julianna Lakers, April 1, 1718/19 called "Chinquepin Ridge" adj sd Sumner, William Arrenton, & Joshua Skinner. Test' Cornelius Moore, George Bains, Caleb Elliott.

No. 161. Isaac, & Lydia Hasket, of Perq, conveyed 29a (one third pt of land) on So Wst Side of Little River, adj Radcliff, unto William Munden. Sept 3, 1770. Test' John Hasket, Thomas Boswell, Zadock Boswell.

No. 162. April 15, 1771. Joseph Jones of Pasq Co, for £20 pd by Joshua Skinner, of Perq, sold 50a "on a creek issuing out of Minsie Creek," adj Benj, & John Harvey, & Aaron Stacks. Test' Charles Blount, Richard Whidbee.

No. 163. July 17, 1770. Thomas Wright, Planter—for £18 pd by John Welch, planter, of afsd—sold 18a on South Side of Little River, & the Pocosin. Test' Thomas Robinson, Margaret Robinson, Helena Elliott.

No. 164. Joseph Sutton, & Miriam his wife, of Perq; Joseph Sutton dec'd, did bequeath unto his son Christopher Sutton dec'd, land "in fee," (gr-father of sd Joseph) who obtained a Writ, which was Ex by William Skinner Esq, Sheriff of Perq; Feb 14, 1771, sold 63a (whereof sd Joseph Sutton the younger, is seized, under the will of Joseph Sutton, dec gr-father of sd Joseph) for £46 pd by Edward Turner, of afsd, "pt of a grt unto George Sutton, Nov 11, 1719," at the head of Deep Creek, called "Rattle Snake Ridge." Mar 2, 1771. Test' Abraham Mullen, William Robins.

No. 165. Joseph Jones of Perq, "heir-at-law of Zachariah Jones," for £20 pd by Benjamin Saunders, of afsd—sold 50a, adj Moses Baker, & the main road that goes to Edenton, & land of John Harmon, down the branch to the Swamp. Feb 4, 1771. Test' John Saunders, Joseph Gilbert, Benjamin Smith.

No. 166. Jacob Hall of Perq, for £24 pd by Green Thatch, of afsd—sold 100a (whereon, formerly lived Sam'l Hall) patented May 17, 1719, adj James Brickley. April 8, 1771. Test' John Thatch, John Gilbert.

No. 167. Feb 16, 1771. Joseph Perrisho of Perq, for £41 pd by Jacob Wyatt, of afsd—sold 41a on north side of Vosses Creek Swamp, adj Robert Bogue, being lands of Joseph purchased of his brother, Josiah Perrisho, & Edmund Maudlin.

No. 168. Zachariah Nixon of Perq, Planter—for £125 pd by Thomas Pearse, Planter of afsd—sold 200a on North East Side of Vosses Creek, formerly belonging to Joshua Davis. April 13, 1771. Test' Thomas Small, Hercules Saint, Zachariah Newby.

No. 169. Joshua Toms, & Elizabeth his wife, of Perq, for £37 s10 pd by Jacob Goodwin, of afsd—sold 50a in Balahack, adj Samuel Williams. April 21, 1770. Test' John Goodwin, George Whidbee.

No. 170. John Clarke, Mariner—& Sarah his wife, of Chowan Co, for £5 pd by Jacob Jacobs, (Hatmaker—of Northampton Co, N. C.) sold 10a in Perq, on So Est Side of Perq River, ⅓ of land, conveyed by John Morgan, to John Henby Jr, Oct 20, 1735. Seal May 4, 1771. Test' Daniel Saint, Robert Avery.

No. 171. July 15, 1771. John Harmon of Perq, for £12 pd by Andrew Knox, of afsd assigned 15a "near Skinners Bridge," on south branch of Castletons Creek Swamp, adj Zephaniah Jones dec, & land of William Scarbrough. Test' William Jones, Ann Jones.

No. 172. Nov 15, 1770. Joseph Sutton, & Miriam his wife, of Perq, for £57 s6 p8 pd by Seth Sumner Esq, of afsd—sold 344a on North East Side of Perq River, which was taken up by Samuel Parsons, Mar 13, 1704. Test' William Barclift, Thomas Robinson, Aaron Moore.

No. 173. Dec 25, 1770. Samuel Johnson of Chowan Co, attorney-at-law, for £29 p5 pd by Jacob Hall, of Perq, sold 212a in Perq, adj John Hopkins, & Daniel Hall. Test' Joshua Skinner, Samuel Skinner.

No. 174. Elizabeth Barclift of Perq, for "love I bear my children: Frances Foster, & Rachel Foster, of afsd, have given 50a of land." Mar 6, 1771. Test' William Robinson, Will'm Leyden, Sarah Foster.

No. 175. James Price of Chowan Co, for £60 pd by Hardy Hurdle, of afsd—sold 95a in Perq, on West Side of Perq River, in the desert, a grt to Robert Riddick Nov 11, 1758. Seal July 5, 1771. Test' Will King, James Price, John Price.

No. 176. James Price, for £15 pd by Hardy Hurdle, conveyed 50a near the head of Perq River, on the north side of Deep Run, adj Simon Stallings, which was taken up by Thomas Speight, July 20, 1717, & sold by him to John Bass, who sold same to James Field, & he gave same to his "son-by-the-law" Jas Price. July 15, 1771. Test' Will. King, James Price, John Price.

No. 177. Benjamin Wilson, & Judith his wife, of Perq, "for love we bear our son Jacob of afsd—do give 180a in the Piney woods," near Indian branch, adj lines, formerly Samuel Perrys, Richard Harrels, & William Kitchens, which was "a gift from our dec'd father Thomas Docton." April 20, 1771. Test' Caleb White, Thomas Wilson.

No. 178. Zebulum Snoden, & Sarah his wife, of Perk, for £190 pd by John Widbee, of same—sold 200a, adj sd Whidbee, & Richard Whidbee. Feb 19, 1771. Test' J. Whidbee Jr, Richard Whidbee.

No. 179. Thomas Hollowell of Perq, for £50 pd by Moses Bundy, of afsd—sold 50a, adj Peter Draper, & sd Bundy. Feb 7, 1771. Test' Matthew White, Job Bogue, Josiah Bogue.

No. 180. Feb 23, 1770. John Pinner, & Chalkey his wife, of Perq, for £62 s10 pd by Gabriel Cosand, conveyed 65a near Suttons Creek, (being half of land pat' by John Henby, & given by him to his gr-dau Chalkey Henby, in his will, now wife of sd Pinner) running down Gum Swamp. Test' Samuel Charles, William Charles.

No. 181. Feb 23, 1770. John Pinner, & Chalkey his wife, for £62 s10 pd by William Charles, sold 65a near Suttons Creek (given sd Chalkey, by her gr-father John Henby in his will May 5, 1752), being the upper half of 130a. Test' Samuel Charles, Gabriel Cosland.

No. 182. Oct 8, 1770. William Wilson, & Sarah his wife, of Chowan Co, & Priscilla Eggerton, for £70 pd by Charles Copeland, of afsd—sold 108a in Perq, on the head of Yeopim River, adj Francis Brown, & Delight Nixon. Test' Jas. Blount, Thos. Ming, John Evans.

No. 183. Oct 21, 1771. James Sutton of Perq, for £15 pd by Benj Scarbrough, sold 30a on north side of Yeopim Creek, near the head of a Swamp issuing out of Franks Creek, sd land given by my gr-father Francis Penrice, to my father James Sutton, Sr, & by his will to me. Test' James Brinkley, James Boush.

No. 184. Charles Blount of Perq, for "love I bear my dau Sarah Harvey, of afsd—do give my son-in-law John Harvey Jr, 5 negroes, & their increase." Nov 16, 1770. Test' John Harvey, Thomas Harvey.

No. 185. July 9, 1771. Charles Blount of Perq, for "love I bear my son Edmund, of afsd—hath given land whereon sd Edmond now lives," 225a on the Sound, & Muddy Creek, adj Richard Clayton, by deeds from Richard Sanderson, & William Reed. Test' Tully Williams, John Reed.

186. Elizabeth Jacocks, with consent of her husband Thomas Jacocks, of Perq, for "love I bear my son John Reed, of afsd—do give goods, & chattels, as

by an agreement before my marriage Jan 18, 1766—also 4 negroes, 1 bed, & furniture, 2 Mares, & colts, called "Spring & Silver Mane" 10 head of cattle, 10 sheep—1 doz pewter dishes, & plates." May 18, 1771. Test' Joseph Hosea, Mary Ripley.

No. 187. Feb 5, 1771. Thomas, & Elizabeth Jacocks, "do give unto William Reed," of Perq, in trust for John Reed (a minor) son of sd Elizabeth, 125a, on the head of land whereon sd Thomas, & Elizabeth Jacocks now lives, adj Joseph Sutton Sr, given to sd John by the will of his father Joseph Reed, dec April 30, 1765. Test' Charles Blount, Richard Sanderson.

No. 188. Oct 2, 1770. William Skinner Esq, Sheriff of Perq; (Execution) Estate of Richard Sanderson, late of Perq, for the sum of £1140, & £6 s5 for cost, did take into his poss' land which sd Sanderson bought of Jeremiah Caruthers, & Joseph Arnold, Charles Blount, & Christopher Towe, John Whidbee, & Joseph Turner, in all 909⅔a, sd land sold to John Hatch, of Onslow Co, N. C. Test' Thomas Jones, Frederick Fonville, William White.

No. 189. Nicholas Stallings, & John Stallings, of Perq, for £100 pd by Jarvis Forehand, of afsd—sold 120a on Southwest side, of the head of Perq River. Dec 27, 1770. Test' Moses Rountree, Job Stallings, Elias Stallings.

No. 190. July 30, 1771. Henry Hall of Perq, for £100 pd by Joseph Creecy, of Chowan Co, sold 125a on Albemarle Sound, near the mouth of Minses Creek, which was purchased by sd Hall, of Richard Sutton dec'd. Test' Eliz'th Bundy, Jno. Bap. Beasley, Joseph Creecy.

No. 191. William Munden of Perq, for £40 pd by Thomas Henby, of afsd—sold 87a on So Wst Side of Little River, adj Wm Boswell, up Fork Swamp. Aug —, 1771. Test' Benjamin Albertson, John Hasket, Joseph Cox. Aug —, 1771.

No. 192. Jacob Wilson of Perq: "Thomas Docton dec'd (my gr-father), did give unto my father Benj Wilson, & Judith his wife, 180a for their natual lives, & to me at their decease," obtained a Writ, & sold same, for £25, pd by Samuel Bagley. Oct 22, 1771. Test' Geo Eason Jr, Jos Riddick, Job Riddick.

No. 193. Elias Stallings Sr, & Elias Jr, of Perq, Yeoman, for £25 pd by Benj. White, of afsd—sold 100a on North East side of Perq River, adj Thomas Winslow, & Cypress Swamp. Aug 5, 1771. Test' John White, Thomas White, Silas White.

No. 194. Mary 23, 1771. George Eason Jr, of Perq, for £50 pd by Osten Nixon, sold 150a near Middle Swamp, adj Wm King, Joseph Hurdle, & Samuel Bagley. Test' Abraham Eason, George Eason.

No. 195. John Powell of Perq, for £100 pd by Jacob Winslow, of same, planter—sold 125a on South west side of Perq River, in the edge of the Pocosin, being the upper corner of a pat' unto Timothy Clare, said land "now in poss' of heirs of William Price." Oct 17, 1774. Test' Jacob Perry Jr, Elias Stallings.

No. 196. Jan —, 1772. Joseph Sutton the younger, & Miriam his wife, of Perq, sold 344a unto Malachi Jones of afsd—land (bequeathed to them in the will of Christopher Sutton Nov 5, 1723/4.) on No E'st Side of Perq River, & East Side of Suttons Creek, down sd Creek to the River. Test' J. Whidbee, J. Skinner, Thomas ———.

No. 197. Daniel Saint, Carpenter—of Perq, for £103 s12 pd by Jesse Winslow, of same, sold 74a sd land "left by will of Samuel Moore to his son Aaron, who sold same to me, Oct 17, 1768, on the banks of Perq River, near Aaron

Moore's dwelling house," adj Seth Sumner. Sept 10, 1770. Test' Mark Newby, Fras. Nixon, Thomas Robinson.

No. 198. Feb 6, 1772. James Sutton of Perq, for £25 pd by Joshua Skinner, sold 50a on north side of Yeopim Creek, adj land belonging to Orphans of Ephrim Sutton, to a branch issuing out of Albemarle Sound. Test' Samuel Penrice, Elizabeth Penrice.

No. 199. Jeremiah Pratt of Perq, for £60 pd by Richard Pratt, Bricklayer—sold 124a on Indian Creek called "Chessons," at the mouth of a Branch issuing out of sd Creek. Mar 5, 1772. Test' Wm Clemons, John Brinkley, John Norcom.

No. 200. Jan 20, 1772. Andrew Collins, & Anna his wife, of Perq, for £50 pd by Christopher Collins, sold 100a, adj Robert Roe, pt of a grt unto William Long, April 1, 1723, & by him conveyed to John Felt, which by his death fell to his son Job Felt, & by his death to his dau Martha Hardin. Test' Robert Roe, Edward Nichols.

No. 201. Thomas Mullen of Perq, Planter—for £50 pd by Captain Joseph Sutton, of same, sold 50a on Suttons Creek. April 12, 1772. Test' Joseph McAdams, Nath'l. Mastyn.

No. 202. Benjamin Harvey of Perq, planter—for £50 pd by Daniel Saint, of afsd—sold 100a on North Side of Perq River, "in the old neck" where Joseph Jessop lived, adj Joshua Moore, John Moore, & Thomas Pierce. Nov 1, 1771. Test' John Harvey, Miles Harvey.

No. 203. Rhoda Elliott of Perq, for £15 pd by William Maudlin, of same—sold 29a on South west side of Little River, "below fork Swamp." May 15, 1771. Test' Elizabeth Parker, George Boswell, ——— Boswell.

No. 204. April 25, 1772. Robert Roe, & Mary his wife, of Perq, for £40 pd by Andrew Collins, of same—sold 200a on Yeopim Creek, "formerly belonging to Samuel Wyatt, & was given by him to his son Jacob, & by sd Jacob dec, to Robert Roe dec'd, & by his death became the property of sd Robert Roe," land adj John Wyatt, John Creecy, John Standin, William Stepney, & Joshua Skinner. Test' Richard Whidbee, Thomas Nichols.

No. 205. Edward Turner Sr, of Perq, for £10 pd by Demsey Turner, of afsd—sold 68½a on a branch of Deep Creek, pt of a grt unto Thomas Collins, July 20, 1717. Seal April 2, 1772. Test' John Whidbee, George Whidbee, Joseph Turner.

No. 206. Feb 27, 1772. William Stepney of Perq, for £40 pd by Robert Roe, sold 100a on South side of Yeopim Creek, adj land sold by sd Stepney to Stephen Harmon, & land of Joshua Skinner. Test' Joshua Skinner, Edward Penrice.

No. 207. George Boswell of Perq, Planter—for an "exchange of land" with Sam'l White, on south west side of Little River, conveyed 41a, on south west side of same River, to "rich neck branch bridge," being pt of land, which George Boswell dec'd, gave to Arnold White, Dec 20, 1740. 11d, 4mo 1772. Test' Charles Morgan, Levi Munden.

No. 208. Jan 20, 1772. Andrew Collins, & Ann his wife of Perq, sold 200a on west side of Yeopim Creek, adj Joshua Skinner, unto Robert Roe, & Mary his wife, "a pat' to Edward Wilson, June 24, 1704, & by his death became the property of his dau Sarah, who married Thomas Williams, who sold same to Richard Bond, who bequeathed same to his sons Edward, & Samuel (who died under age) when sd land descended by hearship to Edward Penrice, & William Arrington, in right of their mother," who sold sd land. Test' Benj. Scarbrough, James Sutton.

No. 209. Benj Wilson of Perq, for "love I bear my son Thomas, of afsd —have given 50a on South west side of Perq River, at a place called the fork path," adj William Newby, & Caleb White, to son Thomas, & his wife Mary & after their decease to gr-son Benj. Wilson." April 20, 1772.

No. 210. Benjamin Snoden, of Pasq Co, for £281 pd by Tully Williams, of Perq, sold 140½a on Muddy Creek, adj Edmund Blount. Nov 21, 1772. Test' Charles Blount, Wm. Layden, Thomas Nichols.

No. 211. John Henby of Perq: "John Henby dec, did bequeath to his son Sylvanus, land of small value, & sd John (son of sd Sylvanus) obtained a Writ, to sell sd land, & William Skinner Sheriff of Perq; executed same Mar 21, 1772, Sold for £120, pd by Job Hendricks: 100a on the mouth of Long Branch, that runs out of Vosses Creek, adj John Lacey, & Joseph Barber. April 9, 1772. Test' John Albertson, Seth Sumner.

No. 212. Feb 24, 1772. William Stepney of Perq, for £26 pd by Stephen Harmon, of same—sold 50a on South side of Yeopim Creek, adj James Williams, & Joshua Skinner, called "Wherry's." Test' Joshua Skinner, Lydia Long.

No. 213. John Nixon of Perq, for £60 pd by Richard Hampton, of Chowan Co, sold 107a on North Side of the head of Yeopim River Swamp, formerly Benjamin Simpsons, adj Mr. Thomas McNight, Delight Nixon, & Charles Copeland. Feb 8, 1772. Test' Thomas Harmon, Delight Nixon, Elizabeth Robinson.

No. 214. Jonathan Moore of Perq, for £55 pd by Caleb Toms, of afsd— sold 50a, adj Moses Elliott, & the mouth of "Reedy branch," on the Swamp, to lines of Francis Toms, & Jacob Elliott. 11d, 3mo 1772. Test' Hercules Saint, Lemuel Ray.

No. 215. Mar 4, 1772. Robert Roe, & Mary his wife, of Perq, for £110 pd by William Haughton, of same—sold 200a on South Side of Minses Creek, adj Joseph Creecy. Test' Joshua Skinner, Edward Penrice.

No. 216. Samuel Bagley of Perq, for £11 pd by John Ownly, of Chowan Co, sold 25a in Perq, adj Job Riddick, Docton Riddick, Abram Eason, & Austen Nixon. Feb 15, 1772. Job Riddick, Thos. Overman.

No. 217. Jan 13, 1772. Benjamin Perry of Perq, for £26 s1 pd by Josiah Rogerson, sold 100a, in sd County. Test' Ann Riddick, Elisha Hunter, Joseph Riddick.

No. 218. Jan 18, 1772. John Moore, & Mary his wife, of Perq, for £45 pd by Jesse Winslow dec'd, sold to Jesse Winslow (son of Jesse) 30a, adj sd Jesse. Test' Mark Newby, Benj. Heaton, Jonathan Phelps.

No. 219. June 20, 1772. John Henby of Perq; "my father Sylvanus Henby bequeathed to me, his son 50a, on the back of William Albertson's line, adj William Charles, & Dempsey Henby, sold sd land to sd William Albertson, for a con."

No. 220. Feb 25, 1771. William Stepney of Perq, Bricklayer—for £30 pd by Hatten Williams, of Chowan Co, sold 40a on North Side of Yeopim River. Test' Wm. Long, Thos. Hoskins.

No. 221. Mar 3, 1772. Joseph, & Mary Farmer of Perq, & John Henby, of afsd, for £16 pd by Wm Albertson, of same—sold 23½a near Suttons Creek, pt of "527a grt unto John Henby 1740, & given to us Sylvanus, & Dempsey

Henby, in the will of our Gr-father 5d 3mo 1762, sd land being the 5pt given to Dempsey Henby, & his heirs." Test' Francis Albertson, John Henby.

No. 222. Aug 25, 1771. Macrora Scarbrough, for £5 pd by Wm Scarbrough, both of Chowan Co, sold two tracts in Perq, one called "Point Pleasant" in Yeopim, another called "Oak Ridge" 201a. Test' John Achison, Nathaniel Allen.

No. 223. Aug 25, 1771. Macrora Scarbrough for £5 assigned "all negro slaves (7), household stuff, impliments, furniture, 1 large Silver Can, Silver Spoons, as delivered to sd William Scarbrough." Test' John Atchison, Nathaniel Allen.

No. 224. Aug 25, 1771. Macrora Scarbrough (Orphan of William), of Edenton, Gent—for £5 pd by Macrora Scarbrough, "doth sell all right to Estate in Perq, unto Wm. Scarbrough, 200a of land devised to Elizabeth Scarbrough (now Eliz'h Painter), by her father Macrora Scarbrough for life, & at her death to her heirs." Test' John Atchison, Nathiel Allen.

No. 225. Jacob Jacobs, & Elizabeth his wife of Perq, for £60 pd by Daniel Saint, of afsd, sold 40a on No E Side of Perq River, adj James Morgan, Isaac Elliott, & Thomas Jessop. Nov 19, 1770. Test' Job Hendricks, Thomas Calloway, Thomas Hendricks.

No. 226. Sept 1, 1772. Joshua Bagley of Perq, for £30 pd by Malachi Chappel, of afsd—sold 50a in "Bear Swamp, called Mulberry Ridge" pt of a pat' unto John Parker, July 28, 1730, adj Jeremiah Cannon, to Cypress Swamp. Test' Thos. Newby, Thos. Robinson.

No. 227. Benj, & Moses Wilson, of Perq, for £50 pd by Caleb White, of same—sold 100a on west side of Perq River, adj Thomas Wilson, & Wm Newby. July 14, 1772. Test' Jacob Wilson, Zachariah Wilson.

No. 228. Oct 13, 1772. Joshua Skinner of Perq, for £80 pd by James McMullen, of same—sold 150a on South Side of Yeopim Creek, at the mouth of Gum Swamp, pt of a pat' to John Cook, 1695, called "Wherrys old field." Test' Samuel Penrice, James McMullen.

No. 229. Richard Cale, & Hannah his wife, of Perq, for £25 pd by Thomas Henby, of afsd—sold 87a on S Wst Side of Little River, adj Wm Boswell, to the head of Long Branch, & down sd branch to fork Swamp. Oct 19, 1772. Test' Levi Munden, Amos Boswell.

No. 230. Edmund Maudlin of Perq, planter—for £60 pd by Joseph Barber, of afsd—sold 105a on "North west side of Joseph Newbys Mill Swamp," adj run of sd Swamp, & lines of Jacob Wyatt, & Robert Bogue. Sept 8, 1772. Test' John Maudlin, Joseph Maudlin.

No. 231. Sept 2, 1772. Ann Davis of Perq, for £7 pd by Joshua Small, of same—sold 5pt of 56a on the Desert, adj lines of Marmaduke Davis, John Gordon, & Jacob Powell, "pt of a pat' in Vir to John Harris, & John Larcum, (888a) & sold by them to John Moseley, who sold sd land to Joseph Redding, who gave same to his son James, & descended from him to his brother John Redding, who willed sd land to his three sisters; one of whom Rachel, married John Davis, from them to their five dau's, one of whom sd Ann." Test' Jesse Eason, David Small.

No. 232. Aug 17, 1772. Wm Stepney of Perq, for £70 pd by John Nixon, of same—sold 56a on N. E. Side of Indian Creek, near the head of Yeopim Creek, on Deep branch, adj Hatten Williams, grt to William Wyatt, April 15,

1745, & sold by him to John Stepney, Oct 29, 1745. Test' Robert Cale, Joseph Pratt.

No. 233. Sept 5, 1772. Joseph Sutton Jr, & his mother Sarah Sutton, of Perq, for £70 pd by sd Sarah, sold 168a on South East Side of Suttons Creek, "on a line that parts sd land from land I sold Malachi Jones, & land where I now live." Test' Thomas Robinson, Margaret Robinson, Helena Elliott.

No. 234. Oct 12, 1772. Benjamin Scarbrough, & Sarah his wife, & James Sutton of Perq, for £25 pd by Joshua Skinner, of same—sold 50a on No Side of Yeopim Creek, adj Orphans of Ephrim Sutton, to a small Creek, called "Franks Creek," sd land formerly James Suttons. Test' Henry Hardin, Martha Hardin.

No. 235. Aug 11, 1772. Joshua Long of Perq, for £30 pd by Joshua Skinner, of afsd—sold 50a "on the Sound side Neck," adj William Wyatt, Benj Harvey, John Harvey, & Luke Sumner, one half of land given my Gr-father Joshua Long, & William Wyatt, by the will of John Wyatt dec'd. Test' Andrew Collins, Robert Roe.

No. 236. Henry Thompson of Chowan, for £130 pd by Thomas Newby, of Perq, sold 200a in Perq, "on Mirey Branch," at the Poly bridge, to Chowan road, & line of Mary Barker, Caleb Elliott, & Joseph Smith. Dec 15, 1772. Test' Hague Elliott, E. Newby, John Bateman.

No. 237. Nov 11, 1772. Samuel Kippin of Chowan, for £20 pd by Joshua Skinner, of Perq, sold 170a on west side of Castletons Creek, "above Skinners bridge, formerly Samuel Phelps, but now possessed by John Painter," sd land pat' by Richard Skinner Nov 22, 1714. Test' Fred'k Norcom, Eleazer Creecy.

No. 238. Jan 16, 1773. Abraham Jannet, & Priscilla his wife, of Perq, for £130 pd by Richard Skinner, of same—sold 186a on So Side of Perq River, adj Jeremiah Doe, Malachi Chesson, John Barrow, David Pierce, Will'm & Thomas White. Test' Joshua Skinner, Henry Skinner.

No. 239. Oct 3, 1772. Tully Williams of Perq, for £78 pd by Edmund Blount, sold 14a on the "head branches of Muddy Creek," pt of a tract sd Williams bought of Benjamin Snoden. Nov 27, 1771. Test' Charles Blount, Demson Barclift.

No. 240. Nov 7, 1772. John Standin of Perq, for £82 s10 pd by Andrew Collins, of afsd—sold 200a on No Side of Yeopim River, adj Jesse Bunch, John Standin & land bought of Richard Banks. July 16, 1746. Test' Levi Creecy, John Creecy.

No. 241. Dec 28, 1773. Jacob Powell of Chowan, for £100 pd by Joshua Small, of Perq, sold 100a "on the Desert side," adj Joseph Gordon, & Jesse Eason, pt of a pat' in Vir to John Haris & John Larcum for 888a, April 21, 1695, & by them sold to John Redding, who willed sd land to his son John, who willed same to his dau Elizabeth, who married James Peartree, & they sold same to sd Powell. Test' Pleasant Jordan, Kadee Powell, Henry Bond.

No. 242. Joseph Sutton of Perq: "Joseph Sutton Dec, bequeathed to his son Christopher 105a, which proved of small value, whereof Joseph Sutton the younger is seized," who obtained a Writ, Ex by William Skinner Esq, Sheriff of Perq, & sold sd land to Malachi Jones, for £62 s10. Oct 19, 1772. Test' W. Skinner, George Whedbee, Seth Sumner.

No. 243. Thos. Nichols of Perq, for £450 pd by George Whidbee, of same—sold 194a, "on the road leading to Nags Head Chapel," adj Joseph Perrishoe,

Abraham Turner, Dempsey Turner, & John Whidbee, Sept 26, 1772. Test' J. Whidbee, Joseph Perrishoe.

No. 244. William Wilson of Perq, for £40 pd by Francis Toms, & Joseph McAdams, of afsd—sold 100a on So Wst Side of the head of Mirey Swamp, including the "Oak Ridge land, bequeathed to me, by Wm Moore dec." Aug 8, 1771. Test' Thos. Robinson, William Arnold, Helena Elliott.

No. 245. William Gordon of Perq, Planter—for £6 pd by Caleb McKee, of afsd—sold 6a on So Wst Side of Little River. Jan 18, 1773. Test' John Stafford.

No. 246. Elizabeth Winslow of Perq, for £50 pd by Isaac Wilson, of afsd—sold 105a in the fork of Cypress Swamp, called "Aarons old field," adj Thomas Newby Jr, along the desert to Pritlow Elliott, & John Parsons line; a dividing line between Robert, & William Wilson. Sept 2, 1772. Test' Jacob Perry Jr, Jacob Winslow.

No. 247. Reuben Brazier, of Craven Co, son of John dec'd of Perq Co, for £20 pd by James Jordan, of Chowan Co, sold 150a in Perq, "whereon Elizabeth Kanier, & John Brazier now liveth, on East Side of Perq River," near Thomas Newby, & William White. Dec 16, 1773. Test' Zachariah Jordan, James Michael.

No. 248. William Scarbrough, of Pasq Co, for £425 pd by Miles Harvey Esq, of Perq, sold 286a between the mouth of Yeopim River & Creek, "which my dec father Macrora Scarbrough bought of Thomas Wyatt, called Point Pleasant" adj John Wyatt. Oct 26, 1773. Test' Matthew Whiteman, F. Norcom.

No. 249. Edward Turner Jr, & Agnes his wife, of Perq, for £270 pd by Richard Whedbee, of afsd—sold 163a, purchased of Joseph Sutton (son of Christopher), on North Side of Deep Creek Swamp. Dec 8, 1772. Test' J. Whidbee, George Whidbee.

No. 250. April 14, 1774. Richard Clayton of Perq, & John Lowry of Pasquotank, for £179 pd by John Whidbee Sen, of afsd, (by virtue of the last will of John Clayton Esq, late of Perq 1769,) doth sell 195a, on No East Side of Perq River, adj sd Whidbee, Rebecca Clayton's dower excepted, (widow). Test' George Whidbee, Joseph Clayton.

No. 251. Nov 24, 1773. Reuben Long, & Penninah his wife, for £25 pd by Joshua Skinner, both of Perq—sold 100a on South side of Mings Creek, adj land of Sam Penrice, & sd Skinner, & lands formerly William Longs, who bought sd land of Francis Penrice, & Christopher Arrenton, part of a pat unto Edward Wilson. Test' Wm Long, Joshua Long.

No. 252. Jan 30, 1773. William Houghton & Mary his wife, for £145 pd by John Taylor, sold 200a, on So Side of Mings Creek, "at the side of Yeopim Road," pat by Edward Wilson, Jun 24, 1704. Test' Joshua Skinner, Wm Morris.

No. 253. April 3, 1773. John Taylor of Perq, for 75a on the Sound Side, conveyed by Samuel Penrice, doth convey 200a, on Lakers, & Mings Creek, adj Edward Hall, Joseph Creecy, Christopher Long, & Reuben Long, sd Land pat' by Edward Wilson June 24, 1704. Test' Joshua Skinner, Henry Hardin.

No. 254. Whereas: Francis Penrice of Perq dec'd, did by his will bequeath unto his son Francis 100a, & sd Francis obtained a Writ from Josiah Martin Esq, & Mr. William Skinner, Sheriff of Perq, did sell sd land, for £75, pd by Joseph Creecy; on Albemarle Sound, adj Edward Penrice, "sd land formerly given by Francis Penrice, to Samuel Penrice, & Christopher Collins." April 19, 1774. Test' Joshua Skinner, John Taylor.

No. 255. Francis Penrice of Perq, "did bequeath unto his son Samuel, 100a on the Sound side, & sd Samuel obtained a Writ, & sold sd land to John Taylor," for £25, adj Joseph Creecy, Christopher Collins, & Orphans of Ephrim Luten. Test' Joshua Skinner, Joseph Turner. April 18, 1775.

No. 256. Sept 11, 1772. Zachariah Toms of Perq, Merch't, & Joseph White of afsd—planter, for £5 pd by sd Joseph, to sd Toms, sold 640a called "Vosses" formerly belonging to Francis Toms, Gr-father of sd Zacharias, & was devised by him to his son Francis Toms. Test' Ralph Fletcher, Caleb Toms, Wm Barber.

No. 257. Oct 2, 1773. Joseph Pratt of Perq, Bricklayer—for £100 pd by Richard Pratt, sold 130a on west side of Indian Creek, adj sd Richard, which was willed to sd Joseph by Jeremiah Pratt Dec'd. Test' Thomas Williams, Robert Cale.

No. 258. May 22, 1773. Reuben Long of Perq, for £60 pd by Joshua Wyatt, of same, sold 50a on East side of the mouth of Yeopim Creek, adj land of Joshua Skinner, & Orphans of Ephrim Luten, on the Sound, called "Smiths Point." Test' Andrew Collins, Elizabeth Long.

No. 259. Joshua Bundy of Perq, for £10 pd by Josiah Bundy, of Pasq, sold 85a, part of 700a grt unto Thomas Nicholson, Sept 1761, which he sold to Ellis Bundy, & sd Joshua, Dec 13, 1761, on Wst Side of Little River, at the mouth of a branch, adj Francis Nixon, plan "where sd Josiah formerly lived." Jan 14, 1774. Test' John Bubdy, Caleb Bundy.

No. 260. Thomas Long of Perq, planter—for £345 pd by Reuben Long, of afsd—sold 464a on the head of Yeopim Creek Swamp, at the head of a small branch issuing out of sd Creek, "on line of my Manor plan." Dec 25, 1773. Test' Joshua Skinner, Jonathan Skinner, Wm. Stepney.

No. 261. Lawrence Lessly, & Miriam his wife of Perq, for £150 pd by Thos. Newby, of afsd—sold 109a by the River Swamp, on line of Pearson. May 23, 1773. Test' Duke Bogue, Josiah Jordan Jr.

No. 262. April 10, 1773. Jesse Bogue of Perq, for £75 pd by Ralph Fletcher, sold 75a on Vosses Creek. Test' Mark Newby, Zachariah Newby, Wm. Baker.

No. 263. Feb 1, 1773. Simon Boswell, & Ann his wife, of Perq, for £45 pd by Chaulkey Albertson, of same—sold 64a on East Side of Long branch of Suttons Creek, "part of land formerly belonging to Joshua Boswell dec'd, given to us in his will." Test' Wm Hill, Wm Albertson.

No. 264. Mark Newby of Perq, for £86 pd by Wm Newby, of afsd—sold 43a at the mouth of a branch on Samuel Newby's Mill Pond, to the main road, between Isaac Elliott, & sd Mark. Jan 17, 1774. Test' Samuel Newby, Gideon Newby, Jos Bogue.

No. 265. July 27, 1773. Charles Rountree of Chowan, for £50 pd by Jarvis Forehand, sold 50a called "Grape tree ridge" part of a pat' to Luke Hollowell, & sold to Thos Jessop, & by sd Jessop to Thomas Rountree, "who willed sd land to his son Charles." Test' Moses Rountree, Abner Hollowell, Luke Stallings.

No. 266. 11d, 4mo 1774. Sarah Clark widow—Ephrim Etheridge, & Miriam his wife, & John Henby, of Perq, for £30 pd by Chalkey Albertson, of afsd—sold 47a near Suttons Creek, "part of a pat' to John Henby, in 1740 for 527a, which was given to Sylvanus, & Demsey Henby, by their Gr-father John

Henby, in his will, May 5, 1752, sd land being ⅖ of that part given to Demsey Henby." Test' Simon Boswell, John Avery, John Bagley.

No. 267. Jan 25, 1773. Jesse Douglas, & Dorothy his wife, & John Henby, of Perq for £16 pd by Chalkey Albertson, of same—sold part of tract, grt to John Henby 1740, (527a) "being ⅕ of land given to Sylvanus, & Demsey Henby by their Gr-father John Henby, in his will May 5, 1752. sd part given to Demsey Henby." Test' Benjamin Albertson, Wm Albertson.

No. 268. William Foster of Perq, for "love I bear my son Frederick of afsd—do set over a parcel of land bought of Samuel Charles, 115a adj Richard Whidbee, & Moses Barber, whereon I now live." Sept 25, 1773. Test' George Hatfield, Gosby Toms, Francis Foster.

No. 269. Zachariah Toms of Perq, for £5 pd by Caleb Toms, of afsd—sold 2a, adj sd Caleb. Jan 5, 1773. Test' Frans. Newby, Foster Toms.

No. 270. Oct 26, 1772. Jacob Jacobs, & Elizabeth his wife, of Northampton Co, & John Henby of afsd—for £16 pd by Wm. Albertson of Perq, sold 23½a, near Suttons Creek, "pt of land pat' by John Henby 1740, & given by him to his Gr-sons Sylvanus, & Demsey Henby in his will, sd land being ⅕ pt of pt given to Demsey Henby." Test' Benj Albertson, Simon Boswell.

No. 271. Joseph Newby, & Elizabeth his wife, for £82 s16 pd by Joseph Guyer, of afsd—sold 92a on West Side of Vosses creek, in the fork of "Cabin Swamp." Feb 3, 1774. Test' Benj Phelps, Jesse Bogue.

No. 272. Jonathan Phelps of Perq, planter—for £80 pd by Richard Goodwin Jr, of afsd—sold 50a in Ballahack, ne'r sd Swamp. Oct 21, 1772. Test' Joseph Elliott, John Whidbee.

No. 273. Jesse Douglas, & Dorothy his wife, of Northampton Co, for £5 pd by Hercules Saint of Perq, conveyed 50a at the head of "Dirty branch," on No Est side of Perq River, adj James Morgan, Isaac Elliott, & Tho Jessop. Jan 28, 1773. Test' Wm. Albertson, Chalkey Albertson.

No. 274. Samuel Perry, & Ann his wife, of Chowan Co, Planter—for £13 pd by Wm. Lilly, of Perq, sold 75a on east side of Chowan Road. April 21, 1773. Test' William Lilly Jr.

No. 275. Feb 13, 1773. Job Riddick, & Prudence his wife, of Perq, for £1108 pd by Joseph Hurdle of same, sold 200a, on No Side of Indian Branch, "which was given James Price, by Thomas Docton, April 11, 1752, & sd Price, sold sd land to sd Riddick, Mar 5, 1762." Test' Stargiss Edvingam, Docton Riddick, Edw Berryman.

No. 276. Silas White, & Christion his wife, for £50 pd by John White, sold 150a on No Est Side of Perq River, pat' by Thomas Jessop, beginning at Newbegun Creek, on John Winslow's line. Jan 25, 1773. Test' Benj White, Thos. White, John Winslow.

No. 277. Charles Moore, Richard, & Joseph Pratt, Exors of Jeremiah Pratt, dec'd; sold land on west side of "Pratts Mill Pond" at public sale, Sept 12, 1772, for £15-s5 pd by Jonathan Haughton, (sd Houghton giving up his purchase to Thomas McNider) pt of a larger tract pat' by Wm Wyatt, April 15, 1745. Seal Feb 20, 1773. Jona Haughton, Deborah Haughton, Thos. Williams.

No. 278. Joshua Bundy of Perq, for £165 pd by Josiah Bundy, of Pasq Co, sold 88a "given to me by my father, in his will, Dec 28, 1760," land on west side of Little River, adj Francis Nixon, River Pocosin, Joseph Ratcliff, & John Henby. Jan 14, 1774. Test' John Bundy, Caleb Bundy.

No. 279. Amos Boswell of Perq, for £42 pd by Jonathan Moore, of same—sold 156a "near Long Branch of Suttons Creek," adj Chalkey Albertson. May 13, 1773. Test' Wm Albertson, Thos. Robinson, Benj Albertson.

No. 280. Feb 16, 1774. Aaron Mizell of Perq, for £75 pd by Samuel Green Jr, sold 100a on the "Main Desert," & line of Willis Riddick, sd land grt to Richard Pierce Dec'd. Test' Benj. Gordon, Samuel Green, Elisha Hunter.

No. 281. Jonathan Moore of Perq, for £42 pd by Spencer Williams, of same—sold 150a on Long Branch of Suttons Creek, which formerly belonged to Joshua Boswell, adj Chalkey Albertson. Nov 12, 1773. Test' Abram. Hosea, Levi Munden, Simon Boswell.

No. 282. Spencer Williams of Pasq Co, for £25 pd by James Davis, of same—sold 50a on So Wst Side of Little River, a pat' unto Robert Cox dec'd. Jan 26, 1774. Test' Jesse Perry, Reuben Griffin, Levi Munden.

No. 283. Richard Goodwin of Perq, for £40 pd by Joshua Deal, of afsd—sold 100a, adj Thomas Wood into the "thick grounds." Aug 11, 1772. Test' John Boyce, Edward Cook.

No. 284. Sept 18, 1773. Mary Godfrey of Perq, for "love I have for my son Joseph Godfrey, doth give 40a, in the fork of a gut, which makes out of Deep Creek, called "Cod" land left him by his father Thomas Godfrey, & all houses." Test' John Gibson, Francis Godfrey.

No. 285. Zachariah Toms of Perq, for £5 pd by Caleb Toms, sold 191a, adj Jesse Winslow, Zachariah Nixon, Andrew Woodley, & Ralph Fletcher. Jan 15, 1773. Test' Frans Newby, Foster Toms.

No. 286. Christopher Nicholson, for £1-s1-p8 pd by my father Thomas Nicholson, sold land in Perq. Sept 18, 1773. Test' William Hill, Caroline Nicholson.

No. 287. June 15, 1773. George Eason Jr, of Perq, for £166 pd by Joseph Riddick, of same—sold 250a, which was grt to Thomas Docton, May 1, 1717, "given in his will to his Gr-son Job Riddick, who sold sd land to sd Eason, lying on west side of the main desert," adj Joseph Hurdle, & Moses Pierce. Test' Simon Stallings, Thos. Hurdle, Seth Stallings.

No. 288. March 24, 1773. John Williams Sr, of Perq, for £40 pd by James Donaldson, of same—sold 100a on west side of Yeopim Creek, up beaver cove, to Spring branch, adj Robert Roe. Test' Andrew Collins, Wm. Townsend, Sarah Branch.

No. 289. May 5, 1774. William Jordan Jr, & Mary his wife, of Bertie Co, for £90 pd by Richard Clayton, of Perq, sold 30a in sd Co, "land whereon sd Clayton lives, ⅓ of 90a, given by Mr Samuel Swann Dec'd, in his will, Jan 8, 1753, to his daughter Mary Clayton, wife of sd Richard," (with all buildings). Test' Chas. Blount, Peter Norcom.

No. 290. Thomas Wright of Perq, for £15 pd by Joseph Sitterson, of Pasq Co, sold 18a in Perq, adj Nathaniel Welch, "where sd Wright lives." Feb 28, 1774. Test' Thos. Robinson, Margaret Robinson, Ann Elliott.

No. 291. Rebecca Clayton, for £25 pd by John Whedbee, conveyed "all right of dower, in a plan' belonging to John Clayton Esq, dec'd, & now the property of sd Whidbee.' July 19, 1774. Test' George Whidbee. And'w. Collins, John Raper.

No. 292. Benj Harvey of Perq, for £8 pd by Dr Benj Bowin, sold unto Dr Nathaniel Merton, of the Town of Hertford, one Lot, or ½a of land. (Reg in Hertford book.)

No. 293. Tho. Nicholson of Perq, Trader—for £6-s10 in "behalf of my gr-sons Thomas, & Joseph Nicholson, Joshua Overman, Will'm Hill, Charles Overman Jr, Pierce Nixon, Thos Robinson, Christopher Nicholson, Nicholas Nicholson, Thos Jordan, Mary Nixon, Barnabe Nixon, Samuel, & Mordica Newby, partners in a Mill Intended over Little River do give right of land around a great Island, & room for a good road, to the main road." Sept 24, 1773. Test' Charles Overman, Robt. Munden, John Smith.

No. 294. May 13, 1774. Joshua Dail of Perq, for £40 pd by John Boyce, of same, sold 100a called "Parmers Cowpens," & "John Parkers old field" adj Thos Ward, up Mirey Swamp, into the "thick ground" which sd Dail purchased of Richard Goodwin. Test' Joseph Smith, Moses Boyce, Josiah White.

No. 295. Mar 2, 1773. Demson Barclift of Perq, "for the benefit, & support of a School," conveyed to William Barclift, & the neighborhood, ½a, on No Est side of the main road, where the School-house is now standing, on line of John Hollowell. Test' Noah Barclift, Francis Foster, John Gibson.

No. 296. William Boyce, Bricklayer—of Perq, for £90 pd by Duke Boyce, Bricklayer of afsd—sold 68a, adj Joseph Jessop. July 16, 1774. Test' Caleb Toms, William Baker.

No. 297. William Trumball of Perq, for £35 pd by John Stanton, of same, sold 17½a on No Est Side of Perq River, on Muddy Creek, adj land where sd Stanton lives. July 9, 1774. Test' John Hollowell, Thom Robinson, Jno Raper.

No. 298. April 20, 1771. William Wilson of Perq, for £13 pd by Wm Arnold, of same, sold 50a on So West Side of "Ballahagen, or Ballahack Swamp," (down the middle of sd Swamp) on line of Joseph Riddick, & Wingate's line, part of land bought of Wm Townsend, & Zachary Chancey. Test' Thos Robinson, Joseph McAdams, John Lowther.

No. 299. Aug 1, 1773. Docton Riddick, of Chowan Co, for £300 pd by Jacob Sumner, of Nansemond Co, Va, sold 640a in Perq Co, a grt to Thos Docton, July 20, 1717. Test' John Powell, Elisha Sumner, John Webb.

No. 300. Jan 19, 1773. Abraham Hosea, & Mary his wife, of Pasq Co, for £30 pd by Simon, & Amos Boswell, sold 300a in Perq, on Long Branch, near Suttons Creek Land formerly belonging to Joshua Boswell, dec'd, & left said Mary for her life. Test' Thomas Henby, John Henby.

No. 301. Oct 21, 1773. John Bateman of Perq, for £32 pd by Joseph Hosea—sold 60a called "Wat Weeks" on North East side of Perq River, in the fork of "Beaver Cove Swamp," which was given in the will of my father William Bateman, to my mother-in-law (step-mother) Betty Bateman. Test' Benj Bateman, Jos Bateman.

No. 302. Benj Wilson of Perq, for "love I bear my son Zachariah, of afsd—do give, pt of a tract of land on So Wst Side of Wilsons Creek," 100a, adj land "I gave my son Jacob," & the land of Ralph Bozman. May —, 1774. Test' Jacob Wilson, Rachel Wilson, Ephrim Wilson.

No. 303. July 18, 1774. Elias Stallings of Perq, & Job Boyce; Whereas Isaac Boyce, in his will gave to sd Stallings authority to sell 150a of land, in the fork of Cypress Swamp, called "The Duck pond," sold sd land to Job Boyce. Test' Joshua Skinner, Benj Scarbrough.

No. 304. Job Kenion of Perq, Wheelwright—for £112 pd by Thomas Winslow, of afsd, sold 150a on No Side of Vosses Creek, adj Will'm. Stone, & Joseph Newby. June 18, 1774. Test' Joseph Newby, Benj. Newby, Joshua Guier.

No. 305. July 5, 1773. Charles, & Edward Blount, in Perq, planters—for £320 pd by Asa Barlift, of afsd—sold 150a at the head of Little Creek, which issues out of Little River, adj sd Barclift, & Tully Williams, called "Maudlins" on So Wst Side of sd River. Test' Demson Barclift, William Stokes.

No. 306. Elizabeth Ranier of Perq, for "love I bear my son John Brasher, of afsd do give after my decease 50a where I now live." May 23, 1774. Test' Duke Bogue, John Robinson.

No. 307. Caleb Mackey of Perq, for £10-s10 pd by George Gordon, of afsd—Planter sold 60a on S. W. Side of Little River. Oct 7, 1774. Test' Moses Jackson, Nath'l Gordon.

No. 308. Whereas; Thomas Long of Perq, dec'd, "did by his will bequeath unto his son Thomas 150a in fee," & sd Thomas obtained a Writ, & sold same to James Brinkley, for £67-10s, land on Indian Creek, called "Mill Swamp" adj Richard French, land grt to Daniel Hall, Aug 16, 1716. Seal Oct 1, 1774. Test' W. Skinner, Elizabeth Skinner.

No. 309. James Perisho of Perq, for £70 pd by Mark Bogue, of afsd—sold 50a on So Wst Side of Vosses Creek, part of a pat to John Lacy 1725. Sept 2, 1774. Test' Joseph Draper, Joshua Hasket, Joseph Hasket.

No. 310. Nov 12, 1773. William Scarbrough of Pasq Co, for £5 pd by Obed Winslow, sold 250a, which was "devised to Elizabeth Scarbrough (now Elizabeth Painter), by her father Macrora Scarbrough, & in default of heirs to his son Macrora, who conveyed sd Right to me." Aug 12, 1771. Test' John Moore, John Painter.

No. 311. July 27, 1773. John Paynter of Edenton, Gent; & Elizabeth his wife, dau of Mac Scarbrough Esq, late of Perq, Dec'd, for £180 pd by Obed Winslow, sold 238a on Perrishos Creek, adj James Perrishoe. Test' Joseph Blount, Joseph Blount Jr.

No. 312. Oct 17, 1774. William Arrenton of Perq, for £35-4s pd by Ezekiel Arrenton, sold 128a, "part of 580a pat by Wm Titterton, Aug 16, 1716, & by him sold to Thomas Long," & by sd Long conveyed to Reuben Long, who sold sd land to sd William Arrenton. Test' W. Skinner.

No. 313. Oct 17, 1774. Reuben Long of Perq, for £75-s8 pd by William Arrenton, of afsd—sold 256a, part of 580a, grt to William Titterton, Aug 16, 1716, conveyed by him to Thomas Long, & by sd Long sold to sd Reuben. Test' Isaac Moore, Caleb Winslow.

No. 314. Oct 14, 1774. Jeremiah Doe of Perq, planter—for £25 pd by Charles Moore, of afsd—sold part of land "whereon I now live." Test' John Hall, Rich. Skinner.

No. 315. Joseph Newby Jr, of Perq, & Elizabeth his wife, for £8 pd by James Elliott, of afsd—sold 10a on East Side of Vosses Creek. Oct 17, 1774. Test' Joseph Draper, Joshua Hasket, Joseph Hasket.

No. 316. Thomas, & Elizabeth Winslow, of Perq, for £254 pd by Elihu Albertson, of afsd—sold 124a on Sou Wst side of Little River, near the mouth of a small branch, adj Roland, & Thomas Robinson, "being part of land grt July 23, 1694, to Wm. Tomblin, & by him assigned to Dennis Collins, & Wm Davis, by sd Davis, sold to sd Thos. Winslow, by sd Thomas Winslow given to my father John Winslow, & by sd John in his will to me." Feb 26, 1774. Test' Thomas Robinson, Wm. Robins.

RECORDS OF DEEDS 239

No. 317. Zachariah Nixon of Perq, & Mary his wife, for £25 pd by Joseph Elliott, of same—sold 240a, adj land of Julius Bunch, & Ephriam Elliott, in Chowan Co. March 24, 1774. Test' Joseph Boice, Moses Stone.

No. 318. Thomas Mullen of Perq, & Ann his wife, for £65 pd by Dempsey Turner, of afsd—sold 55a in sd County. Aug 27, 1774. Test' Francis Penrice, Jacob Mullen.

No. 319. Aug 19, 1774. Simon Boswell of Perq, for £7-s5 pd by Chalkey Albertson, of afsd—sold 7½a on Long Branch of Suttons Creek; part of land "formerly in possession of Joshua Boswell, Dec'd, & by him given me in his will." Test' Wm. Albertson, Joshua Bailey.

No. 320. John Welch, of Bertie Co, for £16-s10 pd by John Lane, Shoemaker—sold 18a on So Wst Side of Little River, which sd Welch bought of Thomas Wright. Jan 26, 1774. Test' Joseph Sitterson, Samuel Jackson.

No. 321. Nov 30, 1773. Henry Hardin, & Martha his wife, of Perq, for £54 pd by Christopher Collins, of same, sold 100a, adj Joseph Creecy, & Samuel Penrice, Reuben Long, & orphans of Ephrim Luten, part of a tract pat by William Long, April 1, 1723, & sold to sd Henry Hardin, by Andrew Collins. Test' Jos. Creecy, Thos. Scarbrough.

No. 322. Tullie Williams of Perq, for £167-s10 pd by Wm. Layden, of afsd—sold 83a near the head of Muddy Creek, which I bought of Benjamin Snowden, Nov 27, 1771, & the other part of John Stokes Aug 31, 1769, adj Sanderson, & Snowden, "over the Great Branch." Aug 26, 1772. Test' Thomas Robinson, Wm. Reed.

No. 323. Cooper Jones of Perq, bricklayer—for £90 pd by Andrew Knox, of the Co of Hertford, Merchant—sold a "negro wench named Mourning, & a negro boy named Brutus, also paid unto sd Knox £48-s7-p5, due by bond, & interest." Oct —, 1774. Test' Wm Newnold, Isaac Moore.

No. 324. Francis Penrice of Perk, Dec'd; did by his "will bequeath to his son Samuel 100a in fee, who sold 45a of sd land to John Lowther," for £96, which land, adj Joseph Creecy, & Christopher Collins, on Albemarle Sound. Oct 27, 1774. Test' Joshua Skinner, Ben Scarbrough.

No. 325. Thomas Newby of Perq, for £200 pd by Josiah Elliott of afsd—sold 109a by the River Swamp. Dec 24, 1774. Test' Joseph Draper, Moses Bundy, Robert Bogue.

No. 326. Marke Bogue of Perk, for £35 pd by Joshua Hasket, Sr of afsd—sold 27a on So Wst Side of Vosses Creek, part of a pat to John Lacy, 1723. Dec 22, 1774. Test' Joseph Draper, Moses Bundy, Robert Bogue.

No. 327. Josiah Elliott of Perk, for £100 pd by Seth Elliott, of afsd—sold 60a on No Wst Side of Vosses Creek, at the mouth of Atkins Swamp, adj Abraham Hasket, Joseph Lacey, & Joseph Newby. Dec 24, 1774. Test' John Robinson, Benj. Elliott.

No. 328. Joseph Newby, Miller—& wife Elizabeth, for £28 pd by Sion Lilly, of afsd—sold 25a on No Side of Mill Swamp, at the mouth of "Cabbin Branch," near Jesse Bogues house, to Reedy Branch. ————, 1775. Test' James Elliott, Zachariah Lilly.

No. 329. James Tatlock, of Pasq Co, for £60 pd by Joseph Williams, Shipwright—of Perq, sold 100a on No Et Side of Perq River. Dec 16, 1775. Test' Joshua Moore, James Williams.

No. 330. Jan 17, 1775. Joseph Williams of Perq, for £35 pd by Andrew Knox, & Co, Merchants—sold 50a in the desert, called "the Oakland" part of 100a, grt Sept 7, 1761 to Andrew Knox. Test' Isaac Moore, Benj'n Smith.

No. 331. Pleasant Winslow, widow of Joseph of Perq Co, & her gr-son Thomas, for £25 pd by Benj Winslow, Planter—of afsd, sold 180a, on No Et Side of Perq River, called "New Neck," adj Solomon Elliott, & Obed Winslow. Oct 19, 1775. Test' John Winslow, Eliab Griffin, Joseph Wilson.

No. 332. Aug 26, 1772. William Layden of Perq, Planter—for £161 pd by Tullie Williams, sold 80¾a adj Benj Snowden. Test' Wm. Reed, Thos. Robinson, Rich. Simpson.

No. 333. John Taylor of Chowan, for £96 pd by Samuel Penrice, of Perq, sold 45a on Albemarle Sound, adj Joseph Creecy, & orphans of Ephrim Luten. Oct 26, 1774. Test' Joshua Skinner, Ben. Scarbrough.

No. 334. Joseph Newby, & Elizabeth his wife, of Perq, for £10 pd by John Pearse, of same—sold 10a on No Wst Side of Vosses Creek, "in Reedy branch," adj Joseph Guyer, to the old road, Jesse Bogue, & Joshua Hasket's line. May 19, 1774. Test' Joseph Draper, Jesse Bogue, Joseph Baker.

No. 335. Jan 3, 1775. John Harmon, of Perq, for £8 pd by Andrew Knox, of same—sold land "I now live on. to the Eastward of Castletons Creek, at Knox'es Mill Swamp" on line of sd Knox, & Valentine Arps. Test' William Arrenton, Isaac Moore.

No. 336. Sept 14, 1774. John Harmon, & Susanna his wife, for "love we bear to his dau Rosanna Smith, and £5, hath given part of a plan' 140a, where she now lives, on Andrew Knox mill pond, at the mouth of Spring branch," adj Theophilus White, & line of Benj Sanders. Test' Andrew Knox, William Jones.

No. 337. Nov 19, 1774. Andrew Knox Exor, of the will of Thos. Halsey, late of Perq, did expose for sale 50a, at a place in the desert called "the Oakland" at the end of Chinquepin Ridge, which was sold to Joseph Williams for £35. Test' Isaac Moore, Ben. Smith.

No. 338. Feb 4, 1774. Demson Barclift, Mary Barclift, Asa Barclift, Noah Barclift, & Wm Trumball, of Perq, (last of Pasq Co) for "love we bear our Sister & Dau-in-law Elizabeth Barnes, do give a negro boy named Will, for her natual life, & at her death, to our Cousin Charlotte Sanderson, the dau of Richard Sanderson dec'd." Test' John Sanders, Edward Blount, Jas Barclift, Tulle Williams.

No. 339. May 3, 1772. Nathaniel Ming of Perq, for £5 pd by Wm. Bennet, of Edenton, hatter—sold 30a adj John Thatch, & Jeremiah Halsey, in Perq Co. Test' Wm. Haughton, Richard Haughton.

No. 340. Joseph Ratliff, & Sarah his wife, of Perq, for £16 pd by Thomas Henby, of same, sold 13a on So West Side of Little River, adj sd Henby, to the main road. Oct 17, 1774. Test' Joseph Cocke, Benj. Morgan, Chalkey Albertson.

No. 341. Samuel Newby, & Elizabeth his wife, & William Newby, & Elizabeth his wife, for £300 pd by Humphrey Park, of Perq, (all of sd Co) sold 143a on West side of Perq River. adj Robert Wilson, to a ditch between sd Samuel, & William Newby, & Isaac Elliott, "along Mill Creek to Jesse Newbys fish pond." Dec 27, 1774. Test' Jacob Wilson, Joseph Bogue, Ann Newby.

No. 342. Oct 7, 1774. Nath'l Williams, & Mary his wife of Hertford, in Perq Co, for £8 pd by Joseph Whedbee, of Edenton, Chowan Co, "sold lot No 1,

HERTFORD PHYSICIANS

A. Dr. G. E. Newby, son of George Durant Newby and Martha Susan McMullen Newby. Born October 31, 1874, in Durant's Neck. Alumnus of University of North Carolina, 1898. Graduated at Jefferson Medical College, Philadelphia, 1900. Formerly practiced in Newport News, Va. Now at Hertford, N. C.

B. Dr. T. A. Cox, son of Dr. David Cox and Sallie White Cox. Born October 11, 1868. Graduate of the University of Maryland, 1892. Practiced in Baltimore. Now located in Hertford.

C. Dr. C. A. Davenport, son of William S. Davenport and Henretta E. Blount. Born October 3, 1897. Graduated at University of Maryland, 1924.

D. Dr. T. P. Brinn, son of J. T. Brinn and Lilly Belle Elliott Brinn. Born November 20, 1899. Graduated at Univeristy of Pennsylvania, 1923.

in the town of Hertford, & water lot fronting opposite." Test' Miles Skinner, Richard Whedbee.

No. 343. Thomas Harvey of Perq, for £250 pd by John Harvey, (my father) sold unto my brother James Harvey, ½ part of "my Mill erected on my plan' whereon I live, & ½ part of my Bake-house, & bottling Mills," with appurtenances. July 21, 1774. Test' John Harvey, John Harvey Jr.

No. 344. David Peirce of Perq, for £50 pd by Wm Skinner, of afsd, sold 180a "which Thomas Peirce in his will gave me." March 25, 1775. Test' Thos. Jones.

No. 345. Aug 6, 1774. Jesse Eason of Perq, for £79 pd by George Eason, of afsd, sold 67a on the main desert, to the great branch. Test' Mills Riddick, Docton Riddick.

No. 346. Roland Robinson of Perq, for £148 pd by Benjamin Roberts, of same, sold 98, & ¾a on South Side of Little River, adj Joshua Albertson. Feb 13, 1775. Test' Levi Munden, ——— Fisher.

No. 347. Aug 6, 1774. George Eason of Perq, for £60 pd by Jesse Eason, sold 22a along the desert side, in the mouth of great branch, "part of a grt unto Richard Pearce 1743, & by him willed to his son Jacob," sold by sd Jacob to George Eason May 16, 1770. Test' Mills Riddick, Docton Riddick.

No. 348. George Walton of Perq, for £18-s7-p6 pd by John Hudson, of sd place, sold 31a adj sd Walton. March 18, 1775. Test' John Hollowell, Jacob Perry Jr.

No. 349. March 18, 1775. John Hudson of Perq, & George Walton, of same; Uriah Hudson in his will, did bequeath to his son John 131a, who sold same to George Walton, for £80-s17-p6. Test' John Hollowell, Jacob Perry.

No. 350. Robert Riddick of Perq, for "love I bear my son Jacob, of afsd— do give 50a of land on the burnt Pocosin" adj Amos Griffin. April 15, 1775. Test' Joseph Riddick, Robert Riddick Jr, John Hollowell.

No. 351. Robert Riddick for "love I bear my son Seth, of Perq Co, do give a parcel of land whereon he lives," 125a, & a tract in the desert, adj Harden Hurdle. April 15, 1775. Test' John Hollowell, Joseph Riddick, Robert Riddick.

No. 352. Nov 23, 1774. Reuben Long, & Pennina his wife, of Perq, for £155 pd by Jonathan Skinner, of same—sold 100a on the head of Yeopim Creek, adj William Stepney, sd land "being the Eastermost part, of a Patent to William Tetterton." Test' Joshua Skinner, Thomas Long.

No. 353. Thomas Nicholson of Perq, Farmer—for £105 pd by Zachariah Nixon Jr, farmer—of afsd—sold 60a on So Wt Side of Little River, adj sd Nicholson, sd Nixon, & John Nixon, "by the side of the road that leads to pine glade." April 5, 1775. Test' Thos. Robinson, Wm. Robinson, Nicholas Nicholson.

No. 354. Joseph Ratliff of Perq, for £50 pd by Thomas Henby, of same— sold 50a on Southwest Side of Little River, on the main road, adj sd Henby, & Seth Morgan. April 17, 1775. Test' Seth Morgan, Nathan Bagley.

No. 355. Joseph Ratliffe, & Sarah his wife of Perq, for £60 pd by Seth Morgan, of Pasq Co, sold 60a on So Wst Side of Little River, adj sd Morgan, & Henley, out to the road. April 17, 1775. Test' Nathan Bagley, Thomas Henby.

No. 356. Joseph Ratliff, & Sarah his wife, of Perq, for £75 pd by Nathan Bagley, of same—sold 75a on South West Side of Little River, adj Thomas Henby, at the road. April 17, 1775. Test' Seth Morgan, ——— Henby.

No. 357. Spencer Williams of Pasq Co, for £20 pd by John Parker, of Perq, sold 45a between Silas Hasket, & Simon Boswell in Perq Co. April 6, 1775. Test' Levi Munden, Morgan Overman, James Davis.

No. 358. Jan 1, 1775. John Lane of Pasq Co, for £16-s10 pd by Joseph Sitterson, of afsd—sold 18a on So Wst Side of Little River, adj John Welch, formerly the property of Thomas Wright. Test' Benj. White, Joseph Bassett.

No. 359. Thomas Robinson of Perq, planter—for £110 pd by William McConnick, of Pasq Co, Merchant "doth sell in open market my negro woman named Mell, (or Miriam) with her two children, George, & Esther." April 12, 1775. Test' Thos. Nicholson.

No. 360. Thos. Newby of Perq, for £15 pd by Mackee Chappel, of afsd, sold 50a "near drinking hole branch" to sd Chappels line. Sept 12, 1775. Test' Job Chappel, E. Newby.

No. 361. Margaret Toms, for "love I bear my son Francis Toms, of Perq, have given one negro man named Aaron, to be delivered to him at the age of 21 years." April 29, 1775. Test' Wm. Albertson, Caleb White.

No. 362. Margaret Toms, for "love I bear my daughters Rebeccah, Margaret, & Elizabeth Toms, have given £45, to be equally divided between them." April 29, 1775. Test' Wm. Albertson, Caleb White.

No. 363. Abraham Mullen of Bertie Co, for £125 pd by Dempsey Turner, of Perq, sold 110a in Perq, on the head of Deep Creek, & line of John Turner, to the line of Jacob Mullen, down to the Swamp. May 3, 1775. Test' Jacob Mullen, John Welch.

No. 364. John Maudlin of Perq, for "love I bear my son John, have given 50a whereon I dwell," adj Joseph Barber, & line of Zachariah Nixon, Ralph Fletcher, & Hercules Saint. Aug 20, 1776. Test' Joseph Maudlin, Joseph Barber.

No. 365. John White of Perq, Yeoman, for £65 pd by John Winslow, of afsd—sold 150a on North East Side of Perq River, & Newbegun Creek, adj sd Winslow line, land "taken up by Thomas Jessop." July 25, 1775. Test' Benjamin White, Thomas White, Miles White.

No. 366. Oct 21, 1773. Joseph Hosea of Perq (who intermarried with Betty Bateman, widow of William, of afsd) for £30 pd by Joseph Bateman, sold 113a (all of sd Betties dower right) whereon sd William Bateman dec'd lived. Test' John Bateman, Benjamin Bateman.

No. 367. April 24, 1775. Thomas Bonner Jr, & Margaret his wife, of Chowan Co, for £245 pd by Julius Bunch, of Perq, sold 300a on north Side of Yeopim River, in Perq Co. Test' Josiah White, Nazareth Bunch, Solomon Bunch.

No. 368. John Hudson of Perq, for £19-17s6p pd by George Walton, of afsd—sold 31a, adj sd Walton; part of 130a "bought by my gr-father John Hudson, of Hannah Bundy, July 21, 1729." Seal Nov 27, 1776. Test' Caleb Winslow, Benj'n Sanders.

No. 369. 4d, 2mo 1775. Ralph Fletcher of Perq, for £75 pd by Gideon Maudlin, of afsd—sold 65a "near the head of Sutton Creek," being part of land, which Francis Newby in his will, gave to his sons; Robert, Marke, Francis, & Jesse, adj Gabriel Cosand, binding on Thos. Hollowells line, & the line of Francis Nixon. Test' Wm Albertson, Sarah Albertson, Mary Albertson.

No. 370. John Turner of Perq, for £62 pd by Josiah Arnold of afsd—sold 50a whereon sd Turner now lives, "at the mouth of Shitten Gut," down to Deep Creek. April 5, 1775. Test' John Gibson Jr, Wm Knowles.

No. 371. Jarvis Forehand of Perq, for £112-s10 pd by Jacob Winslow, of same, planter—sold 125a, part of tract formerly the land of Nicholas Stalling, on No West side of Perq River, adj Elias Stallings. Oct 11, 1773. Test' Moses Rountree, Isaac Griffin.

No. 372. Thomas Henby of Perq, for £33-s19 pd by Joseph Cocke, of same, planter—sold 33a on "South Westerly side of Little River, & Upper side of Maple Glade Road." 21d, 3mo 1775. Test' Jno Hasket, Peter Munden.

No. 373. Joseph Ratcliff of Perq, for £230 pd by Benjamin White, Miller—sold 278a, adj Nathan Bagley, & Seth Morgan. 14d, 6mo 1775. Test' Caleb Toms, Caleb White, Thomas White.

No. 374. Nov 6, 1775. William Long of Perq, planter—"son of William Long Dec'd, & Reuben Long another son of sd William Dec'd, heirs of sd William, July 10, 1758, to Simeon Long (another son of sd William), for £190 pd by sd Simeon, do sell their right in 530a, on East side of Yeopim Creek, at the mouth of Chessons Cove, adj line of John Wyatt, & on South Franks Creek, which was pat by sd William Long Dec'd, Nov 1720." Test' Joshua Long, Thos. Long, Lemuel Long.

No. 375. John Skinner in his will, made bequest; "that his wife for £50" yield up her right of dower to land, & estate given his son Stephen Skinner." Therefore; "I Sarah Skinner relict of sd John, late of Perq, for £50 to me in hand pd by Joshua Skinner, & Wm Skinner Esqs, doth release forever all dower right of sd lands of my late husband." July 8, 1775. Test' John Sanders, Wm White.

No. 376. Caleb Winslow of Perq, for £42-5s-6p pd by George Walton, of afsd—sold 30a bought of John Hudson, adj orphans of Jesse Winslow dec'd, & Uriah Hudson. Dec 12, 1775. Test' Thomas Wilson, Joseph Elliott.

No. 377. June 24, 1775. Wm Skinner, Andrew Knox, & Nathaniel Williams, "by virtue of authority given them by Act of Assembly, March 6, 1773, for regulating the Town of Hertford: for £55 pd them by Charles Moore, have sold, one lot ½a in said Town upon Market Street. Test' Nathaniel Martin, Geo. Whedbee.

No. 378. Samuel Simpson fo Tyrell Co, for £20 pd by Richard Haughton, of Perq, Planter—sold 53½a on "North Side of the head of Yeopim River Swamp," being half of a plan' formerly belonging to Benjamin Simpson, adj sd Haughton, & Chas Cofield. May 15, 1775. Test' Thomas Harmon, Delight Nixon.

No. 379. Dempsey Turner of Perq, for £150 pd by George Whedbee, of afsd—sold 102a on "Deep Creek Swamp," adj sd Whedbee, known by the name of "Edge Hill." May 19, 1775. Test' Wm. Robins, Samuel Barclift.

No. 380. William Barber of Perq, for £130 pd by Gosbee Toms, of same—sold 100a on No Est Side of Suttons Creek, which was sold by Moses Barber, to George Eason, Aug 15, 1752, adj Francis Foster, Nathaniel Nicholson, John Henby, & Samuel Charles. Nov 6, 1775. Test' Thos. Hosea, Foster Toms Jr, Benj'n. Elliott.

No. 381. Aug 15, 1775. Jonathan Phelps of Perq, for £40 pd by Joshua Bagley, sold 2a on the main road, "where James Sitterson fenced, & planted an orchard," adj Wm Townsend, part of land which "fell to me from Wm Phelps, but to Mary Bagley, for her natual life." Test' Hercules Saint, John Brinkley.

No. 382. Mary Moore of Perq, for "love I bear my gr-son Jas Lesley, do give one negro girl named Teresa." Nov 17, 1776. Test' Jno. Stafford, Benj'n. Phelps.

No. 383. Pritlow Elliott of Perq, for £30 pd by Joseph Pearson, of afsd—sold 100a in the fork of Cypress Swamp, called "Aarons Ridge" adj Jas Wilson, Isaac Wilson, & Jesse Copeland, in the Desert. Test' Wm. Townsend, Jas. Wilson.

No. 384. Jeremiah Maudlin of Perq, for £80 pd by John Gibson, sold one negro woman named Pegg. Dec 24, 1774. Test' William Hosea, Jeremiah Maudlin Jr.

No. 385. Mary Moor of Perq, widow—for "love I bear my son-in-law Robert DeCrow, & Sarah his wife, do give to them two negro men named Solomon, & Jack, & two women named Milly, & Amey—one horse—3 cattle—1 bed & furniture, & all personal estate in the house of my sd son-in-law." Oct 25, 1775.

No. 386. Pritlow Elliott, for £35 pd by James Wilson, of Perq, sold tract of land (100a) in the fork of Cypress Swamp, called "Aarons Ridge" adj Isaac Wilson, & sd Elliott. Jan 15, 1776. Test' William Townsend, Joseph Pearson.

No. 387. Reuben Perry of Perq, "do give to my brother Jacob Perry of same, the stream joining my land to build a Mill thereon, & timber to build same, I sd Reuben to draw a share, for work I have done towards building sd Mill." March 12, 1773. Test' Robert Wilson, Joseph Pearson.

No. 388. John Henby of Perq, for £60 pd by Moses Stone, of afsd—sold 50a "near Suttons Creek," part of a tract grt unto Samuel Charles, 1720, on the upper side of lower Gum Swamp, adj John Nicholson. Oct 4, 1774. Test' Simon Boswell, William Albertson.

No. 389. Mary Moore of Perq, for "love I bear my Gr-dau Mary Delano, have given a negro girl, and if she die without issue, to Gr-son Robert Delano." Nov 18, 1774. Test' John Stafford, Benj Phelps.

No. 390. Jan 4, 1776. Jacob Mullen, planter—& Sarah his wife, of Perq, for £55 pd by Joseph McAdams, Andrew Knox, & John Wyatt, of afsd, Merchants—sold 76a, adj Dempsey Turner, John Turner, & Elihu Albertson. Test' Rich Clayton, John Lane.

No. 391. James Sitterson of Perq; "by his will gave unto his dau Hannah 45a & sd Hannah, & her husband John Brinkley sold same," for £95 to Hercules Saint. Dec 16, 1775. Test' Joshua Bagley, Mary Bagley.

No. 392. Jonathan Phelps of Perq, for £100 pd by Jesse Copeland of same—sold 400a on West-side of Perq River, & So side of a creek formerly called "Wilsons Creek," pat Feb 6, 1698. Seal Sept 12, 1775. Test' Thomas Robinson, Ben'n Elliott.

No. 393. Miles Harvey (son of Col John Harvey Esq) of Perq, for £25 pd by Joshua Skinner of afsd—sold a lot ½a in the town of Hertford. Nov 10, 1776. Test' Frederick Norcom.

DEED BOOK I—FIRST PART

No. 3. Elizabeth Cuzens of Perq, for £100 pd by Samuel Swain, of same—sold 300a on South Side of Yeopim Creek, adj Robert Harmon, John Wyatt, & heirs of Andrew Collins. July 30, 1777. Test' John Barrow, John Barrow Jr.

No. 4. Aug 24, 1775. Andrew Collins, & Ann his wife, of Perq, for £45 pd by John Harmon, of same—sold 50a on North Side of Yeopim River, at a Branch on Upper side of Bunch'es Plan' "agreeable to Banks deed, the first Patentee." Test' John Donaldson, Solomon Armstrong.

No. 5. Samuel Skinner, & Sarah his wife of Perq, for s5 pd by James Skinner, of afsd—sold 175a on Minzes Creek, adj Miles Harvey, William Scarbrough, "running up the Swamp to the mouth of Haw-tree branch." July 21, 1777. Test' Edward Hall, John White.

No. 6. Aug 19, 1776. Edward Hall Sr, of Perq, Planter—for £120 pd by Edward Hall Jr, of afsd—Planter—sold 154a on the head of Yeopim River, adj land of Andrew Knox dec'd, purchased by sd Edward Hall Sr, of Thomas Halsey, called "Swanns." Edward Hall, Rachel Hall. Test' Henry Hall, James Hall.

No. 7. Isaac Sitterson of Perq, for £100 pd by William Townsend, of afsd—sold 75a on South east Side of Perq River, adj Hercules Phelps, & sd Townsend, pat' Feb 25, 1696 by Dan'l Snooks, & by him sold to Edward Holmes, & by sd Holmes to John Lilly, which by sd Lilly's death came to his Dau's Sarah Tetterton, & Hannah Sitterson, & by Yedderton Sitterson to his son James," which land was given me by my father James Sitterson in his will." Jan 1, 1778. Test' Samuel Sitterson, John Colson.

No. 8. Hercules Saint of Perq, for £60 pd by Joseph Wood, of afsd—sold 50a on North East Side of Perq River, "at the head of Dirty Branch," to lines of James Morgan, Isaac Elliott, & Thomas Jessop. pt of a tract sold by sd Morgan, to John Henby Jr, Oct 20, 1735. Seal Oct 20, 1777. Test' Humphrey Simons, Thomas Bagley.

No. 9. Sept 27, 1776. Edward Hall Sr, for £115 pd by Henry Hall, of Perq, planter—sold 125a on Minzes Creek, adj Joseph Creecy, & Samuel Penrice. Test' Abraham Depoyster, Edward Hall Jr.

No. 10. William Robins, & Elizabeth his wife, of Perq, for £200 pd by George Whedbee Esq, of same—sold 80a on N. East Side of Perq River, adj "Perrishoe's grave-yard, on Dirt Bridge Branch," to Long Branch. March 1, 1777. Test' Joseph Perishoe Jr, James Sumner.

No. 11. John Moore of Perq, for £45 pd by Ralph Fletcher of same, planter—sold 30a on No Et Side of Perq River. 23, 12mo 1776. Test' Joshua Moore, Thos Robinson, Aaron Moore.

No. 12. Richard Whedbee Jr, & Mary his wife, of Perq, for £307 pd by John Whedbee Sr, of afsd—sold 163a which sd Richard bought of Edward Turner Jr, (which was the land of Joseph Sutton, son of Christopher), on North Side of Deep Creek Swamp. May 24, 1777. Test' George Whedbee, Hanna Whedbee.

No. 13. Charles Blount of Perq, Gent—for "love I bear my Dau Elizabeth Miller, (wife of Andrew, Merchant) and s5 pd by sd Miller, "doth give 150a" adj Tulle Williams, to Little River. Dec 22, 1776. Test' William Littlejohn, Lemuel Blount.

No. 14. Noah Barclift of Perq, planter—for £95 pd by Francis Foster, of same, planter—sold 95a on North East side of Perq River, & the head of "Beaver Dam." Feb 8, 1777. Test' Asa Barclift, Richard Williams. Noah, & Millicent Barclift.

No. 15. Aug 2, 1777. William Stepney of Perq, for £90 pd by Benjamin Scarbrough, of same—sold "plan' on head of Yeopim Creek," adj Joshua Long, & William Nichols. Test' Jonathan Skinner, Delight Nixon.

No. 16. Sept 26, 1777. James Perrishoe of Perq, sold to George Whedbee, of afsd 213a, adj William Robinson, "nigh the grave-yard, & the road that leads to Nags Head Chapel," to line of Abram Turner. James, & Mary Perrishoe. Test' William Hancock, Joseph Perrishoe, Joseph Sutton.

No. 17. Ann Delano of Perq, for £8-s5 pd by Gideon Newby, of afsd, farmer—sold 7a, adj Gabriel Newby. March 24, 1777. Test' Thomas Wilson, Elizabeth Newby Sr, Elizabeth Newby Jr.

No. 18. Joseph Riddick, of Chowan Co, planter—for £100 pd by Seth Riddick, of afsd—sold 200a on West side of "Glissons Ridge," & South-east side of a plain, known by the name of "Smalls peach-orchard," adj John Stallings. Dec 22, 1777. Test' Robert Riddick, Robert Riddick Jr.

No. 19. Joseph Elliott of Perq, for £40, pd by Caleb Winslow, of afsd—sold 240a, (part in Chowan, & part in Perq Co) adj land that Julius Bunch bought of Joseph Nicholson, & Ephrim Elliott. Sept 7, 1777. Test' Jacob Perry, Cornelius Ratliff.

No. 20. Joshua Long of Perq, for £75 pd by Thomas Long, of afsd—sold 100a on North side of Indian Creek, "just above Pratt's Mill." Jan 10, 1777. Test' Benjamin Harvey Jr.

No. 21. Elizabeth Barclift of Perq, for "love I bear my son-in-law Francis Foster, & my dau Rachel his wife," of afsd—do give one half of a tract of land, which was given me by my father Thomas Holloway, Aug 26, 1739, 50a, adj Noah Barclift. Feb 25, 1777. Test' George Whidbee, Joseph Bateman.

No. 22. George Whedbee of Perq, for £5-s10 pd by Joseph Turner Jr, of same, sold 5½a on north Side of "branches of Deep Creek." April 26, 1777. Test' Thomas Roberson, Samuel Barclift.

No. 23. George Whedbee, for £12-s15 pd by Samuel Barclift Jr, of Perq—sold 4a in sd County. April 26, 1777. Test' Thomas Roberson, Joseph Turner Jr.

No. 24. Nathaniel Martin, Doctor; of Perq, for £100 pd by Francis Newby, of afsd sold lot (½a) in the Town of Hertford, (No 21) with common ground, adj the River, being houses & lot which I bought of Col Benjamin Harvey, Dec 30, 1774, & a lot ½a, purchased of William Newbold (in sd Town No 4) between Water St, & the River. July 21, 1777. Test' William Hancock, Jonathan Phelps.

No. 25. Benjamin Bateman of Perq, planter—for £95 pd by Noah Barclift, sold 95a on No Est Side of Perq River, & "head of Beaver Dam." Nov 29, 1776. Benjamin & Mary Bateman. Test' Thomas Robinson, Jacob Kinion.

No. 26. Oct 7, 1777. Thomas Burket, & Mary his wife, & Elizabeth Butler, of Chowan Co, for £32-s10 pd by Richard Hatfield, of Perq, sold 50a on Castletons Creek, in Perq Co, adj John Murdaugh, & John Harmon. Test' John Stafford, Kinchen Gilliam, William Clemons.

No. 27. Roland Robinson of Perq, planter—for £150 pd by William Lane, of Pasq Co, (Silver Smith) sold 145a on South west Side of Little River, adj Thomas Robinson & the Swamp. Jan 25, 1776. Test' Thomas Overman, James Newby.

No. 28. Jan 12, 1778. William Clemons of Perq, for £145 pd by William Barber, of afsd—sold lot in Hertford (No 2). Abigail Clemons, surrenders her dower right in sd lot. Test' John Stafford, Ben. Phelps.

No. 29. John Bateman, & Miriam his wife, for £180 pd by Joseph Perishoe, planter—sold 100a, adj William Robins, & the road that "leads to Beaver Cove

Creek, which was formerly the land of Joseph Perishoe Sr, dec'd, & was given to his dau Miriam in his will." Oct 7, 1776. Test' George Whedbee, William Robins, Joseph Clayton.

No. 30. Jonathan Bateman of Perq, & Mary his wife, & Francis Penrice, & Clarke his wife of same—for £40 pd by Joseph Perishoe Jr, of same—sold 100a, one third of land, formerly belonging to William Tomlin dec'd, (who died intestate) adj Benjamin Sutton, & Elizabeth Albertson. Sept 29, 1777. Test' J. Whedbee, George Whedbee, Isaac Layden.

No. 31. Francis Penrice, & Clarke his wife, & Jesse Burnham, & Milicent his wife, for £75 pd by Joseph Perishoe Jr, all of Perq—sold 100a, two thirds of land, formerly belonging to William Tomblin of afsd, (who died intestate) adj Benjamin Sutton, Joseph Perishoe, & Elihu Albertson. Aug 12, 1777. Test' Thomas Robinson, George Sutton.

No. 32. Zachariah Lilly, & Jane his wife of Perq, planter—for £50 pd by Luke Stallings, of afsd—sold 50a on North East Side of Perq River, "whereon sd Lilly now Dwells, called Hickory Ridge" part of land purchased by Thomas Rountree Dec'd, of Joseph Jesup, & left by sd Rountree, in his will to Jacob Spivey. Jan 13, 1779. Test' Ezekiel Hollowell, William Lilly, Reuben Stallings.

No. 33. Elias Stallings, & Zachariah Stallings, for £5 pd by Luke Stallings, of Perq Co, sold 50a "in the desert," on Juniper Run. Test' Reuben Stallings, Hugh Griffin, Job Stallings.

No. 34. Charles Rountree, of Chowan Co, for £30 pd by Luke Stallings, of Perq, sold 230a, adj Thos. Hobbs, & Simon Stallings. Jan —, 1778. Test' Elias Stallings, Jesse Stallings, Amos Hobs.

No. 35. Sept 4, 1777. Benjamin Arnold, & Sarah his wife, of Dobbs Co, N. C. for £140 pd by Job Parker, sold 100&¾a in Perq Co. Test' Josiah Elliott, Abraham Elliott, Jonathan Pearson.

No. 36. Jan 4, 1778. John Hollowell of Perq, for £100 pd by Josiah Rogerson, of same—sold 100a between sd Hollowell, & Israel Perry, formerly line of William Kitchen, called "burnt ground," pt of a pat' to sd Kitchen, 1719, by him "in his will, given to Christopher Jackson, late of Nanzymond Co Va," & by sd Jackson sold to sd Hollowell. Test' Caleb Winslow, William Hollowell, Thomas Twine.

No. 37. Thomas Nicholson Sr, of Perq, planter—for s30 pd by Jesse Perry, of same planter—sold 4a Swamp, adj Thos Boswell, "through Gum Swamp." Jan 1, 1777. Test' Spencer Williams, Caroline Nicholson, Elphel Scot.

No. 38. Josiah Granbery, of Chowan Co, for £75 pd by Joseph Hurdle, of Perq, sold 80a, adj Henry Hill, & Moses Boyce, Thomas Docton, & Thomas Davis, to the desert, in Perq Co. Reg May 5, 1780. Test' Thomas Hurdle, Simon Stallings.

No. 40. Samuel Bagley of Perq, for "love I bear my son William, do give 150a on South-side of Josiah Rogersons land," formerly property of Benjamin Wilson, adj Joseph Hurdle, called "Brinns Domain pocosin." Oct 25, 1777. Test' Chloe Reddick, Abraham Reddick, Thomas Hurdle.

No. 41. William Newbould, & Grizzell his wife, of Perq, for £600 pd by William Newbould Jr, of afsd—conveyed 3 lots in Hertford, (No. 110-111-129) "with dwelling house, & other Houses appertaining." Aug 26, 1778. Test' Benj Harvey Jr.

No. 42. William Skinner of Perq, for £130 pd by James Skinner, of afsd—sold 180a near Yeopim Creek adj lands of John Barrow, John Skinner, & Richard Skinner. Mar 28, 1778. Test' Elizabeth Cotton, Ruth Davis.

No 43. Robert Bogue of Perq, for £45 pd by Ralf (Ralph) Fletcher, of afsd—sold 45a "near the head of Newby's Mill pond," in a place called the "Beepond" to a gum in "plum tree pond" up the middle of Bee pond. Feb 6, 1776. Test' Jacob Wyate, Josiah Perishoe.

No. 44. April 21, 1778. Reuben Long, & Penninah his wife, for £50 pd by William Arkill, all of Perq, sold 50a, near the head of Yeopim Creek, adj Benjamin Scarbrough, & Joshua Long, to the main road. Test' Thomas Harmon, Simeon Long.

No. 45. July 4, 1778. William Scarbrough, of Pasq Co, Merchant—& Lucy his wife, for £500 pd by Richard Haughton, of Chowan Co, sold 310a, on Perq River, adj Thos Garrett, John Goodwin, & Joseph Burkett. Test' Edmond Standin, Samuel Latamere.

No. 46. July 4, 1778. William Scarbrough, of Camden Co, for £75 pd by Richard Haughton, of Chowan, sold a "small piece of land in Perq," adj Stephen Harmon, sd land bought by Mac Scarbrough, of John Harmon. Test' Edward Standin, Samuel Latimere.

No. 47. John Creecy of Chowan, for £225 pd by Issacher Branch, of Perq, sold 107a on north Side of Yeopim River Swamp, adj Delight Nixon, Thomas McKnight & Charles Copeland, formerly belonging to Benjamin Simpson. Oct 20, 1778. Test' Joshua Skinner, Edward Hall Jr.

*No. 48. Mar 19, 1778. John Stephenson of Perq, for s45, pd by William Newbould, of afsd—sold 1 Lott ½a, in the Town of Hertford (No 112) "upon Church, & Grub St." Test' Tho. Reed, J. Wyatt.

No. 49. July 4, 1778. William Scarbrough, of Camden Co, for £50 pd by Valentine Arps, of Perq, sold 30a on East Side of Lakers Creek, adj "Skinners Bridge" near the mouth of Beaver Dam, where sd Arps lives. Test' Edward Standin, Samuel Latimere.

No. 50. William Baker of Perq, for £50 pd by Benjamin Saunders, of afsd—sold 50a pt of land given by Abraham Saunders, to Judith Boyce, & by sd Judith, & Moses Elliott, her then husband, conveyed to Moses Barber, adj land pat' by sd Abraham, in 1749. Seal Jan 19, 1778. Test' John Stafford.

No. 51. April 21, 1778. Reuben Long, & Penninah his wife, of Perq, for £50 pd by Jonathan Skinner, of afsd—sold land near the head of Yeopim Creek, adj sd Skinner, & William Arrington.

No. 52. John Henby Jr, & Hannah his wife, for £700 pd by William Robins, of Pasq Co, (planter) sold 200a on Suttons Creek, where sd "Henby's Mill pond issues out of Creek Swamp," adj Gabriel Cosand. Dec 29, 1777. Test' George Whedbee, Joseph Perrishoe Jr.

No. 53. Feb 28, 1778. William Scarbrough, of Pasq Co, for £51 pd by William Arrington, of Perq, sold 51a, adj sd Arrington, which was grt to McRora Scarbrough, Nov 26, 1744, & bequeathed by him to his son McRora, who sold same to William Scarbrough. Test' Richard Arrinton, Robert McMorene.

No. 54. Sept —, 1777. William Reed of Perq, Att' for John Hatch, of Onslow Co for £40 pd by Benj Bateman, of Perq, sold 132a on East Side of

---

*(About where the old Baptist parsonage now stands.)

Perq River, adj sd Bateman, & Perishoe. Test' Tulle Williams, Hugh Stevenson.

No. 55. Sept 16, 1779. Hatten Williams, of Chowan Co (Ship-builder) for £1500 pd by John Foster, of Perq, planter—sold 80a on East Side of Perq River, called "Beaver Cove land." Test' Henry Champion, Sarah Knight.

No. 56. Benjamin Smith of Perq, for s40 pd by John White, sold to sd White, William Arrinton, William Jones, William White, Thomas Jones, & William Skinner, land in sd County "whereon a new School House now stands," opposite sd Benjamin Smith, on the main road. July 20, 1778 (Trustees). Test' Wm. Standin, John Goodwin.

No. 57. John Saunders Jr, & Mary his wife, for £140 pd by Caleb Burnham (all of Perq) sold 83a on Muddy Creek, adj Noah Barclift. Feb 9, 1778. Test' Noah Barclift, John Holloway.

*No. 58. Oct 1, 1776. Francis, & Benjamin Albertson, of Perq, for £7 s8 pd by sd Benjamin Albertson, sold 1½a, on west side of Suttons Creek Swamp, "to the road, & the Meeting house land," adj William & Francis Albertson. Test' Simon Boswell, Joseph Jones.

No. 59. April 23, 1777. John Gibson of Perq, planter—for £350 pd by Joseph Jones, of afsd—sold 200a on South-west side of Little River, called "Grassy point, formerly belonging to James Gibson, & by my father sd James, left to me in his will." Test' Chris Bromadge, Barclift Jones.

No. 60. Oct 25, 1776. Margaret Clayton of Perq, for £90 pd by Richard Clayton of afsd—sold 30a "whereon sd Richard now lives, ⅓ of land Given by Mr Samuel Swann dec'd, to his dau Mary Clayton, wife of sd Richard, in his will," Jan 8, 1753. Test' James Moore, John Clayton.

No. 61. April 12, 1779. William Arkill, & Hannah his wife, for £80 pd by Richard Cale, sold 140a on North Side of Yeopim River, whereon William Standin dec'd lived, at the mouth of a small Creek, issuing out of sd River. Test' Benjamin Scarbrough, J. Skinner, Joshua Bagley.

No. 62. Jeremiah Maudlin of Perq, planter—for £250 pd by Joseph Jones Sr, of same, planter—sold 150a on So west Side of Little River, a South west side of "Shitten Gut." Jeremiah, & Sarah Maudlin. Test' Zebulon Snoden, Thomas Sutton.

No. 63. Feb 9, 1789. Richard Cale of Perq, for £75 pd by Benjamin Harvey Jr, sold 50a in Ballahack, adj Jonathan Sherards, & a place called "the Island." Test' John Creecy.

No. 64. July 15, 1778. Robert Bogue of Perq, for £150 pd by Francis Newby, of afsd—sold 100a near Sutton Creek, "formerly land of William Bogue, father of sd Robert, "adj John, & Gosby Toms, & Richard Whedbee. Test' Kezia Nixon, Milicent Newby.

No. 65. Abner Hollowell of Perq, for £200 pd by Hugh Griffin, of afsd, sold 130a, on Juniper Swamp, N. E. Side. March 16, 1776. Test' Will. King, Ben'n. Perry Jr, Job Stallings.

No. 66. Sept 16, 1778. Christopher Collins, & Elizabeth His wife, of Perq, for £150 pd by Zebulon Calleway, of same—sold 100a, adj Joseph Creecy, pt of a tract pat' by Wm Long dec'd, April 1, 1723. Test' Simeon Long, John Wilson.

---

*Suttons Ceek Mo Meeting, about where Newbolds school house now stands.

No. 67. Ephrim Elliott of Perq, planter—for "love I bear my son Caleb," do give 85a, adj Pearson, & Newby. Test' Caleb Winslow, Exum Newby, Josiah White.

No. 68. Benjamin Harvey Jr, & Thomas Harvey of Perq, for 40 barrels of good corn, pd by John Lonsford of above, sold 70a on Skinners Creek, adj Robert Decrow, & Eleazer Creecy. Oct 12, 1779. Test' Wm Barber.

No. 69. Thomas Weeks Jr, of Perq, planter—for £320 pd by Joseph Raper, of Pasq Co, sold 50a on South west side of Little River. Feb 4, 1779. Test' Thomas Weeks, Benj'n. Weeks, Mary Weeks.

No. 70. Elizabeth Branch of Perq, for £100 pd by Thomas Harmon, of afsd—sold 49a—⅓ of 148a, given by deed, from Delight Nixon, to Sarah Harmon, Elizabeth Blanchard, & Orpha Rogers, (in the fork of Mill Swamp) called "McKnight's Mill." Jan 8, 1779. Test' Delight Nixon, Charles Copeland, Orpha Rogers.

No. 71. Dec 14, 1778. Thomas Wilson of Perq, for £500 pd by Robert Decrow, of afsd—sold 50a "Northward from Skinners Bridge, to Rackoon Swamp," & from thence to Castletons Creek Swamp, pt of a pat' to Richard Skinner, Nov 22, 1714. Seal Dec 14, 1778. Test' Reuben Wilson, John Goodwin, Samuel Williams.

No. 72. Elizabeth Person of Perq, for "love I bear my two children, Joseph, & Eleazer Person, do give after my decease, my whole living, & if either should die, the other shall possess the whole estate." April 7, 1779. Test' Benjamin Elliott, Caleb Elliott.

No. 73. John Turner of Perq, planter—for an. "exchange of land on the South Side of Shitten Gut, do exonerate William Knowles," & convey to him 92½a on South side of sd Gut, adj John Stanton, & Joshua Toms. Sept, 7, 1777. Test' ―――――

No. 74. Williams Knowles of Perq, Carpenter—for an "exchange of a plan' on South side of Shitten Gut, with John Turner of afsd"—do ack' myself contented, & do discharge sd Turner," assigned 50a of land on South side of sd Gutt, adj John Stanton, & William Colson. Sept 2, 1777. Test' Moses Jackson, John Abdul.

*No. 75. State of N. C. In con' of 50s for every hundred a, do grt unto William Arkill 50a in Perq, adj William Arrenton. Mar 25, 1780. Richard Caswell Esq Gov, at Kingston. Test' John Franch Pro' Sec. Reg in Perq, by Jos. Skinner.

No. 76. S of N. C. for 50s pd by Richard Arrenton, do grt 150a in Perq, adj William Jones, & John White. (Same as above.) March 25, 1780.

No. 77. S of N. C. for 50s pd by William Skinner, do grt 250a, adj Richard Arrenton, "in Gallberry pocosin." (Same as above) March 25, 1780.

No. 78. S of N. C. for 50s pd by Richard Arrenton, do grt 171a, in Perq, adj Jonathan Skinner, & Wm Arrenton. Mar 25, 1780. (Same as above.)

No. 79. April 5, 1780. John Stephenson, & Elizabeth his wife, of Perq, for £120 pd by Tullie Williams, of same—sold 180a on Southwest Side of Little River, "with all buildings standing." Test' Asa Barclift, Richard Williams. M. G. Skinner Clk.

---

*These grants were probably *bounty land*, for Rev services.

No. 80. Oct 11, 1779. Benjamin Harvey of Perq, for £150 pd by Joseph Elliott, of same, sold 50a in Ballahack, adj Jonathan Sherards, over against a place called "the Island." Test' William Harvey, T. Harvey.

No. 81. William Arkill of Perq, for £5 pd by Ezekiel Arrenton, of same—sold 50a on sd Arrenton's line. Oct 10, 1780. Test' John Goodwin, Isachar Branch.

No. 82. John Robinson of Perq, blacksmith—for "love I bear my sons: Thomas, & Ephrim, assigns all interest in a negro woman, named Peg, which would have been the property of my former wife Keziah, after the death of her mother Sarah Elliott, when the youngest child shall be 21 years of age." Nov 29, 1778. Test' John Skinner, Exum Elliott.

No. 83. Oct 7, 1780. Richard Arrenton of Perq, for £10 pd by William Arrenton, of same—sold 121a adj Jonathan Skinner. Test' Benjamin Smith, Thomas Creecy.

No. 84. Jan 8, 1780. Charles Copeland, & wife Elusia, of Perq, for £1680 pd by Delight Nixon, of same—sold 180a on the head of Yeopim River, adj Francis Brown & sd Nixon. Test' Issachar Branch, Jonathan Skinner.

No. 85. Oct 6, 1779. Miles Harvey, & Mary his wife of Perq, for £250 pd by Thomas Harvey, of same—sold 200a on So Side of Perq River, formerly belonging to Garret, who sold sd land to "our father John Harvey, who in his will gave sd land to sd Miles Harvey," adj Thomas & William White, & James Skinner. Test' ———

No. 86. June 20, 1780. Benjamin Bateman of Perq, planter—for £2000 pd by Charle Blount, sold 63a on No West Side of Perq River, adj Demson Barclift, & John Anderson. Test' Tully Williams, John Clayton.

No. 87. June 3, 1780. Noah Barclift of Perq, Planter—for £250 pd by Charles Blount, of afsd—sold 100a on Batemans Creek, to the mouth of Prows Creek, & a branch called "High Root" & Rapers corner. Test' Tully Williams, John Clayton.

No. 88. John Wingate of Chatham Co, N. C. for £75 pd by Samuel Williams, of Perq, sold 100a on north east side of Ballahack Swamp, adj Goodwin, "formerly the land of Zachary Chancey." Nov 8, 1779. Test' Edward Wingate, Demsey Elliott, Jno. Goodwin.

No. 89. May 12, 1779. Richard Haughton, of Chowan, for £75 pd by Stephen Harmon, of Perq, sold a "small piece of land in Perq," adj sd Stephen, on Beaver Cove. Test' J. Wyeatt, Fred. Norcom, Thos. Robinson.

No. 90. William Bagley of Perq, for £325 pd by Josiah Rogerson, of afsd—sold 150a on No Side of Samuel Bagleys land, adj Joseph Hurdle, formerly Richard Harrels's, called "Brinns domain pocosin." Reg July Court, 1779. Test' Thomas Hurdle, Daniel Stallings, Judah Hurdle.

No. 91. Mar 24, 1780. Thomas Small of Perq, for £80 pd by Charles Moore Sr,—sold lot in Hertford, No. 83. Test' John B. Beasley, W. Newbold.

No. 92. Sept 14, 1776. Jonathan Skinner of Perq, for £55 pd by William Arkill, of same—sold 50a on the head of Yeopim Creek, adj William Stepney. Test' John Creecy, Thomas Harmon.

No. 93. Mar 27, 1780. Henderson Luten, & Sarah his wife, of Chowan Co, for £10,000 pd by Abel Miller, (Shipwright), sold 315a, in Perq, on North West side of Albemarle Sound, adj Joshua Wyatt, & along Sound Side, to a branch that divides sd land, from John Lowthers, to Franks Creek Swamp, down sd Creek to Joshua Skinner's, binding on his land, so as to leave him 100a, at a place called "Suttons." Test' Malachi Miller, Mary Freshwater.

No. 94. Mar 23, 1779. David Taylor of Perq, for £180 pd by Zachariah Webb, of Chowan Co, sold 50a "near Yeopim River," formerly owned by Andrew Collins, & sold by him to William Arkill, & by sd Arkill to sd Taylor. Test' Zachariah Webb, Jr, Robert Bonosen.

No. 95. Benjamin Wilson of Perq for "love I bear my son Zachariah, of same—do give one negro woman named Jane, a boy named Thomson, & a girl named Ferebee. 1 bed & furniture, 3 head of cattle, & other housefold stuff." 1, 8mo 1769. Test' Jacob Wilson, Isaac Elliott.

No. 96. Benjamin Wilson, for "love I bear my gr-son Joseph Anderson, of Perq do give a negro girl named Dinah, now in the hands of Zachariah Wilson." 30, 8mo 1776. Test' William Albertson, Chalkey Albertson.

No. 97. State of N. C. for s50 for every 100a, pd by Stephen Harmon, of Perq do grt 43a in sd County, adj William Standin, Levi Creecy, & Richard Cale. Richard Caswell Esq, Gov, Comd-in-chief, at Kingston, Mar 25, 1780. Josh Skinner Reg. Test' Jno. Franch Pro Sec.

No. 98. John Weeks of Perq, planter—for £2000 pd by Benjamin Weeks, of same—sold 55a on South west side of Little River, adj Joseph Raper, ½ of land which Thomas Weeks bought of Jonathan Sharbo, Jan 12, 1756. Seal April 20, 1780. Test' Benjamin Roberts, Joseph Raper.

No. 99. Isaac Sitterson of Perq, for £95 pd by Jesse Chapel, of same—sold 55a adj William Townsend. Nov 6, 1770. Test' Humphrey Symons, Hezekiah Rogerson.

No. 100. Hercules Saint of Perq, carpenter—for £60 pd by William Pearson, of same—sold 70a on North East Side of Perq River, "pat by Richard Cheaston Sr 1694; who sold 50a to William Bogue, Oct 14, 1768, & was left by sd Bogue in his will to his Dau Miriam, now wife of Gideon Bundy, who sold sd land to me, 20a of same sold to my father, Daniel Saint (by Aaron Wood), Jan 20, 1754, & by him left to me." 10, 6mo 1777. Test' Robert Cale, Peter Pearson.

No. 101. State of N. C. for s50 pd by Benjamin Scarborough, do grt 100a, in Perq, adj John Evans, & William Jones. Richard Caswell Gov, Comd-in-chief, at Kinston Mar 25, 1780. Josh Skinner Reg.

No. 102. John Overman of Perq, planter—for £175 pd by Richard Sanders, of same—planter, sold 75a on Eastmost branch of Suttons Creek, adj Nixon, Charles, & Cosand. 3, 3mo 1777. Test' Thomas Robinson, John Henby Jr.

No. 103. Elijah Griffin of Perq, for "love I bear my Brother's Josiah, & Jesse," of afsd—do assign 50a called "Hickory Neck" adj sd Josiah. Oct 18, 1777. Test' Thos Newby, Exum Newby.

No. 104. State of N. C. for s50 per 100a, pd by John Donaldson, do grt 217½a, in Perq, near Yeopim River, adj Joseph Creecy, & Simeon Long, "on South side of Beaver Cove," to line of Samuel Penrice. Mar 25, 1780 at Kinston. Richard Caswell Gov, & Comd-in-chief.

No. 105. S. of N. C. for s50 pd by Miles Gale Skinner, do grt 160a, in Perq, adj Jonathan Skinner, Richard Arrenton, & John Jones. (Test' same as above.)

No. 106. Joseph Boswell of Perq, for an "exchange, with Spencer Williams" of Pasq Co, & for £16 boot, pd to me by sd Williams, conveyed 100a, on South West Side of Little River Swamp, adj Solomon Roberts, George Boswell, & William Hollowell. Jan 25, 1780. Test' William Hollowell, Soloman Roberts.

No. 107. State of N. C. for s50, per each 100a, pd by Joseph Perry, do grt 391½a in Perq, on the end of a neck of land, known by the name of "long point." Richard Caswell Esq Gov, at Kingston—Mar 25, 1780. Jos. Skinner Reg of Perq. Test' John Franch Pro' Sec.

No. 108. S. of N. C. for s50, per 100a, pd by Phillip Perry, do grt 50a in Perq, on South Side of Perq River, adj his own corner, called "Phillips Ridge." (Test' same as above.)

No. 109. S. of N. C. for s50, per 100a, pd by Jacob Riddick, do grt 70a in Perq, on "west Side of the main desert," near the head of Perq River, adj Phillip Perry, Moses Rountree, to "Throughfare Ridge." (Test' same as above.)

No. 110. S. of N. C. for s50, pd by Simon Stallings, do grt 640a, in Perq on the head of Perq River, adj Robert Riddick. Mar 24, 1780. (Test' same as above.)

No. 111. S. of N. C. for s50, per 100a, pd by Thomas Hollowell, do grt land at the head of Perq River, adj Elias Stallings, & Ezekiel Hollowell. Mar 25, 1780. (Test' same as above.)

No. 112. Feb 19, 1778. Rachel Price of Perq, for £25, pd by Elizabeth Price, of Nancymond Co, Vir, "have made over unto my sister, all my right to land in Perq, (100a) whereon our Father William Price lived, & bequeathed to his two Daus, as named." Test' Sturgess Ederngame, William Lilly Jr, William Lilly Sr.

No. 113. Feb 21, 1776. Samuel Green Jr, of Perq, for £65 pd by Moses Briggs, of Chowan Co, sold land in Perq on northwest" Side of the main desert," pt of tract grt to Richard Peirce dec'd, & by him willed to his son John, who sold sd land to Aaron Meazele, who sold it to sd Green, adj Miles Riddick. Test' Jesse Eason, Alexander Eason, James Jones.

No. 114. Jacob Eason of Perq, for £170, pd by Abraham Sumner, of same—sold 260a, adj Thomas Docton, & Jacob Docton. July Court, 1777. Test' Joseph Riddick, Thomas Hurdle.

No. 115. Nov 7, 1780. John Donaldson of Perq, for £200, pd by John Creecy, of afsd—sold 117½a, adj Zebulon Callaway, & Simeon Long. Test' Stephen Harmon, Jonathan Skinner.

No. 116. Joseph Riddick of Chowan, for £55 pd by Samuel Williams, of Perq—sold 125a, on South West side of Ballahack Swamp, adj a pat' grt unto Zachariah Chancey, Mar 6, 1740, commonly called "Great Branch," adj William Townsend, being part of land formerly William Moore's, & by him sold to William Wilson. Dec 17, 1776. Test' Josiah White, Richard Goodwin.

No. 117. Richard Haughton, & Jemimah his wife, of Chowan Co, for £140, pd by John Creecy, of afsd—sold 107a, on North Side of the head of Yeopim River Swamp, in Perq Co, formerly Benjamin Simpson's, adj Delight Nixon, & Charles Copeland. Sept 16, 1777. Test' George Bains, William Forbes.

No. 118. John Harvey of Perq, for "love I bear my dau Anna do give, 7 negroes, a case of walnut drawers, my bed-stead, 6 Silver table spoons, 6 do tea spoons, 12 Silver handled knives, & forks, reserving my life right in sd negroes, & sd articles." Jan 1, 1777. Test' Thomas Harvey, A. Harvey.

No. 119. Jan 8, 1781. John Creecy of Perq, for "235 bushels of Wheat now pd," by Thomas Harvey, of afsd—sold 100½a, between Minzes, & Yeopim Creeks, adj Zebulon Calloway, & Simeon Long. Test' Joshua Skinner, Kinchia Gilliam.

No. 120. William Skinner of Perq, for £26 pd by Benjamin Saunders, of same, sold 250a, adj John Jones, William Arrington, & Joshua Jones, which was grt to sd Skinner, Mar 25, 1780. Seal Mar 24, 1781. Test' Joshua Jones.

No. 121. Mar 1, 1779. Hatten Williams, & Ann his wife, of Chowan Co, for £80 pd by Frederick Luten, of Bertie Co—sold 200a, on north side of Yeopim River, a grt to John Faulkner, Dec 6, 1770, & sd Williams purchased of John Wilkins, & Timothy Trulove. Test' Elizabeth Williams, William Wilkins.

No. 122. Mar 30, 1776. Jarvis Forehand, of Pasq Co, for £10 pd by Simon Stallings, of Chowan—sold 50a, in Perq, known by name of "Grape tree Ridge" pt of a pat' to Luke Hollowell, Aug 4, 1723, & by him sold to Joseph Jessop, who sold sd land to Thomas Rountree, & sd Rountree "bequeathed it to his son Charles, who in like manner bequeathed it to his son Charles." Test' Wm. Guinn, Job. Lilly, Elizabeth Stallings.

No. 123. William Skinner of Perq, for £100, pd by William Long, of same—sold 250a, adj sd Long, Ezekiel Arrington, William Arrington, William Skinner, & Joshua Long, "on Horse-pen branch." Jan 1, 1781. Test' Ben Phelps, Wm Barber.

No. 124. Ann Williams, of Chowan Co, Extrix of Hatten Williams Dec', for £3533 s10 pd by Richard Pratt, of Perq, (Bricklayer)—sold 156a, on North Side of Yeopim & Indian Creeks. Jan 8, 1781. Test' Reuben Long, Isacher Branch.

No. 125. Mar 1, 1781. Asbury Sutton of Perq, for £2000, pd by William Humphries, of afsd—sold 8a on "South west Side of the new road," adj John Reed, & Thomas Stephenson, orphan of Thomas dec'd. Test' John Reed, Hugh Stevenson.

No. 126. Nov 9, 1780. John Harmon of Perq, for £75 pd by William Jones, of afsd sold 100a "whereon I now dwell." Test' Benj'a. Saunders, Joseph Barrow.

No. 127. Aug 5, 1779. John Turner of Perq, planter—for £200 pd by Joseph Sitterson, of afsd—sold 50a on South west Side of Little River, pt of a tract grt to Richard Whedbee, Sept 27, 1719. Test' Isaac Layden, Zebulon Snoden.

No. 128. Feb 28, 1781. Richard Haugton, for £130 pd by Frederick Halsey, both of Perq, sold 288a, at the mouth of Yates Creek, issuing out of Perq River, adj Benjamin Harvey. Test' Fred. Norcom, Samuel Halsey.

No. 129. July 1, 1775. Andrew Collins, of Perq, & Ann his wife, for £125 pd by William Arkill, of afsd—sold 190a on North Side of Yeopim River, pt of land formerly William Standin's. Test' John Norcom, Miriam Norcom, Moses Wilson.

No. 130. John Henley, & Mourning his wife, of Pasq Co, for £165 pd by Edward Wingate, of Perq—sold 349a "on the River Side." April 15, 1780. Test' Ephrim Wingate, Humphrey Parke.

No. 131. Jan 14, 1778. Edmond Blount of Perq, for £240 pd by Joseph Barclift, of afsd—sold 87a on a branch of Muddy Creek, adj Charles Blount, & William Layden, which sd Edmond bought of Benjamin Whedbee, & Tulle . Williams. Test' Tully Williams, Wilson Weeks.

No. 132. John Twine of Perq, husbandman—for "love I bear my son Thomas of same—do give plan' whereon Martha Asbell, formerly dwelt, on north side of Perq River, adj Joseph Perry, & his own new entry, 50a on the side of the desert." Jan 8, 1780. Test' John Hollowill, Henry Hollowell.

RECORDS OF DEEDS

No. 133. Jan. 12, 1780. William Clemons, Joiner—of Perq, for £200, pd by William Townsend, & Humphrey Park, planters—sold the "Common ground in Hertford (No 2) which was bought of the Directors of sd Town," Jan 22, 1774. Test' Ben. Phelps, Samuel Harrell.

No. 134. Francis Foster of Perq, planter—for an "exchange of 150a, with Frederick Foster" of same, planter—sold parcel of land, 135¼a, on a branch of "Beaver Dam Swamp," on No Est Side of Perq River. Francis Foster, Rachel Foster. Test' Thos Robinson, Joseph Bateman.

No. 135. Caleb Burnham of Perq, for £950, pd by John Stanton, of same—sold 33a on one of the branches of Muddy Creek, running to the middle of "High Root Beach branch." June 16, 1780. Test' John Stanton, Seth Cox.

No. 136. July 13, 1779. Ambrose Knox, of Pasq Co, Merchant—for £100, pd by Thomas Mullen, of Perq, sold 76a on the head of Deep Creek, in Perq Co, adj Dempsey Turner, Abraham Mullen, John Turner, & Elisha Albertson's line. Test' Jonathan Skinner, George Whedbee.

No. 137. Demsey Turner of Perq, planter—for £120 pd by Thomas Mullen, of same—planter, sold 15a on So Wst side of Little River, "in the fork of Deep Creek." Feb 9, 1779. Test' Thomas Robinson, Benjamin Turner.

No. 138. Asa Arnold of Perq, planter—for £114, pd by Thos Sutton, of same, planter—sold 114a on So Wst Side of Little River, "to the Westward of the Table of pines a line mentioned in the will of my dec'd father, William Arnold." Dec 20, 1776. Test' Thos. Robinson, Tully Williams.

No. 139. Asa Arnold, & Susannah his wife, for £32-s3-p9 pd by Thomas Sutton, sold 265a on So West Side of Little River, & Shitten Gut, adj John Nichols, Lawrence Arnold, & Perrishoe. Dec 5, 1777. Test' Thos. Robinson, Wm. Arnold.

No. 140. Benjamin Bateman of Perq, planter—for £11-s10 pd by Joseph Bateman, of same, planter—sold 5¾a on No East Side of Perq River, adj Joseph Bateman. Jan 18, 1778. Test' Francis Foster, Thomas Holloway.

No. 141. Jan 12, 1780. Henry Ross, mariner—for £1016 pd by Wm Townsend, & Humphrey Parke of Perq, sold lot (No 2), in the Town of Hertford. Test' Robert Riddick, William Barber, Samuel Harrell.

No. 142. Joseph Mayo of Perq, for "love I bear my son Joseph of afsd—do give tract of land whereon he now lives," on Deep branch. Oct 30, 1776. Joseph, & Mary Mayo. Test' Duke Bogue, Josiah Jordan Jr.

No. 143. Dec 14, 1780. Joshua Bagley, & Mary his wife, of Perq, for £112 pd by Job Miller, of afsd, sold 100a on the "Swamp which issues out of the head of Yeopim Creek," adj Thomas Long, half mile up sd Swamp, near "Gallberry Desert," pt of land pat' by Peter Jones, Mar 20, 1710. Test' Benjamin Scarbrough, John Creecy, Ezekiel Arrington.

No. 144. Benjamin Morgan of Perq, for £250 pd by William Hollowell, of same—sold 122a on So Wst Side of Little River, adj Isaac Boswell, & James Davis. Jan 15, 1778. Test' Jesse Perry, Seth Morgan, John Hollowell.

No. 145. Robert Harmon of Perq, for £100 pd by Stephen Harmon, of same—sold 50a on Yeopim Creek, adj John Wyatt, William Standin, & land given sd Robert, by "Caleb Harmon in his will." Feb 19, 1781. Test' W. Skinner.

No. 146. Francis Foster of Perq, planter—for £200 pd by Noah Barclift, of afsd—sold 50a, adj land whereon sd Barclift now lives, "being Land whereon my mother-in-law Elizabeth Barclift now lives, & was given to me by sd Elizabeth." Feb 7, 1777. Seal June 5, 1780. Test' John Gibson, Caleb Burnham.

No. 147. Bettie Wilson of Perq, for "love I bear my son Elisha Munden of afsd—do give 30a, on So Wst Side of Little River, near the mouth of Fork Swamp." 21-3mo 1781. Test' Jesse Perry, James Davis.

No. 148. Richard Pratt of Perq, for £100 pd by James Mullen, of afsd, Farmer—sold 100a on Wst Side of Indian Creek, adj Joshua Long. July 21, 1780. Test' William Mullen, Thomas Long.

No. 149. June 27, 1777. Foster Thoms Jr, & Mary his wife, Exors of the will of Malachi Jones, late of Perq, for £200 pd by Edmond Blount, of same—sold 305a, on North East Side of Perq River, & South East side of Suttons Creek, at the mouth of sd Creek, to the "Southward of New Landing," land sold Malachi Jones, by Joseph Sutton Jr, Jan 14, 1772." Test' Joshua Toms, Caleb Toms.

No. 150. Frederick Foster, of Perq, planter—for £300 pd by Francis Foster, of same, planter—sold 135a on No East Side of Perq River, near Suttons Creek, adj Richard Whedbee, sd land "conveyed to me by gift, from my father William Foster." Oct 8, 1779. Test' Thomas Robertson, Joseph Bateman.

No. 151. Joseph Bateman of Perq, planter—for £65-s3 pd by Francis Foster, of same, sold 30a on North East Side of Perq River, & Muddy Creek road. Jan 17, 1778. Test' Benj'a. Bateman, Thomas Holloway.

No. 152. Simeon Boswell of Perq, planter—for £16-s17-p6 pd by John Charles, of same, planter—sold 13½a on the "branches of Suttons Creek, & No East Side of Long Branch," adj sd Charles. Jan 7, 1777. Test' John Henby, Joseph Jones.

No. 153. Foster Toms of Perq, planter—for "¼ part of cost of patenting land, & marking same, by Samuel Charles Dec'd, & Aaron Albertson, Ex of Wm Albertson Dec'd, in behalf of John Charles Jr, (a minor) all of afsd—conveyed to sd Aaron, in trust for sd Charles Jr 55a at the head of Suttons Creek, exclusive of 32a, given to John Henby Jr, by William Charles Dec'd in his will, which sd William bought of Samuel Charles Dec'd, & neither having a conveyance from me, who pat' sd land, June 20, 1749 (348a actual measure), adj sd Foster Toms." Nov 25, 1776. Test' Thomas Robinson, John Toms.

No. 154. Seth Cox of Pasq, for £35 pd by John Bailey, (son of Daniel) of same—& also £12 pd by George Boswell, of Perq, sold 89a, to sd Boswell on So Westerly Side of Little River, adj Robert Cox's pat', & land of Samuel White. Jan 29, 1777. Test' James Morgan, Benjamin Morgan, Nathan Bagley.

No. 155. Joseph Hasket (son of Joshua late of Perq), for s5 pd by "my mother Alice Hasket, of afsd—do set over 50a, as by his will directed to be sold." 19, 10mo 1778. Test' Joseph Draper, Thomas Draper, Silas Draper.

No. 156. Feb 7, 1777. Thomas Small of Perq, for £67 pd by Josiah Granbery, of Chowan Co, sold 80a in Perq, adj Henry Hill, Joseph Hurdle, & Moses Boyce, running to line of Thomas Docton, Thomas Davis, & the desert. Test' Thos. Granberry, Joseph Hurdle, Abraham Small.

No. 157. Keziah Smith, widow—of Perq, for "love I bear my children; Israel, & Elizabeth Smith, doth give 1 feather bed, & furniture—2 Iron Kettles—2 Iron pots, & hooks."————. Jan 5, 1781. Test' Hannah Rogerson, Jesse Rogerson, William Felton.

No. 158. July 28, 1780. Simon Stallings of Perq, for £5 pd by Josiah Rogerson, of same—sold 58a on the head of Perq River (desert land). Mar 25, 1780. Test' Robert Riddick, William Lilly.

RECORDS OF DEEDS

No. 159. Aug 20, 1781. Richard Whedbee of Perq. & Joshua Bagley, of same—for £200 pd by sd Whedbee, assigned land joining Lakers, & Minzes Creek, on lines of Christopher Collins, & John Skinner, (200a) pt of a Pat' unto Edward Wilson, June 24, 1704. Test' Fred. Norcom, Thos. Whedbee Jr.

No. 160. July 16, 1781. Isacher Branch of Perq, for £100 pd by John Johnson, of afsd—sold 50a, near "Doctor Dickinson's Mill pond." Test' Joseph Simpson.

No. 161. Penninah Copeland, for "love I bear my children; Rachel, Sarah, & Jesse, all of Perq, do give to each a feather bed, & furniture, & do promise to give to my sd children, as much Schooling as is reasonable, to fit them for business out of my estate." 16, 11mo 1781. Test' Caleb White, Ben. Albertson, Jr.

No. 162. Isaac Barber of Perq, for £130 pd by John Sanders, (house-carpenter)—of same, sold 104a on N. E. Side of Perq River, adj John Perrishoe, George Fletcher & John Bateman, "me heir of David Sherwood." Oct 9, 1781. Test' J. Whedbee, Asa Barclift.

No. 163. Dec 28, 1779. John Fanning, & Barsheba his wife, of Chowan Co, for £3800, pd by Exum Newby of Perq, sold lots in Hertford, No 133-134-135, "same being the land belonging to the Ferry house, formerly property of Benjamin Phelps, with all water lots, ferry, ferry boats, & every privilege to same, all houses, orchards, & appurtenances to same belonging." Test' Edward Vail, John Stafford.

No. 164. July 29, 1781. Thomas Newby, of Isle of Wight Co, Vir, & Mary his wife, for "$100 Spanish Milled dollars," pd by Isaac Wilson, of Perq N. C. sold 40a in Perq, on So East Side of Perry's Mill Swamp, adj Robert Wilson, & Enoch Jessop. Test' Jacob Randolph, Joseph Scott, Exum Newby.

No. 165. Sarah Nicholson "Relic of Thomas" of Perq, for £70 pd by William Robinson, of same, "sold my husbands right in Twenty partners Mill, with land appertaining" in Pasq Co. 25, 5mo 1781. Test' Thomas Robinson, Charles Overman.

No. 166. Solomon Roberts of Perq, for £10 pd by Spencer Williams, of same—sold 11a, adj sd Williams. 8, 4mo 1782. Test' Jesse Perry.

No. 167. William Robinson of Perq for £13 s6 p8 pd by Sarah Nicholson, of same sold "the Twenty partners Mill, with all land & appurtenances belonging, in Pasq, & Perq Counties." 25, 5mo 1781. Test' Aaron Morris Jr, Charles Overman.

No. 168. William Lane, of Nixonton Pasq Co, for £200, pd by Thomas Robinson, of Perq—sold 100a on So Wst Side of Little River, adj William Roberts, & sd Robinson. Nov 24, 1779. Test' J. Lane, David Bailey.

No. 169. Richard Goodwin Jr, & Mary his wife, of Perq, for £40 pd by Humphrey Parks, of afsd—sold 50a which Richard Goodwin Sr, bought of Joshua Small, adj land formerly Jonathan Sherwood's. 31, 1mo 1781. Test' Samuel Smith, Reuben Wilson, Nathan Parks.

No. 170. Samuel Harrell, & Mary his wife, of Perq, for £16 pd by Humphrey Parks, of afsd—sold 5a, adj sd Harrell, "near Reuben Wilson's path" to the New road. April 9, 1781. Test' John Sanders, Penninah Harrell.

No. 171. Benjamin Newby of Pasq, Tailor—for an "exchange of land with Spencer Williams, & £20 pd by sd Williams, in behalf of John Stanton (of Perq, planter)—conveyed 66a near the head of Little River, (in Perq) adj

Reuben Griffin & Henry White, into Spring Swamp." 25, 3mo 1782. Test' Spencer Williams, Levi Munden.

No. 172. Dec 21, 1779. Abner Hollowell of Chowan, for 40s, pd by Hugh Griffin, of Perq, sold 50a on "North Side of Juniper run, which was given to sd Abner, by Joel Hollowell, in his will." Test' William Griffin, Jarvis Forehand.

No. 173. July 28, 1781. Simon Stallings of Perq, for £5 pd by William Lilly, of same—sold 58a of "Desert land" on the head of Perq River.

No. 174. Sept 20, 1791. Elezar Creecy, & Elizabeth his wife, of Perq, for £200 pd by Joshua Bagley, of afsd—sold 50a, adj Benjamin Phelps, "in a branch issuing out of Gum Swamp." Test' Robert Avery, Thomas Bagley.

No. 175. John Cox, of Pasq Co, for £10 pd by Spencer Williams, of Perq—sold 50a on South West side of Little River, in Perq. Oct 6, 1781. Test' Othneel Lassell, Peter Williams.

No. 176. Benjamin Newby, of Pasq Co, for £55 pd by Henry White, of Perq, planter—sold 66a, near the head of Little River, adj Thomas Boswell. 25, 1mo 1782. Test' Jesse Perry, Thomas Norman.

No. 177. Stephen Harmon of Perq, for £100 pd by Levi Creecy, of same—sold 25a, adj Richard Cale, & Andrew Collins. Feb 14, 1781. Test' John Skinner, William Standin.

No. 178. Peter Pearson, of Dobbs Co, N. C. for £70 pd by Mathew White, of Perq—sold 50a on Cypress Swamp, adj Duke Bogue, & Robert Eason, "formerly Peter Pearsons, & fell to me by heirship." Dec. 11, 1779. Test' Robert Evans, Job Bogue.

No. 179. Delight Nixon of Perq, planter—for £5000, pd by Isachar Branch, of afsd—sold 39a on North Side of "a branch that issues out of Dr. Dickens Mill pond." Mar 19, 1781. Test' Thomas Harmon.

No. 180. July 28, 1781. Simon Stallings, for £5 pd by Thomas Hurdle, of Gates Co—sold 58a, on the head of Perq River.

No. 181. July 23, 1781. Simon Stallings, for £500 pd by Joseph Hurdle, of Gates Co—sold 58a, part of 640a, grt to sd Stallings, Mar 25, 1780. Test' Robt. Riddick, Wm. Lilly.

No. 182. Abraham Elliott of Perq, for £175 pd by Robert Holmes, of same—sold 190a called "Chancey's" adj Jesse Copeland, William Townsend, & Robert Newby, "according to the reputed bounds." Jan 10, 1782. Abraham, & Joshua Elliott. Test' W. Newbould, Samuel Williams.

No. 183. Jan 14, 1781. Caleb Winslow of Perq, for £40 pd by Miles Elliott—sold 240a, adj Julius Bunch, & Ephrim Elliott, "part in Perq, & part in Chowan." Test' Caleb Elliott, Solomon Bunch.

No. 184. Edward Wingate, & Sarah his wife, of Perq, for £175 pd by Abraham Elliott, sold 150a, on "South West Side of Ballahack Swamp," adj Richard Goodwin, sd land grt unto John Moore, & was conveyed by Cornelius Moore, to Joseph Moore (son of John) who died intestate, when title to same returned to sd Cornelius, who conveyed sd land, to William Wingate. Feb 25, 1781. Test' Joseph Smith, Isaac Elliott, Joshua Smith.

No. 185. Mar 15, 1780. Jacob Hall of Perq, for £30 pd by Green Thach, of same—sold 100a "near Pratt's Mill Swamp," adj sd Thach, & Joshua Long, where sd Hall now lives. Test' Joshua Long, James Mullen.

No. 186. July 20, 1781. Zebulon Calloway of Perq, for £3 pd by Christopher Collins, of same, sold 100a, adj Joseph Creecy, Reuben Long, & Abell Miller, part of a tract pat' by William Long dec'd, April 1, 1723. Test' Simeon Long, Robert Roe.

No. 187. Jan 29, 1774. Robert Roe, & Mary his wife, of Perq, for £25 pd by Andrew Collins, of same—sold 50a, known by the name of "Stepney's point" adj James McMullen, "part of a tract taken up by Anthony Wherry, & by him sold to John Stepney, which by his death fell to William Stepney, who sold sd land to sd Roe," on a branch of Yeopim Creek. Test' James Donaldson, Andrew Donaldson.

No. 188. Dec 9, 1776. Aaron Moore of Perq, for £116 s5 pd by Seth Sumner, of afsd—sold 77½a on Perq River, down to Suttons Creek, "formerly belonging to Elizabeth Binford, & her son John, late of Charles City Co Vir, & was sold by them, June 9, 1753 to Samuel Moore, father of sd Aaron, "given to him in his will." Test' Thomas Robinson, Joseph Ratliff, John Moore.

No. 189. Feb 3, 1782. John Harvey of Perq; planter—for £63 (pd by sd Harvey) "Charles Blount doth convey 63a on North east Side of Perq River, where Benjamin Bateman, dec'd, formerly lived, adj Demson Barclift Dec'd, Benjamin Bateman Dec'd, & John Anderson Dec'd, which sd land was purchased by sd Blount, of sd Bateman Dec'd." Test' Thomas Harvey, M. Harvey.

No. 190. Job Branch of Perq, for £100 pd by John Leary, of Tyrell Co, sold 100a, adj John Johnson in Perq. Oct 12, 1782. Test' Thomas Harmon, Isachar Branch.

No. 191. Sept 8, 1781. Orpha Rogers, & Delight Nixon, of Perq, for £20,000, pd by Thos. Harmon, of same, assigns land at the head of Yeopim River, called "Bridge Neck" 177a, adj Samuel Decrow. Test' John Exum, Ann Weston.

No. 192. Mar 11, 1780. Job Branch of Perq, for £120, pd by Stephen Harmon of same—sold 3 cows, & calves, and 46a, "in fork of Samuel Dickerson's Mill Swamp, called Bridge Neck being the 3 pt of Richard Rogers land, that he, & Delight Nixon, purchased of Thomas Ming, son of Joseph, & the part that fell to Elizabeth Branch, wife of sd Job." Test' Isachar Branch, Delight Nixon.

No. 193. Reuben Long, & Penninah his wife, of Perq, for "love we bear Hannah Brinkley, widow of John—do give 60a at the head of Franks Creek, near Felts old field, by the polly bridge." Oct 3, 1781. Test' Joshua Long, Christ. Collins.

No. 194. William Hollowell of Perq, for £10 s18 p9 pd by Isaac Boswell, of afsd—sold 8a on Southwesterly Side of Little River. 23, 10mo 1781. Test' Spencer Williams, Solomon Roberts, Levi Munden.

No. 195. Benjamin Sanders, Sadler—of Perq, for £192 pd by Isaac Lamb, of afsd—sold 40a "up Bull branch," on line of Richard Barnes. Oct 1, 1778. Test' Joseph Scott.

No. 196. Mark Newby of Perq, for £125 pd by Isaac Lamb, of same—sold 200a, adj Robert Newby, & Francis Jones. Mar 26, 1780. Test' Ben. Albertson, Zachariah Newby.

No. 197. July 28, 1781. Simon Stallings of Perq, for £5 pd by John Stallings, of afsd—sold 58a on the head of Perq River, "adj the Desert," pt of 640a, pat' by sd Simon, Mar 25, 1780. Test' William Lilly, Jo. Riddick.

No. 198. July 20, 1781. Simeon Long, & Grizzell his wife, of Perq, for £175 pd by Reuben Long, of same—sold 175a on "South Side of Franks Creek." Test' Zebulon Calloway, Robert Roe.

No. 199. April 17, 1780. John Raper, of Perq, planter, & Blake Barclift, of Camdem Co, planter—for £50 pd by sd Raper, sold land on Northeast Side of Muddy Creek, 50a "on the road, & high root Beach Branch." Test' Noah Barclift, Henry Raper Jr.

No. 200. Nov 22, 1781. Joseph Hosea of Perq, for £150 pd by Nathan Turner, of same—some 68a on north east Side of Perq River, "in the fork of Beaver Cove Swamp," adj Joseph Perrishoe. Test' William Lilly, Daniel Stallings.

No. 201. April 9, 1782. John Lonsford, & Mary his wife, of Perq, for £121 pd by Robert Decrow, of afsd—sold 75a on Castletons Creek, adj Elezer Creecy, & the main road. Test' Thomas Creecy, James Skinner.

No. 202. July 28, 1781. Simon Stallings Sr, of Perq, for £5 pd by Simon Stallings Jr, of Gates Co, assigns 50a on head of Perq River. Test' William Lilly, Daniel Stallings.

No. 203. James Davis of Perq, "in consideration of William Monday, serving in my stead for 3 month in the Malitia, & for £47, pd to him, by Spencer Williams, do convey to sd Williams 50a," on So Wt Side of Little River, adj land of sd Williams. April 12, 1781. Test' Jesse Perry, I. Lane.

No. 204. James Brinkley of Perq, planter—for £100,000 pd by Jacob Hall, of same—sold plan' known by the name of "Carpenters," Arbitraters in behalf of sd Hall, conserning bounds of sd land," (Benjamin Phillips Esq, Joshua Long, Jonathan Haughton, Jeremiah Mixon, William Laster, & Thomas Harmon) sd land, adj sd Jacob Hall. Dec 27, 1780. Test' Reuben Long, Thomas Long.

No. 205. Benjamin Turner of Perq, for £50 pd by George Whedbee, of afsd—sold 70a on Deep Creek, adj Wm. Turner, & Ezekiel Turner his brother, near the Horse Bridge, sd land "given me by my dec'd Father Abram Turner, in his will." Feb 21, 1781. Test' Joseph Perrishoe, Robert Turner.

No. 206. Nov 9, 1780. Christopher Collins, & Elizabeth his wife, of Perq, for £90 pd by Simeon Long, of afsd—sold 180a, at the mouth of Franks Creek, & Spring Branch, (which issues out of Yeopim Creek) "½ of a tract, that William Long gave to his son Thomas, who died under age, when sd land fell to his brother Reuben," & Simeon Long, by the will of their "Father William Long." Test' Samuel Penrice, Robert Roe.

No. 207. Dec. 30, 1780. Lemuel Penrice Sr, & Elizabeth his wife, of Perq, for £150 pd by Joshua Bagley, of afsd—sold 200a on Minzes Creek, adj Henry Hall, Joseph Creecy, Zebulon Calloway, & John Skinner, "whereon we now live," part of a grt to Edward Wilson, June 21, 1704. Test' Christopher Collins, John Brinkley.

No. 208. Sept 15. 1778. Thomas Boswell of Perq, planter—for the "better maintainance of his son-in-law Solomon Roberts, of afsd, planter—hath given 25a," on So Wt Side of Little River, adj Elisha Munden, (minor) son of Benjamin Munden dec'd, the River Swamp, & sd Boswell. Test' Zadock Boswell, Levi Munden.

No. 209. Joseph Cox, of Northampton N. C. planter—for £95 pd by Samuel White, of Perq planter—sold 99a on S. W. Side of Little River, & N. W. Side of fork Swamp, adj John Hasket. Oct 28, 1776. Test' Thomas Henby. Henry White.

No. 210. May 21, 1777. George Eason of Perq, for £100 pd by Abraham Eason, of Chowan, sold 59a on "South Side of the main desert, to Great Branch, & line of Miles Riddick, Moses Bridges, & Jacob Pearson, except 1a, for the use of Jesse Easons Mill." Test' Elisha Hunter, Thomas Walton, Selay? Hunter.

No. 211. Noah Barclift, & Milicent his wife, of Perq, for £100 pd by Blake Barclift, of same—sold 50a on N. E. "Branches of Muddy Creek, by the road, & high root beach branch." Mar 20, 1778. Test' Francis Foster, Caleb Burnham, Thomas Robinson.

No. 212. Richard Sanderson of Perq, planter—for £175 pd by John Henby Jr, of afsd, planter—sold 87a in the fork of Suttons Creek, which was pat' by John Nichols, Feb 21, 1729. 3, 3mo 1777. Test' Thomas Robenson, John Charles.

No. 213. Robert Cox, of Bertie Co, planter—for £25 pd by Thomas Henby, of Perq, planter—sold 96a on "So Westerly Side of Little River," back of Solomon Roberts land, in Perq Co. 20, 10mo 1776. Test' Nathan Bagley, Seth Cox, Levi Munden.

No. 214. Richard Leare (Leary) of Perq, farmer—for "love I bear my wife Ann, of afsd, have given all of my goods, Ready money, household Stuff, all cretures. & all other things to me belonging, as well as a tenement in which I now dwell." Nov 14, 1779. Test' Foster Toms, Martha Hodges.

No. 215. Samuel Wright of Perq, planter—for £4 s6 p8, pd by Joseph McAdams, Merchant, of same—sold 4a, on So Wst Side of Little River. Mar 14, 1778. Test' Rachel Elliott, Anne Wright.

No. 216. July 28, 178—. Simon Stallings, for £5 by Robert Riddick, both of Perq, sold 58a of desert land on the head of Perq River. Test' William Lilly Jr, Daniel Stallings, Thomas Hurdle.

No. 217. Aug 8, 1781. Joseph Perry, for £5 pd by Robert Riddick, both of Perq, sold 62a "near the head of Perq River, on North Side of the River Swamp, adj William Price, to John White's Neck." Test Seth Riddick, Jacob Riddick, Ben Perry.

No. 218. William Skinner, of Perq for £75 pd by Peter Salter, of same—sold 1 lot ½a, in the Town of Hertford, adj William Newbould, which he purchased of Richard Hatfield, Dec 20, 1770, with all houses" June 1, 1782. Test' James Johnson, William Newbold.

No. 219. July 20, 1781. Simeon Long, & Grizzell his wife for £300 pd by Zebulon Calloway, both of Perq, sold 50a on east Side of Yeopim Creek, "part of land formerly belonging to William Long dec'd, in the edge of Franks Creek Swamp."

No. 220. Mar 9, 1782. John Wyatt, & Parthenia his wife, of Perq, for £121 pd by John Lumsford, of same—sold 119a on Yeopim River, up Creek Swamp, to Webbs line. Test' William Arkill, Benj'a. Scarbrough.

No. 221. Joseph Perrishoe of Perq, for £260 pd by Zebulon Snoden, of same—sold 100a, adj Elihu Albertson, & sd Perrishoe, formerly belonging to William Tomlin, adj Benjamin Sutton. Test' George Whedbee, John Bateman.

No. 222. Ezekiel Turner of Perq, for £46 pd by George Whedbee, of afsd—sold 63a "on Deep Creek Swamp, adj William Turner dec'd, & land of sd Whedbee, purchased of Benj'a Turner, where sd Whedbee now lives, sd land given me in the will of my father Abram Turner." Sept 13, 1783. Test' Joseph Turner, Miles Turner.

No. 223. Sept 13, 1782. Jacob Morgan of Perq, for £50 pd by Samuel Maclanahan, of afsd—sold 50a, adj Nathaniel Martin, Joseph Wood, John Modlin, & Ralph Fletcher. Test' Duke Bogue, Joseph Perrishoe.

No. 224. Zebulon Snoden, for £300 pd by Samuel McClanahan, both of Perq, sold parcel of land, adj Benjamin Sutton, Joseph Perrishoe, & Elihu Albertson. Sept 27, 1782. Test' Caleb Toms, Gosby Toms.

No. 225. Oct 15, 1782. "I William Townsend of Perq, have Rec'd of George Whedbee, $221½, for a note he gave William Reed Esq, (for $20) which was sold to Francis Newby, & by sd Newby, transferred to sd Townsend, with interest in full." Test' Francis Newby.

No. 226. William Hollowell of Perq, for £8 pd by Thomas Brinkley, of same—sold 5a on So West Side of Little River, "to Wolfpit Branch." Sept 13, 1782. Test' Joshua Boswell, Isaac Boswell.

No. 227. William Robinson of Perq, for £16 s13 p4 pd by Charles Overman, assigned right of 5/12 part of "Twenty partners Mill." 22, 5mo 1781. Test' Thomas Robinson, Aaron Morris Jr.

No. 228. Moses Bundy, & Jane his wife, of Perq, for £150 pd by Joseph Wood, sold 130a on the "head of Vosses Creek Swamp," adj Thomas Hollowell. Test' Aaron Cornwell, Jos. Newby, Joseph Guyer.

No. 229. Joseph Newby, & Elizabeth his wife, of Perq, for £101 pd by John Winslow, of afsd—sold 70a on Vosses Creek, "near dirt Branch, to Sharbers Branch, thence to lines of Thomas Winslow, Seth Elliott, & John Stone." June 20, 1781. Test' Thomas Winslow, Aaron Cornwell.

No. 230. Joseph Mullen of Perq, for "115 barrels of Corn, to me pd within 3 years from date," by Thomas Wheeler, have given 115a, adj sd Wheeler, Jan 2, 1781. Test' George Sutton, Richard Williams.

No. 231. Caleb Winslow, planter—for £70 pd by Isaac Sitterson, both of Perq, sold 70a, on "Lakers Creek" (commonly called Skinners Creek) beginning at Moore's Landing, (at the mouth of Perrishoes Creek) over the road to Skinners Creek. Nov 6, 1776. Test' Ralph Fletcher, John Saunders.

No. 232. Spencer Williams of Perq, for an "exchange of 50a of land, conveyed to me by William Arkill, of afsd—do convey to sd Arkill 160a, on South westerly Side of Little River," adj William Hollowell. May 17, 1782. Test' Josiah Perry, Levi Munden.

No. 233. Feb 19, 1776. Joseph Riddick of Chowan, for £200 pd by Isaac Riddick, of Perq, sold 197a on South west side of Perq River, & East Side of Denison's Swamp, "where Joseph Riddick dec'd, father of sd Joseph, formerly lived." Test' Robert Riddick, Robert Riddick Jr.

No. 234. July 28, 1781. Simon Stallings for £5 pd by Isaac Lilly, of Perq, sold 60a on head of Perq River (pt of grt 640a) & west side of the "main desert." Test' Robert Riddick, Daniel Stallings.

No. 235. Enoch Jessop of Perq, for £10 pd by Job Chappel, of same—sold 160a known by the name of "Chinquepin Ridge," pat' by William Simpson, & a "few acres bought of Isaac Wilson." Dec 17, 1881. Test' Exum Newby, James Chappel.

No. 236. Francis Pitts, of Chowan Co, for £17 s15 pd by Hatten Williams, of same sold 150a on "South Side of Pratt's Mill Swamp," adj William Wyatt, land pat' by Jacob Caruthers. Oct 19, 1778. Test' William Jones, Simeon Long.

No. 237. Sept 16, 1782. Milly Rogerson, for £80 pd by John Lee, both of Perq, sold 100a on the main road, adj Job Winslow. Test' J. Perry, Jos. Scott.

No. 238. Oct 14, 1779. Benjamin Harvey, for £3400, pd by Thomas & Titus Ogden, (of the Town of Newbern, N. C.) sold a lot, ½a in the Town of Hertford, No 21, with ground joining the River, also lot No 4—½a, with ground opposite, between Water St, & the River. Test' William Harvey, Thomas Harvey, Ben. & Kizzy Harvey (wife of sd Benjamin).

No. 239. Oct 1, 1778. Samuel McClanahan, of Perq, & Mary his wife, for £1500 pd by John Fanning, of afsd—sold "Lots in the Town of Hertford, No 133-34-35, the land & Ferry House, formerly belonging to Benj'n Phelps, with Ferry, & Boats, & all privileges appertaining." Test' Nathan Mastyn, Cornelius Ratliff.

No. 240. Ang 3, 1776. Daniel Rogerson, & Catherine, his wife of Perq, for £40 pd by Israel Perry, of afsd—sold 40a on the River Pocosin, adj "Mill land of Josiah Rogerson." Test' John Hollowell, John Twine, Jacob Perry Jr.

No. 241. Dec 9, 1778. Peter Brinkley, of Perq, for £40 pd by Lewis Jones, of afsd sold 200a, adj John Brinkley, & Luke Sumner. Test' John Wilkinson, Jacob Brinkley, William Bundy.

No. 242. Joseph Mayo of Perq, for £155 pd by Thos. White, of afsd—sold 50a, adj Wm White, & Thomas Robinson. Test' Thomas Exum, Mary Newby.

No. 243. Richard Arrington of Perq, for £200 pd by Thomas Creecy, of same—sold 150a, adj William Jones, Ezekiel Arrington, & Malachi Jones, also tract "whereon I now live, adj land formerly belonging to orphans of Zepaniah Jones, & William Clemmons, (50a) sd land given by John Harmon, to his Dau Susannah, wife of sd Richard Arrington." Nov 9, 1782. Test' William Arrenton, William Arrenton Jr.

No. 244. Jan 6, 1780. James Sumner, of Gates Co, for £65 pd by William Arrenton, of Perq, sold 160a, adj John White, "part of a pat' called Chinquepin Ridge taken up by Juliana Lakers, April 1, 1712, & sold to Hubard, by Scarbrough, & by sd Hubard, to Luke Sumner, "by his death, fell of his son James." Test' Ezekiel Arrenton, William Arrenton.

No. 245. Jan 11, 1783. Joseph Perry of Perq, for £5 pd by Benjamin Perry, of afsd—sold 57a on South Side of Perq River Swamp. Test' Robert Riddick, Jacob Riddick, Robert Riddick Jr.

No. 246. Isaac Sitterson of Perq, for £100 pd by William Townsend, of afsd—sold 75a on Southeast Side of Perq River, adj Hercules Saint, "sd land pat' Feb 25, 1696, by Daniel Snooks, & by him sold to Edward Holmes, & from him to John Lilly, from whom it descended to his two dau's Sarah Tederton, & Hannah Sitterson, & sd Tederton sold his pt to James Sitterson, by his will to his son, James, & was given to me, by my Father, James Sitterson in his will." Jan 3, 1783. Test' William Arrenton, Ezekiel Arrenton.

No. 247. John Harvey of Perq, for "love I bear my wife Elizabeth, & my dau Anna, & Frances Ann Harvey, do give to my brother Thomas Harvey in trust, for sd legatees, my plan' whereon I live, with all negroes, Stock, utensils, Household & kitchen furniture, reserving ⅓ part for the use of my wife." Jan 23, 1782. Test' Peleg Lawton.

No. 248. Nov 26, 1782. Frederick Norcom, & Elizabeth his wife, for £108 pd by Thomas Harvey, of afsd—sold 27⅔a, adj Joseph Harvey, on North Side of Cypress Swamp. Test' John Proctor, Joshua Skinner.

No. 249. Demsey Newby of Perq, for £95 pd by Joseph Newby, of afsd—sold 175a on South west Side of Perq River, "above Haw Tree Island, & along North East Side of Tongue of Reeds, to line of Caleb White." Test' Joseph Bogue, Samuel Elliott, Nathan Elliott.

No. 250. Dec 21, 1782. Spencer Williams, of Pasq Co, for £150 pd by Samuel McClanahan, of Perq, sold 159a on No East Side of Perq River, "near Nags head Chapple." Test' John Earl, Caleb Toms.

No. 251. Luke Stallings of Perq, for an "exchange, with Reuben Stallings, doth acquit sd Reuben" & sold 32a adj Thomas Hobbs, & Simon Stallings, to the River pocosin. May 17, 1780. Test' Ezekiel Hollowell, Daniel Forehand.

No. 252. Joel Barber of Perq, for £53 pd by Zachariah White, of same—sold 43a on So West Side of "Joseph Newby's Mill Swamp," adj Jacob Wyatt, & Moses Barber. Nov 12, 1782. Test' Charles Clary, William Clary, William Bundy.

No. 253. Aug 8, 1781. Joseph Perry of Perq, for £5 pd by Phillip Perry, of afsd—sold 130a, in the mouth of Maple Branch, on South Side of Perq River. Test' Robt Riddick, William Lilly.

No. 254. Luke Stallings for a "swap of Land" with Reuben Stallings, do convey 50a on the North East Side of Perq River, known by the name of "Hickory Ridge." May 17, 1780. Test' Daniel Forehand, Ezekiel Hollowell.

No. 255. Ralph Fletcher of Perq, for £52 pd by William Bundy, of afsd—sold 27a on Vosses Creek, "at the pond side." 4, 12mo 1783. Test' Cornelius Ratclift, Joseph Ratclift, Joseph Draper.

No. 256. William Skinner of Perq, for £60, pd by John Skinner, of same—sold a lot ½a, in the Town of Hertford, (No 9) adj lot of Andrew Knox & Co, & west by the Court House ground, "all that piece of common ground in poss' of sd Knox & Co, where their ware-house stands, to the water." Jan 1, 1783. Test' Joshua Skinner.

No. 257. Jan 2, 1781. William Robins of Perq, & Elizabeth his wife, for £600 pd by Moses Stone, of same—sold 52a. Test' Richard Saunders, Joseph Reed.

No. 258. Oct 18, 1781. Phillip Perry of Perq, for £45 pd by Caleb Winslow, of same—sold 60a, for William Winslow, "orphan of Caleb Winslow dec'd," on Beaver run, adj Rountree. Test' Robert Riddick, William Lilly.

No. 259. April ——, 1783. Francis White, & Lydia his wife, of Perq, for £100 pd by Caleb Winslow, sold "½ of pine land, taken up by Joseph Winslow, 1743 (100a) called point Neck." Test' Ezekiel Hollowell, Jacob White, Francis Newby.

No. 260. July 28, 1881. Simon Stallings for £5 pd by Caleb Winslow, both of Perq, sold "parcel of desert land," 58a, on the head of Perq River. Test' Robert Riddick, William Lilly.

No. 261. Aaron Cornwell of Perq, for £500 pd by Joel Bunch, of same—sold 30a on North Side of Vosses Creek, "at the mouth of Heart Branch." Nov 24, 1782. Test' Charles Chancey, William Clary, Zachariah White.

No. 262. Reuben Long of Perq, for £75 pd by Thomas Long, of afsd—sold 25a on East Side of Indian Creek, adj Joshua Long. 21————1783. Test' John Skinner, Joshua Long.

No. 263. Edward Wingate of Perq, for an "exchange" of land with Spencer Williams, of same—conveyed 349a, at the side of Perq River. 17, 5mo 1762. Test' Josiah Perry, Levi Munden.

No. 264. George Walton of Perq, for £60 pd by Josiah Griffin, of above, sold 25a "near the crook of the road," adj Eliab Griffin. 29, 10mo 1782. Test' Thomas Twine, Uriah Hidson.

No. 265. Joshua Toms of Perq; "am firmly bound unto George Whedbee, & Joseph Perishoe of same," in the sum of £100,000. April 25, 1780. Test' Thomas Robinson.

No. 266. Ephrim Wingate of Perq, for $200 pd by George Whedbee, of same—sold 100a, "New surveyed land," adj Benjamin Suttons old patent. Jan 24, 1783. Test' John Bateman, Joel Kenyon.

No. 267. Frederick Foster, for £300 pd by Gilbert Leigh, of Chowan, sold 135¼a on No East Side of Perq River, on a "Branch of Beaver Dam Swamp." Feb 1, 1783. Test' George Whedbee, John Foster, Wm. Whedbee.

No. 268. Feb 1, 1783. John Foster of Perq, for £183 pd by Gilbert Leigh, of Chowan, sold 80a, which "I bought of Hatten Williams, on North East Side of Perq River, below Nags Head Chappel, called Beaver Cove land." Test' George Whedbee, Fredrick Foster, Francis Pitts.

No. 269. James Harmon of Perq, for £80 pd by Lemont Harmon, (son of Stephen dec'd) sold 50a, on South side of Yeopim Creek, adj John Wyatt, & William Standin. Feb 3, 1783. Test' John Wyatt, Parthania Wyatt.

No. 270. State of N. C. for s50 per 100a, pd by William Skinner, of Perq, do grt 462a, adj John White, & William Arrenton, in sd County. Alex Martin, Esq, Gov, & Comd-in-chief, at Hillsborough, Jan 14, 1783. Jas Glasgow Sec. Reg in Perq, by John Skinner, Reg of Perq Co.

No. 271. S. of N. C. for s50 pd by William Jones, do grt 238a, on South Side of Perq River, "near the head of Calloways Mill pond," adj sd Jones. (Same as above.)

No. 272. S. of N. C. for s50 pd by William Jones Jonne's of Perq do grt 164a, at the head of "Barrows Creek," to Yeopim Creek. (same as above.)

No. 273. S. of N. C. for s50 pd by William Jones, do grt 113a, at the end of "Long point of Spring Branch." (same as above.)

No. 274. S. of N. C. for s50 pd by William Jones, do grt 112a, adj Thomas Newby, & Mary Barker. (same as above.)

No. 275. William Skinner of Perq, for £25 pd by Restore Lamb, "do sell to sd Lamb, & Zachariah Lamb, all land mentioned in above patents, between them." July 17, 1783. Test' Caleb White, Phenias Lamb.

No. 276. Zebulon Calloway of Perq, for £152 s12 pd by Thomas Jones, of afsd—sold 203a, on North Side of Yeopim Creek, adj Andrew Donaldson, William Skinner, & sd Jones. July 24, 1781. Test' Ezekiel Arrenton, Robert Roe.

No. 277. John Chancey of Perq, for £15 pd by John Goodwin, of same—sold 50a, in the fork of Cypress Creek Swamp, & from there to "Cat-tail Swamp," adj Evan Skinner, & Julius Bunch. Jan 17, 1783. Test' W. Skinner, John Wingate.

No. 278. July 15, 1783. Wilson Weeks of Perq, for £200 pd by Joseph Barclift, of afsd—sold 207½a on North East Side of Muddy Creek, adj John Stanton, "whereon William Trumball formerly lived." Test' George Whedbee, John Stafford.

No. 279. Samuel Anderson of Perq, for £59 s12 p6 pd by Joseph Anderson, of same—sold 26a on "Westerly Side of Suttons Creek." 1, 6mo 1782. Test' William Robins, Thomas Hosea, Hevi Munden.

No. 280. May 21, 1783. James Sumner, of Gates Co, for "love I bear my Dau Mary Hunter, of Bertie Co; hath given 215a, in Perq Co, three tracts, formerly Luke Sumners." Test' James Jordan, Christian Sumner.

No. 282. Reuben Stallings of Perq, planter—for a "swap" with Luke Stallings, conveyed 125a, on South Side of Perq River, between sd Reuben, & Job Stalling. July 10, 1783. Test' Jesse Stallings, Hugh Griffin.

*No. 283. State of N. C. for s50, per every 100a, do grt to Abraham Wilson 130a, on West Side of Cypress Swamp. Alex Martin Esq, Gov, & Comd-in-chief, at Danbery Aug 18, 1783. Jas Glasgow Sec. John Skinner, Reg of Perq.

No. 284. S. Of N. C. for s50, pd by Thomas Twine, do grt 66a on North Side of Perq River, adj Joseph Perry. (same as above.)

No. 285. S. of N. C. for s50, pd by Benjamin Sr, do grt 50a on west side of "the great Desert," adj David Riddick, near the head of "Jessops Ridge." (same as above.)

No. 286. S. of N. C. for s50, pd by Joseph Riddick, do grt 500a, on north Side of Perq River, adj Isaac Riddick, John & Simon Stallings. (same as above.)

No. 287. S. of N. C. for s50, do grt to Daniel Stallings 88a, on North west side of Perq River, adj John Powell. (same as above.)

No. 288. S. of N. C. for s50, pd by Jacob Perry Esq, do grt 382a, in Haw Tree Neck," adj Benjamin, & Jacob Winslow, "on East side of sd Swamp." (same as above.)

No. 289. S. of N. C. for s50, pd by Joab Kenyon, do grt 181a, on North West Side of Perq River, "nigh John Whedbee." (same as above.)

No. 290. S. of N. C. for s50, pd by Richard Pratt, do grt 92a, on South West Side of "Pratts Mill Swamp," adj Doctor Dicenson, & Jacob Collins. (same as above.)

No. 291. S. of N. C. for s50, pd by Kinchen (Kinchia) Gilliam, do grt 101a, adj William Townsend, & Miles Harvey. (same as above.)

No. 292. John Creecy of Perq, for £11 pd by Joseph Smith Jr, sold 40a, on South west side of Perq River, at the mouth of Ballahack Swamp, "that issues out of Cypress Swamp." Mar 1, 1783. Test' Robert Cale, Nat. Williams.

No. 293. April 14, 1783. Tully Williams Esq, Sheriff of Perq; "Whereas Zachariah Nixon, & Joshua Foster, were indebted to George Foster, in the sum of £105 s4, & Judgment was obtained agst goods, & chattels of afsd, sd Sheriff, did expose for sale 155a, which was bought by John Anderson," for £82 s9. Test' Thomas Harvey, Kinchea Gilliam.

No. 294. Aug 8, 1781. Joseph Perry, for £5, pd by Jacob Riddick, both of Perq, sold 51a near the head of Perq River, adj Benjamin Perry. Test' Robert Riddick, Seth Riddick, Benj'n. Perry.

No. 295. Aug 20, 1783. Hezekiah Rogerson of Perq, "doth give unto my son John" 25a, adj William Townsend, "on the old road." Test' Sam'l Sitterson, Wm Lane.

No. 296. Aug 18, 1783. Joseph Arnold of Perq, for £15 pd by Joseph Turner Jr, sold 25a, adj sd Turner. Test' Thomas Bateman, Ann ─────?

No. 297. Job Bogue, & Leah his wife, of Chowan Co, for £155 pd by Jacob Goodwin, of Perq, sold 150a, "in a place called the fork," adj Jesse Copeland,

---

*(Note: These grants, are probably *Bounty Land;* given for Rev services.)

& Thomas Newby. Aug 4, 1777. Test' Julius Bunch, Nazareth Bunch, Solomon Bunch.

No. 298. March 8, 1783. Edmond Blount of Chowan, for £350 pd by Thomas Harvey, of Perq, sold 305a on North Side of Perq River, (at the mouth, on East Side of Suttons Creek) late the property of Joseph Sutton, & by him sold to Malachi Jones, & by Foster Toms, (who married sd Jones widow) sold to sd Blount, June 27, 1777. Test' Joshua Skinner, Martha Ann Skinner.

No. 299. Oct 13, 1783. Kinchea Gilliam, & Nancy his wife, of Perq, for £7 s10 pd by Robert Duron (Durant, perhaps), & Hezekiah Rogerson, sold 101a, adj William Townsend, & Miles Harvey. Test' Richard Pratt, Abraham Wilson.

(Note: This is the same land grt to sd Gilliam, by Gov Martin Aug 18, 1783.)

No. 300. Jesse Chapel of Perq, for £130 pd by William Townsend, of afsd— sold 55a "whereon I now live." 17, 3mo 1783. Test' Edmond White, Thos. Lewis, John Rogerson.

No. 301. William Spencer, of Pasq Co, for £5 pd by Thomas Brinkley, of Perq, sold 90a on South west side of Little River, adj Caleb Winslow. 6, 8mo 1782. Test' Zachariah Nixon, Levi Munden.

No. 302. Joseph Perrishoe, for £200 pd by John Bateman, of Tyrell Co, planter—sold 100a in Perq, adj George White, on the mouth of Beaver Cove Creek, part of a tract, belonging to Joseph Perrishoe Sr. Oct 5, 1781. Test' George Whedbee.

No. 303. William Clemons of Perq, for £74 pd by Thomas Creecy, of same— sold 37a on South Side of Perq River, "near the head of Knox'es Mill pond." Nov 18, 1783. Test' Josiah Murdaugh.

No. 304. May 1, 1783. Reuben Long, & Pennah his wife, & Simeon Long, & Grizzell his wife, for £160 pd by James Skinner, sold 160a, in the fork of Franks Creek, by the side of "poly Bridge Branch." Test' Richard Skinner, Robert Roe.

No. 305. John Albertson, of Pasq Co, (Shoe-maker)—for £62-10s pd by Capt Joseph Sutton, of Perq, sold 78a on West side of Suttons Creek. April 27, 1782. Test' Richard Pool, Samuel Small.

No. 306. William Arkill of Perq, for a "swap of 60a with Edward Wingate," of afsd—conveyed 50a, near the head of Yeopim Creek, adj Joshua Long. 17, 5mo 1782. Test' Josiah Perry, Levi Munden.

No. 307. Ralph Fletcher of Perq, for £975 pd by Francis Newby, of same— sold 76½a on South side of Suttons Creek, to line of John Toms. Nov 16, 1779. Test' Thomas Robinson, B. Albertson.

No. 308. Oct 9, 1783. Joseph Riddick, of Gates Co, for £10 pd by Josiah Rogerson, of Perq, sold 225a, on the end of "Crosses Neck," adj Simon Stallings, & Samuel Bagley. Test' Morgan Overman, Reuben Riddick.

No. 309. Aug. 8, 1781. Joseph Perry, for £500 pd by Joseph Riddick, of Gates Co, sold 36a in the mouth of "Hoosin pine Branch," adj Robert, & Isaac Riddick, & John White dec'd. Test' Robert Riddick, Jacob Riddick.

No. 310. Sept 17, 1783. Reuben Hobbs, of Gates Co, for £3 pd by Isaac Lilly of afsd, sold 50a on North West Side of Perq River, adj James Field, & Moses Rountree. Test' William Lilly, William Lilly Jr, John Leigh.

No. 311. State of N. C. for s50, per each 100a, pd by Phillip Perry, do grt 166a, on the head of Cypress Swamp, in Perq. Alex Martin Esq, Gov, & Comd-in-chief, (at Denbury) Aug 18, 1783. Jas Glasgow Sec. John Skinner Reg of Perq.

No. 312. Joseph Bateman, & Ann his wife, for £500 pd by Joseph Hosea, of Tyrell Co, N. C. sold 100a in Perq, "where I formerly lived," near Beaver Dam Swamp, adj John Saunders, & Dempsey Barclift. April 17, 1783. Test' John Bateman, Samuel Hopkins.

No. 313. April 20, 1777. Benjamin Harvey Esq, Sheriff of Perq; "Whereas: Thomas McKnight, was indebted to William Skinner, in the sum of £870 s8 p4, also William White, & Hatten Williams, Exors of John Caloway dec'd, who obtained a Writ, & exposed for sale 600a, in Perq, which was bought by Samuel Dickenson, of Edenton, Doctor of Phisic," for £1330. Test' William Cumming, W. Skinner.

*No. 314. State of N. C. for s50, per 100a, pd by Samuel Dickenson, do grt 531a, in Perq, on North Side of Yeopim River Swamp, adj Thomas Ming, & Thomas Harmon. Gov Alex Martin, Esq, Comd-in-chief at Danbury. Aug 18, 1783. Test' Jas Glasgow Sec. John Skinner Reg, of Perq.

No. 315. S. of N. C. for s50, pd by Ezekiel Arrenton, of Perq, do grt 148a, adj William Skinner. (same as above.)

No. 316. S. of N. C. for s50 pd by Hugh Griffin, of Perq, do grt 160a, at the head of Perq River Swamp, adj Ezekiel Hollowell, & Elias Stallings. (same as above.)

No. 317. S. of N C. for s50, pd by David Riddick of Perq, do grt 200a, on South East Side of "White's Mill pond," up great Branch. (same as above.)

No. 318. S. of N. C. for s50, pd by Jacob Riddick, do grt 118½a, adj Benjamin Perry & John White. (same as above.)

No. 319. S. of N. C. for s50, pd by George Whedbee, do grt 32a, adj Benjamin Sutton, Frederick Foster, & Noah Barclift. Alex Martin Esq, Gov, same date. A. Pearse Pro Sec. Jno Skinner Reg of Perq.

No. 320. S. of N. C. for s50, pd by Charles Copeland, do grt 60a, adj Isachar Branch, "at the end of Long Ridge." (same as above.)

No. 321. S. of N. C. for s50, pd by Elias Stallings, do grt 122a, on East Side of Perq River, at the head of Cypress Swamp, adj Benjamin White, & Phillip Perry. (same as above.)

No. 322. Thomas Nicholson, of Perq, for "love I bear my gr-son Joseph Nicholson, (son of Christopher) of afsd, do give 100a, at the head of a line between me, & Zachariah Nixon." 13, 11mo 1777. Test' Thomas Robenson, Pierce Nixon, Barneby Nixon.

No. 323. 3, 12mo 1783. John Charles, of Wayn Co, N. C. for £100 pd by Benjamin Albertson, of Perq, sold 120a, near Suttons Creek, a pat' to John Henby, & "given by him to his gr-dau Chalkey Henby, in his will, May 5, 1752, now divided for the other half, 55a, being a part of a grt to Foster Toms, June 20, 1749, & was deeded by sd Toms, to William Charles dec'd." Test' Joseph Anderson, Samuel Anderson.

No. 324. William Robins, & Elizabeth his wife, for £439, pd by Onepephous Damason of same, carpenter—sold 155a, in the fork of Suttons Creek. April 12, 1784. Test' John Gibson, John Bateman.

No. 325. Henry White of Perq, planter—for £60 pd by John Parker, of same, planter—sold 90a on South West Side of Little River, & No West Side of

---

*Bounty land.

Fork Swamp, adj George Boswell, formerly belonging to Robert Cox. 9, 8mo 1783. Test' William Boswell, Jacob Boswell.

No. 326. Elizabeth Barclift, widow of Joseph, for s1 pd by Hugh Stevenson, both of Perq, "conveyed three negroes, Joan, Evan, & Judy." Sept, 9, 1783. Test' Benjamin Reed, Asa Barclift.

No. 327. Jacob Perry of Perq, for "good-will I bear my Nephew Israel Perry" (son of Israel), do give 60a Swamp land, adj land "given him by his father," & Benjamin Winslow. Jan 3, 1784. Test' Caleb Winslow, Thomas Twine.

No. 328. Jacob Perry of Perq, for "love I bear my friend Henry Hollowell," do give 50a of Swamp land, "between him & Abraham Twine, pat' by me." Aug 18, 1783. Test' Caleb Winslow, Thomas Twine.

No. 329. Jacob Perry, for "love I bear my nephew John Perry" (son of Israel), do give 35a of Swamp land, adj land "given him by his father, between him, & Caleb Winslow," on line of Henry Hollowell. Jan 3, 1784. Test' Caleb Winslow, Thomas Twine.

No. 330. Jan 3, 1784. Jacob Perry, for £5 pd by Thomas Twine, of Perq, sold 50a, adj him, & Abraham Twine, to line of Joseph Perry. Test' Caleb Winslow, Rachel Perry.

No. 331. Jacob Perry for "good-will I bear my friend Abraham Twine" do give 50a of Swamp land, "pat by me, Aug 18, 1783, adj his father, & Henry Hollowell." Jan 3, 1784. Test' Caleb Winslow, Thomas Twine.

No. 332. Jan 3, 1784. Jacob Perry, for £5 pd by Caleb Winslow, of Perq, sold 50a, "opposite the mouth of Deep Branch, by the side of the Swamp, below Rogerson's Mill dam, pat my me, Aug 18, 1783." Test' Thomas Twine, Rachel Perry.

No. 333. Ezekiel Arrington of Perq, for £31 pd by Thomas Stacy, of same—sold 50a, adj William Arrington, & Joshua Long. Aug 28, 1783. Test' W. Skinner, Penelope Creecy.

No. 334. William Newby, of Guildford Co, for £5 pd by Thomas Wilson, of Perq, sold 50a, adj Joseph, & William Wilson, John & William Moore, & Zachariah Chancey. July 19, 1784. Test' Samuel Harrell, Gabriel Newby, Jesse Wilson.

No. 335. Joshua Bagley of Perq, for £80 pd by William Roberts, of same—sold 50a on Gum Swamp, adj Hezekiah Rogerson, & Benjamin Phelps. Oct 7, 1783. Test' Levi Munden, Roda Munden.

No. 336. Henry White of Perq, "am firmly bound unto Thomas Boswell, of same—in the sum of £1000, for payment of which I bind myself, to abide by a certain bound of land, between me, & sd Boswell," land lying on Oak Ridge. Dec 6, 1782. Test' Jesse Perry, Thomas Brinkley, William Hollowell.

No. 337. Dec 11, 1783. Jeremiah Doe, & Richard Mullen, of Perq, for £50 pd by sd Mullen, sold 50a, a little above "Ralph Doe's Grave yard," adj Richard Skinner, up the Road to Charles Moore's line. Test' James Mullen, Jacob Hollowell.

No. 338. Robert Harmon of Perq, for £100 pd by Robert Nicholson, of same—sold 100a on West Side of Yeopim Creek, & Beaver Cove, adj John Wyatt, Robert Roe, Stephen Harmon, & Zachariah Webb. Mar 18, 1781. Test' William Stanton, R———.

No. 339. Caleb Burnham of Perq, Tailor—for £75 pd by Tully Williams, of afsd—sold 50a on Muddy Creek, adj Noah Barclift. Test' Richard Williams, Asa Barclift.

No. 340. Spencer Williams, of Pasq Co, for £160 pd by William Reed, of Perq—sold 200a on North East Side of Perq River, formerly property of Joseph Arnold. May 27, 1783. Test' Othniel Lessell, Thomas Reed.

*No. 341. State of N. C. for s50, per every 100a, pd by Nathaniel Bratton, do grt 66a in Perq, at the head of "Strawberry Gully." Alex Martin Esq, Gov, Comd-in-chief at Denbury Aug 18, 1783. Jas Glasgow Pro Sec. John Skinner Reg.

No. 342 S. of N. C. for s50, pd by Zebulon, & Thomas Callaway, do grt 407a, on Yeopim Creek, adj William Newbegun. (same as above.)

No. 343. S. of N. C. for s50, pd by John Bratton, do grt 86a, on Pratt's Mill Swamp, adj Joseph Williams. (same as above.)

No. 344. S. of N. C. for s50, pd by John Bratton, do grt 66a, on South Side of Pratt's Mill Swamp. Gov Martin. (same as above.) At Fairfield Oct 11, 1783.

No. 345. S. of N. C for s50, pd by John Bratton, do grt 51a, in the "edge of the pocosin." Alex Martin Esq, Gov, & Comd-in-chief at Danbury Aug 18, 1783. Jas Glasgow Sec. John Skinner Reg of Perq.

No. 346. S. of N. C. for s50, pd by John Bratton, do grt 255½a, near the head of Pratt's Mill Swamp, adj Thomas Thach, & Luke Sumner. (same as above.)

No. 347. S. of N. C. for s50, pd by John Bratton, do grt 55a, adj William Skinner, on "Horse pen branch." (same as above.)

No. 348. S. of N. C. for s50, pd by Isachar Branch, do grt 145a, adj Charles Copeland, in the pocosin. (same as above.)

No. 349. S. of N. C. for s50, pd by Ralph Fletcher, do grt 170a, on South Side of Perq River, adj Jesse Winslow, running to Long Branch. (same as above.

No. 350. S. of N. C. for s50, pd by Jacob Holland, do grt 50a, adj Jacob Hall. (same as above.)

No. 351. S. of N. C. for s50, pd by Joseph Godfrey, do grt 81a, on South Side of Deep Creek, adj Isaac Layden, to line of Tully Godfrey. Alex Martin Esq, Gov & Comd-in-chief at Fairfield Oct 11, 1783. A. Pearse Pro Sec. John Skinner Reg of Perq.

No. 352. S. of N. C. for s50, pd by Reuben Griffin, do grt 92a, in Spring Swamp, adj Charles Morgan, & Levi Munden. Alex Martin Esq, Gov at Danbury Aug 18, 1783. Jas Glasgow Sec. John Skinner Reg of Perq.

No. 353. S. of N. C. for s50, pd by Jesse Perry, do grt 324a, by the side of Little River Swamp. Alex Martin Esq Gov, at Fairfield Oct 11, 1783. A. Pearse Sec. John Skinner Reg of Perq.

*No 354. S. of N. C. for s50, pd by Jesse Perry, do grt 250a, near the head of Little River, adj John Hasket. (same as above.)

No. 355. Tully Williams, planter—for "love I bear Richard Williams, do give 6a, adj Charles Blount, to line of Lockhart Williams, with all houses, timber." April 12, 1784. Test' Ed Blount, John Reed.

---

*Bounty land.

No. 356. Thomas Sutton, & Sarah his wife, for £65 pd by Joseph Mullen, of same sold 128¾a on So Wst Side of Little River, & Shitten Gut, formerly the property of William Arnold Dec'd, adj John Nichols. May 2, 1783. Test' George Sutton, Isaac Mullen.

No. 357. S. of N. C. for s50, pd by James Brinkley, do grt 100a, in Pratt's Mill Swamp, along the edge thereof. Alex Martin Esq Gov, at Danbury Aug 18, 1783. James Glasgow Sec. John Skinner Reg of Perq. (Bounty land.)

No. 358. Thomas Sutton, & Sarah his wife, for £100, pd by Joseph Mullen, of same—sold 114a on So West Side of Little River, formerly property of William Arnold dec'd, on So Wst Side of "Shitten Gut." May 2, 1783. Test' George Sutton, Isaac Mullen.

No. 359. Francis Foster of Perq, planter, & Rachel his wife, for £350 pd by Foster Toms, of afsd—sold 150a, on East side of Suttons Creek, adj the "new road that goes to John Toms," parcel of land pat by Francis Foster Esq, Dec 10, 1780, & by him given to his son William, & by descent came to sd Francis, as heir-at-law of Francis Foster Esq, & sd William." May 15, 1784. Test' Francis Newby, H. Stevenson.

No. 360. Foster Toms, & Mary his wife, of Perq, for £100 pd by John Smith, of Pasq Co, sold 100a in Perq, which was given sd Mary, (then Smith) by Joseph Murdaugh, on North West side of Cypress Creek, at the mouth of a branch below Cypress bridge, adj Benjamin Sanders, to line of Joseph Smith dec'd, (now John Smith's) & Cypress Swamp. May 6, 1784. Test' Francis Foster, John Toms.

No. 361. William Moore of Perq, for £10 pd by John Goodwin, of afsd—sold 50a in Ballahack Swamp, & East side of Creek Swamp, "square with Chancey's patent." Jan 12, 1778. Jacob Goodwin, Miriam Goodwin.

No. 362. William Woodley, for £50, pd by John Woodley, both of Perq, sold 80a on West Side of Suttons Creek. William, & Zilpha Woodley. April 12, 1784. Test' Foster Toms, Zebulon Snoden.

No. 363. Ambrose Knox, of Pasq Co, for £30 pd by John Clary, of Perq, sold 80a on North side of Perq River, at the mouth of Vosses Creek, whereon Benjamin Elliott "formerly lived, & in his will gave to his son Benjamin, which was sold by Ezecution of the Sheriff," to sd Knox. Oct 13, 1783. Test' William Clary, George Whedbee.

No. 364. Joseph Ratliff of Perq, for £331 s13 p4 pd by Humphrey Parke, of afsd, "in gold, & silver," sold 66a on North East Side of Perq River, adj Joseph Pearse, & Benjamin Albertson. ———— 1784. Ralph Fletcher, Cornelius Ratliff, Joseph Park.

No. 365. Joseph Jones of Perq, planter—for £45 pd by Josiah Murdaugh, of same—sold 50a on west side of Perq River, & Southwest side of Castletons Creek, "formerly claimed by Robert Wilson." April 12, 1784. Test' William White, Chalkey Albertson, William Robinson.

No. 366. William Arnold of Perq, for £70 pd by Francis Newby, of same—sold 130a, "betwixt Little River, & Suttons Creek, in the great Body." Feb 20, 1784. Test' Joseph Perrishoe.

No. 367. Sept 15, 1783. Charles Moore, Sheriff of Perq; Benjamin Elliot dec'd, was indebted to William Lane, in the sum of £167 s8, & sd Sheriff, did expose for sale 80a, which was purchased by Ambrose Knox for £170. Test' Will Cummings, T. Vail.

No. 368. Abraham Wilson of Perq, for £40 pd by John Saunders, of afsd—sold 30a, adj Isaac Lamb, "opposite Chinquepin Orchard branch." 18, 3mo 1784. Test' Thos Hollowell, Francis White, Thomas White.

No. 369. Francis Newby of Perq, for £175 pd by Thomas Newby, of same—sold 76a on South Side of Suttons Creek, adj John Toms. Aug 20, 1783. Francis & Rachel Newby. Test' Frederick Nixon, James Nixon.

No. 370. June 1, 1784. George Simmons, of Martin Co, N. C. for £30 pd by Josiah White, of Perq, sold 300a called "Butlers Neck" which was taken up by John Brazier, "where John White now dwells, being all the land held by Elizabeth Raner, & her son John Brazier, & descended to sd Simmons, by heirship." Test' Jas Scott, Abner Harrell, John Smith Jr.

No. 371. June 16, 1784. Benjamin Boyce of Perq, for £10 pd by Josiah White, of same—sold land called "Butlers Neck, where I now dwell, according to the ancient reputed bounds." Test' Thos. Newby, Joseph Scott.

No. 372. Mar 27, 1784. Phillip Perry of Perq, for £5 pd by Benjamin Perry, of afsd—sold 50a near the head of Cypress Swamp. Test' Robert Riddick Jr, Daniel Perry.

No. 373. May 4, 1784. Charles White, & Mary his wife, of Chowan, for £33 s6 p8 pd by Jacob Riddick, of Perq, sold 25a near the "upper Bridge," adj Benjamin Perry Sr, & John White. Test' Benjamin Perry Jr, Ezekiel Hollowell, Jacob Jordan.

No. 374. Thomas Twine of Perq, for £5 pd by Joseph Perry, of afsd—sold 24a taken up, Aug 18, 1783. Seal Jan 9, 1784. Test' Robert Riddick, Jr, Henry Hollowell, Susanna Perry.

No. 375. Mar 27, 1784. Phillip Perry for £5 pd by Robert Riddick, both of Perq, sold 50a near the head of Perq River, adj Benjamin White, & Luke Stallings. Test' Benj'n. Perry, Daniel Perry.

No. 376. April 7, 1784. Richard Bacon, & Joyce his wife, of Perq, for £200 pd by Thomas Newby, of same—sold 130a on South west Side of Perq River, adj William Bond, & Mary Barker. Test' Jos. Scott, Mary Newby, Josiah White.

No. 377. Frederick Nixon, Taylor—for £14 s16 p10 pd by Keziah Pritlow, of Perq, sold 25a, in Pasq Co, adj Francis Nixon dec'd, on "Halls Creek." Aug 29, 1783. Test' Thomas Newby, Francis Newby.

No. 378. Charles White, of Chowan, & Mary his wife, for £200 pd by John White, of Perq, sold 150a, known by the name of "Great bridge Neck" adj Jacob Riddick. May 7, 1784. Test' Jacob Riddick, Eliab Griffin, Francis Toms.

No. 379. April 10, 1784. William Knowles, & Deborah his wife, of Perq, for £215, pd by Francis Newby of same—sold 215a on North Easterly Side of Perq River, "a little below Suttons Creek, at the mouth of Little Creek." Test' Joseph Pierce, John Earle.

No. 380. July 10, 1784. Charles Moore, Sheriff of Perq; "exposed for sale 124a of land, the property of Zachariah Nixon, to satisfy a Judgment obtained by Josiah Granbery," & sd land was purchased by Samuel McClannahan, for £165. Test' J. Whedbee, Francis Foster, Thos Sutton.

No. 381. Nathan Newby, & Peninah his wife, of Perq, for £60 pd by Joseph Smith, of same—sold 150a on South west side of Ballahack Swamp, adj Richard, & Jacob Goodwin, to Cypress Swamp, formerly land of Elizabeth Nixon. Oct 22, 1783. Test' Richard Whedbee, Fred Norcom.

No. 382. Benjamin Scarbrough of Perq, for £125 pd by William Skinner, of same—sold 67a, whereon "I now dwell," near the head of Yeopim Creek, adj Jonathan Skinner, & William Stepney. Mar 5, 1782. Test' Elizabeth Cotton.

No. 383. Nathan Long of Perq, for £110 s12 pd by William Skinner, of afsd—sold 88a near the head of Yeopim Creek, adj William Stepney. June 4, 1784. Test' John Wyatt, Alex'd. Stafford.

No. 384. Robert Homes of Perq, for £250 pd by Nathan Newby, of same—sold 190a, called "Chanceys" on South Side of the River, adj William Townsend, & Robert Newby. Nov 3, 1783. Test' Joseph Baker, Thomas Newby.

No. 385. Alex. Stafford, of Perq, Ex of John Stafford dec'd, for £40 pd by Joseph Sitterson, of afsd—sold 50a near "Nags head Chapel," (according to sd Johns will,) adj William Knowles Mill pond, which was formerly property of William Colson dec'd. May 20, 1784. Test' Thos Whedbee, William Roberts.

No. 386. July 13, 1784. Reuben Long of Perq, for £117 pd by Jain Blair, (surviving partner of Andrew Knox, & Co,) sold 108a on East side of Indian Creek, & Yeopim River. Test' Benj'n. Phelps, John Wyatt.

No. 387. William Colson of Perq, Mariner—for £30 pd by John Stafford, of same, carpenter—sold 50a near "Nags head Chappel," adj Joseph Sitterson, at the head of William Knowles Mill pond, which was purchased by sd Colson, of James Jones. Sept 19, 1783.

No. 388. Joseph Sitterson of Perq, for £16 pd by Thomas Wright, of afsd—sold 18a where sd Wright now lives, adj Nathaniel Welch, & Samuel Wright. Sept 19, 1783. Test' Jno Lane, Samuel Jackson.

No. 389. May 14, 1783. William Clemens of Perq, Carpenter—for £40 pd by John Creecy, Merchant—sold 51½a called "Oakland" in the Desert, adj Thomas Halsey, part of a pat' to Andrew Knox, Sept 7, 1761. Test' W. Newbold, Alex Stafford.

No. 390. July 28, 1784. William Newbold of Perq, Merchant—for £737 s5 p3 pd by Thomas King, of Edenton, Merchant—sold 3 lots in the Town of Hertdord, (No 110-111-112) "now in occupation of sd Newbold, & all houses, outhouses, stables, gardens, belonging to same." Test' Alex Stafford.

No. 391. Samuel Parsons of Tyrell Co, for £10 pd by John Creecy, of Perq, sold 30a at the "River Bank," adj Seth Sumner, & Roger Kinyon. June 16, 1784.

No. 392. Nov 7, 1780. John Donaldson of Perq, for £200 pd by John Creecy, of afsd—sold 117½a, adj Zebulon Calloway, & Samuel Penrice. Test' Stephen Harmon, Jonathan Skinner.

No. 393. Dec 7, 1784. Wm Williams of Perq, yeoman—for £125 pd by Robert Homes, of Chowan, planter—sold 120a in Perq, on N. E. side of Mill Swamp, & Deadmans Swamp. Test' Jonathan Boulton, Joshua Wyatt.

No. 394. Jesse Perry, & Elizabeth his wife, of Perq, for £34 pd by John Hasket, of same, sold 179a on fork Swamp, along Albertsons line, adj sd Hasket. —, 11mo 1784. Test' Seth Morgan, Peter Williams.

No. 395. Ralph Fletcher of Perq, planter—for £235 pd by Mark Newby, of same—sold 100a on North East Side of Perq River, adj Bettie Saint, & sd Fletcher. Nov 27, 1779. Test' Thos. Robinson, Joseph Pearce.

No. 396. Ralph Fletcher, for £40 pd by Mark Newby, sold 20a on North East Side of Perq River, adj William Woodley. Nov 27, 1779. Test' T. Robinson, Joseph Pearce.

No. 397. Oct 2, 1784. Joseph Whedbee, & Thomazzin his wife, of Edenton, N. C. for £10 pd by Ezekiel Arrenton, of Hertford, "sold Lot No 1, in Hertford, also water lots, opposite thereto." Test' Thomas Creecy, Allen Bryan.

No. 398. Matthew Newby, of Dobbs Co, N. C. for £100 pd by Marke Newby, of Perq, sold all "right to land, given by Jesse Newby, to Francis Newby," adj Robert Newby, John Saunders, & Francis Jones. Nov 29, 1779. Test' Ezekiel Arrenton, Elh'a. Ruffin.

No. 399. Thomas Nicholson of Perq, for love I bear my gr-son Thomas, son of Christopher Nicholson, of same—do give 100a, "adj land of Zachariah Nixon, & William Robertson. 13, 11mo 1777. Test' Pierce Nixon, Barnaby Nixon, Jos. Nicholson.

No. 400. Elizabeth Hasket of Perq, for "love I bear my son Jesse, of same—do give a negro man named Mingo." Jan 3, 1785. Test' Solomon Roberts, William Hollowell.

No. 401. Elliot Griffin of Perq, planter—for s40 pd by George Walton, of afsd—sold "40 yards square of the River Swamp, adj the Upper End of the Causway, River Bridge called Thomas Newbys along the Main Road 60 yards, to the Swamp." 31, 3mo 1784. Test' John Hudson, Uriah Hudson.

No. 402. Thomas Nicholson, for "love I bear my son Nicholas Nicholson, of Perq, do give 100a, adj Little River Meeting House, & Charles Overman, where he doth now live." Test' P. Nixon, B. Nixon. 13, 11mo 1784.

No. 403. Thomas Nicholson, for "love I bear my son Nicholas, do give 100a, between Little River Meeting House, & Charles Overmans house, to the fork of Weeks road, & the corner of Thomas Jordans garden, down to the River pocosin." 13, 11mo 1777. Test' Thos Robinson, Pierce Nixon, Barnaby Nixon.

No. 404. Oct 30, 1783. Benjamin Boyce of Perq, for £20 pd by Thomas Newby, of same—sold 100a, adj "Sandy Ridge Road," William Lilly, Caleb, & Job Winslow. Test' Edward White, Robert Evans.

No. 405. William Arkill of Perq, for £70 pd by Jesse Perry, of same—sold 50a on So Wst side of Little River, adj Spencer Williams, & William Hollowell. Sept 8, 1783. Test' Thos Brinkley, William Hollowell.

No. 406. Solomon Roberts of Perq, for £15 pd by George Boswell, of same—sold 29a, adj Elisha Murdaugh. May 7, 1784. Test' William Arkill, Thomas Hasket.

No. 407. William Robins, & John Bateman, Exors of Joseph Perrishoe, late of Perq, have sold (pursuant to his will) 95a, adj George Whedbee, (unto Samuel McClanahan, £166, now dec'd), & Elisha Albertson, to the Road. ——— 1784. Test' John Clayton, William Whedbee, Thomas Sutton.

No. 408. April 26, 1783. Samuel Bagley of Perq, for £3 pd by Isaac Lilly, of afsd—sold 50a, part of a Pat' unto Simon Stallings Sr, Mar 25, 1780. Test' Jacob Bagley, Abr'm. Riddick.

No. 409. Samuel, Miriam, & Thomas Sitterson, of Perq, for £45 pd by Demsey Harrell, of afsd—sold 15a where sd Thomas now lives, on South side of land belonging to Orphans of Hercules Saint, & Jesse Copeland Dec'd. Oct 1, 1784. Test' Joshua Bagley, Robert Cale, Hezekiah Rogerson.

No. 410. Joseph Creecy, of Chowan, for "love I bear my gr-son Frederick Norcom, do give all that land bought of Edward Penrice, & Henry Hall 27a, an Island called Batts Grave." Nov 15, 1784. Test' Mary Creecy, Elizabeth Creecy, Frederick Creecy.

No. 411. Mar 30, 1784. Richard Pratt, & Mary his wife, of Perq, for £82 pd by Frederick Sutton, of same, sold 70a, on North Side of Indian Creek, & head of Deep branch. Test' Thos. Penrice, Reuben Long.

No. 412. Spencer Williams of Pasq Co, for £16 pd by Jesse Perry Esq. of Perq, conveyed 12a on So Wst Side of Little River Swamp, adj William Hollowell. Feb —, 1784. Test' Seth Cox, Thomas Hasket, Joshua Boswell.

*No. 313. State of N. C. for s50, per each 100a, pd by Zachariah Webb, of Perq, do grt 232a, on West Side of "Broad Creek," adj Richard Cale. Alex Martin Esq, Gov, & Comd-in-chief, at Newbern Oct 27, 1784. Jas Glasgow Sec. John Skinner Reg.

No. 314. S. of N. C. for s50, pd by Joseph Godfrey, of Perq, do grt 82a, on Deep Creek, adj Charles Blount. (same as above.)

No. 315. S. of N. C. for s50, pd by Jesse Perry, of Perq, do grt 200a, near Little River, adj Charles Morgan. (same as above.)

No. 316. S. of N. C. for s50, pd by Jesse Perry, do grt 100a, near Little River, adj Caleb Winslow. (same as above.)

No. 317. S. of N. C. for s50, pd by Delight Nixon, of Perq, do grt 96a, on Yeopim River Swamp, adj Isachar Branch. (same as above.)

No. 418. S. of N. C. for s50, pd by Jacob Goodwin, of Perq, do grt 341a, on North Side of Balahack Swamp, adj John Creecy. (same as above.)

No. 419. S. of N. C. for s50, pd by Jonathan Skinner, of Perq, do grt 140a, adj Jacob Hollowell, & Halls corner. (same as above.)

No. 420. S. of N. C. for s50, pd by William Stepney, do grt 63a, adj John Wyatt. (same as above.)

No. 421. Nov 6, 1784. John Creecy of Perq, for £50 pd by Francis Newby, of same—sold 100a on east side of Perq River, formerly land of Joseph Williams, dec'd. Test' Samuel Sutton, Elizabeth Sutton.

No. 422. Feb 19, 1785. Tullie Williams, for "love I bear my Brother Lockheart," doth give land, adj sd Tullie, which I purchased of Mr. John Stephenson. Test' John Brownley, James Sumner, John Reed.

No. 423. Nathan Long of Perq, for £176 pd by Sarah Ashley, of same—sold 100a, "pt of a tract given me by my Father Thomas Long, adj William Skinner, & Andrew Donoldson, whereon I now live." June 11, 1785. Test' Joshua Long, William Arrenton.

No. 424. Sarah Whedbee, for "love I bear my four children; William, James, Martha, & Lemuel Whedbee, do give negroes, bequeathed to me by my Dec'd husband George Whedbee, except Peter, & his wife Judah, & Esther, & Jane." July 27, 1784. Test' Thomas Robinson, Thomas Whedbee, Daniel Parke.

No. 425. Robert Nicholson, & Mary his wife, of Perq for £110 pd by Levi Creecy, of same—sold 111a on West side of Yeopim Creek, adj Jeremiah Collins, Richard Cale, James Willims, & Robert Roe. Sept 8, 1784. Test' Richard Arrenton, Edward Wingate.

No. 426. Jan 7, 1785. John Hatch, of Onslow Co, N. C. planter—for £34 s4 pd by John Creecy, of Perq, sold 64a on No East Side of Perq River, sd land bought by Richard Sanderson, of Christopher Towe. Test' Penelope Reed, George Reed, Thomas Reed.

---

*(Note: These grants are probably Bounty land, for Rev Services.)

No. 427. John Hatch, of Onslow Co for £138 pd by John Creecy, of Perq, sold 230a, on East Side of Perq River, & Beaver Dam Swamp. Jan 12, 1785. Test' Foster Toms, Thomas Stevenson.

No. 428. John Hatch of Onslow, for £66 s13 p4 pd by William Reed, of Perq, sold 250a over the Swamp, adj Samuel Barclift, & Foster Toms, sd land purchased of Jeremiah Caruthers, & wife. Test' Penelope Reed, George D. Reed, Thos. Reed.

No. 429. April 11, 1785. Francis Newby of Perq, for £500 pd by John Creecy of same—sold 442a called "Gums," a pat' to James Thigpen, & sold by him to Thomas Newby, who sold sd land to sd Francis Nov 8, 1728, "now in possession of Samuel Skinner." Test' Henry Hall, James Hall.

No. 430. April 11, 1785. John Creecy of Perq, for £50 pd by Francis Newby of same—sold 66a whereon Cornelius Forehand now lives, adj Joseph Turner, formerly Samuel Parsons, & bought of John Hatch. Test' Henry Hall, James Hall.

No. 431. April 11, 1785. John Creecy, for £80 pd by Francis Newby, sold 150a, adj Seth Sumner, & Joseph Turner. Test' Henry Hall, James Hall.

No. 432. Reuben, & Simon Long of Perq, for £20 pd by William Long of afsd—sold 100a on North Side of Pratts Mill Swamp, "which was bequeathed to sd Reuben in his father William Longs will," adj William Long, & Joshua Long. Nov 9, 1775. Test' William Skinner, Miles Skinner, Lemuel Long.

No. 433. State of N. C. for s50 per 100a pd by John Creecy of Perq, do grt 640a on South side of Balahack Swamp, & North side of Cat-tail Swamp. Alex Martin Esq Gov. & Comd-in-chief, at Newbern, Oct 27, 1784.

No. 434. Jan 11, 1785. John Boyce Sr of Perq, for £40 pd by Abram Wilson of same—sold 100a on South Side of Creek Swamp, called "Palmers Cow pen, & John Parker's Old field" adj Thomas Ward. Test' W. Newbold, Joseph Smith, Abraham Elliott.

No. 435. Dec 21, 1784. Thomas Newby of Vir, Co of Isle of Wight, & Mary his wife, for $500 (Spanished milled), to me pd by Francis Newby, of Perq N. C. sold 542a, as per pat' to James Thigpen, Nov 8, 1728, & by him sold to sd Thomas, "part in Perq, & part in Chowan Co," adj Evan Skinner, in Bear Swamp. Test' John Nixon, Exum Newby.

No. 436. Jan 29, 1785. Thomas Harvey of Perq, for £450 pd by Francis Newby of same, Merchant—sold 305a on East Side of Suttons Creek, bought by sd Harvey of Edmond Blount, & by sd Blount of Foster Toms. June 27, 1777. Test' John Creecy, John Moran.

No. 437. April 11, 1785. John Creecy of Perq, for £150 pd by Francis Newby of afsd—sold 230a On East Side of Perq River, pat' by Edward Turner. Test' Henry Hall, James Hall.

No. 438. Samuel Parsons of Tyrell Co N. C. for £90 pd by Francis Newby of Perq sold 150a on North East Side of Perq River, a grt to Richard Whedbee, & by him sold to ———— Parsons, & "came by descent to sd Samuel, the younger," at the side of Beaver Dam Swamp, adj Seth Sumner. July 5, 1785. Test' Foster Toms, John Creecy.

No. 439. April 11, 1785. Thomas Harvey, for £55 pd by Richard Haughton sold 11a on South Side of Perq River, adj sd Harvey, bought of William Scarbrough. July 4, 1778. Test' William White, Joseph Harvey.

No. 440. Jacob Overman of Perq, planter—for "love I bear my son John, of same, planter—have given 58a on So West Side of Little River," adj Joshua

Boswell, (near the head of little branch) and William Hollowell. 14, 1mo 1782. Test' William Hollowell, Barnaby Boswell.

No. 441. Francis Jones of Perq, planter—& Rachel his wife, for £100 pd by Phineas Lamb, of same—sold 75a on North East Side of Cypress Swamp, near the mouth of Deep Branch. 21, 5mo 1785. Test' Caleb White, Benj'n. White, Milicent White.

No. 442 Benjamin Albertson Sr, of Perq, for £10 pd by John Hasket, of same—sold 10a, in "fork Swamp," adj John Parker, & sd Hasket. —, 2mo, 1785. Test' Nathan White, Samuel Nixon.

No. 443. July 6, 1785. Gosby Toms of Perq, for £50 pd by John Toms, of same—sold 100a, adj sd John Toms, Richard Whedbee, & Francis Newby. Test' Foster Toms.

No. 444. Eliab Griffin of Perq, planter—for £20 pd by Benjamin White, of afsd—sold 50a on North East Side of Perq River, adj Josiah Griffin, Solomon Elliott, & Josiah White. 20, 4mo 1785. Test' Charles White, Josiah Griffin.

No. 445. Gosby Toms of Perq, for £200 pd by Foster Toms, of same—sold 100a on North East Side of Suttons Creek, part of a grt to Samuel Charles, Oct 19, 1768, (by him sold) adj Francis Foster Esq, & Nathaniel Nicholson. May 24, 1785. Test' Edmond Wood, Joseph Turner Jr, J. Whedbee.

No. 446. July 14, 1785. Charles Moore Esq, Sheriff of Perq; Zachariah Nixon, late of Perq dec'd, Joshua Toms, & Caleb Toms, were indebted to William Lowther, & Co; (Judgment was obtained) sd Sheriff did expose for sale 65a, on west side of Suttons Creek, adj Samuel Anderson, William Woodley, & Fras Newby, which was purchased by Thomas Hosea, for £2 s55. Test' Foster Toms, Thomas Jones.

No. 447. Joseph Scott of Pasq, for £34 pd by Thomas Wilson, of Perq, "sold 300a, known by the name of 'Wells Meeting house land' beginning at Spring branch, across Cannons line, to the line of Thomas Jessop, from thence to the River pocosin, & the mouth of Spring branch." 22, 1mo 1785. Test' Joseph Newby, Samuel Elliott, Sam'l. Wallis.

No. 448. William Winslow of Perq, farmer—for £152 s10 pd by Benjamin White, of afsd, Miller—sold 152a on North East Side of Perq River, adj Jesse Winslow, Orphan of Timothy Winslow, Jacob Winslow, Uriah Hudson, & George Walton, to the mouth of Long branch. Feb 21, 1785. Test' Caleb White, Miles White, Seth White.

No. 449. William Wilson, of Randolph Co, N. C. by "power of Att' given me by Thomas Jessop of Guilford Co," for £150 pd by Thomas Wilson, of Perq, sold 294a, at the main road, in Spring branch, adj Jacob Cannon, the River, & the mouth of Spring branch. 17, 1mo 1785. Test' Thomas Draper, Jonah Robinson, Samuel Elliott.

No. 450. Henry White of Perq, for £90 pd by John Overman, of same—sold 50a on "Rich Neck branch," adj John Stanton. 1, 1mo 1785. Test' William Hollowell, Charles Overman.

No. 451. Charles Moore Sr, Sheriff of Perq; in con' of £10 s8 p6 pd by Robert Homes of Chowan, sold land in Perq on Mill Swamp, "as per deed of William Williams, in sd Co, which was sold for debt, due from Joseph Williams Dec'd." April 11, 1785. Test' George Walton, Thomas Newby.

No. 452. 4, 4mo 1785. Thomas Nicholson of Pasq Co, for £180 pd by Benjamin Albertson, of Perq, sold 100a, near Little River Bridge, in Perq, adj Zachariah Nixon, sd land "'conveyed to me by my Gr-father Thomas Nicholson, by deed of gift." Thomas, & Mary Nicholson. 13, 11mo 1777. Test' Joseph Scott, Elliott Scott.

No. 453. John Nixon of Perq, for "love I bear my mother, Keziah Pritlow, do give all my right, of certain parcel of undivided negroes bequeathed to me, in the will of my father, Francis Nixon dec'd." April 5, 1785. Test' Thomas Robinson, Francis Newby.

No. 454. June 13, 1785. Charles Moore, Sheriff of Perq; "John Pierce, late of Perq was indebted unto Thomas Newby, Thomas Hosea, Malachi Jones, Seth Sumner, & Joshua Toms, in the sum of £81 s13 p2, for which a Levie was made against his Estate, & sd Sheriff, did sell 100a, to satisfy same, Land near the head of Newby's Mill pond, up Vosses Creek, adj Charles Clary, Margaret Fletcher, & Zachariah White, which was purchased by William Clary, for £100 s13 p9. Test' Chas. Moore Jr, Joseph Draper, Joseph Harvey.

No. 455. Dec 9, 1783. Reuben Long, & Penninah his wife, of Perq, for £100 pd by William Arkill, of same—sold 50a on Pratts Mill pond, adj Joshua Long, & Thomas Long, taken up by ———— Banks. Test' Thomas Brinkley, Thomas Penrice.

No. 456. Thomas Wilson, & Elizabeth his wife, of Perq, for £110 pd by Thomas Draper, of afsd—sold 100a near "Welses Meeting house," running to the River pocosin. 17, 1 mo 1785. Test' Josiah Robinson, Samuel Elliott, Joseph Gilbert.

No. 457. Miles Gale Skinner, of Perq, for £80 pd by Jonathan Skinner, of afsd—"transferred all right in a certain entry of land, (200) on the head of Richard Arrentons first entry, in Jesse Eason Office," adj sd Jonathan. July 25, 1778. Test' Wm. Newbold.

No. 458. Mar. 24, 1785. John Reed of Perq, planter—for £100 pd by William Reed, of same, planter—sold 25a, in Durants Neck, "part of land left him by his Father Joseph Reed in his will," adj Elizabeth Jacocks, & the "new main road." Test' Charles Moore, Samuel Langston.

No. 459. Joseph Riddick, of Gate Co, for £100 pd by William Robinson, of Perq. in behalf of Charles Overman, Aaron Morris, & Sarah Nicholson, sold 187a, on South west Side of Little River, by Beaver Cove, adj Joseph McAdams, & Weeks. Jan 20, 1785. Test' Reuben Riddick, Edward Beneman.

No. 460. Elizabeth Bogue of Perq, for "love I bear my Dau Elizabeth, of afsd—do give one yoke of oxen, for her right, & benefit." April 5, 1785. Test' John Toms.

No. 461. Isacher Branch of Perq, for £25 pd by Christopher Hodgins (Hudgins), of same—sold 50a on North Side of Yeopim River Swamp, at the head of "Forked Swamp," adj John Johnson. July 9, 1785. Test' Thomas Norman, Ann Liles.

No. 462. John Guyer of Perq, & Abigail his wife, for £25 pd by John Winslow, (son of Joseph) of same—sold 25a, part of a pat' to John Perrishoe, Feb 18, 1775. John & Abigail Guyer. Sarah Morris. Seal 1, 7mo 1785. Test' John Winslow, Simon Lilly, Silas Draper.

No. 463. Isaac Wilson, & Roda his wife, of Perq, for £6 pd by Job Chappel, of same—sold 10a "upon the fork of Mill Swamp, bought of Thomas Newby of Virginia." Oct 21, 1784. Test' Pritlow Elliott, Thos Hollowell.

No. 464. Willis Butler, Admix of Thomas McNider; late of Chowan Co, N. C. pursuant to an Order of Court, of Perq Co, for £20 pd by Joshua Long, of same—sold tract of land in Perq, "on South Side of Pratts Mill Swamp," adj James Brinkley, which was sold by William Wyatt to Jeremiah Pratt, (the elder) & by Jeremiah Pratt Jr, (his son) sold to sd McNider. June 3, 1785. Test' James Mullen.

No. 465. Thomas Robinson, for £1 Sterling, pd by "my Brother William Robinson, with love, & good-will I do bear have given, a parcel of land 310a, which was bequeathed unto my dec'd Brother, Joseph, by my Father Joseph Robinson dec'd, with "provision, if he die without issue," to William Robinson (before sd), part of 4 surveys." 1, 7mo 1785. Test' Elizabeth Robinson, Aaron Morris, Miriam Morris.

No. 466. Joseph Sutton of Perq, farmer—for £111 s17 pd by Chalkey Albertson, of same—sold 78a on West Side of Suttons Creek. May 13, 1785. Test' Seth Sumner, Joseph Perisho.

No. 467. Joseph Sutton, planter—for £81 s1 pd by Joseph Perisho, of Perq, sold 50a on Suttons Creek. May 13, 1785. Test' Seth Sumner, Chalkey Albertson.

No. 468. Capt Joseph Sutton, of Perq, for £17 s2 pd by Joseph Perisho, of same—sold 12½a on West side of Suttons Creek, adj Seth Sumner. May 1, 1785. Test' Chalkey Albertson, Ana Saunders.

No. 469. "I John Barclift hath no right to the land I live on, only as I have leased it, for my life time, sd land entailed on John Turner, & his heirs, so I give up my right to him." June 5, 1784. Test' Moses Jackson, Sam'l. Barclift, Abram Knowles.

No. 470. John Turner Jr, of Perq, Farmer—for £250 pd by Abner Knowles, of afd—sold 75a on South west Side of Little River, adj Elizabeth Barclift, Joseph Mullen, & the pocosin. June 5, 1784. Test' Moses Jackson, Samuel Barclift, John Barclift.

No. 471. Benjamin Gilbert, heir-at-law of Joseph Gilbert Dec'd, for £47 pd by Benjamin Saunders, both of Perq, sold 23a on S. W. Side of Perq River, adj sd Saunders. April 16, 1784. Test' W. W. Barber, Benjamin Smith.

No. 472. Job Branch of Perq, for £150 pd by Isachar Branch, of afsd—sold 88a "in Tyrell Co" ? on Chappel Swamp, along Suttons line to a branch known as "Holly Neck Branch." May 3, 1783. Test' Fred Luten.

No. 473. Isachar Branch of Perq, for £26 pd by Job Branch, of afsd—sold 100a, on North Side of "Samuel Dickersons Mill Swamp." Mar 10, 1785. Test' Fred'k. Luten, Lemuel Long.

No. 474. April 6, 1785. James Chew of Perq, for £60 pd by Richard Skinner, of same—sold 100a, adj sd Skinner, & Charles Moore, "being land my Father bought of Abraham Jennett, & fell to me." Test' Benjamin Saunders, Job Miller.

No. 475. April 11, 1785. Hugh Miller of Perq for £5 pd by Jacob Riddick, of afsd sold 80a, (Swamp land) on South side of River Swamp, adj Stallings, & Powell, "at Hollowells old bridge." Test' Exum Newby, Benjamin Perry Jr.

No. 476. John Barrow, & Martha his wife of Perq, for £50 pd by James Skinner, of same—sold 50a on east side of Yeopim Creek, adj John Skinner. April 13, 1785. Test' Nich's. Skinner, Eri Barrow.

No. 477. Oct 11, 1785. John Wyatt of Perq, Planter—"stands bound" unto Ambrose Knox, Merchant—for the payment of £1900, as by bond, assigns 3800a, slaves, household furniture, horses, cattle, hogs, sheep, & farming utensils. (Bankrupt sale.) Test' William Stepney, J. Lane.

No. 478. Sept 21, 1785. John Wyatt, for £1510 pd by Ambrose Knox, of Pasq Co, sold 4 tracts of land, in Perq, 1st on Southwest Side of Yeopim Creek, (387a) where sd Wyatt now lives, 2d on North side of Yeopim River, called "Stevens" 112a, 3d on North side of Yeopim River called "Phillips," 196a, 4th on North Side of Yeopim River called "Felts Point," 60a. Test' Jas. Iredell, J. Lane.

No. 479. Job Branch of Perq, for £12 pd by Isachar Branch, of afsd—sold 21a, "within lines" of sd Isachar Branch Sr. Mar 10, 1785. Test' Fred'k Luten, Lemuel Long.

No. 480. Jan 5, 1785. John White of Perq, for £7 pd by Jacob Riddick, of same—sold 2½a, on the Side of "Reedy Branch," ad sd Riddick. Test' Seth Riddick, Benjamin Perry Jr.

No. 481. July 27, 1785. Jacob, & Sarah Riddick, for £100 pd by John White, both of Perq, sold 150a, on North Side of Perq River, adj Isaac Wilson, which Robert Riddick bought of Stephen Thomas, formerly Joseph Jessops. Test' Phillip Perry, Benjamin Perry Jr.

No. 482. John Staunton of Perq, for £80 pd by Thomas Layden, of afsd—sold 50a which my "Brother Thomas bequeathed to his son Thomas, & sd Thomas sold to me, ½a, where he now lives, excepting right of Thompeon ? Staunton, widow of my sd Brother," adj Joseph Godfrey. Feb 14, 1785. Test' Foster Toms, Joseph Turner Jr.

No. 483. Mary William, (deed of gift) negroes Daniel, & Hannah, to my Children Milly, John, Mary, Thomas, & Sarah Williams; "my dec'd husband James Williams." Sept 23, 1776. Test' Isachar Branch, John Wilson, Job Branch.

No. 484. Jan 31, 1785. Simeon Long & Grizzell his wife, for £500 pd by Thomas Harvey, all of Perq, sold 260a on North east side of Yeopim Creek, adj John Skinner, James Skinner, & Zebulon Calloway, where sd Long now dwells. Test' John Wyatt, Samuel Penrice.

No. 485. April 12, 1784. Charles Moore, Sheriff of Perq; John Calloway, late of Perq, was indebted unto Ambrose Knox, Admix of Joshua Wyatt dec'd in the sum of £203 s16 p3, & sd Sheriff, did "levy on all lands belonging to sd Calloway, on yeopim Creek, with grist mill thereon," did expose for sale same, which was purchased by Thomas Jones, for £312 s10 p4. Test' Josiah Jordan Jr, Benj'n Saunders.

No. 486. Mar 13, 1784. Richard Pratt, & Mary his wife, of Perq for £170 s12 pd by Reuben Long, sold 108a, on east side of Indian Creek, & Yeopim River, "on the deep branch." Test' Fred'k Luten, Thomas Penrice.

No. 487. Richard Pratt, for £147 pd by Willis Butler, of Chowan, sold 147a on West side of Indian Creek, adj James Mullen. April 12, 1785. Test' Thomas Brinkley, Thomas Penrice.

No. 488. Jan 7, 1784. Jonathan Skinner, & Esther his wife, of Perq, for £60 pd by Nathan Skinner, of same—sold 109a, by the side of Yeopim Creek, whereon John Wilson now lives, which Andrew Collins, bought of James M. McMullen dec'd. Test' William Stepney, Joshua Long.

No. 489. William Skinner of Perq, for £5 pd by Nathan Skinner, of same—sold "all right in land within mentioned." Jan 11, 1785. Test' Nathan Long.

No. 490. Lemuel Barclift of Perq, for £12 pd by Foster Toms, of same—sold 4½a. July 13, 1784. Test' John Toms, Joseph Turner Sr.

RECORDS OF DEEDS

No. 491. Gilbert Leigh, of Chowan, for £10 pd by Joseph Hosea, of Perq, sold 4½a, at the mouth of Muddy Creek, "an Estate of Inheritance." Oct 7, 1784. Test' Joseph Barclift, Z. Snoden.

No. 492. Joseph Jones of Perq, Planter—for £150 pd by Joseph Mullen, of same—sold 153a on So Wst Side of Little River. Feb 11, 1785. Test' William Arnold, Joseph Bedgood, Isaac Mullen.

No. 493. Elizabeth Barclift, & Abner Knowles, of Perq, for £100 pd by Moses Jackson, of afsd—sold 25a on South west side of Little River, adj Samuel Barclift, & Joseph Mullen. June 21, 1784. Test' John Barclift, Joshua Turner.

*No. 494. Jan 8, 1785. John Stevenson, of Pasq Co, for £125 pd by Joseph Mullen, of Perq, sold 100a, on South west side of Little River, known by the name of "Brick House plantation." Test' Othrail Lassell, John Clayton.

No. 495. James Skinner, & Ann his wife, of Perq, for £50 pd by Eri Barrow, of afsd sold 62a on east side of Yeopim Creek, adj John Skinner. April 13, 1785. Test' Richard Skinner, Jno. Barrow.

No. 496. Soloman Roberts of Perq, for £80 pd by "my Mother Mary Roberts" of afsd conveyed 50a, on South west Side of Little River, adj sd Mary, to Winslows & Benjamin Roberts line. 1, 2mo 1785. Test' William Roberts, Benjamin Roberts.

No. 497. Sept 27, 1784. John Reed, & Elizabeth Jacocks, Exors of Joseph Reed, dec'd, & William Reed, planter—all of Perq, for £290, pd by sd William, sold 75a, "near Durants point, opposite the causway," land that sd Joseph, willed to above, adj sd Elizabeth Jacocks. Test' Thomas Stephenson, Mary Reed.

No. 498. Aug 17, 1785. John White, & Huldah his wife, for £40 pd by Josiah Riddick, all of Perq, sold 53½a, on west Side of "Sandy Ridge road," adj Mary Barker. Test' Benjamin Perry Jr, Jacob Riddick.

No. 499. July 27, 1785. John White, & Huldah his wife, for £200 pd by Jacob Riddick, of Perq, sold 100a, on South Side of Perq River Swamp, opposite long point," adj Orphans of John White Sr, dec'd. Test' Phillip Perry, Benj'n. Perry Jr.

No. 500. State of N. C. for s50, per each 100a, pd by Ephrim Wingate, do grt 100a, in Perq, adj Edward Wingate, & Benjamin Sutton. Alex Martin Esq, Gov, & Comd-in-chief, at Newbern Oct 27, 1784.

No. 501. S. of N. C. for s50, pd by Thomas Harmon, do grt 32a, on North side of Yeopim River. (same as above.)

No. 502. S. of N. C. for s50, pd by John Wyatt, do grt 120, on North Side of Perq River, "between bull, & broad creeks, in beaver cove Swamp" adj Zachariah Webb. (same as above.)

No. 503. S. of N. C. for £10, per each 100a, pd by John Hasket, do grt 50a "on bee pond fork, of Vosses Creek Swamp" adj Thomas Hollowell. Feb 16, 1786. Richard Caswell Esq, Gov, & Comd-in-chief, at Kinston. Jas Glasgow Sec. John Skinner Reg of Perq.

No. 504. Feb 12, 1782. Jacob Holland, & Elizabeth his wife, of Perq, for £20 pd by Richard Banks, of afsd—sold 50a, adj Green Thach, & Jacob Hall. Test' Reuben Long, Joshua Long.

---

*A map in one of the Deed Books shows a landing on Little River called "Brick House."

No. 505. Nathan Maudlin of Perq, for £41 pd by Joseph Wells, of same, sold 50a on N. W. Side of Suttons Creek. Oct 6, 1785. Test' Cornelius Ratliff, John Saunders.

No. 506. June 6, 1785. John Creecy of Perq, for "9000 Red Oak Staves," sold land bought of Samuel Pearsons, at R—— Banks, 75a, adj Sumner, & Roger Kinyon. Test' Wm. Clemens, Joseph Morris.

No. 507. July 25, 1785. William Arkill, for £160 pd by Phillip Perry, sold 160a, by the "run of Little River," adj Solomon Roberts, "near the side of the desert," Thomas Brinkley's corner, & Jesse Perry Esq. Test' Jesse Perry, Benjamin Perry.

No. 508. Sept 12, 1785. John Gibson of Perq, planter—for £50 pd by Joseph Mullen, of afsd—sold 60a on West Side of Little River, & South Side of Deep Creek, a "deed of grt, from Joshua Barclift, to my Father, Jas. Gibson, with 40a, between the head of sd land, & Thomas Layden, which was given my Brother Jas. Gibson, in the will of my father." Test' Francis Layden, Lockhart Williams, Geo. Sutton.

No. 509. Peter Hines, of Wayne Co, N. C. for £10 pd by Wm Skinner, of Perq, sold 15a, the South-east part of land grt to Francis Beasley, Oct 8, 1717, adj Miles Harvey, Charles Moore, Richard Skinner, & Joseph Barrow. Sept 17, 1785. Test' Wm. Richards.

No. 510. Thomas Jones of Perq, for £74 pd by William Skinner, of same—sold 111a, "near the head of Thomas Jones Mill pond, on both sides of the great Swamp," adj Alex Lillington, part of a grt to sd Lillington, "nigh a place called Tongue Thicket." Oct 12, 1784. Test' Wm. Richards. (Grt to sd Lillington Mar 13, 1694.)

No. 511. John Pointer, & Mary his wife, (heir of Samuel McClanahan dec'd) for three tracts, to us secured, & £5 pd by Elizabeth Nixon, (the other co-heir) do assign to her 299a, which sd Samuel bought of Caleb Twine, & another tract, purchased by same, of Jacob Morgan 50a, also 120a, contiguous, bought of Charles Moore, Sheriff of Perq; the whole 473a. Oct 1, 1785. Test' Thomas Hosea, Geo Sutton.

No. 512. Thomas Stafford Sr, of Perq, former—for "love I bear my son Thomas of afsd—have given ½a, where I now live," adj John Saunders. April 23, 1785. Test' Henry Raper, Jr., Thomas Bateman.

No. 513. Caleb Bundy, (son of Josiah) of Pasq Co, for £20 pd by Silas Hasket, of Perq, sold 50a, on fork Swamp, which was conveyed to me, by Spencer Williams, adj John Hasket, & John Parker. 11, 3mo 1785. Test' Levi Munden, Thomas Hasket.

No. 514. Rebecca Clayton of Perq, for "love I bear my son John, do give unto sd John's son David, three negroes," Mingo, Shadrick, & Jack. Oct 8, 1785. Test' James Sumner, Elizabeth Clayton.

No. 515. Mary McClannahan, widow of Samuel dec'd, & Elizabeth Nixon, one of the co-heirs of sd Samuel, for "three tracts secured to us," by John Pointer, & Mary his wife (the other heir) transferred to them 100a, near the head of Deep Creek, which sd Samuel bought of Zebulon Snoden, also 95a contiguous to it, sd Samuel bought of Williiam Robins, & 149a, near Nags head Chappel," which sd Samuel bought of Spencer Williams, the whole 344a. Oct 1, 1785. Test' Thomas Hosea, Geo. Sutton.

No. 516. Thomas Staunton of Perq, for an "exchange, with my Father John Staunton, of same—do acquit sd John & conveyed 66a, which my uncle Thomas

Staunton, bequeathed to me in his will," excepting right of Thompeson? Staunton, widow of sd Thomas, her life, 50a, adj Joseph Godfrey, called "Hawkins folly," belonging to Joseph Mullen. 14, 2mo 1785. Test' ———.

No. 517. Aug 6, 1785. Jacob Morgan of Perq, for £50 pd by Francis Newby, of same, sold 80a, called "Charles Morgan's" on Vosses Creek, adj Francis Newby, along the Creek side. Test' Seth Sumner, Jacob Wyatt, Sarah Whedbee.

No. 518. May 11, 1785. Thomas Newby, & Francis Newby, both of Perq, for £250 pd by sd Francis, sold "all my part of a tract of land, left me by my Father Nathan Newby, to be equally divided between us," adj Samuel Mc-Clannahan 200a, also a peice in Currituck given them "in like manner," where Thomas Pugh lived. Test' Richard Skinner, J. Lane, John Mercer.

No. 519. John Stanton of Perq for "love I bear my son Thomas, & for an exchange of land, do give 66a, near the head of Little River," adj John Overman. 14, 2mo 1785. Test' Levi Munden, Thomas Layden, John Bailey.

No. 520. July 28, 1785. Joseph McAdams of Perq, "am firmly bound" unto Ambrose Knox, for the payment of £18-13s-4p as per note, sold 100a, near Deep Creek. Test' J. Lane, Hugh Nox (Knox).

No. 521. Joseph Turner, son of Edward dec'd, of Perq for "love I bear my son Joseph of afsd—do give 200a, on west side of my land," adj Thomas, & James Whedbee, on North East side of Deep Creek Swamp. Sept 4, 1785. Test' Charles Moore, Foster Toms.

No. 522. Sept 18, 1784. Charles Moore, Sheriff of Perq; Whereas: Joseph Jones of Perq dec'd, was indebted unto David, George & Benjamin White, of Pasq Co, & Joseph Sutton & Thomas Whedbee, of Perq, in the sum of £133 s13 p3, & sd Sheriff "to satisfy same, did expose for sale 250a, in Perq," which Joseph Mullen bought, for £101 s16. Test' Joshua Skinner, Nathaniel Williams.

No. 523. Nov 9, 1782. Katherine Creecy, Thomas & Sarah Creecy, his wife, for £200 pd by Richard Arrington, all of Perq, "doth sell 100a, on North east side of Yeopim River," adj John Wyatt, & Richard Cale, sd land given sd Thomas, in the will of his father, John Creecy. Test' William Arrenton, William Arrenton Jr.

No. 524. Feb 14, 1785. Joshua Wyatt of Chowan, for £60 pd by Luke White, of Perq, sold 50a on east side of the mouth of Yeopim Creek, adj Orphans of Ephrim Luten. Test' Wm Standin, Chas Collins.

No. 525. Nov 11, 1758. Right Hon'ble John Earl Granville, for s10, pd by Robert Riddick, hath grt 190a, in Perq on West side of Perq River, adj Lemuel Powell, "in the Parish of Berkeley." Test' Geo Disbrowe, Thos. Jones. John Skinner Reg of Perq.

No. 526. State of N. C. for s50, per each 100a, pd by John Toms, of Perq, do grt 26a, on South East side of Suttons Creek, "including a branch of sd Creek, called Gum Swamp," adj Williaim Bogue, now the property of Francis Newby. Richard Caswell Esq, Gov, & Comd-in-cheif at Kinston Sept 21, 1783. Jas Glasgow Sec. John Skinner Reg.

No. 527. S. of N. C. for s50, pd by John Hasket, of Perq, do grt 100a, on Southeast side of Little River, adj land formerly Robert Cox's. (same as above.)

No. 528. Thomas Caruthers of Perq, for "love I bear my Sons James, William, & Mary, of afsd—do give household furniture." Sept 2, 1785. Test' Mary Maudlin, Elizabeth Albertson, Chalkey Albertson.

No. 529. Thomas Holloway of Perq, for £8 pd by Joseph Mullen, of afsd—sold 52a, "on Landing road," & Samuel Barclift's line. (Brick House Landing on Little River.) Test' Joseph Clayton, Levi Munden.

No. 530. July —, 1758. Whereas: Zachariah Nixon of Perq, was indebted to Joshua Toms, & Judgment was obtained, & the "Sheriff did sell a parcel of land, to satisfy same"—which was bought by Francis Newby, for £25 s7 p4. Charles Moore Sheriff. Test' Zachariah Newby.

No. 531. 12, 7mo 1785. Caleb Trueblood, of Pasq Co, Ex of the will of Thomas Wilson, of Perq, did "expose for sale" land in Perq, which was purchased by Josiah Jordan, for £40 s4 p7; Test' Joseph Scott, Levi Munden.

No. 532. Thomas Jessop of Perq, for £60, pd by Joseph Elliott, (son of Abraham) of same—sold 60a on N. E. Side of Perq River, adj the main road, "opposite to Wells Meeting house." 25, 4mo 1785. Test' John Goodwin, Samuel Harrell.

No. 533. Robert Holmes, & Mary his wife, of Chowan, planter—for £40 pd by John White, of Perq, planter—sold 53½a, adj Mary Barker, on the road. July 26, 1785. Test' Eliaz Griffin, Jacob Riddick.

No. 534. Thomas Robinson, for s1, pd by "my Brother William, for love I bear him, have given 310a, left in the will of my dec'd Father, Joseph Robinson, to my Dec'd brother Joseph, who died without heirs." 1, 7mo 1785. Test' Aaron Morris, Jr, Miriam Morris, Elizabeth Robinson.

No. 535. Richard Pratt of Perq, for £57, pd by James Brinkley, of same—sold 57a on South & West side of "Pratts Mill pond." Aug 8, 1785. Test' Reuben Long, Thomas Long.

No. 536. Dec 6, 1784. Benjamin Newby of Perq, for £60 pd by Abner Harrell, of afsd—sold 40a on North east side of Perq River, "where sd Newby now dwells," adj Nathan Lacey, & John Guyer. Benjamin, & Sarah Newby. Test' Thomas Willson, John Clary, Obed Elliott.

No. 537. June 10, 1785. Charles Moore, Sheriff of Perq; Joseph Perrisho, was indebted unto Foster Toms, in the sum of £581 s3 p9, Admix of Joshua Toms Dec', & sd Sheriff, "took possession of 150a, near Nags head Chappel, & sold same to satisfy sd claims," which was purchased by Edmond Blount, for £449 s 19. Test' Henry Hall, Nathan Long.

No. 538. Jan —, 1786. Jesse Perry Esq, Sheriff of Perq; John Thach late of sd Co dec'd, was indebted to Andrew Knox, & Co, for "recovery of which Jane Blair surviving partner obtained Judgment," & sd Sheriff exposed for sale land on North Side of Indian Creek Swamp, called "Pratts Mill Swamp," now in possession of John Thach, where Joseph Williams formerly lived, purchased by James Bush, for £21. Test' Charles Moore, Richard Skinner.

No. 539. Nov 3, 1784. William Williams of Perq, planter—for £27 s10 pd by John Creecy, "sold land formerly belonging to Joseph Williams, dec'd, which was given in the will of sd Joseph, to sd William," lying on East side of Perq River, adj Francis Newby. Test' Hend'n. Luten, Foster Toms.

No. 540. Jan 9, 1786. Jean Blair, surviving partner, of Ambrose Knox, & Co; William Lindsay, late of the Town of Hertford, Mariner—did sell to Andrew Knox, & Co, 1 Lot in sd Town (No 8) which was "forfeited" to sd Jean Blair. Test' James Iredell.

No. 541. Amos Slack, & Penelope his wife, of Starrington, Co of New London, Conn, for $800 pd by Peleg Lawton, of Perq, sold 50a called "Folly land." Aug 1, 1784. Test' Nathaniel Miner, John Deneson.

No. 542. Peley Lawton of Perq, for £112 s10 pd by Joshua Skinner, of same—sold 50a, near Mines Creek by the name of "Folly land." Sept 28, 1784. Test' Thomas Harvey.

PETITIONS
Alphabetically Arranged

Anderson, Joseph, Gent; Kings Att' by law appointed. Jan 1739.

Arranton, William, for Adix, on Est of Ebinezer Leary dec'd. July 1771.

Arranton, William, for an Audit of Andrew Knox's act Martha Halsey's Est. July 17, 1764.

Arnold, Elizabeth (d of John dec'd) who m Thomas Knoles, for Est, "out of the hands of Sarah Parsons, widow, & Ex of Samuel dec'd." Oct 1745.

Ashley, Joseph, died intestate, John Ashley prayed for Admix. (no date).

Ashley, Joseph, dec'd, William Ashley, for an Order to sell perishables. Apl 18, 1785.

Barber, Aaron, for Est "out of the hands of his Gar, Wm Wood, being 21 years of age." April 23, 1750.

Barber, Mary, Admix of the Est of her Dec'd husband Moses, for an Order to sell "Stock." Oct 16, 1764.

Barclift, Elizabeth, widow of Joseph, for Admix on his Est. July 7, 1760. She relinquished her right of Admix, in favor of John Steverson. April 19, 1762.

Barclift, John, to be appointed Gar to Noah Barclift, Orphan of John. Aprill 17, 1769.

Barclift, John, and Ann his wife. Jan 3, 1739.

Barclift, Joshua, for Admix on Est of George Snowden, "his wife Jane relinquishing her right." Oct 15, 1743.

Barclift, Elender, "has gave up her wright of Admix on Est of Demson Barclift, in favor of Asa Barclift." Apl 12, 1775.

Bagley, Thomas, for his wife Est (Martha) who was widow of Samuel Moore, "now in the hands of Nathan Newby dec'd." Aprill 18, 1763.

Bagley, Thomas, for an Audit of Thomas Bagley Est. (same date).

Bagley, Betty, for Admix on Est of her dec'd husband, William Bagley. (no date).

Barrow, William, dec'd, Dowdy Barrow prays for Admix. April 1762.

Bateman, Thomas, Jr, dec'd (son of Joseph) sale of his Est. May 17, 1763.

Bartlet, Durant (Barclift) & Elizabeth his wife, for an Audit of Thos. Noles Est. Jan, 19, 1768.

Blount, Charles, rented to Capt Joseph Jones a plan' called "Ware Point," prayed for an Audit of his act, —— 1773-77.

Blount, Joseph, for "appraisement of negroes, belonging to Est of Mr. Macrora Scarbrough." Oct 1753.

Bogue, Jesse, for a division of the Est of John Morgan dec'd "who died intestate." Oct 1764.

Boswell, Joshua (age 21), for Est out of hands of James Henley. Jan 1738.

Budget, Daniel, m Ann widow of Will'm Snowden before Oct 1759 (Auditors Act.)

Burns, John, a resident on the Court house lot, house belonging to Joshua Skinner prays for "Licence to keep an Ordinary." July 1758. His "Licence Expiring," he applied for a renewal July 22, 1760, to "keep an Ordinary in the Town of Hertford."

Bush, Ann, for Admix on Est of her dec'd husband William Bush. Apl 17, 1775.

Calloway, Sarah, for gardianship of her son Thomas. (no date).

Calloway, John, Orphan of Joshua, for choice of his gardian. Apl 1744.

Calloway, Joshua, dec'd, Oct. 8, 1742, Elizabeth Admix.

Cannon, Joseph, Orphan of Jacob, in Act with his Gar, Josiah Townsend. Feby 1806.

Charles, John dec'd, wife Margaret Admix. Apl 1740.

Charles, Sam'l, for "an Order to sell perishables." Margaret Henby's Est. Jan 1770.

Charlton, John, m Rachel More (d of Robert) prays for her Est. (no date).

Chancey, Zach (rights) himself; Rebecca, John, Sarah, Penina, Hannah, Edmund. Apl 1742.

Caruthers, Ann, Admix of her dec'd husband Jacob, "to sell perishables." Oct 1759.

Cheston, Richard, for a "Road to be laid out, from Newby's Point, to the Main Road, leading to Morgan's Swamp." Granted. July 3, 1740.

Clayton, John, for "Lycence to marry Rebecca Wood, Virgin Woman under 20 years of age." Sept 20, 1745.

Collins, Nicholas, for leave to "keep an Ordinary at his Now Dwelling House in the town of Hertford." Granted. July 1758.

Collins, Nicholas, "dead without a will," Isaac Sanders prays for Admix. Apl 19, 1762.

Collins, Andrew, m Ann Hall (d of Sam'l dec'd) for her Est out of the hands of John Callaway her Gardian. (no date).

Collins, John, Bricklayer. 1760.

Colson, William, "advanced in years, prays to be Exempt from Tax." Oct 16, 1759.

Conner, Demsey, for "Est of Dorothy Trotter (Orphan of William, & Mary dec'd) out of the hands of Phineas Nixon, her Gardian, now wife of sd Conner." —, 4mo 1747.

Cox, Robert, Ex of Est of Jeremiah Hendrix dec'd. July 19, 1757.

Cox, Joseph, for proper persons to Audit Act of Robert Cox, Admix on Est of Thomas Cox dec'd. Oct 18, 1768.

Creecy, Joseph, & Henderson Standin, for division of Argile Simons Jr, Est (a minor). July 1774.

Davis, John, & Ruth his wife. Aug 21, 1711. (Pasquotank Co Records, deed book A).

Denman, Christopher, "dead without a will, Charles Moor nearest kin," for Admix. (no date).

Denman, Rebecca, for Admix on Est of her husband Charles Denman. July 1737.

Done, Henry, for an Audit of the Act of John Babb's Est. Oct 1764.

Durant, Elizabeth, & George, for "Joseph Blount, Merchant of Edenton, to be appointed their gardian." July 1740.

Eggerton, Sarah, for an Order to sell a "Water Mill on Yawpim River" Apl 1751. (widow of James).

Elliott, Abraham, Planter—died intestate, before July 21, 1766, wife Miriam relinquished her right of Admix, in favor of Cornelius Moore. He was dead Jan 30, 1756.

Elliott, Jacob, "Sheweth that John Collins, Blacksmith, owes him £5.—— 1758.

Elliott, Caleb, Gar of Pleasant, & Elizabeth Elliott (d of Jesse) Elizabeth widow of sd Jesse "refusing to deliver Est to sd Orphans." July 16, 1751.

Elliott, Elizabeth, widow of Isaac, who died intestate, prays for Admix. (no date).

Elliott, Pritlow, "Sheweth that Arthur Croxton in his will bequeathed part of his Est to gr-son Job Elliott; prays to be apt Gar. July 1766.

Elliott, James, m dau of Peter Jones dec'd, prays for Est. July 1758.

Elliott, Pleasant, & Elizabeth of age July 1757 (d of Jesse) for Est out of out of the hands of Caleb Elliott.

Farmer, Joseph, m dau of James Henby, before Apl 19, 1762, "prays for her Est."

Fletcher, Ralph, for Admix" on Est of his Uncle John Gier." July 15, 1754.

Fletcher, Ralph, in behalf of the Orphans of Jesse Winslow dec'd, "Land Entered by Thomas Fletcher for them." Oct 7, 1778.

Flury William, "desires to keep an Ordinary at his house, near Yaw'pim Chapel." Apl 1758.

Gilbert, Joel, Orphan of Josiah dec'd. Aug 20, 1762.

Griffin George, Shipright—"dec'd without a will——Emperor greatest Creitor" prays for an Audit. (no date).

Griffin, Eliab, for Admix on Est of Lydia Griffin, "being next of kin." Apl 17, 1775.

Guyer, John, dec'd, Ralph Fletcher prays for "an Order to sell Perishables." 16, 7mo 1754.

Guy?—— prays for her part of her father Wm Boswells Est. 16, 7mo 1754.

Hall, Ann, for Admix on her husband William Halls Est. July 3, 1739.

Hall, Samuel, to have "Stephen Norcom (s of John) bound to him for 5 years to learn the Coopers trade." July 1735.

Hall, John, m Dorothy widow of William Barrow, who was dead Apl 12, 1764.

Halsey, Jeremiah, for an Audit of Thomas Bonners Est, "who was Gar of Joshua, & Thomas Long (orphans of Thomas) & Wm Stepney (orphan of John)." Oct 20, 1766.

Halsey, Martha, "that William Halsey, made no will" prays for Admix. (no date).

Harmon, Thomas, for division of Est of Thomas Long Jr dec'd. Apl 18, 1774.

Harvey, Thomas, dec'd, 1733/4. He died Sept 20, 1729. (Tombstone at Belgrade).

Hasket, William, that "his Mother-in-law is dead, (Hannah) and hath left two children; Joseph, & Joshua, Infants, prays to have them bound to him." Oct 1736. (dismissed).

Hatch, Edmund, & Lamb, Orphans of Anthony, made choice of Anthony Hatch as their gardian. July 1738.

Henby, James, "dead without a will," Joseph Robinson prays for Admix. (no date).

Hendricks, Jeremiah, & Sarah, for their part of Solomon Hendricks Est. Jan 1744.

Henley, Joseph, prays for his wife Mourning Andersons Est, held by Francis & Elizabeth Nixon, from "Last will of Zachariah Nixon, who was Ex of Joseph Anderson, & Elizabeth Anderson, both dec'd." Jan 19, 1768.

Hosea, Abraham, for a division of his father Robert Hosea's Est; between himself, & brother Joseph. (no date).

Hosea, William, m dau of Thomas Trumball dec'd, prays for her Est, from James Perisho, her Gar. Jan 1739.

Horton, David, & Mary his wife, pray for her Est out of the hands of Richard Skinner. Apl 1744.

Hudson, Mary, widow of John, who died intestate, prays "by reason of her age, that her son John be made Admix, of his Est, in his own name," 15, 1mo 1753.

Hunt, John, of Pasq Co, Gent—"to gr-dau Eliz Evans a negro named Rose; prays that Caleb Bundy be apt her Gar, she being under 14 years of age, if she die to gr-sons: Hunt Evans, John Hunt Evans & Bartho Evans, when 14 years of age" Mar 18, 1796/7. (Records Pasq Co, N.C.).

(Elizabeth Evans was Att' for her husband Ashley Evans, Jan 20, 1712/13.)

Jacobs, Jacob, m dau of James Henby before Apl 19, 1762.

Johnson, William, m Mary Snowden (d of John dec'd) prays for her Est. Apl 19, 1762.

Jones, Daniell. "Edward Wilson dec'd; Sarah Jones wife of Daniel, and Eliza Wyatt wife of Samuel, dau's and heirs of sd Wilson." Sept 2, 1712.

Jones, John, prays for Admix on Est of Mary Jones (his sister)? Oct 21, 1754.

Jones, William, died intestate, Moses Barber "next of kin" prays for Admix. 16, 4mo 1753.

Jones, Zachariah dec'd (intestate) Thomas Jones prays for Admix. Apl 20, 1762.

Zachariah Jones, m Martha, d of Robert Cartright of Pasq Co.

Jones, Thomas, for Admix on Est of Thomas Pierce, "who died intestate." Jan 19, 1757.

Jones, Zephaniah, dec'd, Ann widow. Prays for an Audit of his Est, (d of Joseph Pritchard, & Eizabeth (White). July 17, 1769.

Jones, Thomas, for Admix on Est of Mary Jones; "Several Lawful Claimes" July 17, 1758.

Jordin, Charles, for Licence "to keep an Ordinary in the Town of Hertford, at his now house" April 20, 1762.

Jordan, Joseph, for "licence to keep a public House, at Little River Bridge" which was granted. (no date).

Jordan, Jane, prays for leave to sell "perishable Est" of her dec'd husband Joseph.

Jordan, Joseph, Orphans: Thomas, & Margaret. (Slaves granted them.) June 27, 1761.

Jordan, Matthew O. Jordan, living in Perq 1839, made petition.

Kirby (Cirby) Benjamin dec'd, Dr. John Craven Admix of his Est. Jan 1756.

Kenyon, Joseph, for Est in hands of George Layden. 1757/8.

Kenyon, Hannah, for her part of Est of her father Roger Kenyon. Oct 1768.

Knowles, Thomas, m Elizabeth Arnold (d of John Dec'd) prays for her Est out of the hands of Sarah Parsons, Ex of Samuel dec'd. Oct 1745.

Knowles, Thomas, dec'd, wife Elzabeth prays for Admix. (no date).

Knox, Andrew, prays for an Order to build a "Mill on his own land, on both sides of South Branch of Castletons Creek, adj lands of John Harmon, William Scarbrough, & Est of Zephaniah Jones." July 1771.

Lacey, William, m sister of Timothy Truelove, before Apl 1760.

Lacey, Mary, Exhibited will of her dec'd husband William, 17—.

Lasey, Mary Ann, Exhibited will of her husband Francis Dec'd. July 3, 1739.

Layden, Mary, prays for an Order to sell perishables Est, of her husband (George) July 19, 1762.

Layden, Francis, dec'd, July 31, 1761. Tulle Williams Gar to Orphans. (no date).

Layden, Frances, prays for division of her husband William Layden's Est, "and a part be laid off for Elizabeth, who has since m Richd Jackson." July 19, 1757.

Leary, Sarah, widow of Richard, "who died very much in debt." Oct 1757.

Leary, Sarah, "her former husband, Thomas Long" Apl 1757. She was appointed Gar of her two sons: Joshua, & Thomas Long, Orphans of Thomas, Jan 1756.

Long, William, for a division of Est of Thomas Long, Orphan of William dec'd (intestate) he being nearest of kin. Apl 1, 1761. (Thomas Long a minor).

Long, James (minor), dec'd, Sept 10, 1761, Thomas McNider Admix. (Thomas McNider m Ann (widow of William Long) mother of above James, before this date. (see Long family).

Long, Sarah, widow of Thomas dec'd "who died without a will," before July 1769. She was appointed Gar of children: Joshua, & Thomas Long, Jan 1756, m 2d Richard Leary.

Long, Elizabeth, widow of Joshua, July 1740. Prays for Admix.

Luten, Mary, for an Order to sell perishables Est of her husband, Ephrim. (no date).

Mathias, Joseph, for his Est, in hands of Ann Caruthers, Admix of Jacob. Apl 17, 1769.

Maudlin, Thomas, dec'd, Richard Clayton Admix, for an Audit of Est. Apl 1762.

Maudlin, Elizabeth, for her Est, out of the hands of Peter Jones, & Rebecca Toms, Exrs of the will of Joseph Sutton dec'd. July 1735.

Maudlin, Ezekiel, dec'd; Hannah Chancey, & Thomas Weeks Exrs, for a division by Sam'l Swann, & Richard Whidbee. Jan 1736.

Ming, Thomas, for gardianship of Elizabeth, & Orpha Rogers, Orphans of Richard dec'd. July 1766.

Morris, John "very poor" prays to be exempt from Tax. Apl 1762.

Mullen, Abraham, & Elinor his wife Admix on Est——Apl 19, 1762. He m dau of Abraham Ming, before 1743.

Mullen, Cornelius, for licence to "Keep an Ordinary at his Now Dwelling House, at the Court house" July 1755. (Granted.)

Mullen, Abraham, Jr., that "Joshua Haskett Orphan of Anthony, be bound to him." Apl 1737.

Mullen, Isaac, dec'd, Joseph Turner "nearest of kin" for Admix. Apl 20, 1762.

Mullen, Abraham, for a division of Isaac Mullens Est, "Abraham Hòsea having m Elizabeth widow of sd Isaac," heirs all minors. Jan 1746.

Murdaugh, John, dec'd, Sarah widow; for division of negroes (22). Jan 17, 1764.

Newby, Mary, Admix of Nathan, July 1735. (They lived at Newbys Point across the River from Hertford, & maintained the Ferry on their side.)

Newby, William, for Nathan Newby to be apt his guardian. July 1735 (son of William).

Newby, Joseph Newby Jr, dec'd Jan 1753, wife Elizabeth, for Admix, dau Mary Orphan.

Nichols, Thomas, m Elizabeth (d of Richard Sutton dec'd) for Est out of the hands of Henry Hall her Gar. Apl 1753.

Nicholson, Sarah, Exhibited will of her dec'd husband, Nathaniel. July 1737.

Oates, James, for "Est left him by his gr-father John Wyat, now in hands of Wm Wyatt, & Thos Pierce." (no date) Thought to be son of Joseph Oates.

Oates, Jethro, "sheweth that in the year 1738, John Wyatt in his will, left property to be divided between the children of Elizabeth Oates, his daughter and said Jethro being one of them, is now of age, and prays for his part of Est, in hands of Wm Wyatt." (no date).

Oates, John, for Est left him by will of John Wyatt dec'd, in hands of Thomas Pearce, & Wm Wyatt.

Penrice, Edward, m Sarah Moore (d of Robert lately dec'd) for her Est. (no date).

Perry, Jacob, & John Riddick, for "an Order to build a Grist Mill on a branch of Perquimans River, between Daniel Rogerson, & Thomas Lilly, for the good of the Neighbourhood" Apl 1744.

Perry, Jacob, m before Apl 1755, Ann dau of Thos Lilly, who lived in Piney Woods.

Pettiver, Capt John, complaint against Jacob Perry. Land assigned. Jan 1731/2.

Pratt, Jeremiah dec'd. Orphans: Mary, Jerm'h, Deborah, Richard, & Joseph. Thos Williams Gar. Jan 19, 1716. Elizabeth widow, m 2d Thomas Williams. They had in "their care" four orphans of John Mathias dec'd. July 1754.

Pratt, Jeremiah, for liberty to sell "Perishable Est" of Thomas Callaway dec'd. Oct 3, 1752.

Pratt, Elizabeth (d of Jeremiah (I) m John Mathias. She gave land on Yeopim River "whereon a Chapel is now built, for the worship of the Church of England" of which they were members. This Church fell into decay, and was taken over by the Baptist. Bethel Church was built on the same ground.

Redding, James, "dead without a will," brother John for Admix. Jan 16, 1753.

Reed, Joseph Blount, m Sarah Durant (d of George dec'd, who was son of John, who was son of George (I) before Oct 1741. (Prays for division.)

Reed, Christian, m Mary Durant (sister of his brother Joseph Blount Reed's wife) "for her part of George Durants Est." Jan 1738 He was dead Aug 25, 1747, and his brother Joseph appointed Ex.

Reed, William, & Christian his wife conveyed land in Pasq Co, to Joseph Jordan, Oct 21, 1701 (Pasq Co records, deed book A). Benjamin Reed died intestate before July 1766. George Reed Gent, was dead May 10, 1767, Wm. Reed Ex.

Riddick, Henry, for "an Order to keep an Ordinary, at Loosing Swamp." Apl 18, 1748. (Loosing Swamp was up near the Gates Co Line, if not in the actual county).

Riggs, Abraham, that "Joseph Hasket, Orphan of Anthony, be bound to him, until he be of age, now 13 years old, to learn the Coopers trade." Apl 1736.

Right, Samuel (Wright) gr-son of Hannah Foster, wife of James, for his Est. 1735.

Rogerson, Daniel, for leave to build a "Water Mill on his own land & land of Thos. Lilly dec'd, he living in Piney Woods, remote from any Mill" April 1755.

Sanderson, Hannah, widow of Richard for Admx on his Est, April 1736. "Capt Richard Sanderson died possessed of a considerable personal Est, leaving one son an infant without a Gardian, Joseph Sutton, & Albert Albertson pray to be appointed gardians, Jan 23, 1773; setting forth that said Hannah relict of said Richard Sanderson, "embezzled same to the Injury of said Orphan," prayed the Court that she "be obliged to give an Account to the Court of her proceeding."

Sharod (Sherwood) Elizabeth, for Est from her fathers, "out of the hands of John Jones, Ex to David Sherrod." (no date). Mary Sharrod (Rep' of Elizabeth dec, prays for her part of Mary Jones Est, in hands of John Jones. Apl 18, 1758.

Simpson, Zilpah, for Admix on her husband Benjamin Simpson Est. April, 1762.

Sittersin, Joseph, m Deborah (Relict of Adam Noles) for her Est, "in possession of Moses Jackson." Oct 4, 1796.

---

* The Inventory of Durant Reed is a most interesting paper, and reveals the standing, & great wealth of this family. This document was filed June 26, 1767, and Richard Sanderson, & Tulle Williams appear as Exrs. That he was a gentleman of quality, can be inferred from the number of silver articles there enumerated, among them; 3 Silver Shoe Buckles, 1 pr Silver Knee buckles. He made no will sad to say, therefore his children (if any) are not obtainable. Among Christian Reed's effects, offered for sale Aug 25, 1747: "1 Broad Cloath Coat, & Britches, all trimmed with Gold" shows he was something of a dandy. Joseph Reed, Gent, dec'd Aug 7, 1765, Elizabeth Extrix. She m 2d Thomas Jacocks of Durants Neck. His Inventory shows: "27 negroes, 15 horses, 73 head of cattle, 49 head of sheep," and many valuable pieces of old furniture. The division of William Reed Est, Jan 17, 1802, gives his heirs: 1 George, 2 William, 3 Tulle W. Reed, John, H Reed, & Wilson Reed (sons) and John Mullen, "in right of his wife." (See Reed family in N. C. Hist & Gen Reg, Vol. I-I).

Skinner, Joshua, in behalf of Thos Larrey, Gar of Orphans of John Wyatt dec' "that there is a Copper Still, & one steer, which he prays may be sold, for the benefit of said Orphans." (no date).

Skinner, Evan, for licence to "build a house of Entertainment, on the lott & half of ground laid out for Publick Buildings on Perquimans River, on Phelps Point." Jan 1753.

Smith, Josiah, Orphan of Francis, choose as Gar Robert Wilson. July 3, 1739.

Snoden, Mary, for Admix on her husband Samuel Snodens Est. July 7, 1758.

Snowden, Solomon, died intestate; his widow Mary, for Admix, with his brothers: Wm, & Samuel; and son (a minor) 1746. Solomon m Mary Hawkins, widow of John.

Stepney, John, m dau of Joshua Long, prays for her Est, "out of property left by Leah Long, in account with Jeremiah Pratt." (no date).

Stevenson, John for a division of his "gr-fathers Wm Stevensons Est." July 3, 1739.

Stone, Bethma, for Admix on Est of William, her husband. (no date),

Stokes, William, & wife Elizabeth; Sheweth "that our brother Frederick Snowden, died March Last under age" for Admix. April 1762.

Sumner, Luke, to "sell Perishable Est of James Sumner, decd, and make division between orphans; Robert, William, & Josiah Sumner." April 22, 1754.

Sumner, James, Est divided Sept 10, 1758, among the several heirs: Sons Luke, Seth, David, Robert, William, Josiah. To each £462 s11 p3 3 farthings. (Widow Mary, m 2d Isaac Sanders). He made report on said date that he had received a "full part" of his wife's property. From another loose paper, it appears that James Sumner had also a son James, who is not named in the aforesaid paper. Probably he was an older son, & had already received his part of his fathers Est. Josiah, & Mary Sumner, choose Isaac Sanders as their Gar, Apl 1755.

Sutton, Christopher, Orphan of Joseph, made choice of Peter Jones as his Gar. July 1737.

Sutton, Mary, Orphan of Joseph, made Joseph Sutton as her gar. July 1737.

Sutton, William, son of Richard choose as Gar, Richard Skinner. Oct 1738.

Sutton, Mary, dau of Richard, choose as Gar, Richard Skinner. Oct 1738.

Swain, Elizabeth, Relict of John, for an Order to sell perishables. Jan 22, 1766.

Swann, Henry of Perq, Mer't—appointed Wm, & Thos Swann his Att'. Sept 21, 1709.

Townsend, Wm, to be apt' Gar of his children: Rachel, Wm, & Betty, setting forth that they have received a "Legacy from their gr-father Robert Wilson." April 1759.

Tucker, John, for licence to keep an "Ordinary at his Dwelling House, near Little River." (no date).

Turner, Robert, for an Order to keep an "Ordinary in the house of Evan Skinner, on the Court house Lot" (Hertford.) no date.

Wallice, Josiah of Perq, Schoolmaster. Apl 1760.

Whedbee, Richard, Gar of Zebulon Snoden orphan of Solomon. (no date).

Whedbee, Richard, for Est left him by Solomon Snowden dec'd, "in hands of Wm Snowden."

Whedbee, Joshua, & Thomas, in account with their Gar, Joseph White, orphans of Seth Whedbee, 1805—

Whidbee, Benjamin, (s of Richard) choose Richard Sanderson for his Gar (his bro-in-law). April 1759.

White, Rachel, widow of Theophilus, for Admix. Sept 9, 1734.

Willcocks, John, for Est "left him by his wife Mary (d of Wm Woodley) and a legacy left her by her gr-father Andrew Reid (both dec'd) "now in the hands of Elizabeth Keaton. Jan 20, 1735.

Wingate, Edward, for "cattle belonging to himself, & brother Mitchell, held by his mother Mary, who had m 2d John Bushnall; their father having died intestate." Apl 1745.

Williams, Francis, for his wife Est, from John Callaway, Admix of Wm Wyatt. Apl 19, 1763.

Williams, Tulle, dec'd, Apl 1743. Samuel Scolly Ex.

Williams, Thomas, m Elizabeth, widow of Jeremiah Pratt, before July 1755.

Wilson, Jacob, for an Order to "sell Perishables of Jonathan Sherod, and to be allowed to hire out the negroes, & Rent the Lands, belonging to Peninah Anderson, Orphan to whom he is Gar." Jan 16, 1770.

Wilson, Thomas, marriage contract, to m ——ah (Sarah) Smith. Sept 9, 1734.

Winslow, Thomas, m Elizabeth Phelps (d of Jonathan, & Dorothy) before Apl 18, 1768.

Winslow, Jesse, "Orphan of Thomas" choose as his Gar, Joseph Outland. July 1752.

Winslow, Elizabeth, "Orphan of Thomas" choose as her Gar, Joseph Outland. July 1752.

(Children of Thomas (2) and wife Sarah (Nixon, d of Elizabeth) will 1747.

Winslow, Samuel, of age, for his Est, from Joshua Morris his Gar. July 19, 1769.

Winslow, Timothy dec'd Apl 20, 1772, Mary widow for Admix.

Wood, Mary, to sell Perishable Est of her husband William Wood, "who died without a will,". Oct 17, 1769.

Wright, Samuel, for Admix on Est of Comfort Dowdy, "being nearest of kin." (no date).

Wright, Samuel, "Sheweth that his gr-mother Hannah Foster (wife of James) in her will bequeathed to him sundry Household goods," & he being now 18 years of age, prays for his Est, out of the hands of Geo Gording. July 3, 1735.

DIVISIONS OF ESTATES

Albertson, Joshua, dec'd, Oct 27, 1753. Brothers: William, & Aaron.

Anderson, Sam'l, dec'd, Jan 22, 1765. Heirs: Mary Outland, Peaninah, & Sam'l Anderson Jr.

Ashley, Elizabeth, Admix, Est of her husband William. Oct 17, 1763.

Barber, William, Orphan of Moses dec'd, account of Francis Toms, his Gar. July 19, 1767. (Auditors Act.)

Barclift, Samuel, dec'd July 3, 1788. Heirs: Seth Holloway, John Davis, Mary Holloway, part divided among children of John Holloway dec'd.

Barclift, Joseph, dec'd Aug 9, 1779. Heirs. Deborah Godfrey, Mary, & Susanna Barclift, to each; £157-12-5¾.

Ballard, Abraham, dec'd Jan 12, 1758, Mr. Isaac Hill, & wife Elizabeth Exrs. Heirs: wife Elizabeth, sons: Jethro, Kedah, & Abraham, dau's: Apsilla, Bethsheba.

Barrow, William, dec'd April 12, 1764. Heirs: s Joseph, & dau Sarah, 3d part of Est to John Hall "in right of his wife" (John Hall m Dorothy widow of Wm Barrow). John Hall was Gar to Joseph, & Sarah Barrow, orphans of William, Jan 18, 1768.

Barrow, Orpha, in account with her Gar Eri Barrow. Feb 11, 1806.

Bateman, John, dec'd (no date). Heirs: Hannah, Samuel, & Mary Sutton, Hannah Robins Admix. To them was divided "Cattle at Little River, & a parcell of Smith Tools."

Boswell, Geo, dec'd Jan 1, 1741 (Inventory).

Boswell, Ichabod, dec'd June 12, 1761.

Boswell, Joshua, of age, James Henby Gar. Jan 1738.

Brinn, James, of Chowan, dec'd. Heirs: James Brinn, dau's Sarah, & Charity, wife Elizabeth, Job Chapell, & wife Ann, Jesse White, & wife Elizabeth. (no date.)

Brinn, John, dec'd, ——— 1775. Heirs: John, Joseph, Mary, Jesse, Amey, Josiah, & Ann Brinn.

Brinn, Joseph dec'd. Heirs: Nathaniel Brinn, John Roberson, & wife (not named), 1778.

Brinkley, Michael, dec'd July 30, 1745. Susannah his wife Admix (Inventory) before James Sumner J. P.

Brinkley, Sarah, dec'd July 21, 1799. Heirs: Nancy Arrenton (wife of William) Mary (wife of Thomas Arrenton) Eli, & Miles Brinkley (sons) John (s of John Brinkley) Orphans of Thos Brinkley dec'd, Miriam, & Sally Long, (heirs of Martha Brinkley, who m Joshua Long).

Bunch, America, & Joanna, Orphans of Julius dec'd, in act with Nazareth Bunch their Gar. Feb 10, 1806.

Calloway, John, dec'd Mar 7, 1772. (No legatees named.)

Chancey, John, & Miriam his wife. Jan 16, 1757.

Cotten, Josiah, dec'd May 11, 1797. To Mrs Elizabeth Cotten £408-6-8 & negroes; To Nancy Cotten negroes; to William Blount, in right of his wife Dorothy; £475, & negroes.

Doe, Jeremiah, Orphan of Ralph Dec'd, Jan 16, 1764. Charles Moore Gar. (Auditors act.)

Donaldson, William, dec'd, Sept 13, 1760, wife Mary (m 2d Zachariah Webb, before sd date). He appears as Gar to Orphans, June 20, 1763. (Auditors act.)

Elliott, Thomas, dec'd. Heirs: James, Rachel, & Mary Elliott, Orphans of Thomas Elliott dec'd (Joseph, & Moses) widow Mary, & Ruth Munden (gr-daughter) no date.

Elliott, Thomas, dec'd, Feb 18, 1797. Heirs: Mourning (widow), Miles, Abraham, Peninah, & Docton Elliott, to each £33-3-3.

Felton, Robert, "who died intestate, possessed of 140a of land, adj John Felton, Peter Perry, & Caleb Winslow, which was conveyed by William Felton Nov 2, 1809 to sd Robert, and another tract conveyed by Cader Felton dec'd Dec 1, 1809 to sd Robert, adj John Nixon, on N. Side of Cypress pond, 25a & another parcel 100a in Chowan Co." Claimants for said property: John H. Small, & Maria his wife; Shadrach Felton, Robert Felton, by his Gar Henry Skinner; Thomas Jackson, & Charlotte his wife: "Sheweth that they are joint heirs of Robert Felton dec'd."

Gilbert, Josiah, dec'd, Apl 24, 1762. Heirs: Thomas, & Joel Gilbert, Jemima Cox.

Guyer, John, dec'd July 18, 1754, Ralph Fletcher Admix. (Inventory.)

Gregorie, James, dec'd, Oct 29, 1762. Josiah Granbery Admix.

Hall, John, dec'd Feb 7, 1799. Heirs: Edward, Mary, James Elizabeth, William, Rachel, & Hannah Hall. His widow m 2d ——— Taylor.

Harmon, Thomas, dec'd, July 2, 1774. His division shows that his wife was dau of Thomas Long Jr. Elizabeth Caruthers (d of Jacob) m before this date ——— Harmon.

Harvey, William, dec'd Jan 2, 1798. Heirs: Benjamin F., Julianna, George A. (Negroes to each.)

Harvey, Benjamin Sr, dec'd. Heirs: Thomas, Benjamin F, George A. (s of William, gr-son of Benjamin), Wm M. Harvey. (No date.)

Harvey, Thomas, "Late of Perq dec'd," April 1740, Miles Gale Ex. (Minute book Perq Co 1738.)

Hatch, Anthony, dec'd Jan 14, 1744/5. Relict Elizabeth Admix. (Inventory.)

Hatch, John, of Onslow Co N. C. appointed Wm Reed of Perq Att', Dec 14, 1770.

Hendricks, Solomon, Planter—dec'd, Dec 17, 1744. Sarah his wife Admix, son Jeremiah. (Inventory) Thomas Weeks J. P.

Hosea, Joseph, & William, orphans of Joseph dec'd ——— 1762, with John Stanto Gar.

Hosea, Joseph, dec'd 1758.

Jessop, Thomas, dec'd 12, 12mo 1744. Heirs: Mary, Thomas, Elizabeth, Jonathan, & Enoch Jessop & Joseph Munden.

Jordan, Joseph, dec'd Aug 10, 1760. Wife Jane Admix. Sale of slaves June 27, 1761. Heirs: Thomas, & Margaret Jordan.

Jordan, Mary, dec'd 4, 5mo 1797. Heirs: Elizabeth, Thomas, Josiah, & Mathew Jordan, Robert Watkins, Sarah White (d of Francis) to each £43-12-4.

Exum Newby, & Gabriel White Exrs.

Kinyon, Joseph, d. s. p. Mar 11, 1764, Roger Kinyon Admix. (Auditors act.)

Kinyon, Joab, Orphan of John, dec'd, Thomas Saint Gar, Jan 18, 1768. (Auditors act.)

Knowles, Adam, dec'd, Jan 27, 1762. Wife Sarah Admix, dau's: Deborah and Sarah.

Knowles, John, dec'd, Apl 23, 1773. (Appears to have had no heirs.)

Kirby, Benjamin, dec'd, Oct 1756, Dr John Craven Ex.

Lamb, William, dec'd May 7, 1774. Heirs: Elizabeth Pearson, Miriam, & Mary Lamb.

Leigh Francis, 1801. Heirs: Partheny Barclift, Wm Whedbee, Richard, Thomas, James, & Benjamin Leigh.

Lilly, Thomas, dec'd Oct 12, 1753. Ann Lilly Admix. Inventory.)

Long, James, dec'd, Feb 5, 1762. Heirs: Wm Long; representatives of Sarah Wyatt dec'd, Reuben & Simeon Long, Wm McNider, in right of his mother.

Long, Simeon, Orphan of William, choose Thos McNider as his Gar, Feb 1762. (Thomas McNider, m Ann widow of William Long, before this date.)

Long, Reuben, & Simeon, property sold by their Gar Thos McNider, "at Public Vendue" Sept 11, 1761. Thomas Long (a minor) was dead Sept 10, 1761. James Long also dec'd, same date; Thos McNider Admix.

Martin Stephen, Blacksmith, July 28, 1749.

Maudlin, Ezekiel, Gent, dec'd, 1737. Heirs: Jeremiah, Thomas, Joshua, Hannah.

Maudlin, Ezekiel, dec'd, July 10, 1745, Mary Maudlin, & John Perry Exrs. Among effects, "1 old Bible."

Mullen, Abraham, dec'd Nov 25, 1762. Heirs: Elener widow: £37-17-2, Joseph Turner, in right of his wife; Gideon Maudlin, in right of his wife; Tamer Hassell (dau); Wm Bateman in right of his wife; Miriam, & Deborah Mullen (The last m Christopher Towe). Abraham Mullen was son of Jacob, & brother of Isaac.

Nixon, Zachariah, dec'd, 3, 2mo 1743 (s of Zach) widow Elizabeth, Admix. (She was dau of Francis Toms, m 1st Samuel Phelps, 2d Zach Nixon; she had dau Sarah who m Thomas Winslow (2), and had gr-dau Elizabeth Winslow, named in her will. It is not positively known if this dau was by her Phelps husband, or by Zachariah Nixon.)

Nixon, Delight, dec'd May 11, 1802. Wife Abselah Admix; s John, s Delight, dau Sarah.

Nixon, Phineas, dec'd 14, 4mo 1774. Son Barnable. (Inventory.)

Norcom, Joseph, decd, Nov 28, 1797. Heirs: Frederick, Charles, Martha, & Benjamin Norcom, Sarah Howcott, Elizabeth Beasley, & Mary Hoskins. To each is given £79-12s.

Peirson, John, dec'd, Feb 2, 1761. Wife Elizabeth Admix. (Sale of his Est.)

Peirce, Thomas, dec'd; division by order of Court, Oct 1757. To Alice Calloway (his mother) to Sylvanus Wilson, in right of his wife; John Chancey, in right of his wife; To Mary Barto (Half sister) To Caleb Calloway (half brother) to John Calloway (half brother).

Pierce, Joseph, dec'd, Feb 1806. Heirs: Abraham, Joshua, Margaret, & Elizabeth. (In act' with their Gar William Hollowell.)

Peirson, John, dec'd, Feb 2, 1761. Elizabeth widow, Admix. Sale of Est.

Perrishow, James, dec'd, Jan 2, 1744, Sarah Relict. (Inventory.)

Perry, Phillip, dec'd Apl 10, 1754. Heirs: wife Judith, Sarah, Mary, Jesse, Phillip, Elizabeth, Rachel, Judith, & Miriam Perry.

Perry, William, dec'd, Feb 9, 1802. Heirs: Selah Edwards, Thomas Perry, Penelope Goodwin (wife of William).

Perry, Jacob Sr, dec'd, Feb 27, 1799. Heirs: Miles, & Lawrence Perry, Hephzibah Bogue, Mornica Bunches, to each £25-2-8¾.

Perry, Reuben, dec'd, July 1775. Wife Esther, Admix. Thomas Harvey Clk.

Pratt, Jeremiah, dec'd, Mar 2, 1762; Thomas, & Elizabeth Williams Exrs. Heirs: Children of Joshua Long dec'd; Thomas Long, James Luten, Charles

Blount, Timothy Truelove, Lidia Herron, James Craven, William Wyatt, Joseph White, Jacob Caruthers, Robert Harmon, Henry Warren. Jacob Caruthers made Gar of Orphans of John Mathias (who m Elizabeth Pratt dec'd) Jeremiah Pratt m Elizabeth dau of Robert Rowe, who m 2d Thomas Williams. Jeremiah Pratt dec Nov 9, 1754.

Pratt, Richard, Orphan of Jeremiah dec'd, Jan 22, 1767, Jeremiah Pratt Gar. (Auditors act.) Joseph Pratt orphan of Jeremiah (same date, & Guardian).

Pritchard, Mary, dec'd Apl 9, 1766. Inventory shows 3 negroes, "James, Jacob, & Jude." She bequeathed to her "gr-mother Rachel White a negro man called Jacob," and Rachel White (wife of Thomas, whose will is found in will book C, p 1, Perq. Co) in like manner left said negro Jacob to one of her sons. Her will found behind an old looking glass, by an antique dealer in Suffolk, Va, had never been signed, or probated. (See White family).

Pritlow, Keziah (née Pierce, dau of Thomas, m 1st Nathan Newby, 2d Francis Nixon, 3d Samuel Pritlow) was allowed £13-13-1 for "keeping the ferry from her point to Hertford, on Public days." Signed by William, & Miles G. Skinner. Jan 1781. "Wm Skinner Treasurer of Perq, & Miles G. Skinner Clk."

Reed, Joseph, with sons: Joseph, & Christian, on Joseph Suttons Tax List 1763

Reed, Susannah (d of Benjamin) m Tully Williams, before May 7, 1811.

Redding, John, dec'd Feb 2, 1755; Joshua Small Ex. (Auditors act.)

Robinson, William, dec'd. 4. 3mo 1799. Heirs: William, & Josiah Robinson.

Roe, Robert, dec'd Jan 19, 1756. Francis, & Tabitha Pickering Exrs.

Roe, Robert, dec'd, July 19, 1763 (division). Heirs: Elizabeth Williams, Robert Rowe.

Rowe, Robert, dec'd, Apl 17, 1756 (Audit). Orphans: Elizabeth, John, & Robert. William Skinner Gar.

Rowe, Robert Jr, was 21 years of age July 16, 1770. (Act with his Gar.)

Rountree, Moses, dec'd, Apl 4, 1757. Heirs: Sarah Lilly, Moses, Hannah, Lindy, & Ann Rountree. In the division he left to "son Moses a Bible, & Prayer book."

Saint, Daniel, dec'd. Heirs: Sons Hercules, & Daniel, dau Rachel, Samuel Charles, Cornelius Ratcliff. Jan 18, 1783. He was a Carpenter by trade, and "Exhibited an act in Court July 1756, for Repairing the county Goal."

Saint, Elizabeth, dec'd, Jan 28, 1779. (See Deeds.)

(A sale of perishables belonging to Est of Joseph Ratcliff was made Feb 5, 1761, widow Mary Admix.)

Skinner, Richard, dec'd, Jan 17, 1782. Heirs: son Evan Skinner, heirs of Samuel Skinner; heirs of Joshua Skinner; William Skinner, Steven Skinner, to each is bequeathed 2 negroes.

Snowden, Thomas, dec'd, Dec 1736. Widow Elizabeth. Sons: William, Joseph, George; three youngest children: Sam'l, Solomon, & Lemuel. Richard Whedbee Ex.

Speight, Isaac, dec'd July 27, 1751. Widow Mary. Orphans: Mary, Isaac, & Elizabeth. His Inventory shows: "35 young negroes, 25 old ones in "Bartie County, not yet in his possession," 30 head of Black cattle, 25 sheep, 52 hogs."

Smith, John dec'd, Jan 18, 1766, orphans: Rachel, Peninah, & John. (Auditors act.)

Stepney, John Esq, dec'd July 11, 1761. Orphans: Mary, Rachel, John Jr dec'd; heirs of William Wyatt dec'd; Sarah widow. John Calloway Admix.

Sutton, Joseph Esq, dec'd April 1783. Heirs: Elsbury, & Samuel Sutton. He died before May 14, 1772, when sale of his property, "Ware Point Plantation," was made, which sold for £60.

Sutton, George, dec'd May 2, 1733 .Heirs: Hannah, Samuel, Mary Sutton. Hannah Robins Admix.

Sutton, Samuel, dec'd Aug 8, 1797, Children (not named) widow m 2d Thomas Whedbee.

Swann, Samuel, dec'd June 13, 1771. He appears to be the last of his name in Perq, and no heirs are given.

Toms, Joshua, dec'd 28, 3mo 1783. Heirs: Millicent, & John Toms. He owned 7 negroes.

Towe, Christopher. "Have received from my mother-in-law Elenor Mullen, all Goods, & Chattels Due my wife Deborah, in care of her said mother." Dec 21, 1765 (He m Deborah, dau of Abraham Mullen, & wife Elenor).

Trumball, Thomas, dec'd (no date). Heirs: William, & Mary Trumball.

Tucker, John, on Tax list of Sam'l Barclift (Constable), Oct 20, 1760.

Turner, Thomas, dec'd Nov 9, 1792. Heirs: Benjamin Turner, Anne Charles, Martha (dau) under age, Mary dau, Mary Foster (widow m 2d Elsbury Foster).

Weeks, Thomas Esq, dec'd. Orphans: James, & Wilson Weeks, wife Elizabeth Gar. June 10, 1763.

Wells, Francis, dec'd Aug 10, 1745. Margaret widow Admix. Inventory proven before Joseph Sutton J. P. "83 hogs, 8 horses, 27 cattle, money £13 in hands of John Perry.

Wensley, Henry, was living in Perquimans, June 9, 1742, owned 9 slaves. (Tax List.)

White, Arnold Sr, deed of gift, Pasquotank Co, Apl 19, 1720, (negroes) "to dau Ann a girl Doll, Son Joshua girl Bess, dau Sarah girl Jenny," son Ishmael, dau Parthenia.

White, Anna, dec'd 9, 2mo 1798. Heirs: Martha Sanders, Benjamin, Josiah, & Parthenia White.

White, Henry, of Albemarle, "for love I bear my son-in-law John Morris" conveyed a patent bearing date, Sept 25, 1663. Land adj Robert Lowery, in Pasq Co. He had "liberty to sell said land" Apl 18, 1704. Tho Abington C. C.

White, Henry, s and heir of Henry of (Perq) & Arnold White Jr (s of Henry dec'd) assigned land in Pasq Co, bequeathed to them in his will, unto Aaron Morris of Pasq Co. Jan 18, 1725. (Records Pasq Co.)

White, Joseph, dec'd Oct 1756. Sons: John, William, Thomas, Theophilus. "Isaac Atmore a part of Est."

White, William, dec'd July 1772. His Inventory shows "23 negroes, and £458-2-9 in money." (No heirs are mentioned.)

White, John, dec'd Apl 19, 1774. Rachel & Silas White Exrs. Orphans: Jesse, & James. His division, June 22, 1774. Mother Rachel White (née

Jordan) Benjamin Winslow (brother-in-law) Elizabeth Griffin, brothers: Silas, John, Jordan, Charles, Jacob, & Benjamin White.

Williams, James, dec'd, Feb 7, 1802. Heirs: John Smith, J. B. Williams, John Nixon, Luke White.

Wilson, John, dec'd, Nov 24, 1798. Heirs: Rebecca Webb, Amey Wilson.

Wilson, Elizabeth, dec'd Oct 16, 1802. Heirs: Son John, Nathan, Bagley; heirs of Ephrim Bagley; Zilpah Low, Hannah Ratliff, Elisha Munden, Christopher Wilson, & Sarah Johnson.

Winslow, Jesse, dec'd Jan 11, 1771, Widow Martha, Admix. (Inventory) "12 negroes." Martha Winslow appears to have been dau of Thomas Fletcher. Ralph Fletcher made a petition Oct 7, 1778, "in behalf of orphans of Jesse Winslow, for land entered by Thomas Fletcher."

Winslow, Caleb, "orphan of Timothy," guardian Jacob Winslow (brother) Jan 17, 1768. (Auditors Act.)

Winslow, John, dec'd, 26, 2m 1755, Mary widow Admix. His inventory shows: "5 negroes, 2 horses, 45 cattle, 12 sows, 60 pigs, 19 sheep, 25 geese."

Woodley, John, dec'd 15, 5 mo 1798. Heirs: Pleasant Barber, (widow of dec'd) heirs of William Woodley; heirs of Elizabeth Bundy; Elizabeth Haskit, Moses Stone.

Woodley, Andrew, dec'd, 1762, widow Ann Admix.

Wright, Samuel, dec'd July 16, 1757. Heirs: Thomas, Mary, Hannah, & Samuel Wright, John Chancey, wife Miriam.

Wyatt, William Esq, dec'd. Sale at Public Vendue, Feb 6, 1761. Settlement Jan 21, 1764. Heirs: John, Mary, & Joshua Wyatt (Orphans).

Wyatt, Jacob, dec'd Apl 21, 1791. Heirs: Joshua & Mary (infants) Thomas McNider "intermarried with Ann, widow of William Long; gr-father of said infants, and James Long, one of said orphans of said William died, and said Thomas did possess himself of his Est. and Hatten Williams had taken into his possession two Oxen belonging to said Ann Long." Apl Court 1760.

Marriages

(At Random)

Albertson, Peter, m Ann Jones, before Mar 9, 1703. (Legal papers in Perq.)

Albertson, Nath'l, "uncle of Sarah Harris," Mar 9, 1703. (Legal Papers in Perq.)

Albertson, Josiah, Intention, m with Keziah Tatlock, 16, 1mo 1796. (Pasq Mo Meeting.)

Albertson, Francis (of Suttons Creek Perq), with Caroline Bell, 17, 9mo 1796. (Pasq Mo Meeting.)

Albertson, Benjamin (of Suttons Creek Perq), with Miriam Bell, 19, 8mo 1797. (Pasq Mo Meeting.)

Anderson, Benjamin, with Mary Morris, 21, 2mo 1795. (Pasq Mo Meeting.)

Arnell, Sarah (d of Samuel Parsons), July 1745. (Legal papers in Perq.)

Arnold, Elizabeth (d of John dec'd), m Thos Knowles, before Oct 1745. (Deeds.)

Arrington, William, m sister of Samuel Bond, before Mar 5, 1757. (Deeds.)

Arrington, William, mother Abigail, son Edward, Jan 17, 1763. (Deeds.)

Arrington, Richard, m Susannah Harmon (d of John) before Nov 9, 1782. (Deeds.)

Ashley, Sarah, sister of John Barrow, May 19, 1745.

Ashley, James, m Elizabeth Langley, widow, Nov 1, 1752. (Mar bonds Norfolk Co, Va.)

Bailey, Henry, m Elizabeth Overman, Intention, 18, 1mo 1786. (Pasq Mo Meeting.)

Baker, Moses, m Elizabeth Browne, Jan 12, 1694/5. (Elizabeth City Co, Va.)

Baker, Thomas, m Penelope Williams, Jan 12, 1763. (Edgecombe Co, N. C.)

Barclift, John, m Anne Parish (d of John) before Mar 24, 1738. (Legal papers.)

Barclift, Sarah, (d of Thomas Weeks) Jan 19, 1771. (Legal papers.)

Bateman, John, m Miriam Perrishoe (d of Joseph) before Oct 7, 1776. (Legal papers.)

Bateman, Mary (d of Thos Holloway) Jan 1750. (Thos Hollowells will.)

Beasley, Robt, m Christian Luten (d of Thomas, & Constance) prior to July 19, 1735.

Beasley, Mary, "her dec'd husband Robert Beasley" 1690. (Division.)

Beasley, John, m Sarah Lilse, Sept 30, 1752. (Chowan Mar bonds.)

Bell, John, (Intention) with Sarah Bundy, 21, 11mo 1789. (Pasq Mo Meeting.)

Belman, Esther, "was allowed her freedom from John Turner," at a meeting of Friends in Pasq Co, 21, 12mo 1712. (Symons Creek.)

Barrow, Joseph, m Sarah, widow of Joseph Pritchard Sr, 12, 10mo 1749. She m 2d Edmund Chancey, before 2, 11mo 1768.

Biar, Richard, m Jane Loedman, Jan —, 1682. She m 2d Wm Newby, before 1701.

Blaiton, George, m Mrs Lidia Larker, Jan 21, 1689. (Berkeley Par Reg.)

Blake, David, (s of Thomas, & Mary) m Mary Standridge (d of Thomas, & Margaret) Jan 30, 1784.

Blanchard, Josiah, m Martha Winslow, Nov 3, 1856. (Mar bonds Chowan Co.)

Blount, Joseph, m Elizabeth (widow of Macrora Scarbrough) before July 22, 1755.

"Benjamin, eldest son of said Macrora Scarbrough." (Deeds.)

Bogue, Samuel, m Elizabeth Morgan (Intention) 15, 7mo 1797. (Pasq Mo Meeting.)

Bogue, William (of N. C.) m Sarah Duke (d of Thomas, late of Nansemond Co) 15, 12-1727.

Boice, Epohroditus, m Ann (d of William Carman) no date.

Bundy, Benjamin, (Intention) with Sarah Bell, 21, 9mo 1785. (Pasq Mo Meeting.)

Bundy, Joseph, (Intention) with Elizabeth Henley, 19, 10mo 1785. (Pasq Mo. Meeting.)

Bundy, Caleb Jr, (Intention) with Rachel Nicholson, 19, 10 mo 1785. Pasq Mo Meeting.)

Bundy, Sarah, (Intention) with John Bell, 21, 11mo 1789. (Pasq Mo Meeting.)

Bundy, John, (Intention) with Jemimah Low, 21, 8mo 1790. (Pasq Mo Meeting.)

Bundy, Josiah, (Intention) with Miriam Perisho, 15, 2mo 1792. (Pasq Mo Meeting.)

Bundy, "Miriam Bundy, very much decayed in mind" 21, 3mo 1801. (Pasq Mo Meeting.)

Bundy, Moses, m Elizabeth Jones, (Intention) 15, 12mo 1796. (Pasq Mo Meeting.)

Bundy, Gideon, & Reubin (sons of John dec'd) moved to Back Creek, Randolph Co, N. C. before 6, 10mo 1796. (Minutes of Pasq Mo Meeting.)

Bundy, Jean, (d of John Parish) see his will Perq p April 1759.

Burnley, Thomas, m Hannah Chancey (d of Edmund) before Apl 2, 1684. (She made choice of Matthew Toler, "as her guardian.")

Castleton, George, (s of George, & Mary, of New Castle on line, in England) m Hannah Perishoe (Relict of James) by Mr. Thomas Gordon, 13 ——— 1679. (Berkeley Par Reg.) Hannah Perisho née Hill, it is *thought* m 3d Ezekiel Maudlin.

Chancey, Miriam, wife of John, was dau of Joseph Pierce (or Paine) Oct 18, 1757.

Chappel, Isaac, m Elizabeth Palin (Intention) 18, 8mo 1787.

Chappel, Joseph, m Sarah Squires, (Intention) 16, 8mo 1788. (Pasq Mo Meeting.)

Charlton, John, m Rachel More (d of Robert). (No date.)

Clary, William, m Elizabeth Nicholson (Relict of Joseph) In, 20, 12mo 1786. (Pasq Co.)

Clayton, Elizabeth, (d of Thomas Harvey) see his will p Perq, Nov 10, 1729. (She was wife of Zebulon Clayton 1735.)

Clayton, John, m Rebecca Wood of Virginia "under 20 years of age" Sept 20, 1745.

Clayton, Richard, m Mary Swann (d of Samuel dec'd) before Oct 25, 1776.

Coffin, Francis, m Mary Thurston, July 21, 1692. (Berkeley Par Reg) d May 5, 1700.

Cofield, William, (of Nansemond Co Va) m Elizabeth Sheppard, Jan 5, 1694/5. (E City Co.)

Collins, Andrew, m Ann Hall (d of Samuel) no date.

Cooke, John, m Elizabeth Elker, Feb 20, 1693. (Berkeley Par Reg.)

Copeland, Joseph, came from New England to Isle of Wight Co Va. He was already in that county before the able preacher Thomas Corey made his memorable visit in 1699, and exhibited to the minister his mutilated right ear which had been cut off in New England by the Presbyterians. He m Mary ———, who was dead 27, 3mo 1678. He had probably a son Joseph, who m Elizabeth (d of Thomas Taberer) who is named in his will, p in said Co, Feb 1794. Thomas Taberer left to his gr-son Joseph Copeland "400a called Basses Choice." No connected line can be made, but it seems certain the Copelands in Perq must be a branch of this family.

Copeland, Thomas, m Mary Murrey 18, 11mo 1749. (Pagan Creek Mo Meeting, Isle of Wight.)

Copeland, James, m Martha Johnson, 17, 11mo 1745. (Pagan Creek Mo Meeting, Isle of Wight.)

Copeland, (William, who made his will in N. C. (Co not given) Oct 23, 1720, names sons: William, John, *James*, & Charles, wife Christian.)

Corprew, John, m Euphan Wilson, 3, —— 1756. (Norfolk Co mar bonds.)

Cosand, John, m Sarah Morgan (Intention) 15, 2mo 1792. (Pasq Mo Meeting.)

Cox, Joseph, m Margaret Roberson (d of John, & Ann) no date.

Cox, Joseph M., m Sylvia Cain. (No date.)

Cosand, John, m Sarah Morgan, In, 15, 2mo 1792. (Pasq Mo Meeting.)

Culpeper, Mr John, m Mrs. Sarah Mayo. Ang 23, 1688. (Berkeley Par Reg.)

Collins, Thomas, & Peter were among the living in Warrick Squeake, Feb 16, 1623. (Hotten.)

Collins, John, m Mary Tooke, of Surry Co (at Wm Breden's house in Isle of Wight) 14, 12mo 1682, witnessed by Wm Goodman, and Rebecca Goodman.

Collins, Thomas, m —— Pricklove (Pritlow) in Perq Co, July 4, 1705.

Collins, John, in Ketch Neptune, bound for Carolina. July 2, 1679. (Transportations.)

Davis, Thomas, m Rebecca Wood, In, 20, 2mo 1790. (Pasq Mo Meeting.)

Davis, Joshua, m Miss Sarah Mitchell, Aug 11, 1765.

Davenport, Richard, m Johanna —— issue: Elizabeth, b July 3, 1676— John, b Nov 3, 1677.

Dorman, Richard, m Ann Nicholson (Relict of Christopher) June 26, 1690. Orphans of Christopher Nicholson dec'd, Joseph, John, & Nathaniel, who made choice of "their brother Samuel," as Guardian, Apl 8, 1690. Richard Dorman "Qualified as Gar for Sarah, Elizabeth, Christopher, & Ann, children of sd dec'd," on same date.

Evans, James, m Miriam Jordan, Feb 19, 1785. (Mar bonds Chowan Co.)

Evans, James, m Penelope Gardner, Mar 29, 1801. (Mar bonds Chowan Co.)

Evans, James, m Huldah Chapple, Sept 28, 1807. (Mar bonds Chowan Co.)

Evans, James, m Betsy Asbell, June 4, 1808. (Mar bonds Chowan Co.)

Evans, John, m Elizabeth Asbell, Aug 18, 1797. (Mar bonds Chowan Co.)

Everigin, William, m Elizabeth Henley, In, at Newbegun Creek, Pasq Co, 16, 9mo 1711.

Fendall, John (s of Josias, & Mary) m Elizabeth Lillington (d of Alex, & Elizabeth) Apl 3, 1694/5. John Fendall dec'd, Dec 20, 1695. Elizabeth widow of John, m 2d Samuel Swann, his 2d wife. (See deeds.)

Foster, Francis (of Accomack), s of William, & Margaret, m Mrs Hannah Gosby (relict of John, née Nicholson) Aug 14, 1694, by Mr. John Whidby, Magst. (Berkeley Par Reg.)

Foster, William, m Diana Harris (widow of Thomas) —— 1675, by Rev Mr Taylor.

Foster, John, m Ann Williams, "at Hannah Phillips house, in Perq" May 1, 1689. (Berkeley Par Reg.)

Foster, Robert, "late of this County" died at the house of Thos. Clarke, Nov 24, 1695.

Foster, Ann (wife of John) died Oct 30, 1692. (Berkeley Par Reg.)

Foster, John, m 2d Elizabeth Barclift, ? and had issue: Susannah, b Dec 17, 1695—Elizabeth, b Oct 17, 1698—Richard, b Oct 20, 1701.

Gilbert, Mary, dau of Thomas Bagley, whose will was p in Perq April 1762.

Gilbert, Josiah, m Sarah Outland. In, 15, 11mo 1794. (Pasq Mo Meeting.)

Gilbert, Josiah, m 2d Dorothy Nixon, In, 18, 2mo 1797. (Pasq Mo Meeting.)

Glover, Catherine, widow of Gov Wm Glover, m 2d Tobias Knight, whose will was p in Perq Co, July 17, 1719. She had by first husband one dau, Elizabeth.

Gosbey, John, (s of John, & Mary) m Hanah Nicholson (d of Christopher, & Hannah) July 5, 1685. She m 2d Francis Foster, "of Accomack Co Va" Aug 14, 1694.

Granbery, Josiah T, m Sarah Ann Sawyer, Jan 16, 1826. (Chowan Mar bonds.)

Gray, Thomas, (s of John, & Tabitha) m Sarah Beasley (d of Robert, & Sarah) May 5, 1701.

Grey, John, m Elizabeth Butler, Jan 10, 1703/4. (Berkeley Par Reg.)

Griffin, Josiah (of Piney Woods Perq Co) m Ann Perisho, 16, 9mo 1797. (Pasq Mo Meeting.)

Grimes, William, m Elizabeth Freeman, Dec 24, 1807.

Gumms, Matthew, m Elizabeth (d of Richard Skinner) before Oct 19, 1739.

Gunfalis, Lawrence, m Sarah ———— & had James, b Oct 17, 1684.

Guyer, John, m Abigail Perisho (d of John dec'd) ———— 1787. She was living in Perq Co, 11, 2mo 1806. Sold land on that date, left her by her father.

Hall, Elizabeth, (wife of Moses) was dau of Richard Davis, m before June 14, 1739.

Hall, John, m Catherine ———— before Nov 6, 1690.

Hall, Rachel (sister of James Houghton of Perq, who names her & her children: Edward, Henry, & Mary Hill, in his will) p Apl 1758.

Hall, Samuel, m Margaret Bibing ———— 1676. (Berkeley Par Reg.)

Hall, William, m Ann Mathews (d of George) before Aug 25, 1705. Had dau Sarah b on that date.

Hankok, Stephen, (s of Roger, of Dorset Sheare, in England) m Margaret Drak (d of John, & Mary) "by Mr. Will Nelson, Minister of gospell," Dec 22, 1673. (Berkeley Par Reg.)

Hanbey (Henby), John, m Judith Attaway, July 1, 1688. (Berkeley Par Reg.)

Hog, James, (s of John, of York Sheare in ————) M Ann Kent (d of Thomas, & Ann) "Late of this Co" by ———— June 10, 1679. (Berkeley Par Reg.)

Hopper, Thomas, m Joannah Kinchett, Oct last, 1689. (Berkeley Par Reg.)

Hopkins, John, m Sarah Chaston, Jan 14, 168—. (Berkeley Par Reg.)

Haskitt, Jesse, m Miriam Palin, Intention, 9, 10mo 1785. (Pasq Mo Meeting.)

Haskit, William, m Hannah Bagley, Intention, 20, 7mo 1793. (Pasq Mo Meeting.)

Haskit, Joseph, m Jemima Tatlock, Intention, 17, 7mo 1802. (Pasq Mo Meeting.)

Henley, John Jr, m Keziah Nixon, Intention, 20, 9 mo 1788. (Pasq Mo Meeting.)

Henly, Joseph, m Mourning Anderson, (widow of Joseph) before June 19, 1768.

Hosea, William, m dau of Thomas Trumball dec'd, before Jan 1739. (Legal papers.)

Hosea, Robert, m Sarah Sutton (d of Joseph) before July 15, 1769. (Legal papers.) (Had a dau Elizabeth, who m ——— Mullen, & had Joseph Mullen.)

Hosea, Joseph, m Betty (widow of Wm Bateman) before Oct 21, 1773, she had by first husband s Joseph Bateman.

Jackson, William, m Mary ——— issue: Margery, b Jan 2, 1718—Susannah, b Aug 7, 1723—Parthenia, b Apl 10, 1719—Moses, b Dec 28, 1720—Aaron, b Feb 23, 1725—Ruth, b June 14, 1727—Priscilla, b Nov 8, 1729. (Mary Jackson d of Thos. Barclift.)

Jacocks, Jonathan, of age 1707 (son of Thomas Jacocks of Little River).

Jacocks, Thomas, m Elizabeth Reed, widow of Joseph, née Durant (d of George (2) before May 18, 1771. Deed to son John Reed on said date.

Joiles, Cornelius, m Hannah Vose, Mar 24, 1687. (Berkeley Par Reg.)

Johnson, John, m Sarah Gunfallis, June 1, 1689. (Berkeley Par Reg.)

Jones, Jonathan, m Margaret Vose, Feb 1, 1688. (Berkeley Par Reg.)

Jones, (Peter?), m Elizabeth Waite (Wright, or White) Last of Feb 1693.

Jordan, Solomon, m Eliza Walker, relict of John, prior to Nov 4, 1713. (Col records.)

Kenedy, Joseph, m Jane Ratcliff, 20, 7mo 1696. (Chuckatuck Mo Meeting.)

King, John, m Winifred Conner, Oct 21, 1695. (Mar bonds Elizabeth City Co, Va.)

Knox, Andrew, m Christian (d William, & Martha Halsey) Aug 7, 1756. (Deeds.)

Lary, John, m Abigail Charles, 21——— (Berkeley Par Reg.)

Lawrence, John, m Martha Ricks, 6, 9mo 1740. (Pagan Creek Mo Meeting, Isle of Wight.)

Lawrence, John, of Rich Square N. C., m Margaret Nixon, In, 21, 1mo 1797.

Leper, Thomas, m Ann Kent (widow of Thomas). No date.

Leary, Cornelius, m dau of Richard Bentley, before Apl 24, 1689.

Lerry, Sarah, (wife of Richard?) was former wife of Thos. Long, Apl —, 1757.

Leyden, Francis, m Hariet Godfrey, June 24, 1856. (Mar bonds, Pasq Co.)

Leigh, Edward A., m Grizzell E. Jacocks (both of Perq) July 28, 1857. (Pasq Co.)

Lilly, John (s of John, & Alis) "Late of ——— Sheare, in Ould England" m Jane Swetman (d of George, & Amey, Late of Cheeh Sheare, England) Last of May, 1682.

Lilly, John, m 2d Hannah Phillips (widow) Last of March, 1690. (Hannah Phillips was wife of Henry, in whose house the first Quaker meeting in Perq was held, or rather under the Cypress trees near their home.)

Long, Mary, (d of Francis Penrice) April 1758. (Legal papers.)

Long, Elizabeth, (wife of ——————) m 2d Jeremiah Pratt, 3d Thomas Williams, before 1756. From deeds, and other papers she appears to have been, née Chandler.

RECORDS OF DEEDS

Long, William (s of James, & Ales) m Susan Ames (Relict of George) Jan 28, 1697/8.

Macey, Thomas, m Elizabeth Stanley, Sept 5, 1689. (Berkeley Par Reg.)

Mathes (Mathias), George, had wife Johannah, who died Feb 27, 1695. He m 2d Elizabeth Williams, had dau Jane, b May 23, 1696. (Berkeley Par Reg.)

Maudlin, Elizabeth (d of Joseph Sutton dec'd) 1735. (Petitioned for her Estate.)

Maudlin, Thomas, m Sarah Clayton (d of John). She m 2d John Stokes, before June 4, 1760. Thomas Maudlin called Edward Chancey "brother."

Maudlin, Gideon, m Mary Mullen (d of Abraham, & Elinor) before Oct 9, 1765. (Legal papers.)

Maudlin, Richard, m Polly Morris, Oct 12, 1809. (Pasq Mar bonds.)

Morris, Aaron, m Charity Pritchard, Feb 13, 1770. (Pasq Mar bonds.)

Morris, Joseph, m Sarah Haskit, 19, 4mo 1788 (Intention, Pasq Mo Meeting), son of Benjamin Morris.

Morris, Thomas, (s of Joseph) m Lucretia Henley, 20, 9mo 1794. (Pasq Mo Meeting.)

Morris, Mary, In, with Benjamin Anderson, 21, 2mo 1795. (Pasq Mo Meeting.)

Morris, Joshua, with Margaret Henley, 19, 3mo 1796. (Pasq Mo Meeting.)

Morris, Christopher, with Gulielma Bundy, 18, 2mo 1797. (Pasq Mo Meeting.)

Morris, Aaron Jr, with Lyda Davis, 17, 6mo 1797. (Pasq Mo Meeting.)

Morris, Jacob, with Mary Trueblood, 17, 2mo 1798. (Pasq Mo Meeting.)

Morris, Mark, with Hannah Pritchard, 18, 8mo 1798. (Pasq Mo Meeting.)

Morris, Elizabeth, with Joseph Parker, 15, 2mo 1800. (Pasq Mo Meeting.)

Morris, Thomas, with Rebecca White (married) 20, 2mo 1801. Pasq Mo Meeting.

Morris, Jonathan, with Penelope Symons, 21, 12mo 1785. (Pasq Mo Meeting.)

Morris, Nathan, m Polly Pool, Dec 4, 1809, m 2d Sally Price, Jan 24, 1811. (Pasq Co.)

Morris, John, m Elizabeth Alexander, Oct 8, 1810. (Pasq Co.)

Morris, Isaac, m Pheribe Bundy, 20, 2mo 1802. (Pasq Mo Meeting.)

Morris, Thomas, m Sarah Jordan, 20 3mo 1802. (Pasq Mo Meeting.)

Morris, David, m Drucilla McMeans Williams, Jan 2, 1855. (Pasq Co.)

Newbold, ———, m Mary C. White, July 24, 1863. (Pasq Co.)

Newby, Enoch, Intention, with Mary Nicholson, 21, 11mo 1789. (Pasq Mo Meeting.)

Newby, Joseph, Intention, with Dorothy Nixon, Nov 7, 1794. (Pasq Mo Meeting.)

Newby, William, Intention, with Catherine Melbourn, ——— 178—. (Pasq Mo Meeting.)

Newby, James, Intention, with Ann Bright, Aug 28, 1810. (Pasq Mo Meeting.)

Newby, James, m 2d Millicent Small, Feb 1, 1817. (Pasq Mo Meeting.)

Newby, John, In, with Elizabeth Nicholson, "at Stephen Scotts house" 28 ——— 1701.

Newby, William, with Mary White, 16, 1mo 1802. (Pasq Co.)

Newbold, Miriam, was dau of Ralph Fletcher, whose will was p July 1785, Perq Co.

Overman, John, m Hannah Scott, Dec 10, 1755, issue: Aaron, b Oct 2, 1756—Sarah, b June 8, 1759—Thomas, b Dec 8, 1761—Miriam, b June 1, 1764.

Overman, Mary, dau of Samuel Charles, whose will, Pasq Co, p Mch 12, 1727/8, names her.

Overman, Rachel, wife of Jacob, dau of John Morgan, will Pasq Co, p Mar 29, 1755.

Overman, Ann, dau of Jeremiah Simons of Pasq Co, his will p Xber 13, 1715.

Phillips, Daniel, m Mrs Elizabeth Latham (widow of Paul) about 1697. She was heir of her brother George Latham, and it seems certain that Daniel, & Thomas Phillips, were sons of Henry, & Hannah, who m 2d John Lilly. The two sons made a crop with John Lilly, after her marriage, and there was some litigation in court about it, which was settled in favor of the two Phillips men.

Perisho, James (s of James, & Hannah, née Hill) m Mary Morgan (d of James, & Jan) Feb, 18, 1696.

Palmer, Paul, m Joanna Peterson (widow of Thomas) before 1722. (Col records.)

Palmer, Willis, m "out of Unity" before 21, 4mo 1787. (Wifes name not given.)

Palin, Henry, m Sarah Nixon, Intention, 16, 12mo 1797. (Pasq Mo Meeting.)

Parish, Anne, (dau of John) m ——— Barclift, before Mar 18, 1734. (Loose papers.)

Parker, Joseph, m Elizabeth Morris, Intention, 15, 2mo 1800. (Pasq Mo Meeting.)

Parker, Sarah, is named in the will of Samuel Smith Perq Co, April 1789, as "daughter." He had sons: Job, and Josiah, wife Leah.

Pearson, William, m Elizabeth Penrice, Mch 23, 1772. (Chowan Mar bonds.)

Pearson, Joseph, m Hebe Elliott, Jan 1, 1785. (Mar bonds Perq Co.)

Pearson, Jonathan, m Sarah Elliott (d of Pritlow) before Oct 1787. (Legal papers.)

Pearson, John, m Anne Ormond, May 26, 1789. (Chowan Mar bonds.)

Peirce, John (Perre) s of William, & Margarett, m Alice ? Calloway, widow Nov 3 ——.

Peirce, Joseph, (s of John, & Mary) m Damaris Nixon (d of Zachariah, & Elizabeth) at a meeting at Little River, Aug 11, 1699. He died Nov 16, 1705, when she m 2d Richard Ratcliff. (See their wills, Grimes page 288.)

Peirce, Thomas, m Mary Copeland, 1719, issue: John, b Feb 16, 1720—Mary, b Sept 23, 1722.

Penrice, Edward, m Sarah More (d of Robert dec'd) no date.

Penrice, Francis, m Elizabeth Bond (sister of Samuel) before Jan 17, 1763. (Deeds.)

Phelps, Benjamin (s of Jonathan, & Dorothy nee Jordan, d of Mathew Jordan of Isle of Wight Co Va) m Sarah Knox (d of Andrew, & Christian) before Jan 20, 1776.

Phelps, Margaret, & Elizabeth, were gr-dau's of Daniel, & Elizabeth Saint. Apl 1779.

Phelps, Jonathan, (s of Jonathan, & Hannah) was b Aprill 13, 1687. (Berkeley Par Reg.)

Pike, John, m Sarah Small (Intention) Mar 20, 1802. (Pasq Mo Meeting.)

Perisho, James, m Hannah Hill (Col records) & had issue: Ellener, b Sept 18, 1673—James, b Nov 25, 1676.

Perisho, James, (s of James, & Hannah) m Mary Morgan (d of James, & Jan) Feb 18, 1696.

Perisho, Joseph, m Deborah Wood, Aug 5, 1742. (Mar bonds Perq Co.)

Powell, Samuel, m Margaret Micantuse, Aug 3, 1693.

Pratt, Jeremiah, m Penelope Gilbert, Mch 10, 1772. (Mar bonds Chowan Co.)

Pratt, Elizabeth (d of Richard Whedbee), whose will was p in Perq, 1746.

Pritchard, Mary, m Jesse Hill, Intention, 18, 1mo 1786. (Pasq Mo Meeting.)

Robinson, Thomas, m Sarah Symons, "at Newbegun Creek, Pasq Co, Intention, 16, 9mo 1711. She is named as dau, by Jeremiah Simons of Pasq Co, in his will. Xber 13, 1715. Thomas, & wife Sarah had issue: Joseph, b Sept 14, 1712.

Robinson, Joseph, m Mary ——— & had Thomas Robinson, b Aug 26, 1739.

Robinson, John, dec'd Apl 17, 1758, Inventory. Joseph, & Thomas Robinson Exrs.

Robinson, John, m Keziah Elliott (d of Sarah) Nov 29, 1778, issue: Thomas, & Ephrim.

Roe, Tabitha, widow of Robert, Oct 1756. She m 2d Francis Pickria ? before July 1756. (Minute book Perq Co.)

Rowden, Elias, m Sarah Durant (d of George, & Ann) Aug 14, 1690. (Berkeley Par Reg.)

Russell, John, (s of George, of County Kent, in Ould England) m Deborah Munford, "According to the Cannons of the Church of England" Sept 26, 1679. (Berkeley Par Reg.)

Sanders, Abraham, m Judith Pritlow (d of John, & Elizabeth, will 1728) Issue: Elizabeth, b Dec 22, 1719—Abraham (2) b Dec 23, 1723—Judith, b Feb 28, 1725—John b July 28, 1729. Judith Sanders (d of Abraham m 1st Moses Elliott, 2d ——— Boyce, Jan 19, 1778. Benjamin Sanders, Joiner; April 22, 1766.

Sanders, Abraham, Intention, with Mary Morris (d of Aaron Sr) 20, 8mo 1791.

Sanders, Richard, m Hannah ——— issue: John, b July 28, 1731—Elizabeth, b Apl 27, 1735.

Sanders, John, m Elizabeth ——— issue: Mary, b Dec 4, 1760—Miriam, b Apl 1, 1764—John b Nov 4, 1766—Sarah, b Mch 22, 1769—Elizabeth, b Mch 21, 1771. (Quaker Rec.)

Small, Joshua, m dau of Joseph Redding, before Apl 1754. (Legal papers.)

Small, Joseph, Intention, with Clerkey Perisho, 15, 12mo 1792. (Quaker Records.)

Small, Obadiah, Intention, with Elizabeth Symons, 21, 12mo 1785. (Quaker Records.)

Small, Joshua, m Charity Redding (dau of Joseph, sister of John, & James) before April 7, 1757. (Legal papers.) Thomas Small, Joiner; Jan 30, 1756. (Summons.)

Small, Benjamin, (of Nansemond Co Va) m Elizabeth Belson (d of Edmund, & Mary) b 13, 11mo 1687, had issue: Amey, b 30, 1mo 1702—Hannah, b 31 day of March, 1704.

Small, Obadiah, m Lydia Bundy, "at Symons Creek" Pasq Co, 4, 8mo 1757.

Small, John, (s of John of Nansemond Co Va) m Alce Hollowell (d of Alce, of Elizabeth River (& Thomas dec'd) 25, 12mo 1688, among witnesses, Nathan, & Elizabeth Newby. (Lower Mo Meeting Nansemond Co Va.)

Small, Alice (d of Thomas, & Alice Hollowell, of Nansemond Co Va) was b 16, 12mo 1664. (Lower Mo Meeting, Nansemond Co.)

Small, Joseph, (s of John) m Ann Owen (d of Gilbert) Oct 18, 1722. (Chuckatuck.)

Small, ————, m Joyce Valentine (d of Alexander) before 1782. (Division of Est.)

Small, Tamer, wife of ————, was dau of Thos. Jones. (Division of his Est, 1793.)

Smith, Ann, dau of David Harris, who in a deed of gift, gave her "his Manner Plan called Grassy Point. (Deed book F, No 26 Perq records.)

Smith, Ann, Dept this life, Feb 8, 1693/4. (Berkeley Par Reg.)

Smith, Robert, Dept this life, Mar 4, 1692/3.

Smith, Rosanna, (d of John, & Susanna Harmon) Sept 14, 1774. Her husband not named.

Stacy, Robert, m Elizabeth Henin, by Wm Wilkinson Esq, June 8, 1787.

Stafford, Thos, m Widow of Henry Raper, before Dec 3, 1745. Heirs of sd Raper: John, Enoch, Joseph, & Henry Raper. (Division of Est.)

Stallings, Hepzibah, (d of Jacob Perry) wife of Hardy Stallings. Oct 1777. (Will.)

Stegon, John, m Frances Corwell, Feb 15, 1676, issue: Ann, b May 15, 1677—Mary, b Sept 17, 1679.

Stephens, William, (s of Andrew, & Grace, of Ould England) m Johannah Williams, Feb, 2, 1684, issue: Joshua, b Sept 27, 1685. William Stevens m 2d Mary ———— & had issue: John, b Dec 20, 1704. (Berkeley Par Reg.)

Stephens, Thomas, m Jane ———— issue: Ann, b Mch 5, 1695. (Berkeley Par Reg.)

Steward, John, m Ann Elles, Sept 17, 1688. (Berkeley Par Reg.)

Steward, William, m Elizabeth ———— issue: Mary, b Oct 14, 1686—Johannah, b Aug 25, 1688. He lived near "Frog Hall" in Perq Co, and died before Oct 15, 1733, leaving to his daughters: Elizabeth, & Patience, "land up the Swamp." (See deeds.)

Stokes, John, m Sarah Maudlin (widow of Thomas) June 4, 1760. She was daughter of John Clayton of Perq Co. (Legal papers.)

Stokes, Jonathan, m Elizabeth Etheridge, Mar 11, 1769. (Mar bond Norfolk Co, Va.)

Sutton, Ann, was dau of Francis Penrice, whose will p April 1758, names her.

Sutton, Elizabeth, (d of Nathaniel) m Richard Whedbee, before Mar 30, 1725. (Records.)

Sumner, James, m Mary Blanchard (d of Aaron, & Zilpah) ———— 1758. She m 2d Isaac Sanders of Perq. (See divisions.)

Sumner, Mary, (d of James) m ———— Hunter, of Bertie Co N. C. May 2, 1783.

Swain, John, m Elizabeth Wyatt (d of Samuel) before Mar 2, 1747. (See deeds.)

Symons, Johosaphat, m Sarah Newby, 15, 3mo 1800. (Pasq Mo Meeting.)

Tailor, John, Dept this Life Feb 2, 1688, "at Grassy—Poine?." His wife Julianna (Hutson) Tailor, took up 400a at the head of Castletons Creek, July 29, 1693. She with her sister Johannah, were gr-dau's of Mary Scott, whose will Nov 16, 1691/2, names them.

Taylor, Jonathan, m Elizabeth ———— issue: Elizabeth, b Dec 5, 1693. He died Sept 16, 1698.

Tatlock, Jesse, m Elizabeth Jones, Intention, 16, 1mo 1796. (Pasq Mo Meeting.)

Tomlin, John, & wife Mary ———— issue: William, b Apl 11, 1692. William Tomlin dec'd Dec 1762. Jos. Perisho Ex. (Legal papers.)

Tow, Elizabeth, named in will of Zachariah Toms, April 1774 as daughter.

Tow, Tamer, & Benjamin (children of Deborah) were gr-children of Joseph Sutton, Feb 1794. Deborah Tow was dau of Abraham Mullen. (See deeds.)

Towe, Christopher, m Deborah Mullen (d of Abraham) July 22, 1763. (Mar bonds Perq.)

Therrill, Mr William, of this Co, m Mrs Jean Godfrey, Dec 2, 1676. He m 2d Mrs. Ann Cooke, July 12, 1677. George Durant was one of the Exrs of his will June 3, 1682, sons: William, & Gideon "land on Little River."

Titterton, William, m Margaret Hall, by Mr. Gordon Minister of gospell, Sept 23, 1679. William Tetterton was one of the legatees in the will of Thomas Harvey, p Nov 10, 1729, and Hannah Sitterson in the will of Thomas Harvey will p Jan 1748, is called by him "aunt." Margaret Titterton, & Hannah Sitterson were sisters. (See deeds.)

Travis, Champion, m Elizabeth Bush, Nov 28, 1772. (Mar bonds Norfolk Co Va.)

Trowell, Joseph, m Hona Brian, Oct Last 1683. (Berkeley Par Reg) issue Susannah, b July 9, 1685.

Trueblood, Joshua, m Mary Henley, Intention, 19, 6mo 1790. (Pasq Mo Meeting.

Trueblood, Josiah Jr, m Abigail Overman, Intention, 17, 10mo 1795. (Pasq Mo Meeting.)

Trueblood, Caleb, m Mourning Herriott, 17, 9mo 1763. (Blackwater Mo Meeting, in Va.)

Trumball, William, m Elizabeth Commander, Apl 6, 1798. (Mar bonds Pasq Co.)

Trumbull, Rachel, was dau of Thomas Holloway. (See his will p Jan 1750. Perq Co.)

Turner, George, m Nancy Colson, July 14, 1789.

Turner, Joseph, m Jane Mullen (d of Abraham, & Ellinor) no date. She was sister of Deborah Towe. (See deeds) Joseph Turner is called "Carpenter" in legal papers in Perq. Jane Mullen, had a former husband Abraham Riggs.

Vose, William, (s of Morgan Vose) m Martha Chaston (d of Roger) Aprill 3, 1669, issue: Hannah, ——— 1670—Margaret, b ——— 1671—Winnefret, b ———

1677. Margaret Vose d of William, m Jonathan Jones of Pasq Co (See deeds.) William Vosses land lay on the Creek called Vosses Creek, and ran down to Vosses Point, which is supposed to be the point, just beyond Bear Garden.

Vose, William (2), m Jane Wilkinson, Last of Aprill, 1688. The name of Vose soon disappeared from the records in Perq, probably from the male line dying out, or migration.

Walker, Henderson, m Deborah Green (widow of Walter) April 7, 1686. (Berkeley Par Reg.)

Walker, Capt Henderson, m 2d Ann Lillington (d of Alex, & Elizabeth (Cooke) b June 1, 1679.) Feb 20, 1693. She m 2d —— Jones of Chowan Co.

Walton, George, m Sarah —————— issue: I Elizabeth, b Jan 9, 1768. He m Mary —————— & had issue: 2 Sarah, b Jan 7, 1775—3 Jenima, b Jan 5, 1777—4 George (2), b April 11, 1779—5 Mary, b Aug 17, 1781. This record was found on the Fly-leaf of Fox's Journal, a volume in possession of Dr. Randolph Winslow, of Baltimore Md.

Ward, James, m Miriam Trueblood (d of Thomas, & Lydia) Sept 20, 1770. (Quaker Rec.)

Warde, Richard, m Frances Stanley May 24, 1691. (Berkeley Par Reg.)

Warren, Thos. Gent, of Surry Co Va, m Mrs. Elizabeth Shepard (widow of Maj Robert, of Chippoakes, Surry Co) before Sept 29, 1656. He gave bond on that day, "to deliver cattle unto Anne, John, Robert, & Will Shepard, and to Priscilla, and Susannah Shepard, their full portion of their fathers Est."

Warren, Abraham, m Rebecca Clapper (Relict of John) Jany 23, 1701. (Berkeley Par Reg.) His will Perq, p July 1740, names son: Henry, & wife Sarah (2d wife). Henry Warren (2) moved to Bath. Abraham (s of Abraham, & Sarah) was b Aug 31, 1702. Sarah Warren appears as Extrix of her dec'd husband Abraham, in July 1740, by oath of John Stepney, & John Creecy. (Loose papers.)

Wellwood, Andrew, m Mary Norise, June 10, 1669. (Berkeley Par Reg.)

Wilkinson, John, m Jean White (Relict of Roger) Jan 9, 1686. (Berkeley Par Reg.)

Williams, Thomas, m Sarah Wilson (d of Edward) before Jan 17, 1763. (Loose papers.)

Williams, Hatten, m Ann (widow of Joseph Ming) before Mar 11, 1769. (See deeds.)

Willis, Humphrey, m Mary Moore —————— 22, 1688. (Berkeley Par Reg.)

Wingate, Ephrim, m Elizabeth Williams, Nov 5, 1798. (Mar bonds Chowan Co.)

Wingate, Edward, m Lydia Thompson, Oct 14, 1826. (Mar bonds Chowan Co.)

Wingate, John, was living in Perq precinct 1687, and brought suit in Court on that date. It is thought that the Wingate family in Perq, came from Norfolk Co, Va, where they are found witnessing deeds of Woods, & others, who also moved to N. C.

Wright, John, m Susannah Pendleton, Apl 6, 1807.

RECORDS OF DEEDS

CLERKS OF COURT
Perquimans Co, N. C.
(With time of incumbency, as far as records show.)

Ralph Coates, Clk, Nov 5, 1675. (No Reg given.)

*Thomas Harris, Clerk of Perquimans, is thought to have been son of Thomas (1), who died 1665, leaving a widow Diana, who m 2d William Foster, 1675. She had by her first husband *certainly* a son John, and one dau who m Nathaniel Nicholson. The records are silent about Thomas (2) and David Harris, but it seems to be morally certain they were children of the same couple. Diana Harris m 3d Thomas White, and Court was held at first in her house, and then the house of her 3d husband, presumably at the same place, on several occasions. (See Col Rec.) Francis Foster made his will (no county mentioned, but it was certainly Perq) Oct 9, 1687, naming son Francis, dau Elizabeth, and wife Diana. One of the witnesses was Samuel *Pricklovell* (Pricklove) a known resident of Perquimans precinct.

†Henderson Walker, m Deborah Green (widow of Walter, née Chaston) April 7, 1686. He was later Provincial Governor of N. C. and lies buried in Chowan county. His epitaph on the tombstone marking his grave everlastingly subscribes, that the Colony "knew tranquility" during his reign. He m 2d Ann Lillington (d of Alex. & wife Elizabeth Cooke) b June 1, 1674; married Capt Henderson Walker, Feby 20, 1693, by Thomas Harvey. In his will, p July 4, 1704, only his wife Ann, and one dau Elizabeth are named, she being the child of his first wife. Other legatees: Maj Swann (who m Elizabeth Lillington, sister of his last wife) to whom he left his "swoard," and John, George, & Sarah Lillington.

Richard Plater, Clk, Nov 20, 1690-92. Samuel Pricklove Reg, 1691-92.

Francis Toms, Clk, 1692. Samuel Pricklove Reg. (The last died Apl 20, 1692.)

John Stepney, Clk and "Reg of all Writings for Perquimans Pre'ct" 1692-1702.

Peter Godfrey, Clk, Jan 12, 1702. John Stepney "Reg of all Writings."

Thomas Snoden, Clk, Jan 1703-1709. John Stepney Reg.

Richard Leary, Clk, July 14, 1709-1712. John Stepney Reg.

Richard Clayton, Clk, April 15, 1713-14. John Stepney Reg.

John Lillington, Clk, Aug 10, 1714. John Stepney Reg.

Richard Leary, Clk, Oct 12, 1714, to Apl 14, 1719. John Stepney Reg.

William Havet, Clk, Apl 12, 1720. John Stepney Reg.

Richard Leary, Clk, Jan 20, 1720-1726. John Stepney Reg.

Charles Denman, Clk, Apl 10, 1727. (In behalf of Richard Leary.) John Stepney Reg.

Thomas Crew, Clk, Oct 28, 1729. Charles Denman Reg.

Charles Denman, Clk and Reg, June 1, 1730, to 1736. (Chas. Denman died Apl 24, 1739.)

---

*First Clerk, Thomas Harris; serving from 1665, to 1675, died Sept 1679.

†Henderson Walker, Cler, June 10, 1681-89. Edward Mayo Reg, 1686, Nov 1693. (Edward Mayo sworn in Oct 26, 1685. 2d term July 1693.)

James Craven, Clk, Jan 1736. Charles Denman Reg. (James Craven apt Clk Mar 29, 1735.)

(James Craven, Clk of the Gen'l Court, 1754.)

James Craven, Clk, July 30, 1738-1740. Mac Scarbrough Reg. (The last apt Reg Sept 10, 1737.)

Edmond Hatch, Clk, June 10, 1741, to March 22, 1753. John Harvey Reg.

Richard Clayton, Clk Apl Court 1754, to Jan 29, 1755. John Harvey Reg.

Miles Harvey, Clk, Apl 25, 1755-1768. John Harvey Reg.

Miles Harvey, Clk, May 7, 1772. Thomas Harvey Reg.

M. G. Skinner, Clk, 1778 to Feb 26, 1782. Joshua Skinner Reg, Feb 26, 1780.

M. G. Skinner, Clk (Miles Gale Skinner). John Skinner Feb 26, 1782.

John Harvey, Clk, May 30, 1782. John Skinner Reg. John Harvey Treasurer 1790.

Thomas Harvey, Clk, June 12, 1782, June 22, 1786. John Skinner Reg.

William Skinner, Clk, Oct 25, 1786. Joshua Skinner Reg.

J. Harvey, Clk (John), Jan 29, 1784-1805. Josh Skinner Jr, Reg, Jan 29, 1784.

J. Harvey, Clk, July 22, 1790. Charles W. Harvey Reg. Geo Sutton Treasurer Feb 12, 1798.

J. Harvey, Clk, Feb 18, 1794-Feb 20, 1801. Benjamin Perry Reg.

J. Harvey, Clk, May 16, 1801-1805. Gabriel White Reg.

Thomas H. Harvey, Clk, June 12, 1805. Gabriel White Reg.

John Wood, Clk, Jan 19, 1809. Gabriel White Reg. (Both served until 1824.)

John Wood, Clk, Nov 11, 1824. John Clary Reg.

John Wood, Clk, Nov 23, 1827-1834. Thomas Long Reg.

John Wood, Clk, Feb 16, 1835. A. R. Elliott Reg.

John Wood, Clk, Feb 12, 1840. Milton Hudgins Reg. (Both in office Aug 9, 1841.)

Jos. M. Cox, Clk, Aug 16, 1841. M. Hudgins Reg.

Jos. M. Cox, Clk, Nov 14, 1842. Jos. G. Granbery Reg. (Josiah.)

Jos. M. Cox, Clk, Feb 1848. Jos. H. White Reg.

Jos. M. Cox, Clk, Feb 11, 1851-April 21, 1853. William Henry Bagley Reg.

T. Wilson, Clk, Aug 17, 1853. William Henry Bagley Reg.

T. Wilson, Clk, May 30, 1855. Jos. Wood Reg.

T. Wilson, Clk, Nov 24, 1856. Willis H. Bagley Reg.

T. Billups, Clk, Aug 11, 1857. Willis H. Bagley Reg.

James C. Skinner, Clk, Jan 11, 1858-Aug 15, 1865. Willis H. Bagley Reg.

Jos. R. Wood, Clk, Aug 15, 1865 (Apt July 8, 1865). Jas. M. Mullen Reg.

Jos. R. Wood, Clk, Feb 24, 1866. Jas. M. Mullen Reg. (Nathan Toms Coroner.)

Edw. C. Albertson, Clk, Aug 17, 1868. James M. Mullen Reg.

Edw. C. Albertson, Clk, Aug 22, 1868. U. W. Speight Reg.

Jesse C. Jacocks, Clk, May 18, 1871-Sept 23, 1873. U. W. Speight Reg.

John H. Cox, Clk, elected Sept 23, 1873. U. W. Speight Reg.

Henry Gilliam, Clk, Aug 9, 1877. U. W. Speight Reg.

John Q. A. Wood, Clk, Sept 13, 1878-1889. U. W. Speight Reg.

E. V. Perry, Clk, Dec 1889. W. R. White Reg. 1889-1890.

E. V. Perry, Clk, Dec 1890-1904. R. L. Knowles Reg.

OFFICIALDOM IN PERQUIMANS

A. H. G. Winslow, Clerk Superior Court. Born October 23, 1895. Son of Watson and Ellen G. (Rawlings) Winslow. 317th Machine Gun Battalion, 81st Division, A. E. F. First Lieutenant, 1918-19.
B. W. G. Wright, Sergeant, Company B, 323d Infantry, 81st Division, A. E. F. Elected Sheriff of Perquimans 1920. Still in office.
C. W. F. C. Edwards, Register of Deeds. Born February 7, 1868. Son of John Edwards and E. P. (Goodman) Edwards. 1904-30.
D. James S. McNider. Born January 21, 1880, in Durant's Neck. Son of Thomas J. McNider and Laura (White) McNider. Judge of Recorders Court.

Charles Johnson, Clk, Dec 4, 1906. W. F. C. Edwards Reg. (The last elected Dec 1904 and still holding the Office.)
H. G. Winslow, Clk, elected Nov 1922. (Present incumbent.)

SHERIFFS IN PERQUIMANS CO.

(According to records, and loose papers found in the county, the earliest found being James Morgan. The Provost Marshal probably acted in that capacity, when Perquimans was first open for settlement.)

James Morgan, Com' Sheriff of Perq Co by Gov Gabriel Johnston, Apl 1741, d Oct 1741. Zach Chancey Deputy.
John Stevenson, Apt' Sheriff, by Gov Gabriel Johnston, 1743.
Nathaniel Caruthers, Sheriff, 1746-47.
James Eggerton, Apt' Sheriff, July 20, 1747, by Gov Gabriel Johnston.
John Calloway, Sheriff of Perquimans, Nov 25, 1751.
Mr. Charles Blount, High Sheriff, Oct 1752. John Perry Deputy.
William Skinner, Apt' High Sheriff of Perq, July, 1753, by Hon'ble Matthew Rowan.
John Creecy Gent, Sheriff, July 1757. John Weeks Deputy.
John Calloway, Apt' Sheriff, July 2, 1757, by Gov Arthur Dobbs.
Samuel Sutton, Sheriff, Oct 1760. Andrew Knox Deputy.
Andrew Knox Com' Sheriff, July 21, 1761, and served until 1769.
Benjamin Phelps, Sheriff of Perq, 1778.
Col. Thomas Harvey, Sheriff of Perq, Dec 20, 1780, and again Mar 16, 1782, d 1782. William Skinner, Treasurer for the same period. Perquimans Co.
Joshua Skinner, Sheriff of Perq, 1781. (He was probably Deputy for Col. Harvey.)
Edward Hall, Sheriff, 1786. And again 1798. "Late Sheriff of Perq Co," 1800.
W. Creecy, Sheriff of Perq, 1787.
Richard Skinner, Sheriff, April 14, 1790.
Thomas Hosea, Sheriff of Perq, 1799-1809. James White Deputy, Aug 1803.
Miles Elliott, Sheriff of Perq, 1821.
James Long, Sheriff Mar 20, 1835.
Wm D. Roscoe, Sheriff, Fall Term 1836.
Nathan Bagley, Sheriff, June 4, 1836.
Josiah R. White, Sheriff of Perq, 1858.
Henry White, Sheriff, Oct 1868-1873.
Jesse C. Jacocks, Sheriff of Perq, Oct 1873-1876.
John H. Cox, Sheriff of Perq, Fall Term 1877-78. Resigned in the spring of 1879.
Robert White, Sheriff, Aug 1879-1886.
T. F. Winslow, Sheriff of Perq, Feb 1887, and was Apt' again April 1888.
A. F. Riddick, Sheriff of Perq, 1889, to 1900.
T. F. Winslow, Apt' for second time, spring 1901, served until fall 1904.
B. F. Bray, elected 1904, served until 1920.
W. G. Wright, elected 1920, still in service.

REPRESENTATIVES

(From Perquimans Co.)

1777, Senator, William Skinner. Rep, Benjamin, and John Harvey. (Assembly.)
1778, Senator, Jesse Eason. Rep, Charles Blount, and John Harvey.
1778, Senator, Thomas Harvey.
1779, Senator, Thomas Harvey. Rep, John Whedbee, Jonathan Skinner.
1780, Senator Jesse Eason. Rep, Charles Blount, John Harvey.
1781. Senator, Jesse Eason. Rep, John Whedbee, Jonathan Skinner.
1782, John Whedbee. Rep, Jonathan Skinner, Richard Whedbee.
1783, Senator, Jesse Eason. Rep, John Skinner, John Reed.
1784, Senator, John Skinner, Rep, John Reed, Robert Riddick.
1785, Senator, William Skinner. Rep, John Skinner, Robert Riddick.
1786, Senator, John Skinner. Rep, Foster Toms.
1787, Senator, John Skinner. Rep, Thomas Harvey.
1788, Senator, Thomas Harvey. Rep, Joshua Skinner, Joseph Harvey.
1789, Senator, Joshua Skinner. Rep, Ashbury Sutton, Benjamin Perry.
1791, Senator, Joshua Skinner. Rep, Robert Riddick, Ashbury Sutton.
1792, Senator, Joshua Skinner. Rep, Robert Riddick, Gosby Toms.

THE FAMILY BIBLE

OF

PERQUIMANS CO.

As prepared from County records, Berkeley Parish Register, Quaker records, both in North Carolina, and Virginia, County records, and other records of other Counties in North Carolina, Marriage bonds in Perquimans, and Chowan, also some in Pasquotank and Gates Co, where they were pertinent to Perquimans. Records of Virginia, letters, loose papers, and other documents, wherever found.

Some of this data was submitted by persons living in the Middle West, whose ancestors migrated there from N. C. carrying with them Quaker records of great value. The writer had no opportunity to verify the data thus sent in, but the senders were persons of proven veracity, anxious to serve the public, and gave of their knowledge, a valuable contribution to posterity. These records are true copies of the old ones in Perquimans, which have been destroyed.

The State of N. C. should, and will at some early date, we feel sure, send some competent, careful person on a mission to Guilford College, and make a copy of the *vital statistics*, if no more, the.'e recorded, on the perfectly marvelous Quaker records, kept in the fire-proof safe of said College. That would be a most valuable addition to the great collection already in the Hall of History, Raleigh, N. C. The writer hopes to live to see this accomplished. No State in the Union can boast of more wonderful, or more complete records of any county, than those recorded on the Quaker Mo Meeting of Perq Co. These marriages there written take the early settlers before coming to Perq, in some cases, on down through their migration, to the Rev. and then over the mountains to other States. No more authoritative data could be found, and with the Colonial Records fill in much of interest to any one whose ancestors lived in North Carolina.

Several blank leaves will be found back of each family, to take care of errors, and to afford room for adding new, or unwritten data concerning their family, if so desired.

FAMILIES FOLLOW

Arranged according to the alphabet.

ALBERTSON

Albertson, Penelope, d of Joshua & Mary, b 16, 6mo 1753. Reg of Friends.
Albertson, Mary, d of Elihu, & Jane, b 17, 11mo 1745. Reg of Friends.
Albertson, Caleb, s of Elihu, & Jane, b 24, 4mo 1747. Reg of Friends.
Albertson, Joshua, s of Elihu, & Jane, b 11, 11mo 1749. Reg of Friends.
Albertson, Josiah, s of Elihu, & Jane, b 12, 12mo 1750. Reg of Friends.
Albertson, Miriam, d of Elihu, & Jane, b 4, 12mo 1752. Reg of Friends.
Albertson, Sarah, d of Elihu, & Jane, b 18, 11mo 1754. Reg of Friends.
Albertson, Liddea, d of Elihu, & Jane, b 8, 1mo 1755. Reg of Friends.
Albertson, Abigail, d of Elihu, & Jane, b 24, 2mo 1757. Reg of Friends.
Albertson, Elizabeth, d of Elihu, & Jane, b 24, 3mo, 1759. Reg of Friends.
Albertson, Sarah (d of Elihu) m Benjamin Newby 25, 2mo 1773. He died 28, 9mo 1779.
Albertson, Elias, (s of Elias, & Elizabeth) was b 24, 9mo 1763.
Albertson, Benjamin (s of William, & Sarah) m Sarah Nixon (d of Phineas, & Mary) 19, 10mo 1773. b 17, 12mo 1746/7.
Albertson, Hannah (d of Nathaniel) b 18, 2mo 1719—m John Nixon 10, 3mo 1753; issue: 1 Mary b 16, 12mo 1754—2 Liddea b 14, 3mo 1756—3 Frederick b 4, 11mo 1758—Abigail, (twin to Frederick). (She was 2d wife of John Nixon.) Hannah (Albertson) Nixon d 18, 2mo 1793.
Albertson, Joshua, m Mary Symons (at Symons Creek Meeting) 4, 10mo 1734.
Albertson, William, m Sarah Pritchard (at Symons Creek Meeting) 1, 8mo 1747.
Albertson, Joshua, m Mary Scott (at Symons Creek Meeting) 2, 5mo 1752.
Albertson, William, died 29, 4mo 1803, & "was buried at Suttons Creek Meeting house." (in Perq Co.)
Albertson, Miriam, m Nathan White, (Welles Meeting Perq Co) 6, 4mo 1785.
Albertson, Penninah, m Benjamin Saint, (Welles Meeting Perq Co) 2, 12mo 1789.
Albertson, Phineas, m Rebeccah White, (Welles Meeting Perq Co) 4, 9mo 1793.
*Albertson, Chalkey, m 1st Elizabeth, & had son Zachariah, who died 10, 8mo 1798. m 2d Mary Hollowell, "Suttons Creek Meeting" Perq Co, 18, 8mo 1808, & had issue: 1 Chalkey b 21, 4mo 1809—2 Daniel b 24, 1mo 1811.

---

*It is thought that the name of Chalkey in the Albertson family was for Thomas Chalkey, the celebrated Quaker minister, and in other families through intermarriage with the *Albertsons*.

Albertson, Mary, wife of Chalkey, died 20, 9mo 1812, & "was buried at Suttons Creek Meeting house."

Albertson, Benjamin, (s of Benj of Old Neck dec'd) m Margaret Nixon (d of Nath'l Bagley) all of Perq, 17, 10mo 1811. (Sutton Creek Meeting Perq.)

Albertson, Toms, m Martha Albertson (Symons Creek) 16, 9mo 1810, had issue: 1 Elias b 10, 3mo 1813—2 James b 12, 8mo 1811—3 Mary b 19, 2mo 1815.

Albertson, Benjamin, m Sarah ——— (at Piney Woods Meeting) 12, 10mo 1809, issue: 1 Alfred Parker b 22, 4mo 1811—d 25, 9mo 1816—2 Edmond Peel b 21, 9mo 1813—3 Isabel b 2, 2mo 1816.

Albertson, Nathan, (s of Benj dec'd) m Pheraby Nicholson (d of Nathan) 14, 8mo 1824.

Albertson, Albert, had a grt for land in Perq May 22, 1694—290a by the side of Suttons Creek Swamp. (Land Office Raleigh.)

Albertson, Albert Jr, land grt in Perq Precinct, Sept 1, 1694, on the bank of Perq River, 300a.

Albertson, Albert, appears on Rent Roll in Perq 1700, with 300a on Deep Creek.

ALBERTSON

Birth, Deaths, and Marriages, in Berkeley

Albert Albertson m Mary Gosby, Dec 20, 1668, issue: 1 Albert, b July 15, 1669—2 Susanna, b Feb 19, 1670—3 Esau, b Aug 19, 1672—4 Hannah, b Dec 11, 1675—5 Peter, b Last of June 1677.

Hannah Albertson m Joseph Nicholson, s of Christopher, & Hannah.

Albert Albertson died "att his on house" Feb 28, 1701.

Albertson, Albert Jr, m Elizabeth Mullen, (d of Abraham) who m 2d Wm Bateman, before Oct 18, 1768. (Deed b H-41.)

Albertson, Albert, s of Albert & Elizabeth b ye Nov 23, 1694.

Albertson, John, s of Albert & Elizabeth b Nov 27, 1696.

Albertson, Peter, (s of Albert & Mary Gosby) m Ann Jones (d of Mary Beesly, wid) Aug 27, 1701. issue: 1 Samuel, b Oct 25, 1702—2 Peter, b Oct 7, 1704—3 Joseph, b Feby 5, 1705/6—4 Ann, b Aug 4, 1708—(died young)—5 Mary, b Mch 12, 1710—6 Patience, b Dec 5, 1711—7 Hannah, b June 15, 1715—8 Anne (2d by that name), b Aug 4, 1718—9 Martha, b Aug 15, 1721.

Albertson, Esau, (son of Albert, & Mary Gosby) m Sarah Sexton (d of Darby, & Doroty) ye 27 Jany 1700/1, by Rev Richard French.

Albertson, Esau, (s of Esau, & wife Sarah) b Feb 5, 1703/4.

Albertson, Nathaniel, m Abigail Nicholson (d of Samuel) "at a meeting, at ye house of Samuel Nicholson," July 12, 1704. issue: Sarah, b Nov 2, 1706.

Albertson, Aaron, m Ann Gilbert, July 10, 1729. issue: Nathaniel b Aug 19, 1733. His will Perq Co, p April Court 1782, names wife Anne, Children; Nathaniel, Abigail Cosand (wife of Gabriel) Jean Charles, sons Benjamin, & Nathaniel Exors. Test' Mary Sanders, Mary, & William Albertson. (Perq Co records.)

Albertson, Nathaniel, will Perq Co, p July Court 1785, names sons Joseph, & Jesse, daus Margaret, & Miriam Albertson, Roda Munden, & Anne Moore, son-in-law Levi Munden, wife Mary. (2d wife). Test' Aaron Moore, Anne Moore, Roda Munden.

Albertson, Nathaniel, will Perq Co, p Jan Court 1752/3, names sons Joshua, & William, (Wm, gr-son of Samuel Nicholson) gr-sons Benjamin, & Chalkey, (sons of William) daus Hannah, & Elizabeth Newby, son Aaron, d Lydia Trueblood. Test' Joshua Perisho, James Henbe, Mary Morris.

Albertson, Joshua, will Perq Co, p Oct Court 1753. names son Francis, wife Mary, daus Elizabeth, Mary, & Penelope, brothers Aaron, & William, Exors.

Albertson, William, will Perq Co, p Sept 10, 1784, names sons Benjamin, Chalkey, & William, gr-sons William, & Thomas Hasket, d Mary Anderson, Elizabeth Albertson, wife Sarah. (Who was d of William Newby, by whom she is named, in his will Perq Co, Aug 10, 1782) Exors sons Benjamin, & Chalkey. Test' John, & Samuel Anderson, Josiah Yatton. (Latton.)

Albertson, Albert Sr, will Perq Co, p Apl 14, 1702, names sons Peter, Nathan, Esau, & Nathaniel, son Peter, & wife Ann Exors. son Albert. Test' John Falconer, Nathaniel Nicholson.

ARNOLD

Wm Arnold of Dorset Co England, was bapt June 24, 1587. He "sett sayle from Dartmouth, in Old England, the first of May, & arrived in New England, June 24, 1635." Settled at Hingham, Mass, & became one of the original proprietors of Providence April 1636. He moved to Newport, R. I., 1651, & held many offices in that State. Married Christian Peak. Benedict Arnold was one of his descendants. (Ancestral Records, & Portraits.)

John Arnold had a grt for land in Perq precinct, Jan 1, 1694, 150a on Little River, adj William Barclift.

John Arnold of Conn, New Eng, made a deed in Norfolk Co Va, Aug 21, 1723, sold 300a "which was given by Richard Bowler dec'd, unto his son Richard, he now being likewise dec, Mary Arnold, mother of sd John, heir-at-law." Land on Western Branch.

Thomas Arnold, came to Vir on Ship Culpepper, as Carpenter. In Surry Co Va he apt Mr Robert Perry Merch't Att' to "recover from James Barnett, & Jno. Nichols Ex of Ann Arnold, a plan' formerly belonging to his brother Edward Arnold, of Chickahominy" James City Co Vir, "who did in his will Aug 14, 1679, leave said plan' to her for life, & at her death to next heirs." Mar 17, 1682/3. (Surry Co Records.)

John Arnold on Rent Roll of Perq, prior to 1700, with 150a of land on Little River.

John Arnold, (son of John & Mary) b April 18, 1701. (Berkeley Parish Reg, Perq Co.)

Elizabeth Arnold, (d of John & Mary) b July 22, 1705. m Thomas Knowles, before Oct Court 1745. (Minute book.)

John Arnold (s of Lawrence, & wife Jane) (Richards) b ——— 15, 1703. Berkeley Par Reg.

Joseph Arnold, s of Lawrence, & wife Sarah, b Nov 19, 1745. Berkeley Par Reg.

Jane Arnold, d of Lawrence, & wife Sarah, b Feb 7, 1747. (Berkeley Par Reg.)

One Lawrence Arnold, was dead in Perq before Sept 19, 1694, when his widow, m 2d Jonathan Bateman of Perq Co. He made his will Dec 14, 1691. p Feb 2, 1691 (Old Calendar) naming only one son John, & Lawrence Godfrey. His wife is not named.

John Arnold of Perq, will p July 14, 1724, names sons; John, Lawrence, William & Joseph, d Elizabeth, wife Mary.

John Arnold of Perq, will p July 21, 1735, names son John, & wife Elizabeth, to whom he left "land on Deep Creek." Ex Samuel Parsons.

Joseph Arnold of Perq, d. s. p. will p April Court 1752, dau Mary Ex. Brothers William, & Lawrence. (No other Legatees.)

Edward Arnold made his will in Chowan Co, probated April Court 1752. Son & Ex Edward, d Hannah Stallings, wife Pleasant.

Both Edward Arnold, & John of Perq (1735) have a Crest on their Seals.

Benjamin Arnell m Sarah (d of Jeremiah Cannon) who made his will in Chowan Co, 3, 3mo 1779. She m 2d before Oct Court 1745, Samuel Parsons. Sarah Arnell, is named in the will of sd Samuel, July Court 1745, as dau (step-dau).

The division of Estate of Edward Arnell, Chowan Co, 1777, gives heirs; Sons Wm, John, Edward, & Richard Arnell, dau's Elizabeth Norfleet, Pleasant Knight, Bathsheba, & Esther Arnell.

William Arnold of Perq, m Miriam Newby, (d of Mark). His will p in Perq, Aug Court 1794, names father William, & sons William, & Jonathan, d Mary.

John Arnold, & Thos Holloway, had a joint grt in Perq, April 30, 1703, being "land indented to Priscilla Clay, who died seized of sd land," 18 Xmo 1701.

Mary wife of John Arnold, m 2d Daniel Hall, she appears on Tithe List of Perq, 1740, with "son Lawrence Arnold."

REG OF FRIENDS

Little River, Perq Co.

William Arnold, s of Will'm & Mary b 28, 4mo 1744.
Elizabeth Arnold, d of Will'm & Mary b 19, 4mo 1742.
Benjamin Arnold, s of Will'm & Mary b 27, 4mo 1746.
Mary Arnold, d of Will'm & Mary b 25, 1mo 1749.
Joseph Arnold, s of Will'm & Mary b 1, 4mo 1753.
Asa Arnold, s of Will'm & Mary b 9, 1mo 1755.
Sarah Arnold, d of Will'm & Mary b 27, 11mo 1757.
Thomas Arnold, s of Will'm & Mary b 27 7mo 1759.
Rebekah Arnold, d of Will'm & Mary b 23, 12mo 1763.
William Arnold m Rebekah Cannon, issue: 1 Jemmima b 15, 8mo 1769.
Benjamin Arnold m Sarah Cannon (d of Jeremiah 22, 12 mo 1768, issue Jemmimah b 4, 9mo 1770.
Rebeckah Arnold departed this life 17, 2mo 1773.

BAKER

Lawrence Baker, with his son Lawrence Jr, Elizabeth, John, & Joseph Baker, (all supposed to have been his wife, & children) were Trans' to Isle of Wight Co, Va 1666, by Anthony Matthews. (Hotten.)

The wills in Isle of Wight Co, make plain the fact that descendants of Lawrence Baker, migrated to Gates Co N. C. & from there to other Counties.

Baker, Henry, (died in Isle of Wight) will p Aug 28, 1712. He bequeathed to s Henry, 1800a, "at the Mill, 250a at Somerton" & 25000a at "Buckland," (the last in Gates Co, N. C.) To son James 300a, son Lawrence, "land where I now dwell," 500a, in Nansemond Co; To son William 450a, at "Wickham" daus Mary, Sarah, Catherine, & Elizabeth, wife Mary.

RECORDS OF DEEDS

Baker, Mary, will Isle of Wight, p Oct 23, 1734, Made bequest, to s William 2000a in Nansemond Co, called "Wickham" names her Dec'd husband, Henry Baker, Gent, late of said Co; s Lawrence Ex. Children, Henry, Lawrence, William, d Sarah, & Katherine.

Baker, James, of Isle of Wight Co, in his will, Dec 2, 1756. (d. s. p.) Made bequest to Henry Baker, (s of brother Henry,) of N. C. dec'd. Katherine Baker (d of brother Lawrence,) a negro girl, Richard (s of brother Lawrence) Lands in Isle of Wight Co, & a grist mill, called "Little Mill." Ann (d of brother Lawrence) £25 in money, James (s of brother Lawrence) £25 in money. (James Baker was Clerk of Isle of Wight Co, for a number of years.)

Baker, Lawrence, of Newport Par, Isle of Wight Co, will p July 2, 1761. Names d Katherine, s Richard, d Ann Nelson. To s James, he left "all my lands in N. C." Wife Ann.

Baker, Henry, (s of Henry) will Chowan Co N. C. p May 1, 1739. Sons: Henry (3) John, Blake, David, Zadock, daus Mary, Sarah, Ruth, wife Ruth. Brothers: William, James, & Lawrence. (Wife Ruth was d of Edmund Chancey of Pasquotank Co.) (See will of Edmund Chancey.)

Baker, Blake, was Clerk of Court, in Chowan Co. He resigned Nov 15, 1787.

Baker, Joseph, will Perq Co N. C. p April 1779. Sons: Joel, Moses, & Joseph (2), daus Hannah, Miriam, & Sarah.

Baker, Moses, m Elizabeth Browne, Jan 12, 1694/5. (Elizabeth City Co, Va mar bonds.)

Baker, Moses, will in Chowan Co N. C. p Jan 1724. Sons: Bennett, & William. (No other legatees.)

Baker, Henry, Com' J. P. in Chowan Co, July 15, 1731. His son Henry, made pet' to build a Mill on Sarum Swamp, 1748/9, which was granted.

Baker, William, & wife Elizabeth, sold land in Hertford Co, N. C. 200a, 1717/18.

Baker, Benjamin, m Elizabeth Harvey, Feb 15, 1778.

The Baker family, lived in that part of Chowan which was cut off, & made part of Gates Co, in 1779. Their names do not appear on the Quaker records. They were probably at first Episcopalians. This family figured in a very prominent way in N. C. Many of the male members taking part in the Rev war, & holding offices of rank.

We do not lay claim to either Henry, or Lawrence Baker, whose will was p in Gates Co, Nov 1807, Naming wife Anna Maria, (Burgess) Sons: John Burgess Baker, d Elizabeth Harvey (wife of Col Joseph) daus Agatha, Anna Maria, & Martha Susan, sons: Simmons, James, & Richard (s of brother Wm dec'd). James B. Baker Ex.

Quit Rents for Albemarle Co, from Sept 29, 1729 to Mar 1732, show that Wm Baker Sr, paid on 800a, Wm Baker Jr, pd on 100a, Benj Baker, on 150a, Henry, on 2000a.

Henry Baker of Vir, apt his friend Sam'l Swann Esq, Att. (Col Record.) He pet the Court in 1720, for a "lapsed patent, in Hertford Co, on Wickocon." He was "keeper of a Ferry" over Chowan River, near Menherring. (July 31, 1722.) Henry Baker, Merchant of Vir, brought suit, agst Wm Early, "Att a Court Holden at ye House of Col'o Jno. Hecklefield, (in Perq) Mar 29, 1703." He is also at other times called "Colonel." He was a member of the Assembly Nov 17, 1744. This was Henry (2) as Henry (1) was dec'd at this time.

Another Henry Baker, was member of Assembly, from Hertford Co, April 14, 1778 to Nov 3, 1788, Dec 8, 1789. Allowed £51-9-8 for "traveling 340 miles, with 3 Ferries to cross."

Lawrence Baker, Justice, in Hertford Co. Congress 22, Dec, 1776, District Auditor. In Pro Congress, N. C. at Hillsborough, Aug 20, 1775, from Hertford Co, serving until Nov 13, 1776. Col Lawrence Baker, was appointed a Field Officer of Minute Men, from Hertford Co, Sept 9, 1775. Councillor at Fayetteville, Nov 10, 1788. He Represented Edenton District, Sept 9, 1775.

James Baker, presented a pet' through Wm Wynn, of Hertford Co, Nov 26, 1790. He was living in Bertie Co, 1786, when the inhabitants of sd Co, petitioned for the Court House to be moved to Windsor.

Benjamin Baker, nominated by Committee, "to be returned to the Pro' Congress, agreeable to Resolve." (no date) Hertford Co. He received pay for Army services, £2-8-8, by H. Murfree, at Halifax Sept 1, 1784. (Warrenton Settlement.) He was a private, in Dixons Co, 10 Reg, Abraham Shepard Col. Enlisted April 15, 1781, & served 12 months.

Wm Baker was a private in White's Co, Jan 26, 1776, 3 years service, discharged April 1, 1779, received pay £58-14-6. He was a musician, in Blounts Co, July 20, 1778, 9 months service. In Assembly, from Hertford Co April 14, 1778.

Thomas Baker private, Nelsons Co, Feb 14, 1777. Dec'd Dec 15, 1779.

John Baker private, Ensloes Co, 5 Reg 1777. Deserted Mar 15, 1777.

John Baker, Lt Walkers Co, 7 Reg Nov 28, 1776, promoted to Capt July 1777. P. M. June 1778/79.

James Baker private, Yarborrows Co, 1781-April 22, 1782.

Isaac Baker private, Jones Co, Oct 1, 1781, 12 months services.

Baker Marriages (Chowan Co. Mar Bonds)

Baker, John, m Elizabeth Wilson, Sept 5, 1754. d of James Wilson.
Baker, John, m Martha Cherry, Sept 17, 1790.
Baker, Wm Wilson, m Ferebee Jobe, Aug 24, 1795.
Baker, Levi, m Polly Williford, Aug 24, 1803.
Baker, William, m Polly Bowen, Dec 7, 1805.
Baker, Levi, m (2) Polly Churchwell, June 5, 1806.
Baker, Isaac, m Mary Outlaw, Dec 26, 1807. Sec John Wynns.
Baker, Jeremiah, m Elizabeth Curry, Sept 22, 1808.
Baker, Timothy, m Keziah Parker, Aug 3, 1813.
Baker, Matthew, m Temperance Fullerton, Aug 31, 1824.
Baker, James F., m Rosetta Ward, June 22, 1863.

Baker, Abigail, (wife of Moses,) was d of Thomas Barker, of Edenton, whose will was p in Chowan Co, Oct 16, 1786.

The Bakers drifted over from Gates, into Perq Co, or they may have been in that part of said Co, which was cut off, from Perq in 1779. The County of Perq at one time, embraced part of what is now Gates, almost to the Va line. Gates was formed from Chowan, & part of Perq Counties. Deeds in Perq, call for land around "Orapeake" (Coropeak), & that is just over the Va boundary.

BARROW

John Barrow, had a grt for land in Perq, 300a, "at Yawpim Creeque, Prec't of Berkley, at the mouth of little, or Barrows Creeque." 1681. This land was renewed to him, Apl 24, 1694. He was one of the Justices of Perq, when the precinct was formed, & continued to serve in that capacity, being called Steward, & some time Judge.

John Barrow m Sarah Sutton, Feby 1, 1668, issue: 1 Johannah b July 10, 1669—2 William b Feby 1, 1671—3 John b June 3, 1674—4 Elizabeth b Dec 25, 1676, d Dec 16, 1687—5 Ann b Aug 3, 1679—6 Sarah b Jan 15, 1682-3—7 George b Aug 4, 1685—8 James b Jany 24, 1687—9 Joseph b April 4, 1690.

John Barrow d June 10, 1718. His will p in Perq Co, Aug 1718. Sons: John, Joseph, James. Will proven before Gov Charles Eden.

As he names no other legatees, we are led to believe, his other children, died before this date, also his wife.

Ann Barrow, (d of John) m John Bentley, Nov 6, 1694.

William Barrow, (s of John) m Elizabeth Cook (Relict of John) June 14, 1696. issue: William (2) b Feby 9, 1697.

Elizabeth Barrow b Apl 3, 1710—John b Oct 20, 1713—Mary b Jan —, 1716. These are not placed, from the fact that no father, or mother is mentioned.?

John Barrow (2) m Sarah ——— issue: Sarah b Aug 8, 1712, Rebeckah b June 12, 1714. His will p in Perq, Aug 12, 1719, names son: John (3) dau's Sarah, Rebecca, Elizabeth, & Margaret, wife Rachell. Ex brother Joseph.

John (3) Barrow will Perq, p Mar 5, 1742. d. s. p. To Sisters Sarah Ashley, & Margaret Barrow, bequest. Cousins John, & Joseph Ashley (nephews).

Joseph Barrow m Jeane (Bundy?) issue: 1 Sarah b Dec 20, 1720—2 Joseph (2) b Apl 6, 1724. He m 2d Sarah, issue: 3 John b Jany 30, 1730—4 Orpha b June 20, 1735. Mrs. Jane Barrow died June 13, 1727-8.

Joseph Barrow Will Perq, p Jan 1755. Sons: John, William, dau's Elizabeth Bunday (wife of Josiah), Ann, & Orpah Barrow, wife Sarah, gr-son William Barrow.

William & Mourning Barrow, were Orphans of Joseph Jr, 4, 6mo 1753, Sarah Admix. Joseph, & Sarah Orphans of William, June 20, 1771. Charles Moore Guardian. Orpha, & Ann Orphans of Ann Standin, Eri Barrow Guardian. 1798.

Humphrey Barrow m Sarah, & had Thomas b July 16, 1691.

Joseph Barrow m Margaret Fletcher, 14, 5mo 1807. (Suttons Creek Mo Meeting.)

BARTLETT

(Barclift)

William Barclift had grt for land in Perq 150a on Little River, adj John Godfrey. July 23, 1694.

Bartlett, William (s of William, & Elizabeth) & Ann Duren (d of George, & Ann) were m Oct 6, 1698. issue: 1 Thomas b Sept 25, 1699—2 William b Feby 17, 1700/1—3 John b Feb 15, 1703/4—4 Samuel b May 18, 1706.

Bartlett, William, will Albemarle Co, p July 1698. Eldest son: William, (to whom he left a plan' adj William Arnold) s Thomas, (to whom he left land, adj Thomas Godfrey), Exrs Elizabeth & William Bartlett. Clerk of Court, William Glover. (This was father, of above said William, who m Ann Durant.)

Bartlett, John (s of Wm, & Ann) m Ann Parish (d of John, who names her in his will, Mar 24, 1739) issue: 1 John b May 13, 1724—2 Ann b Dec 16, 1725. Will of John Barclift p in Perq, July 1759. Wife Elizabeth (2d wife). Sons: Asa, Demson, Benjamin, John, & Noah. Dau's Mary. & Elisa Sanderson.

Bartlett, Thomas, (brother of John) will p in Perq, Jan 1750. Names sons: Wm, Thomas, Joseph. Daus: Sarah Bidgood, Elizabeth Wright, Mary Jackson, & Anne Gorden, wife Elizabeth.

Bartlett, William (2), William (1) m Sarah Weeks, (gr-dau of Thomas Weeks Esq, 1771) His will Perq p Dec 19, 1733, Names only one son William (3), & wife Sarah.

Bartlett, William (3), s of William (2) William (1) will Perq, p Jan 1748. Sons: Joshua, Samuel, Joseph, Thomas, John, d Mary Gibson, Gr-son William (4), s of Joshua).

Bartlett, Joshua, will p Perq, Jan 1756. Sons: William (4), James, Blake, daus Miriam & Ann, wife Mary. (She was probably d of Blake Baker, as the name of Blake, appears in that family, as a given name.)

Eliza Sanderson, d of John Barclift, m 2d ———— Trumball (of William) before Feb 4, 1774. John Barclift, in his will bequeathed to his wife, his "brick house." As there is only one very old "brick house" in Perq, the one on the road to Harveys Neck, this may probably be the same one here mentioned. No one seems to know when this house was erected.

Bartlett, Thomas, wife Elizabeth, was d of Thomas Holloway (Hollowell). Bartlett, Rachel, (d of Elizabeth) m Francis Foster, before Feb 25, 1777.

Bartlett, William (4), m Ann Clayton, April 16, 1792. (Mar bonds, Perq Co.)

Ecursus, Foster: "William Foster, & Diana Harris was Married by Rev Mr Taylor, 1675." and had according to his will Oct 9, 1687, son Francis, d Elizabeth.

John Foster, & Ann Williams "were Maried at a Meeting, held at ye house of Hanah Philips, in Perquimans the 1st of May, 1689." m 2d Elizabeth ———— issue: 1 Susannah, b Dec 17, 1695—2 Elizabeth, b Oct 17, 1698—3 Richard, b Oct 20, 1701.

Francis Foster, by wife Frances had issue: 1 Hannah, b Jany 6, 1715—2 Elizabeth, b Apl 1, 1717.

Francis Foster, of Accomack, (son of William, & Margaret) m Mrs. Hannah Gosby, relict of John (née Nicholson, d of Christopher, & Hanah) "were m Aug 14, 1694, by Mr. John Whidby." (Justice.)

Frances Foster (wife of Francis) made her will in Perq, p Jan 27, 1763, naming son William, dau's Elizabeth Barclift, & Frances Hall, gr-dau Elizabeth Foster. (Elizabeth Foster, d of Williiam, & Ann was b Jany 16, 1741/2.)

Frederick Foster (relationship uncertain) will p in Perq, April 23, 1784, names: Brother Francis Foster's children, and children of Gilbert Leigh, Joseph Bateman, children of brother John Foster, sister Sarah Night, brother Ellsberry Foster, sister Winnifred Foster, Francis Pits, Demsey Newby's widow, Mary Bateman's children, Mary Maudlin, widow Stevenson.

John Foster was granted land in Chowan Co (200a) on Yawpim River. Sept 15, 1694.

Francis Foster was granted land 160a in "perquimans precinct," on Suttons Creek, Nov 11, 1719.

William Foster died Oct 10, 1687. His wife Diana m 3d Thomas White (Her 1 husband was Thomas Harris.)

Ann Foster, wife of John, died Oct 30, 1692.

Elizabeth Foster was drowned April 25, 1688.

WILL OF FRANCIS FOSTER

(Minute book, 1755-1761, Perq Co.)

To son William, "plantation whereon I live, and two negro men, a negro woman, & two negro boys." To dau Frances Hall, "a negro wench, and two negro boys. To dau Elizabeth Barclift, "A Negro wench, and a negro woman." Son William Ex. Test' James Gibson, Abraham Riggs, Richard Whidbee. Probated Apl 1761.

BATEMAN

Jonathan Bateman, was granted 400a, in Perq, "on West side of Perq River, in the pocoson, by ye side of Robert Wilsons Creek." 1684.

John Bateman, 250a, on ye North side of Perq River, & West side of Lillys Creek. He had another grt, 145a on North East side of Perq River, adj Atterways Eastermost bounds. Mar 30, 1704.

Bateman, Jonathan, m Margaret ——— issue: 1 Jonathan (2) b Feb 12, 1676—2 John b Nov 2, 1678—3 Thomas b Sept 13, 1688—4 Mary b May 16, 16—.

Bateman, Margaret, wife of Jonathan, died Sept 15, 1688.

Bateman, Jonathan, m 2d Hannah Edge ——— 1692. By Francis Hartley, J. P.

Bateman, Mary, the last child of Jonathan, must have been her child, as she was born after the death of Margaret, his first wife.

Bateman, Jonathan, m 3d Elizabeth, widow of Lawrence Arnold, Sept 28, 1694. She survived him, & is named in his will, which was p in Albemarle, (Perq precinct) Jan 1695-6. He names sons: Jonathan, John, Thomas, & dau Mary. Hannah Bateman Dept this Life, Dec 4, 1692.

A petition was presented to the Court, April 9, 1702, by Jonathan Bateman (2), to "lett Mr Wm Wilkinson, have a pattent for 400a, Surveyed for Mr Sam Swann, in Lillies Creek" he having sold same to sd Wilkinson. This land was later called "Stevensons Point."

Bateman, Jonathan (2), m Elizabeth Holloway, (d of Thomas, & Elizabeth) Sept 23, 1697, issue; 1 Margaret b Oct 20, 1698—2 Nathan b Sept 10, 1702— 3 Jonathan b May 2, 1705.

Bateman, John, d. s. p. will Perq July Court 1750. Nephew: Thomas, to whom he bequeathed plan' called "Broad Neck." Brother Thomas (father of Thomas) Mary Hawkins (d of nephew John Hawkins) Elizabeth Phelps (d of brother Jonathan Bateman) Mary Phelps (d of brother Thomas) Sarah Butterre, (d of brother Jonathan) Exrs Thomas Bateman (brother), William Bateman (nephew).

Bateman, William, m 1st Hannah Mullen, Sept 12, 1759. Jos Barclift sec. m 2d Bettie Mullen, Sept 26, 1760. Father Abraham Mullen. Will p in Perq July Court 1773. Sons: Benjamin, John, Joseph, gr-dau Betty, d of son Benjamin, wife Betty.

Bateman, Thomas, will p in Perq, Oct 1766. Son: William, wife Sarah, d Mary Phelps, gr-son John Phelps Bateman. His perishable Est was sold, by his wife Sarah, May 17, 1763.

Bateman, Thomas (2), m Elizabeth Raper, before Nov 2, 1787. (See John Rapers will.)

Bateman, Benjamin, m Mary Colson, Feb 21, 1765. (Mar bonds Perq Co.)

Bateman, Jonathan (3), m Sarah Hornbee, Dec 30, 1794. (Mar bonds Perq Co.)

BEASLEY

Robert Beasley recorded his mark, in Perq Co, Apl Court 1689. He was married to Johannah Jenkins, Sept 19, 1689. (Berkeley Par Reg.)

He had two grants for land, in Perq, one June 1, 1694, 218a, & the other, May 1, 1694, for 282a. Robert Beasley, had a former wife, Sarah, by whom he had, Francis Beesley, b July 11, 1678, & James, whose age is not given

Robert Beasley appears to have married three times. Mary wid of Robert Beasley recorded the Division of his Est, 1695.

James (s of Robert, & Sarah Beasley) m Mary Cropley (d of John, & Ann) Mar 17, 1675. James Beasley, moved to Bertie Co, where his will was p Jan 1758, his only legatee being William Bentley, son of John, who was probably a gr-son.

Francis Beasley (s of Robert, & Sarah) m Hannah Sutton (d of Joseph, & Deliverance (Nicholson) May 15, 1701. We find him married to Mary ──── before 1704. Francis Beasley, & wife Mary, had issue: 1 James b Aug 4, 1704—2 Robert b Dec 1, 1707. Hannah wife of Robert Beasley, died Nov 7, 1702.

James Beasley was a member of the House of Burgesses, Oct 11, 1709.

Francis Beasley, will Albemarle Co (Perq) p May 20, 1719, names son Jeames, to whom he bequeathed a plan' on S. side of Perq River, To son Robert, land on Morattock River. Wife Mary. Ex Jeams Beasley (brother). This will was p before Gov Eden. James Beasley, m Miss Ann Taylor, Oct 19, 1773. (Mar bonds Perq Co.) James Beasley's Division, Chowan Co 1754. Shows children: John, James, Mary, & Thomas, mother Mary Woolard, John, & Thomas Beasley (probably brothers) Mary Payne, wife of Peter. Thomas Beasley, m Martha ────.

William Beasley, dec'd 19, 1mo 1754, Betty Beasley Admix.

Thomas Beezley, will p July 3, 1733, (no Co given) Sons; John, & Thomas, wife Elizabeth Ex. This will was not made in Perq.

The will of Samuel Beasley, Nov 13, 1735, names brothers; Francis, & Thomas, Mary Beasley (gr-mother) John Beasley, & James Beasley Jr. Witnesses: William Cropley, Thomas Bentley, & Elizabeth Wells. The witnesses, of this will, prove it to be of Perq Co. (See deeds in Perq, for further data.)

BENTLEY

Bentley, Richard, m Jane ──── issue: 1 May b August 29, 1662—2 John b Dec 22, 1665—3 Richards b Feby 2, 1668—4 William b August 15, 1671.

Bentley, Richard, m 2d Lidia Mann, July 3, 1677, by Mr. Wood.

Bentley, Richard (s of Richard) died before May 27, 1697, d. s. p. his will on that date, names as sole legatee, Diana White. Coat of Arms on Seal.

John Bentley, m Ann Barrow, (d of John, & wife Sarah) Nov 6, 1694. (Berkeley Par.)

John Bentley, will Perq, p Nov 1695. Brother William, cousin Elizabeth Leary, wife Ann. Bro-in-law Jenkins Williams, & William Barrow. Sons: John, & Roger.

John Bentley (2) moved to Tyrrell Co, where his will was p June 1754.

Amos Bentley, m Zilpah Simpson, May 3, 1766. (Mar bonds Perq County.) (See deeds of Perq Co.)

BELMAN

John Belman, m Sarah Wilson, (d of Robert, & Ann (Blount, d of Thomas), who came to Perq Co, from Isle of Wight Co Va. John Belmans children are given in Symon Creek Reg, as follows: Sary, b 28, 6mo 1688—Ester, b 22, 1mo 1691—John, b 7, 9mo 1695—Robert, b 2, 12mo 1697—Ane, & Mary (twins) b 13, 1mo 1701—William, b 6, 5mo 1704—Ruth, b 11, 2mo 1707. Hannah, d of John, & Sarah b Aug 28, 1689. Berkeley Reg.)

John Belman, will p in Pasq Co, Jan 1706/7, names only sons: John, & Robert, and wife Sarah.

Robert Wilson in his will, Perq Prect, p Jan 11, 1696, names his gr-children, Sarah, & Ester Belman.

Esther Belman m ——— Turner, at a meeting in Pasq Co. They were allowed to be "free of each, other," & were charged by the Quakers, "not to let it happen again." (See Col Rec, Vol I, Quaker Rec Pasq Co.)

John Belman (2) will Perq Co, p Oct 1740, names as only legatees, wife Mary, & d Sarah. After this the Belman family, disappear from the records, in Perq Co. Probably the male line died out, or they moved to parts unknown.

BLANCHARD

As this family lived until early in 1800, in Gates County, very little can be found on the Perquimans Records about the Blanchards. Mr. Julian Blanchard of New York City, is preparing a lengthy history of this good family, for publication it is hoped, so this book will grant to Dr. Blanchard the privilege of doing his family in his own way, and we feel sure it will be done right, if he follows all the traditions of the Blanchard family. A few stray items will not come amiss, however, and these may have escaped the vigilant eye of said Dr. Julian Blanchard.

The earliest known records of a person by this name, was a grant to Benjamin Blanchard, of 455a "upon Wareck (Warrick) Swamp, at the mouth of Beaver Dam" Oct 16, 1701. This land lay in what is now Gates Co N. C. but was then in the limits of Chowan County.

Sarah Blanchard was daughter of William Walton, of Chowan Co and she was m to ——— before Dec 24, 1760. William Walton was father of Palatiah Walton whose will was p in Chowan Co, Nov 6, 1776.

Mary Blanchard (d of Aaron, & Zilpah) married James Sumner. Aaron Blanchard was dead before 1758, Heirs wife, sons: Aaron Jr, Moses, Mary Sumner, and Sarah Blanchard. Zilpah Blanchard, wife of Aaron, was dau of Mary Speight of Bertie Co. Aaron Blanchard was granted 152a adj George Spivey, Sept 28, 1728. (Land in Gates Co.) He is called at this time of N. C. but the grant is listed on the Nansemond Co Land Book.

Mary Speight of Bertie whose will was p in said Co, May 7, 1743, was wife of Thomas Speight of Perquimans, who in his will, said Co, p Apl 27, 1737, names sons: Moses, and Isaac Speight. Her will names dau Zilpah Blanchard. Zilpah was Admix of her dec'd husband Aaron Blanchard, 1751, children named in his division: Rachel, Monica, Aaron (2) and Moses Blanchard.

Mary Blanchard widow of Robert, 1733. (Records Chowan Co.)

Mary Blanchard Admix of her dec'd husband Abraham, 1749. (Chowan Records.)

Josiah Blanchard was the first to move to Perquimans, and his name is found on Tax List in Perquimans about 1826. He married Martha Winslow, Nov 3, 1856. (Mar bonds Chowan Co.)

From 1832 the Blanchards have been identified with Perquimans Co, their mercantile business being the leading Store in Hertford, and their dealings with the residents of the town and country, always the fairest, have won for them a reputation for honest, square dealing, which makes the Blanchard countersign a solid byword of every one in the county.

BLITCHENDEN

William Blitchenden was granted 50a of land in Nansemond Co Va, Feb 24, 1675/6.

Thomas Blitchenden was granted 53a on Newbegun Creek "perquimans precinct" Nov 11, 1718. Newbegun Creek as the boundaries appear at this time, was in Pasquotank County, but this land was probably in the North Western part of the Co, and might very well be called Perquimans, as the lines were not so well defined as at present. Many tracts of Land in Gates Co, were until 1779 listed for Taxes in Perquimans Co, and the Deeds in Perq show that the boundary of said County stretched as far as, or nearly to the Virginia line.

Thomas Blitchenden made his will in Perq Co, p July 23, 1745, naming sons: John, William, and Abraham, dau Sarah, wife Mary (née Norcom, d of Thomas) They had issue: 1 Thomas, b Sept 15, 1715—2 Sarah, b Jany 14, 1716/17—3 John, b Oct 23, 1718—William, b Jany 23, 1720.

Thomas Blitchenden bequeathed to son John, a "plantation on Sound Side" and to son William, "plantation whereon I now live." (See Deeds in Perq, for further information.)

This family from the name appears to have been an old English one, and they probably came into Perquimans simultaneously with the Norcoms. However that may be, they tarried only a short while, or died out, as the name of Blitchenden soon became extinct. They may have migrated west, as so many Perquimans people did, about 1760, but the writer has no data on the subject.

BLOUNT

Among adventurers to America 1620; John, Richard, & Edward Blount. (Burke.)

Richard Blount settled in Surry Co Va, where his wife Mary, was his "Relict" Sept 19, 1656, Capt Geo Jordan Ex. (Surry Co Rec.)

Thomas Blount, "only son of Richard dec'd" sold land in Surry Co, which was grt unto Robert Warren dec'd, Aug 1, 1649, & was conveyed to sd Richard Blount, Apl 2, 1650, said Thomas Blount "came of age Nov last;" land on Lawnes Creek Surry Co, adj Capt Lawrence Baker. Mar 1, 1677.

Charles Ford "some time of Surry Co, who in his life time was seized of a Divident of land, 250a, which was pat' May 19, 1638 (then in the Co of James City) in Surry Co, adj Sunken Marsh, over against Dancing Point, upon James River, he being the first proprietor" dying intestate, sd land became Escheat, and was reissued to Thomas Blount, & Richard Washington jointly, then orphans, sons-in-laws unto sd Ford, sold sd land unto Jno Goring, Mar 1 1678.

RECORDS OF DEEDS

Thomas Blount was presented by the Gr-jury May 3, 1681, "for not attending Church." He was a Tithable in Sunken Marsh Par, Surry Co, June 1681, (Surry Rec.)

James Blount was living in Isle of Wight Co Va, 1660, moved to Chowan Co N. C. 1664-69. He was the younger son of Sir Walter Blount of Sodington, Worcester, England, who was Capt in the Life Guards of Charles II. In England the family can be carried back for many generations, to and through the Conquest to Normandy, and then for many years. Without doubt they can boast of being "an old family" with perfect right.

With the Conqueror, three young Blounds, sons of Blound of Guisnes, went to England in his train. (See Burke's Heraldry, for descent.)

James Blount who settled in Chowan, is said to have had a brother Thomas, who followed him to N. C. and settled on the Taw, or Pamlico River. This brother Thomas, (3 son of Sir Walter Blount) came to America in 1664, & moved to N. C. 1673, m 1st Ann Wilson, m 2d Mary Scott widow of Joseph of Perq Co. They first took up their residence on Kendricks Creek (now called Mackeys Creek) in Washington Co N. C. issue: Thomas, James, Benjamin, Jacob, Esau.

Thomas Blount (2) m Ann Reading, issue: James, John, & Jacob. William son of Jacob Blount became Gov of Tenn 1790. Jacob Blount, b 1726, fourth son of Thomas & Ann Reading, participated in the battle of Alamance, 1771, & was an Officer in the Rev War. He m Barbara Gray, and 2d Hannah Baker, née Salter. He had issue: William, (Gov of Tenn) Ann, John Gray, Louisa, Reading, m Mary Harvey; Thomas, Jacob, m ——— Collins. Barbara, Willie, Sharpe, m Penelope Little.

James Blount (brother of Thomas) lived at Mulberry Hill Chowan Co. Capt of Militia, member of the Council, and one of the Lords Pro' Dept; m Anne (d of Balthazer Willis of Ipswich Mass, widow of Robert Roscoe of Roanoke) issue: James, Thomas, John, Ann, & Elizabeth. James Blount died 1686. His widow m 2d Seth Sothel Gov of the Province of N. C. After his death she m for her 3d husband John Leah of Nansemond Co Va. (See Blount Gen, in N. C. Hist Reg Vol 1-4)

Edmund Blount (s of Charles Worth Blount, & Mary Clayton) moved to Perq Co, and acquired large tract of land by purchase, & became a man of great influence and wealth, taking part in the official affairs of the county. He m Mary Hoskins d of William, & Sarah née Whedbee) (See Hoskins family N. C. Hist Reg Vol 3.) A detailed account of this family can be found in N. C. Hist Reg Vol 1-4-pp 522-2324, also from Deeds of Perq Co in this book.

BUNDY

William Bundy, the first by that name to appear in Perq, married Mary Pearre (Rellicke of John) Desember 15, 1683. (Berkeley Par Reg, Perq Co.)

Caleb Bundy, (who was a brother of William) m Jane Maners, "at ye quarterly Meeting," July —, 1690.

William Bundy, had previously married Elizabeth ———, probably before coming to N. C., who died Mar 4, 1676, by whom he had one son Samuel, b Feby 4, 1676. Also a dau Mary, who was 1st wife of Timothy Clare. In her marriage bond, she is named as his dau. He had by his 2d wife Mary (née Scott) widow Pearre) a dau, Sarah b Jan 23, 1685, who married Francis Pettitt, of Chowan Co.

William Bundy Dept this Life, Mar 27, 1692. Mary Bundy m (3d) Nicholas Simons, June 30, 1692. (Berkeley Par Reg, Perq Co.)

Bundy, Caleb, will Pasquotank Co, names brothers: William, & John. (No date.) He appears to have died childless, & no wife is mentioned.

Little River, Mo Meeting Reg. Gives the following:

John Bundy's Children: 1 Johnua b 4, 4mo 1717—2 John b 12, 1mo 1719—d 8-2, 1745. 3 Caleb b 12, 5mo 1721—4 William b 21, 1mo 1723—5 Jean b 12, 1mo 1725—6 Benjamin b 12, 12mo 1729.

Bundy, Samuel, (s of William) Planter; of Pasq Co, m Tamer Symons (d of Jeremiah) 5, 10mo 1696, "at the house of Henry White, in Perq." Had son Jeremiah, b July 21, 1725. Samuel Bundy also had a son Samuel, b July 24, 1724.

The will of Samuel Bundy, Pasq Co, p July 1740, names sons: William, Abraham, Gideon, Josiah, d Jane Pike, (wife of Benjamin) Wife Anne. Cousin Samuel Bundy, wife, Ann, & Thomas Nicholsin Exrs.

David Bundy of Perq, will p April 1750, names brothers: Jeremiah, Moses, & Caleb. Uncle Josiah Bundy. (He evidently died without issue.)

Caleb Bundy, of Pasq Co, will April 27, 1721, Sons: John, Benjamin, Samuel, (to whom he left all his land, "up Little River") d Mary Bundy (land bought of brother Samuel) gr-dau Liday Bundy, (d of son William). His wife is not named.

Anne Bundy, will Pasq Co, p Dec 1744. Sons: Gideon, (his wife Miriam née Bogue) Abraham, gr-dau Lydia Bundy. (She was widow of Samuel Bundy.)

Benjamin Bundy, of Pasq Co, names in his will, Pasq Co, p Oct 26, 1728, Wife Hannah, to whom he left a plan' of 1,200a. Brother Samuel Ex.

William Bundy of Perq, will p Jan 1749, names dau Sarah Barrow (wife of Joseph) wife Mary.

The Bundys lived on the edge of Pasquotank Co, & some of them in Perq. They were identified as much with one County, as another.

The children of Samuel Bundy are given in Little River Record, as follows: 1 Mary (d of Samuel Bundy, & Jean his wife), b 24, 2mo 1732—2 Liddah b 23, 7mo 1733—3 Sarah b 5, 3mo 1736—d 19, 9mo 1739—4 Caleb b 28 2mo 1738—d 9, 9mo 1739.

Children of William Bundy: 1 Joseph b 2, 6mo 1745—2 John b 4, 6mo 1752—3 Mary b 28, 6mo 1754.

Joseph Bundy m Sarah—issue: 1 Josiah (no date) 2 William b 15, 11mo 1760—d 27, 11mo 1760.

Josiah Bundy m Elizabeth—issue: 1 Sarah b 22, 8mo 1736—2 Joseph b 26, 10mo 1738—3 Ellis b 1, 7mo 1741—d 14, 3mo 1762—4 Joshua b 18, 4mo 1744—5 Josiah b 12, 4mo 1748—6 Jane b 8, 5mo, 1751—7 Caleb b —, 11 mo 1753—8 Sarah b 18, 9mo 17——.

Caleb, & Elizabeth Bundy,—issue: 1 Dempsey b 16, 4mo 1746—2 John b 10, 11mo 1747—3 Miriam b 1, 8mo 1749—4 Samuel b 28, 3mo 1756—5 Sarah b 9, 1mo 1759.

Bunday, Dempsey m Mary—issue: 1 Zadock b 20, 9mo 1777—2 William b 1, 1mo 1780—3 John b 22, 5mo 1782.

Bundy, Gideon, m Miriam Bogue, (d of William) issue: 1 Lyda b 2, 10mo 1740—2 Samuel b 27, 10mo 1742—3 Sarah b 11, 8mo 1745—4 John b 17, 1mo 1748—5 Miriam b 27, 10mo 1753—6 Christopher b 20, 4mo 1758. Miriam wife of Gideon Bundy d 14, 3mo 1762.

Bundy, Josiah, m Mary Symons, (d of Jehosaphat) 25, 12mo 1766, issue: 1 Lydia b 29, 9mo 1767—2 Elizabeth b 4, 4mo 1769—3 Sarah b 17, 6mo 1770.

Bundy, Joshua, m Elizabeth Bailey, 7, 8mo 1763, issue: 1 Elizabeth b 4, 7mo 1764—2 Sarah b 24, 4mo 1767—3 Ellis b 4, 6mo 1769—4 Hannah, & Penninah, (twins) b 1, 3mo 1773.

Bundy, Caleb, m Miriam (Nicholson) issue: 1 Benjamin b 30, 10mo 1763—Caleb b 16, 5mo 1765—3 John b 24, 10mo 1766—4 Jeremiah b 21, 2mo 1768—5 James b 28, 7mo 1769—6 Hannah b 26, 3mo 1772—7 Moses b 26, 11mo 1774—8 Samuel b 26, 9mo 1776—9 Christopher b 13, 9mo 1777.

Bundy, John, m Lyda Griffin (d of Joseph) issue: 1 Gideon b 31, 3mo 1774—2 Reuben b 25, 11mo 1776.

Marriages

Bundy, John, m Elizabeth Keaton (Newbegun Creek In) 16, 6mo 1716.) (Quaker Records, Perq Co.)

Bundy, William, m Anne Keaton (Newbegun Creek In) 19, 9mo 1719. (Quaker Records, Perq Co.)

Bundy, Sarah, m Joseph Barrow, (Symons Creek), 2, 3mo 1745.

Bundy, Abraham, m Naomi White, (Symons Creek) 3, 1mo 1748.

Bundy, William, m Hannah Morris (d of John & Mary) 6, 10mo 1750.

Bundy, Miriam, Zadock, William, & Mary Bundy, (children of Demsey, received "Unity" in Quaker Meeting, Pasq Co, 19, 1mo 1788.

Bundy, Josiah, was one among those holding slaves, in Pasq Co, 15, 9mo 1787.

Deaths

Bundy, Jane, Dept this Life, 23, 11 mo 1719.

Bundy, Caleb, Dept this Life 31, 11mo 1723 (21?).

Bundy, William, (s of Caleb) Dept this Life 9, 2mo 1721.

Bundy, Caleb Sr, Dept this Life, 4, 3mo 1721.

Bundy, Mary (d of Caleb Sr) Dept this Life, 10, 3mo 1721.

Bundy, Benjamin, Dept this Life, 13, 8mo 1728.

Bundy, John, Dept this Life 22, 2mo 1731.

Bundy, Elizabeth, wife of John, d 17, 3mo 1731.

Bundy, Jean, dau of John, d 30, 1mo 1735.

Bundy, Elizabeth, wife of William, d 7, 10mo 1748.

Bundy, Miriam, dau of sd Elizabeth, d Last of 9mo 1748.

Bundy, Samuel, Dept this Life —— 10, 1750, in the 49 year of his age.

Bundy, Samuel, Dept this Life, 18, 5mo 1753, age 22 years.

Bundy, Gideon, Dept this Life 17, 2mo 1762.

Bundy, Mary, (wife of Caleb) Dept this Life 19, 2mo 1762.

Bundy, John, s of Caleb, Dept this Life 14, 2mo 1762.

Bundy, Miriam, d of Caleb, Dept this Life 13, 2mo 1762.

Bundy, Samuel, s of Caleb, Dept this Life 22, 2mo 1762.

Bundy, Elizabeth, wife of Caleb, Dept this Life 11, 5 mo 1752.

The will of Josiah Bundy, is found in Minute book, 1755-61, (Perq Co Records). Said will dated 28, 12mo 1760. Made bequest to son Joseph, 39a of Wood land, adj where he now lives, To s Gideon all land in Pasq Co, To wife Elizabeth, all land in Perq, "for her Natual life, but not so as to hinder, my sons Ellis, & Joshua, from settling on their part of sd land" also 76a in Pasq Co, on the head of Little River, called "the forks." To s Joshua the other half of land, adj Francis Nixon, & half on a new Survey in Perq. To sons: Ellis, & Joshua, "all Right in 300a in Pasq Co, & all three patents in Perq, taken up by myself, Thomas Nicholson, & Gideon Bundy." To s Caleb 76a in Pasq Co, "which I had of Gideon, & Lydia Bundy." To d Jane a negro girl. Brother Gideon, & sons: Joseph, & Ellis Exrs. Test' Phin's Nixon, Tho Nicholson, Joseph Nicholson.

Pasquotank Mo Meeting

Bundy, Sarah, (Intention) m with John Bell, 21, 11mo 1789.
Bundy, John, (Intention) m Jemmima Low, 21, 8mo 1790.
Bundy, Josiah, (Intention) m Miriam Perisho, 15, 12mo 1792.
Bundy, Moses, (Intention) m Elizabeth Jones, 15, 12mo 1796.
Bundy, Guliema, (Intention) m Christopher Morris, 18, 2mo 1797.
Bundy, Pheribe, (Intention) m Isaac Morris, 20, 2mo 1802.
Bundy, Miriam, was "very much decayed, in mind" 21, 3mo 1801.

CALLOWAY

Richard Calloway, served on the Jury, in Isle of Wight Co Va July 14, 1664. Nothing further found there, about Richard, or his descendants.

Caleb Calloway, was living in Perq Precinct, as early as Mar 1, 1661, when he signed the deed made by the Indian Chief, to George Durant, on sd date. He probably bought land from the Indians, as Durant did, but there is no record of such a transaction, to be found anywhere.

Calloway, Caleb, m Elizabeth Laraunce, 29 ————. She was d of Will Lawrence, & wife Rachell Welsh. b Dec 24, 1655. Issue:

Calloway, William, s of Caleb, & Elizabeth, b Feby 13, 1671/2. d Nov 29, 1692.
Calloway, Dorothy, d of Caleb, & Elizabeth, b Aug 16, 1674.
Calloway, Caleb (2), s of Caleb, & Elizabeth, b Feby 21, 1676. d Dec 16, 1687.
Colloway, Joshua, s of Caleb, & Elizabeth, b July 17, 1679.
Calloway, Mary, d of Caleb, & Elizabeth, b Feb 19, 1681. d June 7, 1698.
Calloway, John, s of Caleb, & Elizabeth, b Sept 13, 1684. d Dec 18, 1687.
Calloway, Karhale, d of Caleb, & Elizabeth, b Feb 16, 1686.
Caleb Calloway died, June 15, 1706.
Calloway, Elizabeth, widow, m 2d John Pearre, (s of Wm & Margrett) 16—— (no date).

Caleb Calloway's will p (in Perq, but Co not given) June 13, 1706. He left to son & Ex Joshua, a "plan' on Yawpim River" names d Rachel, wife of John Wiatt. Gr-dau Elizabeth Wiatt, wife Elizabeth.

It seems from this will, that all his other children were dead. The records do not show what became of Dorothy, & Karhale.

Joshua Calloway m Elizabeth, (thought to have been a d of John Stepney) Issue: Elizabeth b Apl 13, 1716, m Robert Harman (s of Robt, & Elizabeth Freeman).

Ann b Feby 26, 1718/19. (Roman Calendar.)
Samuel b Feby 5, 1731/2.

Joshua Calloway had also a son John, (no record of his birth) who was given liberty April Court, 1744, to "*Chuse* his Gardian." (Minute book Perq Co.)

Joshua Calloway appears on the Tithe List, in Berkeley Parish Perq Co. 1740, with 4 Tithes.

John Calloway was Sheriff of Perq from Nov 25, 1751, to Mar 28, 1758. He was dead Mar 7, 1772. (Loose papers Perq Co.)

Joshua Callaway, will p in Perq Co, July 1742. Names sons: Thomas, John & Caleb, and dau Elizabeth Harman, gr-d Elizabeth Callaway, (d of Caleb) wife Elizabeth.

This will proves that Joshua Calloway had as well as John, a son Caleb, & son Thomas, whose ages are not recorded, in Berkeley Par Reg.

Caleb Calloway (3) m Alice, (widow Calloway m 1st Joseph Pierce—his widow Feb 28, 1729). Issue: Mary b Dec 20, 1737. m ——— Barto. Caleb (4) b Apl 22, 1742.

Caleb Calloway was on the Tithe List in Perq 1740, with 3 Tithes.

Thomas Calloway (s of Joshua) m Isabel Gerratt, Mch 20, 1728. (no record.)

John Calloway m Johanna ———
Issue: Elizabeth b Dec 31, 1750.
Zebulon b Oct 15, 1752.
Joseph b Dec 2, 1757.
Zipporah b Jan 10, 1761.
Sarah b Apl 20, 1766.

Thomas Pierce died before Oct Court 1757. when his Estate was divided, among the several representatives; To Alice Calloway "mother of sd dec'd" one part, to Mary Barto, "sister of the half Blood" to Caleb, & John Calloway, "brothers of the half Blood" each a part.

CHARLES

Jane Charles had a grt for land in Perq 200a on "Southwest side of Western Branch of Yawpim Creek, at a branch that divides sd land from Robert Harmon," Apl 1, 1694. She appears on the Rent Roll of Perq, prior to 1700, with 287a of land. The records do not make plain exactly who this Jane Charles father was. She is named in two of the Charles wills, as a sister. She died d. s. p. 1688.

Charles, William, m Abigail Balie, by Mr. Jefuery Magst, in Rode Island, 14———. Issue: 1 William (2) b July 13, 1661—2 Daniell b Sept 24, 1666—3 John b Nov 22, 1668—4 Jane b Jany 20, 1670, d July 12, 1688—5 Elizabeth b Jan 8, 167——6 Samuel b Mar 22, 1674—7 Isacke b Mar 12, 1676.

Charles, Elizabeth, d of William, & Abigail, m 1st John Long, Aug 11, 1687, m 2d "at a quarterly meeting," Dec 16, 1688, Samuel Nicholson.

Charles, William, Dept this Life Augst 6, 1677. His wife Abigail m 2d John Lary, 21 ———. Issue: Sarah Lary b Sept 15, 1680. Abigail Lury m 3d Francis Toms (1), Jan 6, 1683, issue: Abigail Toms, b Dec 10, 1684. Abigail Toms died Mar 17, 1687.

Charles, William (2), m Elizabeth Kent (b June 1, 1667) Nov 8, 1683, issue: Jane b Oct 1, 1685.

William Charles made his will (Co not given, but certainly in Perq) dated April 7, 1687. He bequeathed to brother John 120a of land, & to dau Jane "plantation I now live on" wife Elizabeth. Ex Francis Tomes (father) stepfather, & Jonathan Philips (Phelps). All of Perq County.

Daniell, Charles, d. s. p. (will Perq) April 17, 1687, names brothers: John, & Samuel, sister Jeane. Ex Francis Tomas (Toms) & Christopher ——— (Nicholson).

John Charles, also d. s. p. His will not dated & no Co given, names brother Samuel.

The will of Jeane Charles, Perq Precinct, July 11, 1688, names only Aunt Marie Stepney, & John Stepney, brothers, & father, but not named. Coat of Arms on Seal.

Charles, Samuel, m Elizabeth Jones, (d of Peter Jones Sr) no date, issue: 1 Jean b Dec 10, 1697—2 Elizabeth b Sept 22, 1700—3 Samuel (2) b Aug 20, 1703—4 John b Dec 22, 1705, m Mary, & had s William (3) b May 27, 1738.

Charles, John, dec'd 28, 3mo 1740, Margaret Relict. (Division of his Est Perq Co.)

Charles, John & William, were gr-sons of Peter Jones Sr, (Will Perq Co April Court 1752.)

Samuel Charles will Perq Co, p Mar 1728, names son Samuel, to whom he left a plan' "on which I live" son John "land on Gum Swamp" son Josuay same, dau's Lidey, Sarah, & Hannaugh Charles. Gr-dau Elizabeth Overman.

Hannah Charles, who was 2d wife of Samuel Charles, also made her will in Perq, p July 1752. She names son Edward Moulin, & dau's Elizabeth White, Sarah Perry, & Ann Cox, son-in-law Robert Cox, gr-dau Mary Moulin, (d of John), & gr-son John Moulin. (She was d of Joshua Toms, m 1 Ezekiel Maudlin, 2 Samuel Charles.)

William Charles (s of John, b 1738) will Perq p Jan 1771. Sons: William, Joshua, Aaron, & John, bro-in-law John Henby, wife Jane, d Margaret, father-in-law Aaron Albertson, Ex.

John Charles, will p Perq Co, Jan 1780. Son Daniel, brother Benjamin, wife Elizabeth, & Ralph Fletcher Exrs.

Samuel Charles m Hannah Davis, Oct 7, 1722, issue: Hannah b Dec 5, 1723.

CHESSON

Spelled variously on the Perq Records. John Cheston had a grt for land in perquimans Precinct, 300a on the mouth of Yawpim Creek, at the mouth of Chestons Cove, adj John Wyate. April 20, 1694. Richard Chaston grant, 200a on Perq River, adj Peter Gray, April 20, 1694.

Chastone, Roger, m Elizabeth, Cowley, May 5, 16—— issue: 1 John b Oct 5, 1661—m Elizabeth Long (d of James, & Elis) Aug 21, 1684. Issue: 1 Sarah b Jany 20, 1663, m John Hopkins Jan 14, 168—. 2 Deborah b Dec 22, 1665, m Walter Green. (No date.)

Walter Green had a grt for land in Perq, 400a, at the mouth of "little Creeque" & Yawpim Creeque, "in precinct of Berkley" 1681.

Roger Chasten Dep this Life April 9, 1669. Elizabeth Chasten m 2d Thomas Harloe (widower) Jan 26, 1672, & 3d Robert Incoson, 167—. He m 2d Ann.

Chaston, John & Elizabeth (Long) had issue: 1 James b May 11, 1692, m 2d Sarah ———. Issue: 2 Elizabeth b May 11, 1692, d Dec 17, 1693.

Chesten, Elizabeth, wife of John d December 24, 1687.

Chasten, John, d May 13, 1695.

Chesten, Richard, m Anne Garrett (sister of Daniel, & Wm) had issue: 1 Sarah b May 17, 1689—2 Daniel b May 3, 1692—3 Daniel (2d by name) b May 1, 1697.

Cheston, Richard, had 200a in Perq prior to 1700. (Rent Roll, Perq Co.)

Cheston Richard (2), m Elizabeth ———— & had issue: 1 Rachel b Sept 8, 1726—2 Richard (3) b Feby 27, 1727/8—3 Elizabeth b Apl 7, 1730—4 Mary b Feby 27, 1731/2—5 Joseph b May 6, 1735.

Cheaston, Richard, will Perq Co p Nov 22, 1715, names son Richard (2) wife Anne, gr-son Daniell Layton. Ex Joseph Jessop, & son Richard.

Anne Chesson, will Perq p Jan 17, 1727. Sons: John, James, & Joshua, sister Esbell Garrett. Ex Daniel, & Wm Garrett, (brothers).

James Chesson (s of John, & Elizabeth, b Nov 8, 1675) m 1st Sarah, & had a dau Elizabeth b May 11, 1692. He m 2d Ann, who was mentioned in his will p in Perq Co, May 19, 1729, naming sons: John, & James (2) & wife Anne. Ex Wm Egerton. (See deeds in Perq, for Chesson.)

John & Richard Chesson were probably brothers, & it is thought that Roger was their father, although they are not named as his children, in Berkeley Par Reg. They migrated from Perq, to Washington Co N. C.

CLARE

Ambrose Clare was grt land in James City Co Va, Oct 15, 1664, "at the head of Spring Branch, adj Hickmans line. (Land book 5—No 28, Richmond Va.) He had another grt, 1155a in Rappahannock Co Va, on N side of Sams Creek, Sept 6, 1667, for trans' Mark Sanders, Tho Jones, Nich Wilson, Sam Wilson & others; and had deeded to him 300a in James City Co, Oct 15, 1664.

John Clare was trans' to Va by Joseph Crowshaw, of York River, Feb 27, 1649. In a grant New Kent Co Va, William Clare names himself "son of Ambrose Clare" who resided in what is now Essex Co Va. The Clare family is of Royal descent. Christopher Cleave was a "subject in the colony at Jamestown," May 23, 1609. (Browns Genesis to America.)

William Cleve is named in the will of Giles Cory, of Lynn Mass, July 25, 1692, as "son-in-law," and Thomas Hire (Hare) of Surry Co Va, in his will, Mar 6, 1704 names Thomas, & William Clare, as his "grand-sons." As the Hares also moved to Perq Co N. C. we may very well say with a certain amount of certainty, that the William here spoken of, is the same which Timothy Clare of Perq, calls "father" in his marriage certificate.

Timothy Cleare granted 473a on Perq River, adj Wm Bundy dec'd. April 25, 1694. Tymo Clare grt 250a "on Perquimans River, adj land whereon he now lives" on E. side of sd River. Feb 4, 1713/4. He purchased of Patrick Kenedy, a plan' on Franks Creek, Feb 15, 1689, and another plan' at the head of Perq River, from Caleb, & Jean Bundy, 25, 2mo 1692/3. His land appears to have been situated on South West side of the Narrows of Perq River. Thomas Harvey of Perq, sold to Timothy Clare 200a on "Upper Vosses Creek," adj John Morgan, & Francis Toms. His land on North side of Perq, was on Brambly Branch, and was called "Round House land." His name is variously spelled on the records in Perq Co; Clare, Cleare, Clear, Clar, but it is each time the same person, as he is the only one of that name in the county, and had no male descendants. The line became extinct when he died. He was Purgess from Perq, Oct 11, 1709, Justice of Peace. (Col Records.) Berkeley Parish Reg gives the date of his marriage as follows:

Timothy Cleare (ye son of Will Cleare) & Mary Bundy (ye dau of William Bundy, & Elizabeth his wife) weare Maried, ye 7 of June 168— and the Quaker records the same, with the date a little different; as follows: "At a Meeting at Jon'a Phelps house, Timothy Cleare, declaring his intention of Marriage with Mary Bundy (d of William) 6, 3mo 1685. Not being familiar with the Quaker marriage rites in this case will not say positively that the dates are the same.

The ages of his children are also given in Berkeley Reg, as follows: Mary, & Elizabeth (twins) b Feb 21, 168—(6), Ann, b Nov 10, 1687, Sarah, b Dec 24, 1683. Mary Cleare (wife of Timothy) died Dec 30, 1694. He m 2d Elizabeth ———— by whom he had no issue—3d Hannah née Larance (widow of Israel Snelling) by whom one dau Hannah; whose age is not mentioned. (See her will, Grimes, page 72.) Timothy Clear's will is found in Deed book E—No 12, in which he names his wife Hannah, and five daughters. This will is a very interesting document, and gives much valuable information. (See deeds, in this book.)

Mary (one of the twins) m Edward Mayo, & had by him: Edward, b 7, 2mo 1703, John b 27, 11mo 1705/6—Mary, b 26, 12mo 1709/10—Ann, b 23, 1mo 1713—Elizabeth, b 21 8mo 1717—Sarah, b 19, 12 mo 1719, & Joseph (no date). She m 2d Joseph Newby, by whom she seems not to have had issue. (See her will Grimes 1739.)

Elizabeth (twin to Mary) m Thomas Winslow. (See *Winslow*, for her descendants.)

Sarah Clare m 1st John White, & had one son John Jr. (See deeds in this book.) m 2d Jacob Elliott (untraced).

Jane Clare, m 1st Joseph Robinson, whose will was p in Perq July 9, 1717, and had son John, & dau Sarah. She m 2d Thomas Jessop. (See Jessop family.)

Of Ann Clares descendants nothing is known. Timothy Clare mentions in his will dau Hepsibeth Perry. She is thought to be a step-daughter, as she is not named in the last part of his will "as daughter." His second wife Elizabeth may have been widow Perry, but there is no proof at hand. Timothy Clare was a Quaker, and wielded a strong influence in the county for the betterment of settlers, and the usefulness of its citizens. He owned large bodies of land in Perq, and there is still extant one original grant to him made in 1709, for 300a on Perq River, which is now in the writer's hands.

COX

Robert Cox appears in Perq very early. He was one of the signers of some of the early petitions for roads in Perq Precinct, and his home was Little River, where he died before Nov 25, 1730. Will probated on that date. Only one son *Robert* (2) is named in this will, and daughters: Sarah Coxe, & Anne Weeks, wife Elizabeth. Test' Mary Collings, John Boswell.

Cox, Robert (2), Robert (1) m Ann ———— (sister of Sarah Hendricks, wife of Jeremiah). His will, p in Perq, June 5, 1768. Sons: Joseph, Robert (3) Seth, gr-son John Cox, gr-dau Sarah Cox, dau Ann Boswell, wife Ann, (Grimes) Robert Cox appears on Tax list of Thomas Weeks, J. P. 1742, 43, 53. Josiah Gilbert, in his will, p in Perq 14, 3mo 1758, names dau Jemima Cox, wife Sarah, sons: Jeremiah, Joseph, Thomas, & Joel Gilbert. Anne Cox died 8, 10mo 1809.

Cox, John, m Miriam, (probably Jordan) and had son Joseph, who m Margaret Rogerson (d of John, & Anne) and had issue: 1 Anne, b 20, 5mo

1809—2 Nathan, & Jordan (twins) b 15, 8mo 1810—3 Mary, b 23, 8mo 1811—4 John, b 11, 9mo 1812—5 Joseph, b 23 8mo 1814—6 David, & Jonathan (twins) b 21, 1mo 1818. Nathan Cox died 21, 9mo 1810, & his twin brother Jordan, died 19, 9mo 1810. Mary Cox, died 9, 9mo 1811. John Cox died 28, 10mo 1813. David Cox died 15, 2mo 1818. Joseph Cox, (s of John, & Miriam) died 10, 11mo 1825. John Cox, died 9, 10mo 1807.

Cox, John, & Miriam, had another son Josiah, who died in Perq 12, 6mo 1808. (Suttons Creek Mo Meeting.) The will of John Cox, probated in Perq, Nov 1807, names wife Miriam, and sons: Jacob, Caleb, Joseph, John, Josiah, & Aaron. Chalkey Draper was one of his Exrs.

John Cox, with his family moved from Pasq Co, to Suttons Creek Perq Co 20, 3mo 1802, with children: Joseph, Jacob, John, Josiah (died 1808), Aaron, & Caleb.

Cox, Joseph (s of John, & Miriam) m Polly Cain (Cane) July 4, 1793. She is named in the will of Nath'l Cane as daughter, whose will was p in Perq, Feb 1800 with her husband Joseph Cox. Joseph Cox m 2d Sylvia Cane (sister of his 1st wife) before 1800. He m 3rd Mary ——— who survived him. His will Perq Feb 1813, names wife Mary, sons: Myles, Willis, Laban, Joseph (2) and dau Lydia Gilly, & Mary Cox. Francis White Ex.

Mary Cox (widow of Joseph) in her will Perq, Mch 30, 1827, names son-in-law Nathan Bagley, dau's: Mary, & Gilly Cox. Benj Toms Ex.

Cox, Caleb, d. s. p. will Perq p Nov 1824, names brother Joseph, Jacob, John, & Aaron, my mother (not named).

Cox, John, m Mary Charlton, Jan 6, 1790. (Mar bonds Chowan Co.)

Another Cox family in Perquimans, is that of Dr. David Cox, who came to Perquimans from Currituck Co N. C. before the War between the States, settling as a young man at New Hope. He later moved to Hertford, where he built up a large practice, and married Miss Sallie White, daughter of Mrs. Ann White, and sister of the wife of Mr. Zach Toms of Hertford. Dr. Cox was a rugged character of great power, and strength, and any word he uttered was accepted as his bond. The writer, to whom he was a family Physician until his health failed, had the greatest admiration for him, not only as a Doctor, but as a man, and reposed in him every confidence, felt herself enriched by his friendship. He introduced the present "pump" into the town and county, being a strong advocate of good water, as a means of good health. Before the advent of these "pumps" the lower counties were stricken each year with Typhoid, Malarial fever, chills, and worst of all Hemorrhagic fever, a fever almost equal to Typhus, and each year the bad climate took toll of many little children, probably from the cause of surface water principally, and much is due Dr. Cox for revolutionizing the water supply of this county. His quaint ways, and sayings are a byword in the county even today, and his memory will always be green in the minds of those who were fond of him.

By his wife, Sallie White, he had issue: 1 Thomas A. Cox, M. D., Hertford, N. C., who also enjoys a good practice and many friends. 2 William (Bill), of Burlington, N. C. the comedian of Hertford for many years in local plays. m Miss Bird. Bill, as he is familiarly called by all his friends, is a prince of good fellows. (David (2), Registered Surveyor, now in partnership with his equally talented son, David (3), one of Perquimans and the elder of Elizabeth City, N. C. 4 Sallie, m Mr. ——— Urquart of Norfolk, Va. 5 Dennis, deceased, who m Miss Nellie Hoskins of Perq, leaving two sons. David Cox (2) has three children, by Nina Parker (d of Mr David Parker), one, of Hertford, and the two daughters of Norfolk, Va. Neither Dr Tom Cox, or his brother Bill have any children.

Dr. David Cox (1) m 2d Clara Small, of Hertford, and had issue: 1 Harriett, m James McNider, Lawyer, of Hertford, and has one son. 2 Nancy. 3 Virginia (both single), school teachers in the City of Norfolk. 4 James Marmaduke, graduate of the University of N. C., single, living in Chicago.

DAVIS

Thomas Davis of Warricksqueake, planter—son of James, late of Henrico, in Vir' dec'd, was granted 300a of land on Warricksqueake Creek, "100 in right of his father, an ancient planter, who came to Va in the "George" 1617, and 100a in right of his mother Rachel, wife of sd James." Mar 6, 1633. Thomas made deposition in Norfolk Co Va 1640. He sold a grant from Sir Wm Berkeley June 1, 1649, to Thomas Maros, who sold sd land 400a unto Robert Bowers, who in like manner gave the land to his dau Mary, wife of Thomas Davis, and was conveyed by them Nov 14, 1708, unto Phillip Reynolds Mer'cht, "lying on W. side of Western Branch," in which deed Thomas Davis is styled, "of Nansemond Co. planter."

Thomas Cook, & Mary his wife "to make good" to John Davis, & Mary his wife, all of Isle of Wight Co, conveyed land to them, on Neck Swamp, Oct 6, 1677. The records of said county, give the will of John Davis "of upper pish" Isle of Wight Co, p June 28, 1714. He names wife Mary, sons: Thomas, Samuel, William, and dau Mary (wife of William Murray) dau's: Sarah, Elizabeth, & Prudence, gr-dau Elizabeth Murray.

Samuel Davis (s of John) will same county; p June 6, 1751. d. s. p. Leg: Mother Amey Jones, to whom he bequeathed "plan' at Meherrin," at her death to sister Mary White, at her death to cousin Ann White, negro girl to sister Sarah Davis, sister Amey Davis, sister Marshillah Davis.

Samuel Davis, planter, "sone of Samuel, late of Isle of Wight Co Vir" appointed Nicholas Cobb, his Att' to dispose of his dec'd fathers Estate, in said county July 23, 1667. Samuel Davis, & Ann his wife removed to Albemarle 1660, and had several children, the eldest being Samuel. (Affidavit of Henry White, who knew them in Isle of Wight Co.) "Samuel Davis of Albemarle in Carolina, heir of Samuel dec'd, and cousin of Ann his wife," sold to John Bond of Isle of Wight Co, 100a of land, which was grt unto Thomas Edghill, by John Harvey, 1637, and by him assigned to William Strange, Mar 2, 1639, "who sold sd land to my father, June 11, 1642." Seal May 12, 1668. Test' Nicholas Cobb, Edward Hickman. (Isle of Wight Rec.) *In Surry Co Va a deed was made by John Davis, & wife Elizabeth "heiress of Roger Rawlings, late of Surry Co," unto Thomas Lane Jr, for 5000 lbs of Tob, sold 50a on Lawnes Creek, "pish of Southwarke, plantation my father died on." Dec 29, 1705. Admix was granted Elizabeth Davis, on Estate of her husband Edward Davis, July 1, 1679. Thomas Davis of Southwarke Parish, sold to James Davis 150a of land on Basses Swamp, Oct 14, 1712. His will Surry

---

*Roger Rawlings, mariner, master of a sailing vessel, m Elizabeth dau of Richard Skinner of Isle of Wight Co. Said Roger was Sheriff of Surry Co Va for years.

Co, Sept 22, 1716, Son: James, dau's: Jane, & Elizabeth Ellis, gr-sons: John, James, & Henry Davis, wife Elizabeth.

Davis, Jeames, (1) first in Perq Co, m "at a Meeting at the house of Henry White," Elizabeth White (d of Henry of Albemarle) 26, 4mo 1690 (s of Wm Davis). Symons Creek Reg gives the ages of their children as follows: 1 William, b 4 4mo 1692—2 Mary, b —, 11mo 1694—3 John, b 14, 1mo 1695—4 Jeams, b 6, 8mo 1698—5 Robert, b 13, 1mo 1701/2—6 Henry, b —, 11mo 1712, d 1, 11mo 1718.

Davis, James, died 14, 12mo 1716. Jeames Davis (Probably son of James) d 24, 3mo 1719. The will of James Davis (no County, or probate) April 22, 1715. Sons: William, James, John, Robert, Henry, Wife Elizabeth.

Davis, Robert, (1) Jeams (1) m Sarah Eager (Eagor) 16, 12mo 1720, "at Symons Creek," issue: 1 Mary, b 4, 12mo 1722—2 Jeames, b 2, 6mo 1726—3 Thomas, b 10, 2mo 1729—4 Joshua, b 1, 1mo 1731—5 Ruth, b 7, 2mo 1737—6 Robert (2) b 22, 11mo 1739.

Davis, William, (2) James (1) William (1) moved to Carteret Co, where his will was p June 1756, Sons: Nathan, Joseph, Wicker, Callip, Beniemen, William, Solomon, dau Abigail, wife Mary.

Davis, Elizabeth, wife of James Davis, m 2d James Newby of Pasq Co, "James Newby & Elizabeth his wife (widow of James Davis bound our son Robert Davis to Jno Symons, to live with him until he be 21 years of age," and said Symons agred to "learn said Davis to weave, & do House carpenter work," also to read, & write, "and sypher as far as sd Symons can do." (Pasq Co. records.)

Davis, John, will Perq Co, p April 1753. Sons: Joseph, William, John, Samuel, dau Sarah Gorden (wife of William.)

Davis, Robert, who m Sarah Eager, will Pasq Co, p Jan 1750. Sons: James to whom he left his "maner plantation" Thomas "plantation next James Lowry," dau's: Elizabeth, & Ruth, wife Sarah.

Davis, Thomas, (1) Robert (1) James (1) William (1) m Lidia Griffin (d of Jeams) 13, 12mo 1752, issue: 1 Thomas, b Aug 13, 1753—2 William, b 7, 5mo 1757—3 Caleb, b Feb 23, 1759—4 Thomas, b Sept 17, 1761—5 Nathan, b Nov 7, 1763.

Davis, Thomas (s of Thomas, & Lydda) died 10, 10mo 1777.

Davis, Thomas (the elder) died 27, 8mo 1781.

Davis, Thomas, of Perq, will p April 1746. Son: Moses, "plantation whereon I live," dau's Elizabeth Davis, & Sarah Bond, wife Elizabeth.

Davis, John, of Pasq Co had wife Dorothy, April 15, 1747. (Pasq Co Records.)

Davis, Thomas, made a deed to his son Arthur Aug 19, 1747. (Pasq Co Records.)

Davis, Thomas, made a deed to his son John, 100a in Pasq Co, Jan 30, 1748.

Davis, Solomon, (s of William) with wife Sarah deed land in Pasq Co, Jan 26, 1713/4. His will said county, p Jan 1739. Dau's: Dorothy, & Elizabeth Davis, Margaret Forster, son-in-law Caleb Coen, gr-son Daniel Coen.

Davis, John, of Perq m Rachel Redding (sister of James, & John) before Oct 12, 1769.

Davis, Joseph (1) John (1) m Elizabeth Sutton (sister of Ashbury) before Feb 1794.

Davis, Thomas, division in Perq (no date) shows sons: Moses, John, William, dau's: Mary, Ruth, Elizabeth, Charity, & Judith. (Loose papers.)

(See deeds in this book, for further data on Davis.)

Davis, Robert, will Perq, p, May 1799. Sons: James, & Caleb, dau's: Mary Davis, & Miriam Albertson, wife Margaret.

Davis, Sarah, will p in Perq, Aug 1717, dau Bethany, Children: Letty, & Alexander.

DRAPER

Thomas, and Sarah Draper are found among adventurers to America, 1620 (Hotten.) Robert Draper was transported in ship Jacob, by John Bainham 1624, age 16. (Researcher Mag.) Henrie Draper came in George 1621, age 14 years. Thomas Draper in Paule of London, July 16, 1635. Joseph Draper in Falcon, Apl 1635 Thomas Draper of Heptonstall Yorkshire, arrived in America 1647. Henry Draper was one among the living at Warrasqueake (Isle of Wight) Feb 16, 1623, when the census was taken after the Indian massacre, of May 22, 1622. (Hotten.)

Joseph Draper was granted 232a of land in Nansemond Co Va, July 12, 1709 "in the Upper Parish, on Poters, and Basses pocoson," and John Draper received a grant for 200a in same locality, July 18, 1709. He was transported to Norfolk Co Va, Mar 19, 1643, by Capt Thomas Willoughby. Richard Draper had 300a granted him, in Currituck Precinct, N. C. Oct 21, 1687, "on East side of North River, adj Robert Swaynes." William Draper was a Tithable in Sunken Marsh Parish, Surry Co Va, 1675, and June 8, 1681. He moved to Pasquotank Precinct N. C. prior to 1704, when he conveyed 100a of land in said county, "which was granted George Cooper, June 24, 1704, and by him assigned to my father Charles Draper." John Akehurst appeared as Att' for John Damon Draper, "Citizen of London" and made release of land, 200a in Pasquotank Co, unto Robert Morgan, and wife Elizabeth, "on which James Williams now Dwells, called Burds folly, said Morgan agreeing to build on said land a dwelling house, 30ft long, by 15 ft wide, at his own cost, and maintain same."

Thomas Draper m in Isle of Wight Co Va, Patience Denson (d of John, who names "dau Patience Draper" in his will, p in said Co, July 1, 1748) at Pagan Creek, 2, 6mo 1739. This Thomas was a son of Peter of Perquimans Co.

Draper, Peter, first in Perquimans, came to N. C. from Nansemond Co Va, at what date is not known. He may have been a son of Joseph, or John of said county, but as the records of Nansemond were burned in 1867, very little of value can be derived from the county records. The Quaker records found there are however of the best, but unfortunately very little is said on those about the Draper family. Therefore it is problematical whether anything further *can* be unearthed about this family, in Nansemond county prior to their coming to Perquimans.

Draper, Peter (1), of Perq, m Hannah Albertson (d of Peter, & Ann, née Jones, who was son of Albert Albertson, & wife Mary. Ann Jones d of Mary Beasley widow, b June 15, 1701, mar Aug 27, 1715). Peter Draper by wife Hannah had issue: 1 Joseph, m Lydia Bogue Aug 1766—2 Millicent, m Benjamin Morris Nov 1772—He was b 20, 8mo 1738, d before 22, 12mo 1796) Millicent Draper Morris, m 2d Jessie Simonds, and died 12, 5, 1809)—3 Silas, m Mary Morris, Feb 1773—4 Thomas, m Lydia Bundy, 2d Mary Newby (d of William Newby, and Jemima née Newby, d of Samuel) Feb 1790.

RECORDS OF DEEDS

Draper Joseph (1) Peter (1) and Lydia née Bogue, issue: 1 Josiah, b 9, 8mo 1768, d 27, 6mo 1837 in Henry Co Ind, m Miriam Newby, b 2 2mo 1772, d 9, 1, 1812, in Highland Co, Ohio. They were m 12, 6mo 1789, issue: 1 Jesse, b 2, 12, 1792, m Delphia Davenport—2 Elizabeth, b 9, 13, 1793, m Jesse Small—3 Joseph, b 23, 11mo 1795, m Biddie Jackson—4 Josiah Jr, b 14, 1mo 1798, m Catherine Pearson, d 10, 12, 1865—5 Miriam, b 13, 9mo 1799 m Ephrim Overman—6 John, b 7, 1, 1801, m Martha Palmer—7 Joshua, b —, 12, 1803, m Huldah Pearson. (All of whom were born in Perquimans Co.) 8 Mary Ann, b 20, 11mo 1810, in Randolph Co N. C. (From old Bibles, and Quaker records, located by Mrs. J. E. McMullen, of Ada, Ohio, and kindly passed on to the writer for publication.)

Josiah Draper kept a diary, that Mrs. McMullen was fortunate enough to come across, which gives the information "I Josiah Draper, and family set of from perquimans county, in State of North Carolina, the 14th of 12mo 1803, to move to Randolph County in same State," and later made another entry in same diary, "Josiah Draper set off from Randolph the 14th of 5th mo 1811, and got to Hiland the 20 of 6th mo 1811, in the Ohio State." He m 2d Jemima Gant, and had dau Rebecca, b 11, 12mo 1811-16.

Draper, Millicent, (d of Peter (1) and wife Elizabeth) b 1745, d 12, 5, 1809, m 1 Benjamin Morris, b 20, 8mo 1738, d before 22, 12mo 1796, when she m 2d Jesse Simons. (For her descendants see Morris.)

Draper, Silas (1) Peter (1) & wife Mary Morris had issue: Joseph, Samuel, Chalkey, Jesse, David, Daniel, & Benjamin, wife (not named) according to his will, p in Perq Co, Feb 1794.

Test' Daniel Willard, Rachel Hasket, Jos Draper Jr.

Draper, Thomas (1) Peter (1) and Lydia Bundy apparently had no issue, m 2d Mary Newby (d of William, & Jemima née Newby, d of Samuel (1) and wife Ann, née Mayo, d of Edward, & Mary née Clare, d of Timothy Clare, and wife Mary née Bundy, d of William Bundy, & wife Elizabeth, all of Perq Co) Feb 1790, issue: 1 John, b 12, 12, 1790, d 1, 6, 1791—2 Achsah, b 4, 6, 1792—3 William, b 7, 10, 1794, d 28, 5mo 1855—4 Jemima, b 12 2mo 1795—5 Gulielma, b ————, d 10, 4, 188- —6 Hannah, b 27, 9mo 1900. Thomas Draper moved with his family to Indiana before 1820.

Draper, Joseph (2) Silas (1) Peter (1), b 3, 11, 1775, m Penninah Bundy, b 24, 1mo 1781, (d of Abraham Bundy) "at Vosses Creek Mo meeting," 2, 6, 1801, issue: 1 Benjamin, & Jesse (twins) b 7, 6, 1805. He m 2d Mary, who died 13, 11mo 1849, issue: 3 Joseph—4 John—5 Alfred, d 3, 8, 1848—6 Hannah, d 20, 12mo 1844, m Jobe Hadley, 22 9mo 1841.

Joseph Draper will Perq Co, p May 1811. Sons: Nathan, & Josiah, dau Rachel Jessop, cousin Isaac Draper, wife (not named).

Test' Daniel Willard, Joseph Willard, Richard Wood.

Draper, Chalkey (1) Silas (1) Peter (1) m Rhoda Willard (d of Martin) 17, 3mo 1803, "at Wells meeting house in Perq Co." All his family migrated to Indiana and settled near White Water Mo Meeting, in said State, before 1820, White Water being the first established in the new territory.

Draper, Samuel (1) Silas (1) Peter (1) m Mary Albertson (d of Josiah, & Kesiah) after 1800, as she is not named as Mary Draper in the will of said Albertson, but is so named in her mothers will, p in Perq Co Feb 1825. In the latters will she is called "daughter Mary Draper," and her husband Samuel Draper, was one of the Exrs of Mary Albertson's will. Samuel Draper died without issue, 1829.

Draper, Rachel, (d of Joseph (2) m Thomas Jessop, 3, 2, 1790.) (See Jessop family.)

DURANT

Of George Durant very little is known before his arrival in Perq Co, but it is an undisputed fact that he landed in Va before 1658. He made deposition in Northumberland Co Va, July 1658, that he "came to Virginia in the ship Potomack, age 25 years." As this book is very much faded with age, all of this statement can not be deciphered. (Northumberland Co record, 1658-66. Archives Richmond Va.) In Berkeley Parish Reg Perq Co, his marriage is given as follows: "George Durant and Ann Moorwood was Married the 4th of January 1658/9, By Mr David Lindsey, Minister of gospel and was Licensed by Mr George Cowbough Magistrate, in Northumberland County Verginia."

He had several grants for land in Va. prior to coming to N. C. One of these 400a in Lower Norfolk Co, on East side of North River, Sept 30, 1670, by Sir William Berkeley, for trans' fourteen persons, and another grant by same authority, on same date, 700a on East side of North River, "which falleth in to Corotock" adj Thomas Tullies land, in what is now Currituck Co N. C. Prior to this date he had taken up land in Perq Co, and was already settled in what is called to this day, "Durants Neck." This deed, or grant from the Indian Chief Kilcocanen, King of Yeopim, for all the land between the River Perquimans, & Roanoke Sound, March 1, 1661, where he had seated a Plan' before Aug 4, 1661. In the second conveyance of the Indian King he spelled his name Cuscutenew, but they are supposed to be one & the same person, and it was the usual procedure at that time, to spell a name just as it sounded to the copiest. This deed is found in Deed book A, No 374, and has as Test' Thomas Weymouth, & Caleb Calleway. Thomas Weymouth was a great navigator, and adventurer, sailing with Capt Pring, and he was among those who started out in 1603, in search of the ill fated colony on Roanoke Island.

How he came to be in Albemarle at this time is not explained. Caleb Calleway was of course already settled in the Province. This deed of the Indian King to sd Durant, is the oldest recorded document in North Carolina. If there were older records they were all destroyed in the uprising of 1677/79. Fifty-five years elapsed between the making of the deed by King Cuscutenew, and its recording on the books in the Reg Office, which was done by John Stepney "Reg of all writings for Perq Precinct" Oct 24, 1716 George Durants Plan' was known by the name of "Wicocombe" and was situated between "two Rivers, Perquimans, & Kototine" (Little River). According to the record George Durant seems to have been a fair minded man, and quite honest in his dealings with both the Indian Chief, and George Catchminy, who set up a counter claim for said land, claiming a prior right, by a grt from Sir William Berkeley, therefore Mr. Durant, "who had cleared a small Peice of Ground," at once "desisted" on hearing the contention of sd Catchmaid, who on Mar 13, 1662 made a bona fide deed to sd Durant for the disputed land. Later the Lords Pro' made a secure deed to Mr. Durant for this land, Dec 26, 1673. No man with the exception of Timothy Clare, is more often, or more honorably mentioned in Perq. He stand out, virile, hardy, opinionated, with a following of all faiths, and from the records died much respected in the community. Some have classed him as a Quaker, but the records do not verify that fact. He was certainly married by an Episcopal Minister (Rev David Lindsey) and his children all but one (Deborah) m into Episcopal families. Not once is his name mentioned in the Quaker records, nor are the ages of any of his children recorded there. It is the opinion of many that he was a Scotchman, and therefore of Presbyterian faith, but his Church affiliations in Perq are uncertain. From the records he appears to have come from London to America. Exactly where this renowned man lies buried is shrouded in mystery. It is said his grave was once to be seen on the bank of a large drain, in Durants Neck, and that in cutting out the ditch, mud from the bottom was thrown out over it, until it disappeared. In the will of William Sherrell, Perq Co, George Durant's place of residence is named as "Berty Point," and the deeds in Perq speak of his "seating" being on a "Point which divides sd land from a Neck called Langleys." His house has long ago disappeared, and even the location is now in doubt. There can be small doubt, however, about its being in the lower part of Durants Neck somewhere near the village of Little River. (See N. C. Hist & Gen Reg, for this family.)

ELLIOTT

John Elliott, son of Bennett of Nasing Essex England, bapt 1604, arrived in America 1631, and settled in New England.

Jacob Elliott, brother of Rev John Elliott the Apostle, who died before 28, 2mo 1651, at which time his will was p in New Eng. He made bequest to son Jacob a "House" and to dau Hannah the same. His Inventory shows wife Margery, and that he had in money £579-23-8, 29, 11mo 1651. Margery wife of Jacob, died Oct 30, 1661, heirs: son Jacob, Theophilus Frary, & wife Hannah, Susannah, & Mehetabel Elliott of Suffolk Mass. (New Eng Hist & Gen Reg, Vol 4-p 257.)

Mehetabel Elliott, m Seth Perry of Boston, before 14, 8mo 1662. Her fathers Est was estimated to be worth £280.

William Elliott was transported to Va by Frances Yardley, Nov 15, 1648. (Lower Norfolk Co Rec.)

He was granted land in Gloucester Co Va, 110a, 1672, and appears as a tithable in Surry Co (Sunken Marsh) June 8, 1681. He was probably a brother of Thomas, of Perq Co. John Elliott came to Va as a headright of Richard Jordan of Surry Co Va, Oct 20, 1689. (Surry Co Rec.) Also thought to be brother of said Thomas.

Thomas Elliott (s of Joseph who d 1697) emigrated to Va, with brothers William, & John, date not given. He acquired large landed Est in Carolina, and served in the Assembly 1696. He was granted 555a in Perq Co, Aug 27, 1714 "on ye N. W. side of Crane Ponds" adj Joseph Smith, & Nathan Newby. John Elliott took up 350a in Anson Co N. C. Feb 25, 1754, adj his own land.

Elliott, (I) Thomas, m 1 Sarah, issue Lydde, b 6, 12mo 1718. This could not have been his first child, as William his son was m to Elizabeth Relph Dec 2, 1690, or this may probably be his brother William who came to America with Francis Yardley. William Elliott had a son Pritlow who was m in 1744, a long period of time between marriages, but he may have married late in life, or been born ten or fifteen years after this date. There is no certain proof of either point.

Elliott, (1) Thomas, m 2d Margaret, who survived him. His will Perq, p Dec 16, 1729. Sons: Caleb, to whom he left "plan' on which I now dwell" Joshua 200a of land, Isaac the "remaining part of tract," William 1 shilling, Thomas (2), Abraham, Solomon, Moses, Joseph, Benjamin, Dau's Mary Brown, & Ursley, wife Margaret.

Elliott, (a) Caleb (1) m Mary Winslow.?
Issue: 1 Ephrim, b July 5, 1731—2 Haig (Hange) b Aug 6, 1735—3 Caleb (2), b Feb 21, 1737—4 Solomon, b Aug 20, 1743—5 Miriam, b Feb 16, 1745—6 Peninah, b Nov 18, 1746, m Joseph Scott, 12, — 1759. Caleb Elliott will p in Perq, Jan, 1777. Sons: Solomon, Ephrim, & Haig, dau Pennah Scott, gr-sons: Elliott Scott, & Winslow Elliott.

Elliott, (b) Joshua, m Anne ————. Issue: Joshua (2) b Mch 24, 1740. (untraced.)

Elliott, (c) Isaac, m Elizabeth Morgan, 18, 1mo 1743. His will p in Perq, April 1789. Sons: Joshua, Isaac (2), Joab, Nathan, dau's Margaret, Rebecca, Miriam, & Sarah Elliott, wife Elizabeth.

Elliott, (d) William, (Thomas (1) m Elizabeth Pritlow, (d of John). Issue: 1 Pritlow (no date), who m Sarah Croxton (d of Arthur) 19, 7mo 1744, m 2d Betty Moore 3, 1mo 1753 and 3d Mary, who survived him. His will p in Perq, Oct 1787. Sons: Pritlow (2), John, Job, Thomas, Jesse, & William, dau's Rachel, Mary, & Elizabeth Elliott, Leah Jordan, Huldah Elliott, & Sarah Pearson (wife of Jonathan), wife Mary. Rachel Elliott m out of Unity, before 5, 12mo 1787. Mary Elliott, m ———— Smith before 5, 9mo 1787.

Elliott (e) Thomas (2) m Mary Morgan (d of John).
John Morgan, who made a deed of gift to her, Jan 12, 1724. (Deed book B—No 192.) He died intestate before July 1752, on which date his Estate was divided, widow Mary Admix, heirs: James, Rachel, Mary, Moses, heirs of son Thomas dec'd, gr-child Ruth Munden.

Elliott (f) Abraham, died "without a will" July 21, 1766, wife Miriam relinquished her right of Admix, and Cornelius Moore became Ex. (Minute book Perq.)

Abraham Elliott Planter, 1756. (Loose papers.) He figures as a householder on Tax list of James Sitterson 1762, with 330a of land in Harveys Neck. On this list he is called Abraham Elliott Sr. In 1764 he appears on same list with son Joseph.

Elliott Abraham (2) m Juliana Wilson (d of Jacob, will Nov 1793) whose will was p in Perq, Feby 1813. Sons: Jonathan W., Benjamin, Ephrim, & Isaac, dau's Achsah Saint (wife of William), Rachel, Keren, & Cynthia Elliott, wife Juliana.

Elliott, (g) Solomon, m Miriam Winslow, issue: 1 Winslow (who had son Exum)—2 Exum—3 Francis—4 Solomon—5 Joseph, b 1775, d 1778—6 Thomas, b 21, 12mo 1779, m three times, d 3, 11mo 1845—7 James, b 1781, m Sarah Toms, 18, 6mo 1807—8 Caleb—9 Haige.

Elliott, (1) Exum (1) Solomon (1) Caleb (1) Thomas (1), m Lydia Parker, 4, 8mo 1790 (2d wife) m first his cousin Sarah Elliott (d of Thomas, & Abigail (Anderson) Elliott) by whom he had a dau Mary Ann, who m James W. Groves, 2d David Copeland.

Elliott, (II) James, (1) Solomon (1) Caleb (1) Thomas (1) m Sarah Toms, (d of John & Mary) at Suttons Creek, 18, 6mo 1807, issue: 1 Benjamin Toms, b 9, 2mo 1809—2 Zachariah Nixon, b 26, 9mo 1811.

Elliott (III) Thomas (s of Solomon dec'd) m Abigail Anderson (d of Joseph dec'd) at Suttons Creek, 17, 4mo 1800, issue: 1 Sarah, b 16, 1mo 1801, m Exum Elliott (her first cousin) 2 Joseph, b 18, 1mo 1803, m Margaret L. White, no issue, m 2d Isabella Parker, issue: 1 William L., b 16, 1mo 1832—2 Joseph P., b 12, 7mo 1833—3 John A. (s of Thomas), 2, 2mo 1806, m Hannah Morris, d 27, 6mo 1829—4 Aaron, b 19, 9 mo 1808, m Mary S. White, issue: David, b 28, 3mo 1829, who m 9, 10mo 1856 Mary Ann Hill—Aaron, m 2d Roda C. Mendenhall (d of James, & Miriam (Hoggott) Mendenhall, issue: 1 Aaron, b 24, 1mo 1844, m Lilly Tyner Manley, 4, 14, 1905—2 James, b 8, 4mo 1847—3 Robert Barclay, b 15, 11mo 1849—4 Sarah S., b 27, 10mo 1851, m Poran Reynold, d 5, 5, 1925—5 Roda C., b 22, 4mo 1854, m Arthur C. Leadbetter—6 Mildred Ada, b 16, 4mo 1856, m ——— Lee—7 J. Gurney, b 19, 7mo 1858.

Elliott, John A., (s of Thomas & Abigail) by Hannah Morris (d of Joshua, & Margaret) (Henly Morris) issue: 1 Abigail, b 1, 12mo 1826, d 1832—3 Mordicai, b 2, 12mo 1828, m Martha Paulin (d of Joseph, & Lydia, (Garrett) Paulin), d 20, 1mo 1892, issue: 1 John E.—2 Mordicai.

Elliott, (h) Moses (1) Thomas (1) m Judith Sanders, issue: according to his will p in Perq, Jan 1756. Joseph, Moses (2) Benjamin, dau Margaret, wife Judah.

Elliott, (i) Joseph, m Hannah Gordon, His will p in Perq, April 1788, gives the issue; as follows; sons Mordicai, Caleb, Dempsey, & Joseph, his dau's Delilah Barrow, Orpha Mayo, & Mary Elliott, wife Hannah.

Mordicai Elliott (s of Joseph) m Leah Smith, 1, 8mo 1778. His will p Perq, Nov 1816, names Gr-children: Peninah, Kesiah, & Martha Elliott (dau's of s Charles) son Willis, d Jemima Speight, Lydia, a gr-dau Lydia Elliott, s Barnabas, & Jesse, wife Leah.

Lydia Elliott (d of Mordicai) will Perq p May 1823, names brother Willis, nieces: Grizzell Speight, & Mary Ann Elizabeth Speight, (br-in-law Noah Speight).

Elliott, Charles (s of Mordicai) lived near Edenton, and was Attorney Gen'l of N. C., he moved to Craven Co, & is buried in New Bern N. C.

Elliott (j) Benjamin Thomas (1) m Sarah. Will p in Perq, Apl 1774, Sons: Josiah, Benjamin (2), Seth, Exum, & Obed, wife Sarah.

Elliott, Ephrim (1) Caleb (1) Thomas (1) will Perq, p Feby 1802. Sons: Caleb, Miles, Townsend, & Josiah, heirs of s Stephen dec'd: Stephen, & Mary Elliott, dau's Mary Wood, Peninah, & Avis, gr-sons Thomas, & Ephrim Roberson.

His wife who was probably dead when this will was probated, was Sarah, (d of William Townsend, by his first wife) who names her in his will 1766. (See other Elliott wills, N. C. Hist Reg Vol 3-8.)

Marriages in Perq

Elliott, Sarah, m Benjamin Hall, at Symons Creek, 6, 9mo 1753.

Elliott, Elizabeth, m Joshua Overman, at Symons Creek, 7, 6mo 1759.

Elliott, James, (s of Thomas, m Mary Jones (d of Peter) 6, 11mo 1754.

Elliott, James, m 2d Martha Winslow (widow of Jesse) 17, 3mo 1781. His will Perq, p Jany 1791, names sons: Nathan, Gabriel, Nixon, dau's Miriam Lou, Sarah, wife Martha. The first wife of James Elliott, was Mary dau of

Phineas Nixon, who in his will p 1772, names "Mary Elliott's three children: Gabriel, Miriam, & Nixon Elliott."

Elliott, Thomas (2) William (1) Thomas (1) m Mourning Wilson, 7, 3mo 1778. (Wellses.) He was dec'd Feb 23, 1797. Heirs: Miles, Abraham, Peninah, & Docton Elliott, wife Mourning Admix. She was dau of Abram Wilson, whose will Perq p May 1795, (names all three of these children, & wife Lydia.) Miles Elliott was Sheriff of Perq Co, 1821. He m Patience Jordan, 1, 10mo 1778.

Elliott, Docton, was of age before 1766, appears on Tax list on that date.

Elliott, Miles, on same list, with 172a of land in Perq, Harveys Neck. His brother Gabriel on same list, 46a in same District.

Elliott, Exum, of age 1792, poll 1, List of James Sitterson.

Elliott, Ephrim, owned 256a in District of Jacob Perry 1792.

Elliott, Pritlow, 650a "on Sipres Creek" in District of Jacob Perry 1792, sons Job, William, 1771.

Elliott, Solomon, 200a called "new neck" in District of Jacob Perry 1792.

Elliott, Sarah, on Vosses Creek, in District of Jacob Perry 1792.

Elliott, Jacob, with 4 Tithables 1748, Joshua with 6. List of James Sitterson. This Jacob was probably the one who m Sarah Clare (d of Timothy, & Mary née Bundy). She m 1st John White, & had son John, m 2d Jacob Elliott.

Marriages

Elliott, Leah, (d of Pritlow) m Josiah Jordan 7, 3mo 1781. (Wellses.)

Elliott, Francis, m Sarah Park, 3, 11mo 179--. (Wellses.)

Elliott, Margaret, m John Barrow, 4, 1mo 1792. (Wellses.)

Elliott, Joshua, m Rachel Sanders, (d of Samuel) 2, 10mo 1793. (Wellses.)

Elliott, Seth, m Mary White, 3, 7mo 1776. (Wellses.)

Elliott, Caleb, m Rachel Jordan, 6, 1mo 1779. (Wellses.)

Elliott, Thomas, m Judith Wells (d of Dorothy) before 1778, and had dau Anne.

Elliott, Nixon, m Rhoda Scott, 12, 2mo 1795. (He son of James; she d of Joseph Scott) "at Piney Woods Meeting house," issue; 1 Penina, b 15, 11mo 1796—2 Job Scott, b 7, 10mo 1798—3 James, b 4, 9mo 1800—4 Elias, b 23, 1mo 1803—5 Mary, b 11, 8mo 1805—6 Nixon (2), b 20, 1mo 1809—7 Henry, b 14, 10mo 1814.

Elliott, Thomas (s of Solomon) m 3d Margaret Cox (widow of Joseph, d of John & Ann Roberson) at Suttons Creek, 19, 12mo 1830. She was b 12, 1mo 1789.

Elliott, Abraham (2) and wife Priscilla with their children were given a Certificate, for removal to Cane Creek Mo Meeting, 14, 7mo 1764.

Elliott, Exum, (s of Jacob, & Zilpha Davenport) b 10, 4mo 1765, m Sarah Pearson, (d of Jonathan & Sarah née Bundy) 19, 3mo 1788. She lived only three months, when Exum, m 2d Catherine Lamb (d of Jacob, & Sarah née Stone) issue: Sarah, b 15, 3mo 1792. (Center Mo Meeting, Guilford Co N. C.)

Elliott, Jacob, (so of Abraham, & Mary) m Hepzibah Stanton (d of Benjamin, & Mary) 24, 5 mo 1804. (Center Mo Meeting.)

Elliott, Exum, moved to Guilford County before 1776, and to Ind in 1815.

Elliott, Rodah, b 3, 3, 1750—Hannah, b 1, 9, 1752. (unplaced.)

Elliott, Haig, was apt Inspector of Perq by Gov Tryon, Jan 23, 1771.

EVANS FAMILY
Descendants of Benjamin Evans, born in Hertford, Perquimans County, North Carolina.

EVANS

The Evan family is of ancient Welsh descent, tracing back to the Roman invasion, and are mentioned in Roman History. Tradition has it that they were originally of Roman extraction, through some intermarriage with a Roman soldier. Mr. Rowland E. Evans of Philadelphia has prepared an elaborate document on the subject, and traces this family through many generations, back to Mervyn Vrych, King of Man, who was killed in battle with the King of Mercia A. D. 864. Mervyn married Essylt, daughter and sole heiress of Conan Tyndaethwy, King of Wales, who died 818-20. Both Mervyn, and Essylt trace their descent from Lludd, King of Britain, brother of Caswallon the chief who resisted the invasion of Caesar, before the Christian era. (Notes made by Mrs Wm Parker Faulke, dec'd.)

The Welsh descent of this line runs as follows:

I. David Goch of Penllech, who appears as a Leaseholder of crown lands in Carnarvonshire, in the 18th year of the reign of Edward II, and was living Nov 9, 1314. He married Maud d of David Lloyd (who traced descent from Owen Gnynedd, prince of Gnynedd; had issue 3 sons: one of whom,

II. Ieven Goch the Graianoe of Penllech, who appears on the jury to take the extent of Cymytmaen 1352. He had titles to certain lands in that period, and m Eva da of Einion ap Cynvelyn (who traced descent from Bleddyn Prince of Wales) issue two sons, the eldest:

III. Evan Modoc (who it is claimed came to America before Columbus) registered in Cwm Amwich pedigree as "ancestor of the gentleman Ysbitty Evan, in Denbigshire" issue:

IV. Diekws duu, who m Gwen dau of Ievan duu (who traced descent from Maelor Crwn head of the 7th noble tribes of Wales) issue:

V. Einion, who m Morvyd dau of Mtw ap Llowarch, issue:

VI. Howel, who m Mali dau of Llewellyn, issue:

VII. Griffith, who m̃ Gwenllian, dau of Einion ap Eivan Lloyd, issue:

VIII. Lewis, who m Ethli dau of Edward ap Ievan, issue:

IX. Robert, who m Gwrvyl dau of Llewellyn ap David of Llan Rwst, Denbigshire, whose 4th son:

X.—Ievan (known as Evan Robert Lewis) living 1601, removed from Rhiwlas, in Merionothshire to Vron Goch, and died there. He had five sons, all after the Welsh custom taking the name of *Evan*. as follows: 1 John ap Evan—2 Cadwalader ap Evan—3 Griffith ap Evan—4 Owen ap Evan—5 Evan ap Evan.

Many of this family immigrated to Va, and from that State to Albemarle at a very early date. The earliest known settler in Va was William Evans, who was a subject in the Colony at Jamestown Jan 1609-Nov 1609. (Browns Geneses to America.) Richard Evans age 35 came to America in "Neptune" 1618. He was probably father, or gr-father of the Richard who died in Perq 1693. Wm Evans passenger for Va, in "Primrose" July 1635, under Comd of Capt Douglas. Jo Evans was transported to Va in Thomas & John from Gravesend Eng, Jan 6, 1635. Richard Evans arrived in Va in "Temperance" from Newfoundland 1619 Comd by Lt Gilbert Peppet. Another Richard was trans' to Accomac Co Va June 25, 1625, by Wm Andrews. Among the living Feb 16, 1623 (after the Indian massacre of Mar 22, 1622) "at Elizabeth Cittye" are to be found the names of the following Evans: Richard, Thomas, William, John, Marke, & George Evans. (Hotten.)

Richard Evans was trans' to Norfolk Co Va, by Richard Parsons 1639. Capt Evans brought over 100 immigrants to Va 1619. Dr George Hacke trans' to Northampton Co Va, Row Evans, & Edward Evans, 1652. Peter Knight trans' William, & Lawrence Evans, to Gloucester Co, Va, July 16, 1652. Thomas Evans arrived in Va, with Wm Jones of Northampton Co, July 24, 1645, and settled on Hungars Creek. (Hotten.) Peter Evans of the Island of Barbados apt' friend Henry Jones of same, his Att' to ack' a "release of land in Isle of Wight Co Va," "unto Levin Buffkin, John Knowles, & Elizabeth Outland, Inhabitants of Virginia." 18, 6mo 1664. (Isle of Wight records.)

Phillip Evans of Plymouth, Mercht made an assignment of goods, in Warrick Crick Bay, Dec 20, 1667. (Isle of Wight records.)

Benjamin Evans, & Faith his wife, of Charles City Co Va, deeded land in Isle of Wight Co, to Thomas Sharp of Surry Co, 365a on Nottoway River. June 12, 1724. (Great Book Isle of Wight Co.)

Abraham Evans with wife Elizabeth was living in Surry Co Va, July 7, 1685. He died about this time & she Executed his Estate.

William Evans had grt for land in Isle of Wight Co, 100a, 1713. (Land book 7-.)

Benjamin Evans had grt for land in Isle of Wight Co, 375a, 1713. (Land book 7-.)

Benjamin Evans had grt for land, 300a in Prince George Co Va, 1705.

Peter Evans immigrated to Va 1650, with the Woolard family, and settled in Northumberland Co, bringing with him wife Elizabeth, and children: Peter (2) John, & Richard, and one dau Sarah. His will was p in Richmond Co 1706, naming the same children, & wife. It is thought that his son Peter moved to Hertford Co N. C. He sold to Charles Merritt, "½ of 600a upon Deep Creek, up Chowanoak River" (Chowan) Mar 16, 1707. (This land was in Hertford Co.), His descendants will be treated later.

John Ewens (Evans) was grt 460a "on Appamattocks" called Bristoll, adj Wm Sanders Nov 10, 1642. He received another grt 50a in Nansemond Co, Oct 28, 1672, formerly granted to Wm Ward.

John Evans, of Sittingbourne Par, Rapp Co Va, will p Jan 29, 1682, names sons: John, & William (not of age) father-in-law William Veale, brother Martin Johnson, God-dau Margaret Ward (d of Bryant Ward) wife Elizabeth.

John Evans was grt 400a in Albemarle, Dec 29, 1718, adj John Jordan Jr. He very probably migrated to Perq Precinct, with the Jordans, who came from Isle of Wight Co. John Jordan Sr m Ruselak Elett (Elliott) Aug 10, 1690. He is thought to be a son of Richard Jordan of Isle of Wight Co Va. A deed was made by him of 50a to "my son and dau John Evans, & Jean his wife," on Ducking Stool Branch, July 15, 1717. He became a Quaker in Nansemond Co, 8, 11mo 1700.

John Evans, who resided in Chowan County will p Jan 15, 1739, names sons: John (to whom he left "plan" whereon I now live") Thomas, & Benjamin, dau's Jane, Mary & Rachel Evans, wife Jane. Wit' by John Evans (son) & Charles Jordan (Probably bro-in-law). John, & Benjamin Evans were both of age before 1718.

Thomas Evans, probably brother of John (1) appeared in Perq simultaneously, & m Dorothy ———, issue: William, b Jan 9, 1689. His will p in Chowan Co Nov 2, 1732, names son: Thomas (2), dau's Alice Williamson, Sarah Broney, & Elizabeth Walker, wife Ellener. (Thomas, & John Evans may have been sons of Thomas & Ann of Essex Co Va.) Thomas (2) Thomas (1) moved to Tyrrell Co, where his will was p June 1745. In this will his mother "Elener Evans" is named. According to this will he had no male descendants.

Richard Evans was grt 240a of land in Perq Precinct 1684, on N. E. side of Perq River, near Castletons Creek. His will p in Albemarle, Oct 2, 1693 names sons: Jonathan, & Richard, dau's Rabakah, & Ann, wife Elizabeth, who m 2d Jeames Old Sept 11, 1694. Elizabeth *Evens* was a headright of John Lee, who received a grt for land in Nansemond Co Va, on E side of Summerton Creek, April 3, 1694. The name "Eivens" according to the old Welsh spelling was used by Richard in his will 1693. He "Departed this Life" May 20, 1693. As no mention of a birth date is given in Berkeley Par Reg, for the three eldest children, we are led to believe they were born in Va, before moving to N. C. Ann (d of Richard Evans, & wife Elizabeth) was b Nov 4, 1685—2 Sarah, b Aug 30, 1693. She being born three months after his death is not named in his will, but her mother in a deed in Perq made provision for her, equal with the others. (See Deeds in this book) Richard, second son of Richard (1) moved to Beaufort Co N. C. (His will, Grimes.)

Jonathan Evans (1) Richard (1) m Mary Luten (d of Thomas, of Chowan Co). His land was situated on the S. W. side of Perq River, adj a place called "Dawsons" (600a) which he sold to Isaac Wilson, Sept 3, 1707. He was grt 141a in Perq, Nov 22, 1714 in the fork of Castletons Creek. He bought 275a from Thomas Harvey, & Elizabeth his wife, on S. W. Side of Perq River, adj Henry Clayton, Elizabeth French, & John Pettiver. Elizabeth French is thought to be his mother, (her 3d husband being Richard French). Court was held at her house in Perq, for a number of years. Court was also held at the house of Jonathan Evans, seemingly the same place. Jonathan Evans certainly had one son William, who is named in his mothers will p in Perq Mar 7, 1723, and other records show that they had two dau's: Mary, m Thomas Burket before Oct 15, 1752, and Elizabeth, who m Thomas Houghton of Chowan Co, before Apl 18, 1743, at which time her father was dec'd.

Thomas Luten of Chowan Co, deeded to his dau Mary Evans, 200a of land in said Co, called "Sandy Point" 1718. She had granted to her 300a in Perq Co, by Lords Proprietors, on Little River, adj Capt John Hecklefield, and her son William was living on said land Jan 4, 1723, to Jan 20, 1728/9. He conveyed this land to John Stepney, Nov 5, 1729 "land patented by my mother Mary Evans April 20, 1719," on Little River, adj William Godfrey. Another deed was made by him of 225a, to Col Richard Sanderson, adj land of Col Hecklefield dec'd. Jonathan & Mary (Luten) Evans, had besides son William, *certainly* one dau Sarah, b Feb 26, 1717/8. (Berkeley Par Reg.) According to these deeds the Evans land lay near the mouth of Little River, around the town of same name, on South west side of the River.

It is an unfortunate fact that neither Jonathan, or William Evans his son made wills in Perq, therefore their descendants are vague, and uncertain. The early persons of this name in Perq, adhered to the Quaker faith, but after a few years they are found with wives of other denominations, and in this way lost caste with the Quaker Church. It is thought, but not proven, that there was at an early date an intermarriage of some Evans with a Harvey lady, or a descendant of some Harvey line, as the name of Miles, and Harvey continued as a given name in the Evans family for many generations. This connection probably came down from Miles Harvey, as both those names figure in the line of Evans, who went west, even to the present day.

As both Jonathan, & William Evans are not available for descent, we have to depend on Peter Evans of Bertie Co for our next move downwards. It seems very *certain* that his descendants came over to Perq, and from them a straight line can be traced. Peter Evans of Bertie, lived near Ahoskie, and sold to William Evans (probably our own William, son of Jonathan) 100a of land on Catawaske Swamp, Hertford Co, April 19, 1715, and also deeded 235a to his son Robert, on So side of Petty Shore (same Co) on same date. Robert Evans with consent of wife Ann, sold 100a on West Shore, to John Wood, "whereon I now live" Mar 19, 1719. He later assigned 640a on South side of Ahosky Swamp, to Peter Parker, Oct 16, 1720. Ann Evans appears as Admix of her dec'd husband Robert Evans, May 1745. Her son Robert, inherited land in Perq, from John Perrisho, and it is probable that he moved to Perq, to take possession of this property. His will, p in Perq Jan 1758, names sons: John, Robert, and dau's: Sarah Griffin, Elizabeth, & Mary Evans, gr-children: Demsey, Aaron, Robert, & Huldah Blanchard.—His inventory, Jan 7, 1758. Robert Evans Ex. This proves that his son Robert was over 21 years of age at this time.

Robert Evans Sr appears on Tax list of Seth Sumner, 1765 with 425a of land in Perq Co. Thomas, John, Joseph, & William Evans on same list, one poll. John Evans had 116a, Joseph 370a, & Thomas 116a in Piney Woods District, 1791.

The division of Robert Evans (3) in Perq Co, May 1797. Heirs: Miriam Pearson, Sarah Woolard, Mary Lacey, and sons: John, William & Benjamin. To each £56, 17s 10½p.

Peter Evans of Bertie Co m Sarah Wynn (d of ———) m 2d Rose ———.

Evans, John (1) Robert (3) Robert (2) Robert (1) m Mariah Forbush, June 9, 1771. He m 2d Miriam Forbes, June 7, 1772 (untraced). One son John (Jack).

Evans, Joseph, (parents uncertain) m Elizabeth Woolard, and his will p in Perq, May 1727, is authority for his children: Wife Elizabeth, son Phineas, dau's: Margaret Moore, Rachel Jessop, Mary Whitehead, Jemima, Annie, Elizabeth, and Minerva Evans. Nathan, & Exum White Exrs.

Evans, Thomas, (parents uncertain) will Perq p Aug 1825, names son Chalkey, dau's: Rhoda, Elizabeth, Mourning Evans, John Clary, & P. Evans Exrs.

Evans, Chalkey (1) Thomas (1) will p in Perq. May 1832. Wife Jemima, dau Margaret. Josiah Bagley and Joshua Jessop Exrs.

Evans, Mary (d of Robert) (3) had sons: Miles, & Evan Lacey.

Evans, Benjamin (1) Robert (3) Robert (2) Robert (1) m Miriam Davis, May 24, 1802, m 2d Rebecca Willard of Perq Co, issue: 1 Charles, m Minerva Grant—2 Margaret, d young—3 Patsy, m Henry Buckner—5 Exum (Axum) m Elizabeth Parks, of York, Ill, 1826—5 William, m ——— Wilhoit—6 Joseph, m Elmira ———7 Nancy, m William Buckner—8 Abigail, m ——— Bardell— 9 Elizabeth, m Sam Prevo, State Rep—10 Rebecca, m Wm Bishop of Kanwakee, Ill—11 Rev Nixon Evans, m Minerva Bartlett of York, Ill—12 William, m Jane Baliff—13 Miles, m Betty Willard—14 Anna, d young—15 Pegga, m Miles Huckabell—16 Martha, d young.

Benjamin Evans m 2d Hannah Lamb (widow Moore) issue: 17 Noah, m Sarah Alberta—18 Mary—19 Malinda, m Col Allen Buckner (s of William Sr) 20 Hannah Ellen, m John Gaynor—21 Robert, d young—22 Silas—23 Henry—24 Sarah Ann.
Thirteen of the first children were born in Hertford, N. C.
Exum (4th son of Benjamin) moved to York, Ill, about 1816 with his family. In 1831 he moved to Plainfield, Ill, where he plyed his trade as a miller, and it is thought he sawed the lumber for the first frame building erected in Chicago. His sons: Milton Harvey, Charles Wesley, and dau's: Sally, Cynthia, Ann, Minerva, & Matilda, the last two twins, were all born in the west.

Harvey Evans (s of Exum, & Elizabeth Parks) had issue: William, Walter A. Evans, Milton Harvey Jr, M. D. (surgeon of Joplin, Mo) Ira Elsworth, and dau's: Mary Ellen, Sarah Adeline, Eunice, m ——— Lockwood, & Carrie Hall, m ——— Pike.

(I am indebted to Dr. M. H. Evans of Joplin, Mo, for the data of Evans in his line who moved west to Illinois.)

FLEETWOOD

Among subjects at Jamestown 1609, can be found the name of Edward Fleetwood Gent. (Brown Genesis to America.) Also listed among "adventurers to America" 1620, Sir William Fleetwood, and Edward Fleetwood Esq. Francis Fleetwood was granted land in Lower Norfolk Co Va, March 1652, adj William Robins, (Norfolk Co records.) He was probably the ancestor of William Fleetwood of Bertie Co N. C. whose will was probated June 12, 1769, naming sons: William, Henry, John, James, Edmond, Hardy, wife Elizabeth (née Ashley). His son Henry Fleetwood, will p May, 1777, in same county, names only one son; William Hooten Fleetwood, dau's Sarah, & Elizabeth, wife Sarah, née Hooten, and bro-in-law William Hooten, cousin William Hardy.

William Fleetwood (3) m Sarah Capehart, Dec 17, 1792. The Perquimans records have nothing to say of the early Fleetwoods, and it seems certain they resided in Chowan Co, until comparatively late years, where many marriages of this family took place. Without county records for reference, one is at sea when trying to work out a family line. The marriages of Fleetwoods in Chowan Co, are as follows:

Jeremiah Fleetwood, m Elizabeth Thompson. Dec 18, 1788. (Mar bonds Chowan.)

Jeremiah Fleetwood, m 2d Mary Pilkinton. July 17, 1790. (Mar bonds Chowan.)

Edmund Fleetwood, m Lydia Bennett. Oct 18, 1813. (Mar bonds Chowan.)

Ashley Fleetwood, m Parthenia Mewborn. Dec 13, 1814. (Mar bonds Chowan.)

From the last named are descended the family, by that name in Perquimans.
Bertie Co, Marriage bonds.

William Fleetwood, m Elizabeth Ashley. Oct 5, 1763.

Jeremiah Fleetwood, m Sarah Fleetwood. Oct 3, 1774.

James Fleetwood, m Penelope Tayloe. Oct 21, 1777.

Edmund Fleetwood, m Winnefred Sparkman. Dec 5, 1785.

Elizabeth Fleetwood, m William Billups. May 23, 1787.

Excursus, Ashley. Subject in Colony at Jamestown, May 23, 1609; John Ashley. (Browns Genesis to America.)

Samuel Ashley came from London to Va in Bonaventure, Jan 1634, age 19. (Hotten.)

John Ashley of Perq, made a deed Nov 21, 1751 unto Joseph Ashley, "land on East side of Yeopim Creek Perq Co, which my mother Sarah Ashley gave me." Joseph Ashley, here named m Sarah Hall, Oct 16, 1787 (Mar bonds Perq Co) William Ashley also lived in Perquimans, and it was his daughter, whom William Fleetwood married, it is thought. James Ashley m Elizabeth Langley (widow) in Norfolk Co Va July 15, 1769 (Mar bonds Norfolk Co). William Ashley, m Hannah Penrice, Apl 19, 1757 (Mar bonds Perq Co). He m 2d Elizabeth Nichols, Mar 25, 1760. Of course neither of these mothers could have been the mother of Elizabeth, who m Wm Fleetwood. William Ashley, m 3d Mrs. Elinth Penrice (widow of Francis) Feb 6, 1764. His first wife was Sarah Harloe, and it seems probable that she is the one mentioned in the deed by her son John Ashley, 1751.

FLETCHER

Ralph Fletcher was living in Perq, prior to 1689. He was one of the early Justices in Perq, serving for years, in that capacity. He is called Steward, or Judge, in the Justice Court Apl 1689.

Capt Ralph Fletcher, had grt for land 370a on Perq River, "at the mouth of a Swamp" adj Jenkins Williams, May 15, 1694.

In an affidavit, made in Chowan Co 1694, he stated that he was b 1632. It is thought that these Fletchers came from Surry Co Va, although no positive proof can be found. Hannibal Fletcher was living in sd Co very early. His wife Elizabeth came to Va, in Primrose of London, 1635, & he is spoken of as "Hannibal Fletcher of Chippoakes Creek." (Surry Co Records.)

Hannah Fletcher was transported to Va, in Middleton, by Capt Adam Thorogood, 1634. Whose wife she was is not shown. (Hotten.)

Berkeley Parish Reg, Perq Pre'ct.
Fletcher births, & deaths,

Ralph (1) Fletcher, m Elizabeth Suton, Mar 11, 167-- —Issue: 1 Elizabeth b Feby 22, 1675—2 Ralph b Dec 24, 1676—3 George b April 4, 1679—4 William b May 10, 1687—5 William (2 by name) b Dec 9, 1688—6 John b Jan 21, 1689, d June 25, 1689, (sons James, & Joshua, ages not given, but named in his will).

Will of Ralph Fletcher, of Perq, p Jan 21, 1728. Sons: Ralph (2) to whom he bequeathed ("my manner house, &-plan'") George, ("my lower house, & plan") Sons: James, & Joshua, Dau's Jane, & Elizabeth.

Elizabeth Fletcher, wife of Ralph, died Jany 21, 1690-1700.

Ralph Fletcher, had also a dau Margaret, who m Thomas Harvey, Jan 27, 1701.

Ralph Fletcher Jr m Jane Morgan (d of James, & Jean) Mch 2, 1698-9, issue: 1 Ralph (3) b April 22, 1703—2 George b June 15, 1705—3 Joshua b Nov 5, 1718.

The Rent Roll of Perq, prior to 1700, shows that Ralph Fletcher possessed 300a in said County.

Ralph Fletcher (3) m Mary Guyer, Dec 23, 1728, issue: 1 Ralph (4) b Feby —, 1729-30 & son Joshua, (age not in Reg.)

His will Perq Co, p July 1752. Sons: Ralph, (to whom he left "my manner plan' ") Joshua, dau's Jane' Miriam, Ruth Fletcher, Mary Ratcliff, (wife of Joseph), wife Mary.

George Fletcher (s of Ralph, & Elizabeth, (Sutton) m Susanna Burtonshall (d of Richard, & Priscilla) Feby 17, 1701.

Ralph Fletcher (4) will Perq, p July 1785. Son Jesse, d Miriam Newbold, d Margaret, s Joshua, & William Skinner Exrs.

William Fletcher, will Perq, p Feby 1827, names brother Zachariah, Winney Harrell's children, Samuel, Francis, Margaret, Ann, & Sarah Nixon Fletcher, sister Margaret White (wife of Aaron) uncle William Jones.

James H. Fletcher, will Perq p Feby 1830, names sister Nancy Skinner, sister Jane Fletcher, wife Grizzell, Exx. (See deeds Perq Co, in this Vol.)

GODFREY

John Godfrey in Norfolk Co Va, conveyed "2 black sows, and one Colt" unto Richard Conquest, for 1216 lbs of Tob," Jan 25, 1646. Matthew Godfrey with consent of wife Dinah, deeded land in Norfolk Co, June 18, 1724, naming his father John Godfrey, & brothers Jonathan, & William. Evan Jones who was granted land, 200a in Princess Anne Co Va, on North west side of Great Cypress Swamp, running into Symons Creek, of North River, Oct 20, 1687, assigned said land (with Consent of wife Dinah) unto Matthew Godfrey of Norfolk Co, Dec 15, 1703. Test' John, and Elizabeth Godfrey. Matthew Godfrey, with Consent of wife Isabella, sold unto John Godfrey (s of Warren) parcel of land purchased of Mr. Evan Jones, on Great Cypress Swamp. June 15, 17¾. Isabella Godfrey appointed her brother George Burges her Att'. June 15, 17¾.

William, & John Godfrey were living in Perq Per'ct, April 6, 1693.

Godfrey, (1) John (s of Francis, & Joan) b Aug 17, 1665, m Elizabeth Bagster (widow of Nathaniel) Feb 19, 1685. Nathaniel Bagster, m Elizabeth (Relict of John Simpler) April 25, 167- —issue: Elizabeth, b Aug 26, 1678. Elizabeth Bagster, widow Simpler, was dau of Thomas Abingdon Clerk of Pasq Co. She m for her 4th husband Capt John Hecklefield of Little River.

Godfrey, (1) John, & wife Elizabeth, issue: 1 Elizabeth, b May 11, 1687. John Godfrey died Aug 24, 1693.

Godfrey, (1) William, m Jane Barrow, issue: 1 John, b Feb 16, 1686—2 Francis, b Aug 12, 1689—3 Mary, b Aug 25, 1691.

Godfrey, Francis (father of above) will Albemarle, p Nov 5, 1675. Sons: William, & John, wife Joane.

Godfrey, (1) Thomas, m Ellener ——— Issue: 1 Thomas, b Mch 11, 1724/5— 2 Joseph, b Feby 14, 1726/7.

Godfrey, (2) Thomas, will Perq, p April 1749. Sons: William, Thomas, Francis, Joseph, dau's: Sarah, & Ellinor. wife Ellinor.

Peter Godfrey was Clerk of Perq, at one time, and returned to Norfolk Co Va, where his will was p 1721.

Godfrey, (3) William (2) Thomas (1) m Frances. He was dead May 9, 1773. (Inventory.)

Godfrey, (3) Joseph, m Mary Hosea, Aug 14, 1786.

Godfrey (3) Tulle, m Mary Pointer, Oct 16, 1786.

Excursus: Hecklefield. (1) Capt. John Hecklefield (son of John) was an Englishman who came to Perq about 1701. He appeared for the first time in Court held "at ye Gran Court House" Oct 14, 1701. The same year he was made Capt of Malitia in Perq Precinct. Court was held at his "House in Little River" Mar 29, 1703, & Oct 26 same year. The Assembly met there Oct 11, 1708, with 26 members in attendance. Mr. Edward Moseley chosen Speaker, William Glover presided as "President."

John Hecklefield m Elizabeth Abingdon (d of Thomas of Pasq Co) & had one son John, who died before Nov 8, 1729. d. s. p. when the name became extinct in Perq. Capt John Hecklefield's land lay around "Little River" a small village, the earliest settlement in the county. He was Dec'd Aug 8, 1721. "Elizabeth Hecklefield Dower Lands," adj Wm Godfrey. He had other land that adj Capt George Clerke, now in the tenure of Abraham Warren, & Mary Evans, widow of said George. Nov 9, 1709. Joseph Godfrey made a deed April 21, 1729, to Ezekiel Maudlin, 150a on So W. Side of Little River, by a small Creek, issuing out of sd River, called "Hacklefields land." Col. John Hecklefield was dead Nov 8, 1729. His land adj William Evans which the latter sold to Col Richard Sanderson. (225a.) John (1) will p in Chowan Co Aug 8, 1721, only one son John is named. The Inventory of this son can be found in the Deeds of Perq, and is a very interesting document.

GORDON

Rev Thomas Gordon appears in Perq as "Minister of gospell" officiating at the marriage of William Titterton, & Margaret Hall, Sept 23, 1679. Berkeley Par Reg is authority for the fact that he came to Perq from Accomac Co Va, but we can not be sure that he was a resident minister in Albemarle. What relationship existed between Rev Thomas, and George Gordon, next to appear in said precinct, if any is not made manifest, nor can it be said with certainty that the last was from the same Co in Va. The children of George Gordin (Gourding) are found in Berkeley Parish Reg, Perq Co, as follows: 1 Sarah (d of George, & Frances) b Jany 19, 1698—2 Elizabeth, b Jany 19, 1700—3 Margaret, b Apl 15, 1702—4 John, b Sept 25, 1705—5 Criston Mary Gordon, b Dec 13, 1707.

What became of these children is not shown. His will p in Perq Jan 1748, names sons: Nathaniel, & George, to whom he left "land I now live on" dau Hanner, gr-dau Tamer. (His wife is not named.)

Gordon, John (1) George (1) will Perq, p April 1758, Sons: John, to whom he left "plantation whereon I now live," son George, gr-children: Mary, and Jacob Gordon, Marmaduke Norfleet.

Gordon, Nathaniel (1) George (1) will Perq, p Jan 1756, sons: Nathaniel (2) & George, dau's: Elizabeth, & Tamer, wife Ann.

Gordon, John, (of Gates Co) will p Feb 1793, names son John, dau Sarah Norfleet. wife Mary, brother George, other children: Judith, Penny, Jeane, Rachel, David, & Beck. Taking into consideration that part of Gates Co was taken from Perquimans in 1779, we may feel sure the Gordons had not moved at all, but found themselves in a new county, when the county lines were changed.

A tradition is prevalent in the family, and they have good foundation for same there can be no doubt; is that three brothers came from Glenbucket,

RECORDS OF DEEDS 353

Scotland to N. C. in 1746, after the battle of Culloden, when they had to flee for safety. This tradition claims that one of them was James (or John) and the records are proof that he was *John* surely, who had son Jacob, and we have seen that he did have a son by that name, and said Jacob married Esther Norfleet, issue:

Gordon, 1 James—2 Joseph—3 George—4 Elizabeth.

Gordon, Elizabeth, m Thomas Granbery (s of Josiah, & Ann Godwin Gregory) issue: Barchia (Bathsheba) Granbery, m James Leigh—Joseph Granbery, m Mary Skinner, 2d Isa Benidicta Gordon (his cousin) Thomas Granbery died unmarried—Wm George, m Sarah Simmons of Currituck Co N. C. Elizabeth, m Benjamin Shananhouse.

Gordon, Jacob, was a Captain in the Continental line.

Gordon, John (1) the Scotchman, had also a son Benjamin, who m Tamer Copeland, issue: John Copeland Gordon, & two daughters. John Copeland Gordon m Mary Wotton, & had nine children, one of whom; George Bradford Gordon, m Elizabeth Anne Jones, issue: 1 John Wotton Gordon, m Annie Pender of Tarboro N. C., died in Richmond Va, soldier C. S. A. 2 Sarah Gordon, d unmarried—3 Benjamin Wotton Gordon, m Maria Louisa Jones, & had Isa Benidicta Gordon, m her cousin Joseph Gordon Granbery. (From papers in possession of Mr Granbery Tucker, Raleigh, N. C.)

George Gordon of Chowan Co, will p Feb 17, 1762, names sons: Josiah, John, George, Dau's Priscilla, Susan, Elizabeth, wife Elizabeth, dau Sarah Hinton.

Gordon, George, dec'd Dec 13, 1758. Inventory shows 112a of land in Perq Co.

Gordon, Nathaniel, Planter, dec'd Jan 15, 1756. Ann Gording sole Extrix. Perq Co.

Gordon, Mary, widow of Robert, 1736. (Loose papers in Perq Co.)

Gordon, Thomas, was granted land in Currituck Co, Nov 20, 1683, 454a called "Gordian Knott on Notts Island.

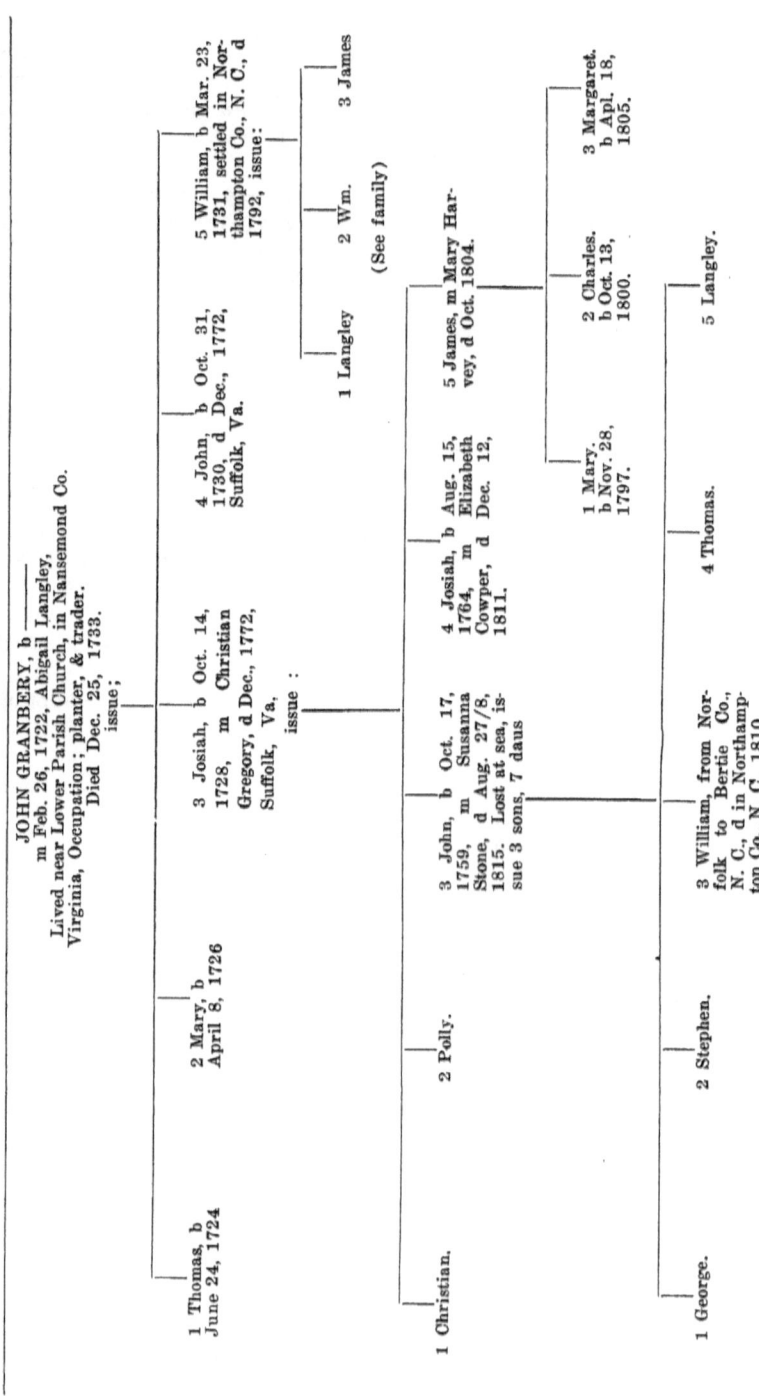

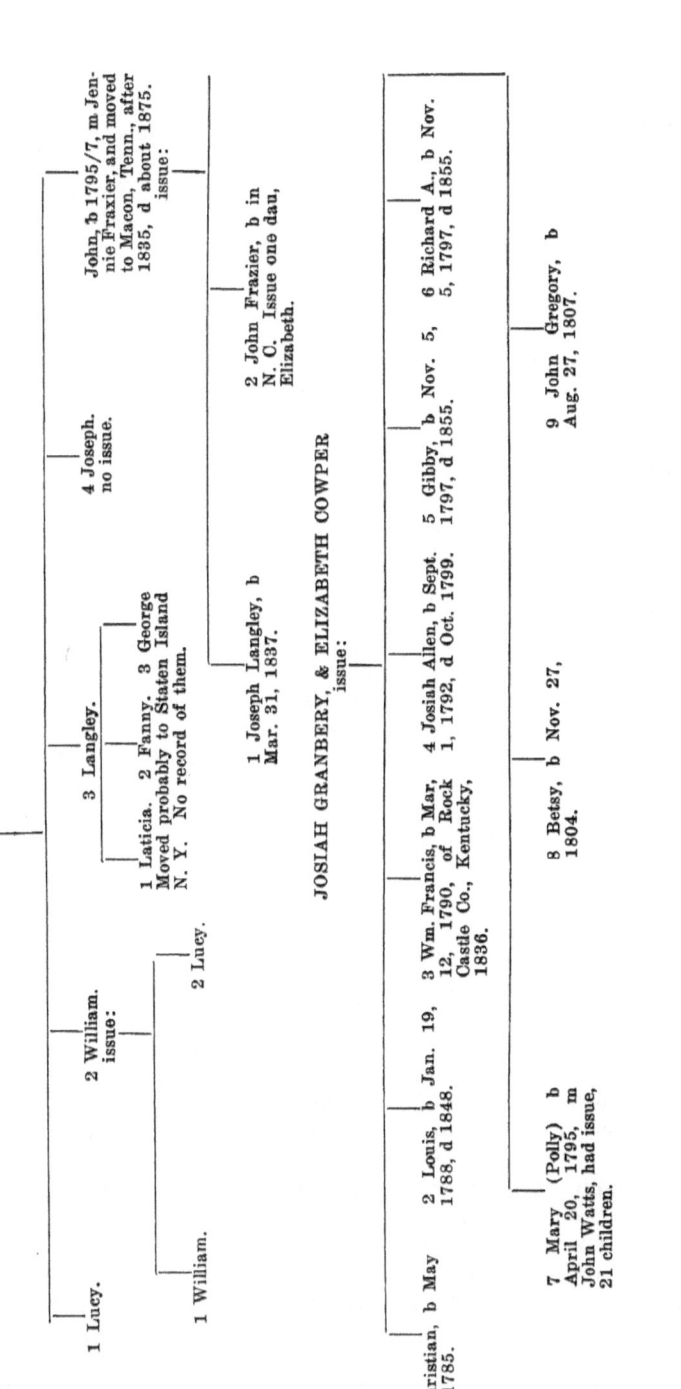

GRANBERY

Samuel Granbery was living in Nansemond Co Va, before —, 11mo, 1706, at which time he attended a convivial party, at the house of one Gresson Cofield, in sd county, where he was "assaulted by John Ewans, who had drunk too freely." The company had met together to "bee merry, drink, & fiddle," but the record is silent as to said Granbery's being in any way at fault. (Early Hist of Quakers.)

William Granbery, appears on the record of Lower Meeting, Nansemond Co, as a witness, to the marriage of Edmund Belson, (s of Elizabeth) of Nansemund, to Mary Crew (d of Mary Tooke, of Isle of Wight) at a Meeting at Pagan Creek, 13, 10mo 1684. John Evans was a Quaker, therefore his Church took him up on going to a dancing party. Samuel Granbery may have been of the same persuasion at this date. There is no way of knowing *certainly* that he was.

John Granbery, made a deed in Lower Norfolk Co Va, with consent of his wife Ann, who names herself sister of Matthew Spivey (s of Matthew, of same county) whom she made her Att' July 15, 1704. "John Granbery, of Nansemond Co, with consent of my wife Ann" sold unto Moses Prescott, of Norfolk Co, Land on Northwest River, in sd county, formerly granted to John Creekmore, by Pat April 20, 1689, & by sd Creekmore, sold to Daniel Browne, June 24, 1691, & by sd Browne, sold to Maj John Nichols, who bequeathed same to Ann my wife," 100a. July 13, 1704. Test' Nath'l Miller, Matthew Spivey, Sarah Spivey. Judith Nichols.

If the Chart made by Mr. Julian Granbery, is correct, & there is no cause to doubt its absolute authenticity, it seems John Granbery had two wives, & that Ann Spivey, was the first. According to the chart mentioned, he m 2d Abigail Langley. Her parents are not given, but the Norfolk Co records, are responsible, for the fact, that Thomas Wright received a grant of 25a in sd county, for trans' three people into the Colony, among them one Robart Langley, Dec 16, 1647. A deed made by William Langley, Lawyer of Norfolk Co, to Jeremiah Langley of same—Gent, sold to him land on Indian Creek, Northwest River, 200a, which "my father, William Langley dec'd, ye Elder, Gent—devised to Abraham Langley, & his heirs, in his will; William Langley being the Elder brother, & heir at law of sd Abraham, who sold sd land for a division, being willing to avoid any dispute." (Norfolk Co Records.)

Matthew Spivey's descendants moved to Chowan county N. C. This family will be dealt with later. Langley appears in Perq, county as a given name, in several families, other than Granbery.

On the Suffolk Parish Vestry book, appear the names of several Granberys, also John, & James Gregorie. John Gregorie was a Vestryman, of Chuckatuck Parish, Mar 24, 1754. Capt James Gregorie, was ordered by the Vestry, to "procession land in Nansemond Co," by Suffolk Parish Vestrymen, Sept 2, 1755. He was one of the Church Wardens, of said Parish, for the year 1755. Benjamin Gregorie appears on the same book, in sd Parish, Nov 1, 1756-57. James Gregorie, died in year 1759, it is thought; his name does not figure on the Parish record, after Nov 13, 1760, at which time Miles King, & Thomas Buxton, were elected Vestrymen, in "room of James Gregory, & James Riddick, Dec'd" Mar 24, 1761.

Two Views of Stockton
Built by Josiah T. Granbery in 1811. Now the home of Mr. R. H. Welch

RECORDS OF DEEDS

John Granbery, was Clerk of Suffolk Parish, Nov 1, 1756-57-58. Wm Granbery was also a resident of the same Parish, & received pay for keeping Allen Rumley, Nov 17, 1757. Thomas Buxton was appointed Clerk, before June 26, 1759, when John Granbery, was ordered to deliver the "papers," to said Thomas, who had become Clerk, in his place. A Vestry meeting was held at the house of John Granbery, for Suffolk Parish May 4, 1762. John Granbery was appointed "as a fit person" to attend to the Ferries, in Nansemond county, Nov 1, 1769.

Thomas Gregorie, appointed "procession Master," May 2, 1768.

The following was copied from a Chart, in possession of Mr. James T. Granbery, of Nashville, Tenn.

John Granbery, b ――― lived near Lower Parish Church, Nansemond Co Va, planter, & trader, died Dec 25, 1733, m Abigail Langley, Feby 26, 1722, issue: 1 Thomas, b June 24, 1724, 2 Mary, b April 8, 1726, d Jany ――― 1814, 3 Josiah, b Oct 14 1728, m Christian Gregory, d Dec 1772 near Suffolk Va, 4 John, b Oct 31, 1730, d Dec 1772, 5 William, b Mar 23, 1731, d in Northampton Co, N. C. 1792.

Josiah (1) & Christian his wife, issue: 1 Christian, d young, 2 John, b Oct 17, 1759, m Susannah B. Stone, lost at sea, Aug 27 or 8, 1815, issue: 1 Polly, m Nath'l Allen, issue: Sheppia, who m Pleasant Sherman. She was the mother of Allen G. Sherman. 2 Josiah (2) b Aug 15, 1764, m Elizabeth Cowper, d Dec 12, 1811, 3 James, b ―――, m Mary Harvey, d Oct 1804, issue: 1 Mary, b Nov 23, 1797, 2 Charles, b Oct 13, 1800, 3 Margaret, b April 18, 1805.

Josiah (2) wife Elizabeth (Cowper) Granbery, issue: 1 Christian, b May 15, 1785, m Thomas Watts—2 Louis, b Jany 19, 1788, d 1848—3 William F., b Mar 12, 1790, was living in Rock Castle Co, Ky 1836—4 Josiah Allen, b Sept 1, 1792, Oct 1799—5 Gibby, b Nov 3, 1797, d 1855—6 Richard Allen, b Oct 3, 1802, died 1855—7 Mary, or Polly, b April 20, 1795, m John Watts, issue: 21 children, 8 Betsy, b Nov 27, 1804—9 John Gregory, b Aug 27, 1807.

John Granbery (2) son of John, & Christian Gregory, by wife Susannah, issue: 1 Betsy, or Elizabeth, b April 13, 1791, m Jonas Hastings, d May 17, 1883, issue: 1 John G. Hastings, b Dec 3, 1812, d Aug 22, 1883, m Ann Chambliss —2 Polly, b 3, 11, 1793, d Oct 1804—3 George, b Sept 9, 1794, d Aug 28, 1815, (lost at sea with his father)—4 Julia, b 1, 17, 1797, d 5, 22, 1851—5 John Gregory, b Oct 1797, d Aug 4, 1799—6 Caroline, b Sept 3, 1800, d June 24, 1889— 7 Augusta, b May 3, 1802, d 1838 in Miss, m Victor M. Randolph, issue: 1 John, b April 8, 1826, d Aug 1852-62—2 Brett—3 Ryland—8 Henrietta, b Sept 2, 1804, d May 9, 1807?—9 Mary Louise, b April 6, 1806, d Dec 18, 1882, m George Hastings, issue: 1 George G. Hastings, who had 1 Edith, 2 Easburn, 3 Ernest.

Richard Allen Granbery, m Mary Ann Leslie Dec 23, 1826, d 1832, issue: 1 Wm Henry, b Sept 23, 1827, m Ann Elizabeth Gonito Dec 12, 1850, issue: Ella Filmore, b 2, 6mo 1853—2 Mary A, b 7, 2mo 1855—3 Chas Wesley, b 11, 27 1857—4 William B, b 2, 2mo 1860—5 Geo B, b Sept 2, 1862—6 Lizzie L, b Jany 14, 1866—7 Ann Estelle, b Jany 22, 1868—8 Carrie M, b Nov 22, 1870— 9 Eva F, b Mar 3, 1876. (Richard Allen, & Mary Ann) issue: 2 John Cowper, b Dec 5, 1829, m Ella Winston (Bishop of M. E. Church South) 1882, 3 George Washington, d in infancy. Richard Allen Granbery m 2d Hariet Griffin, issue: 4 Richard G, b 1835, d 1837—5 George, b 1837, d 1855—6 Hariet Ann, b 1840, d 1842—7 Anna Maria, b 1842, m L. H. Whitehurst—8 Richard F, b 1844, d

1866—9 Albert Burton, b 1847, residence Baltimore Md in 1888—10 Emily Frances, b 1849, m John Francis—11 Asa V, b 1852, d young.

Jonas Hastings, & Elizabeth (Granbery) issue: 1 Wm Henry, C. S. A. killed—2 John, d 1893—3 Robert M, m Julianna C. Granbery.

Henry Augustus, s of John, & Susannah (Stone) m Prudence Mimms of Princess Anne Co, issue: 1 Henrietta A, b Oct 3, 1829—2 Virginia, b Aug 7, 1831—3 Julianna, b June 20, 1840, m Robert M. Hastings, d Nov 3, 1869—4 Wm Henry, b Aug 16,' 1842, m Jennie Herrick—5 Theodore, b May 28, 1844, m Jennie Horn, issue; son Percy (b May 1875)—6 Lelia, b Aug 2, 1846, d May 22, 1850—7 Daniel Walker (Walke?), b Oct 11, 1848, m Mollie E. Peake, issue: Mabel E, b Sept 6, 1880—2 Mary Louisa, b Nov 6, 1851, m Frank L. Jones, issue: 1 Henrietta L, b July 27, 1887—2 Maud V, b Sept 12, 1885.

William Henry, & Jennie (Herrick) issue: 1 Wm Preston, b Jany 11, 1875, d Dec 21, 1888—2 Alice C, b Nov 6, 1876—3 Edwin C, b Feby 23, 1879—4 Eugene F, b July 22, 1881.

John (Greshow)? Granbery (s of Henry Augustus, & Prudence Mimms) b April 17, 1833, d Mar 31, 1895, in Phil Pa, m Mary A. Teague?, issue: 1 Henry A, b June 10, 1858, m Ada Mitchell, issue: 1 Mary W, b April 1, 1880, d July 17, 1881—2 Miriam C., b Nov 17, 1881. 2 John Austin, b July 5, 1861—3 Mary Lee, b Nov 15, 1863, 4 Lelia, b Mar 14, 1866, d April 27, 1866—5 Samuel W, b May 31 1869—6 Julian Hastings, b Aug 28, 1873.

The Perquimans branch of the Granbery family, is represented first by Josiah Granbery, who lived at the "Folly" then in Perq Co, but later 1779, in Gates, after the county was divided. Perquimans at one time embraced the territory as far north as Orapeak (now called Coropeak), & deeds in Perq, are proof of the fact.

This Josiah Granbery, m Ann Gregory (niece of Christian Gregory, wife of Josiah (1) Granbery, of Gates Co) d of James Gregory, & wife Patience Godwin, of Va. Josiah (2) Granbery was one of the Vestrymen of St Pauls Church, Edenton, and a member of the Assembly at Newbern, April 1775, & again at Hillsboro, Aug 25, 1775. (Wheelers History of N. C.)

Josiah Granbery, & Ann had issue: 1 Thomas, 2 John, 3 James, 4 Ann, 5 Elizabeth Granbery.

1 Thomas Gregory Granbery b 1782 m Pherebee Peele Parker, (d of Job Parker of Chowan,) d 1828, issue: Josiah (3) Thomas Granbery, b 1806, m Sarah Ann Baker Sawyer, Jan 16, 1826, d of Willis Sawyer, of Bertie Co, & wife Sarah Baker (d of John Baker, & Mary Wynns, their only child to reach maturity) issue an only child: Mary Isabella, who m Lucius Junius Johnson (a descendant of Elizabeth Gregory, & Rev Daniel Earl). Lucius J. Johnson was a distinguished lawyer of Elizabeth City, N. C. Capt C. S. A. d 1866, she d 1869, issue: 1 Sarah Ann Johnson, 2 Mary Granbery, 3 Charles Earl, 4 Betsy, 5 Granbery, 6 James Madison, 7 Henrietta Martin, Sarah Ann Johnson, the only one now living, in Annapolis Md.

Col Josiah T. Granbery died 1862, in Perq county, where he had lived all his life, & his wife followed him in 1878. He was a large property owner, a successful farmer, & leading citizen. At his home called "Stockton" in Perq, he held sway, as a country gentleman, & great tales are told of the grand doings in the handsome old house, "before the War between the States." None of his children married, so his line ran out with him. He represented the county, in the Assembly, 1835-36, & was President of the Seaboard Agricultural Society, Nov 1857.

2 John Granbery, m Mrs———Cowper, issue: 1 John J. Granbery, 2 George W. Granbery. Both d unmarried. Their names are mentioned in Nansemond Co Va Court, as heirs of Capt John Granbery, Dec 9, 1833.

3 James Granbery, m Nancy Gordon (d of Jacob, & Bathsheba his wife, of Gates Co, whose will is dated Sept 22, 1817) issue: 1 Joseph Gordon, 2 Thomas John, 3 Bathsheba A, 4 William George, 5 Elizabeth Esther Granbery.

(a) Joseph Gordon Granbery, m Isa Gordon (his cousin) (d of Benjamin Wotten Gordon, & Maria Louisa Jones) issue: 1 Mary, b——— 2 Joseph Gordon, b ——— 3 Isa Gordon, 4 Edna Jones Granbery (twins), b ———.

(b) Thomas John Granbery, d unmarried.

(c) Bathsheba A Granbery, m James Leigh, issue one s Richard Leigh.

(d) Wm George Granbery, m Sarah Simmons, of Currituck Co, issue: 1 Thomas, b——— 2 Mary, b——— 3 Lydia, b——— 4 James, b———.

(e) Elizabeth E. Granbery, m Benjamin Shananhouse, moved to Charlotte, N. C. issue:

4 Ann Granbery m William Wood of Perq, whose will was p Nov 1824, in which will he names wife Anne, & son William Edward Wood, & dau's Elizabeth, & Lucy Anne.

(a) Dr Wm E. Wood m Sophie Martin Trotman, (d of Ezekiel Trotman, & Emily Daube, d of Gen'l Peter Daube, of Rev fame) issue: 1 Dr Julian E. Wood, 2 Rev Thomas Granbery Wood, 3 Charles Stanton Wood, 4 Mary Shaw Wood, 5 Annie G. Wood, m J. T. Whitehurst.

(b) Elizabeth Wood, m Rev James G. Hall, moved to Miss. Eight of the family died of yellow fever. Their son Dr William Hall, was a surgeon in the Confederate Army, & his son James G. Hall Jr, was a judge in Tenn.

(c) Lucy Ann Wood died single.

5 Elizabeth Granbery, m Joseph Gordon (s of Jacob, & Bathsheba) issue: 1 Mary G. Gordon, 2 Bathsheba N. Gordon, 3 Jane Gregory Gordon.

(a) Mary G. Gordon, m John G. Harvey (her 1st cousin) issue: 1 Elizabeth Gordon Harvey, 2 Mary Granbery Harvey.

(b) Bathsheba N. Gordon, m 1st John L. Shananhouse, issue: 1 Benjamin G. Shananhouse, 2 Thomas Linch, 3 Nora Gordon. She m 2d Edwin Brace, issue: 4 Elizabeth Granbery Brace, 5 Belle Gordon Brace.

(a) Joseph Gordon Granbery, & wife Isa Benedicta (Gordon) issue: 1 Mary Gordon, b——— m Dr John W. Speight, issue: 1 John Gordon, d young, John Gordon (2) died a lad, 3 Agnes Granbery Speight, m John Calvin Sanford, issue: 1 Agnes Granbery Sanford, 2 John Calvin Sanford.

2 Joseph Gordon Granbery, m Edith Shananhouse, issue: Wm Lee Granbery, Elizabeth Granbery.

3 Isa Gordon Granbery, m Nathan Tucker, issue: 1 Joseph Granbery Tucker 2 Elizabeth Gordon, 3 Mary Gordon, died young, 4 Isa Gordon, 5 Virginia Radcliff, 6 Agnes Granbery Tucker.

4 Edna Jones Granbery, m Thomas Nixon, issue: 1 Julian Granbery Nixon, d unmarried, 2 Dorothy Gordon, m Walter Oakey, issue: Dorothy

Gordon Oakey, 3 Marjory Gordon Nixon, m Loyd Horton, 4 Edna Jones Nixon, m Braxton Dawson.

GREGORY

Rev. John Gregory appears as Rector, of Upper Parish, Nansemond County, Va, in June 1680. It is thought that he was an ancestor of Maj John Gregory, and his brother James. From Duke Creek vestry book said county, the knowledge is gained that Maj John Gregory, James (Gregorie) and his two sons, John, & Thomas were living in that part of the county, on east side of Nansemond River, "Upper Parish," which was added to Suffolk Parish, and the opinion is advanced that Maj John Gregorie was certainly the father of James, before mentioned. He sent in his resignation as vestryman of said Parish, Nov 17, 1757, which was accepted. It is thought he was at this date old, and feeble, and he certainly died soon after. Upper Parish records, and loose papers in Perq, show that he was dead in 1760. John Gregorie's name appears as one of the trustees who by Act of Assembly, were appointed to select a site, and establish a town called Suffolk, May 1742. (5 Henning Statutes 199.)

Mary Gregorie (sister of James) whose will was p in Chowan Co, Nov 25, 1761, made bequest to the children of her brother James, and names her "bro-in-law's" Rev Daniel Earl, and Josiah Granbery, his wife Christian, her niece Ann Gregory and nephews: William, James, Thomas, & John Gregory, children of brother James. This will proves that James Gregory had sisters, Mary, died unmarried, as before seen, Elizabeth, who m Rev Daniel Earl, and Christian who m Josiah Granbery. John Gregory lived in Nansemond Co Va. He was Chairman of the Co Committee of Safety, 1776, and Capt in Continental line, 15 Va Reg. (See Records Land Office Richmond Va.)

James Gregory b Mar 10, 1752, m Mary Wynns d of Col Benjamin, & Margaret (Pugh) and moved to Gates Co, N. C. She was b Nov 8, 1775, which made him 23 years her senior. Margaret Pugh was dau of Col Francis Pugh, & wife Pheribe Savage of Bertie Co, N. C. She m 2d Thomas Barker of Edenton, N. C. after 1736.

James Gregory was Senator from Gates Co. and in the Gen'l Assembly of N. C. 1780-81. He died 1802, leaving wife Mary, and children: Ann, b Mar 3, 1782, m Dr Charles Worth Harvey Oct 28, 1800, d May 28, 1805, issue one son James G. Harvey, who died without issue. 2 Margaret, b Jan 1, 1785, m——— Dickerson, m 2d Dr Isaac Pipkin, and had one daughter Eleanor, who m William Muse. 3 Mary Wynns Gregory, b Mar 17, 1787, m Dr John Burgess Baker of Gates Co, (s of Lawrence Baker, & Maria Burgess, d of Rev Thomas Burgess, of Halifax Co, N. C.)

James Gregory, m Patience Godwin, and had 1st William, m Sarah Moore of Perq Co, N. C. (d of Maj Charles Moore, of the Rev, and wife Sarah Hunter) 2d Thomas, m Mary Benton, July 4, 1767, issue: one son, and two daughters. 3d Ann, m Josiah Granbery (thought to be nephew of Josiah who m Christian Gregory) issue: son George, and dau's: Bathsheba, m Jacob Gordon of Gates Co, N. C. issue: James, George, Joseph, & Jacob Gordon. 4th Elizabeth, m George A. Harvey. 5 Jenny, 6 Mary Hunter Gordon, m Isaac Hunter of Gates Co, N. C.

John Gregory of 15 Va Reg died intestate, d. s. p. Heirs: James G. Harvey, John J. Granbery, George W. Granbery Sr, Mary G. Gordon, Joseph G. Granbery, Thomas J. Granbery, George W. Granbery Jr, Bathsheba A. Granbery, Elizabeth E. Granbery, Ann Wood, Elizabeth Smith, Thomas W. Gregory, Jr., Mary Gregory, Thomas Gregory Jr, John Gregory, Margaret Pipkin, Mary W. Baker, Josiah T. Granbery, Mary Elizabeth Goodman, Jane A. Hodges, Margaret Ann Gregory, & Joseph A. Granbery. The brothers of said John were: James, Thomas, and William.

Other Gregorys in Perquimans, are probably descendants of this same line, but no data bearing on their family has appeared.

Excursus Earl.

"Parson Earl" as the Rev Daniel Earl, Episcopal minister was familiarly called by his many parishioners who loved him very much, officiated in the Churches of Perq as well as Chowan Co. He rode the entire district baptizing the children, performing marriage ceremonies in all the adjacent counties, and ministered to those bereaved by death. He lived in Chowan, where he died before May 31, 1785, will on that date, married first Elizabeth Gregory, sister of Mary (as above) and second Charity Jones, sister of Thomas, who he names in his will, Aug 2, 1775, nieces: Elizabeth, & Ann Earl, "dau's of Rev Daniel Earl."

HOLLOWELL

Of this family nothing is known *earlier* than the Quaker records, in Nansemond Co Va, but no better evidence can be found, for any family data.

Hollowell, Thomas (1) was living in said county,—10mo 1672. He affiliated with Lower Mo Meeting in Nansemond Co, and was one of the witnesses to the marriage of "banns" of Edward Belson, & Mary Crew, 13, 10mo 1684.

Hollowell (1) Thomas, of "Elizabeth rieur" had by wife Alise, issue: 1 Sarah, b 1, 11mo 1647—2 Thomas, b 22, 1mo 1649—3 Henry, b 18, 8mo 1651—4 John, b 22, 4mo 1655, d 10, 3mo 1671—5 Joseph, b 15, 6mo 1657—6 Benjamin, b 28, 12mo 1659—7 Elizabeth, b 9, 7mo 1662—8 Alise, b 16, 12mo 1664—9 Edmund, b 15, 9mo 1667—10 John (second by name) b 5, 9mo 1672.

Hollowell, Thomas "ye Elder Departed this Life" 16, 1mo 1687.

Hollowell, Thomas (s of Thomas) died 15, 2mo 1687.

Alice (widow of Thomas, and Elder in the Quaker Church) died 19, 9mo 1700.

Hollowell (2) Henry, m 1st Elizabeth Cotching (d of Thomas, of Chucktuck dec'd) 7, 8mo 1680. "Father Thomas, mother Alice." He m 2d Elizabeth Scott (intention) 20, 2mo 1693 (d of William Scott Jr, & wife Elizabeth—b Dec 12, 1675).

Hollowell (2) Joseph, (untraced) Joseph (2) probably his son, m Martha Williams, 4-7-174—

Hollowell (2) Benjamin, m Elinor, who was his Admix, in Norfolk Co Va, Feb 17¾.

Hollowell (2) Elizabeth, was first wife of Nathan Newby, (a Quaker minister) who came to Perquimans to live about 1707. He being son of William Newby of Nansemond Co, and she (d of Alice of Elizabeth River) were m

13, 10mo 1678. Nathan Newby m 2d Mary Toms, (d of Francis Jr) of Perq, who survived him, and m 2d Samuel Moore, also of Virginia.

Hollowell (2) Joseph, with wife Grace, assigned land in Norfolk Co, formerly Robert Berrys, May 30, 1701.

Hollowell (2) John, figures as a Quaker, and gave support to the building of the Quaker Meeting house, on Levin Buffkins land, which was proportioned, to be "20 feet long, 20 feet wide, and fitted with seats, at a cost of 3,868 lbs of Tob."

Hollowell (3) Thomas, first in Perq, purchased 100a of land from Jacob Hill, on N East side of Perq River, July 11, 1726. So it can not be said he was one of the *first* settlers in the Province of N. C. Luke Hollowell, from whom descent can be traced, was also in Perq, and well settled Jan 10, 1725/6. His will Perq Co, p April 21, 1736, names sons: Joel to whom he left his "dwelling plantation" William, & John, wife Elizabeth. He devised land in Virginia to son John.

Hollowell (2) Edmund, d. s. p. moved to Bertie Co N. C. where his will was p Oct 20, 1729. Brothers: Thomas, and John.

Hollowell (3) Thomas, of Perq, d. s. p. will p July 1772, names Rachel Wilson (wife of Jacob) cousin Thomas (s of John) wife Sarah. It being often the case that a person making a will called a nephew "cousin" the Thomas here mentioned may have been a nephew, and said John brother of Thomas. There is no way of being positive however.

Hollowell (3) John, m Christian————Issue, according to his will, p in Perq Sept 10, 1784: William, Henry, dau's: Elizabeth Perry, Sarah Riddick, Mary Riddick, Christian White, Ann Evans wife Christian.

Hollowell (4) Thomas, (s of John, according to Thomas Hollowells will) m Mary Lamb, 11, 1 mo 1787, issue: 1 Sarah, b 26, 12mo 1787—2 John, b 12, 3mo 1789—3 Elizabeth b 14, 7mo 1791—4 Polly, b 28, 9mo 1793—5 Thomas, b 27, 4mo 1796—6 Aaron, b 31, 3mo 1799—7 Nathan, b 24, 11mo 1800.

Hollowell, Thomas (father of above) died 27, 9mo 1806. His will, p Nov 1806. Sons: John, b 12, 3mo 1789 Thomas, Aaron, & Nathan, dau's: Sarah, Mary D, & Rebecca Hollowell, wife Mary, her brothers: Preston, & John Lamb Exrs.

Hollowell (5) John, (s of Thomas dec'd) m Mary Jesop (d of Thomas) 12, 7mo 1809. "At Welses Meeting house" in said Co, issue: 1 Betsy, b 1, 6mo 1810—2 Rachel, b 9, 12mo 1812.

Thomas Hollowell, m Sarah Symons, 7, 12mo 1758, d 27, 9mo 1806. (At Symons Creek Pasq Co.)

Joseph Hollowell, m Leah Moore, 6, 11mo 1754.

Hollowell (6) Nathan, m Margaret (d of Christopher Wilson & Pheribee (Parker) and had according to his will: son Wilson, and Dau Eliza. Will p Nov 1829.

HOSKINS

Nicholas Hoskins, b 1589, came to Va in 1616. Temperance his wife in 1620, and had dau Margaret, b in Va 1624. (Hotten) He settled in Surry Co Va, where Robt Canfield made complaint against him, June 25, 1680, that "Nicholas Hoskins had departed this Country" owing him 900 lbs of Tob. An Order of Court was issued Feb 20, 1680, for the seizure of his Est, to satisfy said debt. (Surry Co Rec) Barth Hoskins living in Vir, obtained a grt for land in Elizabeth City Co, Nov 3, 1624. Another (or probably the identical person) Bartholemew Hoskins came to Va, in Safety 1635, age 34. He seems to have settled in Accomac Co Va.

Bartholemew Hoskins, had grt for land in Lower Norfolk Co Va, May 1, 1639, and another grt on Broad Creek, Mar 6, 1648, a 3d grt for 400a on Broad Creek Apl 29, 1653, and a fourth grt on same Creek, 800a, Dec 1, 1654. His grants were it is certain, on Hoskins Creek in Princess Anne Co Va, which Creek is a boundary of the old Moseley tract in said county. (See Map of Moseley Estate, in sd Co.)

Thomas Hoskins, m in Northumberland Co Va, the relict of John Ingram, and made release of her property to sd John, July 26, 1658.

William Hoskins of same, sold to John Garner, half of his grant, Oct 21, 1661.

It is not known which branch of Hoskins furnished the progenitor of the one who first settled in Perq Co, but it seems from the records at hand, that Hannibal Hoskins was the immigrant to this section. He appears first on the Reg of Berkeley Parish, Perq Co, Feb 11, 1689, when he married Margaret Furre (d of Peter). Peter Furre made complaint to the Court that he was being ill used on account of his religion, being a Roman Catholic. (See Col Records) Hannibal Hoskins seems to have died intestate. The next to make his appearance in Albemarle, is William Hoskins, of "Matacomack Creek" who made his will Jan 20, 1692-3, naming as legatees: brother Thomas, and cousin Daniel Cox. The deeds in Perq throw much light on this family, and they have been well written up in N. C. Hist Reg, Vol 3-1, beginning with Richard Hoskins (s of Wm, and Sarah, nee Whedbee.)

The Register carries this family through its many ramifications, well into the nineteenth century.

JESSOP

Not a great deal is known about this family, before coming to N. C. The Virginia records do not yield anything of importance about them, and the Quaker Rec in Nansemond Co, are silent on the subject. They came probably straight from New England, with the Nicholsons, & other families. One ——— Jessop landed in Mass, with———Robinson, from Holland, early after the settlement of the Puritans. This of course is only conjecture, as there is no data at hand to prove the said statement. Without records one can not be *positive* about family movements.

Thomas Jessop, came from London in "Bonaventure" Jan 1634, age 18. (Hotten.)

Edward Jessop settled at Fairfield Conn, 1639, and had son Edward.

Joseph Jessop was granted 190a in Perq Pre'ct, "adj Timothy Clare, through the Dismall" Feb 4, 1713/4. Joseph Jessop was brother of Thomas, and names him in his will, probated in Perq Co, Aug 1735. According to this will, Joseph Jessop had no male descendant. He names his nephews: Thomas, to whom he left "plantation on which I now live" and Timothy, & Jonathan Jessop. He left to gr daughter Mary Mayo, "my plantation at the meeting house," wife Margaret, nieces Mary & Elizabeth (dau's of Thomas). He appointed his brother Thomas Ex. The "meeting" house here spoken of was Wells, which stood across the road from the old Jessop home, and was later moved out on the main road, and is still standing, as part of a barn, owned by Mrs. Jack Trueblood, formerly Jessop. Wells Meeting house was used as a public school house after its abandonment by the Quakers, & was known by the name of "Jessops School house." Mary Mayo here named was a dau of Edward Mayo (son of Edward) who m Mary Clare (d of Timothy). Thomas Jessop from whom descent can be traced, m 1st Jane (widow of Joseph Robinson) dau of Timothy Clare, before Nov 10, 1724, and 2d Mary Ann Martin (d of John of Pasq Co). He died in Perq county before 15, 10mo 1744. Division of his Estate on that date, shows: Wife Mary Admix, children: Thomas (2) Joseph, Munden (part) Elizabeth, Jonathan, & Enoch Jessop, each a part.

Jonathan Jessop was Constable in Perq, July 9, 1766.

The Quaker records of Perq, now at Guilford College, would no doubt throw much light on this family. From that source the following was copied:

Jessop, Jesse, m Sarah————issue: 1 Martin, b 17, 12mo 1822—2 Miriam, b 21, 3mo 1825—3 Sarah (d of Jesse, & wife Mary), b 6, 1mo 1828—4 Jonathan, b 17, 9mo 1829.

Sarah wife of Jesse Jessop died 21, 6mo 1825.
Miriam, d of Jesse, & Sarah, died 17, 5mo 1825.
Jonathan, s of Jesse, & Mary, died 6, 10mo 1830.
Mary wife of Jesse, died 7, 9mo 1831.
Thomas Jessop (son of Thomas) (1) died 14, 12mo 1818.
Rachel Jessop (wife of Thomas) died 3, 3mo 1830.
Anna (dau of above) died 29, 12mo 1831.
Jessop, Joshua (son of Thomas dec'd of Perq) m Rachel Evans, (d of Joseph) 19, 5mo 1819, at Suttons Creek.

Thomas, will Perq, p Feb 1819, Sons: Joshua, & Jesse dau's: Elizabeth Lacey, Mary Hollowell, Anna, & Margaret Jessop, son Thomas, wife Rachel.

Jessop, Rachel, will Perq, p May 1824. Dau's: Margaret Saunders, Mary Hollowell, Ann Jessop, son Joshua, son Jesse, son-in-law Joseph Lacey.

Jessop, Timothy, will Perq, p May 1805. Wife Miriam, child in esse, sister Peninah, and her two children: Thomas, & Mary Willard.

JONES

As everyone knows there are Jones, and then Jones. While it is extremely difficult to decide with absolute certainty the descent of any line of this numerous family, and one is often very much confused by their many Johns, & Peters, yet we can with good grace give the various Peters in Perq with well founded authority. They are well defined on the records, but no mention is made of the place from which they came.

Jones, Peter (1) died in Perq Aug 4, 1679. As he made no will, nothing further can be found. It seems reasonable to suppose that the next by that name was his son. Also it seems probable that there was some connection by marriage, or otherwise, between the Jones' family, & Robert Beasley, where said Peter Jones was buried. He was probably one of the Peter Jones descended from Abraham Jones, of Va, but there is no positive *proof* of this fact.

(2) Jones, Peter (2) Peter (1), m Elizabeth ————. Issue: 1 Rebecca b Mar 14, 1694—2 William, b Sept 28, 1697—3 Peter, b May 7, 1700, Peter Jones, m 2d Mary Overman, issue:. Elizabeth, Margaret, Sarah, John, Hannah, & Mary.

His will p in Perq, April 1752, names children: John, to whom he bequeathed "plantation whereon I now live" & land at "Mile Branch." To son William he left 170a, son Peter "plantation whereon I now live" dau's: Mary, Hannah, & Margaret Jones, Sarah Sutton, Rebecca Denman, gr-son Thomas Sherwood, Exrs son John, & dau Mary.

The division of Mary Jones estate (d of Peter) Jan 1, 1758, makes plain the fact that he had two wives. Heirs of Mary Jones dec'd:

Rebecca Denman, "sister of the half blood."
William Jones, "brother of the half blood."
Peter Jones, "brother of the half blood."
Elizabeth Sherwood, "sister of the whole blood."
Margaret Henby, "sister of the whole blood."
Sarah Sutton, "sister of the whole blood."
Hannah Hinds, "sister of the whole blood."
John Jones, "brother of the whole blood."

By this division the marriages of the daughters are disclosed.

(3) Jones, Peter (3) Peter (2) Peter (1), m Mary Pierce (d of Thomas) (See Pierce) issue: son———b Aug 24, 1723—2 Peter, b Mch 27, 1726—3 Mary, b June 24, 1727—4 Isaac, b Mch 29, 1733—5 Thomas, b Jan 14, 1735—6 Zachariah, b Nov 25, 1740—7 Mahachy, b Oct 1, 1745. (The 1st son probably Zephaniah named in will.)

(2) Jones, William (1) Peter (1), m Priscilla Toms (d of Francis Jr, & Margaret Boge) issue: William, b Apl 27, 1732, d Mch 20, 1753, age 19 years. He was living when his father made his will, p in Perq, April 1752, naming, son William, dau Elizabeth Barber, & Rebeckah Jones, Exrs: Peter Jones (brother) & Moses Barber (son-in-law). As this son died the following year in young manhood, it seems probable that he died unmarried, therefore we are led to believe that William Jones had no male descendants in Perq.

Jones, Peter (3) will Perq p April 1753. Sons: Thomas, Zephaniah, Zachariah, Malachy (land on Mile Branch) dau Mary, wife Mary, gr-son Joseph Jones. Peter Jones Estate was divided Aug 1, 1758, among the several heirs; James Elliott received £81-11-9 "in Right of his wife Mary," Zephaniah, & Malachi Jones same.

The division of Mary Jones Estate, July 1758, a "part to Joseph Jordan, in right of his ward Joseph Jones," other heirs: Thomas Jones, James Elliott "in right of his wife" Zephaniah Jones, Malachi, & Zachariah Jones, each a part. In this division Thomas Jones is said to be the "eldest son of Mary Jones, who died intestate" April 18, 1758.

Thomas Jones m Sarah————issue Elizabeth, b Dec 26, 1730.
Mary Jones, (d of Peter, & wife Anne) b Aug 17, 1754.

Ann Jones (d of Mary Beesley, widow) m Peter Albertson, Aug 27, 1701.

(5) Jones, Joseph (1), (gr-son of Peter 3d) became a Quaker, and his issue is given in their records. He m Mary————"at Little River Meeting

house" 2, 3mo 1768, issue: 1 Margaret, b 9, 12mo 176—2 Sarah, b 15, 2mo 177—3 Elizabeth, b 9, 11mo 177—4 Miriam, b 9, 8mo 1777—5 Huldah, b 15, 11mo 1779, m ———Bundy, d 1, 2mo 1811—6 Joshua, b 6, 1mo 1782—7 Joseph (2), b 17, 1mo 1786, d 22, 11mo 1808—8 Mary, b 18, 1mo 1788—9 Charles b 9, 10mo 1791, m Nancy Wills, 19, 1mo 1811—.

Jones, Joshua, m Pleasant Hasket (d of John) "at Suttons Creek" 13, 7mo 1806. He died without issue, will 1814, wife Pleasant, brother Charles, Pleasant (Hasket) Jones m 2d———Jordan. (See her fathers will, p 1818.)

Jones, Joseph, will p in Perq, May 1819. Son Joseph H. Jones, dau's: Mary Jones, & Margaret Trueblood, sons: Joshua, & Charles Exrs.

Jones, Joseph (2) Joseph (1) m Mary———issue: 1 Joseph (3), b 22, 11mo 1803—2 Huldah Bundy Jones, b 1, 2mo 1811. Mary Jones died 14, 10mo 1813.

Mary Jones, wife of Joseph (1) died———1803.

Jones, Malachi (1) Peter (3) Peter (2) Peter (1) d. s. p. Will p in Perq, Jan 1777. Nephews: Joseph Jones, Nathan Elliott, William Jones (s of Zephaniah) Joshua Jones (s of Thomas) niece Mary Jones (d of Thomas) Exrs wife, brother Thomas, & Caleb White.

Jones, William, will p in Perq, Aug 1794, Wife Ann, dau's: Sarah, Mary, & Margaret, sons: Josiah & Thomas. He lies buried at the Jones farm across "Jones Bottom" near Hertford.

Jones, Miriam (parents not named) m Thomas Nixon (both of Perq) 13, 10 mo 1806.

Jones, Thomas, m Margaret Toms, 5, 4mo 1775. (Welleses).

Jones, William, m Mary Gilbert, 3, 6mo 1737.

Jones, William (s of John) m Jane Albertson, 7, 8mo 1741.

Jones, William, m Rebecca Wiley, Sept 1, 1790.

Jones, Josiah, m Betsey Standin, Nov 3, 1793.

Thomas Jones, will p in Perq, April 1788. Sons: Thomas, William, Zachariah, daus Mary Newby, & Sarah Jones, wife Margaret (nee Toms).

This Thomas Jones was evidently the father of William, of Jones Farm across "Jones Bottom" whose will was p Aug 1794, he being son of Peter (3) and Mary Pierce.

JORDAN

Samuel Jordan arrived at Jamestown with Sir George Somers fleet, 1609. Samuel *Gourden* of Charles City Co, "an ancient planter, who hath abode 9 years in this colony and his wife Cicily, who hath abode 2 years in the colony" received a Patent for 450a in three plantations, part adj John Rolfe (Surry Co) 2pt "abuts the great River, upon a Swamp, adj Martins hope, and 3d pt near Sandys, south upon Ye Great River" Sept 10, 1620. This land lay in the "Territory of Great Weyonoke" and was already planted. Samuel Jordan represented Charles City Co, in the House of Burgesses 1619. He settled at a place called "Jordons Journey" in the present confines of Prince George Co Va, and fortified his house, called "Beggars Bush" and defied the Indians during the massacre of Mar 22, 1622. His wife Sisley arrived in Va, in the Swan, Aug 1610, age 24 years. Among those living at Jordans Journey, Feb 16, 1623 are found, Cicily Jordan, and two children:

Mary age 3, and Margaret age 1, born in Virginia. Cicily Jordan m soon after 1632. Capt William Farrar. Samuel Jordan was living 1632.

Samuel Jordan had three sons, born in England, who came to America, one of them Robert being killed by the Indians, 1622. The other two Samuel, who settled Surry Co, and became ancestor of a branch of Jordans who moved west, and north, Thomas his brother born 1600, came to Va in the ship Diana 1624, age 24. He settled in Isle of Wight Co Va, where he had a grant for 900a of land "at the head of Warricksqueake River" adj Mr Butler Aug 20, 1635. He was a soldier under Sir George Yeardley, and represented Warrasquoke, in the House of Burgesses Oct 1629, 32. His son Thomas (2) patented land in Nansemond Co Va, 1666, and lived in, or near Chuckatuck. In lower Mo meeting records, he is spoken of as "Thomas Jordan of Chuckatuck." He gives the information in these records, that "he was born 1634, and received the truth in ye year 1660, and abode faithful in it unto ye end of his days" (Records Lower Mo Meeting, Nansemond Co.)

Jordan, Thomas (s of Thomas) m Margaret Brasseur (d of Robert) French Huguenot, issue:

(1) Jordan, Thomas (3), b 6, 6mo 1660, m Elizabeth Bough (d of William dec'd) 6, 7mo 1679. He left the Quaker Church, and became an Episcopalian, serving as Vestryman in Nansemond Co, 1702-9; was Sheriff of said county 1708-18; Lieut of Militia 1715, Justice 1732. He had by wife Elizabeth issue; 1 Martha b 22, 11mo 1680—2 Thomas, b 19, 5mo 1681—3 Elizabeth, b 18, 9mo 1683—4 William, b 22, 11mo 1688. Thomas Jordan (4) was a Church Warden of Suffolk Parish, Nansemond Co, year 1757, and was probably dead July 13, 1759, when he is spoken of as a "former Church Warden."

(2) Jordan, John (s of Thomas, & Margaret), b 17, 6mo 1663, m Margaret Bough, in Isle of Wight Co, 8, 10mo 1688. His will p in Isle of Wight Co Va, Feb 1, 1709. Wife Margarett, to whom he left plan' "where I now live, for her Natual life, and at her death to son John," if he die without heirs, to four youngest dau's: Mourning, Elizabeth, Mary, & Susanna. To dau Martha a negro girl "named Moll."

Jordan (a) John (2) John (1) Thomas (1) will Isle of Wight, p Dec 7, 1758, names son John, gr-son Edmund Jordan, d Mourning, d Elizabeth, Tharp, d Margarett Sebill, son Joseph, s Billingsley.

Jordan (b) John (3) John (2) John (1) Thomas (1) will Isle of Wight, p Nov 5, 1778, names his father John Jordan, brother James, sister Patience Jones, brothers Thomas, and William, sister Elizabeth.

Jordan (III) James (s of Thomas, & Margaret) b 25, 11mo 1665, m Elizabeth Ratcliff (d of Richard) In, 9, 12mo 1688, issue 1 John, & James. (twins) b———1689, and dau Elizabeth, who m Stephen Scott of Pasq Co N. C. They were members of Levy Neck Mo meeting Isle of Wight Co. Elizabeth Jordan, wife of James d 30, 6mo 1695 was b 21, 7mo 1668. James Jordan m 2d Anne Roester of Elizabeth River, 28, 7mo 1700. His will p in Isle of Wight Co, Oct 13, 1732, names son John, dau Elizabeth Scott, gr-son James Jordan Scott (s of Stephen, & Elizabeth) son James children, gr-son James Jordan. (Blackabee Terall in his will Isle of Wight, p Aug

27, 1733, left to gr-son James Jordan "all my land at Blackwater," gr-son Joseph Jordan £10 gr-dau Ann Jordan, son-in-law James Jordan.)

Jordan (IV) Robert (s of Thomas, & Margaret) b 11, 7mo 1668, m Christian Outland (widow of William) dau of Thomas Taberer of Trerasoo Neck, Isle of Wight Co) 9, 12mo 1687, issue: Christian, b Jan 25, 1689, m William Scott (s of John dec'd), issue: 1 Mary, b 4, 7mo 1708. Christian Scott died 12, 11mo 1708. Christian Jordan wife of Robert, died 26, 6mo 1689.

Robert Jordan m 2d Mary Belson (d of Edmund, & Elizabeth) b 24, 3mo 1673, married 10, 5mo 1690, issue: 1 Thomas, b 13, 4mo 1692—2 Robert, b 27, 10mo 1693—3 Joseph, b 18, 9mo 1695—4 Mary, b 24, 12mo 1699—5 Margarett, b 12, 2mo 1702—6 Elizabeth, b 17 12mo 1705—7 Edmond, & Belson (twins) b 17, 6mo 1707, Belson died 9, 10mo 1707—8 Samuel, b 29, 4mo 1711.

(a) Robert Jordan (2) Robert (1) m Dorothy Pleasants of Charles City Co Va 3, 6mo 1718. (Weyonoke Mo meeting.) She was his widow 9, 7mo 1718.

Robert Jordan (younger), became a Quaker minister in 1718, serving in that capacity for 17 years. He died 26, 9mo 1735, 40 years of age.

(b) Joseph (1) Robert (1) Thomas (1) became a Quaker minister, and married Ruth Glaister of Pasquotank Co. Children of Joseph Jordan "that great and worthy man, & minister of the Gospel" by Ann his wife, 1 Sarah, b 12, 2mo 1731—2 Abigail, b 19, 7mo 1733—3 Margaret, b "after her fathers Decease ye 29, 10mo 1735." (She d an infant.)

Jordan (V) Richard (1) Thomas (1) b 6, 6mo 1670, m Rebecca Ratcliff (d of Richard) In, 20, 8mo 1706. Richard Jordan of Nansemond Co, died 29, 10mo 1723. Richard Jordan Sr "of Lower pish of Isle of Wight Co, planter" made a deed of gift to his son John of afsd, planter, 100a of Land at the mouth of Cypress Swamp. Mar 30, 1679, Test' Richard, & Alice Jordan. This Richard had m prior to this date Elizabeth Reynolds, sister of John, who bequeathed to his sister, (wife of Richard Jordan) 800 lbs of Tob in his will, Mar 11, 1668. Isle of Wight Co, records.) The Richard here mentioned was probably a brother of Thomas (1) as he could not possibly have been Richard (s of Thomas). It is thought that John son of Richard Sr came to Chowan Co, at a very early date.

Jordan (VI) Joseph (1) Thomas (1) b 8, 7mo 1672. m Sarah. (untraced.) He may have been "Joseph of N. C."

Jordan, Benjamine, b 18 7mo 1674, m Sarah ———. His will Isle of Wight Co, Dec 8, 1715, Wife Sarah, sons: Thomas, Benjamin, dau's: Margaret, & Sarah. Brothers James, Robert, & Richard, Exrs.

Jordan (VII) Matthew (1) Thomas (1) b 1, 11mo 1676, m Dorothy Bufkin (widow of Leaner (Levin) dau of William Newby, & wife *Izabell* ? of Nansemond Co Va) 6, 7mo 1699. His will Isle of Wight Co, p Oct 13 1748. He made bequest to wife Dorothy, "6 negroes, ⅓ of money, and plantation where I now live, with Copper Still, & Utensills" at her death to son Josiah. To sd son "7 negroes, 1 Silver Tankard, 6 Silver Spoons, marked H" To son Mathias "Land bought of cousin Matthew Jordan (nephew) called Bells Point" with all stock, 6 negroes 1 Silver Brecor, 1 Silver Cup, 6 Silver Spoons and ⅓ of money. To dau Charity 4 negroes, 1 Silver Porringer, 1 Silver Tea Cup, & 6 Silver Spoons, To dau Comfort 4 negroes, "1 Silver Porringer, 1 Silver Cupp, and — Large Silver Spoons."

From this will it would not appear that Matthew Jordan, was not a man of spare means. "Disunion" papers were served upon Dorothy Jordan, widow.

17, 3mo 1750, for "Disorderly walking." Soon afterwards she obtained a "Certificate" to the Meeting in Perq Co, and as her two sons Josiah & Matthew had already preceded her, she probably lived a while in N. C. But in Josiah Jordans will p in Perq, he mentions his "mother in Isle of Wight Co Va," sd will p in Perq 1789. She m 2d James Pleasants 7, 12mo 1764.

Jordan (VIII) Samuel (1) Thomas (1) b 15, 2mo 1679, m Elizabeth Fleming, 10, 10mo 1703.

Jordan (IX) Joshua (1) Thomas (1) b 30, 6mo 1681, m Elizabeth Sanbourne (d of Daniel, & Sarah, named in his will). Joshua Jordan will Isle of Wight, p Feb 28, 1717, In his will he "desired that his mother-in-law Sarah Sanborn, shall be Hon'bly taken care of by my wife, and daughter, and shall not want for any thing that can be done for her, likewise shall have a horse & saddle to go to Meeting when she thinks fitt." Wife Elizabeth, Dau's: Sarah, Rachel, Mary, Elizabeth, Margrett, Susanna, sons: Joshua, and Matthew, brothers Robert, & Matthew. Test' Thos. Copeland, Cornelius Ratcliff, Henry Davis. His descendants also moved to Perq Co, N. C.

Matthew Jordan, son of Joshua, was evidently the "cousin Matthew" spoken of in the will of Matthew (1) son of Thomas (1) 1748.

Elizabeth, wife of Joshua, m 2d Cornelius Ratcliff, of Isle of Wight Co Va, 9, 3mo 1721. Their descendants (if any) also came to Perq. (See deeds in Perq.)

Jordan, Matthew (2) Matthew (1) Richard Sr, (son of Matthew, & wife Patience Darden) moved with his "cousin" Josiah to Perq, where his will was p July 1763, naming: Brother Gabriel Newby, sister Anne Jordan, sister Mary Clay, and Elizabeth Newby (wife of Francis) brothers: Francis, Joseph, Benjamin, & Josiah Newby, sister Dorothy Skinner (wife of John) mother Patience Newby (wife of Joseph Sr).

The will of Matthew Jordan, father of Matthew above, Nov 19, 1742, names: son Matthew, dau Dorothy, dau Elizabeth, dau Martha, and wife Patience. His Estate was appraised, May 23, 1743 .(Isle of Wight Co.) Patience Jordan m 2d Joseph Newby of Perq. (See Newby family.) Rebeccah, Richard, Joe, Patience, & Matthew Jordan, heirs of Richard of Isle of Wight Co, Newport Parish, "with consent of our mother Rebeccah, relict of said Richard dec'd." Apl 18, 1739. (Isle of Wight Rec.) Patience Jordan (2) m her cousin James Jordan, and was "disunited" for so doing. Matthew Jordan of Perquimans died without issue.

Jordan, Josiah (1) Joshua (1) Thomas (1) will Isle of Wight Co, Jan 24, 1783, names sons: Thomas "plantation whereon I live" Joshua (2), Robert, and children of "my dec'd son Hezekiah, all Estate I possessed him with in his life time," gr-son Samuel Jordan, dau Doley Brown, son-in-law John Pleasants. "As my son Hezekiah, and dau (not named) have left this life, I give to their representatives, parts as to children." Wife (not named) Son-in-law William Brown, & Jacob Randolph Exrs.

Josiah Jordan m Mourning Ricks 17, 2mo 1746. She was an Elder in Western Branch Quarterly meeting — 11mo 1745. They served as Exrs, Will of Abraham Ricks dec'd, Sept 23, 1745. (Isle of Wight records.)

Hezekiah (gr-son of Josiah) moved to Gates Co, N. C. where he m Mary Cook, and had son Daniel Jordan, m Miss Hunter, Mary Tatum Jordan, m Francis E. Winslow, Susan, who died young. Their descendants also lived in Perq.

Jordan, Rachel (1) Joshua (1) Thomas (1) dau of Joshua, & Elizabeth Sanbourne, of Isle of Wight Co Va, m Thomas White (s of John, of said Co) 13, 7mo 1719, issue: 1 Lydia, b 12, 9mo 1720, m John Robinson of Perq—2 Elizabeth, b 19, 10mo 1722, m Joseph Pritchard of Pasquotank Co—3 Joshua, b 26, 11mo 1727, m Gulielma Jordan—4 Jordan, b 20, 3mo 1729—5 Thomas, b 25, 12mo 1730, m Anne Barrow—5 Rachel, b 25, 12mo 1730 (twin to Thomas) m Benjamin Winslow (s of John Winslow, & Esther Snelling dau of Israel & Hannah, his wife née Larance)—6 John, b 17, 3mo 1733, m Lydia Winslow (d of Joseph Sr & wife Pleasant)—7 Mary, b 29, 2mo 1735, m Joseph Winslow (s of Joseph Sr, & wife Pleasant)—8 Matthew, b 10, 3mo 1738, m Mary Robinson—9 Caleb, b 8, 3mo 1740, m Rebecca Toms (gr-daughter of Francis (1) dau of Francis Jr, of Perq).

Thomas White will Perq, p Jan 1762. Made bequest to son Benjamin (not of age) "plantation on which I now dwell, and water mill," and should not "debar his mother from the dwelling house, and a third of the said plantation." To wife Rachel "chattels, one large looking glass, and a square walnut table," to son Joseph property "I possessed him with" and half of the water mill, until son Benjamin comes of age. Sons John, Matthew, Caleb, same. To dau Mary Winslow "one large looking glass & chattels," dau Sarah White, gr-dau's Sarah, & Mary Pritchard, "negroes which I lent to my dau Elizabeth." Appointed son Thomas, & Benjamin Ex. Test' Thomas Newby, Mary Pritchard, Israel Perry.

Mary Pritchard (d of Elizabeth née White) will Oct 1765, names brother Benjamin Pritchard, to whom she left "all my land," sisters: Elizabeth and Miriam, mother-in-law Sarah Pritchard (step-mother) aunt Sarah Albert—(son) bequest, to gr-mother Rachel White, to whom she left "a negro man named Jacob," at her death to uncle Benjamin White, uncles Joshua, Joseph, Thomas, John, Matthew, Caleb, and Benjamin White, "remainder of Estate." Brother-in- law Zephaniah Jones, and uncle Caleb Exrs.

The will of Rachel White, née Jordan was found behind an old looking glass in an antique shop in Suffolk Va, only a few years ago, with an original grant to Timothy Clare 1707, and another to Benjamin Winslow 1794. As said Rachel (d of Thomas) m Benjamin Winslow, whose will Perq, p Nov 1794, & it seems probable that some of his descendants sold the looking glass to the antique dealer. Benjamin Winslow names in his will sons: Joseph, John, *Jordan*, & Benjamin (2) Dau's: Sarah, and Rachel. Test' Israel, & Lawrence Perry.

The will of Rachel White, found behind the looking glass, was unfortunately unsigned, & not dated, but she names the same children, named in her husband Thomas Whites will p 1762, so there can be no *doubt* of her identity. As this will has never so far been published, the writer gives it in full, for the benefit of future generations.

Will of Rachel White, of Perq Co.

I Rachel White, of the Province of Carolina, and County of Perquimans, being weak of body, But of Sound, and Disposing memory, do think Proper to make and ordain this to be my last Will and Testament, in manner and form following; Firstly I give and bequeath unto my three sons, Joshua White, John White, and Caleb White, my negro girl Called Priscilla, She and all her Increase to them and their heirs forever, also I give unto my son Joshua, one Brass Kittle, and one Stone pot, to him and his heirs; also I give unto my son John, one Small Round table, and two Chairs; also I give unto my son Caleb, one feather Bed, and furniture, and three earthen plates, to him and his heirs forever. Secondly I give, & bequeath unto my son Thomas, my Desk ? and one Cow, and one Walnut framed looking glass, and one Couch, to him and his heirs forever. Thirdly I give and bequeath unto my son Joseph two Cows, and two heifers, one Ewe, and lamb, one Side Saddle, and bridle, one great Chest, and one Pewter Dish, and three plates, two white chairs, to him and his heirs forever. Fourthly I give and bequeath unto my son Matthew, two heifers, one tub and pail, two Ewes, and one looking glass, and one Candle Stick, and one Cofey pot, to him and his heirs forever. Fifthly I give and bequeath unto my daughter Rachel Winslow, one Small Square table, and one brass Candle Stick, and one negro wench Judah, and one old feather bed and some furniture. Sixthly I give and bequeath unto my Daughter Mary Winslow, Eight pounds proc— money, three Earthen plates, and one Earthen *prinah* ? *bole*, one Small Stone mug, to her and her heirs forever. Seventhly I give and bequeath unto my Daughter Sarah Nicholson, one feather bed, and furniture, that Mary *Pritchet* left me, one half *Duzen* Earthen plates, and one punch *bole*, one large pewter Dish, one Deep *puwter* Dish, one *tee* pot, and five *tee* Cups, and *sas*—(saucers) one large Stone pot, one Square table, one Chest, to her and *hers* forever. Eightly and lastly I give and bequeath unto my son Benjamin, one feather bed and furniture, and one Case and bottles, also I give all right of that Negro man Called Jacob, which Mary Prichard left me, to him and his heirs forever. No signature, and no probate, not dated.

A true copy, made by Mrs. Watson Winslow, July 9, 1930.

Rachel White was still living 1774, when her son John (d. s. p. will Perq) made his will said year. The grant to Timothy Clare 1707, called for 300a on Perq River, and it is supposed that the original was kept by some member of his descendants and finally fell into the hands of Rachel White, who hid same behind the old looking glass for safe keeping. Benjamin Winslow who m Rachel White (d of Rachel, and Thomas, as before shown) was ancestor of Jordan Winslow late of Winfall, who was father of Mr. Alonzo Winslow now residing there. Benjamin Winslow was son of John Winslow, and wife Esther Snelling, d of Israel, & Hannah née Larance, who was 3d and last wife of Timothy Clare. The writer has now in her possession an old "square walnut table" which was given to her husband Watson Winslow, by his grandmother, and the question naturally arises, could this table be the same mentioned in the will of both Thomas, and Rachel White? The style of the table proves it to be at least 225 years of age and it may very well be the same. (See other White will; N. C. Hist Reg, Vol 3-3.)

Of Joseph Jordan, who also moved to Perq at an early date, and settled near Little River Bridge, the Quaker records give data as follows:

Jordan, Joseph, departed this Life, 11 11mo 1725. (Reg of Suttons Creek, Perq Co.)

Jordan, Joseph (2) departed this Life —, 12mo 1752. (Reg of Suttons Creek, Perq Co.)

Jordan, Joseph (3) departed this life 4, 7mo 1760. (Reg of Suttons Creek, Perq Co.)

Jordan, Mary (widow of Joseph) died 6, 10mo 1767, and was buried in Friends burying ground at Newbegun Creek, in the 63d year of her age.

Jordan, Jane, (widow of Joseph, dau of Joseph Barrow) died 7, 10mo 1789, age 63.

Jordan, Joseph, Gent, appears first in Perq, with wife *ffelia Christi*, and purchased 200a of land in Pasquotank Co called "Chanceys," where said Jordan "now lives," 1704. ffelia Christi was probably the first wife of Joseph who died 1725, or there may have been a former Joseph who was father of Joseph who died 1725, and this seems to be the most plausible conclusion, taking into consideration the fact that, "Joseph Jordan (s of Joseph of North Car) m Mary Rix (d of Abraham, of Isle of Wight Co Va) in 10, 2mo 1723, therefore we see that Joseph (s of Joseph) m a sister of Mourning Ricks, who m, as before seen, Josiah Jordan of Isle of Wight Co, being cousins once removed, and marrying sisters.

Jordan, Joseph (3) was a Schoolmaster in Perq, teaching perhaps in or near Woodville where he lived, this being the first school spoken of on the records of Perq Co. He petitioned the Court Jan 1756 for license to keep "an Ordinary at his now Dwelling House, near Little River Bridge." He was also a Quaker minister, and probably held forth in the "Little River meeting house" near by on the River by same name.

Joseph Jordan m Penelope Pendleton, at Symons Creek, 7, 3mo 1747. Marriages unplaced.

Robert Jordan, m Elizabeth Carver, 7, 3mo 1765. (Simons Creek, Pasq Co.)

Miriam Jordan, m John Murdaugh, In 7, 2mo 1726.

Jacob Jordan, m Patience Small, 5, 4mo 1751 (Welles, Perq Co.)

Excursus Brasseur.

Robert Brasseur, French Huguenot, was granted 1200a of land in Nansemond Co, Va, April 12, 1653, at the head of Nansemond River, for transporting, himself, his wife Florence, children Mary, Persid, Kathe, Bennet Brassuer, William Wooten, Tho. Parker, Jno. Sutton, Jno. Stephens, ―― Barefield, Elizabeth Paleman, Nicho. Moroise (Morris), Tho Russell, and Ra, Ellis. This grant was located on Southern branch of Nansemond River.

Margaret Jordan (daughter of Robert *Brashare*) b —, 7mo 1642, "united with the truth in her 16th year, who about 63 years of age was taken with an Indisposition of Body, which continued for three years, came to the end 7, 10mo 1708. She was an Elder in Friends meeting at Chuckatuck, and had taken from her by the high Sheriff of Isle of Wight Co, 120 lbs of Tob, 25, 1 mo 1701, she being a widow 11, 7mo 1700. (Sufferings of Quakers.) Thomas Jordan her husband "Departed this Life, ye 8, 10mo 1699, on ye sixth day of the week." He also suffered persecution at the hands of authorities, being imprisoned six weeks for "being at a meeting at his own house" but was released by order of Kings Proclamation. Of the Jordan family too much can not be said, as they seem to be from beginning to end a family of great worth, true, strong, public spirited, every where holding places of honor, and public offices, they have blazed a way for their good name through all generations, since the first intrepid adventurer Samuel Jordan set foot on American soil, down to the present day.

My own husbands mother being of this splendid family, I feel that I can not say too much about them, she herself being a fine example of all that good womanhood stands for in this life.

LAMB

Joshua Lamb in an affidavit made in Perq, asserted that he was "of Mass Bay, in New England." Sir William Berkeley granted to Joshua Lamb of New England "the whole Island of Roanoke" April 17, 1676. Test' James Bray, Darby Maguire, John Culpepper. In this grant he is called "merchant." Joshua Lamb of Roxbury, Co of Suffolk, in New England, Merchant; sold said Island for £150 unto Nicholas Paige, of Boston, same county, Merchant. Sept 29, 1679. Mary Lamb widow of Joshua, returned to Roxbury, where she signed some papers 1690, and calls herself of said town. As Joshua Lamb made no will, so far as the records of Perq make manifest no direct line can be traced from him, but it seems probable that the next to make his entry into the county, may have been his *son*, or *gr-son*.

Lamb, William, (next to appear) made his will in Perq, probated April 1758, naming wife Miriam, and dau's: Elizabeth, Miriam, & Mary. Ex William Newby (bro-in-law). As he named no sons, we are at sea again, as to descent, but he may have "set off" his sons before this date, to use an old Quaker phrase, in use at that day. William Lamb m Miriam Newby 2, 11mo 1751.

Isaac Lamb, (s of Henry) m Elizabeth Nixon (d of Phineas) 18, 2mo 1756. As these two appear to be contemporaries, they were probably brothers. Henry Lambs name appears on Tithe List of James Sitterson J. P. 1744. On List of Masters, & mistresses, between Cypress Bridge, & Skinners Bridge, are found the names of Henry & Thomas Lamb (no date). As Henry Lamb made no will it is not possible to find descent from him, although he surely had children, as shown by his son Isaac.

Lamb, Joseph, (Thought to be son of Isaac) m Lovey Smith, 1, 11mo 1794. His will p in Perq, Nov 1803, names sons: Nixon, & Stanton, brother John Lamb, bro-in-law Hosea Smith, dau's: Mary Sarah, & Nancy Lamb.

Lamb, Zachariah, m Miriam Griffin, 1, 2mo 1785. He also made his will in Perq, p May 1804. Sons: William, & Chalkey, dau's: Mary, & Betsy, wife Miriam.

Lamb, Phineas, m Dorothy ——— & had issue according to his will, p in Perq Feb 1809. Sons: Thomas, Jacob, Josiah, & Isaac, dau's: Lydia, Rebecca, & Elizabeth Lamb, dau Miriam Griffin.

Lamb, Restore, m Millicent Winslow (d of Jacob, & Elizabeth). His will p in Perq, May 1823, names wife Millicent, sons: Stephen, & Caleb, dau's: Sarah Perry, & Mary Lamb, son Jacob, gr-son Thomas Hunter, dau Elizabeth Hunter, dau Kezia Willson, & Gulielma Lamb, son-in-law Sam'l Willson.

LAWRENCE

The supposition seems very plausible, that the family by this name in Perq, came as so many others had done, from Nansemond Co Va, where John Lawrence, was living very early, according to the records of Isle of Wight Co. These records show that Ann Exum of Isle of Wight, wife of Jeremiah, appears to be a daughter of said John Lawrence. No proofs are to be found, but he probably came south with the immigration from New England, where he married Elizabeth Adkinson, 8, 12mo 1653. (Records of Boston.) The Lawrence family appeared in Perq Co, N. C. simultaneously with the Clare's, and others, about 1680-85. The land of John Lawrence adj that of Timothy Clare, July 30, 1701, and said Timothy married for his last, & third wife, Hannah (widow of Israel Snelling, née Larance) before 1705.

Lawrence, William, m Rachel Welsh, issue: 1 Elizabeth, b Dec 24, 1655—2 Will Larance, b July 20, 1661—3 Rachell, b Apl 16, 1665—4 John, b Mar 14, 1667—5 Hannah, b Dec 1, 1669, m 1st Israel Snelling, July 30, 1687, issue: 1 Rachell, b Aug 17, 1690—2 Ester, b Sept 20, 1699, m John Winslow. (See Hannah Clares will, Grimes.) Hannah Lawrence, m 2d Timothy Clare, & had dau Hannah, who m Benjamin Bundy, before Aug 26, 1726.

Lawrence (2) William (William 1) m Margaret Bogue Jany 7, 1689. He died Aug 13, 1694, when Margaret m 2d Francis Toms Jr, son of Francis Sr.

Lawrence (2) John (William 1) m Hannah Bundy, "at a quarterly meeting at Francis Toms ys" 22, —— 1692, issue: 1 William, b Jan 3, 1693—2 Elizabeth, b Jan 12, 1695/6, m Thomas Meriday. (See Deed book A, No 325.) John Lawrence died, Oct 28, 1700.

William Lawrence, son of John, & Hannah, died Aug 27, 1697.

William Lawrence (2) will p in Albemarle (Perq) Aug 1694, names dau's: Jane and Rachell, wife Margaret; Cousin's: Rachel Snelling (sister) and William Lawrence. Exrs: Israel Snelling, & John Lawrence.

LAYDEN

John Laydon, b 1681, came to Va in Susan, 1607, and m in the fall of 1608 Anne Burrus, who had arrived that year, as maid to Mrs. Forrest. She was fourteen years younger than her husband. (Va Hist Mag, Vol 4—p 93.)

Among those alive after the Indian massacre, Feb 16, 1623, "Att Elizabeth Cittye" were John Laydon, Ann his wife, and children: Virginia, Alice, Katherine, and Margaret Laydon. Their marriage was the first marriage solemnized in Virginia, & their eldest dau is thought to have been the first white child born at Jamestown. John Laydon had 200a grt him in the "Territory of Greate Weyonoke, in the Corporation of Henrico 1626." (Hotten), and another grt of 200a on Warwick River, "being an ancient planter" May 5, 1636, 500a and 250a grt Mar 6, 1636, in same Co, also 500a Feb 29, 1631.

No proof is to be found that John Laydon, & wife Anne were the progenitors of the Laydens of Perq county, yet they may prove to be.

Francis Layden of Perq, m Elizabeth —— issue: 1 William, b Aug 12, 1713—2 Mary, b Feby 1, 1715—3 Francis (2), b Oct 26, 1719.

William Layden dec'd Jan 13, 1758, heirs: Elizabeth Gibson, Ann, & Sarah Layden. (Division.)

Francis Layden dec'd Oct 25, 1759, Thomyzin Layden Admix. There were in the division 5 negroes. Thomas Orphan of Francis, guardian Richard Clayton. (Guardian accounts.)

George Layden dec'd Aug 12, 1762, Mary Admix.

Division of Francis (2) Layden Estate 6, 5mo 1799, heirs: Mary, Margaret, and Sarah Layden.

Francis Layden dec'd July 3, 1761, division of his Est Jan 1763, heirs: Mary, Tamer, Isaac, & Thomas. John Clayton Guardian. (John Roberts had the care of the orphans for one year.) Tulle Williams was apt Gar of Thomas orphan of Francis, Jan 7, 1770. (Loose papers.)

LEIGH

Agnes De Leigh dau of Richard De Leigh, great gr-son of Hamon, Lord of High Leigh, temp Henry II. Agnes Leigh m 3 times, her 3d husband being Sir William Venerables, Knt (2d son of William Baron of Kinderton) and had issue: John who took the name of Leigh before the reign of Edward 1st. He m twice, and had by 2d wife, Ellen (d of Thomas De Corona of Adlington) sons: Robert, who became the progenitor of the Leighs of Adlington; Sir William the ancestor of the Leighs of Eisall; Peter founder of Leighs of Becton, 4th: Gilbert De Leigh, who had son: John of Chester, m Cecelia De Townley, ancestor of Lord Leigh, & Gilbert De Leigh (16 Edward 3d) m Alice, dau of Robert Vernon. His son John, m Clara Fenton (d of Thomas) issue: Gilbert De Leigh, of Middleton 1466, issue: Gilbert De Leigh, who m Margaret, 6th child of Walter, & Elizabeth (Mackingfield) Calverly, of Ewel Castle, Surry, England, issue: Francis Leigh of London, who m Alice Lightfoot, had issue: Sir Francis Leigh, Director of the London company, issue: Lawrence of Virginia, who had Col William Leigh of Virginia, who had William Leigh of West Point, King William Co Va, who had Gilbert Leigh of King William, & Westmoreland Co Va, and Perquimans Co, N. C.

In 1608 Henry Dawkes, & his brother-in-law William Leigh both of London, took a bill of adventure from London Company, & settled at Varina in 1632, which was for a long period the county seat of Henrico Co. A son of William Leigh was "Capt Leigh of London," & York Co Va, who died in York Co, 1684/5. He was at the time of his death Admr of the Estate of Phillip Lightfoot, thought to be either his bro-in-law, or uncle-in-law. Elizabeth Lightfoot (wife of John of London) in a will p in London, Dec 24, 1686, names James Leigh as "Son-in-law." It is thought that George, Edward, Capt Francis, & William, were all sons of William Leigh, the emigrant to Virginia. Francis Leigh was a member of the Col Council in Va, 1680.

John Leigh was transported to Va, by Thos Knight, Lower Norfolk Co, Apl 23, 1647.

James Leigh was living on Riverside, & Tanners Creek, Princess Anne Co Va, prior to 1670. This may be the James named in will of Elizabeth Lightfoot of London, as "son-in-law."

Gilbert Leigh of King William, & Westmoreland Co Va. moved to N. C. where he m in Perquimans Co, Elizabeth Foster. Gilbert Leigh was a contractor, & builder, and it is claimed he erected the present Court house in Edenton. He was living in Chowan Co 1765, where he took the contract for many public buildings, and for his enterprises accumulated quite a fortune. In 1774 he purchased lands in Durants Neck, Perquimans Co, where he resided until his death. His will in Perq Co, Nov 27, 1791, names wife Elizabeth, dau Mary Whedbee, sons: Francis, Richard, Thomas, James, & Benjamin. Test' Benj Bedgood, Nicholas Wressell, Sam'l Knight.

Thomas Leigh, & family were residents of Chowan Co, Apl 1711.

Richard Leigh, (s of Gilbert) m Charlotte Spruell, issue: Richard (2) who m & had L. B. Leigh of Little Rock, Ark.

James Leigh (s of Gilbert, of Durants Neck, m 1st ——— Layden, and 2d Mary Barclift, issue: 1 James, m 1st Mary Granbery, 2d ——— Gray—2 Lavinia, m ——— Riddick—3 Martha, m Richard Blount, & had Richard Blount (?), m Rebecca Whedbee, and Martha, m Seth Whedbee—3 Edward youngest child who m 1st Margaret Jacocks, by whom one daughter Susan Jacocks, m Samuel Harrell of Norfolk Va, issue one daughter Margaret, m 1st —— Feribee, m 2d Sager. By Mr. Ferebee three sons. Edward Leigh had by 2d wife, Grizzell Jacocks (sister of first wife) 1 Edward, m Mary Coke (d of Dr Coke of Edenton) 2 Grizzell (unmarried), 3 John, married living north—4 Martha (Mattie) m C. C. Winslow, four children—Maud, m John Dobson of Huntington West Va, three children.

James Leigh (2) James (1) by wife had one son Richard, who died unmarried. By 2d wife Miss Gray one daughter Mary who m Mr. Charles Robinson of Elizabeth City N. C. and had several children, all living.

Martha (Mattie) and husband C. C. Winslow, had issue, 1 E. Leigh Winslow, M Maureen McManus of New Orleans, issue two sons. Ellen Terry, m Clyde McCallum, no issue. Emmett Julian, m Mary Clark, issue one daughter. Caleb Cook Winslow unmarried.

JACOCKS

Excursus, Jacocks.

No records have been found in the lower counties of Virginia throwing light on the Jacocks family, neither are the records in Perq very generous in details about them. The line has been well written up by Mr Hathaway, in N. C. Hist, & Gen Reg, Vol 1-3, page 330. In my work on same line a few stray items have been unearthed which may be of value to searchers after family data. As has been already shown by said Register, Thomas Jacocks was living in "Little River" 1689, with wife Ann. He is said to have been engaged in "farming & merchandising." He died May 2, 1692.

His son Jonathan, m 1st Elizabeth Collins (widow of William) and made his home in Pasq Co, near Newbegun Creek. He was also a merchant, & planter. They had no issue apparently, she dying 1710-11. His 2d wife was Mary Blount (d of John & Elizabeth Davis, b 1696,) both of them dying 1735. A joint deed was made by them, July 20, 1721, to Matthew Pritchard of Pasq Co, 388a in said county, "formerly belonging to William Collins, and bequeathed by him to his nephew Thomas Woodley, and by him conveyed to sd Jacocks." Jonathan Jacocks moved to Bertie Co, and took up 485a on Batchelors Bay, at the mouth of Chowan River, where he died, leaving sons: Jonathan, Thomas, Charles, Worth, Joseph, & dau Elizabeth. Thomas Jacocks (2) was Master of ship Swallow, from Edenton, to Boston, March 26, 1760, and m Rebecca Scolley of Boston.

Joseph Reed in his will, p July 1774, names his "mother Elizabeth Jacocks" who was before marriage a dau of George Durant (gr-son of George, & Ann Marwood) and sister of Mary Durant who m Christian Reed. Joseph Reed here spoken of was son of Joseph Sr, brother of Christian Reed. Thomas Jacocks 2d m Elizabeth, (widow of the elder Joseph Reed) but his issue is uncertain. (See N. C. Hist & Gen Reg, for further data.)

LILLINGTON

No history of Perquimans would be complete without mention of this prominent family, who took such an active part in the early official activities of the colony, and Perq Precinct in particular. Their marriages are found among the highest, and best families, and they wielded a strong hand in

LEIGH HOME, DURANT'S NECK
Built prior to Revolutionary War. Home of James Leigh

the early government of Albemarle. Where they emigrated from to N. C. the records do not make plain, but from the name, one would naturally think from old England. They disappeared from Perquimans almost as mysteriously as they appeared, and only a few deeds are left to give any clue to where they migrated.

Lillington, Alexander (1) m 1st Sarah James, June 11, 1668, "by Mr Taylor Minister," according to Berkeley Par Reg, and had issue: 1 James, b June 5, 1671, d Apl 15, 1692—2 Alexander, b Aug 3, 1674. He m 2d Elizabeth Cooke, June 13, 167— issue: 3 Ann, b June 1, 1679—4 Sarah, b Jany 20, 1681, d last of February 169 —5 Mary, b April 22, 1683—6 John, b June 14, 1687, m Sarah Porter of Beaufort Co N. C. dau of John—7 Sarah (2d by name) b Aug 16, 1690. (Berkeley Par Reg.)

Elizabeth wife of Alexander Lillington, died Mch 29, 1695.

Alexander Lillington died Sept 11, 1697. He m for his 3d wife Mrs. Ann Steward ,—— 19, 1695, by whom no issue.

Lillington, Alexander (2) Alexander (1) m Sarah —— issue: George, b Aug 10, 1693.

Lillington, Elizabeth, (d of Maj Alex Lillington, & wife Elizabeth) m 1st John Fendall, (s of Josiah, & Mary) Apl 3, 1694, by whom one son Robert Fendall. John Fendall died Dec 20, 1695, "at the house of Capt Walker" who was his bro-in-law, having m Ann Lillington sister of Eilzabeth. Elizabeth Fendall née Lillington, m 2d Samuel Swann of Perq, 1698. (See marriage contract, Deeds in Perq Co.)

Lillington, John, of Bath, made a deed in Perq Co, April 9, 1715, naming his "father Alex Lillington" and sold 640a on a Branch of Yeopim Creek, to line of Thomas Carey. (Deed book B, 101.) This land was taken up by said Alexander Lillington (1) Mar 30, 1694, and descended to his son John.

Maj Alex Lillington was born 1643, died 1697.

John Lillington served as Treasurer of Beaufort Precinct, 1719.

Major Lillington had other grants in Perquimans, as follows: 400a "at Bentleys Creeque, fronting ye Sound, at ye mouth of said Creeque, in Berkeley precinct." 1681. (Land book I, p 103) and 49a on Eastermost side of Indian Creek. Mar 31, 1694. (Land book I, p 4.) (See "Grimes N. C. Wills," and deeds in this book.)

LONG

Richard Longe came to Virginia in "London Merchant" with Alice his wife, age 23 and had Richard (2) b in Va. Among the living "Att Elizabeth Cittye" after the Indian massacre, Feb 16, 1623; Richard Long, wife, & infant. (Hotten) William Longe was living at same time "in Elizabeth Cittye."

James Long first in Perq Co N. C. came from Nansemond Co Va. His will p in Albemarle Oct 7, 1680, Names sons: James (2) Thomas, and Giles, wife, (not named).

(2) Longe, James, (2) James (1) was grt 450a in "ye princinct of Berkley, at ye mouth of Beaver Cove, along Yawpim Creek, thence along Yawpim River." 1681. His will p in Chowan Co, July 29, 1712, Names sons: James, Thomas, (to whom he left his "brick house plantation") John "my plantation at Moratock" dau's: Mary, & Elizabeth, wife Elizabeth. James Long had a former wife Ales (Alice) by whom he had son John, b Sept —— 1673.

(2) Longe, Thomas, (1) James (1) "Departed this Life Apl 4, 1688. (untraced)

(2) Longe, Giles, (1) James (1) died before Feb 12, 1691/2. In his will proven on that date he gave all Estate to "Wife and child" but as they are not named, no data can be ascertained about them.

(3) Longe, Thomas, (2) James (2) James (1), m Rabaky Waite (White), Mar 7, 1688/9, issue: 1 Sarah, b Jan 28, 1692—2 William, b Aug 13, 1695—3 Joshua, b Oct 30, 1698. Thomas Long made his will in Perq Co, p Oct 10, 1721. Son: William "land on mill swamp," Joshua, "land on Major Harves Quarter," Thomas "plantation whereon I now live" 470a, dau Sarah Leary (dau-in-law), wife Rebeckah.

(3) Longe, William, (1) James (2) James (1) "son of James, & Ales" m Sarah Johnson, Jan 6, 1697/8 (relict of John Johnson, née Gunfallis d. s. p. will July 1712, wife Sarah, brothers John, & Thomas Long, Nephews: James, & William Long. Sarah Long (wife of William) made her will, proven Perq Precinct, July 8, 1718, naming bro-in-law Thomas Long, sister Mary Perce, bro-in-law Thomas Perce, Cornelius Leary (s of Richard) John Wiatt (cousin) Jonathan, & William Taylor, Joshuway Long, to whom she bequeathed "plantation at creeks mouth" William Long to whom "plantation whereon I now dwell."

(3) Longe, John, (1) James (2) James (1), m Elizabeth Charles, Aug 11, 1687. As he made no will, his line is untraced.

Longe (3) James (2) James (1) made his will in Chowan Co, p April 1734. Sons: James (4) Giles (2) Joshua, John, Andrew, dau Elizabeth. His wife is not named (untraced).

(4) Longe, Joshua, (1) Thomas (2) James (2) James (1), m Elizabeth ——— issue: according to his will, p in Perq Co, July 1741, Sons: Thomas, Joshua (2). He appointed his brother Thomas Long Ex. Joshua Long (2) moved to Tyrrell Co, where his will was p June 1754.

(4) Longe, Thomas, (3) Thomas (2) James (2) Will April 1754. Sons: Joshua, Thomas, wife Sarah. She m 2d Richard Leary.

(4) Longe, William, (2) Thomas (2) James (2) James (1) m 1st Mary ——— issue: 1 Sarah, b Nov — 1720—2 Thomas, b Nov 5, 1723—3 William, b Aug 20, 1725—4 Joshua, (s of William, & Ann), b Nov 30, 1733—5 Thomas (second by name) b Sept 23, 1736—6 Elizabeth, b Dec 13, 1742—7 James, b Mch 3, 1745—8 Thomas (third by name) b Feby 22, 1748/9—9 Reuben, b Apl 17, 1752. William (2) Long died before April 1759. Will p on that date. Sons: Simeon, "manor plantation" Thomas "part of manor Plantation" Reuben "land on Franks Creek" sons William, & James "100a on West side of Minses Creek. gr-sons: Lemuel, & Ichabod Long, & Joshua Wyatt, gr-dau Mary Wyatt, wife Ann Extrix. (Ann Long m 2d Thomas McNider.)

The loose papers in Perq give some further data about the Long family, & leave no doubt that Ann Long (widow of William) m 2d Thomas McNider. It seems also very clear that "daughter Sarah Leary" spoken of in Thomas Longs Will 1721, was a dau-in-law, and not a blood relation, as the Minute book in Perq, gives the fact; "Sarah Lerry, her former husband Thomas Long," Apl 1757. Joshua, & Thomas, Orphans of Thomas dec'd, Jan 1756. Sarah was widow of Richard Leary, July 1757, who "died very much in debt," (Auditors Act Oct 1757). Richard Leary, & Mrs. Sarah Long were m Nov 15, 1756. Thomas Long (a minor) dec'd Sept 10, 1761. His inventory shows a Bible & one Prayer book. William Long Jr dec'd (no date), Wm Wyatt, & Miles Harvey Exors.

James Long Division, Feb 5, 1762; part to William Long, Reubin Long, Simeon Long, representatives of Sarah Wyatt dec'd, William McNider, in right of his mother.

MAUDLIN

Ezekiel Maudlin, first in Perquimans, came from London, according to family tradition. This name does not appear on any of the records of the Lower counties in Virginia, neither do the Quaker records show a person of this name. So the opinion is advanced, that he came straight from England to Perq, or landed first in New England, where he m Hannah Nicholson (d of Christopher, & Hannah ———, b Mch 4, 1667). It is positively known that Christopher Nicholson came to Perq from New Eng, where he had already m Hannah Rednap. The names & ages of his children are recorded in Berkeley Par Reg, but his marriage is not mentioned.

Ezekiel Maudlin, & wife Hannah, issue: 1 Edward, b Feby 11, 1695—2 Ezekiel, b April 2, 1698—3 Mary, b Mar 2, 170-1—4 Elizabeth, b Nov 20, 1703—5 Sarah, b April 28, 1706. Ezekiel Maudlin died Mch 16, 1705-6. (According to the Roman Calendar.)

Hannah (née Nicholson) m 2d Charles. Her will p in Perq Co, July 1752, names son: Edward Moudlin, dau's Elizabeth White, Sarah Perry, & Ann Cox (son-in-law Robert Cox), gr-sons: John Moulin, & John Cox, gr-dau Mary Moulin (d of John).

Ezekiel Maudlin grt for land in Perq, June 20, 1703, which he conveyed to Timothy Clare, April 26, 1705. (Deed book F, No 60.) He evidently died intestate, as no will appears in Perq, made by him.

Hannah Maudlin (above) was 2d wife of Samuel Charles Sr, he had for 1st wife Elizabeth, by whom he had issue, d Elizabeth. (See Charles record in this book.)

Ezekiel (2) Maudlin, m Hannah Toms (d of Joshua, & Sarah née Gosbey, b June 6, 1706), issue: 1 Jeremiah, b Aug 21, 1725—2 Joshua, b Apl 19, 1727—3 Edward, b Apl 7, 1735. Hannah wife of (2) Ezekiel m 2d Edmund Chancey. (2) Ezekiel Maudlin, in his will p in Perq April 17, 1732, names sons: Jeremiah, Joshua, & James, wife Hannah. His son Edward is not named for some reason, & as Edward b April 7, 1735, was born 2 years after the death of sd Ezekiel, we do not see how he *could* have been one of his sons. He is certainly given in Berkeley Par Reg, however, as "son of Ezekiel, & Hannah." (Probably the 2d Ezekiel & Hannah Toms.)

Sarah Maudlin was a legatee in the will of Samuel Charles, Mar 12, 1727-8. (3) Ezekiel Maudlin, is thought to have m 1st Hannah ——— & had Edward, b April 7, 1735; he m 2d Mary ——— issue: 1 Elizabeth, b July 13, 1738—2 Sarah, b March 20, 1741. Ezekiel Maudlin was "Overseer of the Roads" in the district of John Perisho Apl 1740. The division of Ezekiel (2) Maudlin Est, 1737, shows Hannah as his wife, sons: Jeremiah, Joshua, & Thomas.

Among Tithables; May 25, 1743, Edward Modling, Edward Jr, Wm Modling, & Ezekiel Maudlin. Tithables 1768; Mary Modlin, & son Ezekiel, Edmund Modlin, Jacob Elliott & Joseph Draper.

Hannah Chancey, & Thomas Weeks, made petition to the Court, Jan 1736, for a division of the Est of Ezekiel Maudlin Dec'd.

Mary Maudlin widow of Ezekiel, July 1746, John Maudlin petition to sell perishable Est of sd dec'd. Jan 1754.

Edward Maudlin, in a deed Oct 15, 1739, called Thomas Nicholson "cousin." He bought of James Henby Jan 24, 1735, 150a of land, "near the head of Vosses Creek."

(1) Edward Maudlin (Ezekiel (1) m Mary ——— issue: 1 John, b May 26, 1718—2 William, b Feb 27, 1721-2. He was dead Jan 19, 1754, when John Maudlin petitioned the Court for liberty, to sell pt of his Est, which was done Feb 7, 1754.

(1) Thomas Maudlin, will Perq, Nov 16, 1758, names wife, Sarah, son Jeremiah, brother Edmund Chancey, father-in-law John Clayton, bro-in-law Richard Clayton.

(4) Ezekiel Maudlin, m Ann Stafford, Sept 2, 1743, Sec Thos Stafford. (Mar bonds Perq Co.)

(1) John Maudlin m Hannah (dau-in-law of John Stokes, will 1772, Perq Co) issue: (twins) Joseph, & Mary, b Jan 26, 1742/3—2 John (2) b Mch 1, 1745.

John Maudlin moved from Pasq, to Perq Co, 17, 3mo 1787, with children: Hannah, Elizabeth, Jesse, Joseph, Charles, William, Pleasant, & Mary. (Pasq Mo Meeting.)

John Modlin moved from Perq, to Back Creek, Randolph Co, date not known.

Joshua Maudlin Planter, Court 1755.

Edward Maudlin m Sarah Ashley, widow, before July 1745, when an Order of Court was rendered them, to sell Est, & divide with the Orphans.

(1) William Maudlin, will Perq, p Oct 1774, wife Martha, Sons: Miles, Thomas, Jacob & Micajah, dau's Elizabeth, Martha, brother John. Ex.

(1) Gideon Maudlin, m Mary Mullen (d of Abraham) & had issue, see his will Perq p Jan 1777.

McMULLEN

John McMullen born in Dublin, Ireland, 1740, came to Virginia in 1760, where he lived until the fall of 1797, when he migrated with part of his family to Elbert Co Georgia. He had a large family, ten sons and five daughters, all of whom married and became prosperous, living to ripe old age, and themselves rearing large families, who scattered to almost every state in the union. In 1900 when a granite monument was raised to his memory in the family burying ground, on the brow of a hill near the residence of Blackston L. Richardson, in the historic "Valley of Virginia" there were living at that time five thousand persons who owed their strong Scotch-Irish blood to him, through many generations.

"He was a man of noble traits of character, which gave a rich inheritance to those who descended from him. He was a man of strong features, positive convictions, keen intellectual insight, lofty moral ideals, and tireless energy," all of which traits characterized the family. He was a distinguished Virginia Soldier in the Rev War, and it seemed only an act of loyalty, and justice for Judge F. M. McMullen and other of his numerous descendants to thus honor him.

As John McMullen never trod the soil of Perquimans, and the writer has no way of making a detailed line of the ramifications of his family, and the records in Perquimans yielding nothing regarding him or his descendants, we can only write of those who later moved to Perquimans, and have made their home here ever since. John McMullen emigrated to Va at the age of 20 years, and was a tailor by trade. There is a tradition in the family that he made for no less a person than George Washington, his first Military suit. This was a great honor, especially if done well, which bears no shadow of doubt *it was*, knowing the stern rectitude of the maker.

James McMullen (s of John, and Edith Kendall) had son Jeremiah, who m Frances Dabney Shelton, Dec 22, 1830, Greenesville Co Va. He was born in said county Nov 2, 1815, and died at Boydton Va Aug 19, 1873, and was buried there. Frances Dabney Shelton, born in Greenesville Co Va, Nov 8, 1818, died in Hertford N. C. Oct 23, 1880, buried in the cemetery in Hertford. They had issue:

2 Virginia Anne, b Nov 17, 1837, d Oct 2, 1899—2 William Thomas, b May 11, 1841, d July 6, 1918, in Hertford, one of our best beloved citizens, and a man of high integrity, and worth, m 1st Sallie Wood (d of Mr. John S. Wood, & Wife ——— Wood) issue, Dr. Shelton McMullen of Hertford, & Elizabeth City, who m Lydia Palin and had issue: six children; 2 Percy McMullen who m Flora Brockett of Elizabeth City, issue: four children. Mr. Tom McMullen m 2d Mary Wood, and had issue eight children: 1 Sallie, unmarried—2 Roulac, m Miss Mary ——— 3 Frances, m Whit Wright, (Sheriff of Perquimans.) 4 Tom Mac, unmarried, drowned last spring) 5 Mattie, m Julian Jessop of Winfall N. C., issue two children—6 Ruth, m Thomas B. Sumner, of Hertford, no issue—7 Edwin, youngest (unmarried). 2 Percy McMullen, a lawyer of note.

(3) Lucullus Walker (1) Jeremiah (1) James (1) John (1) b June 20, 1843, d Oct 8, 1899, m 1st Mollie Reed, issue four children, m 2d Lina Terris, by whom no issue to live.

(4) Martha Susan, b July 11, 1847, d Feb 26, 1928, m George Durant Newby (a descendant of George Durant pioneer to Perquimans) issue five children. 1 Mary m Mr. C. W. Toms of Durham, & New York, President of the Liggett Myers Tobacco Co. 2 Dr. E. G. Newby of Hertford, one of our best physicians— 3 Evart, m Marion Whedbee of Hertford, Auto dealer, issue five children. 4 Bruce of Los Angeles Cal, m Sophia Capehart of Bertie Co, issue four children. 5 Fanny, m 1st ——— Williams, and had one son Alfred, m 2d Simon Rutenburg, of Hertford.

(5) Frances Katherine, b Mar 15, 1845 (no record) 6 John Henry, b July 7, 1849, d Dec 10, 18— —7 Oscar Gregory, b Dec 4, 1856, d Feb 12, 1918, m Mollie Whedbee (d of Monroe Whedbee of Hertford) issue two children.

(8) John (Jack) Doctor of Hertford, & Edenton, much beloved by every one, white and black, m Lina Tucker, and had 7 children, one of whom is a lawyer of renown in Washington N. C.

(9) Jerry twice married, one child by second wife Elizabeth Anderson of Annapolis, Md.

(10) Minnie Lee McMullen, m Kenneth Rayner Newbold of Perquimans, residence Hertford. She was born in Princess Anne Co Va, where her father had charge of the Methodist Church at that time, he being what was called in old times a "Circuit Rider" and member of the Va Conference. The Churches in Eastern N. C. remained in the said Conference until about 1889-90. This brought to Perquimans Jeremiah McMullen before the War Between the States, and here his daughters, and sons found wives, and husbands, after which they continued to reside in N. C. for many years, until

the children grew up and scattered to other far places, where they have prospered, and reafed families of their own.

Kenneth Rayner Newbold, and Minnie Lee McMullen had issue: twelve children, all of whom grew to maturity. They are all married but one, the youngest, Minnie Mac, who is the mainstay of her parents in their old age. These children have scattered to the four winds, but usually assemble once a year for a family reunion, when great times are seen by the Newbold family. Last year Mr and Mrs Newbold celebrated their "golden wedding" with much ceremony. All the children were here to attend, and the wedding feast was something to marvel at. Mrs. Newbold still retains her full activity, and mental faculties, and her husband bids fair to see many summers again we hope. They have been very fortunate with their children, only losing one, a daughter Edith, wife of Mr. E. B. Skinner, who died about ten years ago, leaving three little girls. Truly it can be said that their children "rise up and call them blessed."

Mr. Thomas McMullen, brother of Mrs. Newbold, was a man of fine traits, true to his friends, honest in business, a splendid father, and devoted husband. He was Mayor of Hertford for some years, later employed in the mercantile business, always respected and highly esteemed, he enjoyed the affection of a large circle of friends. His passing was much regretted, and his memory is a by word in Hertford to this day.

MAYO

Edward Mayo Sr was a resident of Perq Precinct 1684. He is found proving right for himself, son Edward Jr, and dau's Sarah, Ann, & Elizabeth Mayo, John Nixon, Em Nixon, and Anne Nixon (their daughter) and three negroes. (Col Rec Vol I.) On Nov 6, of same year he officiated as Att' in Perq, and May 1693 was appointed "Clarke of this Court." The records in Perq, neither Quaker, or secular, throw any light on his former dwelling place. He held office as Clerk, in Perq for several years.

Mayo, Edward (2) m Mary Clare d of Timothy, & Mary (Bundy) b Feb 21, 1686 (twin sister of Elizabeth, who m Thomas (1) Winslow) issue: 1 Edward (3) b 7, 2mo 1703—2 John, b 27, 11mo 1705/6—3 Mary, b 26, 12mo 1709/10—4 Ann, b 23, 1mo 1713—5 Joseph, b ———6 Elizabeth, b 21, 8mo 1717—7 Sarah, b 19, 12mo 1719.

Mayo (2) Edward, will Pasq Co, p Oct 20, 1724, names son Edward (3) to whom he bequeathed "my plantation," son Joseph, dau's Mary, Ann, Elizabeth, & Sarah. Wife Mary, & brother Thomas Jessop Exrs. (Said Thomas Jessop was his *brother-in-law*, having m Jane Cleare, sister of said Mary.) (See Timothy Clares Will.) Mary Mayo, m 2d Joseph Newby (s of Gabriel) about 8, 5mo 1726. (See Deeds.)

Mayo, Edward (3) Edward (2) Edward (1) m Mary Jessop (d of Joseph) issue: 1 Mary, b 21, 1mo 1727/8—2 Edward (4), b 19, 12mo 1730. Will of Edward (3) also p in Pasquotank Co, Feb 14, 1734, names dau Mary; Wife Mary, & Joseph Jessop Exrs. (wife's father) Joseph Jessop in his will, p in Perq, Aug 29, 1735, names gr-dau Mary Mayo. As Edward Mayo (s of Edward & Mary Jessop) is not named in either his fathers will, or his gr-father Jessops, we may suppose he had passed away.

Mayo, Mary Newby (dau of Timothy Clare, once wife of Edward Mayo) died 27, 10mo 1739. (Quaker records.)

Her will Perq Co, p Jan 1739, Son Joseph Mayo, dau Elizabeth Wilson, son-in-law John Wilson, gr-children: John Wilson, Edward, Jemima, & Isabel Newby niece Elizabeth Winslow (dau of Thomas, & Elizabeth).

Mayo, Joseph, m Elizabeth Newby, (d of his step-father Joseph Newby) before 1766, and shortly after this date, they disappear from Perquimans Co. They probably moved with the Quaker emigration, west.

MOORE

William Moore was transported to Va, in "Primrose" by Rev George White "minister of the word of God" July 27, 1635, age 16, and said White obtained a grant 200a "upon Nancimund River, for transpotations." William Moore, age 32, came to Norfolk Co Va Feb 15, 1648. (Norfolk Co records) Henry Moore, late of Bristol in England, Merc't; now resident of Vir, Feb 6, 1663. Mary Moore (widow of Henry) of the City of Bristol, appointed Richard Penny of James River, to act as her Att'. Nov 25, 1667. John Moore, of Scotland, now in Western Branch, Nansemond Co Vir, m Jane Edwards (d of Peter, of Isle of Wight Co Va, whose will, p Oct 8, 1681, names her). He was trans' to Upper Norfolk Co Mar 6, 1638, by John Ashcomb.

Moore (1) William, recorded his mark in Perq Pre'ct, Sept 1690. With his mother Jean Byer, he proved rights, in Perq, April 1696. Jane Loadman came to N. C. with James Loadman. They came from Surry Co Va, and her mother in said Co, names her later as Jean Newby. Richard Bier, m Jane Loedman, Jan ——— 1682/3. It seems from this record, that she was m 1st to———Moore—2d to Loadman—3d to Richard Bier, & 4th to William Newby, by whom she had no issue. William Newby m 2d Ann———. (Thought to be Ann Mayo.) William Moore was granted 90a of land in Perq, Feby 4, 1713/14, on Perq River, adj Richard Fox, and 100a on N. E. side of Perq River, adj Timothy Clear, Nov 11, 1719 (This last grant was to William 2d it is thought, as the elder William was dec'd, 1717) Margaret Moore, was granted Admix on Est, of her dec'd husband William Moore, April 16, 1717. (Minute book Perq Co) William Moore (1) was Constable in Perq Pre'ct 1700. Margaret was his 2d wife. Berkeley Par Reg gives the children of William Moore, by his 1st wife Elizabeth, as follows: 1 William, b Nov 10, 1699—2 John, b Oct 21, 1702—3 Joshua, b Aug 5, 1705—4 Samuel, b Dec 23, 1707—5 Hezekiah, b Nov 24, 1718. His will, Perq p Oct 31, 1732. Sons: William, John, Joshua, Samuel, & Truman, (to each a plantation) dau's: Elizabeth, & Jane, wife Elizabeth, cousin Robert Bogue.

(3) Moore, William, (2) William (1) m Martha Odome of Henrico Co Va. d. s. p. will Perq p April 1752. Leg: Truman Moore, & William Wilson, wife Martha.

(3) Moore, John, m Ann Denman (d of Charles, Clerk of Perq Co, & wife Sarah) issue: 1 Charles, b Sept 30, 1732—2 Priscilla, b Feby 6, 1734/5. His will Perq, p May 18, 1746. Son: Charles (his plantation) dau Mary, wife Rachel (2d wife). Charles Moore (s of John, & Ann) m Sarah———issue: 1 Ann, b Oct 22, 1756—2 Isaac, b Nov 3, 1757.

Moore (3) Joshua, d. s. p. will Perq, p Feb 24, 1734. Brothers: Samuel, John, Truman, nephew, Cornelius Moore (s of John) niece Elizabeth Nixon, wife Elizabeth.

(1) Moore, Samuel, m Mary, widow of Nathan Newby, née Toms (d of Francis Toms Jr) about 1735/6. His will Perq, p Jan 1752, Wife Mary, nieces: Mary, Hanna, and Martha Moore (dau's of brother John) Leg: Elizabeth Elliot, Francis, & Nathan Newby (s of Nathan, & Mary) He had by Mary, dau Mary, b July 11, 1739.

Moore (3) Truman, Will Perq, p April 1753. Sons: William, Samuel, Thomas, & Jesse, dau's: Jane, & Mary, wife Leah.

(1) Moore, Samuel (2) Samuel (1), m Sarah. His will Perq, p Jan 1756. Sons: Joshua, Aaron, Jonathan, John, dau's: Mary, & Sarah, wife Sarah.

(3) Moore, John (2) Samuel (2) Samuel (1) William (1) m Mary Ratlif (d of Richard, & Damaris Nixon, d of Zachariah Nixon, & Elizabeth Symons). His will Perq, p Oct 21, 1755. Sons: Cornelius, Joseph, (land in Balahack) Gideon, (maner plan'), Dau's: Miriam, Sarah, & Betty Moore, wife Mary. Joseph Ratliff Ex (bro-in-law).

Moore (1) Robert, came to N. C. from the Isle of Man, with Rev Richard Marsden. He m Hannah Manwaring (d of Stephen), issue: 1 James, b Oct 23, 1717—2 Martha b Mch 26, 1726/7—Robert, b Mch 29, 1729.

Hannah Moore Orphan of John dec'd made petition to the Court in Perq, before April 19, 1762, for "her Estate, left her by her gr-father Robert Moore Dec'd, & her uncle Samuel Moore Dec'd, now in the hands of Keziah Newby, Extrix of Nathan Newby Dec'd."

Mary Moore of Johnston Co N. C. discharged Charles Moore of Perq, of his guardianship, Oct 7, 1763.

Joshua Moore of N. C. m Hannah Hargrave, 20, 3mo 1760. (Pagan Creek Isle of Wight Co Va.)

MORGAN

James Morgan emigrant to N. C. came from "Mary Land" where he had married, Jane Knea, Oct 12, 1673. (Berkeley Parish Reg) According to same, they had issue: 1 James, b Feb 2, 1675/6—2 John, b Mar 26, 1678—3 William, b Aug 27, 1679. James (1) Morgan was grt 300a in Perq Precinct, May 22, 1694, "on a Branch of Vosses Creek" adj William Vosse, & Mr Francis Toms. His son John made a deed of gift to his dau Mary Elliott, wife of Thomas Jr, Jan 12, 1724/5, 50a on said Branch. He called this land "Broad Neck," and later it was spoken of as "on Morgans Swamp" and it seems evident that it was situated on the south side of Vosses Creek, where sd Toms land was located, and the Swamp here mentioned, is probably the one just above what is now called Brights Mill, between Winfall, & Brights Creek. (Vosses) James Morgan, (2) James (1), m Jane Martin (d of John of Pasq Co) issue: James (3) b Jany 17, 1707/8. He died intestate, and we have to rely on the will of his wife Jane, for further information. Her will proven in Perq Co, Mar 22, 1742, Sons: John Anderson (son-in-law) & James Morgan, dau Sarah Parsons (wife of Samuel) dau-in-law Ann Morgan (wife of James) gr-daus: Mary, & Miriam Morgan, Elizabeth Cosan, & Jane Anderson.

James Morgan Esq J. P. 27, 8ber 1739. He was Commissioned Sheriff of Perq, by Gov Gabriel Johnston Esq, Apl 1741. Zachary Chancey Dept Sheriff.

Morgan, James, (4) Will'm (1) James (1) m Hannah Overman, who was his Extrix Oct 1741, issue: Rebecca, b May 28, 1739.

(2) Morgan, William, (1) James (1) m Sarah Fletcher (d of Ralph, & Elizabeth) Mch 13, 1699-1700, issue: 1 Sarah, b Jan 8, 1700/1—2 William, b Sept 14, 1703.

Morgan, James, (3) James (2) James (1), wife Ann (née Overman) issue: 1 Elizabeth b Sept 30, 1739—2 Seth, b Sept 16, 1740.

(2) Morgan, John, (1) James (1) m Mary Jones (d of Mary Jones, "ye Relict of Robert Beasley") Sept 2, 1699, issue: 1 Sarah, b Oct 20, 1700—2 John, b Oct 13, 1705—John Morgan will p in Perq Co, Jan 1755. Sons: John (2) & Joseph, dau's: Rachel Overman, Elizabeth Elliott, Mary Elliott, & Hannah Boswell, to them "my manner Plantation," gr-son Joseph Boswell. (No wife is named.)

Joseph Morgan (s of John ? & Mary) was b July 14, 1741.

Morgan (3) James, will Perq Co, names himself "son of William" proven Oct 1741. Sons: Jacob, & Charles, "land on Morgans Swamp" dau's: Elizabeth, & Rebeckah, wife Hannah, & Thomas Overman (bro-in-law) Exrs.

(3) Morgan, William (2) William (1) James (1) m Frances Hendricks (d of Solomon), who made petition July 1747, for "filial Portion" of his Est, out of the hands of Jeremiah Hendricks, her Guar. (Loose papers.)

Morgan (4) James, m Hannah Griffith, 16, 3mo 1768, issue: 1 Millicent, b 1, 1mo 1679—2 James, b 7, 3mo 1771, d 17, 8mo 1774—3 Sarah, b 31, 7mo 1773—4 Charles, b 28, 4mo 1777. Sarah Morgan died 27, 11mo 1780. Hannah Morgan died 27, 11mo 1780.

Morgan, James, m 2d Millicent Symons, 2, 4mo 1783, issue: 5 James, b 22, 12mo 1783—6 Penninah, b 6, 4mo 1785—7 Lydia, b 1, 11mo 1786—8 Margaret, b 18, 11mo 1788—9 Mary, b 14, 7mo 1791—10 Nathan, b 21, 5mo 1793.

(4) Morgan, Charles, (s of James) m Susannah Nixon (d of Barnabe) 1, 5mo 1771, issue: 1 Benjamin, b 1, 7mo 1772—2 Ann, b 18, 2mo 1775—d 18, 10mo 1775—3 Sarah, b 2, 9mo 1776, d 15, 2mo 1777—4 Micajah, b 2, 2mo 1778, d 5, 11mo 1778—5 Penninah, b 26, 12mo 1779—6 Susannah, b 24, 3mo 1782. Susannah wife of Charles Morgan, died 24, 5mo 1783. Charles Morgan (s of James) m 2d Lyda Bundy (d of Josiah) 25, 1mo 1786. (See her will Perq Co, p May 1802; N. C. Hist & Gen Reg Vol 3-3.)

Morgan, Seth, m,Sarah Lindrier, May 18, 1785.

MORRIS

Among passengers in Speedwell of London bound for America May 28, 1635 Richard Morris, age 19 years. Another by same name came to Va from London, the same year age 17. Edward Morris was transported to Va by John Ellis, Apl 1648. (Hotten.)

Mr Richard Morris "Minister of Bristol pish" Henrico Co Va, became later a resident of Isle of Wight Co, and had dau Anne, who was his heir 1678, her uncle Samuel Morris acting as Ex of his Estate. (Isle of Wight records.)

John Morris was living in Lower Norfolk Co Va, 1740. Charles *Moris* whose name is the first to appear on the records of Perq Co N. C. attended a Mo Meeting at Arnold White's house 24, 4mo 1679. He was probably father of John who appears in Perquimans county about 1704, with wife Hannah, they were living in Perq 1716. Little River Quaker Reg, gives most valuable information about this family, and they are always the best of authority.

Morris, John Sr was b 3, 3mo 1680, m Mary Symons (d of Thomas' & Rebecah), b 1687, d 14, 8mo 1745 age 58 years, issue: 1 Aaron, b 14, 7mo 1704—2 Elizabeth, b 6, 9mo 1707—3 Joseph, b 4, 12mo 1709—4 Sarah, b 6, 9mo 1712, m Samuel Moore and was his widow, Jan 21, 1755—5 John, b 21, 12mo 1716—6 Mary, b 24, 11mo 1719. The will of John Morris Sr was p in Pasquotank Co N. C. Jan 1739 Sons: Joseph, and John to whom he bequeathed "my Manner plantation" sons: Zachariah, Isaac, Aaron, dau's: Sarah, and Hannah. Zachariah (s of John) was b 23, 9mo 1722—Hannah (d of John, & Mary) b 23, 12mo 1726. Elizabeth Morris (d of John, & Mary) m William Symons, at Newbegun Creek Pasquotank Co, 5, 7mo 1725. Mary Morris (d of John) m John Robinson, at Symons Creek, 3, 1mo 1738. Elizabeth Morris (d of John) m Wm Symons, 5, 7mo 1725.

Morris, Aaron (1) John (1) m Mary Pritchard—6mo 1724, at Symons Creek, issue: 1 Joshua, b 6, 4mo 1726—2 Benjamin, b 20, 8mo 1728—3 Joseph, b 1, 2mo 1731—4 Miriam, b 4, 3mo 1733—5 Susannah, b 4, 7mo 1735—6 John, b 11, 12mo 1737—7 Mary, b 8, 1mo 1739—8 Sarah, b 5, 1mo 1743, d 26, 7mo 1743—9 Aaron, b 5, 9mo 1744—10 Elizabeth, b 22, 4mo 1747, m Thomas Gilbert, 20, 5mo 1765. Aaron Morris, an Elder in the Quaker Church, died 10, 9mo 1770, age 66. Mary Morris (wife of Aaron) died 12, 10mo 1791.

Morris, Joseph (1) John (1) m Elizabeth Pritchard, at Symons Creek, 2, 10mo 1730. (no record of their children, if any).

Mary Morris (wife of John Sr, dau of Thomas, & Rebecah Symons) died 14, 8mo 1745, age 58.

Morris, John (2) John (1) untraced.

Morris, Joshua (1) Aaron (1) John (1) m Hannah Anderson (d of John) 1, 11mo 1748, issue: 1 Mordicai, b 14, 3mo 1749—2 Clarke, b 29, —1750.

Hannah Morris, died 3, 5mo 1751. Joshua m 2d Huldah Newby, 9, 6mo 1752, issue: 3 Benjamin, b 26, 5mo 1754. Joshua Morris m 3d Mary Winslow, 1, 5mo 1755, issue: 4 Nathan, b 11, 1mo 1757—5 Jonathan, b 7, 7mo 1759—6 Zachariah, b 17, 9mo 1761. Joshua Morris took for his 4th and last wife, Rebeckah Symons, 27, 4mo 1774, issue: 7 John, b 1, 11mo 1774—8 Mary, b 25, 1mo 1776. Mary wife of Joshua, d 13, 3mo 1773.

Morris, Benjamin (1) Aaron (1) John (1) m Mary Bundy (d of Samuel) 6, 10mo 1750, had no issue apparently. He m 2d Elizabeth Overman, 9, 10mo 1763, issue: 1 Joseph, b 25, 8mo 1764—2 Elizabeth, b 27, 12mo 1765—3 Benjamin, b 29, 1mo 1768—4 Rachel, b 2, 4mo 1770, d 16, 8mo 1770. Benjamin Morris m 3d Millicent Draper, 15, 11mo 1772, issue: 5 Peter, b 5, 9mo 1774—6 Ezra, b 3, 5mo 1776—7 Jacob, b 4, 6mo 1778—8 Demcey, b 16, 5mo 1781—9 Eli, b 19, 11mo 1786.

Mary Morris, wife of Benamin, d 18, 5mo 1753, age 22. (d of Samuel Bundy) (Elizabeth wife of Benjamin) d 12, 4mo 1770.) Elizabeth (dau of Benjamin & Elizabeth) d 23, 6mo 1785.)

Morris, Joseph (2) Aaron (1) John (1) m Mary Newby 1, 6mo 1755, issue: 1 Miriam, b 28, 3mo 1756—2 Benjamin, b 5, 10mo 1757—3 John, b 28, 7mo 1759—4 Mary, b 29, 3mo 1761—5 Joseph, b 21, 2mo 1763. Joseph Morris, m 2d Hannah Overman 4, 10mo 1764, issue: 6 Elizabeth, b 19, 7mo 1765—7 Thomas, b 15, 11mo 1766—8 Joshua, (of Joseph, & Elizabeth) b 24, 5mo 1769—9 Sarah, b 6, 9mo 1770—10 Susannah, b 27, 2mo 1772—11 William, b 7, 11mo 1773, d 27, 8mo 1775—12 Chalkey, b 1, 8mo 1775—13 William (2) b 15, 9mo 1777—14 Nathan, b 11, 7mo 1779—15 Ann, b 18, 7mo 1782—16 Penelope, b 3, 1mo 1785—17 Millicent, b 16, 8mo 1787. Joseph Morris (s of Aaron, & Mary, née Pritchard) died 24, 11mo 1798.

Hannah wife of Joseph, nee Overman, died 27, 11mo 1766.

Morris, John (2) Aaron (1) John (1) m Mary Albertson, 20, 1mo 1762, issue: John, & Mary, (twins) b 3, 12mo 1762, died 22, 12mo 1762.

Morris, John (unplaced) m Mary Nicholson, 1, 1mo 1762. (Dau of Thos Nicholson, d 23, 1mo 1772.)

Morris, Aaron (2) Aaron (1) John (1) m Margaret Nicholson (d of Thomas) 30, 11mo 1768, issue: 1 Thomas, b 11, 9mo 1769—2 Christopher, b 18, 10mo 1771—3 Mary, b 31, 3mo 1774—4 Mark, & Ruth (twins) b 9, 1mo 1775—5 Isaac, b 20, 4mo 1780. Margaret wife of Aaron died 17, 12mo 1780. Aaron Morris m 2d Lydia Davis, 27, 2mo 1782, issue: 6 Aaron, b 18, 11mo 1782—7 Pritchard, b 15, 9mo 1784—8 Jehoshaphat, b 17, 8mo 1786—9 Margaret, b 24, 6mo 1788—10 Susan b 24, 6mo 1790—11 John, b 24, 6mo 1794.

Benjamin Morris (s of Aaron, & Mary) died 3, 1mo 1762.

Mary (widow of Benjamin) died 4, 2mo 1762.

Mary (wife of Joshua) died 13, 3mo 1773.

Morris, Joseph (3) m Sarah Sanders, 3, 3mo 1790.

Morris, Jonathan, m Penelope Symons, 21, 12mo 1785 (Pasquotank Co).

Morris, Aaron (3) m Miriam Robinson (d of William) before 1785. (Named in his will.)

Morris, William m Esther Gardner, no date. (Loose papers.)

The will of John Morris, p in Perq Co, Oct 1774, names brother Cornelius, and wife Sarah, two sons (not named).

Joshua Morris will Perq, p April 1777, Wife Rebecca, sons: John, Benjamin, Jonathan, Zachariah, Mordicai, & Nathan, dau's Clarkey Pool, and Mary Morris, father Aaron Morris.

Jonathan Morris will, p in Perq Feb 1796. Sons: Jehoshaphat, and Jonathan nephew John Pool, brother Nathan, & Josiah Bundy Exrs.

Morris, Mordicai (s of Joshua) m Abigail Overman (d of Nathan) 28, 4mo 1773.

Morris, Zachariah, m Ann Williams, 2, 9mo 1752. Ann Morris died same year.

Morris, Demcy (s of Benjamin Morris dec'd) of Pasquotank Co, m Jemima Bogue, (d of Job dec'd) 22, 12mo 1802, at Suttons Creek.

Morris, Mordicai (s of Mordicai) of Pasquotank Co, m Martha Winslow (d of John of Perq) 17, 12mo 1806, at Welses Meeting house in Perq.

Morris, Jacob (s of Benjamin dec'd) m Elizabeth Cornwell (d of Aaron) 22, 12mo 1796.

Marriages (Quaker Records)

Joseph Morris, m Sarah Sanders, 3, 3mo 1790.
Jonathan Morris, m Penelope Symons, 21, 12mo 1785—In Pasq Co.
Aaron Morris, m Miriam Robinson (d of Wm) named in his will July 1785.
William Morris, & Esther his wife, née Gardner. (Loose papers Perq Co.)

Deaths (Quaker Records)

Benjamin Morris, d 3, 1mo 1762. (s of Aaron, & Mary.)
Mary Morris, widow of Benj d 4, 2mo 1762.
Mary Morris, wife of Joseph, d 15, 9mo 1763.
Hannah Morris, wife of Joseph, d 27, 11mo 1766.
Mary Morris, wife of John (d of Thos Nicholson) d 23, 1mo 1772.
Mary Morris, wife of Joshua, d 13, 3mo 1773.
John Morris, will Perq, p Oct 1774, names "brother Cornelius" & wife Sarah, Also 2 sons; not named.
Joshua Morris, will Perq, p April 1777, names wife Rebecca, sons: John, Benjamin, Jonathan, Zachariah, Mordicai, & Nathan, dau's Clarkey Pool, & Mary Morris, father Aaron Morris.
Jonathan Morris, will Perq, p Feb 1796. Sons: Jehoshaphet, & Jonathan, nephew John Pool, brother Nathan, & Josiah Bundy Exrs.

NEWBY

Henry Newby was transported to Va in Thomas, & John Jan 6, 1635. William Newby came from London to New England in Mary, & John Mar 24, 1633, age 24. (Hotten.) The records of Nansemond Co Va show that William Newby was a resident of said county 13, 10mo 1684, being at that date a member of "Chuckatuck" Mo Meeting, where he is found as a witness to a marriage, with wife Izabell. As neither of his three sons, had a wife by that name, and the name of Isobel came down in the family for several generations, among his descendants, it seems natural to suppose that this "Izabell" was William Newby's wife. His sons named on Chuckatuck Reg, were Gabriel, who was the first to migrate to Perquimans, Nathan a Quaker minister about 1707, and Thomas, who is not named on the said Register, but is named in his brother Nathan Newby's will, in Perq. From the records in Perq, it seems that Thomas remained in Isle of Wight Co Va, where his son (presumably) m Mary Pretlow. (Thomas 2.)

Thomas Newby is often called on the records in Perq, "Thomas Newby of Va."

Newby, William (1) and wife Izabell, had issue: 1 Gabriel, b ——— 1659, d—, 12mo 1735, m Mary Toms (d of Francis, & *Pershillah*) b April 27, 1670, married 10, 2mo 1689, issue: I William, b 13, 1mo 1690, m 1st Jean Bier (widow of Richard, née Loadman) July 3, 1701, m 2d Ann ———? and had one son William, born after his death, about 1720. (See deeds in Perq.)

RECORDS OF DEEDS

Newby, Edward (1) Gabriel (1) William (1) b 12, 10mo 1691. d. s. p. Will Perq Co, Aug 6, 1717, names father Gabriel, and brother William Newby.

Newby, Joseph (1) Gabriel (1) William (1) b 7, 9mo 1693, m Elizabeth Nixon (d of Zachariah, & Elizabeth, of Little River) "at Little River meeting house" 9, 11mo 1715, m 2d Mary (widow of Edward Mayo née Clare d of Timothy).

Newby, Francis (1) Gabriel (1) William (1) b 3, 11mo 1695, m Huldah Hunnicutt (d of Robert, & Margaret née Wyke, d of Peter Wyke, & Huldah née Ladd, of Prince George Co Va) Feb 9, 1723, issue: 1 Robert, b Apl 16, 1724—2 Mark, b Mch 25, 1726—3 Margaret, b May 29, 1728—4 Miriam, b Apl 20, 1730. Francis Newby's will p in Perq, April 1744 names sons: Robert, Jesse, Mark, & Francis, dau's: Margaret, & Sarah.

Newby, Jesse (1) Gabriel (1) William (1) b Mar 30, 1704, m Mary Hunnicutt (d of Robert of Virginia, sister of Huldah, his brother Francis' wife) 9, 11mo 1727. d. s. p. Will Pasquotank Co, p Oct 1765, names his brothers.

Newby, Samuel (1) Gabriel (1) William (1) (no birth date), m it is thought 1st Ann Mayo (d of Edward Jr, & Mary née Clare, who m 2d Joseph Newby, son of Gabriel, his 2d wife; Mary Newby's will 1739, names her son-in-law Samuel Newby and three of his children. (See Grimes Wills.) Samuel Newby m 2d Elizabeth Sanders (d of Benjamin & Ann) 1, 8mo 1740 issue: 1 Joseph, b Aug 10, 1741—2 William, b Dec 30, 1743—3 Ann, b Feby 5, 1745—4 Gabriel, b Feby 13, 1747—5 Mary, b Oct 16, 1749—6 Gideon, b Sept 15, 1751—7 Elizabeth, b Mch 16, 1756—8 Miriam, b Oct 16, 1757—9 Samuel, b Mch 25, 1761. It is thought that Samuel Newby had by 1st wife, Ann (supposed to be d of Edward Mayo) dau Jemima, who m her cousin William Newby (s of William, & Ann, b about 1720) Mary Newby née Clare (widow of Edward Mayo) in her will p Jan 1739, names gr-children: Edward, Jemima, & Isabell Newby, who appear to be the children of her "son-in-law" Samuel Newby, and these children are not named among the issue of Elizabeth née Sanders. (See above.)

Newby, William, as seen died before 1720, and is not named in Gabriel Newby's will p in Perq, Mar 1, 1735, but his son William received 300a from his gr-father, in equal division with the sons: Joseph, Jesse, & Samuel; Francis is named but no part allotted to him. He had probably had "set off to him" his share of his fathers Estate. No daughters are named in Gabriel Newby's will, but he had three dau's: Isabel, b 28, 10mo 1697—2 Mary, b 30, 11mo 1699—3 Miriam, b Dec 2, 1701, and a dau Elizabeth (no age given) who m John Nixon, and died 10, 7mo 1730, when John Nixon m 2d Mary———and 3d Hannah Albertson. (See Nixon family.)

Newby, Gabriel (1) of "piquemons" d — 12mo 1735 age 76. His wife Mary née Toms died 2, 9mo 1738, age about 70 years.

Gabriel Newby in his will left to son Samuel his "maner plantation," which was usually given the youngest son, for the better maintenance of the widow, and mother, the younger son usually being single.

Newby, Joseph (1) Gabriel (1) William (1) m 1st Elizabeth Nixon, and 2d Mary née Clare, and had issue (according to his will, p in Perq Oct 1766) Sons: Gabriel, Joseph, Benjamin, and "poor decrepit son Josiah" whom he left "in care" of his other sons, wife Patience (widow Jordan, See Jordan) 3d wife whom he married in Isle of Wight Co Va 15, 12mo 1746. (Pagan Creek Mo Meeting.) Dau's: Mary Thornton, Elizabeth Mayo (wife of Joseph) gr-son Joseph Thurston, gr-dau Mary Newby, Elizabeth Newby (wife of Francis, d of Matthew Jordan, & his last wife Patience) widow Jordan. Brother of Samuel, and son Gabriel Exrs.

Three Joseph Newby's appear in Perq practically at the same time, & this makes quite a bit of confusion, but the writer has turned the leaves of time over, & over to discover proof of each one, and still has some doubt, but of this last named Joseph, she is *sure*.

Joseph Newby (unplaced) made his will in Perq, p April 21, 1735, and names no legatees, but wife Mary. As he left no heirs, he isn't pertinent to this history anyway, so we will dismiss him.

Another Joseph, will p July 1752, wife Elizabeth, and dau Mary. This Joseph in the legal papers in Perq is called Joseph Jr, therefore it seems probable that he was son of Joseph Sr, and gr-son of Gabriel (1). He certainly could *not* have been son of *Samuel*, whose son Joseph, was born 1741, which would have made him only eleven years of age at the time this will was probated. It is thought that Joseph Newby (1) m Elizabeth Turner, (no date however) and had son Samuel who made his will 1737, and probably son Joseph Jr, but no *proofs* appear.

Joseph Newby petitioned the Court Jan 1735 for permission "to build a Mill on Suttons Creek, for the public good." His son Gabriel made the same request on same date "if my father doth not comply with the Law in Building a Mill on Suttons Creek" craved leave to finish it. A final audit of the Est of Joseph Newby, Dec 1777, shows that his son Gabriel died prior to this date. The heirs of Gabriel (2) dec'd were allotted £54, s2, p10½. Other heirs: Joseph, Benjamin, Mary Clary, heirs of Elizabeth Mayo dec'd, Mary Thornton, Dorothy Phelps (step-dau, and daughter of his last wife Patience, by her 1st husband Matthew Jordan of Isle of Wight Co Va. Dorothy m 1st Jonathan Phelps, and 2d John Skinner) Elizabeth, wife of Francis Newby (also step-dau), and one of the heirs being "dead without issue," his part was divided between all the heirs. The supposition is that this dec'd heir was the "poor decrepit son Josiah," as he is not mentioned in this division.

Matthew Jordan (s of Matthew & Patience of Isle of Wight Co Va) will Perq, p July 1763, names "mother Patience Newby, and sisters Elizabeth Newby (wife of Francis) & Dorothy Skinner." (The division of Jonathan Phelps shows that his wife was Dorothy, & loose papers give the fact that she m 2d John Skinner. She had by Jonathan Phelps sons: Jonathan, & Benjamin, and dau Dorothy. (See Phelps.)

Newby, Benjamin (1) Joseph (1) Gabriel (1) William (1) m Sarah Lilly, 1, 3mo 1775. As he died intestate his issue can not be traced.

Newby, Gabriel (2) Joseph (1) Gabriel (1) William (1) m Pleasant White (d of Wm) 5, 12mo 1787. He also died intestate, and can not be traced.

Newby, William (3) William (2) William (1) m Jemima Newby, his cousin, (d of Samuel & wife Ann Mayo) issue: 1 Demsey—2 Anne, b 5, 16, 1750, m John Maudlin 2 — 1769, d in Henry Co Ind about 1845—3 Elizabeth, m Job Bogue, 3 — 1775—4 Isabella, m Truman Moore 10 — 1774—5 Sarah, m Josiah Albertson 3, 8, 1775. d Jan 10, 1793/96—6 Joseph, m Mary White "at Welles in Perq" 4, 8mo 1796—7 William, m Hannah Bundy (d of Caleb) 1, 25, 1797, she d 29, 9mo 1798—8 John (s of William dec'd) m Susannah Tatlock (d of Edward dec'd) of Perq, 22, 10mo 1801 (issue: son John, b 4, 9mo 1802)—9 Mary, b 7, 7, 1768, m Thomas Draper Feb — 1790 (2d wife, they moved to

Ind)—10, Miriam, b 2, 2mo 1772, m Josiah Draper 12, 6, 1789, d 9, 1, 1812 in Highland Co Ohio.

Of Demsey Newby nothing is known. For descendants of Anna Newby, see Maudlin. Job, and Elizabeth Bogue both made will in Perq. (See N. C. Hist & Gen Reg, Vol 3-2). Joseph probably died intestate. Of William, & Hannah, née Bundy nothing is known. For descendants of Mary, & Miriam Newby, see Draper.

Newby, Joseph (2) Samuel (1) Gabriel (1) William (1) m 1st Mary Moore 1, 12mo 1763 issue: 1 Joseph—2 Robert—3 Nathan—4 Ann—5 Jemima Elliott —6 Sarah, all named in his will p in Perq Nov 1814, with gr-children: Samuel and Ann Moore, wife Huldah (2d wife). Joseph Newby died 27, 9mo 1814.

Newby, William (3) Samuel (1) Gabriel (1) William (1) b Dec 30, 1743, d 5 30, 1831, m Elizabeth Ratcliff (d of Joseph) 10, 8, 1766, issue: 12 children, m 2d Elizabeth (Symons) Small, widow, 4 — 1805, issue: four children. 4 Gabriel (son of Samuel) b Feby 13, 1747, m Rachel Townsend (d of William, & Rachel née Wilson, widow of Timothy Winslow, dau of Robert Wilson, & wife Rachel née Pricklove, dau of John Pricklove, & wife Elizabeth)—5 Mary (d of Samuel), b Oct 16, 1749, m Joseph Bogue—6 Gideon, b Sept 15, 1751, d 1, 29, 1816, m Mary Arnold, 1, 1mo 1788, issue: ten children.

Newby, Gabriel (2) Samuel (1) Gabriel (1) William (1) and wife Rachel (Townsend) who were m before 6, 3mo 1776, had issue, according to his will, p in Perq Co 1824. Dau's Rachel Newby, Margaret Cannon (wife of Joseph) gr-children: Mary, & Sophia Cannon, Catherine Baker, & Edwin Newby, Rachel Winslow (wife of Francis (1) and dau of his son William) Achsah Bunch, & Lydia Newby. His wife Rachel is not named in his will, but she was living July 1777, when her mother Rachel (née Wilson) Williams will was probated in Perq, who named her "dau Rachel Newby" and gr-son William Newby (s of Gabriel). (See will of Rachel Williams, N. C. Hist Reg, Vol 3-2.)

Family tradition says that William Newby (s of Gabriel) m Lydia ——— and had among others, dau Rachel, who m Francis Winslow (1) son of William. William Newby's division, shows "a part to Francis Winslow, & wife Rachel.

Newby, Mark (1) Francis (1) Gabriel (1) William (1), m Mourning Phelps, Jan — 1750. His will p in Perq July 1785, names sons: Jonathan, Zachariah, and dau's: Margaret, Arrington, Miriam, Mourning, & Elizabeth Newby. Mark Newby m 2d Keziah Nixon (widow) 6, 12, 1775. Zachariah (s of Mark) m his cousin, Mary Newby (d of Nathan) (2) Nov — 1773. Jonathan, (s of Mark) m Mary Jones, 3, 8mo 1785.

Newby, Robert (1) Francis (1) Gabriel (1) William (1) m Jemimah Pierce (d of Thomas, whose will was p in Perq 1756) 1, 4mo 1748, issue: according to his will p in Perq Apl 1790. Thomas, Robert (2), Wyke, gr-son Willis Newby, dau's: Karin Parker, Mary Walton, Sarah Cosand, Jemimah Cannon (wife of Jacob) and Huldah Newby. Robert Newby (s of Robert) m Mary Moore, 4, 3mo 1789. Thomas Newby (s of Robert) m Mary Saunders, 5, 11mo 1777.

Mary Newby (unplaced) about to move to Back Creek, in Randolph Co, N. C. 3, 12mo 1796. (Quaker records Pasq Co.)

Marriages

Newby, John, m Elizabeth Nicholson (d of Christopher) June 11, 1701. (Quaker Rec.)

Newby, John (s of John), died 4, 1mo 1734.
Newby, Ann, m Francis Mase, at Newbegun Creek, Pasq Co, 5, 11mo 1726. (Quaker Rec.)
Newby, Thomas, m Miriam Nixon, at Symons Creek, Pasq Co, 1, 10mo 1756. (Quaker Rec.)
Newby, Thomas (s of Joseph), m Mary Bogue (d of Duke) at Suttons Creek, 20, 12mo 1797.
Newby, Mary, m Elias Albertson, 7, 12mo 1785. (Quaker records.)
Newby, Gabriel, m Pleasant White, (d of William) 5, 12mo 1787.
Newby, Jesse, m Elizabeth Townsend, 6, 4mo 1791.
Newby, Francis (2) m Elizabeth Jordan (d of Matthew) Nov — 1755.
Newby, Elizabeth (d of John), m John White (s of Henry Sr) Nov 14, 1696.
Newby, Elizabeth (d of Gabriel), m John Nixon (s of Zachariah) Before 1730.
Newby, Sarah, m Barnaby Nixon (s of Zachariah) Jan — 1753. She m 2d Ralph Fletcher, July — 1753.
Newby, Elizabeth, m Daniel Saint, Sept — 1753. She m 2d Esau Lamb, April — 1757.
Newby, Jemima, m Jacob Cannon, Nov — 1778.
Newby, Sarah (d of Thomas), m Josiah Albertson (s of Elihu) 3, 8, 1775.

NEWBY

Nathan Newby (1) William (1) (brother of Gabriel) m in Nansemond Co Va, Elizabeth Hollowell (d of Alice of Elizabeth River, 13, 10mo 1678, among wit Wm Newby, (father) Gabrell Newby, John Hollowell, Dorrithy Newby, Elizabeth Scott, Elizabeth Copeland. Elizabeth, (d of Thomas, & Alice Hollowell) was b 9, 7mo 1662, issue: one son Thomas, age not given, but named in his fathers will.

Nathan Newby was Clerk of the Mo Meeting, at Pagan Creek, Isle of Wight Co Va, 1702. "Att a meeting att Chuckatuck, Co of Nansemond," 9- 8mo 1707, Quakers assembled registered their opinion of Friend Nathan Newby, in these words "to the best of our Judg'mts Nathan Newby, is a man that fears the Lord, we believe his call is to the Ministry, & we desire the Lord to Prosper him, and bee with him, to the end of his daies." Lower Mo Meeting, Nansemond Co Va.)

After coming to Perquimans Co, N. C. Nathan Newby m Mary Toms (d of Francis Toms Jr, & wife Margaret Bogue) issue: 2 Francis (whose will was p in Perq July 1752. Naming "brothers Thomas, & Nathan, & mother Mary Moor." He also names John Robinson, who m his sister Mary)—3 Nathan— 4 Mary (m John Robinson), wife Mary.

Mary Newby née Toms, m 2d Samuel Moore. (Minute book, & division of Estates.)

Thomas (1) Nathan (1) Wm Newby (1) m Sarah Scott (d of Joseph of Va) early in 1700, (date illegible). He is spoken of on records in Perq, as "Thomas Newby of Va."

Ann Scott of Vir, in a deed recorded in Perq, mentions her *"nephew* Exum Newby," & apt's him att' to sell a place belonging to her in sd Co, called "Belvidere." This estate is thought to be the same now called "the old Lamb place" across the River, from the town of Belvidere, & it is probable that the town derived its name from the adjoining plantation. Tradition has made it a *fact*. What relationship existed between Ann Scott, & Joseph, the records do not disclose, but this we do know; William Scott, of Nansemond Co, m Mourning *Exum*, & as the name of Exum continued to be carried down in the Newby, & allied families, in Perq Co, it seems more than probable, that Joseph Scott, was a son of said William. Mourning is also found as a given name of many of the ladies of the family. But as Thomas Newby did not make a will in Perq, no absolute *proof* can be found, to substantiate the fact.

Nathan Newby, lived over the "Causeway" at Bear Garden. He was one of the attendants of the "Ferry" over Perq River, to Phelps Point, & built the first "Goal" in Hertford. He was dead July 1735, "Mary Newby Relict." She petitioned the Court July 1740, that "her tithables be taken off the main Road, to labour on the ferry Road, as it would be more convenient for her to 'set over' people and in that way 'I shall get no Blame.' " The Causeway was at that time called "Newby's Point" later called "Mary's Point." By Act of Assembly July 1755, a public "Ferry was Established, from Phelps Point, to Newby's Point," & Nathan (2) Newby was appointed "Ferryman" on his side, & Jonathan Phelps on his point. They were allowed the stipend of £4 per annum for their services. A ruling was made that they were to "Set over *free;* Inhabitants, of said Co, at Court times; Elections of Assemblymen; Vestry Elections; & Musters."

Nathan Newby (2) Nathan (1) Wm Newby (1) m Keziah Pierce (d of Thomas) 6, 9mo 1752. His will Perq, p Feby 1763, Son Francis (his gr-mother Mary Moore) dau's Mary, Millicent, & Sarah, wife of Keziah, & bro Thomas, Exrs.

Keziah Newby, widow of Nathan, m 2d Francis Nixon, May — 1763.

Francis (3) Nathan (2) Nathan (1) William (1) m 1st Elizabeth Jordan, (d of Mathew, & wife Patience née Darden) Nov — 1755, m 2d Rachel Winslow, (d of Joseph (2) & wife Mary, née White; d of Thomas White, & wife Rachel Jordan; d of Joshua Jordan, & wife Elizabeth Sanborn; of Isle of Wight Co Va.)

Francis Newby, will Perq p May 1807, names sons: Francis (4), Joseph, Nathan (3), & Thomas, dau's Kesiah Sutton, Parthenia, Rachel, & Elizabeth Newby, wife Rachel.

Mary Newby, d of Nathan (2) m Zachariah Newby, Nov — 1772, (s of Mark Newby).

Keziah Nixon née Pierce, m 3d Samuel Pritlow, who took charge of the "Ferry."

Mary Newby (d of Nathan (1) m Jonathan Phelps, & had a dau Elizabeth m Gabriel Newby. Nathan Newby m Keziah Pierce, 6, 9mo 1752. (Deed Perq.)

The Nathan Newby line is better defined, & easier to carry out, than the Gabriel Newby line, and it is evident that they crossed each other many times.

Nathan Newby m Peninah Copeland, 5 12mo 1781.

NEWBY, PASQUOTANK CO.

James Newby, m Sarah Nicholson (d of Christopher), May — 1699, issue: James, b Aug 1, 1702—2 Samuel, b 23, 8mo 1704—3 Benjamin, b 25, 6mo 1707—4 Ann, b 1, 11mo 1708—5 Jeams, b 24, 7mo 1710.

Sarah Newby (wife of Jeams) d 13, 3mo 1718. James Newby m 2d Elizabeth (d of Henry White) she d 1, 12mo 1728, age 55.

Jeames Newby "of the precinct of Pasq," m Elizabeth Daniel (widow) of same, 18, 5mo 1715.

Samuel Newby (s of James, & Sarah Nicholson) m Elizabeth ———— issue: 1 Miriam, b —, 6mo 1726, m William Lamb—2 William, b 22, 7mo 1727—3 Huldah, b 16, 4mo 1729, m Joshua Morris, June 19, 1752—4 Dorcas, b Oct 4, 1730, m John Sanders, Aug — 1751—5 Mary, b July 28, 1732, d 9, 5, 1763, m Joseph Morris, June — 1755—6 Joseph, b Sept 2, 1734, d Aug 2, 1739—7 Dempsey, b Dec 20, 1736, m Mary Ross, Feb — 1760—8 Elizabeth, b Oct 30, 1738, m Esau Lamb, April 1757, or Jacob Jacobs April 1759—9 Pleasant, b Mar 2, 1740—10 Ruth, b Mar 20, 1743, d Mar 2, 1752—11 Samuel, b June 8, 1746, m Rachel Pearson, July — 1766—12 Mordicai, b Jan 8, 1748, m Mary Maudlin, July — 1766. Will probated 1784.

Samuel Newby, & Rachel Pearson, issue: 1 Millicent, b 12, 20, 1766—2 Jesse, b 11, 7, 1768—d 4, 4, 1819, m Elizabeth Townsend, 4 — 1791—3 Elizabeth, b 9, 17, 1771, d 4, 14, 1844, m Benjamin Hill, 12 29, 1787—4 Margaret, b 8, 27, 1773—5 Samuel, b 3, 16, 1776, m Peninah Hobbs, 7, 30, 1801—6 Rachel, b 9, 16, 1779, m Reuben Lamb—7 Anna, b 10, 27, 1781, m Wm Osborn & 2d Obadiah Harris, 2, 17, 1851—8 Jemima, b 4, 5, 1784—9 Nathan, b 2, 22, 1787—10 William, b 7, 16, 1789.

Samuel Newby "worthy minister" died 16, 12mo 1770.

James Newby (s of James) m Naomi White (d of Henry Sr) May 12, 1732, issue: 1 Thomas, b 13, 4mo 1735—2 Enoch, b 19, 10mo 1736—3 Jeams, b 20, 12 mo 1740—4 Elizabeth, b 17, 4mo 1743. James Newby died 1, 11mo 1760, age 50. Naomi Newby d 2, 11mo, 1771, age 68.

Thomas Newby (1) James (2) James (1) m Sarah Overman, 9, 11mo 1763, issue: 1 Nathan, b 20, 7mo 1765—2 Naomi, b 30, 9mo 1767—3 James, b 6, 5mo 1770—4 Jemima, b 22 7mo 1774.

James Newby, m Sarah ———— issue: Henery, b 13, 10mo 1769. He m 2d Keziah Bowles, 22, 6mo, 1774, issue: (unknown).

Benjamin Newby (s of Benjamin) m Ruth Wilson, 13, 10mo 1765, issue: Mary, b 7, 9mo 1768—2 Sarah, b 22, 1mo 1771—. Ruth Newby d 16, 12mo 1771.

Benjamin (1) Newby m Sarah Albertson (d of Elihu) 21, 2mo 1737. He d 28, 9mo 1739.

Joseph (s of Benjamin (1) m Ann ———— issue: 1 Thomas, b 27, 12mo 1759—2 Enoch, b 29, 10mo 1761—3 Miriam, b 29, 1mo 1765—4 Robert, b 18, 10mo 1767—5 Joseph, b 3, 5mo 1770—6 Nathan, b 14, 4 mo 1772.

Thomas Newby (s of Jesse, & Elizabeth) m Nancy Wilson (d of Christopher, & Pheraba) all of Perq, at Suttons Creek, 23, 2mo 1826.

Elizabeth wife of John Newby died 6, 1mo 1720.

Sarah wife of James, d 10, 1mo 1770.

James Newby of Pasq Co, m Elizabeth Davis (widow) May —, 1719.

NICHOLSON

William Nicholson, weaver; of Nor'wch Norfolk Co England, embarked for Boston, Apl 8, 1637, age 33; with wife Anne, age 28, & children, Nicho, Robartt, Elizabeth, & Anne. (Hotten.)

*Christopher Nicholson emigrant to Perq Co, N. C., m before coming to Albemarle Hannah Rednap, issue: 1 Christopher (2)—2 Deliverance, m

---

*Edmund Nicholson, & wife Elizabeth came to New England from Bootle, Cumberland Co England. He died in Marblehead Mass, 1660. Issue: Chris-

Joseph Sutton (s of George & Sarah) Jan 1 —— —3 Samuell, b Mar 12, 1665—4 Hannah, b Mch 4, 1667—5 Joseph, b Sept 28, 1670—6 John, b Dec 17, 1671—7 Nathaniell, b Jany 7, 1675. The ages of Christopher, & Deliverance are not given in the Reg.)

Nicholson, Hannah, wife of Christopher, d Dec 2, 1678.

Nicholson, Christopher (s of Edmund), m 2d Ann Atwood (d of Thomas, of Middlesex," in ould England) Aprill 11, 1680, issue: 8 Elizabeth, b Jan 13, 168— d Sept 11, 1682—9 Sarah, b Aug 5, 1682—10 Thomas, b Feb 7, 1687—11 Ann, b Feb 8, 1689.

Nicholson, Christopher, died Sept 10, 1688. Ann "Relict of Christopher" m 2d Richard Dorman, June 26, 1690, issue: Hannah Dorman, b Mar 30, 1695.

Nicholson, Christopher, the elder, seems to have died intestate.

Nicholson, Deliverance, issue can be found chronicled in the Sutton record.

Nicholson, Samuel, m Elizabeth Charles, at Quarterly Meeting, Dec 16, 1688 (d of Wm & Abigail Charles, b Jany 8, 167—) issue: 1 Abygall, b Sept 24, 1689—2 Hannah, b Aprill 9, 1692—3 Ida, b Nov 10, 1694—4 Elizabeth, b Jan 15, 1697.

The will of Samuel Nicholson, p in Perq Mar 22, 1728, names dau's Sarah, & Elizabeth, son-in-law John Anderson, wife Elizabeth. Samuel Nicholson, d Mar 29, 1727. His wife Elizabeth, m 2d Zachariah Nixon (2). Her Will Perq, p Jan 1748, names, son-in-law John Anderson, Dau's Elizabeth Anderson, & Sarah Jones, gr-sons: Samuel, John, & Joseph Anderson, gr-dau Sarah Anderson.

Nicholson, Hannah (d of Christopher, & Hannah, b Mch 4, 1667, m Ezekiel Maudlin (1).

Nicholson, Christopher (2) m Mary (s of Christopher, & Hannah) issue: 1 Thomas, b June 1, 1715 (loose paper) 2 Mary, b Nov 1, 1717—3 Ann, b Feby 20, 1719. His will p in Perq, July 23, 1723. Son: Thomas, dau's Miriam, Dabora, Mary & Ann; wife Mary & brother Samuel Exrs.

Nicholson, Joseph (s of Christopher, & Hannah) m Hannah Albertson (d of Albert, & Mary, née Gosbey) b Dec 11, 1675, d Jan 2, 1695—m 7, 4mo 1693, issue: Sarah, b Dec 5, 1694. (According to the old Roman calendar.)

Nicholson, Joseph, will Perq, p Jan 1698, made bequest to his brother John, "his plantation on Perq River," other brothers named; Benjamin, Samuel, Nathaniel, & Christopher. (According to this will his dau Sarah, & wife were both dec'd.)

Nicholson, Nathaniel, (s of Christopher, & Hannah) b 1675, m Sarah Harris (d of John, s of Thomas Harris (first Clerk of Perq) & wife Diana) issue: 1 Nathan, b Nov 22, 1716—2 Samuel, b Nov 26, 1722—3 Jonathan, b June 27, 1730. His will Perq, p July 1737, names only one son; Jonathan, to whom he bequeathed his "plantation" dau's Sarah, & Elizabeth, wife Sarah.

Nicholson, John (son of Christopher, & Hannah) b 1671, m Priscilla Toms (d of Francis, & wife Pershillah) Nov 20, 1700. He d June 19, 1718. The division of his Est, April 14, 1719, gives his heirs: d Elizabeth, d Mary, s Samuel, wife Pershillah (who m 2d John Kinsey).

---

topher, b 1638, m Hannah Rednap (d of Joseph, who moved to Perq Co N. C. very early). 2 Joseph, b 1640—3 Samuel, b 1644—4 John, b 1646—5 Elizabeth, b 1649, m Nicholas Anderson—6 Thomas, b 1653. (New England Hist & Genealogical Reg.) See issue of Christopher, above.

Nicholson, Thomas, (s of Christopher (2) m Mary ——— issue: 1 Christopher (3), b Feby 20, 1733—2 Joseph, b Apl 15, 1736—3 Mariah, b May 12, 1738—4 Nicholas, b June 7, 1741—5 Mary, b June 3, 1744—6 Caroline, b Aug 21, 1748—7 Margaret, b Jany 1, 1752—8 Thomas (s of Thomas, & Sarah) b Feby 26, 1774.

Nicholson, Thomas, m Mary Griffin, 7, 6mo 1780. (Quaker records.)

Nicholson, Thomas, m Sarah White, 3, 9mo 1796. (Quaker records.)

Nicholson, Margaret, (d of Thomas) m Aaron Morris (s of Aaron) 30, 11mo, 1768. (Quaker records.)

Nicholson, Samuel (husband of Elizabeth) d 29 — 1727. (Quaker records.)

Nicholson, Joseph, son of Elizabeth, d 10, 1mo 1727. (Quaker records.)

NIXON

Zachariah (1) Nixon (s of Zachariah, of Nottingham, Parish of North Masrom, Eng) m in Perq Co, Elizabeth Page (d of Hask? or Mark Page dec'd, of Albemarle) "according to Quaker rites, 2, 1mo 1681," issue: 1 Damaris, b 8, 6mo 1682—2 Zacharias, b 22, 3 mo 1684—3 Barnabe, b 21, 11mo 1687—4 Francis,? b 20, 8mo 1689. (Quaker Record Pasq Co.)

Nixon, Zachariah, took up 323a of land in Pasquotank Co, 1684 on N. E. side of Little River, "adj lands where Wm Turner now dwells, running to the mouth of said River." Zachariah Nixon, "dying intestate, his son Zachariah surviving him, inherited said land, and cultivated it for several years, who dying bequeathed same to his sons: Zachariah, & Barnabee" the first made choice of that part adj Wm Turner, and Barnabee the part near the main Road, running to the old School House." Zachariah "moving" sold his part 152½a at public vendue, for £100, after having laid out part thereof, in half acre lots, for a Town-ship, and the rest for a common, known by the name of Nixonton, formerly called Wind Mill Point." 9, 5mo 1748. (Records Pasq Co, N. C.)

Nixon, Zachariah (1), died 3, 12mo 1691. Mary Page "Laid down the body," 4, 5mo 1680.

Nixon, Zachariah (3) had a grt for land in Perq county, Jan 21, 1712/3, 105a "in the fork of Little River, adj John Tomlin." Another grt in Chowan Co, 110a "in the fork of Coniby Creek Swamp, adj Edward Moseley." Xber 21, 1712.

Nixon, Zachariah, of Perq Co sold to Aaron Morris of Pasq "two half acre lotts, in Nixonton, on Water Street, adj Jos Newby Jr, con' £38." July 9, 1748.

Nixon, Zachariah, of Perquimans (Planter) and Elizabeth his wife, conveyed to Wm Simpson of Nixonton (Merchant) for "£15-10s, ½a lot in said Town, on the South end, near the Ship-yard." Oct 6, 1750. (Records Pasq Co, N. C.)

Nixon, Zachariah (3), m Elizabeth Symons (d of Thomas, & Rebecca) "at a Meeting at Symons Creek, Pasq Co" 11, 1mo 1707/8, issue: 1 John, b 18, 10mo 1708—2 Phineas, b 7, 1mo 1710—3 Zacharias (4), b 15, 4 mo 1713—4 Rebeckah, b 11, 6mo 1715—(m Francis Toms Jr)—5 Mary, b 25, 6mo 1717—6 Hannah Newby, b —, 1mo 1718—7 Elizabeth, b 23, 4mo 1720—8 Barnabe (2), b 28, 3mo 1724.

Nixon, Zachariah, (s of Zachariah) "father of above children," b 22, 3mo 1684, died 12, 8mo 1739. (Quaker Records Perq Co.) His will, p in Perq

Oct 1739, names sons: John, Phineas, Zachariah, & Barnaby, dau Rebecca Toms, gr-children: Joshua, & Mary Moore.

Nixon, Barnaby (1), appears to have moved to Va, and lived in Prince George Co.

Nixon, John (1), m 1st Elizabeth (d of Gabriel Newby, & Mary née Toms) issue: Elizabeth, b 29, 4mo 1733. He m for his 2d wife, Mary (d of Wm Enervigin) 4, 1mo 1736, issue: 2 Miriam, b 16, 11mo 1736. Mary Nixon, wife of John, died 12, 10mo 1738. By the 3rd wife (name unknown) 3 Zachariah, b 20, 8mo 1744—4 Huldah, b 2, 11mo 1746—5 John, b 20, 5mo 1748—6 Ezra, b 17, 12mo 1751, d 14, 12mo 1773. John Nixon m 4th Hannah Albertson (d of Nathaniel, b 18, 2mo 1719) 10, 3mo 1753, issue; 7 Mary, b 10, 12mo 1753—8 Lidda, b 14, 3mo 1756, d 12, 11mo 1767—9 Frederick, & Abigail (twins), b 4, 11mo 1758. Hannah Nixon d 18, 2mo 1793.

Nixon, Zachariah (5), (s of John) m Mary White (d of John) 15, 9mo 1771, issue: 1 John (2), b 23, 10mo 1772—2 Margaret, b 8, 10mo 1775—3 Zachariah (6), b 10, 3mo 1778—4 William, b 5, 1mo 1781—5 Benjamin, b 19, 8mo 1784—6 Frederick, b 23, 7mo 1791—Sarah, b 14, 7mo 1786—7 Ann Skinner Nixon, b 15, 8mo 1794.

Nixon, Frederick, died 6, 9mo 1793; Sarah, his sister, d 16, 9mo 1793.

Nixon, Phineas, (s of Zachariah, & Elizabeth Symons) m Mary Pierce (d of Thomas, & Mary née Jones, d of Peter, & Mary Jones) issue: 1 Elizabeth, b 18, 12mo 1731/2—2 Mary, b 9, 7mo 1734—3 Rebeckah, b 27, 4mo 1741—Thomas, b 12, 2mo 1745—Sarah, b 17, 12mo 1756/7. Phineas Nixon "an Elder departed this Life" 28, 12mo 1771. His will p in Perq, Mch 11, 1772, names sons: Pierce, Barnaby, & Phineas, gr-sons: Nathan, & Phineas (sons of Thomas) dau-in-law Sarah Nixon, wife Mary, dau's Rebecca Arnold, Sarah Albertson (wife of Benjamin), Elizabeth Lamb, Jemima, Hannah, & Kesiah Nixon, children of Mary Elliott; viz., Gabriel, Miriam, & Nixon Elliott.

Nixon, Thomas, (s of Phineas) m Sarah Smith (d of John) 13, 3mo 1768, issue: 1 Nathan, b 11 5mo 1769—2 Phineas (3), b 28, 11mo 1770. Thomas Nixon (s of Phineas) died 2, 11mo 1771, age 27 years.

Nixon, Pierce, (s of Phineas) m Penninah Smith (d of John) 16, 12mo 1770, issue: 1 Joseph, b 15, 10mo 1771—2 Rachel, b 1, 12mo 1773—3 Thomas (2), b 30, 1mo 1776—4 Mary, b 27, 2mo 1779—5 William, b 26, 10mo 1781—6 Jacob, b 28, 2mo 1784.

Nixon, Peninah "departed this Life" 17, 5mo 1787.

Nixon, Phineas, (s of Thomas dec'd) m Miriam Jones (d of Joseph) 13, 10mo 1808, his will probated in Perq, Aug 1813. Wife Miriam, child in ésse; other Leg: Abigail, Charles, Mary Nicholson (d of Thomas), Huldah Bundy (d of Josiah Jr). George, & Josiah Bundy Exrs.

Nixon, Nathan, (eldest s of Thomas, & Sarah (Smith)) m Lydia Anderson 6, 3mo 1793, "at Welles Meeting house" issue: 1 Thomas, b 23, 1mo 1794—2 Lydia, b 29, 1mo 1797. He m 2d Margaret Bagley (d of Nathan) 14, 6mo 1798, issue: 3 Sarah, b 13, 9mo 1800—4 Phineas, b 2, 14mo 1803. His will p in Perq, Feb 1810. Wife Margaret, son John, Dau's: Sarah, & Pheribe Nixon. Brother Phineas, & Francis White Exrs.

Nixon, Zachariah (6), m Martha Toms (d of Foster) 8, 5mo 1793, issue: 1 Joseph, b 12, 9mo 1794—2 Foster, b 7, 10mo 1796—3 Mary, b 21, 11mo 1798—4 Zachariah, b 16, 9mo 1800, d 7, 7mo 1806—5 John, b 22, 5mo 1803—6 Sarah, b 20, 12mo 1805, d 18, 7mo 1806—7 Toms Nixon, b 14, 5mo 1807—8 Elizabeth, b 27, 7mo 1811.

Nixon, Barnabe, (son of Zachariah, & Elizabeth (Symons)) b 28, 3mo 1724, m Sarah Newby, "at Symons Creek," 1, 1mo 1753.

Nixon, Zachariah, (s of Zachariah, & Elizabeth Symons, b 1713) m Elizabeth Nicholson, June 10, 1734, issue: Francis, b 2, 2mo 1735—2 Mehetebell, b 15, 11mo 1738—3 Zachery, b 10, 10mo 1741. He seems to have died intestate. The will of his wife Elizabeth, is however probated in Perq, July 1769. She names son Francis; gr-children: Joseph Nixon, Zachariah, Miriam, Caroline, Christopher, & Samuel Nicholson; Margaret, Miriam, Jonathan, Mourning, & Elizabeth Newby; gr-sons: Zachariah Newby, & Jonathan Phelps, gr-dau Elizabeth Winslow, Benjamin Phelps, Dorothy Phelps, Mourning Henley & Elizabeth Toms. Sons: Zachariah, & Francis Exrs.

Nixon, Francis (1), m Kesiah Pierce (d of Thomas, & sister of Mary wife of Phineas Nixon). She was a widow Newby when he married her about 1760. (Kesiah m 3d Samuel Pritlow.) His will p in Perq, Jan 1773. Wife Keziah, her former husband Nathan Newby (2) sons: John, James, Samuel, & Thomas.

Nixon, Samuel (1), will p in Perq, Nov 1815, Wife Sarah, daus: Elizabeth Copeland, Margaret, Sarah, Peninah, Mary, Ann, Kesia, & Martha Nixon, sons: Samuel, Francis, brother Wm Jones, son-in-law Henry Copeland Exrs.

Nixon, John, (s of Nathan dec'd) m Anna Henby (d of Thomas) 9, 4mo, 1815.

Nixon, Samuel (2), m Rachel Copeland, 2, 1mo 1793. (Wells Mo Meeting, Perq Co.

Nixon, John, m Ann Morris (Intention) 20, 9mo 1794. (Pasq Mo Meeting.)

Nixon, James, m Sarah Robinson, 17, 10mo 1795. (Pasq Mo Meeting.)

Nixon, John, was made an Elder in Quaker Meeting Pasq Co, 15, 2mo 1786.

Nixon, John, removed to "Wain Co N. C." and was given a certificate from the meeting in Pasq county, to "Contentnea Meeting" in Wayne Co, with children: Lydia, Sarah, Dorothy, Thomas, Josiah, & Mary, 1790.

PEARSON

Peter Pearson, who came to Va from Cumberland, England, about 1701, presented a letter from Friends at Pardshow Cragg, said county, to the Mo Meeting in Isle of Wight Co Va, setting forth the fact that "Peter Pearson the bearer thereof, who hath in Mind to remove to America, is descended of Honest Parents, who hath been Serviceable Among us, and we are Loath to part with him, who has been of Blameless Conversation." (Reg of Friends, Pagan Creek)

The records in Isle of Wight do not disclose a person of this name before this date. A John Person appears at an early date in the county, with wife Frances, who was dau of William Miles. They had a son John Jr, who m Mary Partedg (d of Thomas of Sirry (Surry) Co, 10, 1mo 1692. This person *may* have been a Pearson, & like so many on old records, spelled first one way, & then another, but there is nothing to *prove* this statement. Of Peter Pearson we are *sure*, and also the time he was living in Isle of Wight. He probably remained a very short time in that county, and it is thought he married there Rachel ———— as no mention of his marriage can be found in Perq, although the Quaker records may hold some information, if they were only available. He appears to have been affiliated with Lower Mo Meeting in Nansemond Co, in 1700, and moved to Perq soon after, and as a consequence has no further mention on the Chuckatuck Reg.

Pearson, Peter (1) will Perq Co, p Apl 21, 1735, names sons: Jonathan, Nathan, Peter, John, & Bailey, dau's Rachel, & Mary. His wife is not named, but she survived him 15 years. Rachel Pearson "Exhibited the will of her dec'd husband Peter Pearson, in Court, 1735. (Loose papers, in Perq Co.) The sons: Nathan, & Bailey, are thought to be sons by a former wife as Rachel does not name them in her will. Of course they may have died between the date of his will (1735, 1750) and the time she made her will. Nathan Pearson's name appears on Tithe List Perq Co 1741.

(2) Pearson, Jonathan (1) Peter (1) m Rebecca Elliott, 4, 6mo 1745 (in Perq Co) issue: 1 dau —— m Peacock, 2 dau ——, Coley, 3 Mark, m Elizabeth Lamb (d of William, & Mary (Newby) Lamb) had issue: 1 William, married Elizabeth Chance (Chancey)—2 Rebecca, m Benoni Bentley—3 John, m Hannah ———— —4 Isaac—5 Elizabeth, m —— Chance. (All moved to Ohio.) Jonathan, m 2d Sarah Bundy Oct —— 1765 issue: 4 Elizabeth, b 15, 7mo 1767, m Richard Ratcliff 22, 2mo 1784 in Wayne Co (Contentnea Mo Meeting) died 22, 5mo 1839 in Henry Co Indiana, issue: 1 Anna, b 3, 4mo 1786, m William Maudlin (s of John, & Ann)—2 Joseph, b 8, 3mo 1788, m Rebecca Lamb—3 Jonathan, b 2, 8mo 1791, m Sarah Palmer—4 Nathan, b 9, 6, 1793, m Lydia Palmer—5 Richard, b 8, 11mo 1796, m Catherine Bailey—6 Mary, b 22, 8mo 1799, m John Elliott—7 Gabriel, b 8, 5, 1802, m Catherime Pearson—8 Elizabeth, b 11, 10, 1805, m Exum Pearson.

(3) Pearson, Mark (1) Jonathan (1) Peter (1) m Elizabeth Lamb 6, 3mo 1772 (issue above).

(3) Pearson, Ichabod (1) Jonathan (1) Peter (1) m Miriam Lamb (sister of his brother Marks wife) —, 9mo 1774, issue: 1 Ichabod (2), b —— 1777, d 1845, m Elizabeth Bradbury—2 Abraham, m Senna Lamb—3 Barney—4 Job—5 Rhoda, m John Collyer—5 Margaret, b —— 1788, m Samuel Collier—6 Huldah, m Jesse Maudlin (s of John, & Ann (Newby) Maudlin)—7 Jonathan—8 William, b 22, 9mo 1790, d in Iowa, m Katherine Pickrell.

(3) Pearson, Jonathan (2) Jonathan (1) Peter (1), m Sarah Peele —, 8mo 1780, Contentnea Wayne Co N. C.

(3) Pearson, Rhoda (dau of Jonathan, & Rebecca (Elliott) b —, 4mo 1750, m Reuben Peele (s of Josiah) —, 11 mo 1778, d 11, 24 1833, in Clinton Co Ohio—issue: Jecovey (Howard) Peele.

(3) Pearson, Nathan (1) Jonathan (1) Peter (1), b 10, 28, 1770, m Hulda Lamb (d of Jacob, & Sarah) 6, 12, 1807, in Randolph Co N. C., d 11, 13, 1845, in Henry Co Indiana.

(3) Pearson, Sarah, Jonathan (1) m Exum Elliott, 19, 3mo 1788 (s of Jacob, & Zilpha) d in Randolph Co N. C. 8, 7, 1788.

(II) Pearson, Peter (2) Peter (1) m —— Newby, 10, 3, 1746, and was "disowned for marrying out of discipline," issue: (according to his will p April 1755) sons: Jonathan, Nathan, Peter (3), dau's: Rachel, Mary, Elizabeth. He moved with his family to Wayne Co, from there to Guilford, and from that Co, to the North-West. (Untraced.)

(II) Pearson, John (1) Peter (1), m Elizabeth Croxton (d of Arthur) by "consent of Mo Meeting," 11, 3, 1738. He died intestate, in Perq Co before

June 7, 1760, on which date his widow Elizabeth was made Admx. "Elizabeth Pearson widow."

Peter Pearson petitioned the Court Apl 1766, to be appointed Guardian, for her children: Joseph, Sarah, Eleazer. Peter Pearson appears as guardian of Sarah, Jan 21, 1771, & Enoch Jessop as guardian of Eleazer. (Loose papers, in Perq.)

A Sarah Pearson was dec'd April 17, 1758, John Pearson Ex.

Robert Jordon made a dep' in Surry Co Va, Mar 21, 1758, that "he had known John Pearson for 26 years."

Pearson, Rachel (d of Peter (1) m Robert Bogue (s of Lydia, widow) 8 —, 1738, & had it is thought a dau Lydia, who m Joseph Draper, —, 8mo 1766, and probably other children.

(II) Pearson, Mary, m John Winslow (s of Thomas, & Elizabeth (Clare) Winslow) 2, 9mo 1740. John Winslow died 1754, when Mary m 2d Joshua Morris, s of Aaron & Mary. (See Winslow, for their issue.)

(II) Pearson, Elizabeth (posthumous child) m William Bagley,—5mo 1747, issue: 1 John, b 4, 8, 1749—2 Nathan, b 22, 1mo 1751, m Mary Low (d of George, & Tamer) —, 8mo 1776—3 Ephrim, b 21, 1mo 1752. "Disowned for marrying out of Meeting." 1802.

Pearson, Nathan, (no parents given) m Rebeckah Nicholson (relict of Joseph) at Symons Creek, 26, 12mo 1773, issue: 1 Sarah, b 6, 1mo 1775—2 Anna, b 21, 12mo 1779—3 Huldah, b 4, 8mo 1784, d 22, 9mo 1786. Nathan Pearson with his family moved to Back Creek, Randolph Co N. C. 20, 12mo 1794. Anna his dau, m Stephen Henley, 29, 7mo 1798. Sarah m Benjamin Hill, 1, 8, 1794, d 12, 1, 1794.

Pearson, Nathan, (s of Peter dec'd of Wayne Co N. C.) m Mary Bailey (d of John, of Randolph Co) 3, 7mo 1796, issue: 1 Peter—2 John—3 Ann—4 Levi— 5 Catherine—6 Bailey—7 Stanton—8 Elliott. Most of these moved with the Quaker emigration, to the Northwest Territory, where slavery could not go. Nathan Pearson of the Contentnea Meeting was certainly a son of Peter Pearson Jr. It is thought that Nathan who m widow Nicholson, was a gr-son of Peter Pearson Sr, but no proof is to be found.

Pearson, Joseph, of Perq, will p Jan 1785, d. s. p. Names Heliot Elliott, & Caleb White Exrs. (Untraced.)

Pearson, Eleazer, Will Perq, p May 1795, wife Barsheba, child is esse, daughters; (not named) Caleb Elliott, & Reuben Perry Exrs.

(I am indebted to Mrs. J. E. McMullen of Ada Ohio, for above data.)

Pearson, William (no father named), lived in Piney Woods District, where he paid tax on 60a of land, on East side of Perq River, 1774. He m Miriam Evans (d of Robert), before Dec — 1773. She is named in the division of the Estate of said Robert Evans, May 1777. William Pearson will Perq, p Feb 1807, names son Peter, dau's: Miriam, Lillia, Elizabeth, & Esther Pearson, & Peninah Elliott, wife Miriam, & Thomas White Exrs.

Marriages from Quaker Records

Sarah Pearson (d of Peter) m Joseph Lacey, Sept —, 1757.
Mary Pearson (d of Peter) m Enoch Jessop, April —, 1765.
Rachel Pearson (d of Peter) m Samuel Newby, Mar —, 1766.
Mary Pearson (d of Peter) m John Moore, Nov —, 1769.
Ruth Pearson (d of Peter) m Robert Wilson, Dec —, 1770.

DESCENDANTS OF GEORGE DURANT

A. Thomas Clayton Whedbee, son of Seth Whedbee and Martha (Blount) Whedbee.
B. James Monroe Whedbee, lineal descendant of George Durant. Father of Judge Harry Whedbee and Hon. Charles Whedbee.
C. Judge Harry W. Whedbee, son of James Monroe and Frances (Skinner) Whedbee. Born in Perquimans. Judge of the Fifth Judicial District, Greenville, N. C.
D. Charles Whedbee, son of James Monroe Whedbee and Frances (Skinner) Whedbee. Born in Hertford. Senator for the First Senatorial District, Hertford, N. C.

Peninah Pearson (d of William) m Thomas Elliott (s of Pritlow) April 1, 1796.

Peter Pearson (s of William) m Ann Morgan, Oct —, 1763.

Levi Pearson (s of William) m Elizabeth Bogue, Oct —, 1776.

Rebecca Nicholson (widow) was b June 30, 1743, m 1st John Lane, 2d Joseph Nicholson, 3d Nathan Pearson, all of Perq.

PERRY

Phillip Perry emigrated to Va, and settled in Isle of Wight Co, where he acquired large land holdings. He was uncle of Micajah Perry, London Merchant; who died 1721. The will of Phillip Perry was p in Isle of Wight Co Va, Oct 9, 1669, at which time he gave his age as 70 years. His will names sons: Phillip, & John, "under age" wife Grace. John son of Phillip Perry, conveyed a place called "Whitemarsh" to Col Joseph Bridger, 1673 (Isle of Wight Records). John Perry of "Upper pish of Nansemun Co Vir" for 5000 lbs of Tob, pd by Col Nathaniel Bacon, sold 70a in Lower pish of Isle of Wight Co" May 26, 1675. June 7, 1675, Elizabeth Perry acknowledged her dower to sd land. Phillip Perry had other sons, than Phillip, & John. These sons: James, Jacob, & Joseph, all moved to N. C. James to Chowan, where he made a deed to his brother John Perry of Nansemond Co Va, with consent of wife Patience, land on "Middle Swamp." As Middle Swamp is in what is now Gates Co, then a part of Chowan, it seems certain that this conveyance was in the last named county. Jacob Perry witnessed this deed. The will of Timothy Clare is authority for the fact that said Jacob Perry, m Hepzibath dau of said Clare (step-daughter) and it is thought, but not proven that she was a dau of his 2d wife Elizabeth—(maiden name unknown). All of the children of Timothy Clare are placed without doubt, but *Hepzibeth*, and she is not named in the last clause of his will. His children were by the first wife Mary Bundy, & the last one Hannah, by Hannah née Larance (widow of Israel Snelling). Therefore it seems evident that Hepzibeth Perry was not his *blood child*.

Among emigrants to Va in "Bonaventure" Jan 1634, are found Thomas Perry, age 34, Dorothy Perry age 36, Ben Perry age 4. (Hotten.)

Benjamin Perry Sr, died Mch 11, 1788. Hannah Perry, widow of Benjamin, died Nov —, 1791.

Benjamin Perry Jr (s of Benjamin, & Susan) died Jan 10, 1784. The elder Benjamin Perry was a brother of Micajah, wealthy commission merchant of London. Both Benjamin and Phillip's descendants migrated to Perq Co, at quite an early date. The Tithe, and Tax List in this county show where they lived, and in some cases how much land they owned. Micajah Lowe in his will, 1703, mentions his uncle Micajah Perry of London, who in his will 1721 names "sister Elizabeth Evens," dau Sarah Perry, with her two sons (not named). The Elizabeth Evens here named may have been, wife of Richard Eivens of Perq, who died 1693, naming wife Elizabeth.

Judith, & Thomas Perry are named in the will of Francis West of Nansemond Co, Va, 1715. She m Abram Hill of said County, and they moved to N. C. They sold to John Perry of Bertie Co, 100a, 1756, and to Josiah Granbery land in same Co, which is now situated in Hertford Co. Several of the children of Phillip Perry moved to Perq, as did also some of his brothers.

His gr-son Phillip died in Perq 1751, and names in his will, sons: Jesse, & Phillip, brothers John, Joseph & Jacob. He left to son Jesse "land on Little River" and to Phillip "plantation whereon I now live." dau's: Sarah, Mary, Rachel, Jude, Elizabeth, and Miriam. Jacob (son of Jacob) is made Exor. Witnessed by Benjamin, & Elizabeth Perry.

Jacob Perry Sr (s of Benjamin, & Susan) was brother of Benjamin Perry II. Died 1790, will probated July of said year. He names wife Mary, sons: Miles, Lawrence and Benjamin, Dau's: Hepsebeth, Sarah, & Mary Perry, Maria Bunch, and gr-dau Priscilla Perry (d of Leah). Test' Jacob, & Jos. Riddick, Benj Perry.

Perry, Benjamin (3) m Millicent Riddick, Dec 13, 1785, issue: 1 Mary, b Oct 26, 1786—2 Thomas, b Jan 27, 1789—3 James, b Aug 13, 1792—4 Joseph, b Aug 20, 1796—5 Christian, b Dec 20, 1798.

Perry, Israel (s of John & wife Mary, gr-son of Phillip Sr), died in Perq county 1779, will p May 27, 1779. Sons: Josiah, Israel, John Cader, & Jacob, Dau's: Millicent, Ruth, Rachel, & Ann Perry, dau Priscilla Twine. Wife (not named). His brother Phillip, & Thomas Twine were Exrs. Of these children; Ruth, m Micajah Hill of Perq, May 12, 1763. Rachel, m Richard Skinner, Dec 11, 1770. Priscilla, m Thomas Twine.

Perry, Jacob (s of John, & Mary, brother of Israel, & Phillip) will Perq, p Oct 1777. Sons: Jacob, Israel, & Reuben, dau Priscilla Welch (wife of Dempsey) dau Hepzibah Stallings (wife of Hardy) dau Ann Winslow (wife of Caleb) sons Dempsey, and John, gr-son Isaac Wilson (s of Isaac) wife Ann.

Joseph Perry of Perq died 1801. Jesse Perry the same year.

Perry, Jesse (s of Israel) m Elizabeth Linder. His will Perq p Nov 1801, names sons: Benjamin, John, Josiah, William, & Robert, dau's: Margaret, Christian, Martha, Sally, Asenith, wife Elizabeth, Leg: Mary, Elizabeth, & Millicent Nicholson. Of these children: Sally m 1790 Lemuel Weeks, & had John, James, Hugh, Polly (who m Cornelius Raper) another dau m ——— Benton. Nancy, James, & Hugh died unmarried.

Marriages

Perry, Mary, m William Hollowell, July 6, 1778. (From Judge Benj B. Winbourne's book, on the Perry family.)

Perry, Reuben, m Elizabeth Pearson, Jan 18, 1780.

Perry, Amos, m his cousin, Elizabeth Perry, Feb 10, 1783.

Perry, Elizabeth, m Thomas Stanton, Aug 28, 1784.

Perry, Israel Jr, m Miriam Hollowell, Apl 4, 1785.

Perry, Seth, m Mary Riddick, Dec 29, 1785.

Perry, Susannah, m Moses Howard, June 2, 1790.

Perry, Sarah, m Leverne Garriss, Dec 27, 1791 (d of Jacob Sr).

Perry, Jacob, m Ruth Chappell, Jan 11, 1791.

Perry, Josiah (s of Israel Sr, & wife Priscilla) b in Perq Co, Nov 19, 1741, m Elizabeth Twine (d of John, & Pleasant) lived in Pasq county, and was a lawyer of note, moving from that county to Bertie, where he m 2d ——— Freeman. Marriage bonds Perq Co.

Perry, Reuben, m Dorcas Chappell, Jan 11, 1791. (2d marriage.)

Perry, William, m Ferebe White, Apl 21, 1791.

PHELPS

William Phelps came to America, from Tewksbury England in Mary & John, 1630. Tradition has it that Jonathan Phelps, who settled in Perq Co N. C. was an Englishman, but no record has been found, to prove that fact, and where he came from to Perq, can not be certified by any legal papers. The Land books however give the fact that he took up 400a "in ye pre'ct of Perq, on West side of Perq River, and South side of Wilsons Creek, running down the River 116 perches," 1684. Robert Wilson in a grant to him (same year) names the same Creek, and calls it a "branch" so it was probably a very small stream. This grant is of especial interest, from the fact that it was exactly where the town of Hertford is now located. Seth Phelps was grt "240a in Perq pre'ct, June 24, 1704," on So side of Albemarle Sound, adj Richard Buttenshall. Cuthbert Phelps had land grt him, 300a in Perq prec't, on So side of Albemarle Sound, adj John Jennett. (same date). Samuel Phelps took up 150a of land Feb 10, 1718, on S. W. side of Perq River adj Sarah, & Hannah Lilly. It is a well known fact that Henry Phillips lived on the "Point" and Hannah his wife m 2d John Lilly, leaving several children. Old papers in Perq, show that Jonathan Phelps held land in the same locality, and he sold to the Directors of Hertford land to build a town, called Hertford. Jonathan Phelps petitioned the Court July 1755, for "Lycence to keep an Ordinary at his now Dwelling house" which was granted. An Act of Assembly was passed the same year, for "Establishing A public Ferry, from Phelps point, to Newby's point, whereon the Courthouse Now Stands, on Perq Rier," and agreed to pay said Jonathan "one of said ferry men £4, and Nathan Newby the Other Ferry man," the same, for "setting over ferry free Inhabitants of said County at Court times, Elections, Members of Assembly, Vestry men, & Musters, In said County" Security; James Sitterson, Joseph Ratcliff. Jonathan Phelps, and Nathan Newby prayed for their pay, "for Maintaining a Publick ferry, from Phelps Point to Newby's Point" April 1759, Granted. Jonathan Phelps was dead, July 1759. (Auditors Act.) Dorothy Phelps was granted Admix on Estate of her dec'd husband Jonathan Phelps, April 1759. (Minute book Perq Co.) His Inventory was presented in Court, by Dorothea Phelps, widow, May 20, 1759. Benjamin & Dorothy Phelps Orphans of Jonathan dec'd, in Act with their Guar John Skinner, who intermarried with Dorothy, Relict of sd Jonathan Mar 13, 1761. (Auditors Act.) This Jonathan Phelps was the *third* in descent, from Jonathan (1) in Perq, whose will was p April 4, 1689. His children are given in Berkeley Parish Reg as follows:

Phelps, Jonathan (1) m Hannah ——— & had issue: 1 Sarah, b Jan 15, 1671—2 Elizabeth, b Apl 2, 1679—3 Jonathan, b Nov 6, 1681—4 Samuell, b Aug 6, 1684 (the first Jonathan evidently died, at what date is not given, but he had a second son) Jonathan (s of Jonathan and Hannah), b April 13, 1687. Jonathan Phelps d Feb 21, 1688/9. His will on date above, is much faded and only the son Jonathan, and wife Hannah names are legible. The son Samuel certainly survived him however many years.

(2) Phelps, Jonathan (2) Jonathan (1), m Elizabeth Toms (d of Francis Toms Jr, & wife Margaret Bogue), issue: 1 Henry, b Mch 5, 1724/5—2 Elizabeth, b Aug 29, 1728. His will Perq, p Jan 1732. Sons: Henry, & Jonathan, to whom he left, "my manner plantation" & second, 300a "on Perq River," dau Elizabeth, wife Elizabeth.

(3) Phelps, Jonathan (3) Jonathan (2) Jonathan (1) m Dorothy Jordan (d of Matthew Jordan & wife Dorothy née Newby, of Isle of Wight Co Va) Dorothy Jordans mother, was sister of Gabriel, William, & Nathan Newby, who came to Perq from Nansemond Co Va. She m 2d John Skinner before 1761. (See Auditors Act.) Loose papers, & Minute books in Perq, state plainly Jonathan (3) and wife Dorothy had issue: Benjamin, & Dorothy.

(4) Phelps, Henry, (s of Jonathan (2) m Margaret Nixon (d of Zachariah) issue: Jonathan and Elizabeth, named in his will, p in Perq July 1752. These children were still under age Mar 1758, when Elizabeth chose for her Guar, Robert Newby, and Jonathan (s of Henry) made choice of Mark Newby in the same capacity.

(4) Phelps, Benjamin, m Sarah, & had according to his will, p in Perq, Jan 1785: Dorothy, Margaret, Sarah, & Mary Phelps.

(2) Phelps, Samuel (1), Jonathan (1) will p in Perq, July 1728. Sons: Jonathan, John, William, James. Ex brother Jonathan.

Phelps, Samuel (s of Samuel & Hannah, m Elizabeth Toms d of Francis) b Nov 17, 1706—2 John, b Jan 13, 1716/17. John Phelps was of age Jan 1739, and made petition for his Est out of the hands of Zachariah Elton on that date.

Phelps, William (1) Samuel (1) Jonathan (1) d. s. p. will probated April 1752. Leg: John, Harvey, & James Sitterson (cousins) William Barker, Sarah Eliot, & Samuel Sitterson.

Phelps, Benjamin, petitioned the Court July 1774, for leave to "keep an Ordinary at his now Dwelling house in Hertford," Which was granted. He served as Justice of Peace in Perq Co, 1778.

PIERCE

The name Piers is thought to be derived from a French family by that name. It is variously spelled, on the records in Perq Co, as well as elsewhere.

Peter Piers who lived in the reign of Edward IV, & Richard III, was an adherent of the house of York, & fought at Bosworth field 1485. He was standard bearer of Richard III. John Pierce was Bishop of York. The first grt for land at Plymouth Colony, was given to John Pierce June 1, 1621. Abraham Pierce was the first of that name to settle in New Plymouth, & was called a Freeman 1633. He was a householder 1637. Soldier under Miles Standish 1643, purchased Bridgewater 1645. He died about 1673, when his son Abraham was his Ex. He had also a son John settled at Gloucester 1712. (Ancestral families, & Portraits.)

John (s of John Pierce, & Elizabeth his wife), b 16, 4mo 1643. (Records of Boston.)

Elizabeth (d of John Pierce, & Elizabeth his wife), b 16, 4mo, 1643. (Records of Boston.)

Capt William Pierce, & John Pierce were among the living at James City Feb 16, 1623. (Hotten.)

Capt William Pierce trans to Va in Sea Venture 1620.

Richard Pierce, & wife Elizabeth came in Neptune 1624.

John Pers of No'wch weaver, age 49 years, & wife Elizabeth 36, "about to pass into foreign parts" took passage for Boston April 8, 1637, with children, John, Barbre, Elizabeth, & Judith. (Hotten.)

RECORDS OF DEEDS 405

William Pierce was a Sea Capt, & trans William Edwards to Surry Co Va June 22, 1635. It is probable that the John Pierce mentioned, as living after the Indian massacre May 22, 1622, was a son of Capt William Pierce. His age is not shown, but it seems he would not be too old, to have been the same John Pierce who d in Perq Co 1692. At that time he probably was just a lad, in his 'teens.

There is no proof that he is the same, John, who moved to N. C., but he must have married before coming to Albemarle, as no record of such a marriage was recorded, in the old Berkeley Parish Reg. His wife however, married for her 2d husband, William Bundy Dec 5, 1683. Her marriage is recorded in sd Par Reg, & announces the fact, that she was a dau of Joseph Scott. Her mother Mary Scott, had already passed away, Berkeley Reg, giving the time, as Feb 24, 1681/2, Her father Joseph Scott d Last of Oct 1685.

William Bundy, had 1st wife Elizabeth, by whom he had a son: Samuel b Feb 4, 1682 & by 2d wife Mary Scott, a dau Sarah b Jan 23, 1685, m Francis Pettit, of Chowan. William Bundy d Nov 7, 1692.

Pierce, John, & Mary (née Scott) had issue: 1 Deborah b Mar 5, 1678—2 Rabacka b Aug 9, 1680—3 Mary b May 7, 1682, & Thomas age not given, but he is named in the will of his father John Pierce, Perq Co Sept 13, 1682. Sons Thomas, John, & Joseph, dau Rebeckah, wife not named, William Bundy was made one of the Ex, with Jonathan Phelps.

Thomas Perre, m Mary Kent July 30, 16— Issue: 1 John b July 30, 1691— 2 Thomas b Nov 24, 1693.

Joseph Pierce (son of John, & Mary) m Damaris Nixon (d of Zachariah, & Elizabeth, née Symonds,) at Little River Aug 11, 1699. Joseph Pierce d Nov 16, 1705. Damaris Pierce m 2d Richard Ratcliff of Perq. (See their wills—Grimes.)

His will Perq Precinct, June 6, 1700, names brother Thomas Pierce, & wife Damaris. No other legatees.

John Pierce (2), b July 30, 1691, m Sarah (probably Copeland). His will probated in Perq Co Jan 10, 1726, names sons: Copeland, Thomas, & dau's Mary, Elizabeth, & Hannah, wife Sarah. Brother-in-law Peter Jones. (Peter Jones m Mary Pierce, sister of John.)

Thomas Pierce (Eldest son of John, & Mary (Scott) Pierce), will probated in Perq Precinct Mar 30, 1732. Sons: Thomas, Joseph, & John. Dau Mary Jones (wife of Peter) gr-children Thomas, & Mary Pierce. Son-in-law Peter Jones.

Thomas Pierce (2), (son of Thomas) will p Oct Court 1756, names Dau's Mary Nixon, Sarah Morris, Jamima Newby, Kesiah Newby, Kerrenhappuch Pierce, gr-son Pierce Nixon (son of Phineas & Mary) Brother-in-law Peter Jones. Exors: Phineas Nixon, John Morris, Robert Newby, & Nathan Newby. (Son-in-law.)

Mary Pierce m Phineas Nixon. Her sister Kesiah m 1st Nathan Newby (s of Nathan & Mary Toms) m 2d Francis Nixon, who made his will May 13, 1772, 3d Samuel Pritlow. (See N. C. Hist, & Gen Reg Vol 3—No 2.)

Thomas Pierce (3d) m Miriam, named in his will, Perq Co probated Oct Court 1772. Sons: Joseph, John, David, Abner, Nathan, William, & James. Francis Wright, & Ralph Fletcher Ex.

Nathan Pierce, m Kezia Carter. Aug 19, 170—.

Joseph Pierce, m Elizabeth Barrow. Oct 18, 1780.

Joseph Pierce 2d, m Zebrah Small. Aug 16, 1784.

Abner Pierce, m Mary Roberts. June 17, 1784. (Mar bonds Perq County.)

Division of the Est of Thomas Peirce dec'd, by Order of Court Oct 1757. To Alice Calloway, mother of dec'd, £5-11s-4p. To Sylvanus Wilson, (in right of his wife) £3-11s-4p. To John Chancey (in right of his wife) same. To Mary Bartro (sister of the half blood) same. To Caleb Calloway, (brother of the half blood) same. To John Calloway, (brother of the half blood) same. Thomas Jones Ex.

Peter Jones m Mary Pierce (d of John & Mary) & sister to Thos, & John Pierce (sons of Thomas).

Berkeley Parish Reg, has the following:

Pierce, John, & wife Sarah, had issue
    Mary b Mch 11, 1716/17.
    Copeland b May 11, 1719.
    Elizabeth b May 11, 1721.
    Thomas b Feb 11, 1722/23.
    Hannah b Mch 25, 1725.

Pierce, Thomas Jr, m Mary Copeland 1719, issue:
    John b Feb 16, 1720.
    Mary b Sept 23, 1722.

Pierce, Joseph, & wife Alice, issue: Rebecca b Feb 28, 1729/30, and son Thomas (of Division).

Pierce, James, & wife Elizabeth, issue:
    Hartwell b Jan 22, 1742/3.
    Miles b Feby 23, 1745/6.
    Florella dau b Jany 9, 1747/8.
    Fan son b May 2, 1750.

James Pierce in his will p in Perq Co, April Court 1763, names son: Miles. Wife Susannah, Dau's Kesiah, & Celia. Eldest children, Hartwell, Miles, Florida, & Fen. Test' James, & John Gibson, & Amy Maudlin.

John Pierce, "an Elder," departed this life, 10, 6mo 1812, 80 years of age. (Suttons Creek Mo Meeting.)

PRITLOW—PRICKLOVE

Samuel Pricklove a resident of Perq Precinct, prior to the coming of George Durant 1661, whose land was adj said grant to Durant from the Indian Chief, had his own grant directly from Sir Wm Berkeley. No mention of a grant to Samuel Pricklove can be found in Perq, but the records make mention of the fact that he had a grant from before stated source. Samuel Pricklove is supposed to have come to Perq from Nansemond Co Va, where that family was strongly entrenched. This family was united with the Quaker faith, but Samuel strayed far from the fold, "by taking up arms" and following the rebellion with the redoubtable Durant, at the time Thomas Miller was deposed from the Government 1677-79. For his part in this insurrection, he suffered the disgrace of being in the "Pillory," and had his right ear amputated, and was sentenced to banishment from the Colony. The records do not show whether this drastic punishment was really carried out, but we do know his descendants remained in Perquimans. He was dec'd Apl 20, 1692, without a will, so no definite means can be found to establish his issue; except for one son whose age is given in the Berkeley Par Reg: His wife was Rachel, née Larance, m June 1, 1668, by whom he had son: Samuel b Dec 24, 1674, and it is thought another son (John) born before this date, of whom there is no birth date.

John Pricklove (1) m Elizabeth ——— issue: 1 Leah, b Mch 4, 1695, m Joseph Smith, and had several children, m 2d Thomas Winslow, (see Deeds)—2 Judith, b Dec 2, 1697, m Abraham Sanders—3 Elizabeth, b April 25, 1699, m William Elliott, & had son Pritlow Elliott—4 Rebecca, b Dec 10, 1705, m Zachery Chancey.

John Pricklove, Will p in Perq, May 1, 1728, names Dau's: Rachel Wilson (wife of Robert) Judith Sanders, Elizabeth Eliot, gr-son John Smith, wife Elizabeth.

Pricklove, Elizabeth, will p in Perq July 23, 1728, names Dau's: Leah Smith, Rachel Wilson, Priscilla Sanders, Rebecca Chancey, gr-children: John Smith, Silvanus Willson, Judith, & Priscilla Sanders. As a dau Priscilla is named in her will & not in his, Elizabeth may have been a widow when she m John Pritlow.

Pricklove, John, had a grant for land in Perq, 400a on Perq River, "at the mouth of Wolf pitt branch," adj Jonathan Phelps. Jan 1, 1694. As Jonathan Phelps land lay on the mouth of same branch, up Castletons Creek, we may infer that John Pricklove lived near Hertford.

Pricklove, Samuel, b 1674, m Purina Penrice (d of Francis, & Elizabeth) Mar 25, 1696, issue: 1 Samuel (3) b Nov 6, 1698—2 Francis, b Mch 25, 1702.

His will (no County given, but Perq) p Jan 20, 1702-3, Sons: Samuel, & Francis, wife Peninah.

Pricklove, Samuel, had grant for land in Perq, 400a "at the mouth of a small Creek issuing out of Lillys Creek." Mar 30, 1704.

Pricklove, Francis, had grant for land, 165a "in Perq pre'cs adj Jonathan Bateman. Mar 30, 1704. Both of these grants were in Durants Neck, and were probably taken up by their *mother*, as they were too young to be taking up land. The Perq records show that this was often done.

Pricklove, Samuel, (probably gr-son of Samuel (2) m Keziah Nixon, née Pierce, widow of Francis Nixon) 7, 6mo 1780.

Pricklove, Kesiah, was wife of Nathan Newby, Oct 1756, at the proving of her fathers will on that date. Her husband Nathan (2) Newby, succeeded his father at the Ferry, "on Nathans Point" and was one of the first Directors of the town of Hertford 1759, when it was incorporated. He was dead 1765 when Seth Sumner was made a Director in his place. Keziah his wife m 2d Francis Nixon, who died before Jan 1773, when his will was probated in Perq, whose will makes mention of the fact that Nathan Newby was "former husband" of Keziah. Francis Nixon, & wife Keziah made complaint to the Court 1765, agst Simon Perisho, for debt. Keziah Pritlow was allowed £13-13-1 "for keeping the Ferry, from her point to Hertford on public days." Jan 1784. There can be no doubt that Nathan Newby inherited the Ferry House, & appurtenances on the point opposite to Phelps Point, and that Samuel Pritlow continued the same after he m Keziah.

Pricklove, Rebecca, m Zachary Chancey, who proved rights Apl 20, 1742.

RATCLIFFE

Capt John Ratcliffe arrived at Jamestown with Capt John Smith, in Discovery, April 26, 1607, with 20 other passengers. After Edward Maria Wingfield was expelled for wasting the "stores" he was elected president in his place. John Ratcliffe was one of the Council, "when the Colonists first reached shore" on their crossing to Accomac Co. (History of Accomac Co.) He was living at Jamestown May 23, 1609. (Browns Gen. to America.)

Roger Radclife was living "att West, and Sherlew hundred" Feb 16, 1623. (Hotten.) He arrived in Va, in "George" May 1619, with his wife Ann, age 40, and son Isaac 9 years old. He gave his own age as 44.

Charles Radcliffe had land grt him, in Accomac Co, July 10, 1664.

The History of Grant Co Ind, shows that James & Mary Ratcliffe came from England to Bucks Co Penn, with five children, as follows: 1 Richard, b April 8, 1676—2 Edward, b Aug 14, 1678—3 Rachel, b Feb 16, 1682—4 Rebecca, b Nov 11, 1684—5 James, b 1686/7.

The theory has been advanced that the Richard (s of James & Mary) is the identical one who was such a prominent Quaker in Isle of Wight County Va, but if one will stop to investigate the date thoroughly, it would be seen immediately, that such could not possibly be the case. The Richard in Penn, was only ten years of age when the Richard in Isle of Wight, made his will 1686. May we not more *plausibly* surmise, that Roger of West and Shirley hundred, might be the progenitor of Richard of Isle of Wight, for certainly propinquity would lend color to that version. Again he *could* have been a descendant of John Ratcliffe of Jamestown, however the records do not give any positive proof.

Richard Ratcliffe, first in Isle of Wight Co, made a will in sd county, which was Ack in Court Mar 4, 1686/7. Son Richard (2) to whom he bequeathed 200a of land, "if he die to s Cornelius" son John, dau's Elizabeth, Sara, Mary, & Rebecca, wife Elizabeth, & John Copeland Exrs. Test' Daniel Sandbourne, Wm Outland, Edmund Belson.

The children of Richard are given in Chuckatuck Friends Reg, Nansemond Co, as follows: 1 Elizabeth, b 21, 7mo 1668, m James Jordan (s of Thomas, & Margaret, of Chuckatuck Nansemond Co) 9, 12mo 1688—2 Sarah, b 19, 9mo 1670, m Joseph Kennerly, of Dorchester Co Md, 20, 7mo 1696—3 Richard (2) b 13 7mo 1672, m Elizabeth Hollowell (d of Henry dec'd of Isle of Wight Co) 18, 7mo 1700—4 Cornelius, b 15, 1mo 1674, m Elizabeth Jordan, widow (thought to be Elizabeth Sanborn, wid of Joshua Jordan) of Isle of Wight Co) 3, 9mo 1721—5 Mary, b 5, 2mo 1679, m Thomas Newman, 13, 2mo 1699—6 Rebecca, b, 3, 5mo 1684, m Richard Jordan (s of Thomas of Chuckatuck) 2, 8mo 1706. The marriage Banns name her as "d of Richard Ratcliff of Trerasco Neck" and her *father* appears among the witnesses to the m certificate.

Richard Ratcliffe Sr attended a "meeting at Leavy's Neck, 13, 4mo 1708." Richard and John Ratliff are named in the m certificate of Rebecca (Jordan) as "brother."

How to account for the fact that Richard Ratcliff (1) made a second will in Isle of Wight Co 8, 8mo 1713, p Oct 27, 1718, but from the fact that he names the identical children, and that they had the same husbands, we are led to conclude it was certainly the *same* Richard who made a will 1686, although a period of 27 years intervened. The 2d Richard could not have had a child of marriageable age, at the time the sons and dau's of Richard Ratcliff did marry. Also the issue in the second will is in exactly the same sequence as the first, but the *text* of the will is *different*. Will of Richard Ratcliff of Lower pish Isle of Wight Co, p Oct 27, 1718, gives to son "Richard plan' whereon I now live," after the death of his wife Elizabeth, to her he left 5 negroes for her "Natual life," to be equally divided between his children: Richard, Cornelius, John, Mary, Rebeccah, & the "children of my two dec'd dau's Elizabeth, & Sarah, a childs pt to be divided among them." Son-in-law Thomas Newman (husband of Mary) Richard Jordan (husband of Rebeccah) "a part of my Estate." Test' Wm Best, Humph'ry Marshall, Tho. Copeland.

Cornelius Ratcliff will Isle of Wight Co Va, p Feb 4, 1762. Leg: John Outland, Cornelius Moore, Marthy Winslow (wife of Jesse of Perq Co, (will 1771) John Jordan "over Nansemond River," Richard Jordan & wife Elizabeth, John Newman, Rachel Outland's heirs, Thomas Outland "my plan' in Western Branch" Cornelius Outland (s of Thomas). He gave to Thomas Outland, & Gideon Moore "all ready Money." Test' Charles Driver, Henry Pitt, Samuel Cutchin.

Cornelius, and Gideon Moore were sons of John Moore of Perq Co who made his will Mar 11, 1750. Joseph Ratliff is named in this will as "bro-in-law."

Richard (2) Ratliff moved to Perq Co, where he m for his 2d wife Damaris Nixon (d of Zachariah, & wife Elizabeth Page, d of Mark Page, b 8, 6mo 1682).

His will p in Perq pre'ct, July 14, 1724. Sons: Thomas, Joseph, to whom he bequeathed "lands in Vir, & N. C." Dau's Elizabeth, Mary, Sarah, Huldah, wife Damaris, & brother Cornelius Exrs.

Damaris Ratlif also made her will in Perq, p Feb 24, 1734₁ Son: Joseph. Dau's Mary Moore (wife of John, father of Cornelius, & Gideon) Sarah Winslow, "sons-in-law John More, & Thomas Winslow, gr-dau Betty More.

Joseph Ratcliffe, m Mary Fletcher (d of Ralph) 13, 3mo 1747. He was dec'd Apl 2, 1760, apparently without a will. Inventory on that date. His son Cornelius was bound apprentice to Josiah Jordan of Perq, July 1771, "to learn the Art of a Cordwainer," & Thomas his brother bound at same time to said Jordan. (2) Joseph Ratlif will Perq, p July 1787. Names dau's: Elizabeth, Mary, Peninah, & Catherine, brother Thomas, wife Sarah. Brother Cornelius, & Benj Albertson Exrs.

Joseph (1) Ratliff dec'd Feb 9, 1760; Mary relict. (Loose papers.)

Cornelius Ratliff was heir of Daniel Saint, Jan 18, 1783. (Divisions.)

Joseph Ratliff in Act' with his Guardian Ralph Fletcher, Jan 20, 1771. (Audit.)

Mary Ratliff Admix of Joseph; William Newby who intermarried with Elizabeth Ratlif, petitioned the Court for division of negroes, "given the several Representatives" by Cornelius Ratlif of Va. Jan 19, 1769. (Loose papers.)

Joseph Ratliff m Sarah Newby, 3, 8mo 1774. (Welles Mo Meeting.)
Thomas Ratliff m Hannah Munden, 28, 11 mo 1778. (Welles Mo Meeting.)
Cornelius Ratliff m Elizabeth Charles, — 12mo 1780. (Welles Mo Meeting.)
Daniel Saint, m Margaret Barrow, 15, 6mo 1744. (Welles Mo Meeting.)
Damaris (Nixon) Ratcliff, m 1st Joseph Pierce (s of John & Mary, née Scott) Aug 11, 1699, "at Little River meeting." The Scotts also came to Perq from Nansemond Co Va, and were Quakers.

SCOTT

Joseph Scott of Perq, probably came from Nansemond Co Va, where this family was well entrenched. The Quaker records there, however, fail to mention the ones who evidently moved to N. C.

The will of Joseph Scott, Perq precinct, is so illegible, that it can not be deciphered, only one legatee, being traceable, that a son Joshua. This will is dated Oct 26, 1685. There are however other items of interest, to be found, in the old Parish Reg, of Perq, which is still extant. The first mention in this old book being the death notice of one, Caleb Scott, who Dept this Life, Aug 7, 1679. Probably Caleb was a son of Joseph. He certainly had a dau Mary (m John Pierce).

Mary Scott, Late wife of Joseph, of this Co, Dept this Life Feby 24, 1681-2.

Joseph Scott, Late of Perq, Dept this Life, the last of Oct 1685.

Joshua Scott Dept this Life ye 14 of Jan 16—.

Joshua Scott m Mary ——— & had issue: 1 Grace m Wm Friley of Perq (see deeds), b Sept 21, 1682—2 Sarah b Mar 20, 1685. His will, Albemarle (Perq precinct) Jan 8, 1685/6. Made bequest to dau's Sarah, & Grace, wife Mary Extrix. Test' John Kinsey, Richard Evans, & John Wolfenden.

Two at least of these witnesses came from Va to N. C. John Kinsey from Nansemond, & Richard Evans from Isle of Wight. Wolfenden, was an Englishman, & came it is thought directly from that Country.

Mary Scott, wife of Joshua, Dept this Life May 22, 1692. Her will probated in Perq, Oct 3, 1692, names dau Hepthenia Walker, Julyanah Taylor, & gr-dau Johanah Taylor.

Mary Scott (wife of Joseph) m 2d Thomas Blount (s of James) 1685. On the records, she appears as wife of Joseph, who died 1681-2. Berkeley Par Reg, Perq precinct.)

Joshua Scott, (s of Joshua, & Lidia) b 12, 6mo 1643. New Eng Hist Reg, Vol 2.)

Joshua Scott may have come into Perq with the strong New England migration, which brought hither, Christopher Nicholson, Robert Cannon, Joseph Winslow, & many others.

The Tailor family is represented in Berkeley Par Reg, by the following:

John Tailor, s of John & wife Julianna, b Mch 7, 1690.

Thomas Tailor, Dept this Life, Desember 9, 1687.

John Tailor, Dept this Life febuary 2, 1688, at Grassy ——— (Point).

Elizabeth Tailor, d of Jonathan, & Elizabeth b Desember 5, 1693, died Sept 28, 1694.

Jonathan Tailor, died Sept 16, 1698.

Julianna Tailor, m 2d Benjamin Laker Esq, May 17, 1696. (His third wife.)

Juliana Laker (d of Henry Hudson, & wife Mary) died Dec ——— 1738.

John Hudson, merchant of Boston, New England, died Oct 5, 1733.

Benjamin Laker died, Apl 21, 1701, at his house, on Saseltons (Castletons) Creek.

James Scott, & wife Exelpe, had a d Rachel, b Feby 12, 1738.

Stephen Scott m Hannah Nicholson, Apl 13, 1721. (Second by that name.)

Stephen Scott, will probated Sept 11, 1716 (no Co given), names sons: Edward, to whom he left "land on Newbegun Creek" (Pasq Co), Stephen, &

Henry (plan' to each), John, & Joshua, dau Sarah, & Elizabeth, wife Elizabeth (née Jordan).

Stephen Scott (2) will p in Pasq Co, Jan 1753. Sons: Joseph, Samuel, Dau Mary Conner, (wife of John) Gr-children; Joseph, & Mary Scott, Mary, John, & Cado Conner; Stephen, & William Scott.

John Scott, of Pasq, will p Jan 8, 1738. Dau's: Eliphel, & Hannah, wife Sarah. (See Grimes N. C. Wills.)

SKINNER

As the Skinner family has been well written up in N. C. Historical & Genealogical Register, it will be beyond my power to make a tracing of them which will be fuller, or more adequate. So it is my object only to give some data, not to be found in the above named work, prior to their coming to Perq County. Most of these notes were found in Isle of Wight Co Va, from which in my opinion Richard Skinner emigrated to N. C. A Richard Skinner appears in York Co, at an early date, as "servant of Capt Thomas Thorpe" but there is nothing to prove that he was the same in Isle of Wight, although he may have been identical. Being a "servant" in this case, does not imply an act of servitude, as we are in the habit of applying it. These so called "servants" were often times of a higher station in life than their masters, and were either political prisoners, sent to the Colony for some minor offense against the government, or were merely paying for a passage to this country, by service, for some stated period. And as Thomas Thorpe is mentioned as "Captain" the latter would seem to be the most plausible conclusion, in the case of Richard Skinner of York Co.

Arthur Skinner, was "foreman" of the jury, in Isle of Wight Co Va, April 14, 1664. William Skinner of Bristoll, Eng, Merchant, appears on the Isle of Wight records, as "Att' for Mary Markes of Barbados, Widow; and appointed Robert Ked of Isle of Wight his Att' to Recover from Francis England of Blackwater 5500 lbs of Tob, removed by order of Attorney. 1668. Test' Robert Harris, James Edwards. John Norsworthy of Isle of Wight Co, leased for 14 years, unto Henry Skynner 160a of land in said Co, for the yearly rent of 400 lbs of Tob. Dec 23, 1664. Test' George Norsworthy, Bryan Knowles.

Mary Skinner of "Runnison" Isle of Wight Co widow: sold to George Cripps of Blackwater, for 6000 lbs of Tob, "a dividend of land" on said River 15000a. Test' Edward Poynter, Thos Smyth, Daniel Palmer. June 7, 1680. She was married to John Collins of Upper pish of Isle of Wight Co, before Sept 7, 1680.

Richard Skinner made a deed in Isle of Wight July 11, 1676, and gave "all my lands to my wife and two daughters." Unfortunately they are not named. He also mentions his gr-son Skinner Rawlings. Elizabeth (d of said Richard) m Rober Rawlings, of Surry Co Va, who was a mariner, and owned a "Shipp, which was lying att Warrick squick Bay" July 8, 1677. John Dunford gave bond to pay to Lt Richard Skinner, & James Griffin, 30000 lbs of Tob, July 26, 1674, from Estate of Robert Warren dec'd, of Lawnes Creek. Wit' Wm Edwards, Rog'r Deeke. Roger Rawlings appointed his "father-in-law" Richd. Skinner Att'. Jan 13, 1675.

Mary Skinner made deposition in Surry Co, July 26, 1675, that William Hill, in his will "gave all his property to Wm Edwards."

The Parish Reg of St Peters Church New Kent Co gives the ages of two of the children of Richard Skinner as follows: Rich'd, son of Rich'd Skinner, was bapt Feby 15, 1690—2 Margaret (d of Richard, & Mary) born Aug 6, 1699.

He was in Perq Co, N. C. 1701, and was granted 400a in Perq precinct, "at the punch bowles" adj Nathan Newby, along Bear Swamp. Dec 29, 1718.

As Mary Skinner was a widow in Isle of Wight Co & m 2d John Collins 1680, we are led to believe the Richard who came to N. C. must have been a son of the Richard, who had dau married to Roger Rawlings. He seems a better bet for our emigrant, and the records show that Richard of Isle of Wight was dead 1680. Richard (1) in Perq, in a deed to his dau Margaret Walston (Walton) makes plain he had a dau by that name, & her age is given in St Peters Reg He certainly had a son Richard (2) who m Sarah Overman, issue: 1 James, b 5, 10mo 1715—2 Samuel, & Richard (twins) b 15, 11mo 1717—Evane, b 15, 1mo 1719—4 Joseph, b 11, 8mo 1722—5 Joshua, b 25, 5mo 1724—6 Jonathan, b 13, 7mo 1726—7 William, b 25, 12mo 1728—8 John, b 21, 11mo 1730/1. Joseph (s of Richard) died 15, 9mo 1739. (Quaker Reg.)

A long line of Skinner births can be found in N. C. Hist & Gen Reg.

Richard Skinner, and wife Mary, were still alive in Perquimans, 1722.

Major F. S. Skinner of Providence, R. I., is at work on a book, lining up this old family, which he intends to publish at a future date.

Richard Skinner had land grants in Perq, 400a as above stated, and 356a on Bear Swamp, Nov 27, 1727. William Skinner was granted 600a, adj Ephrim Hunter, Mar 11, 1740. Evane Skinner granted 381a in Bear Swamp, Sept 7, 1761, & 130a, Mar 5, 1780, same location.

SNODEN

Nothing is known of Thomas Snoden prior to his entry into N. C., except an affidavit made by John Foster 1703, that "he knew Thomas Snoden, & Elizabeth his wife in Pennsylvania, where he died, and that his son Thomas came from Maryland to Perq, with his step-father Thomas Hassold." Thomas Snoden according to his own statement, was 24 years old Mar 1703. How long he had been here at that time the records do not show, but he was serving as Clerk of Court 1704. He married in Perq, July 18, 1705 Thomazin Mercer, who appears to have been his 2d wife.

Snoden (Snowden) Thomas and wife Constance ———— issue: 1 Joseph, b Dec 7, 1703, This is the only son by his first wife. His other children being by the second wife Tonsen: 2 Rebeckah, b Nov 23, 1706—3 John, b July 29, 1707—4 Thomas (3), April 18, 1711—5 Willis, b Dec 24, 1713—6 Joseph (2d by name), b Jan 24, 1716/7—7 Samuel, b Feby 6, 1720/1—8 Solomon, b Aug 26, 1724—9 Lemuel, b Feby 26, 1726/7. With all these sons, the name of Snoden could hardly suffer for lack of perpetuation.

Snoden, Thomas (2) will p in Perq, Oct 1736. He bequeathed to son John "land in Bertie Co," and to son Joseph same. To sons: William, George & Samuel "land in Perq Co," sons: Solomon, & Lemuel.

The division of his Estate Dec 1736, by Richard Whedbee, shows heirs: William, Joseph, George, Samuel, Solomon, & Lemuel, to each a part; wife Elizabeth. She is named in the will of John Wilson Aug 6, 1760, as "daughter." From the records it seems that Thomas Snoden had by his third & last wife one daughter, whose name is not mentioned, therefore one can not be certain of the fact. She was widow of Francis Layden whose will was made in Perq, Feb 23, 1727/8, and he names the identical children in his will that she does in hers.

Snoden, Elizabeth, will Perq p Jan 1744, Sons: William, Francis, George, & Isack Layden, gr-dau Elizabeth Layden, gr-sons Robert, & Joseph Warren. Francis Layden possessed 337a of land in Durants Neck 1794, and Mary his wife 100a.

Snoden, Solomon (1) Thomas (1) m Mary Hawkins widow of John (no date). Richard Whedbee petitioned the Court (date not given) "having married Relict of Solomon Snowden" for care of his son Zebulon Snowden, and a division of negroes left by deceased.

Snoden, Jane, relinquished her right of Admix on Estate of her dec'd husband George Snoden, in favor of Joshua Barclift, Oct 15, 1743.

Snoden, Lemuel, dec'd July 7, 1758, widow Mary Admix.

Snoden, William, m Ann Holloway, d of Thomas whose will p Nov 3, 1750, names her. He was dead Oct 1756, Ann Admix.

Snoden, Isaac, gr-son of Mary Sanders of Bertie Co, will 1734. Exrs: George Wynns, Robert Evans.

Snoden, Elizabeth, m William Stokes, before April 1762. They petition the Court on that day for part of "our Brother Frederick Snowdens Estate, who died March last under age."

Snoden, Joseph, d. s. p. will Perq Jan 1740. Brothers: John, George, & William, niece, Thomsen Snoden. The last named was widow of Francis Layden Oct 1756.

SPEIGHT

Francis Speight age 21 years, came to Va, in Thomas, & John, June 16, 1635, from London. He was granted 300a in Nansemond Co Va, Mar 17, 1654, "by a White Marsh." This grant was probably in what is now Gates Co N. C. as the deeds mention land called by that name in said county, and it is positively known that the early Speights lived in Gates before coming to Perq.

John Speight was granted 300a, April 21, 1684, "formerly granted to Francis Speight; and William Speight received a grant for 520a April 21, 1695," on East side of Bennetts Creek. As Bennetts Creek runs through Gates Co, and persons bearing this name were later found there, we are led to believe both these grants were situated in the same locality.

William Speight of Nansemond Co Va, made a deed in Chowan Co N. C., June 26, 1735, to his "son-in-law" Moses Hare, 100a "on Horse Pen Branch," witnessed by Edward Speight, Thos. Speight, and Ann Speight. From legal papers in Perq it appears that Thomas Speight m Mary ——— issue: 1 Isaac—2 Ruth, m Joseph Jordan—3 Zilpah, m Timothy Walton—4 (daughter) m Solomon Sheppard—5 Elizabeth, m Christopher Benn of Isle of Wight Co., Va. Priscilla Speight m Thos. Jordan of Va.

Thomas Speight made his will in Perquimans Co, p April 27, 1737. Sons: Isaac, and Moses, dau's: Rachel, Ruth Jorden, and Zilpah Blanchard (wife of Aaron) wife Mary. (His wife may probably have been ——— Rountree.)

Mary Speight, will Bertie Co, p May 7, 1743, names the identical children, except that she names two gr-dau's Mary, & Elizabeth Speight, but whose children they were is not specified.

Francis Speight of Chowan Co, will p Jan 1749. Names sons: Moses (to whom he left a "plantation at *Contenteny*," (which is in Wayne Co N. C.) John, and Joseph, (to the last, "land in wolfpit valley," (which appears as a location in several deeds in Perquimans Co) Brother William Speight. wife Kathern.

Isaac Speight had issue: Mary, Isaac (2) and Elizabeth.
Joseph Speight m Anne King. Mar 3, 1752. Chowan Mar bonds.)
Isaac Speight m Ann Montfort. July 24, 1764. (Chowan Mar bonds.)
William Speight m Ann Phelps. Aug 8, 1772. (Chowan Mar bonds.)
Josiah Speight m Mrs Elenora Bond. Jan 11, 1775. (Chowan Mar bonds.)
Nancy Speight made her will in Perq Co, p Feb 1834, naming: Sister Celia White, Ruth Elliott, & Margaret Whitehead, brother-in-law Foster Whitehead, brothers: John, & Jeremiah Speight.

SPIVEY

In deed book 10, page 62, Norfolk Co Va, can be seen the will of Matthew Spivey dated Feb 16, 1718. He bequeathed to Extrix "the use of my water Mill, & Rents of my lands, use of Cattle, and old Cows, with my Stock of Hoggs in the hands of Edward Wood, Edward Weston, and William Ward, in the Government of N. C." To said Extrix, use of lands "for bringing up my four youngest Children" dau Sarah, son Matthew, "when he comes of full size, to him my Maner plantation, with Water Mill, at age provided he affirm Saile for tract of Land in the tenor of John Staford, unto my son George Spivey." Children: Sarah, Judith, Tamer, Elizabeth, Matthew, & George Spivey. To Wm Joshson "one coate." Appointed "Mother, Mrs. Judith Nichols, & dau Sarah Extrix" jointly. Test' Hannah Holiday, Robert, & John Bowers, Thomas Maning.

John Granbery of Nansemond Co Va, made a deed in Norfolk Co Vir, "with consent of Ann his wife," unto Moses Prescott of Norfolk Co, "Land on Northwest River," patented by John Creekmore, April 20, 1689, and sold by him to Daniel Browne, June 24, 1691, by said Browne, conveyed to Maj John Nichols, and bequeathed by him to his dau Ann "now wife of said Granbery" 100a. July 13, 1704. Test' Nath'l Wilder, Matthew Spivey, Sarah Spivey, Judith Nichols.

Ann Granbery of Nansemond Co, appointed "brother Matthew Spivey" to act as her attorney, July 15, 1704. (As Judith, mother of Matthew, will 1718, m 2d Nichols, as before seen, Ann was probably a "step-sister" of Matthew Spivey, Jr.)

Matthew Spivey was J. P. in Norfolk Co Va, July 16, 1704.

George Spivey, obtained a grant in Nansemond Co Va, Oct 22, 1666, "near the head of Southern Branch," and John Spivey had a grant Oct 28, 1697, "at a place called 'planters delight'" on E. side of Southern Branch.

Thomas Spivey of Chowan Co N. C. deeded land, 150a to his son Jacob, on west side of Catherine's Creek (Gates Co), and he with wife Mary conveyed 100a on South side of said Creek, unto Moses Hill, Apl 18, 1720. William Hill of Chowan, was "son-in-law" of Thomas Spivey, and had son Moses Hill, wife Mary. (Will Chowan, p 10, 1mo 1750/1.) Thomas Spivey, & wife Mary, sold 200a on North side of Catherine's Creek, called "Meherrin

Neck" unto James Griffin, July 15, 1717. Test' Abram Spivey, Thomas Rountree.

The will of Thomas Spivey, p in Chowan Co, Feb 7, 1729/30. Sons: Benjamin, Jacob, Thomas, & William.

Benjamin Spivey of N. C. sold to John Edwards of "Lower pish" Isle of Wight Co, Va, "for 16 barrels of Tarr, and 600 lbs of Tob" Land in Lower parish, which was part of a patent for 1800a, patented in 1680. Seal April 20 1723.

Thomas Spivey made a deed of gift to his son Benjamin, 496a "as per Patent to me" on N. E. side of Katherine's Creek. 1715/6.

George Spivey, conveyed 100a, on Catherine's Creek, unto Thomas Walton Jr. Dec 4, 1734. Test' Benj Spivey.

Littleton Spivey made a deed in Chowan Co, to John Benton, conveying 40a "where John Spivey, father of said Littleton, lately lived, which he bequeathed to Littleton, & John Spivey his sons." Jane Spivey of Nansemond Co made a deed soon after this, and she is thought to be wife of John dec'd.

Champion Spivey was dead, 1794, division names the following children: John, Dorothy, Delia, & Rachel.

Sarah & Zilpha Spivey were dau's of Palatiah Walton of Chowan Co. Nov 6, 1776.

Marriages

Spivey, John, m Rhoady Ward. May 9, 1790. (Chowan mar bonds.)

Spivey, Josiah, m Orpha Hurdle, Mar 9, 1802. (Chowan mar bonds.)

Spivey, William, m Charity White, Dec 21, 1807. (Chowan mar bonds.)

Spivey, Seth, m Lovey Ward, July 25, 1808. (Chowan Mar bonds.)

Spivey, William, m Louisa Vandermon, Nov 25, 1831. (Chowan mar bonds.)

Spivey, Nathaniel, died 1758. (Records Chowan Co.)

SUTTON

Thomas Sutton, was a subject in the Colony at Jamestown, May 23, 1609. (Browns Genesis to America) Robert Sutton came to America, 1635, age 17 years. (Hotten.)

Nathaniel Sutton, (first in Perq Co) m in Nansemond Co Va, before coming to N. C. Deborah Astine, "by Mr. Babb, minister of gospel" Aug 12, 1668. They became Quakers soon after, arriving in Perq, as we find their names on all the Quaker records.

Sutton, Nathaniel (1), & wife Deborah, issue: George (2), b Mar 2, 1669—Joseph (2), b Aug 6, 1673—Rebecka, b Aug 8, 1676—Nathaniel (2), Aug 29, 1681.

Sutton, Nathaniel (1), died Dec 29, 1682. (His will Grimes, p Mar 12, 1682.) He left to son George, "plan' where I now live," to Joseph plan', son Nathaniel 150a of land, d Rebeckah, cousin John Godby (Gosby). Wife not named, but she survived him, & m 2d John Whedby, May 10, 1685, who died leaving her a widow, when she m for her 3d husband, Dennis Macclenden.

Sutton, Joseph (1), (s of George, & Sarah) brother of Nathaniel, m Delemance Nicholson (Deliverance), (d of Christopher, & Hanah, of New England) Jan 1, 167--, issue: Christopher, b Aug 3, 1685—George (3), b Aug 7,

1687. Joseph Sutton Sr, died Jan 17, 1695. His will, p April 1696, names sons: Joseph (3), Christopher, George (3), & Nathaniel. Wife Deliverance.

Sutton, George, (s of Nathaniel (1) m Rebecka ——— issue: Elizabeth, b Nov 14, 1694—Deborah, b Jan 2, 1699—Richard, b Sept 12, 1697.

Sutton, George (2), will p Mar 11, 1699 (Grimes). Names son Richard (1), d Elizabeth, to whom he left "plan' at Richland," d Deborah, to whom he left, "plan' at the Hickory." His wife is not named in his will.

Sutton, Joseph (2), son of Nathaniel, & Debro) m Parthenia Duren (Durant) (d of George, & Ann) b Aug 1, 1675, m June 18, 1695, issue: George, b Aug 22, 1696—Elizabeth, b Sept 15, 1703—Parthenia, b Aug 8, 1705—Sarah, b Oct 10, 1711.

Sutton, Joseph (2), will Grimes; p Mar 10, 1723. He left to sons: George, & Joseph, plan' "I now live on" d Pashence (Parthenia) d Elizabeth, to whom he left, "6 silver spoons, 1 silver cup, and silver tankard," Gr-son Thomas Sutton. Made brother (bro-in-law) Richard Whidbee Ex.

(Thomas Sutton, gr-son of Joseph, moved to Bertie Co, where his will was p Mar 2, 1750, naming sons: Thomas, William, George, Joshua, & Jasper, Dau's Parthenia, Mary, Elizabeth, & Judith, wife Elizabeth.)

Sutton, Joseph (3), (s of George, & Deliverance) will p Mar 26, 1724. Son: Christopher, Dau's Sarah, & Elizabeth, to d Mary, "land on Suttons Creek" Hannah, "land on Cypress Swamp," wife Rebeckah, brothers, George, & Nathaniel. Peter Jones, & Richard Whidby Exrs. (Rebecca Sutton (née Jones, d of Peter) m 2d Joshua Toms, & 3d Charles Denman.)

Sutton, Mary, (d of Joseph, & Rebecca) in her will, p Jan 1738, names her "mother Rebecka Denman," sisters, Sarah Thomas, & Elizabeth Moulin (Maudlin) cousin & Ex Joseph Sutton.

Sutton, Joseph, called Jr, m Bennett ——— (d of John, & Merry (Bailey) Stepney)? Issue: Hannah, b Jan 6, 1705/6—John, b Dec 23, 1707—Joseph Sutton Jr, died Jan 18, 1723.

Sutton, Richard (1), (s of George, & Rebecka) m Mary ——— issue: William, b Mch 5, 1719.

Sutton, Richard (2), b Dec 9, 1722—Mary, b June 23, 1726—Elizabeth, b Mch 2, 1728—Sarah, b Dec 20, 1730.

Sutton, George (3), m Mary ——— issue: Mary, b Apl 18, 1725—Joseph, b Aug 9, 1727.

Sutton, Nathaniel (2), (s of Joseph, & Deliverance) m Elizabeth Chancey, (named in the will of William Chancey, as "sister" & her children, Joseph, & Deborah as "cousins") had issue: Joseph, b Aug 21, 1727—Deborah, b Mar 13, 1729/30.

Sutton, Joseph (4), m Mrs Rachel Lee, Jan 11, 1732/3, issue: Elizabeth, b Feby 5, 1737/8.

Sutton, Nathaniel, m Elizabeth Chancey, In, 3, 1mo 1726. (Newbegun Creek Mo Meeting.)

Sutton, Samuel (1) (not placed) m Sarah, d of Peter Jones Sr, (see his will in Grimes) issue: George, b Sept 24, 1752, George (2d by name) b Jany 18 1754, John b Jany 31, 1756—George (3) b Nov 16, 1757—Mary b Feb 22, 1760—Samuel (2) b Nov 13, 1762.

Sutton, George, m Sarah Barclift, Dec 27, 1777. (Mar bonds Perq Co.)

Sutton, Samuel (2) m Elizabeth Barclift, Dec 3, 1784. (Mar bonds Perq Co.)

Sutton, Ashbury, m Nancy Reed, (d of Wm, & Penelope) Sept 11, 1779. (Mar bonds Perq Co.)

Sutton, Francis, m Deborah McConnell, Sept 6, 1783. (Mar bonds Perq Co.)

Sutton, George (3), Inventory, May 2, 1733, (Auditors act) Children Hannah, Samuel, and Mary Sutton. Division shows: "Cattle, a parcell of Smith Tools." Hannah Robins Admix.

Sutton, Christopher, will Nov 4, 1723/4, Bequeathed to son Joseph, & wife Miriam, 344a of land, on No Est side of Suttons Creek, down to the River. (Deed of Joseph Sutton, 1772,) Christopher Suttons will, can not be found in Perq, & does not appear to have ever been probated, but this deed mentions the fact that he made one. Miriam Sutton, wife of Christopher, was d of Joshua Toms, named in his will, 1732.

Grants

Sutton, Deborah, (widow) grt 280a "on E. side of Piquemons River" being the Westermost bounds of another tract to sd Deborah, 1684. And 294a on E side of Perq River, "to ye mouth of Little Creek." 1684.

Sutton, George, grt 344a "on ye So East side of Suttons Creek, to ye head of same." (No date.)

Sutton, Nathaniel. 150a "in ye precinct of Perq, on ye East side of Suttons Creek, by a Branch, called 'Eye branch' along Joseph Suttons, line." (No date.)

Sutton, Elizabeth, grt 125a "in precinct of Perq, called 'ye rich thickett' adj Jno Whidby." Aug 19, 1713.

Marriages

Sutton, Hannah, (d of Joseph) m John Keaton, before Oct 27, 1728.

Sutton, Sarah, (d of Joseph) m Robert Hosea (No date).

Sutton, Christopher, m Sarah Jones, July 2, 1745. (Mar bonds, Perq Co, she was d of Peter.)

Sutton, Susanna, d of Abraham Warren, & Sarah his wife, gr-d of Mary Norcom.

Sutton, Ann, d of Francis Penrice, whose will 1758, names her.

Excursus, Wood:

Sutton, Deborah, (d of George & Rebecka) m William Wood May 8, 1718, by Dr Urmstone, of the Church of England. Issue: 1 Richard, b Oct 30, 1720—2 Sarah, b Oct 25, 1721—died Mch 21, 1722/3—3 William, b Sept 3, 1723—4 George, b Sept 2, 1724—5 Deborah, b Mar 25, 1726—6 Rebecca, b June 3, 1727—7 Elizabeth, b Dec 18, 1728. Deborah wife of William Wood, died Dec 18, 1728. Sarah Wood died, Mch 17, 1722/3. (Berkeley Par Reg, Perq Co.)

Wood, Richard, (s of William, & Deborah) m Hannah Lowry, 19, 10mo 1746, issue: 1 Tamer, b 21, 9mo 1747—2 Winnefred, b 29, 3 mo 1749—3 William (2), b 12, 11mo 1750—4 Roda, b 23, 1mo 1753—5 Benjamin, b 16, 4mo 1756—6 Samuel, b 29, 11mo 1758—7 Rachel, b 3, 1mo 1761. Samuel Wood, died 13, 11mo 1782.

Wood, William (2) m Mary ——— issue: 1 Deborah, b 25, 1mo 1764—2 Rebeckah, b 29, 5mo 1765—3 William, b 4, 10mo 1766.

Wood, Richard, m 2d Sarah Morris, (d of John of Pasq Co) at Simons Creek Mo Meeting, 20, 8mo 1764. (Suttons Creek Mo Meeting, Perq.)

This Wood family lived in, & around Woodville, & it is thought the place derived its name from this line of Woods. Another line of Woods, came to the county much later than this date, & made their home near Hertford. Edward & John Wood family who came to N. C. from Norfolk Co Va.

Deaths

Sutton, George (1), Dept this Life, April 12, 1669. (Father of Nath'l, & Joseph (1).

Sutton, Sarah, Dept this Life, March 20, 1677. (Mother of Nath'l, & Joseph (1).

Sutton, Nathaniel, Dept this Life, Dec 29, 1682. (Son of George, & Sarah.)

Sutton, Joseph, Sr, Dept this Life, Jan 17, 1695. (Son of George & Sarah.)

Sutton, George, Dept this Life, April 7, 1700.

Sutton, John, (s of Joseph, & Benet) died Feby 16, 1707/8.

Sutton, Bennett, (d of Joseph, & Benet) died Nov 8, 1711.

Sutton, Christopher, died Nov 27, 1711.

Sutton, Joseph, Jr, died Jany 18, 1723/4.

Sutton, Nathaniel Sr, died Feby 3, 1724/5.

Sutton, Mary, (wife of Samuel), died May 7, 1754.

SWANN

William Swann was grt 1200a in James City Co Va, Nov 5, 1635, for trans 24 persons, some of whom were Richard Jones, John Swann, Nicholas Stallings, Nicholas Foster, Edward Champion, & Richard Perry. This grant was reissued to Thomas Swann, by Sir John Harvey.

Thomas Swann had land grant, Mar 1, 1638, 1200a (as above) on South side of James River, "to half way Neck." Another grt, May 9, 1638, on South side of the James, "at a place called Swanns Bay." He was a member of the House of Burgesses, from James City Co, (Surry) 1645-49, and from Surry Co, 1657-58. In Council 1660-80; d Sept 16, 1680. His home was on Swanns Point, Surry Co Va, & the English sent to suppress Bacons Rebellion, met at his house. He married five times, Miss Codd being his first wife, by whom he had, 1st Samuel, b May 11, 1653, who moved to Perq Co, N. C.

Maj Samuel Swann, "Eldest son of Thomas Swann Esq, of Southwarke pish, dec'd, for £30 pd by Mary Swann Widow of afsd" sold 300a in Surry Co, upon Grays Creek, "part of a grt unto my dec'd father, for 1930a, Oct 4, 1645." Seal Feb 25, 168½. Sarah Swann Ack' sd Deed, Mar 7, 168½. (Surry Co records.)

Sarah Swann, wife of Maj Samuel, (by letter) apt' Capt Thomas Swann of James City Co, her Att' to recover "goods, Chattels, & money due my sd husband." April 30, 1694. Test' Will Foster, Will Gray, Roger Williams. (Surry Co records.)

Samuel Swann "Sone and heir of Thomas," for £75 s4 pd by John Tuke of Surry Co, sold "All Right in Est of my father, the late Capt Thomas Swann," and apt' Maj Arthur Allen Att' Feb 8, 1704. (Surry Co records.)

Samuel Swann "of N. C. gent; sold to Joseph John Jackman of Surry Co Vir" for £450, land called Swanns Point, 1650a, was 300a grt by sd Samuel, by deed, to Mary Swann Relict of Thomas, which was grt sd Thomas "his father" by patent, Feb 15, 1645, in Southwarke Parish, on South side of the

RECORDS OF DEEDS 419

James River. Mar 4 1706. Elizabeth wife of Samuel Ack' her Dower right. (Samuel Swanns 2d wife née Lillington.)

Samuel Swann proved rights for 13 persons, in Perq precinct 1694, & received for importing them 640a of land; himself, wife Sarah (d of Wm Drummond) & sons: William, Samuel, Sampson, Henry, & Thomas, Elizabeth Hunt, & 5 negroes.

He was grt by John Archdale 450a in Pasq Co, Feb 26, 1696, "at the mouth of Newbegun Creek," which he conveyed to said Archdale, the next day.

On Oct 29, 1702 Samuel Swann Esq, was grt 850a, "in ye prect of perquimons, adj Mr Thomas Durant, and Roan Oak Sound, Northerly on Batemans Creek, & Easterly on lands of Geo Katchmaide (now in poss' of Mr Jno Hawkins) being part of 3333a grt by Sir Wm Berkley, late Gov of Vir, to sd Katchmaide, late of the precinct of Perq dec'd." April 1, 1663.

Hon'ble Maj Samuel Swann Sec of State. (At a Gen'l Court in Perq pre't 1700.) The ages of his first children, can not be found in Perq. His wife Sarah, died April 18, 1696. Samuel Swann (1) m 2d Elizabeth née Lillington (d of Alex & wife Sarah née James) widow of John Fendall. (See deeds, for mar contract.) Issue: 1 Elizabeth, b June 26, 1698—2 Sarah, b Dec 29 ——.

Maj Samuel Swann d 7 ber 14, 1707. (Berkeley Par Reg, Perq Co.)

Samuel (1) Swann, m Elizabeth Fendall (widow) before Oct 10, 1698.

John Fendall late of this County, died Dec 20, 1695, at Capt Walkers house. (Capt Henderson Walker, one time Gov of Albemarle m Ann Lillington, sister of Elizabeth, 2d wife of Samuel Swann.)

For the will of Maj Samuel Swann, see Grimes N. C. Wills, p 368, which was p April 20, 1708. He bequeathed to s William "a Bible, & seal ring," to sons: Sampson, Henry, & Thomas, "land between Muddy Creek, & Marshy Gutt" sons: Samuel, & John, dau's Elizabeth, & Sarah; wife Elizabeth.

Henry Swann of Perq, Merchant: apt' Mr William, & Thomas Swann his Att' Sept 21 1709.

Thomas Swann of Pasq Co, conveyed 127a in sd Co, "to his cousin Wm Drummond of Vir, to him & his heirs forever" Oct 18, 1726. (Pasq County Records.)

Samuel Swann of Perq was dec'd 1704. Mary widow & Admix. (Col Rec Vol I.) This could not be Maj Samuel's son, as he names a son Samuel in his will, 1708. If the Samuel who died 1704, left any issue, there is no record of it in Perq.

(3) Samuel (s of Maj Samuel & Sarah née Drummond) m Mary —— (Widow Vail) issue: Mary, b Mch 5, 1726/7, m Richard Clayton—2 Sarah, b Sept 3, 1729—3 Samuel, b Dec 8, 1731.

Samuel Swann (3) will Perq, p April 1753, names his dau Mary "wife of Richard Clayton," to whom he left "land on the Sound side," other dau's Sarah, Ann, Elizabeth, Martha, Jane, Margaret. Exrs John, & Jeremiah Vail (brothers). Test' Susannah Vail, William Woolard.

Thomas Swann (s of Maj Samuel & Sarah Drummond) lived in Pasq Co, where his will was p Aug 9, 1733. Sons: Samuel, & William. He made bequest to Dau's Rebecca, & Elizabeth, "land at Moyock, in Currituck Co," wife Elizabeth.

John & Thomas Swann moved to Hyde County, where their descendants are now living. The county seat of Hyde, Swan Quarter, was probably named for this branch of the family.

(3) Samuel Swann, was Speaker of the Assembly in 1715. Samuel Swann Gent, was sworn in by George Nichols, Att' Gen'l, for the Counties of Currituck, Pasquotank, Perquimans, & Chowan, Oct 3, 1752.

Samuel Swann, & son John were Exrs of the will of Thomas Snowden, p in Perq Oct 1736.

One of Maj Samuel Swanns dau's m John Baptista Ashe, another m Frederick Jones, of Chowan County, Chief Justice of N. C. 1720.

Major Samuel Swanns record in Perq, is without a blemish. The family adhered faithfully to the faith of their fathers, & Samuel Swann was instrumental in establishing a Church according to his belief, the Church of England, believed to be "old Nags Head Chapel" which has long since disappeared. This Chapel, not far from his home, was still unfinished at his death, but it served the people of "Durants Neck" for many generations, finally falling into decay, it was turned over to the Methodist congregation, and it is said the present New Hope Church rests upon the old foundations of Nags Head Chapel. This Methodist Church, is the oldest in the county, so it seems. Here *New Hope* took root upon "old hope" buried in the past.

At the present time there is not a living representative of this influential family in Perq, the last to be found, being Samuel, who was dec'd June 13, 1771, without heirs. Like so many other families, once numerous in our county, they have drifted away, & only the records are a reminder that they at one time wielded a strong hand in the public affairs of this section.

The New Hanover Land Grants, in N. C. show that Samuel Swann, was grt 320a in said county, on East side of the road, from Wilmington, to Brunswick, below his line, Feb 23, 1754, and 300a on same day, same runnings, and 200a on Long Creek, all same date. Thus we see the Swann family continued to migrate ever southward. The Counties of Hyde, Beaufort, & New Hanover, would probably yield valuable information, about this splendid family.

TOMS

After much careful work on this family, in N. C. and Virginia, the writer has arrived at the conclusion, that the Toms emigrant, to N. C., was living in Charles City Co Va, where he sold land in sd County, to Francis Gray, Feb 17, 1656. Only mention of him, so far found, but that is not strange, considering the fact, that nothing remains of the records in that Co, except one book. Gabriel Toms appears on the records in Essex Co Va, but no connection between the two, can be made. However, there may have been, some relationship. It is thought, but not proven, that the Francis who settled in Perq, is the identical one, who is named in sd record, as the dates would bear me out, in that opinion. From Edmundson's Journal, we are led to believe, that he did not embrace Quakerism, until the time of Edmundson's first journey to N. C. 1672. At which time, he & his wife, Mary (d of John Nicholson, sister of William) went over to the new cult. Mary being his 3d wife, by whom he had no issue. Her will p in Perq, 1717, does not name a single one of his children. She was probably a widow before m Francis Toms, as she names in her will, Vesty Lewis, who was wife of Edward Lewis, & probably her daughter.

Francis Toms, m before coming to Perq, Pershillah ———— by whom he had issue: Penelope, b Jan 27, 1670—Francis (2), b Sept 19, 1672—Pershillah, b Mch 19, 1674/5—Joseph, b Nov 16, 1677, died June 6, 1679—Caleb, & Joshua (twins), b Nov 25, 1679.

Toms, Francis, m 2d Abigail Lury (widow of John) Jan 6, 1683, by whom one d Abigail, b Dec 10, 1684. Abigail Toms, Wife of Francis, died Mar 17, 1687.†

Toms, Francis, m 3d Mary Nicholson, who survived him.

Toms, Francis Sr, lived near "Lower Pond, on Reedy Branch, at the head of Vosses Creek." His land adj John Flowers, on western side of "Long Reach" in the "Narrows" of Perq River. The land on Vosses Creek, where his dwelling was erected, adj William Morgan. He had a stretch of land, running from Vosses Creek, to "Middle Swamp" called "Frog Hall." This place still retains its original name, to this day. Francis Toms Jr owned land on S. W. side of Perq River, on "Bull Branch, adj land sold to Henry Grace, June 24, 1714. His land also joined land of William Jones. Francis Toms Sr, made a deed of gift, to Thomas Pierce, Wm Bogue, Isaac Wilson, & Gabriel Newby, 1a of land, "for the Society of Protestant Desenters, Vulgarly called Quakers, whereon a Church is now built," in Perq Precinct, 11mo called Jan, 1705/6. This house of Worship, is supposed to have been Vosses Creek Meeting house, on said Creek, the *exact location*, being lost and uncertain. He was a member of the Council, for many years (see deeds). Clerk of Pasq Precinct Aug 8, 1692 (see will of John Nixon). Dept' to Lord Amey, & his name appears on many grants given by the Lords Pro'r. His oath before the Gov Council, is of interest, to all historians, in its quaint wording, he promised "to Keepe ye Secrett of ye Council, to ye best of my advice, according to my Understanding." This oath was administered in 1706. He had been a member of the Council, since Feb 6, 1683/4. Francis Toms "Collector of Customs" (no date).

On 15, 7mo 1696, he left Perq, on a two months journey (probably to London) but his business is not stated, maybe in the interests of the Quaker Church. Before leaving, he deputized "Wm Glover, his Lov' Friend, to get timber for a big Mill, or a little one, & left it wholely to him, which thee thinks most benificall for me." This was probably the beginning of Toms Mill, on Suttons Creek, in fact if his land ran to Middle Swamp, as before stated, & sd place was called even then, "Frog Hall" we are certain the "Mill" here mentioned, was built on this property. He made a deed, Feb 9, 1688, with consent of wife Abigail, for 300a at the head of Yeopim Creek, "called John Lasy's Plan'," land pat by Wm Charles, June 6, 1683. Another deed Jan 5, 1689/90, with the signature of his last wife Mary. In a deed Mar 24, 1687, he gives the information, that he had been grt 587a in Perq Precinct. (See deeds.)

The Hon'ble Francis Toms, had a grt, in Perq Pr'ct, 640a, adj Capt Ralph Fletcher, & James Morgan, to corner of Wm Voss, & along his line to the River (Perquimans). May 1, 1695. Francis Toms Esq, another grt, in Perq

---

†Note: John Lacey (Lurey) 2d husband of Abigail Balie, in his Will Perq Precinct, Dec 1, 1682, names wife Abigail, & d Sarah. This may be the same Sarah, for whom Foster Toms put in a claim, for her Estate, in 1754. It is thought she m Christopher Denman, but no absolute *proof* is forthcoming.

Pre'ct 375a on North side of Perq River, by beaver dam Swamp. Feb 26, 1696.

Toms, Francis Sr, will Perq, 6, 10mo 1709. Names wife Mary, sons: Francis, Joshua, d Mary Newby (wife of Gabriel) gr-son Francis Newby, father-in-law

John Nicholson, makes bequest to "d Priscilla Kinsey," late wife of John Nicholson.*

Priscilla Toms, had previously m John Nicholson, by whom she had, the children named in their father-in-laws will. He is named in Francis Toms will, also. (See Francis Toms will, & deeds in Perq Co.)

Mary Toms, will p Jan 15, 1717/18, made bequest to Vesty Lewis, & Rachel Laurence, & Elizabeth (d of my brother Wm Nicholson) Joseph Glaister (a Quaker preacher), & wife Mary were made Exrs.

Toms, (2) Francis Jr, (s of Francis & Pershillah) m Margaret Lawrence (widow of Wm, née Bogue) June 8, 1696, "at a meeting at said Lawrence's house," issue: 1 Mary, b 20 —— 1696/7—2 Elizabeth, b Nov 20, 169-- —3 Penelope, b Nov 19, 1702—4 Margaret, b Dec 5, 1707. (Wm Lawrence 1st husband of Margaret Bogue, died Aug 13, 1694.) Francis Toms Jr died 2, 7mo 1729.

Toms, Francis, will Perq p Oct 6, 1729, names: son Francis (3) d Mary Newby, & her husband, Nathan Newby, gr-son Francis Newby, d Elizabeth Phelps, d Priscilla Jones, d Margaret Toms, d Pleasant Winslow, wife Rebecca.

Rebecca, 2d wife of Francis Toms Jr, is thought to be d of Mary Simmons, whose will was p 1724, but no absolute proof exists. She was a d of John Pierce, & wife Mary Scott (d of Joseph) b Aug 9, 1680. (Mary Pierce, m 2d Wm Bundy, 3d Nicholas Simmons.) Rebecca 2d wife of Francis Toms, must have been mother of his son Francis (3), & d Pleasant, who m Joseph (2) Winslow s of Thomas (1) & wife Elizabeth Clare. The age of neither of these two can be found in Berkeley Parish Reg, Perq Co, where the others are recorded.

Toms, Francis (3), m Rebecca Nixon (d of Zachariah, & wife Elizabeth Symons, who lived at that time in Pasq Co, at Nixonton). (See Pasq Co Deeds.)

Toms, Francis, & Rebecca (Nixon) had issue: 1 Zachariah, b Apl 10, 1741—2 Rebecca, b Sept 26, 1743—m Caleb White, of Thomas, & Rachel (Jordan)—3 Mary, b Jany 8, 1745/6—4 Caleb, b Feby 3, 1747/8—5 Elizabeth, b May 25, 1750, m Samuel Phelps, & 2d Zachariah Nixon (2) her cousin.

(3) Toms, Francis, (3) will Perq, p July 1771. Sons: Zachariah, Caleb, dau's Rebecca White, Elizabeth Toms, son-in-law Jos McAdams, & Caleb White.

(4) Toms, Zachariah (1), will Perq, p April 1774, names wife Margaret, sons: Francis, William, dau's Rebecca, & Margaret Tow, bro-in-law Joseph, & Caleb White.

(2) Toms, Joshua, (1) (s of Francis, & Pershillah) m Sarah Gosby (d of John, & Hannah, née Nicholson) b Nov 12, 1687. (See Berkeley Par Reg.) Issue: 1 Sarah, b Mch 5, 1703/4—2 Hannah, b June 6, 1706, m Ezekiel Maudlin (2). Joshua Toms m 2d Rebecca Sutton (widow of Joseph, who was dec'd 1724, née Jones, d of Peter Jones Sr, will 1752). She m 1st Joseph Sutton, 2d

---

*Note: John Kinse (s of John, & Catherine) was b 6, 10mo 1692, in Nansemond Co Va. He m in Perq Co N. C. Pershillah Toms, (d of Francis Sr, & wife Pershillah). John Kinseys will, Perq April 14, 1717, names d Elizabeth, dau-in-law Mary Nicholson, son-in-law Samuel Nicholson, wife Preshillah.

Joshua Toms, & 3d 1737 Charles Denman, Clerk of Perq. Joshua Toms had by Rebecca one d Sarah, b July 4, 1727.

(2) Toms, Joshua, Will Perq, p April 1732, names son, Foster, dau's Sarah, Hannah Maudlin, & Miriam Sutton, son-in-law Christopher Sutton, gr-sons William, & Joshua Sherro (Sherwood). Wife Rebeckah. (Clerk of Court Charles Denman.) The two Sherro children, are thought to be step-gr-children, as Rebecca had a sister, who m Sherwood. (See divisions.)

(5) Toms, Foster, (1) made pet' to the court, Oct 1754, for Est of Sarah Toms, "out of the hands of Charles Moor, Admix of Christopher Denman dec'd."

(5) Toms, Foster, will Perq, p April 1, 1779, Sons: Joshua, John, Gosby, & Foster (2), d Martha.

(5) Toms, Martha, will Perq, p Feby 1794, names sons: John, & Foster, gr-son John (s of Joshua) gr-son Francis Newby (s of Francis) gr-son Zachariah (s of Gosby) gr-son Joshua (s of Gosby). Test' Zachariah Nixon.

(6) Toms, Foster, (2) will Perq, p May 1794. Sons: Joseph, & Samuel, wife Elizabeth. Brothers, John, & Gosby, cousins: Francis Newby, and John Toms Jr.

(7) Toms, John, will Perq, p Nov 1808, names wife Mary, sons: Benjamin, Anderson & John A. Toms, gr-son John White, d Miriam White and her husband Francis, s Foster, dau's Sarah, & Mary.

Francis Toms (2) had land grt him Nov 25, 1714, 200a—which he sold, July 12, 1726, to Thomas Winslow.

Toms, Zachariah (1) s of Francis (3), m Margaret White, (d of William, & Margaret). See his will 1774.

Toms, Zachariah, deed to s Caleb, with consent of wife Margaret. 1775.

Toms, Margaret, made a deed to son Francis, a negro, ——— 29, 1775. The same to dau's Rebecca, & Elizabeth, April 29, 1775. Elizabeth Toms, (d of Zachariah, & Margaret, m ——— Tow).

Toms, Foster, & wife Mary, were Admix of Malachi Jones, (who died without issue) July 1777. Malachi Jones in his will, names niece Mary Jones (d of Thomas).

Toms, Foster, (s of John, & Mary) died 14, 12, 1807. He had no issue. Names in his will, p 1808, Brother Benjamin, sister Nancy Toms, cousin Foster Nixon, and sisters Miriam White (wife of Francis) Martha Nixon, & Sarah Elliott, Exrs brothers: John A. & Anderson Toms. It seems clear that John Toms, father of Foster (above) m Mary Anderson, d of John Anderson. John Anderson, will p in Perq, 1808, names d Mary Toms, & her sons Anderson & John A. Toms.

Toms, Anderson, (s of John dec'd) m Mary Bagley (d of Nathan) "at Suttons Creek Perq Co" 15, 12, 1808. Nathan Bagley in his will, Perq Co, 9, 11mo 1815, names d Mary Toms, & gr-children Mary, & Foster Toms, son-in-law Anderson Toms.

Toms, John Anderson, m Phariby Bagley, (d of Nathan, of Perq) "at Suttons Creek 1, 12mo 1805, issue: 7 Mary, b 24, 11mo 1806—2 Foster, b 5, 3mo 1809.

Toms, Benjamin, (s of John) m Martha Wilson (d of Christopher, & Pheribe) of Perq, "at Suttons Creek" 16, 9mo 1813. He seems to have died intestate. Christopher Willson, will Perq, p Feby 1824, names d Martha Toms, son-in-law Benjamin Toms, wife Pheribe.

Toms, Foster, (1) will 1779, m Martha ——— who for some reason is not named in his will, but she survived him, making a will, which was p 1794.

(Her will already given.) Heirs of Martha Toms dec'd Jan 3, 1798. (Division.) Orphans of Gosby Toms dec'd, John Clary, (in right of his wife Penelope) Samuel Nixon, (wifes part) Jesse Copeland, part—Henry Copeland (.....part) Isaac Barber, (wifes part) Willis Newby part, Nathan Newby part, Francis, Leah, Zach'ry, & Joshua Toms prt, Mary Clary part. (Auditors account.)

Another Audit, Aug 4, 1797, gives to John Toms Sr £58 s14, Foster Toms, Representatives, (same) Francis Newby Jr, (same).

Toms, Leah, account with her Gar, John Clary. Jan 27, 1805.

Toms, Mary (d of Benjamin, & Martha (Wilson) Toms) is buried in the Episcopal Cemetery, in Hertford. She died Sept 1855, age 25 years and 6 months.

Toms, Joshua, (s of Foster, & Martha) m Millicent Newby, —, 8mo 1779. (Welles.)

Toms, Benjamin, in a deed, names d Phereby Blount.

Toms, Zachariah, in a deed to Zach Nixon, 13, 11mo 1804, conveyed "all my part of a Grist Mill, on Suttons Creek, called Toms Mill." In another deed, to Joshua Toms, 14, 5mo 1805, he sold land, "formerly belonging to our father Gosby Toms dec'd."

Toms, Margaret, m Thomas Jones, 5, mo 1775.

TUCKER

John Tucker (spelled variously, Tougart, Tourcart) came to England with William the Conqueror, and fought at Hastings 1066. He was granted Armes by same 1079, and was given an Estate, in South Tavistock, Co Devon, and married relict of Trecareth, who is thought to be the former incumbent of said Estate. His son Stephen was granted permission 1150, to wear his hat in the Kings presence, & also an Estate of Samerton, near Travitock, in Pembroke Co, Wales, which the Tuckers have held for over 400 years (the Sealyham property) and have used the same coat of Arms.

George Tucker, m Maria Hunter of Gaunnte, was a man of note in Milton, next Gravesend, during the reign of Queen Elizabeth, who conveyed to him the "Manor" 1572. He was appointed Jurat July 22, 1562, by said Queen, & Henry Tucker of Bermuda, was Jurat 1639, & Mayor of Gravesend & Milton 1637. They were brothers, and soon after this disappeared from England, and the tradition is generally accepted they they emigrated to America.

Daniel Tucker was a subject in the Colony, at Jamestown 1609. (Brown Gen to America.)

Capt William Tucker was among the living "Att Elizabeth Cittye" Feb 16, 1623. He received a grt of 650a "on East side of the main River, agst Elizabeth Cittie," and 150a at Newport News, 1626, in the Corporation of Henrico. (Land Office, Richmond Va.) He was deputized to go against the rebellious Nansemond & Warrasquicke Indians 1623/4, and served as Burgess from said Co, 1624. John Tucker had a grant for land, Oct 28, 1697, 65a on N. E. side of Western Branch, Nansemond Co, and was living in Lower Norfolk Co Va, Oct 5, 1683, at which time he made a deed unto Capt Wm Robinson, 200a of land which sd Robinson bequeathed in his will, Mar 5, 1695, to Wm Thorogood of Princess Anne Co, who sold sd land to Col Edward Moseley, of same

Co, & he in like manner sold land to Nath'l Tatum of Norfolk Co, Nov 26, 1715, "land on Elizabeth River, at the head of Western Branch, of Indian Creek." The Tuckers settled at a place called "Tucker Town."

Robert Tucker of Weymouth, about 1635 emigrated to Milton Mass, 1662, m Elizabeth Allen, b 1604, d 1682, son Monrasch Tucker, m Waitstill Sumner, b 1654, d 1743, issue Samuel, m Rebecca Leeds, b Milton Mass 1687, d 1758, had son Samuel, m Elizabeth Haywood, b 1719, d 1776, who had son Nathaniel, b 1769.

Mr Robert Tucker of Lower Norfolk Co Va dec'd, Mar 1723. Frances Tucker Admix. "Merchandise belonging to sd Tucker, West India goods, in ye Stores, & Come now in ye Brigantine 'Providence' valued at £450-9-9, in the hands of Mrs Frances Tucker." Three children of sd Tucker, not named.

William Tucker of Norfolk Co, with consent of wife Elinor sold to Richard Tucker his plan' on Deep Creek, "as by a deed from ——— Browne" Nov 13, 1703.

John Tucker, of the Borough of Norfolk, will p Sept 17, 1762. Son: "Henry, negroes, & blacksmith Tools, & £300 in Cash, including money belonging to him from Mr Gristocks Estate, and the Sloop Rebecca, dau Frances Calvert, negroes, & £100 Cash, Son Travis house, & Lott where I now live, son Jno. the land & houses, that was the Glebe, dau Jane £200 Cash, dau Rebecca, & Elizabeth, £100 Cash each, wife Rebecca. My brig 'Three Brothers' to be sold, & money put to Interest, with good security, to be applied to the bringing up & Schooling of my four youngest children, Elizabeth, Travis, Jane, & Jno Tucker. My Sloop Hannah to be hired to the County, & money applied as before." (Norfolk County Records.)

John Hutchings Jr, Christopher Perkins, Edward C. Travis, & Henry Tucker Exrs.

Walter Tucker of Lynn Regis, Dorsett, Mer'cht, Power of Att' to Mr Samuel Tucker of Bristol, to recover Estate of his "cozen John Edwards in Va." Sept 24, 1664. (Isle of Wight Records.) (Samuel Tucker same date, of Ratcliff.) (Isle of Wight Co Va.)

Robert Tucker of the Co of Albemarle, Pro' of N. C., "with consent of my wife Mary," sold to Nath'l Ludgell of Norfolk Co, 150a, part of 300a, for 2000 lbs of Tob. Oct 14, 1704.

Robert Tucker of Norfolk Co, Merchant, att' for John Tucker d. s. p. of Martin Brandon, Prince George Co Va, Aug 18, 1716.

Thomas Parrame in his will, Prince George Co Va, names dau Elizabeth Tucker, and wife Elizabeth. (Court at Merchants Hope.)

Francis Tucker, will Prince George Co Va, Dec 12, 1722. Sons: Francis, John, Henry, Abram, & Mathew, wife Mary. He was dead Jan 13, 1723.

Robert Tucker, m Elizabeth Cleeves in Princess Anne Co, Aug 29, 1750.

Nathaniel Tucker, made his will in Onslow Co N. C. Jan 7, 1750, and names brother Henry Tucker.

John Tucker was living in Perq Precinct 1701.

WHITE

Thomas White was a subject in the colony at Jamestown, 1609. (Browns Genesis to America.)

James White in Va same date, at same place. Henry White of York Co Va, had a son Henry, who moved to Isle of Wight. From the dates it seems probable that this was the identical Henry White who migrated to Perq Precinct N. C., before 1670. He built the first Quaker Church in Perquimans, thought to be Little River Mo meeting, which was about where Woodville is situated. Just beyond the confines of this village can be seen at the present time an old Quaker burying ground, with small stones such as were in common use at that day among the simple Quakers. Meetings were held at the house of Henry White, 26, 4mo 1690, at which time, James Davis (s of William) and Elizabeth White (d of Henry) of Albemarle, took each other as man and wife. Another Quarterly meeting convened at the house of Henry White, 1, 3mo 1695, when it was "agreed that Robert Wilson, Francis Toms, & Henry White, doe write a letter in behalf of the Meeting, to friends at yearly meeting in London." At a meeting held at the house of Arnold White, 24, 4mo 1679, there were present: Henry White, Timothy Meade, Francis Toms, Charles Moris, Jonathan Tailer, Arnold White, George Tailer, Mary White, Rebecka Simons, Solomon Pool, & Margaret White. The children of Solomon Pool were registered at this meeting, as follows: Richard, b 2, 3mo 1680—Ane, b 12, 2mo 1682—Mary, b 15, 10mo 1683—Solomon (2) b 23, 4mo 1687.

As Arnold appears in Perq simultaneously with Henry White, the inference may be drawn with some certainty, that they were brothers, but the records do not mention the fact. John and William White also made their entry into Perquimans about the same time, and they may also be brothers.

White, Henry, children as recorded in the Quaker Reg, of Perq Co, are as follows: 1 Ann, b 5, 10mo 1669—2 Elizabeth, b 29, 10mo 1673—3 Robert, b 2, 11mo 1674—4 James, & John (twins), b 20, 5mo 1676—5 Elkanah, b 2mo 1679—6 Mary, b middle of 8mo 1682—Damaris, b —, 12mo 1684—8 Constant —— —9 Henry (2), b 25, 4mo 1690—10 Arnold, b end of 7mo 1693—11 Mary (2d by name), b —, 7mo 1696—12 Jonas, b 24, 4mo 1700—13 Sarah, b middle of 4mo 1704. His wife was Mary, who died 3, 3mo 1679, and mother of his first five children. His second wife is not given.

The will of Henry White, p in Albemarle, Sept 19, 1706, names the following issue: Henry, Arnold, Isaac, Robert, & John, to whom he devised his "Maner plantation," dau's: Content and Naomy. (No wife is mentioned.) Henry White bought land in Surry Co Va, June 9, 1655 (Surry records). He made an affidavit in Perq Co, 1689, giving his age as 57 years. (Gen'l Court, May 26, 1689.)

White, Arnold Sr, issue: 1 Philliman, b 10, 10mo 1670—2 Arnold, b 29, 4mo 1673—3 Paul, b 20, 1mo 1676. Mary White, wife of Arnold, died —, 1mo 1679.

White, Arnold Jr, (s of Arnold Sr) issue: 1 Paul, b 6, 8mo 1697—2 Ann, b 1, 1mo 1699—3 Joshua, b 28, 12mo 1702—4 Nehemiah, b 25, 12mo 1712—5 Pathenea, b 6, 10mo 1717. Mary wife of Arnold, died 23, 1mo 1680. He m 2d Phereby Nixon, 1, 9mo 1696.

White, John (s of Henry) m Elizabeth Newby (d of John) issue: 1 Abraham, b 3, 12mo 1700—2 Sarah, b —, 11mo 1703—3 Rachel, b —— 1705—4 Jonas, b —, 11mo 1707—5 Elirabe, b —, 1mo 1711—6 John, b —, 11mo 1713—7 Rebecca, b —, 5mo 1716.

White, Arnold, will Perq, Mar 22, 1690. Names d Elizabeth, s Arnold, brother Henry, wife not named.

Marriages

White, John (s of Henry of Little River) m Elizabeth Newby (d of John, & dau-in-law of Matthew Collins of same) 14, 11mo 1696, "at the house of James Davis."

White, Arnold, m Rebeccah Overman, In, at Newbegun Creek, 18, 5mo 1717.
White, Arnold Sr, m Jane Pike (widow, of Pasq precinct) 9, 4mo 1720.
White, Jonathan (s of Robert), m Ann Pike (d of Samuel) 10, 2mo 1729.
White, Abraham, m Sarah Keaton, In, at Newbegun Creek, 9, 9mo 1723.
White, Henry, m Ruth Keaton, In, at Newbegun Creek, 4, 3mo 1727.
White, Nehemiah, m Hannah Overman, at Newbegun Creek, 3, 3mo 1732.
White, Nehemiah, m 2d Martha Pritchard, in, 7, 3mo 1734.
White, Joseph, m Sarah Newby, In, 4, 4mo 1736, at Symons Creek.
White, John, m Susannah Hill, In, 6, 9mo 1746, at Symons Creek.
White, Benjamin, m Miriam Pike, In, 3, 9mo 1761, at Symons Creek.

White, William, was a passenger for Va, in Primrose July 27, 1625, Comd of Capt Douglas. William, and John who came to Perquimans about the same date of Henry's arrival, may have been his brothers. They quickly disappear from the records in Perq. John m Margaret Titerton (widow of William, née Hall), Jan 18, 1685. John *Waite* died Jan 14, 1691. According to his will p in Perq, Apl 4, 1692, he left no heirs. The legatees in said will being wife Margaret, William & Elizabeth Tetterton (Step-children).

White, William, m Margery Williams, *Septemb* 1693. He had by a former wife Rebecka, issue: 1 Sarah, b Oct 13, 1681—2 Thomas, b Nov 17, 1684—3 Samuel, b Dec 2, 1687. William White died Jan 14, 1687. Margery his wife, d Oct 14, 1704.

White, Thomas (probably a brother of John, & William) m Diana Foster née Maners, widow of Wm Foster, m 1675 d Oct 9, 1687. She had by first husband Francis & Elizabeth Foster, named in his will—Oct 9, 1687. Diana White m 3 times, 1st Thomas Harris, Clerk of Perq, 2d William Foster, & 3rd Thomas White. Perq Court was held in the house of Thomas Harris, and after his death, 1679, at the house of Diana Harris, Sept 1679, and still later, at the house of Thomas White, presumably the same house each time. Thomas White in his will Mar 11, 1695, names wife Diana, and William Collins, who it is thought m Elizabeth Harris, d of Diana by her 1st husband.

White, Robert, (s of Henry) will Albemarle, April 19, 1698. Sons: Vincent, Robert, d Mary, friend Thomas Jones. Robert (2) lived in Pasq Co, where his will was p April 16, 1733, Sons: Jonathan, Zapaniah, Joseph, dau's: Ann, Elizabeth.

White, Nehemiah, (s of Arnold Jr) will Pasq Co, p July 1751. Sons: Benjamin, Joshua, dau's: Sarah, Mary, Martha, wife Martha. Joseph Pritchard (bro-in-law) Ex.

White, John, (s of Henry (1) m Sarah Clare (d of Timothy, & wife Mary Bundy). He died before Mar 10, 1730, will p on that date, names son John, and dau's Rachel, Sarah, Elizabeth, Hulde, sister Mary, wife Sarah, who m 2d Jacob Elliott. She was John Whites 2d wife, he having m 1st Elizabeth Newby.

White, Jean, Relict of Roger White, m 2d John Wilkinson, Jan 9, 1686. (Berkeley Reg.)

Henry White made affidavit in Perq 1689, that he "knew Samuel Davis in Isle of Wight Co Va", "where he was an apprentice of Henry White his father" before 1660, said Samuel also migrating to N. C.

White, Edmund, m Millicent Toms, In, 3mo 1788, at Welles meeting house, in Perq. It is not positively known *which branch* of Whites he belongs to. He certainly had one son Edmund (s of Edmund, & Mary dec'd) of Pasq Co, m Margaret Nixon (s of Samuel, & Rachel dec'd of Perq) 15, 5mo 1816, at Suttons Creek meeting house. Margaret wife of Edmond died 14, 11mo 1827.

White, Samuel, will Perq Co p April 1779, names sons: Gabriel, Joshua, William, Benjamin, & Arnold, wife Hepsibee. Henry White, & Levi Munden Exrs.

White, Gabriel, will Perq, p Nov 1824, names wife Abselah, s Andrew Knox White, d Juliana R. White, Sarah, & Martha Ann White. Samuel Nixon Ex.

White, John, (of the Thomas White line) m Mourning ———— issue: 1 Robert, m Rebeckah Albertson (d of Francis dec'd, & wife Caroline) 16, 9mo 1819 at Suttons Creek, issue: 1 Jordan, b 8, 9mo 1821, d 21, 6mo 1822—2 Elizabeth, b 18, 8mo 1823—3 Lucinda, b 19, 2mo 1826—4 William Albertson White, b 15, 2mo 1828.

WHITE

Thomas White Line

In Perquimans Co. there seems to have been two separate, & distinct, lines of this family, that of Henry White, and the descendants of Thomas, of Isle of Wight Co Va. Henry White pioneered to N. C. much earlier than the last named. It is thought, but not proven, that Thomas of Isle of Wight, was a descendant of John White, who came to Va, from New England, & took up land in Norfolk Co.

Elder John White, b 1596 in Essex Co England, arrived in New England, 1632, settled at Cambridge, Mass. John White (uncle of Peregrine, s of William, & Ann (Fuller) White) came to Norfolk Va, 1679, where he m Mary ———— & had John Nicholas, b in Norfolk 1689. John White, of the Southern Branch of Elizabeth River, Yeoman—apt' Anthony Bonford, of Chuckatuck, Nanzimund Co, planter—Att' to sell unto Paul Luke, of Isle of Wight, Land, Cattle, Household stuff, in sd Co, belonging to his wife Edy Lewellin, d of Thomas, formerly of said Co, for 300 lbs of Tob. Apl 23, 1664. (Records Isle of Wight Co.)

White, Thomas (s of John of Isle of Wight) m Rachel Jordan (d of Joshua, & Elizabeth (Sanbourne) Jordan) 13, 7mo 1719. (Elizabeth Sanborn, was d of Daniel, and wife Sarah.) (See the will of Daniel Sanborne Isle of Wight.)

White, Thomas, & wife Rachel (Jordan) had issue: 1 Lydia, b 12, 9mo 1720, m John Robinson—2 Elizabeth, b 19, 10mo 1722, m Joseph Pritchard—3 Joshua, b 26, 11mo 1727, m Guliemma Jordan—4 Jordan, b 20, 3mo 1729—5 Thomas, & Rachel (twins), b 25, 12mo 1730—5 Rachel White, m Benjamin Winslow, (s of John, & Esther (Snelling) Winslow)—6 John, b 17, 3mo 1733, m Mary (d of Joseph, & Pleasant (Toms) Winslow)—7 Mary, b 29, 2mo 1735, m Joseph Winslow (s of Joseph & wife Pleasant (Toms) Winslow)—8 Matthew, b 10, 3mo 1738, m Mary Robinson—9 Caleb, b 8, 3mo 1740, m Rebecca

A. Home of Grandfather Caleb White, near Woodville, N. C. Original home of Francis White, father of Caleb, Miles, Toms, John, Rebecca, Sarah, Martha and Mary White. The present descendants of Caleb White in Perquimans County are Emma H. White, Emma, Elbert, Clara, Margaret and Lucy.

B. Old Toms home on Sutton's Creek. Built on land patented by Hannah Gosby for her daughter Sarah, who married Joshua Toms. Gosby Toms was the last to live in this house, Little H. G. Winslow standing in the door.

C. Courthouse in Hertford. Built in 1824. A former courthouse in Hertford stood on "Phelps Point" and was built in 1722. What became of this structure is not known and if it was situated on this site is another point not definitely settled. Across the street from this courthouse stood ye old "Eagle Hotel," now demolished, where it is claimed General Washington once spent a night.

D. The old Albertson Place. Date of erection unknown. The house of Peter Albertson who owned land on Long Branch of Sutton's Creek. This house has been somewhat modernized, but the real lines unchanged. Situated on the highway between Hertford and Elizabeth City. Now owned and occupied by Mr. Kelly Miller.

Toms (d of Francis (3) & wife Rebecca Nixon, d of Zachariah Nixon, & wife Elizabeth Symons of Pasq Co.)   Rebecca White was b Jan 8, 1743.

White, Thomas, will Perq, book C p 1, p Jan 1762. He bequeathed, to wife Rachel, a negro called Judah, & a negro girl Priscilla, a mare, called "Pink" and a horse, called "Sorrel," 1 large looking glass, and 1 square table. Sons: Joshua, Thomas, Joseph, John, Matthew, Caleb, and Benjamin (not of age), dau's Mary Winslow, (to whom he left a "large looking glass") Sarah, gr-dau's Sarah, & Mary Pritchard.

White, Joshua, (eldest son of Thomas) will Perq, p Apl 25, 1784, names s Jacob, (to whom he left 125a of land, on both sides of Cypress Swamp) s Zachariah, s Joshua (Plan' where I now live) dau's Mourning, Mary, & Elizabeth, wife Mary. (His 2d wife probably) d Margaret Moore, & son-in-law Samuel Moore.

White, Zachariah, will Perq, p Nov 1808, names legatees. Wife Miriam, dau's Margaret, Mary Davis, s Joshua, dau's Miriam, Sarah, s Francis.

White, Jacob, s of Joshua (1) will Perq, p Nov 1816, named wife Miriam, sons: Josiah, Robinson, Theophilus, Joshua, dau's *Jemmimah* Guyer, & Polly White.

White, Joshua, (2) will Perq, p Feb 1831, names son James, wife Sallie, s Gabriel, s Theophilus.

White, Joshua, (3) will Perq, p Nov 1865, Wife Emily, son Joshua W. (Warren) White, Millicent Pearce, Charles Willis Pearce, Mary A. Winslow.

From this line sprang Dr White of Suffolk Va, who is a son of Joshua W. White, named in the last will. (See Jordan family, for Rachel Whites Will.)

White, Mourning, spoken of in the Henry White line, as wife of John White, & mother Robert, (who m Rebeccah Albertson,) may have been a d of Joshua (1) & wife Gulielma. The Whites, & Winslows, crossed so many times, it is difficult to distinguish, one from another. Robert (s of John) died 25, 6mo 1830. This seems all the more to be credited, from the fact that Robert, & Rebeccah had a son named Jordan White, b 8, 9mo 1821, died 21, 6mo 1822.

White, Joseph, (s of Joshua, & Rachel (Jordan) White) is mentioned in his will, but his age is not given. From the fact that five years intervened, between the date of Elizabeth, & Joshua Jordans ages, it is probable that he is the one between. Benjamin White also has no birth date, but we know from his fathers will, that he was the youngest child.

White, Thomas, (twin to Rachel) m Anne Barnes, May 11, 1755, issue: 1 Miles, b Apl 25, 1756—2 Nathan, b Nov 12, 1757—3 Seth, b Mch 1, 1759—4 Orpha, b Sept 25, 1761—Elizabeth, b Oct 27, 1763—Jonathan, b Mch 2, 1766—Miriam, b Oct 25, 1768—d. s. p. 1831. Ann White, wife of Thomas, died Nov 4, 1770.

White, Caleb (s of Thomas, & Rachel (Jordan) White) m Rebeckah Toms, Jan 14, 1761. Issue: 1 Peninah, b Dec 6, 1761—2 Francis, b Feby 24, 1764—3 Toms, b Mch 2, 1766—4 Caleb, b Oct 30, 1768—5 Rebeckah, b Sept 2, 1771—6 Mary, b Nov 12, 1773.

White, Caleb, will Perq, p May 1795, names sons: Francis, Toms, Caleb, James, Josiah, & Elisha, dau's Penina Pritchard, & Rebecca Albertson, Mary, & Betty White, wife Rebecca. Test' Wm Skinner, Caleb Winslow.

White, Francis, m Miriam Toms, 6, 1mo 1790, issue: 1 Toms (2) b 15, 12mo 1790—2 Miles, b 30, 8mo 1792—3 John, b 16, 3mo 1794, died 12, 10mo 1794—4

Caleb (2) b 12, 11mo 1796—5 Mary, b 12, 3mo 1799—6 John (2) b 17, 1mo 1801—7 Rebecca, b 4, 12mo 1802.

White, Francis, will Perq, p Nov 1813. Dau's Mary, Rebecca, Sarah, & Mustia, Sons: Caleb, Francis, Toms, Myles, John, brother Toms White Ex.

White, Miriam, will Perq, 4, 3mo 1831, names sister Elizabeth Griffin, niece Jemima White (d of Josiah, & wife Orpha Robinson dec'd) Martha Jesop (d of Jesse, & wife Sarah) Benj, Jemima, Thomas, Miriam White, Mary Morgan, Mary Jessop, (children of brother Nathan White) Pheribe Wilson, (d of William, & wife Sarah) Anna Nicholson, Rebecca Albertson, Jonathan White, Achsah Nixon, Margaret Wilson, (children of brother Jonathan White), Eliza Ann, & Watson White, (children of Timothy White dec'd) Martha Bogue, (d of Thomas dec'd), Piney Woods Mo Meeting $200. (Miriam d of Thomas, died single.)

White, Nathan, (s of Thomas) m Miriam Albertson, 6, 10mo 1785, at Welles Perq Co.

White, Thomas, (s of Thomas, & Rachel) will Perq, p Aug 1809. Sons: Nathan, Seth, & Jonathan, dau's Orpha Robinson, Elizabeth Griffin, & Miriam White.

White, Seth, will Perq, p Nov 1825—Brothers: Nathan, & Jonathan, sister Elizabeth Griffin, nieces; Sarah Jesop, & Jemima White.

White, Jonathan, m Rachel Winslow, b Nov 9, 1770 (d of Caleb, & Ann (Perry) Winslow, of Perq) issue: 1 Timothy, m Eliza Watkins, & had issue: Eliza, Ann, & Watson, Anna, m Wm Robinson, died 1868, age 71 years, issue: 1 Elizabeth, m Christopher Wilson & had Pharaba Wilson, & Wm Robinson Wilson—2 Rachel Robinson—3 Thomas Robinson. Anna (née White) widow Robinson; m 2d Josiah Nicholson, who died 1852, issue: 1 William (Dr) b 1826, m Sarah W. Newby (née Walton) 1854, 2 Timothy, b Nov 2, 1828, died Sept 15, 1924, age 95 years. He resided in Richmond Ind, m 1st Sarah N. White, Nov 8, 1853, died Sept 26, 1865, issue: 1 Marianna, b 1854, died 1888, m Sept 1877 David Buffmer?—2 John Nicholson, 3 Josiah, died 1908, 4 Thomas, 5 Sarah Ellen, b 1863, died 1864 (age 20mo) 6 Walter, b Aug 1865, died Mar 1867. Timothy Nicholson, m 2d Mary White, April 30, 1868, (sister of Sarah A, who died May 1911), issue: 1 Sarah, 2 Eliza, 3 Josiah (brother of Timothy, b 1831) m Ella Bassett of Rhode Island, 4 John Nicholson, m Mary Winslow, 1833, issue: 1 Ella (single), 2 Edward m ——— George (s of Timothy, & Sarah, b 1835, died 1855.)

White, Rebecca, (d of Jonathan White, & wife Rachel Winslow) m Anthony Albertson, issue: 1 Elias, 2 Edward, 3 Jonathan.

White, Jonathan, (s of Jonathan, & Rachel Winslow) m Mary Twine, issue: 1 Darius, 2 Addison, 3 Caleb. Jonathan White, m 2d Elizabeth Parker (née Skinner) sister of James C. Skinner (father of Thomas, Harry, & Mrs Fanny Whedbee, wife of Mr Monroe Whedbee) issue: 4 Timothy, 5 Jonathan (of Greenville, N. C., called "Jack White") Achsah, 6 child of Jonathan, & Rachel, m 1st Wm Nixon, 2d John W. Wilson. No issue by either.

Margaret White, m John W. Wilson, issue: 1 Alfred, 2 Timothy, 3 Achsah, 4 Christopher, 5 Margaret, 6 Mary Ann, 7 Franklin, 8 Rachel, 9 Horace, 10 Pharaba.

White, Jonathan, will Perq p Aug 1823, names sons: Timothy, & Jonathan, dau's Anna Robinson, & Rebecca Albertson, Achsah & Peggy W White, wife Rachel. Test' Jos White, Nathan Winslow (bro-in-law).

White, Rachel, will Perq, p Nov 1835. Dau's: Anna Nicholson, Margaret W. Winslow, Rebecca Albertson, & Achsah Nixon, gr children: Eliza Ann White, & Watson White, s Jonathan, brother Nathan Winslow.

White, Benjamin, (youngest s of Thomas, & Rachel) will Perq p Aug 1808, names sons: Thomas, John, Jesse, Josiah, Demsey, & Dewey, gr-dau's Martha, & Mary White.

White, Jesse, (s of Benjamin) m Mary Albertson (d of Chalkey) of Perq, 25, 3mo 1802, at Suttons Creek.

White, Jesse, will p in Perq Feb 1814. Son: Cornelius, Chalkey Albertson, dau's: Mary, Elizabeth, Sarah R. White, & Millicent Henley. Brother Thomas White Ex.

White, John, m Lydia Winslow (d of Joseph, & Pleasant née Toms) and had according to his will: (p in Perq Oct 1774) Sons: Francis, John, Samuel, Thomas, & Joseph, wife Lydia, dau's: Dorothy, & Pleasant. The last m Wm Winslow (s of Jacob, & Elizabeth Winslow) 7, 3mo 1787. (Welles Mo Metting.)

(For a continuation of the White family, see wills, N. C. Hist & Gen Register.)

Marriages (Not placed)

White, Joshua, m ——— Cornwell, 15, 1mo 1750. (Pagan Creek, Isle of Wight Co Va.)

White, John (of the Arnold White line) m Mourning White (d of Joshua) no date.

White, Edmund, m Millicent Toms, 3, 3mo 1788. (Welles Mo Meeting.)

White, Jesse, m Abigail Anderson, 2, 4mo 1788. (Welles Mo Meeting.)

White, Charles, (s of John, will 1771), Mary Jones, Nov 21, 1780. (Mar bonds Perq.)

White, Thomas, m Sarah Rountree, Feb 16, 1791, Sec Jesse Rountree. (Mar bonds Perq.)

White, Thomas, m 2d Susannah Palin, Intention, 21, 3mo 1801. (Pasq Mo Meeting.)

White, William, m Elizabeth Robinson, Intention, 21, 3mo 1789. (Pasq Mo Meeting.)

White, Thomas, m Sarah Rolntree, Feb 16, 1791, See Jesse Rountree. (Mar bonds Perq.)

White, Zachariah, m Millicent Nicholson, 30, 2mo 1790. (Pasq Mo Meeting.)

White, Zachariah, m 2d Miriam Elliott, Apl 8, 1795. (Mar bonds Perq.)

White, Edmund, m 2d Mary Morris (d of Aaron Jr) Intention, 21 4mo 1792. (Pasq Co.)

White, Joshua, m Mary Nicholson, Intention, 16, 3mo 1793. (Pasq Mo Meeting.)

White, Robert, m Tabitha Alford, April —, 1702. (Early Quaker records, by Col Olds.) (Col. Fred A. Olds, Raleigh, N. C.)

White, Rachel (d of John) m John Smith, no date. (See deeds.)

White, Francis, m Lydia Winslow (d of Joseph Jr) before Apl 1783. (Legal papers.)

John White dec'd 12, 1mo 1774, will probated by son Thomas, & wife Lida, before John Hollowell J. P. His Inventory shows: 7 horses, 3 cattle, 19 sheep, 13 hogs, 63 hives of bees, 8 punch bowls, 4 dram glasses, 3 "sets of Shoemakers tools" 6 pewter dishes, 8 pewter basins, 27 plates, 24 spoons, &

1 pewter cup, 12 geese, 32 turkeys, "1 cow in the field" rice in the field, parcel of potatoes, (not housed) a barrel of fish, and cash £41 s4, on hand.

Margaret White, (wife of William) in her will p in Perq Jan 1790, names sons: William (2) Josiah, gr-dau Margaret White (d of Margaret Jones) gr-dau Rebecca, Margaret, & Elizabeth Toms, dau Sarah Robinson, gr-children: Edward, Millicent, Elizabeth, & Sarah White, gr-sons: Robert, & William Jordan, gr-dau Margaret Jordan, niece Ann Elliott, gr-son Jesse White (s of Joseph). Test Wm Bond, Job Bond, Exum Newby.

The will of William White, p in Perq Aug 18, 1772, names sons: Joseph (who died before his mother Margaret made her will) William, & Josiah, dau's: Elizabeth Jordan, Margaret Toms, Sarah White, wife Margaret.

Benjamin White, "an Elder," died 16, 11mo 1789, age 53. He had been an elder in the Quaker Meeting for 17 years. (Quaker records.)

WILLIAMS

It would not be a bad statement to say that every county in the State had its family of Williams, at some stage of its history. This county had two families by that name, the older descendants of Lewis Williams of Surry Co Va, and another family represented by Tulle Williams, who came to Perq later, from Currituck Co N. C. The last is well written up in N. C. Historical, & Gen' Reg, therefore we will treat only of the ones who have not had mention.

After much faithful perusal of a great deal of legal matter, some interesting data has been unearthed which throws light on the Williams family living in Perq at an early date.

Roland Williams appears to be the earliest trans' to Va, coming in "Jonathan" 1620, age 20 years. Rowland Williams was granted 70a of land, Oct 20 1704 "at a place called piney Swamp, Warwick Co Va. Rowland Williams was among the living, "Att Elizabeth Cittye" Feb 16, 1623, after the Indian massacre of Mar 22, 1622. From London to Va, in "Thomas, & John" June 16, 1635, Robert Williams, age 44. Roger Williams came in "Truelove" from London, June 10 1635, age 16 years. Thomas Williams arrived in "Transport" from Gravesend, July 4, 1635, age 18. Aboard "Abraham" of London Nov 20, 1635, William Williams, age 25. Thomas Williams was among the living at "West & Sherlew hundred" Feb 16, 1623 (Census). Also Henry, & Mrs. Williams—At James City, Hugh Williams is found among the living, and at "Elizabeth Cittye" William Williams, & Mrs. Williams. William Williams "of great Yarm," age 40 emigrated to New Eng Apl 11, 1637, with wife Alles, & two children. Ann Williams was trans' to Va by John Branch, Aug 27, 1640. John Williams of Isle of Wight Co, in his will, p said Co, Aug 9, 1692, gave his "dwelling plan' to wife Anne for life," and to son John his "Manor plan" names younger son Christopher, made bequest to "William, sone of William Williams, 200a in Newport parish;" To son Thomas land in Surry Co, "where my son John now liveth" son Richard 300a in same Co, "where son John liveth," dau's: Mary, Jane, gr-daus: Ann & Bridgett. (Records Isle of Wight.) Roger Williams & wife Mary deeded land in Surry Co, to Richard Blow, "purchased of Samuel Swann, on Pidgeon Swamp" Mar 1 1680. In another deed same Co, he calls himself "Cooper" & sold 200a to John Watkins, "Land purchased of Maj Samuel Swann, for 261 lbs of Tob, Jan 3, 1681. Christopher Lewis of Southwarke parish Surry Co, in his will, p Aug 20, 1673, gave to

Roger Williams, & son Roger, cattle, and to the elder "my chest with all my cooper tools."

William Williams "Orphan of Lewis dec'd," July 9, 1681. He was bound apprentice to William Newman, July 16, 1683, "until he arrive at age of 21 years" (Surry Co). John Whitley in his will, Isle of Wight Co, Feb 21, 1670, names his "son-in-law John Williams, & dau Ann." Ann Whitley in her will, same Co, names sons: John, Thomas, & William Williams, gr-dau Elizabeth Williams (d of John) Feb 13, 1671. (She was probably wife of John Williams above, & m 2d Whitley.)

George Williams will Isle of Wight, p Oct 9, 1672, made bequest that his three children, "William live with Mr. ——— Cobb, & George, & Elizabeth, with William Bressie, & Susanna his wife." George (2) moved to Northampton Co N. C., and his descendants from there to S. C.

Obed Williams was granted 440a in York Co Va, May 6, 1651, for trans' among them Thomas Williams. Thomas Williams (s of Obediance) was granted 50a in said Co, May 6, 1654. John Williams planter— and Dorothy his wife sold 100a in Nansemond Co Va, "upon New Town Haven River" which was granted by Sir Wm Berkeley to Col Robert Pitt" of Isle of Wight Co, Aug 12, 1665. (Isle of Wight records.)

John Williams of Albemarle N. C. "sold unto Ralph Vickers of Newport parish, Co Isle of Wight" 200a in North end of Surry Co, near a plan' where Wm Williams formerly lived," half of a Pattent to George Pierce, from Sir Henry Cichley, Kt Dept Gov of Vir," April 3, 1681, & by him sold to John & Thomas Williams, Oct 10, 1681. John & Stephen Williams of Albemarle, province of N. C. sold 170a to Richard Williams of Isle of Wight, "on South side of ye main Blackwater," part of a grant, 600a unto William Williams, Oct 28, 1702. Seal Aug 22, 1705.

Arthur Williams of Chowan, made a deed of gift to "loving brother John, 300a where he now liveth, in Lower pish Isle of Wight Co" which was granted John Williams dec'd. Sept 26, 1719.

Thomas Williams (s of Obediance) was granted land in York Co Va, 1663. He had a grant for land in Nansemond Co, Oct 17, 1648, "an Island, called Island Creek." He m Susanna Davis (widow of John) and had sons: Edward, & John.

The Williams family in Perq was first represented by Richard Williams, who m Margary ——— and had issue: Jane, b July 6, 1681—Ruth, b Jan 22, 1686/7. James Penney of Isle of Wight Co, gave to dau Margaret Williams, 500 lbs of Tob, and names gr-son John Williams, wife Lucy (no date).

Jenkens Williams (no parents) m Johanna Barrow, Aug 3, 1690, issue: John, b Oct 12, 1691.

William Williams of Albemarle, will p April 15, 1712. Wife Mary. Sons: Samuel, John (to whom he left "land on Black Water called Littel Town") son Steven. He probably lived in Chowan Co, and his descendants drifted over into Perq. John Williams will Albemarle, Jan 29, 1727/8, names dau Mary, brother Nathaniel (to whom he left a plan') wife Sarah. This will was *certainly* made in *Perq*, as Charles Denman, Clerk of Perq, probated said will.

William Williams above (is thought to be) from all the evidence produced, was the son of Lewis Williams of Surry Co, who was apprenticed to Wm Newman.

Nathaniel (brother of John) m Elizabeth Underwood (d of Thomas) (or Bridger), who is named in the will of said Thomas of Isle of Wight Co, & also in the will of Elizabeth Bridger of same Co, Apl 5, 1717.

Nathaniel, & wife Elizabeth, issue: 1 Timothy, b Dec 2, 1726—2 Sarah, & Ann (twins) b Feb 12, 1727/8—3 John, b Apl 17, 1729—4 James, b May 7, 1732.

Of Timothy we have no knowledge. John Williams (s of Nathaniel) m 1st ―――――, m 2d Rachel Wilson (widow of Wm Townsend, who had for 1st husband Timothy Winslow) by whom he had no issue apparently. His will, p in Perq April 1774, names sons James & John, dau Mary Wilson (step-dau, d of Timothy Winslow) & Anne Donaldson, wife Rachel. Her will same Co, p July 1777, also names dau Mary Wilson. This will is a very interesting document, in that it throws so much light on past history, which would otherwise be baffling to an enormous degree. (See Wilson.)

James Williams will Perq, p Jan 1777. Children: Miriam, John, Sarah, Thomas, & Mary, wife Mary, & Issachar Branch Exrs. One of the witnesses to this will; Anne Donaldson. (For other Williams Wills, see N. C. Hist' & Gen Reg, Vol 3-2—3-3.)

Thomas Williams living in Perq, m before July 1755, Elizabeth Pratt, widow of Jeremiah, and became guardian of Rose, Isaac, Jobe, & Joseph Mathias, orphans of John Dec'd. They jointly petitioned the Court, to sell perishable Estate of said John, & to have possession of it, "out of the hands of Jacob Caruthers." In the division of the Estate of Robert Roe Sr, July 17, 1763, Elizabeth Williams appears as an heir.

WILSON

In "Paule" of London, July 16, 1635, Kathren Wilson, age 28, and children: Robert, age 6—Richard, age 5. (Hotten.)

William Edwards, Clerk of Surry Co Va, was grt (with Rice Davis) 1080a in sd county, for trans' among others, Robert Wilson, & Henry White. July 10, 1648.

William Wilson "of the City of Bristoll, Mercht; apt' son John of Isle of Wight Co, Va Att' Aprill 26, 1666." (Isle of Wight Records.)

George Hardy of Isle of Wight Co, in his will bequeathed, "Land, Housing, my Mill, with all movable Est, to be equally divided between Kinsman George Hardy, & Christopher Willson, after the decease of my wife," He gave also 1000 lbs of Tob toward building a Church in this Parish, "to be Built of Brick." To Christopher Willson "Land in Suit between me & Successors of Justinian Cooper, in case it be restored." (Records Isle of Wight.)

Robert Wilson was living in Chuckatuck, Nansemond Co Va, 9, 12mo 1688, when he witnessed the mar banns of Levin Buffkin, & Dorothy Newby, at the house of Thomas Jordan. He recorded his mark in Perq Co N. C. April 1689, and his son Isaac did the same, May 1689.

At a quarterly meeting at the house of Henry White, in Perq, 1, 3mo 1695 Robert Wilson, Francis Tomes, & Henry White, were apt to "write a letter to friends in London, in behalf of the Meeting."

The will of Robert Wilson, p in Perq Precinct Jan 11, 1696. Son: Isaac, dau Sarah Belman, gr-children: Robert, & Ann Wilson, Sarah, & Ester Belman; wife Ann Extrix. (This will was proven before John Archdale, Daniel Akehurst, Francis Tomes, & Samuel Swann, Justices; at the house of Samuel Swann.)

(1) Robert Willson died "at his own house, up the Narrows of Perq River" Dec 21, 1696. (Roman Calendar.) His wife Ann moved back to Surry Co Va, where her will was p 21, 5mo 1702, reads as follows: "Disposing of worldly Est itt hath pleased God to bestow upon me in Carolina, do bequeath unto Robert Borsman, & Ann, ye son, and dau of John Borsman; & Sarah His wife, except cattle etc, to be equally divided between Robert Wilson, & Ann Wilson, son & dau of Isaac Wilson, & Ann his first wife." Jno Tooke, & Sam'll Cornell Exrs. (Surry Co Rec.)

(1) Isaac Wilson, m Ann ——— issue: 1 Robert, b 10, 8mo 1690—2 Ann, b 16 7mo 1692—3 Benjamin, b 19, 10mo 1694. Isaac Wilson m 2d Ann Parker (d of Robert, & Hannah, "b at Nattensate in Ash Church Parish, in Glouster Sheer") Mch 31, 1701, issue Isaac, b Nov 18, 1702. (The Quaker Rec'ds give the first three, the last are found in Berkeley Par Reg, Perq Co.)

Isaac Willson will Perq, p July 13, 1714. Sons: Benjamin, Robert, Isaac, dau Ann, wife Ann. He was a Burgess in Perq Co, Oct 11, 1709.

(2) Isaac Wilson d. s. p. will p in Perq Dec 29, 1724. Brothers: Benjamin, Robert, nephews: Joseph, & Isaac Wilson, to whom he left a plan' on Perq River "where Capt Pettiver now lives," niece Rachel Wilson, mother Ann Pettiver, uncle Ralph Bozman, other legatees: Joseph, & Thomas Elliott.

(3) Isaac Wilson, will Perq p April 1751. Sons: Robert, James, dau's Rachel, and Miriam Wilson, wife Elizabeth (née Perry, married 2, 12mo 1742).

(1) Joseph Wilson (s of Benjamin) Will Perq, p July 1752. Son: Reuben, dau's Elizabeth, & Mary, wife Mary. Wit' Jacob Wilson, Wm Townsend, Rachel Winslow.

(2) Robert Wilson (s of Isaac & Ann) m Rachel Pricklove (Pretlow) (d of John, and wife Elizabeth). His will p in Perq, June 1758. Sons: Isaac, and Silvanus, dau Rachel Townsend, gr-sons: Reuben Wilson, Obed Winslow, Caleb Winslow, gr-dau's Elizabeth, and Mary Wilson. Exrs Barnaby Nixon, & Jacob Winslow (gr-son).

Rachel Wilson, m 1st Timothy Winslow, issue three sons, & one dau; m 2d William Townsend, issue four children, m 3d John Williams, by whom no issue. Her will Perq county, p July 1777, is a very interesting document.

Isaac Wilson, (s of Benjamin) b Nov 16, 1694.

Robert Wilson, m Martha Gilbert, 4, 1mo 1739. (Quaker Records.)

John Wilson (s of Thos) m Mary Pearson (d of Peter) 20, 9mo 1740. (Quaker Records.)

Thomas Wilson m Elizabeth Newby, 6 8mo 1777. (Quaker Records.)

Isaac Wilson m Roda Chappel. 5, 6mo 1776. (Quaker Records.)

Jonathan Wilson, m Huldah Harrel, 4, 7mo 1795. (Quaker Records.)

William Wilson m Elizabeth Munden 3, 11mo 1765. (Symons Creek Pasq Co.)

Robert Wilson, m Anne Reed 2, 3mo 1752, Suttons Creek Perq Co.

Edward Wilson, came to Va in "Plaine John" May 15, 1635, age 22. He settled in Surry Co, from which place he moved to Perq Co N. C. When or where he married can not be certain, but his wife is given in Berkeley Par Reg.

Edward Wilson, & wife Rachell—issue: 1 John, b Jan 11, 1686—2 Edward, b Last of Feb, 1687/8—3 John (2d by name) b Sept 14, 1693—4 Elizabeth, b Feby 24, 1692—5 Sarah, b July 14, 1695. Edward Wilson died 1712. Dau Sarah m Daniel Jones.

(1) John Wilson, m Elizabeth Mayo (d of Edward (2) & wife Mary née Clare, d of Timothy Clare, & wife Mary née Bundy) & had according to Mary Newby's (née Clare) will 1739, issue: 1 son John Wilson.

(2) John Wilson, m Ann ——— will p April 1785, Wife Ann, dau's Rebecca, & Amey. His division, Nov 24, 1798, shows: dau Rebecca Webb, & Amey Wilson. (See other Wilson Wills in N. C. Hist Reg, Vol 3-2 & 3-3.)

Jacob Wilson (1) m Rachel Hollowell (d of Thomas) m 2d Sarah. His will p Perq, 1793. Son: Jonathan, brothers, Zachariah, & Moses, dau's Misala, Miriam Elliott and Julianna Elliott (buried in Episcopal Cemetery in Hertford, wife of Exum Elliott) Rachel Nixon, sister Sarah Copeland, (wife of Jesse) Jesse Copeland (s of Jesse) d Absala Seymour, kinsman Thomas Hollowell (s of Joseph) Ex.

(3) John Wilson, m Margaret White, 5, 11mo 1828, issue: 1 Alfred, b 9, 1mo 1830—2 Timothy, b 20, 1mo 1832—3 Christopher, b 4, 5mo 1834.

Joseph Wilson, m Sarah Charles, 7, 6mo 1780. (Welles Meeting, Perq Co.)

(1) William Wilson, moved from Pasq Co, to Tyrrell, where his will was p June 1741. Sons: Patterson, William, Thomas, Benjamin, dau's Rebecca, Sarah, & Rosaman Wilson, & Mary Scarbrough, Elizabeth Barclifte. His wife Sarah evidently moved back to Pasq, where her will was p April 1754. Sons William, Benjamin, Thomas, dau's Rebeckah Furbush, Elizabeth Bartlet. Patterson Wilson died in Pasq Co before his mother, so he is not named in her will. His will sd county: p July 12, 1746, names son: William, dau Mary, wife Elizabeth.

(1) Thomas Wilson, will Perq, p April 1785. Sons: Thomas, Samuel, William, wife Elizabeth.

Wilson Grants

Robert Wilson had 450a grt him, "upon ye West side of Perquimons River, near the mouth of Robert Wilsons Creek, to ye South East side of sd Creek, or branch" 1684.

Isaac Wilson, 490a, in Perq pre'ct, to line of Robert Wilson, by Cypress Swamp. May 22, 1694.

Edward Wilson, 250a in Perq pre'ct on the head of Albemarle River (Sound) near the mouth of a Creek. Feby 17, 1696.

William Wilson, 300a in Anson Co N. C. on North side of Broad River, & Dry Creek, Oct 3, 1753.

Capt John Pettiver, 240a in Perq, "by ye side of Perq River, adj Jno Spelman, Xber 10, 1712, and 400a on the head of Bentley Creek (now called Muddy Creek) adj James Cheston, to Spelmans corner, & line of Edward Wilson. Dec 10, 1712, (same) 377a on Cypress Swamp, along ye Indian Swamp. Dec 10, 1712. (same) 220a adj his own land, on Cypress Swamp. Xber — 1712.

John Pettiver was murdered by Joseph Haines. (See deeds.) He m Ann widow of Isaac 1716.

Ralph Bosman (called uncle by Robert Wilson) 166a in Perq Pre'ct, adj Samuel Phelps. Feb 10, 1718.

Marriages

Wilson, Christopher, Intention, with Pharaby Saunders, 15, 11mo 1788. (Quaker Reg.)

Wilson, Jesse, joined the "Baptist Society" and was "out of Unity" 20, 12mo 1788.

A. C. C. Winslow.
C. Edward Daniel Winslow.
B. Watson Winslow.
D. Tudor Frith Winslow.

SONS OF FRANCIS E. WINSLOW AND MARY TATUM JORDAN WINSLOW
COVE GROVE, THE SKINNER HOME IN OLD NECK

RECORDS OF DEEDS 437

Wilson, Thomas, m Martha Pendleton, Mar 31, 1806. (Mar bonds Pasq Co.)
Wilson, Francis, m Nancy Jennings, Nov 19, 1806. (Mar bonds Pasq Co.)
Wilson, John, Intention, with Millicent Trueblood, 20, 7mo 1799. (Pasq Mo Meeting.)
Wilson, Sylvanus, m Rebecca Pierce (d of Joseph, sister of Thomas dec'd) Oct 18, 1757.
Wilson, Sylvanus, (son of Robert, & Rachel (Pricklove) Wilson). (See Robert Wilsons will.)
Wilson, Benjamin, (s of Isaac, & Ann née Parker) m Judith Docton (d of Jacob), & had son Jacob Wilson, whose dau Julianna, m Exum Elliott. (See deeds.)
Wilson, Reuben, (s of Joseph) m Mary Winslow (d of Timothy, & Rachel Wilson, d of Robert, & Rachel née Pricklove) issue: Silvanus, b 8, 9mo 1768— Jacob, b June 12, 1774. Mary, b 8, 1mo 1779—Huldah, b Mar — 1781. (Bible record.)

WINSLOW

For the convenience of those not acquainted with the record, and where the ones needed are to be found, the following is here printed, taken from Winslow Memorial, Vol I, Chart V.

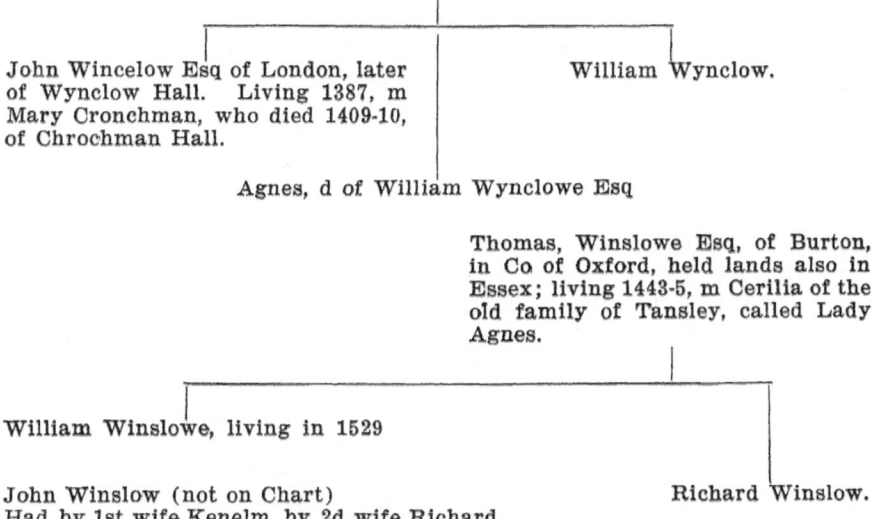

William Wincelowe

John Wincelow Esq of London, later of Wynclow Hall. Living 1387, m Mary Cronchman, who died 1409-10, of Chrochman Hall.

William Wynclow.

Agnes, d of William Wynclowe Esq

Thomas, Winslowe Esq, of Burton, in Co of Oxford, held lands also in Essex; living 1443-5, m Cerilia of the old family of Tansley, called Lady Agnes.

William Winslowe, living in 1529

John Winslow (not on Chart)
Had by 1st wife Kenelm, by 2d wife Richard.

Richard Winslow.

I Kenelm Winslow, who purchased of Sir Richard Newport, an Estate called "Newport Place" in Kempsey, Co Worcester. He had an older Estate, called "Clerkenleap" which was sold by his grandson Richard in 1650. He died 1607, will p Nov 9, 1607, wife Katherine, in Parish of St. Andrews.

Edward Winslow, b Oct 7, 1560 (Parish of St. Andrews) of Droitwich, m 1st Eleanor Pelham, d of Sir Herbert Pelham (no issue) m 2d Magdalene Ollyver, at St Brides Church, London, Nov 4, 1594.

John Winslow, m Agnes (d of John Thogmorton Esq) of Kemsey 1400-20, was father of Kenelm above, issue: Edward, of Kempsey, & Droitwich, Co Worcester, England, b Oct 18, 1575, d May 8, 1655, in Parish of St Andrews, who had issue by 2d wife Magdaline Olliver: 1 Edward, b Oct 19, 1595 (1st Gov of Mass) 2 John, b April 16, 1597, d 1674, age 78, m Oct 12, 1624 Mary Chilton (d of James, who came over in the Mayflower). Her will July 24, 1676.

John Winslow came to New England in the "Fortune" Nov 3, 1621, settled in Plymouth, Mass, and moved to Boston 1656. He was a prominent merchant, and large ship-builder. He had by wife Mary (Chilton), 1 Elizabeth, 2 John, who died 1731, m Abigail Atkinson (d of Theodore) June 18, 1689, issue: 1 Elizabeth, b April 23, 1692—2 John, b Dec 31, 1693, m Sarah Pierce Sept 21, 1721, died Oct 15, 1731—3 Judith, 4 Joseph (age not given) m Sarah Lawrence (d of Major Thomas Lawrence of New Town L. I.) Living in Perq Co N. C. 1677-79, where he served as "foreman of the Petit Jury" when acting Gov Thomas Miller was tried for treason, between the said dates. He is called in the Col Records of N. C. "another New England Traider." The question naturally arises in the mind of any thinking person; would it not be the usual custom for a man of John Winslow's wealth, a merchant and ship-builder, to fit out one of his own ships, with his own goods, and put his son Joseph in command as Captain? Certainly the ship he commanded "Traded" between the Ports of New England, and the ports of Carolina, or he would not have been designated as a "New Eng Traider." This is, however, a moot point, for which no one has been able to find a satisfactory solution. Joseph Winslow, son of John, & Mary (Chilton) had two children whose ages are given in Savages Dictionary, prior to this date, and may we not, with some foundation, come to the conclusion that Thomas Winslow of Perq, who was of age in 1702, may have been his *youngest* son, probably born *after* his death, for Joseph Winslow died in New England 1679. In the absence of proof, we will leave that unsettled question to future generations for solving. No one could serve on a jury, in the Province of N. C. without being a resident of the colony, and having in their possession at least 100a of land, therefore we know he was living in the County, between 1677-79, and it is supposed he would naturally have his family here with him. He probably died in New England on one of his *Trading* trips. However this may be, we pass on to Thomas Winslow, first in Perq according to records still extant. John Winslow had a grant for land in New Kent Co Va 1669. As the records of New Kent have been destroyed by fire, no further mention of said John is made, but it is probable that he was ancestor of the Spotsylvania Winslows, and also the ones found in Essex Co Va, where a Thomas Winslow, with wife Ann, made a deed 1694. Although the writer has made diligent search in Virginia, for some connection between these Winslows, & the family who moved to Perq, no results have rewarded her efforts. The theory still clings that Joseph of New Eng, was the progenitor of the N. C. Winslows, and it seems the most *plausible conclusion*, in face of all the facts.

Thomas Winslow of Perq, proved his freedom "from Timothy Clare" in 1702. He was either an apprentice to said Timothy, or had been imported by him to the Province of N. C., for which he had to serve for a certain length of time. From the fact that he soon after this date m Elizabeth Clare (d of Timothy, & wife Mary (Bundy) we are led to believe he *came of age at that time.* The date of marriage can not be found. For some reason unknown to the writer the Winslows did not have their early marriages recorded, although there was an old record book kept by the Reg of Deeds in Perq, no Winslows appear therein. Therefore no dates can be furnished for them, until they became Quakers, which was not until said Thomas m Elizabeth Clare. The Winslows of New England were Episcopalians, and the supposition is that Thomas adhered to the same faith, & changed on arrival in Perq, from association with his wife's family.

The will of Thomas Winslow, p in Perq, Jan 1745. Sons: Thomas, Timothy, John, Job, to whom he left "a plan' in Pasq Co, near Newbegun Creek," dau's Elizabeth, & Miriam.

According to legal papers in Perq, Thomas Winslow was m to Elizabeth Clear (who was b Feb 21, 1686,) before 1705.

Winslow, Thomas (1) did not have a son Joseph, according to "Grimes," but in N. C. Historical and Genealogical Reg, a variance is noted, which gives said Thomas, a son by that name, and the deeds in Perq make plain the fact that Joseph (1) *was his son*. There is also a difference in the dau's mentioned in these two books, Grimes giving the dau's as: Elizabeth, & Miriam, and Hathaway as: Elizabeth, & Christian. The writer is not up on the daughters, but she is morally certain that Thomas Winslow (1) had a son by the name of *Joseph*. A Thomas Winslow m Leah Smith (widow of Joseph), 1734. (See deeds Perq Co.) She was his widow soon after. Who *this* Thomas *was*, and where he stood in the line of the family, is an unsolved question.

(1) Winslow, Joseph (thought to be *eldest* son of Thomas, & Mary (Bundy)) m Pleasant Toms, b 1710 (d of Francis, & Margaret (Bogue)) 22, 6mo 1729, she died 4, 1mo 1785. They had issue according to his will, p in Perq, Jan 1750; Sons: Joseph, to whom he left "land on Core Neck," dau Lydia, "land at the head of Little River," dau's Miriam, & Mary, "land called Grassy Ridge," wife Pleasant. (See deeds in this book for more information about this family.) Joseph Winslow, had a grt for land in Perq, 225a, granted at a Council in Edenton, Mar 11, 1740. He was living in Balahack, Jan 3, 1745-6 and bought of Samuel Newby 250a, adj "his own line" on that date.

(a) Winslow, Joseph (2) Joseph (1) Thomas (1) m Mary White, (d of Thomas, & Rachel Jordan who were m in Isle of Wight Co 1719; Rachel Jordon d of Joshua, & Elizabeth Sanbourne, d of Daniel Sanbourne, & wife Sarah, of Isle of Wight Co Va, whose will was p in said Co, 16, 12mo 1711.) (See White record.) Joseph (2) will Perq p Oct 1766, Sons: Thomas, John, Joseph, dau's Betty, Pleasant, & Rachel, wife Mary. Exrs John, & Benjamin White (brothers-in-law).

(b) Winslow, Lydia m John White, (s of Thomas, & Rachel (Jordan)) brother of Mary, who m Joseph (2), so that their children were double first cousins. In turn their dau Pleasant crossed over the border again, & m William Winslow, a little further down the line. (See Jacob Winslow line.)

(II) Winslow, Thomas (2) Thomas (1) m Sarah Nixon. His will Perq, p April 1747, Sons: Jesse, Thomas, dau Elizabeth, wife Sarah (née Nixon).

(III) Winslow, Timothy (1) Thomas (1) m Rachel Wilson, d of Robert & wife Rachel (Pricklove, d of John Pricklove, & wife Elizabeth) 9 1mo 1730. His will p in Perq gives his children in the following order: 1 Jacob, 2 Timothy (2), 3 Obed, 4 Caleb, 5 Mary, wife Rachel. His will p July 1752. Test' John, & Mary Winslow (brother, & sister-in-law). Rachel (Wilson) Winslow m 2d Wm Townsend, by whom she had four children, m 3d John Williams.

She is named in her fathers will, 1758, as "dau Rachel Townsend," and in her son Obeds will as "mother Rachel Williams." Her will p in Perq, July 1777, is an interesting document, and clears up many puzzles.

(IV) Winslow, John, m Mary Pearson (d of Peter, & wife Rachel) 20, 7mo 1740, issue: 1 Josiah, 28, 7mo 1741—2 Miriam, b 9, 10mo 1743—3 Thomas, b 8. 1mo 1745/6—4 Samuel, b 10, 4mo 1748—5 Ruth, b 23, 7mo 1750/6—6 John, b 2, 9mo 1754. His will, p in Perq, names sons: Josiah, Thomas, Samuel, & dau Miriam, wife Mary.

Winslow, Mary, m 2d Joshua Moore, "at Symons Creek Pasq Co," 1, 5mo 1755.

Winslow (a) Josiah, m Elizabeth ——— issue: 1 Jonathan, b 28, 7 mo 1768—2 Ezra, b 2, 1mo 1771—3 Josiah, b 10, 9mo 1772—4 Sarah, b 17, 9mo 1774—5 James, b 17, 10mo 177--, and John Woolman, no birth date. (The two last moved to Randolph Co.)

Winslow (b) Miriam, m Bennoni Pritchard, at Symons Creek, 7, 1mo 1762.

Winslow (c) Thomas, (3) John (1) Thomas (1) moved to Randolph Co N. C. where he m 13, 1mo 1768, Elizabeth Phelps, issue: Miriam, b 14, 9mo 1768—2 Henry, b 25, 8mo 1771—3 Eleazer, who died in said county 1843. Married, & had son Nathan, b in Randolph Co, May 23, 1821, d July 30, 1890, issue: Abner Thomas Winslow, who moved to Indiana; ancestor of Mr J. E. Winslow of Greenville, Pitt Co, N. C.

Winslow (d) Samuel, m Ruth Fletcher 13, 3mo 1771, issue: Mary, b 4, 1mo 1772. He probably left the county, as no will appears in Perq made by him. Nothing further can be found on the Perq records, relative to this branch.

Winslow, Henry (1) Thomas (3) John (1) Thomas (1) b 1771, d 29, 1mo 1849, in Randolph Co N. C., m Elizabeth Needham, of Back Creek Mo Meeting, issue: 1 John, b 22, 1mo 1800, d 12 3mo 1830, m Elizabeth Henley (d of Jesse, & Miriam née Bundy) 14, 6mo 1821, issue: 1 Jesse Henley Winslow, b 21 5mo 1822, d 2, 7mo 1875, m Susannah Johnson (d of John Johnson, & Lydia née Falkner) 23, 8mo 1849. They moved to Iowa, where they prospered, and reared a family. From them sprang Mr. E. H. Haskell of Washington, D. C.

TIMOTHY WINSLOW LINE

Winslow, Jacob (1) Timothy (1) Thomas (1), m Elizabeth ———? The ages of his children have not been found, although the Quaker records may hold them. A thorough search of these records, kept in the vault at Guilford College, might reveal much valuable data on the Winslow family, if they were open to the public, and one had plenty of time to examine them. However we have Jacob Winslows Will, which was p in Perq, Jan 1771, with his sons named as follows: William, Jacob (2) Obed, and dau's: Mary, Millicent, Wife Elizabeth.

Nathaniel Welch in his will Perq, p 1789, names "daughter Elizabeth Winslaw, but as several Elizabeth Winslows appear in Perquimans county, it is not positive *proof* that this indicates the wife of *Jacob*. Besides, Jacob Winslows wife Elizabeth, died before this date, and it was not customary for a person to be named in a will, after death. Her will p in Perq, Jan 1785, names dau Mary Saunders, & Millicent Lamb (wife of Restore), sons: William, & Jacob, dau Betty. Benjamin Saunders, & Restore Lamb Exrs. Jacob Winslow lived in "Piney Woods" district, near the Chowan line, and his home, a quaint old residence with many wings, & cubby rooms, was still in use a few years ago, having descended through several generations to Mrs. Elisha Copeland, d of Francis, & Rachel Winslow (s of William Winslow, & wife Pleasant née White). The old rambling house after her death was demolished, and a new and more modern residence arose on the same site.

Winslow (a) William (1) Jacob (1) Timothy (1) Thomas (1) m Pleasant White (d of John, & Lydia, née Winslow (d of Joseph, & Pleasant (née Toms) Winslow) 7, 3mo 1787, issue: Francis, m Rachel Newby (d of William, & Lydia ———) and had issue: Francis (2) m Mary Tatum Jordan (d of Hezekiah, & Mary T. Cook (Jordan)) of Nansemond Co Va, who moved to Gates county, where Mary Jordan resided at the time of her marriage to F. E. Winslow solemnized Nov 19, 1855, issue: 1 Edward Daniel, b Aug 27, 1856, d unmarried May —, 1926—2 Tudor Frith, b Nov 28, 1857, d April 29, 1929, m Mary Wood (d of Charles, & Mary née Skinner) 3 Watson, b July 1, 1859, d Jan 10, 1921, m Ellen Goode Rawlings (d of Walter M. Rawlings, & Marie S. Hughart, of Charlotte Co Va) 4 Caleb Cook, b Mar 19, 1861, d Nov 9, 1909, m Martha Leigh (d of Edward Leigh, & wife Grizzelle Jacocks, of Perq Co.)

Winslow (b) Jacob (2) Jacob (1) Timothy (1) Thomas (1) m Millicent Perry. His will Perq probated May 1807. Sons: Jacob (3), William, & Jesse, Dau's: Sarah, Millicent, & Mary. Wife Millicent.

Winslow (c) Obed, of whom nothing is known. d. s. p.

(V) Winslow, Tudor Frith, (1) Francis (2) Francis (1) William (1) Jacob (1) Timothy (1) Thomas (1) and wife Mary née Wood had issue: 1 Mae Wood (unmarried)—2 Kate, m William Hudson, issue Mary Tudor Hudson—3 Francis Edwards, m Nemmie Parris of Rocky Mount, N. C., issue four children —4 Elizabeth Blount, m Thomas Wilcocks of Norfolk Va, issue three children.

(V) Winslow, Watson, m Ellen Goode Rawlings, b Jan 30, 1869, m Jan 16, 1889, issue Francis Watson, b Feb 7, 1890, d Aug 23, 1891—2 Edward Valentine, b April 11, 1892, d Mar 6, 1907—3 Hillary Goode, b Oct 23, 1895 (Clerk of Perquimans) m Emma G. Pemberton (d of E. L. Pemberton, of Fayetteville, N. C., and wife Katherine Murchison) Dec 2, 1918, issue two children—4 Herman Rawlings, b April 13, 1898, m Ruth Spivey (d of Robert, & Lavinia née Mathews) issue: Watson, & Ruth—5 Walter Frith, b Jan 3, 1903, m Ruth Ayres (d of Wm Ayres, & wife Fanny (Dixon) June 4, 1902, issue: Fanny Lou.

(V) Winslow, Caleb Cook, m Martha Leigh, issue: 1 Ellen Terry, b——— m Clyde McCallum, no issue—2 E. Leigh, b ——— m Maureen McManus, issue two sons, Leigh, & John. 3 Julian Emmett, b ——— m Mary Clark (d of ———) issue: dau Betty, b ———.

William Winslow made his will in Chowan Co, p June 1806. Wife Pleasant, sons: Obed, Jacob, Francis, William, John, Josiah, dau's: Liddy, Mary, & Elizabeth. Exrs, Caleb Winslow, Restore Lamb, Jacob Winslow, & Joseph Copeland. He lived on the edge of Perquimans, and his grand-son Francis (2) made his home in early married life at a place called "Snow Hill" just across the line in Perquimans. Here were born the four little boys, Edward, Tudor, Watson, & Cook, who took an active part in later life in the public affairs of said county. The Winslows are too numerous to trace out all the various family connections, in their many ramifications, and also there is not sufficient data, to make them clear, but this much is certain, both and all branches of this wonderful family, trace back to either Thomas (1) son of Joseph, or John (1) who is supposed to have been brother of said Thomas. Any one wishing to find the data relative to his or her own particular branch, should find no difficulty in tracing them on the splendid records in Perq, where every known Winslow figures at some time or other.

Excursus. Cannon: John Cannon came to New England in "Fortune" with John Winslow 1620. Such records prove that the two families were known to each other before migrating to Perq Precinct. "Robert Cannon of New England died at Mr Durants, Jan 1, 1690." Wm Townsend m Rachel Winslow (widow of Timothy) 4, 4mo 1753, and had dau Betty, who m Joseph Cannon. The last made his will in Chowan Co, p 1785. Wife Betty, brother Jacob, his father Jeremiah Cannon, will in Chowan, 3, 3mo 1779, wife Rachel, her former husband John Smith of Perq Co, d Sarah Arnold (wife of Benjamin), sons: Joseph, & Jacob. Jacob Cannon, m Jemima Newby (d of Robert) is named in his will 1789. Joseph Cannon, Orphan of Jacob, in account with his Guar Josiah Townsend, Feb 1806. Jacob Cannon will, Perq Co, p May 1832, names wife Ann, sons: James, Joseph, and dau: Sally Ann, brother Joseph. Exrs Nathan Winslow, & Allen Saunders. Joseph Cannon was a Lawyer of good repute, and owned "Woodlawn" near Hertford, which was acquired by Mr Charles Wood, and a few years ago met with the misfortune of being burned to the ground. On the place is the old Cannon burying ground, with tombstones, and here was buried Joseph Cannon.

Carleton Cannon, m Martha Winslow (d of Francis, & Rachel (Newby)).

Elisha Copeland, m Mary Jane Winslow (d of Francis, & Rachel).

Jonathan White, m Louise Winslow (d of Francis, & Rachel).

Caleb Winslow (s of Francis, & Rachel) m Sally Cox, & had 1 Hugh Winslow, m Maggie Evans (d of Benjamin) issue Clarrissa. 2 Inez Winslow, m Hugh Pendleton, no issue.

(3) Winslow, Timothy (2) Timothy (1) Thomas (1) untraced.

(3) Winslow, Obed (1) Timothy (1) Thomas (1) d. s. p. Will Perq, p Jan 1775, names brother Caleb Winslow, sister Mary Wilson (wife of Reuben) cousin Sylvanus Wilson, cousin Jesse Winslow (s of Thomas (2) and his brother Jacob Winslows children: Mary, Millicent, William, Jacob, & Elizabeth, sister Rachel White, brother Wm Townsend (half brother), sister Betty Cannon (half-sister) mother Rachel Williams (her last husband).

Winslow, Timothy (father of above sons) will Perq, p July 1752; names sons: Jacob, Timothy, Obed, & Caleb, to whom he bequeathed land "on Little River." Daughter Mary, wife Rachel. They were m Sept 5, 1730.

CALEB WINSLOW'S LINE

Winslow, Caleb (1) Timothy (1) Thomas (1) b Dec 12, 1749, d Mar 3, 1811, m 1st Ann Perry, (d of Jacob) Oct 18, 1769, b Dec 12, 1755, d Feb 4, 1796, age 40 years; he m 2d 1797, Jemmimah Cannon, 3 Jan 29, 1806 Peggy Scott, by whom he had no issue. She d 1822. Caleb Winslow will Perq, p May 1811, names wife Peggy, son Nathan, dau Rachel White (wife of Jonathan) gr-son John Copeland. The ages of his children as given me by Dr Caleb Winslow, son of Dr Randolph Winslow of Baltimore, Md: 1 Rachel, b Nov 9, 1770—2 Jacob, b Apl 9, 1773, d Apl 1775—3 Betsey, b Aug 8, 1775, d July 1775?—4 Timothy, b Aug 4, 1778, d Sept 1783—5 Caleb, b Aug 24, 1780, d 1806, m June 2, 1802, Mary Parker—6 Sarah, b Dec 1782, d Dec 1782—7 Josiah, b Dec 20, 1783, d 1784—8 Esther, b Feb 21, 1786, m ——— Copeland, issue: John—9 Peninah, b Nov 11, 1790, d Sept 1791—10 Obed, b June 7, 1792, d

Aug 1793—11 Nathan, b Jan 4, 1795, d Aug 29, 1873, buried in Friends Cemetery, Harford Rd, Baltimore Md.

Winslow (a) Rachel, m Jonathan White. (See White family.)

Winslow (b) Nathan (1) Caleb (1) Timothy (1) Thomas (1) son of Caleb, & Ann Perry, m Dec 29, 1819, Margaret Fitz Randolph (d of Jacob, & Elizabeth (Pretlow) of Nansemond Co Va, b about 1781, d July 3, 1848, age 67 years, issue: 1 John Randolph, b Nov 8, 1820, d Feb 13, 1866, M. D. (unmarried) buried beside his father in Baltimore—2 Rufus Kinsey, b Jan 22, 1822, d 1843 (drowned when only 19 years of age)—3 Caleb, b Jan 24, 1824, M. D., d June 13 1895, buried beside his father, m Jan 14, 1852, Jane Paxon Parry, b July 23, 1829, d Feb 14, 1910 (d of Oliver Parry, & Rachel Randolph, of New Hope Penn)—4 Margaret Kinsey, b Oct 16, 1826, d 1830, buried on plantation in Perquimans Co, N. C., with her mother.

Winslow, Caleb (2) Nathan (1) Caleb (1) Timothy (1) Thomas (1) m Jane Paxon Parry, issue: 1 Randolph, M. D. b in Hertford N. C. Oct 23, 1852 (resides in Baltimore)—2 Oliver Parry, b Jan 1, 1855, d Apl 18, 1860—3 John Randolph, b June 15, 1856, d, April 20, 1860—4 Nathan, b Dec 4, 1857, killed by a slave, Aug 25, 1858—5 Edward R. Parry, b Oct 18, 1859, d July 9, 1862—6 Julianna Randolph, b in Hertford, Perq Co, May 15, 1861, d Aug 13, 1928 (unmarried)—7 Margaret, Fitz Randolph, b April 1, 1863, d May 8, 1863—8 John Randolph (2d by name) b in Baltimore Md, June 1, 1866, M. D. (residence Baltimore), m Elizabeth Lewis Reed, Feb 6, 1894 (d of Dr Thomas B. Reed, & Mary Campbell, of Philadelphia), no issue.

Winslow, Randolph (1) Caleb (2) Nathan (1) Caleb (1) Timothy (1) Thomas (1) m Rebecca Fayssoux Leiper, b May 29, 1856 (d of John Chew Leiper, & Mary Lewis Fayssoux) m Dec 12, 1877, at Creekside, Ridley Penn, issue: 1 Nathan, b Nov 17, 1878, m Oct 5, 1904, Margaret Kable Massey, b July 29, 1875 (d of J. Llewellyn Massey, of Charlottesville, Va, & Emily Thomas, of Sandy Spring Md) no issue. (Dr Nathan Winslow, residence Baltimore Md.)—2 John Leiper, L.L. B., b Mar 7, 1880, m June 27, 1906, Anne Stewart Tonge, of Bainbridge Ga, b Nov 6, 1877 (d of Wm G. D. Tonge, & Laura E. (Taylor)) issue: 1 Virginia Stewart (d young)—2 John Leiper, b Feb 12, 1911—3 Rebecca Fayssoux, b Nov 5, 1915.) 3 Fitz Randolph, M. D. b July 2, 1881, of Hayden Ariz, m Oct 31, 1913, Florence Isabel Reese, no issue—4 Edward Fayssoux, D Phar, b Nov 23, 1883, m June 6, 1905, Emma White, Garrigues, b Mar 24, 1883 (d of Sam'l M. Garrigues, & Sallie F. (White) issue, 1 Randolph, b Oct 14, 1906—2 Frances G., b Aug 10, 1910 (died same day)—3 Sarah G., b July 22, 1911—4 George Leiper, b Oct 25, 1915 (dead)—5 Mary Fayssoux, b July 7, 1885, in Baltimore, m Sept 11, 1911, James M. Shellman, b Oct 28, 1888 (s of Harvey Jones Shellman, & Josephine Keith, of Westminster Md) Issue: 1 Josephine Keith, b Mar 4, 1916—2 Randolph, b July 26, 1920.

Winslow, Jane Parry, (6th child of Randolph, & Rebecca (Leiper) Winslow) b Nov 7, 1886, m Nov 23, 1910 Herbert F. Carroll of Raleigh, N. C. issue: Herbert F. Carroll Jr, b Sept 16, 1911.

Winslow, Caleb (7th child) b July 1, 1889, m June 21, 1916, Lena Rebecca Gary, b Jan 28, 1888, (d of Col Robert J. Gary, & Vashti Saulsbury) issue: 1 Caleb, b Mar 30, 1918—2 Robert Gary, b Nov 9, 1919—3 Vashti Louise, b May 2, 1922—4 Elizabeth Reed, b Dec 3, 1928.

Winslow, Eliza Leiper (8 child) b Feb 10, 1891, m Oct 23, 1915 John S. B. Woolford, M. D. b Oct 11, 1871 issue: 1 Eliza Leiper, b July 21, 1916—2 Helen Randolph, b Jan 7, 1918. Reside in Roswell, New Mexico.

Winslow, George Leiper, B. S. (9 child) b Mar 4, 1893, m May 5, 1917 Dorothy H. Massey, b Sept 12, 1891 (d of George Massey, & Harriet L. Starr of Philadelphia Penn) no issue.

Winslow, Oliver Leiper (10) b Feb 9, 1895, B. S. m July 19, 1919 Harriet A. Christian, b Oct 22, 1892 (d of Harrison Christian, & Virginia Diamond, of Meridian Miss) issue: 1 Oliver Parry, b Mar 28, 1922—2 Nathan, b June 11, 1926.

Winslow, Richard R. P. Lieut U. S. Army, b May 8, 1897, m April 24, 1919 Anne C. Sherlock of Augusta Ga.

Winslow, St Clair Spruill (12) b April 13, 1899, d Aug 18, 1899.

Winslow (13) Callender Fayssoux, M. S., b Dec 12, 1901, m Dec 14, 1927., Lucy G. Buchanan, b Aug 1, 1905 (d of Herbert Buchanan, & Sarah MacDougal of Norwich, Conn) issue: Luck Gray, b Jan, 1929.

JOHN WINSLOW LINE

John Winslow (1) contemporary of Thomas (1) is thought to be his *brother*, but there is no actual *proof* of the fact. This John m Esther Snelling (d of Israel, & Hannah, née "Larance." d of William Lawrence, & "Rachell Welsh") Hannah Snelling m 2d Timothy Clare, his 3d and last wife, by whom she had one dau Hannah. From this we see that John Winslow m the step-sister of Elizabeth Clare, who was the wife of Thomas Winslow. (See wills of Timothy Clare, 1724, and his last wife Hannah, 1726 (Grimes). John Winslow (brother of Thomas) will p in Perq, Jan 25, 1753, names sons: Benjamin, Israel, John, & Joseph, dau's: Elizabeth, Hannah, & Esther, wife Esther.

The 2d John, whom it seems certain was nephew of John (1), made his will also in Perq Co, p July 1754, naming sons: Josiah, Thomas, & Samuel, dau Miriam, and wife Mary (d of Peter Pearson) therefore we make this distinction, so there will be no confusion of the two Johns, who come so close together. He has been classed as John Winslow (2) to distinguish him from his uncle, by the same name.?

Winslow, Benjamin (1) John (1) m Rachel White (d of Thomas, & Rachel née Jordan) and had issue according to his will: (Nov 1794) Sons: Joseph, John, Jordan, and Benjamin (2) dau's: Sarah, & Rachel. His wife is not named in his will, but she is mentioned in the will of her mother, whose will was located behind an old looking glass, by an antique dealer in Suffolk Va, a few years past. This will is very interesting, but unfortunately is not dated, or signed, positive proof however can be found in the fact that she names the identical children in her will, that her husband Thomas White does in his 1762, p in Perq. (See Perq records.) Mr. Alonza Winslow of Winfall N. C. is a direct descendant of this line of the Winslow family, but the writer has not the data to trace his line.

Winslow, Joseph, was grt 225a in Perq, Mar 6, 1740/1. (Col Rec, Vol 4, p 588.)

Winslow, Timothy, was grt 540a in Perq, Nov 17, 1743. His wife Rachel née Wilson, m 2d William Townsend, and 3d John Williams. (See Townsend, & Wilson.)

Nathan Winslow, Esq.
1795—1873

John Randolph Winslow, M.D.
1820—1866

Caleb Winslow, M.D.
1824—1895
Born in Perquimans County. Died in Baltimore.

Randolph Winslow, M.D.
1852
Born in Perquimans County. Residence, Baltimore.

DESCENDANTS OF THOMAS WINSLOW AND ELIZABETH CLEAR (CLARE) WINSLOW

Winslow, Henry, came to Perq Co, from London about 1740/1. He made petition to the Court Mar 11, 1740/1 for possession of 3333a of land in Perq, called "Birkswear" formerly grt George Catchmaid, & conveyed to sd Winslow. He had no descendants in Perq apparently.

WOOD

The earliest emigrant by the name of Wood, was John, who came from London to Isle of Wight Co, in "Bonadventure" Jan 1634, age 26. He married in said Co, Margaret ——— & had, according to the Quaker Reg of Lower Mo Meeting, Nansemond Co Va, one dau: Elizabeth, b 27, 7mo, 1658. He died soon after this date, and we find his widow married to Thomas Taberer of same Co, by whom she had issue: 1 Christian, b — 9mo 1661—2 Elizabeth b — 10mo 1663. From the fact that there was a *second* dau *Elizabeth*, one would naturally suppose that *John Wood's* dau Elizabeth did not long outlive her father.

William Wood came to Va in "Hopewell" Sept 1635, age 27, Elizabeth, age 24, & Jo Wood, age 26. Another Wm Wood was trans' to Rapp Co Va, July 29, 1650, by Robert Bird. Edward Wood was Trans' to Norfolk Co Va, by John Ashcomb, who was granted 829a of land, "on Langleys Creek, upper Norfolk Co," for transporting emigrants; Mar 6, 1683. With this Edward Wood we are directly concerned, because his descendants moved to Chowan Co N. C.. From Chowan they drifted over into Perquimans. John Wood took up land in Nansemond Co Va, Apl 25, 1667. Whose son he was is not made manifest, but we find in Berkeley Par Reg Perq Co, "Mr John Woode, minister of gospell" performing the rites of matrimony in Perq, as early as June 13, 167—, when he officiated at the marriage of Alex Lillington on that date, and he also married Mr. Wm Therrell, to Mrs. Jean Godfrey, Dec 2, 1676. He is not mentioned as one of the ministers sent out from England by S. P. G., and may very probably be an itinerant, coming down from Va for special occasions. A natural procedure, considering the fact that N. C. for some time after this continued to be a part of Va. If they sent us governors, why would they not also send ministers, to look after the soul's welfare?

There were two distinct families of Woods, in Albemarle, and it is thought that those who settled near Woodville, on Little River, may perhaps be descendants of this earlier branch, but no actual proof has been found. The Woods of Perq, like those of Chowan adhered to the Church of England, proof of which can be found in Berkeley Par Reg, from the fact that William Wood, next found on the record, was married to Deborah Sutton (d of George) May 8, 1718, "by Dr. Urmstone (John) minister of the Church of England." George Sutton however was a strong Quaker, and it seems probable that her family carried over Wm Wood, as we later find the name on the Records of Friends. George Sutton in his will Perq, p Mar 11, 1699, bequeathed to his dau Deborah a "Plantation at the hickory." There is to this day in Perq a place called by that name, on the highway leading to Elizabeth City. William Wood, & wife Deborah had issue: 1 Richard, b Oct 30, 1720—2 Sarah, b Oct 23, 1721, d Mch 21, 1722/3—3 William (2) b Sept 3, 1722/3—4 George, b Sept 2, 1724—5 Deborah, b Mar 25, 1725/6—6 Rebecca, b June 3, 1727—7 Elizabeth, b Dec 18, 1728. Deborah Wood died same day. (A case of too much child bearing.) Sarah Wood died Mch 17, 1722/3. (See Sutton family, this book.)

William Wood dec'd Dec 1, 1769, Mary Wood Admix, before Seth Sumner, J. P., Mary Wood petitioned the Court Oct 17, 1769, for leave "to sell perishable Estate of her dec'd husband William Wood." (Loose papers.)

Wood, Richard (1) William (1) m Hannah Lowry, 19, 10mo 1746, issue: 1 Tamer, b 21, 9mo 1747—2 Winnefred, b 29, 3mo 1749—3 William (3) b 12, 11mo 1750—4 Rhoda, b 23, 1mo 1753—5 Benjamin, b 16, 4mo 1756—6 Samuel, b 29, 11mo 1758, d 13, 11mo 1782—Rachel, b 3, 1mo 1761.

(2) Wood, William (2) William (1) m Mary ———. Issue: 1 Deborah, b 25, 1mo 1764—2 Rebeckah, b 29, 5mo 1765—3 William, b 4, 10mo 1766.

(2) Wood, Richard, m Sarah Morris, "at Simons Creek" 20 8mo 1764. (d of Aaron.)

Wood, Richard, m Cynthia Lassiter, Aug 21, 1800. (Chowan Co marriage bonds.)

Records of Norfolk Co give the fact "that Wm Wood hath departed this country," Oct 5, 1687. From this line are descended Mr John Q. A. Wood of Elizabeth City, & his brother George dec'd. The first for years Clerk of Perquimans county. Mr Wood has always been a fine citizen, and his family highly respected.

John Wood who appears as Clerk of Perq for so many years, probably came to the Co from Chowan. He m Miss Wingfield, and had son Charles Wingfield Wood of Perq Co, who lived at Woodlawn, an old home on the outskirts of Hertford, acquired by his father from Joseph Cannon. Charles W. Wood m Mary (Mollie) Skinner, (d of Benjamin Skinner, and wife Elizabeth Leigh (d of James Leigh, of Durants Neck) and had issue: 1 John, died an infant.— 2 Elizabeth (Bettie) m Mr W. G. Gaither issue: a number of children, all married but two. 3 Mary Wood, m T. F. Winslow of Hertford, issue: 1 Mae Wood, single—2 Katherine Blount, m W. H. Hudson, and had one daughter Mary Tudor—3 Francis E. Winslow, m Nemmie Parish of Rocky Mt N. C., where they reside, issue three girls, and one son. He is a prominent Lawyer of said place, and stands high in his profession. 4 Elizabeth Blount, m Thomas Wilcox of Norfolk Va, issue three children.

Mr. W. G. Gaither and wife Elizabeth Wood, had issue: 1 Charles W. Gaither, m Lula Hayes, and issue a son and daughter—2 Helen (unmarried)— 3 Elizabeth, m Edward Conger of Elizabeth City, N. C. (no issue)—4 Sarah, m C. Burnett Lewis, issue one son—5 William G. Gaither, m Helen Robinson (d of Charles, & Mary Leigh) issue three children—6 Rev Wood Gaither (Episcopal minister) m Penelope Weddell of Tarboro N. C. issue four children —7 Mary, m William Van Eberstein, of Washington, N. C., no issue—8 Nettie Martin, m Wallace Huffines of Rocky Mount, N. C., no issue—9 Louise, unmarried.

EDWARD WOOD LINE

As we have already seen, Edward Wood came to Norfolk Co Va Mar 6 1683. In an affidavit made Jan 1680/1, he gave his age as 38. He was living in Upper Parish Nansemond Co Va, July 18, 1715. Of course he could not be the same, who made his will in Chowan Co, Aug 9, 1691, naming wife Alice, to whom he left "Land at Yawpim." We have to depend for descent from two brothers, Edward, & John Wood, who made a joint deed in Norfolk

Co Va, Nov 1, 1721, as follows: Edward Wood, & Mary his wife, John Wood, & Margarett his wife, of Chowan Co N. C. sold unto Thos. Freeman, & Sarah his wife of Norfolk Co, 100a "where said Edward, & John formerly dwelt" adj land of Thos. Cottell, "for the yearly Rent of one ear of Indian Corne." Test' Tho. Hobgood, Tho. Collett. Another deed same Co, 100a in Elizabeth Parish, Co of Norfolk, "where Edward Wood formerly dwelt," on Spring Mills Creek, adj John Eastwood, Robert Collett, & Edward Wingate. Recorded Dec 1721.

Wood, James, of Perq (connection not apparent) will p Feby 1822, names dau's: Nancy & Sally Wood, gr-daus: Susan, & Sally Norcom (dau's of Betsy dec'd). Sons: Edward, Richard, & James (who moved to Tyrrell Co) sons William, & Edward Exrs. Test' Thomas D. Martin, Mary M. Martin.

Wood, William (1) James (1) will Perq, p Nov 1824, Wife Ann, sons: William E. Wood, Edward Wood, dau's: Elizabeth, & Lucy Ann Wood.

Wood, Edward, (1) James (1) will Perq, p May 1827, names wife Elizabeth, & children (who are unnamed) but his sister Ann in her will, p Feby 1830, gives the names of his children, thus: "Little Edward Wood, son of brother Edward, and James, & William Wood sons of same; she also names niece, Elizabeth S. Hall (d of brother William) sister Sarah, nieces Sarah, & Susan Norcom, sister-in-law Elizabeth Wood (widow of Edward) brother John E. Wood.

Wood, John, was Clerk of Perq 1808.

From this line descended Mr. Charles Wingfield Wood, who made his life-long home in a lovely old place near Hertford, which was only a few years ago destroyed by fire. He has descendants living at the present time in Hertford, Elizabeth City, Rocky Mount, and other points in N. C. This family has from time immemorial stood high in the community, & has sent out into the world many fine representative people.

Marriages

Wood, Samuel, m dau of Robert Smith, prior to May 1, 1693. (Legal papers.)
Wood, Thomas, m Anna Bailey, June 3, 1778. (Mar bonds Pasq Co.)
Wood, William, m Elizabeth Guy, Aug 18, 1804.
Wood, Evan, m Margaret Barber, Jan 4, 1786.
Wood, Elizabeth (d of John Davis of Pasq Co) named in his will, p Apl 1753.

WOOLARD

William Woolard gave a power of Att' to Mr John Cary, "to make Clayme" for the Estate of Justinian Cooper dec'd of Isle of Wight Co Va, Feb 20, 1666.

William Woolard, late of Harwich, in Essex, Mariner, now resident of Isle of Wight Va, M'chant, heir of Justinian Cooper dec'd, 1671. (Isle of Wight records.)

William Woolard m dau of John Philpot, prior to Sept 19, 1694, who names him in his will, on that date. William Woolard will Perq Co, p Feb 2, 1691/2, names only wife Sarah.

Richard Woolard next to appear in Perq, m Jane Richards Feby 1, 1703, issue: Richard (s of Richard, & Jane) b Feby 23, 1704—2 Mary, b Jan 19, 1706/7, d July 20, 1708. From Berkeley Parish Reg we gain the information that he had a former wife Ann, who "died last of Oct 1702." He with wife Ann made a deed in Perq July 24, 1702. Richard Woolard died Feby 4, 1706/7.

The will of Richard Woolard, p in Perq, April 8, 1707. Sons: John, & Richard, dau's: Hannah Boros, & Ann Woolard, wife Jane.

Woolard, William, (2) will Chowan Co, p May 1762, Dau Sarah, wife Mary, other Leg: Jeremiah Frazier, Thomas Beasley, sister Mary Hopkins, Mary, & George Beasley (children of John) wife, & son-in-law John Beasley Exrs. In the Division of the Estate of James Beasley, Chowan Co N. C., Mary Woolard is named as his "Mother." Her will Chowan, p Nov 17, 1788, she names "son John Beasley, dau Mary Bunch, gr-children: Ann, Jeremiah, & Richard Frazier, (children of Jeremiah) gr-son Francis Beasley (s of John) gr-dau Mary Vail, gr-dau's: Sarah Roberts, & Sarah Beasley, gr-son John Frazier (s of Jeremiah), Sarah Woolard, (d of John Evans). Robert Evans had dau Miriam who m —— Woolard. (See division of his Estate.)

WRIGHT

Jeffrie Wright was granted 50a of land in Norfolk Co Va, for his own trans' lying in Linkhorn (Princess Anne Co). John Wright a subject in the Colony at Jamestown, Jan 1609 (Browns Genesis to America). Thomas Wright had 250a of land granted him, Dec 16, 1647, for trans' Peter, & Robert Langley, & Ursula Baylie. He made his will in Isle of Wight Co Va, p Sept 9, 1701, naming sons: John, (who was under age) James, "all my Coopers tools," Thomas, & Joseph, dau Mary, wife Elizabeth. Test' George, & Violet Wright.

Ann, William, & Joseph Wright of Nansemond Co Va, acted as Exrs, of the will of John Wright of Albemarle, Gent; Sept 14, 1694. Ann Wright here mentioned is named in the will of William Townsend of Perq Co, as *daughter*, April 1767. Christopher Wright, & wife Elizabeth of N. C. "late of Princess Anne Co Va," sold to Simon Stone, a plantation on Western Shore of Princess Anne Co, 462½a, 352½a of which was purchased of Cornelius Calvert, & Elizabeth his wife, Nov 1751. Seal Nov 20, 1778. Dr Wright was brother of John, and both were sons of Wm Wright of Nansemond Co, who died 1750. Stephen Wright m Katherine Bond, Aug 13, 1724, in Princess Anne Co. William Wright m Mary Butt, Feb 15, 1744, same county. Samuel Wright petitioned for Adm of Estate of Comfort Dowdy, dec'd, "being nearest kin" (no date). He died in Perq Co, before July 16, 1757, when his Estate was divided; heirs: Thomas, Mary, Hannah, Samuel Wright. His Inventory Dec 3, 1757, Elizabeth Wright Admix. Said Elizabeth is named in the will of Thomas Barclift, as daughter, Jan 1750/1.

Samuel Wright (1) in Perq, will p July 29, 1718, sons: Thomas, & Samuel.

Samuel Wright (2) will Perq, p April 1754. Sons: Thomas, & Samuel, daughters: Mary, & Hannah, wife Elizabeth, one of the witnesses; Jermine Dowdy.

Benjamin Wright, m Ann Townsend, Dec 7, 1762. (Mar bonds Perq Co.)

John Wright, m Tamar Johnson, July 8, 1791. (Mar bonds Perq Co.)

John Wright above was son of Thomas, whose will p in Perq, Jan 1790, names son John, and William, dau's: Sarah, and Ann Biggs, sons: Joseph, & James.

The will of Elizabeth Wright, p in Perq, Jan 1785, names Dau: Elizabeth Wordsworth, gr-son Samuel Wright, dau-in-law Mourning Wright, son-in-law Enoch Raper, gr-dau Fanny Raper, son Thomas.

RECORDS OF DEEDS

RENT ROLL
(Perquimans Co, Prior to 1700)

Thomas Harvey 631a, Alex Lillington Yawpim, 640a, do on Indian Creek 250a, Caleb Calloway 250a on Yawpim Creek. Benjamin Laker, 538a, Jane Charles 287a on Yawpim Creek, Thomas Lepper 470a on Yawpim Creek, John Barrow 300a, John Wyatt 288a on Yawpim Creek, Peter Gray 200a on Perq River, John Gosby (s of John & Hannah) 300a on Suttons Creek, John Spelman 350a, Roger Snell 250a. Sarah (d of Hannah) 200a on Suttons Creek. (This land was situated where the old Toms home still stands on the head of Suttons Creek, now vacant and dilapidated) Robert Harmon 92a, Thos. Pierce 300a. Timothy Clare, Perq River, 473a, John Cheson 300a, Robert Beasley 282a, William Lury 250a, Charles Macdaniel 143a, John Whitby 230a, Richard Cheston (Chesson) 200a, Samuel Nicholson 300a, William Bogue Perq River 200a (His land lay on the River across from Hertford, running down to Vosses Creek, and calls for "Bar Garden," he made a deed of gift of this land to his dau Margaret, who m Jonathan Jones of Pasq Co) Jane Byard 366a, Richard Fox Perq River 200a, James Morgan Vosses Creek 300a, Patrick Canady 210a, James Loadman Perq River 143a, Ralph Fletcher 370a, Jenkins Williams 317a, Albert Albertson 290a (on Suttons Creek, & Long Branch) Isaac Wilson 490a, David Sherwood 350a George Sutton 99a, Lawrence Gonsolvo (Consolvo) 560a, John Fendall 640a. William Barclift Little River 150a William Tomling (Tomblin) Little River 288a, John Hutson Little River 400a, Richard Nowell Little River 400a, John Pierce 300a, John Foster Yawpim (Chowan Co) 200a, John Pricklove Perq River 400a, Jonathan Phelps Perq River 310a, William Man Little River 120a, William Turner Little River 310a, Richard Rooks Deep Creek 150a William Godfrey do 350a, Jno. Godfrey 320a, William Stewart 238a, Jos. Commander Deep Creek 100a, Capt John Hunt Little River (Pasq Co) 450a, John Belman on the Sound Pasq Co, 280a, Albert Albertson Jr 300a on Deep Creek, Cornelius Lurry (Leary) 150a John Arnold Little River 150a, Ann, & Elizabeth Waller 350a (gr-dau's of George Durant (1)) John Cooke 300a Yawpim, Thomas Manwaring 640a, Francis Toms 640a, Edward Holmes 450a, Richard Woolard Yawpim 300a, Lawrence Hunt 200a in Pasq Co, John Willoughby 192a, Thomas Speight (s and heir of Capt William) 320a, also 210a in Chowan, John Hopkins 300a Yawpim, & 300a Indian Creek, Henry White 100a in Pasq Co, George Dear 27a called "Batts Grave" (an island at the mouth of Yawpim River.) Geo. Matthews 200a, James Thigpen 330a, James Fisher Yawpim Creek 225a, John Stepney Sr 293a, Hon'ble Thos. Harvey 300a, Johanah Taylor 164a, Benjamin Laker 187a, James Hibbins and Elinor his wife 284a on Yawpim River.

Vosses Creek is the same now called Brights Creek, about two miles from Hertford. Yeopim Creek, spelled variously Yawpim, Yoppim and Yeopim, is the same Creek each time mentioned. The correct spelling is Yeopim, and it is pronounced, Yoppim.

Also the Creek now called Minsies Creek, was originally Minge Creek, and later called Ming Creek, which in provincial parlance become Minses Creek. This Creek is in Harvey Neck, and is supposed to have been named for James Minge of Surry Co Va, who settled and took up land on said Creek before 1701.

He m Ruth Laker, d of Benjamin who survived him, & m 2d Richard Sanderson. He does not appear to have had issue. (See deeds in this book.)

ORIGINAL WILLS
Found Among Loose Papers in Perq.

Ichabod Boswell of Perq. Land to Lidea Boswell, dau of Thomas. Peter Mundin, & wife "use of Land." Probated Mar 25, 1761. Test, Elisha Parker, John Henby, Rachel Boswell. (Minute book Perq Co.)

Ambrose Knox, of Pasquotank, will probated March 1796. To son John 112a of Land in Pasquotank Co, which I bought of Benjamin White, John, & Seth Hobbs, & Joseph Banks, known by the name of "Dry Ridge" and nine negroes.

Unto nephew Hugh Knox, for the interest of his son Ambrose, my servant Harry, and requests that "he may be well used as long as he lives."

Unto my niece Christian Palin, my horse Paddy, riding chair, & harness.

Unto my nephew Andrew Knox, my Sword, and pistols, "that I bought at his fathers Vendue."

I leave "the use and occupation of four fifths of my Land, and plantation, on Yeopim, Perquimans Co whereon John Wyatt now lives; Known by the name of "John Wyatts patent, to said John Wyatt, and Parthena his wife during their natual lives, & to the longest liver of them (part next to Harmons), also nine negroes, the use of all my stock, & household furniture, plantation, utencils, now in their possession, and unto their heirs lawfully begotten forever."

To my servants that are of age, s10 each (except old Lucy) to whom I give s20. I leave "in Trust with my Exrs my Houses, & Lot in Nixonton, and 100a in Perq Co, which I bought of Joseph McAdams, also eight negroes of the residue of my estate, the interest to be applied to support my son Robert Knox, during his natual life, but in case of reformation of life, and conduct should appear in him, my Exrs shall confirm a fee Simple title to the property, otherwise the said property to descend to my son John Knox."

Bequest to niece Sarah Phelps.

To John Lane Sr s20, as "a Tokan of my Friendship to him."

Appoints nephew Andrew Knox, "Gardian to son John."

Hugh Knox, John Lane Sr Exrs. Dec 23, 1795.   Ambrose Knox. Seal.

Test' William Lans, Wm Jordan, Robt Jordan.

Pasquotank County, March Term 1796.   Enoch Relfe Clk.

Abraham Riggs of Perq, Mar 2, 1759. d. s. p. To wife Jane plantation for life, & at her death to Abraham Riggs (s of John), other legatees: brother John, Elizabeth Bedgood (d of William) Patsy Bedgood, William Bedgood. My kinsman Abraham Riggs, Kinsman Jacob Riggs. Wife, and William Foster, Exrs.

Test' Potsfull Peirce, Joseph Sutton, Joseph Mullin.

John Willson of Perq Co. Aug 6, 1760. To son Joseph, "Land on which I Dwell, after the descease of my wife Elizabeth." To said wife residue of Estate her Natual life, and at her death to be divided between all my children: John, Mourning, Joseph, Elizabeth Leydion, & Hariot Willson. Wife, & son John Exrs.

Test' Tho Newby, Joseph Mayo, Joseph White.

INDEX TO DEEDS

A

Adams, John, G 244.
  Peter, G 244.
Aden, William, G 65.
  Elizabeth, G 65.
  Samuel, G 65.
Akehurst, Daniel, A 147, F 322, 414.
Albertson, Esau, A 177, B 219, C 202, 34, D 152, E 139, 250.
  Peter, B 91, 134, C 72, 143, F 336.
  Arthur, C 72, D 93, E 63, F 304.
  Albert, A 120, B 108, 25, 48, C 51, 175, D 10, 72, 91, 163, F 4, G 25, 56, H 41.
  Nathaniel, A 288, 332, B 134, 48, D 163, F 4, 304, G 184.
  Isaac, E 59.
  Elihu, E 60, F 22, 116, 24.
  Joshua, F 304, H 146.
  William, G 99, H 14, 22, 70, I 153.
  Francis, H 146, I 58.
  Chalkey, H 263, 66, 67, I 466.
Alexander, Anthony, A 161, 67, 68, 210, B 209, D 79.
  Ann, A 167, 68, 210, 217.
Allston, John, B 122, 78, 269, I 305.
  Joseph, B 178.
Ambler, William, C 240.
Anderson, John, A 176, 79, 221, B 154, 87, 314, C 43, 166, D 81, 107, E 56, F 49, G 87, H 115, I 293.
  Jane, A 176.
  Jeane, A 221.
  James, A 207, 33, 331, B 154, C 35, 141, D 107, E 56, F 107.
  Deborah, A 233.
  Elizabeth, D 81, F 44, 48, 49.
  Joseph, I 96, 279.
  Samuel, I 279.
Angley, Elizabeth, B 10, C 17, 22.
Archdale, John, A 114, C 182, F 322.
Archdeacon, William, A 369, B 24.
Arkill, William, I 44, 61, 75, 81, 92, 129, 232, 306, 405, 455, 507.
  Hannah, I 61.
Arline, John, B 261.
Arnell, John, C 77, D 104.

Arnold, Lawrence, A 82, F 22, 120, 23, G 12, 249, 58.
  John, A 180, 384, B 228, C 77.
  William, D 201, 34, F 41, 64, 68, 262, G 12, H 298, I 356, 58, 66.
  Joseph, E 9, F 120, G 249, 56, 57, H 115, 88, I 296.
  Benjamin, I 35.
  Sarah, I 35.
  Asa, I 138, 39.
  Susannah, I 139.
Arps, Valentine, I 49.
Arrington, Christopher, D 66, H 251.
  Abigail, D 66, G 77.
  William, F 222, 41, 67, 98, 310, G 4, 77, 180, 205, 10, H 208, 312, 153, 83, 244.
Arrington, Mary, F. 310.
  Edward, G 77.
  Ezekiel, H 312, I 81, 315, 33, 97.
  Richard, I 76, 78, 83, 243, 457, 523.
  Susannah, I 139.
Asball, Pierce, D 92, F 146.
Asbell, Martha, I 132.
Asbill, Martin, B 197, 261, D 76, 92, F 146.
Asple, Martin, C 115, 190.
  Sarah, C 190.
Ashford, Jonathan, A 53.
Ashley, Sarah, E 25, F 89, G 204, I 423.
  John, E 25, 140, F 89.
  Joseph, E 25, F 89, 344, H 31.
  William, F 344, H 31, 124, 33.
  Rebecca, G 204.
Attkins, Richard, A 149.
Atoway, Thomas, A 9, 64, 179, B 33, C 53, F 245, 52, 214.
  Elleaner, B 33, 35, 124, F 245.
  Mary, B 33.
  Elizabeth, B. 33.
Auston, Robert, A 122.
Avery, Robert, F 167, G 5.
Avingdile, John, A 314.
  Comfort, A 314.
Ayres, Thomas, A. 231.

B

Bacon, James, F 170, 240.
  John, E 141.
  Richard, I 376.
  Joyce, I 376.
Bagley, Thomas, B 1, 5, 6, 67, 68, 71, 74, 87, 266, C 3, 64, 277, D 21, 55, F 17, 19, 39, 125, 228, 318, G 59, 141.
  Susan, B 67.
  Joshua, H 126, 226, I 143, 59, 74, 207, 335.
  Mary, I 143.
  Samuel, E 90, F 209, 29, 76, H 192, 216, I 40, 408.
  William, F 17, 39, I 40, 90.
  Benjamin, G 196, 255.
Bailey, John, I 154.
  Daniel, I 154.
Baker, Moses, F 67, 119, 55, 67, G 5.
Banks, John, A 323, B 57, C 175, 262, F 11, D 36, 49.
  Sarah, B 57, 58.
  Richard, E 72, H 94, 240, I 504.
Barber, William, I 28.
  Moses, I 50.
  Isaac, I 162.
  Joel, I 252.
Barclift, John, B 248, C 177, 84, 248, D 91, 104, 8, 10, 67, E 49, 79, F 29, 30, 143, 45, 216, 47, 71, 395, 96, 400, G 41, 44, 45, 49, 153, 71, H 58, I 469.
  Thomas, B 321.
  Ann, C 162; 248, D 110, G 153, H 58.
  William, C 177, F 143, G 163, H 50, 295.
  Joshua, C 213, D 88, 108, 13, F 65, I 507.
Barclift, Samuel, D 4, 149, F 293, G 141, 192, I 23.
  Elizabeth, D 51, H 174, I 21, 146, 326, 493.
  Sarah, D 108.
  Hannah, F 395, G 131, 218, 326.
  Demson, G 246, 47, H 20, 295.
  Thomas, H 148.
  Asa, H 305.
  Lemuel, I 490.
  Noah, I 14, 25, 87, 146, 211.

Millicent, I 211.
Blake, I 199, 211.
Barnes, Robert, B 7, C 112, 193, 215.
  Elizabeth, B 7.
  Joseph, C 112.
  Mary, C 112.
  Jeremiah, D 91.
Barrow, John, A 74, 381, B 9, D 13, 14, E 25, G 202, H 31, 76, I 476.
  William, A 170, 227, B 157, D 13, 14, 115, F 56.
  Elizabeth, A 170.
  Joseph, C 245, D 13, 14, 66, E 98, H. 31, 52, 76.
  Margaret, D 27.
  Martha, H 76, I 476.
  Eri, I 495.
Barnstable, William, B 50, 80.
Bartlett, William, A 56, 59 (Barclift).
  Thomas, A 189, 286.
  John, B 246, 47, C 133, F 399.
  Samuel, F 184, 228, G 59, 141.
  Bettie, F 188.
Barton, Valentine, A 6, 7.
Bass, John, B 62, C 2, H 176.
Batchler, Richard, A 125.
  Katherine, A 125.
Bateman, Jonathan, A 14, C 43, 530, 31.
  John, A 103, B 33, C 53, D 91, H 41, 48, 301, I 29, 302, 407.
  William, F 92, G 14, 51, 193, 253, 56.
  Bettie, G 193, H 41, 48, 105, 301.
  Joseph, I 140, 51, 312.
  Benjamin, I 25, 54, 86, 140, 89.
  Mary I 25, 30.
  Ann, I 312.
  Miriam, 1 29.
Baudrey, Peter, A 265, 66.
Beasley, Robert, A 50, 55, 177, 262.
  Patrick, A 126.
  Francis, A 161, 67, 68, 97, B 45, 299, I 509.
  Hannah, A 197.
  James, A 226, 177, 262, B 298, C 253.
Bedford, William, D 104, G 185.
  Ann, D 104.
  Thomas, H 37.
Bedgood, William, D 77, F 375.
  Ann, D 77.

Bellamy, Sir Edward, G 221.
Bellman, John, A 44, 178.
Bell, Thomas, B 304, G 107, 212.
Bennett, Joseph, A 130.
  John, A 159, 60, 62, 252, 53, 63, 77, 78, 79, 90, C 122, 313.
  Rose, C 122, 313.
  William, H 339.
Bentley, Richard, A 5, 12, 40, 47, 67, 105, 152.
  John, A 47, 67, 104, B 157, 70, C 229, D 99, F 56.
  William, A 82, 83.
  Francis, A 366.
  Mitchell, B 172.
Berriman, Richard, B 175, F 161, 419.
Beyard, Jane, C 3.
Biggs, Timothy, A 16, 377.
  Thomas, F 397.
  Moses, I 113.
Binard, Jane, H 19.
Binford, Elizabeth, F 107, I 188.
  John, F 107, I 188.
Bird, Thomas, A 191.
Blair, Jain, I 386, 538, 40.
Blake, David, A 50, 101.
Blanchard, Ephrim, D 153.
  Elizabeth, I 70.
Blitchenden, Thomas, A 309, 37, 39, 61, B 6, 195, 97, 233, 44, 45, 61, 72, 79, 97, 323, E 24, 30, 61, 141, 42, C 11, 64, 68, 69, 163, 87, 93, 236, D 18, 21, 75, 79, 97, 112, D 146, 53, 60, F 68, 234.
  Mary, B 272.
  John, D 146, E 24, 30, 53, F 67, 124, 52.
  William, E 24, 30, 53, F 32, 68, 124, G 177.
  Abraham, E 36, F 147, 61.
Blount, Thomas, A 169.
  Mary, A 169.
  James, A 376.
  Charles, E 153, 66, F 79, 87, 150, 51, 311, 98, G 17, 76, 111, 221, 22, H 18, 28, 72, 108, 34, 84, 85, 88, 305, I 13, 86, 87, 189.
  Joseph, E 168, F 160.
  Elizabeth, F 161.
  Edward, H 56, 72, 305.

  Edmund, H 185, 239, I 131, 49, 298, 53, 77.
Boazman, Ralph, F 130.
Boice, Ephroditus, C 113, 72, 79, 269.
  Ann, C 172, 79, 269.
Boiyce, Judah, F 156.
  Judith, I 50.
Boyce, Robert, C 181.
Boyse, John, D 15, 85, 106, F 205, 94, 422, H 294, I 434.
  Susanna, D 15.
  Moses, F 422, G 145, 50.
Boyce, William, H 296.
  Duke, H 296.
  Isaac, H 303.
  Job, H 303.
  Benjamin, I 371, 404.
Bond, Samuel, A 264, 70, 84, 338, B 195, 241, C 46, 59, 67, 187, 245, D 75, E 29, 30, 110, 142, F 53, 68, 241, 48, 49, G 77, H 208.
  Elizabeth, A 284.
  Luke, F 248.
  Richard, B 322, G 77, H 208.
  Edward, H 208.
Bonner, Thomas, F 84.
Bogue, William, A 45, 107, 84, 205, 36, 60, 317, 18, 19, B 27, 67, 237, 68, 309, C 3, 268, D 60, 82, 86, 134, E 13, F 318, I 64, 100.
  Eliner, B 27.
  John, B 126, G 228.
  Josiah, C 278, D 86, 94, 134, 42, 48, E 130, G 200.
  Robert, D 132, G 164, H 22, 79, 101, I 43, 64.
  Deborah, D 148.
  Elizabeth, I 460.
  Jesse, G 200, H 64, 65, 101, 22, 262.
  Joseph, G 224.
  Job, H 143, I 297.
  Ruth, H 143.
  Mark, H 309, 26.
  Leah, I 297.
Bosman, Ralph, A 204, 343, 46, B 169, 285, D 127, E 80, F 352.
Boswell, Thomas, B 83, 134, 35, 36, 202, 312, C 174, D 2, 44, 88, F 269, 372,

G 30, 33, 57, 156, H 27, 156, I 208, 336.
William, B 201, 56, F 97.
James, C 174, D 2, 57.
Charles, D 2.
John, D 2, F 174, 200, 372.
George, D 2, 31, 32, 57, F 27, 31, I 154, 406.
Jane, D 32.
Joshua, D 44, F 251, 74, H 263, 81, 300.
Isaac, G 54, 58, I 194.
Hannah, F 173, 200.
Ichabod, F 372.
Elizabeth, F 372.
Joseph, G 27, 36, 57, 156, I 106.
George, G 33, 34, 35, 58, 233, 34, H 12, 207.
Simon, H 263, 300.
Amos, H 279, 300.
Simeon, I 152.
Bound, Richard, A 358, 66, B 65, F 267, 98.
Abigail, A 366, B 137.
Edward, F. 267, 98.
Samuel, F 267, 98.
Bowin, Dr. Benjamin, H 292.
Branch, Isacher, E 52, F 108, G 244, I 47, 160, 79, 348, 461, 72, 73, 79.
Sarah, F 108.
Arkill, F 108.
Joel, F 108.
Elizabeth, I 70, 192.
Job, I 190, 92, 472, 73, 79.
Brasier, John, G 113, D 122, 172, 79, H 306.
Elizabeth, D 122.
Brazier, Reuben, H 247, I 370.
Bratton, Nathaniel, I 241.
John, I 343, 44, 45, 46, 47.
Brinkley, John, C 54, 91, D 56, 117, F 321, 38, 39, 424, I 193.
Michael, D 118, F 33.
James, F 33, 199, 320, 21, 424, H 308, I 304, 56, 535.
Aphraditus, F 114, 292, G 20, H 157.
Ann, F 321, 38, 39.
Hannah, I 193.
Thomas, 1 226, 301.
Peter, I 241.

Brin, William, B 196.
Bier, John, A 190.
Brooking, Vivian, F 375, G 19.
Brothers, Richard, E 83.
Mary, E 83.
Brown, Francis, F 363, 423, G 114, 48, 68, 201, 29, H 67, 89, 90, 119.
Thomas, H 89.
Bufkin, Ralph, B 40, 111, 206, 70, 78, 83, 85, C 266, D 127.
Bullock, Thomas, E 87, 171, F 28, G 164.
Joseph, F 352.
Thomas, E 80.
Bunch, Jules, D 83.
Julius, F 198, H 4, I 19.
Jesse, H 94.
Joel, I 261.
Burnham, Caleb, I 339, 57, 135.
Jesse, I 31.
Millicent, I 31.
Burkenhead, John, B 1.
Burket, Joseph, C 91, 127, 40, 217, F 114, 202, 92, G 20, H 157.
John, C 91, 211, G 20, H 157.
Thomas, F 54, I 26.
Mary, F 54, I 26.
Burton, Timothy, A 16, 17.
Bush, James, I 538.
Butler, Christopher, A 179.
William, A 108, 132.
Elizabeth, I 26.
Willis, I 464, 87.
Byar, Richard, A 44, 45, 190.
Jeane, A 107, 8, 32, 73.
Byrd, John, C 52.

C

Calldrom, Elizabeth, E 42, F 201, 2.
Calle, Richard, C 148, H 96, 229, I 61, 63.
Calloway, Caleb A, 141, 373, 82, E 170.
Joshua, A 305, 67, B 165, 201, 80, 93, 94, C 1, 10, 51, 76.
Alice, E 170.
Campbell, John, F 193, 94, G 46, 111, 34, 35, 73, 221, 24, 28.
Cannidy, Patrick, B 60.

INDEX TO DEEDS 455

Carman, William, A 322, 40, 49, 54, B 284, 89, C 113, 172, 73, 254, 69, D 46, 122, F 306.
　Elizabeth, B 370.
　Jeremiah, C 160, 70.
Caron, James, A 87.
Carpenter, Francis, A 330.
Carlton, Arthur, A 177, 257, 58.
Cartright, Peter, G 25, 26.
　John, A 134, 256.
　Thomas, A 230.
Caruthers, Nath'l, C 38, 111, 20, 46, 47, D 5, 6, 7, 8, E 21, 71, F 110, 324, 34, 49, H 2.
　Jacob, D 6, E 138, 48, 64, F 110, 68, 348, 49, G 24, H 2.
　James, D 8, E 71, H 2, I 528.
　John, E 21, F 83, 334.
　Ann, F 83, 110, 349.
　Elizabeth, F 110.
　Jeremiah, G 193, 216, F 105, 7, 83.
　Tamer, G 193, H 105, 7.
　Thomas, I 528.
　William, I 528.
　Mark, I 528.
Cary, Thomas, B 101, 2.
　Ann, F 290, 387.
　Robert, F 290, 387.
Castleton, George, A 33.
Catchmaid (Catchmeyd, Catch many), George, A 71, 376, 80, 81, 82, C 218, D 97, G 135, H 127.
　Edward, C 218, D 97, F 193, G 135.
　Thomas, C 218, D 97, F 193, G 135.
Cella, Smith, C 275.
Chancey, Miriam, F 244, 50, G 79, 116, H 58.
　Edmund, H 52.
　Zachery (Zachariah) C 156, 68, D 52, 58, 60, 78, 87, 95, 96, 117, 20, 21, 29, 33, 44, 51, 61, E 1, 3 10, 13, 28, 65, 66, 67, 73, 86, 101, 13, 33, F 111, 391, G 22, H 298, I 88, 116, E 101, 3, 4.
　Stephen, I 277.
　John, F 100, 244, 50, G 79, H 158.
Chandler, Elizabeth, C 218, 19, 20, 22, 23, D 97, 98, 99, 100, 15, F 193, G 135.

Chapman, William, A 9, 10.
Chappel, Robert, B 317, D 145, E 154, F 420.
　Elizabeth, C 197.
　John, F 207, 230.
　Malachi, H 226.
　Mark, G 177, H 360.
　Jesse, I 39, 99, 300.
　Job, I 235, 463.
Charles, William, A 19, 21, 22, 23, G 147, 259, H 146, 52.
　Daniel, A 21, 22.
　Samuel, A 21, 22, 136, 51, C 257, 59, 68, F 132, 195, G 132, 47, H 19, 21, 52, 268, 388, I 153, 445.
　Elizabeth, A 151.
　Jean, B 193.
　Jane, A 273.
　Hannah, E 4.
Chaston (Cheaston, Chesson), Richard, A 1, 94, 315, 16, B 5, 6, 56, 74, 214, 15, 17, 60, C 21, 26, 64, 81, 128, 252, D 21, 34, 55, 61, E 70, 77, F 125, 318, I 100.
　William, H 82, I 153, 323.
　James, B 119, C 90, G 244.
　John, C 257, E 52, G 244, I 152, 53, 323.
Clare, Timothy, A 43, 73, 80, 81, 93, 107, 249, 94, 320, 22, 28, 56, C 1, 3, 8, 48, 88, 94, 96, 113, 49, 258, D 12, 16, 20, 22, 24, 47, 89, 90, 102, E 11, (will) 12, 145, F 8, 60, 63, 72.
　Hannah, B 38, 41, 45, 46, 64, 78, 182, 83, 313, 16, C 38, E 11.
Clayton, Henry, B 54, 223, 40.
　Richard, G 136, 37, H 250, 88, 89, I 60.
　Sarah, B 240, H 170.
　John, F 237, 325, 35, 89, G 110, H 250, 91, I 514.
　Margaret, I 60.
　Mary, I 60.
　Rebecca, H 250, 91, I 514.
　David, I 514.
Clarke, John, H 170.
　Sarah, H 170.
Clemons, William, I 28, 133, 303, 389.
　Abigail, I 28.

HISTORY OF PERQUIMANS COUNTY

Cock (Cox), Robert, B 18, 318, C 30, 78, F 50, 269, H 156, 282, I 154, 213, 325.
  Elizabeth, B 318.
Cocke, Joseph, H 372, I 209.
Cockey, Thomas, A 144.
Coddel, Elizabeth, F 378.
  Henry, C 90, F 381.
Coffin, Mary, A 186, 207.
Coggwell, Henry, A 300,
Coles, James, A 142, 48, 54, 55, 88, 216, 40, 306, 10, B 130, 87, 99, 223, F 201.
  Mary A 148, 88, B 130, 223.
Collerton, Elizabeth, G 122.
Coleston (Colson), William, B 228, F 216, 401, G 189, 93, H 105, I 385, 87.
  Miriam, F 216, G 193, H 105.
  David, G 192, 97, H 45, 206, 20, 27.
  Mourning, H 206, 8.
Cooper, George, C 21.
Cook, John, H 147, 228.
Collins, William, A 106.
  Thomas, B 32, 36, 97, 113, 98, 205, D 21, E 139, F 245, 52, 54, 55, G 190, H 205, I 4, 94, 129, 87, 488.
  Alexandris, B 97.
  Dennis, B 204, D 35, H 316.
  James, C 219, 20 D 21.
  Andrew, F 298, H 116, 200, 4, 8, 40, 321.
  Ann, I 4, 129.
  Anna, H 200, 8.
  Christopher, H 200, 54, 321, I 66, 186, 206.
  Elizabeth, I 66, 206.
  Jonathan, H. 13, 59.
Commander, Thomas, B 96, 171, 200, I 10, 99, C 175, D 72, F 3, 66.
  Conner, Dempsey, F 5, G 22.
Consolver, Lawrence, A 145.
Copeland, Charles, H 182, I 84, 320.
  Jesse, H 392, I 161.
  Elusia, I 84.
  Peninah, I 161.
  Sarah, I 161.
Corbin, Francis, G 151.
Corwell, Aaron, I 261.
Cosand, Gabriel, F 171, G 94, H 180.
Corprew, Thomas, E 168.
  John, G 246, 51, 63, H 20.
  Anne, G 246.
  Sarah, G 251, 63.
Cox, Seth, I 154.
  John, I 175.
Cracofard, William, A 378.
Craven, James, C 169.
Creecy, John, D 28, G 212, I 47, 115, 17, 19, 292, 389, 91, 92, 421, 26, 30, 31, 33, 37, 506, 39.
  Joseph, D 41, 150, 55, F 108, 227, 32, 35, 53, 363, G 77, H 190, 254, I 410.
  Levi, H 62, I 177, 425.
  Eleazer, I 174.
  Elizabeth, I 174.
  Thomas, I 243, 303, 523.
Cretchington, Samuel, B 60, 61.
Crisp, Nicholas, B 105, 20, 21, D 166, E 41.
Cuzens, Elizabeth, I 3.

D

Dail (Deal), Joshua, C 251, E 102, 5, 37, 49, G 145, H 283, 94.
Dameson, Onepephans, I 324.
Dawson, Anthony, A 68, 104, 307, 8, E 146.
Davenport, Richard, A 150, 82, 208, 9, B 145, 47, 287, C 250.
  Johanna, A 182, C 250.
  John, A 208, 9, 237, 38, B 146, 47, 287, C 250.
  Anne, B 147, C 250.
Davis, John, A 376, E 29, F 53, G 162, H 112, 231, I 203.
  Mary, A 367, F 223, 99.
  Thomas, B 126, D 15, F 117, 422.
  Elizabeth, B 126.
  Hugh, B 147, 209, C 250.
  William, B 205, E, 37, F 223, 99, H 316.
  Andrew, C 247.
  Jane, D 15.
  Joshua, F 59, G 209, 32, H 101, 231.
  Moses, F 117.
  Rachel, F 223, G 162, H 112, 231.
  Sarah, G 162.
  Marmaduke, H 43, 61, 112.
  Ann, H 231.
  James, H 282.

INDEX TO DEEDS 457

DeCrow, Robert, H 385, I 71, 201.
   Sarah, H 385.
Deare, George, A 150, B 287.
   Elizabeth, A 150.
Delano, Ichabod, H 70.
   Mary, H 389.
   Robert, H 389.
Denman, Charles, A 361, B 28, 49, 229, 99, C 51, 119, 261, F 35.
Dickson, Elizabeth, C 176.
Dickenson, Samuel, I 313, 14.
Docton, Thomas, N 99, 126, 27, 310, C 41, 42, F 62, 82, 209, 330, 422, G 1, 133, 36, H 24, 26, 177, 92, 287, 99.
   Jacob, C 236, D 116, 133, 276, E 100, 13, F 42, 62.
   Elizabeth, B 127.
Doe, Ralph, C 116, I 337.
   Jeremiah, G 254, H 314, I 337.
Donaldson, Andrew, G 124.
   James, H 288.
   John, I 104, 15, 392.
Dorington, Edward, D 83.
Dorman, Ann, A 65.
Dowers, William, B 71, 37.
Douglas, Robert, A 267.
   Anne, A 267.
   Jesse, H 267, 73.
   Dorothy, H 267, 73.
Dove, Peter, E 139.
Dovewiner, Peter, B 35, 220, 21.
Dowdy, Edward, C 202, 34, G 60, 260.
Drury, Charles, C 192, G 188.
Draper, William, C 21.
   Charles, C 21.
   Peter, F 88.
   Thomas, I 456.
Dudley, Christopher, B 172.
   John, N 217.
   Elizabeth, B 217, 18.
Durant, John, A 26.
   George, A 27, 28, 71, 274, 76, 78, 79, 80, 81, 82, B 168, C 4, 138, D 97, 166, 67, E 41, 168, G 251.
   Thomas, D 100, E 41.
   Mary, E 41.
Duron (Durant), Robert, I 299.

E

Earll (Earl), Patience, H 99.
Eason, William, A 271, F 118, 274.
   George, D 82, E 39, 93, F 1, 67, 192, 98, G 90, 214, 18, 36, H 24, 26, 145, 94, 287, 345, 47, 80, I 210.
   Thomas, E 111, F 118, 192.
   Abner, F 42.
   Moses, F 102, D 90.
   Mary, H 26.
   Jesse, H 345, 47, I 210.
   Jacob, I 114.
   Abraham, I 210.
Edge, Hannah, A 54.
Edwards, William, A 134.
   John, B 90, 109, 10.
   Elizabeth, A 134, B 110.
Eggerton, Patrick, A 289, 91, 92, 93.
   William, A 301, B 114, F 423.
   James, C 61, 230, D 155, E 84, 153, F 79, 301, 423, H 30.
   Priscilla, H 182.
Ellett, William, B 98.
   Elizabeth, B 98.
Ellexander, Anthony, B 49.
Elliott, Thomas, A 387, B 21, 98, 123, 92, 284, C 75, D 1, 63, E 54, 83, F 18, 63, 97.
   William (Ellett), A 387, C 66, D 64, 83, 139, 65.
   Ann, B 123, D 18.
   Mary, B 192, C 75, D 80, F 55, G 113.
   Caleb, B 55, C 75, 266, D 65, 68, 78, E 57, F 18, 203, 4, 5, 25, 38, 353, 60, 73, G 215, 42, H 84, 85, 86, 144, 53, 54, I 67.
   Joshua, C 31, 104, F 133, 80, 211, 58, 85, 92, G 20, H 157, I 182.
   Isaac, C 66, 121, 23, 200, F 315, 74, G 230, H 1, 88, 100, 35, 36.
   Margaret, C 66, 121, 183, F 315.
   Moses, C 157, 241, 64, 66, 75, D 57, 96, 99, F 18, 25, 63, 64, 113, 155, G 5, I 50.
   Hannah, C 241, F 55.
   Abraham, C 264, E 4, 96, 99, I 182, 84, 532.
   Joseph, D 18, F 55, 97, 134, H 317, I 19, 80, 532.

Sarah, D 22, I 82.
Jacob, D 22.
Pritlow, D 165, F 267, 88, H 383, 86.
Benjamin, E 57, F 63, 64, 113, 158, 59, 211, 383, G 38, I 363, 67.
James, F 55, 374, G 113, 158, 59, 211, 383.
Judah (Judith), F 155.
Ephrim, F 353, G 243, H 100, 53, I 67.
Keziah, F 353.
Haig, G 72, H 84. 154.
Cornelius, H 85.
Micajah, H 85.
Solomon, H 86, 154.
Elliott, Mordecai, H 155.
Roda, H 203.
Josiah, H 325, 27.
Seth, H 327.
Etheridge, Ephrim, H 17, 266.
Miriam, H 17, 266.
Evans (Evins, Eivens), Robert, E 147, F 191, 229, G 63, 76, 83, 245.
Jonathan, D 101, 43, B 34, 37, 116, 18, 252, F 54.
Sarah, A 86.
Thomas, A 200, 22.
Mary, A 331, B 143, 60, 62, 232, 300, C 5, 99, D 111.
William, B 232, 300, 5, 7, 14, C 5, 12, 13, 20.
Everard, Sir Richard, G, 140.
Exum, John, B 284.

F

Falconer, John, A 255, 342, B 10, 212, C 17, 18, 22, 23.
Falkner, John, F 334, I 121.
Fanning, John, I 163, 239.
Barsheba, I 163.
Farley, William, A 171.
Farmer, Joseph, H 63, 221.
Mary, H 63, 221.
Felts, Humphrey, B 65.
John, C 245, F 128, H 116, 200.
Job, F 128, H 116, 200.
Felton, Richard Jr, D 126.
Fendall, Josiah, A 27, 28.
Elizabeth, A 143.
John, A 159, 61.
Robert, A 159, 161, 87, B 49.

Field, James, B 263, 65, C 2, 11, 124, 49, 52, E 61, 131, 56, H 176.
Moses, E 96, 99, 156, F 21, 25, 52, 74, 77, 149.
Reuben, F 148.
Sarah, F 148.
Fisher, James, A 128, 66, F 74, 322.
Fletcher, Ralph, A 25, 51, 72, 103, 90, 92, 212, 13, 14, 23, B 113, 211, C 26, 27, D 61, 93, F 245, 52, G 93, 182, H 11, 262, 269, I 11, 43, 255, 307, 49, 95, 96.
George, C 53, F 245, 52.
Flewman, Martha, G 15.
James, G 15.
Flowers, John, A 80, 87, 88, 174, 251, B 16, 164, 211.
Susanna, A 80.
John Jr., B 59, 212, 27, C 53, 152, 78, G 52.
Mary, B 53, 143, 211, 12.
Thomas, C 152.
Elizabeth, C 152.
Flury, William, F 277, 81.
Foans, John, F. 303.
Foones, Thomas, D 76.
Foredice, George, A6.
Forehand, Jarvis, H 189, 265, 371, I 122.
Foster, William, A 13, 14, B 278, F 132, H 268, I 150, 359.
Francis, A 14, 179, 96, 215, B 8, 11, C 51, 191, 257, F 395, 96, H 174, I 14, 21, 134, 46, 50, 359.
John, A 70, 74, 238, B 145, 46, I 55, 268.
James, A 200, 344, 45, C 248, G 45.
Hannah, A 215.
Elizabeth, A 238, B 145, 46.
Rachel, H 174, I 359.
Frederick, H 268, I 134, 50, 267.
Richard, A 378.
Joshua, I 293.
Fourre, Peter, A 87.
Fox, Richard, A 183, 315.
George, A 315, 16, 17.
Foxworth, William, D 56, 118.
Fraser, Robert, A 81.

INDEX TO DEEDS 459

Friley (Fryly, Frilie), William, A 169, 71, 93, 216, B 54, 223.
  Grace, A 169, 93, 216, 223, B 54, E 8.
Fugett, James, A 195.

G

Gale, Christopher, B 240.
  Miles, C 74.
Garrant, Daniel, A 311, 329.
  Jane, A 311.
Garrett, Thomas, C 33, 217, F 202.
  Richard, H 5.
Gennett, Abraham, C 245.
Gews (Gums), Matthew, C 71.
Gibbons, Stephen, B 217, 18, C 34, 35, 36, 37, H 98.
  Jane, C 35. (Gibbens)
Gibson, Stephen, B 79, 308, F 333, 43.
  Jane, B 79, 308.
  John, B 97, H 384, I 59, 508.
  James, C 57, 108, 30, 80, 89, F 375, H 19, I 59, 508.
Gilbert, Josiah, B 295, C 116, 65, 67 D 138, E 144.
  Rebecca, F 338.
  Mary, B 167, 295.
  Joseph, B 295, I 471.
  John, C 98.
  Benjamin I 471.
  Elizabeth, C 98.
Giles, Cornelius, A 88, 89.
  Hannah, A 89.
  Matthew, A 373.
Gilliam, Kitchen, I 291.
  Kinchea, I 299.
  Nancy, I 298.
Gimonson, Elizabeth, E 70.
Givens, Christopher, A 371.
Gilson, Joseph, C 7, 149.
Glover, William, A 147, 64, 269, G 140.
Godbee, Elizabeth, F 378, 81.
  Cary, F 381.
Godfrey (Godfree), Thomas, B 249, C 57, 137, 61, 84, F 199, 200, G 264, H 284.
  Ellinor, C 137.
  Mary, F 199, 200, 350, 51, H 284.
  Joseph, B 262, F 429, G 17, H 284, I 314, 51.

John, B 307, 262, 305, 14, 15, C 184, G 76.
William, A 82, 83, 180, 89, 385, B 213, 32, 49, 50, 62, 305, 14, C 57, 184, D 167, F 350, 51, G 119, 54.
Goodale, Gilbert, A 257, 59, B 228.
Gooding, George, C 78, 125, F 418, H 307.
  John, B 269, C 217.
  Richard, E 10, G 116.
  William, F 418, G 40, 43, H 245.
Goodridge, Jeremiah, A 222.
Goodwin, Richard, D 67, 144, F 275, H 36, 38, 272, I 169.
  Mary, I 169.
  John, A 118, 385, 94, B 250, C 12, 32, 105, D 33, 44, 83, 94, F 275, 414, G 242, H 77, I 277, 361.
  Jacob, G 191, H 129, 31, 69, I 297, 418.
Gordon, John, B 116, F 101, G 238, H 8.
  George, F 418, H 307.
Gourden, John, C 192.
Gosby, John, C 191, E 22, 23.
  Hannah, A 85, C 191.
  Sarah, E 22.
Grace, Henry, A 338, 9, B 55, 195, C 59, 67, 68, E 142.
  Reback, A 339.
Granbery, Josiah, I 38, 156, 380.
Granville, Earl, F 354.
Gray, Thomas, A 197, B 244, 59, C 64, 80, 81, D 21, 112.
  Peter, A 50, 101, 9, 10, 49, 205, D 34.
  Mary, A 109.
  John, A 255.
  Richard, A 341, 40, B 124, D 122, H 41.
  Henry, C 187.
  Tabitha, A 29, 30.
  Elizabeth, A 30.
  Robert, A 29.
Gregory, Samuel, C 61, D 155, E 84.
Green, Fonnyfield, A 145.
  Hannah, A 145.
  Samuel Jr, H 280, I 113, A 48.
Griffin, James, B 44, E 159, F 16.
  James Sr, D 12.
  John, D 12, 122, E 89, 159, F 94, 129, 30.
  William, F 16.

Joseph, F 137, 38.
Humphrey, C 91, F 114, 157, 292.
Reuben, G 239, I 352.
Gums, William, F 221.
Guthry, John, A 280.
Guthrie, Daniel, B 187.
Gohyer, John, D 17, E 155, 69, G 92, 252, I 462.
Guyer, Joshua, G 92, H 5.
Joseph, H 49, 271.
Abigail, I 462.

H

Haire, Thomas, A 194.
John, A 252, 53.
Hall, William, A 155, 60, 88, 97, 359, B 54, 223, 98, C 50, 63, 259, D 9, 56, F 40, 106, 97, 302.
Daniel, A 162, 26, 329, 30, C 54, 65, 259, D 9, 56, F 106, 320.
Rose, A 329.
Clement, C 43, D 91, F 197, 98, 302, G 51.
Samuel, C 261, F 40, 106, H 166.
Jacob, C 65, F 40, 106, 365, H 29, 166, 73, I 185, 204.
Jane, C 65.
Robert, C 234, G 60, 260.
Mary, D 77.
Henry, F 2, 103, 31, H 190, I 410.
Edward, F 131, 297, 394, I 6, 9.
Benjamin, H 27, G 211.
Ann, D 28.
Hallum, John, A 11, 286.
Halstead, Edward, G 43, 44, 45, 91, 148, 68.
Mary, G 148.
Hampton, Richard, H 213.
Hancock, John, B 227, 98, C 253.
Harbort, Jane, A 128.
Hardy, Robert, H 32.
Hare, Lede, A 104.
John, A 202.
Harmon, Robert, A 244, 383, B 155, I 145, 338.
John, C 251, E 109, F 167, 231, I 4, 126, 243.
John Sr, G 261, H 34, 51, 171, 335, 36.
Elizabeth, F 45.

Thomas, I 70, 190, 204, 501.
Susannah, G 261, 336.
Stephen, H 212, I 89, 97, 145, 77, 92, 269.
Caleb, I 145.
Sarah, I 70.
Lemuel, I 269.
Hart, Thomas, A 1.
Harris, David, A 224, 25, 39, 61, 81, B 214, 17, F 26, 218.
Elizabeth, A 224.
William, B 215.
Sarah, B 215, F 218, 19.
John, C 156, 274, F 223, 427, G 158, 62, H 83, 112, 231, 41.
Ann, F 218.
Elijah, F 427, G 158.
Hardin, Henry, H 116, 321.
Martha, H 116, 200, 321.
Harrell, John, B 320, C 215.
Richard, B 320, C 215, E 51, I 90.
Demsey, H 40, I 409.
Susanna, H 40, I 409.
James, H 125.
Abner, I 536.
Samuel, I 170.
Mary, I 170.
Harrison, John, D 116.
Harron, Joseph, F 87.
Harrington, Ann, C 116.
Harvey, Thomas, A 5, 40, 114, 46, 47, 67, 86, 91, 223, 25, 94, B 34, 223, 199, C 28, 32, 74, 105, D 115, 60, F 201, 414, H 28, 343, I 68, 85, 119, 247, 48, 98, 436, 39, 84.
Margaret, A 186, 224, 25.
John, A 378, F 56, 201, 2, 45, 52, 67, 78, 98, G 207, H 93, 343.
Elizabeth, B 34, 199, 223, C 74, I 247.
Miles, C 74, E 42, G 131, 79, 207, H 248, 393, I 85.
Benjamin, C 74, F 57, G 164, 252, H 5, 11, 128, 41, 202, 92, I 24, 63, 68, 80, 238, 313.
Julianna, H 141.
John Jr, H 184, F 161, I 85.
Sarah, H 184.
James, H 343.
Mary, I 85.

INDEX TO DEEDS

Anna, I 118, 247.
Frances Ann, I 247.
Haughton (Houghton, Horton),
    Thomas, A 62, 79, 302, D 101, 143.
Hasket, Anthony, A 49, 94, 101, 9, 49,
    B 74, 129, C 80, D 34, 55.
    Tabytha, A 149, 232.
    Anthony Sr, A 232, 337.
    William, C 252, 63, D 11, 31, F 50,
        G 11.
    Joshua, F 178, H 326, I 155.
    Alice, I 155.
    Abraham, H 42, 70.
    Jemima, H 42, 70.
    Isaac, H 161.
    Silas, I 513.
    John, I 394, 442, 503, 27.
    Elizabeth, I 400.
    Jesse, I 400.
    Lydia, H 161.
    Joseph, I 155.
Hassell, Isaac, F 385, 411, H 107.
    Tamer, F 411.
    Banjamin, F 411.
    James, H 107.
    Abram, F 385.
Haskins, Anthony, A 220.
Hatch, Anthony, B 4, C 176.
    Edmund, F 79.
    John, G 219, H 188, I 54, 426, 27, 28.
Hatfield, Banjamin, G 210, H 82.
    Richard, I 26, 218, 53, E 157.
Hawkins, John, A 82, 118, 221, C 166,
    G 52.
    Anthony, B 72.
    Mary, E 46.
Haynes, Joseph, C 60, 87, 103, 4.
Hecklefield, Elizabeth, A 40.
    William, A 40.
Heggins, Jedideth, C 56.
Henby, John, A 149, B 51, 271, C 37, 97,
    123, 83, 257, D 109, 35, 88, 251, H
    63, 170, 80, 211, 19, 21, 66, 67, 70,
    388, I 8, 52, 130, 53, 211, 323.
    James, B 83, 100, 35, 36, C 34, 97, 99,
        D 30, 119, 64, F 315.
    Elizabeth, C 199.

Hannah, I 52.
Mary, F 138, H 21.
Sylvanus, F 138, H 14, 152, 251, 66,
    67, 70 G 259, H 21, 211, 19.
Dempsey, G 94, 259, H 14, 17, 21, 221,
    66, 67, 70.
Jesse, H 15.
Joseph, H 81.
Mourning, H 81.
Thomas, H 191, 229, 340, 54, I 213.
Hendricks, Solomon, B 257, C 78, 232,
    33, D 69, F 14.
Jeremiah, C 232.
Thomas, F 242, 43, H 98.
Job, F 43, 342, H 98, 211.
Sarah, F 342, 43, H 98.
Elizabeth, H 98.
Hendrickson, George, G 46.
    William, G 46.*
Henley, Jesse, G 84.
    John, H 266.
Henry, Solomon, B 181, D 35.
Hews, Elizabeth, A 40.
    William, A 40.
Hibens, James, A 128.
    Elenor, A 128.
Hicks, Thomas, E 138.
Hill, Henry, A 371.
    Guy, F 7, 272.
    Benjamin, F 290, 387.
    Mary, G 160.
    William, H 12, 93.
    Jacob, B 238.
    Elizabeth, B 238.
    Isaac, F 12.
Hinds, Ann, C 218, 19, 20, F 193, 207,
    316, G 135.
Hines, Peter, I 509.
Hinton, William, H 83.
    Jacob, H 83.
Hobard, Joshua, F 5.
Hobbs, Thomas, B 323, C 11, E 61.
Hobs, Abraham, B 17.
Hobbs, Reuben, I 310.
Hodgens, Christopher, I 261.
Hogg, James, A 78, 145.
    Ann, A 78, 145.
Holden, George, A 378.

---

*(Note: These two are thought to be identical.)

Holland, Jacob, I 504, 350.
　Elizabeth, I 504.
Hollowell, Thomas, B 238, C 270, 78, D 29, 44, 51, 86, 94, 109, 42, E 78, 108, F 88, G 19, H 49, 179.
　Luke, B 41, 237, 63, D 65, 136, H 265, I 122.
　Edward, B 245.
　John, D 53, 54, 103, E 141, 65, F 139, 425, G 19, 241, H 16, 136.
　William, E 128, 31, 32, F 136, 48. I 144, 94, 226.
　Jose, E 128, F 52, 77, 162, 404, H 16, I 172.
　Edmund, E 141.
　Abner, F 136, I 65, 172.
　Miriam, F 162.
　Thomas, I 111.
　Henry, I 328.
Holloway, Thomas, A 385.
　Luke, B 178.
　Elizabeth, B 178.
　Thomas, B 288, C 177, F 150, 375, I 21.
　Edwards, C 69.
　John, F 150, 375.
　Hannah, F 375.
Holmes, Edward, A 157, 82, C 107, I 7, 246.
　Archibald, A 227, 47, 48, 348, 73, B 145, F 296, G 77.
　Robert, I 182, 384, 93, 451, 533.
　Mary, I 533.
Hoode, Peter, A 306.
Horton, Cavey, A 302.
　William, A 302, 170, C 54, D 101, H 252.
　Mary, C 54, H 252.
　Elizabeth, D 101, 143.
　James, F 79, 297.
　Jonathan, H 277, I 204.
　Richard, H 378, I 45, 46, 89, 117, 28, 439.
　Jemima, I 117.
Hosea, Robert, A 203, B 171, 213, 28, C 108, 175, 235, D 72, E 259, F 66, H 68.
　Sarah, C 108, 235, E 2, H 68.

　William, D 72, E 14, 35, F 66.
　Thomas, D 152, E 70, I 446, 54.
　Abraham, E 14, 35, 114, F 3, 66, H 300.
　Joseph, E 70, 114, 143, F 9, 66, 85, 109, H 301, 66, I 200, 312, 491.
　John, E 70, F 39, 66, 76.
　Mary, H 300.
Hoskins, John, E 9.
Howerd, Peter, A 282.
Hubbard, John, F 220, 53, 358.
　Joshua, G 3.
Hudler (Hurdle), John, B 55, 195, C 187, E 142.
　Joseph, F 117, G 133, H 26, 40, 275, I 38, 180, 81.
Huffton, John, A 199, C 180, 234, D 152, E 59, 62, 139, F 101.
　David, D 152, E 59, 60, 139.
Hughes, William, A 5.
Hull, John, E 166.
Humpage, John, C 218, 19, 20, 25, F 193, 207, G 135.
Humphries, William, I 25.
Hunt, Lawrence, A 127, D 80.
　Elizabeth, A 127.
　Susanna, F 55.
Hunter, John, E 166, F 101.
　Williams, D 114, F 101, 78.
　Nicholas, F 101, 78.
　Hardy, F 102, 78.
　Jacob, I 350.
Huntwagger, Daniel, B 229.
Hurdle, William, C 69.
　Thomas, F 284.
　Hardy, H 175, 76.
Hudson, John, B 64, 224, D 153, H 348, 49, 68, 76.
　Uriah, F 60, 129, H 349.

I

Inkerson, Robert, C 17, 22, 110, 44.
Ireland, John, H 5.

J

Jacocks, Thomas, A 41, 42, 56, H 186, 87.

---

* (Note: This may be same as Hollowell.)

INDEX TO DEEDS

Ann, A 56.
Jacob, F 279, 80, H 17, 63, 121, 170, 225, 70.
Elizabeth, H 225, 70, 86, 87, I 497.
Jackson, William, A 95, 228, 29, B 96, 188, 204, 30, 57.
William Jr, A 332, 45, C 16, 78, 125, 232, 49, D 54, E 43, H 100.
Christopher, C 192, D 53, 54, G 241, I 36.
Mary, C 192.
John, D 38, F 14, 140, 262, G 205, H 46, 69, 126.
Edmund, D 50.
Moses, E 43, G 39, I 492.
Sarah, F 14, 140, 262.
Aaron, F 226, 62, G 39.
James, William, A 23.
Francis, C 124, 52, 53, D 34.
Sarah, C 124.
Jennett, Abraham, B 48, C 40, 116, G 144, 254, H 238, I 474.
Priscilla, H 238. (Jennet)
Jenkins, John, A 125, 378.
Henry, A 62, 63.
Jessop, Joseph, A 315, 20, 70, B 2, 27, 78, 122, 58, 77, 84, 85, 234, 36, 76, 77, 301, C 9, 47, 49, 64, 113, 18, 50, 55, 72, 73, 79, 254, 69, D 21, 46, F 73, 266, G 98, 152, H 74, 151, 202, I 32, 122, 281.
Margaret, B 2, 237, 66, 67.
Thomas, B 270, 90, C 8, 73, 118, 50, 83, 258, 60, D 22, 33, 42, 112, 27, 35, 40, E 11, 12, 20, 51, F 93, 94, 95, 192, 402, G 98, H 151, 265, 76, 365, I 449, 532.
Enoch, H 97, I 235.
Jonathan, H 128, 41.
Mary, H 128.
Johnson, John, A 32, I 160.
Gabriel, C 169, 242.
Samuel, H 29, 173.
James, A 54, 55, 72.
Rachel, A 55, 72.
Sarah, A 128.
Jones, Jonathan, A 52, 102, B 30, F 196.
Margaret, A 52.
Peter, A 177, 166, 300, 13, 34, C 90, D 9, 125, F 316, 78, I 143.

Peter Jr, D 79, 101, 20, 43, G 130, 39.
Daniel, A 261, 83, 348.
Sarah, A 348, C 172, 79, 269, D 81.
Arthur, B 79, 308.
William, B 299, C 1, 10, 26, 27, 128, 59, 92, D 61, G 188, I 56, 126, 271, 72, 73, 74.
Thomas, C 172, 79, 269, G 90, I 56, 276, 485, 510.
Frederick, C 211.
John, B 250, 216, 87, D 81, F 35, 119, G 18, 79, 139, 58, 59, 61.
Evan, D 160, E 154, F 420.
Francis, F 122, 312, 13, G 143, H 136, 42, I 441.
Robert, F 290.
Judah, H 142.
Joseph, F 196, H 162, 65, I 59, 62, 365, 492, 522.
Jarvis, F 299, 401, G 25, 26, 40, 41, 43, 55, 56, 60, 64.
Zachariah, G 5, 130, H 165.
James, G 158, H 83.
Willis, G 162.
Mary, G 162.
Samuel, G 167, 223.
Malachi, H 196, 242, I 149, 298, 454.
Cooper, H 323.
Lewis, I 241.
Jordan, John, B 284, D 38, E 18.
Charles, C 105, E 103, 4, F 57, 100, G 118, 20, 21, 79.
Joseph, F 172.
Josiah, G 48, I 531.
Matthew, G 48, H 70.
Sarah, G 118.
Jaoob, G 159, 70, 213, H 36, 69.
James, H 247.
William, H 289.
Mary, H 289.
Thomas, H 293.

K

Kanidy (Kenedie), Patrick, A 195, 205.
Keaton, John, B 322.
Hannah, B 323.
Kellum, John, A 18.
Kelly, Smith, B 180.
Kenedie, Patrick, A 43, 64, 69.
Kenedy, Elizabeth, A 43.

Kent, Thomas, A 24, 25.
Keny, Roger, C 178.
Kenyon, Mary, F 178.
  Joab, I 289.
Kilcocanew (King of Yeopim Indians) A 374, 375. (2d spelled Kiskitando)
Kinion, Job, H 304.
  Roger, C 275, G 37.
King, John, A 126, 374, 75.
  Thomas, I 390.
Kinse, John, A 75, 76, 188, B 130.
  Catherine, A 76.
Kippin, Martha Ann, F 387, G 107, 115.
  Samuel, H 237.
Kitching (Kitchen), William, A 310, 20, 40, 53, B 88, C 48, 114, D 76, 92, 103, 49, 215, F 139, 46, 425, G 96, 100, 241, I 36.
  Margaret, A 353.
Knight, Lewis Alex, A 188, 386, B 130, 31.
  Emanuel, A 188, B 130.
Knoles, Elizabeth, C 214, E 62, F 71, G 109.
  William, C 214, F 264, 405.
  Thomas, E 62 F 71, 264, 405, G 109.
  Adam, F 71.
Knowles, William, I 73, 74, 379.
  Deborah, I 379.
  Abner, I 470, 93.
Knox, Andrew, F 277, 81, 97, 309, 33, 78, 79, 80, G 21, 23, 67, 90, 107, 15, 80, 210, 44, 52, H 5, 11, 25, 46, 82, 134, 60, 71, 323, 30, 35, 36, 37, 77, 90, I 256, 386, 538, 40.
  Christian, F 236, 77, 426.
  Ambrose, I 136, 363, 67, 477, 78, 85, 520, 40.

L

Lacky (Lackee), John, B, 259, 66, 67, 76, C 64, D 21, 112.
  Mary, B 267.
Lacton, James, A 176.
Lacy, John, A 21, D 45, 135, F 141, 336, G 89, H 326.
  Mary, B 180.
  William, B 180, C 143, D 17, F 273, 319, G 52, H 309.
Laker, Benjamin, A 46, 147, B 191, F 415, G 23, 47, 100.
  Jane, A 100.
  Ruth, A 147.
Julianna, B 226, 27, C 134, F 220, 53, 58, 348, 415, G 2, 4, 67, 80, 107, 203, H 160.
  Joshua, I 244.
Lamb, Joshua, A 49, 172.
  Henry, D 23, 131, F 119, 257, 393.
  Thomas, E 19, 105, F 115, 257, 392, 93.
  William, F 176, I 195, 96.
  Isaac, F 288, 93, 94, 307, 74, G 113, 230, H 35, 42.
  Sarah, F 392.
  Restore, I 275.
  Zachariah, 275.
Lancaster, John, G 22,
  Mary, G 22.
Lane, Thomas, F 121, 56, 75, 210, 30.
  John, H 320, 58.
  William, I 27, 168, 367.
Lands, Thomas, C 227, 40.
Larkum, John, C 274, F 223, G 162, H 83, 112, 231, 41.
  Susanna, F 127.
Lasey, Joseph, F 319.
Lassley, Lawrence, H 261.
  Miriam, H 261.
Laster, William, I 204.
Layden, George, F 4, 41.
  Francis, F 66, 85.
  William, H 322, 32.
  Thomas, I 482.
Lawrence, William, A 49, 51, D 27, G 128.
  John, A 172, B 308, 25.
  Michael, C 205, 8, F 27, G 186.
  Susannah, C 205, F 127.
  Henry, G 186.
Lawton, Pelig, I 541, 42.
Leary (Lerre), Cornelius, A 3, 46, 47, 53, 67, 175, D 99.
  Sarah, B 9.
  Ann, I 214.
  Richard, A 273, 74, 75, 76, B 17, 18, 19, 58, 103, 20, 25, 93, 94, C 1, 10, 15, 159, F 287, G 69, 115, I 214.
  John, I 190.
  Mary, A 46.
Lear, John, G 186.
Leane (Lane), Thomas, D 160.

Lee, John, I 237.
Lepper, Thomas, A 26, 78, 119.*
  Ann, A 119.
Leisley, Lawrence, G 141.
  James, H 382.
Lewis, Fielding, G 188.
Leigh, Gilbert, I 267, 68, 491.
Lillie, Thomas, F 46.
Lilly, John, A 13, 99, 129, 57, 58, 63, 337, C 107, D 127, E 165, G 96, H 6, I 7, 246.
  Joseph, F 46.
  William, A 99, D 126, H 16, 274, I 173.
  Hannah, A 136.
  Thomas, B 88, 179, 96, D 18, 126, E 82, 165, F 246, G 96, H 6, 16, 134.
  Isaac, F 234, 65, 84, H 75, I 234, 310, 408.
  Joseph, E 165, F 346, G 62, H 16.
  Timothy, D 112, 26, E 165, F 295, 395, H 16.
  Sarah, F 346.
  Zachariah, G 96, H 150, 51, I 32.
  Joshua, H 6.
  Ann, H 150.
  Simon, H 328.
  Jane, I 32.
Lillington, Alexander, A 8, 98, 290, 323, C 1, H 312, 13, I 510.
  John, A 290, 323, 331, B 101.
  George, A 331, C 99.
Lindsay, William, I 540.
Loadman, Jean, A 31.
  James, A 31, 69, 236.
Long, James, A 4, 79, C 45, 136.
  Alice, A 35.
  Sarah, B 12, 13, C 244.
  Elizabeth, A 372.
  Joshua, B 189, 90, D 36, 115, F 56, H 235, 59, 62, I 20, 204, 464.
  Thomas, A 30, 34, 35, 64, 119, 66, 287, 372, B 157, C 45, 136, D 115, F 56, 106, 287, I 20, 206, 62, 423.
  Reuben, H 251, 58, 60, 312, 13, 52, 74, I 44, 51, 193, 98, 206, 62, 304, 86, 432, 55, 86.
  Peninah, H 251, 352, I 44, 51, 193, 304, 55.
  William, A 145, 56, 66, B 209, D 66, E 106, F 11, 128, 344, H 35, 200, 51, 321, 74, I 66, 128, 86, 206, 19, 432.
  Simeon, H 374, I 198, 206, 19, 304, 432, 84.
  Grizzell, I 198, 219, 304, 484.
  Nathan, I 382, 423.
Lonsford, John, I 68, 201, 20.
  Mary, I 201.
Low, John, C 278.
  Hannah, C 278.
  George, F 193, 207, G 134, 221.
Lowry, John, H 250.
Lowther, William, H 32, I 446.
  John, H 324.
Lovick, John, B 240, C 74.
Luten, James, F 24, 84.
  Ephrim, F 208.
  Henderson, I 93.
  Sarah, I 93.
  Frederick, I 121.
Lytton, James, H 134.

M

McAdams, Sarah, D 110, G 153.
  James, G 153.
  Joseph, G 153, H 58, 148, 244, 390, I 215, 520.
McAlister, John, G 265.
Maccardel, Terrence, C 57, 161.
MacCormick, William, H 359.
Macdaniel, Charles, A 69, 109, 10, 17, B 158, 337.
  Elizabeth, A 110.
Machlenden, Elickander, E 17.
Maclannahan, Samuel, I 223, 24, 39, 511.
  Mary, I 239, 515.
McClanahan, Samuel, I 250, 380, 407.
McClennen, Alexander, F 90.
Magorm, William, F 140, 226, 62.
  Frances, F 140, 226, 62.
McKee, Caleb, H 244.
Mackey, Caleb, H 307.
  William, C 87, 104.

---

*(Thomas Lepper moved to Beaufort County, N. C., where he died.)

Mackiner, Daniel, B 303.
McKnight, Thomas, H 71, 77, 89, 90, 119, I 313.
McNider, Thomas, H 277, I 464.
Mann, William, B 213, 246, C 214, D 110, E 62, G 121.
  John, E 62, F 26, H 148.
Manwaring, Stephen, A 8, 60, 102, 115, 16, 17, 21, 58, 74, B 158, 79.
Marlow, Robert, A 2.
Martin, Josiah, Esq., H 254.
  Dr. Nathaniel, I 24.
Mason, John, A 347.
Mathews, George, A 63, 165, C 276, D 28, 41, 150, G 212.
Mathias, John, C 79, 90, F 236, 77, 378, 79, 81.
  William, F 378, 79, 80.
  Elizabeth, C 79.
Maudlin (Moadley, Modlin), Ezekiel, A 193, 249, B 142, 305, 15, D 12, 48, 137, E 9, F 60, H 73.
Maudlin, Edward, B 51, 203, 312, C 199, 257, 65, 68, D 30, 82, E 48, H 123.
  Abraham, C 142.
  John, D 45, E 4, F 195, 365, 77, G 132, H 364.
  Mary, E 8, G 193, H 105.
  Gideon, F 138, G 189, 93, H 14, 21, 105, 369.
  Joshua, F 151, 282, 398, G 17, 76, H 14, 21, 105, G 66.
  Benjamin, F 188.
  Edmond, H 73, 230.
  William, H 203.
  Betty, G 28.
  Peter, G 28.
Mayo, Mary, B, 243, D 20.
  Joseph, B 243, 290 E 145, F 8, I 142, 242.
  Ann, B 243.
  Elizabeth, B 243, D 20.
  Sarah, B 243.
  Edward, A 35, 37, 39, 61, E 146.
Modlin, Jeremiah, H 384, I 62.
  Sarah, F 239, I 62.
  Joseph, F 239.
  Ashley, F, 239.
  Esbill, F 239.

  Jethro, F 239.
  Nathan, I 505.
Meedes, Thomas, E 70.
Melbourn, William, H 130.
Merton, Dr. Nathaniel, H 292.
Meriday, Thomas, A 325.
  Sarah, A 325.
  Elizabeth, A 325.
Middleton, William, F 120, 23.
Miers, Nathan, G 212.
Miller, Elizabeth, I 13.
  Andrew, I 13.
  Abel, I 93.
  Job, I 143.
  Hugh, I 475.
Minge (Ming), James, A 251, 75, B 191, G 86.
  Ruth, B 191, 279, 81, C 101.
  John, B 279, 81.
  Valentine, B 279, 81.
  Joseph, C 61, D 155, G 86, H 66, I 192.
  Nathaniel, H 339.
  Thomas, G 86, 126, H 66, I 192.
Mizelle, Aaron, G 129, H 280, I 113.
Montgomery, J., C 242.
Morfohey, Nicholas, C 158.
Morgan, John, A 127, B 192, C 241, D 22, 80, H 170.
  John Jr, C 186, 99 D 137, 64, F 23.
  James, A 219, B 268, C 120, 23, 57, 81, 83, 85, 266, D 43, E 57, F 280, G 28, 29, 30, 31, 32, 36, 54, 57, H 17, 63, I 8.
  William, A 219, B 268, C 25, 97, 104, 50, 51, 55, 57, 85, 264, D 43.
  Sarah, C 36, H 98, F 343.
  Joshua, C 88, 92, 155.
  Ann, C 119.
  Robert, C 156.
  Charles, F 377, 416, G 93.
  Seth, H 355.
  Jacob, I 223, 511.
  Benjamin, I 144.
Montague, Thomas, B 25, C 158, D 109, 56, 59.
Moore, Alexander, A 4.
  William, A 107, 132, 73, 236, 318, 19, 28, 41, B 30, 186, 87, 232, 74, 88, C 3, 212, 67, D 34, 42, 51, 55, 60, 73, 74.

INDEX TO DEEDS 467

William Sr., B 89, 92, 179, 206, 9.
William Sr., B 33, 34, 51, 55, 68, 73, 74, 301, C 47, 49, 55, 59, 60, 170, 71, 81, 206, 26, 77, D 122, E 73, 157, F 27, 51, 190, 259, 373, 91, G 22, 42, 242, 44, I 116, 361.
Robert, A 324, B 23, 158, D 52, 62, 87, 95, 117, 20.
Hannah, A 324, B 23, 158.
John, C 3, D 44, E 45, 108, 111, F 127, 88, G 127, 84, H 23, 32, 78, 120, 218, I 11, 184.
Samuel, C 157, 264, D 22, 62, 93, 163, F 107, H 37, 197, I 188.
Truman, C 206, D 129, F 126.
Cornelius, F 188, 89, 387, G 47, 92, 117, 25, 27, 76, 83, 96, 220, 52, 55, H 5, 11, 19, 32, 33, 78, 120, I 184, 367.
Gideon, F 188.
Joseph, F 188, 89, 290, 384, 87, G 38, 127, H 78, I 184.
Darby, F 243, 357.
Margery, F 357.
Mary, F 370, H 120, 218, 382, 85, 89.
Charles, G 90, H 214, 77, 377, I 91, 380, 446, 51, 54, 85, 511.
Ezekiel, G 178.
Jesse, G 229, H 90.
Keron Huppuck, G 255.
Aaron, H 37, 197, I 188.
Jonathan, H 214, 79, 81.
Morris, Richard, A 314, 66, 89, B 3, 29, F 201, 2.
Hannah, B 3.
John, B 26, C 227, F 201, 2, 18.
Zachariah, F 75.
Aaron, I 459.
Morrison, William, A 15.
Morton, Hugh, F 127.
Elizabeth, F 127.
Moses, William, D 127.
Sarah, I 462.
Moseley, Edward, B 69, 284, D 37, 38, 39, E 157, G 253.
John, C 271, 72, 73, 74, F 223, G 162, H 43, 61, 112, 231.
Mullen, Abraham, A 364, B 61, D 17, 19, C 9, 141, 235, D 130, E 15, F 115, 385, 411, G 92, 189, 252, H 41, 102, 18, 41, 363.
Jacob, C 133, D 81, F 4, 41, 206, H 390.
Isaac, D 19, E 2, C 235.
Elizabeth, E 2, G 174, H 68.
Sarah, F 4, H 390.
Joseph, G 151, 157, 74, 85, H 68, I 230, 358, 492, 94, 507, 22, 29.
Elenor, G 194.
Bettie, H 41.
Thomas, H 118, 201, 318, I 136, 37.
Ann, H 318.
James, I 148.
Richard, I 337.
Munden, William, F 212, 13, F 68, H 161, 91.
Benjamin Jr., F 50, G 33.
Hannah, F 213, G 151.
Elisha, G 33.
Peter, G 33, 156, I 147.
Lidah, G 33.
Thomas, G 33.
Murdaugh, John, F 31, 36, 37, 38, 58, G 21.
Joseph, F 249, 412, I 360.
Josiah, I 365.

N

Nerve, Moses, H 5.
Newbold, William, I 24, 41, 48, 390.
Grizzell, I 41.
William Jr., I 365.
Newby, Gabriel, A 77, 136, 37, 38, 51, 260, 62, 333, B 40, 93, 112, 49, 63, 64, 306, 29, 50, 54, C 70, 252, D 34, 48, 55, G 215, H 144.
William, A 173, 236, C 243, E 155, 69, G 108, 78, H 264, 341, I 334.
James, A 200, 1, 18, B 76, 202, 56, 312, D 3, 29.
Joseph, B 72, 243, 90, C 8, 31, 70, 171, 237, 41, 58, D 22, 63, 64, 80, 84, 85, 94, 135, 37, 64, E 54, 62, 140, 58, F 122, 25, 61, 73, 336, G 52, 228, 52, H 271, 315, 328, 34, I 229, 49, 52.
Francis, B 111, 63, 64, 151, 52, 206, 9, 53, 54, C 31, 58, 66, 89, 143, 65, 78, 207, 31, 44, 46, D 39, 109, 56, 58, 59, 200, G 21, 48, 73, 94, 95, 237, H 88, 369, I 24, 64, 225, 307, 66, 69, 79,

98, 421, 29, 30, 33, 435, 36, 37, 38, 530.
Sarah, A 201.
John, A 259, 95, B 247.
Mary, B 40, C 8, 94, 185, 258, E 92, I 164.
Nathan, B 251, C 185, E 92, D 83, F 214, 80, H 121, I 281, 84.
Ann, C 243.
Benjamin, B 311, I 171, 76, 536.
Thomas, C 71, D 63, 64, 139, E 112, 50, F 13, 31, 53, 129, 47, 52, 70, 359, 419, G 95, 223, 24, 45, 52, H 5, 11, 19, 120, 36, 61, 325, 60, I 164, 369, 76, 404, 35, 54, 63.
Samuel, C 89, 244, 46, D 23, 26, 40, E 67, 105, F 27, 123, 94, 270, 312, 13, G 73, 74, 108, 91, H 88, 149, 264, 93, 241.
Jesse, G 73, 94, 237, H 369, I 398.
Robert, G 73, 74, 118, 20, 237, H 88, 149, 369.
Mark, G 73, 74, 94, 172, 237, H 264, I 196, 395, 96, 98.
Keziah, G 94.
Jemima, G 108.
Dempsey, G 177, I 249.
Patience, H. 42, 70.
Elizabeth, H 271, 315, 28, 41, I 229.
Mordecai, H 293.
Gideon, I 17.
Peninah, I 381.
Matthew, I 398.
Exum, I 163.
Nichols, Christopher, B 31.
Nathaniel, C 108, D 82.
George, F 344, H 9.
John, G 60, I 212
Jemima, G 60.
Joseph, H. 4.
Mehitable, H 4.
Thomas, H 45, 124.
Nicholson, Christopher, A 65, 188, 288, B 76, 256, C 270, D 3, 81, 148, 57, F 171, 86, G 189, H 286, 93, I 322, 99.
Nathaniel, A 362, 64, B 48, 148, 53, C 72, 257, 68, D 81, 130, F 4.
Samuel, A 65, 92, 198, 285, B 134, C 97, D 81, F 48, 49.

Joseph, A 65, 92, 139, D 81, H 293, I 19, 322.
Mary, A 288, D 3, I 425.
Sarah, A 362, I 165, 67, 459.
Benjamin, A 363, D 81, 105.
Margaret, B 256.
Thomas, B 265, 70, D 3, 29, 44, 81, 147, 54, E 7, 55, F 187, 235, 91, G 6, 7, 131, 57, 65, 66, 69 H 52, 138, 39, 259, 86, 93, 353, I 37, 165, 322, 99, 402, 3, 52.
John, D 81.
Nicholas, H 293, I 402, 3.
Zachariah, H 22.
Robert, I 338, 425.
Nixon, Barnabe, A 295, H 293, 395.
Zachariah, B 25, 26, 31, 318, C 97, 160, E 108, D 1, 27, 52, 61, 101, 17, 19, 43, 48, F 14, 59, 75, 112, 72, 82, 209, 32, H 101, 13, 38, 39, 68, 317, 53, I 293, 322, 80, 446, 530.
Phineas, D 147, 48, F 153, 406, 7, 8, 28, G 9, 131, 69.
John, D 3, E 55, F 291, 406, 7, G 6, 10, 18, H 67, 138, 39, 213, 32, I 453.
Elizabeth, F 350, I 381, 511, 15.
Francis, G 8, 252, 55, H 5, 11, 32, 33, I 453.
Delight, G 86, 126, H 66, I 70, 84, 179, 90, 417.
Richard, H 66.
Ezra, H 138, 39.
Osten, H 194.
Pierce, H 293.
Mary, H 293.
Frederick, I 377.
Nogell, Jeane, A 39.
Noggins, Lawrence, A 34, 38.
Noles, William, F 386.
Norcom, Thomas, A 156, 81, 234, 35, 74, B 193, 302, C 4, 139, 203, D 9, 97, 98, 99, 115, 166, E 16, 58.
Mary, A 156, 274, B 193.
John, A 243, 44, 46, 327, B 155, 56, C 18, 19, 23, 24, 38, 109, 10, 20, 44, 45, D 146, F 334.
Elizabeth, A 327, I 248.
Susannah, E 16, 58.
Frederick, I 248, 410.

INDEX TO DEEDS 469

Norfleet, Marmaduke, C 192, F 299.
    G 188, H 43, 61.
  Thomas, B 269, D 136, G 188.
  John, D 141.
Norman, Henry, A 67, 175, 87, B 133,
    C 4, 209.
Nowell, Richard, A 120, 24, 228, C 16,
    78, E 43.
  Alis, A 124, B 257.
  Elenor, A 124.

O

Oates, James, A 112.
  Joseph, B 170, C 110, 11, 27, 40, 45,
    46, 47, 211, D 5.
Ogden, Thomas, I 238.
  Titus, I 238.
Oneel, Daniel, A 184.
Only, John, H 216.
Outland, Joseph, F 25, 157, 235, G 20,
    48, 66, 75, 76, H 157.
  Mary, G 75.
  Thomas, H 5.
Overman, Jacob, A 95, B 247, C 30,
    311, D 57, F 376, G 35, I 440.
  Charles, A 357, C 174, 249, D 57, E
    173, F 174 G 7.
  Charles Jr.. H 293, I 227, 459.
  Ann, A 357.
  Ephrim, B 188, 357, C 249.
  Sarah, B 188.
  Joseph, D 2.
  Thomas, D 40, 109, 47, 54, 56, 57, E
    173, F 153, 65, 71, 72, 87, G 248.
  Miriam, F 165, 71.
  John, F 165, I 102, 440, 50.
  Joshua, H 293.

P

Packitt, James, E 110.
Pagett (Pagitt), John, B 304.
  Jane, B 304.
  James, D 75 (Pagdfet), 131, E 18,
    19, 110.
Paine, Stephen, A 70, 74.
  Thomas, F 263.
  Joseph, F 263.
  John, G 139.
Painter, Elizabeth, H 224, 310, 11.
  John, H 237, 311.

Palin, John, C 161.
Palmer, Paul, B 227, 302, C 159, F 391,
    G 69.
  Joanna, G 69.
  Samuel, C 159, G 69.
  Martha, Ann, G 69.
  Joshua, C 159.
  Marthann, C 159.
Pargenter, William, A 254, 342.
Parginter, Ruth, A 342.
Parke, Humphrey, H 71, 341, I 133, 41,
    69, 70, 365.
Parker, Thomas, C 75, D 78, 106.
  James, G 159.
  John, G 159, H 69, 226, 357, I 325.
  Peter, E 64, F 243, 416, G 248.
  Job, I 35.
Parrish, John, A 199, 259, B 200, 13, 47,
    48, C 133, 62, 64, 201, 2, 4, 34, 47,
    F 29, 30, 216, 47, 399, G 41, 55, 60,
    64, 260, H 58.
  Ann, B 213.
Parson, Samuel, A 103, C 141, F 115,
    G 37, I 391.
Patterson, Joanna, G 107, 15.
Paistree (Peartree), James, G 122,
    H 241.
  Elizabeth, G 122, 241.
Pearse, John, G 129, H 334, I 113, 454.
  Richard, G 129, 218, H 145, 280, 347,
    I 113.
  Thomas, H 35, 158, 68.
Pearson, Peter, B 1, 74, 150, 271, C 81,
    I 178.
  William, I 100.
Peavall, Margaret, A 100.
Peirce, Joseph, A 111, C 253, F 244, H
    113, 58.
  Thomas, A 111, 145, 260, 347, B 208,
    20, 98, D 9, 125, E 8, 93, 107, F 244,
    99, G 95, 2-2, H 35, 158, 58, 76, 344.
  Thomas Jr., C 14, 253, 60.
  Potsefull, C 235, E 2.
  James, E 165, F 206, H 130.
  Jacob, G 214, 18, H 145, 347.
  Miles, H 102, 30.
  Susannah, H 130.
  David, H 344.
Peirson, John, A 297.
  Rebeckah, A 297.

Penrice, Thomas, B 81, 82, 84, 286, G 222.
  Francis, B 280, C 86, D 66, F 81, 99, G 77, 88, 204, H 133, 83, 250, 54, 55, 324, I 30, 31.
  Elizabeth, D 66, G 204, H 133, I 207.
  Edward, F 241, 67, 98, G 77, 204, H 132, 208, I 410.
  Samuel, G 88, H 253, 54, H 255, 324, 33.
  Penelope, H. 133.
  Clarke, I 30, 31.
  Lemuel, I 207.
Perrishoe, James, A 33, 48, C 43, D 70, E 74, 76, F 197, G 63, 89, 197, 220, 27, H 43, 55, 57, I 16.
Perrishaw, James, A 60, 115, 16, 310, B 33, 85.
Perrishew, James, B 77, 187.
  John, B 187, C 201, 34, D 110, F 181, 97, 302, G 51, 87, 153, I 462.
Perrishoe, Joseph, C 182, 91, D 4, 91, E 23, 27, 49, 74, 75, 129, F 91, 92, 182, 302, 95, G 14, 51, 87, H 123, 67, 253, 309, I 29, 30, 31, 221, 302, 407, 67, 68, 537.
  Simon, E 74, 75, 76, F 421, G 192, 97, 206, 27, H 45.
  Joshua, F 212, 13, 326, G 151, 253.
  Josiah, F 336, 421, G 89, H 64, 65, 122, 23, 67.
  Samuel, F 302, G 87, 247, 57, H 115.
  Mary, H 122.
  Margaret, I 16.
Person (Pearson), John, D 64, 165, E 112, F 367, 68, G 343, H 1, 100.
  Jonathan, F 17, 39, 184, G 141.
  Joseph, F 367, H 383, I 72.
  Eleazer, F 368, H 100, I 72.
  Elizabeth, I 72.
Perry, Jacob, B, 179, 275, C 47, D 18, 20, 47, 90, E 47, 167, F 137, 42, 305, G 96, 100, 1, 2, 4, 6, 240, H 85, 372, 87, I 245.
  Benjamin, B 274, 75, C 55, D 89, F 10, 162, 66, G 42, 226, H 217, I 245, 85, 372.
  John, B 322, C 35, D 22, 163, 72, F 21, 23, 157, 305, 61, G 100, 55, 240, I 329.
  Samuel, C 41, F 209, H 74, 150, 51, 274.
  Rachel, C 41.
  Phillip, C 55, E 7, I 108, 253, 58, 311, 72, 75, 507.
  Hepsibeth, E 167.
  Israel, E 167, F 142, 305, 61, G 104, 6, 231, 40, I 240, 327.
  Joseph, F 10, 239, 345, G 226, I 107, 217, 45, 53, 95, 309, 74.
  Elizabeth, F 162, 66, I 394
  Reuben, F 204, 307, G 215, H 100, 44, 387.
  Jesse, G 146, I 394, 412, 15, 16.
  Ann, H 151, 274, I 37, 253, 54, 405, 538.
Peterson, Mary, A 140.
  Ann, A 140, 41, 55.
  Jacob, A 153, 55.
  Joanner, B 18, 19.
Petite, Jesterling, A 314.
Pettit, Francis, B 299, C 83, 253.
  Jesse, B 299.
Pettiver, John, A 240, 347, 50, 51, 360, B 28, 66, 121, 73, 74, 207, 9, 11, 12, 33, 36, 52, 58, 87, 93, 94, 95, C 32, 47, 58, 83, 103, 5, 26, 29, 68, 211, 17, D 146, E 107, F 16, 57, 128, 202.
  Ann, B 66, 233, 36, 58, 66, C 47, 59, 126, D 46.
Phelps, Samuel, A 129, 33, 204, B 15, 22, C 181, 256, 67, D 86, 73, F 278, G 80, H 225, 27, 37, 39, 309, C 181.
  Bartholomew, A 217.
  Elizabeth, A 217, C 92, 128, 60, 256, D 68.
  Edward, A 271, 72.
  William, A 303, 4, D 67, E 10, F 130, 210, 78, 391, G 177, H 381.
  Jonathan, B 306, C 128, 56, 256, D 27, 62, 87, 117, 20, F 278, H 272, 381, 92.
  Mourning, C 160.
  Hannah, C 161, 89.
  John, C 255, 56.
  Henry, D 27.
  James, F 278.
  Moses, H 137.

INDEX TO DEEDS 471

Miriam, H 137.
Benjamin, I 239.
Felt, John, D 66, 68. (Phelps)
Phillips, Benjamin, Esq., I 204.
   Thomas, A 90, 91.
   Mary, A 91.
   William, A 40.
Philips, Cuthbert, A 96.
   Frances, A 96.
Philpots, John, A 4.
Pike, Clerk, G 107.
Pinner, John, H 180.
   Charles, H 180.
Pitts, Francis, I 236.
Plato, Thomas, C 62.
Pollock, Thomas, A 264, F 322, 414.
Pointer, John, I 511, 15.
   Mary, I 511, 15.
Poter, John, B 20.
Powell, John, B 144, C 131, D 141, 92, 205, 8 H 195.
   Samuel, D 136.
   Lemuel, E 39, F 6.
   Jacob, F 90, 306, G 62, 101, 22, H 241.
Pratt, Jeremiah, B 53, 189, 90, C 58, 79, 82, 194, 5, 276, D 36, 115, 23, E 34, 77, F 379, H 25, 199, 257, 77, I 464.
   John, C 194, 95, 96, 230, 76, D 41, 123, 50, H 94.
   Jobe, C 194.
   Joshua, C 196, 276, D 41.
   Elizabeth, F 112.
   Mary, F 112, I 411, 86.
   Deborah, F 112.
   Joseph, F 112, H 257, 77.
   Richard, I 124, 48, 290, 411, 86, 87, 535.
Price, Thomas, B 313, E 40.
   Elizabeth, C 42, D 16, I 112.
   James, F, 74, 82, 300, G 235, H 13, 16, 175, 76, 275.
   William, H 275, I 112.
   Rachel, I 112.
Prickloe, John, A 129, 33, 236, 84, E 26, F 100, G 118.
   Keziah, I 377, 453.
Pritchard, Joseph Sr., F 52.
   Sarah, F 291.
   William, F 291.

Pritlow, Samuel, A 26, 42, D 88, 111.
Prottle, Joseph, B 300.
Prows, Charles, A 19, 57.
Plumpton, Henry, G 186, C 205.
Pugh, Theophilus, C 277, F 290, 308, 87.

R

Radden, Joseph, C 271, 72, 73.
Reading, Joseph, D 16. (all the same)
Redding, Joseph, E 113, G 122, H 43, 61, 231.
Raner, Elizabeth, I 370.
Ranier, Elizabeth, H 306.
Ratcliff, Cornelius, A 326, 59, F 369, 70, 71.
   Richard, A 359, B 132, 42, C 260.
   Thomas, B 311.
   Joseph, B 311, C 270, D 31, 109, 58, F 369, 71, G 84, H 340, 54, 55, 56, 73, I 364.
   Mary, F 369, 71, G 84.
   Sarah, H 340, 55, 56.
Rawlings, Anthony, A 297, 98, 99.
   Katherine, A 298, 99.
Ray, William, A 105.
   Alexander, A 237, 48.
Redding, James, F 223, G 162, H 112, 231.
   John, F 223, G 122, 62, H 112, 231, 41.
Reed, Andrew, A 139, 245, B 91.
   Christian, D 99, 166, E 24, 41, 42, 168.
   Mary, E 42.
   Joseph, E 168, G 225, H 187, I 458, 97.
   George, G 173, H 44.
   Elizabeth, G 225.
   William, H 44, 187, I 54, 225, 340, 428, 58, 97.
   John, H 186, 87, I 458, 97.
Rice, John, B 174, 75, 297.
   Edward, C 187, E 29, 142.
Riddick, Joseph, B 316, C 149, E 165, F 15, 69, 70, 74, 111, I 81, 116, 233, 86, 308, 9, 459.
   Robert, B 316, C 149, D 46, E 40, 88, 165, F 69, 70, 74, 231, 300, 40, G 130, H 16, 175, 350, 51, I 216, 17, 375, 481, 525.
   Jesse, C 95, 258, D 24.
   John, D 21, 76, 89, 92, 112, E 17, 165, F 146, 265, 71, 84, 99, H 16.

Margaret, E 17.
David, E 31, F, 409, I 317.
Lemuel, F 127, 307.
Rachel, F 299.
Job, F 340, G 133, 235, 36, H 16, 24, 26, 275.
Mills, H 8.
Prudence, H 24, 275.
Jacob, H 117, 350, I 109, 294, 318, 73, 475, 80, 81, 99.
Docton, H 299.
Seth, H 351, I 18.
Isaac, I 233.
Sarah, I 481.
Josiah, I 498.
Riggs, Abraham, C 108, E 2, 235, G 50, H 65.
Jane, H 68.
Right, Samuel, A 230, 344, C 239.
David, A 241.
Daniel, A 296.
Anne, A 296.
Roberts, Thomas, B 172, 73, 74.
Benjamin, F 357, G 128, 211, H 346.
Solomon, I 166, 208, 406, 96.
William, I 335.
Mary, I 496.
Robenson, John, C 62, 125, 232, 33, E 11, 43, 145, D 50, F 8, 14, 140, 262, I 82.
Roberson, Sarah, B 263, E 11.
Joseph, C 16, 154, D 50, 147, 62, F 140, 86, 235, 62, G 39, 128, 65, 66, I 465, 534.
Robertson, Joseph, C 125.
Robbins, William, C 208, H 55, I 10, 52, 257, 324, 407, 515.
Elizabeth, I 10, 257, 324.
Robinson, Thomas, A 335, B 230, C 78, H 293, 359, I 82, 168, 465, 534.
Susanna, A 270.
Roland, H 346, I 27.
Ephrim, I 82.
Keziah, I 82.
William, I 167, 227, 459, 65, 534.

Roe, Robert, F 80, 105, H 147, 204, 6, 8, 15, I 187.
Mary, H 204, 8, 15, I 187.
Rogers, Richard, G 86, 125, I 192.
Orpha, I 70, 191, G 126.
Elizabeth Coe, G 126.
Sarah, G 126.
Rogerson, Daniel, C 114, 15, D 76, 92, 103, 21, E 141, 165, F 146, 246, 425, G 231, 41 H 16, I 240.
Hannah, D 76.
David, G 231, 41.
Josiah, G 241, H 217, I 36, 90, K 58, 240, 308.
Milly, I 237.
Catherine, I 240.
Hezekiah, I 295, 99.
John, I 295.
Ross, Abel, C 20.
Alex, D 116, E 93.
Henry, I 141.
Rooks, Richard, A 203, 250.
Mary, A 250.
Rountree, Thomas, B 38, 49, 144, 237, 317, C 131, 97, D 136, E 97, G 152, 266, 72, H 111, 51, 74, 265, I 32, 122.
Elizabeth, B 49, 264, 317, D 89.
Francis, Sr., B 49, 264, 65, C 150, 52, 110, D 33.
Moses, B 272, 323, C 11, E 61, 152, F 177, G 181.
William, C 7, 118, 150, D 33, F 15, 34.
Robert, C 48, D 89, G 226.
Joseph, D 151, H 287.
Charles, E 97, H 75, 265, I 34, 122.
Cader, H 95.
Job, H 287.
Rucke, Mary, A 177, 203. Same as Rooks.*
Thomas, B 47, C 133.
Richard, C 133.
Rousham, John, E 148.
Rue, John, C 69.

S

Saint, Daniel, F 125, 218, 19, H 31, 34, 37, 197, 202, 24, I 100.

---

*(The name of Rooks, and Rucke is identical; also Raner and Ranier and Radden, Reading, and Redding. It is thought that Roberson, Robenson, and Robinson are the same name, only spelled differently.)

Thomas, G 209, H 22.
Hercules, H 31, 34, 273, I 8, 100.
Salter, Edward, C 74.
  Peter, I 218.
Sampson, John, B 2, 45, 185, 234, 301, C 150.
  Isaac, B 45, 186.
Sanders, Abraham, B 85, 159, 240, C 165, D 101, 43, E 26, 133, 34, 35, F 156, 76, G 5, I 50.
  Benjamin, B 110, 59, 67, C 31, 58, 66, 104, 200, 67, D 73, 74, E 162, F 179, 94, H 165, I 50, 120, 95.
  William, C 151, 88.
  Richard, D 81, H 110, I 112.
  Joseph, E 161, 62, F 194, 417.
  John, E 161, G 160, H 110, I 162.
  Mary, F 194, I 57, G 114.
  Isaac, F 278, H 67, G 114.
  Leah, G 160.
  Elizabeth, H 110.
  John Jr., I 57, 368.
Sanderson, Richard, A 335, B 4, 286, 87, 88, 92, C 13, 20, 51, 100, 1, 2, 30, 203, D 100, G 134, 35, 36, 37, 40, 73, 95, 219, 21, 66, H 44, 103, 4, 5, 6, 7, 8, 14, 188, I 212.
Sanford, Thomas, A 45.
Scarbrough, Mac Rora, C 45, 134, 36, 216, 17, 28, 42, 75, D 59, 71, 96, E 86, 146, 66, F 5, 160, 268, G 2, 3, 4, H 51, 93, 222, 23, 24, 48, 310, 11, I 53.
  Anna, C 134, 59.
  Benjamin, F 160, 220, 22, 68, 358, 415, G 2, 4, 69, 80, 107, 15, 203, H 92, 93, 183, 234, I 15, 101, 382.
  Elizabeth, F 160.
  Sarah, H 92, 93, 234.
  William, H 222, 23, 24, 48, 210, I 45, 46, 49, 53, 439.
  Lucy, I 45.
Scott, Charles, A 136, 37, 38, 333.
  Joseph, A 65, B 54, H 113, 54, I 447.
  Joshua, A 38, 169, 93, B 54.
  Elizabeth, A 333.
  James, E 51.
  Penina, H 154.

Senicer, Walter, A 41.
Sharbo, Thomas, B 211, C 78, 237, D 69, F 261.
  Rebecca, D 69.
  Jonathan, F 190, 261, I 98.
Sharwood, David, A 133*
  Jane, A 133.
  William, C 72.
Shaw, John, A 218.
Shell, George, F 264, 386.
Sherer, Samuel, B 91.
Sherrod, William, F 339.
  Thomas, F 245.
  Jonathan, F 12, 286, G 61.
  David, C 53, F 245, 314, I 162.
Sherwood, Jonathan, C 104, 70, 71, D 40, 144.
Simpson, John, C 156.
  Elizabeth, C 156, D 11, 20, 59.
Simpson, John, B 227, C 6, 49, 216.
  Elizabeth, C 6, 216, D 52, 87, 93.
  Benjamin, F 169, 301, G 18, H 213, 378, I 47, 117.
  Samuel, F 301, H 67, 378.
  William, H 97.
Simmons, John, F 168, G 24.
  George, A 354, D 122, I 370.
  William, C 269.
  Susanna, A 354.
  Elizabeth, A 354.
Sitterson, James, A 312, C 51, 106, 7, 51, D 59, E 102, 9, F 121, 35, 75, 210, 352, 81, 91, G 22, 177, I 7, 246.
  Hannah, C 107, F 130, 35, 391, I 7, 246.
  Samuel, F 130, 35, I 409.
  Sarah, F 135.
Sitterson, Joseph, H 290, 358, I 127, 385, 88.
  Yedderton, I 7.
  Isaac, I 7, 99, 231, 46.
  Thomas, I 409.
  Miriam, I 409.
Skinner, Richard, A 246, B 70, 199, 225, 26, 27, C 70, 211, D 101, 25, 43, E 41, 88, G 80, 130, 67, H 237, 38, I 71, 474.

---

*(Note: Sharwood, Sherwood, and Sherrod are identical.)

Lewis, B 63, 106, C 215.
Joshua, F 128, G 2, 3, 80, 85, 138, 39,
  61, 67, 202, 3, 52, H 5, 9, 11, 31, 35,
  80, 93, 124, 32, 33, 47, 62, 98, 228,
  34, 35, 37, 51, 375, 93, I 542.
William, F 290, G 157, 207, 12, 20, 52,
  65, I 42, 56, 77, 120, 23, 218, 56, 70,
  75, 313, 82, 489, 509, 10.
John, H 39, 42, 70, 375, I 256.
Joseph, H 54.
Samuel, H 60, 125, I 5.
Sarah, H 60, 375, I 5.
James, H 60, I 5, 42, 304, 476, 95.
Jonathan, H 352, I 5, 92, 419, 57, 88.
Stephen, H 375.
Nathan, I 488, 89.
Miles Gale, I 457.
Esther, I 488.
Ann, I 495.
Slocum, John, A 181.
Small, Thomas, F 422, I 91, 156.
  Obadiah, F 213, G 68.
  Joshua, F 223, G 116, 62, H 38, 112,
    37, 231, 41.
  Charity, F 223, G 116.
  William, G 146.
Smith, Robert, A 58, 59.
  Ann, A 59, B 207, 14, F 219.
  Joseph, A 343, B 21, 22, 233, C 46,
    255, 56, D 65, 68, F 18, 32, 204, 40,
    93, G 21, 71, 72, 143, 60, 201, H 71,
    I 292, 381.
  Francis, A 356, B 44, C 83, 84, D 12.
  Leah, B 21, E 65.
  James, B 66, 207, 8, 9, 14, 89, 93, 94,
    C 127, 40, 63, 73, 254, 69, E 102, 6,
    60, F 73, 81, 99.
  Daniel, B 144, 296, C 35, 240, F 164.
  Sarah, B 144.
  Josiah, B 284.
  David, C 227.
  John, C 266, D 33, E 31, 137, F 208,
    42, 356.
  Rachel, E 31, F 347, 66, G 70, 160.
  Susannah, C 269, F 73, E 160.
  Huldah, E 6.
  Thomas, C 269, F 73, E 160.
  Samuel, E 6, F 179, 80, 81, 258, 347,
    66, G 160.
  Michael, E 160, F 73.

Solomon, F 81, 99.
Benjamin, D 128.
Peninah, G 70, 160.
Rosanna, H 336.
Keziah, I 157.
Israel, I 157.
Elizabeth, I 157.
Snell, Roger, A 146, C 229.
Snelling, Hannah, A 198.
  Esther, A 198.
  Rachel, A 198, 212, 13.
Snoden, Thomas, A 196, 215, 35, 302,
    B 42, 43, 60, 84, 168, G 53, 266.
  Christopher, C 61, G 363.
  George, D 88, 113.
  Jane, D 88.
  Samuel, D 113, D 79.
  William, E 79.
  Sarah, H 178.
  Solomon, E 79.
  Benjamin, H 210, 39, 322.
  Lemuel, F 145.
  Joseph, G 119, 264.
  Zebulon, G 250, 66, H 178, I 221,
    24, 515.
Snooke (Snuke), Daniel, A 29, 53, 91,
    129, 57, 310, 88, C 48, 107, D 18, 89,
    F 136, I 7, 246.
  Margaret, A 240, B 310, D 103, F
    306, 425.
Sothel, Seth, A 15, 16, 17, 71.
Spellman, John, A 425, C 126, 211.
  Mary, A 350, 51, C 126, 211.
Speight, Thomas, B 94, 95, 99, C 2,
    193, H 8, 176.
  Mary, C 193.
  Moses, C 136, D 35, F 42, 69.
  Isaac, G 238, H 8.
  Ann, H 8.
Spivey, George, F 98, 177.
  Jacob, F 266, H 74, I 32.
  Ann, H 74.
Stacy, Thomas, I 333.
Stack, Amos, G 198, H 9, I 541.
  Penelope, G 198, H 9, 541.
Stafford, Thomas, B 193, 221, 22, F 185,
    6, 314, 17, I 512.
  Alexander, I 385.
  John, I 385, 87.

INDEX TO DEEDS 475

Stallings, Lott, B 106, 7, C 193, 215, D 84, E 157.
  Nicholas, B 301, C 8, 49, 50, 94, 95, 96, 131, 258, D 16, 24, 53, E 165, F 78, 396, H 16, 189, 271.
  Daniel, I 287.
  James, C 49, 73, 118, 50, 210.
  Elias, C 94, 197, E 165, 284, 345, F 265, G 62, H 116, 43, 93, 303, I 33, 321.
  Christian, C 95, 96, 258, D 24.
  Henry, C 95, 258, D 24, 25.
  Simon, C 95, E 61, 165, F 234, H 16, 59, I 110, 22, 58, 73, 80, 81, 97, 202, 16, 34, 60, 408.
  Isaac, D 16, 25.
  Samuel, F 1, 373.
  John, H 189, I 197.
  Luke, I 32, 33, 34, 251, 54, 82.
  Zachariah, I 33.
  Reuben, I 251, 54, 82.
Standrick, Richard, A 111, D 125.
Standing, William, B 282, C 245, D 150, E 72, 95, 98, D 81, 82, 83, 85, 138, 98, H 35, I 61, 129.
  Samuel, D 66, 98, E 36, 95, 98, G 81, 82, 83, 85, 138, 98, H 35.
  Henderson, E 95.
  Edward, G 198.
Stanley, Jonathan, A 269, 326, 359.
  Elizabeth, A 326, 359.
Stanton (Staunton), Thomas, F 429, I 482.
  Elijah, B 176, 257, C 78.
  Elizabeth, C 78.
  John, F 144, H 240, 97, I 135, 482, 515.
  Thompson, I 482.
Stephens, Thomas, I 481.
Stepney, John, A 73, 148, 54, 81, 373, B 115, 16, 17, 18, 322, C 19, 24, 38, 238, E 50, F 105, 334, H 2, 147, 232, I 187.
  William, H 206, 212, 20, 32, I 15, 187, 420.
Stevenson, John, F 193, 4, 337, 55, 56, G 19, H 127, I 48, 79, 422, 94.
  Thomas, F 337.
  Elizabeth, I 79.

William, C 138.
  Hugh, I 326.
Stokes, John, G 91, 154, H 18, 114, 322.
  William, G 163, H 50.
  Elizabeth, G 163.
Stone, John, C 275, F 141, 59, 319, 62, 84, 413.
  William, F 141.
  Moses, H 388, I 257.
Sumner, Luke, E 53, 134, 35, F 308, 58, 410, G 149, 86, H 6, 117, 57, 58, 59, 60, I 244, 80.
  Seth, G 90, 251, 63, I 188, 454.
  James, E 83, H 6, I 244, 80. E 125
  Jacob, H 299.
  Abraham, I 114.
Sutton, Joseph, A 32, 93, 190, 386, B 1, 28, 31, 32, 38, 53, 202, 3, C 40, 108, 91, D 29, 105, 30, E 2, 22, 23, 27, F 416, 341, 55, 56, G 56, 84, 97, 140, 89, H 23, 127, 64, 72, 96, 201, 33, 42, 49.
  Deborah, A 32, F 237, G 78.
  George, B 9, 153, 203, C 52, D 124, 49, F 237, 83, 389, 90, H 164.
  Nathaniel, B 141, 311, 22, F 341, 89.
  Elizabeth, C 108, F 2.
  Christopher, D 19, 124, 49, E 56, H 164, 96, 242, 49, I 12.
  Richard, B 137, 40, F 2, 103, 4.
  James, F 99, H 183, 98, 234.
  Susanah, F 104.
  Sarah, C 108, F 103, H 233, I 356, 58.
  Ephrim, F 242.
  Thomas, I 138, 39, 56, 58.
  Samuel, F 382, 89, G 55.
  Benjamin, H 45, 53, 55, 57.
  Miriam, H 196.
  Joseph, I 12, 149, 298, 305, 466, 67, 68, 522.
  Ashbury, I 125.
  Frederick, I 411.
Swain, John, E 94.
  Elizabeth, E 94.
  Samuel, I 3.
Swann, Samuel, A 113, 43, 47, 72, 75, 85, 87, B 69, 133, C 4, 51, 88, D 100, 66, H 289, I 60.
  Elizabeth, A 175.

Thomas, B 69.
John, B 133, C 4.
Sweeney, Terrence, B 288, 92.

T

Tailor, Charles, A 95, C 30, F 140, 262.
Tatlock, James, H 329.
Taylor, John, A 54, F 155, 200, H 252, 53, 55, 333.
  Julianna, A 68.
  Jane, A 68.
  Jonathan, A 119, 67, B 12, 13, E 52, G 244.
  Samuel, B 14, 15, 57, C 259, F 146.
  Lemuel, B 53, 189, C 195.
  Timothy, B 196.
  William, C 56, 259.
  Grace, C 260.
  Susannah, F 200, 35.
  Johanna, G 2.
  David, I 94.
Tetterton, William, A 46, 100, 21, 312, 34, 36, C 14, H 312, 13, 52.
  Sarah, A 336, C 107, I 7, 246.
Thatch, John, F 287, G 69, 115, H 370, I 538.
  Green, H 166, I 185.
Therrell, William, B 4.
Thigpen, James, A 158, 63, 74, 389, B 73, 90, 109, 283, 84, C 70, D 1, 83, 131, F 374, H 4.
  Margaret, A 389, B 52.
  James Jr., B 3, 23, 52, 85, 86, 93, 112, C 71, I 35.
Thomas, James, C 212, 26, 67.
  Stephen, C 251.
Thompson, Henry, H 84, 236.
Tomblin, John, A 84, 95, D 10, 50, 91, E 37, G 26, 56.
  William, B 181, 204, 30, 31, D 10, 50, E 37, G 56, 128, H 318, I 30, 31, 221.
Toms, Francis, A 19, 20, 21, 22, 23, 49, 77, 114, 136, 147, 74, 212, 13, 60, B 20, 52, 89, 100, 64, 241, 42, 51, 306, 8, C 25, 26, 36, 67, 143, 78, 82, 85, D 4, 22, 27, 30, 61, 70, 145, E 99, 108, F 261, 79, 315, 22, 36, 86, 405, 14, G 71, 220, H 121, 244, 56, 361.
  Joshua, B 8, H 169, I 265, 445, 54, 530, 37.

Sarah, B 8.
Foster, C 182, 91, D 4, 19, E 22, 23, 27, 63, 129, F 196, 408, G 132, 259, H 109, I 149, 53, 298, 323, 59, 60, 445, 90, 537.
Martha, E 22.
Margaret, F 315, H 361, 62.
Zachariah, H 121, 56, 69, 285.
Elizabeth, H 169, 362.
Caleb, H 214, 69, 285, I 446.
Rebeccah, H 362.
Gosbee, H 380, 443, 45.
Mary, I 149, 360.
John, I 359, 443, 526.
Tow, Christopher, H 104, 5, 88.
  Deborah, G 193, 99, H 105.
Tromball, William, E 144, F 65, 109, 45, H 297, 338, I 278.
Towe, Christopher, G 189, 93, 99.
Townsend, William, C 6, 107, 56, D 52, 58, 59, 60, 67, 87, 95, 117, 20, 51, E 1, 3, 26, F 135, 256, 391, G 22, 80, H 298, I 7, 133, 41, 225, 46, 300.
  John, C 188, 212, 26, 67, D 73.
  Rachel, F 256.
Tromboll, Simon, B 24.
Trowell (Trowel), Thomas, B 201.
  Joseph, A 79.
Truelove, Timothy, B 291, F 334, I 121.
  Elizabeth, F 334.
  Caleb, I 531.
Turner, William, A 75, 76, 200, C 137, 213.
  Edward, B 198, C 180, 90, D 124, F 116, 254, 55, 89, 222, 390, H 164, 205, 49.
  Abraham, F 252, 314, 17, H 3, I 205, 222.
  John, F 255, 400, G 109, 258, 60, I 73, 74, 127, 469, 70.
  Sarah, F 400.
  Demsey, G 190, H 3, 47, 205, 318, 63, 79, I 137.
  Joseph, F 254, G 50, 189, 93, 94, 99, 216, 49, 58, H 68, 105, 88.
  Joseph Jr., I 22, 296, 521.
  Agnes, H 249.
  Edward Jr., I 12, 520.
  Nathan, I 200.
  Benjamin, I 205, 22.

INDEX TO DEEDS 477

Ezekiel, I 205, 22.
Richard, B 80, D 40.
Jane, G 190, 99, 216.
Ann, A 200.
Twine, John, F 146, 303, G 226, I 132, 330.
Thomas, I 132, 284, 374.
Abraham, I 331.
Caleb, I 511.

V

Varnham, John, A 378.
Vick, Isaac, F 233.
Volloway, John, A 233, 41.
Jean, A 241.
Vosse, William, A 19, 24, 51, 52, 121, 58, 63, 88.
Joan, A 52.
Johanna, A 121.

W

Walker, Henderson, A 4, 142, 47, 59, 61.
Maurice, B 55, F 322.
Wallace, William, G 152.
Charles, G 152.
Walless, Richard, C 209, 29, 51.
Wallis, John, A 90, E 81.
William, E 97, 132, 52.
Wallburton, John, F 114, 292, H 157.
Walton, Timothy, F 253, G 67, H 5.
George, H 348, 49, 68, 76, I 264, 401.
Wanrite, James, D 163.
Ward, James, B 291, G 86.
Thomas, G 213.
John, C, 132.
Mary, C 132.
Warner, Samuel, B 282.
Warring (Warren), Henry, A 244, 51, F 24, 35, 84, G 13.
Elizabeth, A 244, 51.
Abraham, A 331, 63, B 143, 60, 61, 62, 65, C 93, 95, 139, 261, F 24.
Mary, A 363.
Washington, George, G 188.
Watson, Margaret, B 70.
Watrey, Richard, A 380.
Watts, John, A 144, 47.
Weaver, Benjamin, F 214.
Webb, Zachariah, I 94, 413.

Weeks, Thomas, B 231, C 30, 204, D 35, 69, 162, E 62, F 190, 245, 46, 54, 55, 56, 62, 418, G 123, H 148, I 69, 98.
Anne, D 35, 69, 162.
John, G 123, 262, I 98.
Sarah, G 262.
Samuel, G 123.
James, G 123.
William, G 123.
Benjamin, I 98.
Wilson, I 278.
Welch, John B 104, C 76, 77, G 265, H 163, 320.
Nathaniel, C 239.
Wells, Francis, A 226, 62, B 177.
Joseph, I 505.
Wensley, Henry, D 97, 98, 99, 100, 15.
West, William, A 24.
Robert, C 28.
Mary, C 28.
Martha, C 28.
Sarah, C 28.
Wheatley, Benjamin, G 151.
Whedby (Whedbee), John, A 123, D 105, F 282, 83, 89, 397, G 174, H 47, 103, 6, 78, 88, 250, 91, I 12.
Richard, A 123, 372, 84, B 128, 53, 54, C 40, 41, 42, 51, D 105, 30, F 71, 115, 385, 427, G 109, 99, 250, H 80, 249, I 12, 127, 59, 438.
Benjamin, G 221, 22, H 18, 56, I 131.
Debro, A 123.
George, A 123, I 16, 22, 23, 205, 25, 65, 66, 319, 424.
Joseph, H 342, I 396.
Mary, I 12.
Thomezin, I 396.
Sarah, A 384, I 424.
Martha, I 424.
Lemuel, I 424.
William, I 424.
Thomas, I 522.
James, I 424.
Wheeler, Thomas, I 230.
Wherry, Anthony, A 227, 383, B 155, C 112, 238, I 187.
Joshua, C 238.
White, Joan, A 11.
Arnold, A 134, 256, B 188, 312, C 249,

63, 70, D 11, 31, 32, 57, E 38, 81, F 376, 32, 233, 34, 39, H 207.
William, A 135, 266, B 42, 43, C 179, 254, D 11, 140, F 126, 29, G 98, 175, 255, H 35, 86, I 56, 313.
Parthene, A 256.
Anne, A 266.
Thomas, B 183, 296, C 172, 79, D 90, 102, F 72, 149, 60, 64, 215, H 35, 86, 111, I 242.
Henry, B 188, C 249, I 176, 325, 36, 450.
John, B 234, 35, 90, 313, 16, C 7, 8, 48, 94, 150, 258, D 89, 102, E 64, F 149, 215, 68, 402, G 4, 179, 226, H 95, 96, 111, 276, 365, I 56, 370, 78, 480, 81, 98, 99, 533.
Sarah, B 290, 313, 16, C 8, 94, 258, D 89, E 11.
Elizabeth, D 11, 31.
Joseph, E 144, F 54, 58, 164, 263, G 150, H 86, 256.
Joshua, F 148, 215, 404, G 181.
Caleb, F 198, 393, H 227.
Matthew, F 318, G 200, I 178.
Samuel, F 376, G 32, 125, 234, H 10, 11, 207, I 209.
Rachel, G 179.
Theophilus, H 39.
Gulielma, H 86.
Benjamin, H 193, 373, I 444, 48, 522.
Silas, H 276.
Christian, H 276.
Zachariah, I 252.
Francis, I 259.
Lydia, I 259.
Josiah, I 370, 71.
Charles, I 373, 78.
Mary, I 373, 78.
Huldah, I 498, 99.
David, I 522.
George, I 522.
Luke, I 524.
Wiggins, Thomas, C 205, F 6, 134.
Christian, F 134.
Wilcocks, John, C 138, D 101, 38, 43, E 68, 69, 146.
Wilkens, John, F 334, I 121.
Wilks, Charles, B 7, 107, 260, 61, 77, 97, C 64, 193, D 21, 112.

Wilkinson (Wilkson), William, A 1, 2, 3, 165, H 7.
Benjamin, G 42.
Willis, F 134.
Wilkins, Charles, A 289.
Elizabeth, A 289.
Williams, Jenkins, A 97, 130, 90, 92.
Joanna, A 97, 190.
Richard, A 12, 135, 52, 342, I 355.
Nathaniel, C 261, 97, H 342, 77.
John, B 105, 57, 218, 53, C 224, D 101, 15, 43, E 42, F 45, 57, 298, H 288.
Ann, F 43, H 66, 1 121, 24.
Joseph, F 244, G 24, H 329, 30, 37, I 421, 538, 39.
Hatten, F 334, 48, 49, G 187, H 2, 62, 66, 220, I 55, 121, 24, 236, 68, 313.
Samuel, H 81, 129, 31, I 88, 116.
Tully (Tullie), C 100, 2, 29, 30, 203, D 99, H 114, 210, 39, 322, 32, I 79, 131, 293, 339, 55, 422.
Spencer, H 146, 281, 357, I 106, 66, 71, 75, 203, 32, 50, 63, 340, 412, 513, 15.
Sarah, A 358, 73, G 77, H 208.
Thomas, A 358, 73, F 298, G 77, H 208.
Mary, H 342, I 483. (Her children, Milly, John, Mary, Thomas, and Sarah.)
Lockhart, I 355, 422.
William, A 231, 34, I 393, 451, 539.
Jane, A 152.
Ruth, A 152.
Williamson, Richard, A 18.
James, B 102, 3.
Willis, Humphrey, A 62.
Willoby, John, A 206, C 129.
Harris, A 365.
Mary, A 365.
Harry, D 111.
Wilson, Robert, A 151, 64, 78, 343, B 151, 52, 67, 69, 239, C 92, 132, 244, 46, D 62, 138, 39, E 87, 142, 44, 46, 50, 71, F 13, 36, 37, 38, 74, 218, 19, 56, G 49, 142, 45, 215, H 140, 44, 46 I 365.
Isaac, A 164, 236, 60, 97, 98, 355, B 123, 69, 252, 84, C 46, 58, D 18, 46,

INDEX TO DEEDS 479

127, 38, 39, E 47, 146, F 36, 37, 38, 225, I 164, 235, 463.
Ann, A 178, 204, 343, 46, 60, D 18, E 144.
Edward, A 247, F 241, 67, 98, G 77, H 35, 208, 51, 52, I 157, 207.
Benjamin, A 343, B 50, 123, 51, 96, 239, C 42, 58, 104, D 40, 133, 44, 53, E 100, F 67, 260, 359, 88, 92, G 1, 16, 217, H 177, 92, 209, 27, 302, I 40, 95, 96.
Judith, B 123, C 42, F 388, G 1, H 177, 92.
Jacob, C 42, G 16, 217, H 155, 77, 92, 246, 301.
John, C 155, 206, D 20, 140, E 28, I 488.
William, A 257, 360, E 3, 100, F 111, 19, 362, 91, 413, G 61, 116, H 30, 182, 244, 46, 98, I 116, 449.
Joseph, E 87, 171, F 143, G 157.
Sylvanus, E 170, F 244, 63.
Rebeccah, E 170, F 244, 63.
Abraham, F 124, 233, 48, 60, 388, 412, 17, G 1, I 39, 283, 368, 434.
Sarah, F 367, H 182.
James, F 225, H 144, 386.
Thomas, H. 209, I 71, 334, 447, 49, 56, 531.
Mary, H 209.
Moses, H 227.
Zachariah, H 301, I 95, 96.
Bettie, I 147, 456.
Roda, I 463.
Wimberly, John, C 131.
Elizabeth, C 131.
Wingate, John, A 71, I 88.
William, E 1, H 78.
Winslow, John, B 46, D 20, 47, 90, 161, E 11, F 34, 61, 72, 86, 154, 217, 59, 403, G 207, H 316, 65, I 462.
Thomas, B 183, 224, 42, 63, 90, G 8, 39, 94, 124, 53, 58, D 35, 43, 90, 145, 53, 61, E 5, 6, 11, 37, 45, 63, 108, F 7, 16, 34, 61, 72, 149, 55, 215, 72 H 111, 3, 4, 16, 31.
Elizabeth, B 183, 290, C 8, 94, 258, D 90, G 207, H 140, 246, 316.
Joseph, C 158, 241, D 48, 132, 61, E 20, 33, 89, 99, 147, 51, F 7, 93, 94, 95, 133, 215, 86, H 73, 79, 331, I 259, 462.
Timothy, E 11, 33, 151, F 95, 217, 56, G 142.
Jesse, E 11, H 197, 218.
Sarah, E 108.
William, E 113, I 258, 448.
Israel, F 86, 217, 403, G 207.
Pleasant, F 93, 94, 95, 96, 191, H 73, 79, 331.
Miriam, F 96, 155.
Obed, F 95, H 310, 11.
Mary, F 154, G 142.
Josiah, F 154.
Samuel, F 154.
Ruth, F 154.
Henry, F 193, 207.
Benjamin, F 217, 59, 403, G 103, 5, 331.
Jacob, F 403, G 105, H 195, 371.
Caleb, H 376, I 258, 60.
Wood, Richard, D 86, F 237.
Aaron, D 86, 94, E 90, 91, F 19, 125, 26.
Moses, D 134, 42, E 90, 91, C 278.
Joseph, I 8, 228.
William, F 405.
Woodcocke, Edward, F 387.
Woodley, Andrew, D 93, 114, 16, E 63, 69, 93, F 78.
Ann, D 116.
William, E 93, F 101.
Woolard, Richard, A 194, B 114.
Ann, A 194.
John, A 301, B 104, 14, C 76, F 423.
Alice, B 114.
Andrew, C 45, 136.
Williams, F 20, 224.
Mary, F 224.
Wright, Samuel, C 62, I 215.
Thomas, C 62, F 386, G 155, H 163, 290, 320, 58.
Wyatt, John, A 275, 76, 352, B 191, C 44, 76, 198, 229, D 7, 79, F 349, H 2, 235, 390, I 220, 477, 78, 502.
Mary, A 276.
Samuel, A 327, B 137, 56, C 44, E 32, 94, 136, F 80, H 204.

Thomas, A 352, C 44, 135, 36, H 248.
William, A 352, C 44, 276, D 28, 36, 41, 49, 79, 150, E 34, 48, 50, 164, F 20, 24, 224, H 77, 94, 232, 35, I 464.
Wyatt (Wiatt), Elizabeth, A 352, B 137, C 44.
　Jacob, E 32, 94, 136, F 80, H 167, 204.
　Penelope, F. 20.
　Sarah, F 306.

Joshua, H 258, I 485, 524.
Parthenia, I 220.
Wynne, Archibald, C 221, 22, 24, 25.

Y

Yates, John, A 242.
　Elizabeth, A 242.
Yelverton, John, A 278, 79, 91, 92, 93.
　Elizabeth, A 291, 92, 93.

GENERAL INDEX

A

Albertson, Peter, p. 13.
  Albert, p. 13.
  Aaron, p. 13.
  Nathaniel, p. 13.
  Eza (Esau), p. 14.
  Jonathan, p. 22.
  Arthur, pp. 23, 4.
  Family, pp. 315, 17.
Anderson, John, pp. 8, 14, 23, 4.
  Jean, p. 8.
Akehurst, Daniel, p. 10.
Archdale, John, p. 11.
Arkill, William, p. 22.
Arnold, Lawrence, pp. 8, 9, 14.
  Elizabeth, pp. 8, 9.
  John, p. 9.
  William, p. 24.
  Family, pp. 317, 18.

B

Bagley, Thos., p. 23.
Baker, Mr. Henry, p. 14.
  Family, pp. 318, 20.
Banks, Elizabeth, p. 10.
Barclift, Thomas, pp. 9, 24.
  John, Senior, pp. 21, 4.
  Family, pp. 321, 23.
Barker, Anne, p. 15.
Barnstable, William, pp. 15, 16.
Barrow, John, pp. 3, 5, 7, 9.
  Eri, p. 3.
  Arodi, p. 23.
  Family, pp. 320, 21.
Bateman, Jonathan, pp. 7, 9, 10.
  Elizabeth, p. 10.
  John, p. 14.
  Thomas, p. 23.
  Family, pp. 323, 24.
Beasley, Johanna, pp. 8, 9.
  Family, p. 324.
  James, p. 9.
  Robert, p. 8.
  Sarah, p. 9.
Beesley, Francis, p. 15.
  James, p. 14.

Mary, p. 14.
Belman, John, p. 10.
Bentley, John, p. 8.
  Family, pp. 324, 25.
Berry, Edward, p. 9.
Berkeley, Sir William, p. 3.
Biggs, Timothy, p. 3.
Blanchard, Ephrim, p. 31.
  Family, pp. 325, 26.
Blitchenden family, p. 326.
Blount, Thomas, p. 11.
  Family, pp. 326, 27.
Boasman, Elizabeth, p. 15.
  Ralph, p. 15.
Bogue, William, pp. 12, 23.
Bond, Samuel, p. 15.
  Elizabeth, p. 15.
  Mercy, p. 15.
  Susannah, p. 15.
Bonner, Thomas, p. 22.
Boswell, Joseph, p. 23.
Boyce, William, p. 15.
Branch, Mr. Geo., p. 7.
  Isacher, p. 22.
  William, p. 22.
Brasinan, Mary, p. 15.
  Elizabeth, p. 22.
Brasurre, Margaret, p. 30.
Bratton, Nathaniel, p. 22.
  Benjamin, p. 22.
Brickstone, William, p. 8.
Brient, Elizabeth, p. 11.
Brightwell, Mr. Robert, p. 7.
Brown, William, p. 8.
  Francis, p. 22.
Bunch, Jesse, p. 22.
Bundy, Josiah, p. 24.
  William, pp. 24, 32.
  Family, pp. 327, 30.
Butler, Mr. Christopher, p. 7.
  William. p. 8.
  Diana, p. 8.
  Willis, p. 22.
Bush, James, p. 22.
Buyard, Jean, p. 9.
Byrom, John, p. 23.

C

Calloway, Caleb, pp. 2, 7, 8.
    Rachel, p. 12.
    John, p. 12.
    Mary, p. 12.
    Family, pp. 330, 31.
Calleway, Caleb, p. 11, 14.
    Zebulon, p. 22.
Cale, Richard, p. 22.
Cannon, Robert, p. 6.
Carpenter, Rebecca, p. 11.
Carnele, Joseph, p. 15.
Caruthers, Nathaniel, p. 18.
Castellaw, James, p. 21.
Catchmaid, George, p. 3.
Chancey, Zachariah, p. 18.
Chandler, Elizabeth, p. 3.
Charles, Samuel, p. 12.
    Family, pp. 31, 32.
Chastone, Richard, p. 9.
    Sarah, p. 9.
Chesen, James, p. 12.
Cheston, Richard, p. 19.
Chesson family, pp. 332, 33.
Clapper, Jno., p. 11.
Clare, Mr. Timo., pp. 7, 8, 12, 13.
    Elizabeth, pp. 13, 31.
    Family, pp. 333, 34.
Clayton, Henry, p. 8.
    John, p. 17.
Clerks of Court, pp. 311, 13.
Clemons, William, p. 22.
Cock, Robert, p. 23.
Cole, Mr. James, pp. 12, 13, 16.
Collins, William, p. 14.
    John, p. 22.
        Christopher, p. 22.
        Jeremiah, p. 23.
Colson, William, p. 24.
Commander, Mr. Joseph, p. 10.
Corprew, Thomas, p. 32.
Cox family, pp. 334, 36.
Creecy, William, pp. 22, 36, 37.
    Levi, p. 22.
    Thos., p. 23.
Croxton, Arthur, p. 23.

D

Davenport, John, p. 16.
Davis, Mr. John, p. 8.
    Jean, p. 9.
    Family, pp. 336, 38.
Dawson, Mr. Antho, p. 7.
    Capt. Anthony, pp. 10, 12.
Deadman, John, p. 9.
Deal, Malachi, p. 22.
Denman, Charles, pp. 20, 22.
Dewham, Thomas, p. 14.
Divisions of Estates, p. 293.
Docton, Jacob, p. 24.
Doe, Jeremiah, p. 22.
Donaldson, Andrew, p. 22.
Draper family, pp. 338, 40.
Drummond, William, pp. 3, 4.
Duckingfield, William, p. 13.
Durant, George, pp. 2, 3, 4, 6, 8, 9, 22, 32, 36.
    John, p. 7, 8, 10.
    Mrs. Ann, p. 9.
    Thomas, p. 11.
    Family, pp. 340, 41.

E

Eames, Mr. George, p. 8.
Earl, Rev. Daniel, p. 33.
Early, William, p. 14.
Eason, Moses, p. 20.
    Jesse, p. 35.
Edmundson, William, p. 28.
Elliott, Moses, p. 23.
    Abraham, p. 23.
    Joseph, p. 23.
    Jacob, p. 23.
    Family, pp. 341, 44.
Evans, Jonathan, p. 12.
    Thomas, p. 14.
    Mary, p. 14.
    John, p. 14.
    Family, pp. 345, 49.
Evins, Mr. Richard, p. 7.

F

Felton, Richard, p. 36.
Fewox, James, p. 8.
Field, James, p. 23.
Fletcher, Mr. Ralph, pp. 7, 11, 12, 23.
    Family, pp. 350, 51.

Fleetwood family, p. 349.
Forbes, Bailey, p. 22.
  Lamuel, p. 22.
Foster, Mr. Francis, pp. 8, 12, 35.
  William, pp. 8, 10.
  Diana, pp. 9, 10.
  James, p. 14.
Fox, Richard, p. 8.
French, Mrs. Elizabeth, pp. 17, 18.

G

Gale, Mr. Christopher, p. 14.
Gilbert, Joseph, p. 23.
Gilliam, Thomas, p. 10.
Godfrey, William, p. 8.
  Sarah, p. 8.
  John, p. 11.
  Peter, p. 13.
  Thos., p. 24.
  Family, p. 351.
Gording, George, p. 23.
  William, pp. 23, 32.
  Nathaniel, p. 23.
Gordon, Mr. William, p. 33.
  Rev. William, p. 34.
  Family, pp. 352, 53.
Gosby, Hannah, p. 8.
  John, p. 8.
Grace, Luke, p. 15.
Granbery family, pp. 354, 59.
Gray, John, p. 9.
  John, Jr., p. 9.
  Tabitha, p. 9.
  Thomas, p. 9.
Gregory family, pp. 360, 61.
Griffin, John, p. 23.
Guyer, John, p. 23.

H

Hall, Jacob, p. 6.
  Daniel, p. 12.
  Rose, p. 12.
  Edward, p. 22.
  Henry, p. 22.
  Sarah, p. 13.
  David, p. 14.
  Elizabeth, p. 14.
Halsey, Frederick, p. 23.
Hancocke, Thomas, p. 14.
  Mary, p. 14.

Hardy, Thomas, p. 35.
Harloe, Thomas, p. 8.
  Mary, p. 8.
  John, p. 8.
Harmon, Robert, p. 11.
  Thomas, p. 22.
Harris, Thomas, pp. 2, 7, 8.
  John, pp. 6, 9, 11.
  Diana, p. 8.
  Sarah, p. 13.
  David, p. 14.
  Elizabeth, p. 14.
Hartley, Coll. Francis, p. 10.
  Mrs. Susanna, p. 10.
Harvey, John, pp. 5, 17, 19.
  John, Esquire, p. 14.
  Col. John, pp. 21, 22, 23, 25, 35.
  Hon. Thomas, pp. 10, 11, 12, 21, 25.
  Miles, p. 21.
  Benjamin, pp. 21, 22, 23.
  Mary, p. 23.
  Joseph, pp. 22, 23.
  Burton, p. 23.
  Robert, p. 23.
Haskeet, Tabitha, p. 9.
Hasket, William, p. 24.
Haskins, Thomas, p. 10.
Hassold, Thomas, p. 9.
  Mary, p. 9.
  Thomas, Jr., p. 9.
Hatfield, Richard, pp. 22, 23.
Hawkins, John, p. 10.
Hecklefield, John, pp. 13, 14, 16, 17, 35.
  Family, p. 352.
Henby, John, pp. 23, 24.
  Joseph, p. 23.
  James, pp. 23, 24.
  Silvanus, p. 24.
Hendrickson, Jobe, p. 23.
Hendrick, Jeremiah, p. 23.
  Solomon, p. 24.
  Isaac, p. 24.
Hill, Samuel, p. 32.
Hobart, Joshua, p. 24.
Hogg, Mr. James, p. 32.
Holden, John, p. 16.
Hollowell, Thomas, p. 23.
  John, p. 23.

William, p. 23.
Family, pp. 361, 62.
Hooks, John, pp. 15, 16.
Hooper, William, p. 22.
Hudson, William, p. 14.
Huffton, John, p. 9.
  David, p. 24.
Hutson, John, p. 23.
Hyde, Hon. Edward, p. 17.

J

Jackson, William, p. 10.
Jacocks, Ann, p. 9.
  Thomas, p. 32.
  Jonathan, p. 22.
  Family, p. 367.
Jarvis, Thomas, p. 5.
Jenkins, John, pp. 4, 5, 13.
Jessop, Joseph, p. 22.
  Thomas, pp. 24, 30.
  Family, pp. 363, 64.
Johnson, Sarah, p. 15.
  Samuel, p. 22.
  John, p. 22.
Jones, Hon. Francis, pp. 11, 23.
  Peter, p. 11.
  Ann, p. 13.
  Daniel, p. 17.
  Evan, p. 23.
  William, pp. 22, 23.
  Thos., Estate, p. 23.
  Family, pp. 364, 66.
Jooke, Sarah, p. 8.
Jordan, Matthew, p. 19.
  Joseph, p. 29.
  Thomas, p. 30.
  Family, pp. 366, 72.

K

Kenedy, Mr. Patrick, p. 7.
Kennion, Roger, p. 23.
Kent, Ann, p. 8.
Kilcoconen, pp. 2, 36.
Kinsey, Katherine, p. 8.
  John, p. 8.
Kitching, William, p. 35.
Knight, Lewis Alex., p. 14.
  Esther, p. 14.
Knoles, Thos., p. 23.
Knox, Andrew, pp. 21, 24.

L

Lacy, William, p. 9.
  Grace, p. 9.
  John, pp. 9, 23, 24.
Lakar, Benjamin, pp. 10, 11.
Lamb, Mary, p. 10.
  Joshua, p. 10.
  Family, p. 373.
Lawrence, Robert, p. 16.
  Family, pp. 373, 74.
Lawton, Peleg, p. 23.
Layden family, p. 374.
Leah, John, p. 7.
Leary, John, p. 22.
Leigh, Gilbert, p. 32.
  James, p. 32.
  Family, p. 375.
Lillington, Alex., pp. 7, 9, 10, 13.
  Family, pp. 376, 77.
Lilly, John, pp. 11, 13, 23.
Lindsay, Rev. David, p. 4.
Little, Mr. Jno., p. 7.
Lepper, Thomas, pp. 8, 9.
  Ann, pp. 8, 9.
  Sarah, pp. 8, 9.
  Rebecca, pp. 8, 9.
Loadman, James, p. 9.
Long Guyles, p. 8.
  Arthur, p. 8.
  Thomas, pp. 15, 22.
  William, pp. 15, 22.
Long, Joshua, pp. 22, 23.
  Nathan, p. 22.
  Reuben, p. 22.
  Lemuel, p. 22.
  Family, pp. 377, 79.
Lumsford, John, p. 22.
Luten, Frederick, p. 22.

M

Mackey, William, p. 22.
Mannering, Mr. Ste., pp. 7, 9.
Mann, John, p. 24.
Mardlen, John, p. 23.
  Ezekiel, Sr., p. 23.
  Edward, p. 23.
Marriages, pp. 299, 310.
Marsden, Rev. Richard, p. 34.
Mashburn, Mr., p. 35.

GENERAL INDEX 485

Mathews, George, p. 6.
Mathias, Joseph, p. 22.
  Elizabeth, pp. 33, 37.
  John, p. 36.
Maudlin, Ezekiel, pp. 15, 23, 24.
  Hannah, p. 15.
  Edward, p. 24.
  William, p. 24.
  Family, pp. 379, 80.
Mayo, Edward, p. 8.
  Sarah, p. 8.
  Ann, p. 8.
  Elizabeth, p. 8.
  Family, pp. 382, 83.
Mayow, Joseph, p. 23.
McAdams, Joseph, p. 20.
McClenden, Denis, pp. 11, 14, 150.
  Francis, p. 11.
  Thomas, p. 11.
McClenny, James, p. 23.
McMullen family, pp. 380, 82.
Merett, Thomas, p, 8.
Middleton, John, p. 23.
Miller, Thomas, p. 2.
  Charles, p. 23.
Minge, James, p. 16.
  Ruth, pp. 16, 35.
Moline, Robert, p. 10.
  Elinor, p. 11.
Monday, Benjamin, p. 24.
Montague, Thos., p. 24.
Moore, Maurice, p. 35.
  William, p. 12.
  Capt. William, p. 21.
  Elizabeth, p. 12.
  Samuel, pp. 19, 23.
  Charles, pp. 22, 23.
  Family, pp. 383, 84.
More, John, p. 23.
  Truman, p. 23.
  Jno., p. 24.
Morgan, William, p. 14.
  James, Sr., p. 19.
  John, p. 23.
  Jane, p. 24.
  Family, pp. 384, 85.
Morres, John, p. 11.
  Elizabeth, p. 11.
  John, Jr., p. 11.
  William, p. 11.
  Mare, p. 11.
Morris, John, pp. 15, 23.
  Family, pp. 385, 88.
Moseley, Edward, p. 16.
Mullen, William, p. 22.
Murdaugh, John, p. 20.
Murphy, Michael, p. 24.

N

Newbold, William, p. 19.
Newby, James, pp. 14, 15.
  Sarah, p. 14.
  Gabriel, pp. 14, 18.
  Nathan, pp. 17, 18, 19, 20.
  Gideon, p. 18.
  Mary, pp. 19, 23.
  Joseph, p. 24.
  Thomas, pp. 20; 23.
  Francis, p. 20.
  Jesse, p. 24.
  Keziah, p. 24.
  Exum, p. 31.
  Mrs. G. D., p. 36.
  John, p. 15.
  Magdalen, p. 15.
  Elizabeth, p. 15.
  Family, pp. 388, 94.
Nichols, Thomas, p. 11.
Nicholson, John, p. 8.
  Samuel, pp. 8, 11, 12.
  Christopher, p. 8.
  Hannah, p. 8.
  William, p. 14.
  Thomas, p. 20.
  Francis, p. 34.
  Family, pp. 394, 96.
Nixon, John, pp. 6, 8, 22, 24.
  Em, p. 8.
  Zachariah, pp. 19, 23.
  Francis, p. 19.
  Delight, p. 23.
  Phineas, p. 24.
  Family, pp. 396, 98.
Norcom, Joseph, p. 23.
Norfleet, Marmaduke, p. 22.
Nowell, Richard, p. 8.
  Oliver, p. 8.
  Joan, p. 11.

Elinor, p. 11.
Alice, p. 11.

O

Oates, James, pp. 11, 12, 13.
  Joseph, p. 12.
  Elizabeth, p. 12.
Outland, Joseph, p. 24.
Overman, Jacob, p. 11.
  Dorothy, p. 11.
  Jacob, Jr., p. 11.
  Theo., p. 11.
  Ephrim, p. 11.
  Margery, p. 11.
  Ann, p. 11.

P

Parish, Ann, p. 9.
  John, pp. 12, 15.
Parks, Samuel, p. 20.
Parramore, Thos., p. 23.
Peed, Timo, p. 7.
Pearson, Rachel, pp. 23, 24.
  Peter, p. 23.
  Jonathan, p. 24.
  Family, pp. 398, 401.
Pembroke, Dan'll, p. 8.
Penrice, Francis, p. 14.
  Samuel, p. 23.
Perkins, Edmund, p. 9.
Perrisho, James, p. 12.
Perrishaw, John, p. 24.
Perry, Benjamin, pp. 22, 23, 35.
  Phillip, p. 23.
  Family, pp. 401, 2.
Pettigrew, Rev. Charles, pp. 21, 23.
Petitions, pp. 285, 93.
Pettyjohn, Job, pp. 36, 37.
Phelps, Samuel, pp. 15, 16, 22, 35.
  Jonathan, pp. 17, 18, 19, 24, 32.
  Benjamin, pp. 18, 19, 20.
  Dorothy, p. 19.
Phillips, Daniel, pp. 10, 14.
  Henry, p. 28.
  Samuel, p. 13.
Pierce, Mr. Tho., pp. 7, 8.
  Susanna, p. 8.
  John, p. 8, 32.
  Ruth, p. 8.
  Dorothy, p. 8.
  Mary, p. 8.
  Kesiah, p. 19.
  Thomas, pp. 19, 20, 23.
  Family, pp. 404, 6.
Pike, Samuel, p. 8.
  Africa, p. 8.
Plater, Richard, p. 14.
Pollock, Col. Thomas, p. 10.
Potter, Matthew, p. 15.
Pratt, Zebulon, p. 22.
  Mary, p. 23.
  Jeremiah, pp. 33, 37.
Pretlow, Samuel, p. 19.
Pricklow, pp. 2, 9, 14.
  John, p. 12.
Pritlow family, pp. 406, 7.
Prody, George, p. 13.

R

Rainer, Richard, p. 23.
Rainsford, Rev. John, p. 16.
Ratcliffe, Rebeccah, p. 15.
  Joseph, pp. 20, 23, 24.
  Family, pp. 408, 9.
Reed, Joseph, p. 32.
  Christian, p. 32.
Rent Roll, p. 449.
Representatives, p. 313.
Richards, Jean, p. 14.
Ricks, Isaac, p. 15.
  Abraham, p. 15.
Right, Samuel, p. 24.
Roberson, Nicholas, p. 8.
  John, p. 23.
Robinson, Joseph, pp. 20, 23.
  John, p. 24.
Rodman, Edmond, p. 8.
Roe, Robert, p. 22.
Ross, Martin, pp. 36, 37.

S

Sanderson, Capt. Richard, p. 14.
  Richard, pp. 22, 32, 35.
Sanders, Richard, pp. 20, 23.
  Benjamin, p. 22.
  John, p. 22.
Scarbrough, Augustine, pp. 9, 10.
  Macrora, pp. 18, 20, 22.
Scott, Levin, p. 22.
  Ann, p. 31.
  Family, pp. 410, 11.

GENERAL INDEX

Sestion, Walter, p. 12.
Sharbo, Thos., p. 24.
Sheriffs, p. 313.
Simons, Francis, p. 8.
Simmons, Thomas, p. 22.
Sitterson, James, p. 19.
Skillings, Sarah, p. 23.
Skinner, Miss Emily, p. 5.
   Richard, pp. 15, 22, 23.
   William, pp. 19, 21, 22, 23, 25.
   John, pp. 19, 22, 23, 24.
   Evan, p. 20.
   Henry, p. 22.
   Joshua, pp. 22, 23, 36, 37.
   Benjamin, p. 36.
   Charles, p. 36.
   Family, pp. 411, 12.
   Nathan, p. 22.
   Stephen, p. 23.
   Ann, p. 23.
   Harry, p. 25.
   Congressman T. G., p. 25.
Smith, Robert, p. 7.
   John, pp. 8, 22.
   Benjamin, p. 23.
Smythwick, Edward, p. 7.
Snellen, Hannah, p. 13.
   Rachel, p. 13.
   Esther, p. 13.
Snelling, Mr. Israel, p. 7.
Snell, Roger, p. 8.
Snowden, Thomas, pp. 9, 14, 15.
   Constance, p. 14.
   Reverend Mr., p. 36.
Sothel, Seth, pp. 6, 7, 8, 10.
Snoden family, pp. 412, 13.
Speight, Thomas, pp. 11, 22.
   Family, pp. 413, 14.
Spivey family, pp. 414, 15.
Spruel, Gray, p. 23.
Stacey, Thos., p. 23.
Standin, William, p. 23.
Stanton, Margaret, p. 24.
   Moses, p. 24.
Stepney, John, pp. 3, 7, 11, 13, 16, 35.
Stewart, John, p. 6.
Stiball, Richard, p. 11.
Stone, Elisha, p. 22.
   John, p. 23.

Sumner, Seth, pp. 18, 22.
   James, pp. 20, 22.
   Luke, p. 22.
Sutton, Joseph, pp. 4, 8, 15, 21, 22.
   Deliverance, p. 8.
   Christopher, p. 20.
   Ashbury, p. 22.
   Jeremiah, p. 22.
   Francis, p. 22.
   Family, pp. 415, 17.
Swann, Maj. Samuel, pp. 10, 11, 13, 14, 32.
   Elizabeth, p. 133.
   Samuel, Jr., p. 13.
   Mrs. Mary, p. 13.
   Sarah, p. 10.
   William, p. 10.
   Samson, p. 10.
   Henry, p. 10.
   Thomas, p. 10.
   Family, pp. 418, 20.
Symons, Thomas, p. 14.

T

Tailor, Jonathan, p. 11.
Taylor, Jonathan, p. 8.
   Charles, p. 8.
   George, p. 8.
   Mary, p. 8.
   Johannah, p. 15.
Teach (Pirate), p. 24.
Thach, Spencer, p. 22.
   Joseph, p. 22.
Thatch, Thos., p. 22.
Therrill, William, p. 9.
Thigpen, James, pp. 7, 14, 16.
Tomlin, John, p. 6.
   William, p. 24.
Toms, Francis, pp. 8, 10, 13, 20, 28, 30.
   Family, pp. 420, 24.
Tondle, Mr. Thomas, p. 7.
Towe, Martin, p. 20.
Troy, John, p. 9.
Trueblood, Mrs. Jack, p. 30.
Tucker family, pp. 424, 25.
Turner, William, p. 14.

W

Walker, Capt. Henderson, pp. 8, 13.
   Governor, pp. 33, 34.

Ward, Anne, p. 10.
  Francis, p. 10.
  James, p. 11.
  Hannah, p. 11.
  Judge, p. 25.
Welch, Thomas, p. 10.
  Nathaniel, p. 24.
Wells, Francis, p. 14.
Weeks, John, p. 18.
West, John, p. 14.
Weston, William, p. 23.
Whedby, Mr. John, pp. 11, 15.
  Richard, pp. 11, 15.
  Deborah, pp. 11, 15.
Whedbee, John, p. 22.
  Thos., p. 23.
  Judge Harry, p. 25.
  Mr. James, pp. 25, 32.
  Richard, p. 35.
Whidby, John, p. 32.
  Richard, p. 32.
White, Thomas, pp. 2, 10, 23.
  Jeremiah, p. 8.
  Henry, p. 9, 29.
  Robert, p. 10.
  Vincent, p. 10.
  Diana, pp. 10, 11.
  John, pp. 15, 23.
  Alice, p. 15.
  Joseph, 19.
  Luke, p. 22.
  Isaac, p. 23.
  James, pp. 15, 23.
  William, p. 23.
  Sarah, p. 23.
  John O., p. 37.
  Family, pp. 425, 32.

Wilkinson, Col. William, pp. 8, 15.
  Hester, p. 15.
Williams, Roger, p. 5.
  Jenkins, p. 8.
  Abraham, p. 11.
  Anne, p. 11.
  Edward, p. 11.
  John, p. 11.
  Family, pp. 432, 34.
Willoughby, Mr. John, p. 8.
Wilson, Mr. Isac, pp. 8, 15.
  Ann, pp. 8, 22.
  John, pp. 8, 10, 23, 24.
  James, p. 8.
  Alice, p. 8.
  Edward, pp. 16, 17.
  Sarah, p. 17.
  Family, pp. 434, 37.
Wingate, John, p. 22.
  Edward, p. 23.
Winslow, Thomas, pp. 13, 23, 24, 25.
  Thomas, Jr., pp. 24, 31.
  Joseph, pp. 23, 31.
  Timothy, p. 23.
  John, p. 24.
  Job, p. 24.
  Pleasant, p. 31.
  Family, pp. 437. 45.
Wood, Moses, p. 23.
  Family, pp. 445, 47.
Woolard, Mrs. Sarah, pp. 7, 8.
  Family, pp. 447, 48.
Wright, John, p. 10.
  Family, p. 448.
Wyatt, John, pp. 12, 22.
(Wiatt), Elizabeth, p. 17.
  William, p. 22.
  (Same family, spelled both ways.)

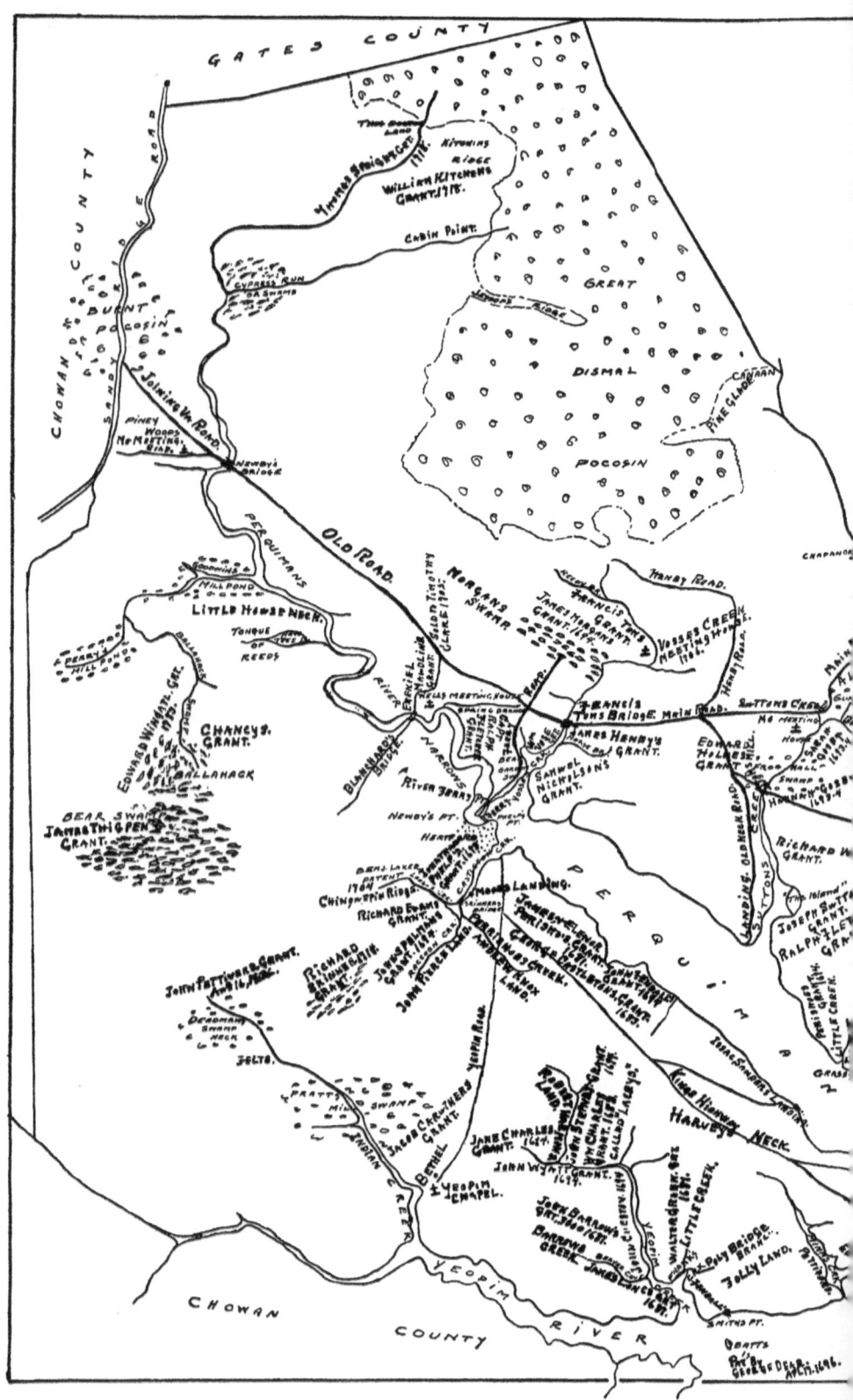

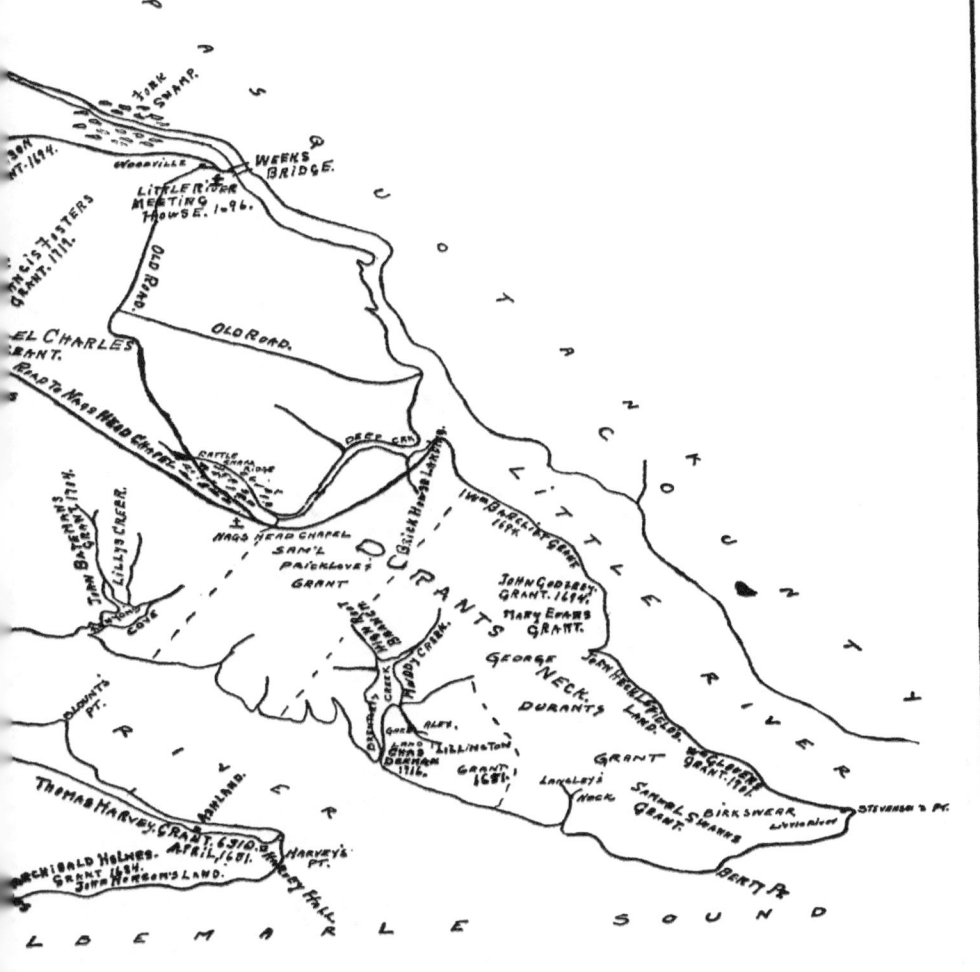

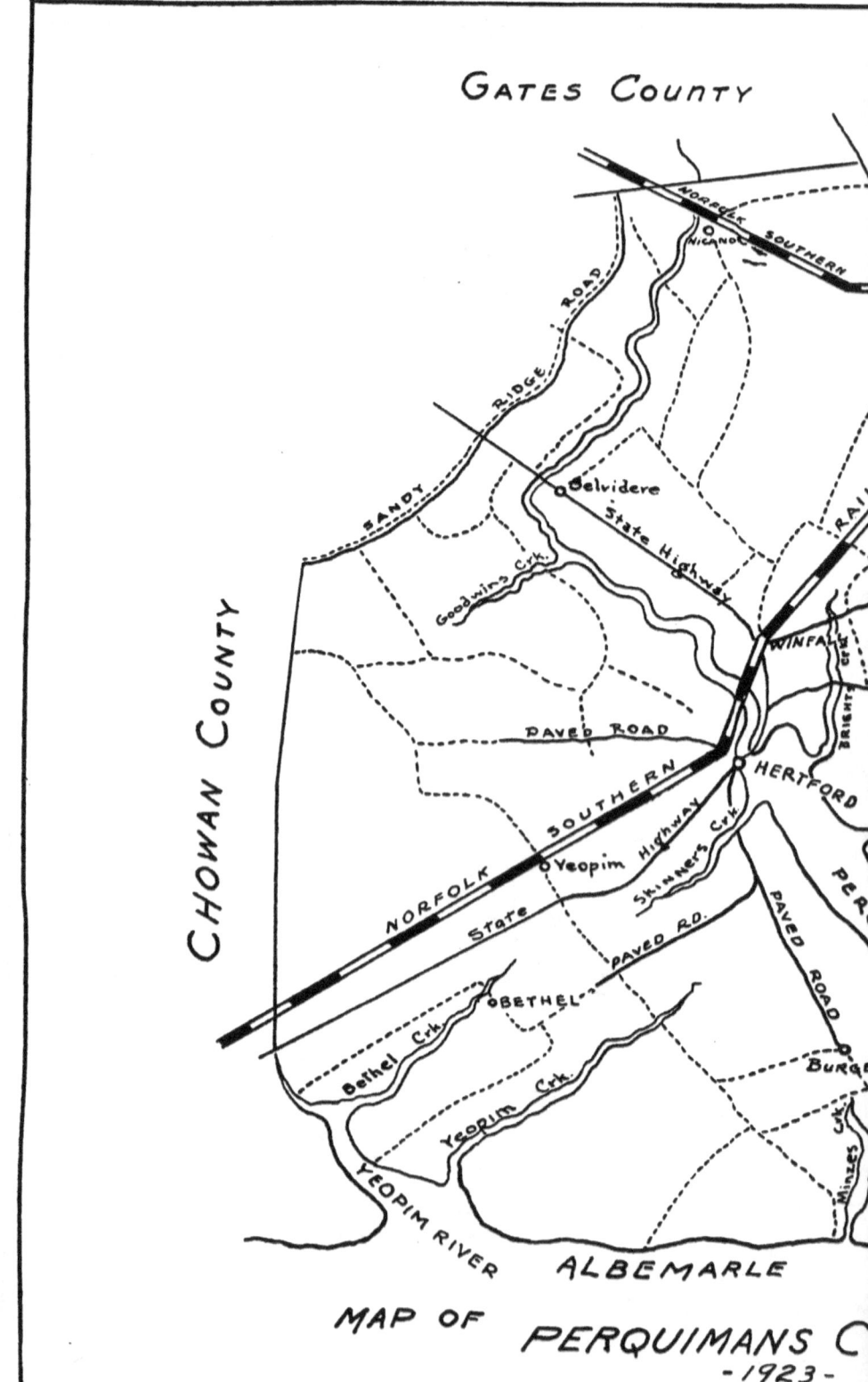

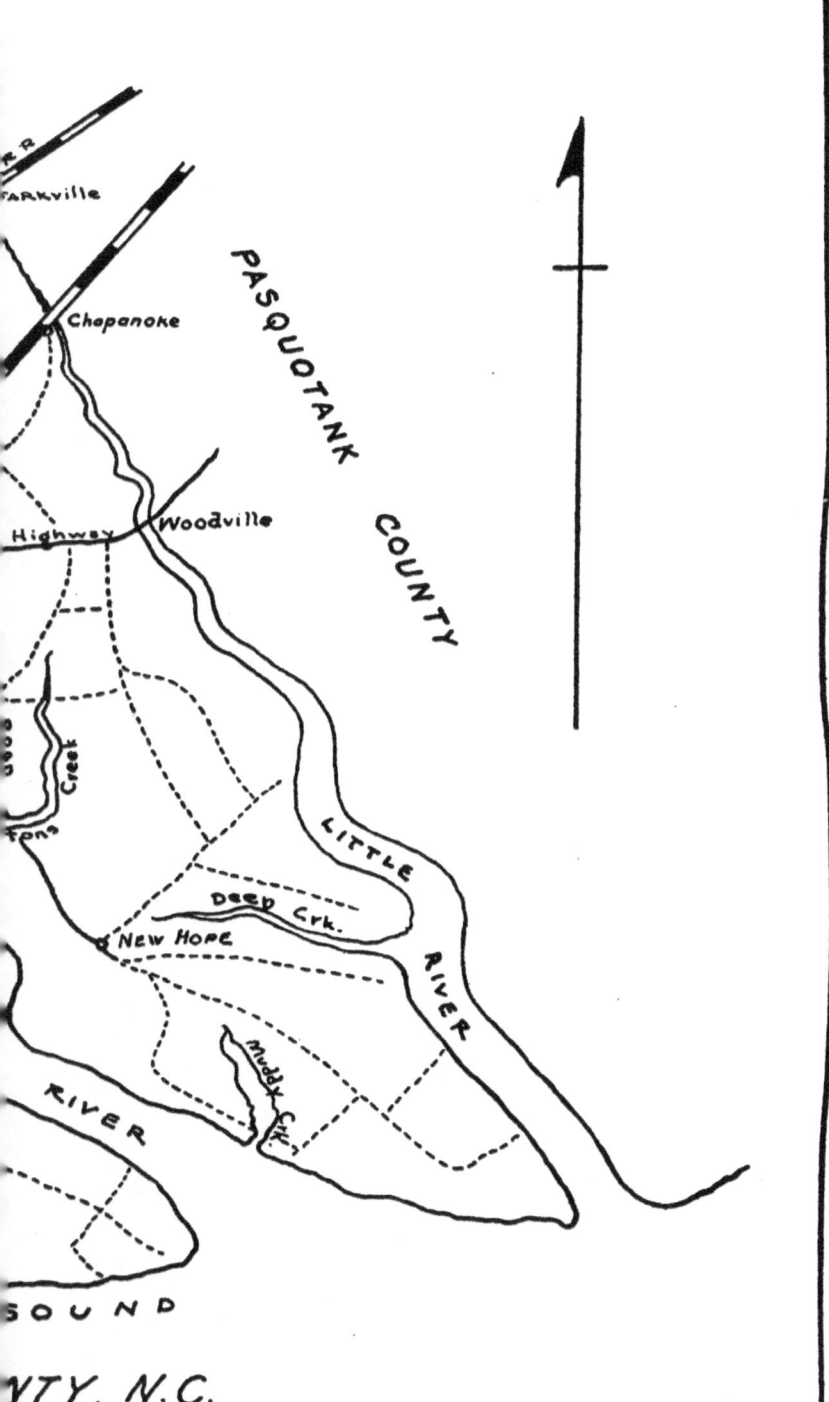

www.ingramcontent.com/pod-product-compliance
Lightning Source LLC
Chambersburg PA
CBHW020633300426
44112CB00007B/96